THE YALE EDITION

OF

HORACE WALPOLE'S

CORRESPONDENCE

EDITED BY W. S. LEWIS

VOLUME THIRTY-THREE

HORACE WALPOLE'S

CORRESPONDENCE

WITH

THE COUNTESS OF UPPER OSSORY

II

EDITED BY W. S. LEWIS

AND

A. DAYLE WALLACE

WITH THE ASSISTANCE OF

EDWINE M. MARTZ

NEW HAVEN

YALE UNIVERSITY PRESS

LONDON · OXFORD UNIVERSITY PRESS

1965

TABLE OF CONTENTS
VOLUME II

LIST OF ILLUSTRATIONS

VOLUME II

HORACE WALPOLE'S CORRESPONDENCE

To Lady Ossory, ca 1778

Erroneously printed in earlier editions as part of HW to Lady Ossory 30 Dec. 1783. The handwriting and the tone of the letter suggest an earlier date (see *post* 19 May 1778).
Address: To Lady Ossory.

YOU accuse me of twenty things that I have no sort of title to, as sense, prudence, entertainment, jollity and mystery. Who would ever think, Madam, of those being features in my character? It is like your desiring me to write, and *promising* me not to say above two words in answer to my letters. Indeed I shall not write on those terms. I have no more vanity than hypocrisy—and if you would only substitute *indifference,* in the place of all the attributes you have so graciously bestowed on me, you would find it the sole key to almost every action of my life for some time past, and I believe for all to come. With neither love nor hatred, with neither avarice nor ambition, it is very seldom that one grows a hypocrite after being the contrary. If I could be vain or forget myself, your Ladyship's compliments would have that effect: but as they have not turned my head hitherto, I trust they will not be able, and then I am sure nothing else will, since I can boast and desire to boast of nothing but being

Yours most faithfully,

HW.

To Lady Ossory, Thursday 1 January 1778

Now first printed.
Address: To Lady Ossory.

Jan. 1, 1778.

THOUGH the fault is not mine, Madam, I am as much ashamed as if I was guilty. It is impossible for me to be at Ampthill tomorrow, and I am forced to plead the last excuse in the world that

I like to make, royal names—nor would I submit to it, if they had any of the appendages. Nay, I am so ashamed of having even the air of wearing the livery of vanity, that I beg you will burn my letter incontinently. The fact is, Mrs Keppel comes to town tomorrow night; the Duchess will positively see nobody but near relations, and as the Duke is so good as to confine himself with her,[1] I have passed the two last evenings with them and her daughters, and as my brother cannot be prevailed on to stir out of his own house[2] even to them, the whole lies on me; and I doubt it would be too brusque and selfish to leave them quite alone merely for my own great pleasure, and even to go away the very day Mrs Keppel comes. I will not fix any other day, because I find how little I am my own master. I will come the moment I can; and should, which is very improbable, our solitary court become a real one, you would find that I should be still much farther from talking like a groom of the bedchamber— but when the Duke is so very indulgent to his wife, it would be very indecent in her relations to be wanting to them. But when I submit to be a courtier, I am sure your Ladyship knows me enough to be certain that I sacrifice myself to propriety. I go to Bedford House tonight from that only motive, as I was asked to meet Princess Amelie, and would not have her think me too much a courtier— Alas! It was not my plan for the end of my life to pass it with princes and princesses! Lady Mary Coke abused me last year before Princess Amelie for being a republican—pray don't call me a royalist at Ampthill. My opinion is, that when one is young, one may please oneself; when old, one must only do what is right—I must confess, that is not always what one likes.

1. The *Public Advertiser* 14 Jan, reported that on Saturday, 10 Jan., 'the Duchess of Gloucester set off with . . . Mrs Keppel . . . for Bath, where the Duke had been some days.'

2. In Wimpole Street. Sir Edward Walpole left the house to Lady Dysart for her life, and then to Mrs Keppel (his will, 57 Rockingham).

To Lord Ossory, Thursday 8 January 1778

Printed in Vernon Smith and Cunningham among the letters of 1777; changed by Toynbee to 1778 on internal evidence.
Address: To the Earl of Ossory at Ampthill Park, Bedfordshire. *Postmark:* 8 IA. FREE.

Jan. 8, 1778.[1]

I WAS very sorry, my dear Lord, that it was too late to write to you last night when I heard the news, that I might immediately make you easy about your friends. It was past eleven when Mrs Howe at Lady Hertford's received a note to tell her that Mud Island was taken *December* 2d,[2] and that only four men were killed and five wounded. This shows that the former accounts of the capture and of the slaughter were totally false. I know nothing more, but conclude the Americans had abandoned the fort—and very probably are gone to New York.[3] The belief of a French war is far from decreasing.[4]

Duke Hamilton[5] most assuredly marries Miss Burrell.[6]

Lady George Germaine was given over yesterday;[7] was rather better at night, but is not so today.

I say nothing about myself, for I am ashamed. The severe cold

1. HW by mistake wrote '1777.'
2. See below.
3. The British remained in possession of New York until the end of the war.
4. 'I have not a shadow of doubt that this Court and that of Madrid are combined against us. . . . The general bent of the nation is more strongly for war than ever it has been within my remembrance' (Stormont to Weymouth, Paris, 28 Dec. 1777, B. F. Stevens, *Facsimiles of Manuscripts in European Archives relating to America,* 1889–98, xx. No. 1809). 'The French ambassador yesterday [9 Jan.] notified that his Court could not consent to the restrictions the English laid on their trade between France and America' (*London Chronicle* 8–10 Jan., xliii. 38).

5. Douglas Hamilton (1756–99), 8th D. of Hamilton, 1769; K.T., 1785; raised the 82d Regiment of Foot, 1777, 'which

distinguished itself in the American War'; lord lieutenant of Lanarkshire 1794–9 (*Scots Peerage* iv. 393–4).

6. Elizabeth Anne Burrell (1757–1837) m. 1 (5 April 1778) Douglas, 8th D. of Hamilton, whom she divorced in 1794; m. 2 (1800) Henry Cecil, 10th E. of Exeter, cr. (1801) M. of Exeter. This marriage is listed in the *Public Advertiser* 12 Jan. as 'on foot, and will speedily be concluded.' Lady Mary Coke's reaction, on hearing the rumour 5 Jan.: 'as there is neither beauty, fortune, or high birth, one must wonder what could be his inducement' ('MS Journals' 6 Jan. 1778).

7. She was 'ill of the measles' (ibid. 27 Dec. 1777), and died 15 Jan. of 'the measles, a distemper which often proves fatal to those whom it attacks at her Ladyship's time of life' (*Morning Post* 17 Jan.).

and fogs frighten me, and I doubt will bring the gout whether I stir or not; I have twice thought it actually come; but it uses me like a coquette that will not part with one, though she does not care for anything but the power. The gout, that can make conquests only of the aged, is still more jealous. I had promised myself a most comfortable week at Ampthill, but I find that the few visions I had left, must vanish like all the rest! A clock has struck that wakes one from dreams!

PS. After dinner. I have now seen the Office account.[8] It says, Mud Island was taken on the 15th of *November;*[9] so I suppose the note to Mrs Howe mistook the date of the letters for that of the surrender; but I am sure of what was in the note, for Lady Mary Coke read it twice with all her importance of accent.[10] The Americans abandoned the fort the night of the attack, leaving all their cannon and stores,[11] and having lost, says the Office, 400 men.[12] Lord Cornwallis on the 10th having passed the Delaware, and being joined by Sir T. Wilson[13] with the troops from New York, attacked Redbank,[14] which the provincials abandoned too, and left their cannon and stores[15]—

8. In the *London Gazette Extraordinary* 9 Jan. with extracts of letters from Sir William Howe to Germain, Philadelphia, 17 and 28 Nov. 1777, and from Lord Howe to the Admiralty 23 Nov. The passages quoted in the notes below are from Howe's letter of 28 Nov.

9. After being bombarded from ship and shore, 'the enemy, dreading an impending assault, evacuated the island in the night between the 15th and the 16th, and it was possessed on the 16th at daybreak by the Grenadiers of the Guards' (ibid.).

10. Lady Mary Coke ('MS Journals' 8 Jan.) records 'that dispatches were received last night from Sir William which mentions the taking of Mud Island and Red Bank with little or no loss.'

11. The 'return' of these is in the *London Gazette Extraordinary* 9 Jan.

12. 'The enemy's loss during the siege is computed to have been 400 killed and wounded. The loss to the King's troops was only seven killed and five wounded' (ibid.).

13. Sir Thomas Spencer Wilson (1726–

98), 6th Bt, 1760; Maj.-Gen. and Col. of the 50th Foot. Because of 'the very critical situation of his private concerns in England,' he had Howe's leave to return and brought the dispatches above mentioned 'by the *Eagle* packet' (ibid.). The *Eagle* arrived at Falmouth on Monday, 5 Jan.; and Wilson had a conference with the King 9 Jan. (*London Chronicle* 8–10 Jan., xliii. 38).

14. In New Jersey on the Delaware, about 7 miles south of Philadelphia.

15. 'On the 18th at night Lord Cornwallis marched with a corps from camp and passed the Delaware on the 19th from Chester to Billings Fort, where he was joined by Major General Sir Thomas Wilson, with a corps that arrived a few days before from New York . . . As soon as the necessary preparations were made, his Lordship . . . [attacked] Redbank. Upon his approach the rebels evacuated the post, and retired to Mount Holly, where they joined a corps of observation, detached from the main army of the rebels, encamped at White Marsh. . . . The entrenchments being demolished, his

so, if you believe authority, they do nothing but supply the King's troops. Sir W. Howe intended to march immediately to Washington,[16] who was at White Marsh[17]—but as his letters are dated *Dec.* 1st[18] and he had taken the island on the 15th, his *immediately* had lasted a fortnight.[19]

I have just received Lady Ossory's, but have not time to answer it.

To Lady Ossory, Saturday 17 January 1778

Now first printed.
Address: To the Countess of Ossory at Ampthill Park, Bedfordshire. *Postmark:* 17 IA.

Arlington Street, Jan. 17, 1778.

I HAVE had nothing worth telling your Ladyship for this week. Yesterday came an account from *New York,* that Sir William Howe has again looked at General Washington, and did not like his looks.[1] There is a report from France that poor Lord Pigot[2] is dead, which some deny, and none agree on the circumstances.[3] Lord

---

corps returned by Gloucester on the 27th, and joined the army in this camp' (*London Gazette Extraordinary* 9 Jan.). The 'return of the artillery and military stores found . . . at Red Bank, the 22nd of November 1777' is ibid.

16. 'A forward movement against the enemy will immediately take place, and I hope will be attended with the success that is due to the spirit and activity of His Majesty's troops' (ibid.).

17. About 15 miles northwest of Philadelphia.

18. That is, 28 Nov. (the private letter mentioned in the first paragraph was 2 Dec.).

19. Cornwallis, however, had returned from Red Bank 27 Nov., the day before Howe wrote his main dispatch, and it could be said that Howe's 'forward movement' would 'immediately take place' after Cornwallis' return.

---

1. At the first look, 'Howe only took a peep at General Washington in the Jerseys, and retreated,' to sail for Chesa-peake Bay; the second look was at White-marsh. Howe returned to Philadelphia 8 Dec. 1777 (*Public Advertiser* 26 Dec. 1777; MASON i. 342 n. 7, 350 n. 15; *London Chronicle* 15–22 Jan., xliii. 62, 73).

2. George Pigot (1719 – 11 May 1777), cr. (1764) Bt and (1766) Bn Pigot; governor and commander-in-chief of Madras 1755–63, and again from 1775, although he was arrested by command of the Council of Madras 24 Aug. 1776 and was illegally confined until his death.

3. 'It was reported yesterday, as from a quarter deserving credit, that an account had been received of the death of Lord Pigot—and it was supposed his Lordship had been taken off by a common Asiatic distemper' (*London Chronicle* 13–15 Jan., xliii. 56). Although this notice does not mention France, the next paragraph in the *London Chronicle* begins: 'Another account says, that a letter from the East Indies, by way of France.' Cf. MASON i. 344 n. 5; *Public Advertiser* 16 Jan.; *Morning Post* 19 Jan. A circumstantial account of his last days was printed

George Germaine is retired to Knowle[4] on his wife's death;[5] and Lord Shelburne, as you must have heard, espouses Miss Molesworth.[6] Thus end the holidays. I conclude by Lord Ossory's letter that he will be at the opening of the parliamentary campaign.[7] I have not heard a word of what are to be the operations of either army: guess I never do, for nothing ever happens as one expects. Experience is so far from guiding me, that the longer I live, the less I trust to my own judgment—not from humility, but from finding how little anybody else possesses. In youth one supposes that there is much wisdom and policy in the world—if one lives, one is undeceived.

They say Voltaire is dead[8]—and so is Craufurd's father.[9] The first would take it very ill to be coupled with so much indifference with a most obscure man—but what is there left to say of him? He has been as much admired and abused as he deserved. His fame and writings will last forever, and those of his antagonists will be forgotten. This is enough for one that was more ambitious of a great reputation, than of a good one.

After dinner.

I was interrupted this morning by Mr Gibbon and George Selwyn. The latter was in good spirits, and did not *mimize*[10] at all. The other told me a very good thing of Hare.[11] The Duke of Northumberland had lost a great cast at Almack's t'other night, and was paying his money round the table. Hare looked at him and said to himself—

London Chronicle 31 Jan.–5 Feb., xliii. 115, 122.

4. Knole, in Kent; the seat of the Sackvilles.

5. 'As she was a good wife and mother and a sensible woman, her death [15 Jan.] was a great blow to him [Lord George] at this moment' (*Last Journals* ii. 91).

6. 'Lord Shelburn's marriage was this day declared with Miss Molesworth' (Coke, 'MS Journals' 8 Jan. 1778). The approaching marriage is also alluded to in the *Morning Post* 21 Jan., but on 24 Jan. 'The match is broke off . . . the beauteous young filly having, within these few days, paid forfeit with her repentant tears,' and on 27 Jan. a reason is suggested, that Lord Shelburne had contributed £100 for the support of American prisoners of war, when she thought the

money might better have been spent on his house in Berkeley Square. But see *post* 18 Nov. 1785, n. 2, for a more plausible explanation.

7. Parliament met 20 Jan. (*Journals of the House of Commons* xxxvi. 584).

8. Voltaire did not die until 30 May. Cf. Mason i. 343.

9. Patrick Craufurd (ca 1704–78) of Auchinames, co. Ayr; father of John and James Craufurd; M.P. Ayrshire 1741–54, Renfrewshire 1761–8. He died at Edinburgh 10 Jan. (Selwyn 137 nn. 2, 4; *Scots Magazine*, 1778, xl. 53).

10. That is, talk about 'Mie Mie,' Maria Emily Fagnani (*ante* 14 June 1774).

11. James Hare (1747–1804), M.P. Stockbridge 1772–4, Knaresborough 1781–1804. Lady Ossory thought his wit 'perhaps of a more lively kind' than Selwyn's (*Eton Coll. Reg.*).

but aloud, 'An ox roasted whole for the benefit of the paupers of Westminster!'[12]

Charles Fox stopped me in the street as I came from Craufurd's[13] and desired I would tell Lord Ossory that he wishes him to come to town very soon, as there is an opportunity of buying a commission for his brother.[14] I was very glad to be charged with such a message, and should have liked to have another to your Ladyship.[15]

To Lady Ossory, Sunday 17 May 1778

Now first printed.

Strawberry Hill, Sunday, May 17, 1778.

AS our Lord is now a Mars,[1] I wish he would step and take a lesson of the King of Prussia, who really does know something of the matter. I found two parsons[2] last night at Mrs Clive's, who were come from town, and said an account was come of a battle between the two great monarchs, and that the Emperor was beaten.[3] I was mortified that the post was gone out, and that I could not show my alert obedience in sending your Ladyship the news incontinently. However to satisfy the rigour of my conscience I put it down on paper directly, as you see; though if I sent it by tonight's post, it would sleep in London, and not be a moment sooner at Ampthill,

12. To whom the Duke was a well-known benefactor. The *London Chronicle* 27–30 Dec. 1777, xlii. 632, reported that 'yesterday the Duke of Northumberland's annual benefactions were delivered to a number of poor of the parishes in Westminster.' The *Public Advertiser* 30 Dec. 1777 mentions his benefactions, which 'may well make his Grace be considered as the Father of the Poor.'

13. In New Grafton Street (*Royal Kalendar*, 1778, p. 56).

14. Richard Fitzpatrick, who had been Lieutenant and Captain in the 1st Foot Guards since 13 Sept. 1772, was promoted 23 Jan. 1778 to Captain and Lieutenant-Colonel in the same regiment, 'on the resignation of Lieut.-Col. West, and Mr Dundas succeeds Mr Fitzpatrick in his lieutenancy. The Earl of Ossory made a purchase of the above commission for his

brother, without the knowledge of the latter, in order to make him a present of it' (*Morning Post* 31 Jan.).

15. To get her 'to come to town very soon.'

———

1. Lord Ossory, as Lord Lieutenant of Bedfordshire, had been Colonel of the Bedfordshire militia since 20 Jan. 1771, but the militia throughout Great Britain was 'drawn out' and organized 26 March 1778 (*Army Lists* 31 March 1782: *Lists of the Officers . . . of Militia. Embodied the 26th of March 1778*, p. [4]; Cobbett, *Parl. Hist.* xix. 969–70). With other colonels of militia, he was made a Colonel in the Army 2 July 1779.

2. Not identified.

3. The report of a battle between Frederick II and Joseph II was false; see below.

than if I carry it to town tomorrow myself, which I shall do,[4] with
a certificate of the truth, or the contradiction—though it is not a
season in which one needs have recourse to such shifts for materials.
The times are fruitful enough of events, and one is not obliged to
prose long about any one of them.

I am very glad the Emperor is beaten, and I should be full as glad
if the King of Prussia was. I should have still more sincere satisfaction if both of them were shot, which would save an ocean of honester
blood. Nay, I am persuaded the mother of one of them[5] would not
totally disagree with me, though she would try to persuade herself
that it was only the death of her enemy that made some amends for
the loss of her son—but truly, heirs apparent that grow up too fast,
are a little inconvenient.[6]

My rurality has not been satisfied; my lilac-tide is not flourishing;
I have heard very few nightingales, and those had not a good shake.
I found this couplet lately in Warton's new volume,[7]

> For mirth of May with skippis and with hoppis
> The birdis sang upon the tender croppis—[8]

but it is not true. Our militia is quartered at Twickenham,[9] and I
believe have been learning their exercise on my poor blackbirds
and thrushes—in short, everything has a melancholy aspect, and
from the first hue of the spring, I forebode that the summer will
be full of disastrous events. I am sorry we do not live in superstitious
times; methinks there was a kind of gloomy consolation in believing
that the elements interested themselves in the politics and fates
of kingdoms. There would be more dignity in consulting the heavens
for the destination of the Toulon fleet,[10] than to believe the lies of

4. The post from London reached
Ampthill every morning of the week
except Monday (*Universal British Directory*, 1791–[1798], ii. 46).

5. Maria Theresa of Austria, mother
of Joseph II.

6. An allusion to the Prince of Wales
as well as to Joseph II; cf. *Last Journals*
i. 554–8.

7. *The History of English Poetry*, Vol.
II, published 6 April (*London Chronicle*
Feb.–April, xliii. 205, 291, 343; Hazen,
Cat. of HW's Lib. 3214).

8. Warton, op. cit. 265; from William

Dunbar's 'Golden Terge' or 'Golden
Targe,' written ca 1508.

9. There were three regiments of Middlesex militia, Eastern, Western, and
Westminster, the last of which was quartered on Hounslow Heath (*Army Lists*
31 March 1782, op. cit. 41–3; *Corr. Geo.
III* iv. 123).

10. A squadron of the French Navy,
based at Toulon and under the command
of the Comte d'Estaing, was reported in
letters from France to have 'sailed for the
Delawar[e] River. The troops on board
. . . to cooperate with Gen. Washing-

the *Morning Post*[11]—but we have lost all taste, and do not seem to have acquired any sense in the place of it. Nonsense for nonsense, I like folly that is built on imagination better than folly that pretends to reasoning. We could not be in a worse situation than we are, if our expeditions had been directed by St Bernard or Peter the Hermit—but *patienza!* I believe we shall soon be good Catholics again![12]

Half an hour later.

The two parsons are wicked liars, and imposed on us poor villagers. I have just seen a layman,[13] who assures me the King of Prussia has not hurt a hair of Cæsar's[14] head.[15] They are within a few miles of each other,[16] with only four hundred thousand men between,[17] and they write notes to one another as often as two misses that are dear friends, and each in love with a different captain; and no minister is trusted on either side. My intelligence says the Toulon fleet has

ton,' etc. (*London Chronicle* 9–14 May, xliii. 454, 462). There were rumours too that it was bound for Gibraltar or to Ireland to supply arms for an Irish Catholic insurrection (ibid. 458; *Last Journals* ii. 142, 168, 171, 175; HW to Mann 31 May 1778; MASON i. 396, 402; *Hibernian Magazine*, 1778, p. 305). On 7 May the House of Lords and the next day the House of Commons had passed a motion that 'all letters relating to the destination of the Toulon Squadron' should be put before them (*Last Journals* ii. 173).

11. The rumours in the *Morning Post* concerning the fleets, political matters, etc., are no wilder than those in other newspapers. The 'lies' are the scandalous rumours in which the *Morning Post* excelled. Cf. *post* 24 Dec. 1778.

12. For HW's fears (on civil rather than religious grounds) of Catholic encroachment, see *Last Journals* ii. 141–2, 172–6; MASON i. 395; COLE ii. 79.

13. Not identified.

14. HW frequently refers to Joseph II as 'Cæsar.' See, for example, HW to Mann 14 April 1769, 16 June 1778, 4 Aug. 1778, 9 March 1779, 28 Dec. 1781. 'For some time it has been the *ton* in our political circles to transmute the appellation of

the *Imperial Joseph* into that of the *Imperial Cæsar*' (*European Magazine*, 1787, xii. 463 n.).

15. Frederick II and Joseph II were in disagreement about Bavaria, Joseph II 'claiming part of the domains of the late Elector of Bavaria' (HW's note on his letter to Mann 17 March 1778). Frederick's reasons for making war against Joseph II are given at length in his manifestos of 7 and 10 July, printed in the *London Chronicle* 18–28 July, xliv. 71–2, 96.

16. A contemporary map of Bavaria and Bohemia and a 'Description of the Principal Places that Have Been or Are at Present the Seat of the War' are in the *London Magazine*, Aug. 1778, xlvii. 369–70, with map facing p. 369.

17. That is, 200,000 on each side. 'Foreign Gazettes say that his Prussian Majesty's army in Silesia, of which the King is to put himself at the head, amounts to 200,000 men. He insists that the whole Bavarian succession be restored to the state in which it was left at the death of the late Elector, and that the several claims be examined and terminated conformable to the usages of the Empire' (GM 1778, xlviii. 189, *sub* 30 April).

not passed the Straits,[18] and that the Irish bills[19] are again compromised,[20] and that the Lords have thrown out the Foley bill,[21] and that Lord Holderness is dead.[22] I fear your Ladyship will have heard most of the articles of my gazette by yesterday's papers; but if you will insist on my sending you news from Twickenham, you cannot expect their arriving very fresh. I can tell you one article that comes a great way farther, and yet will not be blown upon by the *General* or *Public Advertiser*. The Great Duchess[23] has told Mrs Anne Pitt, who is at Florence,[24] that she has received a letter from her father the King of Spain, in which he tells her Great Highness that he disapproves the conduct of France, and will not join her.[25] He certainly did not know Mrs Anne was there, nor how great a politician she is; and yet his fleet looks mightily as if he talked like a parson.[26] However, I am disposed to believe him; especially as I

18. Of Gibraltar. The fleet met with storms and was said to have returned to Toulon (*Last Journals* ii. 177; *London Chronicle* 21–23 May, xliii. 496).

19. Introduced 2 April 1778 to remove restrictions on Irish trade. They were opposed by 'the trading towns on the Western Coast' of England (*Last Journals* ii. 172; MASON i. 395; Cobbett, *Parl. Hist.* xix. 1100–26).

20. See MASON i. 395 n. 9; *Last Journals* ii. 176; *London Magazine*, 1778, xlvii. 262–3.

21. Thomas Foley (1742–93), 2d Bn Foley, n.c., 1777, and his brother, Edward Foley (1747–1803), wished to break the will of their father, Thomas Foley (1716–77), cr. (1776) Bn Foley. Although the will (19 June 1777) made provision for the sons, their income barely paid the interest on their great debts; the estate was so entailed that they could not get control of most of it unless the House of Lords would set aside the will. A petition for a private bill for 'a jointure upon . . . Harriot Lady Foley . . . and to enable the trustees and executors named in the last will and testament of Thomas Lord Foley, lately deceased, to raise money by sale of . . . real estates . . . for payment of certain debts' came before the House of Lords 5 March; the bill was rejected on its third reading 15 May

(*Journals of the House of Lords* xxxv. 341–4, 495; see also MASON i. 383–4, 392–3; *Last Journals* ii. 133–5, 161; Coke, 'MS Journals' 22, 29 Nov. 1777; Mason, *Satirical Poems* 70).

22. He died 16 May at Syon Hill, Isleworth, near SH.

23. Maria Louisa (1745–92), dau. of Charles III (1716–88), K. of Spain 1759–88, m. (1765) Peter Leopold, Grand Duke of Tuscany 1765–90, Holy Roman Emperor (as Leopold II) 1790–2.

24. She returned to England early in September and later in the year had to be confined for insanity (*Gleanings from an Old Portfolio*, ed. A. G. C. Clark, Edinburgh, 1895–8, i. *passim*).

25. This information is in Mann's letter to HW 28 April 1778. Cf. Mann to HW 15 May 1779; *Last Journals* ii. 190. Lady Mary Coke's version: ('MS Journals' 21 June 1778): 'The Great Duchess showed Mrs Pitt . . . a letter she had received from the Princess des Asturies in which she expresses her surprise at the conduct of France and adds that it is not for the interest of Spain to adopt those measures. This Princess . . . takes a great part in the political affairs of that country and therefore may be supposed to know the intentions of the King and minister.'

26. The unreliability of the King's letters to Maria Louisa is mentioned in

wish to keep what I have as long as I live, since the House of Lords
will now let me do what I will with it when I die.[27] I do not desire
the promise of a Garter, which brings ill luck, for they become
vacant before they are received.[28]

I have so supererogated my promise that unless I have any bounc-
ing news, I shall not pique myself on writing again before your
return. Besides I shall live on the road in the interval. I go to town
tomorrow for the Princess,[29] and must return hither on Wednesday
to receive the Duchess of Marlborough who has done me the honour
of desiring a breakfast on Thursday. On Friday you know I go back
to town to meet Lady Ossory, don't I, Madam? Pray when does she
dine here? To be sure this is the life of a stage-coach, but it would
be a very ungallant vehicle, if it complained, when at every stage it
was to find a divinity. Good night, Madam; I shall certainly dream
of being on the road to heaven, though I set out with meeting two
parsons.

To Lady Ossory, Tuesday 19 May 1778

Now first printed.

May 19, 1778.

MY yesterday's letter was gone to the post, and I did not receive
your Ladyship's till I came home at night. I wish I had sooner,
for a line would have answered it, and I have nothing material for
a new dispatch, so your Ladyship will think I only write because I
said I should not, and to be unlike other folks, who promise and
fail.

Mann's letters to HW 7 July 1779, 31
March 1780, 29 Oct. 1782.

27. An allusion to the Foley bill, mentioned above.

28. Lord Holdernesse 'was the second
person to whom the King had long
promised a Garter, who died without
receiving it. Lord Harcourt was the other.'
(*Last Journals* ii. 175). Cf. *ante* 20 Sept.

1777, *ad fin.* According to Lord North's
letter to the King, Holdernesse was to
have been elected 'if he had lived to see
four vacancies in the order' (*Corr. Geo.
III* iv. 144). 'A promise of the Garter
seems to be fatal.' The Duke of Ancaster
was the third to die before receiving it
(Coke, 'MS Journals' 13 Aug. 1778).

29. Princess Amelia.

I am the last person you will persuade that my letters are very sensible, Madam. If I ever had any sense, I have outlived it. It is not of the essence of sense to keep good for threescore years. It is like the productions from warmer climates, and wears out in a certain time, and not in the individual only, but in general. Sense in great countries is like the practice of physic; the practice is totally inverted every fifty years. People in the smallpox used to be kept in an oven; now they are put into a horse-pond. This shows that good sense does not consist in anything certain and settled, but in sudden and violent transitions from one extreme to the other. A whole nation, that is governed by the wisdom of the aggregate body, can make these Pindaric evolutions; but an individual has not such pliable faculties, and is apt to adhere to what was thought sense in his younger days, as he does to the fashion of his clothes, when both are out of date. Nobody has these littlenesses more than I, and as I cannot live fifty years longer, when the present mode of sense will be exploded in its turn, I beg your Ladyship will spare all compliments to my understanding, and look on my silly letters, as they are, newspapers to amuse you for a quarter of an hour in the country. I return to my journal.

The event of yesterday was the apparition of General Burgoyne in the House of Commons.[1] It was literally so in the strict sense of the term; for as spectres, you know, cannot speak unless they are spoken to, and as nobody adjured it in the name of the Father, Son, and Holy to say what it was,[2] it stalked out again, and did not disburthen its mind.[3] I suppose the assembly was a little terrified, for there is no learning certainly whether the weapon it seemed to have

1. Burgoyne had landed at Portsmouth at noon, 13 May, and had arrived in London that evening or the following morning. He was on parole, in order 'to solicit ratification of the convention he concluded at Saratoga with Gen. Gates' (*London Chronicle* 12–19 May, xliii. 464, 466, 474, 480, 486; F. J. Hudleston, *Gentleman Johnny Burgoyne*, Indianapolis, 1927, pp. 286–95; *London Magazine*, May 1778, xlvii. 237).

2. 'The mode of addressing a ghost is by commanding it, in the name of the Three Persons of the Trinity, to tell you who it is, and what is its business: this

it may be necessary to repeat three times; after which it will, in a low and hollow voice, declare its satisfaction at being spoken to, and desire the party addressing it not to be afraid, for it will do him no harm' (Francis Grose, *A Provincial Glossary*, 1787, *sub* 'Superstitions,' p. 12).

3. 'General Burgoyne was yesterday [18 May] in his place at the House of Commons, for the first time since his return from America.—He did not speak' (*London Chronicle* 16–19 May, xliii. 480). He spoke briefly 21 May and again 26 May, when his conduct was examined (ibid. 21–28 May, xliii. 493, 509).

by its side was a sword or a cutlass.[4] *Phantasmato* critics are divided whether a ghost that leaves its prison-house is entitled to seem to wear either. I shall consult Craufurd, and beg him to ask the question of his second-sighted countrymen,[5] and hope to be able to satisfy your Ladyship on Friday.

Lady Holderness is a rich relict. She has £2500 a year, £25,000 in money,[6] the house in town[7] with plate, pictures, furniture, etc., forever, and Sion[8] for life. The lot of the servants is not so bounteous; they have but one year's wages; yet one of them had lived with my Lord thirty years.

I shall send Madame du Deffand an account of the formidable appearance of the Bedfordshire militia, that she may alarm her friend the Comte de Broglie, who is joined with his brother[9] in command.[10] An heroic courtier[11] told me t'other night he wished to see the contest decided here. I am not so brave, nor even gamester enough,

4. HW perhaps meant that no one knew whether Burgoyne, when and if he did speak, would use a thrusting (sword) or cutting and slashing (cutlass) technique.

5. Cf the ironic comment in the *North Briton*, No. 7, 17 July 1762: 'It is a particular mark of the favour of heaven, as all our divines say, to the chosen Scots: I mean the gift of *second sight,* which, though laughed at by every sensible man of every other nation, we all believe to be really possessed in an eminent degree by many of our countrymen, and to be found among us in the highest perfection, where there are no traces, of common sense, nor the first principles of any science.'

6. According to Lady Mary Coke ('MS Journals' 3 June 1778), 'Lord Holdernesse left her the interest of £20,000 that he lent the Duke of Leeds at the marriage of his [Holdernesse's] daughter with Lord Carmarthen, which added to the rest will make her income very considerable.'

7. In Hertford Street (*London Chronicle* 16–19 May, xliii. 479). She died in this house 13 Oct. 1801.

8. Syon Hill, Isleworth, where Lord Holdernesse died. The house was later occupied by George Spencer, 3rd D. of Marlborough (DNB, *sub* D'Arcy, Robert), and had been pulled down when George

James Aungier wrote his *History and Antiquities of . . . Isleworth,* 1840 (p. 228).

9. The Duc de Broglie.

10. This was a false rumour which apparently reached HW from an English source, not from Mme du Deffand, who wrote HW 10 May that the Duc de Broglie 'est nommé généralissime des troupes des côtes de l'océan' (DU DEFFAND v. 43; *Last Journals* ii. 175). On 31 May and again 28 June she wrote that the two brothers would not share the command, but that the Comte de Broglie would command at Metz: 'c'est un grand dégoût, il le sent très vivement' (ibid. iv. 110, v. 44–7, 53). The *London Chronicle* in a letter from 'Paris, May 12,' mistakenly reported that 'Count de Broglio is just appointed commandant-general of the troops on all our coasts of the ocean' (21–23 May, xliii. 496). The Duc de Broglie's official appointment to command the army on the coasts of Brittany and Normandy is dated 29 June (*Rép. de la Gazette*). For a discussion of the French preparations for invading England, and the Channel campaigns of 1778 and 1779, see A. T. Patterson, *The Other Armada,* Manchester, 1960 (information kindly supplied by Mr David Erskine).

11. Not identified.

which would be talking more like a man of the world, to throw a die for all I have, lest France should be as perverse as the House of Lords, and not give it me back to play for again.[12] Seriously I fear France means the worst. She has been sinking in Europe these twenty years. We plumed her in the last war, would it were the last! and three great powers have started up and curtailed her influence. She did not dare to interfere for Poland or Dantzic.[13] She has endeavoured, for one can read her handwriting, to embroil Russia with the Turks.[14] The other two are growling at each other like two bulldogs. We have divested ourselves both of strength and security. What a moment for France to revive![15] While the three rivals are fighting for territory, she may obtain more solid pre-eminence by destroying our Marine and engrossing the commerce of Europe—Oh! if I was King, I would buy off the blow at any price; will you have Gibraltar for Spain, Minorca, Bengal for yourself?—I am a cowardly politician —but then I would not have been so brave, as to send my army and fleet to America—but did not I tell you, Madam, that I am an old fool?—yet not an incorrigible one, for I shall rejoice to find I am so a little more than I think, whatever I say.

To Lady Ossory, ca Thursday 28 May 1778

Missing. See following letter.

12. An allusion to the Foley bill (*ante* 17 May 1778).

13. In the first partition of Poland, 1772, among Austria, Prussia, and Russia.

14. See following note. 'When the last dispatches left Petersburgh, a courier was arrived with advice that a fresh treaty of accommodation was opened which, it was hoped, would prevent the renewal of a war with the Turks, but that otherwise every preparation was making to begin a vigorous campaign' (*London Chronicle* 19–21 March, xliii. 274).

15. Cf. ibid. 28–30 April, xliii. 410: 'The policy of the Court of France was never more conspicuous than at present. They fomented a quarrel between the Court of Russia and the Porte; they have stirred up the Emperor to recover Silesia, and meddle in the succession to the electorate of Bavaria. Not content with disturbing the peace of Europe, they enter into an alliance with the rebel subjects of this country, in expectation that our allies upon the continent will not, from their own affairs, be able to assist us against the designs formed by France.'

To Lady Ossory, Sunday 31 May 1778

Now first printed.

[Strawberry Hill], May 31, 1778.

I DO assure you, Madam, I cannot say how much I am in earnest about the picture,[1] and beg you will not disappoint me about it. I am not at all pleased with its being altered; but if you have any regard for me, you will keep your promise in letting me have it again at any rate on Wednesday, for nothing hurts me so much as not having implicit faith in my friends; and now I have two objects at stake, your promise and your picture.

I have indeed some merit with you, for though you have vexed me very much, and in a way I did not think you would have carried so far, I cannot let my anger (for I must call things by their true names) delay giving you satisfaction on a tender point. Just after I had sent away my letter,[2] Mr St[onhewer][3] came to me with a message from the Duke of Gr[afton] with many apologies for the favour his Grace was pleased to ask of me, and on which he could not insist if I had any objection. It was, to tell me that his Grace had received the most sensible and amiable letter in the world from your Ladyship on a very particular occasion.[4] The Duke was afraid you would

1. The crayon portrait of Lady Ossory by Hamilton (*ante* 13 Aug., 7 Oct. 1773). She had taken it from HW to have the head-dress altered; see following letter.

2. Missing, dated ca 28 May: HW was to see Lady Ossory on Friday, 22 May, in London (*ante* 17, 19 May 1778), and she was still in Grosvenor Place 3 June (see following letter). He would not long delay sending her the contents of this letter of 31 May.

3. Richard Stonhewer (ca 1728–1809), friend of Mason and Gray; under-secretary of state for the north 1765–6, and for the south, 1766; auditor of excise 1772–89; F.S.A., 1787. Since 1766 he had been private secretary to the Duke of Grafton, whose tutor he had been at Cambridge (MASON i. 11 n. 4).

4. Lady Georgiana Fitzroy, Lady Os-sory's daughter by the Duke of Grafton, wished to marry John Smyth, whom she did marry 4 June 1778. The following day Lady Mary Coke at Lady Hertford's 'heard that her niece Lady Georgina Fitzroy had left her father's house the morning before and met Mr Smyth in St George's Church, where they were married. Mr Spencer Stanhope . . . gave her away. They seem to have acted very sillily, for the Duke of Grafton, though he did not approve of her choice, told her that if she would stay six months and was still of the same mind he would give his consent, but she would not wait and has therefore disobliged both her father and her grandfather, Lord Ravensworth' ('MS Journals' 5 June 1778). Cf. *post* 4 Aug. 1778.

take it ill he had not answered it, but begged me to assure you it was by no means from disrespect, or disapprobation of the contents, but from the distress and difficulty of his mind in not knowing how to word his answer properly. So far from any disregard, he begs me to assure your Ladyship, that the best proof he could give of respect for the contents and for you, he had already given by communicating the letter itself to the person concerned,[5] but that he is extremely grieved to tell your Ladyship, that though your opinion agrees *entirely* with his own,[6] neither seemed to be received with any deference.

I told Mr St[onhewer] that upon my honour I had not heard a word of the letter, and that his Grace's orders were of a very delicate nature; but that however I should be so happy to be of any use, or to be able to do any good between two persons who I wished so much should have a just esteem for each other, that I would certainly obey his Grace's commands, and should be overjoyed of the opportunity of satisfying your Ladyship that no disrespect was intended to you. Indeed I trust that the Duke's delicacy will be more pleasing than even a letter would have been; and is an earnest that he will be as reasonable on other occasions hereafter.[7] I undertook the commission the more willingly, as it may make me a happy instrument of contributing to your Ladyship's wishes, as neither you nor the Duke will have any difficulty in searching for a person to convey messages —though I confess, without as much regard as I have, it would not be the office in the world one should canvass for: you, Madam, I trust will not be displeased with my accepting the commission. If I had not thought it too friendly an office to refuse, I was out of humour enough to have excused myself—and yet I think I could not have brought myself to be so unjust even to an enemy.

I have not time to say anything to your news. I expect everything that is bad, and am much provoked that I may suffer myself by the consequence of measures that I always disapproved. The authors[8] deserve everything, and certainly do not deserve the satisfaction of seeing the innocent suffer with them.

---

5. Lady Georgiana Fitzroy.
6. That is, opposed to the marriage.
7. Presumably whenever the two sons of the Duke of Grafton and Lady Ossory should marry.
8. Lord North's administration.

To Lady Ossory, Wednesday 3 June 1778

Now first printed.
Address: To the Countess of Ossory in Grosvenor Place, London. *Postmark:*
4 IV. 2 o'clock.

[Strawberry Hill], June 3, 1778.

I AM not at all ashamed of being ashamed, when I have been in the wrong, Madam, for all the merit there is in sense is to correct one's own folly. I was born with strong feelings, and though the quantity is diminished, the quality of those that remain is still impetuous. Indeed I believe that if ever one has a heart at all, it never grows grey-haired and wrinkled. It is in vain to haggle about it; I was in a monstrous passion at your taking away your picture, and so I am sure will my ghost be, if it is ever removed out of this blue room[1] while poor Strawberry exists. One is an artificial being: I and my friends and this place compose but one idea in my mind, and it is lopping a limb to touch any of the constituent parts—so, how I should not have been angry, I don't know. You have I confess made me more than amends. The picture never did you justice, nor will a picture ever, because your expression, air, grace and dignity are superior to your features; your face is but an earnest of you, and if your whole figure was painted, the motion would be wanting, and you must lose when any essential is absent. I concluded I never should have any picture of you, and that I could not bear—and behaved accordingly. The alteration of the head-dress, though less natural than before, has, I own, made such astonishing improvement, that I could scarce believe it the same picture; nor do I conceive how adding anything to you, unless more of you, should make it more like—but it has got something new of you, a proof of your taste. I now recollect that the air before was *mean;* no wonder it was not like you! It certainly recalled nothing of your figure at the Duke of Richmond's masquerade,[2] when you looked like the Empress of the Universe, and

1. The Breakfast Room, 'Furnished with blue paper, and blue and white linen' ('Des. of SH,' *Works* ii. 421, 425).
2. 6 June 1763, at Richmond House in Privy Gardens. Lady Ossory, then Duchess of Grafton, was dressed as 'Cleopatra —and such a Cleopatra!—' and was a 'glorious' figure (Mann vi. 148).

your Majesty's eyes—but I can draw them no more than if I was a painter.

Pray forgive my late warmth. It would look like the peevishness of age, if I had not been as passionate these hundred years, and always jealous of any slight from those I love—yet in the instant of my greatest anger—but I will not boast—you have seen my heart, and I care not how silly my head is, nor am sorry to have disgraced the one, if I have proved the sincerity of the other. A great addition it will be to my satisfaction, if Lord Ossory excuses the one for the sake of the other. I value his esteem in the highest degree: I wish him to know such good qualities as I have; but with all my faults and defects, I never did, nor ever will, impose myself on him or anybody for merits of any kind that I do not possess. Hypocrisy and vanity aggravate every fault, and depreciate every sort of desert. It is a knave that pretends, or a fool that believes, that he has more virtue or sense than he enjoys.

To Lady Ossory, Tuesday 9 June 1778

Now first printed.

Strawberry Hill, June 9, 1778.

GRATITUDE, I know, is the flower of virtue; but as virtue is like the aloe, a morose plant that defends itself on all sides and does not trouble its head about being pleasing to the eye, touch or taste of others, it does not blossom above once in a century; and yet when its seeds fall on good ground, it produces flowers even out of season. I do not know, Madam, whether you will guess the meaning of this fine figure; but its intention was, if I could have expressed it neatly, to reprove your Ladyship for talking of your gratitude, when I am the person obliged. My wishes, it is true are good, but have I power or talents to confer favours? I accepted an opportunity of doing a good office—but should not I have been a brute to have declined it? You allow me often to wait on you, and to be of a society with the most agreeable people in England—don't I do you a great honour? When an old man is tolerated by those much younger and of much better parts, they are either very good-natured, or very complaisant to his protectress; and he must be blind in either case not to be sensible of his obligation to her. Your Ladyship was always partial to me, and now are charitable, for you not only harbour me still, but would persuade me that my company can be any addition to your circle. I know myself too well to be flattered, though I feel the kindness that dictates the compliment. When I was young, I had rather spirits than parts, but I do not perceive the latter, now the former are evaporated. However as these are subsided, not sunk nor chagrined, I regret nothing I lose by silent degrees, and slide into decline very agreeably, and without pretensions or affectation, while you are so good as not to let me feel any decrease of your friendship. This is the sum total of the account between us, Madam; and if you find me the creditor, you are as bad an arithmetician as a bursar of a college I remember at Cambridge a thousand years ago, who cast up the date of the year at the head of his account, and brought himself in debtor to the society 1738 pounds.

I am not sorry that amidst your bounty in transferring debts to yourself, you have blended a charge of which I am innocent. I do not guess why you think I wished to hinder your seeing the funeral,[1] unless that I was to have inquired of Lord Hertford, and did not? But your Ladyship forgets that the very last thing we agreed on, was, that Lord Hertford could tell nothing more than everybody else, and that therefore it would be needless for me to send to him.[2] Indeed this was your decision, and as I remember it, I should not have forgotten the contrary. What reason upon earth could I have for wishing you not to go? I was very averse to your going to the lying in state,[3] as I am sure it was a mob very unfit for you.[4] Was *that* severity?— but not *right* for you to attend the funeral! In what

1. Of Lord Chatham. He died 11 May; the funeral was held 9 June in Westminster Abbey.

2. As Lord Chamberlain, Hertford would naturally know the plans for the funeral, and the Corporation of London addressed their requests concerning the funeral to him (*London Chronicle* 6–9 June, xliii. 546). Public notice was given on 6 June that 'The nobility, clergy, and gentry who propose to attend the funeral . . . are requested to send their names, titles, or other descriptions to the College of Arms on St Benet's Hill, St Pauls, before four o'clock on Monday next the 8th instant' in order to get their tickets

and to be ranked for the procession from the Painted Chamber to Westminster Abbey (ibid. 4–6 June, xliii. 543).

3. Chatham's body lay in state 7–8 June in the Painted Chamber in the Old Palace Yard, Westminster. The Jerusalem Chamber in Westminster Abbey, first announced as the place for the lying in state, had been found too small to accommodate the crowds that were expected (ibid. 14 May – 9 June, xliii. *passim*).

4. 'The concourse of visitants . . . was incredibly great . . . uncommon crowds of people of all ranks . . . came to take their last view of that political saviour of their country' (ibid. xliii. 546, 550).

light? What absurd idea was it possible for me to have? If you had any curiosity to see a trumpery procession in black cloaks, why should not you? I can turn it in no shape so as to draw an idea of impropriety from it. Your Ladyship does not *affiche* any sentimental melancholy; you was no relation of Lord Chatham; you had not, like several on both sides, emptied jordans on his living head, and strowed his grave with flowers and gold dust.[5] Or do you think I do not hold that you would grace and adorn any solemnity? Do not I always combat your being a recluse?—In short, you are perfectly wrongheaded, and I am glad of it with all my soul. *I* was in a passion last week, *you* was preposterous when you wrote your letter. One is more on a level with folks that *déraisonnent* now and then. You have got into such a train of being perfectly in the right in every action and thought, that you suspect your friends for monitors, when *you* are too *severe,* not they. You know it is my firm opinion that youth may play the devil if it pleases, because everything becomes it; but that when one advances, one should do nothing but what is right and reasonable—but upon my word it never came into my head that one might not go to a funeral. I was not a chicken when I went to the late King's,[6] and should I live to have the misfortune of being witness to such another national calamity, I do not know but I might indulge my grief a second time. Pray, Madam, let me have the honour of attending you thither: my *severity* longs to clear itself.

I will certainly come and make my peace at Ampthill, before you take the field.[7] I would make a Bedfordshire uniform, though I do not think I should look well in it, rather than not show my zeal for the Colonel and Coloneless[8]—but here have I written near four pages

---

5. HW notes in *Last Journals* ii. 173 that Col. Barré, who moved in the House of Commons that Chatham be buried at public expense, 'had first been known by his outrageous attack on Lord Chatham.' 'Lord North . . . gave his hearty consent [to the bill], and would have troubled the House longer, had he had more preparation, and was not so out of breath' (ibid. 174). Cf. ibid. ii. 186; HW to Mann 7 July 1778.

6. For HW's description of George II's funeral, 11 Nov. 1760, see Montagu i. 321–3.

7. With the Bedfordshire militia at its summer encampment. The regiment marched into Winchester 16 June on its 'way to Southhampton, to embark for the Isle of Wight' for the encampment (*London Chronicle* 20–23 June, xliii. 598).

8. HW probably alludes to a new fashion: 'The ladies who attend the military reviews now all dress *en militaire;* the wives of the officers dress in the uniform of the regiment, as did the Duchess of Devonshire and Lady Geo. Sutton some time since at the review of the militia for the counties of Derby and Nottingham' (ibid. 23–26 May, xliii. 498). 'A morning paper says his Majesty has signified to several of the noblemen, commanders in the different regiments of

about nothing! I dined in town today, found your letter when I came to take my chaise in Arlington Street, and brought it with me to answer. I must rise with the lark to receive Lady Spencer at breakfast, but as the Duchess of Devonshire is to come with her, I suppose they will not arrive till moonlight, and then they will think it is the painted glass that makes the house gloomy. I don't care; your picture is in its place again, and I can bear any other vexation.

PS. I recollect how near dying I was at your not walking at the Coronation;⁹ then is it possible I should ever wish not to have you seen?

To Lady Ossory, Tuesday 23 June 1778

Now first printed.
Address: To the Countess of Ossory at Ampthill Park, Bedfordshire. *Postmark:* ISLEWORTH. 23 IV.

June 23, 1778.

DON'T be alarmed at my large paper, Madam: I shall not let my pen take its swing; and as I had none of my smaller size, I only give my pen this vast sheet, and make it promise, as you good parents do when you let a child have a second apple, not to eat it till tomorrow. My reason for writing now is, that I am in a fright lest I may have missed one of your letters. The postman *says* he dropped the bag on Saturday night. In short, we had neither letters nor newspapers on Sunday morning. Some think the mail was taken by an American privateer on Turnham Green; others, that Mr Sayer¹ has been dabbling in a new plot to carry off their Majesties at the foot of Kew Bridge, and that the mail was stopped by authority—Time will show.

militia, his dislike of the appearance of ladies in their several encampments, while military operations were going forward' (ibid. 25–27 June, xliii. 610).

9. 22 Sept. 1761, when she and the Duke of Grafton were at Geneva. HW wrote to Mann 28 Sept. 1761 (MANN v. 537): 'I believe I liked the Coronation the less for wanting the principal figure.' Cf. *ante* 12 Sept. 1761.

1. Stephen Sayre (1736–1818), banker and former sheriff of London; arrested and lodged in the Tower 23 Oct. 1775 on a charge of high treason: plotting to seize the King and overthrow the government; soon released for lack of evidence. Sayre later brought a successful suit against Lord Rochford for false arrest. HW never took the charge seriously (DAB; MASON i. 227, 229, 246).

I doubt I shall not be able to reach Ampthill before your campaign opens. My Royalties are come to the Pavilions[2] for a fortnight, and then remove to Kingsgate. As I am a sad courtier, I doubt it would look ill if I went away at this moment; I think your Ladyship named the beginning of July for your march. Pray tell me—and pray, this hot weather don't walk at the head of your regiment. Boadicia, I know, did not mind being tanned, and Lady Mary[3] would rejoice to add freckles to freckles for her King and country, but as your picture has been made more like you, I entreat that you will remain like your picture, as you value

Your devoted

HW.

To Lady Ossory, Saturday 27 June 1778

Now first printed.
Address: To the Countess of Ossory at Ampthill Park, Bedfordshire. *Postmark:* ISLEWORTH. 27 IV.

Strawberry Hill, June 27, 1778.

I AM exceedingly concerned, Madam, at the account you give me of poor Lady Holland. Lord Digby called here the day before yesterday and told me he feared she was very ill. Though I interest myself so very much for your Ladyship and Lord Ossory, I am sincerely grieved too for Lady Holland herself, of whom I never heard a fault, and who has all the sense that makes virtue meritorious. I shall go to the Pavilions this evening, and shall then know when I shall be at liberty to wait on you. It is very flattering to say I can give you any comfort. I can give you none but that of knowing how much I feel for you.

Lord and Lady Hertford made me a visit yesterday evening, and

2. 'At the extremity of the gardens [of Hampton Court Palace], opposite Thames Ditton, is the lodge belonging to the Duke of Gloucester, as Ranger of Hampton Court Park. It is called the Pavillion [*sic*], and is a neat little structure' (*Uni-* *versal British Directory*, 1791–[1798], iii. 499). See also Ernest Law, *History of Hampton Court Palace*, 1885, vi. 313–14, 487–8.

3. Coke.

confirmed the account I had received from Madame du Deffand[1] in the morning of the engagement between two of Keppel's[2] frigates and three of the French.[3] The latter fired first[4]—but what matters which? Lord H. thinks the war now determined by them, and I need not say, has most gloomy apprehensions. *We* that have been in the right, shall not have much more cause to exult—I have not time to say a word more—nor could you attend to it. Real grief cannot be amused; the fictitious is amused with its own parade.

PS. Mr Almack has wrote to me on Lord O[rford]'s debt,[5] who, I think, has been very formal.

To Lady Ossory, Tuesday 7 July 1778

Now first printed.
Address: To the Countess of Ossory at Ampthill Park, Bedfordshire. *Postmark:* 7 IY. EK.

Strawberry Hill, July 7, 1778.

I HAVE not written for some days, Madam, from total uncertainty about your Ladyship's situation and my own: I mean the former with regard to Lady Holland. General Conway was here the night

1. Her letter of 21 June 1778 (DU DEF-FAND v. 51–2) quoted a report of a five-hour battle between two frigates, *La Belle Poule* and the *Arethusa*. According to this report, the English frigate 'a été fort maltraitée,' and the French captain was 'très content de son équipage.'

2. Augustus Keppel (1725–86), cr. (1782) Vct Keppel; Admiral of the Blue 29 Jan. 1778; commander-in-chief of the grand fleet, 22 March 1778 – 18 March 1779; M.P.; lord of the Admiralty.

3. According to Keppel's three dispatches to the Admiralty 18 and 20 June, from aboard the *Victory*, at sea (*London Gazette* No. 11886, 23–27 June), the English fleet on 17 June sighted 'two ships seemingly reconnoitering the fleet, with two tenders accompanying them.' The British gave chase, and the frigate *Licorne*, and a 'schooner' (the 'lougre, le *Coureur*,' *Mercure historique*, 1778, clxxxv. 146) were captured; the other frigate, *La Belle*

Poule, was towed to safety at Brest. On the 19th another French frigate, the *Pallas*, of 32 guns, was captured. See also *Last Journals* ii. 186–8.

4. The garbled account in the *London Chronicle* 25–27 June, xliii. 614, is headed 'HOSTILITIES *commenced by* FRANCE.' It appears from Keppel's dispatches that both the *Licorne* and *La Belle Poule* fired broadsides after the British had fired across their bow: the commanders of both French ships were requested to go to Admiral Keppel, 'who wished to speak' with them (*London Gazette*, loc. cit.). The French considered that the British had 'fired first'; they 'lay the aggression entirely at our door,' and charged that the English fired the first broadside (ibid.). A correspondent discusses these contra-dictory claims in the *London Chronicle* 14–16 July, xliv. 53.

5. Presumably a gambling debt at Almack's; the letter is missing. Lord

before last from town, and told me there were more hopes of her. I most fervently hope there are, and that they will increase fast.

My own motions float every day—and well they may at such a solemn moment. The Duke has at last been so good as to let himself be persuaded not to risk the Duchess and his children on the sea-shore,[1] whence even a smuggling vessel under American colours might carry them off.[2] As I have joined my entreaties, I cannot decently leave them myself. Indeed and to confess the truth, I think every hour so important that I can take no resolution of absenting myself. Every considerate person thinks our very being as a nation at stake; and they who look most earnestly for grounds of confidence find no wisdom to rest it on. In short, the alarm is not in proportion to the danger. Early fear is sage; its superfœtation subsides; and a degree of despair hardens into firmness. Insensibility cannot be prepared for action; and surprise, where indifference is not founded on courage but levity, becomes a panic—Such has been the case of all great countries that have been lost in a moment. Superior Providence has been better to us than our own: the West Indian and Mediterranean fleets are arrived. They prevent bankruptcy and give us sailors[3]—but is not it offensive that we must labour for those very ministers that have brought us to this pitch of ruin? and who yet will call themselves politicians, if they are not torn to pieces. Yes, we must. I have none of that Jewish perverseness to be squabbling with the Pharisees, when the Romans are at the gates. I am not angry

Orford, however, had suffered an attack of insanity April 1777 – March 1778, and after his recovery apparently remained in Norfolk until he came into waiting on 29 July as lord of the Bedchamber to George III, 'his Lordship being recovered from his long illness' (ibid. 28–30 July, xliv. 103).

———

1. At Kingsgate, in Kent (*ante* 23 June 1778). The Duke of Gloucester visited the encampment at Coxheath on Sunday, 12 July, and reviewed the troops there the following day (*London Chronicle* 11–16 July, xliv. 48, 51).

2. John Paul Jones's attempts in April to burn the shipping at Whitehaven and to kidnap the Earl of Selkirk are largely responsible for HW's fears (ibid. 25–30 April, xliii. 406, 410, 414; *Last Journals*

ii. 169–70). Illustrative of the general fear of American and French privateers is the account from Hull of a ship thought to be a French privateer; after causing great alarm it was found to be a ferryboat unable to make its way against wind and tide (*London Chronicle* 17–19 Nov., xliv. 488).

3. Under 6 July HW wrote (*Last Journals* ii. 189): 'The West India and Jamaica fleets arrived. It was very astonishing that France had not endeavoured to intercept them; not only for the great blow it would have been to our trade, but as out of them the Government got 1300 sailors to man more men-of-war.' The ships expected from the East Indies arrived in early August (ibid. ii. 195–6; *London Chronicle* 6–8 Aug., xliv. 134).

at the French whom we have tempted, forced to undo us—but I forget domestic enemies when I have foreign. *That* is the difference between patriotism and faction. No Briton is my foe, if a French marshal lands on either island. From Broglio I would protect Lord Mansfield or Lord George Germain; to me

> Alike or where they shone or where they shine,
> Or on the *Rubicon*, or on the *Rhine*.[4]

These are my politics, Madam, and I am sure are Lord Ossory's.[5] Our country will revive again—perhaps know its true friends. Whether it does or not, we must deserve it should—but it will. I have always indulged myself in half superstition; that is, encouraged myself to believe in good omens, *never* in bad. The arrival of the two fleets of merchantmen I accept as a happy augury of our affairs mending. We shall have a naval victory or a peace. *We shall.* Your Ladyship is tied to allow me the gift of prophecy. *You have been among the prophets.* Your prediction last year of Philadelphia is verified; it is evacuated.[6] I look on you as Deborah, and depend on your delivering Jabin King of Canaan into our hand.[7] Tell me, Madam, when you shall go down from Mount Tabor,[8] and pray send me good news of dear Lady Holland.

---

4. Pope, *Essay on Man*, iv. 245-6 ('Alike or when or where, they shone or shine . . .').

5. Cf. HW to Mason 18 July 1778, MASON i. 416.

6. 'By a letter in town from Philadelphia, dated June the 5th . . . [it is reported that the evacuation] . . . was fixed for the 12th of June' (*London Chronicle* 2–7 July, xliv. 14, 19). In his dispatch of 5 July Sir Henry Clinton reported that, 'pursuant to his Majesty's instructions, I evacuated Philadelphia on the 18th of June, at three o'clock in the morning' (*London Gazette Extraordinary* 24 Aug.).

7. It was not Jabin but Sisera, the captain of Jabin's army, of whom the Lord had said 'I will deliver him into thine hand' (Judges 4. 7, 14).

8. In Palestine, whence Deborah with Barak and his army descended to conquer the Canaanite oppressors.

To Lady Ossory, Sunday 12 July 1778

Now first printed, except for part of the first paragraph which appeared in W. S. Lewis, *Horace Walpole*, 1961, p. 41.
Address: To the Countess of Ossory at Ampthill Park, Bedfordshire. *Postmark:* ISLEWORTH. 13 IY.

Strawberry Hill, July 12, 1778.

I WAS in my chaise yesterday morning going to see Osterley Park with a party of my neighbours,[1] when I met the postman and opened your Ladyship's letter first. It more than damped all my entertainment—I was not prepared for so dreadful an account of poor Lady Holland, nor had heard a word of it! As I have been conversant so much in scenes of the like shocking kind, it made me feel double for her brothers and sisters[2] and your Ladyship. I certainly wish her total recovery—or should not know what to wish. It is one of those solemn moments, in which nothing is left to us but resignation and silence. What vicissitudes for Mr Fitzpatrick![3] what variety of trials for his good-nature and his firmness! Life seems to me as if we were dancing on a sunny plain on the edge of a gloomy forest, where we pass in a moment from glare to gloom and darkness—but reflections are endless. I know not what comfort to give you, Madam. There is none for real grief, but the two that were providentially given to us in spite of ourselves, Hope and Time.

With such unavoidable woes, how provoking it is, when the folly of a few can squander the happiness that millions enjoy! I sit here waiting to see whether this summer is to bring desolation, or we are to consume in detail. The politics of the Court I do not comprehend. They have brought us to a pass that we must accept a humiliating treaty,[4] *now,* or submit to what shall be imposed when we are in a

---

1. Among them was the Rev. Norton Nicholls (ca 1742–1809), Gray's correspondent, who was probably visiting his uncle, William Turner, at Richmond (HW to Mason 16 July 1778, Mason i. 413–14). The others have not been identified.

2. Lady Louisa Fitzpatrick and the

three Vernons, Lady Holland's half-sisters.

3. Richard Fitzpatrick had returned from America about 1 June, to find his sister very ill (*London Chronicle* 2–4 June, xliii. 536; Jesse, *Selwyn* iii. 286–7; *Last Journals* ii. 185).

4. With the American colonies. The three commissioners to act with the Howes

much worse condition. It is not possible that we should gain anything by a war with France. Yet the ministers seem to be more afraid
of recanting their language with France, than with America—and
yet every hour increases their danger. Had the West India fleet been
taken, the storm had begun here. I am told there had been a secret
council of the merchants, in which they had determined to go to
the King, and demand the sacrifice of Lord Sandwich. Every blow
will heighten the discontents, and the sufferers will not be afraid
of a government, that has everything else to apprehend. There is
another mischief in their half-measures: many are lulled asleep. They
neither make peace with France nor rouse the country against it—
I will not prophesy any more for them, if they do not merit my patronage.

I am not at all sorry that Mr Selwyn is discontent. I should be
much concerned if he were.[5] I love him too well not to wish that his
intoxication may evaporate.[6]

Should there be any amendment at Old Windsor,[7] I am sure your
Ladyship will be kind enough to let me share in your joy. If not, I
shall be glad of your removing to camp.[8] You would not easily prevail
on Lord Ossory to amuse himself by anything but his duty, but it
is very graceful to waive private for public feelings. I do not admire
those who can ruin a nation and joke, which is very silly. One should
be a very great man, before one can afford to be a very little one.

To Lady Ossory, Wednesday 22 July 1778

Now first printed.
Address: To the Countess of Ossory at Ampthill Park, Bedfordshire. *Postmark:*
23 IY.

Arlington Street, July 22, 1778, late at night.

IN the present suspense of public and private[1] calamity, Madam,
I have not known what to write. I am sure you do not suspect me
of not thinking of your melancholy position; and I am as sure that

(Sir William Howe was replaced by Gen.
Clinton) in conciliating the colonies had
sailed in April (ibid. ii. 168).

5. Word evidently missing; read 'were
not' or 'were content.'

6. Selwyn was at Milan making arrangements to bring Maria Fagnani to England

(Jesse, *Selwyn* iii. 286, 294, 313, 321).

7. Where Lady Holland was living
(*Leinster Corr.* ii. 234).

8. The camp of the Bedfordshire militia
on the Isle of Wight (*ante* 9 June 1778).

1. The illness of Lady Holland.

you would have communicated your satisfaction.to me, had you any yourself.

I came to town today, and find no reason for believing that France has declared war.[2] What was mistaken for a declaration seems to have been the reading the *ordonnance* about prizes.[3] For these last five or six days everybody has been expecting news of an engagement between Admiral Keppel and the Brest fleet[4]—a solemn moment indeed! As an Englishman or as a man, what must one feel!—it is not necessary to have the additional horror of those who have brought on such a crisis! I find today that it is rather the opinion that the French are retired into port.[5] Should it be so, I shall not comprehend the reasoning, if we are not industrious to endeavour peace. What could victory give us but a weakened navy? Is the crown of England to be gamed for like the thirteen provinces, and at great disadvantage?

The vision of pacification with America is vanished like all our other drunken dreams. Yesterday came advice of the commissioners[6] being arrived at Philadelphia,[7] of having notified their commission

2. Someone had told HW on Saturday evening, 18 July, that France had declared war, and the *Public Advertiser* 20 July reported 'the French Court having made a declaration . . . in form against Great Britain on Tuesday last.' Neither France nor England made a formal declaration, but both nations considered themselves at war. Cf. HW to Mason 18 July 1778, Mason i. 414, 422.

3. Cf. *Last Journals* ii. 190, *sub* 19 July: 'The ministers received intelligence of war having been declared by France; but it was a mistake, occasioned by the *ordonnance* for privateers being read in some seaport towns.' The *London Chronicle* 18–21 July, xliv. 70 prints a report from Boulogne 'that an order hath been issued for privateers to put to sea immediately. This order hath been read on the Exchange, by the Commissary of the Marine. . . . The orders are signed by M. de Sartine, and they are addressed to the commandant of Boulogne.' The *ordonnance* of 24 June, registered 14 July, is in the *Mercure historique*, 1778, clxxxv. 148–75.

4. The Brest squadron, commanded by Comte d'Orvilliers, had sailed 8 July

(*Sandwich Papers* ii. 10). The engagement between the two fleets occurred 27 July; see *post* 4 Aug. 1778.

5. A letter from Paris, 20 July, in the *London Chronicle* 21–23 July, xliv. 80, reported the Brest fleet on 9 July off Ushant, where the engagement of 27 July took place.

6. Five commissioners had been appointed to treat with the American colonies: Lord Carlisle, chairman; Lord Howe; Sir William Howe; William Eden (1744–1814), cr. (1789) Bn Auckland, M.P.; and George Johnstone (1730–87) naval officer, M.P. at this time for Appleby. Lord Carlisle, Eden, and Johnstone had sailed from Portsmouth to join the Howes, who since 1776 had been joint commissioners to America. Sir Henry Clinton succeeded Sir William Howe as commissioner (*London Chronicle* 11–13 Aug., xliv. 151–2; *Annual Register*, 1778, xxi. [323–8]; B. F. Stevens, *Facsimiles of Manuscripts in European Archives Relating to America*, 1889–98, xi. No. 1075, xxiv. No. 2101).

7. 6 June (Carlisle to George Selwyn 10 June 1778, in Jesse, *Selwyn* iii. 280; Stevens, op. cit. xi. No. 1109).

to the Congress—and of having received not a syllable in reply.[8] Lord
Howe, too, I hear, has refused to act as commissioner[9]—when shall
we think we have received *dementis* enough? We have not Christian
cheeks enough to turn to all those that slap us.

London is the most desolate place I ever saw. Its few inhabitants
talk of an inundation last Monday, that drowned all their kitchens.[10]
The weather however still keeps up its spirits like a good Englishman. I own I have enjoyed this jubilee summer.[11] However as I
came, I remarked symptoms of our poverty. I seldom ever was a fortnight absent, but I found some new building on the road. Today,
though I have been five weeks absent,[12] I could not discover a soupçon of brick and mortar, not a skeleton of a new bow-window. Opulence is no more! Want of money is in everybody's mouth,[13] and
indeed in everybody's hands, for with all the recruiting and pressing
and camping, there are robberies every evening. My neighbour

8. 'The day before yesterday [21 July]
dispatches arrived from the Commissioners, in twenty-five days from Philadelphia. Before these were sent off, they
had been ten days in that city; but,
though they had sent a message to the
Congress immediately on their arrival,
there was then no answer received' (*London Chronicle* 21–23 July 1778, xliv. 78).
The letter of the Commissioners, dated 9
June, was first read in Congress 13 June,
and on 17 June the reply to be sent was
approved by Congress. The 'idea of dependence,' on which the letter, commission, etc., was based the Congress found
'utterly inadmissible' (Stevens, op. cit. xi.
Nos 1104, 1110; *Journals of Congress*,
Philadelphia, 1777–88, iv. 347–53).

9. See MASON i. 421 n. 10. Lord Howe's
letter of 7 June to the commissioners,
declining to serve (Stevens, op. cit. xi.
No. 1099), reached London 21 July. He
and his brother Sir William, while still
commissioners under a previous patent
of 6 May 1776, had both applied for relief
from their commands, and Sir William
had arrived 2 July in London (*Daily
Advertiser* 3 July). Lord Howe turned
over his command to Admiral Gambier
12 Sept. and sailed for England late in
September (ibid. 14 Aug.; *Carlisle MSS* 367,
387; *London Chronicle* 24–27 Oct., xliv.
406).

10. 'A terrible storm of thunder, lightning, and rain did a great deal of damage
in London and its neighbourhood' (GM
1778, xlviii. 331). Details of the damage
are given in the *Annual Register*, 1778,
xxi. [192]; *London Magazine*, 1778, xlvii.
332–3. The kitchens, being usually in
the basements, would be the first to be
flooded.

11. That is, a summer the like of which
came once in fifty years. 'The hot weather
has much exceeded our usual summers'
(*London Chronicle* 4–6 Aug., xliv. 125,
where high temperatures during the summer are recorded; GM 1779, xlix. 274). 'In
many parts of Hertford, Bedford, Cambridge, Berks, and Buckinghamshire, the
harvest is already begun; a circumstance
not known in this kingdom so early for
fifty years before' (*London Chronicle* 21–
23 July, xliv. 79). Cf. ibid. 14–16 July,
xliv. 51.

12. HW was in London 'for a moment'
on 19 June (HW to Mann 16 June).

13. The great increase in the number
of bankruptcies from 1740 to 1777 is
shown in a table in the *London Chronicle*
5–7 Nov. 1778, xliv. 446: 'our *Gazettes*
teemed with bankruptcies, generally doubling and trebling in number whatever
had been usually known,' but at the same
time fortunes were being made (*Annual
Register*, 1778, xxi. 36).

Judge Perrin[14] was robbed two nights ago at his own door. His Worship's own son[15] went off last week for debt.[16] We are a virtuous, civilized, sober people! and must be the admiration of all Europe. Our gallantry in truth is not that of the ages of chivalry. Instead of defending oppressed damsels, our newspapers teem with nothing but abuse on all the handsome women in England, who, if you believe those daily biographers, are errant street-walkers. These scandalous chronicles are our diurnal amusement in the midst of a civil war, and at the eve of a war with France—and the principal historian is a divine, and the pensioner of a pious Court![17] Four days ago a person I know sent to the Lord High Admiral's[18] to ask if there was any account of the fleet. The answer, in writing, was, 'Lord S. says there is nothing new; catches[19] are going round.' This will sound but silly, when we are quite undone. I conclude Dr Franklin told the French how childish we were, and was not believed. I figure him reading our papers at Versailles, and saying. 'You thought I ex-

14. Sir Richard Perryn (1723–1803), Kt, 1776; sergeant-at-law, 1776; baron of the Exchequer 1776–99. His 'small house' was on the London Road, near the outskirts of Twickenham (Edward Ironside, *History and Antiquities of Twickenham*, 1797, p. 106, in *Bibliotheca Topographica Britannica*, Vol. X; R. S. Cobbett, *Memorials of Twickenham*, 1872, pp. 363–5).

15. Perryn certainly had four and probably five sons. Three of them (the first, third and fourth) are identified in *Old Westminsters:* 1) Richard Perryn (ca 1754–1825), of Christ Church, Oxon (B.A., 1776, M.A., 1779); rector of Standish, Lancs, 1779–1825; 3) John Perryn (ca 1758–1805), army officer (his monument, according to Cobbett, op. cit., 97, calls him third son); 4) James Perryn (ca 1760–96), also in the army. The unidentified Perryn who was at Westminster School 1767–9, and the Perryn who was there ca 1773–5 are probably the second and fifth sons.

16. Inasmuch as a creditor could get a life sentence for a debtor if the debt was over 40s., absconding for debt was common. Cf. A. S. Turberville (ed.), *Johnson's England*, Oxford, 1933, i. 324–6.

17. Rev. Henry Bate (from 1781, Dudley), editor of the *Morning Post*. 'Some years ago Mr Garrick agreed with Mr Bate that for a pension and hopes of prefer-

ment, he should keep a newspaper open for all writings in favour of Government . . . To do Mr Bate justice, he was a very constant, diligent, zealous and able, though perhaps too warm a writer on the part of Government' (North's memorandum to the King, 1782, in *Corr. Geo. III* v. 471). The pension of £200 a year ended when Bate left the *Morning Post* in 1780, and in 1781 Lord North paid him £3250 from secret service money 'in extinction of all his claims on the head of pensions or preferment.' The King refused to reimburse North for the £3250 paid 'to that worthless man Mr Bates' 'an article that never was stated to me, and therefore for which I cannot stand indebted' (ibid. vi. 7), and North became personally responsible for the £3250.

18. Lord Sandwich's.

19. 'The chief promoter of the Catch Club was the well known John Montagu Earl of Sandwich' is HW's MS note in his copy (now WSL) of Sir John Hawkins, *A General History of the Science and Practice of Music*, 1776, v. 420; the note is on the following passage: 'In . . . 1762 a society for the improvement of vocal harmony was established by a great number of the nobility and gentlemen, met for that purpose at the Thatched House Tavern in St James's Street, Westminster.'

aggerated, and now you see all I told you, was exactly true. You *would* take the English for a grave nation; they are the foolishest people upon earth'—but I will not repeat half he must say—

To Lady Ossory, Tuesday 4 August 1778

Now first printed.
Address: To the Countess of Ossory at Ampthill Park, Bedfordshire. *Postmark:* ISLEWORTH. 4 AV.

Strawberry Hill, Aug. 4, 1778.

I WAS engaged to dine in town yesterday, and was not sorry, as it gave me opportunity of inquiring more about our sea-battle,[1] which had been swelled into a naval triumph.[2] I found extreme disappointment the fashion. For my own part I love the French so little, and value the lives of men, nay, of ships, so much, that I am contented with the former running away, and the others being saved;[3] for I think the French showed spirit and abilities enough to prove that a great victory would have been dearly purchased.[4] As we have somewhat more to fight for than fame, security is the first object. The Admiral is returned to Plymouth.[5] I hear the French have dispatched six ships to intercept our Indiamen, and that Keppel has sent five after them.[6] Byron's[7] fleet has suffered considerably by

1. On 27 July the English fleet, commanded by Keppel, and the French by d'Orvilliers, each fleet consisting of thirty ships, met in an indecisive engagement west of Ushant. Cf. MASON i. 415, 425 nn. 1–3.

2. See HW to Mann 4 Aug. 1778; *Last Journals* ii. 195. The French also claimed the victory (*London Chronicle* 20–22 Aug., xliv. 184).

3. In the night following the battle, 'the whole French fleet went off, and got into Brest . . . It was evident the French had orders not to risk a battle' (*Last Journals* ii. 195). Cf. MASON i. 425 nn.

4. Official reports showed 133 English killed and 373 wounded; 150 French killed and about 600 wounded (*London Chronicle* 1–4, 20–22 Aug., xliv. 113, 184).

5. 'Yesterday morning advice was received express at the Admiralty Office

from Admiral Keppel, with an account of the safe arrival of all his fleet off Plymouth the 31st of July, and would proceed immediately for Portsmouth' (ibid. 1–4 Aug., xliv. 118).

6. 'It is said the Brest fleet detached two sail of the line and six frigates to the westward in search of our homeward-bound fleets, and that five sail of the line from Keppel's were sailed to prevent their design upon them' (ibid. 4–6 Aug., xliv. 123). In *Last Journals* ii. 196 HW uses the figures of six French and five English ships.

7. John Byron (1723–86), vice-admiral, 29 Jan. 1778, the grandfather of the poet, had sailed from Plymouth 9 June with a squadron designed to intercept the Toulon fleet under d'Estaing, which had sailed 13 April for North America. Byron and Admiral Parker left Plymouth 'with 13 sail

a storm.[8] The Canadians have sent to desire union with the Congress.[9] Every event is a counterpart to 1759![10]

I don't know whether your Ladyship has yet left Ampthill; I think you would have told me to change my direction.

May not I please myself with what I have heard of your father's[11] kindness to your daughter? It must be a sweet consolation to you, Madam, in the midst of your other distress.[12]

It is an anxious moment with me too, but the prospect is more favourable. The Duke of Gloucester has been reduced to ask permission to make the campaign with the King of Prussia,[13] but it is thought the Emperor has begged peace.[14] I am rejoiced in a public light too that one of the partitioners of Poland is scourged by another. The *bon homme* King Poltis[15] had none of those mortifications.

of the line . . . to be joined by some more from St Helen's' (*London Chronicle* 11–13 June, xliii. 566).

8. 'The whole of his fleet have suffered inconceivably by storms. Many of the ships have been dismasted; others have lost their rudders. The Admiral himself, and five of his ships, had not been heard of for several days when the last advices left America' (ibid. 1–4 Aug., xliv. 114, 118). See also *post* 7 Aug. 1778.

9. This was a false rumour which HW included in *Last Journals* ii. 195, *sub* 1 Aug. 1778: 'It was . . . said that the Canadians had sent a deputation to the Congress to propose union.' A report that 'a revolt had taken place in Canada' appeared shortly after this date and was denied (*London Chronicle* 13–18 Aug., xliv. 158, 163).

10. When France and England were fighting in Europe and in North America.

11. Lord Ravensworth's.

12. The illness of Lady Holland.

13. The Duke of Gloucester, who was a General in the army and Colonel of the 1st Foot Guards, had been informed that the King 'had no occasion for his service.' On 25 July the Duke had asked for and had received permission from the King 'to go as a volunteer to the King of Prussia' (*Last Journals* ii. 191–2), but Frederick II was displeased, for reasons given in his letter to Comte Finckenstein,

8 Aug. (Frederick II, *Politische Correspondenz*, 1879–1939, xli. 324–5). Rumours concerning the Duke's going into Prussian service and George III's declining the Duke's services are in the *London Chronicle* 28–30 July, 4–6 Aug., xliv. 102, 126. Cf. *post* 6 Sept. 1778.

14. On 18 July, according to a report from Berlin, 20 July, the Emperor sent a flag of truce with the message that he 'was from a sense of humanity led to spare the lives and blood of his innocent subjects and was ready to settle the Bavarian affairs upon the principles proposed by his Prussian Majesty, in the course of the late negotiation'; he was ready to begin 'a fresh negotiation' (*London Chronicle* 30 July – 1 Aug., xliv. 112; *Last Journals* ii. 192). It was not Joseph II but Maria Theresa who, unknown to her son, had 'begged peace.' See her letter of 12 July and her '*propositions*' to Frederick II in his *Politische Correspondenz*, xli. 265. The negotiations terminated 3 July with the Prussian declaration of war against Austria (ibid. xl. 313, *passim*; xli. 1–241).

15. 'Poltis, that gen'rous King of Thrace,' hearing of the war between the Greeks and the Trojans because 'Paris took Atrides' wife,' said:

'With ease I could compose this strife . . .
Now I have two right honest wives,
For whose possession no man strives:

Having nothing else to say, but what would branch out of these topics, and fearing you do not even wish for amusement, I will send away a short letter rather than disturb you, Madam. I need not add how much I am

Your Ladyship's devoted

HW.

To LADY OSSORY, Friday 7 August 1778

Now first printed.

Strawberry Hill, Aug. 7, 1778.

I AM very glad, Madam, that I anticipated your telling me, and showed my joy on Lady Georgina's good fortune before I heard it from your Ladyship. I renew my congratulations most cordially on your glimpse of Lady Holland's recovery.[1] You have reason to expect it on any favourable appearance. Her disorder[2] was an accident, and not hereditary—then indeed the intervals are more terrifying than the fit! I hear rumours that make me think it will not be long before I have bad news from Norfolk.[3]

One to Atrides I will send;
And t'other to my Trojan friend. . . .
The wrath of gods and man shall cease;
And Poltis live and die in peace.'
—Matthew Prior, 'Alma,' ii. 91–120, in Prior, *Literary Works*, ed. Wright and Spears, Oxford, 1959, i. 487–8, with commentary at ii. 965, referring to Pope's note on the *Iliad* ix. 450; Pope's source was Plutarch.

1. Lady Ossory to Selwyn ('chez le Marquis Fagniani à Milan') 2 Aug. 1778: 'Poor Lady H. since her attack six weeks since has been in a constant state of *delirium* more or less, and her refusing to take proper food and medicines made her case almost hopeless; nor could anybody persuade her to either, but lately the disorder has taken a more favourable turn; and since a *new nurse* has attended her, she has been much more tractable, and Dr Elliot has now hopes in time she

may be restored to the situation she was in before this attack. You know what that was, and our opinions alas! agreed. I have been at Old Windsor within this fortnight, just saw Lady H. or rather her *spirit*, for no flash appeared. She knew me, and that was all—so rests this unhappy case. The poor children are well' (MS in possession of the Society of Antiquaries, London).

2. Her tuberculosis was accompanied by high fevers and delirium, alternating with intervals of apparent recovery: 'Her poor head is certainly affected by the delirium, for it seems they find the sight of her friends hurt her' (Lady Sarah Lennox to Lady Susan O'Brien 4 Aug. 1778, in Lady Sarah Lennox, *Life and Letters* i. 270; cf. ibid. i. 267).

3. HW had heard of Orford's strange activities in relation to the Norfolk militia, and probably of the plan to sell the pictures at Houghton to Catherine of

I fear the dispersion of Byron's fleet is but too true.[4] Déstain[5] is certainly safe in the harbour of Boston.[6] I believe I told your Ladyship in my last that I am content with Keppel's not having lost a single ship, and with the flight of the French. There is no law in the marine code, that forbids a fleet running away; and as folks are satisfied when an army runs, is it more honourable in a navy? I am very sorry there are suspicions of Spain;[7] I was quite easy on that head[8]—but I comprehend nothing; we have knelt to America[9]—That was the *comble* of humiliation—is it more disgraceful to fall prostrate to France?—I don't speak for myself—I should not have thrust myself into such a scrape; but when I had hectored and crouched, I should not haggle about a little more or less—nor do I believe the person would, who has been so condescending to Lord O[ssory] at

Russia (R. W. Ketton-Cremer, *A Norfolk Gallery*, 1948, pp. 183–4; HW to Mann 18 Dec. 1778).

4. Cf. *ante* 4 Aug. 1778, n. 8. The fleet, poorly equipped and manned, was dispersed by storms ca 4 July: some ships arrived at Sandy Hook beginning ca 30 July (just after d'Estaing had left), others (including Byron's) at Halifax and Newfoundland; and one was driven back to England. The fleet was not reassembled at Sandy Hook until 18 Sept., and did not put to sea to search for the enemy until 18 Oct. (DNB, *sub* Byron, John; *London Chronicle* 8 Aug.–8 Sept., xliv. 138–9, 146, 158, 234).

5. Jean-Baptiste-Charles d'Estaing (1729–94), Comte d'Estaing; Vice-Adm., 1777; in command of the Toulon fleet, which reached the Delaware 8 July. See John J. Meng, *D'Estaing's American Expedition 1778–1779*, New York, 1936.

6. A false report. An American ship arrived at Brest reported having met d'Estaing's fleet 12 June, 'exactly twenty leagues from Boston' (*London Chronicle* 14–16 July, xliv. 56), and a paragraph from Paris 10 July reported that D'Estaing had sent ahead two fast frigates to Boston 'to announce his speedy arrival there' (ibid. 18–21 July, xliv. 70). Instead of going to Boston, he arrived at the Delaware 8 July, appeared off Sandy Hook 11 July (bottling up Howe's fleet), sailed for Rhode Island 22 July, remained there until 22 Aug., when, having suffered by

a storm, he sailed for Boston to refit (Meng, op. cit. 4–6; *Annual Register*, 1778, xxi. 227*–36*).

7. 'There was reason to believe . . . [Spain] wished to acquire Florida, part of the Newfoundland fisheries, and Jamaica' (W. M. James, *The British Navy in Adversity*, 1926, p. 91). Recent rumours concerning ship movements, Spain's neutrality, or preparations for war are in the *London Chronicle* 4 July–6 Aug., xliv. *passim*. Actually Spain remained neutral until June 1779.

8. HW relied on reports of revolts in Mexico to keep Spain occupied (HW to Mann 31 May 1778) and the recent arrival of a new ambassador from Spain, together with the report from Mrs Anne Pitt, had assured him (*ante* 17 May 1778; *Last Journals* ii. 190), but 'I have heard enough to make me change my mind about Spain, who I believe will join in the *mêlée*, unless we are awed into peace' (HW to Mason 10 Aug. 1778, MASON i. 425).

9. By sending the five commissioners to America in accordance with Lord North's plan for conciliating the colonies. HW refers to 17 Feb. 1778, the day North 'opened his conciliatory plan,' as 'A day for ever memorable as one of the most ignominious in the English annals,' and analyzes the shame of the administration in reversing itself and stooping 'to beg peace of America *at any rate*' (*Last Journals* ii. 110, 115, 110–25).

W[inchester].[10] Was not Lord O. ashamed for him? There is nothing puts one so much out of countenance as people that ought to be so. Meanness in adversity after insolence in prosperity, is as natural, as for poplars to turn the black side of their leaves in a storm, which appear all white in fair weather. I am perfectly in a state of indifference from not knowing what to wish. We want incredible fortune, and yet we want calamity too to bring us to our senses. I love my country, I do not love France as a rival—but as I said long ago, I should love my country more, if it was not for my countrymen. We have gone out of our character; we were *les fiers anglais,* but we never were insolent till within these five or six years. The late Duchess d'Aiguillon said to me at Paris in 1766, 'You English have beat us everywhere; and yet I never heard one of ye brag.' We have bragged of late years—but indeed not *after* victory[11]—but let us talk no more of it—I cannot bear to think, still less to write on it.

It is most true that the Duke[12] was going to the King of Prussia, on finding it impossible to obtain any command at home. We flatter ourselves the journey will not take place, as it is believed that the Emperor has submitted—We may bend, when Cæsar[13] does, since he bends when we did.[14] Though I hate the King of Prussia, I am rejoiced at Cæsar's mortification—One could not hope both should be punished, and here is dramatic justice; the aggressor is chastised, and not, as generally happens, his people for him. I wished that the two first shots should carry off both their heads, and save the lives of so many thousand honester men. If the pacification does not ensue, I shall tremble in all lights for the Duke! I know a physician[15] who thinks it impossible that his R.H. should stand an autumnal campaign—yet he is determined to go, if the war reblazes. I need not describe the agony of the Duchess, but I must mention her regard for his honour. She has not attempted to dissuade him. She looks

10. The Bedfordshire militia, of which Lord Ossory was colonel, was encamped on Winchester Downs. See below, n. 29.

11. An allusion to the ministry's early estimates of American cowardice and ineffectiveness and to Gen. Burgoyne's bombastic manifestoes preceding his defeat at Saratoga. Cf. *ante* 8 Aug. 1777.

12. Of Gloucester.

13. 'The Emperor,' Joseph II.

14. That is, Joseph II, indifferent to law and equity while his power was superior, had occupied Bavaria but was forced to bend when Frederick II and Prince Henry of Brunswick intervened and occupied Bohemia. The British, HW suggests, likewise ignored American charters and rights until forced to bend when France signed the treaty of alliance with the colonies.

15. Probably Dr Richard Jebb.

at the children[16] and weeps, when he is not present. If he escapes this journey, I shall begin to think him immortal; and her, contrary to my expectation, born to be happy. Till all was settled, it was a profound secret. I had often this summer found her in tears, and was astonished, as so many things had happened in her favour, and the Duke's fondness seemed increased—but his R.H. had resolved not to be dissuaded. She had obeyed him, as she always does, so implicitly, that I had not the smallest suspicion, till he had written to the King of Prussia, on obtaining the King's permission.[17] As his struggle to leave the Duchess and his children must have been the worst part, he deserves as much honour as if he returned covered with glory. Men can be heroes on much cheaper terms.

There is nothing so true, Madam, as what you say, that no experience but one's own is worth a straw. I am sorry Mr S[elwyn] will obtain that brat.[18] When he could leave it a month sooner than he designed, the passion was waning.[19] I am persuaded the parents[20] saw it did—and that convinces me that their withholding it before, was to draw him to Milan. Their whole conduct appears to me so abominable and infamous, that I shall be heartily glad to see him again alive. When they could brand their own child, at least hers, in so foul a manner, there can be no sentiments; and where there are no sentiments and no law, what check is there? Ask the Emperor and the King of Prussia, not forgetting the Legislatress of Russia, their accomplice in Poland. If the Fagnanis were sovereigns, a manifesto would tell us that Mr S. died of an hemorrhoidal colic;[21]

16. Princess Sophia Matilda and Prince William Frederick.

17. The Duke read the letter to HW, 'and very sensible it was. He said that being desirous to serve his country, he knew he could learn the science of war nowhere so well as in his Majesty's army; and that as his brother had no objection, he asked leave to attend his Majesty as a volunteer' (*Last Journals* ii. 191). For Frederick II's comments, see his *Politische Correspondenz*, Berlin, 1879–1939, xli. 324–5.

18. Maria Fagnani. When Selwyn left Italy it was agreed that in April 1779 her parents would bring her to Lyons, where Selwyn would place her in a convent (DU DEFFAND v. 77).

19. When Mme du Deffand saw Selwyn in Paris 16 Oct. 1778, she wrote HW that Selwyn 'n'a que sa petite dans la tête. L'amour le plus violent, la passion la plus effrénée, n'ont jamais produit une si extrême folie' (ibid.).

20. Giacomo, Marchese Fagnani, m. (1767) Costanza Brusati (d. 1804) (ibid. n. 2).

21. After Alexis Orlov had strangled Peter III of Russia in 1762, Catherine II issued a manifesto in which his death was attributed to a severe hemorrhoidal colic (MANN vi. 64 nn. 4, 6). Selwyn wrote to his niece, Mary Townshend, from Milan, 15 June 1778: 'I hope that Lady M[iddleton] has not been made to believe by Mr W[alpole] that they [the

and D'Alembert[22] and Diderot[23] would celebrate their clemency.[24]

I have been so indignant in this letter, that to sweeten it a little, I will send you some very pretty lines; old, but never printed. They were repeated to me this spring on memory by the old Lady Brown,[25] not my Catholic neighbour,[26] and were made by Rowe the tragic poet on Lady Hervey when Miss Lepelle, with whom he was in love, as everybody was then.

> I counted o'er the long, long score
> 　Of laughing Cloe's lovers;
> Which, sad to see! besides poor me,
> 　Full forty-nine discovers.
> But Cupid cries, 'Her nimble eyes
> 　Will quickly end your sorrow:
> Fifty a day, for that's her play,
> 　She kills—you'll die tomorrow.'

Lady Brown told me she once asked Lady Hervey, towards the end of her life, if she remembered them? 'Do you think,' replied my Lady Hervey, 'that we women ever forget flattery?' Lady Brown assured me the verses were made extempore[27]—I wish, as Lady Holland mends, that Mr Fitzpatrick, who alone can, would make some as

Fagnanis] will poison me. Of all the ideas which ever come [came] into a man's head, who knew the world, and me, I think that was the most absurd; upon any supposition which could have been the foundation of it. But his historic doubts, and his historic certainties, have always appeared to me to have something more singular in them than those of any other person. But the fact is, il ne parait s'en douter désiré, il n'y [a] point de secret impénétrable pour lui.' And on 16 Sept. 1778 he wrote her: 'I shall leave the country without being poisoned or pillaged' (S. Parnell Kerr, *George Selwyn and the Wits*, 1909, pp. 235, 246).

22. Jean le Rond d'Alembert (1717–83).

23. Denis Diderot (1713–84).

24. The English Ambassador at St Petersburg, Lord Cathcart, 'writes in a sour strain: "All his [Diderot's] letters are filled with panegyrics of the Empress, whom he depicts as above humanity"' (John Morley, *Diderot*, 1878, ii. 127). Cf.

the Duchesse de Choiseul to Mme du Deffand ca 12–14 June 1767, in Mme du Deffand, *Correspondance complète*, ed. Sainte-Aulaire, 1866, i. 110–20.

25. Margaret Cecil (ca 1696–1782) m. Sir Robert Brown, cr. (1732) Bt. HW mentions her in his letter to Mann 13 Feb. 1743 OS (MANN ii. 166).

26. Frances Sheldon (1714–90) m. 1 (1736) Henry Fermor; m. 2 Sir George Browne, 3d Bt. She was HW's occasional correspondent (MORE 49, n. 4, and *passim*).

27. This paragraph to this point was first printed in Dorothy Margaret Stuart, *Molly Lepell Lady Hervey*, 1936, p. 37. The verses and a variant of this anecdote as they appear in HW's 'Book of Materials,' 1771, p. 61, are in MORE 418. Another copy of the verses in HW's hand, 'Extempore on Lady Hervey by Nich. Rowe,' is in the Huntington Library among the Jerningham Papers, JE 753 (Mr Tyrus G. Harmsen to WSL 29 Nov. 1956).

genteel to the same metre. The world is just to him on his lovely attention to his sister.[28]

I don't love camps, but I love the Colonel and Coloneless so well, that I do not swear I will not visit the Bedfordshire militia,[29] if the Duke does not go abroad—I had other matters to tell you, but they were about myself, and this letter is as long as the French line of battle already.[30] Pray drink Lord Richard's[31] health.

To Lady Ossory, Tuesday 11 August 1778

First printed in *Letters of Horace Walpole,* selected by W. S. Lewis, 1951, pp. 192–6.

Strawberry Hill, Aug. 11, 1778.

I HAD neither room nor time, Madam, to tell you in my last how much I am ashamed to hear the kind things you are so good as to say to me. Very moderate friendship and good-nature would incline one to try to amuse such reasonable grief as yours, especially if letters could effect it, and letters from one that is so accustomed to write them, that they cost but the mere half hour. The remnant of an useless life is dedicated to my friends; I have no other employment; and the long and invariable favour your Ladyship has shown me, entitles you to every suit and service I can perform. You cannot lessen yourself in my eyes by disparaging yourself—nay, though I dislike it, it exalts you; it adds to my esteem. Vanity is to me the most ridiculous of all human faults. Humility, if not a virtue, is a love of virtue, and a respect for truth. The Pharisee and the Magdalen is the most

28. Corroboration of his solicitude is found in Lady Sarah Lennox, *Life and Letters* i. 265–6, 271, and in a letter from Lady Ossory to Selwyn (Jesse, *Selwyn* iii. 295).

29. Encamped at Winchester, although Lord and Lady Ossory were in Southampton. Lord Ossory's arrival there is announced in the *Morning Post* 24 June, in a letter from Southampton dated 20 June. Lady Ossory and their two daughters had arrived early in August.

30. Lists of the French line of battle and of the Brest and Toulon squadrons had recently appeared in the newspapers and magazines. See, for example, the *London Magazine,* May 1778, xlvii. 223–4; *London Chronicle* 30 June – 2 July, xliv. 2.

31. Lord Richard Cavendish (1752–81), brother of the D. of Devonshire; M.P. Lancaster borough 1773–80, Derbyshire 1780–1. He 'had gone a volunteer with his friend Captain Walsingham, and was on deck of Keppel's ship [the *Victory*] the whole time' of the action off Ushant 27 July (*Last Journals* ii. 195; *London Chronicle* 4–6 Aug., xliv. 122–3, 128; *Morning Post* 30 June).

beautiful story in the New Testament.[1] Your last has realized what Rousseau's presumption thought nobody but himself could dare to achieve. I have got his preface to his memoirs:[2] it is the superlative of arrogant eloquence; it would be the sublime of madness, were the madness real. As it is not, it is the affectation of singularity pushed to distraction. Not content to be unlike all mankind, he hopes at the Day of Judgment to be sent to Bedlam[3]—it is even shocking! He aims at extorting a confession—it is not right to say how far his vanity goes—that he was the most extraordinary mortal ever created.[4] To glory in confessing our crimes, and to brave mankind to imitate him, has more of Diogenes, than of the penitent Magdalen. I will send you this frantic piece of meditated extravagance, but beg you not to give a copy. It will get about, but I should not like to be the disperser.

I told you, Madam, that I had some history of myself for you; consequently very insignificant to anybody; but it will amuse you for a moment. In the first place I have been printing for Lady Craven a translation of her *Somnambule,*[5] and that you shall have too.[6] It is not ill done; but if it were, she is so pretty and good-humoured,[7] that I am pleased to please her.[8]

---

1. In his letter to Mason 10 Aug. 1778 (MASON i. 427) HW also refers to the Pharisee-Magdalen story, comparing its true humility with the false humility of Rousseau.

2. What HW calls the 'preface' is generally printed as the beginning of the first chapter of Rousseau's *Confessions.* HW had received his copy from Mme du Deffand in her letter of 2 Aug. (DU DEFFAND v. 64), and had quoted it in full in his letter to Mason 10 Aug. (MASON i. 426–7). Books I–VI of *The Confessions* were not published until 1782 (Théophile Dufour, *Recherches bibliographiques sur les œuvres imprimées de J.-J. Rousseau,* 1925, i. 238). See also MASON i. 426 nn. 6, 7, 9.

3. The phrase 'to be sent to Bedlam' goes beyond the text; see MASON i. 426.

4. 'Je ne suis fait comme aucun de ceux que j'ai vus; j'ose croire n'être fait comme aucun de ceux qui existent; je ne vaux pas mieux ou moins, je suis autre.'

5. *Le Somnambule,* by Pont-de-Veyle (*ante* 12 Sept. 1775, n. 4). The translation by Lady Craven was printed (75 copies) at SH 24 June – 30 Aug. under the title *The Sleep-Walker, A Comedy: In Two Acts. Translated from the French, in March, M.DCC.LXXVIII,* with four lines by HW to Lady Craven on the verso of the title-page (Hazen, *SH Bibl.* 114–15; COLE ii. 111; *HW's Fugitive Verses* 170–1).

6. The copy HW gave the Ossorys has not been traced.

7. 'She is a very pretty woman, and has more manner, politeness, and sense than anybody of her own time of life that I am acquainted with, and though her conduct was at one time a little censurable she soon corrected herself and makes a good wife and one of the best mothers that I know' (Coke, 'MS Journals' 30 June 1779).

8. See also HW's eight lines of verse, 'To Lady C——. 1778,' printed in *Works* iv. 395 and in *HW's Fugitive Verses* 82.

The next chapter is not so agreeable to me. Contrary to my determination, I have been writing again for the public. I have a horror for the stage of authors, which they call their *senilia*, and which therefore they ought not to write, for what can age produce that is worth showing? My present case is not of choice, but necessity.[9] Somebody has published the poems of Chatterton the Bristol boy,[10] and in the preface intimates that I was the cause of his despair and poisoning himself, and a little more openly is of opinion that I ought to be stoned.[11] This most groundless accusation has driven me to write the whole story—and yet now I have done it in a pamphlet of near thirty pages of larger paper than this, I think I shall not bring myself to publish it.[12] My story is as clear as daylight, I am as innocent as of the death of Julius Cæsar, I never saw the lad with my eyes,[13] and he was the victim of his own extravagance two years after all correspondence had ceased between him and me[14]—and yet I hate to be

9. The remainder of this paragraph (except for one sentence, 'I intend . . . Ladyship.') was printed in DALRYMPLE pp. xxx–xxxi.

10. *Miscellanies in Prose and Verse; by Thomas Chatterton*, ed. John Broughton (d. 1801), attorney of Bristol who signed the Preface 'J.B.' (CHATTERTON 177 n. 1).

11. 'One of his [Chatterton's] first efforts, to emerge from a situation so irksome to him, was an application to a gentleman well known in the republic of letters; which, unfortunately for the public, and himself, met with a very cold reception . . . perhaps he [the reader] may feel some indignation against the person to whom his first application was made, and by whom he was treated with neglect and contempt' (pp. xviii–xxi). For further details, see MASON i. 423; CHATTERTON 345 and illustration.

12. *A Letter to the Editor of the Miscellanies of Thomas Chatterton*, of which 200 copies were printed at the SH Press in Jan. 1779 to be distributed to friends and others interested in the Chatterton affair ('Short Notes,' GRAY i. 50–1; Hazen, *SH Bibl.* 116–18; CHATTERTON 121–2; MASON i. 423). HW also mentions his hesitancy to print in his letters to Mason 24 July, 10 Aug. 1778 (ibid. i. 424, 425) and to Cole 15, 22 Aug. 1778 (COLE ii.

105–6, 109). Broughton had in effect suggested that HW write an account of his conduct: 'It were to be wished that the public was fully informed of all the circumstances attending that unhappy application; the event of which deprived the world of works which might have contributed to the honour of the nation, as well as the comfort and happiness of their unfortunate author' (*Miscellanies . . . Chatterton*, p. xxi).

13. Catcott, Langhorne (on the authority of Catcott), and Warton had stated or implied that HW had seen Chatterton after the latter had come to London late in April 1770 (COLE ii. 50 and n. 3; *Monthly Review*, April 1777, lvi. 259; Thomas Warton, *The History of English Poetry*, Vol. II, 1778, pp. 141–2). Four years later Warton corrected his statement (*An Inquiry into the Authenticity of the Poems Attributed to Thomas Rowley*, 1782, p. 109 n.). Broughton (*Miscellanies*, pp. xviii–xix) indicates that Chatterton applied to HW before leaving Bristol.

14. Chatterton died during the night of 24–25 Aug. 1770; his last letter to HW is dated 24 July 1769, and shortly thereafter HW returned all the papers he had received from Chatterton (CHATTERTON 116–17).

the talk of the town, and am more inclined to bear this aspersion, than to come again upon the stage. I intend to consult every friend I have before I resolve, and of course, Lord Ossory and your Ladyship. It is impossible to have a moment's doubt on the case. The whole foundation of the accusation is reduced to this—If I had been imposed upon, my countenance might have saved the poor lad from poisoning himself for want, which he brought on himself by his excesses.[15] Those few words are a full acquittal, and would indeed be sufficient—but the story in itself is so marvellous, that I could not help going into the whole account of such a prodigy as Chatterton was. You will pity him, as I do; it was a deep tragedy, but interests one chiefly from his extreme youth, for it was his youth that made his talents and achievements so miraculous. I doubt, neither his genius nor his heart would have interested one, had he lived twenty years more. You will be amazed at what he was capable of before eighteen, the period of his existence—yet I had rather anybody else were employed to tell the story.

As I have taken such an aversion to the character of author, I have fallen into a taste that I never had in my life, that of music. The swan, you know, Madam, is drawing towards its end, when it thinks of warbling, but as I have not begun to sing myself, I trust it is but distantly symptomatic. In short, I have only lived with musicians lately and liked them. Mr Jerningham[16] is here at Twickenham, and sings in charming taste to his harp. My niece Miss Churchill[17] has been here with her harp, and plays ten times better and sings worse —but I am quite enchanted with Mr Gammon,[18] the Duke of Grafton's brother-in-law.[19] It is the most melodious voice I ever

15. Cf. Broughton (*Miscellanies*, p. xviii): 'He possessed all the vices and irregularities of youth, and his profligacy was, at least, as conspicuous as his abilities'; E. H. W. Meyerstein, *Life of Thomas Chatterton*, 1930, p. 77; COLE ii. 205.

16. Edward Jerningham (1737–1812), poet; HW's correspondent; 'the Charming Man' of the HW-Berry Correspondence.

17. Sophia Churchill (d. 1797), dau. of Charles Churchill by Lady Mary Walpole, HW's half-sister; m. (1781) her cousin, Hon. Horatio Walpole, styled Bn Walpole 1806–9, 2d E. of Orford of the 3d creation, 1809. Lady Mary Coke thought her

'a fine young woman and well behaved' ('MS Journals' 31 Oct. 1778). 'The Cecilia of the present age; but since she is wedded, her friends have seldom been favoured with her performance on the harp' ('Musical Amateurs' in the *London Chronicle* 30 Jan.–1 Feb. 1787, lxi. 111).

18. Richard Grace Gamon (1748–1818), cr. (1795) Bt; M.P. (GM 1818, lxxxviii pt i. 570; William Betham, *Baronetage*, 1801–5, iv. 290–1; Burke, *Peerage*, 1953, p. 904, *sub* Grace).

19. Gamon's first wife was the D. of Grafton's half-sister (d. 1794), dau. of James Jeffreys by Lady Fitzroy; see below; Musgrave, *Obituary*; GEC.

heard; like Mr Meynell's, but more perfect. As I pass a great deal of time at Hampton Court,[20] in a way very much like the remnant of the Court of St Germain's[21] (—and I assure you, where there are some that I believe were of that Court), I was strolling in the gardens in the evening with my nieces,[22] who joined Lady Schaub and Lady Fitzroy,[23] and the former asked Mr Gammon to sing. His taste is equal to his voice, and his deep notes, the part I prefer, are calculated for the solemnity of Purcel's[24] music, and for what I love particularly, his mad songs[25] and the songs of sailors.[26] It was moonlight and late, and very hot, and the lofty façade of the palace, and the trimmed yews and canal, made me fancy myself of a party in Grammont's time—so you don't wonder that by the help of imagination I never passed an evening more deliciously. When by the aid of some historic vision and local circumstance I can romance myself into pleasure, I know nothing transports me so much. Pray, steal from your soldiery, and try this secret at Bevis Mount[27] and Nettley Abbey.[28] There are Lord and Lady Peterborough[29] and Pope to

20. HW was there on the night of 1 July (Lady Elizabeth Laura Waldegrave to Anne Clement 1–2 July, MS wsl).

21. Through the generosity of Louis XIV, James II lived with his Court in exile (1688–1701) at St Germain-en-Laye.

22. Sophia Churchill and his great-nieces, the three Ladies Waldegrave.

23. The 3d D. of Grafton's mother, Elizabeth Cosby (d. 1788), m. 1 (1734) Lord Augustus Fitzroy; m. 2 (1747) James Jeffreys, commissioner of customs. Although her proper title was Lady Augustus Fitzroy, her son's becoming in 1747 the heir-apparent to the Dukedom of Grafton probably led to her being called 'Lady Fitzroy,' the title used in the notice of her second marriage (MONTAGU i. 108 n. 27; GM 1747, xvii. 591).

24. Henry Purcell (ca 1658–95) composed many of his songs for the exceptionally low and versatile voice of John Gostling, basso profundo, one of the most celebrated bass singers of his time.

25. 'Those curiosities of the Restoration period known as mad songs in which the phases of temporary insanity are represented by variations in tempo and style' (Jack A. Westrup, Purcell, 1937, p. 153; Allardyce Nicoll, Restoration Drama, Cambridge, 1923, pp. 15–19, 59–63). In Sir John Hawkins, General History of . . . Music,

1776, v. 179, HW marked in his copy (now wsl) a footnote apropos of 'a song called New Mad Tom,' by George Hayden: 'Songs of this kind, such as Tom of Bedlam, and others set by Lawes, of which there are perhaps more in the English than any other language, were frequently sung in character.'

26. Such as 'Come away, fellow sailors,' 'Arise, ye subterranean winds,' and 'Blow, Boreas, blow,' the last mentioned by Charles Burney, General History of Music, 1776–89, iii. 493–4, as a favourite in his time.

27. Bevois Mount, Hants, in 1778 a seat about a mile north of Southampton, east of the Winchester-Southampton road; now a part of Southampton. Lord Peterborough bought the seat and 'converted it into a kind of wilderness, through which are various winding gravel walks' (Richard Warner, Collections for . . . Hampshire, 1795, i pt ii. 81; BERRY, i. 80 n. 22).

28. Netley Abbey, a Cistercian foundation ca 1239, long in ruins when HW saw it in 1755 (HW to Bentley 18 Sept. 1755). In 1790 he remembered it as 'charming Netley' (BERRY i. 80 and n. 23).

29. Charles Mordaunt (ca 1658–1735), 3d E. of Peterborough, 1697; commander-in-chief of the Allied forces in Spain,

people the former scene,[30] and who you please at Nettley—I sometimes dream, that one day or other somebody will stroll about poor
Strawberry and talk of Lady Ossory—but alas! I am no poet, and
my castle is of paper, and my castle and my attachment and I, shall
soon vanish and be forgotten together!

To Lady Ossory, ca Thursday 20 August 1778

Missing. See following letter.

To Lady Ossory, Saturday 29 August 1778

Now first printed.
Lady Ossory was at Southampton; cf. *post* 6 Sept. 1778.

Strawberry Hill, Aug. 29, 1778.

GRAMERCY, Madam, for your lenity! I was afraid you would
have dismissed me from your service, when I was become poet
laureate to the Sibyls.[1] Sure it is from my being the bellman, that
you recommend to me to make verses on my royal niece. You cannot
be serious: you cannot imagine that I, who scarce ever name my
purple relations to my most intimate friends, for fear of being vulgar, would trumpet that connection in a ditty, if I were as elegiac as
Ovid and made it my profession to write lamentations for all the
unfortunate princesses in Christendom. I feel seriously for the
Duchess, and too seriously, to make an amusement of her story, which
you know is my only reason for writing of late;[2] and I take care that

1705; diplomatist. His second wife (m.
1722 or 1735) was Anastasia Robinson
(d. 1755), a famous singer (Burney, op.
cit. iv. 244–9). According to HW, Peterborough was 'One of those men of careless wit and negligent grace, who scatter
a thousand bon mots and idle verses . . .
His enmity to the Duke of Marlborough
and his friendship with Pope will preserve
his name, when his genius, too romantic
to have laid a solid foundation for fame,
and his politics, too disinterested for his
age and country, shall be equally forgotten' (*Royal and Noble Authors, Works*
i. 438–9).
    30. Pope was a frequent visitor at Bevis
Mount, and one of the walks there was
called 'Pope's Walk.'

1. In a missing letter HW evidently
had sent Lady Ossory a copy of his verses,
'A Card to Lady Blandford,' dated 15
Aug. 1778, and first printed in *Works*
iv. 391 (*HW's Fugitive Verses* 80–1; a MS
copy in HW's hand is in one of HW's
copies of *Des. of SH*, 1774, now wsl). In
these verses HW invites Lady Blandford,
aged over eighty, to meet five other
ladies, ranging in age from about fifty
(Lady Malpas) to about seventy-five
(Lady Margaret Compton); hence HW's
'the Sibyls.'
    2. HW forgets *A Letter to the Editor
of the Miscellanies of Thomas Chatterton*,
which he had written 'not of choice, but
necessity' (*ante* 11 Aug. 1778).

both my subjects and style should be too foolish to be suspected of having any view but momentary pastime.[3] We do not yet know the Duke's fate: the King of Prussia's answer is not arrived.[4]

The American war draws indeed to an end; the fleet and the relics of the army may very possibly be taken in a net.[5] Your cousin[6] says there are barely provisions for nine weeks at New York.[7] To varnish this, Byron and two more ships have been swelled to ten[8]— but these little cobwebs are brushed away as fast as they are spun; and ruin stalks on so fast, that perhaps by Christmas we shall know what law France and Spain will dictate to us. Our eyes will open, but it will be too late, and will

> Serve only to discover sights of woe!
> Regions of sorrow! doleful shades![9]

In truth there seems little more wanting to throw the nation into convulsions. I hear of nothing but dissatisfaction and discontent from all quarters. Perpetual disappointments and the general want of money sour the most zealous; and though I live in the most ministerial of all districts, one would think they were the headquarters of Opposition. All blame is thrown as high as it can go—you would

3. In 1778 HW wrote a translation of a French riddle on *portrait*, 'Riddle, A Looking-Glass,' 'A Card to Lady Bland-ford,' the four lines prefixed to Lady Craven's translation of *Le Somnambule*, and 'To Lady C[raven]. 1778' (*HW's Fugitive Verses* 79–82, 169–70).

4. See *post* 6 Sept. 1778.

5. When Sir Henry Clinton and his army reached New York from Philadelphia, 'they found Lord Howe blocked up in the port by Monsieur d'Estaing, and provisions in the town for only nine weeks, so that, unless they could be relieved, both the army and the fleet were likely to be starved into a surrender' (*Last Journals* ii. 197–8, *sub* 23 Aug. 1778; *London Gazette Extraordinary* 24 Aug.; *Daily Adv.* 25 Aug.; Lord Carlisle to Selwyn 22 July in Jesse, *Selwyn* iii. 299–302). D'Estaing's fleet left New York for Rhode Island 22 July; the news from Lord Howe reached England 13 Sept. (*Last Journals* ii. 199; *London Chronicle* 15–17 Sept., xliv. 265).

6. Probably Lord Carlisle, then in New York as one of the commissioners; Lady Carlisle was Lord Ossory's first cousin.

Cf. Jesse, *Selwyn* iii. 301; *Carlisle MSS* 355–8.

7. Carlisle does not mention 'nine weeks' in the letters cited above, although he mentions starvation as possible. The *London Chronicle* 1–3 Sept., xliv. 218, comments: 'New York must at all events be relieved . . . if they have no relief but what is yet to go from hence, such assistance will come too late.'

8. '24th [Aug.]. News came that Admiral Byron, with three of his ships, had been met within 150 leagues of New York. The Court immediately gave out that he had ten ships with him' (*Last Journals* ii. 198). Cf. *London Chronicle* 25–27 Aug., xliv. 195: 'Yesterday [24 Aug.] a messenger was sent from the Admiralty to his Majesty at Windsor with an account of Admiral Byron's fleet being safe arrived within 150 leagues of New York, consisting of ten sail of the line, with very little damage; and as the wind was then fair, they expected to be at New York in a few days.' See also *Corr. Geo. III* iv. 197–8; *London Chronicle* 15–17 Oct., xliv. 370.

9. *Paradise Lost* i. 64–5, adapted.

think the servants intended to impeach their master. 'He was told this would happen; my Lord M.M. or N.N. endeavoured to dissuade him, but he would'—This is the language every day, especially on every new disaster—Well! the French are not more satisfied; here is a good ballad that I borrowed to copy when I was in town on Wednesday, where I had not set my foot for a month and stayed but one night, and died of the heat, and now I am shivering—I hope this Pindaric transition will banish all your Ladyship's *ailmentelle.*

À M. le Duc de Chartres,[11]
Sur l'air, Chanson, Chanson.

1.

Vous faites rentrer votre armée;
L'Angleterre très alarmée
    Vous en louera.
Et vous joindrez à ce suffrage
Les lauriers et le digne hommage
    De l'Opéra.

2.

Quoi! Vous avez vu la fumée!
Quel prodige! La renommée
    Le publiera.
Accourez vite; c'est bien juste
D'offrir votre personne auguste
    À l'Opéra.

3.

Pour avoir la toison fameuse
Jason sur la mer orageuse
    Se hasarda.
Il n'en eut qu'une; et pour vos peines
Je vous en promets des douzaines
    À l'Opéra.

4.

Chers badauds, courez à la fête,
À l'envie criez à tue-tête,
    Brava! brava!

11. 'Paris, Aug. 10. The Duke de Chartres, commander of the blue squadron in the naval combat off Ushant [27 July], took the opportunity of coming to this capital with the King's leave, while his squadron continued in Brest road [to see his father, wife, and two sons] . . . Wherever the Duke appeared

Cette grande action de guerre
Est telle qu'on rien voit guère
   Qu'à l'Opéra.

5.

Grand Prince, poursuis la carrière,
Franchis noblement la barrière
   De l'Opéra.
Par de si nobles entreprises
À jamais tu t'immortalises
    À l'Opéra.

I beg my own pardon, for on transcribing, I don't think it is a good ballad, but I have seen nothing tolerable so long, that I don't wonder I was mistaken.

Mr Craufurd gave me a much better account of Lady Holland than you do, Madam. He had not seen her, but had been at Old Windsor the day before with Mr Fitzpatrick.

You don't mention Lady Anne, nor her observations on camps, and the sea, and so many new objects. You give so much of your affection to my Lord's sisters,[12] that you are a perfect stepmother to your own children. I allow Miss Vernon is a nymph of the first water; nay, she does not want foils; but is not Lady Gertrude a nymph too in a cockle-shell? I have been dancing the hays[13] this evening with my own charming nieces[14] for the entertainment of her Highness Sophia, and a minuet with her—there is not quite fifty-five years' difference in our ages, I assure you. My nieces laughed a little irreverently, though I told them that I was a very fine dancer be-

he was received with the greatest acclamations, on account of his intrepidity shown in the late naval fight. He returned on the 4th to his command at Brest' (*London Chronicle* 13–15 Aug., xliv. 158). 'The Duke de Chartres behaved like a hero; he received no wound' ('Extract of a Letter from Paris, Aug. 9,' in *Public Advertiser* 24 Aug.). A second look at his conduct indicated that it was not intrepid, perhaps indeed was cowardly, and his going to his favourite opera so frequently at this particular juncture became the subject of ridicule. For a full and unfriendly account of his conduct, and his aspirations for the post of Grand Admiral,

see *La Vie privée du Duc de Chartres, aujourd'hui Duc d'Orléans*, 'Par une Société d'Amis du Prince' (attributed to Anne-Gédéon La Fite de Pellepore, and Charles Thévenot de Morande), 1790, pp. 31–51. The text of the ballad there printed, pp. 47–8, differs slightly from HW's and the air is given as '*Des Revenants.*'

12. Lady Holland, Lady Louisa Fitzpatrick, and the 'three Vernons.'

13. 'A country dance having a winding or serpentine movement, or being of the nature of a reel' (OED).

14. The Waldegraves.

LADY GERTRUDE FITZPATRICK, AFTER REYNOLDS

fore I had the smallpox.[15] I was in great danger last week of being drowned with the three Waldegraves, Miss Keppel, Lady Dysart and Lady Bridget Talmache. We were crossing the river in a boat no bigger than a toothpick-case, to see the Goldsmiths' barge[16] that was coming with a shoal of boats, one of which, a giant to ours, and full of drunken giants, ran upon us on purpose, struck the middle of ours with its prow, and gave us a bang that I believe turned us quite over, for we found ourselves just where we were—thus I divided myself between antediluvians and leading-strings.

To Lady Ossory, Sunday 6 September 1778

Now first printed.
Address: To the Countess of Ossory at Southampton. *Postmark:* 8 SE.

Strawberry Hill, Sunday, Sept. 6, 1778.

I SHOULD not trouble your Ladyship with a letter today, when I have exactly nothing to tell you, but to prevent my receiving a mortification, or, which would be more civil to say, to prevent Mr Fitzpatrick giving himself the trouble of coming hither when I am absent, which I shall be after Wednesday, as I have promised to be at Park Place on Thursday.[1] As he may have left you, I shall endeavour to find him in town and let him know it, for his visit would flatter me so much, that, though I do not often encroach upon the good-nature of young people, I must indulge my vanity for once, and shall claim his promise when I can receive it. Nay, dangerous as he is, my pretty nieces shall do the honours for me—am not I an old wretch? I should scold like Billingsgate, if they looked at a captain of their own accord, and I expose them to an irresistible Dorimant[2] for my own interest!

15. HW was inoculated for smallpox in 1724, when he was seven.

16. 'The new-built barge belonging to the goldsmiths' company.' On 22 Aug. it 'ran foul of a coal barge and was greatly damaged' (*London Chronicle* 29 Aug. – 1 Sept., xliv. 216).

1. 10 Sept.; he returned to SH 16 Sept. Although he does not mention the death

of Lord William Campbell until the following letter, he probably had the news 5 Sept. (cf. Coke, 'MS Journals' 5 Sept. 1778) and was going to Park Place to be with Lady Ailesbury and other members of the family.

2. A rake modelled on John Wilmot, Earl of Rochester, in Sir George Etherege's *The Man of Mode, or Sir Fopling Flutter,* 1676.

The papers have told you, Madam, of the King of Prussia's gracious excuse to the Duke.[3] It was so gracious, and tender, that his R.H. is quite satisfied. I would have compounded for much less.

The delay of the sea-fight makes every moment more important and more dreadful. The Duke has an apprehension, that shows his great good sense, and ought to strike everybody. Capt. Walsingham[4] has sent his R.H. a confirmation of the report of a Portuguese ship delivering M. d'Orvilliers's[5] message to Admiral Keppel that he was waiting for him[6]—yet as he does not seem to have waited for him, the Duke fears the plan is to draw Mr Keppel southward till he falls into the jaws of the Spanish squadron, or is enclosed between them and the French[7]—and then what is to guard all the coasts of these two islands? If Mr Keppel has positive orders to follow the French,[8] can he avoid it, knowing that they who have given those orders, would be unmerciful, if to save the nation he brought the fleet back? He is greatly to be pitied—and so are we!—would not one think there was

---

3. 'The Duke of Gloucester received a letter from the King of Prussia on Wednesday [2 Sept.] and a packet, the contents of which have not transpired. We find, however, by the orders given yesterday morning that his Royal Highness's journey is deferred for the present; and seeing the very impoverished state of the seat of war, England has reason to rejoice that this valuable Prince is not likely to be exposed to the severe trial of such a winter campaign, before his health and constitution are perfectly re-established' (*London Chronicle* 3–5 Sept., xliv. 226). The substance of the letter is ibid. 8–10 Sept., xliv. 246; *Last Journals* ii. 199. See also *ante* 7 Aug. 1778, n. 17.

4. Hon. Robert Boyle Walsingham (1736–80), Capt. R.N., 1757; son of 1st E. of Shannon; M.P. Knaresborough 1758–61, 1768–80, Fowey 1761–8; took the name of Walsingham in 1756; commanded at the Battle of Ushant the *Thunderer*, on which he was lost in a hurricane in the West Indies (Burke, *Peerage*, 1953, p. 1907, *sub* Shannon; GM 1781. li. 343; *Public Advertiser* 4 Aug., 3 Sept.; *London Chronicle* 17–19 Feb. 1780, xlvii. 176).

5. Louis Guillouet (1708–92), Comte d'Orvilliers; son of the governor of French Guiana; commandant of the Brest Fleet,

22 July 1778; superseded or resigned because of health in Sept. 1779; dismissed from the service in 1783; retired to a seminary; left France in 1790 (NBG; *London Chronicle* 25 Sept.–7 Oct. 1779, xlvi. 302, 318, 336).

6. 'Extract of a letter from Falmouth, Aug. 27 . . . I am just now told that the French fleet have been seen from the Land's End, but I doubt it. It is likewise said that they brought-to a Portuguese ship bound for England, and bid them tell Keppel if they met him, that they were waiting for him' (ibid. 29 Aug.–1 Sept., xliv. 216).

7. 'The first important news received, it is thought, will be of a junction between Count d'Orvilliers and the Spanish fleet from Cadiz' (*Public Advertiser* 10 Sept.; cf. *London Chronicle* 12–15 Sept., xliv. 262).

8. His orders were to engage the French fleet but not to leave the 'Channel approaches unguarded unless he received definite information of the enemy.' Consequently he could send only a few of his ships to search for the French, and no contact between the two fleets was made (W. M. James, *The British Navy in Adversity*, 1926, pp. 137, 121–58).

more eager desire to sacrifice the Admiral, than to save the kingdom? Will any man in opposition trust himself to such treachery?[9]

To Lady Ossory, Wednesday 16 September 1778

Now first printed.

Strawberry Hill, Sept. 16, 1778.

THE Bedfordshire militia I implicitly believe, Madam, is the finest corps in the army; but I cannot much commend the discipline of the commanders. If Colonel Caractacus goes a-partridge-shooting,[1] when so many coveys of French are hatching; and Boadicia flies to expel the stench of a pig-sty by smelling to mignonette, instead of fitting scythes to her postchaise and mowing down legions, I shall despair of the Republic. The country might respire, if only ministers, who make nothing but blunders, indulged themselves in holidays when the fate of England is at stake.[2] All is lost, if the unpaid are remiss. Your next step will be to joke on a civil war,[3] or to go to Montem[4]—Scipio, who was as comical and as idle as anybody, never played at leap-frog till he had demolished Carthage.

After this reproof, I will do justice to your visit at Windsor,[5] and

9. Keppel, M.P. for Windsor, was of the Opposition. After the Battle of Ushant 27 July, 'The Court affected to be greatly disappointed at not having gained a complete victory, in order to blame Keppel' (*Last Journals* ii. 195, 186-8). 'Senior naval officers shunned appointments, as they had no confidence in the government and knew they would be made scapegoats on the first sign of failure to achieve the impossible' (James, op. cit. 142).

1. The season opened 1 Sept. Lady Ossory wrote to Selwyn about this time: 'Lord Ossory has forsaken the Red Coats, to attend the partridges' (undated letter in Jesse, *Selwyn* iii. 295).

2. Lord North's partiality for holidays was well known. For Lord George Germain's week-end which was responsible for instructions not reaching Howe to make a junction with Burgoyne, see Alan Valentine, *Lord George Germain*, Oxford,

1962, pp. 282-5. Neither Sandwich nor the Secretary of the Admiralty was in town when the news of the Battle of Ushant reached London (*Last Journals* ii. 187).

3. As the King had done; see *Last Journals* i. 346, ii. 80-81; cf. *ante* 22 July 1778.

4. The Eton festival, which the King and Queen had attended on 9 June (*Public Advertiser* 29 June, detailed account signed 'Etonensis'; Sir H. C. Maxwell Lyte, *History of Eton College*, 1911, pp. 499, 505-7; W. L. Collins, *Etoniana Ancient and Modern*, 1865, pp. 145-6).

5. To visit Lady Holland. In the letter quoted in n. 1, Lady Ossory wrote: 'I have seen Lady Holland in her drawing-room in her riding dress, and I have heard of her airing twice a day. She has received me in the most affecting manner . . . , but she is worn to a shadow; her voice is gone, and she spits and coughs much, though they still entertain hopes that her lungs are not deeply

to your quest of Lady Louisa.[6] The rarer virtues and feeling are, the more beautiful. It is commonly the mark of a degenerate age, that it produces some shining characters. I want my friends to be brilliants, when everybody else chooses to be foils. The scene at Windsor goes to one's soul; and you have painted it, Madam, in a manner to make the most profligate ashamed of their insensibility. A few drops called forth by pathetic distress, would drown and silence a volley of folly and laughter, though a prime minister were the jester. How earnestly must one wish that poor Lady Holland may be restored to such an affectionate family!

I am just returned from another melancholy theatre, where others of my friends have displayed equal tenderness. I went to Park Place[7] to keep Mr Conway and Lady Ailesbury company on the death of Lord William,[8] as they can have nobody with them, for Lady William[9] and her three beggared orphans[10] are there. Lady William had an estate of £800 a year of her own in Carolina,[11] which is confiscated

affected. It is apparent that she gains strength; her appetite is good, and those about her think she gains flesh; but she begged me to lead her to bed, and to see her undressed; and to feel her poor heart beat! Oh, my God! I never can forget that, and her embrace, when I left her!'

6. Lady Ossory 'went to ask leave of that *worthy woman* [the Duchess of Bedford], which was very kindly granted, for Lady Louisa Fitzpatrick to come and spend three weeks with me here' (ibid.).

7. Lady Mary Coke noted that HW, 'at Park Place,' was among those not at Lady Blandford's Sunday evening 13 Sept. ('MS Journals').

8. Lady Ailesbury's brother, Lord William Campbell (ca 1732 – 4 Sept. 1778), an officer in the navy (post-captain, 1762); M.P. Argyllshire 1764–6; governor of Nova Scotia 1766–73 and of South Carolina from 1773 until the outbreak of the American war of independence; volunteer on board the *Bristol* at the attack on Charleston, 1776; commander of the *Lion* 26 March 1778; died at Southampton after a long illness; buried 'Monday evening,' 7 Sept., 'in a very solemn manner in St Anne's Church, Soho' (*Scots Peerage* i. 385, ix. 25; DAB; *Scots Magazine*, 1776, xxxviii. 667; Coke, 'MS Journals' 23

June, 21 July, 5 Sept. 1778; *Public Advertiser* 10 Sept.; James T. Rutnam, 'The Conway Letters to Horace Walpole,' unpublished essay, 1955, p. 5).

9. Sarah Izard (d. 1784), dau. of Ralph Izard of Charleston, South Carolina, m. (1763) Lord William Campbell (*Scots Peerage* i. 385). At the time of her marriage she was 'esteemed one of the most considerable fortunes in the province' (*South Carolina Gazette* 23 April 1763, quoted in *South Carolina Historical and Genealogical Magazine*, 1901, ii. 235 n.). Her father was 'wealthy and influential' and her 'relatives were all patriots' (DAB).

10. 1) Caroline Campbell (1764–89). 2) Louisa Campbell (1766–1852), m. (1799) Alexander Johnston, Kt, 1809. 3) William Conway Campbell (1773–1856), British naval officer. Another daughter, Anne, had already died (*South Carolina Historical and Genealogical Magazine*, 1901, ii. 235 n.; *Scots Peerage* i. 385, ix. 25; *Scots Magazine*, 1799, lxi. 495; Kearsley's *Peerage*, [1796], ii. 243; HW to Conway 5 Oct. 1777; Coke, *Journals* iii. 123, 417–18, and 5 July 1777; Daniel Lysons, *Environs of London*, Vol. III, 1795, p. 375; Rutnam, op. cit. 5, 7, Appendix B; GM 1852, n.s. xxxvii. 638).

11. Lands owned by the Izard family are described in Henry A. M. Smith,

by the Americans and depopulated.[12] Lord William lost fifteen thousand pounds besides his government. This is one sample of what the Court has cost its friends! The poor Lady was two days ago seized with the gout. I was alarmed by it the same day, and returned for fear of making their house a complete hospital; but as mine has shifted to two or three parts, I flatter myself it will go off for the present.

This memento checks me, or I should have plunged over my ears in a promise about October, which your Ladyship so kindly asks. I must give it *sous le bon plaisir de mon tyrant*, and leave inviolable engagements to youth, though seldom better kept than those of decrepitude. I am just now summoned to Nuneham, and pro- pro- propose—to intend—to go thither on Monday, but the Lord Gout knows whether he will dispense with my absence.[13]

I dined yesterday at Caversham,[14] but could not walk out, though it was a halcyon day. The house is made an excellent one: has no display of taste, but has no crime against it. All is sensible and handsome and comfortable. The place I have seen more than once before. It has a noble air, glorious trees, and a rich comely prospect—but one regrets not seeing the river, when it is so very near. My elderly nephew and his young wife are delighted with one another and their joint production.[15] The eldest son[16] was there, and a very melancholy sight to me, who know so much of madness. He is a fine handsome

Baronies of South Carolina, Charleston, S.C., 1931, pp. 135–40, but Lady William's estate is not specified. In the will of her father, Ralph Izard, 13 Sept. 1757, proved 10 Feb. 1761, she and her sister Rebecca were left plantations 'at Wasmesaw left me by my father-in-law Jos. Blake, Esq., and my father Walter Izard, Esq.' (*South Carolina Historical and Genealogical Magazine*, 1901, ii. 233).

12. MS reads 'depoplitated.' The estate apparently was restored to her (her son later lived on maternal South Carolina lands, according to *Scots Peerage*, loc. cit.). Shortly before Lady William's death Lord Frederick Campbell, her brother-in-law, wrote to the Duchess of Argyll, 7 Aug. 1784: '[She] has not, as I understand, any pension, but is only allowed a part of the money given by the public to support American sufferers' (*Intimate Society Let-*

ters of the Eighteenth Century, ed. 9th D. of Argyll, 1910, i. 212).

13. HW made the visit as planned, and spent four days at Nuneham (HW to Lord Harcourt 17, 27 Sept. 1778).

14. In Berkshire, near Reading; the seat of Lord Cadogan.

15. Hon. (from 1800, Lady) Emily Mary Cadogan (31 May 1778–1839) m. (1802) the Duke of Wellington's brother, the Hon. and Rev. Gerald Valerian Wellesley (COLE ii. 306 n. 3; Kearsley's *Peerage*, [1796], i. 182). 'Lord Cadogan told me he was very much pleased with his daughter, but it is not often that they are so welcome' (Coke, 'MS Journals' 20 June 1778).

16. Charles Henry Sloane Cadogan (1749–1832), 2d E. (n.c.) Cadogan, 1807; sometime an officer in the army; at his death 'had been insane for more than 25 years' (GEC).

strong young man, very civilized, and now quite reasonable—but now and then there was a look in his eyes!—he is again going into the army,[17] which I do not comprehend.

You have seen the accounts from the two fleets,[18] Madam. My own belief has long been, that the Brest fleet will not engage till they know the fate of Destain's. All our commercial fleets are arrived so miraculously, that I begin to think a camel can thrid the eye of a needle.[19] It is an innuendo that we ought to stick to our trade, and not go a-conquering.

When I went to Park Place, I took a Prior[20] in the chaise with me, and was excessively struck with a passage to which I beg your Ladyship to turn. In this age of applications from Shakespeare,[21] etc., I have seen nothing half so apposite, and for so long a tirade. It is towards the end of the third book of *Solomon*, beginning

The child to whose success thy hope is bound,

and the thirteen following lines.[22] The grandsire[23] comes in so opportunely that it makes one start like a ghost.

17. As Capt. in the 61st Foot, stationed at Minorca; his date of rank in the regiment is given as 18 June 1778 in *Army Lists*, 1779, p. 128. He had been Lt and Capt. in the 3d Foot Guards (ibid. 1775, p. 3, where his name is crossed out by a contemporary hand in the Yale copy).

18. 'Lord Howe . . . joined by one of Byron's squadron, was gone with that and seven others after D'Estaing, but it was thought with too small a force. It was said Sir P. Parker, with six of Byron's, was seen very near New York' (*Last Journals* ii. 199). Howe's dispatches of 18, 26, 31 July are in the *London Gazette* 12–15 Sept., No. 11909. According to the *London Chronicle* 12–15 Sept., xliv. 264, Adm. Hyde Parker, 'with six sail of the line, was seen off Nantucket shoals.' Capt. Venture, of the *Hannah* sloop, who brought Lord Howe's dispatches, 'when he came off the *Lizard*, saw Admiral Keppel's fleet, all well, in search of the French squadron, who were said to be off Cape Finisterre the day before' (*Daily Adv.* 15 Sept.).

19. '13th [Sept.] The Lisbon and Jamaica fleets arrived; thus all the trade was come home safe, having almost

miraculously escaped so many enemies' (*Last Journals* ii. 199). 'The arrivals of yesterday may be considered the greatest known for many years past; the fleets having all safe arrived at the following places: at Bristol, the Jamaica fleet; at Plymouth, the Leeward Island fleet; and in the Downs, the Lisbon and Oporto fleets; also the Straits fleet' (*London Chronicle* 12–15 Sept., xliv. 264).

20. HW had the 3-vol. 1725 edn of Prior's *Poems*, now at Wolterton, and the folio edn of 1718, now wsL (Hazen, *Cat. of HW's Lib.* 1877, 2047).

21. Such as *Modern Characters from Shakespear. Alphabetically Arranged*, 1778, and *Modern Characters for 1778: By Shakespeare. Part II*, [1778], both containing passages from Shakespeare applied to individuals and topics such as 'Degeneracy of the Times,' 'The Congress,' etc. In the first book, p. 34, are applications to 'Hon. Capt. F——zp——k' and 'Lady Louisa F——zp——k,' both highly laudatory; cf. *Morning Post* 21 Feb.

22. Prior's *Solomon*, Book III, lines 736–48.

23. Line 745.

There is another excerption might be made, not less just, in the preceding book, beginning

And now I leave the true and just supports, etc.,

to the end of that paragraph[24]—but it is sad to be forced to amuse oneself with quotations for the calamities of one's country!

To Lady Ossory, Sunday 27 September 1778

First printed in *Letters of Horace Walpole,* selected by W. S. Lewis, 1951, pp. 196–9.

Strawberry Hill, Sept. 27, 1778.

ON my return from Nuneham[1] I find your Ladyship's too partial letter, in which you repeat the prejudices that I perceive you have instilled into Lord Ossory. But even if they were well founded, I should beg you never would let me know them. I have long been aware, Madam, that you keep my letters; to continue to write them under that impression is a tacit conviction of vanity. I have no excuse, but that having vowed myself your gazetteer, I was too far dipped to retreat; and might plead that I trusted to the numerosity of my letters for their overwhelming themselves; and as they are stuffed with private history and allusions, I am sure great part of them must be unintelligible to most readers. But I will speak very honestly, and give your Ladyship a substantial reason for never commending me. I do try to be both as humble and as natural as I can. I cannot be the first, if *you* flatter me; and it is impossible to be quite easy and simple, while one thinks one's letters will be read more deliberately than they are written. Nay, one contracts a visionary dignity, and grows so proud and conceited of the imaginary rank of worship one expects to hold in the republic of *epistles,* that, for fear of forfeiting it, one suppresses a thousand trifles and nonsenses that make the delights of correspondence. I trust I have not been very guilty in that respect—and yet I am naturally so foolish and careless, that I am persuaded my letters would have entertained you better, if you had never commended them. Can I say everything, that comes

---

24. Book II, lines 691–701.

1. On the date of this letter (HW to Lord Harcourt, same date).

into my head, to Lady Ossory, if Posterity stands behind my chair
and peeps over my shoulder? Depend upon it, I shall be very affected,
if you make all Futurity your confidants—However, Madam, I think
by this time your Ladyship must be possessed of such a stock of my
invaluable MSS, that the devil will be in any printer that has courage
to undertake them; and as the English language will be obsolete
before he can get to the year 1778, I shall write with less apprehension for the future, for whatever wants a commentary is sure of being
admired.[1a]

Thus much for me and my letters. If you commend me any more,
Madam, it will be tautology. Let me go on in my own way, and do
not make me screw myself into a writer of fine letters. Men are but
too apt to be above trifles; and I think I shall be a prodigy, if I resist
all your spoiling.

I have passed four most agreeable days at Nuneham. Mr Mason,
Miss Fauquier,[2] and Sir Joshua Reynolds with his two nieces[3] were
there, besides accidents. I visited my passion, Oxford, one morning.
Mr Wyat[4] has built a handsome gateway to Christ Church,[5] taken,
I think, from Claudius's arch;[6] and is building an observatory,[7] of

1a. Cf. More 224–7.

2. Jane Georgiana Fauquier (d. 1823),
m. (1786) George Venables-Vernon, 2d Bn
Vernon, 1780, Lady Harcourt's half-
brother and Lord Harcourt's first cousin.
She is frequently mentioned in the *Harcourt Papers*.

3. Mary Palmer (ca 1750–1820), dau. of
Sir Joshua's sister Mary, m. (1792) Mur-
rough O'Brien, 4th E. of Inchiquin, 1777,
cr. (1800) M. of Thomond; and her sister,
Theophila ('Offy') Palmer (ca 1756–1848),
m. (1781) Robert Lovell Gwatkin. The
first was Sir Joshua's amanuensis and chief
heir; he painted both several times
(Graves and Cronin ii. 721–6, iv. 1381;
Sir Joshua Reynolds, *Letters*, ed. F. W.
Hilles, Cambridge, 1929, p. 78, and
passim; idem, Portraits, ed. F. W. Hilles,
[1952], p. 27).

4. James Wyatt (1746–1813), who super-
intended the building of the Offices at
SH in 1790, executed from designs by
James Essex ('Genesis of SH' 82).

5. Wyatt worked on various buildings
at Christ Church from 1773 to 1801. In
1778 his Doric gate to the Canterbury
Court at Christ Church was built in
Burford stone (Reginald Turnor, *James
Wyatt,* 1950, p. 29, with illustrations at
pp. 56–57 of Wyatt's gate and the one it
replaced).

6. HW is probably thinking of the
Arch of Titus at Rome, which has a
general resemblance to the Canterbury
Gate though the columns are Corinthian
and the other details somewhat different.

7. The Radcliffe Observatory, begun in
1772 from designs by Henry Keene. At
Keene's death in 1776 only the ground
floor and Observer's house were complete.
Wyatt was called in to finish it but work
was for some time suspended and it was
not completed until 1798. Wyatt had
probably added little to Keene's work by
1778, but Wyatt's octagonal tower 'pulled
the whole scheme together . . . Without
disparaging Keene, one feels tempted to
give the building to Wyatt, whose ability
it expresses so well' (Turnor, op. cit. 30,
and illustration on p. 58; DNB, *sub* Keene,
Henry).

which I have some doubts. As I had never seen General Guise's[8] collection,[9] I did expect something, but so execrable an assemblage my eyes never beheld. There are three or four vast chambers covered from head to foot. Not six I believe ever were originals—at present the whole collection, whether Raphael's, Rubens's, or Carlo Maratt's, are of the selfsame colours, Bonus's son[10] having been retained at 15*s.* a day to new-paint the whole legacy.[11] I behaved sadly in the Hall, where there is so exact a resemblance of Welbore Ellis,[12] that it gave me a fit of laughter, that scandalized all the Society—he is in the attitude of saying, 'Oui, Sire.'[13]

You have spelt *Matson*[14] rightly, Madam, though you would not, if you had remembered Dick Edgcumbe's[15] *MadSon,* and *Damn'd Son.*[16] I doubt George deserves to inherit the former manor, as I am sure he did not the latter.[17] Madame du Deffand gives me just the

8. John Guise (1682 or 3 – 1765), B.A. Oxon. 1702; army officer under Marlborough; Gen., 1762 (W. G. Hiscock, *A Christ Church Miscellany,* Oxford, 1946, Chapter VII).

9. HW wrote to Mann 1 Aug. 1760 that Guise 'has notified to Christ Church, Oxford, that in his will he has given them his collection of pictures' (MANN v. 429). A catalogue of the collection when it was still in Guise's possession appeared in *London and Its Environs Described,* 1761 (actually published in 1760), iii. 18–36. HW included it in his SH publication, *Catalogues of the Collections of Pictures of the Duke of Devonshire, General Guise, and the Late Sir Paul Methuen,* 1760, pp. 11–25; cf. Hazen, *SH Bibl.* 52. For other lists of the pictures, see *A New Pocket Companion for Oxford,* Oxford, n.d. (ca 1770), pp. 93–4; *The Oxford University and City Guide,* new edn, Oxford, 1824, pp. 147–52; Tancred Borenius, *Pictures . . . in the Library of Christ Church, Oxford,* Oxford, 1916.

10. Richard Bonus, who is described (probably incorrectly, see n. 11 below) as 'old' Bonus. In the Red Bedchamber at SH was 'A moonlight on copper; by Bonus, jun.' for which HW paid a guinea (*Des. of SH,* 1774, p. 40 of HW's annotated copy, now WSL; *Works* ii. 437); sold SH xxii. 49.

11. In a note on his letter to Mann 1 Aug. 1760, MANN v. 429 n. 24, HW wrote that 'the University employing the son of Bonus, the cleaner of pictures, to repair them, he entirely repainted them, and as entirely spoiled them.' Hiscock, op. cit. 78, says that the pictures were restored by Richard Bonus of Oriel Street, Oxford, between 1770 and 1773 for £450. He is described (probably incorrectly) as 'old' Bonus (ibid.) but the elder Bonus apparently lived in Oxford Road, London (HW to Lort 4 June 1779, CHATTERTON 184).

12. Who had been an undergraduate at Christ Church; D.C.L., Oxford, 1773. The portrait was painted by Gainsborough in 1763.

13. Cf. *ante* 11 Aug. 1771.

14. George Selwyn's seat near Gloucester.

15. Richard Edgcumbe (1716–61), 2d Bn Edgcumbe, 1758; intimate friend of HW and Selwyn.

16. Danson Hill 'near Wellend,' Bexley, Kent, was a seat of the Selwyn family, as Matson also was (unpublished Selwyn corr. now WSL: Maynard to Selwyn 24 Sept. 1748; Mathias to Selwyn 26 July 1742, 11 Nov. 1742, etc.).

17. Col. John Selwyn 'hired' Danson Hill (*Archæologia Cantiana,* 1880, xiii. 397).

same accounts of his letters that your Ladyship does.[18] However, I shall rejoice to see him again.[19]

I ought not to have answered your letter so paragraphically, Madam, but to have commenced with your honours at the least of all little courts.[20] I am glad of them, and of your campaign,[21] as I flatter myself they will together have dispelled your recluseness. It is time to inure yourself to a world where your daughters will want you. The Duchess of Cumberland I should think is a sensible woman.[22] I am sure she has given a sample by seeking your Ladyship.

In military lore I am totally unread. Every profession has its own idiom. Common sense, with the aid of political conjecture, would make me conclude that *the Colonel* was *not* excepted[23]—but perhaps the order was meant to be oracular, that our Lord might be blamed in whichever sense he should interpret it.[24] Were I in his place I would do whichever I thought became my duty and me best, and not trouble myself about comments.

Your Ladyship's account of Lady Holland is so dreadful, that, as on our political situation, I know not what I wish—nor would I remind you of it. This will arrive when you are in the midst of Io Pæans and loyal effusions, and all those endearments that must pass between a great Prince and his people, when both are so worthy of each other![25] Far be it from me to intrude; my little epistle cannot expect an audience before next morning, when the fumes of loyalty are a little evaporated. I have been so long out of hearing even of the

18. Mme du Deffand had written 23 Aug. 1778, 'Il me parait plus fou que jamais,' and to the same effect on 20 Sept. (DU DEFFAND v. 67, 72).

19. See *post* 21 Oct. 1778.

20. As indicated later in the paragraph, the court of the Duke and Duchess of Cumberland, who had a country seat near Southampton to which they had gone 9 June (*Morning Post* 11 June).

21. That is, of her going to Winchester with Lord Ossory and the Bedfordshire militia.

22. HW seldom praised the Duchess, but he thought her 'certainly very sensible' (*Last Journals* i. 241–2, *sub* 12 July 1773), and more 'discreet' than the Duchess of Gloucester (ibid. ii. 157, *sub* 2 April 1778). His account of her in Feb. 1781 is much

less favourable (*Last Journals* ii. 350–4), and so is the Duchess of Gloucester's (*ante* 4 Dec. 1771, n. 4).

23. That is, HW thought that the Colonel, Lord Ossory, *should* mount guard with the detachment of Bedfordshire militia assigned to guard George III at Winchester: 'The Bedfordshire militia have received orders to march, and do duty on his Majesty while he remains at Winchester' (*London Chronicle* 26–29 Sept., xliv. 307). See also *post* 9 Oct. 1778.

24. Lord Ossory was a member of the Opposition, and whatever he did could be interpreted to his disadvantage.

25. The King and Queen arrived at Winchester 28 Sept.; the King reviewed the troops 29 Sept.

echo of politics, that I do not know whether the Court is in weepers for the capture of Mr Stuart,[26] or not. I returned but to dinner, and shall not sally into my neighbourhood till tomorrow, as I have letters and newspapers of a whole week to read and answer; so I have yet seen no soul but Mr Raftor,[27] who told me an excellent story of his old sister Mrs Mestivyer.[28] She is both a great politician and natural philosopher. Mrs Clive happened to say she never saw the Thames so low[29]—'And don't you know why it is so?' said Mrs M.—'It is occasioned by the vast quantities of beer that have been brewed for the camps.'

I forgot to mention what taste has penetrated to Oxford. At St John's College they have demolished a comely old square garden of about an acre, and bestowed upon it three yards of serpentine shrubs, five loose trees that are hopping about between four walls;[30] and I suppose will have an irregular lake of a hogshead of water—when the brewing season is over!

Your Ladyship's most etc.,

H. W.

26. Hon. Charles Stuart (1753–1801), K.B., 1799; Lord Bute's 4th son; Lt-Col. 26th Foot, 1777 (stationed in America); eventually Lt-Gen., 1798, and governor of Minorca, 1799 (*Army Lists*). His sister, Lady Louisa Stuart, in a letter to Lady Caroline Dawson, 28 Oct. 1778, apologized 'for having given you a fruitless uneasiness about the foolish story of Charles being taken' (*Gleanings from an Old Portfolio*, ed. A. G. C. Clark, Edinburgh, 1895–8, i. 91).

27. James Raftor (d. 1790), actor who lived at Little SH with his sister, Kitty Clive.

28. —— Raftor, m. —— Mestivyer; she lived with Mrs. Clive at Little SH, and was alive in 1783 (*Harcourt Papers* viii. 169, 173; HW to Harcourt 10 June 1780, 18 May 1781, 5 Aug. 1783; Percy Fitzgerald, *Life of Mrs Catherine Clive*, 1888, pp. 103, 104).

29. 'The water in the River Thames is lower than ever was known by the oldest man living either at Windsor or Eton' (*London Chronicle* 8–10 Sept., xliv. 243;

later reports of the drought are ibid. 19–22, 22–24 Sept., xliv. 288, 295).

30. 'The gardens belonging to this [St John's] College are extremely agreeable, very extensive, and well laid out. They still retain the names they formerly had, when they had nothing to boast of but a plantation of elms, viz., the *outer* and *inner grove*. But now the outer one is disposed in regular walks and grass-plots. The inner grove is of quite a different cast to this, being so contrived as not to satiate the eye at once, but its various parts present themselves gradually to view. No spot is calculated to yield a more pleasing variety' (*A New Pocket Companion for Oxford*, new edn, 'corrected and much enlarged,' Oxford, n.d., ca 1772, pp. 67–8). HW presumably refers to the Inner Grove. Although he preferred a natural garden to a formal one, he here regrets the loss of something that was good of its kind (the formal garden) for something that is not good of its kind, for the 'natural' garden in this instance is more artificial than the formal one. Cf.

To Lady Ossory, Friday 9 October 1778

Now first printed.

Arlington Street, Friday night late, Oct. 9, 1778.

I CANNOT express how infinitely grateful I am for your Ladyship's writing to me in your great distress.[1] I wanted to write, and
did not know how to begin; I was afraid of breaking in upon your
grief too soon and of putting you to the trouble of an answer, when
you had a thousand melancholy duties to take up your thoughts.
I knew you would be satisfied how thoroughly I interest myself in
whatever affects you, and would impute my momentary silence to
the true cause. I will not pretend to suggest comfort—you have the
best and only consolation to real concern, attention to Lord Ossory
and his family. You will conquer yourself for them—and though
you condescend to ask my advice, you do not want it. I shall approve
whatever you do, for I shall be sure you determine according to the
preponderating weight in the scale of duties; and when you are
guided by the judgment of Lord Ossory and Mr Fitzpatrick, there
can be no doubt of your choosing the right part. Lord Ossory's coolness and good nature are your Ladyship's best guides, and you should
mind no other, were I capable of advising; but I know no more what
is proper to do on such an occasion, than to form a decree in Chancery. I did smile indeed at your *impetuosity* with your children. I
should have assigned the orphans[2] to you, because I thought you
preserved the exact medium between too much indulgence and too
little[3]—how one may be mistaken!

I feel exceedingly, Madam, for poor Lady Louisa. She sees early
the instability of human happiness—her sister and Lady Thanet[4]

HW's 'The History of the Modern Taste
in Gardening,' which in 1778 was printed
but not published, and the discussion in
Isabel W. U. Chase, *Horace Walpole:
Gardenist*, Princeton, N.J., 1943. Cf. *ante*
11 Aug. 1771.

———

1. Lady Holland died 6 Oct. For Lady
Ossory's letter to George Selwyn on this
occasion, see Jesse, *Selwyn* iii. 327–8. Cf.
ibid. iii. 330–1.

2. Lady Holland's two surviving children: Hon. Caroline Fox (1767–1845),
and Lord Holland, aged almost 5. For the
arrangements concerning them, see the
following letter.

3. Lady Sarah Lennox hoped that Lady
Ossory, because of her uneven temper and
unkindness to Caroline Fox, would not
have charge of the girl (Lady Sarah Lennox, *Life and Letters* i. 270, 274).

4. Mary Sackville (1746 – 30 Sept. 1778),

taken away in one week! The latter seemed to have as full a share as
the world could bestow; youth, beauty, riches, virtue, and a husband
sensible of her merit. If life was not chequered with tragedy and
comedy, how such events would strike! They do in small villages,
where an event is remembered for years. We live in such a multiplic-
ity, that in a quarter of an hour we run from one topic to another—
nay, and ask for more news the next moment. I have tonight heard
your two relations mentioned, and the Duchess of Chandos's[5] christening[6] and Dr Hay's[7] death, who the day after his keepers left him,
walked deliberately into the Thames[8] at noon in the sight of fifty
persons, and when he had waded up to his chin, deliberately plunged
his head down and was suffocated, before he was taken out. This is
an alarming catastrophe to me, who must tremble for one,[9] that his
keepers have quitted too.

You did not tell me, Madam, whether the Colonel mounted guard,
or obeyed the countermand;[10] nor whether he dined with his Sovereign Lord[11]—you see, I too am asking for more news.

dau. of Lord John Philip Sackville by
Lord Ossory's and Lady Louisa's aunt,
Lady Frances Gower, m. (1767) Sackville
Tufton (1733–86), 8th E. of Thanet, 1753.
She died of fever. On her marriage the
Duchess of Northumberland wrote, 'Beauty
without Art had in this case its reward'
(*Diaries of a Duchess*, ed. J. Greig, New
York, 1927, pp. 76–7, quoted in GEC xii.
697 n.).

5. Anne Eliza Gamon (d. 1813), sister
of Richard Gamon (*ante* 11 Aug. 1778),
m. 1 Roger Hope Elletson; m. 2 (1777)
James Brydges, 3d D. of Chandos, 1771.
Lady Mary Coke reports that the Duchess's
conversation at the christening mentioned
below 'was by all accounts very vulgar.
The Queen said to her, "I suppose your
Grace will go out of town as soon as you
can?" to which her Grace replied that it
was her intention or purpose to receive
the homage of her neighbourhood' ('MS
Journals' 9 Oct. 1778). Cf. MASON i. 446.

6. Her daughter (Charlotte or Georgiana: the name is variously given) was
born on 'Sunday evening,' 6–7 Sept., at
the Duke's 'house in Chandos Street, near
Portman Square' (*Public Advertiser* 8
Sept.), where the christening took place
on Thursday evening, 8 Oct.; 'the spon-

sors were their Majesties in person, and
the Princess Royal Charlotta Augusta;
after which a grand entertainment was
given to a great number of nobility present on the occasion.' The state bed,
canopy, and other decorations for the
christening are said 'to have cost upwards
of £3000, besides the apparel of the child
during the ceremony, being of the richest
laces, to the amount of £700.' The child
died on 9 or 10 Oct. (*London Chronicle*
17–19 Sept., 8–13 Oct., xliv. 280, 347, 351,
356; *Annual Register*, 1778, xxi. 205; Coke,
'MS Journals' 28 Sept.–11 Oct.; William
Betham, *Baronetage*, 1801–5, iv. 290–1).

7. Sir George Hay (1715–6 Oct. 1778),
Kt, 1773; D.C.L., Oxford, 1742; M.P.;
jurist and orator. He refused appointment
in the spring of 1778 as one of the commissioners to treat with the United States.

8. At Battersea, where he lived (*London
Chronicle* 3–8 Oct., xliv. 336, 340; *Carlisle
MSS* 372).

9. Lord Orford.

10. Lord Ossory, as Colonel of the Bedfordshire militia, had received orders to
furnish a guard for the King during part
of his stay at Winchester 28–30 Sept. to
review the militia regiments stationed on
the Downs. The 'countermand' was evi-

The rise of the stocks persuades most men that peace is on the anvil[12]—I doubt it will be but an awkward performance. The Spanish minister[13] has formally declared his master[14] will not acknowledge the independence of America, till its *late* monarch does.[15] Methinks this will not advance peace, for *we* shall not be disposed to make that acknowledgment, if the King of Bantam will keep us in countenance.

I should have instantly obeyed your Ladyship's orders about Mr Berrisford,[16] but choose to submit to him whether he will not stay till the spring, as I always pack up the chief curiosities and all the miniatures the beginning of October, for fear of damps and housebreakers, and he would see Strawberry now to great disadvantage. I came to town today and return tomorrow, but will send him the order, if he still should desire it.[17]

dently an explanation that the colonel of the regiment need not mount guard, and Lord Ossory did not. For the two nights the King and Queen were at Winchester, the West Kent militia began the watch and was relieved by the Bedfordshire militia, the guard in each instance consisting of 'a captain, two subalterns, and 100 men.' On Wednesday morning, 30 Sept., the captain of the Bedfordshire detachment, Charles Ventris Field, was knighted (*London Gazette* No. 11914, 29 Sept.–3 Oct.).

11. 'Several general officers, and the colonels of the line, had the honour of dining with his Majesty' on Tuesday, 29 Sept. (ibid.).

12. 'Within these few months the three-per-cent consols have risen upwards of 6 per cent. If therefore the public funds are a true political barometer, there must be some secret negotiations for peace; and indeed the decisive operations of the two grand fleets seem to countenance this opinion' (*London Chronicle* 6–8 Oct., xliv. 343). Stocks had taken a sharp dip in the first quarter of the year but had by this time regained much of the loss; see the summaries at the end of each

issue of GM. Cf. MASON i. 448 and n. 29.

13. Pedro Francisco Luján Silva y Góngora (1727–94), 6th Marqués de Almodóvar; cr. (1780) Duque de Almodóvar; Spanish representative in Russia 1761–3, Portugal 1763–77, and ambassador to England 1778–9, who had been in England since 13 July (*Enciclopedia universal ilustrada*, Barcelona, 1905–33, xxviii. 2788, xxxi. 685; *Repertorium der diplomatischen Vertreter aller Länder*, Vol. II, ed. Hausmann, Zurich, 1950, p. 393; Juan Moreno de Guerra y Alonso, *Guía de la grandeza*, 2d edn, Madrid, 1917, p. 57; HW to Mann 3 July 1779; *London Chronicle* 3–5 Nov. xliv. 434).

14. Charles III.

15. HW makes a similar statement in his letter to Mason 11 Oct. 1778, MASON i. 448. The basis for this rumour has not been found, and less than a month later another rumour of opposite import prevailed; see *London Chronicle* 3–5 Nov., xliv. 434.

16. Probably Benjamin Beresford (ca 1750–ca 1819); see *post* 3 Nov. 1782.

17. He apparently waited; see *post* 24 July 1779.

To Lady Ossory, Wednesday 21 October 1778

Now first printed.

Strawberry Hill, Oct. 21, 1778.

I AM very unworthy of so long a letter from your Ladyship, for I am in such a state of ignorance about everything in the world, that if I made my answer of a length in proportion, I should be reduced to fill it chiefly with the personal history of that most insignificant personage myself. Not but three or four most important events have happened or are in agitation in my microcosm, and have occupied the interior government extremely—but as they regard nobody but the sovereign himself and his subjects (my servants) I shall be brief on them, though, had not your Ladyship's affliction[1] intervened, I could have made a considerable chapter on the first article—at present it is so old and out of my head, that I will only tell you that a fortnight ago I gave my nieces[2] a most brilliant assembly.[3] My whole castle was illuminated, and the palace of Armida[4] was not more enchanting. This adventure produced another that was of the dolor-

1. The death of Lady Holland.

2. The three Waldegraves and Anna Maria and Laura Keppel (Mason i. 445). Lady Elizabeth Laura Waldegrave wrote to her cousin Anne Clement 6 Oct. 1778: 'My dearest Nancy, I write by Mr Walpole's desire to beg of you and Mrs Clement [the grand-aunt of the Waldegraves and Keppels, and aunt of Anne Clement] to come to Strawberry Hill on Thursday the 8th of October to his assembly. He says he can give you both a bed if you will come. He desires me to insist upon your coming if Mrs Clement cannot . . . I should think there could be no objection. Pray send me an answer, that I may let Mr Walpole know. Yours most affectionately' (MS wsl).

3. The detailed description that normally would have gone to Lady Ossory went to Mason 11 Oct. 1778 (Mason i. 445–8). A letter from Lady Horatia Waldegrave to Anne Clement 10 Oct. 1778 (MS wsl) supplements that account: 'I am sorry that you was not able to be

at Mr Walpole's assembly. There was not so many people as I expected but le toute [sic] ensemble was very well. The Gallery looked charming. There was six card tables, I believe two loo tables, two whist, and two quadrille. The two latter tables and one of the whist were in the Gallery; the other whist and one of the loo tables was in the Round Room at the end; and the other loo table was in the Tapestry Bedchamber. It was very well light[ed] up. None of us played at cards. So we did nothing but parade about the rooms, so to show our authority. We got with Miss Anne North into a room where Mr Walpole locked us up with General Fitzwilliams [sic; one of the 'two ancient Generals' mentioned in Mason i. 447]. Was not that very wicked? However, Maria was the only one who profited by him, for he paid her such fine compliments.'

4. In Tasso, La Gerusalemme liberata, XVI, passim, or possibly in the opera Armida mentioned ante 14 Nov. 1774.

ous kind. My courtesy was so general and flowing, that it produced a rheumatism, and a very painful one, but that is gone too and you shall hear no more of it. The adventures of the second volume are linked also: Lord Orford having renewed the composition with his creditors, commenced before his last disorder, has not only concluded it, but has terminated his affairs with my brother and me too.[5] We have signed and sealed,[6] and it is an object to me worth seven thousands pounds, for though I do not get a sixpence at present, four thousand pounds are secured to me, with interest,[7] and I am discharged from paying above three thousands for my house,[8] which I expected I should be forced to do.[9] We see some snakes under this crop, but as they respect a futurity that we are too wise to expect,[10] we do not trouble ourselves about it, and enjoy the good of the present moment.

This opulence—to come, has very naturally made me extravagant directly. I am buying a house,[11] and a charming one, I mean for the situation, and a very good one intrinsically. If my hopes do not gallop too fast, I shall inhabit it incontinently. I am not at liberty to say more yet—nor will I tell you, that if I had a disposition to attend to

5. HW apparently did not at this time know the details of Lord Orford's settlement with his creditors. In HW's letter to Mann 11 Feb. 1779 it appears that HW consented to the sale of the Houghton pictures to Catherine of Russia, only to discover that Lord Orford did not need to sell them to raise the £15,000 required to settle his grandfather's debts, and he had no intention of paying his father's debts. See also Lord Orford to HW 1 Oct. 1778, and HW's reply 5 Oct. 1778.

6. On Tuesday 13 Oct. 1778 (Mason i. 445).

7. By the terms of his father's will ('Short Notes,' Gray i. 15 n. 96) HW was to receive £5000; by 1782 he had received only £1000 ('from my eldest brother'—therefore by 1751), and the £4000 without interest in 1786 ('Account of My Conduct,' Works ii. 365; HW to Mann 28 March 1786).

8. In Arlington Street, left to HW by Sir Robert Walpole for the unexpired term of the lease, to 1781. Presumably at the time of Sir Robert's death the lease was not entirely paid for, and Lord Orford now agreed to discharge this debt. Cf. 'Short Notes,' Gray i. 15 n. 96.

9. Probably when the lease expired in 1781.

10. HW and Sir Edward agreed 'to renounce their claim to the inheritance of Houghton, in return for the payment of the money due to them under their father's will . . . although the step might have proved highly disadvantageous to their interests' (R. W. Ketton-Cremer, A Norfolk Gallery, 1948, p. 183). If Lord Orford predeceased them, Sir Edward and HW, as the next in line to succeed to the earldom, might not inherit Houghton with the title, or might inherit it in an impoverished state, since Lord Orford was now free to do as he pleased with estate.

11. In Berkeley Square, his town house from 14 Oct. 1779 until his death. The deed of assignment was dated 25 March 1780 (Toynbee x. 341 n. 3, on information from Vernon Watney, the owner of the house in 1904). For a summary of the legal problems connected with the purchase, see Mason i. 453 n. 1; post Appendix 7.

vexations more than to advantages, I need not be so expensive, for I have had a loss of seven hundred pounds that I must pay next week[12]—not at play nor by my own fault I assure you, but it would be paltry indeed to feel seven hundred and not seven thousand—and so I am very rich and content.

Having thus expatiated on myself, it will be but civil to come to your Ladyship. I congratulate you (you particularly, Madam, for you are gathering the fruits of the education you sowed), on Lady Warwick's adoption of Miss Fox. It is in every light the properest disposition that could have been made, and as poor Lady Holland would approve it, one great burthen is taken off your mind.[13] Lord Holland will be as lucky too,[14] but boys do not, and should not demand equal attentions from tenderness, to replace a mother; nor is he of an age to feel like Miss Fox. He will not be spoiled, which will be very happy, though Lord Ossory will err on that side sooner than on the opposite.

I have not the most slight acquaintance with *your* Court[15] or its connections. Of the Duchess's good sense I have no doubt—Her attentions to your Ladyship confirm my opinion; and whatever forces the entrenchments you cast up round you, falls in with my wishes. Pray do not pique yourself on an obstinate defence.

Alas! for your chintzes, muslins, and wet drapery, Madam! My £700 knows how to feel for them—if Lord Ossory wins a sweepstakes,[16] and you are like me, you will bespeak an embroidery. I do

12. 'I am come to town . . . on disagreeable business with my brother . . . a clerk in our joint office [in the Custom House] having chosen to dispose of some money entrusted to him, à la macaroni' (HW to Harcourt, 9 Oct. 1778; to Mason 11 Oct. 1778, MASON i. 445 and n. 7; 'Account of My Conduct,' *Works* ii. 364–5; 'Short Notes,' GRAY i. 15).

13. 'Lady Louisa Conolly and the Duke of Richmond have both offered to take the two children under their protection, and Ossory seems inclined to the latter. They are both such good offers that it does not much signify which he prefers' (James Hare to Carlisle 28 Sept. – 5 Oct., *Carlisle MSS* 371). 'Lord Ossory has determined to give Caroline to the care of Lady Warwick, which is a sad disappointment to us all, who wished so much to have

her in our family: but at least it's a comfort that since she is to be with theirs they have pitched on the most like her mother of the whole set, for I hear she is gentleness itself; I only hope she will have spirit enough not to let Lady Ossory govern her' (Lady Sarah Lennox to Lady Susan O'Brien 26 Oct. 1778, in Lady Sarah Lennox, *Life and Letters* i. 281). In 1781 the Duchess of Bedford took her 'into her care . . . I know not the *whys* or the *wherefores* that she leaves Lady Warwick' (same to same, 9 April 1781, ibid. i. 321).

14. 'Lord Ossory takes Henry' (ibid. i. 281). Charles James Fox assisted with the boy's education.

15. That of the Duke and Duchess of Cumberland (*ante* 27 Sept. 1778).

16. Lord Ossory raced at the New-

not equally pity Lady Holderness; she is the Queen of Smugglers,[17] and must stand the chances of her warfare.

George Selwyn is at Paris.[18] La Mimie is on the point of being a Duke's daughter,[19] for the Duke of Queensberry is dying of a mortification in his leg.[20] George is to be here on the 15th of next month.[21]

Are you not diverted, Madam, with the treaty between the Courts of Luton and Hayes?[22] They say, there are to be answers.[23] I would offer my press, if I thought it would be accepted.

market Second October Meeting, 12–17 Oct., but he won no sweepstakes (James Weatherby, *Racing Calendar*, 1778, pp. 138–44).

17. 'A most superb court-dress, belonging to a lady of quality [Lady Holdernesse], has been lately seized and carried to the Custom House. . . . The principal piece of silk is said to have been intended as a court-dress for her Ladyship's daughter [Lady Carmarthen]' (*London Chronicle* 15–17 Oct., xliv. 371). HW mentions Lady Holdernesse's smuggling activities in his letters to Anne Pitt 19 Jan. 1766, MORE 98, and George Montagu 7 Sept. 1769 (MONTAGU ii. 288), and especially in *Last Journals* i. 108 n. 2, *sub* May 1772.

18. He arrived there 12 Oct. (DU DEFFAND v. 76–8).

19. Maria Fagnani's reputed father, Lord March, became 4th D. of Queensberry 22 Oct., succeeding his cousin. In the *Oracle* 27 Jan. 1791 she is called 'the Duke of Queensberry's natural daughter.'

20. He died 'this morning [22 Oct.] between three and four o'clock . . . at his house in Burlington Gardens' (*London Chronicle* 20–22 Oct., xliv. 392). 'He came to town in order to be at the Drawing-Room on Thursday [8 Oct.] . . . and in getting in or out of his chaise he broke his shin, which immediately became very bad, and he is now attended by three surgeons and there is much fear

a mortification will take place' (Lady Mary Coke, 'MS Journals' 11 Oct. 1778). The *London Chronicle* 15–17 Oct., xliv. 371, reported the illness 'a violent inflammation in his leg, owing to the unskilfulness of an operator in cutting a corn upon one of his Grace's toes.'

21. He delayed his departure from Paris until 19 Nov. (DU DEFFAND v. 82–7).

22. That is, the supporters of Lord Bute (Luton Hoo) and Lord Chatham (Hayes). Under 16 Oct. in *Last Journals* ii. 200 HW wrote: 'Lady Chatham published Lord Bute's negotiation with her Lord by the intervention of Sir James Wright and Dr Addington, on Lord Bute's having employed Samuel Martin to show a letter which imputed overtures to Lord Chatham.' The pamphlet HW mentions, *An Authentic Account of the Part Taken by the Late Earl of Chatham, in a Transaction Which Passed in the Beginning of the Year 1778* (though printed in the *London Chronicle* 13–15 Oct., xliv. 364–5, *sub* 14 Oct., it was not advertised as published until 17 Oct., ibid. 15–17 Oct., xliv. 375). The pamphlet is not recorded in HW's library. Other references to the affair are ibid. 13–22 Oct., xliv. 364–5, 380, 389.

23. As indicated ibid. 389. HW discusses these answers in *Last Journals* ii. 201–2; see also *Annual Register*, 1778, pp. 244–64, for texts and extracts.

To Lady Ossory, Wednesday 28 October 1778

Now first printed.

Arlington Street, Oct. 28, 1778.

WELL, I have agreed for my house, Madam, and am come to sign and seal.[1] It is no less than Sir Cecil Bishop's[2] in Berkeley Square, in my eye the cheerfulest and most agreeable situation in London, and yet I buy it very cheap.[3] In truth it is plain and homely, but I am charmed with it, as men pretend to be when they marry a dowdy for convenience—and I shall return to my mistress Strawberry with double pleasure, when the honeymoon is over.

It is pity the town is so empty, for there is enough to talk on. There is Lord Mount Stewart's manifesto,[4] Lord Howe and Governor Johnstone from America,[5] a quarrel and reconciliation at Court, Admiral Keppel come in,[6] and the Brest fleet come out,[7] and Lord March new boiled, and issuant a young Duke.[8] The apparition of Lord Howe is a little untoward, as he has not brought Monsieur Destain prisoner, which we were positive last week he would do.[9]

1. HW's agreement to buy the house is dated 2 Nov. 1778 and is signed by HW and the auctioneer. See Appendix 7.

2. Sir Cecil Bisshopp (d. 15 June 1778), 6th Bt, 1725, of Parham, Sussex; M.P.

3. For £4000, not including the fixtures, which were 'to be taken at a fair valuation.' See Appendix 7.

4. A four-column letter ('Hill Street, Oct. 23') from Lord Mount Stuart 'To the Printer of the *London Chronicle*,' in which Mount Stuart denied that his father, Lord Bute, had initiated or fostered negotiations for a union between Chatham and Bute. He quotes a letter from Bute to Lady Chatham, 16 Aug. 1778, and concludes, 'I do not intend to set up for a newspaper author, or to answer questions, objections, or observations, or to engage in printed altercation with anybody' (*London Chronicle* 24–27 Oct., xliv. 401–2; also in some of the daily papers of 26 Oct.). See also *Last Journals* ii. 201–3.

5. Both arrived at Portsmouth on Sunday, 25 Oct. in the ship *Eagle* from New York (Supplement to the *London Gazette* No. 11921, 24–8 Oct.).

6. Keppel, having made no contact with the Brest fleet, came into Portsmouth 25 Oct. with about 20 ships, several badly damaged by a storm, and other ships of the fleet arrived within a day or two. He went ashore 27 Oct. and arrived in London 2 Nov. (ibid. 27 Oct – 5 Nov., xliv. 415–16, 418, 434).

7. It was reported 'from Brest that all the captains of the ships there under 80 guns have received orders to get ready for sailing' (*Daily Adv.* 22 Oct., sub 'Paris, Oct. 9'). D'Orvilliers' fleet had returned to Brest 18 Sept. (*Gazette de Leyde* 9 Oct.). On 23 Oct. it was still there: 'Les vaisseaux de guerre dans le port de Brest, qui avaient ordre de mettre en mer, n'avaient pu encore appareiller le 23 à cause de mauvais temps' (ibid. 6 Nov., sub 'Paris . . . 30 octobre').

8. Of Queensberry.

9. The manœuvres of the two fleets are described in A. T. Mahan, *Major Operations of the Navies in the War of Amer-*

His Lordship has taken nothing but his leave[10]—What care I? says your Honour; tell me about the quarrel at Court. Why, Madam, you know the Duchess of Argyll[11] was to come into waiting, and she had resolved to be quite well, and look as well as she could, and carry her last rays to Lord Petre's.[12] 'No,' said our gracious Queen; 'Lady Egremont, you shall go with me to Lord Petre's.' 'Madam,' said the Queen of Scots, 'if you meant to affront me, you might have taken another method'[13]—Now methinks one way of affronting is as good as another. Says the Countess of Hertford, 'Duchess, I shall leave the key (the golden key)[14] with you'—'Leave it with Lady Egremont, she is the favourite,' said the angry dame—and home she goes, swears she will resign, and sits down to write. The Duke, who did not think that all ways of scolding a Queen were equal, insisted on penning the letter, and so he did, and it was copied and sent, and moderate enough no doubt, for the answer was, 'Desire her to consider on it'— and so she did[15]—and so ends my story—but the beginning is still wanting, and that everybody supplies as they please by conjecture. But I do not profess recording guess-work, and who can tell why two ladies fall out?[16]

Lord March has everything;[17] Mr Douglas[18] is to get something,[19]

ican Independence, Boston, 1913, pp. 69–81, and in Howe's dispatch of 17 Aug., in the London Gazette 24–28 Oct., reprinted in the London Chronicle 27–29 Oct., xliv. 411–15.

10. HW uses the same phrasing in his letter to Mann 30 Oct. 1778.

11. HW gives a more detailed version of this affair in Last Journals ii. 202–3, saying that the Duchess of Argyll 'had long aimed at being the King's mistress . . . and behaved so familiarly with the King, even at Chapel, and behind the Queen's chair, that the latter was determined to affront her.'

12. The King and Queen spent two nights, 19–20 Oct., at Lord Petre's seat, Thorndon Hall, in Essex, 'contiguous to Warley Common,' where the King reviewed on 20 Oct. the troops encamped there (London Chronicle 17–27 Oct., xliv. 384, 399, 402; London Gazette No. 11920, 20–24 Oct., Mason i. 446 and n. 14). Lord Petre's journal before and during the visit is printed in Maude D. Petre, The Ninth Lord Petre, 1928, pp. 40–48.

13. 'The Duchess of Argyll did not attend her Majesty to Lord Petre's, which is rather to be wondered at, as she was in waiting and able to go' (Coke, 'MS Journals' 21 Oct. 1778).

14. Of the Queen's Bedchamber.

15. Lady Louisa Stuart was at Court 30 Oct. 1778: 'The Duchess of Argyll was in waiting, which they reckoned an event, as there has been a great fracas between her and the Queen, and she resigned; but now it is all made up' (Lady Louisa to Lady Caroline Dawson 30 Oct. 1778, in Gleanings from an Old Portfolio, ed. A. G. C. Clark, Edinburgh, 1895–8, i. 93–4).

16. In Last Journals ii. 202–3 HW suggests that the 'Queen had early been jealous of her, and had used her so ill that she had thought of resigning; but the Duke loved money better than her, and was not jealous.'

17. From the late Duke of Queensberry, who had died 22 Oct.

18. Archibald James Edward Douglas (1748–1827), cr. (1790) Bn Douglas of

if Lord March gets nothing;[20] a Sir John Douglas[21] is to be Earl of
Drumlanrig with part, if the same nothing happens,[22] and the Duke
of Buccleugh, much the nearest relation,[23] has not even a chance.[24]
The house at Petersham with everything in it, not much, and £1000
are left to Lady Jane Scott,[25] for which I am glad, though I doubt
whether she can afford to live in it.[26] The Marchesina[27] is not come
to Paris, but George is to fetch her in April.

I wrote all this last night, Madam, having destined this morning
to a survey of my new palace, I should say *a review*, but I am confined today to my old one by the gout in my foot, which was so slight
yesterday that I thought it would go off. It is still so inconsiderable,
that I rather encourage it, in hopes of paying but so moderate a fine
for the winter. Besides, it is very becoming just now, and gives me a
very opulent look, as I expect a Jew broker[28] to sell some stock for me,
and a lawyer[29] to make the conveyance. It is so like a rich old alderman to be sitting with a large shoe and buying a house when one
should be thinking of one's coffin!—but I have saved five and forty
pounds by the rise of stocks since yesterday; and as the gain of five
and forty pounds would banish any alderman's philosophy, why

Douglas; the subject of the Douglas cause
in the 1760's; M.P.

19. See below, fourth paragraph from
the end of this letter.

20. That is, if the 4th Duke of Queensberry ('Lord March') died without lawful
issue.

21. (ca 1708 – 13 Nov. 1778), 3d Bt, 1733,
of Kelhead; M.P. (*Scots Peerage* vii. 150).

22. Sir John Douglas's grandson, Sir
Charles Douglas (1777–1837), 5th Bt, 1783,
in 1810 succeeded the 4th D. of Queensberry ('Lord March' of this paragraph)
in the titles of Marquis and Earl of
Queensberry, Viscount Drumlanrig, and
Lord Douglas (*Scots Peerage* vii. 150–2).
The earldom of Drumlanrig went with
the dukedom to the Duke of Buccleuch;
see below.

23. The 4th Duke of Queensberry was
the grandson of the 3d Duke's uncle,
William, 1st E. of March. Archibald
James Edward Douglas, even more distantly related, had been befriended and
partly educated by the 3d D. of Queensberry. The Duke of Buccleuch was the
grandson of the 3d Duke's sister.

24. In 1810, however, on the death of
the 4th D. of Queensberry ('Lord March'
of this paragraph), unmarried, the D.
of Buccleuch became 5th D. of Queensberry and inherited the Douglas estates in
Dumfriesshire (GEC, *sub* Buccleuch and
Queensberry).

25. His niece.

26. After dining with Lady Jane at
Douglas House on 3 June 1779, Lady Ossory wrote to Selwyn: 'The house is just
such a one as I should have supposed
the Duke of Queensberry to have contrived. The place is as ugly as it can be
in that very beautiful part of the world'
(Jesse, *Selwyn*, iv. 175).

27. Maria Fagnani.

28. Gomez; see below.

29. John Tilly (ca 1715–90), 'attorney,
15 Poultry,' 'many years an eminent solicitor,' died at his house at Walthamstow 17
June 1790 (*New Complete Guide to All
Persons Who Have Any Trade or Concern
with the City of London*, 1783, p. 306; GM
1790, lx pt i. 577; *London Chronicle* 19–
22 June 1790, lxvii. 586). HW agreed
with Samuel Clayton the auctioneer, on

should I be more a Stoic? Indeed I look upon myself as the most rational of all philosophers: I have never valued money, and yet had prudence enough to keep myself independent and at ease; and even my new purchase is a stroke of worldly wisdom, for I raise a house at least over my head if the stocks should leave me in the lurch.

Pray, Madam, direct your next missive to town, for I shall certainly be more resident here for some time than at Strawberry, for my new mansion is so ready that the moment I can take up my bed, I may walk thither. I forgot to tell you that in the second storey there is a vast nursery, that held the late Sir Cecil's whole bench of Bishops.[30] I bought an ancient cradle some years ago;[31] so if anybody would leave me a dukedom, I might set about procreation without loss of time.[32]

I had actually sealed my letter and directed it to Southampton, but it was luckily not gone to the post, when I received your Ladyship's from Ampthill. You will find how impossible it is for me to stir or even think of stirring; I was brought down into the dining-room today by two servants. However I think it will be a short fit, and that I possibly may be free in few days; nay, I shall be more courageous after a fit than when I might expect one, as I have had none for near two years.[33]

I have told your Ladyship the outlines of the Duke of Queensberry's will. He has given the English estate[34] to Mr Douglas, if the present Duke has no lawful Mimis.

Having not seen a creature today but old Gomez[35] the broker, I can add nothing to my gazette. The town is so silent that I suppose there is nobody in it.

If my gout goes off, and my purchase is finished, I shall be very happy to make a visit to Ampthill for a day or two the end of next week—but an ancient's promises are as brittle as a boy's, and therefore I always speak with an if.

2 Nov. 1778, to purchase the Bisshopp house 'if Mr Tilly my attorney approves of the title'; see Appendix 7.

30. He had twelve children; three of the eight daughters died young (William Betham, *Baronetage of England*, 1801–5, i. 195).

31. On 14 Aug. 1774 but 'was ashamed to bring it away, as having no babe to put into it' (COLE i. 343; BERRY ii. 155).

32. As rumour suggested the new Duke of Queensberry would do (Coke, 'MS Journals' 28, 31 Oct., 15 Nov. 1778; Lady Sarah Lennox, *Life and Letters* i. 284, *sub* 26 Oct.).

33. His last fit was from Dec. 1776 to Feb. 1777.

34. Amesbury in Wiltshire (*Scots Peerage* i. 211).

35. Probably A. Gomez, who in 1796

My poor nephew, I hear, intends to bring in a bill to authorize the militia to invade the coasts of France.[36] I am serious—but somebody knocks and I must again seal my dispatch.

To Lady Ossory, Monday 9 November 1778

Now first printed.
In Kirgate's hand.
Address: To the Countess of Ossory at Ampthill Park, Bedfordshire. *Postmark:* 9 NO.

Arlington Street, Nov. 9, 1778.

ALAS! Yes, Madam, I am again on the gridiron, and have been so ever since I wrote last; nor are any of the bars cool yet. In short, my dear Lady, I have been confined to my bed with the gout ever since Thursday was sennight,[1] in both feet and knees, and in my left hand and elbow. On Friday and Saturday I thought myself recovering, and sat up for two hours each day, but on Saturday night the enemy resumed all its posts, and, which is forty times worse, has made a lodgement in my right hand.

In this forlorn state, Madam, am I at present; and therefore it would be unpardonable to tire anybody else with an old story so often repeated, and which signifies nothing but to the sufferer, as there is no danger in it, and it is even called renewing one's lease.[2] If it is, I am sure it is as bad to hold of the gout as of the Church, for both screw one to the uttermost.

You will excuse my brevity, Madam, when you know that it costs me an effort to dictate. Perhaps some few days may make a favourable change.

---

bought £4500 of 3 percent consols for HW (Gomez to HW 2 May 1796); or 'old Gomez' may be the father of A. Gomez.

36. No record has been found that Lord Orford introduced such a bill.

---

1. 29 Oct.
2. It was believed that following a regular fit of the gout, 'the patient's good habit of body and appetite return in proportion to the severity of the pain in the last fit; and in the same proportion the next fit will be either accelerated or retarded; for, if the last fit was very severe, the next will not come on in less time than a solar revolution' (*Encyclopædia Britannica*, Edinburgh, 1771, iii. 126).

To Lord and Lady Ossory,
Wednesday 18 November 1778

Now first printed.
In Kirgate's hand.
Address: To the Earl of Ossory at Ampthill Park, Bedfordshire. *Postmark:*
18 NO. FREE.

Arlington Street, 9 o'clock, Nov. 18, 1778.

My good Lord and Lady,

PHILIP has just shown me your very kind note, and its kindness tells me that an answer from myself will be more satisfactory. I am inded a vast deal mended since yesterday morning, and General Conway, who came up to me yesterday, is so satisfied with the change in me that he has just left me, and returns to Park Place tomorrow morning. I am actually out of bed, and have been so this half hour, and bear it extremely well. I will say nothing of what is past, for it is over, and I will forget it, if I can; but I cannot stand many such recoveries; though I own the note to Philip is a precious cordial, and I heartily thank both for it.

To Lady Ossory, Friday 20 November 1778

Now first printed.
In Kirgate's hand.

Arlington Street, Nov. 20, 1778.

IT may be a work of supererogation, Madam, but my gratitude for your Ladyship's and Lord Ossory's goodness is so warm, that I cannot help thanking you step by step as I mend, as if every change were owing to you as much as to me it seems to be. Seven of my joints are already expecting their deliverance, and it is only the right hand, which I want most, that is yet sullen and will not acknowledge your influence.

Mr Fitzpatrick has been so good as to call here, but I was not only not able to see him, but have refused so many of my own family, that I did not dare to receive others; for when one is ill, one's consolations are to take precedence according to the act of succession, and not by the measure of one's own feelings; just as one is sometimes forced to have a low fever turned into a high one, before one is to have the comfort of a cure.

Apropos to Mr F. I am glad there is some poetic justice left in the world, though her prose sisters may all be retired. In one of your Ladyship's letters at the beginning of this month, which I received a week too late, you told me that you had betrayed one of mine to Mr Fitzpatrick; and the very letter in which you told me so, fell first by your own fault into the hands of a wrong H.W.[1] In short, it was carried to *Woolterton*,[2] which I suppose was taken for *Arlington*, as your Ladyship has a magnificent style of sketching ideas of the alphabet rather than of drawing any precise likeness of the letters.

Mars's bastard, the god of duels, has been very pert this week; Colonel Ackland, after all his escapes in America, is killed by an officer[3] in Devonshire;[4] and the Vicomte du Barri[5] by his friend[6] at

1. Hon. Horatio Walpole (*ante* 22 April 1777), son and heir of HW's first cousin Horatio (1723–1809), 2d Bn Walpole of Woolterton, 1757, cr. (1806) E. of Orford, n.c.

2. Woolterton, Norfolk, the seat of HW's first cousin Horatio.

3. Said to be 'Lieutenant Lloyd, a brother-officer, in which he [Acland] defended the Americans against the aspersion of cowardice' (W. L. Stone, *Ballads and Poems Relating to the Burgoyne Campaign*, Albany, N.Y., 1893, p. 316). In 1775 John Lloyd had become lieutenant of the 20th Foot (of which Acland was major); he became captain in the same regiment, 1787.

4. Acland died 15 Nov. (31 Oct. and 22 Nov. are incorrect) 'as a result of a duel, the precise details of which are not clear' (Dyke Acland in *Devon and Cornwall Notes and Queries*, 1932–33, xvii. 13). Conflicting reports were current. The *London Chronicle* 19–21 Nov., xliv. 494, attributed it to 'a contusion received in his head by a fall a few days before as he was going to his farm.' Lady Sarah Lennox on 23 Nov. was 'very glad he did not lose his life in a duel' but on 12 Dec. wrote that he 'was killed by a fall on his head in a duel' (Lennox, *Life and*

Letters i. 285; *Leinster Corr.* ii. 265). According to W. P. Courtenay in DNB, Acland 'escaped without a wound' from the duel, but 'the exposure brought on a severe cold, from the effects of which he died.' Cf. *Bulletin of the Fort Ticonderoga Museum*, July 1934, iii. 167.

5. Jean-Baptiste du Barry (1749 – 18 Nov. 1778), known as Vicomte Adolphe du Barry; son of Jean-Baptiste du Barry (1722–94), Comte du Barry, nephew (by marriage) to Mme du Barry, who had been his father's mistress before she became the King's mistress and was married to Vicomte Adolphe's uncle (Marius Tallon, *La Vicomtesse Adolphe . . . et les du Barry*, Privas, 1892; DU DEFFAND, *passim*). Mrs Damer had met the Du Barrys at Spa in the summer of 1778, had accompanied them to Bath late in October, and after the Vicomte's death accompanied the Vicomtesse to Paris (Tallon, op. cit.; Coke, 'MS Journals' 30 Oct., 26 Nov. 1778; *Liste des seigneurs et dames, venus aux eaux minerales de Spa, l'an 1778*, Liége and Spa, [1778], *sub* 2, 8, 24 July for the arrival of Rice, the Du Barrys, and Mrs Damer, in that order).

6. James Louis Rice (ca 1730–1801), son of Thomas Rice of Ballymacdoyle, co. Kerry; went to the Irish Pastoral

Bath. This friend, alias toadeater, is a sharper, not of the first order. They quarrelled at the tavern, took a coach at three in the morning, and sat in it very sociably till daylight, when they fought; Orestes was killed on the spot, and Pylades dangerously wounded.[7]

I live in hopes of seeing Lord Ossory next week,[8] but do not build upon your Ladyship before Christmas; a less loss than ever, as I cannot expect to make so distant a journey as Grosvenor Place for some weeks.

To Lady Ossory, Tuesday 24 November 1778

Now first printed.
In Kirgate's hand.
Address: To the Countess of Ossory at Ampthill Park, Bedfordshire. *Postmark:* 24 NO. EK.

Arlington Street, Nov. 24, 1778.

YOUR Ladyship's letters are so agreeable that I can never repent contributing to make them more legible, though they fully answer the pains of deciphering. I order a few lines to you because you talk of not writing till bidden; commands I will certainly give, if they will be minded. Think what an event a letter from you is in my miserable state! And yet my situation is highly mended. I am swung out of bed, and lie upon my couch for eight or ten hours before I am put into my cradle again; and all this without pain. But this rapid advancement from my bed to its water-gall my couch, does not flatter me that I shall be fit for Christmas gambols, and for promoting jollity at Ampthill;

College at Louvain; entered the Austrian army and became the friend of Joseph II, who made him a Count of the Holy Roman Empire; became acquainted with Du Barry at Paris in 1774; tried at Taunton at the Lent assizes, 1779, for the death of Du Barry and acquitted of manslaughter; planned to rescue Marie Antoinette during her imprisonment and convey her to Ireland; died in Spain (Richard Hayes, *Biographical Dictionary of Irishmen in France*, Dublin, 1949, pp. 274–5; GM 1801, lxxi pt ii. 1212; *Annual Register*, 1778, 1779, xxi. 211, xxii. 204–5; *London Magazine*, 1779, xlviii. 187–8).

7. HW's account approximates that in an 'Extract of a Letter from Bath, Nov. 18,' in the *London Chronicle* 19–21 Nov., xliv. 490, and further details are ibid. 21–26 Nov., 19–22 Dec., xliv. 498–9, 509, 593, and in Tallon, op. cit. The cause of the duel is variously given as a misunderstanding connected with gambling or a jealousy caused by Rice's attentions to the Vicomtesse.

8. Parliament was to meet 26 Nov.

The days of folly and of fond delight
Are wasted all and fled; those that remain[1]

are doomed I doubt to anguish, at least to feebleness and a narrow circle. I have broken too many promises to dare make more; and though my limbs are all broken to pieces, they must be boiled in Medea's kettle[2] if I recover my jollity and Ampthillity. I have another certain mark of age which makes me think I shall grow very rich: my dread of a relapse has made me at last submit to be dirty. I have neither had my room mopped every day, as I used to do in the gout, nor changed my sheets above once a week; so, as dirt is the foundation of wealth, I don't see why I should not come into Parliament again, at least for any Scotch borough, except the shire of *Air*.

Lord C.'s[3] stories diverted me extremely, especially that of the dinner in the Island of Barrataria[4]—but what will they signify? Facts will not counteract credu*ll*ity, which ought to be the orthography of credulity in the present age, that believes no truth but every lie, however clumsy.

I hope poor Miss Fox is recovered,[5] and that I shall see our Lord soon, and then, though I cannot caper, and have scarce any voice left, I will sing an Io Pæan inwardly. Adieu, my dear Madam, you see I have nothing to tell you or entertain you with, and only write to extract letters from you; the world will amuse you better in a day or two,[6] if ruin, disgrace, folly, and squabbles amongst the actors, can put you into a merry mood.

Your most devoted

H.W.

---

1. Quotation not traced.
2. 'Get thee Medea's kettle and be boiled anew' (Congreve, *Love for Love,* IV. xv).
3. Not identified.
4. Possibly a reference to a dinner given by the Lord Lieutenant in Ireland, from *Baratariana* (*ante* 30 Dec. 1773, 5 Jan. 1774).
5. Her illness was probably the stone, an attack of which nearly killed her a year later; see *post* 27 Oct. 1779, n. 7.
6. Parliament was to meet 26 Nov.

To Lady Ossory, Saturday 5 December 1778

Now first printed.
In Kirgate's hand.

Arlington Street, Dec. 5, 1778.

YOUR Ladyship's goodness quite overcomes me; and as I can dictate a few words today, they cannot be so well employed as to thank your Ladyship for your new goodness in your letter to Philip. I had begged Lord Ossory to make my excuses for not answering your Ladyship's last obliging letter; and as he returns to Ampthill today, I knew he would tell you how ill I have been again, though perhaps he will not tell you that he has been as friendly to me as you yourself could have been.

In truth I have been very foolish, and much to blame. The moment I am out of pain, and see those I love, my spirits run away with me, and I exhaust myself with talking. I talked all day for three days, and in consequence was five whole nights without a wink of sleep. I got a high fever, the gout came again in both knees, and my breast was so weak, that I could not speak to be heard. General Conway scolded me, as one deserves to be when one is a baby of six years old, or sixty—and it was time: I kept my bed for two days without being able to have it made, and on Thursday at four o'clock when my Lord Ossory left me, I was so extinct that I ordered my doors to be shut up and no creature to be admitted. Instead of departing, at five o'clock I fell asleep, and between that and past nine the next morning I got very near fourteen hours of sleep out of the sixteen—*pas mal çela*—I was so well yesterday morning that I rose at noon, and saw company till ten at night; and my want of voice, and a good deal of fever still, prevented my chattering. I have had another perfectly good night, have not the smallest degree of fever left, and can even bear to sit near the fire which I had not seen for six weeks—but what a long story I am telling, and what fine proofs of taciturnity I give! Your Ladyship will think it is my nurse is answering your letter to Philip. In a word, Madam, I have peeped again into the grave, but am returned, as Sam. Martin was luckily not behind me, to give me a tip with the edge of his target.[1]

1. Another reference to Martin's reversion of HW's ushership of the Exchequer and his having practised at a target before he fought a duel with Wilkes (HW

I will not pretend to answer a word of your last till I can write myself, nor to tell you news of any sort, as you will learn all more agreeably from our Lord. I shall now employ all my attention and care to refit my old hulk for another voyage into the world—of my friends —a mere coasting voyage of a no great length, nor far from the shore. Adieu, my best Madam; be assured, though so little remains of me, that my gratitude and attachment remain as entire in that small fragment, as they were in the whole, before any part was consumed.

To Lady Ossory, Saturday 12 December 1778

Now first printed.
In Kirgate's hand.
Address: To the Countess of Ossory at Ampthill Park, Bedfordshire. *Postmark:* 12 DE. EK.

Arlington Street, December 12, 1778.

I PERCEIVE and feel the kindness of your Ladyship's reason for not answering my last, and I will not suffer you to write again to Philip. I have been very ill indeed ever since this day sennight, and in great danger of an inflammation on my breast,[1] but it is quite over; and so is my gout, all but in my right hand. I have not been permitted to see but a few of my own family and one or two friends, and scarce to speak to them. Tomorrow I am to see a few more, under Sacrament of being very prudent: the better day the better deed.

Poor Mr Craufurd has got the gout.

Quelles nouvelles depuis deux jours![2]—but I must not talk, and you will see today's papers.

Adieu both!

PS. I shall not attempt to write before the middle of next week.

to Mann 18 Jan. 1764, MANN vi. 198 n. 8; *post* 16 Aug. 1788).

1. A more detailed account of this illness is in HW's letter to Mann 18 Dec. 1778.

2. On 10 Dec. the Lords of the Admiralty issued orders for holding a court martial on the conduct of Admiral Keppel at Ushant 27 July based on charges preferred by Sir Hugh Palliser. On 11

Dec., Temple Luttrell introduced a motion in the House of Commons that Palliser be court-martialled for failing to obey Keppel's orders at Ushant. The debate was long and heated, and both Keppel and Palliser spoke (*London Chronicle* 10–12 Dec., xliv. 566–8; *Journals of the House of Commons* xxxvii. 42; Cobbett, *Parl. Hist.* xix. 1377–87, xx. 53–73; *Last Journals* ii. 214–15, 223–6).

To Lady Ossory, Saturday 19 December 1778

Now first printed.
In Kirgate's hand.

Arlington Street, Dec. 19, 1778.

MY weak voice has no hand, and my weak hand no voice yet, so I shall attempt no great achievements today, Madam. Perhaps a better reason were, that I have nothing new to tell you. My recovery is in a very prosperous way, and more owing to nature, than to my own intended prudence: patience is the only real possession I have, and I shall employ it till I am quite as well as I was two months ago, intending to keep my whole merry Christmas in this room. I cannot adjourn to Ampthill, and I will not deign to accept any succedaneum.

The court martial[1] seems to have awakened part of this drowsy country at last, and is the first flagrancy that has caused any sensation; but I never answer for the next minute. The letters received by Colonel Stuart[2] were by no means welcome, and so they go on lying about divisions in America, and so they will, till people are tired of believing.

1. Of Admiral Keppel. It was held at Portsmouth 7 Jan.–11 Feb. HW discusses the trial and its background and consequences in *Last Journals*. A bill, 'to enable the Lord High Admiral . . . to order court martial of sea officers to be held,' brought in by Admiral Pigot 16 Dec., was rushed through and passed in the House of Commons the next day, and sent to the Lords on the 18th. It received the royal assent 24 Dec. as 19 Geo. III c. 6, the title revised to read, 'An act to authorize the lord high admiral, or the commissioners for executing the office of Lord High Admiral for the time being to order any court martial which may be appointed on the charge of Sir Hugh Palliser against the Honourable Augustus Keppel, to be holden on shore' (*Journals of the House of Commons* xxxvii. 54–5; *Journals of the House of Lords* xxxv. 541–5; *Statutes at Large*, ed. Owen Ruff-

head, 1763–1800, xiii. 311). The Admiralty's order for the trial is dated 31 Dec. (text in *Minutes of the . . . Court-Martial . . . for the Trial of . . . Admiral Augustus Keppel*, 1779, pp. 1–2).

2. On 17 Dec. 'Col Stuart, son of the Earl of Bute, arrived at the Plantation Office with dispatches from Gen. Clinton at New York' (*London Chronicle* 17–19 Dec., xliv. 585; *Public Advertiser* 19 Dec.). Letters, with enclosures, from the peace commissioners were also brought; the commissioners announced their intention of sailing home, feeling that their mission was fruitless (B. F. Stevens, *Facsimiles of Manuscripts in European Archives Relating to America*, 1889–98, *passim*). Nevertheless the *Daily Advertiser*, 18 Dec., reported that 'several of the southern colonies have accepted the terms of reconciliation offered them by his Majesty's commissioners.'

The Duke of Richmond is quite recovered:[3] he was in much danger last Sunday, and the Duchess sent an express for Lord George.[4]

The King of France has been in earnest; the Queen thinks herself big with twins.[5] She grew frightened, and her debts came into her conscience; she sent for Monsieur Necker,[6] told him she owed four hundred thousand livres, did not know how to pay them, and was afraid to tell the King. The Protestant Comptroller replied, he would pay them with his own money, and the King should never know it. I doubt there was as much policy as Protestant *grandeur d'âme* in this, for by mere accident the King heard the story, and will pay the debt himself.[7]

There is a stupid play come out of Fielding's,[8] without nature, character, probability, wit or humour. It has an advertisement prefixed,[9] which ascribes the long loss of this treasure to its being lent to poor Sir Charles Williams,[10] who, it supposes with dull pertness,

3. Lady Sarah Lennox to the Duchess of Leinster, 15 Dec. 1778: 'My brother has been very ill, but is now . . . out of danger. I was so much alarmed as to come to town . . . His complaint is what they call spasms in his bowels, which occasioned a bloody flux with such violent pain nothing ever equalled it. But as there was no inflammation or fever . . . the danger is past . . . Dr Heberden has attended him and says he need not come any more' (*Leinster Corr.* ii. 265–6, with references to his recovery at pp. 266–9; Coke 'MS Journals' 17 Dec. 1778).

4. The Duke's brother, Lord George Lennox.

5. Her daughter was born on the day this letter was written: Marie-Thérèse-Charlotte (1778–1851), 'Madame Royale,' m. (1799) Louis-Antoine de Bourbon, Duc d'Angoulême.

6. Jacques Necker (1732–1804), Swiss banker, Director-General of Finance 1777–81, 1788–90.

7. This anecdote, not in DU DEFFAND, came from Mrs Damer, who was in Paris 4–9 Dec. Lady Mary Coke, in her 'MS Journals' 17 Dec. 1778 reports having seen Mrs Damer after her Paris visit, and continues, 'the Queen of France was not then [9 Dec.] brought to bed but very big and expecting every day. She thought herself she should have two children.'

Cf. DU DEFFAND v. 88, 90; *Leinster Corr.* ii. 265. The Queen's debts were estimated at 1,500,000 livres by the *London Chronicle* 7–9 Jan., xlv. 31.

8. *The Fathers: or, The Good-Natur'd Man*, first acted at Drury Lane 30 Nov., and published 12 Dec., the day of the ninth and last performance (Genest vi. 77–88; *London Chronicle* 28 Nov.–3 Dec., 12–15 Dec., xliv. 528, 533, 572; W. L. Cross, *The History of Henry Fielding*, New Haven, 1918, i. 372–3, iii. 99–109; F. Homes Dudden, *Henry Fielding*, Oxford, 1952, i. 217–21, ii. 1066–8). HW's copy, now WSL (Hazen, *Cat. of HW's Lib.* 1810. 29. 9), has two notes in Kirgate's hand: at the foot of the title-page, 'December'; on the verso of the title-page, apropos of the statement in the Advertisement that Sir Charles Williams died in Russia: 'This is not true; Sir Charles returned from Russia, disordered in his senses, and died so in England.' In the Prologue, written by Garrick, HW marked one couplet, apropos of the public's demand for portraits and statues of a departed 'son of fame' and also a line describing Sophia in *Tom Jones*.

9. It was probably written by Sir John Fielding, who wrote the dedication to the Duke of Northumberland (Cross, loc. cit.; Dudden, loc. cit.).

10. Sir Charles Hanbury Williams

laid it aside[11] lest it should interrupt his political negotiations—I don't hold the latter very high in general, but at least they are of as much importance as a paltry comedy. Sir Charles, continues the preface, *died in Russia,* and so the piece was lost for many years. Could one believe this could be asserted already, when everybody knows he came home from Russia out of his senses, and died in a mad-house here?[12] A reflection that might have checked the ill nature, if not the ignorance.

Pray, Madam, let me hear of your holidays, if I cannot partake them; but I will look forward to your coming to town.

To Lady Ossory, Thursday 24 December 1778

Now first printed. A corner of the MS has been broken off and lost.

Dec. 24, 1778.

I CAN make no better use of the resurrection of my right hand, Madam, than in answering your Ladyship's las⟨t.⟩ It touched me, it charmed me, it hurt me, it displeased me. H⟨u⟩mility and contrition springing from the reflections of good sense are amiable, are respectable—but they may be pushed too far, and then they approach to the humiliation of a bigot or enthusiast. Is it just, is it rational to confound yourself, or to imagine that I confounded you, with women who brave public censure, or level themselves to the most abandoned of their sex? I did not name the two ladies in question,[1] because, though there are shades in their conduct, I think the

(1708–59), K.B., 1744; verse-writer; diplomatist; M.P.; HW's correspondent.

11. Since Fielding embarked on 26 June 1754 for his voyage to Lisbon, he could have sent the MS of the play to Williams at any time between Aug. 1753 and June 1754. Apparently the MS remained at Williams's country house, Coldbrook Park, in Monmouthshire, where his nephew discovered it in 1776 (Earl of Ilchester and Mrs Langford-Brooke, *Life of Sir Charles Hanbury-Williams,* 1928, pp. 279–88; Cross, op. cit. iii. 100).

12. Williams left St Petersburg 1 Sept. 1757, broke down at Hamburg in Jan. 1758, arrived in England 26 Feb., was placed under Dr Batty's care in a house in Kensington for five weeks, improved, was released, but in March, 1759, was placed under the care of Dr John Monro and was confined until his death. At 'the end of July he was living in Lord Bolingbroke's house at Chelsea. He was then temporarily quieter and better, but never fully recovered his senses, and died on November 2' (Ilchester and Langford-Brooke, op. cit. 417–28; MANN v. 183; SELWYN 322–3).

1. Lady Carmarthen and Lady Derby. Lady Carmarthen's affair with John Byron began in November 1778, and on

behaviour of both disgusting: and when a party is made to support one of them² in defiance of all laws of decorum,³ I could not think on one who has almost hid herself even from her nearest friends, unless to admire the contrast, and not to draw a comparison.⁴

Indeed in general I do not love to talk of young people, ⟨when there⟩ is no occasion to commend them. Condemnation looks like ⟨the bitter⟩ness of old age—and besides, not connecting with them, ⟨they often⟩ make very slight impression on my memory, and very seldo⟨m take⟩ up my thoughts when I am writing a letter. If there were ⟨any⟩ imagination, or novelty in the style of the present race, I should be entertained with the report, without envy or detraction; but what amusement is there in hearing that Sir Charles This

13 Dec. she eloped with him. Divorced by Act of Parliament in May 1779 for adultery, she married Byron 9 June 1779 (*Trials for Adultery*, 'Taken in Short-Hand, by a Civilian,' 1779–80, Vol. II, Libel of the M. of Carmarthen vs. the Marchioness of Carmarthen; *Corr. Geo. III* iv. 232–4; *Public Advertiser* 18, 25 Dec.; Coke 'MS Journals' 29 Nov., 15, 22 Dec. 1778). Lady Elizabeth Hamilton (1753–97), m. (1774) Edward Smith-Stanley, 12th E. of Derby, 1776. In 1778 she had an affair with the Duke of Dorset, the father of her daughter Lady Elizabeth Henrietta Stanley, born in 1779. Lord and Lady Derby were separated by early December, but Lord Derby refused to give her a divorce. HW refers to both affairs in his letter to Lady Browne 18 Dec. 1778, and to the second in his letter to Mann 29 Jan. 1779 (MORE 193–4; Lady Sarah Lennox, *Life and Letters* i. 290–2; *Intimate Society Letters of the Eighteenth Century*, ed. the D. of Argyll, [1910], i. 267–89; Coke, 'MS Journals' 28 June, 2–22 Dec. 1778, 26 Jan. 1790; *Public Advertiser* 12, 26 Dec.; *Morning Post* 16, 24, 26 Nov., 7–8 Dec.).

2. Lady Derby.

3. Lady Derby's mother, the Duchess of Argyll, 'declares highly that she will protect Lady Derby' (Coke 'MS Journals' 22 Dec. 1778). 'There is a sort of party in town of who is to visit her [Lady Derby] and who is not, which creates great squabbles' (Lady Sarah Lennox to Lady Susan O'Brien, Feb. 1779, in Lennox, *Life*

and Letters i. 291). Both HW and Lady Mary Coke indicate that Lady Carmarthen repented her conduct, that Lady Holdernesse would 'receive her daughter on any terms,' but 'I don't hear she [Lady Carmarthen] desires to see company or that she intends to brave the world; however bad she may be, at least there is some appearance of shame' (HW to Lady Browne 18 Dec. 1778, MORE 194; Coke, 'MS Journals' 22 Dec. 1778).

4. In spite of her retirement, Lady Ossory was the subject of gossip: 'Lady Ossory has taken a fancy to Mr Steuart, Lady Bute's second son [James Archibald Stuart, later Stuart Wortley Mackenzie (1747–1818), M.P. 1768–1806], who is Lieutenant Colonel to her Lord's regiment of militia. They have been together at Southampton all this summer, and their intimacy is not doubted by any of those who have been in their company. I think she has good courage and no shame, for if Lord Ossory discovers this affair and that she is a second time divorced she can't expect any more protection' (Coke, 'MS Journals' 12 Nov. 1778). 'Lady Ossory's inclination for Mr Steuart is now much talked of' (ibid. 29 Dec. 1778). Lady Louisa Stuart wrote 17 Nov. 1778 to her sister, Lady Caroline Dawson, that their mother, Lady Bute 'tells me that a little piece of scandal goes about, which is likely enough to be true; that Lady Ossory is violently in love with James' (*Gleanings from an Old Portfolio*, ed. A. G. C. Clark, Edinburgh, 1895–8, i. 104).

is run away for debt, or my Lady That turned street-walker? In short, there is nothing but vice without taste, great villainy for little objects, and more pleasure in losing money than in spending it.

⟨I⟩ should totally disapprove your Ladyship's *retaining* Curtius.[5] ⟨I⟩ should scorn being defended against the *Morning Post*.[6] There is a silent dignity in your conduct that is the only answer you should deign to give to ill nature, and which ill nature alone will reject. There are passages in Curtius well written, and others in which he attempts innovations in language that are more than he can wield —but if he wrote better, I would not employ him; yet I would send him a civil answer, not to set a new dog barking.

The Commissioners are returned,[7] and do not confirm the disposition of the Americans to treat—indeed their return is sufficient proof of the contrary.

Nothing can be kinder than your Ladyship's invitation—but alas! nobody can be less able to accept it—today for the first time ⟨I have cra⟩wled about my room a little with a stick; but my weakness ⟨is still great⟩, and I was frightened at seeing in the glass how I am emaciated. ⟨My greate⟩st ambition will be to reach Grosvenor Place: I must be ⟨content wi⟩th the satisfactions that are left, and not aim at those that fly me.

To Lady Ossory, Sunday 3 January 1779

The portion containing the address and postmark has been torn off; cf. last paragraph.

Strawberry Hill, Jan. 3, 1779.

YOUR Ladyship may be surprised at my dating hence, till you know my reasons. I mended so slowly in town, that I hoped change of air would do better—but I moved with as much circum-

---

5. William Jackson (ca 1737–95), clergyman turned editor of the *Public Ledger*, was the reputed author of letters signed 'Curtius.' See DNB; *Notes and Queries*, Feb. 1961, n.s. vii. 43–7, 266–7; David Garrick, *Letters*, ed. Little *et al.*, Cambridge, Mass., 1963, iii. 1255–7. Cf. MANN i. 240, iv. 236.

6. The *Morning Post*, 17 Dec., had said: 'Grosvenor Square is, without doubt, the happiest spot . . . in this metropolis, the air being perfectly favourable to the votaries of *Venus*; a subscription, we are

informed, is set on foot, to ornament the centre, by building a temple dedicated to that goddess, in which, to give preference to the inhabitants of the Square, those who are best initiated in the mysteries of love, will be appointed priestesses of the temple—Lady Oss——y, Lady Gr——r, Lady D——y, Lady D——y, and the Marchioness of C—— are already appointed.'

7. In the *Roebuck* man-of-war. Lord Carlisle arrived in London from Ports-

spection, as if General Washington was watching me.[1] I took the air four times in Hyde Park, before I began my march, and had this house baked for a week previously, and stayed for the frost.[2] All these precautions have answered—negatively—that is, I have not suffered. I move but from the red to the blue room,[3] and cannot walk even those three yards yet—but my spirits are better, which always flag when the fever is quite gone; so all my vivacity when I was at the worst was a little light-headed. In truth I was so weary of town which is a desert, and saw so very few people for the last week, that I could not bear it. I had no books or papers or dogs or cats to amuse me, so I was swaddled up—and here I am—if I had any thing else to say, I would have spared you this preface on myself, Madam.

The year commenced indeed with a very significant tempest:[4] I grieve for the Cross at Ampthill,[5] but if storms have any meaning, I believe they do not come to give hints to individuals, but to nations. That on the New Year's morning was a very general declaration, and legible from Arlington Street to this place. The road was strewed with tiles, pales, bricks and trees; I counted seven of the latter down, two entire garden walls at Brentford, as Mr Whitchurch's[6] and Mr Franks's[7] are here. My skylight was demolished in

mouth on Monday night, 21 Dec., and Eden probably on 22 Dec., after a delay caused by his wife's illness 'on the road from Portsmouth' (London Chronicle 22–24 Dec., xliv. 602, 608). Johnstone had already returned (ante 28 Nov. 1778), and Sir Henry Clinton remained in America.

1. Cf. ante 17 Jan. 1778.

2. HW went to SH 1 Jan., returned to Arlington Street 6 Jan., 'and was neither the better nor the worse for it' (HW to Conway 9 Jan. 1779).

3. The Blue Bedchamber and the Red Bedchamber, described in HW's 'Des. of SH,' Works ii. 435–8, were on the principal floor of SH (the floor plan is ibid. ii. Pl. IV, facing p. 512) and therefore more convenient for him during illness than his own bedchamber on the floor above (ibid. ii. 452–3).

4. 'The new year was ushered in by a violent tempest of wind, which began in

the night precisely as the old year ended. Ancient historians would have regarded it, and the destruction of a considerable part of the Royal Hospital at Greenwich by a fire the same day, as omens of political storms' (Last Journals ii. 234). Accounts of the damage are in the London Chronicle 31 Dec. 1778 – 5 Jan. 1779, xlv. 6, 8, 10.

5. 'The top of our cross . . . at Ampthill was thrown down, as I hear from Lady Ossory this morning' (HW to Cole 3 Jan. 1779, COLE ii. 135).

6. James Whitchurch (living in 1784; d. 1785 or 1786). His house, purchased about 1740, was York House, near Twickenham Church. 'Lord Clarendon lived at the great house, fronting the water, now Mr Whitchurch's. It was called Hyde Farm' and later York Farm or House ('Book of Materials' 1759, pp. 4, 25; R. S. Cobbett, Memorials of Twickenham, 1872, pp. 217–21; Daniel Lysons, Environs of London, Vol. III, 1795, pp.

town, and here I have lost two beautiful elms in a line with this bow-window[8]—Lady Jersey would not grieve more if she had lost two of her pretty foreteeth. One of the stone Gothic towers at Lady Pomfret's house (now Single-Speech Hamilton's)[9] in my street fell through the roof, and not a thought of it remains. There were only two maids in the house, who luckily lay backwards—but the greatest ruin is at my nephew Dysart's at Ham, where five-and-thirty of the old elms are blown down. I think it no loss, as I hope now one shall see the river from the house.[10] He never would cut a twig to see the most beautiful scene upon earth.

Don't you like the remonstrance of the twelve admirals?[11] and did you expect a rebellion in Wales?[12] The ministers are not lucky in their attempts to raise a revenue; nor indeed in raising anything but rebellions. I begin to think we shall revert into a heptarchy.[13] I was

563–4; Edward Ironside, *History and Antiquities of Twickenham*, 1797, p. 144, and map, *Bibliotheca Topographica Britannica*, Vol. X; Twickenham Rate Books).

7. Moses Franks (1718–89), of Teddington, near the boundary between Twickenham and Teddington. His wife was the daughter of Aaron Franks of Isleworth, at whose house HW heard Leoni sing in 1774 (*ante* 14 Nov. 1774; Hilda F. Finberg, 'Jewish Residents in Eighteenth Century Twickenham,' in *Transactions of the Jewish Historical Society of England*, 1952, xvi. 130). In his 'Book of Materials' 1759, p. 26, HW noted, 'Mr Moses Franks began to inhabit his house in Teddington Lane, 1766.'

8. In the Blue Bedchamber.

9. William Gerard Hamilton (1729–96), M.P. 1754–96. 'The Gothic house of the Countess of Pomfret in Arlington Street, was designed by Mr [Sanderson] Miller of Radway' (HW, *Anecdotes of Painting*, Vol. V, ed. F. W. Hilles and P. B. Daghlian, New Haven, 1937, p. 161). Hamilton occupied it from 1766 to 1787 or 1788 (*Royal Kalendar*; COLE ii. 135 n. 3; E. B. Chancellor, *Memorials of St James's Street*, 1922, p. 84, where the house is confused with Pelham's).

10. Ham House, near Petersham, Surrey; across the Thames from SH. Cf. BERRY ii. 175.

11. A 'strong remonstrance against the conduct of the Admiralty in ordering the court martial on Keppel' (*Last Journals* ii. 229; HW to Mann 5 Jan. 1779). The text of the 'Memorial presented last week [30 Dec. 1778] to his Majesty by the Duke of Bolton' with the names of the twelve signers appears in the *London Chronicle* 2–5 Jan. xlv. 11; *Annual Register*, 1778, pp. 310–12. As indicated in the *Annual Register*, 1779, p. 109, this was not a party measure, for at least two thirds of the signers were not connected with the Opposition.

12. Lord Bulkeley and Sir Watkin Williams Wynne, who had been supporters of the administration, led a protest against reform measures designed to increase the revenue from Wales. Wynne 'now flew off [from the administration] at once, and the Welsh proprietors held assemblies in London, and were determined to oppose the invasion of their property, however legal' (*Last Journals* ii. 213–4; *London Chronicle* 29–31 Dec. 1778 – 20–23 March 1779, xliv. 626, xlv. 82, 130, 278). As a result of these protests the lords of the Treasury ordered the measures not to be put into effect 'till further orders' (ibid. 11–13 March, xlv. 244), but they were later enforced (ibid. 16–18 Sept., xlvi. 269).

13. As the government of Britain was at various times from the sixth to the ninth century.

diverted last week with a speech of Lord Townshend; he was coming out of Lord North's levee, where he had *extorted* some favour, and met an acquaintance going in. 'Well,' said he, 'what are you going to ask?' The person was shy: 'Come, come,' said the Viscount, 'I am sure you want something: here, I'll lend you my pistols.'[14]

You certainly laugh at me, Madam, when you propose my writing for you to Curtius. I have not his direction here, or would send it to you; but to be sure a letter for him to be left at his printer's would do.

I intend returning to the capital on Tuesday,[15] if I am able to go abroad; or else shall stay here, where I have more comforts, and can divert myself better than by waiting for accidental visits; for I make it a rule never to ask anybody to come to me, which is intercepting them from something they would like better—if I end in my armchair, it shall be a punishment to nobody else. I cannot get to Ampthill—the next bes⟨t place of all.⟩

To Lady Ossory, Thursday 14 January 1779

Address: To the Countess of Ossory at Ampthill Park, Bedfordshire. *Postmark:* 14 IA.

Jan. 14, 1779.

BY not hearing from me for a fortnight, you may imagine, Madam, that I go out, and have been diverting myself, to repair lost time—Oh! my life is very giddy and dissipated! My exquisite enjoyment has consisted in two returns of pain and lameness; my expeditions, taking the air, with the contrast of new confinement; and my *menus plaisirs*, a few sprinkled visits of charity, from a few friends that remained in town. My silence therefore has proceeded from suppression of lamentations, and from having nothing to place in their stead.

By Monday I expect company and events; but as I hope you and Lord Ossory will be in the former class,[1] I shall have no occasion to

14. He had fought a duel with Lord Bellamont (*ante* 4 Feb. 1773).
15. He returned on Wednesday, 6 Jan. (HW to Mann 5 Jan. 1779; to Conway 9 Jan. 1779).

1. Parliament was to convene on Tuesday, 19 Jan.

send you the latter. I have heard nothing but what cannot interest your Ladyship or me, that Lady Priscilla Bertie is to marry Mr Burrel,[2] and that an Irish Lady Kingsborough[3] has introduced the fashionable fashion of elopements at Dublin.

There is in sooth a charming novelty today of a very different kind; an answer from Mr Gibbon to the monks that have attacked his two famous chapters.[4] It is the quintessence of argument, wit, temper, spirit, and consequently of victory.[5] I did not expect anything so luminous in this age of Egyptian darkness—nor the monks neither —Alas! how can he have any of the leaven left?

Did you see Mr Anstey's verses at Bath Easton?[6] They were truly more a production of this century—and not at all too good for a schoolboy. In the printed copy they have omitted an indecent stanza or two on Mrs Macaulay.[7] In truth Dame Thucydides has made but an uncouth match;[8] but Anstey has tumbled from a greater height

2. On 23 Feb. 1779 she married Peter Burrell (1754–1820), Kt, 1781; 2d Bt, 1787; cr. (1796) Bn Gwydir; M.P.

3. Caroline Fitzgerald (1755–1823), m. (1769) Robert King, styled Vct Kingsborough 1768–97, 2d E. of Kingston, 1797. She had been separated from her husband 'for some years before his death' in 1799 (GEC).

4. *A Vindication of Some Passages in the Fifteenth and Sixteenth Chapters of the . . . Decline and Fall*, 1779, published 'Jan. 14,' as HW noted in his copy, now WSL (Hazen, *Cat. of HW's Lib.* 1609: 39.10), where he made several marks of approval and identified 'a gentleman' (p. [147]) as 'Mr Ayre a Roman Catholic.' The 'monks' are Henry Edwards Davis (1756–84), of Balliol College, Oxford, who attacked Gibbon in the spring of 1778 (see also *post* 9 Feb. 1779); East Apthorpe (d. 1816), of Jesus College, Cambridge, rector of St Mary Le Bow 1778–92, prebendary of St Paul's 1790–1816; Richard Watson (1737–1816), Regius Professor of Divinity at Cambridge, later Bishop of Llandaff; James Chelsum (1738–1801) of Christ Church, Oxford; Thomas Randolph (1701–83), President of Corpus Christi College and Margaret Professor of Divinity at Oxford; and Francis Eyre (ca 1732–1804) of Warkworth, Northants (Venn, *Alumni Cantab.*; Foster, *Alumni*

Oxon.; BM Cat.; *Scots Peerage* vi. 455). In 1778 Gibbon had asked HW about the propriety of answering Davis, and in December sent HW the printed *Vindication* to read but not to keep, since the pamphlet was not yet published (HW to Gibbon ca May 1778, 25 Dec. 1778). For a detailed study of the controversy see S. T. McCloy, *Gibbon's Antagonism to Christianity*, 1933, *passim*.

5. The '*Vindication* can still be read as an example of deadly polemic. Gibbon's prose was never more forceful' (D. M. Low, *Edward Gibbon*, 1937, p. 263).

6. 'Winter's Amusement. The Late Bath Easton Prize Ode,' printed in the *London Chronicle* 2–5 Jan., xlv. 13; the eleventh stanza refers to Mrs Macaulay's recent marriage. Read at Mrs Miller's 3 Dec. 1778, the poem was printed, with minor changes, in the fourth volume of *Poetical Amusements at a Villa near Bath*, Bath, 1781, pp. 19–23, and in Anstey's *Poetical Works*, ed. John Anstey, 1808, pp. [259]–62. Cf. R. A. Hesselgrave, *Lady Miller and the Batheaston Literary Circle*, New Haven, 1927, pp. 62–4.

7. The 'Epode, repeated by the author on being asked to read the preceding ode a second time' (*Poetical Amusements*, iv. 24–6; Anstey's *Poetical Works*, pp. [263]–5).

8. Mrs Macaulay, aged 47, had married,

than she—Sense may be led astray by the senses—but how could a man write the *Bath Guide,* and then nothing but doggerel and stupidity?

Mr Craufurd has come in as I was writing: he tells me, everything goes *swimmingly* for Admiral Keppel,[9] which he is very glad of—but he is very sorry for Palliser[10]—I cannot be so equitable, if it is unjust to rejoice that a scoundrel is odious—besides, it will give a hint that it is not absolutely safe to be so.

To Lady Ossory, Monday 1 February 1779

Feb. 1, 1779.

WHEN Lord Ossory is in town, Madam, I do not presume to think of writing. He is more in the world, and hears everything sooner than I do—nor would it be fair to him, to divide a moment of your time with him. However there were such interesting topics in the letter I had the honour of receiving this evening, that I must answer it directly—But I shall waive the first subject, which concerns myself, to come to the last that touches your Ladyship—and can I but admire your goodness in thinking of me, when an angel[1] is inoculated? You must now continue it, for you have promised I shall hear how she goes on. Sweet little love! you must be anxious, though inoculation now can scarce be called a hazard. It is as sure, as a cheat of winning, though a strange run of luck may once in two thousand times disappoint him.

14 Nov. 1778, William Graham (ca 1758–1845), aged under 21, the younger brother of James Graham the quack doctor. Graham, who was then a 'surgeon's mate,' on his second marriage (1797) was 'the Rev. William Graham, M.A., of Misterton in Leicestershire.' He is probably the William Graham who matriculated at St Edmund Hall, Oxford, 13 March 1789, aged 30, and graduated B.A. 1792, M.A. 1795 (Foster, *Alumni Oxon.;* GM 1797, lxvii pt i. 524; 1845, n.s. xxiv. 319; *Town and Country Magazine,* 1778, x. 623–4; BM, *Satiric Prints* v. 355, No. 5598; *Annual Register,* 1845, lxxxvii. 284; *London Chronicle* 28 Nov.–1 Dec. 1778, xliv. 523).

9. The court martial of Keppel on charges preferred by Palliser had begun at Portsmouth 7 Jan. and had continued daily, except Sunday, 10 Jan. The five charges of misconduct and neglect of duty and the testimony appeared in the newspapers and magazines. See also *Last Journals* ii. 234–6, 240–50; *The Proceedings at Large of the Court-Martial, on . . . Keppel,* 'Taken in short hand by W. Blanchard,' 1779.

10. Sir Hugh Palliser (1723–96), cr. (1773) Bt; Rear-Adm., 1775; Vice-Adm., 1778; Adm., 1787; lord of the Admiralty 1775–9; commander of a division and third in command under Keppel at the Battle of Ushant, 27 July 1778.

1. Lady Gertrude Fitzpatrick.

The pictures at Houghton, I hear, and I fear, are sold[2]—what can I say? I do not like even to think on it. It is the most signal mortification to my idolatry for my father's memory, that it could receive. It is stripping the temple of his glory and of his affection. A madman excited by rascals has burnt his Ephesus.[3] I must never cast a thought towards Norfolk more—nor will hear my nephew's name, if I can avoid it. Him I can only pity; though it is strange he should recover any degree of sense, and never any of feeling!—I could have saved my family, but cannot repent the motives that bound my hands.[4] If any unhappy lunatic is ever the better for my conduct and example, it is preferable to a collection of pictures.

Yes, Madam, I do think the pomp of Garrick's funeral[5] perfectly ridiculous.[6] It is confounding the immense space between pleasing talents and national services. What distinctions remain for a patriot hero, when the most solemn have been showered on a player?—but when a great empire is on its decline, one sympton is, there being more eagerness on trifles than on essential objects. Shakespeare, who *wrote* when Burleigh counselled and Nottingham[7] fought, was not rewarded and honoured like Garrick, who only *acted,* when—indeed I don't know who has counselled and who has fought.

I do not at all mean to detract from Garrick's merit, who was a

---

2. To Catherine II of Russia for £40,555. The details of the sale were not completed until later in the year (COLE, *passim; London Chronicle* 24–27 April, xlv. 398).

3. Erostratus or Herostratus, hoping to acquire eternal fame if only by committing a great crime, burnt the Temple of Diana (Artemis) at Ephesus, according to tradition on the night in 356 B.C. when Alexander the Great was born.

4. If Lord Orford had been declared a lunatic, the estate would have been placed in Chancery and might have remained intact, but the income from Orford's Court positions would have been lost.

5. Lord Ossory's memorandum, quoted in Vernon Smith, i. 330–1 n.: 'In Italy I became acquainted with Garrick, and from my earliest youth having admired him on the stage, was happy to be familiarly acquainted with him, cultivated his society from that time till his death, and then accompanied him to his grave as one of his pall-bearers. He and Mrs Garrick (I think it was in 1777) have been with us in the country; Gibbon and Reynolds, at the same time, all three delightful in society. The vivacity of the great actor, the keen sarcastic wit of the great historian, and the genuine pleasantry of the great painter, mixed up well together, and made a charming party. Garrick's mimicry of the mighty Johnson was excellent.'

6. Garrick died 20 Jan. and was buried at the foot of Shakespeare's statue in Westminster Abbey 1 Feb., the date of this letter. Cf. *Last Journals* ii. 237; *London Chronicle* 2–4 Feb. 1779, xlv. 115; Carola Oman Lenanton, *David Garrick,* 1958, p. 374: 'the most magnificent funeral that London had ever witnessed.'

7. Charles Howard (ca 1536–1624), 2d Bn Howard of Effingham, 1573, cr. (1597) E. of Nottingham; Lord High Admiral when the Spanish Armada was defeated in 1588.

real genius in his way, and who I believe was never equalled in both tragedy and comedy. Still I cannot think that acting, however perfectly, what others have written, is one of the most astonishing talents —yet I will own as fairly, that Mrs Porter[8] and Mlle Dumenil[9] have struck me so much, as even to reverence them. Garrick never affected me quite so much, as those two actresses, and some few others in particular parts, as Quin[10] in Falstaff, King[11] in Lord Ogleby, Mrs Pritchard in Maria in *The Nonjuror*,[12] Mrs Clive in Mrs Cadwallader,[13] and Mrs Abingdon in Lady Teazle.[14] They all seemed the very persons—I suppose that in Garrick I thought I saw more of his art —yet his Lear, Richard, Hotspur (which the town had not taste enough to like),[15] Kitely[16] and Ranger,[17] were as capital and perfect as action could be. In declamation I confess he never charmed me; nor could he be a gentleman;[18] his Lord Townley[19] and Lord Hastings[20] were mean, but then too the parts are indifferent, and do not call for a master's exertion. I should shock Garrick's devotees, if I uttered all my opinion—I will trust your Ladyship with it—it is, that

8. Mary Porter (d. 1765), who acted at Lincoln's Inn Fields as early as 1699, later at the Haymarket and Covent Garden, but chiefly at Drury Lane from 1708 to 1743, when she retired. Dr Johnson said, 'Mrs Porter in the vehemence of rage, and Mrs Clive in the sprightliness of humour, I have never seen equalled' (Boswell, *Johnson* iv. 243).

9. Marie-Françoise Dumesnil (1711–1803), the famous tragedienne, whom HW had seen several times at Paris in 1765, finding her 'admirable,' acting 'in the highest perfection' (DU DEFFAND v. 265, 277, and *passim*). She retired in 1776 and acted in a final benefit in 1777.

10. James Quin (1693–1766) first played Falstaff in *The Merry Wives of Windsor*, 1720; in *Henry IV, Part I*, 1722 (both at Lincoln's Inn Fields); and in *Henry IV, Part II*, 1736, at Drury Lane (Genest iii. 53, 73, 476, iv. 376–9). His farewell performance in 1753 was in *Henry IV, Part I*.

11. Thomas King (1730–1805), the original Lord Ogleby in Garrick's and Colman's *Clandestine Marriage*, 1766; Sir Peter Teazle in *The School for Scandal*, 1777; and Puff in *The Critic*, 1779.

12. A comedy by Colley Cibber (1671–1757), first acted at Drury Lane, 1717.

13. In Foote's *Author*, first produced at Drury Lane, 1757, with Foote and Mrs Clive as Mr and Mrs Cadwallader; she 'was not inferior to Foote' (Genest iv. 480).

14. In Sheridan's *School for Scandal*.

15. 'Yet I think he excelled himself in it—but he did not please the town' (HW's MS note in his copy, now WSL, of Thomas Davies, *Dramatic Miscellanies*, 1783–4, i. 225, on the passage 'The person of Garrick was not formed to give a just idea of the gallant and noble Hotspur'). Garrick played Hotspur five times in Dec. 1746 and 'never resumed the part' (Genest iv. 212).

16. In Jonson's *Every Man in His Humour* (altered by Garrick, 1751).

17. In *The Suspicious Husband*, 1747, by Benjamin Hoadly (1706–57) and his brother John Hoadly (1711–76).

18. 'Garrick acted every part admirably except a common man of fashion' (*Letters of Lady Louisa Stuart to Miss Louisa Clinton*, 1st ser., ed. Hon. James Home, Edinburgh, 1901, p. 343, *sub* Dec. 1823).

19. Lord Townly in Vanbrugh's and Cibber's *Provok'd Husband*, 1728.

20. In Rowe's *Jane Shore*.

Le Texier is twenty times the genius—What comparison between the powers that do the fullest justice to a single part, and those that instantaneously can fill a whole piece, and transform themselves with equal perfection into men and women, and pass from laughter to tears, and make you shed the latter at both? Garrick, when he made one laugh, was not always judicious, though excellent—What idea did his Sir John Brute[21] give of a surly husband?—His Bayes[22] was no less entertaining—but it was a garreteer-bard—Old Cibber preserved the solemn coxcomb; and was the caricature of a great poet, as the part was designed to be.

Half I have said I know is heresy, but fashion had gone to excess, though very rarely with so much reason. Applause had turned his head, and yet he was never content even with that prodigality. His jealousy and envy were unbounded; he hated Mrs Clive till she quitted the stage, and then cried her up to the skies to depress Mrs Abingdon. He did not love Mrs Pritchard, and with more reason, for there was more spirit and originality in her Beatrice than in his Benedict.[22a]

But if the town did not admire his acting more than it deserved, which indeed in general it was difficult to do, what do you think, Madam, of its prejudice even for his writings? What stuff was his Jubilee Ode,[23] and how paltry his prologues and epilogues![24]—I have always thought that he was just the counterpart of Shakespeare; this the first of writers and an indifferent actor; that, the first of actors, and a woeful author—Posterity would believe me, who will see only his writings; and who will see those of another modern idol, far less deservedly enshrined, Dr Johnson. I have been saying this morning, that the latter deals so much in triple tautology, or the fault of repeating the same sense in three different phrases, that I believe it would be possible, taking the ground-work for all three, to make one of his Ramblers into three different papers, that should all have exactly the same purport and meaning, but in different phrases. It would be a good trick for somebody to produce one and

21. In Vanbrugh's *Provok'd Wife*, 1697.
22. In Buckingham's *Rehearsal*, 1672.
22a. Cf. Genest iv. 261.
23. *An Ode upon Dedicating a Building and Erecting a Statue to Shakespeare at Stratford Upon Avon*, 1769. HW's copy (Hazen, *Cat. of HW's Lib.* 3222:10),

now in the Harvard Library, has on the title-page in HW's hand, 'Garrick, September.'

24. He wrote 165 prologues and epilogues (Mary E. Knapp, *A Checklist of Verse by David Garrick*, Charlottesville, Va., 1955, Nos 270–434).

read it—A second should say, 'Bless me, I have this very paper in my pocket, but in quite other diction'; and so a third.[25]

Our Lord has been so good as to call on me again, and found me; but I take for granted will make his little Gertrude a visit tomorrow, though probably not bring your Ladyship with him till she is recovered. I am in no pain even for her beauty.

As the court martial is likely to end this week,[26] I suppose the parliamentary campaign will be warmly renewed the next[27]—but what campaign will restore this country to its greatness? It is blotted out of the list of mighty empires; and they who love processions, may make a splendid funeral for it!—but indeed it was buried last year with Lord Chatham, at whose interment there were not half the noble coaches that attended Garrick's!

To Lady Ossory, Tuesday 9 February 1779

Hitherto printed as a continuation of the letter of 1 Feb.

Feb. 9, 1779.

I AM thoroughly concerned, Madam, for yours and Lord Ossory's disappointment,[1] and very sorry you trusted to a surgeon in the country, as they must have less experience. However, if a second trial should fail, you may be very easy, for I believe there is scarce an instance of the smallpox naturally after two inoculations. The late Lady Lothian,[2] who was in that case, I know never had it. For your

25. Part of HW's 'General Criticism on Dr Johnson's Writing,' first printed in *Works* iv. 361–2, parallels this passage. The MS, now in the British Museum (Add. MS 37728, fol. 34–35v.) differs appreciably from the text in *Works*, and most of it was written some years before 1779, as indicated by the spelling 'Dr Johnstone's' and 'Johnston's' and by the handwriting. HW's MS at the end of his 'Criticism' in *Works* reads: 'This fault is so usual with him, he is so apt to explain the same thought by three different sets of phrases heaped on each other, that if I did not condemn his laboured coinage of words, I would call, I would call it

Triptology.' Immediately underneath this passage HW wrote 'his threefold inundation of parallel expressions.' Similar remarks are in *Walpoliana* i. 34–5.

26. The court martial of Keppel lasted until 11 Feb.

27. There was little action in Parliament during the court martial (*Last Journals* ii. 236–7).

1. Lady Gertrude Fitzpatrick's inoculation for smallpox had not taken effect.

2. Caroline Darcy (d. 15 Nov. 1778), m. (1735) William Henry Ker, styled E. of Ancram 1722–67, 4th M. of Lothian, 1767.

perfect tranquillity I still wish it may appear; she will certainly have very few, with so little disposition to infection.

You are both so very partial to me, Madam, that I dare not gulp your commendation of the pamphlet.[3] I wrote it, just to say I had cleared myself, and have given very few away,[4] and had rather it was soon forgotten, as it is likely to be in such distracted times. I sincerely do not recollect why I did not return the first papers;[5] I have spoken strict truth to the best of my memory, and cannot tell whether I forgot or reserved them to transcribe.[6]

You blame my humility, and therefore I will not give the answer you expect; especially as I have others ready. In the first place I have not impartiality enough for such a work as Mr Elmsley[7] thinks me fit for. In the next, it would be an imitation—and there even my humility fails me—and the last and strongest plea is that I am twenty years too old to write what if well written, would demand twenty years to write, allowing the necessary time for collecting materials[8] —but I have already scribbled a vast deal too much—I must publish my fourth volume of painters[9]—and then intend the world shall hear my name no more.

The weather has been disagreeably too hot, but I cannot say has affected me *en bien ou en mal*. I certainly recover more slowly than ever, as is natural—and therefore conclude reasonably that one more severe fit will totally confine me. I go nowhere but into very private rooms, nor think of others—and now dispense with my saying any more of myself, Madam. You forbid me humility, and yet all I say

3. HW's *Letter to the Editor of the Miscellanies of Thomas Chatterton*, 200 copies of which were printed at SH in January 1779 (Hazen, *SH Bibl.* 116–19).

4. The earliest reference to a presentation copy of the printed pamphlet. Cole's copy reached him 14 Feb. (ibid.).

5. Which HW had received from Chatterton.

6. This passage is apropos of a paragraph on p. 36 of *A Letter* . . . , part of HW's letter to Bewley 23 May 1778 (CHATTERTON 128 and nn. 65–6).

7. Peter Elmsley (1736–1802), bookseller in the Strand, who declined to publish Gibbon's *Decline and Fall* (Boswell, *Johnson* iii. 97 n. 3).

8. The nature of Elmsley's project for HW is not clear. Since Elmsley was one of the literary club of booksellers responsible for Johnson's *Lives of the English Poets* (Elmsley's name is not on the title-page of the original edition, 1779–81, but is on that of the four-volume edition of the *Lives*, 1781), he may have had in mind a similar work, perhaps concerned with artists, for HW—hence HW's comments about 'an imitation' (perhaps of Johnson's *Lives* or Vasari's, or both), and the great amount of time it would require.

9. The fourth volume of *Anecdotes of Painting* had been printed in 1771, but HW delayed publication until 9 Oct. 1780 (Hazen, *SH Bibl.* 63–5).

and do is founded on the consciousness of my own weakness, and on the dread of being blind to my own defects.

We are in greater confusion than all the world hears. Last night came an account of a serious insurrection at Edinburgh, where the mob has burnt two mass-houses and threatened some lives.[10] The state of Ireland is still more alarming—Lord Buckingham is coming away.[11] There are rumours of changes, and certainly overtures for them. It is declared that Lord Suffolk desires to retire.[12] We may have novelties—but where is there any hope?

I give your Ladyship my word that I know of no offers that my nieces have refused, or even received.[13] Lies are so rampant, that they may have been involved in the havoc—one would think there were sad subjects enough of all sorts to glut the maw of ill nature, but like Craufurd it had rather dine where it is not asked, than where invited. Your Ladyship's words imply no malicious account in what you have been told; but falsehood is predominant, and not a hundredth part of what one hears every day is true.

I long to hear that you are at ease about Lady Gertrude; and then I will indulge the hope of seeing you. In the meantime pray permit me in my turn to tax your Ladyship's humility. Pray read all Mr Gibbon's pamphlet, and do not fear not understanding it. It is lumi-

10. The Catholic lords, Lord Traquair and his son Lord Linton, and Robertson, principal of the University. HW gives an extended account of this incident in *Last Journals* ii. 241–3. Only one mass-house was burned, but the contents of another, including a library of 9,000–10,000 volumes, were destroyed. Other damage done by the mob is described in *A Memorial to the Public, in Behalf of the Roman Catholics of Edinburgh and Glasgow*, 1779.

11. Lord Buckinghamshire, Lord Lieutenant of Ireland, was not recalled until 1780. *Last Journals* ii. 245: 'The ministers were angry at Lord Buckingham for having encouraged the Irish *Protestants* to arm. It was declared that he had desired to be recalled—but it may be presumed he had been ordered to desire it.' Lady Mary Coke ('MS Journals' 4 Jan. 1779) records: 'I am sorry to say Lord Buckingham is much disliked in Ireland; the two faults most complained of are his pride and avarice.'

12. Suffolk died in office, secretary of state for the North, 7 March 1779, although by the end of 1778 he had indicated to both George III and Lord North his 'determination to resign,' provided he was made Lord Steward in place of Lord Talbot (*Corr. Geo. III* iv. 239–40).

13. Sophia Churchill had been mentioned as a possible wife for the Duke of Queensberry (Lady Mary Coke, 'MS Journals' 31 Oct. 1778). When the Duke of Ancaster died 8 July 1779 he was engaged to marry Lady Horatia Waldegrave (*post* 20 July 1779). Lady Ossory wrote to Selwyn 3 June 1779: 'The Lady Waldegraves have been about marrying the whole town, but are not married' (Jesse, *Selwyn* iv. 177).

nous as day, with clearness one of his brightest talents. I am sure
the whole will delight you. It is Mr Gibbon *that can make the dryest
subject interesting and entertaining*,[14] and his reply to Davis[15] is the
strongest evidence that can be given.

To Lady Ossory, Wednesday 17 February 1779

Address: To the Countess of Ossory at Ampthill Park, Bedfordshire. *Postmark:*
17 FE.

Feb. 17, 1779.

I ACCEPT Lady Gertrude's single pustule,[1] Madam, in full of all
accounts: it is an ambassador that completely represents its
principal, and is authorized to sign *peace* in its name. I could almost
imagine that you had sent me the pimple itself, *for* I found a rosebud
and two cowslips in your letter, which would be a prettier transformation than any in Ovid.

I am not fond of mobs, Madam, though I like the occasion,[2] and
can but compare the feel I had from them, with what I should suffer
were the illuminations for the conquest of America. After putting
out those lights, we should have heard

And then put out *the* light.[3]

Liberty has still a continent to exist in—I do not care a straw who
is minister in this abandoned country—It is the *good old cause of
freedom* that I have at heart—and the vexation and mortification that
I have seen for these last days tell me what we have escaped—if I did
not know it before. We had a most brilliant Westminster last night,[4]

14. Probably from Lady Ossory's letter,
quoting Elmsley.

15. Davis first attacked Gibbon in *An
Examination of the Fifteenth and Sixteenth Chapters of Mr Gibbon's History
of the Decline and Fall of the Roman
Empire . . .* , 1778, and he followed
Gibbon's *Vindication* with *A Reply to
Mr Gibbon's "Vindication,"* 1779. HW's
copy of Davis's second pamphlet, now
wsl, contains no notes. Cf. *ante* 14 Jan.
1779; Hazen, *Cat. of HW's Lib.* 1609:39.10,
1609:41.1, 3188.

1. From her second inoculation for
smallpox.

2. The acquittal of Admiral Keppel,
the news of which reached London in
the evening of 11 Feb. (*Last Journals* ii.
247).

3. *Othello* V. ii. 7.

4. Admiral Keppel 'arrived at his house
in Audley Square' from Portsmouth about
4 P.M. on 16 Feb. 'In the evening all the
houses at the west end of the town were
illuminated (some with a particular ele-

and guns and squibs till six in the morning—but the City, I hear, was not illuminated.[5] Lady Greenwich, looking uglier than ever with rage, said, she would go out of town, since she could not be safe in her own house.[6] I replied, 'Madam, I believe your Ladyship must not go to Edinburgh to be quiet, for the tumults there are a little more serious than ours.'[7] In truth, I, who was born in an age of mobs, never saw any like those of this week;[8] they were, as George Montagu said of our earthquakes, *so tame you might have stroked them.*[9] I drove through the whole City to beyond the Royal Exchange on Friday night with my nieces to show them the illuminations, and back through Holbourn and St James's Square where was the greatest concourse, and passed as quietly as at noonday. I own I was diverted to see fear surmount pride. The Duke of Northumberland, who on the eve of accepting his place,[11] would have drenched the populace with beer and ale, would not put out lights till midnight, and then was forced to hang out flambeaux—and so was Lord Weymouth,[12] who has been in a charming panic, for he has no spirit even when he is drunk.[13] It is pleasant to see those, who condemned the towns of America to fire and sword, terrified with crackers.

I found Admiral Keppel at the Duchess of Richmond's this morning: he looks ill and quite exhausted with fatigue. He has not been

gance and beauty), and every possible demonstration of joy and zeal displayed which so judicious, so brave, and so worthy an officer merited' (*London Chronicle* 16–18 Feb., xlv. 162; *Last Journals* ii. 252).

5. 'On Tuesday night, . . . a great number of people . . . came into the City a little after 12 o'clock and obliged the inhabitants in Fleet Street, etc., to illuminate their houses' (*London Chronicle* 16–18 Feb., xlv. 166).

6. No. 11, Bruton Street (*Directory to the Nobility, Gentry . . . 1793*, p. 23).

7. See preceding letter.

8. HW noted that on the night of 11 Feb., following the news of Keppel's acquittal, 'the mob was far more temperate than usual, the Opposition having taken no pains to inflame them, nor even furnished them with any *cri de guerre*' (*Last Journals* ii. 247).

9. HW quotes this, with acknowledgment to Montagu, to Hertford 10 Jan.

1765; to Montagu 26 May 1765; to Sir William Hamilton 13 Aug. 1773; and to Lord Strafford 1 Aug. 1783. For an account of the damage done by the mob, which was greater than HW here suggests, see the *London Magazine*, 1779, xlviii. 92.

11. As Master of the Horse, a post he had asked for. He was appointed 27 Nov., kissed hands and was sworn 3 Dec. 1778 and retained the position until 1780 (*post* 26 Nov. 1780). HW thought it 'a ridiculous promotion: he was afflicted with the stone, and very lame with the gout, and at least sixty-five' (*Last Journals* ii. 212; *London Chronicle* 3–5 Dec. 1778, xliv. 537; *Morning Post* 2 Dec. 1778).

12. Who was HW's neighbour in Arlington Street (*Royal Kalendar*, 1779, p. 20; HW to Montagu 1 Dec. 1768, MONTAGU ii. 271).

13. 'Rank fear was Weymouth's predominating characteristic. . . . Weymouth passed the night in drinking with Charles Fox' (*Last Journals* ii. 246, *sub* Feb. 1779).

at Court[14] or the House of Commons[15] yet, and will go out of town as soon as he can[16]—for my part I shall not light another candle till Lady Gertrude arrives in full beauty.

To Lady Ossory, Tuesday 23 February 1779

Address: To the Countess of Ossory at Ampthill Park, Bedfordshire. *Postmark:* 23 FE.

Feb. 23, 1779.

AS you bid me write again before your arrival, and do not name the day, I hurry to obey you, Madam, though I have nothing to tell you, but how happy I shall be to see you. Were I a good courtier, to be sure I should announce *the great news,* as called, of the capture of Santa Lucia[1]—I did say, there was great want of good news, when this conquest was so dignified![2]—I think the last King of Great Britain should thence be called Lucius, as the first Christian King of it was. *My humility* does not stoop to exultation on such pigmy victories—but it does find matter of triumph on seeing that when your Ladyship pretends to vanity, you are still forced to borrow your proofs from humility; for is not it being lowly in mind to be proud of agreeing in opinion with others, and not depending on your own

14. On 19 Feb. 'at two o'clock Admiral Keppel . . . attended the levee at St James's. Admiral Keppel and some other of the admirals had a conference with his Majesty' (*London Chronicle* 18–20 Feb., xlv. 173). The King 'received him civilly, but took not the least notice of what had passed relative to him, nor showed him any particular distinction' (*Last Journals* ii. 253; Cobbett, *Parl. Hist.* xx. 154).

15. On 18 Feb. 'Admiral Keppel being come to the House, Mr Speaker acquainted him that the House had on the 12th instant ordered that the thanks of this House be given to him for his distinguished courage, conduct, and ability . . . last summer . . . and . . . particularly for his having gloriously upheld the honour of the British flag on the 27th and 28th July last' (*Journals of the House of Commons* xxxvii. 139, 150. See also *Last*

Journals ii. 253; Cobbett, *Parl. Hist.* xx. 131–3; *London Chronicle* 18–20 Feb., xlv. 169–70).

16. He went to Bath 12 March (*London Chronicle* 13–20 March, xlv. 254, 270).

―――――

1. British forces landed on Santa Lucia in the French West Indies 13 Dec. 1778, and the island capitulated 30 Dec., the day after d'Estaing, who had been blocking the harbour, sailed away. The news reached London 22 Feb. (*London Chronicle* 20–25 Feb., 23–25 March, xlv. 184–5, 284–6; A. T. Mahan, *The Major Operations of the Navies in the War of American Independence*, Boston, 1913, pp. 100–105).

2. In *Last Journals* ii. 255 HW calls the taking of Santa Lucia 'more important' than the success of General Campbell in Georgia, and it 'took off much uneasiness for the West Indies.'

taste? Your Ladyship's example will sooner confirm me than your arguments cure me—nay, I beg you will leave me one virtue, lest I should not be worth one. I have at the same time a supreme reverence for pride; for that honest pride that makes one respect oneself, and prevents one's wading through every kennel to keep one's place. Oh! that it should be possible to be insolent on the strength of majorities, and when the tide turns, to crouch to those one has insulted, and beseech them to accept of treachery to one's friends as an atonement![3] Humble or not, I would burst with pride rather than so debase myself.

The winter has, indeed, Madam, been worthy of last summer. On the contrary, Sir Horace Mann tells me,[4] they have skating on the Arno. I went to Strawberry on Saturday to enjoy the sun, and to avoid the squibs and crackers.[5] There was a great deal of glass shed at night,[6] and they say the illuminations are to be repeated on Thursday, when the admiral is to dine with the West India merchants.[7]

The rejoicings have produced exceeding ill-humour, which being very productive of the same temper in its adversaries, I think the nation will awake a little from its slumbers. Whenever the thorough *reveil* does come, it will be very serious!

Poor Mrs Brand[8] is dead of a sore throat,[9] Lady Priscilla Bertie is married today,[10] and the Queen has produced another prince.[11]

3. In *Last Journals* ii. 246–7 HW describes the 'triple treachery' of Rigby, Lord Weymouth, and the Chancellor, Lord Thurlow: 'they meant to betray their associates, and dealt separately with the two squadrons of Rockingham and Grafton.' When the trial of Keppel went against the administration, they renewed their negotiations. See also HW to Mann 25 Feb. 1779.

4. In his letter to HW 16 Jan. 1779.

5. On Saturday afternoon, 20 Feb., Admiral Keppel was presented with 'the freedom of the City, enclosed in a box made of heart of oak' (*London Chronicle* 20–23 Feb., xlv. 180, where a full account of the procession, ceremony, and 'a general illumination' after dinner, is given).

6. The illuminations in the City 'spread to Westminster after midnight, when the mob was much more riotous than the preceding nights, and far more windows broken; but it was believed to be at the

instigation of the Court to make the Opposition sick of those rejoicings, for many windows of the Opposition were broken, particularly Charles Fox's' (*Last Journals* ii. 255; *London Magazine,* 1779, xlviii. 92–3).

7. 'In these tumults Admiral Keppel excused himself from dining with the West-India merchants (as he had been invited to do), that he might give no occasion to more disturbances' (*Last Journals* ii. 255; HW to Mann 25 Feb. 1779; GM 1779, xlix. 100). A letter of thanks from the merchants for his protection of their ships, and his reply, are in the *London Chronicle* 20–23 Feb., xlv. 180.

8. Hon. Gertrude Roper (1750–1819) m. (1771) Thomas Brand (the younger) of The Hoo, Herts; Bns Dacre, s.j., 1794 (COLE i. 198).

9. A false report.

10. By special licence her marriage to Peter Burrell was performed at the house

Pray make my Io Pæans to Lady Gertrude upon her recovery from renoculation; and tell Lady Anne that

> C cannot claim Castalia's choicest lay,
> As Ann and Ampthill ask it all for A.[12]

PS. Mr Beauclerc has just called and told me a shocking history. Sir Hugh Palisser has a sister[13] at York, whom he supported. As if the poor woman was not wretched enough with his disgrace and ruin, or accessory to his guilt, the mob there has demolished her house, and she is gone mad—What a bill would the authors of the American war have to pay, if they were charged, as they deserve, with all the calamities it has given date to!—however, I do believe they are as sorry, as if they were penitent!

To Lady Ossory, Thursday 8 April 1779

This letter was enclosed with the following one. See last paragraph.
Address: To the Countess of Ossory at Ampthill Park, Bedfordshire.

April 8, 1779.

I DID not answer your Ladyship's letter, as I generally do, the moment I received it, because I had nothing to tell you but about the remnant of myself, which is the worst subject in the world. I have been six days at Strawberry Hill, and I think the soft southwest did me good; but I have a constant feverish heat that seems to be undermining my ruins; however, its progress is very slow, and so if you please, we will say no more of it—but your goodness in inquiring is written on my heart's last tablet. Mr Mason was with me for two days: he is printing the third book of his *Garden*.[1]

of her mother, the Duchess of Ancaster, in Berkeley Square.

11. Octavius (1779–83), born between 3 and 4 A.M., 23 Feb. (*London Chronicle* 23–25 Feb., xlv. 185).

12. This couplet is presumably apropos of some alphabetical rhymes by Lady Anne. Cf. preceding letter, first paragraph.

13. Palliser had three sisters: Rebecca (d. before 1789) m. William Walters, a major in the army who died 28 Feb. 1789; Alice m. John Clough of York; and Ursula (ca 1722–96) m. John Fletcher (William Betham, *Baronetage*, 1801–5, iii. 401).

1. *The English Garden: a Poem. Book the Third*, 1779, published 10 May (*London Chronicle* 8–11 May, xlv. 444; Philip Gaskell, *First Editions of William Mason*, Cambridge, 1951, p. 24).

Lord Harrington is gathered to his fathers[2]—or rather, is taken from his *mothers*.[3] Lord Beauchamp's son[4] is well again. Lord Harrington has left my Lady £2500, besides her jointure of £1500 a year: to Lady Anna Maria[5] £6000; £5000 to Mr Stanhope,[6] and an estate of £150 a year—but there are so many debts, that the legacies are more magnificent than generous.[7] The charming house at St James's[8] is to be sold; but it is supposed the present Earl will purchase it.[9]

This is all I have heard, Madam, since I came to town yesterday, which is perfectly empty; the grass grows in the streets, though nowhere else, for the climate is turned to as Asiatic as the government,[10] and it is to be hoped that in time there will be elephants and tigers of our own growth in the Sultan's gardens, to the great satisfaction of Sir William Chambers.[11] I was pleased yesterday to see that, though everything old-fashioned is going out of date, we have still resources. If our trade decays, we have new handicrafts. At Turnham Green I read on a large board, *Manufacture of Temples*. I suppose the Arch-

---

2. He died 1 April.

3. The 'mothers' here are the women in his 'harem.' Cf. BM, *Satiric Prints* v. 213, No. 5322; *Town and Country Magazine*, 1772, iv. 9–11.

4. Francis Charles Seymour-Conway (11 March 1777–1842), styled E. of Yarmouth 1794–1822, 3d M. of Hertford, 1822; M.P. In 1798 he married Maria Fagnani.

5. Lady Anna Maria Stanhope (1760–1834), m. 1 (1782) Thomas Pelham-Clinton, styled E. of Lincoln, 1779–94, 3d D. of Newcastle-under-Line, 1794; m. 2 (1800) Lt-Gen. Sir Charles Gregan Crawfurd, G.C.B.

6. His younger son, Hon. Henry Fitzroy Stanhope (1754–1828), army officer; M.P. (*Eton Coll. Reg.*). In 1783 he was acquitted in a court martial for his conduct in the surrender of Tobago to the French (*London Chronicle* 22 May–28 June 1783, liii. 496, 541, 562, 578, 616).

7. Harrington 'mentioned in his will that his house and furniture, etc., at Petersham are to be disposed of, and the money to be appropriated towards discharging his debts' (ibid. 6–8 April, xlv. 334).

8. In the Stable Yard, St James's Street, where Harrington died (ibid. 1–3 April, xlv. 319).

9. He did; and it remained his town house until his death in 1829 (*Royal Kalendar* 1779–1829).

10. An allusion to the growth of the King's power: 'He had attained what pleased him most—his own will at home. His ministers were nothing but his tools —everybody called them so, and they proclaimed it themselves' (*Last Journals* ii. 244, *sub* Feb. 1779). HW probably has in mind also the latter part of Mason's *Heroic Epistle to Sir William Chambers*, ll. 101–46, especially ll. 101–2, 138–9 (Mason, *Satirical Poems* 51–2).

11. Chambers, 'Comptroller General of His Majesty's Works,' had published in 1772 *A Dissertation on Oriental Gardening*, in several passages of which he had described the animals placed in Chinese gardens: 'menageries for all sorts of tame and ferocious animals.' Mason, in his *Heroic Epistle to Sir William Chambers*, 1773, ll. 71–6, satirizes these passages; HW in his notes to the poem says: 'To recommend the introduction of bears, monkeys, elephants, etc., into our gardens was identically what had been practised on our stage; and whether his Majesty or the mob would be delighted with such sights at Kew or Drury Lane, the idea

bishop of York will set up looms in his diocese for Popish chapels,[12] and Manchester weave dungeons for the Inquisition. The Pope's bull against the dissenters' bill[13] is actually issued from the Clarendon printing-house[13a]—I was interrupted by the strangest story I ever heard, and which I cannot yet believe, though it is certainly true.

Last night as Miss Wray[14] was getting into her coach in Covent Garden from the play,[15] a clergyman[16] shot her through the head— and then himself. She is dead; but he is alive to be hanged—in the room of Sir Hugh Palisser. Now, Madam, can one believe such a tale? How could poor Miss Wray have offended a divine? She was no enemy to the church militant or naval, to the Church of England or the church of Paphos.—I do not doubt but it will be found that the assassin was a dissenter, and instigated by the Americans to give such a blow to the state. My servants have heard that the murderer was the victim's husband—methinks his jealousy was very long-suffering! *Tantæne animæ cœlestibus iræ!*[17]—and that he should not

is barbarous, and never to be admitted into our beautiful real landscapes' (Mason, *Satirical Poems* 43, 49, 60).

12. Archbishop Markham recognized the need for the Roman Catholic Relief Bill of 1778 (Sir Clements Markham, *Markham Memorials*, 1913, ii. 8, 32).

13. Following the Relief Act for Roman Catholics in 1778 (18 Geo. III c. 60), a bill 'for the further relief of Protestant dissenting ministers and schoolmasters' (19 Geo. III c. 44) was ordered 17 March, and it passed without debate 30 April (*Journals of the House of Commons* xxxvii. 259, 360; Cobbett, *Parl. Hist.* xx. 239–48, 305–22).

13a. A petition of the University of Oxford, passed in full convocation at Oxford 22 March, was presented 30 March in the House of Commons against the 'bill now depending in Parliament' (*Journals of the House of Commons* xxxvii. 299; *London Chronicle* 30 March–1 April, xlv. 309). It called the bill 'injurious and dangerous' to Church and State for making no provision of 'any profession whatever of . . . belief in the fundamental doctrines of Christianity, or even the authority of the Holy Scriptures . . . and that without some such provision, dissenting ministers and schoolmasters of all

denominations will be at liberty to preach any doctrines,' etc. The petition was presumably published with the imprint 'Oxford, at the Clarendon Printing-House,' used for publications *auctoritate Universitatis* (cf. R. W. Chapman, *Some Account of the Oxford University Press*, Oxford, 1926, pp. 42, 54). The allusion to the 'pope' is presumably to the Archbishop of Canterbury, Frederick Cornwallis.

14. Martha Ray (ca 1745–79), dau. of a staymaker in Holywell Street, London, was Lord Sandwich's mistress from about 1761 until her death (DNB, *sub* Hackman, James; Boswell, *Johnson* iii. 532).

15. *Love in a Village*, by Isaac Bickerstaffe (d. 1812?).

16. James Hackman (1752–79), who was indicted 9 April for murder, tried at the Old Bailey 16 April, and hanged at Tyburn 19 April (*Boswell Papers* xiii. 239–44, and *passim*). For his military and clerical career, see the following letter. In HW's library was *The Case and Memoirs of the Late Rev. Mr James Hackman*, 8th edn, 1779, now WSL (Hazen, *Cat. of HW's Lib.* 1609. 40. 1).

17. Virgil, *Æneid* i. 11: 'Can heavenly spirits cherish resentment so fierce?' *Animæ* is HW's error for *animis*.

have compounded for a deanery! What trials Lord Sandwich goes through![18]—he had better have one for all.

Friday 9th.

I gave David this letter yesterday, and had forgotten to seal it, which he did not perceive till I was gone out for the evening. Instead of sealing it, he kept it for me till this morning, after I had written my second. I send both to show I had been punctual, though all the novelty is evaporated, and my intelligence is not worth a farthing more than the newspaper.

To Lady Ossory, Friday 9 April 1779

Hitherto printed as part of the letter of 8 April.

April 9, 1779.

LADIES, said a certain philosopher, always tell their minds in the postscript. As that is the habitation of truth, I send you, Madam, a little more truth than there was in my narrative of yesterday, which was warm from the first breath of rumour—yet though this is only a postscript, I will not answer for its perfect veracity. It is the most authentic account I have yet been able to collect of so strange a story, of which no doubt you are curious to know more.

The assassin's name is Hackman; he is brother[1] to a reputable tradesman[2] in Cheapside, and is of a very pleasing figure himself, and most engaging behaviour. About five years ago he was an officer in the 68th[3] regiment,[4] and being quartered at Huntingdon, pleased so much, as to be invited to the oratorios at Hinchinbrook,[5] and

18. Sandwich, in addition to the death of his mistress, was (as first lord of the Admiralty) involved in the trials of Keppel and Palliser. His wife had long been insane.

1. That is, brother-in-law.
2. Frederick Booth, attorney of No. 3 Craven Street in the Strand. Through him Boswell tried unsuccessfully to see Hackman in prison (GM 1779, xlix. 213; *Universal British Directory*, 1791–[1798], i. 371; *Boswell Papers* xiii. 218–41, *passim*;

London Chronicle 8–13 April, xlv. 340, 347).
3. The words 'in the 68th' are badly blotted; hitherto printed 'in the 66th.'
4. Hackman was ensign in the 68th Foot 20 May 1772, and lieutenant 10 July 1776, but retired from the army at the end of 1776 to prepare himself for the church.
5. Hinchingbrooke, the seat of Lord Sandwich, to the west of Huntingdon. Lord Sandwich was particularly fond of music, and Miss Ray was 'of a remarkable

much caressed there. Struck with Miss Wray's charms, he proposed marriage—but she told him she did not choose to carry a knapsack. He went to Ireland, and there changed the colour of his cloth, and at his return, I think not long ago, renewed his suit, hoping a cassock would be more tempting than a gorget—but in vain[6]—Miss Wray, it seems, has been out of order and abroad but twice all the winter. She went to the play on Wednesday night for the second time with Galli[7] the singer. During the play the desperate lover was at the Bedford Coffee-house and behaved with great calmness and drank a glass of *capillaire*. Towards the conclusion he sallied into the piazza, waiting till he saw his victim handed by Mr Macnamara.[9] He came behind her, pulled her by the gown, and on her turning round, clapped the pistol to her forehead and shot her through the head. With another pistol he then attempted to shoot himself, but the ball only grazing his brow, he tried to dash out his own brains with the pistol, and is more wounded by those blows than by the ball.

Lord Sandwich was at home expecting her to supper at half-an-hour after ten. On her not returning an hour later he said something must have happened—however, being tired, he went to bed at half-an-hour after eleven, and was scarce in bed before one of his servants came in, and said Miss Wray was shot. He stared, and could not comprehend

judgment and execution in vocal and instrumental music' (*The Case and Memoirs of . . . Hackman,* 8th edn, 1779, p. 2). 'Soon after he obtained his commission he was quartered on a recruiting party at Huntingdon' (ibid. 1).

6. She agreed to marry him 'and desired to cease all further intercourse with him until it was completed. This they agreed to, and as he almost immediately after went to Ireland with his regiment, the marriage was suspended till his return' (ibid. 3–4). On his return, apparently a short time before the murder, Signora Galli told him that Miss Ray 'was tired of him, and had resolved to quit him.' After leaving the army, Hackman was ordained priest 28 Feb. 1779 at Park Street Chapel, Grosvenor Square, and on 1 March 1779 was presented to the living of Wiveton, Norfolk. HW's account generally agrees with that in the *London Chronicle* 13–15 April, xlv. 356.

7. Catherine Rinni Galli (ca 1724–1804), mezzo soprano; came to England in 1743; 'the last of Handel's scholars.' 'After

quitting the stage she resided as a companion' with Miss Ray (GM 1804, lxxiv pt ii. 1250; Daniel Lysons, *Supplement to . . . The Environs of London,* 1811, p. 111; Richard Edgcumbe, 2d E. of Mount Edgcumbe, *Musical Reminiscences,* 3d edn, 1828, pp. 7–8). She was Miss Ray's music teacher and may have been hired by Lord Sandwich partly to watch her and break off the connection with Hackman, who paid Galli well to see Miss Ray (*The Case and Memoirs of . . . Hackman,* 8th edn, 1779, pp. 3–4).

9. Probably John Macnamara 'a young Irish Templar' whom Hackman watched 'coquet it at the play' with Martha Ray just before her murder (Rev. John Warner to Selwyn 13 April 1779, in Jesse, *Selwyn* iv. 68; *London Chronicle* 20–22 Jan. 1780, xlvii. 79); 'a very respectable character of Lincoln's Inn,' on whose right arm she was leaning when she was shot, as he was escorting her to her carriage (*The Case and Memoirs of . . . Hackman,* 8th edn, 1779, pp. 8–9).

what the fellow meant—nay, lay still, which is full as odd a part of the story as any—at twelve came a letter from the surgeon[10] to confirm the account—and then he was extremely afflicted.

Now upon the whole, Madam, is not the story full as strange as ever it was? Miss Wray has six children,[11] the eldest son[12] is fifteen, and she was at least three times as much.[13] To bear a hopeless passion for five years, and then murder one's mistress—I don't understand it. If the story clears up at all, your Ladyship shall have a sequel. These circumstances I received from Lord Hertford, who heard them at Court yesterday from the Lords of the Admiralty. I forgot that the Galli swooned away on the spot.

I do not love tragic events *en pure perte*. If they do happen, I would have them historic. This is only of kin to history, and tends to nothing. It is very impertinent in one Hackman to rival Herod, and shoot Mariamne—and *that* Mariamne, a kept mistress! and yet it just sets curiosity agog, because she belongs to Lord Sandwich at a critical moment—and yet he might as well have killed any other inhabitant of Covent Garden.

To Lady Ossory, Thursday 6 May 1779

Dated by the reference to Conway.
Address: To Lady Ossory.

Thursday.

I CANNOT think of going to the play tonight,[1] Madam; nor can be out of the way of hearing the first news that shall come. I have done what was right; I approved and applauded Mr Conway's

---

10. Dennis Obrian (GM 1779, xlix. 212), perhaps Dennis O'Bryen (1755–1822), a surgeon who later became a pamphleteer.

11. She had nine children by Lord Sandwich, five of whom survived her: Robert (see below); Basil (1770–1851), legal writer; John (b. ca 1771), naval captain; William (d. young); Augusta (d. 1849) m. (1789) Francesco Giuseppe Maria Enrico di Viry, Conte di Viry (as 'Henry Speed') (*Sandwich Papers* i. 10; *London Magazine*, 1779, xlviii. 188; George Martelli, *Jemmy Twitcher*, 1962, p. 177; Venn, *Alumni Cantab.*; Vittorio Spreti, *Enciclopedia*

storico-nobiliare italiana, Milan, 1928–36, vi. 924).

12. Robert Montagu (1763–1830), who had begun his naval career in 1778 and who became an admiral in 1810 (GM 1830, c pt ii. 643; John Marshall, *Royal Naval Biography*, 1823–35, i. 135–6; *Sandwich Papers*, loc. cit.; *London Chronicle* 10–13 April, xlv. 347).

13. According to the inscription on her coffin-plate, she was 34 (DNB, *sub* Hackman; Boswell, *Johnson* iii. 532).

———

1. Probably to Covent Garden, where Hannah More's tragedy, *Fatal Falsehood*,

going instantly;[2] but I cannot pretend to be easy now he is gone. My feelings for my friends are stronger and more sincere than my philosophy; and great is the difference between advising them to act as they ought, and being indifferent to the consequence.

To Lady Ossory, Tuesday 22 June 1779

Strawberry Hill, June 22, 1779.

YOUR Ladyship's reproaches would be very just, if my pleas of excuse were not too valid. I have been in town but one half day since I had the honour of seeing you;[1] and my own pastime is too insipid to send you. I have a more weighty apology too to urge, which increases every day, and which I will give you in the moving words of one, almost my cotemporary, Dan Lydgate,[2] who in his last piece complains of his trembling joints, and declares that age having benumbed his faculties, had deprived him *of all the subtyltè of curious makyng in Englysshe to endyte*.[3] You will think me torpid indeed, Madam, when I tell you that I have not set my foot in London even since the delivery of the Spanish ambassador's sour rescript.[4] In truth

was acted for the first time (Genest vi. 83, 100–102; Allardyce Nicoll, *A History of Late Eighteenth Century Drama 1750–1800*, Cambridge, 1927, p. 288).

2. On 1 May there were reports that the French were going to attack Jersey, and on Monday, 3 May, when the rumours were confirmed, Conway, the governor of Jersey, set out for the island. News that the invaders had been repulsed at their attack on 1 May reached London on Thursday (the date of this letter), 'but it was not till late in the night of Friday that an account came of the retreat [to France], and I did not learn it till Saturday morning' (HW to Mann 9 May 1779). Conway arrived at Portsmouth Tuesday morning and 'embarked on board the *Cabot* sloop of war' for Jersey (*London Chronicle* 4–6 May, xlv. 430).

———

1. In a letter to Selwyn 3 June 1779 Lady Ossory refers to 'the last time I dined at Strawberry' (Jesse, *Selwyn* iv. 174).

2. John Lydgate (ca 1370–ca 1451).

3. HW is following Thomas Warton, *A History of English Poetry*, ii (1778). 70: 'Lydgate appears to have been far advanced in years when he finished this poem [*The Fall of Princes*]: for at the beginning of the eighth book he complains of his trembling joints, and declares that age, having benumbed his faculties, has deprived him "of all the subtylte of curious makyng in Englysshe to endyte."' Warton's note on the quotation is 'B. vii. Prol. fol. i.b. col. 2. ad calc. He calls himself older than sixty years.' The only Lydgate item in HW's library was a volume (now WSL) containing some illuminated drawings copied for HW from the MS of Lydgate's 'Life of King Edmund' in the Harleian Library (Hazen, *Cat. of HW's Lib.* 3505).

4. Almodóvar, the Spanish ambassador, delivered to Lord Weymouth on 16 June the 'sour rescript' of the same date. In it were detailed the grievances and reasons for Spain's taking the part of France in the American war. The following day in the Houses of Lords and Commons,

I concluded the eruption of a third war would call Lord Ossory to town;[5] and then I knew your Ladyship would have more authentic intelligence than I could send you by rebound.

The ruin of my country is certainly no matter of joy to me. Perhaps I have long thought it undone; and then one may be allowed to prefer one mode to another. A nation cannot perish entirely. Foreign enemies seldom destroy a country, and then only by total conquest. In my opinion the subversion of a happy constitution, which is only effected by domestic enemies, is a worse evil, certainly a more permanent and more mortifying one, than defeats by strangers. If calamities restore the spirit of our constitution, which had exalted us from a little trading island to the rank of a great empire, we may be a mighty people once more; for it is liberty alone, not titular authority and prerogative that can aggrandize small countries. If we will be emperors, it will be without empire. The majesty of the people of England was no joke—for they maintained their dignity—but a Grand Signor of this diminutive islet, without its trade, which is never an appendage of despotism, would be crushed amidst the real potentates that now exist in Europe—and two of their Majesties seem to think the hour is come for sweeping us from the roll of monarchs.

These are not professions, but have always been my opinions, Madam. I think the national character lost, or we should not be where we are at this moment, trusting to precedents of former miracles for preservation—but miracles are not such matters of chance, as to contradict calculation. Only Turks believe that fools are inspired. If Providence interposes its omnipotence in politics, at least it selects wise men for its agents—or if not wise men, a genius. I sit here, waiting till the star appears that is to conduct those sages—I know not from what quarter, east, west or south they are to come—I am sure they have not set out from the north. My utmost wish, not my expectance, is to live to see my country escape tolerably from this menacing darkness. I am too inconsiderable to give advice, and too old to contribute anything else; and therefore sit silently here awaiting the working of the tempest—shipwreck or miracles are soon learnt anywhere.

the manifesto (in translation) and the King's reply were read (*Journals of the House of Lords* xxxv. 801–3; *of the House of Commons* xxxvii. 452–4). HW went to London 15 June and returned to SH the following day (HW to Conway and to Mann 16 June 1779).

5. Parliament remained in session until 3 July.

I have wandered beyond my intention, but you set my pen a-prating, though I have told it I will have it hold its tongue. My private story is very brief. My health is much better for quiet and total idleness, and my fevers gone. Lady Ailesbury and Lady William Campbell passed one night here,[6] and last week the Duke of Richmond and the Duchess of Leinster dined with me. On Friday[7] I dined at Princess Amelie's,[8] and was so unfortunate to my confusion as to arrive after she was set down to table, but as her R.H. had a great cold, I took occasion to go and inquire after her the next day and made my submission. There were the Duchess of Bedford, their Ladyships Ailesbury, Holderness, Mary Coke,[9] Margaret Compton, Anne Howard, Betty Delme,[10] Mrs Howe, Lords Hertford and Dillon, Lords Pelham[11] and Edgcumbe and their wives, and Mr Morrice, who looked dreadfully ill indeed.[12]

I hear Lord Carlisle has resigned,[13] and conjecture why;[14] and that Lord Shelburne is going to be married[15]—perhaps your Ladyship

6. 'Your Countess was here last Thursday,' 10 June (HW to Conway 16 June 1779).

7. 18 June.

8. At Gunnersbury.

9. HW also saw her at Lady Blandford's Sunday evening, 20 June (Coke, 'MS Journals').

10. Lady Elizabeth Howard (1746–1813), 3d dau. of Henry, 4th E. of Carlisle by his 2d marriage, m. 1 (1769) Peter Delmé (1748–89), m. 2 (1794) Charles Garnier (1770–96), Capt. R.N.; painted by Reynolds (A. E. Garnier, *Chronicles of the Garniers of Hampshire*, 1900, pp. 28–9, with Plate, 36–7; Collins, *Peerage*, 1812, iii. 508).

11. Thomas Pelham (1728–1805), 2d Bn Pelham of Stanmer, 1762; cr. (1801) E. of Chichester; m. (1754) Anne Frankland (ca 1734–1813).

12. Coke, 'MS Journals' 18 June 1779: 'There was a great dinner today at Gunnesbury House. I pitied the Princess, for she was very ill with a violent cold, pain in her head, and feverish. We were seventeen at dinner, and in the evening there was two parties at loo and one at whist. The Princess stayed till after ten o'clock, and when she went away desired the company would stay as long as they pleased, and if they had a mind of supper they might call for it, but many of them went

away intending to go to the Duchess of Beaufort, who was at home and was to have music.'

13. He was treasurer of the Household from 1777 until 16 July 1779, when he resigned and was succeeded 1 Dec. by Lord Onslow (*London Chronicle* 22–24 July, xlvi. 78; Jesse, *Selwyn* iv. 216; *Daily Adv.* 2 Dec.).

14. According to Lady Mary Coke, 'Lord Carlisle wanted to be secretary of state and was supported by Lord Gower [his father-in-law] and some others; the rest opposed it, and Lord Carlisle said he would resign and 'twas feared others would in consequence, but his Majesty came to town on Monday [21 June] and sent for them all and by some means or other has reconciled all their differences. Lord Carlisle and his friends are contented with some promise that has been made him but is however to resign his white stick [as treasurer of the Household]' ('MS Journals' 27 June 1779). George III told North 6 April that an 'office of business of a secondary kind' should be found for Carlisle (*Corr. Geo. III* iv. 325), and George III's memorandum, ca 11 June, suggests Carlisle as first lord of trade (ibid. iv. 353).

15. To Lady Louisa Fitzpatrick on 19 July; see below. In the National Library

knows to whom—unless you tell me to the contrary, I shall be very glad.

Shall I make you smile, Madam, in this ugly hour? You know my Swiss David's solemnity and uncouth pronunciation, which he thinks perfect. He came into my room t'other day very composedly and dangling his arms said, 'Auh! dar is Meses Ellis want some of your large flags[16] to put in her great O'—I cried, what! though I could scarce question him for laughing—at last with much ado I discovered that Mrs Ellis's wants lay in her grotto.[17]

That beautiful spot, Mr Hindley's, is to be sold by auction next Monday.[18] I hear Mrs Coke,[19] the mother of him of Norfolk,[20] intends to be the purchaser—and I hope so; for I do not know her, which is a good circumstance in a next neighbourhood; and a dowager[21] is a quiet sort of neighbour, and don't keep hounds. I pray for the peace of my little Jerusalem, since I have long been cured of having any other object.

Wednesday noon.

I had sealed my letter for the post, when I received your Lady-ship's second, for which I give you a million of thanks. I am delighted with the confirmation of Lady Louisa's match. My acquaintance with Lord Shelburne is very slight—but two essential points are gospel, that he is a man of sense, and that he made an excellent husband to

of Ireland, Fitzpatrick MSS, are six letters from Lord Shelburne to Lord Ossory concerning the marriage: the first, dated 'Sunday night,' in June, announcing his proposal to Lady Louisa, which he hopes Lord Ossory will approve, and mentioning his readiness to prepare the marriage settlement; and the others (2, 10, 12, 15, 17 July) concerning the settlement.

16. Or irises.

17. The Welbore Ellises lived at Twickenham in Pope's villa, which Ellis had inherited through his first wife, her father, Sir William Stanhope, having purchased it in 1744; Stanhope had added a second grotto (BERRY i. 41 n. 22; London Museum, Sept. 1770, ii. 139–42). This anecdote is in HW's letter to Conway 5 June 1779, the date the incident occurred.

18. The house, with seven acres of land, was advertised for sale by auction

by Skinner 28 June, but it appears (post 6 June 1780) that the highest bid, £4600, was below the reserve price, and Hindley bought it in. Five parcels of land, a total of fifteen acres, were to be sold separately, and the pictures were advertised for sale by auction by Skinner 5–6 July (Daily Adv. 28, 29 June).

19. Elizabeth Denton (formerly Chamberlayne) (ca 1732–1810) m. Wenman Coke (formerly Roberts), nephew of Lord Leicester (MONTAGU i. 209 nn. 8, 9; C. W. James, Chief Justice Coke, 1929, p. 220 and genealogical table).

20. Thomas William Coke (1754–1842), cr. (1837) E. of Leicester; 'Mr Coke of Norfolk,' 'the first Commoner of England'; M.P.

21. Her husband had died in 1776 (MONTAGU, loc. cit.).

a wife[22] far inferior to Lady Louisa in beauty.[23] There is a third, which though negative, I reckon a capital merit at present. He is not a gamester.

George Selwyn is suddenly returned,[24] and as Lord Ossory is in town too, I think I shall go to town tomorrow.

To Lady Ossory, Tuesday 6 July 1779

Address: To the Countess of Ossory at Ampthill Park, Bedfordshire. *Postmark:* ISLEWORTH. 6 IY.

July 6, 1779.

I SHOULD not have waited to owe you a letter, Madam, had I not had a substantial reason for silence. I had the gout in my foot for two days at the beginning of last week: it went off at once, but at night came into my left eye, and remained there four or five days. To whither Old Truepenny, like the ghost in *Hamlet,* will shift its quarters next, I cannot tell, but I see it will never quit me till it makes a ghost of Horatio. In the meantime it lays such an embargo on me that I never dare engage myself or promise anything that I am to perform personally, lest I seem capricious—but I am so much worse company than usual when I am not well and struggle to hide it, that I determine never to bind myself for a minute but conditionally.

I have done talking politics, Madam, as I should if I lived at the foot of Vesuvius and the mountain grumbled.[1] If the lava takes a contrary direction and my cottage escapes, I will look about me and see what is left. How can you mind what passes in Parliament? The vestry at Ampthill is of as much consequence. Nothing happens there but contradictions. I observe the Speech gives the lie to all the late assertions of hopes in America, of which it speaks dolefully.[2] I do

---

22. Lady Sophia Carteret (1745–71), m. (1765) William Petty, 2d E. of Shelburne.

23. 'He made the best of husbands to his first wife' (Coke, 'MS Journals' 8 Jan. 1778).

24. He had arrived in Paris 14 April, then had gone to Lyons to meet Maria Fagnani, whom he had brought to Paris and placed in a convent, but as soon as the Fagnanis gave permission for her to come to England, he obtained a passport,

with Mme du Deffand's help, and left Paris 15 June, expecting to reach London 21 June (S. Parnell Kerr, *George Selwyn and the Wits,* 1909, pp. 256–65; DU DEFFAND V. 131–51).

1. Its latest eruption was on 22 May (*London Chronicle* 19–22 June, xlv. 585).

2. In his speech from the throne 3 July the King said: 'It is impossible to speak of the continuance of the rebellion

not think your neighbour so much in the wrong in apprehending a rebellion if Lord North was turned out. The nation would be consequent in resenting it—in short I believe I am really Xo Hoho,[3] a Chinese that comprehends nothing he sees or hears.[4]

Pray let me know when you come to your wedding,[5] that I may get a peep of you. Of weddings in my own tribe[6] I am as tired as of politics, and have put cotton into all my ears. Be the events of Empress Chance obeyed; nobody but her Majesty has any decision. I leave everything to her, have abandoned all my principles, and am governed by nothing but *De par la Reine*.

George I have seen.[7] He embarked in an instant on receiving a warrant to carry off his prize,[8] as if she had been the heiress of the Indies and he had feared a retractation. I did not ask to see her. Would you ask to see the moon, if Endymion told you he had married her?

Lord Bolinbroke I hear will live. At first they thought he had taken laudanum.[9] It would have been monstrous injustice in opium to kill him, when it will not dispatch Beauclerc.[10]

in North America without the deepest concern; but we have given such unquestionable proofs of our sincere disposition to put an end to those troubles, that I must still hope that the malignant designs of the enemies of Great Britain cannot long prevail against the evident interests of those unhappy provinces, and that they will not blindly persist in preferring an unnatural and dangerous connection with a foreign power, to peace and reunion with their Mother Country' (*Journals of the House of Commons* xxxvii. 460).

3. An allusion to HW's *A Letter from Xo Ho, a Chinese Philosopher at London, to His Friend Lien Chi at Peking,* [1757] (Hazen, *Bibl. of HW* 39–42).

4. 'I pretend not to account for the conduct of Englishmen; I told thee before, they are *incomprehensible*' (*A Letter from Xo Ho, Works* i. 207, 209).

5. On 19 July, of Lady Louisa Fitzpatrick and Lord Shelburne. The *London Chronicle* 8–10 July, xlvi. 27, prematurely announced it as having taken place 8 July.

6. There were rumours that Lady Maria Waldegrave would marry Lord Egremont

and that Lady Anna Horatia Waldegrave would marry the Duke of Ancaster (Coke, 'MS Journals' 10, 22, 27 June, 4, 9 July).

7. Probably on 23 June; see the last paragraph of the preceding letter.

8. Maria Fagnani.

9. 'Lord Bolingbroke has been dying, some say of a natural disorder but more are of opinion he had taken something to put an end to his life. . . . the physician says there is every reason to suppose he had taken laudanum, an opinion that will gain credit from his having distressed his circumstances and being that sort of man so void of all principles that he was very likely to put an end to his existence the moment his life was no longer agreeable' (Coke, 'MS Journals' 27 June 1779). 'Lord Bolingbroke is still alive but never in his senses. The physicians now think the miserable state he is in was not the effect of laudanum but a palsy upon the brain' (ibid. 10 July). This second view is supported by Lord Pembroke's letter to Lord Herbert 1 Jan. 1780, in *Henry, Elizabeth and George,* ed. Lord Herbert, 1939, p. 371.

10. An allusion to Beauclerk's ill treat-

In my neighbourhood there is no talk of the fleets.[11] All we think of is the new tax on posthorses,[12] which they say will produce more disturbances than the ballot for the militia would have done,[13] and a million of broken heads. I suppose that was the object (as it seems to be of all our measures) and that as the demand for plasters will be infinitely increased, it may furnish pretext for a heavy gabel[14] on diaculum[15]—adieu! Madam, if we are digged out alive, when the conflagration is over, we will chat over old times. I do not design to embark like Pliny, and probe the nature of earthquakes.[16]

PS. Harold, my venerable cat that was found on the Goodwin Sands fifteen years ago or more, died last night in a good old age. I am not grieved, for I have not strength to have carried him out of Troy like Anchises on my shoulders.

To LADY OSSORY, Wednesday 14 July 1779

Arlington Street, July 14, 1779.

TO show your Ladyship that I do not always wait for provocatives, I begin a letter tonight, without well knowing what it is to contain. I came to town this morning about my house in Berkeley Square, of which at last I begin to have hopes—though I am in Chancery for it[1]—but it is by a mode of my own. I have persisted in com-

ment of his wife, Lady Diana, who had first been married to Lord Bolingbroke. See also SELWYN 267, 269, 275.

11. On 16 June, the day the Spanish rescript was delivered, thirty-five ships of the Channel Fleet put to sea to cruise under the command of Admiral Sir Charles Hardy.

12. The Posthorse Act (19 Geo. III c. 51), which took effect 5 July, imposed a tax of a penny a mile on each horse hired for travelling post and required a five-shilling licence for postmasters and innkeepers who kept horses for hire, etc.

13. Lord North's 'Additional Militia Bill' (for augmenting the militia), as passed in the House of Commons 24 June, provided for doubling the number of men in the militia, but on 30 June the House of Lords objected, and on 2 July

passed the bill merely for raising additional volunteer companies. After further debate the bill was accepted in the House of Commons 2 July and received the royal assent (19 Geo. III c. 76) the following day (*Journals of the House of Commons* xxxvii. 455–9; *Journals of the House of Lords* xxxv. 813; *Annual Register*, 1779, pp. 169, 171–2; for the debate, see Cobbett, *Parl. Hist.* xx. 915–62, 969–1018).

14. Or gabelle, i.e., tax.

15. Or diachylum or diachylon, an adhesive plaster.

16. The elder Pliny lost his life observing the eruption of Vesuvius 24–25 Aug. 79, which buried Herculaneum and Pompeii (Pliny, *Letters*, VI. xvi).

1. See Appendix 7.

plimenting and flattering my parties, till by dint of complaisance and respect, I have brought them to pique themselves on equal attentions; so that instead of a lawsuit, it has more the air of a treaty between two little German princes who are mimicking their betters only to display their titular dignities. His Serene Highness Colonel Bisshopp[2] is the most obsequious and devoted servant of my Serenity the Landgrave of Strawberry.

His Royal Highness of Sion,[3] who is Lord Paramount of Strawberry,[4] has acquainted the College of Electors of Westminster that they are to be invaded by the French forthwith, and has subscribed £2000 for the defence of his Palatinate.[5] Governor Johnstone is said to be gone to destroy the embarkation[6]—I hope he will do it as completely as he has demolished his own character.[7] The town does not seem to be much alarmed, and the courageous stocks don't value it a fraction;[8] so it does not become us poor little princes to be more frightened than our superiors.

I met Miss Wrottesley[9] this evening at my niece Cholmondeley's,[10] and she told me Mr Dunning[11] has found a flaw in the settlements,[12] and that they must be drawn again.[13]

2. Thomas Bisshopp (ca 1737–1805), son of Sir Cecil Bisshopp, 5th Bt, the former owner of the house (*ante* 28 Oct. 1778); Capt. and Lt-Col., 1774, and Col., 1780, in the 2d Foot Guards; died in Chester Street, Grosvenor Place (William Betham, *Baronetage*, 1801–5, i. 195; E. Kimber and R. Johnson, *Baronetage*, 1771, i. 193; *Army Lists*; GM 1805, lxxv pt i. 91; HW to George Hardinge 4 July 1779).

3. The Duke of Northumberland.

4. 'The parish of Twickenham is in the manor of Sion, of which the Duke of Northumberland is lord' (Edward Ironside, *History and Antiquities of Twickenham*, 1797, p. 8, in *Bibliotheca Topographica Britannica*, Vol. X).

5. At a meeting of 13 July, reported in the *London Chronicle* 13–27 July, xlvi. 42–3, 56, 87; at the second reference the Duke's subscription of £2000 is mentioned. The church wardens in each parish were to go 'to everybody's house to collect voluntary subscriptions' (Coke, 'MS Journals' 20 July 1779).

6. That is, the embarkation point of the French in their expected invasion of England. On 16 May he had been appointed commodore and commander-in-

chief of a small squadron, with which he sailed from Portsmouth 9 July. 'Their destination is unknown' (*London Chronicle* 10–13 July, xlvi. 38, 40).

7. Because of his hot temper, duelling, scurrility, etc. Cf. *ante* 28 Oct. 1778.

8. HW's statement is borne out by the 'Prices of Stocks' given in the *Gentleman's Magazine*.

9. Dorothy Wrottesley (1747–1822), sister of Harriet Wrottesley (*ante* 3 April 1773), m. (1780) Christian, Baron von Kutzleben, envoy extraordinary and minister plenipotentiary from Hesse-Cassel (BERRY i. 346 n. 19).

10. Mary Woffington (ca 1729–1811), sister of the actress Peg Woffington, m. (1746) Rev. Hon. Robert Cholmondeley, HW's nephew (DU DEFFAND i. 299, and *passim*; *Town and Country Magazine*, 1777, ix. 625).

11. John Dunning (1731–83), cr. (1782) Bn Ashburton; solicitor-general 1768–70; M.P.; friend of Lord Shelburne.

12. The marriage settlement for Lady Louisa Fitzpatrick (Miss Wrottesley's first cousin) and Lord Shelburne.

13. These difficulties may have caused the postponing of the wedding from Satur-

Are not you sorry, Madam, for the poor Duke of Ancaster,[14] especially since he made so noble and sensible a will?[15] I think his attention to his mother[16] must half kill her.[17] I hear he has left a legacy to
a very small man that was always his companion, and whom, when
he was drunk, he used to fling at the heads of the company, as others
fling a bottle. Lord Bolinbroke, I suppose you know, is not dead.

Lady Jane Scott, to whom I made your Ladyship's compliments,
has found in a cabinet at Ham[18] a most enchanting picture in enamel
by Zincke[19] of the Duchess of Queensberry, which the Duke always
carried in his pocket. It is as simple as my Cowley,[20] in white with the
hair all flowing, and beautiful as the Hours in Guido's 'Aurora,'[21]
and very like her to the last moment.[22]

I dined on Saturday with my cousin T. Walpole[23] at Carshalton[24]

day, 17 July, to Monday, 19 July (Coke,
'MS Journals' 14, 17 July 1779).

14. Robert Bertie (1756–8 July 1779),
4th D. of Ancaster, 1778. He died of scarlet fever (Coke, 'MS Journals 8–9 July
1779).

15. Lady Mary Coke thought his will
'the most sensible and reasonable action
of his whole life. He has left to his uncle
the present Duke of Ancaster, Grimsthorpe
and five thousand pounds a year, the
remainder to his sons or wherever the
title goes to. His mother's jointure he
makes up three thousand pounds a year
and the house in town, furniture, etc., to
her forever,' etc. ('MS Journals' 15 July
1779). For other details of his will, including provision for his natural daughter
by Rebecca Krudener, see Robert D. Bass,
Green Dragoon, New York, 1957, pp. 42–
3 et passim.

16. Mary Panton (d. 1793), m. (1750)
Peregrine Bertie, 3d D. of Ancaster, 1742.

17. He had increased her jointure by
£1800 a year, repairing the injustice of
his father's 'absurd' will (HW to Mann
16 July 1779).

18. In the house at Petersham (within
the manor of Ham) that she had inherited
from the Duke of Queensberry (ante 28
Oct. 1778).

19. Christian Frederick Zincke (1685–
1767), of whom HW gave an account in
Anecdotes of Painting (Works iii. 475–6,
and Anecdotes of Painting, ed. Ralph N.
Wornum, 1849, iii. 749–50; Thieme-Becker;

George C. Williamson, History of Portrait
Miniatures, 1904, ii. 62–4).

20. Zincke's 'masterpiece, and perhaps
the finest piece of enamel in the world'
('Des. of SH,' Works ii. 475). It was in
the Cabinet in the Tribune and was sold
SH xiv. 51 to P. and D. Colnaghi for
Robert Holford for 60 guineas.

21. The vast fresco of 'Phoebus and
the Hours Preceded by Aurora,' painted
in 1614 in the Casino Rospigliosi Pallavi-
cini in Rome.

22. Lady Jane Scott left this portrait to
Lady Greenwich (Coke, 'MS Journals'
26 Nov. 1779). Now in the possession of
the Duke of Buccleuch at Montagu House,
it is reproduced as the frontispiece to
Violet Biddulph, Kitty, Duchess of Queens-
berry, 1935. A copy of it by HW's friend,
Lady Lucan, is in the possession of the
Duke of Portland at Welbeck Abbey
(Richard W. Goulding, 'Welbeck Abbey
Miniatures,' Walpole Society, 1914–15, iv.
159, No. 233).

23. Hon. Thomas Walpole (1727–1803),
son of Horatio, 1st Bn Walpole of Wolterton; banker in London and Paris; HW's
correspondent.

24. In Surrey, eleven miles from West-
minster Bridge. Walpole owned Carshalton
House 1768–85 (H. S. Vade-Walpole,
'Notes on the Walpoles,' Genealogical
Magazine, 1898–9, ii. 392–6; Carlisle MSS
487). HW mentions the visit in his letter
to Lady Ailesbury 10 July 1779 and to
Mason 9 Aug. 1779, Mason i. 456.

where, though so near London I never was in my life. It is as rural a
village as if in Northumberland, much watered with the clearest
streams[25] and buried in ancient trees of Scawen's Park[26] and the
neighbouring Beddington.[27] I had long wished to see the latter, the
seat of one of my ancestors Sir Nicholas Carew,[28] whose head, as he
was Master of the Horse and Knight of the Garter, flew off in one of
the moods of Henry VIII. Madam Bess I think often visited his son[29]
there.[30] It is an ugly place, with no prospect, a large very bad house,[31]
but it was burnt, rebuilt wretchedly after the Restoration and never
finished. Nothing remains of the ancient fabric but a brave old hall,
with a pendant roof copied by Wolsey at Hampton Court, a vast
shield of arms and quarterings over the chimney, and two clumsy
brazen andirons, which they told us had served Queen Elizabeth in
the Tower, but look more as if they had served her for cannon to
defend it. There is an almost effaced picture of Sir Nicholas, that
seems to have been painted by Holbein, and for which, perished as
it is, I longed.[32]

25. 'The River Wandle passes through
the parish, and being increased by other
streams and several springs which rise
there, forms a large sheet of remarkably
clear water, in the centre of the village,
which gives it a singular, and in the summer a very pleasing appearance' (Daniel
Lysons, *Environs of London,* Vol. I, 1792,
p. 122).

26. Sir William Scawen (d. 1722) purchased part of the manor of Carshalton
in 1712 and the remainder shortly thereafter.

27. For an account of Beddington at
about this time, see Lysons, op. cit. 49–
67, 545–6.

28. (d. 3 March 1539), K.G., 1536;
master of the horse to Henry VIII 1522–
39; condemned for treason and beheaded
on Tower Hill. His daughter Mary m.
Thomas, Lord Darcy, from whom was
descended Catherine Darcy, Lady Philipps,
grandmother of HW's mother ('Pedigree
of Walpole . . . 1776' in HW's extra-
illustrated 'Des. of SH,' 1784, now wsl).

29. Sir Francis Carew (ca 1530–1611), Kt,
1576 (Lysons, op. cit. 56–60).

30. 'In . . . August 1599 Queen Elizabeth paid a visit to Sir Francis Carew at
Beddington, for three days, and again in
the same month the ensuing year; the

Queen's oak and her favourite walk are
still pointed out' (Lysons, op. cit. 57 and
n. 34). In HW's copy of Lysons (now wsl)
four pages of HW's MS notes are bound
in, including one referring to this visit:
'A pane of glass was preserved past the
beginning of the present century, in the
house at Beddington, on which were
written with a diamond, I.C.S: X.O.Q.PU:
supposed to mean scandalously on Queen
Elizabeth, "I see (for saw) Essex occupy
you." '

31. It is described in Lysons, op. cit. 53.

32. John Milbourn made a copy of this
picture for HW, who placed it in the
Great North Bedchamber ('Des. of SH,'
Works ii. 497); it was sold SH xx. 111
to H. Rodd for £5.15.6. A print from this
copy appears in Lysons, op. cit. facing p.
54. The original 'fine portrait of Carew,
painted on board, was preserved at Beddington till about twenty years ago [i.e.,
ca 1866–7], when the house was sold and
the pictures were disposed of' (DNB: James
Gardiner). Although Holbein painted a
portrait of Carew, now in the possession
of the Duke of Buccleuch, the painting
HW mentions is not attributed to Holbein
(Arthur B. Chamberlain, *Hans Holbein
the Younger,* New York, 1913, *passim*).

I shall terminate this letter of scraps and nothings with a good epigram which Mr Jerningham gave me t'other day;

> Ce Marmontel[33] si lent, si long, si lourd,
>   Qui ne parle pas, mais qui beugle,
>   Juge la peinture en aveugle,
> Et la musique comme un sourd.
> Ce pedant à si sotte mine,
>   Et de ridicules bardé,
> Dit qu'il a le secret des beaux vers de Racine—
>   Jamais secret ne fut si bien gardé.

The first line put me in mind of an excellent satiric epitaph on the General Lord Cadogan,[34] of which I have forgotten all but the last couplet,

> Ungrateful to th' ungrateful man he grew by,
> A bad, bold, blustering, bloody, blundering booby.

They were Bishop Atterbury's,[35] who was glad to kill the Duke of Marlborough[36] with the same stone.

---

33. Jean-François Marmontel (1723–99), man of letters.

34. William Cadogan (1672–1726), cr. (1716) Bn and (1718) E. Cadogan; army officer under Marlborough; M.P.; master of the robes to George I 1714–26; envoy 1714–16 and ambassador 1716–20 to The Hague.

35. Francis Atterbury (1662–1732), Bp of Rochester 1713–23; deprived of his offices and banished in 1723 for his connection with the Jacobites and an attempt to restore the Stuarts; intimate friend of Pope. In Atterbury's *Epistolary Correspondence*, ed. John Nichols, 1783–4, ii. 414 n., is 'the communication of a correspondent': 'the following lines which Atterbury is said to have repeated with great emotion on a noble Lord's quitting his apartment, after proposing and improperly pressing some terms which the Bishop had rejected with disdain:

"Unmov'd by pity, and by shame unaw'd
The genuine spawn of bully and of bawd;
Ungrateful to th' ungrateful wretch he grew by,
A baseborn, blundering, blustering, bloody, booby!" '

In his copy (now WSL) HW identified the 'noble Lord' as 'Lord Cadogan, the General,' and 'ungrateful wretch' as 'D. of Marlborough.' For the last line he wrote, 'or thus—A bad, bold, boisterous, bloody, blundering booby.' A different occasion for the lines and variant versions appear in Joseph Spence's *Anecdotes*, ed. Singer, 1820, pp. 155–6, and in his *Observations, Anecdotes, and Characters*, ed. Malone, 1820, pp. 169–70 and n.

36. John Churchill (1650–1722), 1st D. of Marlborough.

To Lady Ossory, Tuesday 20 July 1779

Address: To the Countess of Ossory at Ampthill Park, Bedfordshire. *Postmark:*
ISLEWORTH. 20 IY.

Strawberry Hill, July 20, 1779.

IT would have been impossible for me, Madam, to have met your
Ladyship in town yesterday, had it been proper; but when you
was there but for one day, and that a nuptial one,[1] I should have
been unreasonable to expect you to bestow a twinkling on me. In
fact I was detained here; poor Lady Ailesbury was come to me all
terror and distress. Her daughter[2] was really taken prisoner,[3] and she
had been told her husband and his island[4] were captive too.[5] The
Duchess of Leinster, Lady William Campbell and Mrs Damer were
actually taken by a privateer, the captain of which was no doubt a
Paladin in disguise; he not only treated them with the continence of
Scipio, but with disinterest, a virtue still more rare in a freebooter.
He would not touch a pin; and they were told they were mistresses
to go whither they pleased.[6] Mr Conway has been as little molested
—*Acharnement* is left only to us. A courtier said yesterday, 'We must
act offensively.' I replied, I thought we had done that sufficiently

1. The marriage of Lady Louisa Fitzpatrick to Lord Shelburne.
2. Mrs Damer.
3. She and the others mentioned below
were in the packet boat *Prince Frederick*
going from Dover to Ostend when they
were captured (*London Chronicle* 15–20
July, xlvi. 54, 59, 62; DU DEFFAND v. 160;
GM 1779, xlix. 378; 1781, li. 194).
4. Conway was governor of the Isle of
Jersey.
5. A false report (*London Chronicle*
17–22 July, xlvi. 64, 72).
6. 'At Lady Blandford's [18 July] Mr
Walpole confirmed to me a report I had
heard yesterday . . . [of the three] all
being taken in the packet; a very disagreeable circumstance for themselves and their
friends, though Mr Walpole does not seem
to make much of it . . . I pity her [Lady
Ailesbury] excessively, for we have had
another ugly report of Jersey being taken
which though it is certainly not true, 'tis

highly probable it will be attacked if
we can't destroy the transports and flat
bottom boats which are collected at the
different ports in France' (Coke, 'MS
Journals' 18 July 1779). On the following
day Lady Ailesbury told Lady Mary Coke
the three were safe, 'but their danger
was very great, for the packet by endeavouring to escape was stranded, and the
other packet which got off received two
or three broadsides which might have
sent them to the bottom, so they really
ran a great risk, both of being drowned
or shot. They were treated with civility,
not only by being released but in having
all their baggage returned them. Lady
Ailesbury goes back to Park Place tomorrow' (ibid. 19 July 1779). Anna Maria
Keppel wrote to Anne Clement 20 July
1779, apropos of the capture: 'They have
met with very great civility from the
French; I dare say the *rest* of the *ton* set
envy Mrs Damer excessively' (MS WSL).

already, for we had offended all the world. There were letters in the City on Saturday that say Gibraltar is besieged—I have heard no more of it since; but it is very probable.[7]

It is true that my niece Horatia[8] has put on mourning for the Duke of Ancaster:[9] it is on precedents, and with the approbation of the Duchess Dowager, who has written to her in the kindest manner, acknowledging the intended marriage, lamenting not having her for a daughter and offering to come to her as soon as she is able. Lady E. Burrel has written in the same style; and the new Duke and Duchess[10] have sent compliments of condolence. Lady Horatia has behaved in the most reasonable manner, shown very proper concern, but nothing romantic or extravagant.[11]

Your Ladyship exacts a *petit mot* on Canopus,[12] but I have not a

7. Gibraltar was blockaded by the French and Spanish from 21 June 1779 to 1783, but the English managed to relieve it and keep it in their possession throughout the war.

8. Lady Horatia Waldegrave.

9. 'Poor little Horatia looks very ill still; she finds herself a little better, and much easier since she has got her mourning on' (Anna Maria Keppel to Anne Clement 20 July 1779, MS WSL).

10. The late Duke's uncle, Brownlow Bertie (1729–1809), 5th and last D. of Ancaster; m. (1769) Mary Anne Layard (1743–1804).

11. At the Drawing-Room on Thursday, 15 July, Lord Robert Bertie, uncle of the late Duke of Ancaster, told several people 'that the Duchess of Gloucester had sent a message to the Duchess of Ancaster to let her know that perhaps she might not have been acquainted with her son's intention of marrying her youngest daughter, but that it was to have been a match, and that Lady Horatia had given the Duke of Ancaster a lock of her hair, which she desired might be returned to her, and also she desired the Duchess of Ancaster would order a lock of the Duke's hair to be cut off and sent to her daughter as she intended to mourn for him. Did you ever hear of such nonsense, or such folly? But as the message comes from the House of Folly it is less surprising. Lord Robert added the Duchess of Ancaster had never heard her son had offered himself [n]or is it to be sup-

posed he had; all he had said upon the subject to his mother was this, that as such a marriage might take place he hoped it would not displease her, if it did, which certainly did not imply that the affair was settled' (Coke, 'MS Journals,' 17 July 1779). 'Mr Walpole I thought was not in good spirits. Is it possible, do you think, that he can approve of all this excessive nonsense of the Pavillions?' (ibid. 25 July 1779). '. . . by all I now hear there is much reason to think the marriage being agreed upon was nothing but the invention of Gloucester House' (ibid. 29 July 1779). Lady Horatia wrote to Anne Clement 4 Aug. 1779: 'At sixteen my prospect of happiness is over, for I can never be quite happy whilst I remember him, and when I should forget him I should be *too* ungrateful as the last eleven weeks that I remained in London I was perfectly happy, and it was him that made me so. I now feel as if I had lost everything in the world and have not a wish beyond my sisters' being happy' (MS WSL).

12. Twenty lines of heroic couplets, 'To the Seamen of Old England,' are signed 'Canopus' in the *London Chronicle* 29–31 July, xlvi. 99, but they may have appeared in another newspaper before 20 July. The import is:
'We are true hearts of oak, and lords of the main,
As we beat them before, why not beat them again?' (ll. 5–6)

word to say. I have lived till all the maxims and axioms that I learnt in my youth are grown as superannuated as I am. The sages I was taught to worship have been exploded, and the experience of past ages contradicted. Ministers become more popular in proportion to their miscarriages: debts, taxes, losses, strengthen government. Saws and proverbs, formerly esteemed the quintessence of wisdom, are inverted—for instance: rats of old abandoned a sinking ship—now they run into it. As we have chopped our old system to pieces and thrown it into the kettle to give it new life, be sure it will come out with fresh vigour and bloom—however, obstinate I *wait for the echo* —Let us see what is left, when we come to sue for, and do obtain peace. A map then and a pen and ink will decide who have been in the right.

I hope and do not doubt, Madam, but your new Countess[13] will be very happy. Lord Shelburne made an admirable husband to a wife much less handsome, and apparently, for I did not know her, less agreeable. He I am sure will be out of luck if he is unfortunate, for I must do the Duchess of Bedford the justice to say that a Spartan dame never launched more excellent wives than she has done.

This was only meant as an answer, and I will not swell it into more. I see one is to be kept upon the *qui vive* all the summer with reports and alarms true or false; but I have prepared myself by disbelieving every one till it has been contradicted backwards and forwards two or three times. We have not arrived at a word of truth these four years, till by a new lie becoming necessary, its predecessor is forgotten and suffered to appear stark naked.

To Lady Ossory, Saturday 24 July 1779

Address: To the Countess of Ossory at Ampthill Park, Bedfordshire. *Postmark:* ISLEWORTH. 24 IY.

Strawberry Hill, July 24, 1779.

YOU will be tired of seeing my hand, Madam, yet it would be indecent, neither to accept your kind invitation, nor tell you why I do not. Yesterday I received notice from my attorney[1] that the Master of the Rolls[2] has with epigrammatic dispatch heard my cause

13. Lady Shelburne.

1. John Tilly.
2. Sir Thomas Sewell (ca 1710–84), Kt,

and pronounced a decree in my favour. Surely the whip of the new driver Lord Thurlow[3] has pervaded all the broad wheels of the law and set them galloping. I must go to town on Monday, and get my money ready for payment—not from impatience to enter on my premises, but though the French declare they are coming to burn London, bank-bills are still more combustible than houses, and should my banker's[4] shop be reduced to ashes, I might have a mansion to pay for, and nothing to pay with. If both were consumed, at least I should not be in debt.

I will own fairly too that the moment is so huge, I do not care to stir. It is pretty certain that France, vociferous as her threats, and ready as her preparations, will await the decision of the empire of the sea. We have, I doubt, one prong less to our trident than she and Spain;[5] yet I think the grapple will be tough. Were I Neptune or Æolus, or—I forget who was the classic god of sea-fights, or whether they ever deified any Twitcher[6] after his reception into Olympus, I should perhaps make a pretty impartial division of the damage, and lay it so heavy on both sides, that Madam the House of Bourbon should be glad to leave off playing with fire, and Madam Great Britain should learn to treat mediators with more civility.[7] Every man John of the latter lady's boys are confident of success, and when all other arguments fail, cry, Providence has always saved us; which argument, I suppose, is built on this simple hypothesis, that God made Great Britain, and the devil all the rest of the world. To be sure I heartily pray for victory—but I would not have it quite so round, as to turn our heads, and encourage us to pawn our last fig-leaf. Obstinacy has brought us to the precipice; and after squandering America, we stake ourselves rather than own we have lost it—but

1764; M.P. Harwich 1758–61, Winchelsea 1761–8; Master of the Rolls 1764–84.

3. Who had been Lord Chancellor since 3 June 1778.

4. Croft and Backwell of Pall Mall in 1777 (the names of the partners at various times included Hart, Darell, Devaynes, Dawes and Noble of 39, Pall Mall). Most of HW's dealings appear to have been with Richard Croft until Croft died in 1793 (MANN vi. 278 n. 1, 279 nn. 3, 4; Mann to Richard Croft 8 June 1774, now

WSL; A. Gomez to HW 2 May 1796; London directories, *passim;* HW's MS Account Book, Jan.–July 1794, now WSL).

5. When d'Estaing and Byron met off Georgetown, Grenada, on 6 July 1779, Byron was defeated.

6. For Sandwich's nickname see MONTAGU ii. 153 n. 4.

7. Before breaking off diplomatic relations with Great Britain, Spain had offered to mediate between Great Britain and France.

I forget—what is all this to my going next week to Ampthill or not? Why, this all, our all, is the reason I do not go. Public, private considerations fetter me. I am no hero, nor any of the fine things your Ladyship says of me, and yet I must stay and comfort those that are weaker than myself. Lady Ailesbury is impressed with a thousand terrors, and not without cause. I tremble myself lest Mr Conway should have an opportunity of being romantic and defending a pebble, because he has nothing else to defend—but *dabit Deus his quoque finem*.[8] I have lived to see the rebels at Derby[9]—and I am mighty apt to think that everything will end as I wish. I know no reason why I should be favoured with Fortune's smiles;—but she takes fancies; and in gratitude and deference I have thrown myself entirely upon her. But two days ago she delivered me from a deluge. There was a torrent of rain; all the pipes were stopped, and the inundation burst into six places of my house. The Gallery was overflowed, pictures and damask soaked, the Star Chamber drowned, and the staircase was a cataract. I sent up all the servants, and in a quarter of an hour the waters ceased, and I dreamt that a rainbow rested on the battlements and assured my castle should never be drowned again. Pray, Madam, learn my visions; they are very comfortable, and founded on gratitude not presumption.

I have heard much of Mr B.'s[10] being a second Cosmo Gordon[11] and a third Parson Bate. It is a worthy occupation for a man and a gentleman! but too ⟨conte⟩mptible to dwell on!

⟨A card⟩[12] shall be left for Mr Berrisford in Grosvenor Place on Monday.

My gout entered like love, but I assure you did not retreat like love, or at sixty-two I doubt the fit would have been longer.

---

8. Virgil, *Æneid* i. 198: 'To this, too, God will grant an end.'

9. In 1745.

10. Not identified.

11. Hon. Col. Cosmo Gordon (ca 1737–1813), son of William, 2d E. of Aberdeen; army officer until he resigned his commission, 1783, after a duel in which he had killed a fellow officer. In 1776 it had been learned that he 'was the person who for two years together has put in so many scurrilous paragraphs in the *Morning Post* about Lady Sarah [Lennox Bunbury] and Charles Fox, D. [of] Dorset and the Lady Derby, D[uches]s of Devonshire and the Duke, and D[uches]s of Gordon and many, many others' (John Baker, *Diary*, ed. Yorke, 1931, pp. 375–6, 263, 275; *Scots Peerage* i. 91; *Army Lists*; *Boswell Papers* xviii. 229; J. M. Bulloch, *The Gay Gordons*, 1908, pp. 159–64; GM 1813, lxxxiii pt i. 387; E. R. Curtis, *Lady Sarah Lennox*, New York, 1946, pp. 233–4; Coke, 'MS Journals' 30 Nov., 1 Dec. 1776; *Notes and Queries*, 27 June 1931, clx. 462).

12. Of admission to SH.

To Lady Ossory, Saturday 7 August 1779

Address: To the Countess of Ossory at Ampthill Park, Bedfordshire. *Postmark:*
7 AV. ISLEWORTH.

Aug. 7, 1779.

I HAVE had a double excuse for not having written to your Ladyship for above a week; a return of the gout in my eye, and the
completion of the purchase of my house, for which I have been no
fewer than three times in town since last Sunday.[1] Fortune has again
smiled on me: I think myself most lucky to have paid my money—
the house might be burnt, I obliged to buy it, and have nothing to
pay for it—at least I shall not be in debt for the ashes—Well! Fortune has smiled on more than an individual, by conducting home
our West Indian fleet.[2] Huffed, rebuffed and driven off as she has
been, she is likely to be our best ally—The rest, as ill-treated, are not
so forgiving. Whether the French will come, is another matter: they
certainly meditate it, and great destruction: they give out, to burn
London. Lord North said publicly at a large dinner at Lord Hertford's on Tuesday last, that he expected them in a week—Not having
the Duchess of Bedford's shrewdness, I cannot discover cleverness in
such a notification, unless he had bragged too that he had invited
them. Still my mind does not *misgive* me, which is a comfortable
resource, when one has not much grounds in reason. I take what precautions I can in my own affairs, and then resign myself to good
fortune.

Your Ladyship will see Lord Grantham,[3] and probably Lord Mac-

1. Lady Mary Coke noted HW's absence
from Lady Blandford's on Sunday evening
1 Aug., and two weeks later, when he was
there, he 'did not seem well' ('MS Journals' 1, 15 Aug. 1779).

2. 'Bristol, July 31. Yesterday arrived
. . . 17 sail of West India ships. They
parted with the ships bound to London,
etc., off Scilly all well. This vast fleet,
amounting to 265 ships, valued at near
two millions sterling, sailed from St Kitt's
the 15th of June . . . Providence hath
been remarkably kind since this American
dispute in favouring the arrivals of the

British fleets' (*London Chronicle* 3–5 Aug.,
xlvi. 118).

3. Thomas Robinson (1738–86), 2d Bn
Grantham, 1770; M.P.; ambassador to
Madrid 1771–9; first lord of trade 1780–
2; foreign secretary 1782–3. Following the
break in diplomatic relations with Spain,
he arrived in London from Madrid, via
France, on 3 Aug. (ibid. 3–5 Aug., xlvi.
114). HW's *Collection of Prints, Engraved
by Various Persons of Quality,* now WSL,
contains three etchings by Grantham and
other etchings from his drawings.

cartney.⁴ Our friends are returned on our hands from all quarters
—would to God I were as sure of seeing Mr Conway in safety! I do
not desire to have him achieve an Iliad in a nutshell.⁴ᵃ This I dare say
to you, Madam, though not to him. Do not wonder then that forty
or twenty miles nearer to news are important to me. If Sir Charles
Hardy's⁵ navy does not beat one a third more numerous,⁶ and with
little loss too, Jersey will be swallowed on the road to England. All
that will remain to the few will be, to cry, you cannot say we did it
—though they do say so. This may sound small consolation—but
weigh it against what we should feel if we had an empire lost and all
the lives and all the disgraces on our consciences, and then, Madam,
is inculpability no *douceur?*—Well! we must shut our eyes on all this
at present, and defend our last stake, and not scold like the perverse
Jews when the Temple totters. I could be amazed at many things, if
I had leisure—as why, after stooping to beg pardon of the Congress,
we rejected the mediation of Spain—why, after beseeching France not
to dabble in America, we do not treat now and save what we can, as
any peace signed today would be preferable to what we shall possibly
sign two months hence—but we have stridden from blunder to
blunder, and as at chess when the game is deplorable, the king and

<hr />

4. That is, HW expected the fall of
Grenada. 'It is said that the French landed
upon the island of Grenada on the 20th
of June. As there is no force on the island,
Lord Macartney, who is the governor,
must instantly surrender' (*London Chronicle* 3–5 Aug., xlvi. 118). Macartney was
forced to surrender unconditionally on
4 July and was taken prisoner to France
(Helen H. Robbins, *Our First Ambassador
to China*, 1908, pp. 107–15; *London
Chronicle* 4–9 Sept., xlvi. 232, 234, 238).
4a. 'Their low mechanical notions remind me of an absurd problem proposed
by the famous Monsieur Huet, whether
the Iliad might not be written upon vel-
lum in so small a hand, that the whole
might be contained within a nutshell?
This important question is said to have
engaged . . . the French Court, and . . .
the Dauphin, and his train, are for putting
the Iliad into a nutshell' (Lord Cork and
Orrery, *Remarks on the Life and Writings of . . . Swift*, 3d edn, Dublin, 1752,
p. 172; Hazen, *Cat. of HW's Lib.* 43).

5. Sir Charles Hardy (ca 1714–80), Kt
1755; Admiral of the Blue, 1770. Keppel
was forced to resign 18 March 1779, on
which day Hardy, the senior admiral,
succeeded him (George III to Sandwich
17 March, *Sandwich Papers* ii. 196, 236).
On 29 July he was ordered to remain at
sea to prevent an invasion by the combined French and Spanish fleets (Admiralty orders 29 July, *Corr. Geo. III* iv.
400).
6. On 5 Aug. Hardy had 37 ships of
the line and 23 other vessels (Hist. MSS
Comm., *Stopford-Sackville MSS*, ii [1910].
137; GM Aug. 1779, xlix. 422; *London
Chronicle* 17–19 Aug., xlvi. 168). According to Dutch letters, there were 66 ships
of the line in the combined French and
Spanish fleet (Lord North to Sandwich 18
July, *Sandwich Papers* iii. 6, 47–8). '62
sail of the line and about 40 inferior
sail' were sighted off Falmouth 16 Aug.
(*Daily Adv.* 21 Aug.).

the castle change places, the one is reduced to a corner, and the other, who is called rook too, may not bring him back without being check-mated.

To Lady Ossory, Sunday 5 September 1779

Address: To the Countess of Ossory at Ampthill Park, Bedfordshire. *Postmark:* ISLEWORTH. 6 SE.

Strawberry Hill, Sept. 5, 1779.

YOUR Ladyship and I seem to think alike, that when things are very bad, *il n'y a rien à dire.* For my part I have put most of my senses and intellects under an interdict. There is little use of them, when one can neither believe one's ears or eyes, nor can comprehend what is doing or not doing, nor can judge on anything like nineteen in twenty of those one meets. Now and then indeed I do meet with a person or two, who is so candid as to say, 'Well, I own I was mistaken.' So civil a concession stops one's mouth, and prevents one's saying, 'You lie; I know why you chose to mistake.' Yes, Madam, I have been silent, for I did not know what to say; nor am a jot wiser now. Our fleet is at Portsmouth[1] —nor do I form an opinion:[2] I have seen how foul it is to pronounce on manœuvres at sea. Who this time twelvemonth conceived the merits of Admiral Keppel?

I scarce guess where you are, and direct this at random to Ampt-hill. I have passed a miserable summer, and like a joist of an old mansion am mouldering with it. The gout has passed great part of its *villeggiatura* in my left eye, and now seems settled for autumn in my hip, but incog. under the name of rheumatism. I should be ashamed of complaining with such an exemplar of fortitude hard by, as my

1. Where it arrived 3 Sept. to receive victuals (*London Chronicle* 2–9 Sept. xlvi. *passim*).

2. Lady Mary Coke was less reticent: 'You can't imagine what a damp it has struck upon everybody's spirits the fleet's returning into port without having done anything, and leaving the fleets of Spain and France masters even of our Channel and in their power to take all the islands and insult our coasts' (Coke, 'MS Journals' 5 Sept. 1779; Lady Mary was at Southampton). 'I think the spirit of our people, the honour of our fleet, and perhaps the safety of the country depend upon our not remaining here more than is inevitably necessary' (Lord Mulgrave to Sandwich, Spithead, 3 Sept., *Sandwich Papers* iii. 92).

poor old friend Lady Blandford. It will be three weeks on Tuesday since she was seized with a disorder in her bowels. At once, according to all her doctrine and all her practice, she determined to die and would take nothing to assist nature, but told me when I expostulated with her, that the machine was worn out, and that life was of no value when uncomfortable. She has persisted, perfectly cool and in her senses, begging for laudanum, suffering dreadfully, and the more, as you may imagine, from our late more than West Indian heats.[3] She was alive this morning,[4] for Nature was determined to prove that she might have lived, if she had pleased, though eighty-four.[5] Consider, too, Madam, that it is not the fashion to wish to die, as it was with the Romans. Miss Stapylton,[6] who is also a Virtue personified, has tended her from the moment she heard of her illness, and has literally scarce been in bed since—Miss Stapylton has £30,000, and Lady Blandford nothing[7]—I wish we had some of these exalted characters in breeches! These two women shine like the last sparkles in a piece of burnt paper, which the children call the parson and clerk[8]—alas! the rest of our old ladies are otherwise employed; they are at the head of fleets and armies.[9] Pray tell me something of yourself and concerns, Madam.

3. 'Owing to the excessive heat of the weather, all the springs in Windsor are dried up' and the river 'is lower than ever was known' (*London Chronicle* 14–16 Sept., xlvi. 259).

4. She died in the morning of 7 Sept. at her house at Sheen (ibid. 7–9 Sept., xlvi. 235).

5. Read *eighty-two*. Four years earlier (*ante* 23 Nov. 1775) HW gave her age as 78, which agrees with other references (*ante* 23 June 1771).

6. Catherine Stapleton (ca 1733–1815) (MORE 170 n. 2, and *passim*).

7. 'Lady Blandford died richer than was at first thought. I think she left about fifteen thousand pounds' (Coke, 'MS Journals' 26 Sept. 1779).

8. See MORE 283 n. 3.

9. Sir Charles Hardy and Lord Amherst: Jeffrey Amherst (1717–97), cr. (1776) Bn Amherst, commander-in-chief of the army 1778–82. 'Two dotards are at the head of the only fleet and only army that are to decide our fate' (MASON i. 453); *Last Journals* ii. 221, *sub* 7 Dec. 1778: 'Lord Amherst was now found out, and allowed to be, a man totally void of parts.'

To Lady Ossory, Saturday 11 September 1779

Address: To the Countess of Ossory at Ampthill Park, Bedfordshire. *Postmark:* ISLEWORTH.

Strawberry Hill, Sept. 11, 1779.

THE British flag is indeed strangely lowered,[1] Madam—I used to say the English flag; but since disgrace is our lot, I am very willing that the Scotch, who have occasioned, should partake of it. The accounts from the West Indies are much more creditable,[2] and the loss of the enemy much the more considerable—at least the *Gazette* is to say so tonight.[3] For my own part, I am not at all sorry for Sir Charles Hardy's inaction,[4] not loving a *va-tout*.

You may imagine how much my feelings sympathize with your Ladyship's. Jersey rankles the most of all.[5]

This is all I can write at present, having no use but of my right arm. The other is all gout, but I flatter myself it will not be a long fit, though my nights have been very painful. Your kind invitation to Ampthill, Madam, adds to my woes. I do not think I shall ever be able to go any whither on pleasure more. I never now have a week of perfect health together, nor have strength to recover in the inter-

1. By Byron's losses and Hardy's inaction mentioned below.

2. Vice-Admiral Barrington arrived at the Admiralty 9 Sept. with dispatches from Vice-Admiral Byron about his engagement with d'Estaing at Grenada on 6 July; other reports appeared in the *London Chronicle* 4–11 Sept., xlvi. *passim*. Byron with 21 ships of the line had attacked D'Estaing with 25, and had been defeated (*London Gazette* No. 12012, 7–12 Sept.; A. T. Mahan, *Major Operations of the Navies in the War of American Independence*, Boston, 1913, pp. 105–13).

3. The *London Gazette*, loc. cit., contains dispatches from Byron dated 8, 17 July and 3 Aug. In the first Byron reported, 'I am convinced they [his ships] did the enemy great damage, although their masts, rigging and sails appeared less injured than ours.' The British casualty list included 183 killed and 346 wounded. In the dispatch of 3 Aug. he reported (on the authority of 'two gentlemen who left Grenada about a week ago') that the French killed were 'three captains, eighteen lieutenants, and 1200 men' and 'the wounded amounted to nearly 2000.' The official French report was 190 killed and 759 wounded (ibid.; GM 1779, xlix. 466–8; A. T. Mahan, op. cit. 112).

4. The Channel fleet anchored at Spithead 3 Sept. and the combined French and Spanish fleets anchored at Brest 14 Sept. Although detachments from each fleet went on cruises outside, the two main fleets did not engage. The *London Chronicle* Sept.–Oct. contains many rumours that Hardy was on the point of sailing.

5. That is, HW feared that Jersey would soon be lost because the Channel fleet was inactive and apparently too weak to command the Channel. Jersey was not further molested until Jan. 1781 (*post* 9 Jan. 1781).

vals. There is nothing shocking in decay, when one has outlived the glory and prosperity of one's country.

To Lady Ossory, Friday 24 September 1779

Address: To the Countess of Ossory at Farming Woods near Thrapston. *Postmark:* ISLEWORTH.

Strawberry Hill, Sept. 24 at night.

I CAN learn no more of Lord Maccartney, Madam, than your Ladyship sees in the papers, that he is near Rochelle.[1] I have written to Madame du Deffand[2] to beg she will do him any service in her power, though he must have more powerful mediators—but sometimes by accident a straw may be more useful than a white wand.

There was a *Gazette*[3] this morning that will frighten the combined fleets out of their senses. We have destroyed a whole navy of walnut-shells at a place as well known as Pharsalia, called Penobscot.[4] If Great Britain was taken, and we reconquered an ait in the Thames, I believe the *Gazette* would think the latter only worth mentioning —but all we do and do not, is too silly and contemptible to dwell on!

Poor Lady Lincoln[5] has a new misfortune,[6] and has lost her son.[7] Lord Thomas[8] the successor is in America[9] and has more chances than one against returning.

I was in town yesterday for the first time of my going out these

1. His dispatch dated 'Near La Rochelle, France, Sept. 4' was in the *London Gazette* No. 12015, 18–21 Sept., reprinted in the *London Chronicle* 21–23 Sept., xlvi. 281. He had arrived at La Rochelle 3 Sept.

2. 23 Sept. (DU DEFFAND v. 175).

3. A *London Gazette Extraordinary,* 24 Sept.

4. On 14 Aug. Commodore Sir George Collier with five ships entered Penobscot Bay on the coast of Maine and attacked the American fleet there. Of the ships, ranging from 32 guns to 10 each, 14 were blown up by the Americans to prevent their falling into his hands, 4 were taken, and 1 was burnt; and 24 transports were burnt (Collier's dispatch, 20 Aug., ibid.;

HW to Mason 28 Sept. 1779, MASON i. 467 and nn. 8–9).

5. Lady Frances Seymour-Conway (1751–1820), dau. of Lord and Lady Hertford, m. (1775) Henry Fiennes Pelham-Clinton, styled Lord Clinton 1752–68 and E. of Lincoln 1768–78.

6. Her earlier misfortune was the death of her husband 18 Oct. 1778 in his 28th year.

7. Henry Pelham-Clinton (23 Dec. 1777 – 23 Sept. 1779); styled E. of Lincoln after his father's death; died at Brighton, 'where he was sent to be bathed in the sea' (*London Chronicle* 23–25 Sept., xlvi. 294; Coke, 'MS Journals' 23 Sept. 1779).

8. Pelham-Clinton.

9. A captain in the First Regiment of

weeks; as my left hand is still muffled. I went to give some orders about my new house, with which I am much pleased, now it is painted and papered, though in the plainest manner possible. You are so good, Madam, as to mention the air of Southampton to me— I believe the sea air would do me good, if anything would—but at present I am too low and too weak to determine on anything, or to bear anything but perfect quiet. You would not know me, for instead of being perpetually occupied about some trifle or other, I lie and doze half the day on the couch, and at night count the day gone with satisfaction.

It is very foolish or very vain, probably both, to fill half a letter with one's self at such a moment—but is the public a better theme? Where can one descry a prospect that promises a gleam of hope? Flying from D'Orvilliers,[10] beaten by Destain,[11] and comforted by gathering a wreath of sea-weeds at Penobscot! How low is a nation sunk, when its understanding may be so insulted! Whenever the King of Prussia was beaten, he said he was beaten—he never sang Te Deum for putting to flight a handful of hussars. Adieu! Madam, I am sick of the times, and sick of myself, and so I doubt are you too.

To Lady Ossory, Thursday 14 October 1779

Printed from the MS now WSL; sold at Sotheby's ('Other Properties') 30 July 1940, lot 570 (with two others from HW to Lady Ossory); later sold by Maggs to WSL.

For the date, see the following letter, second paragraph, where this note is mentioned.

Address: To Lady Ossory.

Thursday morning [14 Oct. 1779].

I AM come to town to take possession of Berkeley Square; and your Ladyship's letter of the 9th which N.B. I received *but* yesterday, gives me great hopes of finding you in town. How happy I shall be if you are, and that I may catch a glimpse of you after dinner!

Foot Guards, he served as A.D.C. to General Sir Henry Clinton 1779–80.

10. After sighting the combined fleet under d'Orvilliers off the Lizard 31 Aug., Hardy stood in, instead of pursuing, because he preferred giving battle in the Channel. The next day, he began tacking eastward, hoping d'Orvilliers would follow him (*Sandwich Papers* iii. 7–8, 89–91).

11. At Grenada 6 July.

To Lady Ossory, Thursday 14 October 1779 *bis*

Written over the sheet with the address are sixteen lines of verse (in an unidentified hand) beginning
>'Ye British dames by folly led
>Under the name of fashion . . .'

Address: To the Countess of Ossory.

Berkeley Square, my inauguration day, Oct. 14, 1779.

I CAME to town this morning to take possession of Berkeley Square, and am as pleased with my new habitation, as I can be with anything at present. Lady Shelburne's being queen of the palace over against me[1] has improved the view since I bought the house, and I trust will make your Ladyship not so shy as you was of Arlington Street.[2]

I stopped at the turnpike,[3] and sent to Grosvenor Place—but no tidings of you—however, as I shall stay in town till Saturday, I do not despair, having left a note for you. On Saturday I must return, as my royalties leave the Pavilions on Sunday, and go to Blackheath.[4]

The catastrophe of the poor old lady that you killed with kindness, has touched me exceedingly—not on her account, for having been cotemporary of Lady Gowran,[5] I conclude she was ancient—and then is not it charming to be smothered with joy? but I feel tenderly for your Ladyship who must have suffered for your most innocent good nature.

I know nothing of the authenticity of Lord Maccartney's and

1. Shelburne House, on the south side of Berkeley Square; better known, from 1784, as Lansdowne House. Begun in 1762 by Robert Adam for Lord Bute, it was sold before completion to Lord Shelburne in 1768. The remaining portion of the house is now the Lansdowne Club (E. B. Chancellor, *Private Palaces of London,* 1908, pp. 275–90; *Short Guide to London,* ed. L. R. Muirhead, 1956, p. 42).

2. In which her former husband, the Duke of Grafton, lived.

3. At Hyde Park Corner.

4. A house known as Blackheath or Wricklesmarsh, in the hundred of Blackheath, at Charlton, in Kent; until 1775 the seat of Sir Gregory Page (see *post* 14 Nov. 1779). For the history of the house see Daniel Lysons, *Environs of London,* Vol. IV, 1796, p. 329; *The Ambulator; or The Stranger's Companion in a Tour round London,* 1774, pp. 14–17). The Duke of Gloucester took the house 'for his principal place of residence during the summer' (*London Chronicle* 12–15 July 1777, xlii. 55; ibid. 6–8 April 1779, xlv. 330, HW to the Duchess of Gloucester 9 July 1787).

5. Lord Ossory's grandmother: Anne Robinson (d. 1744), m. (1718) Richard Fitzpatrick, cr. (1715) Bn Gowran. She brought the estate of Farming Woods into the family.

D'Estain's letters,[6] but believe they are thought genuine. Madame du Deffand in a letter[7] I received yesterday, tells me they are very angry with the former for his great indiscretions on shipboard.[8] He is at Limoges,[9] where the Comte de Broglie has seen and commends him. I have written again tonight to my friend in his favour, and have told her that Lord M. has always been *deservedly* a great favourite of the ladies, and that as women govern in France, she must interest them in his behalf—I hope Lady Maccartney will forgive me if he earns his release.

It is firmly believed that Destain is gone with fourteen ships of the line to New York,[10] where Arbuthnot[11] has but seven.[12] This will exceedingly shorten the American war. The combined fleets, now said to amount to seventy,[13] are expected forth again[14]—France, I am persuaded, is impatient to shorten the whole war. I have heard

6. With his dispatch of 5 July 1779 to Lord George Germain concerning the loss of Grenada, Macartney enclosed copies of a letter from d'Estaing 3 July demanding the unconditional surrender of the island, and Macartney's crisp reply of the same date: 'Lord Macartney is ignorant of the Count d'Estaing's force; he knows his own and will defend the island to the utmost of his power' (John Barrow, *Some Account . . . of the Earl of Macartney*, 1807, i. 57–8, 427–36; BM, Egerton MS 2135.9; ff. 54–72).

7. 1–2 Oct. 1779 (DU DEFFAND v. 177–9).

8. 'On est ici fort prévenu contre lui; il a tenu des propos dans le vaisseau qui l'a amené en France, qui ont extrêmement choqué, et qui effectivement sont très imprudents' (ibid. v. 178). According to a letter from Bordeaux 9 Sept. Macartney was brought to France on *La Diligente* (*London Chronicle* 23–25 Sept., 7–9 Oct., xlvi. 291, 337). An Englishman who was at Grenada when it was taken reported that 'The French officers in general behaved very politely to the English, except D'Estaign, who treated Lord Macartney and the other prisoners very ill' (ibid. 2–5 Oct., xlvi. 321).

9. 'Paris, Sept. 17 . . . Lord Macartney has been sent to Limoges; he desired to go to Paris, but was refused' (ibid. 25–28 Sept., xlvi. 302; DU DEFFAND v. 177).

10. He sailed from San Domingo 16 Aug. not to New York, but to Savannah; after the siege, his squadron returned piecemeal to Brest (Pechot's 'Journal' and 'Epoques et événements' in B. F. Stevens, *Facsimiles of Manuscripts in European Archives Relating to America*, 1889–98, xxiii. Nos 2010, 2023; see also Joannès Tramond, *Manuel d'histoire maritime de la France*, 1927, pp. 494–6). It had been reported, however, in the *Public Advertiser* 13 Oct., and *London Chronicle* 12–14 Oct., xlvi. 360, that his fleet had 23 ships of the line and 11 frigates, and that his final object was to act with Washington against the British in New York.

11. Marriot Arbuthnot (ca 1711–94), Rear-Adm., 1778; Adm. of the Blue, 1793. Appointed to the command of the North American station in Feb. 1779, he arrived at New York 25 Aug. In his dispatch of 8 Oct. from Sandy Hook he said he expected d'Estaing's fleet of 24 ships of the line and 14 frigates unless some of them had been disabled by storms (*London Chronicle* 27–30 Nov., xlvi. 513, from the *London Gazette*).

12. 'Admiral Arbuthnot arrived at New York on the 25th of August with six ships of the line and one frigate' (*Public Advertiser* 14 Oct., 3 Nov.).

13. '54 ships of the line, followed by a corps de reserve of 16 ships of the line under the Spanish Admiral Don Cordova', according to report from The Hague of 19 Aug. (*Daily Adv.* 30 Aug.; see, however, *ante* 7 Aug. 1779, n. 6). '51 ships of the line' and 'the squadron of observation of 16 men of war,' were reported at Brest,

tonight at an Irish house, whereon I do not entirely pin my faith, that Lord North says he fears the Irish, more than the English Parliament.[15] At the same place I was told that an American negotiator is here offering treaty, on condition of total silence on the word *independence,* and that his offer has been rejected[16]—By an odd collision of circumstan⟨ces,⟩ I did discover one truth, whatever the rest were. The Bishop of D⟨erry⟩[17] had said there, that *he* had proposed to the administration to take off the test in favour of the Catholics.[18] I do know that he has said that it was to be taken off; which I do not believe.

Now I am sending coals to Ireland,[19] I must add an excellent story I was told at the same place. That Lilliputian, Lady Newhaven,[20] arriving at Tunbridge desired Mrs Vesey to explain to her and instruct her in the customs and news of the place. A man arrived ringing a bell—for what? said my lady. 'Oh!' replied Mrs V., 'to notify your arrival.' At that instant the man bawled out, 'At one o'clock at Mr Pinchbeck's[21] great room will be shown the surprising tall woman.'

I hope these Hibernian tales will satisfy your Ladyship in the

14 Sept. (ibid. 28 Sept., *sub* Paris, 21 Sept.).

14. The combined fleet did not put to sea again; d'Orvilliers was superseded 16 Sept. by Du Chaffault (ibid. 9 Oct.; DU DEFFAND v. 176); the Spanish squadron left Brest 9 Nov. (Tramond, op. cit. 480–1). See *post* 1 Nov. 1779.

15. The crisis in Anglo-Irish relations is described in H. Butterfield, *George III Lord North and the People 1779–80,* 1949, and T. H. D. Mahoney, *Edmund Burke and Ireland,* Cambridge, Mass., 1960, pp. 84–9.

16. No support for this rumour has been found. Congress had resolved 8 May to 'agree to a treaty of peace with Great Britain,' and a committee 'to prepare instructions for the minister plenipotentiary . . . for negotiating a peace' was appointed 4 Aug.; the instructions were approved 14 Aug. (*Journals of the Continental Congress, 1779,* Washington, 1904–37, xiv. 565, 920–4, 952, 955–62). John Adams was appointed 27 Sept. minister plenipotentiary (ibid. xv. 1113), but he did not sail until 13 Nov. (*Adams Papers,* ed. Butterfield, Cambridge, Mass., 1961–, Ser. I, *Diaries,* ii. 400).

17. Frederick Augustus Hervey (1730–1803), Bp of Derry, 1768; 4th E. of Bristol, 28 Sept. 1779. In 'Mem. 1783–91,' 11 Feb. 1784, HW refers to him as 'that infamous and half-witted incendiary . . . active in the prosecution of his vile and unprincipled schemes in Ireland,' who 'stuck at nothing—no, nothing, to promote' his political views, including 'toleration of popery.'

18. He wrote to Lord George Germain ca 10 Sept.: 'If something . . . be not speedily effected to pacify both the Papists and Presbyterians, we risk a general insurrection' and that a repeal of the Test Act should be moved (W. S. Childe-Pemberton, *The Earl Bishop,* 1925, i. 238; see also MASON i. 469).

19. That is, Lord Ossory, of an Irish family and with estates in Ireland, would already know the state of affairs there.

20. Frances Allen (d. 1801), m. (1758) William Mayne, cr. (1763) Bt and (1776) Bn Newhaven; 'a little lively sort of a fairy, not very conversant with the great world' (Mrs Delany to Mrs Dewes 22 Feb. 1755, *Delany Corr.* iii. 334).

21. Christopher Pinchbeck the younger (ca 1710–83), inventor and toyman, a

room of the Middlesex election,[22] of which I know no more than the man in the moon.

The invitation to Farming Woods will not want the codicil of Fotheringay,[23] which I have seen,[24] and Kirby[25]—I forget whose—if ever I recover my youth and spirits—or at least the latter, which is not very probable, while I remember the happy days of my spring, and the glorious days of my autumn! When the chill of winter is sharpened by the blasts of national disgrace, the only comfort of age is, that there are no more seasons to follow. I know I do not wish for one more summer, if I am to pass it like the last! Nor can I see on what to build for expecting that the next will be more comfortable.

To Lady Ossory, Wednesday 27 October 1779

Address: To the Countess of Ossory at Ampthill Park, Bedfordshire. *Postmark:* ISLEWORTH. 28 OC.

Strawberry Hill, Oct. 27, 1779.

I AM fortunate, Madam, that you have had a parenthesis of Bedfordshire neighbours between *fixed air, electricity, solar microscopes* and every topic in and out of creation; and my barren narrow conversation, which is confined to few ideas and less knowledge than any man's who has lived so long, had opportunities of seeing so much, and yet has stored up but a heap of indigested trifles, and fathomed no earthly thing to the bottom, nor any heavenly one to the top—which in truth I believe can be done a very little way—however, I honour natural philosophers in every one of their walks. They aim at enlightening mankind; most other professions at deceiving.

favourite of George III; son of the inventor of copper and zinc alloy associated with the name. He had a shop in Cockspur Street, St Martin's in the Fields, and he owned one of the two sets of assembly rooms at Tunbridge Wells (Margaret Barton, *Tunbridge Wells,* 1937, p. 4; Selwyn to Lord Carlisle 3 Aug. 1775, *Carlisle MSS* 283; Mason, *Satirical Poems* 96 and *passim*).

22. A candidate was to be elected on 28 Oct. to fill the vacancy made by the death of John Glynn on 16 Sept.

23. The castle and church of Fotheringhay in Northants, about 8 miles from Farming Woods.

24. In 1763. See *Country Seats* 58 and HW to Montagu 23 July 1763, MONTAGU ii. 90–1. For a full account see John Nichols, *History . . . of Fotheringay,* 1787, in *Bibliotheca Topographica Britannica,* Vol. IV.

25. Kirby Hall, Northants, the seat of the Hattons, from whom it passed to the Earls of Winchilsea (*post* 25 Dec. 1780, 30 Aug. 1786).

I have always heard that Bowood[1] was magnificent—you will not wonder that accounts of noble palaces raise a sigh in my breast, not of envy, but remembrance!—but alas! what will all our seats be but monuments of past splendour? As I should not like to die in an unfinished moment, though perhaps preferable to the catastrophe, I wish for peace, to know what is to be left. I doubt, many turbulent scenes are to pass first: and though one expected them much sooner, it is plain that causes have at last their effects; and though one is often disappointed in the calculations of wisdom, folly and presumption produce their natural consequences. These multiply daily; and, being so numerous and so repugnant to each other, the medicines, that would, as in bodily distempers, cure some, are prejudicial to others. For instance, can your Ireland be redressed, without danger of producing insurrections here? Can the two islands jar, and not facilitate the views of France and Spain? I have reason to believe that the combined fleets will again appear before the conclusion of the campaign, though the Government thinks not. They still talk at Paris of invasion;[2] and having threatened it so often vainly, may have rendered it more facile by our incredulity—but what signify conjectures?—as Cato says, Plato cannot end them and the sword must.[3]

My constitution which sat out under happy stars, seems to keep pace with the change of constellations, and fail like the various members of the empire. I am now confined with the rheumatism in my left arm, and find no benefit from our woollen manufacture which I flattered myself would always be a resource.[4] On Monday I shall remove to Shelburne Square,[5] and watch impatiently the opening of the Countess's windows; though with all her and her Earl's good-

1. Bowood Park, in Wiltshire, seat of the Earl of Shelburne (later Marquess of Lansdowne), who had recently married Lord Ossory's sister.

2. 'Paris, Oct. 15 . . . We have accounts from Brest that the King has wrote to M. Du Chaffault that no reason whatever shall make him alter his intention of having the fleet sail as soon as possible, and that all he wants of his navy is to land 80,000 men in the enemy's country' (*London Chronicle* 23–26 Oct., xlvi. 398).

3. In Addison's *Cato*, V. i, Cato, with 'Plato's book on the Immortality of the

Soul' in his hand and a 'drawn sword on the table by him,' soliloquizes:

'It must be so—Plato, thou reason'st well!—
Else whence this pleasing hope, this fond desire,
This longing after immortality? . . .'

Then, 'laying his hand on his sword,'
'I'm weary of conjectures—This must end 'em.'

4. As the bootikins had helped him in fits of the gout.

5. I.e., Berkeley Square.

ness to me, I doubt I shall profit little of either. I do not love to be laughed at or pitied; and dread exposing myself to numbers of strange servants and young people who wonder what Methusalem does out of his coffin. Lady Blandford is gone;[6] her antediluvian dowagers dispersed; amongst whom I was still reckoned a lively young creature. Wisdom I left forty years ago to Welbore Ellis, and must not pretend to rival him now when he is grown so rich by the semblance of it. Since I cannot then act old age with dignity, I must keep myself out of the way—and weep for England in a corner.

I am glad the appearances in Miss Fox are better.[7] The elder Lady Albemarle[8] has had a stroke of palsy,[9] but is better. Lady Sarah came to town with her, and still looks prettier and fresher than an angel of Correggio.[10]

Whither are your next motions, Madam? You lately talked of not seeing London till the roses appear. That is a little perverse; and very uncomfortable to me, since, seldom dining abroad, I should be happy to sit by your fire in the long evenings; but you scarce arrive, till the *tourbillon* of Ranelagh surrounds you. Well! I must have done with wishes, which are foolish but in youth, when time *may* accomplish them.

To Lady Ossory, Monday 1 November 1779

Address: To the Countess of Ossory at Ampthill Park, Bedfordshire. *Postmark:* GC.

Berkeley Square, Nov. 1 too late for the post.

YOU bid me send you all the news. Pray, of what sort would you have, Madam?—or do you act the innocent, and ask, though you know more than I do? Most likely, for I know no more than the

6. She had died 7 Sept.

7. Lady Sarah Lennox wrote to the Duchess of Leinster 5 Nov. 1779 that Caroline Fox 'has been ill, it seems, a long time with the stone, an uncommon disorder for a child. Lord Warwick . . . has no reason to expect her to live, as she is given over by all the physicians that attend her. Poor Lady Warwick is to be pitied most excessively' (*Leinster Corr.* ii. 298).

8. Anne Lennox (1703–89), m. (1723)

William Anne van Keppel, 2d E. of Albemarle.

9. When she was visiting Lady Sarah Lennox at Goodwood. Reports on her illness and recovery are in Lady Sarah's letters in *Leinster Corr.* ii. 291–309.

10. 'Mr Walpole looks very old, but he was in great spirits, and was very entertaining' (Lady Sarah Lennox to the Duchess of Leinster 5 Nov. 1779, apropos of HW's visit to Lady Albemarle and Lady Sarah ca 20 Oct., ibid. ii. 295, 297).

herb-women in St James's Market.[1] But I have no objection to being
a dupe, if you have a mind I should be one. It is but one step below
ignorance—So then you do not know that the lord president of the
Council,[2] such an age ago as last Wednesday, would not attend to
swear in Lord Stormont,[3] but walked in the Park during the solemnity, to the great scandal of all true Catholics.[4]

In the next place your Ladyship, poor soul, does not know that
the paymaster of the Army[5] holds all you poor souls very cheap who
do not know that Lord Gower is *out*—Why, has he resigned? has he
resigned?—no, not yet, the King has not been in town.[6]

I can gratify your Ladyship's curiosity or finesse no farther, for I
truly know no more. Nay, I hold this state machinery or mystery
in the same light as the Middlesex election. Objects that are gigantic
on some horizons, are straws on others. When every part of the
fabric totters, who can care whether a board starts in the floor of the
drawing-room or closet, except some *joiner* who hopes his bill will
be paid before the palace tumbles? Contrary to Lord Sh[elburne]'s
opinion, there are reasons to think that the combined fleets will, if
not yet sailed, still leave Brest to the amount of fifty-two sail;[7] Sir
Charles Hardy has forty-three[8]—but come the blow this year or not,

1. Near St James's Square, on the west
of the Haymarket about midway between
Charles Street and Jermyn Street, displaced when Regent Street and Waterloo
Place were laid out, 1813–20. (Wheatley,
London Past and Present ii. 283–5, iii.
158–9, 453–4).

2. Lord Gower, uncle to Lord Ossory,
had been lord president since 23 Dec.
1767.

3. As secretary of state for the North.
The post had been vacant since the death
of Lord Suffolk 7 March 1779.

4. Stormont was nephew and heir to
Lord Mansfield, who was known to be
sympathetic to Catholic emancipation.

5. Richard Rigby (1722–88), paymaster
general of the land forces 1768–84; M.P.
Castle Rising 1745–7, Sudbury 1747–54,
Tavistock 1754–88; in his youth a friend
of HW.

6. Although the King had been at
Windsor and Kew most of the time since
his levee on 20 Oct., he had been at the
council when Stormont was sworn 27 Oct.

and at the levee 29 Oct. (*London Chronicle* 19 Oct.– 2 Nov., xlvi. 382, 406, 414,
417). On 11 Nov., when Jenkinson saw
Gower, the latter had offered his resignation but 'did not say a word of his
desire to be out of his office at any particular time' (*Corr. Geo. III* iv. 482).

7. The *Daily Adv.* 26 Oct., prints (*sub*
'Paris, Oct. 15') an account 'from Brest,
that the King had wrote to M. Du
Chaffault . . . his intention of having the
fleet sail as soon as possible, and that
all he wants of his navy is to land 80,000
men in the enemy's country.' Hardy heard
that 'the enemy's combined fleet was
ready to sail on the 31st October' (*Sandwich Papers* iii. 105). 'The greatest number of ships they can possibly send to sea
does not exceed 52 sail of the line' (*London
Chronicle* 30 Oct.–11 Nov., xlvi. 418, 449).

8. The fleet sailed from Spithead 22
Oct.: 37 ships of the line, 9 frigates, 3
sloops, and 8 fireships (*Daily Adv.* 26
Oct.).

what is to amend our situation? Will more losses in other parts? Will greater difficulties and dissatisfactions at home? Will Ireland discourage France? Will new taxes encourage England? Will perseverance in measures that open new calamities everywhere, close them? Where can France or Spain be wounded by us? When we cannot protect Jamaica,[9] can we reconquer America? When ministers begin to be afraid of keeping their places, will they intimidate others—except by their example? If *anybody*[10] will be his own minister,[11] will he not be his only minister? They have long thrown all the blame on him, and now it looks as if they would throw their offices on him too.[12]

I met Lady Bute this evening; she expects Lord Maccartney every hour.[13] Thank you for the sight of Lady Maccartney's letter,[14] Madam; but as I do not visit her, I cannot possibly on this occasion: it would look like assuming merit on good offices,[15] which I could only attempt, but which I have not the smallest reason to think contributed to his return. Pray, Madam, do not call this or anything of the kind, modesty and humility—it is only humiliation, which is but pride mortified. I see myself a poor invalid threatened with a painful and irksome conclusion, and mortified at seeing the decay of my country more rapid than my own: ambition I never felt, but was content with being an individual in so free and splendid a nation —'Tis all gone, Madam—and methinks one sinks in one's own estimation in proportion.

When I mention my woes however, it is to excuse my frequent excuses, not to complain of my lot, which has been singularly happy

9. The need for additional soldiers in Jamaica and convoys to reduce the number of ships captured by privateers is suggested in the *London Chronicle* 16–23 Oct., xlvi. 370, 386, 392. The exposed situation of Jamaica led shortly to rumours that it had been captured (following letter) but despite a threat of conquest in 1782 it remained in British hands throughout the war.

10. The King.

11. 'I think it was in this debate [4 Dec. 1778] that Lord George Germaine asserted that the *King "was his own Minister"* ' (*Last Journals* ii. 220).

12. The King complained that 'Lord Gower has not pointed out the most distant shadow of the means of forming a more efficient ministry, that till that was produced by someone, I could not think of parting with what I had' (George III to Jenkinson 7 Nov. 1779, *Corr. Geo. III* iv. 477).

13. 'On Tuesday night [2 Nov.] Lord Macartney arrived at his father-in-law (Lord Bute's) house in Audley Street, from France, on his parole' (*Public Advertiser* 4 Nov.; *London Chronicle* 16 Oct. – 16 Nov., xlvi. 376, 430, 470).

14. Missing.

15. That is, HW's request to Mme du Deffand to intercede for Macartney (*ante* 14 Oct. 1779).

and fortunate. I am so at this moment; for I expect General Conway this week;[16] and I shall think him as much recovered, as if I had seen a bomb in the air over his head.

Nov. 2d.

I have heard nothing new today. If you can explain what I have been telling you, and if you are not in the secret—nay, if you are, perhaps you may not understand it, be so good as to decipher to me —but I am in no hurry—When Titus was at the gates of Jerusalem, can one read with patience the squabbles of the Pharisees?

PS. I must commend the honesty of your Milesians, Madam. If forty thousand Scots were in arms asking redress,[17] do you think they would have let the E. Indian fleet depart from Limerick before they were satisfied?[18]

To Lady Ossory, Saturday 6 November 1779

Address: To the Countess of Ossory at Ampthill Park, Bedfordshire. *Postmark:* 6 NO. GC.

Saturday evening, 6th.

IF there is a sprig of truth left growing in Bedfordshire, I entreat your Ladyship to spare me a cutting, for there is not a leaf to be had in town for love or money, everything is so dear! and yet falsehood bears a still higher price. Jamaica is taken, and it is not;[1] the combined fleets are sailed, and they are not.[2] The East Indiamen

---

16. See *post* 21 Nov. 1779.

17. The number of men armed for the defence of Ireland against invasion at this time is variously given. In the House of Commons 6 Dec. 1779 Lord Ossory and Fox reported 42,000 (Cobbett, *Parl. Hist.* xx. 1198, 1221–2), an estimate accepted by W. E. H. Lecky (MASON i. 469 n. 3). The Irish were agitating for free trade as a means of economic relief.

18. News of the safe arrival of eight East India ships at Limerick reached London 7 Sept. A convoy was sent to escort the ships to the Downs, and a false report of their arrival had been received 1 Nov.

'This fleet is said to be the richest ever known to arrive at one time' (*Public Advertiser* 22 Oct., 2, 3, 6, 11 Nov.; *London Chronicle* 4–7 Sept. – 13–16 Nov., *passim*).

———

1. 'Various reports were again propagated yesterday [5 Nov.] at the west end of the town in regard to the taking of Jamaica by the French, but no credit was given to any of them, the whole being supposed to be destitute of foundation' (*London Chronicle* 4–6 Nov., xlvi. 438, 440; cf. ibid. 2–4 Nov., xlvi. 432).

2. 'Early this morning [6 Nov.] an express arrived from Sir Charles Hardy,

are arrived, and are not. Lord Gower is out, and is not. Lord Northington is dead and is not.[3]

The edition of Gower, privately printed at Glasgow,[4] says he has been out these three weeks—but the critics say that cannot be so, for etc.

Lord Weymouth's servants say he is to resign.[5] Some say, Lord Bathurst is to be president,[6] and Lady Cranborne says, her Lord.[7] Lord Maccartney is come,[8] but we have missed each other. They say he is dismally lean and black. George and the Signorina arrived last night.[9] Lord Mount Stuart is at Paris—or not.[10]

You see how friendly I am, Madam. Nobody tells you anything, and I tell you both sides of everything.

Your humble servant,

JANUS.

PS. Very good sport in Nubia.[11]

dated at sea, within sight of Brest, Thursday, the 4th instant . . . the combined fleets . . . were out, and lay off Brest Harbour' (ibid. 4–6 Nov., xlvi. 440). This report was denied ibid. 6–9 Nov., xlvi. 446, and no action ensued.

3. Reports and denials of his death appeared in the *Public Advertiser* 5 and 9 Nov.

4. That is, rumours about Lord Gower among Scots in London.

5. Weymouth, secretary of state for the South, resigned 24 Nov. For references to his resignation, including the King's letter of 5 Nov., asking him not to resign and offering him the presidency of the Council, and Weymouth's reply of 6 Nov., see *Corr. Geo. III* iv. 471–99, *passim*.

6. Bathurst was sworn 25 Nov. as lord president of the Council, succeeding Lord Gower (*Public Advertiser* 22, 26, 29 Nov.).

7. Lady Cranborne is said to have zealously used 'her wit, her audacity, and her social talent . . . for the furtherance of her husband's parliamentary influence' (Lady Gwendolen Cecil, *Life of Robert, Marquis of Salisbury*, 1921–32, i. 2).

8. 2 Nov.; see preceding letter. He

brought Mme du Deffand's letter of 24 Oct. to HW (DU DEFFAND v. 183–4).

9. Selwyn and Maria Fagnani had been at Matson.

10. Mount Stuart, appointed envoy to Sardinia 13 Oct. 1779, passed through Canterbury 19 Oct. and landed at Ostend 25 Oct. 'Notwithstanding all the interest possible was made by the Sardinian ambassador to get a French passport for Lord Mountstewart to travel through France in his way to Turin . . . it was not to be obtained' (*Public Advertiser* 28 Oct.; *London Chronicle* 14–28 Oct., xlvi. 362, 390, 406; Horn, *Diplomatic Representatives* 126).

11. Possibly an allusion connected with James Bruce or George III. Bruce had travelled in Nubia, and a pamphlet (11 pp.) was published in London ca 1780, *Copy of a Letter from Bologna, Dated March the 15th in the Year 1778, Wrote by a First-rate Designer Who afterwards Unexpectedly Came to England*, about the collection of Asiatic and African antiquities exhibited by him (BM Cat., *sub* Bologna, Appendix). George III, like Augustus after the conquest of Egypt (and Ethiopia, including Nubia) in 30 B.C., was having difficulty with America,

To Lady Ossory, Sunday 14 November 1779

Berkeley Square, Nov. 14, 1779.

I MUST be equitable; I must do the world justice; there are really some hopes of its amendment—I have not heard one lie these four days—but then indeed I have heard nothing—well then, why do you write?—Stay, Madam; my letter is not got on horseback yet; nor shall it mount till it has something to carry. It is my duty as your gazetteer to furnish you with news true or false, and you would certainly dismiss me, if I did not at least tell you something that was impossible. The whole nation is content with hearing anything new, let it be ever so bad. Tell the first man you meet that Ireland has revolted; away he runs and tells everybody he meets—everybody tells everybody—and the next morning they ask for more news—well, Jamaica is taken—Oh! Jamaica is taken—Next day, what news? Why, Paul Jones[1] is landed in Rutlandshire and has carried off the Duchess of Devonshire, and a squadron is fitting out to prevent it—and I am to have a pension for having given the earliest intelligence;[2] and there is to be a new farce called *The Rutlandshire Invasion*,[3] and the King and Queen will come to town to see it, and the Prince of Wales will not, because he is not old enough to understand pantomimes.

Well, Madam; having dispatched the nation and its serious affairs, one may chat over private matters. I have seen Lord Maccartney, and do affirm that he is shrunk and has a soupçon of black that was not

viewed by the King (as Augustus had viewed Egypt) as his personal realm. The reference may also include the King's addiction to hunting at a time of national crisis; cf. the *London Chronicle* 30 Oct.– 2 Nov. 1779, lxvi. 422; BM, *Satiric Prints* v. 345–6, No. 5574, where George III is presented as oriental despot and staghunter.

1. John Paul Jones (1747–92) had attracted great attention for his exploits in 1778 at Whitehaven, etc. (*ante* 7 July 1778).

2. When Major Cuyler, aide-de-camp to General Howe, brought Howe's dispatches on the taking of Long Island, it was re-

ported, 'His Majesty, we hear, has made Major Cuyler a very valuable present' (*London Chronicle* 17–19 Oct. 1776, xl. 382).

3. A title suggested to HW by two recent farces apropos of the threatened French invasion, Edward Neville's *Plymouth in an Uproar*, 1779, with music by Charles Dibdin, and Frederick Pilon's *The Invasion; or A Trip to Brighthelmstone*, 1778 (Genest vi. 88–9, 140–1; Allardyce Nicoll, *A History of Late Eighteenth Century Drama 1750–1800*, Cambridge, 1927, pp. 290, 297). HW's copies, now WSL, are Hazen, *Cat. of HW's Lib.* 1810. 31.2 and 29.7.

wont to reside in his complexion. George is so engrossed by the Board of Trade,[4] that I have seen him but the morning after his arrival. Mr Beauclerc has built a library in Great Russell Street[5] that reaches halfway to Highgate. Everybody goes to see it; it has put the Museum's[6] nose quite out of joint.

Now I return to politics. Sir Ralph Paine and Dr Johnson are answering General Burgoyne,[7] and they say the words are to be so long that the reply must be printed in a pamphlet as large as an atlas, but in an Elzevir type, or the first sentence would fill twenty pages in octavo. You may depend upon the truth of this, for Mr Cumberland told it in confidence to one with whom he is not at all acquainted, who told it to one whom I never saw; so you see, Madam, there is no questioning the authority.

I will not answer so positively for what I am going to tell you, as I had it only from the person himself. The D[uke] of Gl[oucester] was at Bath with the Margrave of Anspach.[8] Lord Nugent[9] came up and would talk to the Duke and then asked if he might take the liberty of inviting H.R.H. to dinner?—I think you will admire the quickness and propriety of the answer—The Duke replied, 'My Lord, I make no acquaintance but in London'—where you know, Madam, he only has levees—The Irishman continued to talk to him even after that rebuff. He certainly hoped to have been very artful —to have made court there, and yet not have offended anywhere

4. Selwyn's office was in the Board of Works (*post* ii. 169), but his friend, Lord Carlisle, had kissed hands as first lord of the Board of Trade and Plantations 10 Nov. (*Corr. Geo. III* iv. 469; *London Chronicle* 9–11 Nov., xlvi. 454).

5. His house is now No. 99, Great Russell Street, Bloomsbury, but the library, a separate building behind the house, no longer exists. It had upwards of 30,000 volumes and was sold by S. Paterson, 9 April 1781 and forty-nine following days, for £5,011.

6. Montagu House in Great Russell Street, purchased in 1759 as the 'general repository' of the British Museum.

7. *A Letter from Lieut.-Gen. Burgoyne to His Constituents, . . . Relative to His Return to America* had been published 6 Nov. (*Public Advertiser* 3, 6 Nov.). HW's copy (Hazen, *Cat. of HW's Lib.*

1609. 40. 4) has his note 'Nov. 6' on the title-page and in the pamphlet of 38 pages five other notes, corrections, and marks by him. Five editions appeared in 1779 (BM Cat.). Answers in the newspapers had already appeared; see, for example, the *Public Advertiser* 12, 13 Nov. 1779.

8. Christian Friedrich Karl Alexander (1736–1806), Margrave of Brandenburg-Ansbach, 1757, and of Bayreuth, 1769; abdicated 1791, in which year he married Lady Craven. Following his arrival at the Grand Hotel, Covent Garden, on 16 Oct., he had been visited by the Duke and they had been together at Salisbury on 27 Oct. See the *London Chronicle* 16 Oct.–2 Nov., xlvi. 374, 422; *Public Advertiser* 22 Oct.– 26 Nov.

9. Robert Nugent (1709–88), cr. (1767) Vct Clare and (1776) E. Nugent; M.P.

else by not going in town, which would have been a gross affront to the Duke had he accepted the invitation. I was at Blackheath[10] t'other morning where I was grieved. There are eleven Vander-werffes[11] that cost an immense sum: half of them are spoiled since Sir Gregory Page's[12] death by servants neglecting to shut out the sun. There is another room hung with the history of Cupid and Psyche in twelve small pictures by Luca Jordano,[13] that are sweet. There is too a glorious Claud,[14] some fine Tenierses,[15] a noble Rubens and Snyder,[16] two beautiful Philippo Lauras,[17] and a few more, and several very bad.[18] The house is magnificent, but wounded me; it was built on the model of Houghton, except that three rooms are thrown into a gallery.[19]

Now I have tapped the chapter of pictures, you must go and see Zoffanie's[20] 'Tribune at Florence,'[21] which is an astonishing piece of

10. *Ante* 14 Oct. 1779. A catalogue of the 118 pictures at Sir Gregory Page's appears in *London and Its Environs Described,* 1761, i. 315–22, with the name, dimensions, and artist for each picture; and in *The Ambulator; or, The Stranger's Companion in a Tour round London,* 1774, pp. 14–17, without the dimensions.

11. Adriaen van der Werff (1659–1722). 'Sir Gregory Page . . . was the personal friend of Vander Werff. . . . eight of the Vander Werffs (there were twelve in all) were bought for the Louvre at the price of 33,000 francs' (Cunningham). The twelve pictures are listed in *London and Its Environs,* i. 319–20; *The Ambulator,* p. 16.

12. Sir Gregory Page (ca 1695 – 4 Aug. 1775), 2d Bt, 1720, of Greenwich, Kent (*London Chronicle* 5–8 Aug. 1775, xxxviii. 131). His collection was sold in 1775, 1783, and 1787; his great-grandnephew, Sir Gregory Page-Turner, had sales in 1815 and 1824 (Lugt i. *passim*).

13. Luca Giordano (1632–1705); listed in *London and Its Environs,* i. 316; *The Ambulator,* p. 15. They were later at Hampton Court (Cunningham; Thieme and Becker).

14. 'A landscape, with figures—Claude Lorrain' (*London and Its Environs,* i. 317; *The Ambulator,* loc. cit.). It is identified by M. Röthlisberger (*Claude Lorrain,* New Haven, 1961, i. 477–8) as 'View of

the Trinità de'Monti in Rome,' 1632, now in the National Gallery, London.

15. David Teniers (1610–90), two landscapes 'with many figures, a fair at Ghent —Sir D. Teniers' (*London and Its Environs,* i. 320; *The Ambulator,* p. 17).

16. Frans Snyders (1579–1657), 'Rubens, two figures, fowls, and fruit—Rubens and Snyders' (*London and Its Environs,* i. 315; *The Ambulator,* p. 15).

17. Filippo Lauri (1623–94), both pictures listed as 'Venus, Cupid, and Satyrs' (*London and Its Environs,* i. 316; *The Ambulator,* loc. cit.).

18. 117 pictures, including 13 copies, are listed, ibid. 14–17, and in Thomas Martyn, *The English Connoisseur,* 1766, ii. 91–6.

19. In his account of John James (d. 1746), the architect of the house, in *Anecdotes of Painting,* HW says that 'the idea . . . was taken from Houghton' (*Works* iii. 435). For views and plans of the house, see the references cited in DNB, sub James, John; *British Magazine and Review,* 1783, ii. 269–70, and plate facing p. 269.

20. John Zoffany (1733–1810), who had been in Florence for most of the time between 1772 and 1779 and had just returned to England. HW has an account of him in *Anecdotes of Painting,* Vol. V, ed. Hilles and Daghlian, 1937, pp. 83–4.

21. See MANN viii. HW wrote to Mann

work, with a vast deal of merit. There too you will see a delightful piece of Wilkes looking—no, squinting tenderly at his daughter[22]— it is a caricatura of the Devil acknowledging Miss Sin in Milton.[23] I do not know why, but they are under a palm tree,[24] which has not grown in a free country for some centuries.

15th.

With all my pretences there is no more veracity in me than in a Scotch runner for the ministry. Here must I send away my letter without a word in it worth a straw. All the good news I know is, that the devil of a winter is come in that will send armies and navies to bed, and one may stir out in November without fear of being tanned. I am heartily glad that we shall keep Jamaica and the East Indies another year, that one may have time to lay in a stock of tea and sugar for the rest of one's days—I think only of the necessaries of life, and do not care a rush for gold and diamonds and the pleasure of stealing logwood. The friends of Government, who have thought of nothing but of reducing us to our islandhood, and bringing us back to the simplicity of ancient times, when we were the frugal temperate virtuous Old English, ask how we did before tea and sugar were known—better, no doubt—but as I did not happen to be born two or three hundred years ago, I cannot recollect precisely whether diluted acorns and barley bread spread with honey made a very luxurious breakfast.

I was last night at Lady Lucan's[25] to hear Misses Bingham[26] sing

about it on the day he first saw it at Zoffany's studio, 12 Nov. 1779. It was exhibited at the Royal Academy in 1780, was bought several years later by Queen Charlotte, and remains in the Royal Collection.

22. Mary Wilkes (1750–1802). Zoffany's portrait of her and Wilkes was exhibited at the Royal Academy in 1782; it is illustrated in Lady Victoria Manners and G. C. Williamson, *John Zoffany*, 1920, facing p. 72, with an account of it at pp. 73–4, 176–7; it was then in the possession of Sir George Sherston-Baker, 5th Bt, a direct descendant of Wilkes's niece, Dinah Hayley, who married Sir Robert Baker, 1st Bt.

23. In 1820 Lady Louisa Stuart told

Miss Louisa Clinton: 'Horace Walpole said to Lady Louisa, after Wilkes and his daughter, who was very plain, had passed by at a party, "There goes Sin with his daughter Death"' (as summarized from Louisa Clinton's journal by Hon. James A. Home in his edition of *Letters of Lady Louisa Stuart to Miss Louisa Clinton*, Edinburgh, 1901, p. 87).

24. 'Walpole is unfair in one part of his criticism, if not in all. The tree does not bear the least resemblance to a palm' (Manners and Williamson, op. cit. 74).

25. In Charles Street, Berkeley Square (*New Peerage*, 2d edn, 1778, iii. 312).

26. Presumably the two elder daughters of the Lucans. Lavinia Bingham (1762– 1831) m. (1781) George John Spencer,

Jomelli's[27] *Miserere,* set for two voices.[28] There were only the Duchess of Bedford, Lady Bute, Mrs Walsingham,[29] the Brudenels,[30] Keenes, Lord Maccartney, George Selwyn, Mr Jerningham and half a dozen Irish. The service lasted near three hours, and was so dull, instead of pathetic, that I was rejoiced that *the worst was over,* and *the two women had left the sepulchre.* The Duchess told me that a habit-maker returned from Ampthill is gone stark in love with Lady Ossory, on fitting her with the new dress, I think they call it a Levite,[31] and says he never saw so glorious a figure—I know that; and so you would be in a hop-sack, Madam—but where the deuce is the grace in a man's nightgown bound round with a belt?

Good night, Lady! I hope I shall have something to tell you in my next, that my letter may be shorter.

To Lady Ossory, Monday 15 November 1779

Address: To the Countess of Ossor⟨y⟩ at Ampthill Park, Bedfordshire. *Postmark:* 15 NO. GC.

Codicil to my today's, viz., Nov. 15, 1779.

I ENCLOSED the above to Lord Ossory, because it was not worth sixpence, and had sent it to the post, and then went to Bedford House, where lo! enter Lady Shelburne,[1] looking as fresh and ripe as Pomona. N.B. Her windows were not open yesterday, and today there was such a mist, ermined with snow, that I could not see. I find it was not a habit-maker that was smitten with your Ladyship as a

styled Vct Althorp 1765–83, 2d E. Spencer, 1783. Her sister Louisa died unmarried (George Kearsley *Peerage,* 1796, ii. 401; John Debrett, *Peerage,* 1817, ii. 1041).

27. Niccolò Jommelli (1714–74), composer of operas, oratorios, cantatas.

28. This composition, his last, completed shortly before his death, is a setting for two female voices of Saverio Mattei's Italian paraphrase of Psalm 51.

29. Charlotte Hanbury Williams (1738–90), 2d dau. of Sir Charles Hanbury Williams, m. (1759) Hon. Robert Boyle-Walsingham (*ante* 6 Sept. 1778; MORE 251 n. 2.).

30. James Brudenell (*ante* 10 July 1776)

m. (1760) Lord Dartmouth's sister Anne Legge (d. 1786).

31. 'A loose dress, so called from its supposed resemblance to the dress of the Levites' (OED). This passage from HW's letter is the only one quoted to illustrate the word, which is marked *obsolete.*

————

1. The Duchesses of Bedford and Grafton presented her to the King and Queen at the Drawing-Room 18 Nov. Her brother Richard Fitzpatrick was also present (*London Chronicle* 18–20 Nov., xlvi. 481). For the birth of her first child, see *post* 12 July 1780.

pig in a poke, but somebody else; but as her Grace's[2] mouth has lost one tooth, and my ear, I suspect, another, I have not found out who the unfortunate man is.

Next enters your Ladyship's letter. I have seen my dignity of minister to Spain[3]—many a fair castle have I erected in that country; but truly never resided there. Voltaire's *Dom Pèdre*[4] is a poor performance indeed!

Mr Cartwright, who, I humbly apprehend, is Mr Carteret,[5] is, I also apprehend, no better informed than his elder brother.[6] So far from being gone to Cadiz, the French fleet I believe is gone to the hospital.[7] Mr Conway is not come—I trust from the obstinacy of a contrary wind. It blustered violently on Saturday night, and made me very uneasy—but I think it was a wind full in his teeth. I have expected him for this fortnight—three days before the frigate[8] sailed. This is long enough for a codicil, in which one has nothing more to give.

To Lady Ossory, Sunday 21 November 1779

Address: To the Countess of Ossory at Ampthill Park, Bedfordshire. *Postmark:* NO. GC.

Berkeley Square,[1] Nov. 21, 1779.

I AM sorry, Madam, to inform you, if you have not heard it, that the troubles in Ireland ripen. An express came yesterday, that the independent army had invested the House of Commons and forced the members to take an oath of voting for free trade and a

2. The Duchess of Bedford's.

3. Lord Grantham, recently returned from Spain (*ante* 7 Aug. 1779).

4. *Don Pèdre*, a tragedy, begun in 1761 and published in 1774, printed in Voltaire's *Œuvres*, ed. Moland, 1877–85, vii. 237–304. Apparently Mme du Deffand sent it to HW in 1775 (DU DEFFAND iv. 170). The hero of the tragedy is Don Pedro, king of Castille; HW's *Historic Doubts* is cited in one of the prefaces.

5. Hon. Henry Frederick Thynne (from 1776, Carteret) (1735–1826), cr. (1784) Bn Carteret; M.P.; joint postmaster general 1770–89; assumed name of Carteret in 1776 on inheriting some of the Carteret family estates.

6. Lord Weymouth, whose resignation as secretary of state is mentioned in the following letter.

7. On returning to Brest 10–15 Sept., the French fleet 'disembarked more than eight thousand sick, many of whom died soon after' (A. T. Patterson, *The Other Armada*, Manchester, 1960, p. 210 *et passim;* cf. *London Chronicle* 30 Oct.– 2 Nov., xlvi. 418: 'upwards of 15,000' sick at Brest). Fever, smallpox, and various illnesses caused by inadequate provisions and poor water supply had weakened both French and Spanish fleets, but especially the French, since midsummer.

8. *Champion,* which arrived at Portsmouth 20 Nov.; see following letter.

1. HW first wrote 'Strawberry Hill.'

short money bill.[2] The mob too *Palisser'd*[3] the houses of the Attorney-General Scott[4] and Sir Henry Cavendish,[5] who had ventured to plead a little for the English government.[6] This is all I know yet, for I have been confined again these three days with the gout in my foot, and was not out of bed today till three o'clock.

Lord Weymouth has resigned and quits his *bureau* tomorrow.[7] This I suppose was what your Ladyship meant by saying you heard *the sheath was absolutely thrown away*—if it is, I believe Lord Weymouth will run after it—for I think the sword will never be his weapon. Nor can I admire any, who after doing all the mischief they could, cry out Fire! That they will go to extremities, I do not doubt—what principle should restrain them?

A few answers to your last, and I have done, for I am a little in pain. I have not seen the prologue and epilogue to *The Critic*,[8] but am now very impatient, for I hear they are Mr Fitzpatrick's,[9] and

2. The events of this paragraph occurred on 15 Nov. In order to force the English to accept free trade, the Irish supported a short money bill, that is, for six months instead of the usual two years. The 'mob,' after attacking Scott's house, 'returned to the Parliament House and swore all the members whom they could find going in to be true to Ireland, and vote for a short money bill' (*London Chronicle* 20–23 Nov., xlvi. 490, 496). The short money bill (for 25 Dec. 1779 – 24 June 1780) was passed in the Irish House of Commons 27 Nov. (*Journals of the House of Commons . . . of Ireland*, 1779–80, xix. 154–7).

3. On the night of 11 Feb. 1779, after the news of Keppel's acquittal reached London, the mob attacked an empty house in Pall Mall belonging to Palliser, broke the windows, and 'demolished whatever remained' (*Last Journals* ii. 247).

4. John Scott (1739–98), cr. (1784) Bn Earlsfort, (1789) Vct Clonmell, and (1793) E. of Clonmell; M.P. (Ireland); solicitor-general 1774–7 and attorney general 1777–82 for Ireland; chief justice of the Court of King's Bench in Ireland 1783–98. The mob broke the windows of his house in Harcourt Street, Dublin, and did considerable damage, for which Parliament later paid (*London Chronicle* 20–25 Nov., xlvi. 490, 496, 500–1).

5. (1732–1804), 2d Bt, 1776; parliamentary reporter; M.P. (Ireland); receiver general for Ireland and P.C., 1779; deputy vice-treasurer of Ireland, 1795.

6. 'Advices were received on Saturday that a tremendous mob . . . had threatened the lives' of Scott and Cavendish, who in the Irish Parliament had 'defended the English nation from the charge of being avaricious and oppressive in its disposition towards Ireland and endeavoured to stem the torrent of popular clamour, and to oppose moderation and good sense to the vehemence of factious oratory' (ibid. 20–23 Nov., xlvi. 490).

7. He delivered the seals of his office to the King 24 Nov. (*Corr. Geo. III* iv. 495).

8. Sheridan's *The Critic*, first performed 30 Oct. 1779 at Drury Lane; published 1781. HW's copy, now WSL, is Hazen, *Cat. of HW's Lib.* 1810. 33. 5.

9. His prologue (there was no epilogue), 'said to be the production of a man of fashion, was well spoken [by King] and well received' (*London Chronicle* 30 Oct. – 2 Nov., xlvi. 421). Genest (vi. 126) thought it 'a particularly good one.' In a letter of 2 April 1782 Sheridan referred to Fitzpatrick as 'my very particular friend, next to Fox himself' (W. Fraser Rae, *Sheridan*, 1896, i. 383).

will answer I shall admire them. If your Ladyship has copies, I beg you will let them be transcribed and sent to me incontinently.

The story you have heard of a royal amour,[10] I fancy, was founded on a letter that has made much noise and was delivered by mistake to a wrong person. The circumstances are too numerous for a letter and were only the gossiping of two girls,[11] who did not expect to have their correspondence rehearsed to the ladies of the Bedchamber.

La Signorina[12] I have not seen, and in truth did not ask to see her. I love David too well, not to be peevish at an Abishag of eight years old.

Should I hear anything before tomorrow night, it shall make a PS., but I wrote today, lest I should not be able to tomorrow.

PS. 22d, from my bed.

I have had a bad night, though I expected a most tranquil one, for about eight in the evening, as Lady Ailesbury and Mrs Damer were sitting with me, the door opened, and entered General Conway.[13] As the wind had been violent, I was comforting myself that it was contrary; but he had landed at Portsmouth the night before,[14] after

10. Lady Mary Coke explains HW's reference in her 'MS Journals' 7, 15 Nov. 1779: 'I told you . . . the Prince of Wales helped the ladies to mount on horseback, and every little attention of his Royal Highness is it seems so flattering that each lady construes everything as a preference to herself; a niece of Sir George Howard's lives in the [Windsor] Forest, and has been honoured with some notice, from which she concludes she has his R.H.'s affection, and being too much flattered to conceal her good fortune, she imparted it in a letter to a friend, who in answer wished her joy of her conquest and wrote a great deal about her noble lover. The letter was directed to New Lodge, the name of General Hodgson's house, but the letter by mistake came to the house built by His Majesty at Windsor, which is called the Lodge, and the letter was given to Mrs Hogerdon [Hagerdorn, one of the Keepers of Robes to the Queen], a name resembling Hodgson, one of her Majesty's German women,

who not being perfect in the English language did not understand it, but easily comprehending it concerned the Prince of Wales, hurried with it to the Queen, who when she read it showed it to the King, and here my story ends. All Windsor, however, talks about it, and poor Miss Hodgson is exposed to a good deal of ridicule, and in my opinion has more reason to be angry with the post office than ever you had for the unhappy wandering of her letter.'

11. Miss Hodgson was presumably the elder of the two daughters of Gen. Studholme Hodgson by Catherine, sister of Sir George Howard (DNB, *sub* Studholme Hodgson). Her correspondent has not been identified.

12. Maria Fagnani, Selwyn's ward.

13. 'On Tuesday [Monday, according to HW] evening Gen. Conway arrived in town from . . . Jersey, was yesterday [Wednesday, 24 Nov.] at Court, and laid before his Majesty the state of that island on his departure, which is now so strongly

being blown to Plymouth. After his servants and baggage were embarked, the frigate was very near being lost.

I have seen nobody but him today, so cannot tell any more news.

To Lady Ossory, Monday 29 November 1779

In Kirgate's hand.
Address: To the Countess of Ossory at Ampthill Park, Bedfordshire. *Postmark:* 29 NO.

Berkeley Square, Nov. 29, 1779.

THOUGH you[1] command, Madam, it would be impertinent and ridiculous to talk of myself, when at the same time the post will bring you Lord Ossory's account of Mr Fox's duel.[2] Could such an old story as the gout expect to fill a cranny of your attention at such a moment? Would not you hate anybody or letter that could not answer fifty questions you want to ask in a breath? I would answer them beforehand if I were not just got into bed with a little return of pain[3]—Oh, and Lord Lyttelton[4]—in about three hours your Ladyship will want to know all about him too.[5] Would I could satisfy you, but just now I am not able, and therefore, after thanking you a thousand times, I must bid myself good night, and will answer your letter as soon as it is in my power.

fortified that they are under no apprehension of another visit from the French' (*London Chronicle* 23–25 Nov., xlvi. 502).

14. 'Portsmouth, Nov. 21. Yesterday morning arrived the *Champion* frigate, Capt. Hamilton, from Jersey. Gov. Conway is arrived in this ship' (ibid. 20–23 Nov., xlvi. 494).

————

1 MS reads 'your.'
2. On 29 Nov. Fox fought a duel with William Adam (see following letter), in which Fox was slightly wounded. Adam had suggested in the House of Commons 25 Nov. that, bad as the administration might be, it was preferable to the Opposition. Fox taunted Adam for supporting North and his ministry, a support which, Fox suggested, Lord North could hardly be grateful for. Richard Fitzpatrick was Fox's second. A detailed account of the

duel is in MASON i. 481–3. See also the *London Magazine*, 1779, xlviii. 553–4, 556–8, 575–6.

3. From HW's letter to Mason 29 Nov. 1779, MASON i. 482, it appears that he 'was in the other room from twelve till six today, when my pains returned [and he went to bed]; yet finding them easier at nine,' he had 'been writing in bed till eleven at night.'

4. 'On Saturday evening died, at a quarter past eleven, at his seat . . . Pitt Place, Epsom . . . Lord Lyttelton' (*London Chronicle* 27–30 Nov., xlvi. 514). His dream or premonition that he would die within three days, which he did, was much talked of; see MASON i. 480–1, 487; *London Magazine,* 1779, xlviii. 534–6 (with a print facing p. 534).

5. Unexplained.

TO LADY OSSORY, Thursday 2 December 1779

In Kirgate's hand.

Thursday evening, Dec. 2, 1779.

YOUR Ladyship must excuse another short answer to the letter I have this moment received, for I am extremely weak and low, the consequence always of the fever going off. My pains are gone everywhere but in my right arm and hand, which last is uneasy enough; but then I sleep and doze exceedingly; a most fortunate faculty in one that is so long decaying.

I am vexed that Lord Ossory or your Ladyship should think it necessary to make an apology for his not calling on me before he went: I thought he called very often in so short a space; and I am always upon my guard not to let my tiresome illnesses torment others too. How should Lord Ossory, who comes but for a moment, and has a thousand friends, amusements, and politics to drink at a draught, have time to come and sip my dregs of gout? Surely, surely, Mr Fox's duel was sufficient to occupy him wholly for two days. Of all duels, on true or false record, this was the most perfect! So much temper, sense, propriety, easy good humour, and natural good nature, on a base of firmness and spirit, never were assembled. For Mr Adam,[1] I cannot describe him, as I never extracted malevolence out of the fogs of the Highlands.

Of poor Lady Jane,[2] I own I did not care to speak to your Ladyship; as I knew how you would lament her; nor can I tell you much now about her death or will. I think her low spirits began before Lady Blandford's death;[3] yet that might increase them. They increased to the greatest degree, and at last she died of obstinately refusing nourishment.[4] The *Green Which*[5] did pretend to take care

1. William Adam (1751–1839), nephew of Robert and James Adam; M.P. Gatton 1774–80, Wigtown burghs 1780–4, Aberdeen burghs 1784–90, Ross-shire 1790–4, Kincardineshire 1806–12; solicitor-general, 1805; P.C., 1815. After the duel he became a close friend and supporter of Fox, and Richard Fitzpatrick proposed him for membership in Brooks's Club; he was elected 5 March 1788 (*Memorials of Brooks's from . . . 1764 to the Close of the Nineteenth Century*, 1907, p. 39).

2. Lady Jane Scott, who had died at 1 a.m. on 26 Nov. (Coke, 'MS Journals' 26 Nov. 1779).

3. On 7 Sept. 1779.

4. Lady Mary Coke visited her 18 Nov., when she was 'indeed very bad. She has

of her, I don't know whether she did,[5a] but I know she talked brutally about her. I have heard that Lady Jane has left her fortune to Lady Frances,[6] but am not sure.[7]

I have heard Mr Tickell's[8] poem[9] read once, and thought the beginning very bad. The allusions are not at all just, but forced into the service by vile puns. Towards the end there seems some very pretty lines—but upon the whole, *à quoi bon? à quel propos?* I believe it was meant for a satire, but the author winked, and it flashed in the pan.

I have not seen the prologue,[10] Madam, but should seriously take it very kindly if you would send me a copy—indeed I want amusement.

I have not breath to dictate more, and must take my leave.

To Lady Ossory, Monday 6 December 1779

In Kirgate's hand.

Berkeley Square, Dec. 6, 1779.

I RETURN both poems, Madam, with the fidelity and gratitude which they, the author, and your Ladyship deserve from me. The lines to Delia are very poetic, dressed with all the genteel ease of Mr Fitzpatrick.[1] The prologue is charming, and a short, just, and compendious history of the English stage.

eat nothing these last ten days, but I persuaded her to take some broth. I cannot think she will hold out long, but she is as much in her senses as I am. I mention this as I am sure you will hear otherwise, and the report is cruel and without foundation' ('MS Journals' 18 Nov. 1779).

5. Lady Greenwich, whose first husband was Lady Jane's brother.

5a. Lady Mary Coke found Lady Greenwich at Lady Jane Scott's on the afternoon of 25 Nov.; 'at three o'clock she returned to Sudbrook' ('MS Journals' 25 Nov.).

6. Her niece, Lady Frances Scott (1750–1817), sister of Henry, 3d D. of Buccleuch, m. (1783) Archibald James Edward Douglas, cr. (1790) Bn Douglas of Douglas.

7. See following letter.

8. Richard Tickell (1751–93), dramatist,

poet, and pamphleteer; grandson of Addison's friend Thomas Tickell. Although Tickell at this time had a pension of £200 a year for writing in support of the ministry, he subsequently supported Fox.

9. *Epistle from the Honourable Charles Fox, Partridge-Shooting, to the Honourable John Townshend, Cruising*, published 9 Dec. 1779 (*Public Advertiser*); in line 128 Richard 'Fitzpatrick's wit' is mentioned. HW's fully annotated copy is now at Harvard (Hazen, *Cat of HW's Lib.* 3222. 16. 23). HW dismisses the poem to Mason 11 Dec. 1779, MASON i. 487.

10. Richard Fitzpatrick's prologue to Sheridan's *The Critic*.

———

1. The phrasing of this sentence suggests that the 'lines to Delia' may have been written by someone other than Fitz-

I am told my account of Lady Jane's will was wrong, and that she has left her original £10,000 to the Duke of Buccleugh,[2] and to Lady Frances, only £250 a year, Petersham[3] and £1000 in money;[4] so the public had made a better will for her.[5]

I lament not being able to be today where I seldom wish myself, in the House of Commons[6]—but if I opened the current of regrets, they would soon swell to a torrent, and I had better bid your Ladyship good night, since I have nothing new to tell you.

To Lady Ossory, Tuesday 14 December 1779

Address in Kirgate's hand.
Address: To the Countess of Ossory at Ampthill Park, Bedfordshire. *Postmark:* 14 DE. GC.

Berkeley Square, Dec. 14, 1779.

WHEN Lord Ossory is in town, my dear Madam, my letters are useless; and when I can only dictate, they are not only *gênées* and insipid, but force me to exert my faint voice more than I can afford. I am now trying to scratch out a few lines with my muffled hand; and the effort must be accepted in lieu of length. In fact I am impatient to thank your Ladyship and Mr Fitzpatrick for his intended offering to the Armoury at Strawberry,[1] where it shall be

patrick, although 'the author' in the first sentence, if not an error for 'authors,' would preclude this interpretation. If not Fitzpatrick's, the lines might be Sheridan's 'Stanzas' or 'Damon to Delia,' which, with Mrs Sheridan's reply, appeared in the *Annual Register*, 1788, pp. 196–7; cf. Sheridan, *Plays and Poems*, ed. Rhodes, New York, 1929, iii. 228–9.

2. Lady Jane Scott 'has left the Duke of Buccleugh [her nephew] ten thousand pounds of the fifteen she had on an estate of his in Scotland, for which he paid her five hundred pounds a year' (Coke, 'MS Journals' 26 Nov. 1779).

3. The house Lady Jane had inherited from the Duke of Queensberry (*ante* 28 Oct. 1778).

4. 'Five thousand pounds to Lady Frances for her life [at five per cent,

the interest would be £250 a year] with the house of Petersham and everything in it at her own disposal' (Coke, 'MS Journals' 26 Nov. 1779).

5. Lady Mary Coke gives other details of the will, including the bequest of 'the beautiful picture of the Duchess of Queensbury to Lady Greenwich' (ibid.; for the picture, see *ante* 14 July 1779).

6. 'Lord Ossory has given notice for a motion on Monday next [6 Dec.] in the House of Commons' (*Public Advertiser* 4 Dec.). See following letter.

———

1. HW's 'Des. of SH' records no gift from Fitzpatrick. What follows suggests that the intended gift was possibly the bullet from Adam's first pistol which wounded Fox 'slightly in the belly' (*London Chronicle* 27–30 Nov., xlvi. 518).

consecrated on the fourth of November,[2] a more solemn holiday there than the fifth.[3] I recollect a story of James I, who being seized with the colic as he was hunting, stepped into a cottage, and, complaining, the good woman of the house recommended a bullet to him to swallow, which she assured him had done wonders, and had often passed through her whole family. I will preserve Mr Fitz's present carefully, that so *sovereign* a medicine may have a chance of returning whence it came; and in case of need, of going through all the Scots that deserve it.

You know, Madam, I can give you no account of new beauties, but what I hear: Miss Gore[4] is much admired. Miss Lenox[5] is said to be very well, but no more. Lord Ossory's speech[6] was thought very sensible and proper, and to have no fault but its brevity, which is never charged on speeches that are not liked. Hitherto all goes well for Ireland—I fervently hope the Irish will be as reasonable.

Recommend books to you, Madam!—why, the manufacture is lost both in England and France! I believe nothing will be printed soon but ship news; and Wilkes's and Temple Lutterel's speeches, which they print themselves.[7]

If Lord O. is returned today as I conclude, pray tell him, Madam,

---

2. The anniversary of the birth of William III.

3. Guy Fawkes Day.

4. Emily Gore (ca 1756–1832), dau. and heiress of Charles Gore of Horkstow, Lincs; elder sister of Lady Cowper; lived abroad (Italy, Switzerland, the Netherlands, etc.) with her family most of her life; in England ca 1779–ca 1782; friend of Goethe from about 1787; died at Leghorn (*Notes and Queries*, 1912, 11th ser., vi. 402–4, 423–5; Lady Victoria Manners and G. C. Williamson, *John Zoffany*, 1920, pp. 52–3, with illustration facing p. 52).

5. Maria Louisa Lennox (1760–1843), eldest dau. of Lord George Lennox (Burke, *Peerage*, 1953, p. 1776, *sub* Richmond; Collins, *Peerage*, 1812, i. 209). Lady Sarah Lennox wrote to the Duchess of Leinster 15 Dec. 1779: 'Louisa Lennox . . . looks very pretty and as yet has been only moderately admired, which I think promises that she will be properly admired,

that is, upon acquaintance, will charm all those who know her and who have taste, and will escape vulgar admiration' (*Leinster Corr.* ii. 305, and *passim*).

6. On 6 Dec. in the House of Commons 'Lord Ossory supported motion of Lord Shelburne on criminal neglect of Ireland' (*Last Journals* ii. 258); that is, Lord Ossory introduced the motion in the Commons. It was rejected 192 to 100 (Cobbett, *Parl. Hist.* xx. 1197–8, 1241; *Journals of the House of Commons* xxxvii. 493; *London Chronicle* 4–7 Dec., xlvi. 542–3).

7. In *Last Journals* i. 434, *sub* 13 Feb. 1775, HW noted: 'Temple Luttrell, brother of the Duchess of Cumberland, a wit and a poet, spoke against the motion [for providing 2000 additional seamen] in a style both turgid and flat. He printed his speech in the newspapers, which was much abused.' A collected edition of Wilkes's speeches had appeared in 1777; some were published individually.

that I shall have a gallery of Dusseldorp[8] for him at the original rate of six guineas.

You see, Madam, there was no such miracle in Buckinger writing with his stump! I have some notion that all the limbs and members may serve as coadjutors to the others; but I will not surmise how far that may be carried, lest old folks like me should, as they are apt, attempt ridiculous experiments.

To Lady Ossory, Thursday 23 December 1779

In Kirgate's hand.

Berkeley Square, Dec. 23, 1779.

ALAS, Madam, I am very unlikely to enjoy even a more agreeable prison at Ampthill: all my advancement is retrograde: again, I can neither walk nor write. The deluge, which your Ladyship calls mild weather, as I suppose Noah did the moment his pair of peacocks ceased croaking for more rain, has brought back my gout particularly into my right hand; and as I had no reason to expect a return, I have still less for guessing when it will depart. Lord Bristol[1] died yesterday morning of the same distemper in his stomach: not three months ago he made a visit to the Duke and Duchess at the Pavillions, and good-naturedly called on me on his return, to persuade me to leave off the use of the bootikins, and to recommend a system of applications, I forget what, that had done wonders for him. I rose and stamped hard with both feet on the marble, and said, 'This is what the bootikins do for me: your Lordship, though now free from the gout, has been brought into my room by two servants: I will not blame your Lordship's method, but can I exchange my own for it?' —However, as Lord Bristol is delivered from the gout, and I am not,

---

8. By Nicolas de Pigage (1723–96): *La Galerie électorale de Dusseldorff, ou Catalogue raisonné et figuré de ses tableaux . . . , contenant 365 petits estampes rédigées et gravées d'après ces mêmes tableaux,* engraved and published by Christian de Méchel (1737–1817), Basle, 1778 (BM Cat.; NBG). HW's copy is Hazen, *Cat. of HW's Lib.* 3513.

1. Augustus John Hervey (1724–79), 3d E. of Bristol, 1775; naval officer from

it may be a moot point whether Martha or Mary has chosen the better part.

Lord Coventry and Col. Hervey[2] are Lord Bristol's executors.[3] He has left an estate of £800 a year that he had purchased,[4] to Mrs Nesbitt,[5] for life, paying £300 a year to his natural son[6] by Mrs Clarke (the Kitty Hunter),[7] till of age, and £400 afterwards, he to have the whole if surviving her;[8] if not, she and Col. Hervey to have the property of the whole. His personal estate, estimated at £30,000, Lord B. divides between Mrs Nesbitt and the aforesaid son. I do not hear of another legacy, not even to his sisters.[9] To Col. Hervey he had in his life given their mother's house in St James's Place.[10]

1740; lord of the admiralty 1771–5; groom of the Bedchamber 1763–72; M.P. 1757–75.

2. Hon. William Hervey (1732–1815), 4th son of John, Bn Hervey of Ickworth, and younger brother of the 2d, 3d, and 4th Earls of Bristol; M.P. Bury 1763–8; entered the army, becoming Gen., 1798 (Venn, *Alumni Cantab.; Old Westminsters; Army Lists;* John Philippart, *Royal Military Calendar,* 1815, i. 45–6; William S. Childe-Pemberton, *The Earl Bishop,* 1925, *passim*).

3. Mrs Nesbitt, mentioned below, was also one of the executors (Hon. William Hervey, *Journals . . . from 1755 to 1814,* ed. S. H. A. Hervey, in *Suffolk Green Books, No. XIV,* 1906, p. 293).

4. Lessingham, near Sleaford, Lincolnshire (Childe-Pemberton, op. cit. i. 251, ii. 437; Hon. William Hervey, op. cit. 245, 511).

5. Lord Bristol's mistress from about 1771 until his death: Mary —— (d. 1815 or later) m. —— Nesbitt, a young banker who died before 1775; the 'Circe' painted by Reynolds (Childe-Pemberton, op. cit. i. 100, 251, ii. 437; Augustus Hervey, 3d E. of Bristol, *Journal,* ed. David Erskine, 1953, p. xxx; *Town and Country Magazine,* 1775, vii. 9–12, with print facing p. 9; Graves and Cronin ii. 690–1; D. M. Stuart, *Molly Lepell, Lady Hervey,* 1936, pp. 356–7). She was 'a lady not unknown in the political world' whose villa 'near the Horns in Norwood' was 'late the

Earl of Bristol's' (*European Magazine,* 1788, xiii. 297).

6. Augustus Hervey (b. ca 1764–5, d. 1782), at this time at Bury St Edmunds Grammar School, entered the Navy and was killed in action at Gibraltar (Hon. William Hervey, op. cit. p. xxxvi, and portrait facing p. 324; Augustus Hervey, op. cit. p. xi; Stuart, op. cit. 355–8).

7. Elizabeth Catherine Hunter (d. 1795), dau. of Thomas Orby Hunter of Crowland, Lincs, m. (1770) Alured Clarke, later K.B. and Field Marshall. Before her affair with Lord Bristol she had eloped (1762) with Lord Pembroke and had borne him a son in that year (MONTAGU ii. 14–17; Graves and Cronin, ii. 498–9).

8. That is, if he survived Mrs Nesbitt, not Mrs Clarke; cf. MONTAGU ii. 14 n. 8.

9. He had four sisters, all of whom were given the rank in 1753 of an earl's daughter: Lady Lepell Hervey (1723–80), m. (1743) Constantine Phipps, cr. (1767) Bn Mulgrave; Lady Mary Hervey (1725–1815), m. (1747) George Fitzgerald of Turlough, co. Mayo; Lady Emily Carolina Nassau Hervey (1735–1814); Lady Caroline Hervey (1736–1819) (Hon. William Hervey, op. cit. pp. xxxviii–xl; Augustus Hervey, op. cit., *passim;* MONTAGU i. 150 n. 2).

10. This house, overlooking the Green Park, was built for Lady Hervey in 1748, and was destroyed in an air raid, 1941 (MORE 416 n. 15). By the terms of her will it was to come to Col. Hervey if he

I know no more of our new victories than your Ladyship reads in
the newspapers and gazettes;[11] nor can one add to the ridicule which
the Court itself has thrown on the business in Georgia,[12] by firing
guns,[13] by efforts at illuminations, and by their method of retailing
the intelligence, by an anonymous letter,[14] and by suppressing every
syllable from Gen. Prevost[15] himself, etc. They had better have stuck
to their triumphs on the Mosquito shore,[16] which were heroic and
perfect in every light, and the narratives of which seem to me the
clearest relations of any battle or siege I ever saw.

The prospect does seem to clear up happily in Ireland[17]—Oh, that
we may come a little to our senses, and be softened into some wisdom
by good fortune, as we have long been hardened in folly and obstinacy, by disappointment and disgrace!

You are to know, Madam, that I have in my custody the individual
ebony cabinet in which Madame de Sévigny kept her pens and paper
for writing her matchless letters. It was preserved near Grignan by
an old man who mended her pens, and whose descendant gave it

survived his brothers George and Augustus. He sold it in 1782 to Lord Northington for £7000 (Hon. William Hervey, op.
cit. 303; COLE i. 325–6).

11. HW records in *Last Journals* ii.
259–60, *sub* Dec. 1779: '18th. Account of
Col. Dalrymple and Capt. Luttrell taking
the fort of Omoa from the Spaniards, and
two register ships: *vide Gazette*. 20th.
Extra *Gazette* on the repulse of D'Estaing
at the Savannah in Georgia.'

12. The blockade and siege of Savannah
11 Sept.–18 Oct.

13. The news of the failure of D'Estaing's main attack on 9 Oct. and the
termination of the 'general engagement
. . . in favour of his Majesty's troops . . .
was communicated to the public by the
firing of the Park and Tower guns, and
his Majesty received the compliments of
the nobility on the occasion' (*Daily Adv.*
21 Dec.).

14. In the *London Gazette Extraordinary*, 20 Dec.

15. Maj.-Gen. Augustine Prevost (1723–
86), a Swiss formerly in Sardinian service
who entered the British army, 1756; Maj.-
Gen., 1779 (*Dictionnaire historique et
biographique de la Suisse*, Neuchâtel,
1921–34, v. 344; GM 1787 lvii. pt ii. 660;

Army Lists). Extracts from his dispatch
of 1 Nov. were published in the *London
Gazette* No. 12042, 21–25 Dec. According
to the *Public Advertiser* 24 Dec., they
were to have appeared in the previous
Gazette, 'but owing to the dispatches
being kept at the Queen's Palace, his
Majesty having that day gone to Windsor
. . . [it] is unavoidably postponed till tomorrow evening.'

16. In a dispatch headed 'St Fernando
de Omoa, Oct. 21, 1779,' from Capt. W.
Dalrymple, 'Commandant of the Loyal
Irish Volunteers,' to Lord George Germain,
and in another headed '*Charon*, in the
Harbour of Omoa, October 27, 1779,'
from the captain of the *Charon*, Hon.
John Luttrell, is the account of the
capture of Omoa in the gulf of Honduras
that HW alludes to in n. 11 above (*London Chronicle* 16–21 Dec., xlvi. 585–9,
from the *London Gazette* 18 Dec.; *London
Chronicle* 28–30 Dec., xlvi. 621). Dalrymple
and his men had come from the 'Mosquito
shore' at the mouth of the Black River
(Rio Negro) on the north coast of Honduras to join forces with Luttrell to
capture Omoa.

17. See following letter.

last year to Mr Selwyn,[18] as truly worthy of such a sacred relic.[19] It wears, indeed, all the outward and visible signs of such venerable preciousness, for it is clumsy, cumbersome, and shattered, and inspires no more idea of her spirit and *légèreté*, than the mouldy thighbone of a saint does of the unction of his sermons. I have full powers to have it repaired and decorated as shall seem good in my own eyes, though I had rather be authorized to enclose and conceal it in a shrine of gold and jewels, as princely bigots serve the skulls and shrivelled corpses of their patron saints.

Lord Macartney is gone to Ireland;[20] and as many others are dispersing themselves, my circles will be very thin, though I must depend upon them for some time, for last night and this morning I have had pretty sharp pain in my hand. At the beginning of this fit your Ladyship commended my patience; alack! it is what I am reduced to ingraft upon temperance, which did not avail me. If I live to an hundred, I suppose I shall acquire all the other virtues, but the one, which longevity makes a sinecure, and consequently requires no institution.

To Lady Ossory, Saturday 1 January 1780

Address in Kirgate's hand.
Address: To the Countess of Ossory at Ampthill Park, Bedfordshire. *Postmark:* G⟨C?⟩.

Berkeley Square, Jan. 1, 1780.

I ASSURE you, Madam, I have no affectation of philosophic indifference to life. I like to live whenever I am free from pain, or do not look forward—but I have so comfortless a prospect before me

18. Who wrote about it to Mary Townshend 2 and 5 Oct. 1778, concluding, 'if there should be any historical doubt about it, Horry shall clear it up for us' (S. Parnell Kerr, *George Selwyn and the Wits*, 1909, pp. 249, 251). In the letter of 2 Oct. Selwyn commented: 'I was going to write to my Lady Ossory, who is as well as yourself a professed admirer of Mme de Sévigné, but when I reflected upon her kind of devotion and yours, I thought that besides *les droits de parenté*,

je pouvais entrevoir dans votre spiritualité . . . plus de quiétisme pour ainsi dire, que dans la sienne et qui mérite, à mon estime, la préférence' (ibid. 248).

19. Mme du Deffand had stored the cabinet for Selwyn before he brought it to England (DU DEFFAND v. 80, 82, *sub* 24, 30 Oct. 1778).

20. 'Lord Macartney has just left me; he returns in two days to England where he will deliver his ideas respecting the present state of this kingdom' (E. of

—if I have any prospect before me, that it is no counterfeit levity when I speak with coolness of a moment that may spare me many sufferings, and what I dread still more, helpless decrepitude—but you shall hear no more of thoughts that I confess ought not to pass my own bosom, and which Lord Bristol's death suggested. You are equally kind, Madam, in being affected at what I said, and in recommending Bath; but indeed I cannot listen to that advice: Bath is excellent for those who are *in travail* of the gout, and seek a fit as a composition for subsequent health—but I certainly have no occasion to accelerate the attacks; they are made without any declaration of war, and I find myself a prisoner, as happened six weeks ago, when I thought myself most secure of a truce by the short fit in September. In short, my dear Lady, Bath might give me the gout, but cannot cure it. My management of myself is formed on the best observations I can make on my own constitution after long experience: I certainly have less quantity of pain and have shorter fits than formerly: I recover the use of all my limbs tolerably in the intervals, and my spirits still more; and therefore, when I am reckoned deaf to all advice, it is not from obstinacy, but from never having known one, who, doomed to an incurable disorder, had better success; or who, though Herculean to me, preserved his inside so strong, or his head and stomach so totally unattacked. I would not have said half so much, if gratitude for your Ladyship's singular goodness had not obliged me to give you a rational account, to compensate for the idleness of what you dignify by calling it wit and phrases; though my expressions are but the colours with which I would skin over the reflections that arise in long illnesses, and that will sometimes slip into the pen, when they are floating on the mind.

I gladly congratulate your Ladyship and our Lord on the pacification of Ireland, which seems assured by the cordial reception given by both Houses there to the Quieting Bill.[1] Their expressions are

Buckinghamshire to Lord George Germain, Dublin, 10 Jan. 1780, Hist. MSS Comm., *Lothian MSS*, 1905, p. 360; cf. Macartney to Buckinghamshire 21 Jan. 1780, ibid. 361).

———

1. 20 Geo. III (23 Dec. 1780) c. 6, 'An act to repeal certain acts made in Great Britain which restrain the trade and commerce of Ireland' (these acts had restricted Irish exports); it was based on the first two of three propositions for the relief of Irish trade outlined by Lord North 13 Dec. (*Journals of the House of Commons* xxxvii. 508–11, 517, 522; Cobbett, *Parl. Hist.* xx, 1272–85). 'In the House of Commons in Ireland, on Monday Dec. 20, Mr Forster . . . observed that the propositions brought into the English House of Commons contained

even pathetic and heroic, for instead of exulting on having extorted redress, they accept it with humility and gratitude. It now appears that that alarming struggle was fortunate: it has obtained what England ought to have conceded earlier, and what may enrich both countries; and it leaves a sturdy army there, ready in the spirit of its hero of the Boyne,[2] to resist France, or, arbitrary power—a better guard, than toleration of papists to protect a Protestant constitution!

Methinks I am sorry, Madam, that you did not accept for me even with thanks, as I should have done myself, Lady Shelburne's condescension in apologizing for not answering my card,[3] which was totally unnecessary: mine was a mere *how d'ye*—sure she will not think me capable of having complained! I should be as peevishly ceremonious as your great viceroy, Lord Buckingham, who, I see is grown popular, with Lord Hilsborough[4] and Lord North[5]—the same insects do not thrive in both countries.

Lord Bristol has left a paper, or narrative of the Lord knows what, that is to be padlocked till his son is of age—nine years hence[6]— and then not to be published while *whom God long preserve*[7] is alive—This was leaving the boy a fortune indeed, if both live nine years!—There too is another noble author—not for me, but for a supplement—I had rather the Earl-Bishop[8] would publish his father's[9] memoirs.[10]

not only all we could reasonably desire, but more than we could expect' (*Daily Adv.* 29 Dec. 1779). The two resolutions which he moved were unanimously adopted (Henry Grattan, *Memoirs*, 1839, ii. 13; cf also *Last Journals* ii. 260, *sub* 27 Dec. 1779, on 'two votes of the House of Commons of Ireland expressing *nem con.*, satisfaction with the act passed here for their free trade').

2. William III. In the Battle of the Boyne, 1 July 1690, he defeated James II.

3. Missing.

4. Who had succeeded Weymouth as secretary of state for the South 25 Nov. 1779 (*Corr. Geo. III* iv. 479–99).

5. 'Private letters from Corke mention that there was a meeting of the merchants held there on the arrival of the news that the Irish bills had passed the British Parliament; when it was proposed, and unanimously assented to, that the freedom of that City should be presented to the

Right Hon. Lord North and to the Earl of Hillsborough' (*London Chronicle* 30 Dec. 1779 – 1 Jan. 1780, xlvii. 8).

6. As HW says, at the end of the next letter, it was Lord Hervey's papers and memoirs, not Lord Bristol's own, which were restricted. By this reckoning Augustus Hervey would have been born ca 1768, whereas he was probably born earlier, ca 1764–5; see preceding letter. When Lord Bristol's will was made, 20 May 1779, Augustus was in school at Bury St Edmunds; at Bristol's death the boy was said to be a midshipman in the Navy (Hon. William Hervey, *Journals . . . from 1755 to 1814*, ed. S. H. A. Hervey, in *Suffolk Green Books, No. XIV*, 1906, p. 517; *London Chronicle* 30 Dec. 1779 – 1 Jan. 1780, xlvii. 3).

7. George III.

8. The 4th E. of Bristol.

9. John, Lord Hervey (1696–1743); Pope's 'Sporus.' His *Memoirs* were not

Last year began with a hurricane;[11] this commences with a fog as thick as butter—I hope, an omen of our adversity softening, as mists never blow down trees nor blow away islands, and may clear up. This is a new species of divination, and may be called *the comparative:* and as every man is partial to a system he invents, however nonsensical, you will take it as a compliment, I hope, Madam, if I wish you a happy new fog, and a thousand of them!

PS. All my letter but on this page[12] was written last night; the improvement of my hand is owing to having exchanged my bootikin for a glove—so the fog has been of service to me, and will consequently convince me of the reality of my discovery. Formerly the same prognostics foretold the downfall of the Turk and the cure of the toothache.

To Lady Ossory, Monday 3 January 1780

Address: To the Countess of Ossory at Ampthill Park, Bedfordshire. *Postmark:* 3 IA. GC.

Berkeley Square, Jan. 3, 1780.

WELL! Madam, I shall love a fog as long as I live; it is the best weatherglass in Christendom—and then I spell[1] it so well! Nostradamus[1a] was a baby to me. Nay, I now understand that text, which I never comprehended before, of *seeing as in a glass darkly.* Here has Captain Fielding[2] brought in the whole Dutch fleet,[3] with the life and soul, veins, arteries, blood and nerves of the squadron

published until 1848, and then not completely.

10. The Earl-Bishop did not possess them; see following letter.

11. *Ante* 3 Jan. 1779.

12. The preceding paragraph and the postscript.

---

1. Interpret; cf. OED, V², I. 2a.

1a. Michel de Notredame or Nostredame (1503–66), called Nostradamus, astrologer and physician, author of the controversial *Prophecies,* 1555. HW's copy, *The True Prophecies and Prognostications of Michael Nostradamus,* 1685, is Hazen, *Cat. of HW's Lib.* 2177.

2. Charles Feilding (1740–83), grandson of Basil, 4th E. of Denbigh; captain, Royal Navy, 1760–83 (MASON ii. 2 n. 12; Collins, *Peerage,* 1812, iii. 279; GM 1740, x. 316; GM 1783, liii pt i. 94).

3. 'Seven Dutch merchant ships, laden with hemp, iron, cables, pitch, ropes, and tar' (MASON ii. 2 n. 13). They were part of a convoy 'of five ships and frigates of war' which 'sailed from the road of the Texel' 27 Dec. (*London Chronicle* 4–6, 6–8 Jan., xlvii. 17, 26). The engagement took place 'Friday last [31 Dec.], off Portland' (*Daily Adv.* 5 Jan.). See, however, the third paragraph of this letter.

at Brest, which will now be a *caput mortuum*. The Dutch made no resistance—This is all I know yet, but that their admiral[4] is prisoner too—Now you expect a Dutch war[5]—no such thing—at least you are a bad courtier if you conclude so. It is supposed, that the French town of Amsterdam refused to pay taxes unless they might trade with France, but that the rulers of the Republic declared they would not *protect* such illicit trade—and some whispers, not very low, say, that Sir Joseph Yorke[6] advised this capture,[7] persuaded that Holland would not resent it—Such is the creed of the morning—I answer for nothing but being glad of the crippling of the French navy.

Here is another fresh piece of intelligence for which I do not love my friend the fog so much, though I believe it gives as much pleasure at St James's. The back settlers in Carolina have risen, since Prevot's victory, to the amount of three thousand, have seized a town,[8] and declared for the old government—Whatever contributes—and a straw will—to encourage the prosecution of that ruinous war, is very unpropitious.

—Oh dear! I fear my fog was but a mist! The Dutch admiral fired a broadside, but struck on Fielding's first gun, and is brought in with all—but what we wanted—naval stores.[9] If this last state, and not

---

4. Lodewijk van Bylandt (1718–93), Graaf van Bylandt; rear-admiral (*Nieuw Nederlandsch Biografisch Woordenboek*, Leyden, 1911–37, iv. 383–6; A. J. van der Aa, *Biographisch Woordenboek der Nederlanden*, Haarlem, 1852–78, i. 523–4; *London Chronicle* 6–8 Jan., xlvii. 26). He figures in a number of Dutch and English prints; see BM, *Satiric Prints* Vol. V, Nos. 5628, 5712*, 5714*, 5719*, 5724*. His account of the incident appears in the *London Chronicle* 29 Jan. – 1 Feb., xlvii. 111 and in GM 1780, l. 94–5. Bylandt was not actually a prisoner: Feilding took the merchant ships, and the admiral chose to accompany his convoy to Spithead, whence he sailed 27 Feb.

5. War between Great Britain and the Netherlands was postponed until Dec. 1780 (*post* 25 Dec. 1780).

6. (1724–92), K.B., 1761; cr. (1788) Bn Dover; ambassador (1761–80) to The Hague; M.P.

7. The *London Chronicle* 13–15 Jan., xlvii. 54, reported that 'Sir Joseph Yorke,

about the 14th of Dec., presented a private memorial to the Stadtholder, in which was explicitly set forth the determination of our Court, at all events to persist in searching their ships.' Feilding's instructions of 12 Dec. (*Sandwich Papers* iii. 10–11) were 'to visit the . . . Dutch ships . . . and if you find that they are carrying naval stores to the enemy, you are . . . to cause them to be intercepted.' HW's account is in *Last Journals* ii. 262–3.

8. 'Advice had . . . been received that a large body of Highland emigrants (said to be about 3000 men) had assembled in the back settlements of Carolina, and made themselves masters of the town of Cambden, in which they had found a considerable booty, the inhabitants of Charlestown having conveyed their most valuable effects thither, when they were apprehensive of a visit from General Prevost' (*London Chronicle* 28–30 Dec. 1779, xlvi. 617). HW records the incident in *Last Journals* ii. 260.

9. 'Capt. Fielding desired permission to

the first, is the truth (for remember, Madam, I write as anybody passes by and only stops to tell me something; and therefore warrant nothing), the ministers may have blundered us into another war;[10] and then it will be they, and not I, that have seen in a glass darkly.

Well! I shall not pique myself, Madam, on adjusting the more or less of this event, which will be discussed, contradicted, affirmed in every newspaper. My office is to dispatch away my letters with nine post-horns blowing before them on the first singularity. The truth or falsehood is to follow after at their leisure in the state-coach, and Don Welbore Ellis[11] may then hand them out in ceremony if he pleases. The pleasure of a letter in the country is hearing something unexpected that sets everybody to chattering, guessing, reasoning in the dark and wanting to hear more—and that more when it comes, is generally far short of the expectation—so you shall have no second parts from me.

My last intelligence was wrong; Lord Bristol's codicil, now printed,[12] seems to relate entirely to his father's papers, to nothing of his own; nay, it seems rather civilly than rudely meant as to the hour of publication, and to prevent disagreeable truths appearing with regard to the late P. of W.[13]

visit the merchant ships, which was refused. Upon sending his boats to visit them, they were fired at; upon which he fired a shot ahead of the Dutch admiral, who returned a broadside; Captain Fielding did the like; and then the Dutch immediately struck their colours' (*London Gazette* 3 Jan., quoted in *London Chronicle* 4–6 Jan., xlvii. 17). 'To the great disappointment of the captors and ministers, no stores were found but hemp and iron' (*Last Journals* ii. 263).

10. According to the *London Chronicle* (n. 7 above), at the Cabinet Council 28 Dec., 'Lord North was for avoiding anything that would probably involve . . . war with Holland; Lord Hillsborough and Lord Amherst were of the same opinion; but the Chancellor, Lord Sandwich, and Lord George Germaine con-

tended . . . that if the Dutch were permitted to supply the French . . . we should feel all the disadvantages of a war without any of its returns; that it was consequently better to . . . continue to search, but at the same time to avoid a war as far as possible.'

11. Treasurer of the Navy 1777–82; noted for his formality and punctiliousness.

12. In the newspapers, e.g., in the *London Chronicle* 30 Dec. 1779–1 Jan. 1780, xlvii. 7.

13. Frederick (1707–51), Prince of Wales, father of George III. In the codicil Bristol left 'strict injunctions . . . never to print or publish' Lord Hervey's manuscripts or memoirs 'during the reign of his present Majesty.'

To Lady Ossory, Saturday 8 January 1780

Address: To the Countess of Ossory at Ampthill Park, Bedfordshire. *Postmark:* 8 IA. GC.

Berkeley Square, Jan. 8, 1780.

THOUGH I am always afraid of writing too often (however contradictory my practice may be), especially when I have nothing to tell you, Madam; still it is impossible not to thank you for Mr Fitzpatrick's verses, which are written with the ease of his common conversation, and in which the rhymes seem the most proper words that could have been chosen to express his thoughts; the reverse of which is generally the case. The progress of cold and hot fits in female education are as naturally described; and your Ladyship must allow, that if morality may disapprove, truth, who is less a party woman, must give her *imprimatur* to the contents—and therefore I cannot conceive why the author should be shy of letting his poem be seen. As Macduff says,

He has no children!

I have been out to take the air, and am going to Strawberry for a day or two to season myself, before I return into a bit of the world, into which I shall step as reluctantly and timidly as a boy into cold water. I am so demolished, decayed, and so nervous, that the clapping of a door makes me quiver like a poplar. My spirits, if I did not struggle, are disposed to sympathize with my nerves; but I think while one has any sense left, one may keep one's mind under government.

I do not agree, I confess, with our Lord and his brother about Ireland. The present calm may perhaps not be very permanent, that is, when the people shall find, that trade does not enrich in a year or two, like a voyage to the East Indies. But as it is my opinion, that, except on accidental tumults, the people never have any strong operative passions, but when actuated by artful interested leaders, I think those who set the late vehemence in motion, will be very cautious how they play with such two-edged tools. The leading gentlemen of the country, I am persuaded, were overjoyed at having a pretence for being satisfied, *for* they were within a fortnight of seeing their authority slip out of their hands, and pass to those, who having no opportunity of reaching English ministers, would have discovered treason in the estates and property of their own landed superiors.[1] This is human nature. The great plead the distresses of the people —but when they have nursed up the people to a consistency, somebody or other has shrewdness enough to discover that the great are the cause of the distress. This was on the point of happening in Ireland—but I am running into speculation, which is mighty apt to deviate into prediction, when I only meant to answer a paragraph of your Ladyship's letter.

I know nothing more of the egg of a Dutch war that we laid last week, but that Count Welderen was at the King's levee on Wednesday, which surprised me. It was vexatious to have been disappointed of making the important seizure.[2] My first object in politics is to demolish the French marine. My Whig blood cannot bear to part with a drop of the empire of the ocean. Like the Romans I would have Rome domineer over the world, and be free at home. The old man in me is sensible there is little equity in this, and that a good patriot is a bad citizen of the world[3]—but a citizen of the world, as the world is constituted, would be the most useless animal in the creation, and as much *isolé* as the worthy man in the *Spectator* who passed his time in playing with his cat and taking a walk to Islington.[4] To be of any use in a community one must act within a possible sphere, and the smaller the province one chooses, the more good one can do. I am persuaded that a good justice of peace, who confines himself to his own parish, is a more beneficial member of society than Brutus or Cato—however, there would be nothing but Tarquins and Cæsars, if there was nothing but justices of the peace; and therefore one must not refine too much. I never did give loose to my own disquisitions, but I found it as well to come back to my own common sense, and to the common routine of thinking.

1. 'The principal Irish gentlemen, even those in Opposition, as Mr Gratton [Grattan], certainly took so warm a part as they did *for* England, on the reception of the Bill, from their having been in danger of seeing their influence and popularity wrenched out of their hands by the mob. An attempt had even been made at Cork to divest Lord Shannon of the command of his volunteer regiment, for having voted for new taxes'

(*Last Journals* ii. 260, *sub* 27 Dec. 1779).

2. That is, the 'masts and timber' the English expected to find on the Dutch ships (MASON ii. 2; *Last Journals* ii. 262).

3. 'Of all modern virtues patriotism has stood the test the worst' (HW, *Royal and Noble Authors, Works* i. 386).

4. The 'sober citizen, who died a few days since,' whose journal is quoted in *Spectator* No. 317. 'Playing with his cat' is HW's addition.

To Lady Ossory, Thursday 13 January 1780

Berkeley Square, Jan. 13, 1780.

YOU are very suspicious and very unjust, Madam; and I must have been the most ungrateful of men, and the most blind to my own faults, I who am so writative and so talkative to those I love, if I had meant the most indirect reproof for your Ladyship's frequent and kind letters. I do not in the least guess what word you could interpret as a reproach. I know very little what I have written, but I will swallow my Bible, if I was guilty.

I return the verses[1] as you command. I should like to have kept them, but have not even taken a copy without permission.

For three days I have been at Strawberry Hill, and was the better for it, though the weather was so sharp. I now go out, but like it so little, that I think I am not so well: my spirits do not stand mixed company—but how should I not be out of order? I have this morning been visiting a Royal Duke, a Serene Margrave,[2] and a King's daughter[3]—Think what a constraint upon nerves, that for two months have been seeking repose on cushions and couches! and could scarce find it there!

The print of the Sultan is not new to me; I had it four months ago.[4] *The Critic,* I own, was not so new as I expected;[5] and then my being ill versed in modern dramas, most of the allusions must have escaped me. Does not half the merit of *The Rehearsal* depend on the notes?[6] Excuse me, if I write no more, for I am fatigued—and pray do not suspect me of what I never could mean.

1. By Richard Fitzpatrick.
2. The Margrave of Anspach.
3. Princess Amelia.
4. A print of George III wearing a turban; designed to suggest a parallel with an oriental tyrant. One version is titled 'The Patriot,' another 'Ecce Homo.' In BM, *Satiric Prints* v. 328, these are listed as Nos 5544–5, and the date for the first is suggested '? before 10 July 1779.' The same allusion is ibid. Nos 5546 (published 10 Nov. 1779), 5574 (Dec. 1779), 5635 (10 Feb. 1780).
5. HW had read *The Critic* in manu-
script; see his letter to Mason 11 Dec. 1779, Mason i. 487. There is no record that he had seen it played.
6. 'A key to *The Rehearsal* was published by Sam Briscoe in 1704 [in Buckingham's *Collected Works,* 1st edn], and this was appended to nearly every subsequent edition of the play' (*The Rehearsal,* ed. Montague Summers, Stratford-upon-Avon, 1914, p. vi). HW's edition of Buckingham's *Works* was in two volumes, 1715 (Hazen, *Cat. of HW's Lib.* 39).

To Lady Ossory, Monday 17 January 1780

Address: To the Countess of Ossory at Ampthill Park, Bedfordshire. *Postmark:*
17 IA.

Berkeley Square, Jan. 17, 1780.

THE letter I this moment receive, Madam, is a great mark of
confidence indeed, and I wish I could repay it by reasons for
dispelling your uneasiness. One of your apprehensions I think not
a very solid one, at least a minute one in comparison of the greater
clouds that threaten; I mean your dread of abuse. I know not why,
nor how it can be directed personally to one amongst so many.

That the scene grows very serious there is no doubt; nor do I as-
sume vanity from having possessed the spirit of prophecy; a most
useless talent, as predictions never serve as warnings. We know
prophets are not honoured in their own country—where then should
they be honoured? Where they are not known? Where probably
they never are heard of? I believe your Ladyship has heard me say
that whenever the tide should turn, it would be terrible; and that
they who had been fools, would, to excuse themselves, say they had
been cheated.

Still I do not presume on having judged rightly once, nor shall
pretend to go on divining; though I can guess at some things that
will happen,[1] but which are not so proper for a letter; and yet you
might decipher some of my home-opinions from what I said in my
last on the leaders in Ireland. In general, I think, there is great
confusion toward—nor can I foresee what its march will be—the end
of its end is but too well to be guessed, which is very rarely consonant
to its intentions; and therefore, even if necessary, not to be anxiously
wished.

Age and illness naturally make me more tranquil than I should be
at such a moment, if younger. *Esto perpetua!* is always at my heart
to say to my country and its constitution—but the hand of my
climacteric clock rusts at the hour of peace, and will let me wish
nothing but to hear *that* strike. As I am as unlike Oliver Cromwell
as possible, I do not like to depart in a storm[1a]—nay, if anybody would

1. Probably an allusion to the beginning
of the petitioning movement; cf. HW to
Mason 11 Dec. 1779, MASON i. 487–8.

1a. Cromwell died 3 Sept. 1658, the day
after a great storm, but tradition had
long placed his death and the great storm

listen, I would preach moderation—but the superannuated can only sit quiet and observe the progress of the hurricane!—or be swept away with it.

I did not write your Ladyship an account on Saturday, as at first I had a mind to do, of Mr Stanley's[2] horrid exit, as I hoped it would prove one of those common ill-natured expositions of sudden deaths —but it was too true. He was found yet alive, and had given his throat two gashes, but was dead before the company could be fetched from the house.[3] His will made in July was so reasonable, that it looks almost as if having satisfied reason, he thought himself at liberty to indulge his frenzy—but in fact the delirium was almost instan[tan]eous. At eleven he had written letters, and left an unfinished one open on his table; and then issued into the road to act his tragedy, where he was found.

He leaves his estate, about £5000 a year, equally between his sisters,[4] and to the survivor, with a jointure of £500 a year to either husband if surviving. He gives the estate at Chelsea, that came from Sir Hans Sloane,[5] about half of the whole, to his next relation Lord Cadogan;[6] the residue to Mr Sloane,[7] with his library at present and

on the same day: 'On which day there happened the most violent storm of wind that had ever been known, which some men fancy to have been preternatural' (George Smith Green, *Oliver Cromwell: An Historical Play*, 1752, pp. 53, 129–34; Mark Noble, *Memoirs of the Protectorate-House of Cromwell*, Birmingham, 1784, i. 147–8).

2. Hans Stanley (ca 1721–13 Jan. 1780), diplomatist and politician.

3. 'Mr Stanley cut his throat in a walk that leads from Lord Spencer's park at Althorp to the village. . . . He was found by one of Lord Spencer's servants, not then dead, and most probably might have been recovered had his throat been sewed up before they had moved him, but the ignorance of those about him did not suggest to them that method; they took him up, and the effusion of blood which followed soon put an end to his existence' (Coke, 'MS Journals' 10 Jan. 1780). Further 'authentic particulars' are in the *London Chronicle* 22–25 Jan., xlvii. 88.

4. Anne, married to Welbore Ellis

(*ante* 14 Sept. 1774) and Sarah Stanley (ca 1726–1821) m. (*ante* 1774) Christopher D'Oyly (ca 1717–95), barrister, M.P. Wareham 1774–80, Seaford 1780–4. For the D'Oylys, see BERRY ii. 58 n. 33, and *passim*.

5. (1660–1753), cr. (1716) Bt; the physician whose bequest to the nation was the beginning of the British Museum. His estate was divided between his two surviving daughters: Hans Stanley's mother and the mother of the 3d Bn Cadogan.

6. A letter from Lord Cadogan 15 Jan. 1780 to Lord Buckinghamshire, one of the trustees under Stanley's will, confirms HW's account. 'He died at Althorp and left me at Caversham but a few days ago in the greatest appearance of health and tranquillity of mind I ever saw' (Hist. MSS Comm., *Lothian MSS*, 1905, pp. 360–1). Further details of his 'very sensible will' are in the *London Chronicle* 20–22 Jan., xlvii. 80, where it is suggested that Mrs Ellis and Mrs D'Oyly probably would give the Welsh estate to Rice's children; see below.

7. Hans Sloane (Sloane-Stanley after

the choice of four pictures; and a small estate in Wales to a most distant cousin (v. note at the end of my *Historic Doubts*)[8] the late Mr Rice,[9] who being dead before him, the bequest is disputable.[10] His not having altered that disposition is another proof that the madness was very recent. Nay, the evening before his death or that very morning he had expressed to one of the company his satisfaction in the way of life at Althorpe—in short, it is a most shocking story, and with his father's[11] catastrophe, dreadful to the two sisters!

To Lady Ossory, Saturday 29 January 1780

Berkeley Square, Jan. 29, 1780.

THE weathercock Marquis[1] has taken his part, or rather his leave, and resigned his key on Thursday.[2] But there was a more extraordinary phenomenon in the Closet the same day. Lord George Gordon[3] asked an audience, was admitted, and incontinently began

---

1821) (1739–1827), of South Stoneham, Hants, later of Paultons, Hants; M.P. Newport 1768–80, Southampton 1780–4, Christchurch 1788–96, Lostwithiel 1796–1806 (Burke, *Landed Gentry*, 1952, p. 2389). He was great-nephew of Sir Hans Sloane and first cousin once removed of Hans Stanley.

8. The 'Addition,' p. [135] of *Historic Doubts*, containing a 'notice, obligingly communicated to me by Mr Stanley,' about the descendants of Perkin Warbeck's widow, among them 'Hans Stanley, Esq.; George Rice, Esq., etc.' Although the note is inaccurate, Perkin Warbeck's widow having had no children in her four marriages (*Scots Peerage* iv. 530–1), the descent and relationship of Stanley and Rice (from a daughter of Sir Matthew Cradock) is not affected.

9. George Rice (ca 1724–3 Aug. 1779), of Newton, Carmarthenshire; M.P. Carmarthenshire 1754–79; lord lieutenant of Carmarthenshire 1755–79 (GEC, *sub* Dinevor; Burke, *Peerage*, 1953, p. 698, *sub* Dynevor).

10. Rice's predecease made it, 'I conclude, a lapse legacy' (Lord Cadogan's letter, quoted in n. 6).

11. George Stanley of Paultons, Hants,

who 'cut his throat . . . in bed with his wife' 31 Jan. 1734 (HW to Mason 17 Jan. 1780, Mason ii. 5).

---

1. Of Carmarthen.

2. '27th [Jan.] The Marquis of Carmarthen . . . resigned his key of Chamberlain to the Queen. He had written to the Committee at York that he approved of their meeting. He was a light, variable young man, of very moderate parts, and less principle' (*Last Journals* ii. 266–7). The Yorkshire Association, which opposed the American war and advocated Parliamentary reform and economy, is frequently mentioned in Mason. For countenancing the Association, Carmarthen was dismissed 8 Feb. from his post as Lord Lieutenant of the East Riding of Yorkshire but was restored in 1782 under the Rockingham ministry. For his own account of his conduct, see his *Political Memoranda*, ed. Oscar Browning, in Camden Society, n.s., Vol. XXXV, 1884, pp. 18–23, 65.

3. (1751–93), the agitator, who had become president of the Protestant Association late in 1779. A detailed variant of the anecdote HW tells about him is in the *London Chronicle* 7–9 March, xlvii.

reading his Irish pamphlet,[4] and the King had the patience to hear him do so for above an hour, till it was so dark that the lecturer could not see. His Majesty then desired to be excused, and said he would finish the piece himself. 'Well!' said the lunatic apostle, 'but you must give me your honour that you will read it out.' The King promised, but was forced to pledge his honour. It puts one in mind of Charles II at Scoon before his restoration.[5] It is hoped this man is so mad that it will soon come to perfection—unless my plan is adopted, of shutting up in Bedlam the few persons in this country that remain in their senses. It would be easier and much cheaper than to confine all the delirious.

Your Ladyship asked me in your last, whether it was the situation of public affairs that affected my nerves—to be sure there would be more Roman dignity in answering, yes—but something less than truth. I fear one's country is never so near one's heart, that the clapping of a door gives it a palpitation. My total weakness and variety of pains, and the trepidation that the least surprise causes on my nerves, make me so occupied with self, that I doubt the case of poor crazy old England does not affect me so entirely as it ought; and as she, however crippled, will hobble on somehow or other; and as my option lies only between suffering and extinction, the surviving world is but a secondary consideration. Nay, I am often divided between contrary shames—sometimes I blush at attending more to myself than to my *patria;* and sometimes, at being anxious about a scene in which I can take so little part, and which I must quit so soon! This incertitude is very natural—but as I have no time for affectation, I let myself go according as the several sensations rise uppermost—and the Whig, or the superannuated invalid predominates, as the weather-glass of my health mounts or sinks.

235, almost one column; in the *Political Magazine,* 1780, i. 95; etc. See also *Last Journals* ii. 266.

4. Not written by Gordon but by Francis Dobbs (1750–1811), Irish politician and eccentric: *A Letter to . . . Lord North, on his Propositions in Favour of Ireland,* Dublin, 1780; another edition, London, 1780. On 24 Jan. Gordon had thinned the House of Commons from about 200 to 40 by reading the entire pamphlet to the House despite many protests. On the following day he started

to read it again to the House, declaring that 'the pamphlet was really so excellent that it ought to be read every day in the week,' but in response to protests he desisted (Cobbett, *Parl. Hist.* xx. 1307–14; *London Chronicle* 22–27 Jan., xlvii. 87, 89). The pamphlet does not appear in HW's library.

5. To ensure Scottish support Charles II at his coronation at Scone 1 Jan. 1651 had to swear to both the covenant and the solemn league and covenant of 1643.

I enclose a copy of verses, which I have just printed at Strawberry, only a few copies,[6] and which I hope you will think pretty. They were written three months ago[7] by Mr Charles Miller,[8] brother of Sir John,[9] on seeing Lady Horatia at Nuneham. The poor girl is better. Sir Richard Jebbe pronounced her in a consumption; but he is such a raven that I did not believe him, nor do. The moment she came to town, the Duchess of Ancaster carried her for two days to Lady Eliz. Burrel's; and as she returned better, and not worse as I expected from such a scene, I am little alarmed for her.

When may one expect to see you in town, Madam?—or are you learning to skate *à la royale?*[10] Apropos, I was diverted with your Ladyship's calling my princes and princesses *my royal society*—It was as little in my calculation or plan to pass the end of my days with Highnesses as with philosophers. *Encore à propos;* Princess Amalie told us an excellent story t'other night of Lady Mary Coke. Her R.H. dines once a week at Lady Holderness's with only the party for the evening loo.[11] Lady Mary asked the same honour.[12] The Princess insisted on a very small dinner, as she has on those occasions —but found a banquet. As she sat down, the groom of the chambers presented to her, as she thought, an empty gilt salver—for what purpose she could not guess—but on it lay (what she had not seen, being so purblind) two gold pins to pin her napkin, as is her way.

---

6. '1780. At the end of January printed 150 copies of Mr Charles Miller's verses to Lady Horatia Waldegrave on the death of the Duke of Ancaster to whom she was to have been married' (*Journal of the Printing Office* 19; HW to Mason 22 Jan. 1780, Mason ii. 7–8; Hazen, *SH Bibl.* 220).

7. 'A.D. 1779.' is printed at the end of the verses.

8. (d. 1781), son of Sir John Miller (d. 1772), of Chichester, 4th Bt; brother of Sir Thomas Miller (1731–1816), 5th Bt, and of Ann, Cts of Albemarle, at whose house at Hambledon, Hants, he died 13 Oct. 1781; equerry to the D. of Gloucester (*London Chronicle* 16–18 Oct. 1781, l. 371; Burke, *Peerage*, 1953, p. 1458). A letter from him to Lord Harcourt 7 June 1780, describing the Gordon riots, is in the *Harcourt Papers* viii. 290–3, printed as by 'O. Miller.'

9. HW's error. The only Sir John Mil-ler living at this time apparently had no brother Charles: Sir John Miller (from 1780, Riggs-Miller) (d. 1798), cr. (1778) Bt; M.P.; the husband of Lady Miller of Batheaston fame (*ante* 14 June 1774; DNB, *sub* Miller, Anna; Ruth A. Hesselgrave, *Lady Miller and the Batheaston Literary Circle*, New Haven, 1927, *passim*).

10. In his letter to Mason of the same day HW mentions George III's skating (Mason ii. 9).

11. Lady Mary Coke's 'MS Journals' indicate that the weekly party, for dinner and loo or whist or commerce, was at Princess Amelia's on Tuesdays; Lady Holdernesse had the group for dinner 17 Dec., but this was not a regular occurrence (Coke, 'MS Journals' 16–17, 25 Dec. 1779, and *passim*).

12. 'The Princess Amelia dines with me on Thursday [13 Jan.] and stays the evening' (ibid. 10 Jan. 1780).

Still she did not perceive they were of gold; and after dinner flung them away; when to the eternal disgrace of magnificence, Lady Mary retired to hunt for her pins.

I forgot to ask you, Madam, if you are not glad that Lord G. Gordon is a Scot? Would one deny them the benefit of the Union, and monopolize lunacy ourselves? I was once talking to Craufurd on our frenzy; and he replied, 'We are not mad.' 'No,' said I, 'but you know we are, and profit of it.'

To Lady Ossory, Wednesday 2 February 1780

Feb. 2, 1780.

I CANNOT tell your Ladyship precisely the story of the Duke of Ancaster's presentiment,[1] for I have forgotten it, having heard it but once imperfectly, and being not apt to listen attentively to dreams and auguries—all I remember was, that once walking with her, he said something of foreseeing he should not live long.

I send your Ladyship, as you order, Lady Craven's novel,[2] which is, being very short, full of one long name, but not of long names. It is scarce a story, and I am told, is a translation;[3] but it is very prettily told, and has, I will swear, several original expressions, that are characteristic, and must be her own. There is no mystery or secret about it, except that it was one to me for four-and-twenty hours, being sent to me anonymously, and I was all that time before I guessed the author. The reason of my not naming it, Madam, you will find in my character, which abhors anything that looks like

1. In Charles Miller's 'To Lady Horatia Waldegrave, on the Death of the Duke of Ancaster' is the passage
> '. . . where, strange to tell!
From his young lips the dire prediction fell.'
(ll. 23–24)
2. *Modern Anecdote of the Ancient Family of the Kinkvervankotsdarspraken-gotchderns: A Tale for Christmas 1779.* 'Printed for the Author; And sold by M. Davenhill' *et al.*; dedicated to HW 30 Nov. 1779; see Hazen, *Cat. of HW's Lib.* 2364.
3. HW is keeping up Lady Craven's

joke in the dedication where she says, 'this anecdote . . . was prettily written in French by a German lady who passed some time in England with the late Madame Poushkin Moushkin,' etc. HW called it 'a sort of imitation of Voltaire, and yet perfectly original' (HW to Mason 17 Jan. 1780, MASON ii. 7). The *Monthly Mirror*, July–Dec. 1801, xii. 9, reports: 'But the fact is, this production was not the offspring of . . . [her] fertility; it was literally a German anecdote, which she augmented considerably, and adorned by many little whimsical ideas.'

vanity. Though I am very proud of it, do I ever boast of your goodness to me? It is certainly very glorious

> To have contending Queens at dead of night
> Forsake their down—[4]

and write for me or to me—but honours to me are never unaccompanied by retrospect to myself, where I behold nothing but a wretched skeleton, conscious of a thousand faults and defects, ill-skinned over with one or two studied and negative virtues, and at my best time possessed of only mediocre and commonplace talents —which being a true picture, you will be so good, Madam, as not imagine that I wish to have it retouched, and therefore do not send it me back varnished, I beseech you.

I must certainly agree with you, Madam, about the two mad lords you mention, for you know I have long thought the whole nation out of its senses. I go farther now, for I am of opinion that, like some animals who by instinct medicine themselves, we are going to apply that remedy of insanity, letting ourselves blood. Had the petitions[5] been the tide of an universal torrent, they might have done what good they pleased—but I fear with you that that is not the case.[6] Lord Cholmondeley[7] told me that in Cheshire not one of the Whig gentlemen would sign the petition.[8] In Norfolk, the county I know the best, there is scarce a name, except Mr Coke's, of any of the great Whig or Tory families to the first signature.[9] Nor can I believe,

4. Quotation not found.

5. Following the lead of the Yorkshire Association, other counties had held meetings and had circulated petitions critical of the administration. See Last Journals ii. 265, 268, 271, and passim; H. Butterfield, George III, Lord North, and the People, 1949, passim.

6. Lady Ossory's comments probably had included a reference to a recent meeting called at Bedford by Lord Ossory, Lord Lieutenant of the county, 24 Jan. and mentioned in the London Chronicle 18–20 Jan., xlvii. 67. A petition complaining of the expenditure of the public money was voted and was read with others in the House of Commons 10 Feb. (Journals of the House of Commons xxxvii. 586–7; Butterfield, op. cit. 337).

7. George James Cholmondeley (1749–1827), 4th E. of Cholmondeley, 1770, cr.

(1815) M. of Cholmondeley; HW's grand-nephew; Lord Lieutenant of Cheshire 1770–83; Chamberlain of Cheshire 1770–1827.

8. Butterfield, op. cit. 212, supports this view, but the London Chronicle 18–20 Jan., xlvii. 67, reported that the petition was 'signed by all present at the meeting [at Northwich 13 Jan.], except six.'

9. That is, those who signed the Norfolk petition at the meeting at Norwich 29 Jan. The petition was later circulated for additional signatures, and there were complaints that 'alterations' were made 'after it was signed by some of the petitioners.' A counter-petition was also drawn up and signed at the meeting and circulated for additional signatures (Butterfield, op. cit. 212–13, 247, 250; London Chronicle 3–5 Feb., xlvii. 125).

when three parts in four of England were with the Court, that even half have changed their opinions in one year, giddy as multitudes are. The Court has been thunderstruck with what has been already done; but will recover its spirits—and have a firm back game, for I do not find that one Scotch county has petitioned.[10] If the petitioning committees receive no satisfaction, they will grow outrageous—and then—but I do not care to be a prophet. I like petitions; it is a Whig measure. I wished for and recommended them five years ago, when they might have checked at least infinite mischief, and prevented the waste of buckets of blood and treasure—but some heads of Opposition were still too much in hopes of passing into the Closet without breaking open the door! though Yorkshire could have been led to petition then as easily as now. Well! we must still hope the best. Principles are or ought to be permanent things; and if they are right, must not be influenced by temporary events. We must only take care not to mistake passions for principles, nor let the latter be the aggressors, especially when the path leads to blood. I dread the spilling of blood for itself. I dread drawing it, because though the person may suffer, the Crown nine times in ten is the gainer—and I dread it more particularly now, because my Whiggism was taught to consider France as our capital enemy, and she will be most advantaged by our domestic feuds. The Court deserves everything that a ruined and dishonoured nation can inflict, and has left itself without excuse. Who could plead for it, when its own accomplices and tools fly from it?—but I do hope our friends will remember that we have enemies at sea as well as at land, and that the temple will not be taken by the Romans, while we are pulling down the Pharisees.

PS. I write thus freely, because my letter goes by the coach[11] with Lady Craven's book—It should not whisper my fears to the lowest courtier in the Post Office, because it is better the Court should be alarmed and bend. Its *raideur* would produce all I apprehend.

10. Nor did any petition later.

11. The regular Ampthill carriage left London on Tuesday, Friday, and Saturday at noon (*New Complete Guide to All Persons Who Have Any Trade or* *Concern with the City of London,* 15th edn, 1777, p. 136), but a carriage to Bedford was scheduled for Monday and Wednesday (ibid. 139).

To Lady Ossory, Sunday 6 February 1780

HW may have written a letter to accompany 'A True Love Story,' in Kirgate's hand, dated 'Feb. 6, 1780,' now among the letters of HW to Lady Ossory in the possession of Mrs Vernon. The text differs only in minor details from that in HW's *Hieroglyphic Tales*, SH, 1785, where it is the sixth and last tale.

To Lady Ossory, Saturday 12 February 1780

Address: To the Countess of Ossory at Ampthill Park, Bedfordshire. *Postmark:* 12 FE. GC.

Berkeley Square, Feb. 12, 1780.

I OBEY, Madam, as far as writing, to show my obedience; but I certainly cannot amuse you. Politics I disclaim, when Lord Ossory is in town; he sits at the fountainhead, and I can get no purer a draught, than what is adulterated by Betty[1] or Macpherson[2] for their different customers. Yet when nothing is stirring but politics, what can I send? Oh! old Egerton[3] is dead, and has left the Duke of Bridgwater[4] but one thousand pounds of all his millions. They go to a sister[5] and her children,[6] and then to a Miss Sykes[7]—and if she does

1. Elizabeth Munro (or Neale) (ca 1730–97), the 'celebrated fruit-woman in St James's Street, who took great liberties with the Court in her conversation—her shop was consequently much frequented by the Opposition' (HW's note in Mason, *Satirical Poems* 66–7; MONTAGU i. 109; MASON i. 81).

2. James Macpherson (1736–96), 'the Ossianite, had a pension of £600 a year from the Court, to supervise the newspapers, and prevent the publication of truth or satire' (*Last Journals* i. 524, *sub* Feb. 1776). See also MASON i. 431 n. 8.

3. Samuel Egerton (1711 – 10 Feb. 1780), of Tatton Park, Cheshire; M.P. Cheshire 1754–80 (Joseph Foster, *Pedigrees of County Families of England*, Vol. I, Lancashire, 1873, *sub* Egerton; GM 1780, l. 103; Burke, *Commoners* iii. 39). 'Mr Egerton is supposed to die possessed of the greatest landed property of any com-

moner in England. The misfortune he received in the loss of an only daughter [*ante* 13 Nov. 1776] . . . who lately died in childbed is generally imagined to have been the cause of his death' (*London Chronicle* 12–15 Feb., xlvii. 154).

4. Francis Egerton (1736–1803), 3d and last D. of Bridgwater, 1748; 'the founder of British inland navigation'; second cousin to Samuel Egerton, both being great-grandsons of John, 2d E. of Bridgwater (Foster, loc. cit.).

5. Hester Egerton (d. 9 July 1780) m. (1747), as 2d wife, William Tatton of Withenshaw (Wythenshawe), Cheshire; resumed her maiden name 9 May 1780, by sign manual, on becoming heiress to her brother (Foster, loc. cit.; Burke, *Commoners* iii. 41; *London Chronicle* 9–11 May, xlvii. 449).

6. William Tatton Egerton (1749–1806), M.P.; and Elizabeth Tatton (d. 1803),

not become a duchess, then to the above said Duke. Another legacy of £5000 is given to Mrs Grey[8] by her husband's sister Lady Di. Middleton.[9]

Everybody is full of Mr Burke's yesterday's speech,[10] which I only mention as parent of a *mot* of Geo. Selwyn. Lord Geo. Gordon, single, divided the House,[11] and Selwyn set him down afterwards at White's,[12] where he said, 'I have brought the whole Opposition in my coach; and I hope one coach will always hold them, if they mean to take away the Board of Works.'[13]

Lord Ossory assures me your Ladyship will be here next week; it will be a red-lettered day in my almanac, from which the gout has expunged most of the festivals. Another shall be *Innocents' Day*, for the Ladies Anne and Gertrude—and I believe my devotions at my chapel of ease in Grosvenor Place will be as sincere, mind, I do not say, fervent, as Lady M. Fitzgerald's[14] at the Lock Hospital[15] in the neighbourhood.

m. (1770) Christopher Sykes, 2d Bt, 1783 (Foster, loc. cit.; Burke, *Peerage*, 1953, p. 2045, *sub* Sykes of Sledmere; Burke, *Commoners* iii. 41).

7. Daughter of Mrs Sykes mentioned in n. 6: Decima Hester Beatrix Sykes (1775–1843) m. (1795) John Robinson Foulis, 2d son of Sir William Foulis, 6th Bt (William Betham, *Baronetage of England*, 1801–5, i. 179, iv. 132; Burke, *Peerage*, 1953, p. 2045).

8. Lucy Danvers (d. 1799), dau. of Sir Joseph Danvers, 1st Bt, m. (1748) Hon. John Grey (ca 1724–77), son of Henry, 3d E. of Stamford, M.P. Bridgnorth 1754–68, Tregony 1768–74, clerk comptroller of the Board of Green Cloth 1754–77 (Montagu i. 344 n. 21; GM 1799, lxix pt i. 535; Collins, *Peerage*, 1812, iii. 368; Venn, *Alumni Cantab.;* Burke, *Peerage*, 1953, p. 1981). Lady Mary Coke mentions her occasionally in her *Journals.*

9. Lady Diana Grey (d. 14 Jan. 1780) m. (1736) George Middleton of Seaton, near Aberdeen, Scotland (Collins, loc. cit.; Musgrave, *Obituary;* Coke, *Journals* iv. 139).

10. His celebrated *Speech . . . on Presenting to the House of Commons . . . A Plan for the Better Security of the Independence of Parliament, and the Œconomical Reformation of the Civil and Other Establishments*, published by Dodsley 6 March 1780, although John Hay had brought out an unofficial version 17 Feb. (*Public Advertiser*). HW's copy of the Dodsley version (now wsl; Hazen, *Cat. of HW's Lib.* 1609. 40. 10) shows that he read it with the greatest care; his marks are in the margin of almost every page.

11. On Burke's motion for leave to bring in his bill, Lord George Gordon argued 'that a more unconstitutional speech had never been delivered in that House,' called for a division, and was alone in opposition to the motion. Lord Ossory was one of those named to prepare and bring in the bill (Cobbett, *Parl. Hist.* xxi. 72–3).

12. Selwyn had been a member of White's Club since 1744, but Lord George Gordon's name is not listed in W. B. Boulton's *History of White's*, 1892, ii. part 2; cf. Percy Colson, *White's 1693–1950*, 1951.

13. Which had been one of the objects of Burke's attack (Burke, op. cit. 46–7). Selwyn's post of Paymaster of the Works was abolished in 1782, but he received an equally lucrative appointment in place of it.

14. Her funeral sermon (1815) by the Rev. Thomas Scott, who had known her

To Lady Ossory, Thursday 1 June 1780

Address: To the Countess of Ossory at Ampthill Park, Bedfordshire. *Postmark:* ISLEWORTH. 1 IV.

Strawberry Hill, June 1, 1780.

I THINK it my duty to give your Ladyship a faithful account of Lady Warwick and her sisters, from an eye-witness who did not know it would be transmitted to you. Mr Couslade[1] is returned from Warwick Castle, and I questioned him minutely. He thinks the Countess will recover, but it will be long and slow.[2] He saw her but twice, and that as she was airing, for the least thing disorders her nerves. Miss Vernon[3] is better, and he thinks, though very delicate, in no consumption. He commends both her and Miss Elizabeth extremely, and says he never saw more proper modest behaviour, and that both are very reserved.

This is all I really have to say, Madam. Nay, though so proud of the honour of being your Ladyship's gazetteer, I foresee I shall be obliged to resign my office, for a reason that the present ministers

since 1786, indicates that her religious fervour had been constant since about 1765; she was 'an attendant on' Scott's ministry at the Lock Chapel 1786–1803 (Scott, *Works,* ed. John Scott, 1823–5, vi. 505–51, especially pp. 505, 510; H. C. Marillier, *A Bit of Eighteenth Century Romance,* The Sette of Odd Volumes, No. xxxix, 1910, *passim,* especially pp. 71–2, giving information that Sir Robert Walpole was her godfather). A lady of the Bedchamber to Princess Amelia 1775–86, she is frequently mentioned in Lady Mary Coke's 'MS Journals' (*Royal Kalendar; London Chronicle* 16–18 Feb. 1775, xxxvii. 166).

15. Founded in 1747 'for the cure of females suffering from disorders contracted by a vicious course of life,' Lock Hospital was in Grosvenor Place, near Hyde Park Corner. It was supported by voluntary contributions. In 1764 the Chapel, to which HW alludes, was founded as a means of income (from the rental of pews) to the Hospital. In 1842 the Hospital and the Chapel were re-moved to Westbourne Green, Harrow Road (Wheatley, *London Past and Present* ii. 412–13; *London and Its Environs Described,* 1761, iii. 322–6).

———

1. John Cowslade (d. 1795), of Donnington, Berks; HW's occasional correspondent; commissioner for appeals and regulating duties in the Excise Office 1763–95; gentleman usher to the Queen 1761–95 (quarterly waiter 1761–74, daily waiter 1774–90, gentleman usher of the private chamber 1790–95); living in Berkeley Square ca 1773 and in South Moulton Street, Westminster, at the time of his death (*Annual Register,* 1763, p. 126; ibid. 1790, p. 238; *London Chronicle* 11–14 April 1795, lxxvii. 357; Montagu i. 251 n. 1; *Royal Kalendar, passim*).

2. She had given birth to a son 5 April: Hon. Charles John Greville (1780–1836), K.C.B., 1815; Maj.-Gen., 1819 (Burke, *Peerage,* 1953, p. 2174; *Army Lists; London Chronicle* 11–13 April, xlvii. 355).

3. Caroline Maria Vernon.

will think a very bad one—my being totally unfit for my place. It is too hard on a poor writer of an evening post to be forced to labour in his vocation only in summer. Mr Bates had rather lie than speak truth; and for fear he should even be suspected of veracity, he has chosen the Duke of Richmond for the hero of his abuse[4]—but I, who have no invention, and confine myself to matters of fact, cannot relate what never happened. Campaigns are out of my depth. I neither understand Lord Amherst, nor what he ought to understand, the army. I do not know a first rate from a tenth; nay, nor how many rates there are,[5] nor how small a large ship may be. I cannot expound a gazette after all the pains in the world have been taken to make it unintelligible; and as our whole war consists in confounding the truth, I am not qualified to register King Mars's or Earl Neptune's campaigns. Since poor Lady Blandford's death I shall have no opportunity of meeting Lady Greenwich and hearing her break her bulk of scandal. There is not so untittletattling a village as Twickenham in the island; and if Mr Cambridge did not gallop the roads for intelligence, I believe the grass would grow in our ears.

I have some other employments that I could wish to resign too; more exalted, though not so flattering; but having no salaries annexed to them, I should gain no patriot credit by giving them up. Nobody ever felt the slavery of Court attendance more than I did on Monday. The country was gushing with verdure and beauty, the day was sultry, and Strawberry as cool as a grotto—yet I was forced to go to town to a birthday and a ball![6]

4. On 25 Feb. 1780 twelve 'Queries Addressed to his Grace the Duke of R——.' and signed 'An Inquirer' appeared in the *Morning Post*, of which Bate was editor. On 24 and 28 April informations against the printer and Bate were moved in the Court of King's Bench for a libel (a charge of high treason) against the Duke of Richmond. Bate was found guilty 22 June and was committed to the King's Bench Prison 25 June 1781, but his twelve-months' sentence was shortened at the Duke of Richmond's request. Bate denied responsibility for the 'Queries.' See *The Trial (at Large) of the Rev. Henry Bate,* 'from Mr Gurney's Shorthand Notes,' 1780; W. T. Whitley, 'An Eight-eenth Century Art Chronicler: Sir Henry Bate Dudley, Bart.,' in the *Walpole Society,* 1924–1925, xiii. 42–3.

5. 'The British fleet is . . . distributed into six rates, exclusive of the inferior vessels' (William Falconer, *Universal Dictionary of the Marine,* 2d edn, 1771). First-rates (100 guns), and the second, third, and fourth-rates (90–98, 64–80, and 50–60 guns respectively) were ships of the line; fifth and sixth-rates (32–44 and 20–28 guns) were called frigates (*Court and City Register,* 1779, pp. 142–7; D. Lescallier, *Vocabulaire des termes de marine anglais-français,* 1799). Cf. OED, *sub* rate, III. 9. b.

6. A 'great ball and supper at Glouces-

Oh! 'tis the sweetest of all earthly things
To live with Princes and to talk of Kings!
Then happy man who shows the tombs! said I![7]

This last line was certainly written for me, who love Westminster Abbey much more than levees and circles, and—no treason, I hope —am fond enough of kings, as soon as they have a canopy of *stone* over them.

On Tuesday I was asked to a conversation-piece at Lady Clermont's, and there I found that Thalestris, the Princess Daskiou[8] and her son[9] and daughter.[10] The lad is a tolerable Pompey; the daughter, a perfect Tartar. The mother who I hoped had forgotten me, recollected our having passed an evening together at Northumberland House,[11] as she told Lady Clermont; but as she did not claim me, I shall not leave my name at her lodgings in blood-bowl alley.[12]

ter House' for Princess Sophia Matilda of Gloucester, born 29 May 1773 (*London Courant* 2 June 1780; HW to Mason 28–31 May 1780, MASON ii. 47).

7. Pope, *Satires of Donne*, Satire IV, ll. 100–102. The second line should read 'To gaze on Princes . . .' HW quoted the third line to Conway 26 Dec. 1774.

8. Ekaterina Romanovna Vorontsova (1743–1810), m. (ca 1758–60) Prince Mikhail Illarionovich Dashkov; Russian littérateuse and friend of Catherine the Great; director of the Academy of Arts and Sciences in St Petersburg 1782–96; first president of the Russian Academy 1784–96 (MANN vi. 65 n. 13; MASON ii. 59 n. 37; Günther Schlegelberger, *Die Fürstin Daschkowa*, Berlin, 1935). She and her son and daughter had been presented to the King and Queen on 25 May (*London Chronicle* 25–27 May, xlvii. 506, her name there given as *Dauffendoff*), and were at Bath in July (ibid. 27–29 July, xlviii. 91–2).

9. Prince Pavel Mikhailovich Dashkov (1763–1807), who had been presented to George III a few days after his arrival in England, Oct. 1776; M.A., University of Edinburgh, 1779; travelled extensively with his mother and sister; became a general and was for several years an influential friend of Czar Paul I (*The Russian Journals of Martha and Catherine Wilmot*, ed. Londonderry and Hyde, 1934, p. 46, and *passim*; Schlegelberger, op. cit.

73–85, 228, and *passim; London Chronicle* 8–10 Oct. 1776, 22–24 April 1779, xl. 350, xlv. 392).

10. Anastasia Mikhailovna Dashkova (1761–1830) m. General Scherbenin; disinherited by her mother, with whom she had frequently quarrelled; brought up her brother's illegitimate children (*The Russian Journals of Martha and Catherine Wilmot*, pp. 172–3 *et passim*, Schlegelberger, op. cit. *passim*). Mrs Damer made 'A small profile in terra-cotta' of her (BERRY ii. 272).

11. Princess Dashkov had been in England in 1770 to place her son in Westminster School (HW to Mann 4 Oct. 1770) and again in 1776, when she was presented at St James's on 3 Oct., a few days after arrival, and on 7 Dec. she passed through Newcastle 'on a tour through Great Britain' after having been 'received at Alnwick Castle with all the honours due to her rank, by orders from the Duke of Northumberland' (*London Chronicle* 1–5 Oct., 14–17 Dec. 1776, xl. 328, 335, 584). As the Duchess of Northumberland continued to entertain until a few days before her death on 5 Dec. 1776, HW could have met the Princess in either 1770 or 1776.

12. Princess Dashkov was implicated in the death of Peter III of Russia (MONTAGU ii. 38–9; MANN vi. 65).

Your Ireland, I find, has spoken out, though professing much decorum. The Chancellor[13] is for firmness—as if frowns would pass more current in Ireland than in America. The heir-apparent of the seals,[14] out of contradiction both to the Chancellor—and to his own treatment of Dr Franklin,[15] takes the side of acquiescence; and probably will prevail,[16] for Lord Thurlowe is in so bad a way, that if he lives, he is not likely to be able to execute his office.[17]

Yesterday's papers say the Church of England is to assemble to-morrow in St George's Fields and to follow their metropolitan Lord George Gordon to the House of Commons, to demand that the Defender of the Faith should be forced to part with his Whore of Babylon[18]—so his triple crown is in as much peril as his other diadems!—but your Ladyship can read the papers as well as I, and when I recur to them, you must yourself be weary of a

MERCURIUS RUSTICUS.

13. Lord Thurlow.

14. Wedderburn. Attorney-General 1778–80, he kissed hands 9 June on being appointed lord chief justice of the Common Pleas (*Daily Adv.* 12 June; *Corr. Geo. III* v. 78). From April to December 1783 he was first commissioner of the Great Seal and from 28 June 1793 to 14 April 1801 he was lord chancellor, a post he had long coveted.

15. On 29 Jan. 1774 'Dr Franklin was again heard by counsel before the Privy Council. Wedderburn, solicitor-general [1771–8], made a most bitter and abusive speech against him, which was much admired. He made no reply. . . . The ministers determined to turn Franklin out of his place of postmaster of America, which could but incense him and drive him (a man of vast abilities) on farther hostilities, and recommend him as a martyr to the Bostonians. This place was all he had, and it was taken away' (*Last Journals* i. 284–5). HW's note on the first sentence of the above-quoted passage: 'This event, a capital one in giving date to the American war.'

16. 'The Irish Mutiny Bill, being granted here, was received in Ireland and passed' (ibid. ii. 327, *sub* 11 Aug. 1780). This bill tacitly acknowledged 'that an Act of Parliament passed in England has not been able to bind Ireland' (*London Chronicle* 10–12 Aug., xlviii. 144).

17. On 15 May 'the Lord Chancellor set out for Tunbridge Wells to use the waters, by the advice of his physicians' (ibid. 13–16 May, xlvii. 472). References to his improvement, relapse, improvement, and journey to Bath on 8 June are ibid. 18 May – 10 June, *passim*. He was at Court 16 June 'for the first time since his illness' (ibid. 17–20 June, xlvii. 585). *Last Journals* ii. 305, *sub* 26 May, parallels this paragraph.

18. On 30 May Lord George Gordon gave notice in the House of Commons that on 2 June he would present 'the petition of the Protestant Associations of London, Westminster, and Southwark, praying the repeal of the late act in favour of popery in England. He acquainted the House that the whole Association proposed to assemble in St George's Fields and to accompany their petition to the House' (*London Chronicle* 30 May – 1 June, xlvii. 521, 523). HW cut from an unidentified newspaper an account (now WSL) of the meeting of the Protestant Association at Coachmakers' Hall on 29 May and wrote at the top 'Wednesday—May 31, 1780.'

To Lady Ossory, Saturday 3 June 1780

Berkeley Square, June 3, 1780.

I KNOW that a governor or a gazetteer ought not to desert their posts, if a town is besieged, or a town is full of news—and therefore, Madam, I resume my office—I smile today—but I trembled last night[1]—For an hour or more I never felt more anxiety—I knew the bravest of my friends were barricaded into the House of Commons, and every avenue to it impossible. Till I heard the Horse and Foot Guards were gone to their rescue,[2] I expected nothing but some dire misfortune—and the first thing I heard this morning was that part of the town had had a fortunate escape from being burnt after ten last night—you must not expect order, Madam; I must recollect circumstances as they occur—and the best idea I can give your Ladyship of the tumult, will be to relate it as I heard it.

I had come to town in the morning on a private occasion, and found it so much as I left it, that though I saw a few blue cockades[3] here and there, I only took them for new recruits. Nobody came in; between seven and eight I saw a hack and another coach arrive at Lord Shelburne's, and thence concluded that Lord George Gordon's trumpet had brayed to no purpose. At eight I went to Gloucester House; the Duchess told me there had been a riot, and that Lord Mansfield's glasses had been broken,[4] and a bishop's,[5] but that most

---

1. When the Gordon riots began. See also HW to Mason 4 June 1780, MASON ii. 51–5, and HW to Mann 5 June 1780 for detailed accounts of what follows.

2. After marching from St George's Fields to the House of Commons the rioters pressed into the lobby of the House of Commons and attempted to force the doors of both Houses. 'The petitioners would attend to nobody but their leader. . . . For five hours together this scene of confusion continued . . . till about half past nine o'clock, when the guards coming with fixed bayonets, it [the lobby] was soon cleared' (*London Chronicle* 1–3 June, xlvii. 536).

3. At the meeting of the Protestant Association on 29 May it was unanimously passed, on Lord George Gordon's motion,

'that they might know their friends from their enemies [when the petition was presented on 2 June] . . . that every real Protestant, and friend of the petition, should come with blue cockades in their hats' (ibid. 30 May – 1 June, xlvii. 523).

4. 'Lord Mansfield had the glasses of his carriage broken, the panels beat in, and narrowly escaped with life' (Cobbett, *Parl. Hist.* xxi. 656).

5. The Bishop of Lincoln's; see below. 'The wheels of the Bishop of Lincoln's carriage were taken off, and his Lordship escaped with life, being obliged to seek shelter in the house of Mr Atkinson, an attorney, where he changed his clothes and made his escape over the leads of the adjacent houses' (ibid.). His 'carriage was broken, he himself taken into a Mr

of the populace were dispersed. About nine his R[oyal] Highness and Colonel Heywood[6] arrived—and then we heard a much more alarming account. The concourse had been incredible, and had by no means obeyed the injunctions of their apostle, or rather had interpreted the spirit instead of the letter.[7] The Duke had reached the House with the utmost difficulty,[8] and found it sunk from the temple of dignity to an asylum of lamentable objects. There were the Lords Hilsborough, Stormont, Townshend, without their bags, and with their hair dishevelled about their ears, and Lord Willoughby[9] without his periwig, and Lord Mansfield, whose glasses had been broken, quivering on the woolsack like an aspen.[10] Lord Ashburnham had been torn out of his chariot, the Bishop of Lincoln ill-treated,[11] the Duke of Northumberland had lost his watch in the holy hurly-burly,[12] and Mr Mackinsy[13] his snuff-box and spectacles. Alarm came that the mob had thrown down Lord Boston[14] and were

Atkinson's . . . in a fainting fit, and . . . obliged to escape in disguise' (ibid. 665; GM 1780, l. 267).

6. Nathaniel Heywood (d. 1808), Lt-Col. 25 May 1772; equerry 1769–80 or '81 and groom of the Bedchamber 1780 or '81–1805 to the D. of Gloucester (GM 1808, lxxviii pt i. 566; Army Lists; Royal Kalendar). In a letter (now in the possession of Lord Waldegrave at Chewton House) from Heywood and Mrs Heywood to William Frederick, 2d D. of Gloucester, 26 Aug. 1807, on the death of the Duchess of Gloucester, Heywood refers to his 'service of near forty years.'

7. At the House of Commons on 2 June Lord George had told his followers 'to be decent and orderly, at the same time to keep to their purpose! to insist on an answer to the petition that night' (London Chronicle 30 May – 3 June, xlvii. 523, 535–6). See also MASON ii. 52 n. 5.

8. But according to the London Chronicle 1–3 June, xlvii. 536, 'His Royal Highness the Duke of Gloucester, and the Dukes of Devonshire, Richmond, Roxburgh, Earl of Shelburne, Lord Camden, Bishop of Peterborough, and many other patriotic noblemen had their carriages conducted with great respect and honour to the door of the House.'

9. John Verney (later Peyto-Verney) (1738–1816), 14th Bn Willoughby de Broke, 1752.

10. 'Lord Mansfield was exceedingly terrified, and said to the Duke of Gloucester this country was undone, *that a change of administration might be good, if any coalition be made*' (*Last Journals* ii. 307). Nevertheless, when there was talk of the House of Lords' going in a body, with Lord Mansfield (who sat on the woolsack and was Speaker *pro-tempore* during the illness of the Lord Chancellor) at their head, he 'expressed his readiness if their lordships thought it proper' (Cobbett, *Parl. Hist.* xxi. 669).

11. Thomas Thurlow (1737–91), Bp of Lincoln 1779–87, of Durham 1787–91; Dean of St Paul's 1782–7; younger brother of the Lord Chancellor.

12. 'There was a gentleman with his Grace in the carriage, which gave rise to a false report that the gentleman was a Jesuit. His Grace was forced out, and in the scuffle, he lost a valuable watch and his purse' (ibid. 666). According to the *London Chronicle* 1–3 June, xlvii. 536, he 'was much ill-treated, and had his pocket picked of his watch.'

13. Hon. James Stuart Mackenzie (ca 1719–1800), brother of Lord Bute.

14. Frederick Irby (1749–1825), 2d Bn Boston, 1775; F.S.A., 1778; lord of the Bedchamber 1780–1825.

trampling him to death—which they almost did.[15] They had dis-
wigged Lord Bathurst on his answering them stoutly,[16] and told him
he was the Pope and an old woman—thus splitting Pope Joan into
two. Lord Hilsborough, on being taxed with negligence, affirmed
that the Cabinet had the day before empowered Lord North to take
precautions, but two justices[17] that were called, denied having received any orders.[18] Col. Heywood, a very stout man and luckily a
very cool one, told me he had thrice been collared, as he went by the
Duke's order to inquire what was doing in the other House; but
though he was not suffered to pass, he reasoned the mob into releas-
ing him—yet, he said, he never saw so serious an appearance and
such determined countenances. About eight the Lords adjourned,
and were suffered to go home; though the rioters declared that if
the other House did not repeal the bill, there would at night be
terrible mischief. Mr Burke's name had been given out as the object
of resentment.[19] General Conway I knew would be intrepid and not
give way—nor did he, but inspired the other House with his own

15. Cf. Cobbett, *Parl. Hist.* xxi. 656, 668–9.

16. He was 'pushed about in the rudest manner, and kicked violently on the legs' (ibid. 656).

17. 'Mr Justice Wright' and 'George Reid, Esq.' (*London Chronicle* 1–3 June, xlvii. 535): Sampson Wright (d. 1793), Kt, 1782; J.P. for Middlesex, Essex, and Surrey; successor to Sir John Fielding as magistrate of the Bow Street Public Office (BERRY i. 253 n. 16; Cobbett, *Parl. Hist.* xxi. 669, 671, 675, 684–6). George Reid (fl. ca 1780–?1810) was a merchant of 18 Argyll Street, Golden Square; his house was threatened during the Gordon riots, as he reported 8 June 1780 from his 'District of St George's, Hanover Square and St Marylebone' (*New Complete Guide to All Persons Who Have Any Trade or Concern with the City of London*, 1783; J. P. de Castro, *Gordon Riots*, 1926, p. 160; GM 1810, lxxx. 376).

18. On 3 June in the House of Lords, Chamberlain, solicitor of the Treasury and messenger for Lord North, 'informed the House that he went with a message from Lord North to Sir John Fielding on Thursday [1 June], whom he found at

Brompton; and Sir John told him he would be in town early the next morning, and appoint proper persons to attend in St George's Fields, to give him intelligence if there was any appearance of disturb-ance, and he would take measures accord-ingly' (*London Chronicle* 3–6 June, xlvii. 540; Cobbett, *Parl. Hist.* xxi. 686). Wright again testified that he had received no orders (ibid.).

19. 'Though the fact was little known the Address [presented to George III 1 May 1778 and signed by 207 Roman Catholics] emanated from the pen of Edmund Burke' (De Castro, op. cit. 6). Burke did not participate in the debate on the Catholic Relief Bill of 1778, but on 18 March 1779 he presented to the House of Commons a petition from Roman Catholics in Scotland (Cobbett, *Parl. Hist.* xix. 1137–45, xx. 322–7). During the riots on 2 June Lord George Gordon, speaking to the petitioners, 'in-formed them of the bad success their petition was like to meet with, and marked out such members as were oppos-ing it, particularly Mr Burke, the member from Bristol' (ibid. xxi. 657).

resolution. Lord George Gordon was running backwards and forwards, and from the windows of the Speaker's Chamber denouncing all that spoke against him to the mob in the lobby. Mr Conway tasked him severely both in the House and aside,[20] and Col. Murray[21] told him he was a disgrace to his family.[22] Still the members were besieged and locked up for four hours, nor could divide, as the lobby was crammed. Mr Conway and Lord Fred. Cavendish, with whom I supped afterwards,[23] told me there was a moment, when they thought they must have opened the doors and fought their way out sword in hand.[24] Lord North was very firm, and at last they got the Guards and cleared the pass.[25]

Blue banners had been waved from tops of houses at Whitehall as signals to the people, while the coaches passed, whom they should applaud or abuse. Sir Geo. Saville's[26] and Ch. Turner's[27] coaches were demolished. Ellis, whom they took for a popish gentleman, they carried prisoner to the Guildhall in Westminster, and he escaped by a ladder out of a window.[28] Lord Mahon[29] harangued the people from the balcony of a coffee-house and begged them to retire—but at past ten a new scene opened. The mob forced the Sardinian minister's[30] chapel in Lincoln's Inn Fields,[31] and gutted it. He saved

20. Conway's resoluteness is further described in De Castro, op. cit. 40.

21. James Murray (1734–94) of Strowan, brother of John, 3d D. of Atholl; cousin to Lord George Gordon; Col., 1777; governor of Fort William, 1780; Maj.-Gen., 1782; M.P. Perthshire 1773–94 (Scots Peerage i. 484).

22. See also Last Journals ii. 306–7; GM 1780, l. 269.

23. Not at Gloucester House, 'as General Conway did not go to the Duke's Court' (Last Journals ii. 317, sub 10 June 1780); possibly at Conway's or the Duke of Richmond's.

24. The House of Commons 'was in great danger from their fury for four hours, and Colonel Luttrell proposed to open the doors, which were locked, and cut their way sword in hand' (ibid. ii. 307).

25. At about 9:30 p.m. (De Castro, op. cit. 41; Last Journals ii. 307; London Chronicle 1–3 June, xlvii. 536).

26. Sir George Savile (1726–84), 8th Bt, 1743; M.P. Yorkshire 1759–83. He had

introduced the Roman Catholic Relief Bill in the House of Commons on 14 May 1778.

27. Charles Turner (?1727–83), cr. (1782) Bt; M.P. York City 1768–83 (Venn, Alumni Cantab.). He had supported Savile's bill in 1778, and on 11 April 1780 had referred in the House of Commons to Lord George's 'twist in his head . . . if anything relative to religion was mentioned' and his being 'a laughing-stock and . . . make-game of the whole House' (Cobbett, Parl. Hist. xix. 1143, xxi. 386–7).

28. For details see De Castro, op. cit. 37; Cobbett, Parl. Hist. xxi. 657; London Chronicle 1–3 June, xlvii. 536.

29. Charles Stanhope (1753–1816), styled Vct Mahon 1763–86; 3d E. Stanhope, 1786; scientist and politician.

30. Vittorio Amadeo Sallier de la Tour (1726–1800), Marchese di Cordon; Sardinian envoy to England 1774–84 (MORE 194 n. 16).

31. The chapel of SS. Anselm and Cecilia in Duke Street (now Sardinia Street), Lincoln's Inn Fields. For addi-

nothing but two chalices;[32] lost the silver lamps, etc., and the benches being tossed into the street, were food for a bonfire, with the blazing brands of which they set fire to the inside of the chapel, nor, till the Guards arrived, would suffer the engines to play. My cousin T. Walpole fetched poor Madam Cordon,[33] who was ill,[34] and guarded her in his house[35] till three in the morning, when all was quiet.

Old Haslang's[36] chapel[37] has undergone the same fate, all except the ordeal.[38] They found stores of mass-books and run tea.[39]

This is a slight and hasty sketch, Madam. On Tuesday the House of Commons is to consider the Popish laws[40]—I forgot to tell you

tional details concerning the destruction there, see MASON ii. 51–2 nn. 3–4.

32. Mrs Ann Roberts (ca 1764–1857) 'took the sacred plate from the sacristy. . . . to the priest that was hiding at the Ship Tavern, at the corner of Turnstile, Gate Street, Holborn' (The Lamp, n.s., July–Dec. 1857, p. 238).

33. Carolina d'Hoensbroeck m. (1770), as 2d wife, Vittorio Amadeo Sallier de la Tour, Marchese di Cordon (MORE 194–5 n. 16).

34. 'The lady of the Sardinian Ambassador was so frighted when the rioters set fire to the Chapel which joins to his Excellency's dwelling-house that she fainted away; and, what must greatly add to her sufferings, her Excellency is with child' (London Chronicle 3–6 June, xlvii. 538). The London Courant 12 June reported her 'much recovered of her late fright.'

35. In Lincoln's Inn Fields (HW to Mann 5 June 1780).

36. Josef Franz Xaver von Haszlang (ca 1700–83), Freiherr (later Graf) von Haszlang, Bavarian minister to England 1741–83 (MONTAGU i. 185–6 n. 25). His epitaph in Daniel Lysons, Environs of London, Vol. III, 1795, p. 358, was annotated by HW: 'Nothing was ever less deserved than the encomiums in the epitaph of that worthless man. For thirty years he kept forcible possession of a house he had taken in Jermyn Street, and being a foreign minister, the landlord could not arrest him. Once the owner untiled part of the roof to drive him out, and even that not availing, offered to forgive all the rent due, if he would but quit the house—but all in vain. I wonder the old

miscreant was not honoured with a velvet coffin above ground in Westminster Abbey, like two other ambassadors, on whom that idle punishment was inflicted for not having paid their debts.'

37. The Bavarian Chapel, though entered from Warwick Street, was behind Haszlang's house, 24, Golden Square, and had formerly been the Portuguese Chapel (Registers of the Catholic Chapels, Vol. I, ed. Weale, 1941, pp. xxi–ii, Catholic Record Society, Vol. XXXVIII).

38. About midnight the rioters stripped the Chapel 'of the various ornaments, books, etc., and made a bonfire of them in the street, but did not set fire to the building; a party of the guards were sent there also, upon which the mob went away' (London Chronicle 1–3 June, xlvii. 536). Cf. OED, sub 'ordeal' 3.

39. ' 'Tis said there were found under the altar of the Romish Chapel in Warwick Street by the mob on Friday night 16 bags of tea and a quantity of lace, worth £500, which were destroyed' (ibid. 3–6 June, xlvii. 538). 'Haslang . . . maintained himself for above thirty years by gaming, smuggling, and selling protections against arrests' (Last Journals i. 107–8, sub 1772; Town and Country Magazine, 1770, ii. 513 ff.).

40. On Tuesday, 6 June, was passed Conway's motion to consider the petitions as soon as 'the tumults subside that are now subsisting.' The House adjourned to 8 June, and on that day adjourned to 19 June (Cobbett, Parl. Hist. xxi. 663–4; Journals of the House of Commons xxxvii. 902–3).

that the Bishops not daring to appear, the Winchester Bill, which had passed the Commons, was thrown out.[41]

No saint was ever more diabolic than Lord Geo. Gordon. Eleven wretches are in prison for the outrage at Cordon's,[42] and will be hanged instead of their arch-incendiary. One person seized is a Russian officer[43] who had the impudence to claim acquaintance with the Sardinian minister and desire to be released. Cordon replied, 'Oui Monsieur, je vous connaissais, mais je ne vous connais plus.'[44] I do not know whether he is an associate of Thalestris, who seems to have snuffed a revolution in the wind.

I hear there are hopes of some temperament in Ireland.[45] Some-

41. The bill 'for exempting the city of Winchester, the county of Southampton, the town of Shrewsbury, and the county of Salop, out of the provisions of . . . "an act for regulating the quartering of soldiers during the time of the elections of members to serve in Parliament." ' It was sent by the Commons to the Lords, 1 June; on 2 June, a motion to adjourn the second reading for three months lost, 26 to 13, and it was ordered to be read a second time on 6 June, which was done (*Journals of the House of Lords* xxxvi. 140, 142, 144–5; *London Chronicle* 1–3 June, xlvii. 535). HW apparently thought the lost motion was for the second reading, not the postponement. The bill passed the Lords 22 June and received royal assent the next day (*Journals of the House of Lords*, xxxvi. 151, 154).

42. Thirteen people were arrested and were examined by Justices Addington and Wright at the Bow Street Office 3 June. William Reeves 'gave security for his future good behaviour'; Thomas Inwood 'put in bail for his appearance on Wednesday next'; and the remaining eleven were recommitted (to Clerkenwell Prison) for examination on 7 June. They were examined 5 June, when all were discharged but three who were freed by the mob 6 June (*London Chronicle* 3–8 June, xlvii. 538, 543, 545).

43. Princess Dashkov's 'natural brother Rantzau was taken in Mons. Cordon's chapel, and was reclaimed by Simonin [Simolin, Russian minister to England], and released' (HW to Mason 9 June 1780,

MASON ii. 59–60). Lady Mary Coke wrote in her 'MS Journals' 16 June 1780 that Princess Dashkov 'is suspected to have had some hand in this business. . . . as her natural brother, an officer . . . in the Russian service, was actually taken setting fire to the . . . chapel and confined. The Russian envoy demanded him the next day and he was released, as at that time there was not sufficient evidence to condemn him, since which they have entire proof, and a very strong remonstrance is gone to the Russian Court, but he made his escape the moment he got his liberty.' In the *Political Magazine*, Nov. 1780, i. 729, he is identified as 'Ronzoff,' 'natural brother to the Princess Dashkoff, and after being discharged . . . he went home to Petersburgh, where he was instantly committed prisoner to the Castle, by an order from the Empress.'

44. In the House of Lords on 23 June Lord Loughborough, who witnessed the meeting between Cordon and the Russian officer, testified that 'although the Russian claimed an acquaintance with him [Cordon] . . . and said he had dined with him, [Cordon] did not recollect to have seen him' (Cobbett, *Parl. Hist.* xxi. 750).

45. Heads of a 'bill for punishing mutiny and desertion and for the regulation of the army' were brought in the Irish House of Commons 25 May by G. P. Bushe; on 2 June the title was changed to a 'bill for the better accommodation,' etc. (n. 46 below). The bill was first read 12 Aug. (*London Chronicle* 1–3 June, xlvii. 536; *Journals of the House of Com-*

body, I forget who, has observed that the English government pretends not to *quarter* soldiers in Ireland, and therefore must be glad of a bill[46]—It is time some of our wounds should close!—or I believe, I shall soon have too much employment, instead of wanting materials for letters.

To Lady Ossory, Tuesday 6 June 1780

The last paragraph is now first printed.
Address: To the Countess of Ossory at Ampthill Park, Bedfordshire. *Postmark:* 7 IV.

Strawberry Hill, June 6, 1780.

YOU will think me amazingly callous to politics, Madam, when you see my date is from the country. In truth I came hither on Sunday to avoid the Birthday;[1] and stay, because Mr Hindley's house[2] is again to be sold by auction in half an hour;[3] and—if one ever is to have a tranquil moment again, it is very important to know who is to be my Ucalegon[4] and live at next door. I write a few lines, because I have this instant received two letters at once from your Ladyship, and must thank you for the old protest which has contracted the hue of a MS—and to answer a few of your questions, or to tell you that I am not qualified to satisfy them.

I know no more of Saint George Gordon, but that I would change

mons of . . . Ireland, 1779–80, xix. 427, 439, 488; *Statutes at Large . . . Ireland,* Vol. XI, Dublin, 1786, pp. 523–41, 19 & 20 Geo. III, c. 16).

46. Clauses III–VI in the bill referred to the billeting and quartering of soldiers.

---

1. 5 June, observed as the King's birthday. 'The Court at St James's . . . was by far the thinnest in point of number that has been remembered for years past' (*London Chronicle* 3–6 June, xlvii. 542).

2. Hindley, 'having imprudently engaged himself in large sums of money with one Ca———r, an East India captain, hath thereby ruined himself, and his seat at Twickenham, pictures, etc; are now upon sale' (J. C. Brooke to Richard

Gough, 21 June 1780, in Nichols, *Lit. Illus.* vi. 396–7).

3. 'To be . . . sold by auction by Mr Skinner . . . [6 June], at twelve, on the premises, in eight lots, that distinguished villa on the bank of the Thames . . . formerly the seat of the late Right Hon. John Earl Radnor deceased' (*Daily Adv.* 1, 6 June 1780). The 'furniture . . . plate . . . books, and other valuable effects' were sold by auction 24–26 July 1780, the sale having been postponed from 21–23 June, 3–5 July, and 17–19 July (ibid. 9, 20 June, 1, 17, 24–26 July 1780). The house was sold again at Christie's in 1792 (*World* 14 June 1792).

4. A Trojan elder whose house stood next to that of Deiphobus and was burned with it (*Æneid* ii. 311—12).

his last name into Cordon, and baptize him with a halter. We have reports here of some continuance of riots, but of late I credit nothing till after two or three rebounds. All I gleaned more of the tumult on Friday was, that the Archbishop of York, who was above stairs in a committee, hearing of Lord Mansfield's danger, flew down, rushed through the crowd, and carried off his friend in Abraham's bosom.[5] The Duke of Richmond told me this with great approbation. A Mr Holroyd,[6] a member, told the Gordon that he ought to be sent to Bedlam, but that he himself would not quit him a moment, sat by him, followed him up into the gallery—and in short, prevented his farther addresses to the mob.[7]

You ask about Mr Selwyn; have you heard his incomparable reply to Lord George Gordon, who asked him if he would choose him again for Luggershall?[8] He replied, his constituents would not—'Oh yes, if you would recommend me, they would choose me if I came from the coast of Africa'—'That is according to what part of the coast you came from: they would certainly, if you came from the Guinea Coast.'—Now, Madam, is not this true inspiration as well as true wit? Had one asked him in which of the four quarters of the world Guinea is situated, could he have told?

I knew nothing of my nephew Cholmondeley's lending or dismissing his encumbrances.[9] I shall rejoice in both. I do not allow

5. Archbishop Markham's letter describing the Gordon Riots, including this incident, is in Sir Clements Markham, *Markham Memorials*, 1913, ii. 32–5.

6. John Baker-Holroyd (1735–1821), formerly Baker, cr. (1781) Bn Sheffield, (1816) E. of Sheffield; army officer; friend of Gibbon; M.P. Coventry 1780–4, Bristol 1790–1802.

7. For this incident, which is variously reported, see also J. Paul de Castro, *Gordon Riots*, 1926, p. 40; Cobbett, *Parl. Hist.* xxi. 657; *Last Journals* ii. 307; GM 1821, xci pt i. 563.

8. Selwyn controlled the nomination for both seats for Ludgershall (L. B. Namier, *The Structure of Politics at the Accession of George III*, 2d edn, 1957, p. 148). Lord George Gordon was returned with Lord Melbourne on 11 Oct. 1774, and Selwyn and Lord Melbourne on 12 Sept. 1780.

9. The chief of Lord Cholmondeley's

many mistresses ca 1774–ca 1785 was Mrs Elliott: Grace Dalrymple (ca 1758–1823) m. (1771) John Elliott, cr. (1776) Kt and (1778) Bt, from whom she was divorced for adultery in 1774. According to Lady Mary Coke's 'MS Journals' 23 June 1778, Lady Elliott 'now lives with Lord Cholmondeley. She is with child and 'tis thought he intends to marry her.' The paternity of her daughter born in 1782 was also claimed by the Prince of Wales (BERRY i. 255–6 n. 27; *Town and Country Magazine*, 1777, ix. 625–8, where Cholmondeley is associated with 'variety [in women] without discrimination, and intrigue without attachment'; *Notes and Queries*, 1916, 12th ser. i. 233; Robert D. Bass, *The Green Dragoon*, New York, 1957, pp. 192, 385). The reference here is possibly to her going to France: she returned in June 1781 (*Carlisle MSS* 498, 509.)

that there was anything execrable in *the play*[10] but the actors.[11] I was charmed with both prologue[12] and epilogue,[13] and with the delivery of both.[14] I have read neither: but liked the latter full as well as the former. I may change my opinion on examining them.

I do believe there is some truth in Miss K.'s story.[15] I know no more of the haggle between Lady I.[15a] and your cousin Duke, nor a syllable of her daughter, not even who the baronet is. In fact, I do not look at all after the next generation and their valentines, except my own tribe, and they are so numerous, and there have been so many contretemps about them, that I abstract my attention as much as I can, and leave the private as well as the public to chance, who at least has some decision, which I see in nobody else.

We had an exceedingly pretty fire-work last night on the bank of the Thames at that most beautiful of all spots that was Mr Giles's[16]

10. Lady Craven's *Miniature Picture*, first acted at Drury Lane 24 May 1780. HW saw it with the author and a group of friends on the second night, 26 May; see his letter to Mason 28 May 1780, MASON ii. 43–5. For HW's copies of the play (the first of which is now WSL), see Hazen, *Cat. of HW's Lib.* 1810. 33. 2; 2363.

11. The cast is given in Genest vi. 134.

12. By Sheridan, who thought so well of it himself that he later 'took the first 30 lines and added 2 more' to make the prologue to his *Pizarro* (ibid. 135; MASON ii. 44 n. 12).

13. By Joseph Jekyll (1754–1837), wit and politician (ibid. ii. 44 n. 16).

14. The prologue was 'spoken in perfection by [Thomas] King' (ibid. ii. 44). HW liked the epilogue 'still better'; it 'was full as well delivered by Mrs Abington' (ibid.).

15. Possibly Anna Maria Keppel, HW's grandniece born in 1759; she did not marry until 1790. The 'story' probably concerns Lord Ossory's first cousin, the 3d D. of Dorset, who was 35 and unmarried. Lady Mary Coke wrote ('MS Journals' 23 June 1779): 'a person not long ago told me that Lady Irwin was grown very gay . . . it was observed she made up to the Duke of Dorset thinking perhaps her great income might tempt him to marry her.' Lady Irvine, however, had four marriageable daughters

(the eldest being already married to HW's cousin, Lord Beauchamp): her youngest daughter married in 1787 Sir John Ramsden, 4th Bt; this match was rumoured in 1785 (Coke, 'MS Journals' 16 Nov. 1785), and Sir John and the Duke of Dorset may have been considered as prospects for the elder daughters.

15a. Or *J.*: HW's *I* and *J* at this time are identical.

16. Daniel Giles (ca 1725–1800), silk merchant of 21, Old South Sea House and of New Bond Street; lived in New Broad Street, London; director of the Bank of England from 1778, its deputy-governor 1793–5, and governor 1796–7. His villa at Twickenham, Little Marble Hill, was the cottage, remodelled and enlarged, occupied by Mrs Clive before she came to Little SH ca 1754. She was succeeded by —— Barlow, Giles (who left the house after his wife died in Nov. 1778), Franco, and Lady Diana Beauclerk (*Court and City Register; Royal Kalendar;* GM 1800, lxx pt ii. 798; *New Complete Guide to All Persons Who Have Any Trade or Concern with the City of London,* 1783, p. 237; *London Chronicle* 10–12 Nov. 1778, xliv. 459; R. S. Cobbett, *Memorials of Twickenham,* 1872, pp. 245–6; MASON ii. 272; BERRY ii. 36 n. 4; HW to Mann 12 Oct. 1776; Hilda F. Finberg, 'Jewish Residents in Eighteenth-century Twickenham,' in

and is now one Franco's[17] a Jew, who gave the entertainment in honour of the day. I carried Lady Browne thither; my horses were frightened at the rockets, and we stepped out of the chaise and stood by the river, till we were blighted by the east wind, and smothered by the smoke, for our *freeborn weather,* that on Monday and Friday was as hot as Lord George, is now as cold as the Duke of Devonshire.

I shall go to town tomorrow, and you see, Madam, do not decline my duty, when I have a word to say—but not having a grain of penetration, I did apprehend my summer letters would be very barren. I have been so far wise, that I never would embark in anything that made it expedient to maintain a character, which is a horrid burthen on an Englishman. I may mistake and guess wrong, and change my mind, or talk nonsense, with impunity. I shall not be thought more trifling than usual. And is not it some comfort not to be the worse for wear?

⟨Mr Hin⟩dley's is sold for £3600, just one thousand less than was offered last year. My new neighbour is a Mr Webbe[18]—I do not know him—and that is better than somebody I might have known—and not liked.

To Lady Ossory, Wednesday 7 June 1780

Address: To the Countess of Ossory at Ampthill Park, Bedfordshire. *Postmark:* 7 IV. GC.

Wednesday, five o'clock, June 7, 1780.

I AM heartily glad I am come to town, though never was a less delicious place; but there was no bearing to remain philosophically in the country, and hear the thousand rumours of every hour,

Transactions of the Jewish Historical Society of England, 1952, xvi. 130).

17. Probably Raphael Franco (d. 1781), 'of the firm of Jacob, Moses, and Raphael Franco, City merchants of Fenchurch Street'; painted by Gainsborough ca 1780 (Finberg, op. cit. 130–1; E. K. Waterhouse, *Preliminary Check List of Portraits by Thomas Gainsborough,* in the *Walpole Society,* 1953, xxxiii. 41; Cobbett, op. cit. 245, who gives the name as 'David Franco').

18. Nathaniel Webb (1725–86), of Saville Row; M.P. Taunton 1768–75; Ilchester 1775–80 (*Court and City Register,* 1779, p. 66; GM 1786, lvi pt ii. 1001). In the Twickenham Rate Books for 1783 and 1784 there are the entries: 'Webb, late Hindley Fred[eric]k for house and land' and 'Webb Nath[anie]l Esq., late Hindley, for house and land.' The Rate Books 1778–82 are missing. The house (Radnor House) was sold ca 1784 to Sir Francis Basset, who appears in the Rate

and not know whether one's friends and relations were not destroyed. Yesterday Newgate was burnt, and other houses,[1] and Lord Sandwich near massacred.[2] At Hyde Park Corner I saw guards at the Lord President's[3] door, and in Piccadilly met George and the Signorina, whom I wondered he ventured there. He came into my chaise in a fury, and told me Lord Mansfield's house is in ashes,[4] and that 5000 men were marched to Kanewood[5]—It is true, and that 1000 of the Guards are gone after them. A camp of 10,000 is forming in Hyde Park as fast as possible,[6] and the Berkshire militia is just arrived. Wedderburne and Lord Stormont are threatened, and I do not know who.[7] The Duchess of Beaufort[8] sent an hour ago to tell me Lord Ashburnham had just advertised her that he is threatened, and was sending away his poor bed-ridden Countess[9] and children;[10]

Books under 1785: 'Bassett, Sir Fra[nci]s, late Webb Esq.' (see also Edward Ironside, History . . . of Twickenham, 1797, p. 142, Bibliotheca Topographica Britannica, Vol. X; MORE back end-paper; Cobbett, op. cit. 293–4; BERRY ii. 222, and passim; Daniel Lysons, Environs of London, Vol. III, 1795, p. 574).

1. Eye-witness accounts of the fires are quoted in J. Paul de Castro, The Gordon Riots, 1926, pp. 69–109, passim. This book is the chief source for the annotation about the riots in this and the following letters. See also Christopher Hibbert, King Mob, Cleveland, Ohio, 1958.

2. On his way from the Admiralty to the House of Lords his chariot was stopped at the corner of Bridge Street and Parliament Street. To escape from the mob he took refuge in a coffee-house and the Guards protected him. His face was cut (De Castro, p. 79).

3. Lord Bathurst's, Apsley House, escaped destruction, although it was one of the buildings named to Lord Stormont as threatened (ibid. 74).

4. The mob attacked Mansfield's house in Bloomsbury Square about 11 P.M.; the house was first pillaged and then burned (letter by Abp Markham, Mansfield's neighbour, cited ante 6 June 1780, n. 5; MASON ii. 57 n. 20). Mansfield later took Topham Beauclerk's house in Great Russell Street, Bloomsbury Square (London Courant 21 Aug.; post 17 Dec. 1780).

5. Caen Wood, Lord Mansfield's seat, between Highgate and Hampstead. The numbers 5000 and 1000 are gross exaggerations: 'Knowing that Kenwood is threatened with . . . destruction, I have wrote to Lord Amherst for a detachment of Light Horse to be sent there to guard the avenues' (Stormont to George III 11 A.M., 7 June, Corr. Geo. III v. 75).

6. The Hertfordshire militia marched into Hyde Park and pitched their tents, the encampment consisting of the Royal Scots, the Queen's, and four regiments of militia. The forming of the camp and the arrival of the Hampshire militia are mentioned in the London Chronicle 6–10 June, xlvii. 550–3.

7. Stormont wrote to George III (loc. cit.) that 'my house was to be attacked next.' In his note to the War Office 6 June, he names people and buildings threatened, and adds: 'There is also reason to suspect that the houses of Lord North, and his Majesty's other ministers may be threatened' (De Castro, p. 74).

8. The Dowager Duchess: Elizabeth Berkeley (ca 1719–99), m. (1740) Lord Charles Noel Somerset, 4th D. of Beaufort, 1745. She was HW's neighbour in Berkeley Square (ante 27 Dec. 1775 n. 6).

9. Elizabeth Crowley (ca 1728–81), m. (1756) John Ashburnham, 2d E. of Ashburnham, 1737. She had been an invalid since 1776: 'since she went into the

and the Duchess begged to know what I proposed to do. I immediately went to her, and quieted her, and assured her we are as safe as we can be anywhere and as little obnoxious; but if she was alarmed, I advised her to remove to Notting Hill, where Lady Mary is absent.[11] The Duchess said the mob were now in Saville Row; we sent thither and so they are, round Col. Woodford's[12] who gave the Guards orders to fire at Lord Mansfield's, where six at least of the rioters were killed.[13]

The mob are now armed, having seized the stores in the Artillery Ground.[14]

If anything can surprise your Ladyship, it will be what I am going to tell you. Lord George Gordon went to Buckingham House this morning and asked an audience of the King—Can you be more surprised still?—He was refused.[15]

I must finish, for I am going about the town to learn and see and

country, [she] was seized so suddenly with either the gout or rheumatism in her head as to deprive her entirely of her senses' (Coke, 'MS Journals' 8 Aug. 1776). During the riots she 'was carried out in the night in blankets' (ibid. 10 June 1780).

10. A son, aged 19, and four daughters, aged 21, 18, 17, and 14; see George Kearsley, *Peerage*, [1796], i. 101; Burke, *Peerage*, 1867, p. 42.

11. Lady Mary Coke was returning from a visit to Lord and Lady Strafford in Yorkshire; she wrote to them at 4 o'clock on Thursday, 8 June, from Notting Hill, shortly after her arrival (Coke, 'MS Journals' 7–8 June 1780).

12. John Woodford (d. 1800), Capt. and Lt-Col., 1st Foot Guards, 1776, and Lt-Col. of the 6th (Gordon) Fencible Infantry (*Scots Peerage* iv. 555; DNB, *sub* Woodford, Sir Alexander George; De Castro, pp. 99, 187). According to the *London Chronicle* 22–24 June, xlvii. 606, his house was saved by an alert servant, who, hearing some of the rioters planning to destroy it, 'ran home . . . and . . . tore the brass plate with his master's name on it, from the door, shut up every window in the house and wrote and stuck up a bill, "This house to let." '

13. Woodford, who received his orders from Durden, a magistrate for Middlesex, gave the order to his soldiers between 4 and 5 A.M. on 7 June, but it was not until later in the day that the military was given discretionary power to preserve order (De Castro, pp. 99, 172–5). The number killed is variously reported.

14. A letter from Lord Hillsborough to Lord Amherst 7 June 1780 (De Castro, p. 135) shows an awareness of the rumour: 'If the mobs are possessed of the Artillery Arms it will be necessary to have upon each bridge end two 4-inch howitzers with grape shot.' The New Artillery Ground, to which HW here refers, was 'near the upper end of Moorfields' (*London and Its Environs Described*, 1761, i. 202–3).

15. George III's minute (partly in his own hand, the rest in Stormont's) reads: 'It is impossible for his Majesty to see Lord George Gordon until he has given sufficient proof of his loyalty and allegiance by employing those means which he says are in his power to quell the present disturbances and restore peace to this capital.' It is endorsed by George III: 'Substance of this minute to be declared by Lord Stormont to Lord G. Gordon in the Porter's Lodge. June 7th, 1780' (*Corr. Geo. III* v. 76). Cf. *London Chronicle* 6–8 June, xlvii. 550.

hear—Kane Wood is saved; a regiment on march met the rioters.[16]

It will probably be a black night—I am decking myself with blue ribbands like a May-day garland[17]—horsemen are riding by with muskets. I am sorry I did not bring the armour of Francis I to town, as I am to guard a Duchess Dowager and an heiress[18]—will it not be romantically generous if I yield the latter to my nephew?[19]

From my garrison in Berkeley Square.

PS. The pious insurgents will soon have a military chest. They took forty-five guineas from Charles Turner yesterday.[20]

To Lady Ossory, Thursday 8 June 1780

Second letter dated 7 June, actually written at 2 A.M. on 8 June.

Wednesday night, past two in the morning, June 7 [i.e., 8], 1780.

AS it [is] impossible to go to bed (for Lady Betty Compton has hoped I would not this very minute, which, next to her asking the contrary, is the thing not to be refused) I cannot be better employed than in proving how much I think of your Ladyship at the

16. A detachment of Light Horse (n. 5, above). According to the report of Lt Bygrove, 16th Light Dragoons, he with 27 men 'marched . . . on Wednesday 7th inst. to Caen Wood, where I dispersed about 60 of the rioters who had an intention of setting fire to Lord Mansfield's house. I returned from this duty at 8 o'clock in the evening of the same day' (De Castro, pp. 112–13). On 11 June 100 men were stationed at Caen Wood (ibid. 265).

17. 'The cockade was adopted by many for self-preservation' (ibid. 54). On Thursday, 8 June, was circulated a handbill urging people to 'abstain from wearing blue cockades, as these ensigns are now assumed by a set of miscreants whose purpose is to burn this city and plunder its inhabitants' (London Chronicle 8–10 June, xlvii. 558).

18. The Duchess of Beaufort's granddaughter, Lady Elizabeth Compton (1760–1835), m. (1782) Lord George Augustus Henry Cavendish, cr. (1831) E. of Burlington.

19. Lord Cholmondeley; cf. post 4 July 1781.

20. The 'whole city was laid under contribution' (Thomas Holcroft, A Plain and Succinct Narrative of the Gordon Riots, ed. G. G. Smith, in Emory University Publications: Sources and Reprints, 2d ser., Atlanta, 1944, p. 26), exactions being made on the pretext of burying the dead, 'for the honour of religion,' to prevent damage or destruction to property, etc. (London Chronicle 8–10 June, xlvii. 554; Mason ii. 57–8). As Turner was leaving the House of Commons on 'Wednesday,' 7 June, he 'was exceedingly insulted and ill-treated by the mob, some of whom robbed him of his watch and purse, containing upwards of twenty guineas, and a bank note, also two rings, one of which belonged to one of his ancestors, who was Lord Mayor of London at the time of the great fire

most horrible moment I ever saw. You shall judge. I was at Gloucester House between nine and ten. The servants announced a great
fire; the Duchess, her daughters[1] and I went to the top of the house,
and beheld, not only one but two vast fires, which we took for the
King's Bench[2] and Lambeth;[3] but the latter was the new prison,[4]
and the former at least was burning at midnight. Colonel Heywood
came in and acquainted his R.H. that nine houses in Great Queen
Street had been gutted and the furniture burnt; and he had *seen* a
great Catholic distiller's[5] at Holbourn Bridge broken open and all
the casks staved—and since the house has been set on fire. At ten I
went to Lord Hertford's,[6] and found him and his sons charging
muskets. Lord Rockingham[7] has 200 soldiers in his house and is
determined to defend it.[8] Thence I went to General Conway's,[9] and
in a moment a servant came in and said there was a great fire just
by. We went to the street door and thought it was St Martin's Lane
in flames, but it is either the Fleet prison[10] or the distiller's. I forgot
that in the court of Gloucester House I met Col. Jennings who told
me there had been an engagement at the Royal Exchange to defend

in 1666' (*London Chronicle* 8–10 June,
xlvii. 560). Probably HW and the newspaper refer to the same incident, despite
the discrepancy of one day in the two
accounts.

———

1. The three Ladies Waldegrave.
2. The King's Bench prison, Southwark
(MASON ii. 55 n. 2).
3. The Archbishop of Canterbury's
palace at Lambeth was marked for destruction, but escaped damage because a
heavy guard was posted there from 6
June.
4. The New Bridewell, Surrey, a short
distance from the King's Bench (*London Courant* 9 June).
5. The distillery on Holborn Hill of
Thomas Langdale (ca 1713–90) (MASON
ii. 56 n. 16; Catholic Record Society, Vol.
XII: *Obituaries*, 1913, p. 38), who received
almost £19,000 for damages (George Rudé,
Wilkes and Liberty, Oxford, 1962, p. 4).
6. In Grosvenor Street (*Royal Kalendar*, 1780, p. 19). For Hertford's six sons,
see Burke, *Peerage*, 1953, pp. 1047–9.
7. Who had introduced the Roman
Catholic Relief Bill of 1778 in the House
of Lords.

8. 'The situation of Lord Rockingham's
house in Grosvenor Square carries with
it every appearance of its being a seat
of war. Every front room of the house
is full of soldiers, prepared for the reception of the mob, and his Lordship's
stables are turned into barracks, in which
troops of cavalry are continually in
readiness for action' (*London Chronicle*
8–10 June, xlvii. 553). The Marquess of
Carmarthen was in Rockingham's house
'most parts of the nights of Tuesday and
Wednesday the 6 and 7. We had a hundred soldiers there, and near as many
more gentlemen, servants, etc., armed'
(D. of Leeds, *Political Memoranda*, ed.
Browning, Camden Society, n.s., Vol.
XXXV, 1884, p. 33).
9. In Warwick Street, Charing Cross
(*Royal Kalendar*, 1780, p. 56).
10. The mob had started to burn the
Fleet Prison about 1 A.M. on June 7
but had delayed action to permit the
prisoners to remove their effects (J. Paul
de Castro, *Gordon Riots*, 1926, pp. 110,
136–7).

the Bank[11] and that the Guards had shot sixty of the mob; I have since heard seventy,[12] for I forgot to tell your Ladyship that at a *great* council held this evening at the Queen's house at which Lord Rockingham and the Duke of Portland[13] were present,[14] military execution was ordered,[15] for in truth the justices dare not act. After supper I returned to Lady Hertford, finding Charing Cross and the Haymarket and Piccadilly illuminated from fear, though all this end of the town is hitherto perfectly quiet, lines being drawn across the Strand and Holbourn to prevent the mob coming westward. Henry and William Conways[16] [*sic*] arrived and had seen the populace break open the toll-houses on Blackfryars Bridge and carry off bushels of halfpence which fell about the streets, and then they set fire to the toll-houses.[17] General Conway's porter has seen five distinct conflagrations.[18]

Lady Hertford's cook came in, white as this paper. *He is a German Catholic;*[19] he said his house had been attacked, his furniture burnt,

11. There were two attacks on the Bank of England: the first, to which HW refers, between 11 and 12 P.M., 7 June; the second, between 3 and 4 A.M. 8 June (MASON ii. 56–7 n. 17).

12. There are no accurate figures of the casualties at the Bank; see the discussion ibid., and Kirgate's estimate of 'not above a dozen' below.

13. William Henry Cavendish Bentinck (1738–1809), 3d D. of Portland, 1762; M.P., lord chamberlain of the Household 1765–6; lord lieutenant of Ireland, 1782; first lord of the Treasury (prime minister), 1783, 1807–9.

14. 'All Privy Councillors, though in Opposition, were summoned. Lord Rockingham and the Duke of Portland went.' At this meeting 'it was determined not to shut up the courts nor proclaim martial law, but to empower the military to act at their discretion, on which Lord Rockingham and the Duke of Portland left the Council' (*Last Journals* ii. 311).

15. The second Privy Council of 7 June ordered 'the military to act without waiting for directions from the civil magistrates and to use force for dispersing the illegal and tumultuous assemblies of the people' (*New Annual Register*, 1780, 'Principal Occurrences,' p. 53). The news-papers interpreted this order as 'putting the cities of London and Westminster under martial law' (*Daily Adv.* 9 June), but this was not legally the case (De Castro, op. cit. 172–5, 126–8, 185–6; MASON ii. 58 n. 27).

16. Hon. William Conway (later Seymour-Conway) (1760–1837), Lord Hertford's sixth son; M.P. Coventry 1783–4, Downton 1785–90, Orford 1790–6 (Burke, *Peerage*, 1953, pp. 1047–8; Collins, *Peerage*, 1812, ii. 565–6; birth notice in GM 1760, xxx. 489, which incorrectly records a daughter).

17. Which were 'reduced to ashes.' On the following morning 'a party of the mob were busily employed in carrying away their hats and pockets full of halfpence, which they dug out of the ruins of the toll-gatherers' houses on Blackfriars Bridge' (*London Chronicle* 6–10 June, xlvii. 552, 554). See also MASON ii. 56 n. 10.

18. 'Last night there were no less than fourteen places on fire at one time, in different parts of the town' (*London Chronicle* loc. cit.).

19. An error for 'Protestant'; see HW to Mason 9 June 1780, MASON ii. 56. Vernon Smith followed the MS and printed 'German Catholic'; Cunningham, followed

that he had saved one child and left another with his wife whom he could not get out; and that not above ten or twelve persons had assaulted his house. I could not credit this, at least was sure it was an episode that had no connection with the general insurrection, and was at most some pique of his neighbours. I sent my own footman[20] to the spot in Woodstock Street;[21] he brought word there had been eight or ten apprentices who made the riot, that two life-guard-men had arrived and secured four of the enemies.[22] It seems the cook had refused to illuminate like the rest of the street. Tomorrow I suppose his Majesty King George Gordon will order their release; they will be inflated with having been confessors, and turn heroes.

On coming home I visited the Duchess Dowager and my fair ward —and am heartily tired with so many expeditions, for which I little imagined I had youth enough left.

We expect three or four more regiments tomorrow, besides some troops of horse and militia already arrived. We are menaced with countersquadrons from the country.[23] There will, I fear, be much blood spilt before peace is restored. The Gordon has already surpassed Massaniello,[24] who I do not remember set his own capital on fire. Yet I assure your Ladyship there is no panic. Lady Ailesbury has been at the play[25] in the Haymarket, and the Duke and my four nieces[26] at Ranelagh this evening. For my part, I think the *common*

by Toynbee, silently corrected to 'German Protestant.' The cook was Ferdinand Schomberg of Woodstock Street, Oxford Road. Enoch Fleming and John Morris were found guilty 3 July 1780 of 'feloniously entering [Schomberg's house] . . . and burning and destroying the furniture thereof.' On 8 June 1781, in a suit to recover £800 for damage done to his house during the riots, Schomberg was awarded £400 (*London Chronicle* 1–4 July 1780, 9–12 June 1781, xlviii. 6, xlix. 554).

20. David Monnerat or James Sibley.

21. South of Oxford Street and west of New Bond Street.

22. Justice George Reid reported at noon 8 June: 'At about two this morning a small house in Woodstock Street was plundered and set on fire. Capt. Mosely of the 17th was very active in his endeavours to save it, and took two men in the act of plundering and burning whom he

brought to me and whom I immediately conveyed to the Guard. Soon after I took two more whom there was great reason to suspect had been concerned in the same business. They were all directed to be conveyed to the Tilt Yard Guard' (De Castro, op. cit. 160).

23. There were reports, which proved false, that the rioters would be joined by Lord George's supporters from Birmingham, Essex, Kent, and Scotland (ibid. 195; *Last Journals* ii. 311–2).

24. Tommaso Aniello (1620–47), called Masaniello, a Neapolitan fisherman who in 1647 led a successful revolt of the Neapolitans against Spanish misrule (*Enciclopedia italiana*).

25. Home's *Douglas*, Colman's *Manager in Distress,* and Garrick's *Miss in Her Teens* (*London Chronicle* 6–8 June, xlvii. 547).

26. The three Ladies Waldegrave and probably Anna Maria Keppel.

diversions of these last four-and-twenty hours are sufficient to content any moderate appetite; and as it is now three in the morning, I shall wish you good night and try to get a little sleep myself, if Lord George Macbeth has not murdered it all—I own I shall not soon forget the sight I saw from the top of Gloucester House!

Thursday morning after breakfast.

I do not know whether to call the horrors of the night greater or less than I thought. My printer[27] who has been out all night and on the spots of action, says, not above a dozen were killed at the Royal Exchange, some few elsewhere; at the King's Bench he does not know how many[28]—but in other respects the calamities are dreadful. He saw many houses set on fire, women and children screaming, running out of doors with what they could save, and knocking one another down with their loads in the confusion. Barnard's Inn is burnt,[29] and some houses, mistaken for Catholic. Kirgate says, most of the rioters are apprentices, and plunder and drink have been their chief objects, and both women and men are still lying dead drunk about the streets—brandy is preferable to enthusiasm. I trust many more troops will arrive today. What families ruined! What wretched wives and mothers! What public disgrace!—ay! and where, and when, and how will all this confusion end? and what shall we be, when it is concluded?—I remember the Excise, and the Gin Act,[30] and the rebels at Derby, and Wilkes's interlude,[31] and the French at Plimouth[32]—or I should have a very bad memory—but I never till last night saw London and Southwark in flames!

After dinner.

It is a moment, Madam, when to be surprised is not surprising. But what will you say to the House of Commons meeting by twelve

27. Kirgate.

28. 'Two or three persons are said to have perished in the King's Bench Prison during the conflagration there; they were drinking in the cellar, and got so intoxicated that they were unable to come out' (*London Chronicle* 8–10 June, xlvii. 553).

29. An inn of Chancery; it was only partly burnt (De Castro, op. cit. 134, 238–9).

30. The Excise scheme of 1733 and the Gin Act of 1736 were unpopular measures which provoked loud opposition (MANN i. 187 n. 32; iv. 48 n. 17).

31. In 1768, when the cry of 'Wilkes and Liberty' accompanied rioting in the Middlesex election.

32. In 1779, when the combined French and Spanish fleet entered the Channel and might have taken Plymouth had it dared.

o'clock today, and adjourning, ere fifty members were arrived, to Monday sevennight![33]—so adieu all government, but the sword!

Will your Ladyship give me credit when I heap contradictions on absurdities—will you believe such confusion and calamities, and yet think there is no consternation?—well, only hear—My niece Mrs Keppel with her three daughters drove since noon over Westminster Bridge, through St George's Fields, where the King's Bench is smoking, over London Bridge, passed the Bank, and came the whole length of the City! They have been here, and say the people *look* very unquiet—but can one imagine that they would be smiling? Old Lady Albemarle who followed me in few minutes from Gloster House, was robbed at Mrs Keppel's door in Pall Mall between ten and eleven by a horseman.[34] Sparrow,[35] one of the delivered convicts, who was to have been hanged this morning, is said to have been shot yesterday as he was spiriting up the rioters. Kirgate has just heard in the Park, that the Protestant Association disavow the seditious, and will take up arms against them[36]—If we are saved, it will be so as by fire.

I shall return to my own castle tomorrow—I had not above four hours' sleep last night, and must get some rest. General Conway is enraged at the adjournment,[37] and will go away too. Many coaches

33. 19 June (*Journals of the House of Commons* xxxvii. 903; *Last Journals* ii. 312; Cobbett, *Parl. Hist.* xxi. 664; *London Chronicle* 8–10 June, xlvii. 553, which reports 'about 80 members' present).

34. The horseman 'asked for her purse which she says had in it five and forty guineas; after she had given it him, he said he would go with her home for that no farther harm should happen to her' (Coke, 'MS Journals' 9 June 1780).

35. John Sparrow was freed by the rioters 7 June when Newgate was burnt. He had been convicted on 5 April of assault and robbery (*London Chronicle* 4–6 April, xlvii. 333; MASON ii. 60 n. 43; *post* 10 June 1780). 'On Wednesday evening the Hertfordshire militia stopped two men at Barnet, on suspicion of their being deserters; but they proved, by their own confession, to be Sparrow, late sergeant of the first regiment of foot guards, and his companion, who were to have suffered yesterday [8 June] at Tyburn. They were both safely lodged in Hertford

gaol. . . . One of the persons who was to have been executed yesterday is said to have been shot on Wednesday night last' (*London Chronicle* 8–10 June, xlvii. 553). He apparently escaped, was recaptured and committed to New Prison in May, 1782, and in Dec. 1782 was pardoned 'on condition of serving in one of his Majesty's regiments of foot in the West Indies' (ibid. 9–21 May, 24–26 Dec. 1782, li. 452, 486, lii. 611).

36. In a notice distributed on 7 June, probably by the Protestant Association, the rioters were denounced as 'a set of miscreants whose purpose is to burn this city, and plunder its inhabitants,' and who wore blue cockades 'to screen themselves.' All 'peaceable and well-disposed persons' were accordingly asked not to wear the blue cockades. The rumour of taking up arms against the seditious was probably derived from this notice.

37. He had 'intended to move to repeal' the 'popish laws' on 8 June (*Last Journals* ii. 312).

and chaises did leave London yesterday. My intelligence will not be so good nor so immediate—but you will not want correspondents. Disturbances are threatened again for tonight, and some probably will happen, but there are more troops, and less alacrity in the out-laws.

To Lady Ossory, Friday 9 June 1780

Address: To the Countess of Ossory at Ampthill Park, Bedfordshire. *Postmark:* 9 IV.

Berkeley Square, June 9 at noon, 1780.

ALL has been quiet tonight as far as we know in this region—but not without blood being spilt yesterday. The rioters attacked the Horse Guards about six in Fleet Street and not giving them time to load, were repelled by the bayonet. Twenty fell, thirty-five were wounded and sent to the hospital where two died directly. Three of the Guards were wounded and a young officer named Majoribank.[1] Mr Conway's footman told me he was on a message at Lord Amherst's[2] when the Guards returned and that their bayonets were steeped in blood.

I heard too at my neighbour Duchess's whither I went at one in the morning, that, the Protestant Associators, disguised with blue cockades as friends, had fallen on the rioters in St George's Fields and killed many[3]—I do not warrant the truth, but I did hear often in the evening that there had been slaughter in the Borough,[4] where a great public-house had been destroyed, and a house at Redriffe and another at Islington. Zeal has entirely thrown off the mask and owned its name, Plunder.[5] Its offspring have extorted money from several houses with threats of firing them as Catholic. Apprentices and

1. Apparently the John Majoribanks who was ensign in the army 12 Nov. 1779 and in the First Foot Guards 3 Feb. 1780 (*Army Lists*).

2. Lord Amherst, as commander-in-chief of the Army, had quarters in the Horse Guards, Whitehall.

3. This rumour, which HW repeated in his letter to Mason 9 June 1780 'at night' in less guarded terms, has not been corroborated.

4. That is, Southwark.

5. The *London Courant* 10 June 1780, after mentioning some of the wilder rumours of the day, said that 'Men of common observation . . . honestly confessed that all the tumults and all the outrages had been committed by less than 500 men, whose principle was impiety and whose object was plunder.'

Irish chairmen and all kind of outlaws have been the most active. Some hundreds are actually dead about the streets with the spirits they plundered at the distiller's; the low women knelt and sucked them as they ran from the staved casks.[6]

It was reported last night that the primate George Gordon is fled to Scotland[7]—for aught I know he may not be so far off as Grosvenor Place. All is rumour and exaggeration—and yet it would be difficult to exaggerate the horrors of Wednesday night: a town taken by storm could alone exceed them.

I am going to Strawberry this instant, exhausted with fatigue, for I have certainly been on my feet longer these last eight-and-forty hours than in forty days before. I forgot to tell your Ladyship that as I came to town I saw in chalk on a hack at Hammersmith, *God blast the Pope*—now the soldiers tear away blue cockades[8]—and when I return next, I expect to read on the walls, *De par le Roi, Regiment de Picardie.*[9]

Adieu! Madam: allow my pen a few holidays, unless the storm recommences—

To Lady Ossory, Saturday 10 June 1780

Strawberry Hill, Saturday night, late.

WAS not I cruelly out of luck, Madam, to have been fishing in troubled waters for two days for your Ladyship's entertainment, and to have come away very few hours before the great pike

6. 'Numbers . . . died with inebriation, especially at the distilleries of the unfortunate Mr Langdale, from whose vessels the liquors ran down the middle of the street, was taken up by pailfuls, and held to the mouths of the besotted multitude; many of whom killed themselves with drinking non-rectified spirits, and were burnt or buried in the ruins. . . . The same scenes of beastly drunkenness happened in many other places' (Thomas Holcroft, *A Plain and Succinct Narrative of the Gordon Riots*, ed. G. G. Smith, in *Emory University Publications: Sources and Reprints*, 2d ser., Atlanta, 1944, p. 29).

7. A false rumour.

8. 'People were yesterday evening ordered to destroy their blue cockades, and several men who did not immediately comply have been wounded by the troops. The order has taken full effect, and no person with that badge appears' (Col. Charles Stuart to Lord Bute [9] June 1780, quoted in De Castro, *Gordon Riots*, 1926, p. 183).

9. There were rumours that the French had fostered the riots and would invade England: 'Orders were sent down to Admiral Geary to Portsmouth last night to put to sea immediately, for fear the enemy should take advantage of our intestine commotions and attempt to land a body of troops on this island' (*London Chronicle* 6–8 June, xlvii. 552).

was hooked?[1] Well, to drop metaphor, here are Garth's lines reversed.

> Thus little villains oft submit to fate,
> That great ones may enjoy the world in state—[2]

Four convicts on the eve of execution are let loose from Newgate,[3] and Lord George Gordon is sent to the Tower. If he is hanged, the old couplet will recover its credit—for Mr Wedderburne is Chief Justice.[4]

I flatter myself I shall receive a line from your Ladyship tomorrow morning: I am impatient to hear what you think of *black Wednesday*—I know how much you must have been shocked, but I long to read your own expressions; when you answer, then one is conversing. My sensations are very different from what they were. While in the thick of the conflagration, I was all indignation and a thousand passions. Last night when sitting silently alone, horror rose as I cooled—and grief succeeded, and then all kinds of gloomy presages. For some time people have said, where will all this end? I as often replied, where will it begin?—It is now begun, with a dreadful overture; and I tremble to think what the chorus may be! The sword reigns at present—and saved the capital! What is to depose the sword? —is it not to be feared on the other hand, that other swords may be lifted up?—What probability that everything will subside quietly into the natural channel?—nay, how narrow will that channel be,

1. HW left London for SH shortly after noon 9 June, after writing to Lady Ossory. Lord George Gordon was taken into custody at his house in Welbeck Street about five o'clock and was taken to the Horse Guards for examination before being lodged in the Tower.

2. 'Where little villains must submit to fate' (Samuel Garth, *The Dispensary*, 1699, Canto i. 9–10). HW also modifies this couplet in his letter to Mason 27 May 1775, Mason i. 204.

3. Three (*London Chronicle* 1–3 June, xlvii. 534; Coke, 'MS Journals' 13 June 1780) or four (HW; *London Courant* 7 June) convicts under sentence to be hanged at Tyburn 8 June were freed by the rioters when Newgate was burnt 7 June. The names of the three are given in the *London Chronicle*, loc. cit. One of them, John Sparrow, is mentioned *ante* 8 June 1780. James Earley was re-

taken 'at a house in George Street, Bethnal Green,' 11 June and hanged 22 July (*London Courant* 14 June; *London Chronicle* 15–18 July, xlviii. 50). The third, John Carr, may be the unnamed convict under sentence of death who was hanged 9 June after being captured while trying to destroy some of the remains of Newgate (*London Courant* 10 June) or shot by the soldiers (Coke, 'MS Journals' 13 June 1780; *London Chronicle* 8–10 June, xlvii. 553). For the crimes for which the three were convicted, see Mason ii. 60 n. 43.

4. On 9 June, the day Lord George Gordon was arrested, Wedderburn was appointed lord chief justice of the Common Pleas and sworn a member of the Privy Council (*London Chronicle* 13–15 June, xlvii. 569). HW implies that Wedderburn was a greater villain than Lord George.

whenever the prospect is cleared by peace! What a dismal fragment of an empire!—yet would that moment were come, when we are to take a survey of our ruins!—That moment I probably shall not see. When I rose this morning, I found the exertions I had made with such puny powers, had been far beyond what I could bear; I was too sick to go on with dressing myself. This evening I have been abroad, and you shall hear no more of it. I have been with Lady Di at Richmond,[5] where I found Lady Pembroke,[6] Miss Herbert[7] and Mr Brudenel. Lord Herbert[8] is arrived. They told me the melancholy position of Lady Westmorland;[9] she is sister of Lord George Gordon, and wife of Colonel Woodford, who is forced to conceal himself, having been the first officer who gave orders to the soldiers to fire, on the attack of Lord Mansfield's house. How many still more deplorable calamities from the tragedy of this week that one shall never hear of!—I will change my style, and like an epilogue after a moving piece, divert you with a bon mot of George Selwyn. He came to me yesterday morning from Lady Townshend, who terrified by the fires of the preceding night, talked the language of the Court, instead of Opposition. He said she put him in mind of removed tradesmen, who hang out a board with 'Burnt out from over the way.' Good night, Madam, till I receive your letter.

5. In April 1780, after her husband died, Lady Diana Beauclerk took a house at Richmond, apparently until 1781 or 1782, when she removed to Little Marble Hill, Twickenham. From about 1790 she lived at Devonshire Cottage, Richmond (ante 6 June 1780; BERRY i. 148, 163, ii. 36 n. 4; Henry, Elizabeth and George, ed. Lord Herbert, 1939, p. 464).

6. Who had lodgings at this time in Richmond Park (ibid.).

7. Georgina Herbert (1747–99), dau. of Hon. William Herbert; niece of Henry, 9th E. of Pembroke; sister of Henry Herbert, cr. (1780) Bn Porchester and (1793) E. of Carnarvon; bedchamber woman to the Queen 1786–99. Lady Louisa Stuart called her 'An excellent being, one of those original characters that have something answering to the French word piquant . . . a great deal of humour . . . a certain bluntness . . .

warm feelings. . . . Friendly and generous to excess. . . . She died of dropsy 1799' (ibid. 135 n. 1, and passim; Gleanings from an Old Portfolio, ed. A. G. C. Clark, Edinburgh, 1895–8, i. 115, and passim, for many references to her and some of her letters; Royal Kalendar; GM 1799, lxxix pt i. 534; Coke 'MS Journals,' passim).

8. George Augustus Herbert (1759–1827), styled Lord Herbert till 1794; 11th E. of Pembroke, 1794; army officer; M.P.; vice-chamberlain of the Household 1784–94. In 1787 he married his first cousin, Elizabeth Beauclerk, Lady Diana's second daughter. For his travels, see Henry, Elizabeth and George, passim. He arrived at Margate from Ostend 5 or 6 June 1780 (ibid. 558).

9. Lady Susan Gordon (ca 1746–1814), m. 1 (1767) John Fane, 9th E. of Westmorland; m. 2 (1778) Lt-Col. John Woodford.

Monday morning the 12th.

Disappointed! disappointed! not a line from your Ladyship—I will not send away this till I hear from you. Last night at Hampton Court I heard of two popish chapels demolished at Bath[10] and one at Bristol.[11] My coachman has just been in Twickenham and says half Bath is burnt; I trust this is but the natural progress of lies that increase like a chairman's legs by walking—mercy on us! we seem to be plunging into the horrors of France in the reigns of Charles VI and VII![12]—yet, as extremes meet, there is at this moment amazing insensibility—within these four days I have received five applications for tickets to see my house![13] one from a set of company who fled from town to avoid the tumults and fires. I suppose Æneas lost Creüsa by her stopping at Sadler's Wells.

13th.

The letter I have this moment received is so kind, Madam, that it effaces all disappointment. Indeed my impatience made me forget that no post comes in here on Mondays. Today's letters from town mention no disturbance at Bristol, or anywhere else. Every day gained is considerable, at least will be so when there has been time for the history of last week to have spread and intelligence from the distant counties to be returned. All I have heard today is of some alteration to be made to the Riot Act,[14] that Lord George cannot be tried this month,[15] and that the King will go to the House on Mon-

10. One Roman Catholic chapel and 'about six or seven' houses were destroyed in riots at Bath on Friday night, 9 June. A second chapel and other houses were threatened but were saved when order was restored. See accounts in COLE ii. 224 n. 3; *London Chronicle* 10–15 June, xlvii. 563, 568, 571, 573. For this riot John Butler was convicted at the Wells assizes and was hanged on 28 Aug.; seven others were acquitted (ibid. 26 Aug.–2 Sept., xlviii. 198, 207, 211, 215).

11. Riots were prevented at Bristol by the placing of troops 'throughout the principal streets' of the city (ibid. 13–15 June, xlvii. 571, 574).

12. Charles VI (1368–1422), King of France 1380–1422, and Charles VII (1403–61), 1422–61.

13. One request was from Mrs Abing-

ton; see HW's letter to her 11 June 1780. Another may have been from the Princess Dashkov (*post* 29 June 1780).

14. 1 George I (1714) st. 2 c. 5 ('An act for preventing tumults and riotous assemblies, and for the more speedy and effectual punishing the rioters'); it prohibited the unlawful assembling of twelve or more persons to the disturbance of the peace. A motion was made (and defeated) in the House of Commons, 27 June 'that it is the undoubted right of his Majesty's Protestant subjects to be armed for their own defence, without any commission for that purpose' (*Journals of the House of Commons* xxxvii. 928).

15. The King did not notify the Commons of Lord George's arrest until 19 June (ibid. xxxvii. 903). In July, the trial was set for November (HW to Mann 24

day.[16] I will now answer what is necessary in your Ladyship's, and take my leave, for as you observe, the post arrives late, and I have other letters that I must answer—Mr Williams interrupted me, and has added a curious anecdote—and a horrible one, to my collection of the late events. One project of the diabolic incendiaries was to let loose the lions in the Tower,[17] and the lunatics in Bedlam. The latter might be from a fellow-feeling in Lord George, but cannibals do not invite wild beasts to their banquets. The Princess Daskiou will certainly communicate the thought to her mistress and accomplice, the Legislatress of Russia.

George, I think, need not fear Mimy's being reclaimed—when parents can give up a child, I have no notion of their caring what becomes of it.

My cousin the Miss Townshend[18] whom your Ladyship mentions is quite a stranger to me. My nephews, nieces and cousins compose such a clan, that with all my genealogic propensities, I never saw all of them, though it seems this young lady is one who, according to the proverb, knows Jack Pudding.[19] She shall certainly command a ticket for Strawberry, and I actually enclose one; but when you talk of enthusiasm, Madam, it is impossible to make an acquaintance on that ground; it would be Jackpudding—ing myself in good earnest.

I do not know whether I am glad or sorry that you must remove from Grosvenor Place[20]—That will depend on your future habitation—but I must finish, and would, if I dared, return the *Dearest*— but there would be a soupçon of the Jack Pudding in that too, and therefore I don't.

PS. I like an ironic sentence in yesterday's *London Courant*, which says, all our grievances are *red-dressed*.[21]

July 1780); it did not take place until 1781.

16. For the King's speech on the Gordon Riots to both houses of Parliament 19 June, see *Journals of the House of Lords* xxxvi. 147; *London Chronicle* 17–20 June, xlvii. 590.

17. A squib in the *London Courant* 27 June, 'A Caution to the Public,' an imagined freeing of the beasts in the Tower, may derive from this rumour. For the ten lions and other beasts in the Tower, see David Henry, *Historical Description of the Tower of London*, 1778, pp. 12–27.

18. Probably Mary, eldest of the three unmarried daughters of HW's first cousin, the Hon. Rev. Edward Townshend (Collins, *Peerage*, 1812, ii. 472; Burke, *Peerage*).

19. 'Jack Pudding' ordinarily means a mountebank (OED); the proverb has not been found.

20. Presumably the Duke of Atholl declined to renew the lease because he wished to inhabit the house himself. Cf. *ante* 12 Jan. 1775.

21. The red uniforms of the soldiers. 'INTELLIGENCE EXTRAORDINARY: The tumults have happily subsided in and about

To Lady Ossory, Friday 16 June 1780

Address: To the Countess of Ossory at Ampthill Park, Bedfordshire. *Postmark:* 17 IV. [?GC].

Berkeley Square, June 16, at night.

DEPEND upon it, Madam, you will always find my conduct simple and void of mystery. I have but two reasons for silence, ignorance, or from what secrets I know being those of others, not my own. The former was the cause of my not mentioning the reconciliation of the King and his brothers.[1] I knew nothing of it but common report till Tuesday last,[2] when Miss Keppel told me in a postscript[3] that the Duke of Gloster had asked an audience and been graciously received.[4] On Thursday the Duchess herself sent me word of it, and desired me to come to town.[5] I came today and have been with her this evening, and when I came away just now, which was past eleven, the Duke was not come back from Kew, where he had been to pass the evening with the Prince of Wales. Not a word has passed between the brothers about the Duchess.[6] But you may understand that the two Dukes have different ideas, for the Duke of Cumberland was at the Drawing-Room yesterday without his Duchess, and the Duke of Gloster was not. For the command of the army, I believe his R.H. expects it no more than I do.[7] This is the naked truth, and which I could not have told you six hours ago: in my last, to have talked vaguely of what I did not know, would really have looked mysterious.

The conquest of Charles Town[8] is a great event at the present

town! and it is now all peace and quietness. The petitions of the people have been duly considered and attended to, and all their grievances are now perfectly RED-DRESSED!' (*London Courant* 12 June).

---

1. HW gives a detailed account of the reconciliation in *Last Journals* ii. 313–19.

2. 13 June. The *London Courant* 12 June, the *London Chronicle* 10–13 June, xlvii. 561, and other newspapers reported the reconciliation.

3. Her letter is missing.

4. On 11 June.

5. Her letter is missing.

6. In the King's letter of 11 June he had 'told the Duke he should be glad to *see him and his children,* but there must be no mention of the Duchess' (*Last Journals* ii. 313).

7. When the Duke suggested that '"there ought to be one person intrusted with the care of the capital"' during the Gordon Riots, the King replied, '"Oh . . . I will take care of that myself"' (ibid.).

8. '15th [June 1780]. Arrived the Earl of Lincoln, with account of the capture of Charlestown [12 May] by Sir Henry Clinton and Admiral Arbuthnot, with

moment—not a good one, if it ensanguines us against peace. I neither understand military details nor love them for that reason. But this success is coupled with a very remarkable event. A Colonel Scott,[9] I think a prisoner, says the Americans are sick of the war, but have been buoyed up by Spanish gold, and *by French promises of the conflagration of London*[10]— a hellish sort of war, but who set the precedent? The Court talk much of a plot, and this anecdote is corroborative.[11] Indeed I cannot at all agree with Mr F.[12] in wishing Lord George Gordon may not be found guilty.[13] He is so black in my eyes already, that though I have infinite compassion for criminals, I never heard of one I should pity less. If he is the source of our being ruled by an army, I shall abhor him still more. Have you heard, Madam, that the common soldiers style one another *your worship,* as being the only justices of peace?

I have sent to inquire after Mr Fox, and hear he is better with great pleasure.[14] General Conway was setting out for Jersey, but the alarm was ill-founded.[15] I know nothing of Lord Beauchamp's deposition against the Lord Mayor,[16] but what I saw in the papers.[17] Mr

little loss, the Provincials being forced to surrender for want of provisions. The Court was much elated . . . and gave out that they should be soon masters of the southern colonies' (ibid. ii. 319–20; *London Gazette Extraordinary* 15 June).

9. Brig.-Gen. Charles Scott (ca 1739–1813) was captured at Charleston, and remained on parole until his exchange near the close of the war; he was governor of Kentucky 1808–12.

10. It was reported that Sir Andrew Hammond 'declared in the Drawing-Room at St James's on Thursday, that an American officer of the name of Scott, who was made prisoner at the capture of Charlestown, told him that Congress had with the utmost difficulty prevailed on the Americans to support the expense and inconvenience of the present campaign, and that the chief reason which induced them to enter upon it was a confident assertion that the cities of London and Westminster would be laid in ashes this summer' (*London Chronicle* 15–17 June, xlvii. 584, and a similar report in the references cited in n. 8).

11. De Castro, in *Gordon Riots,* 1926, pp. 216–37, considers the rumours, and

finds no concerted plot or plan. Apropos of the trial of the rioters, HW noted that 'nothing came out of any plot or plan having been formed' (*Last Journals* ii. 322, *sub* 28–29 June 1780).

12. Richard Fitzpatrick.

13. He was tried 5–6 Feb. 1781 and acquitted.

14. His illness is reported in the *London Courant* 13, 14, 21 June. 'Last night Mr Fox was a good deal better' (ibid. 14 June).

15. His departure on 9 June for Portsmouth to embark for Jersey was reported by Lady Mary Coke in her 'MS Journals' 10 June 1780, and by the *London Chronicle* 10–13 June.

16. Brackley Kennett (d. 1782), lord mayor 1779–80. He was said to have been 'a waiter at the King's Arms, a notorious house of ill-fame: he afterwards had a brothel of his own; then kept a tavern; then commenced wine merchant, and afterwards became alderman and then first magistrate of the first city in England' (A. B. Beaven, *Aldermen of the City of London,* 1908–13, ii. 133, 200, and *passim*).

17. HW records under 7 June that

Duane,[18] I believe, is not yet settled at Twickenham, as the house and court are full of workmen—but I have had no time yet to make my visits, or think of them. Nor have I seen Miss Vernons, nor have I been to the twilights at Bedford House. In truth I have thought of nothing but that horrible Wednesday and its consequences. Those that I immediately apprehended, insurrections and like tumults in the country, seem, thank God, not likely to ensue. My disorder was merely fatigue, and a sick mind. I long to sink into calm stupidity. These tempests brush me up and revive me for a moment, but I had rather wear out quietly with my dowagers of Twickenham at tredrille.[19] This country cannot recover its splendour—it will be for some time the seat of distractions; and when exhausted, be an insignificant solitude under a bashaw. I have no loftier wish than to be one of the owls that hoot in an obscure village in the evening, and leave desolated cities to vultures and beasts of prey.

To Lady Ossory, Friday 23 June 1780

Address: To the Countess of Ossory at Ampthill Park, Bedfordshire. *Postmark:* 23 IV. GC.

Strawberry Hill, June 23, 1780.

I ENTREAT your Ladyship not to suspect yourself of impertinence, when you are obliging; nor me of indirect meanings, when I speak plainly. I did see Lord Ossory on Tuesday, and you will find that, though I avoided details, my answer was the outline of what had passed.[1] It is a subject on which I never love to write; because

'The Justices were afraid to act, and the Lord Mayor Kennet and Sheriff Pughe behaved shamefully' (*Last Journals* ii. 310). The newspapers reported that Kennett was examined by the Privy Council on Friday evening, 9 June, and was dismissed (*London Chronicle* 10–13 June, xlvii. 562, 566; *London Courant* 13 June; De Castro, *Gordon Riots*, 1926, pp. 51–6).

18. Matthew Duane (1707–85), coin collector and antiquary; frequently mentioned in the HW-Mann Correspondence. 'He has the whole management of the affairs of Lord Ossory, one of my particular friends' (HW to Mann 4 Dec. 1781). His house, near the centre of Twicken-

ham, had formerly belonged to Edmund Waller (d. 1771), grandson of the poet, whose heirs presumably sold it to Duane (Edward Ironside, *History . . . of Twickenham*, 1797, p. 78, *Bibliotheca Topographica Britannica*, Vol. X; MORE back endpaper; R. S. Cobbett, *Memorials of Twickenham*, 1872, pp. 256–9; BERRY ii. 102 n. 3).

19. As he had just reported to Strafford 12 June 1780.

———

1. Presumably the continuation, from the last letter, of the story of the reconciliation of the King and his brothers. For details, see *Last Journals* ii. 317–19.

to begin it, has the air of an air, which I dislike; and when one answers, one cannot, at every sentence, say, 'Pray don't repeat this'; or, 'This may be repeated.' And yet that is necessary on points that occasion discussion, and on which one does not like to be quoted.

Considering what a crop there is of discordant opinions, and the quantity of matter that enters into head-dresses at present, it will be very serious, Madam, if the ladies come to pulling caps. The fields of battle will be strewed with strange fragments!—but everything seems to be returning to chaos! I am come back to this little nook, in hopes it will escape the general hurly-burly. Lord Ossory agreed with my sentiments more almost than any man I meet with. Mine about this country, I own, are total despair: nor do I see from our present position, our present generation of actors, and from our present enemies, whence aught but ruin should come, either to the nation or constitution, and probably to both—and if either is undone, what signifies the other? The felicity of universal confusion encourages a war within a war; and the attention to the internal one will absorb all regard to the other; and by the time absolute power is attained, it will, like abstract powers, be charming in speculation, but prove to be nothing but the *vis inertiæ*—I am weary of such scenes and prospects, and have quitted them. There may perhaps be farther combustions—but whether expected or not, we shall affect to expect them, and prepare—not to prevent, but to profit of them; which, I doubt, was a little the case lately. Have you never known a chambermaid, Madam, that would tick[2] at a chandler's shop to the amount of six or seven shillings, rather than part with a favourite crown-piece?

I have got the print of Lady Gertrude,[3] but it is poorly executed and faint and unfinished—however it is sweetly pretty, though it has not half the countenances of the original. Pray tell me, when you

2. That is, deal on credit.

3. Vernon Smith's note: i. 417: 'From Sir Joshua Reynolds' picture of her as a child in my possession.' The print of Lady Gertrude as 'Collina' or the 'little mountaineer,' engraved by J. Dean, was not published until 8 Nov. 1780, but HW probably had an early or proof copy before the inscription was added. This print is not to be confused with one published 10 June 1780, engraved by J.

R. Smith after Sir Joshua Reynolds, showing a child with grapes, and erroneously called 'Lady Gertrude Fitzpatrick'; it is Lady Anne. See the illustrations; John Chaloner Smith, *British Mezzotinto Portraits*, 1884, i. 163, iii. 1267; Graves and Cronin i. 313–16, iv. 1310; BM, *Cat. of Engraved British Portraits*. A print of 'Lady Gertrude Fitzpatrick' was in the London sale, No. 679, but no print of Lady Anne is listed.

have taken one, where your new house is. Do you really move, like a pawn, only an inch farther in Grosvenor Place?

My hay is cut and it has rained all day—well, Madam, is not it better to have only annual distresses, than to attend to old Madam England's cancers and amputation of limbs?[4] I am trying to learn all the doctrines of selfishness, and to care for nothing but my own enjoyments. If it is true, that the love of one's country and such virtues are but emanations of self-love, is not it wise to lop them when they no longer flatter one's vanity?—In short, to speak with the dignity that becomes every man who prefers himself to all the world, if my country is ever worthy of me, I will think on it again: if the prodigal does not return and repent, I will eat the fatted calf by myself.

To LADY OSSORY, Thursday 29 June 1780

Address: To the Countess of Ossory at Ampthill Park, Bedfordshire. *Postmark:* ISLEWORTH. 29 IV.

Strawberry Hill, June 29, 1780.

IF your Ladyship did not give me themes, I should certainly not think of writing, for I know nothing but what the *Morning Chronicle* said yesterday, and have thought on nothing but my hay, though I have not a load half so big as a lady's head-dress; but the weather is so benevolent, that I sit amongst the reapers till nine at night, and do not wish myself on the parade.

I had heard of Lord Grantham's match,[1] and suppose he has contracted some Spanish ideas, and minds blood more than beauty. If the lady ceases to be your neighbour,[2] she will become more your acquaintance. I know no more of the Duchess of Ancaster's mis-

---

4. Satirical prints on the loss of British possessions were current. See, for example, BM, *Satiric Prints* v. 387, No. 5649: 'The English Lion Dismember'd,' 12 March 1780, showing a paw labelled 'America' cut off.

———

1. Lord Grantham, ambassador at Madrid 1771–9, m. (17 Aug. 1780) at her father's house in St James's Square, Lady Mary Jemima Yorke (1757–1830). The

engagement had been announced 14 June (Coke, 'MS Journals' 22 June). A letter from Lord Grantham 23 June informed Lord Ossory of the approaching marriage (MS in National Library of Ireland: Fitzpatrick MSS).

2. Lord Hardwicke's country seat was Wrest Park, Beds, four miles southwest of Shefford and about four miles from Ampthill. HW described Wrest Park in *Country Seats* 70–1.

fortunes, and heard before I came out of town that Lady Willoughby was out of danger.[3]

The Princess Daskiou was here this morning with her horde of Tartars, but I kept out of sight, having nothing to regale her but one old horse. I have paid my visit to Lord and Lady Sefton,[4] who do not suit me quite so well as poor Lady Blandford.[5]

Have you heard, Madam, that on Lord Effingham's[6] coming to life,[7] report has shot old Lord Godolphin?[8] The Monument[9] to be sure would as soon head a riot.

I have deferred my journey to Malvern[10] for a fortnight or three weeks; I shall regret Strawberry less in August; and besides have been remarkably well for this last fortnight, and besides find it mighty difficult to set about anything, so totally is all my activity gone. I think there is nothing but your Ladyship that has not lost influence over me. You can make me exert even a talent I never had, as I am going to give you a proof. The lines are indifferent enough; but prompt obedience like charity can cover a dozen bad verses; and as I scribbled them while the Tartars were in the house and send them by the return of the post, you may be sure I do not think them fit to be shown, and beg you will not let them go out of your hands. The theme was too good not to be better treated; and what will do in a private letter, will not stand criticism; and still less, if taken for a cool design of venting indignation—but here they are, and if they

---

3. 'Lady Willoughby, who had been dangerously ill for some time, is pronounced by her physicians to be out of danger' (*London Courant* 1 July). Fever and delirium continued, however, and she did not recover until about 22 July (Coke, 'MS Journals' 9, 22 July).

4. Charles William Molyneux (1748–94), 8th Vct Molyneux, 1759, cr. (1771) E. of Sefton; M.P. (Daniel Lysons, *Supplement to the First Edition of . . . the Environs of London*, 1811, p. 189). For Lady Sefton, see *ante* 27 March 1773.

5. They were living in the house at Sheen occupied by Lady Blandford until her death in 1779; cf. *ante* 23 June 1771.

6. Thomas Howard (1747–91), 3d E. of Effingham, 1763; army officer 1762–82; governor of Jamaica 1789–91.

7. 'There are numberless stories circulating about, the chief part void of all foundation. The last related to Lord Effingham. It was reported that being one of the rioters he was shot by the military. This did not gain much credit. It was then said that being engaged in the late insurrections he was gone off; this some people chose to believe, but today I am told he is peaceably at his house in Yorkshire' (Coke, 'MS Journals' 27 June 1780). See also Lord Albemarle, *Memoirs of the Marquis of Rockingham*, 1852, ii. 407–8; HW to Mason 14 April 1782, MASON ii. 235–6.

8. Francis Godolphin (1706–85), 2d Bn Godolphin, 1766; M.P.; governor of the Scilly Islands 1766–85 (*Eton Coll. Reg.*).

9. In Monument Yard, Fish Street Hill; designed by Wren and erected 1671–7 to commemorate the Great Fire of London, 1666.

10. HW did not go (MASON ii. 49, 69).

will provoke Mr Fitzpatrick to write better, you and I shall both be better satisfied.

> When mitred masters o'er a groaning land
> Extend the Church's all-usurping hand,
> No more our woods are ours; our mansions slide
> To glut some pontiff's patriarchal pride;
> And star-chambers in law's defiance grant
> Whate'er the Gospel's appetites can want.
> Hence then—nor longer o'er the genial room
> Shall Laud's ill-omen'd aspect hurl its gloom.
> No tyrant Stuart shall to crosiers give,
> And borrow from the gift, Prerogative.
> Each free-born lord shall his own rights assert,
> Nor vassals be enchain'd but by the heart;
> While each calm Ossory's benignant smile
> Diffuses old good-humour round our isle.[11]

Heart and *assert* are bad rhymes, and do not agree in sound or sense, but are like an address that echoes a royal speech with the unfelt protestations of slaves.

Pray send me directions to your camp[12]—do the Infantas make the campaign? The report here is that the Parliament is immediately to be dissolved,[13] in hopes of another phoenix rising out of the ashes of London. In that case I conclude Lady Gertrude will remain at Ampthill to keep open house. The *province* of Bedfordshire I trust will stick close to the house.

To Lady Ossory, ca Wednesday 12 July 1780

HAD I known whither to direct, I should not have waited for your Ladyship's congratulations (which I owed you on Lady Shelburne's delivery)[1] but should have announced Lady Maria's

---

11. Printed in *HW's Fugitive Verses* 172.

12. The Bedfordshire militia was encamped on Buckland Down, near Plymouth (*London Chronicle* 10–12 Aug., xlviii. 142).

13. On 8 July Parliament was prorogued to 24 Aug., when it was further prorogued to 28 Sept., but on 1 Sept. it was dissolved (*Journals of the House of Commons* xxxvii. 939, xxxviii. 3).

---

1. Of a son, Henry Petty (after 1818, Petty-Fitzmaurice) (2 July 1780–1863), 3d M. of Lansdowne, 1809.

approaching coronet.[2] It has many agreeable faces (after some shades). The best, next to the splendour, is the satisfaction which all Lord Egremont's family express on the occasion. Lady Egremont, Count Bruhl,[3] Mr Herbert[4] and Lady Elizabeth have been presented at Gloucester House, and Mr Marsham[5] and Lady Frances are coming to town on purpose. You will, I believe, approve, that having full powers to treat with Lord Egremont, I told him the Duchess would leave the terms to him, that no advantage would be taken of his passion, and that he should decide what he should think was proper for his widow, and the Duchess's daughter. Lady Egremont very handsomely told me, that if it was left to the lawyers, they would be guided by *her* jointure, which is but two thousand; but as the times are more extravagant and more dear now, she thought Lady Maria ought to have three. It is pleasant to deal in this way, and not commence union with a family as if one was undermining it—So now I am to have Sir William Windham's[6] grandson for one of my numerous nephews! I believe I shall live to be the world's uncle.

You have lost your neighbour Mrs Page,[7] I hear, Madam, and that she has made a very reasonable will and dispensed her money pretty equally amongst the Howes.[8]

July 18.

I wrote the preceding page some days ago on receiving your Ladyship's last, and in expectation of a direction; but it is arrived so late, that it has made all I have said stale; however I send it, as it tells you what relates to our great wedding; except that my modera-

2. For more than a year there had been rumours of Lady Maria Waldegrave's engagement to Egremont (Jesse, *Selwyn* iv. 177; Coke, 'MS Journals' 10, 22 June, 4 July 1779, and 9 July 1780).

3. Lord Egremont's step-father: Hans Moritz (1736–1809), Graf von Brühl, of Saxony, had married Lady Egremont 6 June 1767. He was Saxon ambassador to London 1764–1809 and was well known as an astronomer; see DNB.

4. Henry Herbert (1741–1811), cr. (17 Oct. 1780) Bn Porchester and (1793) E. of Carnarvon; m. (1771) Lady Elizabeth Alicia Maria Wyndham (1752–1826), 1st dau. of Lady Egremont.

5. Hon. Charles Marsham (1744–1811),

3d Bn Romney, 1793; cr. (1801) E. of Romney; m. (1776) Lady Frances Wyndham (1755–95), 2d dau. of Lady Egremont.

6. Sir William Wyndham (ca 1687–1740), 3d Bt, 1695; M.P. Somerset; friend and follower of Bolingbroke. Despite Wyndham's Jacobitism and his opposition to Sir Robert Walpole, HW called him 'the great Sir William Windham' (*Mem. Geo. II* i. 80). Wyndham's second wife, by whom he had no children, was HW's friend Lady Blandford.

7. She died 2 July at her seat at Battlesden, in Bedfordshire (*London Courant* 7 July), without issue.

8. Lord Howe and Gen. Howe were her nephews.

tion has not been adopted, but the jointure is to be four thousand, and the pin-money, one. The wedding we think will be in about three weeks.

I am glad your Ladyship bathes in so beautiful a prospect—though I think the Tritons enjoy a better, when you bathe. Glastonbury I never saw; the Peter Burrel, the proprietor,[9] I suppose is either the uncle of Mr Burrel, the present Lord Consort of Willoughby, or he himself; I know the grandfather's name was Peter. You are too hard, I think, on the remarried widower.[10] His marrying again so soon is in my opinion a better proof of his love for his last wife, than his erection of a monument for her. He was impatient to be as happy as he had been. It requires more philosophy to venture a second time, when the first marriage is unprosperous. Your account of the Bishop's tomb at Glastonbury, Madam, seems typical of what is coming. The Bishop was kicked into the Abbot's kitchen, you say, and then defaced by the soldiers.[11] Abbots mayhap may grow luxurious on the spoils of bishops, and the army complete the depredation—Most of the present bench deserve such a fate.

Your Lady Jacob[12] reminds me of what happened to myself five-and-twenty years ago.[13] I went to see the painted glass of Messing Church in Essex,[14] and dined at an ale-house. The landlady entertained me with bon mots of *Mr Charles,* just as if I had known him—and was much surprised I had never heard of him. He was a Mr Charles Luckyn,[15] a younger brother or uncle of the late Lord Grimston,[16] had been dead some years, but had been the George Selwyn or Hare of that village—such is fame! This is a copy in miniature of that admirable chapter in Voltaire,[17] where a Chinese goes

9. HW had misread the letter; see below.

10. Not identified.

11. For an account of the abbey and kitchen ca 1780, see John Collinson, *History and Antiquities of the County of Somerset,* Bath, 1791, ii. 240–62.

12. Not identified.

13. Actually in 1749; see HW to Montagu 20 July 1749, Montagu i. 91–2, where HW gives a variant of this story.

14. Three and a half miles SE of Coggeshall. The seventeenth-century painted glass HW saw is still there.

15. (ca 1694–1745), rector of Pebmarsh

and vicar of Messing (Montagu i. 92 n. 11).

16. James Grimston (1711–73), 2d Vct Grimston, 1756. Charles Luckyn was his uncle. The first Lord Grimston, the adopted heir of Sir Samuel Grimston, had changed his name from Luckyn to Grimston.

17. 'Entretien avec un Chinois,' in his *Dictionnaire philosophique,* under 'Gloire, Glorieux,' Section III (Voltaire, *Œuvres* xix. 267–70). HW refers to the passage in his letter to Cole 23 July 1782, Cole ii. 332, and *post* 11 Oct. 1788. In the second reference HW again parallels the

into a bookseller's shop, and they are mutually astonished at each other's ignorance of the great names in their different regions.

I am forced to comment your paragraphs, Madam, for I have nothing to send you in return. The only novelty I know, is, that we have had a riot of our own at Richmond, where an embankment for barge horses being carried before Mr Colman, the manager's, garden by the City,[18] he, feeling himself, like Agamemnon, a king of kings, behaved with equal hauteur, and levied a mob to destroy the works, which they did with hatchets last week in open daylight. The City, three days after, sent a naval force, consisting of one barge with a committee on board, who seized thirteen of the rioters, and sent them to London, where they were bailed—but the barge remains *encamped* near the bridge, according to the precedent in London— yet, notwithstanding the terror spread through Europe by the camps in the two parks[19] and by the barge at Richmond, fifteen Russian men-of-war are arrived at Copenhagen, and are expected southwards, with no friendly dispositions towards us[20]—but what signifies any credit we lose abroad, while we are all puissant at home, and can bestow the diadem of Greenwich Hospital on Sir Hugh Palisser?[21]

Luckyn anecdote and the passage from Voltaire.

18. According to the Act of 17 George III, c. 18 ('for enabling . . . the City of London to purchase the present tolls . . . for navigating upon the River Thames'), a tow-path for barges was to be built on the Richmond, rather than the Twickenham, side of the Thames. Colman had later lost a suit against the City to prevent its construction. See HW to Mason 15 July 1780, MASON ii. 69–71, where additional details of Colman's feud with the City are given, and the *London Chronicle* 18–20 July, xlviii. 62, for two long paragraphs concerning the affair. Paragraphs opposing the proposed tow-path and a reference to Colman's quarrel with the City are in the *London Courant* 21, 22, 27 July. Further disturbances connected with the tow-path are mentioned in the *London Chronicle* 19–21 Oct., xlviii. 378.

19. Hyde Park and St James's Park, in which soldiers remained encamped following the Gordon Riots.

20. 'One of the Baltic fleet, which made a running voyage from the Sound to England (there being no men of war to conduct the trade from thence) is arrived in the river, and brings an account that fifteen Russian ships of the line, and seven frigates, were assembled at the Sound. These ships were to join ten sail of Swedish and twelve sail of Danish men of war, in order to defend the neutral commerce of the northern potentates; and a large fleet of Swedish and Danish merchantmen, loaded with naval stores, were expected soon to sail from the Sound' (*London Courant* 15 July). These ships, with others to total 50, were expected to conduct a fleet of merchant ships (loaded with naval stores for France and Spain) to the Channel, and there was speculation as to what would happen if Great Britain continued its policy of searching neutral ships for war materials (ibid. 20 July; *London Chronicle* 13–15 July, xlviii. 46).

21. His appointment (supported by Sandwich) as governor of Greenwich Hospital was announced 15 July (ibid. 13–18 July, xlviii. 46, 49; *Corr. Geo. III* v. 28). 'There never was so bare-faced a

Is not it more eligible to be emperor of ten miles round London, than to extend our empire, as Lord Chatham did, from the Oronooque to Japan?

I shall conclude this rhapsody with a dismal adventure that happened to me yesterday. The door opened and Margaret entered with her apron spread over both arms, as a midwife presents a child to be baptized, and bearing, as I thought the longest leanest naked babe I ever beheld—As she approached, I perceived that master or miss had no head, but a bloody neck—'Christ!' said I, 'what have you got there?'—'A friend of mine has sent me a fawn, if your honour pleases to accept it'—'For heaven's sake,' said I, 'take it away, I could as soon eat a child'—However, I did call her again, and begged her pardon for having treated her present so brutally—but one must have been a cannibal to have ever borne the sight of it again.

The Duchess told me tonight at the Pavilions that your aunt is going to carry her grandson[22] abroad, and takes the two Misses Vernon,[23] and not her niece Dorothea[24]—whence comes that dereliction?

I am sorry I have no talent for piscatory eclogues, since your fishermen are so polished and harmonious, and their fishwives such flageolets. Eelinda and Salmonia would be musical names, and Turbotto and Jan Dorado of no harsh sound—but you say, *when you climb the hills*—alas! I can climb still less than write poetry—oh! on looking again at your Ladyship's description, I see I have made a mistake, and that you ask not what Mr Burrel, but what Mr Bladen is proprietor of Glastonbury[25]—in truth, I know not—I know *I* am

mockery of the public opinion, or so gross an insult on the Navy of England, as the appointment of Sir Hugh Palliser to the government of Greenwich Hospital' (*London Courant* 18 July). Even Lady Mary Coke, a staunch supporter of the administration, said 'I must acknowledge that nothing at this time could be more improper' ('MS Journals' 20 July 1780).

22. The Duke of Bedford.

23. The Duchess of Bedford had also presented Caroline Maria Vernon to the King and Queen at Court on 15 Feb. 1778 (*Morning Post* 16 Feb. 1778).

24. Dorothy Wrottesley (*ante* 14 July

1779), whose approaching marriage might explain her not going with the Duchess. See *post* 23 Sept., 11, 17 Dec. 1780.

25. In 1733 the estate of Glastonbury Abbey was purchased for £12,700 from the Duke of Devonshire, by Thomas Bladen (ca 1698 – 2 Feb. 1780), M.P.; deputy governor of Maryland 1742–6. At his death the property went to his daughters, Mrs Henry St John and Lady Essex, who sold it in 1799 for £40,500 (*Old Westminsters* and *Supp.*; W. Phelps, *History and Antiquities of Somersetshire*, 1839, i. 540).

proprietor of the chair of Joannes Arthurus the monk of Glastonbury,[26] and once made the present Archbishop of Canterbury sit in
it at breakfast[27]—but I will reserve it now for a real abbot—It is
too much honour for a renegade. If the Pope sends us a genuine
Austin, well and good.

I do now expect all the Martinico ships safe in Torbay[28]—not because Sir Hugh is president of crippled sailors, but because *Venus
orta mari mare præstat eunti*.[29] Good night, Madam.

To Lady Ossory, Tuesday 1 August 1780

Address: To the Countess of Ossory at Ampthill Park, Bedfordshire. *Postmark:*
ISLEWORTH. 3 AV.

August 1, 1780.

Y OUR Ladyship's last letter and mine might have curtsied and
bowed on the road, for they certainly passed each other; nay,
they might have chatted over their own contents, as they were both
full of the same subject. I shall not resume it, as you may imagine
how thoroughly I must be tired of it. I will only add, that the
Duchess, however offended, had antecedently taken such an aversion to her future son-in-law, that she is delighted the match failed[1]

26. In the Holbein Room at SH: 'A
very ancient chair of oak, which came out
of Glastonbury Abbey; on it are carved
these sentences, *Joannes Arthurus Mona-
cus Glastonie, salvet eum Deus: Da pacem,
Domine: Sit Laus Deo*. Lord Bathurst had
several chairs copied from this' ('Des. of
SH,' *Works* ii. 455).

27. Cf. *ante* 7 Oct. 1773.

28. Admiral Geary's squadron on 3
July captured 12 French ships from
Martinique and San Domingo. Some of
them had already been brought in to
Plymouth, and four more arrived there
19 July. For details, see the *London
Chronicle* 13 July – 1 Aug., xlviii. *passim*;
Jesse, *Selwyn* iv. 345. HW supposes they
will be brought in to Torbay in tribute
to Lady Ossory, who was there (or had
been there) on a tour from Plymouth,
near which the Bedfordshire militia was
encamped (*ante* 29 June 1780).

29. Ovid, *Heroides*, xv, 'Sappho to
Phaon,' l. 213, where HW's 'eunti' (way-
farer) reads 'amanti' (lover): 'Venus who
rose from the sea makes way on the sea
for the lover.' Cf. BERRY ii. 204.

1. Details concerning the breaking of
the engagement are in HW's letter to
Mann 24 July 1780. Lady Melbourne,
Lord Egremont's mistress, caused the
rupture (*Last Journals* ii. 351). Three
fairly accurate paragraphs and 'A Supposed Tête-à-Tête' on the affair are in
the *London Chronicle* 27–29 July, xlviii.
92, 94–5, and one less accurate ibid. 5–7
Sept., xlviii. 226. Lady Ossory's letter to
Selwyn 3 June 1779, on Egremont's intended rupture, prompted Lady Louisa
Stuart to hint at Egremont's 'home con-
nexions' (*Notes . . . on George Selwyn*,
ed. W. S. Lewis, New York, 1928, p. 49).
Lord Melbourne informed Anthony Storer

—and I will swear that the abandoned is no mourning bride, but far more gay than during his preposterous courtship. Still, I allow they are unfortunate girls to have missed so many splendid marriages as they have been flattered with.[2] They are like the prints of Edward V, and have had coronets hanging over their heads that never lighted on them.[3] They have been with me here since last Friday, and on Monday received a visit that gave them great joy. Their heroic cousin William[4] arrived before any of us came down to breakfast, and I made them keep him to dinner. They could not receive a proposal with more modesty than he did my compliments on his late victory. He has promised to dine with us again tomorrow; but did not forget to desire I would make his compliments to your Ladyship the first time I should write.

Though *our* story has made so much more noise, it is not touching and melancholy like the silent one your Ladyship tells me of poor Mrs Byng.[5] I remember to have heard at the time that Lord Torrington[6] was the sole cause of his brother's[7] ruin.[8]

I find my materials run so short, that I shall postpone my letter

that the Duchess of Gloucester demanded 'a larger settlement than Lord Egremont had proposed'; cf. *ante* ca 12 July 1780, first and third paragraphs (Storer to Carlisle 20 July, *Carlisle MSS* 436).

2. 'Each [of the three] has missed one of the first matches in this country; Lady Laura Lord Carmarthen, Lady Maria Lord Egremont, Lady Horatia the Duke of Ancaster, after each had proposed and been accepted' (HW to Mann 24 July 1780).

3. For prints of him, see James Granger, *Biographical History of England*, 5th edn, 1824, i. 27; Rastell's *Chronicle*, not mentioned by Granger, which contains a woodcut depicting the crown over Edward V's head; *Vertue Notebooks* iv. 146 and Index; COLE i. 308. See also HW to Mann 22 April 1751, MANN iv. 245.

4. Also Lord Ossory's cousin, Hon. William Waldegrave (1753–1825), cr. (1800) Bn Radstock; Capt., 1776, in the Navy; Vice-Adm., 1795; Adm., 1802. On 4–5 July, in command of *La Prudente*, he and Capt. Cadogan of the *Licorne* had captured a French frigate of 44 guns which was so badly damaged Waldegrave

had to burn it. For details, including testimony on his bravery and calmness, see the *London Chronicle* 20–25 July, xlviii. 72–3. At the time he was at SH his ship was being repaired (*London Courant* 24 July).

5. Bridget Forrest (d. 1823), m. (1767) Hon. John Byng, 5th Vct Torrington, 1812.

6. George Byng (1740–1812), 4th Vct Torrington, 1750; minister plenipotentiary at Brussels 1783–92.

7. John Byng (1743–1813), 5th Vct Torrington, 1812; army officer; diarist.

8. In Aug.–Sept. 1781 Lady Mary Coke saw Lord and Lady Torrington in Brussels. She refers to their former extravagance, his being deeply in debt to the Duke of Portland, their quiet and reformed manner of life, and his acquiring of information which would be useful in a diplomatic post ('MS Journals' 4 Aug.–20 Sept. 1781, especially 10, 11 Aug., 20 Sept.). She does not mention the brother, but she had written, 23 Dec. 1777, that he and the Torringtons were 'ruined people' and 'all gone abroad.'

to another post. These last ten days have been totally engrossed by my own family: when once one has told the story, it is not fair to tease others with impertinent collateral circumstances, that are important to nobody but the concerned.

Wednesday 3d.[9]

William *the Prudent* kept his word, stayed all night, and left us this morning before breakfast. I do not wonder his cousinesses are so fond of him: if he is Mars at sea, he is smooth as a calm at land. He tells us from Navestock[10] that the Parliament is to be dissolved next week, which I find is the general opinion.[11] My nieces leave me tomorrow, and are to be woodland nymphs for the rest of the season.[12] I shall go to Park Place next week[13] for a few days, and perhaps to Nuneham if the Lord and Lady are there,[14] of which I am not certain; nor shall I, if there is a general election, for I abhor hearing details of elections.

The Countess Cowper is at the point of death with a cancer.[15] This is all the news our region furnishes.

To Lady Ossory, Wednesday 16 August 1780

Strawberry Hill, Aug. 16, 1780.

NO wonder you was charmed with Mount Edgcumbe, Madam. You have described it justly by saying, 'It has the beauties of all other places added to peculiar beauties of its own.' You must

9. Wednesday was 2 Aug., but HW's letter is postmarked 3 Aug. According to the *London Courant* 3, 4 Aug. Waldegrave was presented to the King on 2 Aug., before he returned to SH for dinner, and to the Queen on 3 Aug.

10. Lord Waldegrave's seat in Essex.

11. The *London Chronicle* 27–29 July, xlviii. 91, reported that 'The dissolution of Parliament has been agitated in Council, and it is imagined will take place in a few days.' Parliament was dissolved 1 Sept.

12. Lady Elizabeth Laura wrote to Anne Clement, from Hackwood Park, the Duke of Bolton's seat in Hants, 7 Aug.: 'My sisters and myself came here on Friday [4 Aug.], and propose staying here till Thursday [10 Aug.]. . . . Direct your

letters for me at Iron's Hill near Lyndhurst in the New Forest, Hants' (MS wsl). Lady Mary Coke heard that the family were going to the New Forest, of which the Duke was warden, ('MS Journals' 30 July, 6 Aug. 1780), and that 'the three Lady Waldegraves are gone to the Duke of Bolton's in Hampshire' (ibid. 6 Aug. 1780).

13. On 9 Aug. (HW to Mason 8 Aug. 1780, Mason ii. 72).

14. HW postponed his visit because he heard that Lord and Lady Harcourt were leaving Nuneham on 10 Aug. for a visit (HW to Mason 8 Aug. 1780, Mason ii. 72–3; HW to Lord Harcourt 2 Sept. 1780).

15. She died 21 Aug. at her house at Richmond (*post* 23 Aug. 1780, n. 12).

have felt too for its Lord and Lady, who last year beheld above an hundred ancient oaks, growing exactly where they ought, felled to make room for a battery![1] I was not less pleased with your phrase of the old gentlewoman's 'open-armed way of receiving you.' You must have been touched with her cordiality, when you express it so significantly, for you have given a picture in one epithet, that is more pathetic than a description. I have no prospects, no adventures, to send your Ladyship in return. My own little landscape is brown and parched. A sultry east wind has reigned for eight-and-twenty days, and left us neither grass nor leaves. This is the third summer that our climate has been growing as Asiatic as our government; and the Macphersons and Dalrymples, I suppose, will hail the epoch of the introduction of camels and dromedaries in lieu of flocks of sheep—yet a Russian fleet riding in the Downs[2] is a little drawback on our Ottoman dignity.

Lady Barrymore is not dead, as I told you,[3] Madam, but better.[4] The Parliament too, I hear, is not to be dissolved till next month.[5] We newswriters cannot always warrant our goods—nor are falsities

1. 'Plymouth, August 24 . . . Everybody is sorry for the devastation produced in the beautiful woods of Mount Edgcombe. It is an entire falsehood that his Lordship objected to their being cut down, for on a proper representation of the circumstances by Lord Shuldham and others here, that it was very possible that these groves might be made use of as a place of concealment for the enemy, in an attack upon the dockyard, all that his Lordship said . . . was this, "If it be absolutely necessary for the preservation of the dockyard that Mount Edgcombe be destroyed, you have my ready consent, even to the last shrub. No private interest can have the smallest influence when set in balance with an object of the magnitude you mention; but I would beg leave to remark, gentlemen, that without your fears are very well founded, I am entirely averse to the destruction of these groves" ' (*London Chronicle* 26–28 Aug. 1779, xlvi. 194). HW had been at Mount Edgcumbe in 1745 (SELWYN 92–5; MANN iii. 92). For the problem of defending Plymouth, Lord Edgcumbe's part therein, and the importance of Mount Edgcumbe, see A. T. Patterson, *The Other Armada*, Manchester, 1960, pp. 136–48 (information kindly supplied by Mr David Erskine).

2. 'By letters from Deal, dated August 11, we learn, "That last night five Russian ships of the line and a large frigate arrived in the Downs. . . . the most probable conjecture is that they are sent to protect the neutral trade in the North Sea, but were driven into the Downs by contrary winds' (ibid. 15–17 Aug., xlviii. 154). Thirteen ships arrived in the Downs on 18 Aug., sailed the following day, and the original six ships left on 21 Aug. (MASON ii. 76 n. 9; *London Courant, passim*).

3. If HW's memory is correct, he refers to a missing letter or to a conversation. None of his recovered letters before this one mentions Lady Barrymore's death.

4. She died 5 Sept. 1780 in France; the news reached London on the 21st (Coke, 'MS Journals' 23 Sept.). 'Letters from Paris mention the death of Lady Barrymore, after a lingering disorder' (*London Chronicle* 23–26 Sept., xlviii. 291).

5. 1 Sept.

a discredit to the profession. Paragraphs of news are like roasted chestnuts; not one in twenty is sound. They are like mottoes too wrapped in sugar, which everybody breaks, finds nothing worth reading, and yet goes on cracking.[6]

I was not so much misinformed about Miss Ingram's[7] match. Lord William is gone to Temple Newsham[8] *en famille,* and, they say, Lady Irwin[9] is to pay his debts.[10] I enlarge my QU. instead of effacing it.

It is not decent to trouble his Majesty's postman with such a scrap as this, filled only with recantations and repetitions; and therefore I shall reserve it till the wind changes, when we expect cargoes of novelties, and such victories, as nothing but a new Parliament is worthy of hearing.

6. 'The Game of Mottos, or English Jokes. In imitation of but far superior to those French mottos or jokes usually sold at the confectioners' at 1s. the dozen. These jokes were invented abroad, as an agreeable amusement after dinner and supper, by enlivening and entertaining a company at a trifling expense. Ladies choose for gentlemen and gentlemen for ladies, and it frequently happens that accident or chance disposes of or applies a joke in so apt a manner as to be productive of the greatest mirth or humour. . . . Price 6d. a dozen, or 3s. 6d. the hundred. The celebrated French jokes are sold at the same price. N.B. The first collection imported, being by many gentlemen and ladies thought too grave and serious, the proprietor has got a new collection composed, and what are selling now are all of a lively and facetious turn' (ibid. 21–23 Nov. 1769, xxvi. 499; an earlier version of the advertisement is ibid. 25–28 Feb. 1769, xxv. 195, etc.). Cf. OED, *sub* motto, 1c, 6.

7. Hon. Frances Ingram Shepheard (1761–1841), 2d dau. of Charles, 9th Vct Irvine; m. (1 March 1781) Lord William Gordon, despite the opposition of Lord Chancellor Thurlow, her guardian (*Scots Peerage* iv. 554, v. 19; J. M. Bulloch, *The Gay Gordons,* 1908, pp. 116–23).

8. Templenewsam, in Yorkshire, near Leeds; the seat of Lady Irvine.

9. Frances Gibson Shepheard (1734–1807), m. (1758) Charles Ingram (1727–78), 9th Vct Irvine, 1763; 'spent a long and beneficent life at Temple Newsam'

(*Scots Peerage* v. 18; GEC). According to a story Lady Mary Coke heard at Margate the marriage was the result of 'Lady Ingram's gaming at Gloucester House': 'you must have heard that she used to play at that House till two or three o'clock in the morning and as she carried her daughters with her they were left to amuse themselves and make acquaintance with any men who frequented the house, among others Lord William Gordon, who is certainly very clever and . . . an old practitioner in gallantry' ('MS Journals' 12 Aug. 1780).

10. In Lord William Gordon's first proposals for a settlement he asked for £10,350 in South Sea annuities, presumably to pay his debts. He 'was not seized or possessed of any estate or fortune such that he could do anything,' according to his petition to Chancery. His income was £500 a year allowance from his brother the Duke of Gordon, £100 from the deputy rangership of the Green Park, and £300 from his commission as Lt-Col. of his brother's regiment of Northern Fencibles. His petition was not granted, and the case went to the House of Lords on his appeal 29–31 Jan. 1781, and was denied 9 Feb. 1781 (information from R. W. Hale to WSL 29 Jan., 2 Oct. 1934). On 26 Nov. 1780 Lady Mary Coke recorded the rumour that the marriage 'is broke off upon Lady Irvine finding his debts were too considerable for her to undertake the payment,' but Lady Frances Scott was sure it was not broken off ('MS Journals').

If the Russian squadron happens, like other folks, to insult Plymouth, I suppose you will go to see it, unless the very names of the commanders terrify you, for they sound as if selected to affront us. What think you, Madam, of Captains Cocuffsoff,[11] Boscarcuff, Huncuff, and Melnicuff? I wish such tremendous appellations do not imprint terror enough to recall the camps into the two Parks![12] They are at least as terrible as the schoolboys,[13] the black maid[14] and the servant girls[15] that have been hanged for obliging both Houses of Parliament to adjourn, and for burning London about the Government's ears.

This morning I made my annual visit to the Norths, and was received by my Lady, with whom I found that superlative jackanapes Mr Eden. He flung himself upon the settee, and thence distributed airs of protection, as far as was consistent with giving himself no sort of trouble. The contrast was perfect. Lady North was all humility and civility; the *commis parvenu*[15a] seemed to be giving audience.

Friday night 18th.

I dined at Ditton[16] today, and though Lord Beauchamp, a great news-merchant, was there, I did not learn a tittle. We have had

11. In command of the *America*. His name and the names which follow are in a list of captains of the Russian fleet, only one squadron of which had at the date of HW's letter reached the Downs (*London Chronicle* 15–17 Aug., xlviii. 154; *London Courant* 17 Aug.).

12. The encampment in Hyde Park broke up on 10 Aug. and in St James's Park on 15 Aug. (*London Chronicle* 5–25 Aug., xlviii. 115–152, *passim*).

13. 'It is worthy of remark that of the several persons, male and female, executed on account of the late riots, seventeen of them have been under 18 years of age, and three not quite 15' (newspaper cutting from the *London Courant* 14 Aug. inserted by HW in *Last Journals* ii. 327, *sub* Aug. 1780). For a list of those executed, see the *Annual Register*, 1780, pp. 277, 285–7; *London Chronicle* 8–10 Aug., xlviii. 135.

14. Charlotte Gardiner or Gardner, convicted at the Old Bailey 4 July for leading a mob, in June, to demolish John Lebarty's house in St Katharine's Lane,

and to threaten St Katharine's Hospital nearby. She and Mary Roberts, hanged on Tower Hill 11 July, were the first women executed for the Gordon Riots (ibid. 4–11 July, xlviii. 12, 18, 23; A. C. Ducarel, *History of the Royal Hospital . . . of St Katharine*, 1782, p. 33, *Bibliotheca Topographica Britannica*, Vol. II).

15. Two other women, Mary Cooke, aged about 25, and Elizabeth Collins, aged about 17, were hanged in St George's Fields on 9 Aug. (*London Chronicle* 11 July–10 Aug., xlviii. 37, 47, 99, 134).

15a. Shelburne in the House of Lords 6 March had called Fullarton a *commis* (clerk), a term resented by Fullarton; the two fought a duel on 21 March; see *post* 14 Jan. 1781. Fullarton had been secretary to Stormont at Paris; Eden was chief secretary to Lord Carlisle in Ireland 1780–2 and had been under secretary of state for the North 1772–8, 'Lord Suffolk's deputy' (*Last Journals* ii. 178).

16. Lord Hertford's seat at Thames Ditton, Surrey.

rain and a west wind, but as it is again turned to the N.E. we must still wait for the fate of the West Indies—but as my letter might be quite stale—no, I think, it could not be less interesting if it lay in my drawer this month—well, it shall go. One cannot be always in the year '59, and have victories fresh and fresh for every post-day. We have camps at home instead of conquests abroad, and Lady Amherst's[17] assemblies on the Parade[18] in lieu of French cannon in Hyde Park. I remember an old ironic song of Estcourt[19] with this passage:

How with bloody French rags he has litter'd poor Westminster Hall,
O slovenly John Duke of Marlborough![20]

Future Scotch historians will have no occasion to decry our present commanders; nor treaties of Utrecht and Paris, to refund our conquests! So the present glorious era will at least wipe off one national reproach, our woeful talent at negotiation. Nobody can say Mr Eden made a shameful peace.[21]

17. Elizabeth Cary (ca 1740–1830), m. (1767) Sir Jeffrey Amherst, cr. (1776) Bn Amherst.

18. 'In St James's Park. The open space before the Horse Guards [where the Amhersts lived]; part of the old Tilt Yard at Whitehall' (Wheatley, *London Past and Present* iii. 28). 'Thursday night [10 Aug.] Lord Amherst had a grand military route at his house, Whitehall' (*London Courant* 12 Aug. 1780).

19. Richard Estcourt (1668–1712), actor and mimic; friend of the Duke of Marlborough; praised by Steele in the *Tatler*, No. 51, 6 Aug. 1709, and the *Spectator*, No. 468, 27 Aug. 1712.

20. To the account of Estcourt in HW's copy (now WSL; Hazen, *Cat. of HW's Lib.* 3912) of David Erskine Baker's *Biographica Dramatica*, new edn, 1782, HW added a note at i. 148: 'Estcourt's chief merit lay in his political ballads, which were excellent: particularly, the "[Full] Trial and Condemnation of John Duke of Marlborough," and the "Jewel of the Tower," on Sir R. Walpole. They were printed in a vol[ume] of State ballads, but without the names of the particular authors.' The quoted passage from stanza 14 of 'Full Trial' should read

'You see with his pitiful French bloody rags,
How he 'as litter'd poor Westminster Hall . . .'

It is in *A Pill to Purge State-Melancholy: or, A Collection of Excellent New Ballads*, 1715, p. 163 (now WSL; Hazen, *Cat. of HW's Lib.* 2446); the label on the spine is *State Ballads*; the ballad consists of twenty five-line stanzas, pp. 161–4. In his copy, HW did not identify Estcourt as the author, although he expanded *P——t* to *Paulet* in stanza 17.

21. Because, as one of the commissioners to treat with the American colonies in 1778, he made no peace at all.

To Lady Ossory, Wednesday 23 August 1780

Strawberry Hill, Wednesday, Aug. 23, 1780.

I WENT to town yesterday, Madam, and arrived just time enough to learn the desolation of Jerusalem. Our whole outward-bound fleets for East and West Indies are taken by the Spaniards[1]—as in a drag-net; though *they* are not reckoned able fishers. Seven companies of General Rainsford's[2] new-raised troops for Jamaica,[3] and two of Lord Macleod's,[4] and two ordnance-ships for the East,[5] are included in this great prize. I could not send you the virgin account in time,[6] for Lord Maccartney told me your Ladyship had ordered him to direct his letters to Ampthill, and that you should stop at Bowood. As the waters are so troubled, I conclude your host[7] will resume *his* fishing-tackle.[8] The Parliament, it is now said, will not be dissolved.[9]

1. 'Yesterday [22 Aug.] the lieutenant of the *Thetis* arrived at the Admiralty express, with the disagreeable intelligence that the fleet of outward-bound West India ships, which sailed from England on the 29th of July, and the outward-bound East India fleet, which sailed at the same time, under convoy . . . had fallen in with a squadron of Spanish and French men-of-war . . . on the 9th instant, a little way from the island of Madeira. . . . Fifty-two of the West India ships, and five East Indiamen, are all taken' (*London Chronicle* 22–24 Aug., xlviii. 177; *Sandwich Papers* iii. 277). Later reports revealed that the total number of ships lost was 63. See Robert Beatson, *Naval and Military Memoirs*, 1804, v. 148–54.

2. Charles Rainsford (1728–1809), Maj.-Gen., 1777, Gen., 1795; aide-de-camp to George III, 1777; equerry to the Duke of Gloucester ca 1768–ca 1781; M. P. Maldon 1773–4, Berealston 1787–8, Newport 1790–6 (*Court and City Register, passim*). At the date of this letter he was in command of the camp at Blackheath (*London Courant* 14 Aug.).

3. On 2 June 1780 Rainsford became the first colonel of the 99th Foot, raised for service in Jamaica (Mason ii. 77 n. 14), a post he held until 4 May 1781

(*Army Lists*). The *London Chronicle* 22–24 Aug., xlviii. 182, refers to the 'loss of the Jamaica regiment' as 'by far the greatest we can sustain by the late capture' because it might lead to the loss of Jamaica, and implies that the regiment consisted of '1000 men.' According to a return made by Don Luis de Cordóba, the Spanish commander who took the ships, there were 667 soldiers going to the West Indies, including 303 specifically designated for Jamaica and 64 for Jamaica and St Lucia; an additional 19 were for the 'American squadron' (*London Courant* 19 Sept., reprinted from the *Madrid Gazette* 29 Aug.).

4. John Mackenzie (1727–89), styled Lord Macleod; Baron Macleod and Count Cromarty in the Swedish peerage; M.P.; see Mason ii. 76–7 nn. 10, 12.

5. 'On board the five East Indiamen [*Royal George, Godfrey, Hillsborough, Gatton,* and *Mountstuart*] were a great supply of all kinds of naval stores. . . likewise 80,000 stand of arms, and military stores in abundance' (*London Chronicle* 22–24 Aug., xlviii. 178, 184).

6. That is, before she left Plymouth on her return to Ampthill.

7. Lord Shelburne.

8. HW may imply that Shelburne, instead of fishing in troubled waters, is

The pendulum of our councils seems to vibrate very irregularly.

In the evening I went to Dr. Graham's.[10] It is the most impudent puppet-show of imposition I ever saw, and the mountebank himself the dullest of his profession, except that he makes the spectators pay a crown apiece. We were eighteen. A young officer of the Guards affected humour, and tired me still more. A woman, invisible, warbled to clarionettes on the stairs. The decorations are pretty and odd, and the apothecary who comes up a trap-door—for no purpose, since he might as well come upstairs, is a novelty. The electrical experiments are nothing at all singular, and a poor air-pump, that only bursts a bladder, pieces out the farce. The Doctor is like Jenkinson[11] in person, and as flimsy a puppet. I hope his brother, whom Mrs Macaulay married, is not such a wooden thing on wires.[11a]

The Countess Cowper is at last delivered from her misery.[12] She died with consummate courage, and at the same time with the weakness of trying to conceal the cause[13] of her death. I have heard no particulars of her will. I believe she had little to bequeath, nor has given but trifling legacies from her son.[14] This is an important event only in this neighbourhood, and that only as it serves for conversation. If you correspond with a villager, you must now and then, Madam, take up with our gossipry. Another on our list of burials is

returning to *his* fishing at Bowood. In fact he retired there, indignant at negotiations with Rockingham for a new ministry, and did not come to Parliament when it reopened (*Last Journals* ii. 332–3; Lord Fitzmaurice, *Life of William Earl of Shelburne*, 2d edn, 1912, ii. 73).

9. This was the latest of many rumours: 'It is said that it is at last finally determined upon in the Cabinet not to dissolve Parliament till their next meeting about the Christmas recess' (*London Chronicle* 19–22 Aug., xlviii. 176). Although prorogued to 28 Sept., Parliament was dissolved 1 Sept. (*London Gazette* No. 12114, 29 Aug.–2 Sept.).

10. James Graham (1745–94), quack doctor, had an elaborate establishment called the 'Temple of Health' on the Royal Terrace, Adelphi. Colman's 'theatrical extravaganza,' *The Genius of Nonsense,* satirizing Graham's quackery and entertainment, opened 2 Sept. (Eugene R.

Page, *George Colman the Elder,* New York, 1935, pp. 267–8; *London Courant* 1 July, 4 Sept.).

11. Charles Jenkinson (1729–1808), cr. (1786) Bn Hawkesbury, (1796) E. of Liverpool; political follower of Bute and George III.

11a. Mr Ketton-Cremer has kindly pointed out that HW is quoting Congreve, *Way of the World,* III. i, Lady Wishfort to Peg: 'Why dost thou not stir, puppet?—thou wooden thing upon wires!'

12. She died 21 Aug. at Richmond (*London Chronicle* 24–26 Aug., xlviii. 187; Musgrave, *Obituary*). GEC gives 25 Aug., but Lady Mary Coke, who was at Margate, heard of her death on 23 Aug. ('MS Journals').

13. Cancer (*ante* 1 Aug. 1780).

14. Earl Spencer (*ante* 17 July 1776), her only surviving child. He and her stepson, Lord Cowper, 'Each gets a

a Sir Patrick Hamilton.[15] His history is curious. He has an estate of
£1800 a year in Ireland, but has lodged at Twickenham for three or
four years, watching impatiently an ancient uncle[16] who has some
money. The old gentleman, formerly a captain in the Scotch Greys,
is now eighty-eight, but as beautiful and sleek as Melchizedeck, when
he was not above two hundred; and he walks four or five miles every
day, and looks as if he would outlive his late heir for a quarter of a
century more. Sir Patrick was knighted when Mayor of Dublin.[17]
His lady[18] is still more parsimonious. In his mayoralty he could not
persuade her to buy a new gown. The pride of the Hamiltons surmounted the penury of the Highlands. He bought a silk that cost
five-and-fifty shillings a yard, but told his wife it cost but forty. In
the evening, she displayed it to some of her female acquaintance.
'Forty shillings a yard! Lord, Madam,' said one of them, 'I would
give five-and-forty myself.'—'Would you, Madam? You shall have it
at that price.' Judge how Sir Patrick was transported when he returned at night, and she bragged of the good bargain she had
made!

Mr Brown has shown me his designs for improving Belvoir
Castle.[19] They show judgment, and *would be* magnificent.[20] I asked
whence the funds were to arise, for I hear the Duke's exchequer is

jointure by her death' (HW to Mann 24
Aug. 1780).

15. Sir Patrick Hamilton (ca 1716–80),
Kt, 1761; Lord Mayor (1760–1) of Dublin;
died 22 Aug. and was buried at Twickenham 27 Aug. 1780 (MONTAGU i. 393 n. 1;
R. S. Cobbett, *Memorials of Twickenham*,
1872, p. 71; Daniel Lysons, *Environs of
London*, Vol. III, 1795, p. 583; George
Hamilton, *History of the House of Hamilton*, Edinburgh, 1933, p. 977; information
kindly supplied by Mr David Erskine).

16. Charles Hamilton (ca 1693–1784)
lived at No. 12, Montpelier Row, Twickenham, and was buried at Teddington.
He became Capt., 10th Dragoons, 1743
(retired, half-pay, 1754), but he was never
in the Scotch Greys (2d Dragoons) (Cobbett, op. cit. 375; Lysons, op. cit. 508;
G. Hamilton, loc. cit.; Everard Hamilton,
Hamilton Memoirs, 2d edn, Dundalk, 1920,
pp. 26–7; Mr David Erskine).

17. He was 'late lord mayor' when
dubbed by Halifax on 30 Oct. 1761 (W.
A. Shaw, *Knights of England*, 1906, ii.
291).

18. Elizabeth Meredith, dau. of Richard
Meredith of Greenhills, co. Kildare, m.
(1747) Patrick Hamilton (G. Hamilton,
loc. cit.; Mr David Erskine).

19. The D. of Rutland's seat in Leicestershire.

20. In HW's 'Book of Materials' 1771,
p. 84, is an account of Brown, quoted in
Toynbee, *Supp.* ii. 163–4: 'A year before
his death [Brown died 6 Feb. 1783] he
had made a great design for improving
the house at Belvoir, and for laying out
the ground there; but it was not begun
to be executed.' For Brown's plans, which
he placed in a MS book, his 'executors
received £300. The Castle was subsequently altered by James Wyatt' (Dorothy
Stroud, *Capability Brown*, 1950, p. 214).

extremely empty.[21] Sir Sampson Gideon[22] follows him round Cambridgeshire, and discharges the bills his Grace leaves unpaid.[23]

I have been writing letters and soliciting votes for Lord Macartney to be governor of Madras;[24] and yet can scarce wish to succeed—yet there is merit in not despising twenty thousand a year,[25] in an age when commands over Indian mines, and foreign embassies are thought below the acceptance of the beggars at Brooks's.

Friday, 25th.

Lady Hertford has brought me a *Morning Post,* in which are mighty compliments to *me,* yes, to *me.*[26] This shows the value of praise and abuse, and how judiciously they are dispensed! The Duke of Richmond, the living temple of virtue, is the object of calumny, I of commendation!—yet methinks my principles do not entitle me more to panegyric from a pensioner than the Duke's. It

21. The Duke's father had died intestate, leaving debts of over £60,000 which the present duke had assumed (W. E. Manners, *Some Account of the . . . Marquis of Granby,* 1899, pp. 392–3).

22. (1745–1824), cr. (1759) Bt, (1789) Bn Eardley; M.P.

23. 'His present Grace [of Rutland] . . . will I am persuaded never be out of debt, for neither he or she has any idea of proportioning their expenses to their income' (Coke, 'MS Journals' 31 May 1779).

24. None of these letters has been found. The *London Courant* had reported 21 July that 'Lord Macartney is soliciting the government of Madras, expecting that Governor Rumbold will speedily be recalled,' and had noticed some opposition to him (ibid. 12, 18, 21 Aug.). Appointed governor and president of Fort St George, Madras, in Nov. 1780, he arrived at Madras 22 June 1781, resigned in June 1785, and arrived in England in Jan. 1786. He refused an offer to succeed Hastings as governor-general of India.

25. Madras 'is £16,000' a year, Bengal '£25,000' (Macartney to Lord Ossory 31 Jan. 1783, in Macartney's *Private Correspondence,* ed. C. C. Davies, 1950, Camden Third Series, lxxvii. 214). Macartney's letters to Lady Ossory 19 Aug., 13, 28

Oct. 1780 mention problems in his getting the appointment and her good offices in obtaining Shelburne's support. With an estate of 'above £2400' a year, Macartney owed '£12,000, the greatest part of which would have been discharged by this time had it not been for my losses at Grenada' (19 Aug.; MSS in the National Library of Ireland: Fitzpatrick MSS).

26. The *Morning Post,* 24 Aug., includes a book review, signed 'Candour,' of '*A Retreat for the Gods,* a poem, inscribed to the elegant Genius of Strawberry Hill. The invocation is warm and animated; the images are mostly from the Gothic fable, but in the true spirit of poetry. After follows a description of the building, which, for singularity of taste, and simplicity of design, does honour to the hand which raised and ornamented it. The few lines prefixed to this little performance inform us, that the master of this elegant mansion is a private gentleman, whose good taste, and particularity of genius, do honour to the country which gave him birth. He further says, that his erudition is great, his knowledge extensive, and that his researches, which have turned upon anecdotal antiquity, have proved themselves both of entertainment and use for society in general.'

talks too of my extensive learning, which always makes me laugh—
no mortal's reading has been more superficial.

I heard last night that the Russian fleet only lifted up its leg
against us, and is returned;[27] and tonight that Lord Vernon[28] is
dead. If I receive no orders tomorrow from your Ladyship, I shall
send this to Ampthill. On Monday I shall go for two or three days
into Kent to visit Mr Barrett,[29] and see Knowle again,[30] and some
other places.[31]

Saturday.

My Lady says nothing; go to Ampthill, letter!

To Lord Ossory, Thursday 31 August 1780

Address: To the Earl of Ossory at Ampthill Park, Bedfordshire. *Postmark:*
31 AV. GC.

Berkeley Square, Aug. 31, 1780.

My dear Lord,

AS I told Lady O. in my last that the Parliament was *not* to be
dissolved, I write one line to contradict myself, for though you
are in no danger, I hate to give false intelligence. It is to be dissolved
tomorrow.

I returned from Kent last night, and am going to Strawb[erry]
as fast as I can, to avoid hearing of elections. When the Russian
fleet was candidate for the Downs, and the Court dared to set up
nobody against it, it is not worth inquiring about petty boroughs.
I should as soon care about what passes at a vestry. When we are

27. The fleet had sailed on 19 and 21
Aug. (*ante* 16 Aug. 1780, n. 2). The squadron which had first arrived in the Downs
returned to cruise in the North Sea. It
reached St Petersburg ('the road of Cron-
stadt') on 19 Oct. for the winter; the two
other squadrons were to winter at Lisbon
and Leghorn (*London Chronicle* 25–28
Nov., xlviii. 505).

28. Lady Harcourt's father, George
Venables-Vernon (1709–21 Aug. 1780), cr.
(1762) Bn Vernon; M.P.; died at Sudbury,
Derbyshire.

29. Thomas Barrett (?1743–1803), of
Lee, near Canterbury; HW's occasional
correspondent. HW went to Lee on Monday, 28 Aug., and returned 30 Aug. For
HW's description of Lee, see *Country Seats*
76–7 (COLE ii. 237 n. 4; BERRY i. 59 and
n. 5; MASON ii. 77–8).

30. For his earlier visit, see HW to
Bentley 5 Aug. 1752; for the visit in 1780,
see *Country Seats* 77.

31. Deane (see *post* 1 Sept. 1780), St
Albans, and Barfreston Church (*Country
Seats* 77).

quite prostrate, I suppose we shall have *the* member of Parliament, as there is still *the* senator at Rome.[1]

Yours most etc.,

H. W.

To Lady Ossory, Friday 1 September 1780

Strawberry Hill, Sept. 1, 1780.

THERE have been twenty cross-purposes, Madam, and I have been a sufferer by them all. Lord Maccartney told me your Ladyship had ordered him to direct to Ampthill; accordingly so did I. Then you stayed in the West, and I went into Kent. You directed your letter to me here, and here it waited for me, and here I found it today, and learn that you are to be in town today in a new house, still in Grosvenor Place, for you move no farther than a pawn. I am as sorry for poor Mrs Crayle[1] as G. Selwyn was for poor Mrs Craufurd[2] whom he had never seen; and a good deal more sorry for his muscular pains,[3] but do not at all interest myself about his election,[4] nor any other body's election, while nobody will interest himself about anything else for these six weeks. I heard as I passed through the town that the Parliament was to be dissolved—a curious moment to be sure[5]—but I suppose it is a measure to make the whole

1. 'The municipality of Rome is represented by a municipal body of 48 councillors (besides the two ecclesiastical deputies of the secular and regular clergy); 8 of these with the name of *Conservatore di Roma* form the Roman magistracy, besides the chief called *Senatore di Roma*' (Gaetano Moroni, *Dizionario di erudizione storico-ecclesiastica*, Venice, 1840–79, lxiv. 30–1, *sub* Senato Romano, translated).

———

1. Perhaps the wife of Crayle Crayle (d. 2 Oct.) of Acton, Middlesex (Daniel Lysons, *Environs of London*, Vol. II, 1795, p. 9; GM 1780, 1. 495); or a resident of Bedfordshire.

2. Perhaps Hon. Sarah Sempill (d. 1751), dau. of Hew, 12th Bn Sempill, m. (1750) as 2d wife, Patrick Craufurd of Drumsoy

and Auchinames (*Scots Peerage* vii. 563). See also HW to Selwyn 6 Sept. 1757, SELWYN 137 and n. 2, where this reference appears also.

3. 'I am at present in a weaker state of health from a present disorder than I ever was' (Selwyn to Lord North 22 Aug., in Jesse, *Selwyn* iv. 363).

4. Selwyn wrote to Lord North from Matson, 22 Aug.: 'It is my intention . . . to resign all thoughts of being a candidate at the next election for the City of Gloucester. . . . The difficulties are greater, and the probability of success less, than it ever was on other occasions of a similar nature' (ibid.). He was persuaded to make a canvass but declined the poll (*post* 23 Sept. 1780).

5. When it had been so recently prorogued from 24 Aug. to 28 Sept. (*ante*

nation drunk, lest it should be afraid of the French and Spanish fleets! or regret the two[6] that we have lost! It is certainly wise to lay ourselves open to every kind of attack, for every one that is missed counts for a victory on our side. We should not be half so glad of the arrival of the ships from the Levant,[7] if we had not lost those that were going to the East and West. This sort of wisdom must captivate *me,* it is so like my own. I believe I have told your Ladyship that I reckon it is five to one better for me that my hay should be spoiled than not, because as I have five cows and but one horse, the cows will eat bad hay, and the horse will not. However, you may be sure I admire the verses,[8] and perfectly agree with them: the ministers are full good enough for the people. You may depend, Madam, on my neither showing nor naming; not only from fidelity, but because coarser dainties than pearls are good enough for swine.

I have not been capering at balls in the torrid zone like your Ladyship's neighbourhood, but I have been jolting over stony roads in the midst of Africa; at least I thought so, though in the heart of Kent. I have seen nothing very charming, and little new. One place struck me much, but more from recollection of old passages, than from any curiosity in itself. This was Deane,[9] a *trist* old seat of the Oxendens, now deserted—but it was long the residence of Sir George,[10] who in my very youth was the fine gentleman of the age— extremely handsome, a speaker in Parliament, a lord of the Treasury, very ambitious, and a particular favourite of my father—till he became so of my sister-in-law[11]—That, and a worse story,[12] blasted all his prospects, and buried him in retirement—

29 June 1780, n. 13). 'The English Parliament was suddenly dissolved. It was said that the ministers consulted Lord Loughborough, who was on the Northern Circuit, and he advised it, as he said he found the Court was losing ground again every day' (*Last Journals* ii. 329).

6. The fleets of East and West Indies merchantmen (*ante* 23 Aug. 1780).

7. The Lisbon and Oporto fleets, 'about 24 sail' (*London Chronicle* 26 Aug.– 2 Sept., xlviii. 200, 202, 210).

8. Not identified.

9. Or Dene Park, north of Tonbridge; built in the sixteenth century; then in the possession of Sir Henry Oxenden, 6th Bt (*Country Seats* 77).

10. Sir George Oxenden (1694–1775), 5th Bt, 1720; M.P.; a lord of the Admiralty 1725–7 and of the Treasury 1727– 37; groom of the Bedchamber to the P. of Wales, 1742.

11. Lady Orford, when Lady Walpole, had an affair with Sir George, who was said to be the father of her only child, George, later third Earl of Orford. HW himself is reported on 26 May 1796 to have said: 'I am well convinced . . . that [George] was not the son of my brother. Sir Henry [George] Oxenden was his father' (Joseph Farington's diary, in DALRYMPLE 324). See also GEC, *sub* Orford; John, Lord Hervey, *Memoirs,* ed. Romney Sedgwick, 1931, iii. 740–3; HW to Thomas

For when a courtier's out of place,
The country shelters his disgrace.

Portraits of him,[13] and some heroines[14] of the time—now totally forgotten, but fresh in my memory, seemed a waking vision—it was like Æneas's meeting Dido in the shades—I could not have conceived that scenes in which I was not in the least interested, could have made so strong an impression—yet they really affected me as if I was beginning the world again. I could not shake off the sensations till I came to Knowle—and that was a medley of various feelings! Elizabeth and Burleigh and Buckhurst[15]—and then Charles,[16] and Anne Dorset and Pembroke,[17] and Sir Edw. Sackville[18]—and then a more engaging Dorset,[19] and Villiers[20] and Prior—and then the old

Walpole 19 Sept. 1780 for a veiled reference).

12. He 'had two children by his wife's sister [Arabella Dunch], who was married to his most intimate friend Mr [Edward] Thompson, from whom, upon Sir George Oxenden's account, she was separated, and died in childbed not without Sir George's being suspected of having a greater share in her catastrophe than merely having got the child' (Hervey, op. cit. 741–2).

13. His portrait by Thomas Hudson (1701–79) was, in 1907, owned by the Oxendens, whose seat at that time was Broome (H. A. Tipping 'Broome Park, Kent,' Country Life, 1907, xxii. 24).

14. Mrs Thompson's portrait was also at Broome in 1907 (ibid. xxii. 25).

15. Thomas Sackville (ca 1536–1608), cr. (1567) Bn of Buckhurst, (1604) E. of Dorset; poet, dramatist, and statesman; succeeded Lord Burghley as Lord High Treasurer, 1599. Queen Elizabeth granted him the reversion of Knole, which he was the first Sackville to own (Victoria Sackville-West, Knole and the Sackvilles, 1931, pp. 28–47).

16. 'He [HW] means Richard' (ibid. 181, where this passage is quoted): Richard Sackville (1589–1624), 3d E. of Dorset, 1609; friend and patron of Beaumont, Ben Jonson, Fletcher, and Drayton (ibid. 48–81). It is more likely that 'Charles' is Charles I; see n. 18 below.

17. Anne Clifford (1590–1676), m. 1 (1609) Richard Sackville, 3d E. of Dorset; m. 2 (1630) Philip Herbert, 4th E. of Pembroke, 1st E. of Montgomery; Bns Clifford, s.j.; included in Royal and Noble Authors, Works i. 485–6. Cf. Montagu i. 125; Sackville-West, op. cit. 48–81.

18. Edward Sackville (1590–1652), K.B., 1616, 4th E. of Dorset, 1624; K.G., 1625; M.P. Sussex 1620–2; killed Edward Bruce, Lord Bruce of Kinloss, in a duel, 1613; painted by Van Dyck (the portrait HW saw at Knole); a devoted follower of Charles I, as was his wife, the governess of Charles I's children. His second son, Hon. Edward Sackville, was taken prisoner by the parliamentary forces in 1646 and murdered by a soldier (Collins, Peerage, 1812, ii. 164–5; Sackville-West, op. cit. 82–110).

19. Charles Sackville (1638–1706), 6th E. of Dorset, 1677, cr. (1675) E. of Middlesex; rake and poet; 'the finest gentleman in the voluptuous court of Charles the Second, and in the gloomy one of King William' (Royal and Noble Authors, Works i. 425).

20. George, 2d D. of Buckingham. The sixth E. of Dorset, according to HW, 'had as much wit as his first master [Charles II], or his cotemporaries Buckingham and Rochester, without the royal want of feeling, the Duke's want of principle, or the Earl's want of thought' (ibid.).

Duke and Duchess[21] and Lady Betty Germaine[22] and the court of George II!

The place is stripped of its beeches[23] and honours, and has neither beauty nor prospects.[24] The house extensive as it is, seemed dwindled to the front of a college, and has the silence and solitude of one. It wants the cohorts of retainers, and the bustling jollity of the old nobility, to disperse the gloom. I worship all its faded splendour, and enjoy its preservation; and could have wandered over it for hours with satisfaction; but there was such a heterogeneous housekeeper[25] as poisoned all my enthusiasm. She was more like one of Mrs St John's abigails, than an inhabitant of a venerable mansion; and shuffled about in slippers, and seemed to *admire* how I could care about the pictures of such old *frights* as covered the walls!

When the coast is clear and your elections over and gone drunk to bed, I shall be very happy, Madam, to wait on you at Ampthill. I have been better for these three months than in the last five years; and though I do not allow myself to draw notes upon futurity, I like to employ my moments of health to the best advantage. Those I gladly give to the few I love—sickness and pain one should keep to oneself.

21. Lionel Cranfield Sackville (1688–1765), 7th E. of Dorset, 1706, cr. (1720) D. of Dorset; m. (1709) Elizabeth Colyear (d. 1768).

22. A close friend of the Duke and Duchess, she had three rooms assigned to her at Knole, where she lived much of the time after her husband's death in 1718. At his request she left Drayton (and part of her fortune) to a younger son of the Duke and Duchess, Lord George Sackville, who took the name of Germain (Sackville-West, op. cit. 12–13, 169–72, and illustrations facing pp. 168, 172).

23. 'Great havoc of the fine old woods by the late Duke' (*Country Seats* 77),

Charles Sackville (1711–69), 2d D. of Dorset, 1765, who held the title for less than four years. For a more detailed account of the park and house, see HW to Bentley 5 Aug. 1752.

24. Gibbon in 1761 thought Knole 'a noble pile, very much upon the plan of Sissinghurst; the park finely wooded and the ground disposed by nature but the place wants prospect and water' (*Gibbon's Journal to January . . . 1763*, ed. D. M. Low, 1929, p. 27, *sub* 5 June 1761).

25. A 'trapes of a housekeeper' (HW to Mason 31 Aug. 1780, Mason ii. 78; Sackville-West, op. cit. 189–90).

To Lady Ossory, Tuesday 12 September 1780

Address: To the Countess of Ossory at Ampthill Park, Bedfordshire. *Postmark:* ISLEWORTH. 12 SE.

Sept. 12, 1780.

WHEN the Bedfordshire election is over, and Lady Spencer has been chaired at St Alban's,[1] I shall be ready to steal to Ampthill, Madam; but would not for the mines of Golconda[2] find myself in the midst of one of those combustions: I should be, according to the incomparable and picturesque simile, like a dog in a dancing-school. I was like anything still more awkward and confused last week. Coming out of Lady Di's in the dark, I missed my way and pitched headlong down a perpendicular bank into a brick pavement laced with orange tubs and flower pots: broke two of the latter to powder, and yet only bruised my hand, and slightly hurt my hip. Had I weighed more than gossamer, I must have been dashed to pieces.

Your Ladyship has been very charitable to Mr Byng—but what must Lord Torrington feel, if he has any feeling, to know his brother eats the bread he has, from a minister[3] whom the elder always opposed![4] This I should think would wound one to the quick.

Admiral Keppel is thrown out at Windsor;[5] but though all the royal bakers and brewers and butchers voted against him, you must not imagine it was by mandate,[6] whatever Ramus[7] the page might

1. In the election of 1780, a 'strong contest is expected for . . . St Alban's, between Lord Grimstone and Colonel Sloper, who stands upon the interest of Lord Spencer' (*London Chronicle* 5–7 Sept., xlviii. 226). Lord Spencer was ill at Wimbledon during the election.

2. 'The old name of Hyderabad, formerly celebrated for its diamonds, used as a synonym for a "mine of wealth"' (OED, where this passage is quoted).

3. Lord North.

4. 'On leaving the Army in May of 1780, it seems probable that he [George Byng] went almost immediately into his monotonous duties in the Inland Revenue at Somerset House, or some similar work,

although there is no record of his being at Somerset House till 1782' (*The Torrington Diaries,* ed. C. Bruyn Andrews, 1934–8, i. p. xxix).

5. He was defeated 8 Sept. by Hon. John Montagu (Hussey-Montagu) and Penyston Portlock Powney, the votes being for Montagu, 214; for Powney, 174; and for Keppel, 158 (*London Chronicle* 9–12 Sept., xlviii. 242). He had represented Windsor since 1761. On 27 Sept. he was returned for Surrey.

6. 'The King is said to have canvassed for votes in person against the Admiral. One elector, a silk-mercer, and a stout Keppelite, stated that his Majesty, in canvassing him, said in his usual quick

say; for his M[ajesty] himself told the Admiral that he hoped he would carry his election[8]—how saucy in his own servants to thwart his wishes! I know nothing at all worth writing: of all dull letters a short one is the best.

To Lady Ossory, Saturday 23 September 1780

Address: To the Countess of Ossory at Ampthill Park, Bedfordshire. *Postmark:* ISLEWORTH. 23 SE.

Strawberry Hill, Sept. 23, 1780.

THOUGH I care so little about elections, Madam (because I have such a contempt for the aggregate when it is assembled), I feel for the vexation your civil war produces and will produce to your Ladyship and Lord Ossory;[1] and take it as a mark of your persuasion of the interest I must adopt in all your affairs, that you are so good as to communicate the detail. I hope you will triumph at least; which is very consolatory, when one has no more than the disappointment of antagonists to lament. You will be so glad

manner, "The Queen wants a gown—wants a gown—No Keppel!—No Keppel!" ' Prince Augustus, aged seven, later Duke of Sussex, 'himself told me that he had been locked up in the nursery at Windsor for wearing Keppel colours.' The Prince of Wales and Prince Frederick showed their satisfaction when Keppel was returned for Surrey (Lord Albemarle, *Memoirs of the Marquis of Rockingham*, 1852, ii. 424–5).

7. William Ramus (d. 1792), page of the Bedchamber to the King 1762–89, and at his death described as 'formerly first page to his Majesty' (GM 1792, lxii. pt ii. 869; *Royal Kalendar* 1762–91). According to an account from Windsor, 8 Sept., 'Mr Ramus and some of the musicians were put to bed the night before the election to become inhabitants' so that they could vote against Admiral Keppel (*London Courant* 11 Sept.).

8. 'The King was making the strongest interest at Windsor against Admiral Keppel, yet, meeting him on the Terrace there, told him he hoped he would carry his election. Keppel lost it, but the coun-

ties of Surrey and Suffolk immediately offered to elect him, and he accepted the former. (Prince of Wales took great part for Keppel, and would not speak to Col. Egerton, who voted against him)' (*Last Journals* ii. 329). Other suggestions of the King's intervention in the election are in the *London Courant* 13 Sept. See also BM, *Satiric Prints* v. 419–20, 424, Nos 5700, 5701, 5708.

1. On 27 Sept. Lord Ossory was returned for Bedfordshire, but Lord Ongley, who had represented the county since 1761, was thrown out (*Members of Parliament*; *Last Journals* ii. 330). In the *London Courant* 15 Sept. (and following days) appeared an advertisement signed by Lord Ossory: 'Lord Ongley having declined soliciting your votes and interest, I beg leave to request them' for the Hon. St Andrew St John, friend of Fox and supported by the Bedford interest. In a joint advertisement the two solicited votes. 'It is thought [they] will be elected . . . without opposition' (ibid.).

to see your house empty for a day or two, and have the empty bottles removed, that I will not encumber you the only moment you can breathe. Indeed I could not well, for I have advertised my long-delayed last volume of Painters to come out,[2] and must be in town to distribute it. I seized this opportunity to publish it, because I was sure nobody would think of it or me, and that it will have a favourable chance for being taken no notice of. It is a debt I owed, and I will take care to incur no more. My cousin and namesake[3] is come into Parliament,[4] which baptizes me *the old H.W.*—and then one must not play the fool. Charles Fox, I have just heard has beaten Lord Lincoln from the hustings,[5] of which I am very glad. George Selwyn has been here for a moment this morning on the road from *his* defeat.[6] I did not quite enjoy him, as his errand was to give a glimpse of my house to the Signorina and the official Signora Madre,[7] and he would point out twenty things to them of which they had no more conception than of the Apocalypse; yet he entertained me with some of his calamities; they hanged him in effigy, and dressed up a figure of Mimie, and pinned on its breast these words alluding

2. *Anecdotes of Painting*, Vol. IV, was advertised for publication 'On Monday, October 9' (*London Chronicle* 26–28 Sept., xlviii. 304). All but a few pages of it had been printed since 1771. See Hazen, *SH Bibl.* 63–5, where the reasons for the delay are discussed.

3. HW's first cousin once removed, the Hon. Horatio Walpole (1752–1822), 2d E. of Orford (n.c.), 1809.

4. He had been returned for Wigan on 11 Sept.

5. 'At the close of the poll yesterday [22 Sept.] for the City and Liberty of Westminster, the numbers were . . . : For Sir George Brydges Rodney 5298, Hon. Charles Fox 4878, Lord Lincoln 4257' (*London Chronicle* 21–23 Sept., xlviii. 287). 'Lord Lincoln having last night [22 Sept.] given up the contest for Westminster, by declining the poll,' Rodney and Fox were returned. 'Lord Lincoln then demanded a scrutiny, which is to begin on the 10th of October' (ibid. 288). On that date, Lincoln then declining the scrutiny, Rodney and Fox were officially returned (ibid. 10–12 Oct., xlviii. 347). After the polls were closed on 22 Sept. Fox and Admiral Young (as proxy for

Rodney) were chaired; among the people in the procession were 'Lord Ossory, the Hon. Mr Fitzpatrick . . . Mr Burke' (ibid. 21–23 Sept., xlviii. 288).

6. As early as 4 Sept. the *London Courant* reported that 'John Webb, Esq., and Dr Barrow certainly come in for Gloucester, and Mr Selwyn is thrown out.' This prediction proved true. Selwyn and Sir Andrew Hammond made a canvass and 'declined the contest,' and Webb and Barrow were elected without opposition on 14 Sept. (ibid. 6–18 Sept.). Anticipating this outcome, Selwyn, who had represented Gloucester since 1754, had had himself returned for the family borough of Ludgershall on 12 Sept. See also 1 Sept. 1780, n. 4; Selwyn to Lord Carlisle 11 Sept., *Carlisle MSS* 442–3.

7. Mrs Bethia Webb, Selwyn's housekeeper, styled 'governess' to Maria Fagnani in his will, is probably the 'governess' referred to below; 'Nanny' was apparently a nurse or governess under Mrs Webb's direction (S. Parnell Kerr, *George Selwyn and the Wits*, 1909, pp. 258, 261, 263, 325; Jesse, *Selwyn* iv. 48, 326, 342, 359, 362, and *passim*; Bernard Falk, 'Old Q's' *Daughter*, 1937, p. 25).

to the gallows, 'This is what I told you, you would come to.' From Gloucester he went to Luggershall, where he was received by ringing of bells and bonfires—'Being driven out of my capital,' said he, 'and coming into that country of turnips where I was adored, I seemed to be arrived in my Hanoverian dominions.' *This* paid for the burthen of the governess and child!—There are other folks who would feel more comfortable among their turnips just now, than in their Castle, having been treated on the terrace with the sight of crape-cockades inscribed, 'For Admiral Keppel'[8]—If *Ich Dien*[9] does not wear one, he at least, I hear, *boudes* those who voted against the admiral[10]—so, victories may be bought too dear!

I am trembling at every letter I receive from Paris. My dear old friend I fear is going![11] The last,[12] which was on Tuesday, had left her at the twentieth day of a fever. To have struggled for twenty days at eighty-four[13] shows such stamina that I have not totally lost hopes—but yet that letter was worse than the three preceding,[14] which had much flattered me. It will be a grievous loss—but when one is old oneself, one cannot have many such misfortunes!

Miss Wrottesley's £5000[15] will purchase a princely turnippery; but I doubt even that nor a baron[16] will indemnify her for the capital

---

8. 'The people of Windsor wore crape favours with Keppel's name, in the King's face, on the Terrace' (*Last Journals* ii. 330, *sub* 22 Sept. 1780).

9. The Prince of Wales.

10. In the election for Windsor; the poll for Surrey did not take place until 27–28 Sept. (*London Chronicle* 26–30 Sept., xlviii. 303, 309).

11. Mme du Deffand died on the date of this letter (DU DEFFAND v. 250).

12. Wiart to HW 10 Sept. 1780, ibid. v. 246–7.

13. She would have been 84 on 25 Sept.

14. Wiart to HW 30 Aug., 3, 6 Sept. 1780, ibid. v. 244–6.

15. Her marriage portion: 'We talked of Miss Dolly Wrotsley's marriage [25 Nov. 1780] with the Hessian minister, not a very advantageous one certainly but 'tis a husband and some people think any is better than none. The Duchess of Bedford gives her three thousand pounds and she had two of her own; the Baron I should think could not make great

settlements' (Coke, 'MS Journals' 17 Sept. 1780; *post* 17 Dec. 1780).

16. Christian Moritz Wisner (ca 1735–98), Baron Kutzleben; son of Maria Margrethe Wisner; adopted 19 Aug. 1755 by Johann Gottfried, Bn Kutzleben (probably his father) and on 20 April 1763 was authorized to take the name and arms of Kutzleben; entered the Hessian army, 1752, and distinguished himself; sent to London, 1774, by the Prince of Hesse-Cassel to receive payment for Hessian forces employed by the British; minister (1776–81) and envoy extraordinary and minister plenipotentiary (1781–9, 1791–8) from the Landgrave of Hesse-Cassel; recalled for military duty 1789–92 as colonel of the Ditfurth regiment (GM 1798, lxviii pt ii. 813; *London Chronicle* 12–15 Nov. 1774, 2–9 July 1776, 5–7 Nov. 1789, xxxvi. 467, xl. 16, 26, lxvi. 442; *Times* 7 Nov. 1791; *Les Papiers de Calonne*, ed. Christian de Parrel, Cavaillon, 1932, pp. 123–8).

she quits—and yet, £5000 will soon I believe buy a principality in England.

To Lady Ossory, Wednesday 27 September 1780

Address: To the Countess of Ossory at Ampthill Park, Bedfordshire. *Postmark:* ISLEWORTH. 27 SE.

Strawberry Hill, Sept. 27, 1780.

I REJOICE in your triumph, Madam, though I cannot partake of your fireworks. Not only had I ordered my books[1] to be advertised, but have a more melancholy cause that detains me. The letters that I have received today from Paris bid me be prepared to receive an account of my dear old friend's death. I knew she had been very ill, but till these two last posts, I had been flattered that she was recovering. Today her own secretary,[2] and Mr T. Walpole pronounce that there are no hopes.[3] I had sent James's powder, and had begged my cousin if possible to obtain her trying it[4]—but alas! I knew France too well, and physicians too, and *their* physicians still more, to have much hope of its being given—but it is too shocking to be told that the physician[5] has laid aside all medicines, and yet would not suffer her to take it! When is it best to try it, but in despair? and when, if not at eighty-four? He said, it would vomit her, and kill her —is not he killing her himself by trying nothing! and by not trying the powder in that case? This is a horrible thought, though she could not be immortal; and the terror I have been under for some time of her becoming deaf, added to blindness, had made me more reconciled to her great age, and to the probability of losing her— She retains, that is, did retain her senses,[6] did not suffer, knew her situation, and was perfectly tranquil, and spoke little—but by the whole description she appears to me to have been almost worn out— I tremble for the next letter[7]—though it is just as if I had already

---

1. *Anecdotes of Painting,* Vol. IV.

2. Jean-François Wiart, Mme du Deffand's secretary and valet-de-chambre (DU DEFFAND, *passim*).

3. His letter to HW is missing; HW answered him 28 Sept. 1780.

4. HW to Thomas Walpole 6 Sept. 1780.

5. Michel-Philippe Bouvart (1717–87), who had been Mme du Deffand's physician since 1775 and probably for a longer period. See DU DEFFAND, *passim.*

6. She had entries made in her journal up to and including 10 Sept. (ibid. v. 461).

7. In the next letter Wiart wrote that

received it—Another friend gone! I scarce have one left of above my own age. It is these memorandums, that at the same time reconcile one to one's own departure—what can one expect but to survive one's friends if one lives long?—in this unhappy mood, Madam, I should be bad company. Can I care about elections? If an opponent's[8] death could set Mr Burke to moralizing on the hustings at Bristol,[9] how must the loss of so dear a friend affect me! The savage physician exasperates me—what transport should I have felt, if I could have saved her, though but for six months! Perhaps I could not—I will not be unjust; it is probable that I should not—but oh! not to let me try! It augments my abhorrence of physicians and professions. Long ago I said that the Devil's three names, Satan, Lucifer and Belzebub, were given to him in his three capacities of President of Priests, Lawyers and Physicians. I repeat it now with rancour: Belzebub and Bouvard are synonymous terms in my lexicon. Five years ago I loved the wretch, for he saved her, as I thought, in my presence[10] —Did that give him a right over her life? Has not he cancelled my gratitude? Can one love and hate at once? I would if I could—yes, I do thank him for prolonging her life for five years—but oh! professions, professions! how *l'esprit du corps* absorbs all feelings!—and how prejudice becomes principle! Dear old woman! she is now, I fear, no more!—I can write no more, Madam, for I can write on no other subject, and have no right to torment you with my concern. You shall hear no more of it. Nature takes care that hopeless griefs should not be permanent; and I have seen so much affectation of lamentation where little was felt, and I know so well that I have often

'la tête est totalement perdue, les idées entièrement éclipsées' (ibid. v. 249), but it did not reach HW until 7 Oct., when the news of her death also arrived (ibid. v. 250; HW to Hon. Thomas Walpole 8 Oct. 1780).

8. Richard Combe (ca 1728–8 Sept. 1780), M.P. Milborne Port 1772, Aldeburgh 1774–80 (Foster, *Alumni Oxon.*; *London Chronicle* 12–14 Sept., xlviii. 250). He intended to stand for Bristol in the election, the return of which was made 20 Sept.

9. In Burke's speech at Bristol 9 Sept., when he declined to stand for the city which he had represented since 1774, he said: 'Gentlemen, the melancholy event

of yesterday reads to us an awful lesson against being too much troubled about any of the objects of ordinary ambition. The worthy gentleman who has been snatched from us at the moment of the election, and in the middle of the contest, whilst his desires were as warm and his hopes as eager as ours, has feelingly told us what shadows we are, and what shadows we pursue' (ibid. 14–16 Sept., xlviii. 260; GM 1780, 1. 618–19, where the speech is misdated 19 Sept.; Burke, *Works*, 1803, iii. 433).

10. About 20 Sept. 1775 (HW to Conway 6 Oct. 1775; 'Paris Journals,' DU DEFFAND v. 350).

felt most where I have discovered least, that I will profane my affection to my lost friend with no ostentation—much less to those who never knew her. I live enough in solitude to indulge all my sensations, without troubling others.

PS. Since I wrote my letter, I have had another shock; General Conway has broken his arm! Lady Ailesbury assures me there is as little bad as there can be in such an accident,[11] and that I shall hear again tomorrow—Still I shall go to him on Friday.[12]

To Lady Ossory, Tuesday 10 October 1780

The MS has been torn at the top right-hand corner and has deteriorated on the right side. The mutilated or omitted words have been restored from Vernon Smith's text.

Address: ⟨To⟩ the Countess of Ossory at Farming Woods near Thrapston. *Postmark:* HENLEY. 12 OC.

Pa⟨rk Place,⟩ Oct. 1⟨0, at midnight, 1780.⟩

I SIT down after the family here are gone to bed, to answer your Ladyship's letter, which I received this morning as I was getting into my post-chaise; and tomorrow I go to Nuneham; a visit I could not refuse, as it is but sixteen miles off, and that I have not been there these two years—o⟨ther⟩wi⟨se⟩ I am in no mood to seek or to contribute to amusement.

You did me justice, Madam, in imputing my silence to my unhappiness. My dear old friend is gone! I had been told to expect it; but the contrary wind kept me twelve days in anxious misery! and I could not help h⟨aving⟩ moments of hope—now they are all destroyed!—Mr Conway's acciden⟨t, too⟩, though he is in the fairest way possible, did not diminish my con⟨cer⟩n—my spirits are so naturally good, that I know they will recover withou⟨t ef⟩forts⟨; yet⟩

11. 'Lady Hertford told me that General Conway had fallen down one of his hills at Park Place and broke his arm, but before I left St James's I had the satisfaction of reading a letter from Lady Aylesbury to Lady Hertford where she says Mr Conway has no fever and but little pain and that he was in all respects as well as it was possible to be after such an accident; it is broke just above the elbow' (Coke, 'MS Journals' 29 Sept. 1780; HW to Thomas Walpole 8 Oct. 1780).

12. 29 Sept., when HW stayed only one night at Park Place. He returned on 10 Oct., the day after the publication of the fourth volume of *Anecdotes of Painting,* and stayed another night (HW to Harcourt 3 Oct. 1780; following letter).

frequent losses of friends remind one of the discomforts of old age —bu⟨t⟩ one should not attrist those who are at a distance from the precipice—

I have not heard Lady Charlotte Finch's[1] bon mot—nor anything else till last night, when I learnt Lord Cornwallis's victory[2] from those most concerned. I passed the evening with Lady Hertford at Mrs Keene's.[3] Lord and Lady North were there, *en cour plénière*, with Miss,[4] the Queen Mother Drake,[5] Mr Williams, and Brydone,[6] the Sicilian traveller, who having wriggled himself into Bushy, will I suppose soon be an envoy, like so many other Scots.[7] As Lord North's poppies had been just jerked with sprigs of laurel, he was very good company, and my partner at cribbage. He has just been in Somersetshire and let a house to a woman who petitioned for a piece more of land, as her tenement had no backside. I said he had certainly not sold her a good *bargain*.[8] This suited his humour, and he told us several more good stories. ⟨I say nothing o⟩f the victory over my godson[9]—It is all in the *Gazette,* and I suppose, m⟨ore⟩. 'Tis sufficient to make us relapse into our American frenzy, which the last cargo of bad news had cooled. The conqueror talks of severity to the late renegades[10]—he forgets his own protest on the Stamp Act[11]—or perhaps chooses to wash it out with blood.

1. Lady Charlotte Fermor (1725–1813), m. (1746) Hon. William Finch; governess of the royal nursery 1762–93 (GM 1813, lxxxiii pt ii. 93; *Royal Kalendar,* 1793–4; MANN i. 4 n. 23). She had been at Eastbourne from 12 June to 9 Oct. with the Princesses Elizabeth and Sophia, and Princes Edward and Augustus (Coke, 'MS Journals' 12 June 1780; *London Chronicle* 3–10 Oct., xlviii. 326, 341).

2. On 16 Aug. 1780, at Camden, South Carolina, over the American forces commanded by Gen. Gates. For details, see HW to Mann 7 Oct. 1780; Cornwallis's dispatch, dated 21 Aug., in the *London Gazette Extraordinary* 9 Oct.

3. At Richmond (BERRY i. 148 n. 10).

4. The eldest daughter of the Norths: Hon. Catherine Anne North (1760–1817) m. (1789) Sylvester Douglas, cr. (1800) Bn Glenbervie.

5. 'Gilly' Williams's sister, Anne (d. 1782), m. 1 (1726) Sir William Drake (d. 1733), 6th Bt; m. 2 George Speke, by

whom she was the mother of Lady North.

6. Patrick Brydone (1736–1818), author of *A Tour through Sicily and Malta,* 1773 (Hazen, *Cat. of HW's Lib.* 2810); comptroller of Stamp Duties 1779–1818.

7. Lord Mount Stuart, the son of Lord Bute, was the most recently appointed envoy.

8. 'To sell any one a bargain: to make a fool of him, to "sell" him' (OED).

9. Horatio Gates (1727–1806), in command of the southern department of the American revolutionary forces (S. W. Patterson, *Horatio Gates,* New York, 1941, pp. 4, 398). He had been defeated at the battle of Camden; as a result Congress ordered an investigation. Gates's account of his defeat, from the *New Jersey Gazette,* 13 Sept., was reprinted in the *London Chronicle* 16–18 Nov., xlviii. 473–4. For HW's account of his being godfather, see *Last Journals* ii. 110; HW to Mann 7 Oct. 1780.

10. Toward the close of his dispatch of

Lady Surrey[12] is not only confined, but for some time was tied down in her bed. She now walks about the house, but sometimes herself asks for the strait waistcoat.

The Duchess of Gloucester is certainly not going abroad to my knowledge—at least the Duke is amazingly recovered by the sea air,[13] and looks, they tell me, remarkably well.

I believe these are answers to all your Ladyship's questions, except on Lady Granard's[14] ⟨mat⟩ch. I did not know it or her.[15] The last query is very kind; Boughton[16] and D⟨ra⟩y⟨ton⟩[17] I have seen and Kirby I should like to see,[18] but you will be returned and the season gone, ⟨be⟩fore I could reach Farming Woods. At present I will wish you good ⟨ni⟩ght, ⟨Mad⟩am, after thanking you again for your kindness about my poor ⟨lost⟩ friend! her not having taken James's powder adds to my sorrow, and I cannot forget it—but I have promised to say no more on that terrible subject.

21 Aug. Cornwallis says: 'The rebel forces being at present dispersed, the internal commotions and insurrections in the province will now subside. But I shall give directions to inflict exemplary punishment on some of the most guilty, in hopes to deter others, in future, from sporting with allegiance and oaths, and with the lenity and generosity of the British government.' He gave orders 17 Aug. 'to seize the most violent people' (*London Gazette Extraordinary* 9 Oct.). See also *post* 16 Nov. 1780.

11. He 'had been one of five who voted for the repeal in the House of Lords' (*Last Journals* i. 498); that is, on 10 Feb. 1766 he and three others had supported Lord Camden in opposing a resolution asserting the right of the Crown to tax and bind America 'in all cases whatsoever' (*Correspondence of Charles, First Marquis Cornwallis*, ed. Charles Ross, 1859, i. 11; HW to Mason 28 Nov. 1781, MASON ii. 168; Cobbett, *Parl. Hist.* xvi. 165–70).

12. Frances Fitzroy-Scudamore (1750–1820), m. (1771) Charles Howard, styled E. of Surrey 1777–86, 11th D. of Norfolk, 1786. She 'had become a lunatic soon after marriage' (GEC).

13. At Weymouth; see following letter.

14. Lady Georgiana Augusta Berkeley (1749–1820) m. 1 (1766) George Forbes, styled Vct Forbes 1765–9, 5th E. of Granard, 1769, who had died 15 April 1780; m. 2 (Jan. 1781) in Dublin, Rev. Samuel Little, D.D. Her last child by her first husband, Lady Elizabeth Forbes, was not born until Nov. or Dec. 1780 (George Kearsley, *Peerage*, [1796], ii. 343; Collins, *Peerage*, 1812, ix. 324).

15. HW had met her at Paris in 1765–6, shortly before she eloped with Lord Forbes ('Paris Journals,' DU DEFFAND v. 271, 294).

16. In Northamptonshire. See HW's account of his visit there with William Cole in 1763, in *Country Seats* 54–5; Cole's account in MONTAGU ii. 340–1; HW to Montagu 23 July 1763, ibid. ii. 89.

17. In Northamptonshire. It was the seat of Lady Elizabeth Germain when HW and Cole were there in 1763; see *Country Seats* 55–8; MONTAGU ii. 89–90, 341–3.

18. Lady Ossory had already invited HW to see Kirby (*ante* 14 Oct. 1779).

To Lady Ossory, Wednesday 1 November 1780

Address: To the Countess of Ossory at Ampthill Park, Bedfordshire. *Postmark:* 1 NO.

Berkeley Square, Nov. 1, 1780.

I HAVE suspected for some time, Madam, that I am growing superannuated, and now I am sure of it, for I don't know what I say. I certainly did not, if I told your Ladyship that I was going to Nuneham for a *fortnight*. I meant to stay but two nights, and literally did stay but three; and the reason I gave you, not having been there in two years, was the worst reason I had to give, another proof of dotage; for besides the visit to Lord and Lady Harcourt, to whom I certainly have great obligations, my journey comprehended two visits (going and coming), to Mr Conway, who still kept his bed; and moreover I was to meet Mr Mason at Nuneham.[1] All this is not an excuse of myself, but an accusation. Your Ladyship's is not quite so just. You know I offered myself at Ampthill first, and your election, and then your immediate removal to Farming Woods, prevented my paying my first duty to your Ladyship and Lord Ossory; and when I pleaded a debt to Lord Harcourt, I did and could mean nothing but the specific moment in which I was to go to him. Different fits of illness and close confinement have interrupted several intended journeys to Ampthill; and all last year I was literally not out of my own house once, no, not once, I mean, not to sleep anywhere else. I certainly am better at present than I have been these five years, and if it continues, will indubitably wait on you; it shall certainly be the first visit I will pay anywhere.

As I have been returned above a fortnight, I should have written, had I had a syllable to tell you—but what could I tell you from that melancholy and very small circle at Twickenham Park,[2] almost the only place I do go to in the country, partly out of charity, and partly as I have scarce any other society left which I prefer to it—for, without entering on too melancholy a detail, recollect, Madam, that I

1. Mason did not arrive until after HW had left Nuneham (MASON ii. 83–4).
2. At this time in the possession of the Duchess of Montrose (*post* 25 July 1781).

For its history, see R. S. Cobbett, *Memorials of Twickenham*, 1872, pp. 224–36; HW to Lady Suffolk 17 July 1766, MORE 123.

have outlived most of those to whom I was habituated, Lady Hervey, Lady Suffolk, Lady Blanford—my dear old friend,[3] I should probably never have seen again—yet that is a deeper loss indeed! She has left me all her MSS[4]—a compact between us—in one word I had at her earnest request consented to accept them, on condition she should leave me nothing else—She had indeed intended to leave me her little all, but I declared I would never set foot in Paris again (This was ten years ago) if she did not engage to retract that designation. To satisfy her, I at last agreed to accept her papers, and one thin gold box with the portrait of her dog.[5] I have written to beg her dog[6] itself, which is so cross, that I am sure nobody else would treat it well; and I have ordered her own servant,[7] who read all letters to her, to pick out all the letters of living persons, and restore them to the several writers, without my seeing them.[8]

Were I vainglorious, to be sure I might have boasted of passing a second evening with Lord and Lady North—nay, at their own palace.[9] Perhaps you will think I am going to be swaddled in ermine in my dotage like old Brudenel[10]—but be assured, Madam, that I do not design to have robes and a coronet laid on my death-bed like Lord Hunsdon.[11]

3. Mme du Deffand.

4. They are described and their history is given in DU DEFFAND i. pp. xliii–xlviii.

5. Tonton. For this section in her will (dated 24 Jan. 1780; there were earlier wills in 1771 and 1773 in which the bequest of her papers was mentioned), see ibid. vi. 7. The gold box with the portrait of Tonton, now WSL, is illustrated in MASON ii. facing p. 145; for details concerning the box, see DU DEFFAND v. 2, 201, vi. 26; HW to Thomas Walpole 26 Oct. 1780.

6. As early as 1 Jan. 1774 Mme du Deffand had asked HW to take Tonton after her death, and he had written to Wiart asking that it be brought to him by his cousin, Thomas Walpole (DU DEFFAND iv. 2, 5, v. 201, 253).

7. Jean-François Wiart.

8. HW's letter to the Marquis d'Aulan, Mme du Deffand's nephew and executor, probably written 31 Oct., is missing but is alluded to in his letter to Thomas Walpole 26 Oct. 1780. See also DU DEFFAND i. p. xliv.

9. Bushey House, in Bushey Park, of which Lady North was ranger 1771–97.

10. Hon. James Brudenell (*ante* 10 July 1776), aged only 55, had been created Bn Brudenell of Deene 17 Oct. 1780; in 1790 he succeeded his brother as 5th E. of Cardigan.

11. Henry Carey (1526–96), cr. (1559) Bn Hunsdon; first cousin (and possibly half-brother) to Queen Elizabeth. He had hoped to be Earl of Wiltshire, the title Sir Thomas Boleyn, his maternal grandfather, had held. 'When he lay on his death-bed, the Queen gave him a gracious visit, causing his patent for the said Earldom to be drawn, his robes to be made, and both to be laid down upon his bed . . . "Madam (said he), seeing you counted me not worthy of this honour whilst I was living, I count myself unworthy of it now I am dying"' (Thomas Fuller, *History of the Worthies of England*, 1662, pt ii. 24).

I came to town on Sunday to pay my duty to the Duke of Gloucester, who however did not arrive[12] till last night. I never saw him look so well, and so robust. He returns on Saturday to stay till after Christmas: so shall I, but for only two or three days, as all my few acquaintance have left my neighbourhood, and as I do not think it prudent at this critical time of the year for me to be much in the country. I may be in a busy scene here for aught I know, but I take care to have no business with it. Another phoenix just like its predecessor is risen from the ashes of the last Parliament[13]—and I suppose will have the final honour of consuming its own nest. Lord Ossory I conclude is arrived and will tell you particulars, of which I am informed only by the newspapers.

George I have seen in his paternal mansion[14] and drank tea with him and his adopted babe,[15] and its governess[16] and Mr Storer. He goes every night at nine to the new Irish Queen's[17] *couchée.*[18]

Your Barbary traveller[19] is probably an ape of Mr Bruce, and

12. From Weymouth. 'The Duke of Gloucester came to town for a few days and is now returned to Weymouth, where they are to stay till the middle of January; if they were wise and honest they would not come to town till they had paid all their debts, but such a reformation in them is not to be expected' (Coke, 'MS Journals' 5 Nov. 1780). 'This day . . . the Duke and Duchess of Gloucester will receive the compliments of the nobility at their house in Upper Grosvenor Street, it being his Highness's birthday' (*London Courant* 25 Nov.).

13. The new Parliament had met 31 Oct.: 'The King's Speech very vague, and like former ones; but it declared for another year of war' (*Last Journals* ii. 332); and as HW wrote to Mann 2 Nov. 1780, 'il ne valait pas la peine de changer' the old Parliament for the new.

14. The house in Cleveland Court, St James's (the address is sometimes given as Cleveland Row or Cleveland Square; the house may have been at the corner of Cleveland Court and Cleveland Row), in which Selwyn died, had belonged to his father. About 1768 George Selwyn let it to his nephew Thomas Townshend and took a smaller one in Chesterfield Street, but he had now returned to Cleveland Court because, with his adoption of Maria

Fagnani, he needed larger quarters (S. Parnell Kerr, *George Selwyn and the Wits*, 1909, pp. 17, 305–6; Wheatley, *London Past and Present* i. 421–3; E. B. Chancellor, *Memorials of St James's Street*, 1922, pp. 116–18; *Royal Kalendar* 1768–91; *Carlisle MSS* 472–3, and *passim*).

15. Selwyn had 'adopted' Maria Fagnani in that her parents had agreed to let her live with him in England and he had agreed to make her his heir.

16. Mrs Webb.

17. Lady Carlisle's. Her husband's appointment as Lord Lieutenant of Ireland, to succeed the E. of Buckinghamshire, had been officially announced 13 Oct. (*London Gazette* No. 12126, 10–14 Oct.).

18. At her house in St James's Street (*London Courant* 15 Dec.). Lady Carlisle's daughter Lady Elizabeth Howard, later the Duchess of Rutland, was born on 13 Nov. 1780.

19. Probably Eyles Irwin (ca 1751–1817), author of *A Series of Adventures, in the Course of a Voyage up the Red Sea, on the Coasts of Arabia and Egypt; and of a Route through the Deserts of Thebais, hitherto Unknown to the European Traveller . . . MDCCLXXVII*, 1780; 2d edn, June 1780 (*London Chronicle* April 15 – 24 Aug., xlvii. 372, 395, 555, xlviii. 65, 81, 177). Irwin attributes many of the diffi-

hopes to lie himself into £7000.[20] I can sooner believe that savages eat living beefsteaks,[21] than that they imitate our pitiful European vice of insincerity. The impulse of nature may make us knock out the brains of an enemy; but it must be long tutored, and civilized and polished and refined, before we sell our country and posterity for a mess of pottage.

As your Ladyship has long had the bulk of my book,[22] my last volume (and *last* volume it shall be), it was not worth while to send it to you for the addition of two or three pages;[23] but since you desire it, if I am so lucky as to see Lord Ossory, he shall have it.[24]

To Lady Ossory, Thursday 16 November 1780

Address: To the Countess of Ossory at Ampthill Park, Bedfordshire. *Postmark:* 16 NO. GC.

Berkeley Square, Nov. 16, 1780.

IT will, I am sensible, Madam, look like paying your Ladyship for your compliments;[1] and that will look like swallowing them greedily; and yet I must instantly tell you how very much I am

culties in his journey to the falsehood and treachery of the Arabs. HW's copy is Hazen, *Cat. of HW's Lib.* 2884.

20. 'Mr Bruce, who is lately returned from his travels in Abyssinia, has received from the King five thousand guineas for his drawings, reserving at the same time the use of them for his work, which we understand he has disposed of for two thousand guineas more' (*Oxford Magazine*, 1776, xiii. 95). Bruce's biographer, Alexander Murray, mentions that 'Mr Bruce received a gratuity for these drawings. Letter from Whitshed Keene, Esq. to Mr B. London, Dec. 4, 1775,' but does not give the amount (*Account of the Life and Writings of James Bruce*, Edinburgh, 1808, p. 115 n.).

21. 'We are informed that Mr Bruce, lately returned from Abyssinia . . . represents that nation as very barbarous and savage . . . that they eat raw meat taken from a beast when alive . . .' (report from 'Salisbury, July 18,' in *London Chronicle* 19–21 July 1774, xxxvi. 66). HW's disbelief of this report appears in his letters to

Mann 10 July 1774 and to Selwyn 10 Aug. 1774 (SELWYN 260). When Bruce published his *Travels to Discover the Source of the Nile* in 1790, he referred (iii. 296) to the 'violent outcry' which 'was raised in England at hearing this circumstance, which they did not hesitate to pronounce *impossible*,' although the Jesuits and earlier travellers had mentioned the same practice.

22. *Anecdotes of Painting*, Vol. IV.

23. 'The Advertisement, on half-sheet b and leaf c₁, dated 1 October 1780, was printed just before the volume was published. The cancelled Advertisement, comprising leaf a₂ and half sheet b (pp. [v]–ix, and [x] blank), was printed in October 1773' (Hazen, *SH Bibl.* 65). For a few other pages that might not have been in Lady Ossory's earlier copy, see ibid. 64–5.

24. No later record of either copy has been found.

———

1. On the *Anecdotes of Painting*, Vol. IV; see below.

charmed with and applaud your letter[2] to Mr Stonhewer.[3] I cannot select such apt words as your own; it was *noble, simple, genuine.*[4] Those epithets belong to handsome actions, not to trifling writings. I do not know what the House of Lords will do; nor have I heard that they know yet. They have appointed a committee on the affair.[5]

Mr Fitzpatrick's last reply to Adam was excellent[6]—but methinks the man on the white horse in the Revelations,[7] whose name I think was Death,[8] is gone forth!—I am sorry it is *a white horse.* That did not use to be the colour on which revenge rode[9]—but everything is so confounded now, that one does not know a white horse, from a white rose.[9a]

2. Missing.

3. Who had been named in connection with the quarrel between the Earl of Pomfret and the Duke of Grafton; see below.

4. Presumably Lady Ossory had used these words to describe some part of the *Anecdotes of Painting,* Vol. IV, probably the Dedication to the Duke of Richmond, which she would have seen for the first time if HW had given the Ossorys their first copy of the volume between April 1771, when the printing of the body of the book was completed, and Oct. 1773, when the Dedication and the original Advertisement were printed. See the discussion in Hazen, *SH Bibl.* 63–5.

5. On 22 Oct. 1780 the Duke of Grafton received a challenge from the Earl of Pomfret accusing the Duke of taking under his protection 'a man who has swore destruction to my property and the lives of my children' (*Journals of the House of Lords* xxxvi. 188–9). Pomfret wrote that his discharged gamekeeper, Langstaff, had taken revenge by various attacks on Pomfret's family, and had been appointed to a minor post in the excise through the application of the Duke's friend, Stonhewer. All the Duke's attempts to explain his ignorance of the affair and Stonhewer's having acted in good faith failed (ibid. xxxvi. 189–90). On 3 Nov. the House of Lords ordered the two to be in their seats in the House on 6 Nov., on which date Pomfret was judged guilty of a contempt of the House of Lords and was committed to the Tower. He was released 17 Nov.

on his pledge of good conduct. For details, see ibid., *passim; Last Journals* ii. 334–6; HW to Mann 2 Nov. 1780; Cobbett, *Parl. Hist.* xxi. 854–67; *London Chronicle* 2–18 Nov., xlviii. 432–80, *passim.*

6. In the House of Commons on 13 Nov., 'Adam, the Scotch duellist [*ante* 2 Dec. 1779], complained of a severe advertisement from the Westminster Association, who said they would guard Charles Fox's invaluable life, as those who attacked him and other patriots . . . were sure of being rewarded. He was severe on Fox's private life . . . and said they who adopted such advertisements were infamous. Fox made a temperate answer, denied having known of the vote of the Committee, and imputed it to their zeal for him. Fitzpatrick said the same of his absence, but that he approved the vote. "Then," said Adam, "he comes under my description." Fitzpatrick replied cleverly, that he had not applied the words to Adam, and if he applied these words to himself he could not help it. As they stood, he did approve them' (*Last Journals* ii. 335). For the text of the advertisement, the speeches of Adam, Fox, and Fitzpatrick, etc., see Cobbett, *Parl. Hist.* xxi. 844–54.

7. Revelation vi. 2.

8. Death rode the 'pale horse' (Revelation vi. 8); a galloping white horse is the device of the House of Hanover.

9. For the red horse, see Revelation vi. 4.

9a. The emblem of the Jacobites.

A good courtier yesterday sang the praises to me of that atrocious villain Arnold,[10] who, he said, till he heard of Andrée's[11] execution, would not discover the persons at New York, with whom Washington was in secret correspondence; then indeed he did.[12] Christ Jesus! only think of the monster! I hope he will be a Privy Councillor! betraying to Sir Harry Clinton in the height of his indignation for Andrée the wretched poor souls cooped up in New York, who are guilty of that correspondence. When I expressed my horror at such bloody treachery, and said I did not doubt but Lord Cornwallis's savage executions[13] had hurried on Andrée's fate, and were, besides cruel, indiscreet; the same apologist said, 'Oh! we have more prisoners of theirs, than they have of ours.'—How tender to their *own friends*, who they do not care if hanged, provided they can spill

10. Sir Henry Clinton's 'circumstantial detail,' of Benedict Arnold's decision to join 'the King's standard' (by boarding the *Vulture* 25 Sept. in Tappan Bay), together with the account of André's capture, trial, and execution, reached London 13 Nov. (*London Gazette* No. 12135, 11–14 Nov.; *Daily Adv.* 14 Nov.). Clinton's accompanying dispatch of 11 Oct. contained copies of the letters concerning Arnold's treason (texts in Carl Van Doren, *Secret History of the American Revolution*, New York, 1941, pp. 475–6, 482–95).

11. John André (1751–80), Capt., 1777; Major, ca 1780. As adjutant-general to Clinton he carried on the correspondence with Arnold, was captured at Tarrytown 23 Sept., was tried and convicted as a spy 29 Sept., and was hanged 2 Oct. (DNB; *Last Journals* ii. 334–5; *London Chronicle* 30 Nov.–2 Dec., xlviii. 526–7; *Army Lists*; *Proceedings of a Board of General Officers, Held by . . . Gen. Washington . . . Respecting Major John André*, Philadelphia, 1780).

12. Arnold had written to Washington 1 Oct., that if André were executed, Arnold would 'retaliate on such unhappy persons of your army as may fall within my power' and called 'Heaven and Earth to witness that your Excellency will be justly answerable for the torrent of blood that may be spilt in consequence' (*London Chronicle* 2–5 Dec., xlviii. 534, reprinted

from the account authorized by Congress). His retaliation failed because the identity of Washington's chief New York spies and correspondents Abraham Woodhull and Robert Townsend was not revealed until some 150 years later. Maj. Benjamin Tallmadge, the head of Washington's secret service, wrote to Washington 11 Oct. 'that though he [Arnold] knows not a single link in the chain of my correspondence, still those who have assisted us in this way are at present too apprehensive of danger to give their immediate usual intelligence' (Morton Pennypacker, *General Washington's Spies*, Brooklyn, N.Y., 1939, pp. 4–12, 184). Townsend reported to Tallmadge 20 Oct.: 'I am happy to think that Arnold does not know my name. However, no person has been taken up on his information' (ibid. p. 186).

13. According to *Last Journals* ii. 335, Cornwallis 'hanged 120 Carolinians,' but the *London Chronicle* 10–12 Oct., xlviii. 345–6, reports merely the hanging of '10 of the rebels that were found in arms after having taken the oaths.' Arnold admitted 'that forty of the principal inhabitants of South Carolina have justly forfeited their lives . . . hitherto spared by . . . Clinton' (Van Doren, op. cit. 491). For Cornwallis's defence of his executions, see *Correspondence of Charles, First Marquis Cornwallis*, ed. Ross, 1859, i. 56, 58, 60, 72–3.

more buckets of blood! I know nothing of poor Andrée[14]—he is much commended,[15] but so he would be, if as black as Arnold.

I am far from guessing why Mr Sherlock[16] does not write in his own language,[17] unless it is for the reason your Ladyship so luckily guesses. I should think everybody in this age could write best in his own. Formerly, before the babel of languages that overwhelmed the Latin, were settled into some idiom, folks wrote better in the tongue of the Romans, than they could in their own hodge-podge; but that is no longer the case. Mr Sherlocke's Italian is ten times worse than his French, and more bald. He by no means wants parts—but a good deal more judgment.

I am not got abroad again yet, but think I shall in two or three days: nor have I heard anything new or more than I tell you; except its being said now that Lord George Gordon will not be tried this term.[18]

14. In *Last Journals* ii. 334 HW mistakenly refers to him as 'Major-General St André, son of St André, the surgeon . . .' The *London Chronicle* 11–14 Nov., xlviii. 464, also refers to 'Major St Andree.'

15. See the *London Chronicle* 14–16 Nov., xlviii. 465, 469.

16. Rev. Martin Sherlock (ca 1750–97), Irish-born traveller and author; chaplain to Frederick Augustus Hervey, 4th E. of Bristol and Bp of Derry, ca 1777; surrogate of Killala and Achonry, 1781; vicar of Castlecomer and Kilglass, 1782; rector of Skreen, 1788; archdeacon of Killala, 1788. See also COLE ii. 301–2; MASON ii. 104.

17. His books had been written in French and Italian: *Lettres d'un voyageur anglais*, Geneva, 1779 (translated into English by John Duncombe, 1780); *Consiglio ad un giovane poeta*, Naples, 1779 (partial English translation from the French version, 1786); *Nouvelles lettres d'un voyageur anglais*, Paris and London, 1780 (English translation, 1781). The only work he published originally in English was *Letters on Several Subjects*, 1781. For HW's editions of these works, see Hazen, *Cat. of HW's Lib.* 3050, 3373, 3051, 361. 6.

18. On 10 Nov. 'The grand jury found the bill of high treason against Lord George Gordon.' On the 13th, 'It was determined not to try Lord George Gordon till the next term' (*Last Journals* ii. 334, 336). Michaelmas Term began on 6 Nov. and ended 28 Nov.; he was tried 5–6 Feb. 1781 during the next term, Hilary Term, which began 24 Jan. and ended 12 Feb. 1781 (Rider's *British Merlin*, 1780, 1781). On the first day of Michaelmas Term, Lord George had filed a petition that he might be tried during that term (*London Chronicle* 4–7 Nov. xlviii. 440).

To Lady Ossory, Sunday 26 November 1780

Address: To the Countess of Ossory at Ampthill Park, Bedfordshire. *Postmark:*
27 NO. [?GC].

Sunday, Nov. 26, 1780.

MY aches are not so mighty, Madam, as to merit your obliging inquiry after them; they come and go, and are rather omens of crippletude, than positive evils. One should not mention marks of decay as illness, for is there a remedy for old age? I do not condemn Medea, who knew there was no other than chopping her father into cutlets.[1] Miss Vernon's disorder is of consequence; beauty and youth should be tended—I am sure she will want no attention at Ampthill.

I may totter as much as I please; I believe the dowagers on either hand of me have a very different idea of me; at least if they keep watch and ward at their windows, as dowagers sometimes do. Two mornings ago they might have seen me receive, first, Dr Hunter,[2] and a moment after, Lady Craven—a man-midwife, and so pretty a woman are very creditable—and yet alas! he came to talk to me about Greek medals,[3] and she of a new comedy she is writing.[4]

A still odder thing happened at night—I asked Lady Bute who this Prince Callimanco[5] is (for so I am sure the mob will call him)

1. Not her father, Æetes, but her father-in-law, Æson, the father of Jason.

2. William Hunter (1718–83), M.D., Glasgow University, 1750; anatomist and obstetrician; brother of the more eminent John Hunter (cf. *ante* 3 Dec. 1776); physician to Queen Charlotte 1764–83; F.R.S., 1767; F.S.A., 1768; professor of anatomy to the Royal Academy, 1768; HW's occasional correspondent. For HW's relations with Hunter, which were friendly until they were cooled by political differences, see Jane M. Oppenheimer, *New Aspects of John and William Hunter*, New York, 1946, pp. 145–56. Hunter attended Lady Ossory at the birth of Lady Anne Fitzpatrick.

3. Hunter left his medals and his other collections to his nephew for twenty years and then to Glasgow University, where

they comprise the Hunterian Museum. See Charles Combe, *Nummorum veterum populorum et urbium, qui in museo Gulielmi Hunter asservantur, descriptio figuris illustrata,* 1782, in which HW is mentioned at p. ix.

4. Probably *The Silver Tankard,* an unpublished musical farce, presented at the Little Theatre in the Haymarket on 18 July 1781 and acted for six nights (Genest vi. 201). For a summary, see the *London Chronicle* 17–19 July 1781, l. 63.

5. From 'calamanco': a glossy checked or striped material—'a Spaniard is a Camocho, a Calimanco' (OED). Francesco d'Aquino (1736–95), Principe di Caramanico; envoy extraordinary from the Two Sicilies 1780–5; viceroy of Sicily, 1786 (Vittorio Spreti, *Enciclopedia storico-nobiliare italiana,* Milan, 1928–36, i. 411;

who is coming from Naples. 'Lord!' said she, 'don't you know? Why, he is the favourite of the Queen of Naples[6]—' 'That I should have thought,' said I, 'would rather be a reason for his *not* coming.' 'Oh!' said she, 'I suppose she is tired of him'—Should one have expected that of all living beings *that* would have [been] a topic for Lord Bute's wife to have tapped![7] The same night at Lady Holderness's I saw Lady Grantham—as she is not *my* wife, I really think her very tolerable. She was well dressed, behaved like a human creature, and not like her sister,[8] or a college tutor. Her lord is to kiss hands to-morrow as First Lord of Trade.[9]

I do not find that Lord Deerhurst[10] is dead yet, nor has lost his eye; but the surgeons despair of him.[11]

Enciclopedia universal ilustrada, Barcelona, [1905]-33, xi. 688). He was Grand Master of the freemasons (Harold Acton, *Bourbons of Naples*, 1956, p. 151).

6. Maria Carolina (1752-1814) of Austria, dau. of the Empress Maria Theresa and sister of Marie-Antoinette, m. (1768) Ferdinand IV, K. of Naples 1759-1806, 1812-25, and of Sicily 1759-1825 (Ferdinand I of the Two Sicilies). Caramanico was her favourite until displaced by Sir John Acton (ibid. 151, 271); Sir John was rumoured to have poisoned him (ibid. 272).

7. Because Bute had been the favourite of the Princess of Wales.

8. Her elder sister, Lady Amabel Yorke (1751-1833), succeeded her mother as Bns Lucas of Crudwell, 1797, cr. (1816) Countess de Grey of Wrest, m. (1772) Alexander Hume-Campbell, styled Vct Polwarth from 1750, cr. (1776) Bn Hume of Berwick, who died 9 March 1781.

9. A post he held until 1782. He succeeded the Earl of Carlisle, who had been appointed lord lieutenant of Ireland.

10. George William Coventry (1758-1831), styled Vct Deerhurst 1758-1809, 7th E. of Coventry, 1809; went to New York during the American war, 1777, stayed about two weeks, and there sold his commission for £500, which Richard Fitzpatrick is said by Lady Mary Coke to have received from him in return for a worthless draft on a London banker. His marriage in 1777 and his 'extravagance and worthlessness' and 'bad conduct' had

led to strained relations with his father, who had refused to support him and was erroneously reported to have disinherited him. A reconciliation took place as a result of the accident mentioned below (GEC; Coke, 'MS Journals' 15 July, 6 Oct. 1777, 22, 25, 28-9 Nov. 1780; *Last Journals* ii. 135, *sub* March 1778; *Carlisle MSS* 450, 474-5, 753, and *passim*).

11. While hunting near Wooton in Oxfordshire with the Duke of Beaufort on 18 or 20 Nov. (*Delany Corr.* and *London Chronicle*, cited below), Deerhurst forced his horse to attempt to jump a 'five-barred gate.' The horse fell on him and Deerhurst's 'right eye was beat into his head, his nose broke and laid flat to his face,' and he was 'much mangled.' He was reported dead. On 27 Jan. 1781 he 'found a difference' between light and dark, and there was some hope that his left eye might be saved, but in 1785 he wore a green silk patch over it, and in 1809, when he succeeded to the earldom, he had 'for many years been totally deprived of sight' as the result of this accident (*London Chronicle* 21 Nov.-7 Dec., xlviii. 496, 513, 542; Coke, 'MS Journals' 22, 25, 28-9 Nov. 1780; *Carlisle MSS* 448-50; Mrs Boscawen to Mrs Delany 27 Nov. 1780, *Delany Corr.* v. 582-3; *Betsy Sheridan's Journal*, ed. Le Fanu, 1960, p. 41; GM 1809, lxxix pt ii. 892). About a month before this accident, he had shot himself in the leg (*London Chronicle* 19-21 Oct., xlviii. 384).

We and Holland grow very fractious.[12] We bully, and so we have done before, and then drew in our horns—They will not mind, nor I dare to say go to war with us—but do us all the hurt they can. They have offered us another bitter pill[13]—and I am sure we kecked at that with all possible temper. His Majesty asked his Lordship Master Fred[14] the new Lord Lieutenant, whether he should swallow it. Master Fred, who has been Lord Lieutenant about six thousand —seconds, advised King George not to take such a nasty potion, and so King George has begged to be excused—and so I suppose the Dutch agent[15] will go to Ireland, whether they will or not; and Master Eden[16] will be ready to offer to make it up, as he did in America. *Ma foi, vive la dignité!* We have bullied ourselves, as the vulgar say, out of house and home, and solve all by saying, I won't say I have been in the wrong.

There is a new comedy, called the *Generous Impostor,*[17] which Mrs Crewe and all Sheridan's protectors protect,[18] though he did not

---

12. HW noted in *Last Journals* ii. 337, *sub* 20 Nov.: 'Great apprehensions of war with Holland, it having been discovered from Lawrence's [i.e., Henry Laurens's] papers that the city of Amsterdam had entered into a treaty with the Americans. Sir J. Yorke was ordered to present a new imperious and peremptory memorial [9 Nov.], though we had been so put to shame on that sent by Lord Suffolk.' HW adds that 'the Dutch envoy [Welderen] demanded that a Dutch agent should reside in Ireland, which was saying that Holland looked on Ireland as become independent. The King replied that he had consulted his Lord Lieutenant [Carlisle], who advised against it.' The Dutch had also protested insults to their ships. England published a declaration of war on Holland 20 Dec. 1780 (MASON ii. 89–90 and n. 1; *London Chronicle* 21–23 Nov., xlviii. 494, and *passim*).

13. Welderen's letter of 24 Oct. 1780, in which he reported on the refusal of the request to have a Dutch agent recognized in Ireland, appeared in the *London Chronicle* 21–23 Nov., lxviii. 496.

14. Lord Carlisle, whose appointment had been announced 13 Oct.

15. 'James French James,' appointed 'Commissary General in . . . Ireland'

(Welderen's letter cited in n. 13; in the same letter the agent is twice called 'Mr French').

16. Eden and Carlisle had been commissioners to treat with the American colonies in 1778 (*ante* 22 July 1778), and Eden had recently been appointed principal secretary to Carlisle as Lord Lieutenant. They both kissed hands on their appointments on 18 Oct. (*London Chronicle* 17–19 Oct., xlviii. 374).

17. By Thomas Lewis O'Beirne (ca 1748–1823), divine and Whig pamphleteer; Bp of Ossory, 1795, of Meath, 1798. The play was first acted at Drury Lane 22 Nov. and ran for seven nights (Venn, *Alumni Cantab.*; Genest vi. 177–8). When HW wrote this letter, the play had appeared for four consecutive nights, 22–25 Nov.; the last performance was 13 Dec. (GM 1780, l. 580).

18. When the play was published in 1781, O'Beirne dedicated it 'To Mrs [Frances] Greville, [daughter of Mr Maccartney, and wife of Fulk Greville, Esq.] and Mrs Crewe, [her daughter]'; the bracketed additions are by HW, in his copy now WSL (Hazen, *Cat. of HW's Lib.* 1818. 34. 1). On the title-page HW noted 'November,' and he has made minor corrections on pp. 15 and 84. The Duchess

write it; but I hear it is most indifferent.[19] It is a translation or imitation of *Le Dissipateur*.[20]

Lord Maccartney's speech pleased much at the India House,[21] and I hear his chance improves, of which I am very glad.[22] It is said that the Nabob of Arcot[23] has literally bought four members of Parliament, to guard his interests[24]—I thought he had taken much higher precautions.[25] I like this purchase—as we are grown perfectly

of Devonshire and her sister (soon to be Lady Duncannon) and Lady Craven 'and many others of the first quality and fashion' attended on opening night (*London Courant* 23 Nov.).

19. On opening night, '*The Generous Impostor* was received very favourably upon the whole, although in the fourth act the audience expressed a strong desire to condemn it. The plot and the incidents are much too serious for comedy, and yet . . . it owed its success last night chiefly to the fifth act's being almost direct tragedy. The whole fable is meagre, and more adapted to the taste of the French than of the English stage' (*London Chronicle* 21–23 Nov., lxviii. 495). 'The truth is, that the circumstances of the play, though partly gleaned from Plautus and Destouches, are neither sustained by pleasantry nor conducted with art; and there is but little comic force in the characters or dialogue' (*Monthly Review*, Feb. 1781, lxiv. 146).

20. O'Beirne's comedy 'is avowedly founded on a piece written by Destouches [in 1736], called *Le Dissipateur, ou l'Honnête friponne*, which was presented for the first time at the theatre of Paris in 1753' (*London Chronicle*, loc. cit.). O'Beirne makes no acknowledgment to Philippe Nericault Destouches (1680–1754) in the printed version of *The Generous Impostor*, which Genest calls 'only a French piece adapted to the English stage' (vi. 177).

21. On 23 Nov. at a Proprietary Court, when the proprietors were debating whether the new governor of Madras should be 'one of their own servants' or not; the motion to limit the appointment lost. During the discussion Lord Maccartney, who was not one of the company's servants, 'in a very sensible and modest speech' said 'that though it was his utmost ambition to aspire to that

appointment, he should scorn to gain it by any illiberal or low arts' (*London Chronicle* 23–25 Nov., xlviii. 500, where other points in his speech are given).

22. His nomination by the directors of the East India Company on 14 Dec. was confirmed at a meeting of the proprietors on 20 Dec. 1780 (ibid. 14–21 Dec., xlviii. 576, 591; *Last Journals* ii. 340). Miss L. S. Sutherland in *The East India Company in Eighteenth-Century Politics*, Oxford, 1952, p. 351, says that his appointment, 'pushed through in the teeth of the Company and Parliament Opposition, was certainly a good one.'

23. Muhammad Ali Khan Walajah (1717–95), Nawab of the Carnatic after Clive took Arcot on his behalf in 1751, and puppet of the British government at Madras. See C. E. Buckland, *Dictionary of Indian Biography*, 1906, p. 74; James M. Holzman, *The Nabobs in England*, New York, 1926, p. 55.

24. The *London Courant* 25 Nov. reported that Paul Benfield, newly elected M.P. for Cricklade, 'boasts . . . that he has brought *nine* members into Parliament, at the trifling expense of *seventy thousand pounds* of the Nabob's money.' HW also refers to the rumour in his letter to Mann 18 Jan. 1781, where he gives the number as nine, and to Mason 30 March 1781, Mason ii. 123. Thomas Townshend alluded to it in the House of Commons 30 April 1781 (Cobbett, *Parl. Hist.* xxii. 122; *London Chronicle* 28 April–1 May 1781, xlix. 414). 'At a time when this impoverished prince could not even pay his agents their salaries, the Opposition believed that he had purchased the direct control of seven or eight seats in the House of Commons' (Sutherland, op. cit. 323, citing Add. MSS 29143, ff. 272–3; Holzman, op. cit. 108–10, 134).

25. By gaining the interest of the King

ridiculous and contemptible, the more we grow so, the more diverting. When we have Cardinals, I suppose they will be protectors of different nations as at Rome: Cardinal Hurd of the Duke of Mecklemburgh,[26] and Cardinal Cornwallis of the Pope.

Monday.

Keith Stewart[27] arrived on Saturday, in a dismal way, and with a dismal account. He was forced to push to England to save his ship[28] from foundering, saw three others of Rowley's[29] fleet dismasted, and four missing.[30] All this is hushed up as much as possible, lest we should be frightened and not continue to knock our heads against stone walls and wintry oceans, and fatal climates.[31] We tremble too in whispers about Destain's and Guichen's[32] junction.[33]

The D[uke] of Northumberland, who never was old ⟨till a fort⟩night ago, had an audience on Friday, ⟨to have lea⟩ve to resign[34] from infirmity—but as that is no incapacity, he was pressed to stay —and was convinced.[35]

and Queen, by means of Lord Sandwich, as suggested in HW to Mason 30 March 1781, MASON ii. 123 and n. 6, and in Last Journals ii. 244–5, sub Feb. 1779.

26. The reigning Duke was the Queen's brother: Adolphus Friedrich III (1738–94), D. of Mecklenburg-Strelitz, 1752.

27. Hon Keith Stewart (1739–95), son of Alexander, 6th E. of Galloway; Capt., 1762; Rear-Adm., 1790; Vice-Adm., 1794; M.P. Wigtown burghs, Feb.–April, 1762, Wigtownshire 1768–84; receiver general of the land tax in Scotland, 1768 (Scots Peerage vi. 165–6; John Charnock, Biographia navalis, 1794–8, vi. 471–3).

28. The Berwick, of 74 guns, which he had commanded since 1778.

29. Joshua Rowley (1734–90), cr. (1786) Bt; Rear-Adm., 1779; Vice-Adm., 1787. He had been sent to Jamaica with ten ships of the line to reinforce Sir Peter Parker, protect Jamaica, and convoy ships bound for England (Burke, Peerage, 1953, p. 1822).

30. As reported in the London Chronicle 25–28 Nov., xlviii. 506 (a similar account is in the London Courant 27 Nov.).

31. Cf. London Chronicle 9–11 Nov., xlviii. 454: 'A vessel from Jamaica, lately arrived at Corke, brings an account that

the expedition to St Juan, on the Spanish Main, has been fatal to many British officers, as well as common men . . .' Twenty-one officers are named 'and 503 privates' are also said to have died.

32. Luc-Urbain du Bouexic (1712–90), Comte de Guichen; entered the navy, 1730; as Rear Admiral of the Channel Fleet fought in the Battle of Ushant, 1778; commanded the fleet at Brest, 1779, and at Martinique, 1780; fought three battles with Rodney in the West Indies, 1780, and one with Kempenfelt off the Azores, 1781.

33. On 16 Aug. 1780, Guichen had sailed for Europe. 'Sealed orders, opened at sea, directed him to proceed to Cadiz, where he anchored on the 24th of October.' D'Estaing was then at Cadiz to bring the French fleet back to Brest; with thirty-eight ships, including Guichen's, he sailed from Cadiz 7 Nov. 1780 and arrived at Brest 3 Jan. 1781 (A. T. Mahan, The Major Operations of the Navies in the War of American Independence, Boston, 1913, pp. 148, 158, and passim; London Chronicle 9–11, 28 Nov.–2 Dec., xlviii. 456, 520, 528).

34. As Master of the Horse.

35. Two paragraphs ibid. 28 Nov.–2 Dec., xlviii. 520, 528, support HW's inter-

I dined with the Lucans[36] yesterday. After dinner Lord Clermont informed us that in the course of his reading he had found that Scipio first introduced the use of toothpicks from Spain.[37] I did not know so much; nor that his Lordship ever did read, or knew that Scipio was any body but a racehorse.[38] His classic author probably is Marsh[39] upon the Gums. Lord Melbourne is to be a viscount[40]— and in time will read. *En voilà pour aujourd'hui!*

To LADY OSSORY, Tuesday 5 December 1780

Address: To the Countess of Ossory at Ampthill Park, Bedfordshire. *Postmark:* 5 DE. [?GC].

Berkeley Square, Dec. 5, 1780.

I HAVE the best of all excuses, Madam, and that which a saint might make, for not having mentioned[1] the pictures of Hogarth at Bristol,[2] of which Lord Shelburne is so good as to inform me. I should have specified, if I had known of, them, because, being in a church, they are considerable enough: otherwise, I confined myself to his pictures, that were not portraits, the latter being too numerous; and to the prints from his works, for the use of collectors. I am much flattered by Lord Shelburne's approbation, though I am sorry he gives himself time to read such idle books; and I am obliged by your Ladyship's haste to acquaint me with my omission; though, I assure you, I shall not be pressed to repair it, as it will be long, I believe, before there is occasion for a new edition.[3] I printed 600,

pretation. Temporarily 'convinced,' the Duke of Northumberland resigned on 27 Dec.

36. In Charles Street, Berkeley Square (*ante* 14 Nov. 1779).

37. The only mentions of toothpick (*dentiscalpium*) in Roman writings are in Martial, where no origin is given (*Thesaurus linguæ Latinæ*, sub 'Dentiscalpium'; Martial, *Epigrams*, VII. liii, XIV. xxii). Petronius mentions picking the teeth with a silver quill (*Satyricon* 33).

38. Classical names for race-horses were common (see MANN v. 490 n. 29: 'Cato')

39. John March (d. 1802), a Swede formerly in the French army, practised dentistry in Ireland and later in England; Lady Louisa Stuart considered him a

charlatan (GM 1802, lxxii pt i. 92–3; Lady Louisa Stuart, *Notes . . . on George Selwyn*, ed. W. S. Lewis, New York, 1928, pp. 34–5).

40. Peniston Lamb (1745–1828), 2d Bt, 1768; cr. (1770) Lord Melbourne, (11 Jan. 1781) Vct Melbourne.

———

1. In *Anecdotes of Painting*, Vol. IV.

2. An altar-piece in three panels, in the manner of Raphael, painted in 1756 for St Mary Redcliffe. It is now in the Bristol Art Gallery, and is illustrated in R. B. Beckett, *Hogarth*, 1949, pp. 63, 77, and Plates 181–3.

3. HW wrote in a notebook dated 1780: 'In St Mary Ratcliffe Bristol are two [*sic*]

to supply the purchasers of the two editions of the former volumes.[4] Not above a quarter are sold yet[5]—and I have no right to settle in my bookseller's[6] shop: one should only pass through it, or not go thither. I remember a story of poor Dr Chapman,[7] one of Dr Middleton's[8] antagonists,[9] but I have so entirely forgotten his works[10] that I shall tell it very lamely. He went to his bookseller,[11] and asked how his last work had sold?—'Very indifferently indeed, Sir'—'Ay! why how many are gone off?'—'Only five, Sir'—'Alack!—and how many of my *Eusebius*[12] (I think it was) have you left?'—'Two hundred, Sir!'—'Indeed! well, but my book on (I don't know what)—how many have you of them?'—'Oh! the whole impression, Sir'—'Good now! good now! That is much!—Well! Mr——, I cannot help it— I do my duty, and satisfy my conscience; I will write on'—Not being so conscientious as Dr Chapman, I shall accept, or take my quietus —but as we are only among ourselves, I will tell your Ladyship another old story apropos to Lord Shelb[urne]'s reading idle books.

After Sir Paul Methuen[13] had quitted Court,[14] the late Queen,[15]

historic pictures by Hogarth' (*A Note Book of Horace Walpole*, ed. W. S. Lewis, New York, 1927, p. 1), but he did not add a reference to them in his account of Hogarth for the editions of 1782, 1786, and for *Works* iii. 453–73.

4. That is, HW had printed 300 for each of the earlier editions of *Anecdotes of Painting* and the *Catalogue of Engravers*. See Hazen, *SH Bibl.* 55–6.

5. 'I believe not a third part is sold' (HW to Cole 30 Nov. 1780, COLE ii. 248).

6. John Bell (1745–1831), at the 'British Library, in the Strand,' (Stanley Morison, *John Bell*, Cambridge, 1930; *London Chronicle* 7–10 Oct., xlviii. 339; Hazen, *SH Bibl.* 56, 103).

7. John Chapman (1704–84), of Eton and King's College, Cambridge; D.D., Oxford, 1741; said to have been tutor 'for a short time' to HW at Cambridge (John Hutchins, *History . . . of Dorset*, 3d edn, 1861–70, i. 122), although HW does not mention him in 'Short Notes,' GRAY i. 5–6.

8. Conyers Middleton (1683–1750), D.D., author and controversialist; HW's correspondent; see DALRYMPLE 1–25.

9. For Chapman's controversies with Middleton, see DNB; DALRYMPLE 297–8, 304.

10. Three of Chapman's works were in HW's library: *Miscellaneous Tracts Relating to Antiquity*, 1742; *Property the Bane of True Letters*, 1746; and *A View of the Expediency and Credibility of Miraculous Powers among the Primitive Christians*, 1752 (Hazen, *Cat. of HW's Lib.* 1398, 1337, 832).

11. The London bookseller for Eusebius and other books by Chapman was William Innys (fl. 1711–56), although Samuel Birt (d. 1755) published a much greater number of Chapman's writings (BM Cat.; H. R. Plomer *et al.*, *Dictionary of the Printers and Booksellers . . . 1668 to 1725*, Oxford, 1922, pp. 167–8; ibid. *1726 to 1775*, Oxford, 1932, p. 26).

12. *Eusebius: or, the True Christian's Defence against a Late Book Entitul'd 'The Moral Philosopher'* [by T. Morgan], Cambridge and London, 1739–41.

13. (1672–1757), K.B., 1725; M.P.; diplomatist and art collector (MANN i. 243, ii. 366; Hazen, *SH Bibl.* 52). A variant of the following anecdote is in *Horace Walpole's Marginal Notes, Written in Dr Maty's Miscellaneous Works and Memoirs of the Earl of Chesterfield . . . 1777*, ed. R. S. Turner, *Miscellanies of the Philobiblon Society*, 1867–8, xi. 10–11.

14. Methuen was treasurer of the King's

who thought she had that foolish talent of playing off people, frequently saw him when she dined abroad during the King's absences at Hanover. Once that she dined with my mother at Chelsea, Sir Paul was there as usual. People that play off others, generally harp on the same string. The Queen's constant topic for teasing Sir Paul was his passion for romances, and he was weary of it, and not in good humour with her—'Well, Sir Paul, what romance are you reading now?'—'None, Madam; I have gone through them all'—'Well! what are you reading then?'—'I am got into a very foolish study, Madam; the history of the Kings and Queens of England'—perhaps Lord Sh[elburne] thinks romances as wise a study.

I know nothing of yesterday's debate[16] more than you will see in the papers, Madam; nor of anything else; no, not the title of Lady Craven's play, which not being quite born, perhaps is not christened.

When you write to Lady Warwick, I wish your Ladyship would persuade her (with her Earl's leave) to bring to town a most curious book, which I once looked over in his father's[17] time.[17a] It is a folio by one John Thorpe,[18] in the reigns of Elizabeth and James I, and contains many ground plans and a few uprights of several goodly mansions of those days; of some of which John Thorpe was the architect. This is not mere personal curiosity: I have found in my notes[19] that in that book is a plan of *the old house* at Ampthill, altered by

Household 1725–30. Thereafter he held no Court appointment, but after his resignation 'he went too often to Court to be well with the Opposition, and too seldom to Parliament to be well with either side' (John, Lord Hervey, *Memoirs,* ed. Sedgwick, 1931, i. 102).

15. Caroline (1683–1737).

16. On 4 Dec. in the House of Commons 'Sir Hugh Palliser took his seat . . . read his defence—dull. Keppel's spirited answer, disdaining compromise, and declaring he would call him nothing but Governor of Greenwich. Lord North's warm defence of Palliser, and owning his recommendation of him, though probably not true' (*Last Journals* ii. 339). The occasion for this exchange was the introduction of the Navy estimates for 1781, and Fox's assertion that he would approve them only on condition that an inquiry would be made into the conduct of Lord Sandwich; see Cobbett, *Parl. Hist.* xxi. 908–49; *London Chronicle* 5–7 Dec., xlviii. 540–1.

17. Francis Greville (1719–73), 8th Bn Brooke, 1727, cr. (1746) E. Brooke, (1759) E. of Warwick.

17a. 1771 (Hamilton to HW 15 Sept. 1771).

18. (ca 1563–1655), a surveyor rather than an architect; son of a Northamptonshire mason; in the Office of Works ca 1583–ca 1601; thereafter a land-surveyor. HW was the first to draw attention to him, in a supplement to the *Anecdotes of Painting,* 3d edn, 1782, i. (*Works* iii. 144–5). See also John Summerson, *Architecture in Britain 1530 to 1830,* 1953, p. 27, and *passim.* The folio, 'probably the most important document relating to Elizabethan architecture which we possess' (ibid. 27), was sold in the library of Hon. Charles Greville, mentioned below, and was bought by John (later Sir John) Soane; it is now in the Soane Museum.

19. Missing.

John Thorpe.[20] I want to see whether that Ampthill is your Ampthill or Houghton.[21] It is pity the book is not engraved: being only
lines, it could not cost much; indeed many persons would be glad to
subscribe for it. As Mr Charles Greville is a *savio*,[22] I marvel he does
not promote it. Did I ever tell you, Madam, that Eliz[abeth] Duchess
of Exeter,[23] sister of our Ha⟨rr⟩y IV, and her second husband Sir J.
Cornwall Lord Fanhope, lived at Ampthill, and he died there?[24]
Their portra*itis* in painted glass were in the church; whence there
is a pretty print in Sandford's *Genealogic History of the Kings of
England*[25]—but I dare to say that I have told you this before,—*et
que voilà de ma radoterie*—it is a proof at least that I dote on Ampthill.

To Lady Ossory, Monday 11 December 1780

Address: To the Countess of Ossory at Ampthill Park, Bedfordshire. *Postmark:*
11 DE. EK.

Berkeley Square, Dec. 11, 1780.

WHETHER you are glad, or sorry, or neither, my Lady, the
Empress-Queen is dead,[1] and Miss Bingham is to succeed her
—oh! no, I mistake; the latter is only to be Lady Althorpe at present[2]

20. In *Anecdotes of Painting*, 3d edn,
1782, i. [288–9], HW mentions that the
book contains 'ground plans of . . .
Ampthill (now called Houghton); and
Ampthill old house, another spacious
palace in which Catherine of Arragon
some time resided, and of which he says
he himself gave the plan of enlargement.'
According to Campbell Dodgson in DNB
'the words "enlardged per J. Thorpe,"
on the plan of Ampthill . . . probably
mean drawn to a larger scale by J.
Thorpe,' not that Thorpe enlarged the
building.

21. See *post* 25 Dec. 1780.

22. Or connoisseur. His collections were
sold in 1810, the year following his death:
paintings, sculptures, prints, jewels, etc.,
in two sales by Christie, 31 March and 4
April; and his library by Leigh and
Sotheby, 11 June (Lugt, Nos 7743, 7745;
*List of Catalogues of English Book Sales
1676–1900 now in the British Museum*,
1915, p. 125).

23. Elizabeth (d. 1425), m. 1 (1386) John
de Holand, cr. (1388) E. of Huntingdon,
(1397) D. of Exeter; m. 2 (before 12 Dec.
1400) Sir John Cornwall (d. 1443), K.G.,
ca 1409, cr. (1432) Bn of Fanhope, (1442)
Bn of Milbroke.

24. On 10 or 11 Dec. 1443.

25. Francis Sandford (1630–94), herald
and genealogist, wrote *A Genealogical
History of the Kings of England*, 1677;
HW's copy (now WSL) is Hazen, *Cat. of
HW's Lib.* 581. The print is on p. 252,
and the account of the Duchess of Exeter
and her husbands on pp. 251–3. HW's
'portrait*is*' suggests that he is following
Sandford's spelling, but Sandford (p. 253)
refers to 'Her Portraiture . . . and that
of the Lord Fanhope.'

---

1. The death of Maria Theresa on
29 Nov. at 'about 9' p.m. at Vienna was
announced in the *London Gazette* No.
12142, 5–9 Dec. 1780.

2. On 6 March 1781 Hon. Lavinia Bing-

—but I believe another Empress-Queen[3] will feel her crown totter a little by this match. It was declared at Devonshire House on Saturday[4] after the opera,[4a] and the Emperor—stay, I mean Admiral Darby[5] was to beat Monsieur Destain yesterday,[6] and everybody was in such spirits on these three great events, for the Emperor is to march directly into Lorrain,[7] and Lord Spencer is to convoy—Lord bless me, I heard so much of all those matters, that I do nothing but confound them, and don't know one from t'other, so I will say no more on them.

I saw Madame la Baronne[8] last night at Madame de Welderen's,[9] ay, and the Baron too: he is well enough, and she looked very well.

ham married George John Spencer (1758–1834), styled Vct Althorp 1765–83, 2d E. Spencer, 1783; lord privy seal July–Dec. 1794; first lord of the Admiralty 1794–1801; book collector. He 'preserved all his letters though he was seen to be throwing away those of his wife, the beautiful Lavinia, into a clothes-basket for burning' (Hist. MSS Comm., *Bulletin of the National Register of Archives*, 1964, p. 24).

3. Probably Lord Althorp's sister, the Duchess of Devonshire.

4. 'Last Saturday Lord Althorp's marriage with Miss Byngham, Lord Lucan's daughter, was declared. 'Tis his own choice, and the young lady being very much accomplished and well behaved Lord and Lady Spencer are perfectly satisfied though she has no fortune; indeed in that family it was not wanted' (Coke, 'MS Journals' 12, 15 Dec. 1780).

4a. *Ricimero*, a 'serious opera . . . The music by several celebrated composers,' presumably including Jommelli and Majo, who composed operas of this title (Alfred Loewenberg, *Annals of Opera*, 2d edn, Geneva, 1955, i. 196, 237; *London Courant* 9 Dec.).

5. George Darby (ca 1720–90), Vice-Adm., 1779; Rear-Adm., 1781; M.P. In Sept. 1780 he became commander of the Channel Fleet and lord of the Admiralty. Darby was president of the court martial which acquitted Palliser, and owed his advancement to Lord Sandwich (*Sandwich Papers* iii. 278, 292–303).

6. 'A report was current on Saturday, and generally believed, that advice had been received that the grand fleet under Admiral Darby was in sight of the combined fleet; but upon inquiry it was found that no such intelligence had been received at the Admiralty' (*London Courant* 11 Dec.). Darby thought his fleet too weak for a battle (Darby to Sandwich 10 Dec. 1780, *Sandwich Papers* iii. 309; *London Chronicle* 9–12 Dec., xlvii. 560).

7. It had been rumoured in 1766 that Joseph II would demand the restitution of Lorraine, which his father had once ruled (Mann vi. 395).

8. The Baroness Kutzleben.

9. Anne Whitwell (1721–96), dau. of William Whitwell by Anne Griffin, 2d dau. of James, 2d Bn Griffin; went to Holland as maid of honour to Anne, Princess of Orange; m. (1759) Jan Walrad, Count van Welderen, Dutch envoy to England (Montagu ii. 139, n. 9; GM 1807, lxxvii pt ii. 679). The Welderens lived in St James's Square (*Court and City Register*, 1781, p. 92). 'At Madame de Welderen's there was two parties, one at whist and the other at half-crown loo. Mr Walpole was there. I asked him when he had heard from Madame du Deffant and was quite surprised when he told me she died in September last. She will be a great loss to the English who go to Paris, as she was one of the few who piqued herself upon showing them civilities' (Coke, 'MS Journals,' 12 Dec. 1780, the date Lady Mary incorrectly gives for the party; cf. ibid. 14 Dec. 1780).

I know nothing else upon earth or water, but I have sent your Ladyship enough to spread upon many slices of conversation, and that is the great use of letters in the country.

To Lady Ossory, Sunday 17 December 1780

Berkeley Square, Sunday, Dec.17, 1780.

NO, Madam, I have been much out of order. As the outworks have for some time been in ruins, I thought the citadel itself was at last, to use an old word, beleaguered. In short, for some days I had a pain in my stomach, and never having had it there nor knowing how it feels there, I concluded it was the gout. But it took another turn, and became a disorder that has been fashionable and was almost gone out of fashion; just the time when the ancient generally adopt modes. I am pretty well again, but look ruefully, as you may believe, for I can afford to part with very little of *my embonpoint*.[1] You ask if I shall pass my Christmas in town; I know and feel it is a kind question; but I must answer alas! yes. I am grown an Astracan lamb,[2] and vegetate in one spot. George Selwyn says he told your Ladyship that I am out of spirits. I did not know it particularly, nor have any cause; but I am sensible they often flag; and one reason for my reluctance to going anywhere is, that if I am not perfectly quiet all the morning, I am exhausted before night. This, with twenty other decays of which I am sensible, makes me shun what I am not fit for.

I will return Lord S.'s[3] letter when I have the honour of seeing your Ladyship. I do not know whether he judges rightly of certain persons just at present. It has been their mood, and may be so still; and I know *one*[4] that having tried others and been rejected,[5] is will-

---

1. This word is written in letters about one third the size of those in the remainder of the letter.

2. The barometz, or Scythian or Tartarian lamb, a 'vegetable lamb' described by travellers in the Middle Ages as eating plants within its reach. See BERRY ii. 140 n. 4; *post* 15 Jan. 1788, where HW calls it 'African lamb'; OED, *sub* barometz. In his notes on Bayle's *General Dictionary*, 1734–41, vi. 557–8, HW wrote,

'The Scythian lambplant, a fiction. 558' (MS Commonplace Book, 1750, now WSL, p. 31).

3. Shelburne's. Cf. *ante* 5 Dec. 1780.

4. The King.

5. In *Last Journals* ii. 307–9, 324–6, HW describes overtures made in June and July 1780 to Conway and then to Rockingham for a new ministry. In the first plan 'Lord North was to have been the sacrifice'; in the second 'he was the

ing, nay desirous of trying with those Lord S. means, what he tried last year[6]—but I should wonder if they were accepted now, unless to expose them, which is not worth while. Nobody blots flimsy blotting paper out of spite.

My old acquaintance, or rather, my acquaintance old Lady Shelburne, I see by the papers, is dead.[7] How has she left her fortune, once so great, but which with superabundant cunning she had rendered almost as crazy as she was latterly?[8]

Your aunt[9] was charming about Madame la Baronne,[10] till *almost* the last minute, and told me they would have very little[11]—but indeed when people were in love with one another! However—I suppose to accustom them to economy, she did not give the Baron a dinner even on the wedding-day,[12] and he begged one of the parson that was to marry them. The kitchen was as cold the next day, and the turtles pecked on the same parson's board.

Mr Morrice has been in England above these two months.[13] I have not seen him, for he has been laid up with the gout at Chiswick from within a week of his arrival, when, I hear, he looked as ill as

negotiator and was to be preserved' (ibid. ii. 324). On 9 July, Rockingham reported George III's *decisive disinclination* to almost every idea, on which (I thought) a government . . . could be formed' (to John Lee, in Lord Albemarle's *Memoirs of the Marquis of Rockingham*, 1852, ii. 420).

6. In Feb. 1779, negotiations were started with Rockingham and the Duke of Grafton, perhaps without the King's knowledge, although both thought 'by warrant from the King.' The King's 'sole view . . . was to divide the Opposition' but the collapse of negotiations 'served to make a firmer union between the several factions in Opposition' (*Last Journals* ii. 244–7, 252). Rockingham wrote to Keppel, Nov. 1779, that George III's 'intending to *open a negotiation* with me . . . was to serve some purpose of creating jealousies *somewhere*' (Albemarle, op. cit. ii. 385).

7. She died 9 Dec. at Llewenny Hall, co. Denbigh (*London Courant* 15 Dec.; *London Chronicle* 14–16 Dec., xlviii. 570).

8. According to the *London Chronicle* loc. cit., 'Her . . . jointure devolves upon . . . the Earl of Shelburne; and her real

and personal estate, being very considerable, she hath given to her youngest son, the Hon. Thomas Fitzmaurice, and appointed him sole executor'; he 'comes into the possession of £8000 per annum, besides a large personal fortune' (ibid. 16–19 Dec., xlviii. 578).

9. The Duchess of Bedford, who was also aunt of Baroness Kutzleben.

10. The Duchess had given her 'two hundred pounds for her clothes' as well as £3000 for her marriage portion (Coke, 'MS Journals' 16 Nov. 1780; *ante* 23 Sept. 1780).

11. According to Lady Mary Coke, the income of the Kutzlebens was £1000 a year, and £10,000 'is settled upon her and the children, though she told the Duchess that if there was any they must go to Hesse' ('MS Journals' 16 Nov. 1780).

12. They were married on 'Saturday evening,' 25 Nov., 'at Bedford House' (*London Courant* 28 Nov.).

13. He had left for Italy on 30 July 1779 and had returned to England by 15 Sept. 1780 (Coke, 'MS Journals' 1 Aug. 1779, 22 July, 15 Sept. 1780; HW to Mann 24 July, 19 Sept. 1780).

when he went abroad.[14] I thought Lord John[15] much broken before he went out of town.

The crapaudines[16] begin to discover amazing charms in Miss Bingham. One of them, as Lord Althrop was talking to her, went up to him, and holding up her fan that Miss might not *see* what she said, told him, 'She is a *sweet* creature!' Another of them repeated this—and yet I would not swear was not the very person that said it—for if a court is no bigger than an egg-shell, it is equally full of jealousy and treachery. I wish the inhabitants of any court would write comedies—if they could speak truth. They would need but to write down what they have seen and heard—and there would be character with a witness! Lord Hervey did leave a Dialogue of one whole day in the late King's reign, that is, of what commonly passed there.[17] It was not I believe exactly what I mean, but rather a ridicule on the individuals of the *dramatis personæ;* I never saw it, but Lady Hervey told me it was the best thing he ever wrote—However, those would be transient ridicules. I would only have general Nature, when it has been refined and strained through the thousand sieves of self-love, ambition, envy, malice, mischief, design, treachery, falsehood and professions, glazed over with perfect ease, good-breeding and good-humour, and the passions only evaporating through invisible pores, but the angles of the atoms as sharp as needles, and mortal as diamond dust—but how could one describe smiles that assent away another's favour, or a bow purposely omitted, and then recollected as designedly to tell a person he is in disgrace, before he knew it himself? Could a pit or gallery comprehend the importance assumed by a bed chamber-woman or a page of the back stairs in denying some arrant trifle that was a secret in the morning and is to be in the *Gazette* at night? I caught Lady S[pencer] t'other night in one of these mysteries—It was two nights before Lord Althrop's match was owned[18]—but I had supped at Lord Lucan's with

14. Morice, who lived at The Grove, Chiswick, called on Lady Mary Coke on 15 Sept., 'saying he is quite recovered of the complaint for which he went abroad, but he is very lame' ('MS Journals' 15 Sept. 1780).

15. Cavendish.

16. Toad-eaters, toadies. Cf. OED, *sub* crapaud, crapaudine.

17. 'The Death of Lord Hervey, or A Morning at Court. A Drama,' written for the amusement of Queen Caroline in the summer of 1736, during George II's visit to Hanover; published with Hervey's *Memoirs* in 1848. Sir Robert Walpole is one of the characters. See the *Memoirs,* ed. Sedgwick, 1931, ii. 574–5, 585–96.

18. That is, on 7 Dec.; the engagement was announced on 9 Dec. (*ante* 11 Dec. 1780).

the whole court of Spencer, and Lord A. had sat at a side-table with the two girls,[19] Miss Molesworth[20] and old Miss Shipley.[21] I knew if I asked directly, I should be answered, 'Upon my word *I* know nothing of the matter'—so after supper sitting by Lady S. on a settee, I said, 'Pray, Lady S., is it owned that Lord A. is to marry—Miss Shipley?' She burst out a-laughing, and could not re-compose her face again.

I fear, by your Ladyship's account, that Miss Vernon ought to go abroad; and, if she ought, surely no time should be lost. Old Dr Monro[22] told my father that he scarce knew anything that asses' milk and change of air would not cure, and that it was better to go into a bad air, than not to change it often.

My being confined and idle has made me scribble a volume about nothing. I hope you will be as *désœuvrée* when you are to read it.

Just as I had finished my letter, I learnt the dreadful calamity that happened at the Opera-house last night—don't be alarmed, Madam; not a life is lost—yet. There *was* a fire, and it is not yet extinguished. The theatre was brimful in expectation of Vestris.[23] At the end of the second act[24] he appeared; but with so much grace, agility and strength, that the whole audience fell into convulsions of applause: the men thundered, the ladies forgetting their delicacy and weakness, clapped with such vehemence, that seventeen broke their arms, sixty-nine sprained their wrists, and three cried bravo! bravissimo! so rashly, that they have not been able to utter so much as *no* since,[25] any more than both Houses of Parliament. I do not

19. Hon. Lavinia and Hon. Louisa Bingham.

20. Their first cousin.

21. Although she was only compara-tively 'old,' Anna Maria Shipley (ca 1749–1829), m. (1783) Sir William Jones, Kt, seems to be indicated here. 'The eldest [daughter of Bishop Shipley], Anna Maria, was of a stern character . . . and lived principally with her cousin [first cousin once removed], Lady Spencer, at Althorpe' (A. J. C. Hare, *Memorials of a Quiet Life,* New York, n.d., i. 89; GM 1829, xcix pt ii. 91).

22. James Monro (1680–1752), M.D., Oxford, 1722; fellow of the College of Physicians, 1729; physician to Bethlehem Hospital 1728–52.

23. The younger Vestris, Marie-Auguste Vestris-Allard (1760–1842), natural son of Gaetano Appollino Baldassare Vestris, was beginning a brilliant career as 'principal dancer at the King's Theatre.' With him in London was his father, who did not dance until the son's benefit (Gaston Capon, *Les Vestris,* 1908, *passim;* BERRY i. 218; *London Chronicle* 16–19 Dec., xlviii. 580; *London Courant* 16, 18 Dec.; *Political Magazine,* 1780, i. 792).

24. Of *Ricimero* (ante 11 Dec. 1780). He also danced at the end of the third act (*London Courant* 16, 18 Dec.).

25. 'It is decided in the *ton* that *the Vestris* is to be quite *the rage* this year. Nothing else is talked of in the polite circles. When he dances the ladies leave

love to exaggerate, but the shouts were so loud that they reached Great Russell Street, and terrified Lord Mansfield,[26] who thought the mob was coming again, and fled to Kane Wood—but though the true cause was soon discovered, there is to be a camp in the Meuse[27] every opera night, and nobody suffered to appear there, but gagged and handcuffed, for really if people are at liberty to applaud what they approve, there is an end of all government!

As folks in the country love to hear of *London fashions*, know, Madam, that the reigning one amongst *the quality*, is to go after the opera to the lottery offices, where their Ladyships bet with the keepers. You choose any number you please; if it does not come up next day, you pay five guineas; if it does, receive forty—or in proportion to the age of the *tirage*. The Duchess of Devonshire in one day won nine hundred pounds. General Smith,[28] as the luckiest of all Mites, is of the most select parties, and chooses the numeros.

To Lady Ossory, Monday 25 December 1780

The address has been torn off.

Christmas Day, 1780.

THOUGH you order me to give you an account of myself, Madam, I shall not obey, for I cannot give you a good one; and **one is** so apt to talk of oneself, and by the courtesy of self-love to

their boxes and come into the front of the pit, where they exercise their hands in clapping as violently as the men' (*London Chronicle* 23–26 Dec., xlviii. 603).

26. After the destruction of his house in the Gordon Riots, Mansfield had taken the late Topham Beauclerk's house in Great Russell Street, Bloomsbury Square (*London Courant* 21 Aug.). For his fears, cf. *ante* 3 June 1780 and n. 10.

27. The King's Mews, Charing Cross, on the site of the present Trafalgar Square.

28 Richard Smith (1734–1803) served in India 1753–69, retiring as Brig.-Gen.; M.P. Hindon 1774–5, 1776–7, Wendover 1780–4, Wareham 1790–6; said to be the 'Sir Matthew Mite' of Foote's *Nabob;*

elected to Brooks's 1779 on Richard Fitzpatrick's nomination; died 'in an advanced age, leaving a very large fortune' (GM 1803, lxxiii pt ii. 696; *Memorials of Brooks's*, 1907, p. 25; *Town and Country Magazine*, 1776, viii. 345–7, where he appears as 'Sir Matthew Mite' with Mrs Armistead; BM, *Satiric Prints* v. 230, vi. 709, Nos 5352, 7692; J. M. Holzman, *The Nabobs in England*, New York, 1926, p. 162; *Carlisle MSS, passim;* L. S. Sutherland, *The East India Company in Eighteenth-Century Politics*, Oxford, 1952, *passim*). He won and lost large sums and was said to play 'deeper than any man in the kingdom' (*Morning Post* 23 June 1778).

think every trifle of importance, that I will boldly be out of order if I please, without being responsible to anyone; no, not even to a friend.

We have so many enemies, and subdue them so rapidly, that I did not think it was worth while to notify to your Ladyship the new war with Holland.[1] Lord Cornwallis, I suppose, will step over and dispatch it in a parenthesis of six weeks, and still be as likely as ever to conquer America. Who is to burn Amsterdam I have not yet heard.

Lord Warwick has already sent me John Thorpe's book, Madam, and a most obliging letter.[2] *The* Ampthill is not Houghton-Ampthill, but the individual palace that stood in your paddock where the cross is, and in which Queen Catherine *lay*,[3] as royal folk did then, though now they, and everybody else, only *sleep*—and a spacious and goodly mansion it was. There is not the elevation, nor of Kirby Hatton,[4] built by the dancing Chancellor[5] in 1570; but there is the ground plan. I remember wanting to make the last Chancellor Bathurst dance at one of Monsieur de Guines's balls.[6] He came thither very

1. '21st [Dec.]. The King's manifesto against the Dutch [dated 20 Dec.] published in an *Extraordinary Gazette*, letters of marque granted, and an embargo laid on all Dutch vessels in our ports' (*Last Journals* ii. 340; *London Gazette Extraordinary*, 21 Dec.).

2. Missing.

3. HW made the distinction between the two Ampthills in his account of Thorpe in *Anecdotes of Painting*, 1782, i. Supplement, p. [2]; *Works* iii. 144. In 1783 or later he glossed a reference to 'the Earl of Elgin's House at Ampthill': 'now called Houghton, a seat of the Duke of Bedford. The other Ampthill, where Queen Catherine of Arragon resided, is at a small distance, and now the seat of the Earl of Ossory' (MS note in his copy, now WSL, of Thomas Pomfret's *Life of the . . . Countess Dowager of Devonshire*, 1685, p. 66).

4. Kirby Hall, Northants, begun in 1570 by Sir Humphry Stafford of Blatherwycke, at whose death in 1575 the house was incomplete. Thorpe was not the architect, although he says he laid the first stone in 1570, when he was about seven; his father

(d. 1596) may have been the principal mason. For an account of the house and two views of it, as well as a reproduction of Thorpe's ground plan, see John Summerson, *Architecture in Britain 1530 to 1830*, 1953 pp. 36–8, Plates 20A, 21A.

5. Sir Christopher Hatton (1540–91), 2d son of William Hatton of Holdenby, Northants; lord chancellor 1587–91. On the line, 'My grave Lord-Keeper led the Brawls' in 'A Long Story' Gray added the note: 'Hatton, preferred by Queen Elizabeth for his graceful person and fine dancing.' On this note HW added in his copy of *Designs by Mr R. Bentley, for Six Poems by Mr T. Gray*, 1753, (now WSL): 'In Ant. Bacon's papers published by Birch is an extract of a letter on the news of the Court, in which one Capt. Allen tells Mr Bacon, that at the marriage of the Chancellor's nephew Sir William Hatton, his Lordship danced the measures, and left his gown on the chair, saying "Lie there, Chancellor." Vol. I. p. 56.'

6. Cf. *ante* 3 April 1773, where HW mentions one of de Guines's balls attended by Bathurst and HW.

THE CROSS AT AMPTHILL PARK

drunk, and as somebody wished to see the Scotch *reel,* I proposed that my Lord Chancellor should dance it.

I am uncommonly glad, Madam, that Mr Coxe[7] is destined for Mentor to your Telemachus.[8] His travels[9] are by far the most sensible of all those late publications, and his principles of the old rock.[10]

Your heroine[11] at Bath, Madam, is from the same quarry in another light, and the counterpart to Cato himself, who accommodated a friend with his own wife, for the sake of virtue, and took her again with as much decorum as possible. Pray read the description in Lucan,[12] or, if you affect not understanding Latin, in Rowe;[13] you will see with what staid gravity those matters were transacted, when good patriots desponded about the commonwealth. I have not a Lucan in town, or would refer you to the spot.

My nieces[14] are indubitably not going abroad, nor do the Duke and Duchess think of it. They will be in town at the end of next month.

Lord Maccartney I hear is to sail before that time:[15] Lady Maccartney does not go with him. I remember what a quarto my last letter was, and restrain this within bounds.

PS. I shall not attempt to see Vestris till the weather is milder, though it is the universal voice that he is the only perfect being that has dropped from the clouds within the memory of man or woman —but then indeed nobody allows memory much retrospect, lest they

---

7. Rev. William Coxe (1747–1828), historian, biographer, and traveller; author of *Memoirs of Sir Robert Walpole,* 1798.

8. Lord Ossory's nephew, Lord Holland, seven years old at this time; cf. *ante* 21 Oct. 1778. He was at Eton from 1781 to 1790, and there is no record that Coxe was his tutor. Coxe had been tutor to the sons of the Duke of Marlborough and travelling tutor to Lord Herbert (*ante* 10 June 1780) 1775–9 (*Henry, Elizabeth and George,* ed. Lord Herbert, 1939, *passim*).

9. At this time Coxe had published two volumes of travels: *Sketches of the Natural, Civil, and Political State of Swisserland,* 1779; *Account of the Russian Discoveries between Asia and America,* 1780; 2d edn, revised and corrected, 1780, 4th edn, 1804. Neither appears in the records

of HW's library. For HW's favourable opinion of one of Coxe's later travel books, see HW to Conway 21 May 1784, *post* 15 Jan. 1788.

10. That is, Whig.

11. Not identified.

12. *Pharsalia,* ii. 326–91.

13. Rowe's translation, 2d edn, 1722, of Lucan's *Pharsalia* is Hazen, *Cat. of HW's Lib.* 1875; the passage is Book II. 508–612.

14. The three Ladies Waldegrave.

15. On 15 Jan., 'attended by his secretaries and suite,' he 'set out for Ireland in order to embark from thence to his presidency of Madras' (*London Chronicle* 18–20 Jan. 1781, xlix. 66; *Daily Adv.* 19 Jan. 1781). He arrived at Madras 22 June 1781.

should seem old themselves. When the Parliament meets,[16] he is to be thanked by the Speaker.

To Lady Ossory, Tuesday 2 January 1781

Berkeley Square, Jan. 2, 1781.

MERCY on the poor men that are to be in love with Lady Anne, when she comes to maturity of tyranny! If she begins already with enjoining such tasks to her slaves, what will she do, in the full career of her power! The Sphinx was a harmless dicky-bird in comparison. To send one four quipos,[1] and only a hint at an alphabet, and bid one construe four Peruvian verses, without one's having ever learnt a syllable of the language, is despotism unparalleled. She might as well have ordered me to read an Egyptian obelisk, and tell her what was meant by animals so ill drawn that they are like nothing in the creation. My penance is ten times worse; I am to find out rhymes in colours, and thoughts in knots, and cadence in a jangle of oughts and ends! I am a sibyl if I believe that any being but a lady's chambermaid can understand the sense of minced ribbands, or discover sentiments in a salmagundi of black and blue and red and purple and white. A piece of a tippet may be very good poetry in Lima for aught I know; and such a genius as Dryden would soon have written a whole birthday gown from as small a sample as Lady Anne has sent me; but for my part I cannot unsew a single stitch of such millinery versification; and though I will not contemptuously return such silken lines directly, I despair of unravelling them, and will only retain them, till I have *effilé'd* them for a whole morning, since it seems that a mistake in a single shade may occasion a blunder, or perhaps a *double entendre*.

Your Ladyship's New Year's wishes are infinitely kind, though the *molti e felici* are compliments I can only accept as I would flowers strewed on my urn. I am well again; but my late disorder was I be-

---

16. The House of Commons met 23 Jan. 1781, the House of Lords 25 Jan.

---

1. Quipu, 'a device of the ancient Peruvians and others for recording events, keeping accounts, sending messages, etc., consisting of cords or threads of various colours, knotted in various ways' (OED). 'Quipos were made familiar to eighteenth-century readers by the *Lettres péruviennes* of Madame de Graffigny, published in 1749' (Toynbee). The earliest use cited in OED is 1704.

lieve a little of the gout in my stomach; and when once the flaw begins there, where my only strength lay, it would be silly not to know how precarious the tenure is.

Never deluding myself on that chapter, you will not wonder, Madam, that I am little qualified to resolve any questions about the dawn of the next reign. I attend to what is said about the Prince's family[2] no more than I should to a prophet, who should offer to lay before me a vision of the whole next century. Can I forget that I kissed the hand of this Prince of Wales's great-great-grandfather, the night but one before he left England for the last time?[3] and that I was then ten years old? Antiquated dukes may hobble into and out of golden chariots, if they think their corpses look well in them[4]— I should not like to lie in state before I am dead.[5]

Methinks the nation itself is fond of a magnificent funeral, and chooses to call in all countries to its burial; or at least to provoke them to dispatch it. *Et tu, Brute,* even Holland is to give us a stab.[6] The elements too have joined the armed neutrality. What a catastrophe that of Barbadoes![7]—yet we are all gaiety, nay delighted with the Dutch war.[8] We lose provinces and islands, and are comforted

2. A partial establishment for the Prince of Wales (his 'family') headed by Lord Southampton as Groom of the Stole had been announced, under date of 29 Dec. 1780, in the *London Gazette* No. 12149, 30 Dec.–2 Jan. 1781; for the list, see the *London Chronicle* 2–4 Jan., xlix. 10. HW recorded the event and some of those appointed under 28 Dec. in *Last Journals* ii. 340–1.

3. HW describes the occasion in *Reminiscences*, ed. Paget Toynbee, 1924, p. 11. He mentions it to Mann 13 Feb. 1767, 25 Feb. 1782, and to Mary Berry, 25 Sept. 1793. George I left England 3 June 1727, when HW was nine years old (his tenth birthday was 24 Sept. 1727 OS).

4. The Duke of Montagu, aged 68, had just succeeded (29 Dec. 1780) the Duke of Northumberland, aged 66, as Master of the Horse (*London Chronicle* 30 Dec.–2 Jan., xlix. 3).

5. The same general sentiment, much expanded, appears in the third paragraph of HW's letter to Mann 31 Dec. 1780.

6. Since the accession of William and Mary in 1689, Holland and Great Britain had had no war, and much of the time had been allies. By a vote of 4 to 3 the States General on 20 Nov. 1780 had resolved to join the armed neutrality promoted by Catherine II of Russia (Sir Francis Piggott and G. W. T. Omond, *Documentary History of the Armed Neutralities,* 1919, p. 247).

7. The *London Gazette* No. 12148, 26–30 Dec. 1780, contained a detailed description of 'a most violent hurricane which began on Tuesday the 10th instant [October] and continued almost without intermission for near forty-eight hours.' Many people were killed, and property damage was great: 'scarce a house is standing in Bridgetown; whole families were buried in the ruins of their habitations.'

8. 'The war with the Dutch never could have happened at a better time than it has, for from every seaport we have intelligence of their ships being taken and sent in' (*London Chronicle* 30 Dec.–2 Jan., xlix. 3). 'A Dutch war must inevitably enrich a British marine' (advertisement for marines in the *Daily Adv.* 1 Jan.). See also *Last Journals* ii. 341–2.

by barrels of pickled herrings! Then, Madam, what a brave string of
Irish peers![9] they put me in mind of the chain of galley-slaves in *Don
Quixote*.[10] Like them, I dare swear, their new Lordships would one
and all assure one, they are honest men![11]

The ancient sovereigns of this isle are come to a *non plus* too.
The Countess of Albany[12] is retired into a convent.[13] You know
they live at Florence. Last St Andrew's Day,[14] who is the favourite
saint *there too*, the Count got so beastly drunk, that at night every
filthy consequence ensued. The Countess complaining, he tore her
hair and endeavoured to strangle her. Her screams alarmed the
family and saved her. She privately acquainted the Great Duke,[15] and
by his authority and connivance she contrived to take shelter in a
convent,[16] declaring she will never return to her husband again, who
has in vain reclaimed her from the Great Duke.

Having nothing better to offer as a New Year's gift, I shall add
a nuptial ode that I made for Lady Lucan.[17] It would be presumption to hope it, but if Lady Anne would be so good as to translate
it into a wisp of parti-coloured silk,[18] and stuff a pincushion with
it, I should flatter myself with my work being immortal.

I

Hymen O Hymenæe!
To Althorp and Bingham!
Ye bards come and sing 'em,
And all the bells ring 'em
With ding, ding a dong.

9. Five were created barons; nine were
raised from baron to viscount; and two
from viscount to earl. The list is in the
London Gazette No. 12146, 19–23 Dec.
1780.

10. Don Quixote sees coming down the
road 'some twelve men in a company on
foot, inserted like beadstones in a great
chain of iron that was tied about their
necks' (*Don Quixote*, tr. Thomas Shelton,
1725, Book III, Ch. 8, i. 182; HW's copy,
now WSL, is Hazen, *Cat. of HW's Lib.* 3999).

11. The galley-slaves describe their
crimes in the best light possible by using
euphemistic language (tr. Shelton, i. 182–
94).

12. Luise Maximiliane of Stolberg-
Gedern (1752–1824) m. (1772) Charles

Edward Stuart (1720–88), the Young Pretender, titular Earl of Albany (BERRY,
passim).

13. HW's account which follows is
based on Mann's letter to him 12 Dec.
1780.

14. 30 Nov., the festival of St Andrew
the Apostle, the patron saint of Scotland.

15. Leopold (1747–92), Grand Duke of
Tuscany 1765–90, Holy Roman Emperor
(as Leopold II) 1790–2.

16. Of the White Nuns in the Via del
Mandorlo (H. M. Vaughan, *Last Stuart
Queen*, 1910, p. 59).

17. For the approaching marriage (6
March 1781) of her daughter Lavinia to
Lord Althorp.

18. That is, a quipu.

II

To Althorp and Bingham!
But pray do not ding 'em
With this or that thingum
That may call up in Bingham
  A blush all day long.

III

Your best wishes bring 'em,
Your best roses fling 'em
O'er the hammock, where Bingham
And Althorp shall swing 'em
  With ding, ding a dong.

PS. I am sorry to add so serious a PS. as that poor Lady Foley died this morning.[19]

To Lady Ossory, Thursday 4 January 1781

Jan. 4, 1781.

I RETURN the quipos, Madam, because if I retained them till I understand them, I fear you would never have them again. I should as soon be able to hold a dialogue with a rainbow by the help of its grammar a prism, for I have not yet discovered which is the first or last verse of four lines that hang like ropes of onions. Yet it is not for want of study, or want of respect for the Peruvian manner of writing. I perceive it is a very soft language, and though at first I tangled the poem and spoiled the rhymes, yet I can conceive that a harlequin's jacket, artfully arranged by a princess of the blood of Mango Capac,[1] may contain a deep tragedy, and that a tawdry trimming may be a version of Solomon's Song. Nay, I can already say my alphabet of six colours, and know that each stands indiscriminately *but* for four letters, which gives the Peruvian a great advantage over the Hebrew tongue, in which the total want of vowels left every word at the mercy of the reader; and though our salvation depended upon it, we did not know precisely what any word signi-

---

19. In childbed, at Foley House, Chandos Street, Marylebone (*London Chronicle* 2–4 Jan., xlix. 11; *Daily Adv.* 3 Jan.).

---

1. Manco Capac, legendary founder of

the Inca empire in Peru. 'Mango Capac, the son of the sun, is as authentic a founder of a royal race, as the progenitor of the Heraclidæ' (HW, *Historic Doubts*, 1768, pp. iii–iv; *Works* ii. 105).

fied, till the invention of points, that were not used till the language
had been obsolete for some thousands of years.[2] A little uncertainty,
as where one has but one letter instead of four, may give rise to many
beauties. Puns must be greatly assisted by that ambiguity, and the
delicacies of the language may depend on an almost imperceptible
variation in the shades; as the perfection of the Chinese consists in
possessing but very few syllables, each of which admits ten thousand
accents, and thence pronunciation is the most difficult part of their
literature.

At first sight the resemblance of blue and green by candle-light
seems to be an objection to the Peruvian; but any learned mercer
might obviate that by opposing indigo to grass-green, and ultra-
marine to *verd de pomme*. The more expert one were at nuances,
the more poetic one should be or the more eloquent. A vermilion *A*
must denote[3] a weaker accent, or even passion than one of carmine
and crimson, and a straw-colour *U* be much more tender than one
approaching to orange.

I have heard of a French perfumer[4] who wrote an essay on the
harmony of essences. Why should not that idea be extended? The
Peruvian quipos adapted a language to the eyes, rather than to the
ears. Why should not there be one for the nose? The more the senses
can be used indifferently for each other, the more our understand-
ings would be enlarged. A rose, jessamine, a pink, a jonquil and a
honeysuckle might signify the vowels; the consonants to be represented by other flowers. The Cape jessamine, which has two smells,
was born a diphthong. How charming it would be to smell an ode
from a nosegay, and to scent one's handkerchief with a favourite
song! Indeed, many improvements might be made on the quipos
themselves, especially as they might be worn as well as perused. A
trimming set on a new lutestring would be equivalent to a second
edition with corrections. I am only surprised that in a country like
Peru, where gold and silver thread were so cheap, there was no

2. 'Before the invention of points, only
a few learned men read Hebrew. 104'
(HW's note in his 'MS Commonplace
Book,' p. 49, on Pierre Bayle's *General
Dictionary*, 1734–41, x. 104 n.; in Bayle
a quotation from Brian Walton, 1600–
1661, suggests that points were introduced
about 500 years after Christ).

3. HW first wrote 'express.'
4. Perhaps La Faye, author of *Catalogue
et almanach du goût et de l'odorat, donné
par La Faye, marchand, pour 1772* (Comte
Robert de Montesquiou, *Pays des aromates*,
1900, p. 112).

clinquant[5] introduced into their poetry. In short, Madam, I am so pleased with the idea of knotting verses, which is vastly preferable to anagrams and acrostics, that if I were to begin life again, I would use a shuttle instead of a pen, and write verses by the yard. As it is, I have not been idle; nay, like any heaven-born genius, I have begun to write before I can read; and though I have not yet learn[ed] to decipher, I can at least cypher like Atahualpa[6] himself. As a proof of my proficience, pray, Madam, construe the following colours,

> Brown, blue, white, yellow green yellow yellow white, red brown brown
>   blue white.[7]

As I was writing this last line, I receive your Ladyship's interpretation of the verses. Whoever made them they are excellent, and it would have been cruel to have deprived me of them, till I could have unravelled them. Pray tell me who made them, for they are really good and sterling. I am sorry I expressed myself so awkwardly, that you thought I disapproved of the quipos. On the contrary you see how much they have amused me. In good truth I was glad of anything that would occupy me and turn my attention from all the horrors one hears or apprehends. I am sorry I have read the devastation of Barbadoes and Jamaica etc., etc., etc., etc.,—when one can do no good, can neither prevent nor redress, nor has any personal share by one's self or one's friends, is not it excusable to steep one's attention in anything?—I fear, Madam, you and Lord Ossory have a suffering friend! poor Mr James, I hear, is totally ruined—his whole property swept away![8]—There is another dreadful history less known —The expedition sent against the Spanish settlements is cut off by the climate, and not a single being is left alive.[9] The Duchess of Bedford told me last night that the poor soldiers were so averse, that

5. Tinsel, foil.

6. Atahuallpa (ca 1502–33), 'the last of the Incas' of Peru, murdered by the Spaniards.

7. HW gives the meaning, *je vous aime,* in the following letter.

8. James Hare to Lord Carlisle 29 Dec. 1781: 'Boothby has just told me that James finds himself in such bad circumstances that he is obliged to sell all his horses, and give up hunting entirely; but as James is in town, and has not said one word to me about it, I am in hopes that

it is not exactly so' (*Carlisle MSS* 556). See also the following letter.

9. 'An account of the expedition sent by Governor Dalling from Jamaica, of 1500 men, against the Spanish settlements having been destroyed to a man, with 25 officers, by the climate. On this the Government said not a word' (*Last Journals* ii. 343). See also HW to Conway 3 Jan. 1781; to Mason 4 Jan. 1781, MASON ii. 91 n. 10, from which it appears that about 380 of 1800 men survived.

they were driven to the march by the point of the bayonet, and that besides the men, twenty-five officers have perished.

Lord Cornwallis and his tiny army are scarce in a more prosperous way.[10] On this dismal canvas a fourth war[11] is embroidered; and what I think, threatens still more, the French administration is changed, and likely to be composed of more active men, and much more hostile to England.[12] Our ruin seems to me inevitable. Nay, I know those who smile in the Drawing-Room, that groan by their fireside—They own we have no more men to send to America, and think our credit almost as nearly exhausted. Can you wonder then, Madam, if I am glad to play with quipos—Oh no! nor can I be sorry to be on the verge—does one wish to live to weep over the ruins of Carthage?

To LADY OSSORY, Tuesday 9 January 1781

Address: To the Countess of Ossory at Ampthill Park, Bedfordshire. *Postmark:* 9 IA.

Jan. 9, 1781.

YOUR Ladyship takes so kind a part in all that concerns me, that, though I could not have told you how thunderstruck I was yesterday with news of the loss of Jersey,[1] and alarmed for General Conway who was but two hours in town, and had not time

10. 'Lord Cornwallis . . . had been very ill [with a fever], and was marched 150 miles into the country with only 1300 men, and was then in great danger of being cut off, Washington having detached 3000 men to reinforce Gates.' Colonel O'Hara wrote to Conway, 'declaring he trembled for Lord Cornwallis . . . and professing his firm belief of the impossibility of our recovering America' (*Last Journals* ii. 341, *sub* 30 Dec. 1780). At the date of HW's letter, Cornwallis was 130 miles from Charleston at Winnsborough, South Carolina (Sir Henry Clinton, *Observations on Some Parts of the Answer of Earl Cornwallis,* 1783, pp. 39–51; *Correspondence of Charles, First Marquis Cornwallis,* ed. Ross, 1859, i. 64–81, esp. p. 68, where Cornwallis says that if he were 'to penetrate into the further parts of North Carolina, my small army would have been exposed to the utmost hazard'). The *Daily Adv.* 1 Jan. reported that 'he

had penetrated very far into North [*sic*] Carolina.'

11. With the Dutch, in addition to the conflict with France, Spain, and the American colonies.

12. HW noted the change in *Last Journals* ii. 342, *sub* Dec. 1780: 'The Queen's influence prevailed: she obtained the dismission [18 Dec.] of the Prince de Montbarrey [secretary at war], and got the Duc du Châtelet, one of our bitterest enemies, to succeed him. And it was thought M. de Vergennes would fall, too, the only one who had supported the Americans, for all the other ministers did not like them, though they wished to hurt us, and had much neglected them; and Dr Franklin was grown old and indolent, and had lost all credit at Versailles. Yet they had a mind to support the Americans enough just to ruin us by another year's war.'

1. An expanded version of the attack

to see me, and set out with a broken arm not quite recovered,[2] yet I must communicate the sudden transition to joy, and relief from the worst part of my alarm. The troops in Jersey made a stand, gained a complete victory, and took all the remaining French, that had landed, prisoners.[3] Mr Conway, I conclude, will proceed, and thank his little army, who, without detracting from their merit, certainly owe some of it to his discipline—Well, Madam, *je respire!* These rapid revulsions are a little too much for such harassed nerves as mine —but you forbid me—and I am silent.

I received two packets from your Ladyship last night, and at almost any other moment should have enjoyed them. I can now go over them again, and with pleasure, except the article of Miss Vernon. Your picture of her is very alarming—I tremble for your Ladyship and for her brothers and sisters!—but alarms of every kind will be the lot of all that have any feeling for some time; and even hearts of rock will groan at last, for gold lies in the hearts of those rocks and is as sensitive as the most shattered nerves. Nor will ducal coronets or portraits of Lord and Lady Spencer console them, if the mines of ore and diamonds are swept away. I had not heard that anecdote of Cunningham.[4] It is one of those traits, that whatever is said of comedy, nay, of the exaggeration of farce, would be too strong for the stage. The bombast passion of a lover in a romance might be carried to such an excess—but a governor writing on the ruins of a whole island levelled by the most fatal of all hurricanes, that his chief misery was the loss of—what?—his bracelets with the portraits of his idols[4a]—who would dare to bring such a revolting hyperbole on the stage?

on Jersey and the repulse is in *Last Journals* ii. 343–4, *sub* 8–9 Jan. About 800 French troops landed at Jersey on 6 Jan., captured the lieutenant-governor in his bed, but were repulsed in a battle in which both French and English commanders were killed. An extract from Lt-Gov. Corbet's report, 6 Jan. 1781, is in the *London Gazette Extraordinary* 9 Jan.; see also GM 1781, li. 42.

2. 'The express [from the Council ordering Conway to Jersey] went to him at Park Place at eleven; he was in town by three, though with a broken arm not quite recovered, and set out in two hours for Portsmouth' (*Last Journals* ii. 343).

3. On 9 Jan., 'At noon an express from Guernsey that the troops in Jersey had rallied, attacked the ['near 2000'] French, gained a complete victory, taken 500 prisoners, and driven 400 into the sea' (ibid.).

4a. Corroboration of this anecdote has not been found.

4. James Cuninghame (ca 1731–88), Maj.-Gen., 1777; Lt-Gen., 1782; M.P. East Grinstead 1786–8. He was governor of Barbados 1780–3; arrived at Barbados 12 July 1780; recalled because of his arbitrary actions (Robert H. Schomburgk, *History of Barbados*, 1848, pp. 337–47, 685). The legislature of Barbados had petitioned for his recall a few months after he arrived (John Poyer, *History of Barbados*, 1808, pp. 474–6).

Excuse me, Madam, but I do believe there is a great flaw in my memory—I cannot recollect what you allude to by *pigs*. Pray tell me, and which you have not done, the author or authoress of the verses on the quipos. The explication of mine, is—if I ciphered it right, *Je vous aime*. Perhaps I ought to have told you it was French.

Somebody knocks, I must finish—but it is not necessary to make excuses for short letters, when I so often send you such long ones—It was Mr Cambridge to ask news of Jersey, and to trumpet a victory of Carleton[5] the Lord knows where, at t'other end of the world[6]—I neither satisfied his curiosity, nor listened to his gazette.

PS. Mr Craufurd has called on me too, and tells me Mr James's loss will be but about £15,000, and that he can bear it; but the Storers are totally undone, and so G. Selwyn says too.[7] I pity them!

I forgot to tell your Ladyship that I met Mrs Montagu t'other night at a visit. She said, she had been alone the whole preceding day, *quite hermetically sealed*—I was very glad she was uncorked, or I might have missed that piece of learned nonsense!

To Lady Ossory, Sunday 14 January 1781

Berkeley Square, Jan. 14, 1781.

I BEG we may correspond no more in Peruvian, Madam, for it would take less time to send our letters to Lima to be interpreted, **than** to decipher three words. I return the alphabet, and humbly hope you had forgotten your A B C, for the words as I read them are, *On vous aimons*, which so good a grammarian as your Ladyship could not have written, if you remembered your colours—unless, which is much more probable, I have not expounded them rightly, for I certainly have no genius for so brocaded a language, which is

5. Christopher Carleton (1749–87), nephew of Sir Guy Carleton (*ante* 27 Dec. 1775); Major 29th Foot 14 Sept 1777; Lt-Col., 1783 (Collins, *Peerage*, 1812, viii. 112; *Army Lists*).

6. General Haldimand, Governor of Quebec, in a dispatch to Lord George Germain, Quebec, 25 Oct. 1780, reported that Major Carleton on 10–11 Oct. had taken Fort Ann and Fort George, and had returned to Crown Point (*London Gazette* No. 12150, 2–6 Jan.).

7. Thomas Storer (ca 1717–93), the father of Anthony Morris and Thomas Storer, had considerable property in Jamaica. In 1774 Charles Howard wrote that A. M. Storer's property was in Antigua, which had suffered from the same hurricane. They recovered from their losses (*Carlisle MSS* 280).

like a piece of silk, all confusion, till it is unfolded. I will tell you what is of more importance. I asked the Duchess of Bedford t'other night at Princess Amelie's how she found Miss Vernon? 'Oh,' said she, 'I never saw her look so pretty; the journey[1] had given her a charming colour. Dr Warren was with her three times yesterday, and says if she does not go to three assemblies in an evening, she will be very well.'—In truth, I do not much depend on this account; the glow might be hectic, and three visits in one day did not sound well; and besides her Grace is apt [to] see everything *couleur de rose*—still I think your own tenderness made you think her worse than she may be—I hope so.

You have seen Mr Fox's combat with highwaymen in the papers[2] —at first I concluded they were not highwaymen, but Highlanders, and that Messrs Adam and Fullerton[3] were ambitious of farther preferment.[4]

I know nothing farther of Jersey, so contrary is the wind; nor anything else, but that Lord Carlisle is laid up with the gout in his red heels.[5]

1. She had been visiting the Ossorys at Ampthill (*ante* 26 Nov., 17 Dec. 1780, 9 Jan. 1781).

2. 'On Thursday evening [11 Jan.] as the Hon. Charles Fox was coming to town, he was stopped by a highwayman who, with the severest menaces, demanded his money, which, as soon as the footman perceived, he immediately fired; the robber instantly returned it, and had not his accomplice kept at a distance, it is supposed there must have been murder, as the second shot went through the servant's coat, and Mr Fox was resolutely bent not to be robbed. The highwayman is thought to be wounded, as he rode off full speed towards Finchley Common as soon as Mr Fox discharged a double-barrel pistol at him' (*London Chronicle* 11–13 Jan., xlix. 48; *Daily Adv.* 15 Jan., slightly abridged).

3. William Fullarton (1754–1808), army officer and politician; secretary to Lord Stormont's embassy at Paris 1777–8; M.P. Plympton 1779–80, Haddington 1787–90, Horsham 1793–6, Ayrshire 1796–1803. In 1780 he raised the 98th Regiment at his own expense. His appointment to command the regiment caused a duel 21 March 1780 with Lord Shelburne, who had spoken against the practice of giving 'occasional rank' in the army to untrained men. See MASON ii. 12–14; *Last Journals* ii. 288–94.

4. Adam's duel with Fox (*ante* 2 Dec. 1779) and Fullarton's with Shelburne (Fox and Shelburne were in opposition to the ministry) led HW to associate Adam and Fullarton as courting perferment: 'Fullerton being a Scot, as well as Adam, renewed much national animosity' (*Last Journals* ii. 292, *sub* 24 March 1780); he called the second duel 'a second part to the history of Adam and Charles Fox,' and 'Mr Adam and Mr Fullerton attempted to stab in open daylight' (to Mason 22 March, 1 Nov. 1780, MASON ii. 12, 87); he noted that the same pistol wounded Fox and Shelburne, Adam having borrowed Fullarton's (to Mann 8 April 1780).

5. Lord Carlisle's foppishness was the subject of much contemporary satire. On 9 March 1778 the Duke of Richmond in the House of Lords, commenting on Carlisle as one of the Commissioners to

Your Ladyship's history of Mr Whitebread the brewer[6] and his insolent wealth came very apropos to what the Princess said t'other night. She was talking of the crew of Irish peers, and said to the Duchess of Bedford, 'I would not give a straw to be a peer in this country—no, give me a good brewhouse; *that* is what makes one considerable here'—I doubt, if we brew as we bake, nothing will make us considerable long!

May not I ask, Madam, if you do not begin to think of London? Shall not Lady Anne learn of Vestris,[7] while you have a shilling left? Pray let her be fit to make a curtsy like a Christian, in case the French should land. You will really keep her and yourself in the country, till you will feel for your friends that are undone by hurricanes, or till you lament the war with Holland, though you might have a share in a privateer,[8] and though John St John[9] has a contract

treat with the American colonies, referred to 'his Lordship in his red-heel shoes, and all that elegance of dress which is so exceedingly proper to his Lordship' (*London Chronicle* 7–10 March 1778, xliii, 240). The red-heeled shoes are also mentioned in a satirical print, 'America to Her Mistaken Mother,' published by M. Darly 11 May 1778 (BM, *Satiric Prints* v. 289, No. 5475; reproduced in *American Heritage*, 1956, viii, 45; other references to his foppishness appear in BM, *Satiric Prints* v. 286–9, Nos 5473–4; *Last Journals* ii. 130, *sub* 9 March 1778; Cobbett, *Parl. Hist.* xix, 867; MASON i. 421). According to the *Macaroni and Theatrical Magazine*, Jan. 1773, p. 146, Charles Fox was responsible for 'the renovation of that fashion laid aside since the beginning of the present century—red-heeled-shoes: C——s, appearing in these on a Birthnight about three years ago, brought them into fashion; and they are now frequently worn by what the macaroni world call a *well-drest man.*'

6. Samuel Whitbread (1720–96), eldest son of a dissenting 'yeoman of Bedfordshire,' 'said to have died worth a million at least . . . his private benevolence . . . is said to have exceeded £3000 per annum' (GM 1796, lxvi pt i. 531); M.P. Bedford borough 1768–74, 1775–90, Steyning 1792–6 (Burke, *Landed Gentry*, 1937, pp. 2418–19; GM 1787, lvii pt ii. 632–3; Bed-

fordshire Parish Registers, ed. F. D. Emmison, Vol. VIII: *Cardington*, Bedford, 1934, pp. vii, 28, 113).

7. The elder Vestris, Gaetano Appollino Baldassare Vestris (1729–1808), father of the dancer mentioned *ante* 17 Dec. 1780, taught ballet at the rate of 'Six Guineas Entrance and a Guinea a Lesson,' as suggested by one of the satirical prints dealing with him; see BM, *Satiric Prints* v. 535–7, Nos 5908–11, especially v. 535–6, Nos 5908–9. The Prince of Wales told Mrs Keppel 'he loved Cholmondeley dearly, he was such an honest good fellow, but he must go and laugh at him for learning to dance of Vestris' (Laura Keppel to Anne Clement 21 Jan. 1781, MS WSL; cf. *post* 25 July 1781). On 26 May 1781 Lady Mary Coke at the Duchess of Beaufort's 'saw Lady Betty Compton take her lesson of Monsieur Vestris' ('MS Journals').

8. As in the Seven Years War, some privateers for the American war were fitted out by subscription or the purchase of shares by ladies (Gomer Williams, *History of the Liverpool Privateers*, 1897, pp. 122, 225; *London Chronicle* 30 Jan.–1 Feb., xlix. 112).

9. Hon. John St John (ca 1746–93), 3d son of John, 2d Vct St John; M.P. Newport (Hants) 1773–4, 1780–4, Eye 1774–80; surveyor-general of the land revenues of the Crown 1775–84; pamphleteer and

for furnishing us with play-thing coaches,[10] that are neater than the Dutch ones, and as cheap as Mr Atkinson's[11] rum. Do but come to town, and you will not have a fear or a care left. The serene house of Brudenel will steep your senses and feelings in a delicious lethargy, and you will see everything through an eternal mist, as the Scotch do, and which they call second sight, not having the first gift of sight, which is, to see things as they are.

I was much diverted with your setting Mrs Montagu on her head, which indeed she does herself without the help of Hermes. She is one of my principal entertainments at Mrs Vesey's, who collects all the graduates and candidates for fame, where they vie with one another, till they are as unintelligible as the good folks at Babel—I am again interrupted—all one's letters, one's time, one's occupations are cracked by alarms! Col. Conway[12] is just arrived; his uncle and he were overtaken, nay, sailed[13] in a tempest—they saw a transport with sixty poor men perish, and fear the cutter, that preceded to notify their arriving to Jersey is lost.[14] The *Emerald*[15] was tossed for two days and nights, and General Conway's broken arm was hurt[16]— Capt. Marshal,[17] a stout sailor, gave them up, the sailors were lashed

dramatist (Foster, *Alumni Oxon.;* Berry ii. 29).

10. Books on coaches do not explain what these were.

11. Richard Atkinson (1738–85), member of the Goldsmiths' Company; alderman of London 1784–5; M.P. New Romney 1784–5; director, East India Company 1784–5; satirized in *The Rolliad.* 'He belonged to a City firm [Hutchinson Mure] which traded chiefly with Jamaica. During the American War he contracted to supply the troops with rum. The rum he provided was new, and did great harm amongst the soldiers, many of whom died from the effects of it' (Toynbee; A. B. Beaven, *The Aldermen of . . . London,* 1908–13, ii. 137, 201, and *passim;* GM 1785, lv pt i. 407. For further details of his contracts and loans, see Mason i. 437, ii. 192; Cobbett, *Parl. Hist.* xx. 1287–9; BM, *Satiric Prints* vi. 75–6, No. 6485. Lord Shelburne in the House of Lords 15 Dec. 1779 had charged Lord North with having given Atkinson a 'contract . . . for 5,000 hogsheads of rum at a price actually double what it could be purchased for on

the quays of London' (Cobbett, loc. cit.; *Last Journals* ii. 259, 410).

12. Hon. (after 1793, Lord) Robert Seymour-Conway, 3d son of Lord Hertford (*ante* 21 June 1773).

13. From Portsmouth, 8 Jan. (preceding letter).

14. This information remains unchanged in HW's letter to Mann 18 Jan. 1781.

15. A repeating frigate in poor condition (*Royal Kalendar,* 1780, p. 143; *Last Journals* ii. 345; *Sandwich Papers* iv. 71–3).

16. HW to Mann 18 Jan. 1781: 'a goodnatured sailor, seeing him awkward at getting up the ladder into the frigate, and not knowing, or not considering that he had a broken arm, gave it such a kind tug, that he almost broke it again.'

17. Samuel Marshall (ca 1740–95), Lt, 1760; Master, 1762; Capt., 1771–ca 1793; Commissioner of the victualling office 1787–93; extra commissioner of the Navy 1793–4; deputy comptroller of the Navy 1794–5; died at his house in Holles Street, Cavendish Square; of Berry House, Hants

or could not stand to their work—the wind changed providentially, or they were lost on the rocks, and carried them to Plimouth, where the Conways landed—Col. Conway found his wife miscarrying—Oh! I could fill my paper with distresses—but the Parliament will meet in two or three days,[18] and vote that we are all felicity and glory! General Conway is stopped at Park Place to cure his bruises, as his island is safe—I have not time to say more—

Monday.

Col. Conway was with me an hour this morning and has given me such an account of their voyage as makes me shudder; and I have since received a note from Lady Ailesbury to tell me her husband is in bed with the rheumatism and fatigue, but I fear with his arm, for his nephew says it was very painful to him, though neither the pain nor their peril made the smallest impression on his calmness, which astonished even his nephew, who knows him. Thank God that he is alive. It is a time to feel any blessing to oneself, when so many are in anguish!

To Lady Ossory, Thursday 25 January 1781

Address: To the Countess of Ossory at Ampthill Park, Bedfordshire. *Postmark:* 25 IA.

Berkeley Square, Jan. 25, 1781.

YOU know I never pretend to continue my gazette, Madam, when Lord Ossory is in town.[1] I can only send the dried skin of news, and he can give you the marrow. He was so good as to sit with me two hours yesterday morning.

I certainly do love and have for forty years loved General Conway as my dearest friend, and consequently am very uneasy about him. He is extremely out of order still; and had I not been deceived about

(GM 1785, lv. pt i. 323; GM 1795, lxv. pt ii. 881; *Court and City Register* and *Royal Kalendar, passim*). 'Captain Marshall is so good an officer that he lets everyone cry out before he even notices himself' (Darby to Sandwich 21 Oct. 1781, *Sandwich Papers* iv. 71). Although he is frequently called 'Sir Samuel Marshall, Kt,' in the 1790's,

his name is not in W. A. Shaw's *Knights of England.*

18. The House of Commons 23 Jan., the House of Lords 25 Jan.

1. He had come to London for the meeting of the House of Commons on 23 Jan.; see preceding letter.

him on his return, and if I did not every day expect him to be brought to town, I should have gone to him. I am now waiting for the post, which I hope will bring me a more satisfactory account.

My gaming losses, Madam, have been trifling, and my luck as usual fluctuating, so as to make very little difference. Still I do not decline the purse,[2] which I shall value, though it should not have an enriching virtue.

I have seen Vestris—and remain in my senses.

To Lady Ossory, Wednesday 31 January 1781

Address: To the Countess of Ossory at Ampthill Park, Bedfordshire. *Postmark:* 1 FE. GC.

Berkeley Square, Jan. 31, at night, 1781.

IT is not to save myself, I assure your Ladyship, that I decline writing when Lord Ossory is in town. I do write when he is not, because I am aware that any intelligence, that is not quite bad, and that takes care not to be false, is acceptable in the country. But when our Lord is here, and hears all that passes in Parliament, and at Brooks's all that passes, how chilled must sound the little that I learn in my own room, or in the small circle to which my acquaintance is reduced, or to which I have reduced it! I go little into the fashionable world, and less among politicians of either side; and to no public places: and of the young world, except of my own family, I determine to know nothing; or, if I cannot help it, to say nothing. One of the *reigning* topics (I have improperly used almost a treasonable word) is the Prince of Wales. With him I am positive never to occupy myself. I kissed the hand of his great-great-grandfather—would not it be preposterous to tap a volume of future history, of which I can never see but the first pages? I am sensible that those persons are happier, who do not feel what is improper for their age; but having always had a horror for juvenile ancientry, I will not make an exception in my own favour; nor should have any comfort in it. It is an absurd saying, that none know themselves—what the deuce then do they know? Do they think they bound, when they totter, or mistake

2. Apparently a present from Lady Ossory brought to HW by Lord Ossory.

wrinkles ⟨for beauty, and⟩ want of memory for thoughtlessness?

I have had another cause of silence too, Madam; I have been at Pa⟨rk Place⟩ to see General Conway. I suspected he was worse than I was told, ⟨and⟩ found he had been much worse than I suspected. He still has fever, and still rheumatism; his hands are swelled, and his face and legs emaciated; nor has he yet been out of his bedchamber. In short, he is much broken, and I doubt will be long before he recovers his strength.[1] I came back but today to attend the Princess,[2] and know absolutely nothing. I believe there is nothing new, for the Duchess of Bedford was there—oh! yes, Capt. Waldegrave has taken some rich Dutch prizes,[3] for which I am very glad, as I like him much, and his cousins love him extremely.

Thank your Ladyship for the account of Sir Walter Raleigh's and his wife's[4] pictures,[5] but I shall not meddle with them. I have neither room nor money for more purchases. The stocks are so terribly fallen,[6] that what trifles I had saved *from myself* for others, would not now pay the legacies I have given; and I must endeavour, if I live, to hoard

1. He had returned to London when HW wrote to Mason 3 March 1781: 'I dined the other day with Mr Conway' (MASON ii. 116).

2. Amelia.

3. In a letter 'from the Hon. Capt. Waldegrave, Commander of . . . *La Prudente*, to Mr Stephens, dated Spithead, the 29th inst.,' Waldegrave reported that his ship and the *Ambuscade*, which had sailed together from Cork 18 Jan. on a cruise, had captured circa 22 Jan. 'a Dutch brig, loaded with sugar and tobacco,' from Curaçao and on 26 Jan. '*L'Americaine*, a private ship of war, mounting 24 nine-pounders on her maindeck, and 8 three-pounders on her quarter-deck, complement 245 men' (*London Chronicle* 20–23 Jan., 30 Jan.–1 Feb., xlix. 78, 106). The '*Elizabeth and Sophia*, from St Eustatia, a prize to . . . *La Prudente*,' arrived at Plymouth 24 Jan. (ibid. 27–30 Jan., xlix. 102).

4. Elizabeth Throckmorton or Throgmorton (1565–1647), dau. of Sir Nicholas Throckmorton, and maid of honour to Queen Elizabeth until her attachment to Raleigh was discovered, m. (1592) Sir Walter Raleigh (ca 1552–1618).

5. Two oval pictures in 'crayon' or 'watercolour,' with an inscription in gold on Lady Raleigh's portrait, 'Videtor et vere est. Ano Dm^{no} 1602.' Both pictures are described in detail in a letter from an unknown correspondent from 'Bath, October ye 5th' (perhaps 1780), to Lord Harcourt, in the *Harcourt Papers* viii. 100–3. The pictures and a letter were in the possession of 'Mrs Ralegh,' 'the only daughter of his [Sir Walter's] great-grandson,' who wanted to sell the three items 'almost for subsistence' (p. 101). Mrs Ralegh 'will thankfully accept of the offer your Lordship makes of doing her the honour to name these pictures to the Duchess of Portland, or anybody you think proper, and will be happy to follow your Lordship's opinion with regard to the disposal of them. For my own part I was half glad and half afraid when I heard the name of Mr Walpole, I have an idea of so much depending on the *ton* he takes in speaking of a thing of that sort' (ibid.).

6. For example, 3 per cent consols had declined more than 22% between Jan. 1776 and Jan. 1781, from 87½ to 58. For details, see the tables in the *Gentleman's Magazine* for each month.

the deficiency.[6a] This is an uncomfortable reflection—but who that reflects, has not some such to make? The nation, like a great boy, does not allow itself a moment's thought. It engages every day to support new wars, though it cannot manage one of them—ere long, to use the sublime nonsense of a Secretary of State, *it will be stunned into its senses*[7]—but what good will its senses do then?—This was a letter of obedience, but I fear, ill-conducted to enliven your solitude.

To Lady Ossory, Wednesday 13 June 1781

Address: To the Countess of Ossory in Grosvenor Place, London. *Postmark:* [? 6] O'CLOCK. 14 IV. ISLEWORTH.

Strawberry Hill, June 13, 1781.

THE Beauty Room, Madam, is the Yellow Bedchamber[1] hung with Jarvis's[2] small copies of Sir Peter Lely's beauties, which chamber is on the ground floor here, next to the Little Parlour. I placed your screen[3] there *pour cause,* and because it accords with the chimney-piece, which is black and yellow. Had it inhabited the Blue Room in which I chiefly live, it would not have lasted even *my time.* In Berkeley Square it would have looked as if in disgrace and in exile; just as French ministers, when under a cloud, feel miserable, though suffered to ⟨dwe⟩ll in Paris itself, if not permitted into the heaven of heavens ⟨Ver⟩sailles.

Mr Storer has just left me;[4] I have showed him such hosts of portraits of the dead, that if he retains their names, he would make a good vice-chamberlain to Proserpine on a *Birth-night,* if there were any such fête in the shades below; but as ceremonies are of the essence

6a. HW's will in 1781 is missing. Payment of about £100,000 in legacies left no residuary estate. See SELWYN 344–77.

7. Lord Stormont in the debate on the King's message relative to the rupture with Holland 25 Jan. in the House of Lords: 'We had very wisely determined not to procrastinate any longer; we had given them the first blow, and would probably stun them into their senses' (Cobbett, *Parl. Hist.* xxi. 1006).

1. HW had already explained this (*ante* 20 June 1776).

2. Charles Jervas or Jarvis (ca 1675–1739), whose paintings HW had earlier described as 'wretched daubing' (*Anecdotes, Works* iii. 410).

3. 'A fire-screen worked by Lady Ossory, 1781' ('Des. of SH,' *Works* ii. 419), possibly one of the screens sold SH xvii. 62.

4. George Selwyn to Lord Carlisle 13 June: 'Storer is coming here to dinner. He lives now with Mr Walpole; has his lodging at Strawberry Hill, as an antiquarian' (*Carlisle MSS* 497).

of all courts, I suppose there they keep death-nights, and then he will be more at home in a ballroom than even Lord Brudenel.

I direct this to Grosvenor Place, for though you named today for your leaving town, nobody sets out at the time they intended. I shall be obliged to go thither oftener than I wish. When your Ladyship found me at the Grove,[5] it was to inform Mr Morrice, that Lord Orford has named me and Mr Skrine[6] to be referees with him to compromise my Lord's claims on Cav. Mozzi[7] for money due from my Lord's mother. I do not admire the pursuit of that claim, and tried to avoid being employed in it; but, though cast off when I am of no use, they come to me when any drudgery is to be done!

I have been reading a book as heterogeneous from my pursuits as Mr Storer's new profession from his: Mr Beckford's[8] on hunting[9]— and as I always reckon that any book pays me in which I find *one* passage that pleases me or tells me something new (I mean that I care to learn, for as to novelty, every book of science could tell me what I don't know), I found one jewel in Mr Beckford, for which I would have perused a folio. His huntsman christened one of his hounds *Lyman*. 'Lyman!' said the squire; 'why, James, what does *Lyman* mean?'—'Lord! Sir,' said James, 'what does *anything* mean?' I am transported with James's good sense and philosophy. ⟨It⟩ comforts me for all the books of science which I do not understan⟨d, and⟩ is an answer to all the pretended knowledge upon earth; and if M⟨r⟩ Beckford were a classic (as he will be one to those *who know of none*) I would change my motto of *Fari quæ sentiat*[10] for, *What does anything*

5. The Grove, or Grove House, at Chiswick, Middlesex; the seat of Humphry Morice. 'Soon after' the death of Lady Frances Elliot, 1772, Morice purchased the house and 80-acre grounds, 'made considerable additions to the house, and built a large riding-house, with excellent stables for thirty horses' (Daniel Lysons, *Environs of London*, Vol. II, *Middlesex*, 1795, p. 197, where a detailed history is given). HW's ambiguity is in part explained *post* 17 July 1781.

6. 'Mr Skrine had begged to be excused, but my Lord [Orford] insisted' (HW to Mann 5 July 1781). 'It seems Cav. Mozzi, by a letter to Mr Sharpe, rejects Mr Skrine' (HW to Mann 13 July 1781).

7. Cavaliere Giulio Giuseppe Mozzi del

Garbo (1730–1813), poet and mathematician. For his connection with Lady Orford and his long dispute with Lord Orford about Lady Orford's will, see the HW-Mann Correspondence.

8. Peter Beckford (?1739–1811), sportsman and master of foxhounds; M.P. Morpeth 1768–74 (*Old Westminsters*).

9. *Thoughts on Hunting. In a Series of Familiar Letters to a Friend*, Sarum, 1781; published 31 May (*London Courant*). HW placed a large cross in the margin where the following anecdote appears on p. 62 of his copy, now wsl (Hazen, *Cat. of HW's Lib.* 2796). Beckford attributes the story (slightly adapted by HW) to the 'huntsman of a friend of mine.'

10. Speak what you think.

mean? as more expressive of *quæ sentio*—I have gone through Sir R. Worseley's[11] *Isle of Wight*,[12] which is in my own way—and yet alas! I did not find *one* diamond in that dunghill—no, James for my money!

To Lady Ossory, Wednesday 20 June 1781

Address: To the Countess of Ossory at Ampthill Park, Bedfordshire. *Postmark:* 21 IV.

Strawberry Hill, June 20, 1781.

I SHALL not be able to wait on your Ladyship yet, for my niece Lady Maria,[1] who has had a bad cold that has turned to a cough, is coming to me for the air. I expect Mr Mason too, who has long promised me a visit.[2] If unengaged, I should be very glad to meet the company you propose to me; not that I want additional allurements to Ampthill.

It is not common for me, Madam, to send you news from Court, or to contradict what is said to be transacting there; but for once I will be important—only because I have nothing more insignificant to tell you—Be assured therefore that the Emperor is not going to marry the Princess Royal.[3] I have been at the Pavilions this evening with the Duke and Duchess: his R[oyal] H[ighness] is already returned from his extempore jaunt to Brussels,[4] and has *not* settled the marriage articles. If his Highness has retained Cæsar in our pay, like his

---

11. Sir Richard Worsley (1751–1805), 7th Bt, 1768; M.P.; F.R.S. and F.S.A.

12. *The History of the Isle of Wight,* 1781; dedication to the King signed 4 June 1781 (COLE ii. 272; MASON ii. 147; Hazen, *Cat. of HW's Lib.* 3220).

---

1. Waldegrave; she left SH 3 July (*post* 4 July 1781).

2. Mason planned to go to SH on Monday, 9 July, or shortly thereafter (MASON ii. 148 n. 3).

3. Charlotte Augusta Matilda (1766–1828), eldest dau. of George III, m. (1797) Frederick I (Charles William), K. of Württemberg, 1805. The Duchess of Chandos had 'proposed the Princess Royal to the Emperor' (*post* 12 Sept. 1781). The

Public Advertiser 20 June mentioned this marriage as 'very improbable.'

4. The Duke of Gloucester, travelling as a private gentleman, left London 12 June. Landing at Ostend a few hours after the Emperor had landed, the Duke followed to Bruges, where they had a conference. The Duke left Bruges for Ostend 15 June and returned to London 17 June without having had to go to Brussels (*Daily Adv.* 15, 20 June; *London Chronicle* 12–21 June, xlix. 568–9, 584–5, 592). According to HW, it was not a 'political visit,' though 'it was supposed that he went on some negotiation from the King' (*Last Journals* ii. 365, 366), perhaps concerned with trade (*London Chronicle* 19–21 June, xlix. 592).

ancestor Maximilian,[5] it is more than I am at liberty to disclose.[6] I dare go no farther than to advise you not to buy into the stocks upon that presumption. Mr Wraxhall[7] may be more explicit, even in the House of Commons, though he knows no more of it than I do.[8] However I should not like to be thought totally ignorant, as I observe the depth of politics in the present times is to seem to know the contrary of all that is true—yet why should I affect more honours than I enjoy? Do not they seek me in my humble cell? Do not I want all my philosophy to combat the fumes of pride?—In a word, Princess Sophia has invited Tonton[9] to the Pavilions—and, will it be believed, I have consented to carry him!—how weak is mortal man! That *I* should live to let my dog be a courtier!—I do not know how others feel on such occasions, but for my part I cannot act this renegade part with *an unembarrassed countenance*.[10] I tremble lest Mr Fox should write a note[11] to record my fall in my *Royal and Noble Authors,*

5. Maximilian I (1459–1519), Holy Roman Emperor, 1493; served as volunteer under Henry VIII in defeating the French at Guinegate near Thérouenne ('the Battle of the Spurs') in 1513, and accepted payment from him.

6. In *Last Journals* ii. 366 HW records the friendliness of the Emperor to England: 'The Emperor told his Royal Highness he had a great inclination to come to England, but it would give too much jealousy to the other European powers; and he added, "If one wished to serve *you* (meaning England) it would be to no purpose, you are too obstinate" . . . The Emperor told the Duke that we had offered Gibraltar to Spain for a separate peace, but it had been rejected.'

7. Nathaniel William Wraxall (1751–1831), cr. (1813) Bt; M.P.; memoir writer.

8. In his first speech in the House of Commons, 25 Jan. 1781, on the King's message relative to the rupture with Holland, Wraxall argued that England greatly needed an ally on the Continent and that the Emperor was the best possibility. HW's 'explicit' is explained by Wraxall's many historical references and his detailed reasons why the Emperor would be a valuable ally. Wraxall drew 'a most animated character of Joseph, and described and dwelt on his virtues and qualifications

with all the warmth of a passionate admirer' (Cobbett, *Parl. Hist.* xxi. 1097, the entire speech reported on pp. 1090–1100).

9. Thomas Walpole the younger had brought Tonton to HW shortly before 30 April (HW to Hon. Thomas Walpole 30 April 1781).

10. An allusion to the political ballad of that name, published in 1746, and possibly written by Sir Charles Hanbury Williams. See HW to Montagu 12 June 1746, MONTAGU i. 30.

11. Fox's MS note upon Gibbon's political volte-face in 1779 (in a presentation volume of the *Decline and Fall,* seen among Fox's books before they were sold ca 15 June) had been printed in the *Public Advertiser* 20 June (a variant appeared in the *London Courant* 29 June). See George Hardinge to HW ca June 1781, in Nichols, *Lit. Illus.* iii. 212–13; *Last Journals* ii. 367, where the *Public Advertiser* cutting, inserted and dated 'June 20, 1781' by HW, is printed as HW's text; *Carlisle MSS* 488–9, 501; *Memorials and Correspondence of Charles James Fox,* ed. Lord John Russell, 1853–7, i. 265–6; *Notes and Queries,* 1 Oct. 1853, 1st ser., viii. 312; D. M. Low, *Edward Gibbon,* 1937, pp. 282–3.

where my Whiggism is the most apparent. My father is reported to have said that every man has his price.[12] You see, Madam, my dog was *my* vulnerable part. I have resisted bribes for myself—I was not proof against honours for Tonton—Do not give me quite up, dear Lady. Make it your own case; if Prince Octavius was to offer Lady Gertrude his hand and his rattle, could you find in your heart to refuse your consent?—I will quit this tender subject, and tell you an anecdote, that you will have as much difficulty to believe as if it was in the *Gazette*.

A few evenings ago I was invited by the old Lady Fitzwilliam[13] at Richmond[14] to see some pictures[15] and Japan that were her father's Sir Matthew Decker.[16] I asked her if she had ever happened to hear a ridiculous story that I had been told in my youth, and which I concluded had only been a joke. It was, that Sir John Germaine,[17] Lady

12. HW is not certain whether his father said it. In *Mem. Geo. III* i. 283, *sub* 1764, a passage which he wrote in 1768 and recopied ca 1775, he accepts it: 'so true was the maxim of Sir Robert Walpole, that *every man has his price.*' To Cole 4 May 1774 he writes: 'My father is said to have said . . .' (COLE i. 325), and to Mann 26 Aug. 1785, 'a maxim ascribed to him by his enemies.' In his 'Book of Materials' 1759, p. 44: 'In 1781, the Duke of Montrose asked my brother Sir Edward Walpole, whether it was true that my father Sir Rob. Walpole said that every man has his price. My brother replied that he had often heard that saying imputed to his father, but had never heard him himself say so: (nor did I ever hear him say so).' In *Walpoliana* i. 88 Pinkerton quotes HW: 'I never heard him say, that all men have their prices; and I believe no such expression ever came from his mouth.' HW's final view may be that reported by Coxe: 'The political axiom generally attributed to him, that *all men have their price*, and which has been so often repeated in verse and prose, was perverted by leaving out the word *those*. Flowery oratory he despised; he ascribed to the interested views of themselves or their relatives, the declarations of pretended patriots, of whom he said, "*All those men have their price*," and in the event, many of them

justified his observation' ('From Lord Orford [HW] and the late Lord John Cavendish') (William Coxe, *Memoirs of the Life and Administration of Sir Robert Walpole, Earl of Orford*, 1798, i. 757).

13. Catherine Decker (d. 1786), m. (1744) Richard Fitzwilliam, 6th Vct Fitzwilliam, 1743.

14. 'The house upon Richmond Green . . . was formerly the seat of Sir Charles Hedges, secretary of state to Queen Anne, and afterwards the property of . . . Sir Matthew Decker' (Daniel Lysons, *The Environs of London*, Vol. I, 1792, p. 453).

15. 'In this house are the paintings of Richmond abovementioned [one by Vinkeboom, another 'said to be the work of one of Rubens's scholars'], some good pictures of the Flemish school, and a painting of a pineapple' (ibid.). The pictures HW saw were among the 144 bequeathed in 1816 by Lady Fitzwilliam's son to Cambridge University as part of the foundation of the Fitzwilliam Museum (*Handbook to the Fitzwilliam Museum, Cambridge*, Cambridge, 1952, p. 14).

16. Matthew Decker (1679–1749), cr. (1716) Bt; merchant; born in Amsterdam; came to England, 1702; connected with the East India Company, of which he was governor 1725–6, 1730–3; M.P.

17. Sir John Germain (ca 1650–1718), Kt and Bt, 1698; soldier of fortune who

Betty's husband, had been so exceedingly ignorant that he believed his countryman Sir Matthew (they were both Dutch) was author of St Matthew's Gospel. She replied directly, 'It is so true, that Sir John had thence conceived such a reverence for my father's piety, that he left him £200 to be distributed amongst poor Dutch'[18]—now, Madam, what story is improbable after this?—nor is it possible to add anything after it.

To Lady Ossory, Wednesday 4 July 1781

Address: To the Countess of Ossory at Ampthill Park, Bedfordshire. *Postmark:* ISLEWORTH. 4 IY.

Strawberry Hill, July 4, 1781.

I EVERY day grow too wary, Madam, to dip myself in promises of visits at the least distance of place or time, and expect to make **few** more, so little I can depend on my health, though for the last six months it has been very flourishing; but at present it has pulled me by the sleeve, or rather by the knee, where I have got the rheumatism by putting on thinner stockings on sultry Saturday and sauntering in the dew till between nine and ten. I thought it would have obliged me to receive on my couch a stately visit yesterday from the upright[1] Dowager of Beaufort and Lady Betty Compton, who breakfasted with me; and as everybody is a candidate for the latter's hand, it would have been mortifying to be lame when I had so fair an

---

in 1701 married Lady Mary Mordaunt, the divorced wife of the Duke of Norfolk. After her death in 1705 he married Lady Elizabeth Berkeley (*ante* 5 Dec. 1769).

18. HW recorded the anecdote in his 'Book of Materials' 1771, pp. 75–6, on 15 June 1781, after his visit to Lady Fitzwilliam, and added: 'Frances Lady Browne, widow of Sir Geo. Browne, was present when Lady Fitzwilliam told me this, whom I name, the story being almost incredible.' A little later HW added: 'Another instance of Sir J. Germaine's ignorance to confirm the former, told me by the Earl of Huntingdon from the late E. of Chesterfield, July 1st, 1781. As Sir John was dying, his wife Lady Betty pressed him to take the sacrament. He

asked her if she thought it would do him good. She replied, Yes; and he took it. A little time after, he called to her, and said, "Betty, you told me the sacrament would do me good, yet I feel as weak as before" ' (ibid. 76). This story appears in *Walpoliana* i. 120; the first anecdote, sometimes badly garbled, later appeared in *Walpoliana* i. 119–20; Mary Berry, *A Comparative View of Social Life in England and France*, new edn, 1844, i. 226–7; Sir James Prior, *Life of Edmond Malone*, 1860, pp. 442–3; Elizabeth Foster, Ds of Devonshire, *Anecdotes and Biographical Sketches*, 1863, p. 25.

---

1. HW wrote this word in large upright letters.

opportunity of entering the lists. However I made shift to go through every room of the house, and should not have despaired, if unluckily Lady Hertford had not proposed to go to the Chapel in the garden, which reduced me to use my stick, and I doubt left the prize still to be contended for by Lord George Cavendish,[2] Lord Fairford,[3] and my great-nephew Cholmondeley, who I hear t'other day forgot himself, and squeezed the mother's hand instead of the daughter's—oh! what consequences might have ensued, had such a fit of absence seized him with another Duchess Dowager of B![4]

My niece[5] left me last night, quite recovered. Her sisters fetched her away; Captain Waldegrave came to us the evening before and returned with them. He is fallen away, and shows how hard his service has been. In short all one sees and hears from the returned is a tale of distresses beyond belief! T'other day I was told of a letter from an officer in the *victorious* army of the conqueror Cornwallis,[6] which said, 'I expect to date my next from the prison at Boston!'

Did your Ladyship hear of a Prince Sulkowski,[7] who was lately in England? He was competitor with the present king[8] for the crown of

2. Lord George Augustus Henry Cavendish (1754–1834), cr. (1831) E. of Burlington; M.P. He married Lady Betty Compton on 27 Feb. 1782, despite her mother's opposition (Coke, 'MS Journals' 1781, *passim*, and 3 Jan. 1782).

3. Arthur Hill (1753–1801), styled Vct Kilwarlin 1756–72, Vct Fairford 1772–89, and E. of Hillsborough 1789–93; 2d M. of Downshire, 1793; M.P.

4. Bedford. Gibbon wrote to his stepmother 3 July 1775: 'You know I am not a writer of news but I cannot forbear telling you that the Duchess of Bedford made regular proposals of marriage to the young Earl Cholmondeley and was as regularly refused. Poor as he was (he replied to Mr [Richard] Fitzpatrick the ambassador), he was not quite poor enough to accept them' (Gibbon, *Letters*, ed. J. E. Norton, 1956, ii. 79). The proposal is also mentioned in the account of the Duchess of Bedford in Charles Pigott's *The Female Jockey Club*, 1794, pp. 76–7.

5. Lady Charlotte Maria Waldegrave.

6. On 15 March Cornwallis had 'obtained a signal victory' over Greene near Guilford, North Carolina, but was unable

to follow it up (his own letter of 17 March to Lord Rawdon shows 1924 men before the battle, and casualties of 532). He says that Greene's forces numbered 'about 5000 or 6000'; official American returns showed casualties of 1307, with others, not estimated but 'very considerable,' among the artillery, and missing men in the militia. The news reached London on 4 June and was reported in the *London Gazette* No. 12195, 2–5 June. Cornwallis himself thought the victory was of doubtful value, as it proved to be (Cornwallis, *Correspondence*, ed. Ross, 1859, i. 85–93, 502–10; idem, *An Answer to . . . Sir Henry Clinton*, 1783, p. v; *London Chronicle* 2–21 June, xlix. 536–41, 557, 575; *Last Journals* ii. 364), but in the *London Magazine*, 1781, l. 252, it was called 'the most glorious of any that has been obtained by the King's forces since the commencement of the American war.'

7. August Casimir Sulkowsky (1729–86), D. of Bielitz, 1762 (*Europäisches Genealogisches Handbuch*, ed. C. F. Jacobi, Leipzig, 1800, [pt i]. 539; John Lind, *Letters Concerning . . . Poland*, 1773, pp. iii–iv).

8. Stanislas II (Stanislas Augustus Ponia-

Poland, is hideous, and covered with brilliants. G. Selwyn said, he had never before seen a monster set in diamonds. This opulent Palatine came about a fortnight ago, with his *reine manquée*,[9] to see Strawberry, and was admitted without a ticket, as all foreigners are. I was not here: he left a card with all his titles, as **Prince of Thiski**, **Duke of Thatski** etc. to thank me in the name of all Europe for the free ingress of strangers. It seems the part of his revenues in specie (for it would be cumbersome to give a handful of peasants to every housekeeper) is rigidly economic (unless you reckon the list of titles on his cards); on Margaret he bestowed four and sixpence, having appropriated but five shillings to this visit, of which, prudently reflecting that he might be overturned or lose a wheel, he retained one sixpence—however, being asked like the Duchess of Beaufort to visit the Chapel, he surmounted his sage reserve, and generously conferred that sixpence on the gardener!

> The Crown of Poland, venal twice an age,
> To just three millions stinted modest Gage[10]—

I suppose it is cheaper since the partition.[11]

I do not in the least know who Perlin[12] was that wrote travels,[13] of which it is necessary to unriddle the names.[14] Pray tell me who he was, and—as I suppose he lived ages ago, what he expended on *concierges*. Lord Ossory shall certainly have Hentzner,[15] and as soon as he pleases, if your Ladyship will tell me how to send him.

towski) (1732–98), King of Poland 1764–95; lover of Catherine II of Russia and elected through her intervention.

9. Louise Mniszech (b. 1745), dau. of Johann Mniszech, Grand Chamberlain of Lithuania, m. (1766) August Casimir Sulkowsky, Duke of Bielitz (Jacobi, loc. cit.).

10. Pope, *Moral Essays*, Epistle III (To Bathurst), ll. 129–30. Count Joseph Edward Gage (ca 1678–1766), in later years a Spanish grandee and general, offered in 1719 to pay £3,000,000 for the crown of Poland; the king, Augustus II, refused. The Polish nobility, 'venal twice an age,' had elected a king of Poland in 1696 and 1707, and in 1709 and 1733. See also 'Paris Journals,' du Deffand v. 288–9; Pope, *Poems*, Twickenham edn, iii pt ii. 101–2; HW, *Notes on the Poems of Alexander Pope*, ed. Sir W. A. Fraser, 1871, p. 19: 'Monsieur de Gage, a Spanish general,

brother to Lord Viscount Gage'; Selwyn 215.

11. Poland lost in the First Partition, 5 Aug. 1772, about a third of its territory and about half of its inhabitants.

12. Estienne Perlin, an ecclesiastic who visited England and Scotland in the early 1550's.

13. *Description des royaulmes d'Angleterre et d'Escosse*, 1558.

14. Richard Gough had edited this work in 1775 together with *Histoire de l'entrée de la Reine Mère dans la Grande Bretagne*, 'par De la Serre, Paris, 1639,' 'Illustrated with Plates, English Notes, and Historical Prefaces.' HW had no copy in French, but he had an English translation with Gough's notes in the *Antiquarian Repertory*, 1775–84, i. 221–39 (Hazen, *Cat. of HW's Lib.* 3850).

15. Paul Hentzner (1558–1625), *Journey into England . . . in the Year 1598*, SH,

Do not be afraid, you shall not be plagued with Tonton, though I assure you he has a very decent privy purse for his travels—but I recollect that my uncle Horace used to say, that Mademoiselle Furniture does not love dogs; which makes me allow Tonton handsomely, that he may silence such tattling housekeepers as Margaret.

To Lady Ossory, Tuesday 17 July 1781

Address: To the Countess of Ossory at Ampthill Park, Bedfordshire. *Postmark:* ISLEWORTH. 17 IY.

Strawberry Hill, July 17, 1781.

I DID not mean, Madam, that I should be confined *to London* till Lord Orford's business is settled;[1] if I did say so, I expressed myself ill, as I wrote in a great hurry. On the contrary, as Mr Morrice is so much nearer to me, I believe our meetings will be at the Grove, unless when necessary to go to town to see the lawyers,[2] who have not yet given in the respective claims, for which we are waiting.[3] Cavalier Mozzi has complained so much of delays, that I did not care to be out of the way and have any imputed to me. Indeed at present it is impossible for me to stir; Lady Ailesbury comes to me tomorrow, and I am still so lame with my rheumatism, that it is near three weeks that I have not been round my own garden. Your Ladyship and Lord Ossory are very kind to think on me, but I am grown such old lumber, as to be fit for nothing but a garret. Were I as young as my brother, who is eleven years older, I might be amusing. I sat in admiration of his spirits and humour for two hours t'other night,[4] when I was scarce able to open my lips. He described having been to see his new house at Isleworth,[5] after not having been out of his own

---

1757; 220 copies printed. Vernon Smith's note ii. 42: 'Paul Hentzner's Journey in England in the year 1598, now in my possession, printed at Strawberry Hill.' In this copy, now wsl, is Vernon Smith's note in pencil: 'Sent to Lord Ossory 1781 by HW.' See also Hazen, *SH Bibl.* 31–3.

---

1. See *ante* 13 June 1781, third paragraph.

2. Joshua Sharpe (*ante* 7 July 1773), representing Cav. Mozzi, and Charles Lucas (living in 1797), of 7, New Inn, London, in 1791, representing Lord Or-

ford (HW-Mann Correspondence; *Universal British Directory*, 1791–[1798], i. 382). HW had been in London 12–13 July to consult them (HW to Mann 13 July 1781).

3. 'Lucas will not be ready to give me in the list of my Lord's demands these ten days' (HW to Mann 13 July 1781).

4. 'I saw Sir Edward yesterday morning. He looks handsomer than ever and was in very good spirits' (Lady Horatia Waldegrave to Anne Clement 3 Nov. 1781, MS wsl).

5. On 20 July 1781 Sir Edward Walpole

doors since April twelvemonth. He said he was so surprised himself, that he could not believe he was there, and asked who *that* was, and that they assured him it was he himself[6]—for my part, I shall sooner take myself for nobody, than for anybody else—perhaps when I am a ghost, I shall take myself for something, and *walk* at Ampthill; and even Lady Gertrude will not be frightened, as I shall be very little less than I am.

To Lady Ossory, Wednesday 25 July 1781

Address: To the Countess of Ossory at Ampthill Park, Bedfordshire. *Postmark:* ISLEWORTH.

Strawberry Hill, July 25, 1781.

POOR human nature, what a contradiction 'tis! today it is all rheumatism and morality, and sits with a death's head before it: tomorrow it is dancing!—oh! my Lady, my Lady, what will you say, when the next thing you hear of me after my last letter, is, that I have danced three country-dances with a whole set forty years younger than myself! Shall not you think I have been chopped to shreds and boiled in Medea's kettle? Shall not you expect to see a print of Vestris teaching me?[1]—and Lord Brudenel dying with envy?[2] You may stare

---

purchased from the 'trustees in the settlement made on the marriage of Willoughby Lacy, Esquire, with Maria Ann Lacy his now wife' the house at 'the Rails Head,' 'by the waterside,' 'built [about 1750] by James Lacey, Esq., patentee of Drury Lane Theatre.' Sir Edward left the house to his daughter Mrs Keppel, and it was 'pulled down . . . some years' before 1840 (Daniel Lysons, *Environs of London*, Vol. III, 1795, p. 100; Sir Edward Walpole's will, 57 Rockingham; BERRY i. 320–1 and n. 15; George James Aungier, *History and Antiquities of Syon Monastery, the Parish of Isleworth*, 1840, pp. 232–3).

6. Lady Elizabeth Laura Waldegrave to Anne Clement 7 Sept. 1781: 'The account you give me of Sir Edward's good looks and spirits makes me quite happy; it gives me great pleasure to hear that he goes so much out. This country house

will I hope add many years to his life' (MS WSL).

———

1. 'Regardez-Moi,' by Gillray, one of the satirical prints dealing with Vestris's ballet lessons, shows HW's nephew Lord Cholmondeley as a goose being taught the ballet (BM, *Satiric Prints* v. 536–7, No. 5911; *ante* 14 Jan. 1781). HW's earlier variant of this print (reversed), entitled 'L'Entrée' and dated 1781, with his identifications of Vestris and Cholmondeley, is in the New York Public Library. The *Morning Post* 21 March had reported that Dr Johnson 'was learning to dance of Vestris' (Boswell, *Johnson* iv. 79; *Boswell Papers* xiv. 180). Richard Marlay wrote to Lord Charlemont 27 Jan. 1782 that the elder Vestris 'teaches all the town to bow and to walk gracefully. . . . Lord Edgcumbe and Lord Dudley are much improved by him' (Hist. MSS Comm., 12th

with all your expressive eyes, yet the fact is true. Danced—I do not
absolutely say, *danced*—but I swam down three dances very gracefully with the air that was so much in fashion after the battle of
Audenarde,[3] and that was still taught when I was fifteen, and that I
remember General Churchill[4] practising before a glass in a gouty
shoe.

To be sure you die with impatience to know the particulars. You
must know then—for all my revels must out—I not only went five
miles to Lady Aylesford's ball last Friday,[5] but my nieces the Waldegraves desired me there to let them come to me for a few days,[5a] as
they had been disappointed about a visit they were to make at another place—but that is neither here nor there. Well, here they are,
and last night we went to Lady Hertford at Ditton. Soon after, Lady
North and her daughters[6] arrived, and besides Lady Elizabeth and
Lady Bel Conways,[7] there were their brothers Hugh[8] and George.[9]
All the *jeunesse* strolled about the garden. We ancients with the
Earl[10] and Colonel Keene retired from the dew into the drawing-
room. Soon after the two youths and seven nymphs came in, and
shut the door of the hall. In a moment we heard a burst of laughter,
and thought we distinguished something like the scraping of a fiddle.

Rep., App. x, *Charlemont MSS*, 1891, i.
396).

2. The younger Vestris 'dances like
an angel of light (as Lord Brudenell
says)' (ibid.).

3. Oudenarde, a battle won 11 July
1708 by Marlborough and Prince Eugene
over Vendôme and the Duke of Burgundy.

4. Charles Churchill (ca 1679–1745),
Lt-Gen., 1739; M.P. Castle Rising 1715–
45; father of HW's brother-in-law, Charles
Churchill (ca 1720–1812) (COLE ii. 292 n.
9; MANN i. 139 nn. 8, 10; DNB, *sub* Churchill, Charles, 1656–1714; *An Historical
Description of the Church . . . in Bath
Commonly Called the Abbey*, Bath, 1778,
p. 41).

5. 20 July. 'Lady Aylesford is going to
give another [ball] at Putney' (Anthony
Storer to Lord Carlisle 18 July, *Carlisle
MSS* 514).

5a. They stayed until Friday or Saturday (n. 18 below). They 'arrived at Mr
Dickens's [at Branches Park, Suffolk, 12
miles from Bury St Edmunds] on Satur-

day night [28 July]' (Lady Elizabeth Laura
Waldegrave to Anne Clement 1 Aug. 1781,
MS WSL).

6. Her two elder daughters: Hon.
Catherine Anne North (*ante* 10 Oct. 1780),
and Hon. Anne North (1764–1832), m.
(1798) John Baker-Holroyd, cr. (1781) Bn
and (1816) E. of Sheffield (BERRY i. 114 n.
11). For the third daughter, see *post* 21
June 1782.

7. Lady Isabella Rachel Seymour Conway (b. 1755), m. (1785) George Hatton
(*post* 17 Sept. 1785; John Debrett, *Peerage*,
1817, i. 103; Collins, *Peerage*, 1812, ii.
565).

8. Hon. Hugh Seymour Conway (1759–
1801), Lord Hertford's 5th son, known
from 1794 as Lord Hugh Seymour; naval
officer; a lord of the Admiralty 1795–8
(BERRY i. 261–2 nn. 2–4).

9. Hon. George Seymour Conway (1763–
1848), the 7th son, known from 1794 as
Lord George Seymour; M.P.; army officer
(BERRY ii. 40 n. 11).

10. Of Hertford.

My curiosity was raised, I opened the door and found four couples and a half standing up, and a miserable violin from the ale-house. 'Oh,' said I, 'Lady Bel shall not want a partner'— I threw away my stick, and *me voilà dansant comme un charme!* At the end of the third dance, Lord North, and his son[11] in boots, arrived—'Come,' said I, 'my Lord, you may dance, if I have'—but it ended in my *resigning my place* to his son.

Lady North has invited us for tomorrow, and I shall reserve the rest of my letter for the second volume of my regeneration—however, I declare I will not *dance:* I will not make myself too cheap; I should have the Prince of Wales sending for me three or four times a week to hops in Eastcheap.[12] As it is, I feel I shall have some difficulty to return to my old dowagers at the Duchess of Montrose's,[13] and shall be humming the 'Hemp-dressers,'[14] when they are scolding me for playing in flush.[15]

Friday, the 27.

I am not only a prophet, but have more command of my passions than such impetuous gentry as prophets are apt to have. We found the fiddles, as I foretold—and yet I kept my resolution and did *not* dance, though the Sirens invited me, and though it would have shocked the dignity of old Tiffany Ellis,[16] who would have thought it an indecorum. The two younger Norths[17] and Sir Ralph Payne supplied my place. I played at cribbage with the matrons, and we came away at midnight[18]—so, if I now and then do cut a colt's tooth,

11. Hon. George Augustus North, who succeeded his father as 3d E. of Guilford in 1792 (*ante* 13 Nov. 1776).

12. A parallel with Prince Hal and Falstaff in *Henry IV*, Part I.

13. Lady Lucy Manners (ca 1717–88), m. (1742) William Graham, 2d D. of Montrose, 1742. She lived at Twickenham Park, for the history of which see More 123 and R. S. Cobbett, *Memorials of Twickenham*, 1872, pp. 224–36. HW's visits to her helped to fill the gap in his social life left by the death of Lady Blandford in 1779.

14. The music and the directions for dancing the Hempdresser, taken from *The Compleat Country Dancing Master* published by J. Walsh in 1718, are in the *Delany Corr.* iv. 169. References to the

dance are also in Coke, *Journals* ii. 366, iii. 361, iv. 21–2, 26–7, 31, 37, 43.

15. 'A rush of emotion or passion; elation or excitement arising from this, or from success, victory, etc.' (OED, *sub* flush sb². 3).

16. A derogatory reference to Welbore Ellis as flimsy or transparent; see *tiffany* in OED. For his decorum, cf. James Hare to Lord Carlisle 11 Feb. 1782: 'Mr Ellis, commonly called the Duke of Alva' (*Carlisle MSS* 574).

17. Hon. Francis North (1761–1817), 4th E. of Guilford, 1802; entered the army, 1777, becoming Lt-Col., 1794; and Hon. Frederick North (1766–1827), 5th E. of Guilford, 1817; M.P. Banbury 1792–4.

18. Lady Elizabeth Laura Waldegrave to Anne Clement 1 Aug. 1781: 'We went

I have it drawn immediately. I do not know a paragraph of news—the nearer the minister, the farther from politics.

PS. My next jubilee dancing shall be with Lady Gertrude.

To Lady Ossory, Tuesday 7 August 1781

Address: To the Countess of Ossory at Ampthill Park, Bedfordshire. *Postmark:* ISLEWORTH. 7 AV.

Strawberry Hill, July [Aug.] 7, 1781.

YOU must be or will be, tired of my letters, Madam—every one is a contradiction to the last; there is alternately a layer of complaints, and a layer of foolish spirits. Today the wind is again in the dolorous corner. For these four days I have been confined with a pain and swelling in my face. The apothecary[1] says it is owing to the long drought—but as I should not eat grass, were there ever such plenty, and as my cows, though starving, have no swelled cheeks, I do not believe him. I humbly attribute my frequent disorders to my longevity, and to that Proteus the gout, who is not the less himself for being incog. Excuses I have worn out, and therefore will not make any for not obeying your kind invitation again to Ampthill. I can only say, I go nowhere, even where Tonton is invited—except to balls—and yet though I am the last Vestris that has appeared, Mrs Hobart did not invite me to her *Sans Souci*[2] last week, though she had all my other juvenile cotemporaries, Lady Berkeley, Lady Fitzroy, Lady Margaret Compton and Mrs French,[3] etc. etc. Perhaps

last Thursday to Lady North's. We danced till twelve o'clock; it was not a regular ball, as we had but six couple, but I never had more pleasure. We were all in spirits. I own I left Strawberry Hill with regret, we passed our time so very comfortably' (MS wsl).

1. Sterling Gilchrist (d. 1791), surgeon and apothecary at Twickenham after his retirement from the army as surgeon of the Third Regiment of Dragoon Guards 1761–5 (Berry i. 369). 'I believe he is a very good apothecary' (Lady Euston to Anne Clement 21 Aug. 1785, MS wsl).

2. Her villa on Ham Common, later the setting for amateur theatricals and various entertainments (*post* 10 Nov. 1782; Berry i. 290, 294). 'The site of the villa is now covered by Hobart Place' (*The Beautiful Lady Craven*, ed. A. M. Broadley and Lewis Melville, 1914, i. p. lxxiv n. 2).

3. Katherine Lloyd (d. 1791), dau. of Richard Lloyd, lord chief justice of Jamaica; m. (several years before 1743) Jeffrey French, sometime M.P. HW had known her since about 1740 (Berry i. 57 n. 17, and *passim;* Mann ii. 135–6; BM, *Satiric Prints* v. 635, No. 6090).

you do not know that the lady of the fête, having made as many conquests as the King of Prussia, has borrowed the name of that hero's
villa for her hut on Ham Common, where she has built two large
rooms of timber under a cabbage.[4] Her field officers, General French,
General Compton etc. were sweltered in the ball-room, and then
frozen at supper in tents on the grass. She herself, as intrepid as King
Frederic, led the ball, though dying of the toothache, which she had
endeavoured to drown in laudanum—but she has kept her bed ever
since the campaign ended.

This is all I know in the world, for the war seems to have taken
laudanum too and to keep its bed.

I have received a letter today from Sir Horace Mann,[5] who tells me
the Great Duke has been making *wondrous improvements* at Florence.
He has made a passage through the Tribune, and built a brave new
French room of stucco in white and gold, and placed the Niobe in it;
but as everybody is tired of her telling her old story, she and all the
Master and Miss Niobes, are orderly disposed round the chamber,
and if anybody asks who they are, I suppose, they answer, Francis
Charles Ferdinand Ignatius Neopomucenus, or Maria Theresa Christina Beatrix etc.—Well, Madam, have I any cause to sigh that the
pictures at Houghton are transported to the North Pole, if the Tribune at Florence is demolished by Vandals, and Niobe and her progeny
dance a *cotillon?* Oh! sublunary grandeur, short-lived as a butterfly!
We smile at a clown who graves the initials of his name or the shape
of his shoe on the leads of a church in hopes of being remembered;
and yet he is as much known as King I-don't-know-whom, who built
the Pyramids to eternize his memory. Methinks Anacreon was the
only sensible philosopher: if I loved wine, and should look well in a
chaplet of roses, I would crown myself with flowers, and go drunk to
bed every night *sans souci.*

4. That is, Mrs Hobart had borrowed
the design as well as the name: Frederick's
one-story palace had a semicircular cen-
tral pavilion (Mrs Hobart's 'cabbage') projecting above the roof line.

5. See Mann to HW 24 July 1781 and
HW's reply 23 Aug. 1781.

To Lady Ossory, Tuesday 4 September 1781

Address: To the Countess of Ossory at Ampthill Park, Bedfordshire. *Postmark:* 4 SE.

Strawberry Hill, Sept. 4, 1781.

I AM sorry your Ladyship is so like Dr Johnson as not to understand the Grecian graces of odes,[1] but to require them to be indited in as Dunstable[2] prose as a bill in Chancery. Do you think as he does, that prose only should be encumbered with learning and a hash of languages, and that poetry should be as plain as the hornbook? I believe I could expound all your Ladyship's difficulties in Mr Jones's[3] ode[4] if you had specified them. *Curled smiles,* the sole instance you produce, is not so beautiful, as the next expression, *the bubbling tear;*[5] but is very intelligible to anyone who has seen an angel of Correggio, whose mouth is generally curled into a crescent, and in truth I think strains grace into almost a grimace.[6] The clan of Howes would certainly have been more profuse on the transcendent qualities of their sovereign lady; but I believe Mr Jones is not so zealous an idolater at that shrine.[7] However if the ode is not perfect, still

1. Johnson in his life of Gray, published 17 May 1781 but seen by HW in January, had said that he 'would gladly find the meaning of the first stanza of the Progress of Poetry,' and had objected to a number of passages in it and 'The Bard' (Mason ii. 97, and *passim*).

2. Direct and plain, with no turns; from the straightness and evenness of the road from London (Edgeware Road) to Dunstable, Bedfordshire, a part of the Roman Watling Street (OED).

3. William Jones (1746–94), Kt, 1783; Oriental scholar and jurist. He had been private tutor to Lord Althorp 1765–70. HW had met him in 1780. See Mason ii. 35–6 and n. 33.

4. *The Muse Recalled, an Ode, Occasioned by the Nuptials of Lord Viscount Althorp and Miss Lavinia Bingham, Eldest Daughter of Charles Lord Lucan, March VI, M.DCC.LXXXI*, SH, 1781; printing of 250 copies finished 11 Aug. (Hazen, *SH Bibl.* 119–21).

5. 'Each morn, reclin'd on many a rose,
   Lavinia's pencil shall disclose
   New forms of dignity and grace
   Th'expressive   air,   th'impassioned
           face,
   The curled smile, the bubbling tear,
   The bloom of hope, the snow of
           fear . . .'
                                    (pp. 5–6).

6. One of HW's favourite contrasts: '. . . all Correggio's grace, and none of his grimace' (HW to Mann 18 Nov. 1771); '. . . his grace touches upon grimace; the mouth of the beautiful angel at Parma curls up almost into a half-moon' (HW to Mary and Agnes Berry 26 Nov. 1790, Berry i. 149–50 and n. 19; cf. Mason i. 176 and n. 5 for 'grimaces . . . Graces,' suggested by Mason and adopted by HW).

7. The Howes, like the Binghams, were Irish and would have praised the bride more effusively than Jones had. A strong Whig, violently opposed to the American war, Jones might have objected to Lord

the eighth, ninth and tenth stanzas have merit enough to shock Dr
Johnson and such sycophant old nurses, and that is enough for me.
How precious is any line of Demosthenes that offended King Philip
and the whole Court of Macedon!

Your other question, Madam, of who was Lady Elizabeth *Thimbleby*,[8] I cannot so well resolve: I only guess that she was no relation
of the Maid of Honour of Queen Elizabeth who died by pricking her
finger with a needle.[9]

The Library[10] I have read. There are some pretty lines, and easy
verses; but it is too long. One thought is charming, *that a dog though
a flatterer, is still a friend.*[11] It made me give Tonton a warm kiss, and
swear it was true.

I have heard of Lady Derby's imperial conquest[12]—nor should I
wonder if her mother was immediately to transport her own rags of
beauty to Vienna, since there is a monarch that can take up with
remnants of charms, that indeed never were very charming.

I direct this to Ampthill, as you name no day for quitting it; yet if
you have any remains of fever, you cannot change the air too soon. I
have had a letter[13] from Mr Morrice who tells me that he has received
some of our judicial papers,[14] but cannot open them, as he has been
confined to his bed ten days by the gout. I should have said that it
was only a note by another hand. Mine still writes with difficulty,

Althorp's alliance with Lord Lucan, a
supporter of the administration. Other
possible grounds of his objecting to her
—her cleverness, coarseness, asperity,
abuse, intolerance, etc.—are suggested in
GEC xii. 155 nn. b, c.

8. Elizabeth Thimbleby or Thimelby,
dau. of —— Thimelby, Esq. of Lincolnshire, m. Hon. Henry Lumley (1660–1722),
brother of Richard, 1st E. Scarbrough
(Collins, *Peerage*, 1812, iii. 711).

9. A monument in Westminster Abbey
of a young woman pointing her index finger at a skull on which her right foot is
resting caused guides to tell people she
died from pricking her finger. The legend
is mentioned in the *Spectator*, No. 329,
and the *Citizen of the World*, No. 13
(kindly communicated by Mr Ketton-
Cremer). The monument is to the memory of Elizabeth Russell (1575–1600), dau.
of John, Lord Russell; goddaughter of
Queen Elizabeth (John Dart, *Westmonas-*

terium, 1742, i. 111–12, with illustration
facing p. 111; GEC ii. 77 n.c).

10. By George Crabbe (1754–1832), published 24 July 1781 (*London Chronicle*
24–26 July, l. 85; *Public Advertiser* 24
July). HW's copy is in his 'Poems of
George III,' now in the Harvard Library;
on the title-page HW noted, 'By Mr Crab,
bred an apothecary' (Hazen, *Cat. of HW's
Lib.* 3222.17.3).

11. 'And see a favourite tribe mankind
    attend,
      And in the fawning follower find
        the friend'   (ll. 195–6).

12. Lady Derby had come to the notice
of the Emperor at Spa. For references to
her and the Emperor see *Intimate Society
Letters of the Eighteenth Century*, ed.
9th D. of Argyll, 1910, i. 279, 272–89; Coke,
'MS Journals' July–Aug., 23 Nov., 24
Dec. 1781.

13. Missing.

14. On the Mozzi-Orford lawsuit.

though almost well;[15] but having replied to your Ladyship's queries, and having nothing new to tell you, it shall take its leave.

To Lady Ossory, Wednesday 12 September 1781

Address: To the Countess of Ossory at Farming Woods, Northamptonshire. By Thrapston bag. *Postmark:* ISLEWORTH. 13 SE.

Wednesday night, Sept. 12, 1781.

I WOULD not answer your last, Madam, till I could tell you something on better authority than my own—yet that something is but another's conjecture. I have been at Ditton this evening, where Lord Hertford told me that he thinks the combined fleets are retired.[1] A neutral ship has met them sailing westward[2]—and it is hoped they have suffered by a storm[3]—This is war! One sits at home coolly *hoping* that five or six vessels full of many hundreds of men are gone to the bottom of the deep! Can one look back on the last six years and not shudder at the devastation deliberate love of power has committed—to the utter loss of power! The fleets have been seen off Kingsale[4]—but Lord H. could not be easy if he expected any attempt on Ireland. He flatters himself the Czarina will make peace for us— but she must first make us make peace.[5] As to any landing here, it has not been apprehended—The enemies have no transports with them—but indeed we have no intelligence neither. They have landed

15. 'A finger of my right hand has opened with an explosion of chalk-stones; five have come out, and it is still big with another' (HW to Mason 9 Sept. 1781, Mason ii. 152).

———

1. The combined French and Spanish fleet, consisting of 49 ships of the line, had escorted the Minorca expedition past Gibraltar, and then turned northward to the Channel. The fleets had separated on 5 Sept. and had made for their respective ports, Brest and Cadiz (*Sandwich Papers* iv. 10–14, 50–67; *Last Journals* ii. 372, 374; Mason ii. 151–2; *London Chronicle* 11–13 Sept., l. 256).

2. To Ireland, as was feared; actually, the Spanish fleet was returning to Cadiz.

3. 'We have just received information that in the course of last week there were

no less than three severe storms in the latitude now occupied by the combined fleets, and that they suffered very much in the gales' (ibid. 6–11 Sept., l. 240, 248).

4. 'Letters have been received at one of the most respectable houses in the city that the combined fleets have been seen off Kinsale,' near Cork (ibid. 11–13 Sept., l. 250). There were rumours that troops would land in Ireland, and Cork was preparing for invasion (ibid. 8–15 Sept., l. 248, 250, 259; HW to Mann 7 Sept. 1781).

5. For HW's comments on various offers and suggestions for peace at this time, and the King's refusal to accept them, see *Last Journals* ii. 373, 375–6, 384. HW mentions both Joseph II and Catherine II as possible intermediaries.

on Minorca,[6] and Gen. Murray's[7] wife[8] and family,[9] with other English women have escaped to Leghorn[10]—It must have been a shocking
separation! There is little chance, I believe, of the island's being
saved. We shall be pared to the quick, while we are dreaming of recovering America—we might as sensibly pursue our claim to the
crown of France. Have you seen this epigram, which for aught I
know may have been in the newspapers?

> O England, no wonder your troubles begin,
> When blockaded without, and blockheaded within.[11]

I am glad I have been a physical prophet, Madam, and that change
of air has cured your fever.

I have met Miss Loyd at Lady Di's. She is superlatively inflated
with the odours that flowed from the Emperor on her and Lady
Clermont.[12] 'We sat round him, and he put us[13] quite at our ease.'
'He would not have put me so,' said I; 'I have seen a good deal of
princes in my day, and always found, that if they put themselves at
their ease, they did not at all like that I should put myself so.' I

6. On 20 Aug. a force of 16,000 French
and Spaniards under the Duc de Crillon
landed at Port Mahon and blockaded
Fort St Philip. Gen. Murray, the governor, with 2,016 regular troops (of whom
400 were invalids) and 200 seamen, held
out till 5 Feb. 1782. In Oct. 1781 Murray
indignantly refused Crillon's bribe of a
million sterling to capitulate (DNB, sub
Murray, James, ca 1719–94). A letter from
Murray, St Philips Castle, 19 Aug. 1781,
sent by Sir Horace Mann to Lord Hillsborough and received 11 Sept., reported
that the forces were preparing to land
(London Gazette No. 12223, 8–11 Sept.).

7. Gen. Hon. James Murray (ca 1719–
94), Maj.-Gen., 1762; Lt-Gen., 1772, and
Gen., 1783; governor of Quebec 1760–6
and of Canada 1763–6; governor of Minorca 1774–82 (Scots Peerage iii. 515–17).

8. Anne Whitham or Witham (ca 1761–
1824), dau. of Abraham Whitham, Consul-
General of Majorca, m. (14 March 1780)
as 2d wife, Gen. Murray. His first wife
had died without issue 26 June 1779
(ibid. iii. 516).

9. The Murrays at this time had only
one child.

10. They 'escaped to Leghorn last
night' (Mann to HW 1 Sept. 1781), having 'embarked the very day the enemy
landed and in 12 days got safe to Leghorn' (ibid. 4 Sept. 1781). Similar information was given in the London Chronicle
15–18 Sept., l. 266.

11. This epigram, HW's own, appears
in the MS of Last Journals, sub Sept.
1781, signed 'H.W.,' and in A Note Book
of Horace Walpole, ed. W. S. Lewis, New
York, 1927, p. 15, where HW's heading
is 'On the combined fleets of France and
Spain off Scilly Sept. 1781.' HW quoted
it to Mason 25 Sept. 1781 as 'a new
epigram that came to my hand t'other
day' (MASON ii. 156). It has not been found
in 'the newspapers.'

12. They had gone to Brussels early in
June, where they had seen the Emperor.
Later they had gone to Spa, where Lady
Mary Coke saw them, and they left Spa
on 15 Aug. to return to England (Coke,
'MS Journals' 9, 15 June, 9, 10, 13, 15
Aug. 1781).

13. Us is written in letters twice the
usual size.

demurred too to the great admiration—I remember when the
Lady Clermonts of that time wept for the departure of the Duke of
Lorrain, the late Emperor[14]—and yet he proved an oaf. This man
announces too much—we shall see. Then came the Archduchess[15]
and then Duke Albert—'You know he is to be inaugurated four
times'[16]—'God forbid I should know it,' said I. 'I should be sorry to
know how often a German prince is to go through a ceremony.' The
Duke of Richmond[17] told me a much better story, a sequel to the
Duchess of Chandos's history, which you have heard, and how she
proposed the Princess Royal to the Emperor.[18] Mr Fitzherbert[19] told
her he had heard of a great marriage on foot. Her Grace was mysterious—'What match?' He told her. 'Why, surely,' replied she, 'the
Emperor has not divulged it yet!—I really beg your pardon, Mr
Fitzh[erbert], for interfering in your province—but I will make you

14. Francis I (1708–65), Holy Roman
Emperor 1745–65, had been Duke of Lorraine 1729–35. After the War of the Polish
Succession, at the insistence of the Emperor Charles VI, he surrendered the
duchy of Lorraine for the right to that
of Tuscany, to which he succeeded in
1737.

15. Maria Christine (1742–98), dau. of
Francis I and Maria Theresa, and sister
of Joseph II, m. (1766) Albrecht Kasimir
August (1738–1822), D. of Saxe-Teschen,
son of Augustus III of Poland; Austrian
general (Mann i. 433 n. 9). He had
recently been appointed governor of the
Austrian Netherlands. Many references
to her and Duke Albert are in Lady Mary
Coke's 'MS Journals' July–Aug. 1781.

16. Their inauguration at Brussels was
set for 17 July (Gazette de Leyde 10, 13
July); on 31 July at Ghent, 'Monseigneur
le Duc, représentant l'Empereur, reçoit la
prestation du serment de fidélité, comme
Comte de Flandres, de la part des États
de la province' (ibid. 7 Aug.). Probably
the ceremony was repeated at other places
during their tour, which lasted until 14
Sept. (ibid. 18 Sept.).

17. Who had just returned from Spa:
Lady Mary Coke mentions his being
there 16 Aug., and she saw him at Ostend
4 Sept., when his vessel left several hours
before hers.

18. The Duchess of Chandos 'was here

[at Brussels] when the Emperor returned
from his tour in Holland and the Archduchess to please everybody that was here
had a Court that they might all be
presented to him. The Emperor, who is
very polite, had said something civil to
her when she told him in very bad French
that so charming and amiable a Prince
as he was ought to marry the Princess
Royal who she assured him was a delightful Princess, that she thought there could
be no objection but the difference of
religion and that might easily be adjusted.
The Emperor, though never at a loss,
was surprised, and told her whatever he
might think he fancied the Princess
Royal would not like to marry any person old enough to be her father. "That
is nothing," replied her Grace, "I married
to my first husband an old man and it
did very well." Lady Torrington was
present at this conversation and I have
repeated it exactly as she told me. The
Emperor has mentioned it more than
once with some surprise' (Coke, 'MS Journals' 5 Aug. 1781).

19. Alleyne Fitzherbert (1753–1839), cr.
(1791) Bn St Helens; son of William Fitzherbert (ante 6 Jan. 1772); minister resident at Brussels 1777–82 and minister
plenipotentiary 1782–3; later held many
diplomatic posts in France, Russia and
Holland.

all the amends I can: I shall certainly be appointed to conduct the
Princess to Vienna, and I will ask for you to accompany us.'

I have at last received all (I shall ever have) of Mad[ame] du Deffand's papers. *All* I know there are not, for I miss some—but there
are some very curious, and some of her own dear writing, admirable.

I have made some purchases too at Mr Sheldon's,[20] very cheap
indeed, and shall go to town on Friday to see them. I have made a
goldfish pond[21] too—in short, I am as busy and trifling, as if I were
still Lord of the Ocean—I do not know but I may soon go a-hunting
in a white hat lined with green.[22] Your Ladyship, I suppose, goes
a-shooting in the absence of Lord Ossory,[23] lest the pheasants and
partridges should think you are alarmed. It is the modern way: we
souse into diversions to conceal our panics. All the watering-places
are thronged: one would think this was the most unhealthy country
in Europe. On the contrary: this proves it is the most healthy, for
nineteen go to amuse themselves, for one that goes for illness. Mercy
on us! how we shall stare, if ever we come to our senses again!

PS. Lady Mary Coke has had an hundred distresses abroad,[24] that
do not weigh a silver penny all together.[25] She is like Don Quixote,
who went in search of adventures, and when he found none, imagined
them. She went to Brussels to see the Archduchess, but either had
bad intelligence, or the Archduchess very good, for she was gone,

20. William Sheldon (d. 1780), of Weston, Long Compton, Warwickshire, whose
collection was sold at Weston in two sales
by Christie and Ansell, 27 Aug.–11 Sept.
and 7–12 Sept. Among HW's purchases
were four pictures that he gave to Cole
(Cole ii. 327–8 nn. 5, 7; Chatterton 195
n. 2). His most important purchases were
tapestry maps, for which see HW to Harcourt 1 Sept. 1787.

21. 'Sept. 29 pd for the Pump, bason
[the goldfish pond] in the flower garden,
draining the lawn in that garden and
cleaning the ponds 32–19–7' (*SH Accounts*
18, 174).

22. The King's 'disregard of national
disaster, provided he can still go "a
hunting"' is satirized in a print published
16 Feb. 1782, 'The Royal Hunt, or a
Prospect of the Year 1782' (BM, *Satiric
Prints* v. 559–61, No. 5961, Nos 5574,
5675–6, 5850, 5964, and 5988 also suggest

the King's preoccupation with hunting
1779–82). Mr Ketton-Cremer suggests that
HW is echoing 'a song or nursery rhyme.'

23. The Bedfordshire militia, of which
he was colonel, was encamped at Coxheath (*London Chronicle* 24–26 July
1781, l. 85).

24. She left for Brussels 31 July, arrived
there 3 Aug., stayed there, except for
several days at Spa, until 1 Sept., and
arrived at her country house, Notting
Hill, on 6 Sept. ('MS Journals' 26, 30
July, 4 Aug.–6 Sept. 1781). HW's information may have come from the Duke of
Richmond; at Ostend on 4 Sept. Lady
Mary had 'told him of what had happened
to me' (ibid.), and her journal does not
refer to her having seen HW.

25. She was overcharged for transportation, unnecessarily delayed, and frustrated
in various ways.

when Lady Mary arrived.²⁶ So was the packet-boat at Ostend,²⁷ which she believes was sent away on purpose by a codicil in the Empress Queen's will.²⁸

You must get some standard pomegranates,²⁹ Madam. I have one now in this room, above five feet high in a pot, in full blow. At Paris they mix them with their orange trees.

To Lady Ossory, Thursday 27 September 1781 or Thursday 4 October 1781

Missing. See 7 Oct. 1781, n. 14.

Lady Mary Coke noted in her 'MS Journals' 30 Sept. 1781: 'I saw Mr Walpole at General Fitzwilliam's. He seems in spirits but I think does not look well.'

To Lady Ossory, Sunday 7 October 1781

Strawberry Hill, Oct. 7, 1781.

I BEG your Ladyship's pardon for not returning the *History of Fotheringay*,¹ which I now enclose.

The new Veres² have been returned to England these six weeks,³

26. That is, when Lady Mary returned to Brussels after visiting Spa. She was presented to the Archduchess and Duke Albert at Brussels 5 Aug. and dined with them 9 Aug. Lady Mary left for Spa 13 Aug. and returned 24 Aug.; the Archduchess had left Brussels that morning for a three-week tour of Flanders. 'You know I am very just; I shall always acknowledge the Archduchess has been very civil, but she certainly has avoided seeing me alone and I have some reason to think she left Brusselles at least a day sooner than she intended on purpose that she might not give me a private audience, which she could not have refused when I was to take leave' (ibid. 4–5, 9, 24, 29 Aug. 1781).

27. On Monday, 3 Sept., 'I was up early and immediately engaged a vessel. The tide served at a little before one o'clock, when I promised myself to go on board, but as something very particular always attends me, between eleven and twelve, when my equipage was to be shipped,

the captain came and told me he had engaged himself to another person.' She was unable to leave until 5 Sept., at 2 a.m., and was extremely sea-sick on the passage.

28. For Lady Mary's imagined persecutions by Maria Theresa, see *ante* 10 Aug. 1775.

29. That is, 'not dwarfed or trained on a wall' (OED).

———

1. Perhaps the *'unpublished record* of Dugdale, in the possession of George Finch Hatton, Esquire' (H. K. Bonney, *Historic Notices in Reference to Fotheringhay*, 1821, p. vii). The Hattons' seat, Kirby, was near Farming Woods, which the Ossorys owned.

2. Aubrey Beauclerk (1740–1802) succeeded his father 2 Oct. 1781 (see below) as 2d Bn Vere of Hanworth; 5th D. of St Albans, 1787; m. (1763) Lady Catherine Ponsonby (1742–89).

3. They had arrived in Brussels 28 Aug. and had left the following day for

and I visited them at their palace (as it really was of Henry VIII)[4] at Hanworth not long after their arrival. All their near kin have done so too, and *tout s'est passé comme si de rien n'était.*[5] Their fellow-traveller[6] is left behind.[7] We live in such an awkward unfashionable nook here, that we have not yet heard Lord Vere's[8] will,[9] nor know whether Lord Richard Cavendish is dead or alive.[10] *I* am so much awkwarder still; and treasure up scandal so little, that, though I heard the Brighthelmstone story,[11] I have quite forgotten who the

England (Coke, 'MS Journals' 29 Aug. 1781). HW thought they had been in Italy earlier (HW to Mann 3 Oct. 1781).

4. Hanworth House was in Henry VIII's possession as early as 1519. He settled it on Queen Catherine Parr, who lived there after his death. The manor was purchased in 1670 by Sir Thomas Chamber, whose daughter in 1736 married Lord Vere Beauclerk, and through her it came to him. Hanworth House was destroyed by fire 26 March 1797, and rebuilt by the 5th D. of St Albans. The manor was sold by the 6th Duke (Daniel Lysons, *Historical Account of Those Parishes in . . . Middlesex . . . Not Described in the Environs of London,* 1800, pp. 92–6; Burke, *Peerage,* 1953, p. 1841; GEC xi. 290 n.).

5. 'Lord Vere died on Monday, so I suppose the Beauclerks will come out of their retirement. Lord Bessborough [father of the new Lady Vere] went to Hanworth as soon as ever he returned from Yorkshire and all the neighbourhood of Richmond, Twickenham, etc., intended waiting on Lady Catherine' (Coke, 'MS Journals' 4 Oct.).

6. Thomas Brand (1749–94), of The Hoo, Herts; son of HW's correspondent, Thomas Brand; M.P. Arundel 1774–80 (COLE i. 198 and n. 1).

7. Lady Mary Lowther told Lady Mary Coke 4 June 1778 'that Mr Beauclerke, Lady Catherine, and Mr Brand were gone together abroad, being so in debt they found it troublesome staying at home. She made some remarks upon Mr Brand going with them and leaving his wife behind.' 'Mr Brand of all his great fortune has only remaining to spend two thousand pounds a year; one he gives his wife to maintain herself and the children. The

other he chooses to spend abroad with the Beauclerks; it is not a pretty story' (Coke, 'MS Journals' 4, 11–12 June 1778). On 29 Aug. 1781 Lady Mary Coke supposed the Beauclerks' return to England 'was a sudden resolution, for I heard they had no intention of going back while Lord Vere lived; possibly he may have desired them to return.' Lord Torrington 'inquired if anybody was with them and was told only their children, so I suppose Mr Brand has determined to continue some time longer abroad or at least thinks it more proper not to arrive in England at the same time' (ibid.).

8. Lord Vere Beauclerk (1699–2 Oct. 1781), 3d son of Charles, 1st D. of St Albans, cr. (1750) Bn Vere of Hanworth.

9. Lady Mary Coke on 7 Oct., the date of HW's letter, 'could not learn anything of Lord Vere's will,' but on 13 Oct. she reported to Lord and Lady Strafford: 'Lord Vere's will is now known. Hanworth with the estate is given to the present Lord and everything else he died possessed of to Lady Vere for her life and at her death a thousand pounds a year to his eldest grandson and two hundred a year to the second [both grandsons were sons of the new Lord Vere and subsequently became 6th and 8th Dukes of St Albans], six thousand pounds to Lady Charles Spencer [the deceased's daughter] and all the rest to Lord Vere' (ibid.).

10. The *London Chronicle* 4–6 Oct., l. 336, reported his death 'at Naples about the 12th [i.e., 7th] of September last.' See also [?William Fawkener] to Lord Carlisle 14 Oct. 1781, *Carlisle MSS* 522; Venn, *Alumni Cantab.;* Collins, *Peerage,* 1812, i. 360; GM 1781, li. 490; MASON ii. 161 and n. 6.

11. Not found.

principal personage was—so you will not fear my repeating it. I do not design to know a circumstance about Admiral Rodney[12] and Admiral Ferguson.[13] We are to appearance at war with half Europe and a quarter of America, and yet our warfare is only fending and proving, and is fitter for the Quarter Sessions than for history. It costs us seventeen or eighteen millions a year to inquire whether our generals and admirals are rogues or fools, and since most of them are only one or t'other, I would not give half a crown to know which. The nation is such an oaf as to amuse itself with these foolish discussions, and does not perceive that six years and above forty millions, and half our territories have been thrown away in such idle pastime. How the grim heroes of Edward III and Henry V would stare at hearing that this is our way of making war on France!

The night I had the honour of writing to your Ladyship last, I was robbed[14]—and as if I was a sovereign or a nation, have had a discussion ever since whether it was not a *neighbour* who robbed me[15]—and should it come to the ears of the newspapers, it might produce as ingenious a controversy amongst our anonymous wits, as any of the noble topics I have been mentioning. *Voici le fait.* Lady Browne and I were as usual going to the Duchess of Montrose[16] at seven o'clock. The evening was very dark. In the close lane under her park pale, and within twenty yards of the gate, a black figure on horseback pushed by between the chaise and the hedge on my side. I suspected

12. Sir George Brydges Rodney (1719–92), cr. (1764) Bt, and (1782) Bn Rodney; Adm., 1778; commander-in-chief of the Leeward Islands and Barbados fleet from 1779 to 1 Aug. 1781, when ill health forced him to resign his command to Hood and sail for home. In *Last Journals*, Sept. 1781, ii. 374 HW noted, 'Sir George Rodney arrived in England,' that is, at Plymouth on 19 Sept., and at his house in London on 24 Sept. (*London Chronicle* 20–25 Sept., l. 282, 285, 294, 296).

13. Not 'Admiral' but 'Governor' Ferguson: George Ferguson of Jermyn St, London, Lt-Gov. of Tobago 1779–81 (H. I. Woodcock, *History of Tobago*, Ayr, 1867, pp. 45–55). On 2 June the British forces at Tobago capitulated to French forces under the Comte de Grasse and the Marquis de Bouillé. The articles of capitulation appear in the *London Gazette* No.

12226, 18–22 Sept., (see also the *London Chronicle* 4–7 Aug., 22–25, 27–29 Sept., 9–11 Oct., l. 122–3, 289–90, 306, 345, and *passim*). Rodney had intimated that Ferguson was at fault, but a Board of General Officers reported 31 March 1783 that 'he did everything that was proper for the defence of' Tobago (ibid. 26–29 April 1783, liii. 406).

14. HW's letter of Wednesday, 12 Sept., was postmarked 13 Sept. He was robbed on a Thursday night (HW to Mason 9 Oct. 1781, MASON ii. 160), and his letter to Mason on 9 Oct. implies that the robbery occurred on the preceding Thursday night, 4 Oct., or no more than a week earlier, 27 Sept. A letter from HW to Lady Ossory 27 Sept. or 4 Oct. is therefore missing.

15. See following letter.

16. At Twickenham Park.

it was a highwayman, and so I found did Lady Browne, for she was speaking and stopped. To divert her fears, I was just going to say, 'Is not that the apothecary going to the Duchess?' when I heard a voice cry, 'Stop!' and the figure came back to the chaise. I had the presence of mind, before I let down the glass, to take out my watch and stuff it within my waistcoat under my arm. He said, 'Your purses and watches!' I replied, 'I have no watch.' 'Then your purse!' I gave it to him; it had nine guineas. It was so dark, that I could not see his hand, but felt him take it. He then asked for Lady Browne's purse, and said, 'Don't be frightened, I will not hurt you.' I said, 'No, you won't frighten the lady?'—He replied, 'No, I give you my word I will do you no hurt.' Lady Browne gave him her purse, and was going to add her watch, but he said, 'I am much obliged to you, I wish you good night,' pulled off his hat and rode away. 'Well,' said I, 'Lady Browne, you will not be afraid of being robbed another time, for you see there is nothing in it.' 'Oh! but I am,' said she, 'and now I am in terrors lest he should return, for I have given him a purse with only bad money that I carry on purpose.'[17] 'He certainly will not open it directly,' said I, 'and at worst he can only wait for us at our return; but I will send my servant back for a horse and a blunderbuss,' which I did. The next distress was not to terrify the Duchess, who is so paralytic and nervous. I therefore made Lady Browne go into the parlour and desired one of the Duchess's servants to get her a glass of water while I went into the drawing-room to break it to the Duchess. 'Well,' said I laughing to her and the rest of the company, 'you won't get much from us tonight—' 'Why,' said one of them, 'have you been robbed?' 'Yes, a little,' said I. The Duchess trembled—but it went off. Her groom of the chambers said not a word, but slipped out, and Lady Margaret[18] and Miss Howe[19] having servants there on horseback, he gave them pistols and dispatched them different ways. This was exceedingly clever, for he knew the Duchess would not

17. Hon. Augustus Hervey, later 3d E. of Bristol, told Casanova in 1763 or 1764, 'We English always carry two purses on our journeys—a small one for the robbers and a large one for ourselves' (Jacques Casanova, *Memoirs,* tr. Arthur Machen, 1928, ix. 170). Johann Wilhelm von Archenholz describes the common precaution of carrying two purses, one to be given to the highwayman if necessary (*A Picture of England,* 1789, ii. 80).

18. Compton.

19. Hon. Juliana Howe (ca 1732–1803), sister of Hon. Mrs Howe (*ante* 27 March 1773), General Howe, and Richard, Earl Howe. She lived at Richmond (Berry i. 112 n. 13).

have suffered it, as lately he had detected a man who had robbed her garden, and she would not allow him to take up the fellow. These servants spread the story, and when my footman arrived on foot, he was stopped in the street by the hostler of the George[20] who told him the highwayman's horse was then in the stable—but this part I must reserve for the second volume, for I have made this no-story so long and so tedious, that your Ladyship will not be able to read it in a breath; and the second part is so much longer, and so much less, contains so many examinations of witnesses, so many contradictions in the depositions, which I have taken myself, and I must confess, with such abilities and shrewdness that I have found out nothing at all, that I think to defer the prosecution of my narrative, till all the other inquisitions on the anvil are liquidated, lest your Ladyship's head, strong as it is, should be confounded, and you should imagine that Rodney or Ferguson was the person who robbed us in Twicken-ham Lane. I would not have detailed the story at all, if you were not in a forest,[21] where it will serve to put you to sleep, as well as a news-paper full of lies; and I am sure there is as much dignity in it, as in the combined fleet and ours popping in and out alternately like a man and woman in a weather-house.[22]

To Lady Ossory, Wednesday 17 October 1781

Address: To the Countess of Ossory at Farming Woods, Northamptonshire. By Thrapston bag. *Postmark:* ISLEWORTH. 17 OC. 18 OC.

Strawberry Hill, Oct. 17, 1781.

MY story is grown cold, Madam, and I am tired of it, and should make nothing of it now. In short, though it has had a codicil, it has ended no how, and is only fit to entertain the village where it happened. The quintessence was that a great corn-factor, who is in bad odour here on the highway, arrived at the George a moment

20. The George Inn, near the intersec-tion of London Street and Church Street, as shown in 'A Plan of Twickenham . . . from an actual survey by Samuel Lewis, 1784,' the back endpaper to MORE.

21. Farming Woods.

22. See *Last Journals*, Sept. 1781, ii. 372–4, for HW's elaboration of this point.

Early in September Admiral Darby was at Torbay. His fleet was too weak to venture against the combined fleets off Scilly. Then when the combined fleets had left and Darby's fleet had been increased from 22 to 26 sail, he 'sailed from Torbay, but the enemy was gone some time be-fore he appeared off Scilly.'

after or before our robbery, and was suspected, and my footman thought he could swear to the horse—and then Zoffanii the painter was robbed, and his footman was ready to take his Bible to the person of a haberdasher, intimate of the corn-factor; but Mr Smallwares proved an alibi, and the corn-factor gave a ball—and none but the dancers acquit him—and so much for an idle story. Your Ladyship's idiot was more tremendous than our corn-wayman.

I am not likely to hear of a place, Madam, for your *raccomandée,* but will propose her if I should.

I see Graves[1] and Hood[2] have been tolerably beaten;[3] I do not wish Hood unthrashed, but I had rather it was Commodore Johnstone, that had met with a drubbing, instead of a rich booty.[4] I read too that Lord Cornwallis is trying to house his tattered laurels at New York;[5] and for that I am not much grieved neither. Since we are to be cuffed from one end of Europe to t'other end of America, I am glad when renegades are our representatives. I hope Lord Dunmore[6] is going to have his dose.[7]

1. Thomas Graves (1725–1802), cr. (1794) Bn Graves; Col. of Marines 1775–9; Rear-Adm., 1779; Vice-Adm., 1787; Adm., 1794; commander-in-chief at Plymouth 1786–9; received with the peerage a pension of £1000 a year; M.P.

2. Sir Samuel Hood (1724–1806), cr. (1778) Bt, cr. (1782) Bn and (1796) Vct Hood; Rear-Adm., 1780; Vice-Adm., 1787; Adm., 1794; received with the viscountcy a pension of £2000 a year for himself and two successors.

3. Graves's dispatch of 14 Sept. in the *London Gazette Extraordinary* 15 Oct. reported that he and Sir Samuel Hood on 5 Sept. with 19 sail attacked the French fleet of 24, under De Grasse, at the mouth of the Chesapeake, and was defeated with a loss of 90 killed and 246 wounded and a 74-gun ship. Hood's division, being in the rear, was unable to take part in the engagement. The inability of the English fleet to dislodge the French from their blockade of the Chesapeake was a contributing factor to Cornwallis's capitulation at Yorktown.

4. On 21 July Johnstone had captured in Saldanha Bay four Dutch East India-men, one from Bengal and three from China; a fifth ship, from China, had been fired by the Dutch and could not be saved. A detachment from his fleet had also captured on 1 July and had brought in on 9 July a Dutch East India ship 'loaded with stores and provisions, and about forty thousand pounds in bullion' (Johnstone's dispatch of 21 Aug., in the *London Gazette Extraordinary* 15 Oct.). The six prizes, including the one lost, were estimated at a 'million of specie' (*London Chronicle* 16–18 Oct., l. 376). 'On Wednesday last [5 Sept. 1782 the prizes were] . . . finally condemned at the Admiralty' (ibid. 7–10 Sept. 1782, lii. 243).

5. 'Philadelphia, July 25. We are assured that Lord Cornwallis has detached the whole of his cavalry, and part of his infantry, under Colonel Tarleton, for South Carolina. It is supposed Lord Cornwallis intends to embark with the remainder of his army for New York' (Boston newspaper of 9 Aug. quoted in the *London Chronicle* 13–16 Oct., l. 368).

6. John Murray (1730–1809), styled Vct Fincastle 1752–6, 4th E. of Dunmore, 1756; representative peer 1761–74, 1776–90; governor of New York 1769–70, of Virginia 1770–6, and of the Bahamas 1787–96.

7. Dunmore, who had been in England since 1776, sailed for Virginia on 7 Oct. (ibid. 4–9 Oct., l. 334, 343). Cf. MASON ii. 184.

I heard at Park Place[8] that the Prince of Wales has lately made a visit to Lady Cecilia Johnstone,[9] where Lady Sarah Napier was.[10] She did not appear, but he insisted on seeing her, and said, 'She was to have been there,' pointing to Windsor Castle. When she came down, he said he did not wonder at his father's admiring her, and was persuaded she had not been more beautiful then.

Lord Richard Cavendish is indubitably dead, and so I see is Lord Kelly.[11] As this is but a postscript to my last, your Ladyship will excuse its brevity.

To Lady Ossory, Friday 26 October 1781

Oct. 26, 1781.

IN good sooth, Madam, I do not know who is the grandmother of Charity, unless it means the present Duke of Montagu, in whose breasts I conclude there is not a drop of the milk of charity left, *vu* the dirt he has discovered in his transactions with Lady Beaulieu,[1] since the death of Tisiphone her sister.[2] Old Marlborough,[3] or old Duchess Montagu[4] could not be that grandmother, unless they may be called the grandames of charity children, who would willingly have left some of their own children to the parish.[5] The friend who wrote the verses was perhaps Bishop Hurd,[6] or Lord Brudenel or Lady Greenwich or one of the King's footmen.

8. Where HW went 11 Oct. (Mason ii. 161).

9. Lady Henrietta Cecilia West (1727–1817), m. (1762) Col. (afterwards Gen.) James Johnston. At this time she was living at Petersham.

10. Lady Sarah's second husband, Hon. George Napier, whom she had married on 27 Aug. 1781, was a nephew of Gen. Johnston (Lennox, *Life and Letters* ii. 4, 13; Burke, *Peerage*, 1953, pp. 1536–7).

11. Thomas Alexander Erskine (1732–9 Oct. 1781), styled Vct Fentoun to 1756, 6th E. of Kellie, 1756; 'the musical Earl,' praised by Dr Burney; died of a putrid fever at Brussels following a paralytic stroke as he was returning from Spa to England (*London Chronicle* 13–20 Oct., l. 368, 382).

---

1. Isabella Montagu (d. 1786), 1st dau. and coheir of John, 2d D. of Montagu, by Mary Churchill, dau. of John, 1st D.

of Marlborough, m. 1 (1723) William Montagu (1700–39), 2d D. of Manchester, 1722; m. 2 (1743) Edward Hussey (from 1749, Hussey-Montagu), cr. (1762) Bn Beaulieu and (1784) E. of Beaulieu; the Isabella of Sir Charles Hanbury Williams's 'Isabella; or, The Morning.'

2. The Duchess of Montagu, who had died in 1775 (*ante* 15 Aug. 1776).

3. Sarah Jennings (1660–1744) m. (1678) John Churchill, 1st D. of Marlborough. HW in his letter to Mann 10 Dec. 1741 OS, Mann i. 235, refers to her as 'Old Marlborough.'

4. The Duchess of Marlborough's youngest dau., Mary Churchill (1689–1751), m. (1705) John Montagu, 2d D. of Montagu, 1709.

5. The younger Ds of Montagu 'never would lend the Duke a shilling' (HW to Montagu 20 July 1749, Montagu i. 95).

6. On the death of Cornwallis, Archbishop of Canterbury, in March, 1783,

I have heard a very indifferent account of poor Mr Morrice from Lady Margaret Compton,[7] who says Dr Turton[8] has a bad opinion of him. He is at Bath and that delays our consultation on Cav. Mozzi's affair. Of my nephew[9] I have received just such accounts as Lord Ossory gives. I wish he would fix on his Isthmus of Corinth[10] for the scene of an exploit he has got in that head which all the world finds so sensible. He is going to set up *at Leghorn* a monument for his mother and has sent me the epitaph for my opinion. It says, she died *universally lamented.*[11] Oh! that he would translate it into Greek or Coptic,[12] or any *lingo* that every English sailor could not understand! I have answered very respectfully,[13] as becomes a dutiful uncle without giving any opinion or advice at all, for to contradict a madman is to persuade him. If he thinks I approve, he may change his mind.

In the meantime, while Mr Morrice is incapable of attending our Court, I have been transacting another knotty affair, of which I despaired, but have brought to an amicable hearing. Mr Jephson's play on my *Otranto*[14] has been committed to my care on and off for these twelve months.[15] But he had chosen other guardians too. A lady

'The King . . . immediately offered it to his most favoured of the bench, Dr Hurd, Bishop of Worcester, lately preceptor to the Prince' (*Last Journals* ii. 504).

7. HW may have seen her at Lady Harrington's whist party on Sunday, 21 Oct. (Coke, 'MS Journals').

8. John Turton (1735–1806), M.D., University College, Oxford, 1767; Fellow of the Royal College of Physicians, 1768; physician to the Queen's household, 1771; physician in ordinary to the Queen, 1782; physician in ordinary to George III and the Prince of Wales, 1797.

9. Lord Orford.

10. Unexplained.

11. 'Universalmente compianta' (*Miscellanea genealogica et heraldica*, 1898, 3d ser. ii. 151, where the epitaph and arms are given). HW gives details concerning the monument and quotes the proposed epitaph in his letter to Mann 18 Oct. 1781.

12. It is in Italian.

13. The request for HW's opinion had come from Lucas, Lord Orford's lawyer (HW to Mann 18 Oct. 1781). Lucas's let-

ter and HW's reply are missing.

14. *The Count of Narbonne*, acted at Covent Garden 17 Nov. 1781; dedicated to HW. HW's copy of the first edition, 1781, is in the Merritt Collection at Harvard; his copy of the Dublin edn, 1781, is now WSL (Hazen, *Cat. of HW's Lib.* 1810. 33. 6, 2402).

15. See HW to Jephson 25, 27 Jan. 1780 for HW's suggestions on the MS, which had been submitted to Thomas Sheridan, father of R. B. Sheridan. HW read the MS twice at this time. For his efforts to bring the play to the stage, see HW to Henderson 18 July, 26 Aug., 15 Oct., and to Jephson 7, 10 Nov. 1781. Mr C. B. Hogan has kindly called our attention to a report in the *Public Advertiser*, 1 Nov.: 'The management of *The Count of Narbonne* is . . . under very good care: Mr Horace Walpole, with a fondness nothing less than fatherly, directs that part of the affair which respects the scenes and dresses, while Mr Henderson takes charge of the rehearsals and the casting of inferior parts . . . [Henderson] is to wear

genius[16] persuaded him to give it to Mr Sheridan,[17] who having the opera and the nation to regulate besides,[18] and some plays to write, neglected the poor Irish orphan.[19] Then I was desired to recommend it to t'other house.[20] Unfortunately a third guardian[21] was appointed, and though your Milesians have hearts unsteady as the equator, they have always an ecliptic that crosses their heads, and gives them a devious motion. When I applied to Mr Manager Harris,[22] it came out that the Hibernian trustee[23] had originally engaged the play to him, and when Mr Harris complained of the breach of promise, he was not softened by the too zealous friend. There had been twenty other mismanagements, and Mr Harris would not hear the play named. As I have seen other negotiators[24] of late miscarry by bullying first and bending afterwards, I took the counterpart, and in two days so softened the majesty of Covent Garden, that he has not only engaged to act the tragedy, but by the beginning of December,[25] when my utmost hopes did not expect to see it before spring.

Nor was this my only difficulty. Mrs Yates[26] is dying,[27] and the sole

a dress which is lent him from among the antiquities at Strawberry Hill.'

16. Possibly Lady Harcourt (formerly Lady Nuneham), to whom Jephson had dedicated his *Braganza*, and whose husband had aided him politically in Ireland.

17. Richard Brinsley Sheridan had been manager of Drury Lane since 1776, in succession to Garrick.

18. In 1778 Sheridan and Thomas Harris (see below) purchased the patent of the Opera House (King's Theatre, Haymarket); in 1779 Sheridan took over Harris's share, and in 1781, before 20 Dec., Sheridan disposed of the patent to William Taylor (BERRY i. 191 n. 12; MASON i. 362–3 n. 12; Michael Kelly, *Reminiscences*, 2d edn, 1826, ii. 359–60; Walter Sichel, *Sheridan*, 1909, i. 47 n. 2, 529 n. 2, ii. 391). In 1780 Sheridan had been elected M.P. for Stafford borough.

19. R. B. Sheridan 'perfectly agreed with me [Thomas Sheridan] in opinion as to the excellence of the play, but he was under absolute engagement for two tragedies to be brought out this season; however that *The Count of Narbonne* should have the preference of all others for the next' (Thomas Sheridan to Jephson

11 Jan. 1780, quoted in part in *The R. B. Adam Library Relating to Dr Johnson and His Era*, 1929–30, iii. 219).

20. Covent Garden.

21. Edmond Malone, the editor of Shakespeare; HW's occasional correspondent. Some of the problems relating to *The Count of Narbonne* are mentioned in the HW-Malone Correspondence.

22. Thomas Harris (ca 1738–1820), a proprietor (1767–1820) and stage manager of Covent Garden (GM 1820, xc pt ii. 374–5).

23. Malone.

24. The Government, in conducting American and foreign affairs.

25. It opened 17 Nov.

26. Mary Ann Graham (1728–87), m. (ca 1756) Richard Yates; tragic actress. She appeared at Drury Lane 1754–67, 1774–9, and at Covent Garden 1767–73, 1779–83 (C. B. Hogan, *Eighteenth-Century Actors in the D.N.B. Additions and Corrections*, 1952, p. 20; Genest, *passim*).

27. 'Mrs Yates lies dangerously ill, with so alarming a fit of the stone, at her house in Pall Mall, that her life is despaired of' (*London Chronicle* 16–18 Oct., l. 374).

remaining actress Miss Young[28] refused the part of the mother, because, as she said, Mrs Crauford[29] had refused it. Mr Harris begged me to write to Miss Young. I did,[30] and to turn aside what I guessed to be the real motive of the refusal, I told her, I would not suspect that Mrs Crauford declined the part from preferring that of the daughter, because Mrs Crauford must know the world too well not to be aware that when a gentlewoman of middle age appears in a very juvenile part, it does but make that middle age more apparent.[31] There was so much sugar strewed over this indirect truth, that even there I have succeeded too, and Miss Young has complied.[32] I am to attend rehearsals,[33] and give advice on scenes, dresses etc., and so must be frequently in town. In short, my uncle[34] never negotiated with more abilities. Pray, Madam, respect my various talents. I have lately acted as a justice of peace;[35] am to sit as chancellor in a court of equity on my nephew's dispute with Mozzi, and have now been plenipotentiary to the sovereign of a theatre! What pity that I should have cut my abilities so late! Well! thus I unwrinkle my old age with whatever pastime presents itself, instead of growing ill-humoured or covetous, the resources of longevity.

Your Ladyship however seems to think that I have a good deal of wrongheadedness in my composition. I confess I have not that verbal patriotism which bids one say one wishes what one does not wish. I confess I do wish better to the Americans than to the Scotch, because the cause of the former is more just. The English in America are as much my countrymen as those born in the parish of St Martin's-in-the-Fields;[36] and when my countrymen quarrel, I think I am free to wish better to the sufferers than to the aggressors. I do look on Lord

28. Elizabeth Younge (ca 1744–97), m. (1785) Alexander Pope (1763–1835), actor and painter.

29. Ann Street (1734–1801), m. 1 (1753) —— Dancer (d. 1759); m. 2 (ca 1768) as 2d wife, Spranger Barry (1719–77); m. 3 (ca 1778) Thomas Crawford (ca 1750–94) (C. B. Hogan, op. cit. 5).

30. See HW's letter to her, 22 Oct. 1781.

31. HW had also suggested to Miss Younge that Mrs Crawford had declined the mother's part 'from resentment on her husband's account, whom Mr Jephson had undervalued.'

32. Her letter to HW, mentioned in

HW to Jephson 7 Nov. 1781, is missing.

33. On 10 and 16 Nov. (HW to Jephson 10 Nov. 1781; post 15 Nov. 1781).

34. Horatio Walpole (1678–1757), cr. (1756) Bn Walpole of Wolterton; statesman and diplomatist.

35. A reference to HW's activity in 'examinations of witnesses' and 'depositions, which I had taken myself' connected with the robbery (ante 7 Oct. 1781).

36. A reference to the alleged legal fiction that the English overseas were technically in the parish of St Martin's-in-the-Fields (HW to Mann 2 Feb. 1774, 23 Jan. 1783, 30 April 1786).

Cornwallis as a renegade. He was one of five who protested against the Stamp Act.[37] He therefore had no principles *then,* or has none now; and neither in compliance with the vulgar or the powerful, will I say I approve him.[38] If an alderman's son,[39] not content with a decent fortune[40] and a large portion of well-deserved immortality,[41] is proud of becoming toad-eater to a Scotch Chief Justice,[42] of having a few more words said to him at a levee than are vouchsafed to Dr Dominiceti,[43] and of being ordered to pen memorials for such boobies as Lord Suffolk[44] and Lord Hilsborough,[45] I do not wonder. But when a gentleman, a man of quality,[46] sells himself for the paltry honours and profits that he must quit so soon, and leave nothing but a tarnished name behind him, he has my utter contempt; nor can I see how my love of my country obliges me to wish well to what I de-

37. See *ante* 10 Oct. 1780.

38. Lady Ossory wrote to Selwyn, 'Monday,' [5 Nov. 1781]: 'You do not mention Col. Conway's arrival [on 3 Nov.; see following letter]. I hope he brings tidings favourable, I mean with regard to Lord Cornwallis. If Mr Walpole talks to you on that subject he will put you in a rage —I never *will allow* he can be in earnest though he swears it' (MS WSL).

39. Edward Gibbon, the historian, was the son of Edward Gibbon (1707–70), alderman of London, Vintry Ward, 1743–5; M.P. Petersfield 1734–41, Southampton borough 1741–7, (MASON i. 243 n. 16; *Old Westminsters*).

40. In 1778 Gibbon 'was still burdened with his father's debts, and his own expenses were certainly not sinking. Perhaps he could count on £700–£800 in a good year. He was spending over £1000.' His appointment to the Board of Trade in 1779 had brought him a net increase of £750 a year (D. M. Low, *Edward Gibbon,* 1937, pp. 277–8; Gibbon, *Letters,* ed. Norton, 1956, ii. 327).

41. The first three volumes of his *Decline and Fall* had been published (Vols II–III on 1 March 1781).

42. Lord Loughborough, who had been instrumental in getting Gibbon appointed a lord of Trade, July 1779 (Low, op. cit. 278; MASON ii. 99 and n. 25; Gibbon, op. cit. *passim*).

43. Bartholomew Joseph Alexander de Dominiceti (fl. 1750–82), 'Lord de Cete et de Cortesi, Knight of the Holy Roman Empire and Noble of Venice,' quack doctor who came to England in 1753, practiced at Bristol 1753–64, at Millbank 1764–5, and at Chelsea 1765–82; bankrupt, 1762, 1782; treated patients, including the King's brother, the Duke of York, and Sir John Fielding, in 'baths, fumigatory stoves and sweating chambers' (Reginald Blunt, *In Cheyne Walk and Thereabout,* 1914, pp. 137–55; Boswell, *Johnson* ii. 99–100, 489; Daniel Lysons, *Environs of London,* Vol. II, 1795, p. 124; BM Cat.; BM, *Satiric Prints* vi. 595–6, No. 7514; GM 1762, xxxii. 243; GM 1782, lii. 456). His son, Hector Rodomonte Francis di Dominiceti (1756–1817), a physician, was also treating patients at this time (*Eton Coll. Reg.; London Courant* 30 July, 19 Oct., and *passim*).

44. At the time of his death, 7 March 1779, Lord Suffolk was secretary of state for the North.

45. Secretary of state for the South, Nov. 1779 – 2 March 1782. There is no record that Gibbon wrote for him, but, at the request of Lord Weymouth, Hillsborough's predecessor, and Lord Thurlow, Gibbon wrote in the summer of 1779 (the first draft was finished by 10 Aug.) his only work of this kind, a *Mémoire justificatif* in answer to a French manifesto (Low, op. cit. 281–2; J. E. Norton, *A Bibliography of Edward Gibbon,* Oxford, 1940, pp. [22]–35).

46. Cornwallis.

spise. Your Ladyship is more charitable, or more patriotic, or perhaps your sentiments may not be so rooted as mine, who do prefer
the liberties of mankind to any local circumstances. Were I young
and of heroic texture, I would go to America. As I am decrepit, and
have the bones of a sparrow, I must die on my perch—and when you
turn courtier, I will peck my bread and water out of another hand.

For France, I have no predilection for it; nor is my respect for it
augmented. It does so little, it makes so poor a figure, that one would
think Lord North was minister there as well as here. In truth, Madam,
I have no platonic passions. I cannot love what I do not esteem. We
have forfeited all titles to respect. I appeal to the unalterable nature
of Justice whether this war with America is a just one—if it is not,
can an honest man wish success to it? and I appeal to posterity whether
it can find in all our annals so disgraceful a period as the present.
You, Madam, as a sound patriot may wish that Admiral Darby with
an inferiority of two thirds had beaten the combined fleets[47]—which
he did not attempt to beat—but give me leave to say that you should
recur to your piety. Piety believes in miracles; miracles alone can
counterpoise superior weight of metal, or counteract folly, which
has thrown away the empire of the ocean. It is true, we have still the
jaw-bone of an ass left—but somehow or other it has lost its wonder-
working efficacy—but come, Madam, I will show that I can be impartial too. I do assure you I have not the smallest apprehension
from Lord Cornwallis's victorious arms; and I do pray for the duration of the present ministry, for I am sure they will never conquer
America nor any thing else.

I had heard the story of Lady Sarah[48] and the Prince,[49] and know it
is true. The spindle tree I have—paper enough I have not to reply to
other articles in your Ladyship's letter. I beg your pardon for the
length and tediousness of this, but I could not bear not to justify myself in your eyes; I have spoken the truth, I do not know whether
with any success. My sentiments have always been the same, *and* I
believe firmly will never alter.

---

47. Early in September 1781 the combined fleets, anchored off Scilly, consisted
of 47 ships of the line, whereas Darby
had only 22 ships of the line in Torbay

(*Last Journals* ii. 372; HW to Mason 9
Sept. 1781, Mason ii. 151 and n. 5).
48. Napier.
49. Of Wales.

To Lady Ossory, Tuesday 6 November 1781

Address: To the Countess of Ossory at Ampthill Park, Bedfordshire. *Postmark:* ISLEWORTH. 6 NO.

Strawberry Hill, Nov. 6, 1781.

I BELIEVE I am very dull, or quite blinded by prejudice, for I confess I do not feel the force of your Ladyship's arguments. Are men in the right to take up arms in self-defence, and in the wrong to declare themselves independent? Is resistance *by force* a thing indifferent, and the declaration *in words,* a crime? Methinks by that rule all who joined the Prince of Orange were justifiable, but ceased to be so the moment King James was dethroned. Thus men ought to offend a king, but never to punish him!—I believe their Majesties would agree to that compromise.

I can as little subscribe to the position that it is the duty of an officer to obey his king, whatever may be the officer's opinions. Were that maxim true, no conscientious man can accept a commission, if it dissolves the obligation of his conscience. Those very loyal instruments, the bells of a parish church, do allow a precedence to God— Fear God, honour the King[1]—but I am talking politics, and arguing —two things I do not love. I am almost afraid to tell you news on that subject, as I doubt your Ladyship is less and less likely to recover your share of sovereignty over America. Lord Graham[2] and Lord Sefton, who have been in town, tell me that the accounts brought by Colonel Conway[3] are very bad indeed.[4] I did see him himself on Saturday at

1. I Peter 2. 17; the motto inscribed on the bells. Cf. HW to Mann 28 Dec. 1781.
2. James Graham (1755–1836), styled M. of Graham to 1790; 3d D. of Montrose, 1790; M.P.; holder of numerous Court appointments.
3. He left New York 1 Oct. and arrived in London 3 Nov. (*London Gazette* No. 12239, 3–6 Nov.).
4. Lady Mary Coke's account in 'MS Journals' 3 Nov. parallels HW's: 'While we were at dinner at Lord Hertford's . . . Col. Conway came in; he went in February to America where he has served in the army of Lord Cornwallis, but being

made aide-de-camp to Sir Henry Clinton is sent back home with his dispatches. 'Twas natural to ask him whether he brought any news, to which he answered a great deal but none very good. He confirms the report of the French having landed 3600 men and that they are very strong at sea; our frigates have counted six and thirty sail, but three are supposed to be frigates, so their fleet is three and thirty sail of the line and we are only three and twenty, but he removes the fears we were in for Lord Cornwallis by saying that if he should judge his post not sufficiently strong to withstand an

Ditton on his way to Windsor,[5] but he was so discreet as to say nothing, but that what he brought was not very good: that the French have thirty-seven ships,[6] and we twenty-three;[7] that the former have landed 4000 men,[8] and evacuated Rhode Island,[9] and taken *two* of our best frigates; the papers say *three;*[10] but it is not true that two regiments have been cut to pieces,[11] for the 45th,[12] one of the named, is in England. He did say, that your friend Lord Cornwallis has the back country open to him,[13] and he did not add, what Lord Sefton tells me is said, that he had provisions but for six weeks.[14] We shall

attack he can always go farther into the country without any danger of his army being surrounded.'

5. 'Col. Conway had sent Sir Henry Clinton's dispatches to the King at Windsor, and when the dinner was over he set out himself to wait on his Majesty. It seems it is the rule for every officer to send the dispatches some hours before they go themselves' (ibid.).

6. The French fleet of 28 ships of the line under the command of the Comte de Grasse arrived in Chesapeake Bay late in Aug. and with the arrival early in September of the squadron under the Comte de Barras from Rhode Island (with additional troops) there were 36 ships of the line, including two 50-gun ships (*London Chronicle* 3–20 Nov., l. 439, 445, 461, 487; Cornwallis, *Correspondence,* ed. Ross, 1859, i. 119, 121; idem, *An Answer to . . . Sir Henry Clinton,* 1783, p. 197).

7. 'Our fleet consists of twenty-three sail of the line and two 50's' (Hon. H. Broderick to Right Hon. Thomas Townshend, New York, 30 Sept. 1781, in Cornwallis, *Correspondence,* i. 121).

8. Cornwallis to Clinton, Yorktown, 8 Sept. 1781: 'The French troops landed at James Town are said to be 3800 men' (ibid. i. 117–18).

9. On 28 Aug. Sir Henry Clinton learned that Barras with his squadron had sailed from Rhode Island. Earlier Rochambeau had marched his army from Rhode Island to join Washington (Clinton, *Narrative . . . Relative to His Conduct,* 1783, pp. 15–17).

10. 'Sir Henry [Clinton] in his dispatches . . . takes notice of the loss of the *Iris* frigate of 32 guns, Capt. George

Dawson, the *Richmond* of 32 guns, Capt. Charles Hudson, and the *Guadaloupe* of 28 guns . . . Capt. Robinson; these ships having fallen in with M. de Grasse were unfortunately captured' (*London Chronicle* 3–10 Nov., l. 433, 449).

11. The *London Chronicle* 3–6 Nov., l. 433, reported that 'upwards of 400 privates, principally British, were killed' at New London, Conn. According to Arnold's official return, two regiments bore the brunt, the 40th having 31 killed and 55 wounded, and the 54th having 15 killed and 78 wounded (ibid. 3–10 Nov., l. 437–8, 441, 452).

12. Presumably the 54th; '45th' may be a typographical error in a newspaper.

13. Cornwallis's letter to Clinton 20 Oct. 1781, announcing his capitulation at Yorktown, indicates that he had considered two alternatives: 'to escape to New York by rapid marches from the Gloucester side,' or to attack the enemy 'in the open field,' but 'being assured by . . . [Clinton] that every possible means would be tried by the navy and army to relieve us, I could not think myself at liberty to venture upon either of those desperate attempts' (Cornwallis, *Correspondence,* i. 510).

14. The *London Chronicle* 3–6 Nov., l. 433, referred to letters from Cornwallis to Clinton (not quoted in the *London Gazette*) in which the former reported 'that he had nearly two months' provisions with him, and that he made no doubt of receiving a fresh supply before his stock was exhausted.' Cornwallis wrote to Clinton 16 Sept. 1781: 'By examining the transports and turning out useless mouths, my provisions will last at least

close, I believe and hope, Madam, in wishing an end to this destruction of the species; nor can the most loyal, I suppose, think that even the dependence of America was worth purchasing at the expense of thousands of lives, of forty millions of money, of the sovereignty of the sea, and of the loss of America itself. We were naturally tradesmen, and had better have borne a few affronts, than asserted the point of honour at so dear a rate.

It is very far from true, Madam, that I write either prologue or epilogue to the *Count of Narbonne*.[15] I could no more compose twenty verses than I could dance a hornpipe. My faculties are as *délabrées* as my limbs, and these are deplorable. My nerves are so shattered, that the clapping of a door makes me tremble; and this poor hand that is writing to you, has long lost the use of three of its joints, and I fear will quite desert me. I have now, and have had all the summer the gout in the fourth finger. Thus my person is as antiquated as my political opinions!

I have not seen Mr Selwyn for half a century. He has *the malapropos* almost as strongly as *the apropos*. Others, with more malice, say they perceive a likeness to *the* Lord William[16]—Miss Loyd is full as like to Lady Sarah. Miss Bunbury has a great deal of the Lenoxes, not so handsome, but with a much prettier person than any of the females of the family.

Genealogist as I am, I cannot make out, Madam, how Miss Sackville is Lord Mansfield's niece.[17] You say you do not entirely believe that his Lordship gave away his niece. *Cela me passe*. To weep at weddings I know is of ancient custom, as much as *double entendres*; a ceremonial, the former, of which I never knew the origin. The more and

---

six weeks from this day, if we can preserve them from accidents' (Cornwallis, *Correspondence*, i. 119).

15. The *London Courant* 30 Oct. had reported that HW was writing the epilogue. See also MASON ii. 162 and n. 8; *post* 15 Nov. 1781.

16. Lord William Gordon, the father of Louisa Bunbury, mentioned below. Selwyn wrote to Lord Carlisle 26 Oct. 1781: 'Miss Bunbury pleased me much, a mixture of the Richmonds and of Lord William. I had not seen her till the other day since I assisted at her christening for old Lord Holland' (*Carlisle MSS* 523).

17. Lady Ossory's remarks were presumably about two different marriages, but HW assumes that they refer only to that of Elizabeth Sackville (b. 1762), dau. of Lord George Germain, m. 21 Oct. at Drayton, Northants, Henry Arthur Herbert (1756–1821), later M.P. Lord Mansfield's niece (actually his wife's niece) Harriet Frances Charlotte Finch-Hatton (1752–1821), m. 18 Oct. Sir Jenison William Gordon, 2d Bt, 1780 (GM 1781, li. 489; Collins, *Peerage*, 1812, vi. 318; Burke, *Peerage*, 1953, pp. 2254–5; *London Chronicle* 20–23 Oct., l. 387; Alan Valentine, *Lord George Germain*, 1962, p. 476).

the longer a fashion prevails, the less sense there commonly is in it. Thence solutionists, like etymologists, seldom hit on the true foundation, both hunting for some meaning.

I recollect how prolix my last was; and though you are too civil to tell me, Madam, of that other symptom of my dotage, I am aware of it myself, and wish you good night.

To Lady Ossory, Thursday 15 November 1781

Address: To the Countess of Ossory at Ampthill Park, Bedfordshire. *Postmark:* 16 NO.

Berkeley Square, Nov. 15, 1781.

I DON'T know whether I shall be able to go through a letter, Madam, for I have a new swelling on one of my fingers, which must be lanced, and my hand trembles so much that I often cannot write a line. In this uneasy situation I am again come to town to attend a rehearsal. This play I confess plagues me a good deal, for our Lord's ecliptic countrymen undo as fast as I do. The manager[1] was going to hurry on the performance last Saturday, before actors, scenes or anything was ripe. I trusted to accidents and bore that haste. I had no sooner done so, than one of your Milesians[2] took fire and wrote an angry letter[3] to Mr Harris in resentment of the precipitation—Well! that quarrel I made up. Today, after I had begged Mr Harris to procure an epilogue and he had got one,[4] Mr Jephson had written to this Mr O'Quarrel, who is a poet too, to write one, and so he has;[5] and now, on Thursday night with the play to come forth on Saturday, we don't know which is to be preferred. I am to be at the theatre to-

1. Thomas Harris.
2. Edmond Malone.
3. Missing.
4. From Richard Jocelyn Goodenough (d. 22 Dec. 1781), author of *The Cottagers*, 1768, republished as *William and Nanny*, 1779. His epilogue was used the first two nights only; thereafter Malone's was used (GM 1781, li. 595; *London Chronicle* 22–25 Dec., l. 605; Jephson, *The Count of Narbonne*, 1781, pp. [83–4]). The *London Chronicle* 17–20 Nov., l. 484, reported his epilogue 'was very happily adapted to the events of the preceding play, and contains

many good and nervous lines, which were admirably delivered by Miss Younge.' Malone wrote to Lord Charlemont 8 Jan. 1782: 'My poor brother epilogue-writer, Mr Goodenough, who lived just near me [in Queen Anne Street, Cavendish Square], shot himself a few days ago' (Hist. MSS Comm., 12th Rep., App. x, *Charlemont MSS*, 1891, i. 395; *London Courant* 22–24 Nov., 24, 25 Dec.).
5. Malone's epilogue, like Goodenough's, was published with the play, pp. [81–3]; it appeared in the *London Chronicle* 22–24 Nov., l. 502.

morrow by eleven, and Lord knows what will happen! I will tire
your Ladyship no more with my grievances, but will take care how
I promise and vow for a play again. I want to be quiet in my own
Strawberry again—indeed I am fit to be nowhere else, and have a
great mind to fix there.

I heard a great deal of French news t'other day by one[6] just come
from Paris. I don't answer for one syllable being true. My historian
says the Queen seemed to be resolved, *à la* Marie d'Este,[7] that her
babe should be a dauphin. Her reckoning and her person shifted
backwards and forwards, and the last time having put off her delivery
for a fortnight, and sent the King to hunt, he was fetched back in a
quarter of an hour to see a son.[8] Then there is a delightful episode of
a Mademoiselle Diane de Polignac,[9] a friend of the favourite Duchess,[10] who was Dame to Madame Elizabeth, and who was so very pious
and had so bemethodized her mistress, that they feared the Princess
would follow her aunt Louise into a convent,[11] and they would have
dismissed the saint, if the Queen would have consented, and if the
saint herself had not one *beau matin* had the misfortune to have a
little one.[12] For fear of any more virgin-mothers, the Queen and the

6. Not identified.

7. Mary of Modena (Maria Beatrice
. . . d'Este) (1658–1718) m. (1673), as 2d
wife, James II of England. On the birth
of her fourth daughter (the daughters
and a son all having died young), it was
rumoured that the substitution of a male
child had been considered; and in 1688,
when her second son, James Francis
Edward, was born, there were doubts
(disproved by an investigation) of the
genuineness of the birth.

8. Louis-Joseph-Xavier-François (22 Oct.
1781 – 4 June 1789), the Dauphin.

9. A daughter of Louis-Melchior Armand, Vicomte de Polignac: either Diane-
Françoise-Zephyrine de Polignac (b. 1740
or 1746), or Diane-Louise-Augustine de
Polignac (b. 1742 or 1748). She was styled
Comtesse de Polignac; lady of honour to
Mme Élisabeth 1778–89; emigrated with
her brother and sister-in-law (mentioned
below), in July 1789; but in 1796 was on
the Continent according to her *Mémoires
sur la vie et la caractère de Mme la duchesse
de Polignac*, London, 1796 (La Chenaye-
Desbois; *Almanach royal*, 1789, p. 144;

Vicomte Albert Révérend, *Titres . . . de
la Restauration*, 1902–6, v. 391; Jean-
Pierre-Louis de la Roche du Maine, Marquis de Luchet, *et al.*, *La Galerie des
États-Généraux*, 1789–90, iii. 102–7, where
she appears as Ténésis; Auguste Cabanès,
La Princesse de Lamballe intime, n.d.,
pp. 388–9; BERRY ii. 227). She was said to
be living in 1817 at St Petersburg (Charles-
Joseph, Prince de Ligne, *Mémoires et
lettres*, 1923, p. 335).

10. Gabrielle-Yolande-Claude-Martine de
Polastron (ca 1749–93) m. (1767) Armand-
Jules-François, Comte and (1780) Duc
de Polignac; the favourite of Marie-Antoinette, who generously rewarded her;
emigrated in July 1789, first to Switzerland, then to Italy, and finally to Austria;
died in Vienna (Diane de Polignac, op.
cit.).

11. The daughter of Louis XV, Madame
Louise, had become a Carmelite nun in
1770 (*ante* 11 Aug. 1774, n. 3).

12. 'La Duchesse de Polignac était
gouvernée par la Comtesse Diane de
Polignac, sa belle-sœur . . . méchante et
laide. Née avec un esprit supérieur et

Duchess have produced an old Madame Dandelot,[13] who was exiled in the last reign for having taken a very different way to convert Madame Adelaide,[14] by lending her a strange book[15] of which I protest I know the name no more than your Ladyship. One anecdote more, and I will not ask my hand to say a word more. The Comte d'Artois carried his eldest boy the Comte d'Angoulême to see the Dauphin. The child said, 'Il est bien petit.' The Prince replied, 'Patience, mon enfant, vous le trouverez bientôt trop grand.'[16]

I don't know whether your Ladyship can read all this tittle-tattle; it does not signify if you do not. I know nothing else, nor could write more if I did. Soon mayhap I must write upon a slate; it will only be scraping my fingers to a point, and they will serve for a chalk pencil.

Friday.

I have been at the theatre[17] and compromised the affair of the epilogues; one[18] is to be spoken tomorrow, the friend's[19] on the author's night. I have been tumbling into trap doors, seeing dresses tried on in the green room, and directing armour in the painting room, and all this with such a throbbing hand, that I was tempted to

fertile en vues et en moyens, elle était l'auteur de la fortune de sa maison. . . . Elle avait obtenu un brevet de chanoinnesse, et quoiqu'elle fût demoiselle, et repoussante tant par la fierté et la roideur de son caractère, que par la difformité de sa figure, elle donnait, chaque année, un nouvel enfant à l'état. De la dernière place, à la cour, qu'elle avait obtenu en 1775, en qualité de dame de compagnie de la Comtesse d'Artois, elle était devenue dame d'honneur de Madame Élisabeth, qui avait bien moins d'autorité dans sa maison que Madame Diane de Polignac. Le Roi, lui-même, redoutait . . . la Duchesse et Diane' (Jean-Louis Giraud Soulavie, *Mémoires historiques et politiques du règne de Louis XVI*, 1801, vi. 31).

13. Paternal aunt of the Duchesse de Polignac: Marie-Henriette de Polastron (d. 1792 or 1793), m. (1736) François-Léonor, Comte d'Andlau, army officer. 'Elle [la Duchesse de Polignac] en devait beaucoup à la Comtesse d'Andlau sa tante, qui lui avait servi de mère et l'avait élevée avec soin dès sa plus tendre en-

fance; elle n'a cessé de lui rendre ceux d'une tendresse et d'un respect vraiment filials.' Louis XVI and Marie-Antoinette gave her 'une pension de six mille livres' (Diane de Polignac, op. cit. 4–5, 9, 58; La Chenaye-Desbois i. 480, xvi. 11; *Dictionnaire de biographie française*, 1933–, ii. 862).

14. Marie-Adélaïde (1732–1800), 4th dau. of Louis XV. HW had met her in Paris in 1765 (BERRY i. 207 and n. 15).

15. *Histoire de Dom B——, portier des Chartreux, écrite par lui-même*, Rome, n.d., by Jean-Charles Gervaise de la Touche (1715–82); the incident, which was then recent, is described by Charles-Philippe d'Albert, Duc de Luynes, *Mémoires*, vii. 332–3, *sub* 24 June 1746. For the book, see MANN i. 273 n. 25.

16. This last anecdote, in slightly different phrasing, is in Cornelia Knight, *Autobiography*, 3d edn, 1861, ii. 310.

17. Covent Garden.

18. Goodenough's.

19. Malone's.

rest myself in Covent Garden Churchyard, and bilk both the great stage and the little one.

To Lady Ossory, Thursday 22 November 1781

Address: To the Countess of Ossory at Ampthill Park, Bedfordshire. *Postmark:* ISLEWORTH. 22 NO.

Strawberry Hill, Nov. 22, 1781.

I AM angry with myself, Madam, for having dropped a word that gave you any concern; nor shall I forgive my guilty self, though it has produced such new proof of your Ladyship's goodness. I have not suffered at all by my campaign at the theatre, but *like weeds that escape the scythe,* I do not catch cold where a giant would. It is true, I am so nervous, that the least surprise or sudden noise agitates me from head to foot—but I will not say a word more on my debility. An aspen leaf can give an oak no idea of its sensations—and why should it? I have such a dread of seeming not to be apprised of my antiquity and decay, that very likely I carry it to affectation, for it is difficult to keep to the medium of simplicity and common sense on any occasion. Having therefore put in my caveat against being suspected of any imaginary robustness, you shall hear no more of any cracks that happen to the premises.[1]

After all my pains Mr Jephson is not quite satisfied.[2] Though I had begged him (and he had promised) not to communicate to his Irish friends the approaching exhibition of his tragedy,[3] he had, as I told your Ladyship, written to one[4] of them here, who, as I told you too, quarrelled with Mr Harris, and then, I believe, with me about his epilogue.[5] To punish me, he wrote to Mr Jephson[6] that I had given

1. An echo of Waller; see *post* 1 July 1782, and n. 7.

2. See HW to Jephson 21 Nov. 1781, to Malone 23 Nov. 1781, and to Mason 26 Nov. 1781, Mason ii. 167.

3. HW alludes to this understanding in his letter to Jephson 7 Nov. 1781: 'I must act about the impression [that is, having the play printed] just the reverse of what I did about the performance, and must beg you would commission some friend to transact that affair.'

4. Malone.

5. Malone wrote to Lord Charlemont 8 Jan. 1782: 'I have lately become acquainted with your friend, Mr Walpole, and am quite charmed with him. There is an unaffected benignity and good nature in his manner that is, I think, irresistibly engaging' (Hist. MSS Comm., 12th Rep., App. x, *Charlemont MSS*, 1891, i. 395).

6. The Jephson-Malone correspondence is missing.

up a material point of the decoration of the last scene, and had consented that the statue of Alphonso should be cumbent, though Mr
Jephson had called it *standing*⁷—which by the way was wrong.⁸ The
truth was, we had not time to remedy that contradiction, unless by
altering the word, which Mr Friend would not allow, nor could we
have placed an erect statue in the scene prepared—and if we could,
it would have spoiled the great effect of the last scene—In short, Mr
Jephson has written me a pressing letter⁹ to amend that disposition,
when it is too late.¹⁰ Well! I am content with having brought so
beautiful a play on the stage; and as it is never too late to learn, I
will take care how I undertake such an office another time.

My sage nephew Lord Orford, is, I hear, drawing up a code of laws
—for coursing—for the use of her Imperial Majesty of Russia—a
fitter code indeed for a despot, than a general system of legislation.
I hope Diderot and D'Alembert will celebrate her humanity in not
allowing poor hares to be hunted to death, but according to law. You
see, Madam, she has sent her son¹¹ to travel¹²—shall you be prodigiously surprised if he was to die suddenly by eating ice when he was
overheated?¹³

7. The last half of Act V, Scenes vi–xv, takes place in 'The inside of a convent, with aisles and Gothick arches, part of an altar appearing on one side; the statue of Alphonso in armour in the centre' (*The Count of Narbonne*, 1781, p. 70). Austin says, 'There stands his statue' (Scene vii, p. 71), and the Count, 'Pointing to the statue of Alphonso,' says: 'Like their great monarch, he stands rais'd above them' (Scene x, p. 73).

8. That is, in the time and place of the action of the play, the statue would be on the tomb and would therefore be recumbent. Jephson, however, as HW mentions in his letter to Jephson 21 Nov. 1781, 'made a distinction between the statue and the tomb.' In Act V, Scene ii, Austin tells Theodore of

'The statue of thy grandsire
. . . .
. . . which the people's love

Rear'd near his tomb, within our convent's walls.'

9. Missing.

10. HW's letter to Jephson 3 Dec. 1781 indicates that the change was made in later representations: 'I was sorry you took so much to heart an alteration in the scenery of your play, which did not seem to me very material; and which, having since been adjusted to your wish, had no better effect.'

11. Paul, Grand Duke of Russia, who succeeded her in 1796 as Paul I.

12. In 1781–2 he and the Grand Duchess toured western Europe.

13. As early as 1764 Lord Buckingham-shire, envoy to St Petersburg, had reported rumours that Catherine II might, except for fear of the consequences to herself of a second palace crime, attempt to assas-sinate her son, and he himself had some fears for his life.

To Lady Ossory, Tuesday 18 December 1781

Address: To the Countess of Ossory at Ampthill Park, Bedfordshire. *Postmark:* 18 DE.

Tuesday noon, Dec. 18, 1781.

I HEARD our parenthesis of good news[1] too late last night, Madam, to give you an inkling of it; and I doubt whether if we should receive a complete wreath of sea-flags, I shall have time to send you a leaf today, as I am to dine with Princess Amelie, and shall not be dismissed before the post departs. As American liberty is safe, I shall like prodigiously to have crushed a quota of the French navy, and shall love Admiral Kempenfeld[2] as much as Lord Sandwich himself can. The East Indian triumph is firmly believed.[3] If we only conquer at t'other end of the world, and lose all our nearer possessions, we shall be like a trapes in the Strand that one sees with short petticoats and a long train.[4] I will keep my letter open, till the coach comes to the door, in hopes of a fortunate express, as I have begged Lady Hertford to send me the earliest news.

I was diverted last night at Lady Lucan's; the moment I entered, she set me down to whist with Lady Bute—and who do you think were the other partners? the Archbishopess of Canterbury[5] and Mr Gibbon. I once saved Lady Suffolk at the Dowager Essex's[6] from playing at the same table with Lady Yarmouth.[7] I saw Lady Suffolk ready to sink, and took her card from her, saying, 'I know your Ladyship hates whist, and I will play instead of you.'

1. HW noted in *Last Journals* 17 Dec. 1781, ii. 390–1: 'Came an account of Sir Eyre Coote having gained a great victory over Hyder Ally.' News of Kempenfelt's naval victory came the same day. For details of the two battles, 1 July and 12 Dec., see the *London Chronicle* 15–20 Dec., 1. 584–5.

2. Richard Kempenfelt (1715–82), Rear-Adm., 1780; drowned in the *Royal George*.

3. An extract of a letter from Sir Eyre Coote to Col. Braithwaite 6 July 1781 describes his victory over Hyder 'Ali near Porto Novo 1 July (*London Gazette* No. 12251, 15–18 Dec.).

4. HW's memorandum, 'Street walker,' on Mason's letter to him 16 Dec. 1781 probably refers to this simile; see MASON ii. 168.

5. Mrs Frederick Cornwallis.

6. Elizabeth Russell (d. 1784), m. (1726) William Capell, 3d E. of Essex.

7. Amalie Sophie Marianne von Wendt (1704–65), m. (1727) Gottlieb Adam von Wallmoden, from whom she was divorced in 1739; cr. (1740) Cts of Yarmouth; successor to Lady Suffolk as mistress of George II.

If I am too late, should any account come, I conclude Mr Fitz-patrick will write.

I have been listening impatiently for the Park guns[8]—but it is past two, and they are dumb—I fear their office is almost grown a sinecure like the Laureate's, who only chants anniversaries, whether glad or sorry!

To divert my impatience, I will tell your Ladyship a story that George Selwyn told us t'other day after dinner at Lord Hertford's,[9] and you will allow the authority very good. When Mr de Grey[10] became Baron of Walsingham he felt that so high a rank and a title so illustrated could not consort with commercial commissioners. He resigned his seat at the Board of Trade. Lord Carlisle obtained it for Storer, who kissed hands, vacated his seat, and was re-elected[11]— but lo! the great Baron of Walsingham cried 'Hold!—I am above the place[12]—but till I have another as lucrative, I will not relinquish the salary'—that is, livery and labour degrade; wages for doing nothing, do not—and so poor Storer has already lost four hundred pounds, because a peer blushes to be in the red-book below his rank, but not to take another man's pension who works for it![13] Do not you like,

---

8. The guns in St James's Park, to announce the victory.

9. On 15 Dec.: 'Mie Mie and I dine on Saturday at Lady Hertford's, and she carries us to the opera afterwards' (Selwyn to Lord Carlisle, Tuesday, 11 Dec. 1781, *Carlisle MSS* 549.

10. Thomas de Grey (1748–1818), 2d Bn Walsingham 9 May 1781; M.P.; a commissioner of the Board of Trade and Plantations, 1777 – 22 Dec. 1781 (see n. 13 below); joint vice-treasurer of Ireland 1784–7; joint postmaster general 1787–94.

11. Storer, M.P. for Morpeth 1780–4, was notified of his appointment to the Board of Trade on 18 July; on the same day he kissed the King's hand, vacated his seat in Parliament, and a writ for a new election at Morpeth was given out. On 26 July he was re-elected (*Members of Parliament* 166; *London Chronicle* 17–19 July, l. 62).

12. Many peers sat on the Board of Trade from its beginning in 1660 until its suppression in 1782; see Robert Beat-

son, *Political Index*, 3d edn, 1806, iii. Supplement, pp. vii–xv.

13. Because Walsingham refused to vacate his seat on the Board until he had drawn additional salary (Selwyn wrote Carlisle 30 Nov. that £200 was the desired amount), both Storer and Sir Adam Fergusson, who had been named at the same time, were unable to take their seats and draw salary until 22 Dec., when a new patent, replacing one drawn up before 18 July but withheld, was issued. Because of this irregularity it was thought that Storer might have to go through another election. By refusing to vacate his seat from 18 July to 22 Dec., Walsingham received payment of about £420 and cleared about £315 (the annual salary was £1000 less expenses of about £250 a year; see *ante* 26 Oct. 1781, n. 40). The details of this affair are in *Carlisle MSS* 513–14, 536, 539–40, 547–9, 552. Had Walsingham been willing for a new patent to be issued showing him still a member of the Board in July 1781, Lord North could have

Madam, to see a grandee hopping with one foot on the *haut du pavé,* and t'other in the kennel, *partie per pale,* ermine and mud?

It is just four—I must seal my letter, and go—

To Lady Ossory, Wednesday 19 December 1781

Address: To the Countess of Ossory at Ampthill Park, Bedfordshire. *Postmark:* 19 DE.

Dec. 19, 1781.

THERE! Madam, there! one cannot for a moment expect success, but one is in a scrape and involved in disgrace! Runners come forth in swarms, buzz about one's ears, cry 'Victory! transports taken! an expedition defeated! the West Indies saved!'—and one is such a driveller as to believe them, and to die with impatience for half a dozen French men-of-war towed into Portsmouth, and as many sunk, with the loss of only a leg or arm to some of one's particular friends—next night comes out a *Gazette*[1] and coolly tells you, yes, we had taken a few transports, though somehow or other we have dropped half a dozen by the way;[2] and as to destroying the enemy's fleet, why, they happened to be an over-match for us,[3] as they had five little vessels of 110 guns each,[4] which had been concealed behind a mole-hill, out of sight of any of our cutters; and so we contented ourselves with our day's sport, and hope you will not be much disappointed.[5] Well, but what have you done with the West Indies?—Oh! they will go—but you have got the East Indies in their stead, and sure diamonds and gold are preferable to sugar; and had not you

arranged for both Storer and Fergusson to begin their duties and salaries (*Corr. Geo. III* v. 256).

1. The *London Gazette* No. 12251, 15–18 Dec., contained Admiral Kempenfelt's dispatch of 14 Dec., which HW, with some licence, paraphrases below.

2. Several transports 'struck to us; the exact number I cannot acquaint you with (and am apprehensive that some which struck were not taken possession of, the evening coming on, and it blowing fresh with thick weather)' (Kempenfelt's dispatch).

3. 'At daylight the next day we saw them to leeward, upon which I formed the line; but perceiving their force so much superior to my squadron, I did not think it advisable to hazard an action' (ibid.).

4. The *Bretagne, Invincible, Majesteux,* and *Terrible* of 110 guns each, and the *Royal Louis* of 112 guns (ibid.).

5. The *London Gazette* 19 Jan. 1782 listed fifteen of the prizes which had arrived at various English ports (*London Chronicle* 19–22 Jan. 1782, li. 73).

rather our gracious Sovereign was Great Mogul, than master of two
or three islands almost as small as Mecklemburg? I wish you good-
night, Madam; I have done with politics, they make me sick!

To LADY OSSORY, Saturday 22 December 1781

Address: To the Countess of Ossory at Ampthill Park, Bedfordshire. *Postmark:*
22 DE.

Berkeley Square, Dec. 22, 1781.

YOUR inquiries about Miss Keppel are very kind indeed, Madam.
Till within these four or five days I was not at all alarmed about
her, and thought from her embonpoint that a cough would be of no
consequence—but Mrs Keppel is so terrified by the many fatal disorders that have carried off almost all the house of Albemarle,[1] that
she has frightened me too, and but this morning by the Duke's command I proposed to her to carry her daughter abroad, to which she
immediately consented, and I believe will, if upon farther consultation it is judged right.

In answer to your Ladyship's other question, in good truth my
serenity is not at all ruffled; nor would it be yet, were it ever likely to
be. It would be as ruffleable as a porcupine, had it set up its quill yet,
for hitherto I am only reading both Bryant[2] and Milles[3] by deputy.
I skimmed the former's second volume,[4] and dipped into one or two
pages of the latter, but though I have tough patience at a tedious
book, I doubt I shall never compass all the ancient lore in Mr Bryant's
first volume, and still less its *caput mortuum* in the Dean's. I let
Lady Ailesbury carry Bryant to Park Place before I had finished a
quarter of what I intend to read, and have lent t'other to a clergy-

1. 'Miss Keppel is so ill that the
Dowager Lady Albemarle says she is
going in the same way as all her daughters, but Mrs Keppel I suppose does not
see the dangers, for she goes everywhere
and does not appear in the least dejected.
She is a strange vulgar woman in manners
and expressions' (Coke, 'MS Journals' 25
Dec. 1781).

2. Jacob Bryant (1717–1804), *Observations upon the Poems of Thomas Rowley:
in Which the Authenticity of Those
Poems Is Ascertained*, 2 volumes (actually
two parts, paged consecutively); published

1 Dec. 1781 (CHATTERTON 236 n. 5). HW's
annotations in his copy are printed ibid.
351–7.

3. *Poems Supposed to Have Been Written at Bristol, in the Fifteenth Century.
By Thomas Rowley.* 'With a Commentary
in Which the Antiquity of Them Is Considered, and Defended. By Jeremiah
Milles, D.D., Dean of Exeter,' 1782, a
quarto volume published 8 Dec. 1781
(ibid. 237 n. 9). HW's annotations are
printed ibid. [331]–43.

4. That is, pp. 306–[598].

man.[5] Mr Conway says, Mr Bryant has very nearly convinced him, and he (Bryant) certainly has ingenuity enough to be a formidable adversary, whether one is in the right or in the wrong—yet where I have looked into him, I thought I saw weak places[6]—however, I am unalterably determined not to write a word more on the subject. I have declared I would not in my defence of myself;[7] and have determined besides not to write more on any subject, and least on this, because having unwillingly taken a part, I must be prejudiced. But in fact I look on this controversy, as I do on other problems of faith which can never be cleared up to the satisfaction of everybody; and I do not believe that the salvation of my understanding depends on crediting legends, when it requires so much learning to prove it probable that the supposed author ever existed; and if he did exist, that he was inspired; which Rowley must have been. The corporal evidence I had seen before, and very vague and inconclusive it is— but shall not I be doubly out of luck, Madam, if Rowley is pronounced Gospel? I believed in Ossian,[8] who is now tumbled into the Apocrypha; and I doubted of Rowley, who is now to rank with Moses and the prophets!—I doubt, I have very bad judgment.

As to Lord Maccartney, whom your Ladyship describes with the Arabian eloquence of Scheherezade, and with much more wit, when you make him ride on three elephants at once like Astley;[9] I own, since his paltry behaviour to me about Lady Mary Wortley's letters,[10]

5. Not identified.

6. All but two of HW's notes on Bryant are in the second volume; the notes indicate the 'weak places.' See also CHATTERTON 236 and n. 6.

7. 'Having thus fulfilled what was due to the public and to myself, I declare I will never trouble myself any farther about Chatterton and his writings; much less reply to any anonymous persons that shall choose to enter into the controversy. I do not think myself of consequence enough to take up the time of the public; and I have probably too few years to live, to throw away one of the remaining hours on so silly a dispute' (A Letter to the Editor of the Miscellanies of Thomas Chatterton, SH, 1779, p. 48; Works iv. 229–30). Although HW printed nothing further on the Chatterton controversy, he left some additional material for publication; see Works iv. 234–45.

8. In A Letter to the Editor, pp. 20–1,

HW had written: 'I might urge in excuse for my caution, that this was the second time that I had been selected, I know not why, for communicating revelations of the Muses to mankind. . . . In short, sir, I was one of the first intrusted with specimens of Ossian's fragments, which though I implicitly credited, I had not found universally received. I had not zeal enough to embark a second time in a similar crusado' (Works iv. 216). See also COLE ii. 206 and nn. 8–9; DALRYMPLE 64–5.

9. Philip Astley (ca 1742–1814), equestrian performer, whose Amphitheatre Riding House was at the foot of Westminster Bridge, in Lambeth (GM 1814, lxxxiv pt ii. 502; Wheatley, London Past and Present i. 76–7).

10. Macartney's mother-in-law, Lady Bute, had inherited most of the letters of her mother, Lady Mary Wortley Montagu, but not Lady Mary's letters to Lady Mar. Copies of them had been lent to HW

I take no part in his triumphs, nor care whether he rises in the east
or sinks again in the west. He was treacherous to me at the very
moment he had been greatly obliged to me.[11] I have not equal faith
in Lady Derby's triumphs[12]—yet, as I have been telling you, I had
rather believe anything than contest it; and were I to hear that Dr
Hunter was sent to Versailles to make a new treaty of Paris with the
Queen's accoucheur[13] (who you say, Madam, is made free of the
theatre) I would not dispute it—nay, I should rejoice; for considering
how many *miscarriages* we have had, it could not be so scandalous a
peace as the last.

To Lady Ossory, Tuesday 25 December 1781

Address: To the Countess of Ossory at Ampthill Park, Bedfordshire. *Postmark:*
25 DE. [?GC].

Christmas Day, 1781.

I ALWAYS answer immediately, Madam, if I have time, because,
as letters ought to be nothing but extempore conversations upon
paper, if the reply is not speedy, the curiosity that prompted the
question, may be passed, before the answer arrives. Nothing then
can be farther from my thoughts than[1] accompanying my niece[2]
abroad, if she should go, which is not determined, as her disorder
seems to be an inflammation on her breast and not a tendency to
consumption. For me, who only pendulate from Berkeley Square to
Strawberry, and think Ampthill as far as the Antipodes, and who was
near dashing my brains out on Saturday night by missing a step at

by Lord Ossory, who had obtained them
from Lady Mar's grandson. Lady Bute,
'hearing that Lord and Lady Ossory read
these letters to their acquaintance, was
much offended,' and got the copies from
them (Lady Louisa Stuart to the 2d M.
of Bute 16 March 1824, copied by the present Lord Bute's librarian for Mr Robert
Halsband). Perhaps Lady Bute had sent
her son-in-law to collect the letters from
HW. According to Lady Louisa's letter,
Lady Bute obtained the copied letters
'some time after Lady Frances Erskine's
death' (i.e., after 1776).

11. HW had supported Macartney's ap-

plication for the governorship of Madras
(*ante* 23 Aug., 26 Nov., 25 Dec. 1780).

12. At Vienna; cf. *ante* 4 Sept. 1781.

13. Charles-Thomas Vermond of the
Rue Beaurepaire, brother of the Queen's
reader and confessor, the Abbé Vermond
(*Almanach royal*, 1781, p. 592; NBG *sub*
Matthieu-Jacques de Vermond; Louis
Petit de Bachaumont *et al., Mémoires
secrets*, 'Londres,' 1777–89, xii. 197, xxv.
295–6, *sub* 18 Dec. 1778, 25 April 1784).

1. MS reads 'that.'

2. Anna Maria Keppel.

Mrs Keppel's door, if David had not catched me in his arms like a baby thrown out of window when a house is on fire, is it possible that I should think myself able to convoy anybody else? Oh! no, Madam; nor were I as brawny as Commodore Johnstone, would I set my foot on the Continent at present, when every country in Europe, except we ourselves, must be sensible of our shame!

For your Ladyship's other question, why I do not publish my letter on Chatterton?[3] What, because I don't know who in the newspaper wants to see it![4] My resolutions must be light as gossamer if such a breath could make them waver. I flattered myself that you knew me enough to be sure that when I have once made a resolution, it is not the easiest thing in the world to shake it: much less such an idle controversy as whether Rowley or Chatterton was Rowley; which is as indifferent to me, as who is churchwarden of St. Martin's parish—And now, can I care now what is thought about it? When I have outlived all the principles and maxims purchased for us *by the noble army of martyrs*, and when there is nothing so foolish and absurd that is not believed and adopted, what matters whether Ossian or Rowley or Mother Goose's Tales are canonized as classics? Thank my natal stars, I was born in a better age, and had much rather be, what I was, an author of a very inferior class twenty years ago, than the brightest luminary that is bound in morocco and gold and presented to the library in the Park[5] at this disastrous era—to be elbowed by Scotch metaphysics, and lied out of my senses by Scotch historians; and not get a wink of sleep on my shelf, though a forgotten author, from hearing Dr Hunter teach the youngest Prince[6] his Erse alphabet, or being stunned by a dialogue half Highland and half German, between the librarian[7] and Madame Schwellenberg!—Lady, now lettest thou thy servant depart in peace, for my eyes see no salvation!

3. *A Letter to the Editor of the Miscellanies of Thomas Chatterton*, SH, 1779. Although no trade edition was published, HW allowed the complete pamphlet to be reprinted serially in the *Gentleman's Magazine* in 1782. See HW to John Nichols [Sept. 1782].

4. In a 'Review of Writers on Rowley's Poems,' addressed to the printer of the *St James's Chronicle* from 'Lincoln's Inn, Nov. 28, 1781' and printed in that newspaper for 20–22 Dec. 1781, the anonymous author mentions Warton, Tyrwhitt, Croft,

Bryant (for whom the article is a puff), and 'the Honourable Horatio Walpole, who, as I am credibly informed, has both written and printed two long letters on this very subject; though for reasons best known to himself he has not yet vouchsafed to make them public.'

5. The Royal Library in the Queen's House (Buckingham Palace), St James's Park.

6. Alfred, then aged fifteen months, who died on 20 Aug. 1782.

7. Frederick Augusta Barnard (ca 1743–

To LADY OSSORY, Monday 7 January 1782

Address: To the Countess of Ossory at Ampthill Park, Bedfordshire. *Postmark:* 8 IA. [?GC].

Monday night, Jan. 7, 1782.

I WAS angry, I am angry; but, the gods know, not with you, Madam—nor with anybody else in particular. I am aggrieved by nobody. Mine is an honester and an unselfish indignation. I am hurt to see all prospects annihilated, that would have made one care about what is to survive one. Nothing will be left of England but the vestiges of its grandeur: and what shocks one already, is, that the vandalism that overspreads ruined empires has anteceded our last moments. Bad taste, spite, calumny, pert dulness, and blundering affectation of humour have taken place of everything agreeable. I would not quote such vulgar records as the newspapers, if they were not the oracles of the times, and what everybody reads and cites. Besides Macpherson's daily column of lies,[1] is there a paragraph that is not scandalous or malevolent? Even in those that are set apart as a tithe for truth, half of each is replete with error and ignorance. If a family has a misfortune of any kind, it is cast in every mould in ill-nature's shop, and the public is *diverted* in every way in which it can be misconstrued—I need instance but in the late melancholy adventure of Lord Camden's daughter.[2] Is not a country more savage than Hottentots where all

1830), K.C.H., 1828; said to have been son of Frederick, Prince of Wales; librarian to George III and IV; F.S.A., 1789; F.R.S., 1790 (Boswell, *Johnson* ii. 480; Nichols, *Lit. Illus.* iv. 699; W. A. Shaw, *The Knights of England*, 1906, i. 456; GM 1830, c pt i. 571; Edward Edwards, *Lives of the Founders of the British Museum*, 1870, pp. 468–74). Since Barnard would hardly speak a Highland dialect, HW probably refers to Barnard's assistant, William Graham, 'Clerk in the Library' 1773–91 (*Royal Kalendar*).

———

1. That is, paragraphs favouring the ministry, written by or under the direction of Macpherson and sent by him to the newspapers. See *ante* 12 Feb. 1780; MASON i. 431 n. 8.

2. Frances Pratt (ca 1751–1833), Lord Camden's eldest dau., m. (1775) Robert Stewart, cr. (1789) Bn Londonderry, (1795) Vct Castlereagh, (1796) E. and (1816) M. of Londonderry. According to the *London Courant* 25 Dec. 1781, on 21 Dec., at her father's seat at Chislehurst in Kent she was seized by 'two strange men' who 'carried her off through fields and by-ways, woods, and other unfrequented places, until her fright deprived her of her senses and her recollection. . . . In the morning, however . . . recovering herself from her delirium, [she] found herself in a wood, robbed of her purse, her watch . . . and with the utmost difficulty found her way home in a very deplorable condition.' This account appeared also in the *Public Advertiser* 26

private distresses are served up the next morning for the breakfast and entertainment of the public?[2a] When you have waded through the scandal of the day, the next repast is a long dissertation on two contending pantomimes,[3] while a mixture of losses of ships and armies and islands is a glaring mark of the insensible stupidity of the age, which is less occupied by national disgrace and calamity, than by slander that used to be confined to old maids, and follies only fit for children. A week's newspapers preserved to the end of the next century will explain why we are fallen so low. They would supply Voltaire with a chapter on *les mœurs du temps*. I think I have justified myself and my contempt for the times I live in, Madam, and why I am not ambitious of having it remembered that I belonged to them.

I cannot answer your Ladyship's question about Lord Essex's[4] trial; indeed I do not remember the circumstance.

Miss Keppel is much better. Sir Richard Jebbe is confident of its being a bilious case.

I have been this evening at Miss Monckton's[5] to see Mademoiselle Theodore[6] dance a minuet with young Edgcumbe;[7] and tomorrow I

Dec. and, without her name ('a young lady'), in the *London Chronicle* 22–25 Dec., l. 608. On 27 Dec. 1781 Lady Mary Coke talked with the Duchess of Bedford about this 'extraordinary story' and wrote that 'some people recollecting the unhappy disorder in her mother's family are of opinion that some part may have been imaginary, but there is no doubt that she was absent the whole night' ('MS Journals').

2a. See MORE 267 for HW's similar comment in 1788.

3. *The Choice of Harlequin; or, The Indian Chief* had been first performed at Covent Garden 26 Dec. 1781 (printed, 1782), and *Lun's Ghost; or, The New Year's Gift* at Drury Lane 3 Jan. 1782 (Allardyce Nicoll, *A History of Late Eighteenth-Century Drama 1750–1800*, Cambridge, 1927, pp. 322, where the first performance of *The Choice of Harlequin* is misdated, and 334; *London Chronicle* 25 Dec. 1781 – 8 Jan. 1782, *passim*).

4. Robert Devereux (1566–1601), 2d E. of Essex, 1576; Queen Elizabeth's favourite, tried for high treason 19 Feb. 1601

and beheaded on Tower Hill 25 Feb. 1601.

5. Hon. Mary Monckton (1748–1840), dau. of John, 1st Vct Galway, m. (1786) as 2d wife, Edmund Boyle, 7th E. of Corke, 1764; 'well known for her literary parties in imitation of those of Mrs Montagu and Mrs Vesey' (Toynbee xii. 143 n. 2).

6. —— Crépé (d. 1798), known as Mlle Théodore, m. (1783) Jean Bercher, called Dauberval; a member of Noverre's ballet troupe, formerly of the Opéra at Paris (when she lived in the Rue Poissonnière), who came to London with Noverre and others in 1781 (D. Lynham, *Chevalier Noverre*, 1950, pp. 101–4, 187–8, and *passim*; *Spectacles de Paris*, 1779, xxviii. 16; *Enciclopedia dello spettacolo*, Rome, 1954–, iv. 206).

7. Only son of HW's friends, Lord and Lady Mount Edgcumbe: Richard Edgcumbe (1764–1839), styled Vct Valletort 1789–95, 2d E. of Mount Edgcumbe, 1795; author of *Musical Reminiscences of an Old Amateur, Chiefly Respecting the Italian Opera in England*, 1827; 4th edn, 1834.

shall go to the opera[8] for the first time this year to see her and hear the Allegranti[9]—as Queen Elizabeth's reign is over, and there is no likelihood of there being any trials. I do not believe that even her ghost condescended to peep at the ball that was given at Hatfield[10] last Thursday to the county of Hertford.

Pray do not forget Lord Chandos[11] at Woburn.[12] Mine is in black profusely laced with silver, a white waistcoat much slashed, and a round black hat with a rich jewel.[13]

Tuesday.

My project of going to the opera is addled. I have got the rheumatism in my left arm, and cannot put on my coat. It is not the gout; I know his tooth too well to mistake his bite.

---

8. Anfossi's *I Viaggiatori felici*, advertised in the *Public Advertiser*, 8 Jan.

9. Teresa Maddalena Allegranti (b. ca 1754, living 1801), Italian soprano who first appeared at Venice in 1770 and in London 11 Dec. 1781 in Anfossi's *Viaggiatori felici*. She was in London 1781–3. For the success of her first season and for a description of her voice, see Hermann Mendel, *Musicalisches Conversations-Lexicon*, 1870–9; Mason ii. 174; HW to Mann 7 Feb. 1782; Edgcumbe, op. cit. 3d edn, 1828, pp. 26–7. Her portrait by Cosway was engraved by Bartolozzi and published 4 June 1783. She is said to have married ca 1798 'an Englishman called Harrison and retired to Ireland, where she died' (Sir George Grove, *Dictionary of Music*, 5th edn, ed. Blom, 1954).

10. 'The Earl of Salisbury gave a most superb supper and ball a few days ago at his seat at Hatfield. There were five hundred guests present, invited from all parts of the country, and among them the first nobility and gentry. Several private gentlemen officiated for their noble host as masters of the ceremonies, ushers, and stewards, and in their several capacities conducted the departments assigned to them with the utmost regularity and elegance' (*London Chronicle* 5–8 Jan., li. 26). In Queen Elizabeth's time Hatfield was in the possession of the Crown and

had been her residence before her accession to the throne, but James I in 1607 exchanged Hatfield for Theobalds, the seat of the first Earl of Salisbury. Lord Salisbury then began the building of Hatfield House, but he died before it was completed.

11. Giles Brydges (b. 1547 or 1548, d. 1594), 3d Bn Chandos, 1573; M.P.; entertained Queen Elizabeth at Sudeley Castle, 1592.

12. A portrait of him, by Hieronymus Custodis of Antwerp, is described by HW in *Notes to the Portraits at Woburn Abbey*, 'By H.W. 1791,' 1800, p. 12, No. 78, as 'Giles, Lord Chandos, *ætat*. 43.' Cf. George Scharf, *A Descriptive and Historical Catalogue of the Collection of Pictures at Woburn Abbey*, 1877, pp. 30–1; *A Descriptive Catalogue of the Portraits . . . at Woburn Abbey*, 1834, p. 14; Thieme-Becker.

13. HW purchased his portrait, also by Custodis, 40½ by 28 inches, at the Sheldon sale (*ante* 12 Sept. 1781) and later gave it to Lord Harcourt, in whose family it remained until sold by auction by Christie, Manson & Woods, Ltd., on 11 June 1948, Lot 101, for £42 to Mr M. R. Schweitzer of New York City, in whose possession it remained in May, 1952. The portrait is mentioned in Scharf, op. cit. 31.

To Lady Ossory, Saturday 12 January 1782

In Kirgate's hand.
Address: To the Countess of Ossory at Ampthill Park, Bedfordshire. *Postmark:*
12 I[A]. GC.

Berkeley Square, Jan. 12, 1782.

YOUR Ladyship will excuse my employing Kirgate, as I am not able to write myself. One would have thought that I had been too well acquainted with the gout's voice to mistake his accent for a stranger's; but as the pain began on the inside of my elbow, I flattered myself that it was only rheumatic. Next morning I was cured of my mistake, and at present my poor lean hand is colossal. I have had much less pain than fever, but three restless nights have convinced me so much of my extreme weakness, that should the gout take a fancy, as it did some years ago,[1] of making the grand tour of my person, I should little expect to get through it; indeed I cannot now attempt even to dictate an answer to above one or two paragraphs in your Ladyship's letter: much less is my head clear enough to tell you the whole strange story of Mrs Steuart. The family themselves neither are nor can ever be certain in their belief; but upon the whole it seems to me to have been a sudden fit of lunacy with which she had been afflicted.

Captain Waldegrave was so very obliging and good-natured as to call on me this morning, and I was happy to see him look so much better than I expected after all his vexations, disappointments[2] and illness: he talked of being at Ampthill I think on Monday next.

Doctor Dee's[3] black stone[4] was named in the catalogue of the collec-

1. In December, 1774; see HW to Mann 9 Jan. 1775.
2. The nature of these is not clear. He had been in command of *La Prudente,* a fifth-rate frigate of 36 guns, but later this year was transferred to the *Phaeton,* a new ship of 38 guns (*London Chronicle* 22–25 June, li. 605; *Royal Kalendar,* 1783, p. 144).
3. John Dee (1527–1608), mathematician and astrologer, held in high esteem by Queen Elizabeth.

4. In the Great North Bedchamber at SH: 'A speculum of kennel [cannel] coal . . . used to deceive the mob . . . It was in the collection of the Mordaunts, Earls of Peterborough, in whose catalogue it is called, *the black stone into which Dr Dee used to call his spirits* . . .' ('Des of SH,' *Works* ii. 501). It is called an obsidian in *Proceedings of the Society of Antiquaries of London,* 1907, 2d ser. xxi. 383.

tion of the Earls of Peterborough,[5] whence it went to Lady Betty Germain,[6] she gave it[7] to the last Duke of Argyle,[8] and his son Lord Frederic to me, H. W.[9]

To Lady Ossory, Saturday 19 January 1782

Address: To the Countess of Ossory at Ampthill Park, Bedfordshire. *Postmark:* 19 IA.

Berkeley Square, Jan. 19, 1782.

I HAD seen in the papers the epigram your Ladyship has sent me today, and liked it so much that I cut it out.[1] Like well I did too the Ampthillian lines[2]—It was the subject[2a] alone that I disapproved in them; and though you say I had no right to take exception, as there was no compliment to my roses and lilies,[3] I do maintain that my complexion is likely to last as long as my fame, and therefore if I should have been in the right to be displeased at a compliment to the more durable of the two, I might justly protest against one to the shorter-lived of the twain. Nay, as much as your Ladyship may disparage my looks (which I believe you did out of revenge), I have no doubt but the outside of my head will survive the inside; and therefore as I may last till I am a fine man of my age, I beg you will let me enjoy what I

5. HW to Mann 22 March 1771: 'You must know that last winter, being asked by Lord Vere to assist in settling Lady Betty Germaine's auction, I found in an old catalogue of her collection this article, *The Black Stone into which Dr Dee used to call his spirits.'*

6. Her husband, Sir John Germain, left to her the property he had inherited from his first wife, Lady Mary Mordaunt, only surviving child of Henry, 2d E. of Peterborough.

7. Or she sold part of the collection and the Duke of Argyll purchased the stone at auction (HW to Mann 22 March 1771).

8. John Campbell (ca 1693–1770), 4th D. of Argyll, 1761; army officer; Lt.-Col., 1712; Gen., 1765; M.P.

9. In the winter of 1770–1 (HW to Mann 22 March 1771). It now (1963) belongs to Sir Osbert Sitwell, Bt.

1. The copy Lady Ossory sent is missing. The epigram may be one of the following: 1. 'Epigram on Matrimony,' six lines; 2. 'Epigram on the Serpents carved on each side of the stair of Physicians Hall, Edinburgh,' both newspaper cuttings pasted in HW's 'Book of Materials' 1771, pp. 74–5, with material of approximately this date; 3. 'Epigrammatick,' twenty-four lines, pasted on the front end-paper of a volume of HW's 'Theatre of George 3' containing plays of 1781–2.

2. Apparently (see below) verses by Lady Ossory; missing.

2a. HW himself.

3. His complexion: 'Lilies and roses will quickly appear'; 'Roses and lilies her cheeks disclose' (John Gay, *Beggar's Opera,* I. iv. Air III; II. iii. Air XXI; the second reference kindly communicated by Mr Ketton-Cremer).

can, instead of nursing me with visions of what I shall never attain.

It is my belief, though still a problem, that Lord George Germaine has resigned;[4] which is signing his confession at least that America is lost. The King has had a violent bleeding at (his own) nose, which returned yesterday at the Drawing-Room.[5] Scarce any great ladies, except those immediately attached to the Court, were at the Birthday,[6] in resentment for not having been asked to the Queen's balls last year. Upon my word I believe everybody will have spirit at last in England, except the two Houses of Parliament.

So Lord Ossory comes on Monday[7]—and your Ladyship—very early *next* winter!

To Lady Ossory, Saturday 9 February 1782

Address: To the Countess of Ossory at Ampthill Park, Bedfordshire. *Postmark:* 9 FE.

Berkeley Square, Feb. 9, 1782.

LORD Ossory says that your Ladyship complains of my not writing; but he could have told you that I have scarce an inch of finger left. One of those with which I am now writing, is but recovering of a new explosion of chalk. I believe they look in little like the channels of lava from Vesuvius. Indeed when our Lord is in town, you know it is my compact not to write. He lives at Brooks's, where politics are sown, and in the House of Commons where they come up. I go scarce anywhere, see few people, and know nothing of the new generations that have been hatched since I went to roost. When I do write, if I had not a sovereign command over my pen, I should talk of nothing but my own caducity, which, as if one's country was a something of which one is part, keeps pace with the body politic, and

4. Lord George remained secretary of state for the Colonies until 11 Feb. 1782, when he was created Vct Sackville and was succeeded by Welbore Ellis.

5. On 12 Jan. the King had caught cold at a review, and the levee for 16 Jan. was cancelled. On 17 Jan. he 'having been extremely indisposed . . . was twice let blood,' and on 18 Jan. 'he was seized with a bleeding at the nose in the Drawing-Room, which obliged him to retire very

soon after three o'clock, before half the customary ceremony of the day [the Queen's birthday] was gone through.' He 'did not appear in the Ball Room in the evening' (*London Chronicle* 15–19 Jan., li. 64, 69).

6. For a partial list of those present, see ibid. li. 69.

7. When the House of Commons met, following its adjournment on 20 Dec. 1781 for the holidays.

loses a joint or a faculty every month. As I have not recovered the use of my left hand, so Great Britain is losing her right one, Lord George Germaine—yet I suppose, like Widdrington[1] in 'Chevy Chace,' she will continue fighting on upon her stumps[2] Lords Stormont and Hilsborough[3]—nay, what may she not recover with the semblance of a new secretary, who has all the activity of an Aulic councillor, the circumstantial minuteness of a churchwarden, and the vigour of another Methusalem—even the respectable Ellis![4] What enterprises will be set on foot by this dashing old Parr,[5] and his cotemporary my Lord President Jenkins![6]—Well! I shall expect to be sent for, since the empire is to be recovered by antediluvians.

Our Lord to be sure has told you, Madam, how in one day one culprit[7] was whitewashed in one House,[8] and another[9] blackened in the other.[10] I do not approve the treatment of the latter—the courtiers are ready enough to vilify him now he is fallen—but the Opposition never hit on a right scent—like mongrels they only worry hunted game. If they were true bull-dogs, they would fasten on that bloody caitiff the Lord Advocate,[11] who proposed *en passant* to starve

1. 'Rog. de Widrington,' as conjecturally identified in Thomas Percy, *Reliques of Ancient English Poetry*, 1765, iii. 333–4; 2d edn, 1767, i. 33. HW had both editions (Hazen, *Cat. of HW's Lib.* 2919, 3455).

2. 'For when his leggs were smitten off,
   He fought upon his stumpes'
(Percy, op. cit., 1765, i. 244, the later version of 'Chevy Chase').

3. Secretaries of state for the North and the South, respectively. In the *London Chronicle* 2–5 Feb., li. 128, appeared the rumour that Germain 'has resigned' and that 'American affairs will in future be transacted by' Hillsborough.

4. Welbore Ellis, secretary of state for America and the Colonies from 11 Feb. to 27 March.

5. Thomas Parr (d. 1635), supposedly born in 1483.

6. Earl Bathurst, lord president of the Council 1779–March 1782, was 67; Ellis, 68. Henry Jenkins (d. 1670), called the 'modern Methusaleh,' asserted that he had been born in 1501.

7. Lord Sandwich.

8. In the House of Commons, Fox, 'in a motion on the abuses of the Navy, was

not less personal to Lord Sandwich, whom, of late, he had pursued with much violence. I told him of it, and of his wasting his fire on a secondary character, whom all the rest were willing to sacrifice. I advised him to make his push at Lord North, as, if the keystone could be removed, the whole edifice would fall. He owned I was in the right, and he took my advice. The motion against the Admiralty was rejected by 288 [205] to 183' (*Last Journals* ii. 399, *sub* 8 Feb., HW's mistake for 7 Feb.). For details, see the *London Chronicle* 7–9 Feb., li. 138–141; I. R. Christie, *The End of North's Ministry, 1780–1782*, 1958, pp. 299–313.

9. Lord George Germain.

10. On 7 Feb. by Lord Carmarthen, who held 'that any person labouring under a heavy censure of a court martial should [not] be recommended to the Crown to be raised to the dignity of the peerage. . . . The motion was in every light odious, and tended to destroy the best prerogative of the Crown, that of pardon' (*Last Journals* ii. 398–9). See also the *London Chronicle* 7–9 Feb., li. 137–8; Cobbett, *Parl. Hist.* xxii. 999–1022.

11. Henry Dundas (1742–1811), cr.

five thousand fishermen and their families as a preliminary,[12] and has now got £6000 a year for condemning the American war,[13] which I suppose he will now promote again as advantageous to his new post[14] —and then we fast to beg a blessing on such wars and such war-makers![15] When Lord North told Lord George Germaine that he must go out, he replied shrewdly, 'And pray, my Lord, why are you to stay?'[16]—undoubtedly for his modesty and philosophy. When one of the subscribers to his new loan[17] asked him, if we were near peace, he replied, 'A year nearer than we were, and a year nearer to destruction.' I hope our historians Sir John Dalrymple and Macpherson will parallel[18] this indifference with that of the Roman magistrates[19] who expected the Gauls in their curule chairs in the Forum.[20] Our dictator would be less sad. Cannot you figure him, Madam, in the midst of St James's market,[21] not in a curule, but a very easy chair, with a circle

(1802) Vct Melville; lord advocate of Scotland 1775–83. He had forced the resignation of Germain, being 'satisfied with *one human sacrifice,*' as Jenkinson wrote the King 3 Feb. 1782; that is, Germain and not Sandwich also (*Corr. Geo. III* v. 359; Christie, op. cit. 283–304; Mason ii. 176–7 and nn. 5–11).

12. In his speech in the House of Commons 6 March 1775; hence his nickname of 'Starvation' Dundas. See Mason ii. 135 n. 11.

13. That is, by forcing the retirement of Germain, who had publicly said that he would refuse to recognize the independence of the colonies.

14. The rumour was that Dundas would succeed Ellis as treasurer of the Navy (*London Chronicle* 7–9 Feb., li. 141–2). Although Dundas was offered the post, the nominal salary for which was £2000 but in time of war was considerably greater, he refused it because his demand of life tenure as keeper of the Signet of Scotland rather than tenure at the King's pleasure (as he had held the appointment since 1779) was not met. On the formation of Shelburne's ministry in July 1782 the demands were met, and Dundas became treasurer of the Navy, a post he held until April 1783 and again from Dec. 1783 to 1800. See Mason ii. 177–8, 258. Isaac Barré succeeded Ellis.

15. See *A Form of Prayer to Be Used in All Churches and Chapels . . . upon*

Friday the Eighth Day of February, Being the Day Appointed by Proclamation [9 Jan. 1782] *for a General Fast . . .* [with prayers]: *For . . . Blessing and Assistance on the Arms of His Majesty by Sea and Land.* In Scotland the fast was observed on 7 Feb. (*London Chronicle* 8–10 Jan., li. 40).

16. A variant of this anecdote is in *Last Journals* ii. 396, *sub* Jan. 1782.

17. North's request for a new loan of £13,500,000 was approved by the House of Commons, in a Committee of Ways and Means, on 25 Feb. The loan of 1781 had been open to a large number of individuals; that of 1782 was open to only a few, although Lord North reported on 25 Feb. that 2469 people had offered to subscribe a total of £73,290,000 (Cobbett, *Parl. Hist.* xxii. 1052–64; Mason ii. 192 and n. 6).

18. In the manner of Plutarch.

19. 'Consuls' in HW to Mann 10 March 1755, Mann iv. 469.

20. The Romans who 'had held curule magistracies . . . put on the stately robes . . . and, thus habited, seated themselves on ivory chairs in the middle of their houses,' which were in the Forum (Livy V. xli. 2–8).

21. HW had used the comparison with St James's Market in his letter to Mann, loc. cit. He imagines the Roman magistrates as being outdoors, not in their houses.

of butchers round him, splitting their sides with laughing at his jokes, and telling them it was true he had undone them, but should continue a good customer still, whoever should be their or his master; it was all one to Punch.

To Lady Ossory, Saturday 23 February 1782

Address: To the Countess of Ossory at Ampthill Park, Bedfordshire. *Postmark:* 23 FE.

Feb. 23, 1782.

I NEVER remonstrate, Madam, against the behests of Dame Prudence, though a lady I never got acquainted with till near my grand climacteric. I approve of your giving no handle to suspicions; but is it necessary to banish yourself? must you be able to prove an alibi? and may not your staying in the country be surmised as calculated for seeing your son more secretly? It avails nothing to cure a jealous mind of one object of distrust—you do not cure it of jealousy. I shall certainly not open my lips on one of your Ladyship's motives and measures—but as to your fixing a time for coming, and though Lord O. says it will be next week, I have little faith; nor shall expect you before the Greek Calends,[1] a certain time of a month in which the Athenian ladies, who never kept their words, used to come to town.

This was all I had to say, for our Lord will write to you himself no doubt from the field of battle. Perhaps I ought to congratulate you on his being almost, almost victorious; at least it was a drawn battle, when the enemy had a majority but of one.[2] I confess I expected the Opposition would have lost ground, as I thought Lord Sandwich more unpopular than the War,[3] and that the deserters, as

1. That is, never, since the Greeks used no calends in their reckoning of time.

2. On 22 Feb. Conway in the House of Commons moved an 'address . . . earnestly imploring . . . that the war on the continent of North America may no longer be pursued for the impracticable purpose of reducing the inhabitants of that country to obedience by force'; the motion was rejected 194 to 193 (*Journals of the House of Commons* xxxviii. 814;

Cobbett, *Parl. Hist.* xxii. 1028–48; I. R. Christie, *The End of North's Ministry 1780–1782*, 1958, pp. 319–28).

3. On 20 Feb. Fox had 'moved an inquiry into Lord Sandwich's mismanagement of the Navy during 1781. . . . The motion was rejected by a majority of 19 [236 to 217]—a small one, but prognosticating the downfall of the ministry' (*Last Journals* ii. 403–4; Cobbett, op. cit. 934–46; Christie, op. cit. 313–19, 378–82).

usual of late, would make their peace by returning to their colours[4]—but it seems I little understand how interest operates on men. It appears that it acts again as it used to do formerly, and conducts its mercenaries to the increasing side—Still it is my opinion, though I do not boast of my penetration, that the present face of affairs will produce nothing but new confusion. Though the Court should take panic, or be actually beaten, it will recover its ground. The Opposition will not agree, and one little faction or other, will grow, or pretend to grow, more enraged at its competitors, than at the enemy, and will accept the places against their late friends, which they cannot obtain by the acquiescence of those friends.

This, I imagine, will be the case, if it comes to a treaty—but should an alteration and a new Administration take place, what can they do, ruined as the country is?—no—I shall tremble for them, not rejoice—especially as their old antagonists turned into an Opposition, will be very different opponents, and not conscientious and moderate as they have been—I foresee much more that I will not express—nor will I say more, when it would only be conjecturing—I have no opinion of my own sagacity—and what signifies my guessing what is to happen, when I shall probably see so little of the crowd of events that are coming on?—I shall leave my country afloat, struggling for existence, and then in quest of a new constitution, for I do not see a shadow of probability of the old being restored. To that my attachment was, and I care little indeed about any other that will not resemble it. Perhaps this is not the language of a man rejoicing in the success of his friends—but *places* for them was never what I was solicitous about—On one point I do heartily rejoice—the pursuit of the American war must stop[5]—aye, and for a while at least despotism must pause—and though it may be England's fate at last, it will not be America's!

I beg your Ladyship's pardon for talking so much politics—no, I do not—I could talk to no man more capable of understanding them—and it would be impertinent to treat *you* with trifles at such a moment, which made me write, though Lord O. is in town—but I have

4. For the divisions of 20 and 22 Feb., see ibid. 376–83, 389–405.

5. Conway's motion on 27 Feb. 'that the further prosecution of offensive war on the continent of North America for the purpose of reducing the revolted colonies to obedience by force will be . . . fatal to the interests both of Great Britain and America' was carried 234 to 215 (*Journals of the House of Commons* xxxviii. 861; *Last Journals* ii. 410–11).

not anticipated what he will tell you. He is too young not to regard triumph as a good—it is the property of sedentary age to balance the different aspects of prospect.

To Lady Ossory, Thursday 28 February 1782

Printed from MS now wsl; sold at Sotheby's 30 July 1940 ('Other Properties'), lot 570, to Maggs, who sold it to wsl.

In Toynbee xii. 187–8, the letter is dated 5 March 1782, the day after 'a resolution proposed by Conway condemning the prosecution of the American war was allowed by the government to pass without a division.' If Lady Ossory arrived in London 'next week' after the preceding letter of 23 Feb., the date of 28 Feb. for this letter is preferable, Conway's victory of 27 Feb. being even more significant than his victory of the following week.

Address: To Lady Ossory.

[Berkeley Square, 28 Feb. 1782].

I WAS very ill, Madam, after I left your Ladyship, and I am well again, without having done anything to occasion either. I only mention this to show you that my disorders are of no consequence, nor worth minding: and therefore, good as you are, I do beg of you to take no notice of them, for it makes me appear very ridiculous to myself, as I can give no account of what is the matter with me. It will indeed oblige me seriously, if you will never say anything about it, for if it is fancy, I do not desire to be indulged in it.

I wish your Ladyship joy on last night's victory,[1] General Conway has just been here in great spirits and told me of it.

1. Conway's motion of 27 Feb. that 'reducing the revolted colonies to obedience by force will be the means of weakening the efforts of this country against her European enemies' was debated until between one and two o'clock of the following morning, and a motion to adjourn was defeated by 234 to 215. A resolution for an address to George III was passed the same morning (*Journals of the House of Commons* xxxviii. 861; *Last Journals* ii. 410–11). HW calls this 'a decisive blow' to the administration, whereas he barely mentions (ii. 414) the resolution moved by Conway on 4 March declaring that 'this House will consider as enemies to his Majesty and this country all who shall endeavour to frustrate his Majesty's paternal care . . . by advising . . . the further prosecution of offensive war on the continent of North America'; the resolution was passed without a division (*Journals of the House of Commons* xxxviii. 868; Cobbett, *Parl. Hist.* xxii. 1064–1101).

From Lady Ossory, ca Thursday 21 March 1782

Printed for the first time from MS now WSL; purchased from Mrs Richard Bentley, 1937.

This note, apparently the only one from Lady Ossory that has survived, was no doubt removed from the rest of her letters by HW because of his memoranda for his *Last Journals* on the third side:

March 21.[1]

Ld North's letter.[2] Late K. yielded & was glorious.[3]

Ld H.[4] to Mr C.[5] K. spoke of Ch. F.[6]

Chanc[ellor][7] saying K. would not part with army impeachable.[8]

Forth[9] to France to treat.[10] Ld Mansfield.[11]

That Dss insisted on going to Court.[12]

1. Most of these notes were intended for *Last Journals,* but HW used few of them. Under 20 March HW reports North's announcement concerning the fall of his ministry and then goes into a general discussion of the problems of forming the new ministry. 'In short, not to dwell on days and hours, the King consented to take Lord Rockingham, and . . . 27*th,* Lord Rockingham was admitted to an audience of the King, and accepted the administration' (ii. 422–5).

2. North to the King [18 March 1782], in *Corr. Geo. III* v. 394–7. 'He wrote a letter, that was commended, to the King to take his leave' (*Last Journals* ii. 422).

3. North, attempting to persuade the King to permit him to resign, wrote: 'Your royal predecessors (particularly King William the Third and his late Majesty) were obliged to yield to it ['the deliberate resolution of the House of Commons'] much against their wish in more instances than one. . . . Your Majesty . . . can lose no honour if you yield at length, as some of the most renowned and most glorious of your predecessors have done, to the opinion and wishes of the House of Commons' (*Corr. Geo. III* v. 395).

4. Probably Hertford.

5. Conway?

6. Charles Fox. The Duke of Richmond and Fox 'were the two he [the King] had most wished to exclude' from the new ministry (*Last Journals* ii. 426).

7. Thurlow.

8. Lord Amherst, commander-in-chief, was succeeded by Conway.

9. Nathaniel Parker Forth (1744–after 1792), a friend of the Duc de Chartres (Amédée Britsch, *Lettres de L.-P.-J. d'Orléans à . . . Forth,* 1926, pp. x–xv).

10. A reference to the attempt in the last days of the North ministry to 'patch up a peace with America [and France], without the intervention of the future ministers' (*Last Journals* ii. 422; *Corr. Geo. III* v. 431–3, 442–3). Forth was ordered to Paris on a secret mission in Feb. 1782, and conferred with Vergennes on 12 March, without effective result (Britsch, op. cit. 8; idem, *La Jeunesse de Philippe-Égalité,* 1926, p. 399).

11. He had been in France in 1774, perhaps on a secret mission (*Last Journals* i. 373).

12. The Duke of Gloucester was considered as commander-in-chief of the army, but HW was 'persuaded . . . that he would not have accepted, unless the King would have received the Duchess' (ibid. ii. 434). 'The Duke of Gloucester won't be commander-in-chief for two reasons; one is, that the Duchess can [not] be admitted at Court; and the second is that Lord Rock[ingham] will not permit it' (Selwyn to Carlisle 23 March, *Carlisle MSS* 604).

K. would not send for Rock[ingham] on Thursday 21 and Frid. 22, though had only to next Mond. when House to meet again, to form an administr[ation][13] and though it was known that Russia and Holland on point of making alliance with America,[14] and though on 21st news that all grand juries in Ireland had joined the volunteers, and declared for independence[15] and so did Conolly[16] in Parl[iament].[17]

Jenyns's book.[18]

Bate & Mcpherson.[19] Macph[erson]'s 2 advertisements.[20]

March about 21. Ld Loughborough who had been lying by, had now, probably by threats of joining Oppos[ition] got grant of £1000 a year with a salary from time had been Chief Justice, but Ld Chanc[ellor] would not sign it.[21]

Address: To the Honble Mr Walpole.

[ca 21 March 1782]

I AM sorry my note arrived too late for the purpose proposed of giving you the *first* intelligence[22]—I will hope the best, but on all occasions a certain degree of caution is useful (except with tried friends)—I hope you heard I called on Tuesday m[orning], but on hearing *one* Mr Stonhewer was with you went away; thinking all *three* would feel awkward if he stayed, and that my company would not make amends for driving Mr S. away.[23]

13. Negotiations with Rockingham were carried on by Thurlow and Shelburne, and the King did not see him until noon on 27 March, the day the new ministry took office (*Last Journals* ii. 423–5; *Corr. Geo. III* v. 412–13, 418–21).

14. 'Hague, March 9. Their High Mightinesses have agreed to enter upon a negotiation for peace with the ministers from Russia' (*London Chronicle* 19–21 March, li. 274).

15. HW noted in *Last Journals* ii, 418, *sub* 10 March: 'The Court had had secret intelligence that the volunteers [in Ireland] were already negotiating with France. To America they were so propense that they had made illuminations on the success of General Conway's motion to address the King for peace.'

16. Thomas Conolly (?1737–1803), politician and landowner; M.P. Malmesbury 1759–68, Chichester 1768–80, Londonderry (Irish House of Commons) 1761–1800; married to Lady Louisa Lennox, sister of the D. of Richmond.

17. In the debate on 12 March in the Irish House of Commons, over the bill 'to enact English statutes, where the

kingdom of Ireland and Great Britain enjoyed equal benefits and equal rights,' Conolly 'declared he had for a series of years resisted a declaration of rights, but he now acknowledged himself of the same sentiments with the gentleman who had spoke last'—this was Ogle, who maintained that 'a declaration of rights . . . must . . . in the end be obtained' (*London Courant* 21 March).

18. *Disquisitions on Several Subjects,* 1782, published anonymously; discussed in Mason ii. 198–9, 203, 225, 229, 244.

19. Both writers for the North ministry; for North's arrangements with them, see *Corr. Geo. III* v. 414, 471.

20. Not found.

21. 'It is said that a patent is prepared but not yet sealed (on account of the present unsettled state of the ministry) which gives Lord Loughborough £1000 per annum additional salary' (*London Chronicle* 14–16 March, li. 260). He had been lord chief justice of the Common Pleas since June 1780.

22. Of the fall of North's ministry; see HW's reply 21 March.

23. Lady Ossory's avoiding Stonhewer

I am sorry my Note
arrived too late
for the purposes proposed
of giving you the first
Intelligence — I will hope
the best, but on all occasions
a certain degree of caution
is useful (except with
tryed friends) — I hope
you heard I called on Tuesday m[orning] but on
hearing one Mr Stonhewer
was with you went away;
thinking all three would feel

ANNE, COUNTESS OF UPPER OSSORY, TO WALPOLE
CA 21 MARCH 1782

To Lady Ossory, Thursday 21 March 1782

Address: To the Countess of Ossory.

March 21, 1782.

IT was most obliging, Madam, to send me the news,[1] though I happened to be gone to the Princess.[2] I did not indeed expect to live to see the administration demolished—I hope I shall not be mistaken in thinking the moment not ripe for their fall. Their having laid down their arms, before a capitulation made, is a very favourable circumstance; and if their successors are wise, may be turned to good account, if, instead of paying court for pardon, they take care to be above wanting it. If they imitate the last ministers, they will make way for them again, and will fall less pitied, and still less deserving pity.

To Lady Ossory, Thursday 13 June 1782

Address: To the Countess of Ossory at Ampthill Park, Bedfordshire. *Postmark:* 13 IV. GC.

Berkeley Square, June 13, 1782.

THOUGH it was being ungrateful for your kind note, Madam, I could not bring myself to write when I had nothing to tell you but about myself. What can be said of a lame old creature but that he is still alive?[1] I have been for two days[2] at Strawberry to sleep in the air, which was literally all I could do, for it rained every minute, and unless I had had a pair of Mrs Noah's clogs, I could not have set my foot out of the ark. I found every mortal at Twickenham as ill as they

is explained by his connection with the Duke of Grafton, who had asked Stonhewer on 30 June 1768 to inform Lady Ossory, then Duchess of Grafton, that the Duke had sufficient evidence of her adultery to entitle him to a divorce (*Trial* 136–7).

1. On 20 March Lord North, to avoid a motion for the removal of the ministers,

announced that the administration was dissolved (Cobbett, *Parl. Hist.* xxii. 1214–32).
2. Princess Amelia.

1. 'Mr Walpole has just now been with me and seems quite recovered' (Coke, 'MS Journals' 16 June 1782).
2. 10–12 June (HW to Mann 10 June 1782).

have been in town.[3] Both Lady Di's daughters[4] were in bed, Lady Browne very bad, and Mrs Clive, I think, in a still worse way. Then it was so cold, I had no inclination to stay. Of my spring delights, lilacs, apple-trees in bloom, and nightingales, the two last are over, and the first going. My orange trees still keep their beds; and for roses, there was not even a white one on the 10th of June[5] (except in the conservatory at Kane Wood),[6] though they used to blow as religiously on that day as the Glastonbury thorn. In short, the season seems to sympathize with my decay, as poets say it does with them when their Phillis is absent. I don't believe you found Ampthill very sultry, Madam; you had better return to town like me, and put an erratum at the end of your almanac, *for June read January*. Summer was made to be felt and enjoyed, not to be taken for better for worse like a spouse in whom one has no pleasure any longer.

I found nothing new in town, but a marriage or two, as many deaths, a house-breaking and a murder—if they are novelties. Lord Lewisham[7] marries his cousin Lady Frances Finch,[8] Lord Aylsford's[9] sister; Lady Grandison is dead at Spa;[10] her body arrived before her death was known; her steward received a letter from Margate from her maid, to say they had got in there with her Lady after a disagreeable passage—he went to look for a house for her, and an hour after learnt that it was the corpse. Sir Thomas Frankland's[11] house was broken open last night in Bond Street close to St James's Street,

3. An epidemic of influenza had reached its height in London about the fourth week in May (Theophilus Thompson, *Annals of Influenza*, 1852, pp. 117–99, esp. pp. 118–20; MASON ii. 249 and n. 1).

4. Mary Beauclerk (1766–1851), m. (ca 1795) Graf Franz von Jenison zu Walworth; Elizabeth Beauclerk (ca 1767–93), m. (1787) her first cousin, George Augustus Herbert, styled Lord Herbert until 1794, 11th E. of Pembroke, 1794 (DALRYMPLE 320 nn. 28–29; *Betsy Sheridan's Journal*, ed. William LeFanu, 1960, pp. 176–7).

5. The birthday of the Old Pretender. The Jacobites adopted the white rose (the symbol of the Yorkists) supposedly because the Old Pretender's father, James II, had been D. of York (*Notes and Queries*, 1926, 13th ser. cli. 123).

6. Caen Wood, Lord Mansfield's seat at Highgate; a reference to Mansfield's alleged Jacobite sympathies.

7. George Legge (1755–1810), styled Vct Lewisham until 1801, 3d E. of Dartmouth, 1801; M.P.; lord of the Bedchamber to the Prince of Wales 1782–3; lord warden of the Stannaries 1783–98.

8. (1761–1838), m. (24 Sept. 1782), at her mother's house in Grosvenor Square, Lord Lewisham. His great-grandmother (Anne, Cts of Dartmouth) was Lady Frances's great-aunt.

9. Heneage Finch (1751–1812), 4th E. of Aylesford, 1777; M.P.; lord of the Bedchamber 1777–83; lord steward of the Household 1804–12.

10. She died at Spa on 29 May 1782 and was buried at Youghal, co. Cork.

11. Sir Thomas Frankland (1718–84), 5th Bt, 1768; M.P.; naval officer, becoming finally (1756) admiral.

though his wife[12] and servants were in town; and as Lady Chewton and her sisters[13] came from the Opera, they saw two officers fighting in Pall Mall next to Dr Graham's,[14] and the mob trying to part them. Lord Chewton and some other young men went into the house and found a Captain Lucas[15] of the Guards bleeding on a couch. It was a quarrel about an E O[16] table, I don't know what: this officer had been struck in the face with a red-hot poker by a drawer, and this morning is dead.[17] So are hundreds of peach and apricot trees of the influenza —but methinks I am writing a letter like the casualties at the end of a reign in Baker's *Chronicle*. He would have interpreted them into judgments and portents—now they are only common occurrences, and will be forgotten tomorrow, without disturbing civilized society. Religious times breathe a browner horror[18] on everything; philosophers write folios against immoral times; but when a nation is perfectly well bred and indifferent, no enormities shock anybody; and when they have made an article in the newspaper, are mentioned no more than the clothes at the last Birthday. I should not have ventured to tell you half my paragraphs, Madam, if you were not a country body of a week's standing.

12. Sarah Rhett (1722–1808), dau. of William Rhett of South Carolina by Mary Trott, m. (1743) in South Carolina, Thomas Frankland, later (1768) 5th Bt (Burke, *Peerage*, 1928, p. 973; *South Carolina Historical and Genealogical Magazine*, 1903, iv. 38; GM 1808, lxxviii pt i. 374).

13. Lady Charlotte Maria and Lady Anne Horatia Waldegrave.

14. Schomberg House, Pall Mall, to which he had moved in the spring of 1781, finding his Adelphi establishment (*ante* 23 Aug. 1780) too expensive; he called it the 'Temple of Health and of Hymen.' See DNB; Wheatley, *London Past and Present* iii. 220–1.

15. The only Lucas in the *Army Lists* dated 30 April 1782 and not in the 1783 *Army Lists* is William Lucas, who had become Lieutenant (not Captain) in the 18th (or Royal Irish) Regiment of Foot on 12 Nov. 1779.

16. That is, 'even and odd, a game of chance said to have been invented by

Beau Nash [see DNB]. It had lately become popular with all classes, as it was supposed to be beyond the reach of the laws against games of chance' (Toynbee xii. 267 n. 3). On 5 June 1782 leave had been given in the House of Commons to bring in a bill to prevent gaming, chiefly EO; the bill was passed on 27 June. See Cobbett, *Parl. Hist.* xxiii. 110–13.

17. 'Tuesday night a violent fracas happened at a house in Pall Mall, famous for the pernicious custom of E.O. playing; and is said to have originated from some offence given to three officers; the consequence of which was, all the windows in [Dr Graham's] The Temple of Hymen were destroyed, and it is said one of the guards, who were called to assist in quelling the riot, lost his life, in attempting to rescue the officers from their opponents' (*London Chronicle* 11–13 June, li. 566).

18. 'And breathes a browner horror on the woods' (Pope, 'Eloisa to Abelard,' l. 170; cf. *post* 30 Aug. 1786).

To Lady Ossory, Saturday 22 June 1782

Dated by the second part of the letter, 28 June: 'I had begun this letter a week ago here.' HW did not go to SH until 22 June (HW to Cole 21 June 1782, COLE ii. 327).

[22 June 1782].

THE weather, I confess, did change, Madam, as suddenly and unexpectedly as the administration, and both probably for a short time. His majesty the sun, who had not shown a good while, came out in a very warm mood, and everybody was impatient to kiss his hand— but in three days his chancellor the east wind turned those halcyon days to a storm, and I look upon the bloom of summer as gone. I have been twice at Strawberry,[1] but shall not settle there till next week, when my Court removes over sea,[2] and leaves me at liberty, which I shall enjoy as much as the Duke of Manchester[3] or Lord Ludlow[4] do a Drawing-Room. My nephew Lord Cholmondeley, you know, Madam, is going to Berlin[5]—he refused Russia, which I should have thought he would have preferred, as he is more formed to succeed with a gallant Empress than with a peevish old politician, and could carry better credentials.[6] They say the Prussian King is at last well disposed to us and huffs the Dutch *à notre intention*[7]—if after

1. 10–12 June and again on 22 June, when presumably he is writing this letter.

2. 'The Gloucesters set out the twenty-ninth' (Coke, 'MS Journals' 13 June 1782). The *London Chronicle* 4–6 July, lii. 18, reported that the Duke and Duchess 'set off' on 4 July 'for Margate, to embark for Ostend, on their way to the German Spa.'

3. George Montagu (1737–88), 4th D. of Manchester, 1762; styled Vct Mandeville 1739–62; lord of the Bedchamber 1762–70; lord chamberlain of the Household (succeeding Lord Hertford on 10 April) 1782–3; ambassador to Paris 1783–4 (cf. *post* 17 April 1783).

4. Peter Ludlow (1730–1803), cr. (1755) Bn Ludlow, (1760) E. Ludlow; comptroller of the Household 1782–4.

5. On 14 June Cholmondeley had been appointed 'envoy extraordinary and min-

ister plenipotentiary to the Court of Berlin' (*London Gazette* No. 12304, 11–15 June); on 21 Sept. Sir John Stepney was appointed 'envoy extraordinary at the Court of Berlin' (ibid. No. 12332, 17–21 Sept.).

6. Cholmondeley's gallantry and virility inspired much humour and satire: see BM, *Satiric Prints* v. 305, 536–7, vii. 195–6, Nos 5497, 5911, 8679. *The Torpedo, a Poem to the Electrical Eel*, 1777, was dedicated to him.

7. Lusi, the Prussian emissary in London, wrote 12 March to Frederick II that 'on est bien fâché ici d'apprendre que la Hollande, au lieu de penser à la paix, est sur le point de s'unir plus étroitement à la France et à l'Amérique.' Frederick replied, 29 March, that 'les Hollandais assistés de la Russie se flattent bien par sa médiation d'être restitués *in integrum*,

all we do not sink, English vanity will conclude more than ever that Providence dotes upon us, and never will let us be ruined, let us play the fool as much as we will. I have a better opinion of Providence, and, unless it originally bestowed good luck on fools as a balance and compensation, I do not believe that it employs itself in remedying blunders. My countrymen, with their leave, are exceedingly contemptible. They have for these seven years been applauding and encouraging the Court to persist in all its frenzy and obstinacy, and now it rains addresses of thanks to his Majesty for changing his administration[8]—though they have no reason to thank him or themselves for the change.

Strawberry Hill, June 28.

I had begun this letter a week ago here, in answer to your Ladyship's last, was interrupted, and left it here in my table drawer—yet though it is superannuated, it will be as new as anything I could tell you. Besides Lord Ossory has been in town,[1] and carried you all the novelties of the week, if there were any. Lord Rockingham was said to be better yesterday, but that is a very ancient date in the health of a first minister[2]—What would Lord Shelburne think of my want of curiosity, who came out of town this morning without inquiring? I am to dine tomorrow with Princess Amelie at Gunnersbury,[3] must return on Sunday for the last Drawing-Room at Gloucester House— and on Thursday shall be sovereign of myself again, which is much more important to me than who is to be first lord of the Treasury, if the Marquis is carried off in his second dictatorship. Three hours ago I saw just the reverse of what is passing in Lord Rockingham's ante-

quelques possessions qu'ils ont perdus. Puis-je leur conseiller en bonne foi de renoncer à cette espérance . . . ?' (Frederick II, *Politische Correspondenz*, Berlin, 1879–1939, xlvi. 576, 577). Charles Fox told Lusi that if Holland remained under French influence, England would beg for Frederick's aid (Lusi to Frederick, 4 June, quoted by M. L. Brown, *American Independence through Prussian Eyes*, Durham, N.C., 1959, p. 34).

8. Frequent notices of these addresses of thanks appear in the newspapers.

1. Parliament was still in session.

2. 'The Marquis of Rockingham now lies dangerously ill. He seemed to be in a fair way of recovery a few days ago, but has since had a relapse' (*London Chronicle* 25–27 June, li. 616).

3. Gunnersbury House, Ealing, Middlesex, Princess Amelia's summer residence, purchased in 1761: 'pleasantly situated . . . an extensive and beautiful prospect. It was built for Serjeant Maynard, in the year 1663, by Webbe, a pupil of Inigo Jones. . . . The whole of the premises consists of about 95 acres, surrounded with a lofty brick wall' (Daniel Lysons, *Environs of London*, Vol. II, 1795, p. 226). See also *post* 4 Nov. 1786.

chamber. It was Lady North, her three daughters[4] and one of her sons[5] taking a solitary promenade on the river, and landing to stroll on the shore, without a single Rosencrans or Guildenstern attending. Forty years ago[6] I myself was one of the *dramatis personæ* in such a scene; and as even then I was perfectly indifferent to the change of decorations, it is not surprising that I should look on them now with much composure—but it was constitution not philosophy: philosophy is only a command of muscles. I never could command mine, when I really cared; and should have made a miserable politician, had I ever felt a sensation of ambition.

I believe there is some apprehension of a visit in the Channel from the united squadrons.[7] I heard a good deal about them t'other night, and dreamt the French had landed at *Torbay*,[8] which I loved myself for, as it showed what a preference there is at my heart to *Torbay*.[9] At least I am sure that I had paid little attention to the idea of an invasion,[10] but a great deal to a modicum of King William's coat taken out of his wound after the battle of the Boyne,[11] and set in a crystal locket, which Mrs Walsingham showed me a week ago, and which probably gave the colour to my dream.

The Bishop of Salisbury[12] is dead; I conclude Bishop Shipley[13] will succeed him, nor can have above one competitor, Bishop Hinchliffe[14]

4. Hon. Catherine Anne North (*ante* 10 Oct. 1780), Hon. Anne North (*ante* 25 July 1781), and Hon. Charlotte North (1770–1849), m. (1800) Hon. Lt-Col. John Lindsay; she was later the intimate friend of Mary and Agnes Berry (BERRY i. 114 n. 11).

5. She had three sons living at this time: Hon. George Augustus North (*ante* 13 Nov. 1776), Hon. Francis North, and Hon. Frederick North (*ante* 25 July 1781).

6. When Sir Robert Walpole's ministry fell.

7. The *London Courant* 18 June reported that 'Lord Howe will certainly be in full force to oppose the combined fleets in the middle of July,' and, the next day, that 'we hear from Madrid, that Don Cordova hoisted sail the 23d of May, with 27 ships, and the division of Count de Guichen.'

8. On 5 Nov. 1688 King William III landed at Brixham, south of Torbay.

9. That is, William III stood for the Whig principles which HW cherished.

10. 'The French still keep up the alarm of invading this island, at least in appearances' (letter from Jersey, 12 June, in *Daily Adv.* 19 June).

11. In the Battle of the Boyne, 1 July 1690, William III was slightly wounded in the shoulder.

12. John Hume (ca 1706 – 26 June 1782), Bp of Bristol 1756–8, of Oxford 1758–66, and of Salisbury 1766–82 (Foster, *Alumni Oxon.*; S. L. Ollard and Gordon Crosse, *A Dictionary of English Church History*, 2d edn, 1919, p. 542). He was succeeded by Hon. Shute Barrington (*post* 30 June 1785).

13. Jonathan Shipley (1714–88), Bp of Llandaff, 1769, and of St Asaph 1769–88; of strong Whig principles; friend of Benjamin Franklin, Burke, and Reynolds.

14. John Hinchliffe (1731–94), Bp of Peterborough 1769–94; Master of Trinity College, Cambridge, 1768–88; friend and possibly a correspondent of HW (COLE ii. 156 n. 1; CHATTERTON 196 and n. 2). Like Shipley, he supported the American

—unless your *beau-frère*[15] is immediately premier, and names the Chancellor's brother[16]—I suppose tonight I shall dream of Bishop Hoadley[17]—for you see, Madam, I am an old Whig even in my sleep, and that the powers of darkness cannot affect my principles.

To Lady Ossory, Monday 1 July 1782

Address: To the Countess of Ossory at Ampthill Park, Bedfordshire. *Postmark:* 1 IY. GC.

Berkeley Square, July 1, 1782.

UNDOUBTEDLY you will have as early intelligence as I can send you, Madam, of today's great event—Lord Rockingham died at one o'clock at noon.[1] Unless I could tell you what is to be, it would be idle to add more, or to talk of any other subject than what this event will produce; and as I have neither the honour of being a prophet, nor am of the drawer of any cabinet, I will not pretend to say what will be, nor (like a thousand others who know no more than I, and, who will not be more consulted) what should be, though I am perfectly clear what ought to be; but as the Crown is lapsed to King George again, and as he may not happen to be of my opinion, I shall keep it to myself, and be ready, like the Vicar of Bray, to admire the choice, whatever it shall be.[2]

They say there has not a *howd'ye* as big as a silver penny been sent from Windsor, nor any inquiry made[2a]—and yet I should think there

cause, although in 1775 he temporarily advised coercion rather than conciliation. The *London Chronicle* 27–29 June, li. 621, reported the rumour that Hinchliffe would succeed Hume, and Shipley would succeed Hinchliffe. The Duke of Grafton and Lord Camden thought the translation of Hinchliffe to Salisbury 'fixed,' but Shelburne supported the King's choice of Barrington (Grafton, *Autobiography and Political Correspondence*, ed. Anson, 1898, pp. 18, 325–7, 329).

15. Lord Shelburne, married to Lord Ossory's sister.

16. Thomas Thurlow, Bp of Lincoln 1779–87, of Durham 1787–91. Through the influence of his brother, Lord Thurlow, he had become Dean of St Paul's earlier in 1782, despite the opposition of Lord North (MASON ii. 192).

17. Benjamin Hoadly (1676–1761), Bp of Bangor, 1715, Hereford, 1721, Salisbury, 1723, Winchester, 1734; 'a true Whig' (*Walpoliana* i. 62). 'I have a real affection for Bishop Hoadley; he stands with me in lieu of what are called *the Fathers*' (HW to Pinkerton 30 Sept. 1785, CHATTERTON 282–3).

———

1. HW received this information from Lord Cholmondeley shortly before 4 o'clock (HW to Harcourt 1 July 1782).

2. The chorus of 'The Vicar of Bray.' See MASON ii. 132 and n. 5.

2a. 'The King showed his aversion to Lord Rockingham so indecently and so

was care taken to have minute intelligence. I can give you some very good of the negative kind, Madam. Though there is a mitre vacant,[3] and it is now six o'clock, I have not seen a divine knocking at a pair of gates[4] in this square, nor are any marrowbones and cleavers[5] yet arrived.

It will be a singular year if the next six months produce as strange events as these six have; a total change, the caterpillars,[6] the influenza and the death of a prime minister—apropos, I was forced last Saturday to have two bird-cherries at Strawberry Hill cut down and burnt; they were totally covered with webs, like a sheet, full of well grown caterpillars—as I have prodigious faith in nature's prognostics, I am persuaded that we are not yet secure against an inundation of Scotch ministers. I picked up a caterpillar myself that had as many colours as a plaid. You that have no superstition, Madam, may laugh at me for telling you of my dreams and omens—to be sure, I did not use to be so credulous; but remember,

> The soul's dark cottage, battered and decay'd,
> Lets in new light through chinks which time has made.[7]

I have so many of those inlets, that no wonder my faith increases—but adieu, Madam, I will go and hear what the world says—

PS. Oh! I have got a new omen, that tells me Lord Shelburn will be Minister—Premiers always live where I do. In Arlington Street, my father, Lord Granville,[8] Mr Pelham, the Duke of Grafton. It is odd that their star and mine should *domicilier* together—but the nearer the church[9]—

meanly that, though he had accepted him for his minister, he did not once send to inquire how the Marquis did when he was dying' (*Last Journals* ii. 445).

3. The bishopric of Salisbury. See *ante* 22 June 1782.

4. Lord Shelburne's.

5. That is, 'the mob' who with the 'rough music' of marrowbones and cleavers would herald Shelburne's becoming prime minister; see HW to Mann 1 Nov. 1742 OS, MANN ii. 96.

6. Comments on the heavy infestation of caterpillars appear in the *London Chronicle* 2–18 April, li. 318, 327, 373.

7. Edmund Waller (1606–87), 'Of the Last Verses in the Book' (or 'On the Foregoing Divine Poems'); a favourite couplet of HW's; see MONTAGU i. 228; BERRY i. 364, and *ante* 22 Nov. 1781.

8. John Carteret (1690–1763), 1st E. Granville, 1744; secretary of state for the North 1742–4, 10–14 Feb. 1746, and lord president of the Council 1751–63. In 1742–4 he was virtual prime minister under Wilmington and Pelham.

9. 'The nearer the Church the further from God' (Bishop Lancelot Andrewes, *Sermon on the Nativity before James I*, 1622, cited in the *Oxford Dictionary of Quotations*, 1941, p. 4).

To Lady Ossory, Sunday 7 July 1782

Address: To the Countess of Ossory at Ampthill Park, Bedfordshire. *Postmark:* 8 IY.

Sunday evening, July 7, 1782.

YOU will not be surprised, my dear Madam, that either I do not write, or do not know what to write. What I think and feel, I can best tell you by what I said to Mr Fitzpatrick[1] last night. I met him in the passage of the playhouse;[2] he said, 'I fear you do not approve us.' I replied, 'I feel concern so much more than disapprobation, that I call it only concern.'[3] He said, 'It was coming fast to this point *before* Lord Rockingham's death'[4]—'Yes,' I answered, 'but I wish it had not come to this point these three months!'[5] These sentiments might be rolled out into a long commentary, but they contain the pith.

I have no hesitation in saying that I think Mr Fox[6] the fittest man in England for prime minister; I say it aloud and everywhere. But there are points in question at this moment far more important than

1. Who was chief secretary for Ireland during the lord lieutenancy of the D. of Portland 8 April – 15 Aug. 1782. Fitzpatrick had arrived in London from Ireland on 20 June (*London Chronicle* 20–22 June, li. 600).

2. The Little Theatre in the Haymarket, where HW saw George Colman's *English Merchant* and John O'Keeffe's *Agreeable Surprise.* He mentions the latter *post* 4 Aug. 1782.

3. Some of the Rockingham party (notably Fox, Burke, Lord John Cavendish, and Fitzpatrick) had resigned when the King made Shelburne and not the Duke of Portland first lord of the Treasury. 'The paucity of followers was a sad lesson to the designers ['resigners' in MS] of their ill-digested precipitation. Fox grew sensible of it, and confessed it. Richard Fitzpatrick, his friend, . . . though his sister was Lord Shelburne's wife, chose to follow the fortune of his friend rather than of his brother-in-law. Meeting me at the play on his return from Ireland, he said to me, "I hear you disapprove us, and indeed I do not know whether we

have not been in the wrong." I replied, "Mr Fitzpatrick, I feel too much concern to have any room for blame"' (*Last Journals* ii. 452).

4. Hearing of Shelburne's appointment, Fox on 4 July 'carried the seals to St James's, declaring that the day before the death of Lord Rockingham he had notified his intention of resigning, unable to endure the treacheries of Shelburne, and his interference in his (Fox's) province' (ibid. ii. 449; HW to Mann 7 July 1782; *Memorials and Correspondence of Charles James Fox,* ed. Lord John Russell, 1853–7, i. 435, 438–9).

5. That is, 'till the peace with America was concluded, Ireland settled, alliances concluded on the continent, and perhaps reconciliation with Holland' (HW to Mason 8 July 1782, Mason ii. 263).

6. Apparently Lady Ossory sent him all or part of this paragraph from HW's letter; see *post* 3 Nov. 1782. HW analyzes Fox's strengths and weaknesses as possible prime minister in *Last Journals* ii. 446, 450.

who shall be premier. The pacification of America and the negotiations on the anvil are of dearer moment; and ought not, cannot wait for domestic contests. Every man too has his own feelings. I have been called a republican[7]—I never was quite that, as no man ever was quite of any of the denominations laid down in books. But if never a republican quite, I never approached in thought, wish, inclination or reasoning towards being a partisan of an aristocracy.[8] What! not be a republican, and yet approve a republic of tyrants! I never admired Lord Rockingham—shall his self-elected executors tell me that I am to take the oaths to Lord Fitzwilliam,[9] I who was a nonjuror in the uncle's time! I see a very good reason why Mr Fox should say that that imaginary King never dies—but, as I told him t'other night,[10] my Whiggism is founded on the Constitution, not on two or three great families, who are forced to have virtue for a claim to their dignity, and any able man they can find to execute the office for them. My Whiggism is not confined to the Peak of Derbyshire.[11]

In my tiny sphere I have been labouring to prevent disunion: to very little purpose truly. Mr Fox[12] has suffered me with his usual and unalterable good humour to talk to him very freely—not on the general rupture, for I am neither vain enough nor foolish enough to suppose that I can persuade him by *my* arguments out of his own; nor do I talk to a politician on his duty to his country, because a master-genius feels something in himself, which inferior mortals cannot feel, and which tells him that whatever hurt he does, he can repair the moment he is possessed of full power—but my point has been and shall be to endeavour to preserve good terms between him and his

7. By Lady Mary Coke, for example (*post* 22 Jan. 1783); see also COLE ii. 189–90 n. 22.

8. 'My reflections led me early towards, I cannot quite say republicanism, but to most limited monarchy . . . a quiet republican, who does not dislike to see the shadow of monarchy . . . who approves the name of a king, when it excludes the essence; a man of such principles, I hope, may be a good man and an honest' (*Mem. Geo. II* i. 376–7).

9. William Fitzwilliam (1748–1833), 2d E. Fitzwilliam, 1756; nephew and heir of Rockingham; friend of Fox at Eton. On 6 July some of the Rockingham Whigs had met at Fitzwilliam's and had decided

not to support Shelburne; see HW to Mann 7 July 1782.

10. When Fox 'came to expostulate with' his uncle, the Duke of Richmond. HW, at Richmond's request, remained and tried to keep the discussion moderate (*Last Journals* ii. 450).

11. That is, to the Cavendish family, whose seat, Chatsworth, is in Derbyshire, near Kinder Scout, 'the Peak.' On Rockingham's death, Lord John Cavendish, according to HW, thought that 'the house of Cavendish ought to have the exclusive right of naming a prime minister' (ibid. ii. 446), namely, the Duke of Portland, who had married into the family (ibid. 446–9).

12. Vernon Smith at this point inserted

uncle-Duke. Even in that I may fail at present, but they are both too good-natured not to forgive on the first opportunity.[13]

There is a world more of topics for talk, but the tide is too rapid at present not to hurry the present moment away, and supply its place before the post can arrive. I have sketched my thoughts, as it would look like want of confidence, or political mystery, if I was silent. I am apt to be too frank, and thank my stars have no secrets to conceal. I like and dislike and say so, and readily avow my purposes. I long to get to Strawberry, where I shall have no purposes at all. When this vision of a Whig administration, so unlikely ever to be realized, had acquired substance—not then likely to last, has vanished so instantaneously, what a dotard should I be, if again I looked forward! Adieu! Madam—I do not believe you enjoy the crisis more than I do—but I beg you not to suppose that I desire an answer. It cannot be pleasant to you to talk on points that touch you more nearly— but I am a creature *isolé*, and what I think or say is of no consequence.

To Lady Ossory, Thursday 11 July 1782

Address: To the Countess of Ossory at Ampthill Park, Bedfordshire. *Postmark:* 12 IY.

Berkeley Square, July 11, at midnight, 1782.

I AM this minute come from Lady Mary Coke's at Notting Hill, where I dined with the present Commander-in-Chief[1] and the late Chancellor of the Exchequer,[2] and though the party had been made before the rupture, nothing could pass more amicably[3]—nay,

(ii. 95–7) Lord Ossory's 'Character of Mr Fox.' See Appendix 8.

13. At the meeting between Fox and Richmond, 'I did prevent any warmth, and they parted civilly, though equally discontent with each other' (*Last Journals* ii. 450).

1. Conway, one of the Rockingham Whigs who had not resigned. For HW's discussion of Conway's relations with the Rockingham party and his reasons for not resigning, see *Last Journals* ii. 451–2.

2. Lord John Cavendish, who had re-signed, although he continued to perform duties of office until he was replaced on 13 July. Cf. ibid. ii. 453–4.

3. Lady Mary Coke noted in her 'MS Journals' 11–12 July: 'I have company at dinner and a party at loo in the evening, the late Chancellor of the Exchequer and the Commander-in-chief; my party was fixed before the ministry broke, but I hope these two though now divided in the political line are still friends . . . My company left me before eleven o'clock. We played half-crown loo, and Mr Walpole and Mrs Lloyd won con-

Lord John left us to sup at Richmond House.[4] All this is mighty well; and I might compliment myself on having contributed to preserve appearances[5]—yet I see how little they will last, when any opportunity offers of discovering what is under the embers. Nay, I believe, what moderation remains, proceeds from perceiving already how ill the late precipitation is generally taken. Very ill indeed, by all not immediately connected with the principal actors.

On my table I found your Ladyship's letter, and sit down to answer it, late as it is, because I shall leave London tomorrow with no thoughts of seeing it again in haste; for though my two friends have acted rightly, I am far from being enamoured of anything else. It flatters me much to find that I am so fortunate as to agree with your Ladyship and Lord Ossory, and to find you so full of confidence on a point on which I had no right to expect any. You may be assured nothing you have said, will pass my lips—indeed I shall see nobody tomorrow, and am going to vegetate only among my dowagers.

It is self-evident that the sole way of preventing much evil was by remaining. Nor is it less certain that the rash steps taken must please infinitely in a place[6] where dissension was always cultivated. What could the opening of so many doors produce but the introduction of some of the late discarded? It will not in truth surprise me if the introductor himself[7] is at last sent to graze: nor was I in the wrong when I said in the first moment that power was *lapsed* back again.[8] Some very disgraceful circumstances that have just come

siderably. He told her she had taken Miss forever.'

4. The Duke of Richmond remained Master-General of the Ordnance March 1782 – April 1783, Dec. 1783 – Jan. 1795. For his reasons for not resigning with Fox, Lord John Cavendish, *et al.*, see *Last Journals* ii. 449–51.

5. In addition to HW's attempt to keep peace between the Duke of Richmond and Fox, 'In a conversation with Lord John Cavendish . . . I told him frankly that I should rejoice that Mr Conway had retained his post. He had pledged himself to the House of Commons and to the public that America was disposed to make peace with us; was not his honour

then at stake to endeavour to realize his engagements?' (ibid. ii. 452).

6. The King and his inner circle.

7. Fox, the first to resign.

8. To the King. At the time of the resignations, 'the temperate did see the mischief of disunion in the party, and apprehended that it would tend to a restoration of the old ministry, and consequently to a revival of the American war. The King, no doubt, exulted (as he often did in events that soon heaped new humiliations on himself) in having divided a party that had often thwarted his views, and had so lately compelled him to receive them on their own terms' (ibid. ii. 449).

out will repay what has been lost, with usury, for all credit in patriotism must be lost when its wages are so high.[9]

Your private lamentation, Madam, is equally well founded, though the relapse will be much more dangerous to Mr Fox than to Mr Fitzpatrick, whose stamina are of stouter texture; the former, I fear, will destroy himself. I was on the point of saying to him t'other morning, 'Well, but you must not go and play at taw again!'—but I thought it would be impertinent. What can one suggest that he does not know and must have thought?—I did flatter myself that he now was on the high road to all he ought to attain—he would have attained it—but he will neither live to reach the goal, nor, when Parliament is not sitting, take the least pains to promote his own views—but I blame myself for expatiating, when you, Madam, have comprised in a short fable the quintessence of all I could say. It is so just, that I wish Mr Fox had seen it *last Wednesday* sevennight[10] —I do confess it is he on whose account I am mortified.[11] I had pleasure in thinking that old as I am, I should yet see a first-rate minister, who would revive this country. That vision is over, and every other! I have been shown a glimpse of a new Jerusalem: I waked, and found it was a dream!—here conclude my politics—All will run back into the old channel—a miracle happened—and might almost as well not. At sixty-five it is too late to look forwards again. I am as much disappointed as if I had had personal views—but I confess that I find it more easy to comfort myself from having had none. I can wish well to England, as I did before, but when one can neither do good nor prevent mischief, it is allowable to leave the public to itself. It will be a capital loss to me, if your Ladyship and Lord

9. Edmund Burke had attempted to get the clerkship of the Pells for his son Richard, and Shelburne had obtained a pension of £3,200 a year for Col. Barré. See Richard Burke to HW 7 July 1782 and Burke's proposal of the same date in Cunningham ix. 523–4; *Last Journals* ii. 452–7; *Carlisle MSS* 633; *post* 4 Aug. 1782, n. 20.

10. 3 July; Fox resigned on the 4th (*ante* 7 July 1782, n. 4; *Corr. Geo. III* vi. 74–5; *Memorials and Correspondence of Charles James Fox*, ed. Lord John Russell, 1853–7, i. 460–3).

11. Fitzpatrick wrote to Lord Ossory 5 July: 'All persons who have any understanding, and no office, are of opinion that Charles has done right. All persons who have little understanding, are frightened. And all persons who have offices, with some very few brilliant exceptions, think he has been hasty' (ibid. i. 461; see also Christopher Hobhouse, *Fox*, new edn, 1947, p. 128: Fox's resignation 'was the mistake of his whole life which cost him dearest').

Ossory adhere to your purpose of going abroad;[12] but I cannot be so selfish as to disapprove it. Next winter, I am persuaded with you, will be very disagreeable, and to you an anxious one.[13] What one cannot remedy, it is best to avoid.

Thank you exceedingly once more, Madam, for your letter and fable, and be assured wherever you are, that while I remain here, I shall be most unalterably

Your Ladyship's most faithful humble servant,

H. W.

To Lady Ossory, Sunday 4 August 1782

Address: To the Countess of Ossory at Ampthill Park, Bedfordshire. *Postmark:* ISLEWORTH. 5 AV.

Strawberry Hill, Aug. 4, 1782.

I SHOULD have written, Madam, had I had anything to tell you; but what can I send from hence, but repetitions of the samenesses of every summer? I pass most of my evenings at the hospital of the poor Montroses;[1] Cliveden is little less an infirmary. I have dined again with Princess Amelie,[2] and twice with the Hertfords at Ditton, and see a great deal of my family, who are cantoned round me like those of a patriarch when tribes began to increase and remove to small distances. My brother is at Isleworth, Lady Dysart at Ham,[3] the Keppels at the Stud,[4] the Waldegraves at the Pavilions,

12. They did not go.

13. Lord Ossory and Richard Fitzpatrick were allied with Fox, although their sister was married to Lord Shelburne. Lord Ossory had refused the advances of Shelburne, who could have obtained for him the English peerage he so much desired. See Lord John Russell, ed., op. cit. i. 462–4, especially Shelburne to Ossory 4 July, and Ossory's reply.

1. William Graham (1712–90), 2d D. of Montrose, 1742, had become blind and deaf.

2. At Gunnersbury, where he had dined on 29 June (*ante* 22 June 1782).

3. Ham House, near Petersham.

4. The Stud House in the House Park at Hampton Court. The Duke and Duchess of Gloucester 'have lent the Pavillions at Hampton Court to the Lady Waldegraves, and the Stud Lodge to Lord and Lady Chewton' (Coke, 'MS Journals' 4 July 1782). While the Duke and Duchess were abroad, the Ladies Waldegrave had lived there during the summer (Lady E. Laura Waldegrave correspondence, 9 Jan. 1775, and *passim*, MSS wsl). For an account of the Stud House, see Ernest Law, *History of Hampton Court Palace*, 1885, vi. 313, 315, 491.

and Lady Malpas[5] in the Palace;[6] but I am not the better stocked with materials for letters; nor, though the neighbourhood is enriched by some invention, as Lady Cecilia Johnston's at Petersham, and Lady Bridget Tolmache's on Ham Common, is my gazette at all flourishing, since we have ceased to be on the high road to intelligence. Lord North, finding Bushy Park too solitary, since his sun was set, is gone on a progress into the Tory regions of Oxford and Staffordshires;[7] and Mr Ellis has moulted his French horns[8] with the seals.[9] The events of our district have been confined to the death of Mr Prado,[10] the marriage of Miss Pococke,[11] the death and will of Mr Child,[12] which have occupied us more than the hide and seek of the hostile fleets.[13] Bankruptcies, houses to be sold or let, and robberies every night, fill up the gazette of our neighbourhood, but would make dull journals into another county. I have forsworn politics, and have no connection with the next generation. I know nothing of what the P[rince] of W[ales] does; and for him who only *undoes,* I am like his laureate, and talk of anything rather than of him.[14]

George and La Mimie called on me half an hour ago; he is gone to pass a day or two with Col. Keene on Hampton Court Green—so the fall of a party can make people as fond of one another, as

5. Hester Edwardes (ca 1727–94), m. (1747) HW's nephew, George Cholmondeley, styled Vct Malpas.

6. Hampton Court. On 7 June 1782 she had been granted Suite XVIII in the Gold Staff Gallery, where she lived until her death in 1794 (ibid. vi. 465; *post* 6 Oct. 1794).

7. On 6 Oct. he wrote from Walmer Castle, Kent, to thank the City of Exeter for granting him the freedom of the City (*London Chronicle* 22–24 Oct., lii. 397). Wroxton Abbey, near Banbury, Oxfordshire, was the seat of his father, Lord Guilford.

8. Perhaps an allusion to Marshall Botta at Florence, who used to have French horns played in his courtyard to proclaim victories won by the Austrians (Mann to HW 25 Aug. 1759, MANN v. 317, and *passim*).

9. Ellis had been secretary of state for America and the Colonies from 11 Feb. to 27 March 1782.

10. At Twickenham 26 July (GM 1782, lii. 406).

11. Sophia Pocock (d. 1811), m. (22 July 1782) at her father's house in Charles Street, Berkeley Square, London, John Poulett (1756–1819), styled Vct Hinton 1764–88, 4th E. Poulett, 1788. The groom's father, Lord Poulett, had a villa at Twickenham, and the bride's father, Admiral Pocock, lived in the house there later known as Orleans House.

12. Robert Child died 28 July. The chief provisions of his will are given in GM 1782, lii. 406; BERRY ii. 72 n. 28.

13. Lord Howe was unwilling to risk an engagement with the superior force of the combined fleets (HW to Mason 10 July 1782, MASON ii. 266 and n. 21).

14. In Whitehead's 'Ode for His Majesty's Birthday, June 4, 1782,' there is only one reference to the King: 'The Monarch's fondest wish' for peace (*London Chronicle* 1–4 June, li. 535).

two Englishmen that are perfect strangers, if they happen to meet in China![15] George is all afflictions; the Duke of Queensberry has broken a tendon, and Mrs Webbe is dying.[16] I love him so well that I hope he will never have greater calamities.

Lady Chewton is a very good young woman, Madam, and I rejoice that Lord and Lady Waldegrave[17] are satisfied with her.[18] Lady Sefton's politics must be admirable: Mrs Bouverie,[19] I hear, is a great politician too. The trade will grow more entertaining, if the ladies make it the fashion—it was become as much a profession of calculation as that of a banker's shop. I do not know what it would not become, since *honest* Colonel Barré[20] has established a drawback[21] for principles.

I was indeed, Madam, excessively diverted with *The Agreeable Surprise:*[22] it is excellent nonsense, and very original. Whatever is so, has great merit in my eyes: I would not give sixpence a ream for what Mr Hayley[23] and such copyists write. I am sorry you are to

15. Selwyn had been on friendly terms with Keene for several years, at least since 1775. Keene, through his wife, was closely associated with Lord North, whose ministry had fallen in March, and Selwyn had consistently supported North and the Court party. Selwyn gives a friendly but somewhat condescending estimate of Keene in a letter to Lord Carlisle 1 April 1782 (*Carlisle MSS* 621, and *passim*).

16. Mrs Bethia Webb, 'governess' to Mimi; she was living in Sept. 1790 (ibid. 691–2; codicil, 11 June 1788, to Selwyn's will proved P.C.C. 12 Feb. 1791). See also *ante* 23 Sept. 1780.

17. John Waldegrave (1718–84), 3d E. Waldegrave, 1763, m. (1751) Lord Ossory's cousin, Lady Elizabeth Leveson-Gower.

18. Lady Chewton had been their daughter-in-law since 5 May 1782.

19. Henrietta (Harriet) Fawkener (ca 1751–1825), m. 1 (1764) Hon. Edward Bouverie; m. 2 (1811) Lord Robert Spencer; an accomplished woman and one of the beauties of the day. See BERRY i. 163 n. 9; *Genealogist*, n.s., 1884, i. chart facing p. 128.

20. Isaac Barré (1726–1802), soldier and politician. At Shelburne's request, the commissioners of the Treasury had approved shortly before Rockingham's death an annual grant of £3200 for Barré, then treasurer of the Navy, the grant to take

effect when Barré ceased to hold that or another office under the King. The grant, designed to compensate for Barré's loss of army preferment, was discussed in the House of Commons 9 July, when a motion to censure those responsible for approving the grant was proposed but withdrawn. HW in *Last Journals* ii. 456 called Barré's defence of himself in the House 'still more impudent than his acceptance of the grant. He pleaded having lost his commission in the army for having opposed the Court [regarding general warrants] from conscience. . . . The House accepted that brokerlike apology.' A satirical print, 'Date Obolum Belisario,' published 24 Aug. 1782, shows Shelburne handing Barré a paper inscribed 'Pension £3000 pr Ann.' (BM, *Satiric Prints* v. 610, No. 6028); HW's copy, with his MS identification of the two, is in the New York Public Library.

21. 'An amount paid back from a charge previously made; . . . originally, the action of drawing or getting back a sum paid as duty' (OED).

22. By John O'Keeffe (1747–1833). HW had seen it at the Little Theatre in the Haymarket 6 July (*ante* 7 July 1782), but did not own a copy (first edition, 1783).

23. William Hayley (1745–1820), poet and biographer.

pay half as much for this letter,[24] Madam, but [what] can I do? I
have condemned myself to pass the end of my life as insipidly as
I possibly can; and yet, since you will have the goodness to recollect
me, I cannot give up gratitude, as I have all entertainment; but
when I have told you that I am grateful, I have nothing else worth
telling you of your

Ever devoted

H. W.

To Lady Ossory, Thursday 15 August 1782

Address: To the Countess of Ossory at Ampthill Park, Bedfordshire. *Postmark:*
ISLEWORTH. 15 AV.

Strawberry Hill, Aug. 15, 1782.

I AM greatly proud, Madam, of having formed so able a scholar
as your Ladyship. Be assured that you will every day find more
comfort in becoming an antiquary. The study of antiquity has a
multitude of advantages over other pursuits. All its discoveries produce new lights and no disappointments. They are not doubtful like
the fruits of sciences that depend on reasoning. Is it not charming
too that one may choose one's field of inquiry? You may pursue the
conquest of France with Edward and Henry, humble Spain with
Queen Bess, or with her treat the Dutch with haughty kindness. You
may plant colonies in America with Drake, Raleigh and Cavendish;
subdue Tyrone,[1] and fetch the regal chair from Scone—instead of
being on the point of restoring it.[2] Then by choosing your period,
you may choose your party; and in the Wars of the Roses change
according to the prevailing side, with every revolution. All this naturally follows, if you dive into the secrets of old families. You grow

24. A single letter cost 1*d.* for each post
stage, or 3*d.* from Twickenham to Ampthill.

———

1. In the days of the first and second
Earls of Tyrone in the sixteenth century,
and again in 1641, Tyrone was the seat
of insurrection against English rule.
2. A letter to the Society of Antiquar-

ies of Scotland, printed in GM Oct. 1781,
li. 452–3, mentions a treaty in 1328 and
a recently discovered writ of 1 July 1328,
ordering the return of the stone (brought
to England by order of Edward I in 1296)
to Scotland. HW, however, is referring to
the prominence of the Scots in English
politics.

interested about their heroes, and forget our cotemporaries and the present state,

—from what height fallen![3]

—but I will proceed to your interrogatories, Madam. The shield certainly contains the arms and quarterings of a Sydney. Quarter 1st is Sydney, 2d Dudley, 3d Somery, or, two lions in pale azure, 4th Gray, 5th Beauchamp, 6th Old Warwick, or and azure, with a chevron ermine, always quartered by the Beauchamps.

The shield therefore I conclude to belong to a female Sydney, who married an earl, and thence perhaps[4] Frances Countess of Sussex,[5] foundress of Sydney College.[6] There are, I believe, instances of ladies who have given only their own arms; or such a shield might answer to another of her husband, in which were only his arms. Had she impaled his, they would have been impaled, not quartered, on the man's side; but could not possibly be in the last quarter. Nor could the shield, even without the coronet, represent Sir Henry Sydney's widow,[7] who would have impaled her own arms, or if she had borne her own alone, would have given them alone, and not her husband's alone.

Thus, a little too like a genuine antiquary, I have answered your Ladyship's questions, without satisfying your curiosity. Nor could I ever unravel to my own satisfaction the history of Ampthill-Houghton. By the busts in the house, and by the crests in the frieze without, it is certain that it was possessed by the Sydneys. The new-discovered shield confirms it; and perhaps does, connected with your Ladyship's postscript, which I have since received by itself, explain the whole. As you have found that Robert the first Earl of Leicester[8] was steward of the manors of Anne of Denmark, and that Ampthill

3. Milton, *Paradise Lost*, i. 92.

4. HW first wrote 'probably.'

5. Frances Sidney (ca 1531–89), dau. of Sir William Sidney of Penshurst, Kent, and sister of Sir Henry Sidney, mentioned below, m. (1555), Thomas Radcliffe (ca 1525–83), 3d E. of Sussex, 1557.

6. In her will, 1588, she left £5000 and some goods for 'the Erectyon of a newe Colledge in the Universitie of Cambridge, to be called the Ladie ffrauncis Sidney Sussex Colledge,' the foundation-stone of which was laid on 20 May 1595 (C. W.

Scott-Giles, *Sidney Sussex College*, Cambridge, 1951, pp. 13, 20).

7. Sir Henry Sidney (1529–86), Kt, 1550; K.G., 1564; lord deputy of Ireland, m. (1551) Lady Mary Dudley (d. 1586), dau. of John, D. of Northumberland.

8. Robert Sidney (1563–1626), cr. (1603) Bn Sydney, (1605) Vct Lisle, and (1618) E. of Leicester; the younger brother of Sir Philip Sidney; chamberlain to Anne of Denmark and surveyor-general of her revenues 1603–19.

was a jointure manor of queens,[9] and as one of the busts is of his sister, Mary Countess of Pembroke,[10] the Arcadian, is not it possible, that as the greater Ampthill was the manor-house, Houghton-Ampthill might be a lodge, which he lent or obtained a grant of, to his sister Lady Pembroke, who being a Sydney, and more proud of her brother Sir Philip and her own family, than of her husband, might decorate the house with her own emblems, and as a sort of foundress leave a shield of her own arms only with the coronet to testify her dignity? I think we used to doubt whether the male bust was her husband's or her brother's, Sir Philip. I prefer this hypothesis to my first idea of the shield belonging to Lady Sussex.

Mightily I am pleased with Mr Leveson's[11] legacy[12] to Captain Waldegrave; we do not seem in a course that will enrich him by prizes. I had no curiosity about Monsieur de Grasse,[13] though I was in town for two days[14] while he was the object of the moment. To be sure he was something of a sight;[15] but formerly beaten French admirals were no rarity to us.[16]

9. The manor of Ampthill came into the possession of Henry VII in 1508. In 1542, by act of Parliament, the royal honour of Ampthill was created, from the profits of which Henry VIII 'made provision for Anne of Cleves. James I settled it on the Prince of Wales, who in turn assigned it as portion of the dower of Queen Henrietta Maria.' After her death the honour was leased, and its connection with the Crown ended in 1881 (Vict. Co. Hist. Beds, ii. 38–9, iii. 271).

10. Mary Sidney (1561–1621) m. (1577) Henry Herbert (ca 1538–1601), 2d E. of Pembroke, 1570. Her brother Sir Philip Sidney wrote the Arcadia for her. James I granted her Houghton Park in 1615, and she had the house built.

11. Lord Ossory's uncle, Hon. Baptist Leveson-Gower (?1703 – 4 Aug. 1782), great-uncle of Capt. Waldegrave; M.P. Newcastle-under-Lyme 1727–61; commissioner of Trade and Plantations 1745–9; died at the D. of Bridgewater's in Cleveland Row, London (Venn, Alumni Cantab.; Old Westminsters; London Chronicle 8–13 Aug., lii. 139, 150).

12. £3000 (Coke, 'MS Journals' 29 Aug. 1782).

13. François-Joseph-Paul de Grasse

(1722–88), Comte de Grasse, Marquis de Grasse-Tilly, after being in battles at Dominica, Saint Lucia, Tobago, and St Kitts, was in April 1782 defeated at the Battle of the Saints and captured by Rodney. Brought prisoner to Portsmouth on 31 July, he arrived in London on 3 Aug. at the Royal Hotel, Pall Mall, and on 12 Aug. left for Dover to embark for France. In London he attracted much attention and was treated with respect: he dined with Sir Peter Parker, walked in St James's Park, was at the Drawing-Room on 8 Aug., dined with Lord Keppel at the Admiralty, visited the Bank of England, etc. (London Chronicle 30 July–13 Aug., lii. passim; Annual Register, 1782, lxxv. 216; W. M. James, The British Navy in Adversity, 1926, pp. 332–55).

14. 5–6 Aug. (HW to Mason 4 Aug. 1782, MASON ii. 270–2).

15. 'The Count de Grasse is about six feet four inches high, of an athletic person, fine manly carriage, and of a most heroic aspect. He dresses in the naval uniform of his country, appears remarkably cheerful, and is very fond of walking' (London Chronicle 3–6 Aug., lii. 122).

16. 'Count de Grasse . . . is the first commander-in-chief of a French army or

Mr Morrice is gone to some mud-baths, I forget where.[17] Having been turning over my books since your postscript arrived, I must hurry my letter, for I am not dressed, my dinner is ready, my cousin Mr T. Walpole is with me, and I shall not have time to say more after dinner.

To Lady Ossory, Saturday 31 August 1782

Address: To the Countess of Ossory at Ampthill Park, Bedfordshire. *Postmark:* ISLEWORTH. 31 AV.

Strawberry Hill, Aug. 31, 1782.

IT is very strange indeed, Madam, that you should make me excuses for writing, or think that I have anything better, or even more urgent, to do, than to read your letters. It is very true that the Duchesse de la Valière, in a hand which I could not decipher,[1] has recommended Count Soltikoff[2] and his wife[3] to me—but, oh! my shame, I have not yet seen them. I did mean to go to town today on purpose, but I have had the gout in my right eye-lid, and it was swelled yesterday as big as a walnut—being now shrunk to less than a pistachio, I propose in two or three days to make my appearance, and plead my eye's big belly. Luckily the Comtesse was born in England, the daughter of the former Czernichew,[4] and she is in such terrors of highwaymen, that I shall be quit for a breakfast —so it is an ill highwayman that blows nobody good. In truth it

fleet who has been prisoner in England since the reign of Queen Anne, when Maréchal Tallard was taken by the Duke of Marlborough, and confined to . . . Nottingham. Maréchal de Belleisle, indeed, and his brother the Chevalier, were prisoners with us the war before last, and were confined in Windsor Tower, but they were not in command when taken' (ibid. 1–3 Aug., lii. 118).

17. When HW dined with him at Chiswick on 19 July, Morice had 'totally lost the use of his legs and feet.' 'He set out immediately [after 22 July] for some German mud-baths' (HW to Mann 21 July, 20 Aug. 1782).

———

1. Her letter is missing.

2. Count Ivan Petrovich Saltykov, presumably the one (1736–1805) who was Marshal and governor of Moscow (NBG sub Soltikov; Varvara N. Golovina, *Memoirs*, tr. Fox-Davis, 1910, p. 388).

3. Daria Petrovna Chernyshev, m. Count Ivan Petrovich Saltykov (Golovina, op. cit. 71, 388).

4. Petr Grigor'evich Chernyshev (1712– 67), Russian minister to England 1746– 55 (*Repertorium der diplomatischen Vertreter aller Länder*, Vol. II, ed. Friedrich Hausmann, Zurich, 1950, p. 320; V. A. Bil'basov, *Geschichte Katharina II*, Berlin, 1891–3, ii pt i. 613). Ivan Chernyshev (HW to Mann 2 Dec. 1768) was a more recent Russian minister to England.

would be impossible in this region to amass a set of company for
dinner to meet them. The Hertfords, Lady Holderness, and Lady
Mary Coke did dine here on Thursday, but were armed as if going
to Gibraltar,[5] and Lady Cecilia Johnstone would not venture even
from Petersham, for in the town of Richmond they rob even before
dusk—to such perfection are all the arts brought! Who would have
thought that the war with America would make it impossible to stir
from one village to another? yet so it literally is. The colonies took
off all our commodities down to highwaymen. Now being forced
to mew and then turn them out like pheasants, the roads are stocked
with them, and they are so tame, that they even come into houses.
I have just been reading a most entertaining book, which I will
recommend to you as you are grown antiquaries—I don't know
whether it is published yet, for the author sent it to me. Part was
published some time ago in the *Archæologia*,[6] and is almost the only
paper in that mass of rubbish that has a grain of common sense.[7] It
is Mr E. King[8] on ancient castles.[9] You will see how comfortably and
delectably our potent ancestors lived when in the constant state of
war to which we are coming. Earls, barons and their fair helpmates
lived pell-mell in dark dungeons with their own soldiers, as the poor-
est cottagers do now with their pigs. I shall repent decking Strawberry so much, if I must turn it into a garrison.

Mr Vernon was your Ladyship's informant about the Soltikoffs—
but he gave me more credit for my intended civilities than I deserved. The French do not conceive when they address strangers to
us, that we do not at all live in their style. It is no trouble to them,
who have miscellaneous dinners or suppers, to ask one or two more:
nor are[10] they at any expense in language, as everybody speaks French.
In the private way in which I live, it is troublesome to give a formal
dinner to foreigners, and more so to find company for them in a

---

5. See n. 14 below.

6. 'Observations on Ancient Castles. By
Edward King, Esq. Read at the Society
of Antiquaries, March 21, 28, and April
18, 1776,' in *Archæologia*, 1777, iv. 364–
413. The remainder of the book appeared
in *Archæologia*, 1782, vi. 231–375.

7. HW wrote to King, 27 Aug. 1782: 'I
was extremely pleased with your account
of ancient castles, and thought it the most
sensible and satisfactory of all the papers

published by the Antiquarian Society.'

8. Edward King (ca 1735–1807), miscellaneous writer; F.R.S., 1767; F.S.A., 1770;
P.S.A., 1784–5.

9. *Observations   on   Ancient   Castles.
Sequel to the Observations on Ancient
Castles*, 1782. 'Reprinted with the original
Plates from Vols. 4 and 6 of the "Archæo-
logia"' (BM Cat.; Hazen, *Cat. of HW's
Lib.* 544).

10. MS reads 'at.'

circle of dowagers, who would only jabber English scandal out of the *Morning Post*.

Mr Fitzroy Scudamore[11] by a very old will gives everything to his daughter,[12] consequently to Lord Surry, who gets above £40,000. An estate of £1200 a year, goes to Lord Southampton,[13] if Lady Surry has no children. To two or three very old servants he has not left a farthing—it is no excuse that the will is of ancient date—why did not he make a later?

You are not serious, Madam, that Mr Fox is going to Gibraltar![14] Is he to be Alexander at Oxydracæ,[15] as well as at Statira's[16] feet?[17] —but he may save himself the trouble; I should think the town gone by this time—which is more than our fleet is[18]—just this moment I hear the shocking loss of the *Royal George!*[19] Admiral Kempenfelt is a loss indeed—but I confess I feel more for the hundreds of poor babes who have lost their parents! If one grows ever so indifferent,

11. Charles Fitzroy-Scudamore (formerly, to 1749, Fitzroy) (ca 1713 – 19 Aug. 1782), of Holme Lacy, Herefordshire; natural son of Charles, 2d D. of Grafton; M.P. Thetford 1733–54, 1774–82; Hereford City 1754–68; Heytesbury 1768–74; officer in 1st Foot Guards 1734–48 (*London Chronicle* 20–22 Aug., lii. 179; Burke, *Peerage*, 1953, pp. 165–6, *sub* Beaufort; *Old Westminsters*).

12. Lady Surrey, who was insane (*ante* 10 Oct. 1780).

13. Nephew of Fitzroy-Scudamore.

14. He did not go. Gibraltar was besieged by powerful Spanish and French forces. Fox would have gone as an observer, as did Lord Effingham, who returned to London on 18 Nov. after accompanying Howe: 'His Lordship sailed with the Grand Fleet . . . in company with several other persons of the first distinction' (*London Chronicle* 19–21 Nov., lii. 491).

15. The Oxydrakai (Kshudrakas) were one of the confederation of free tribes in northwest India, whom Alexander defeated at the end of 326 B.C. He is said to have leaped alone into their citadel (*Cambridge History of India*, Vol. I, ed. E. J. Rapson, New York, 1922, pp. 375–6 and Map 4).

16. Alexander the Great m. (324 B.C.) Barsiné or Statira, dau. of Darius Codo-

mannus, K. of Persia. According to Plutarch, she was put to death by Roxana, soon after Alexander's death; elsewhere it is stated that she was killed, some fourteen years later, by Cassander (Justin, *Historiæ Philippicæ*, XI. x, XV. ii).

17. Mrs Mary Robinson, at this time Fox's mistress and formerly the Prince of Wales's, had first played Statira to Lucy's Alexander in Racine's *Alexander the Great* (Ozell's translation, 1714) at Drury Lane on 17 Feb. 1777.

18. 'Gibraltar, I am persuaded, will follow Minorca, if not already gone. So far from the fleet being sailed to its relief, part is gone in pursuit of the Dutch to the Baltic, though the Dutch are really in the Texel. I truly do not know what has occasioned this strange management' (HW to Mann 30 Aug. 1782). Howe's fleet sailed 11 Sept. to relieve Gibraltar (W. M. James, *The British Navy in Adversity*, 1926, p. 372).

19. On 29 Aug. the *Royal George*, Kempenfelt's flagship, was being slightly careened for repairs, with the officers and men and a large number of visitors on board. Suddenly it sank, being so rotten that a piece of the bottom gave way under the strain. About 1000 persons were drowned, including Kempenfelt (W. M. James, op. cit. 371; *London Chronicle* 29 Aug. – 3 Sept., lii. 216, 220).

some new calamity calls one back to this deplorable war! If one is willing to content oneself in a soaking autumn with a match broken or with the death of a Prince Duodecimus,[20] a clap of thunder awakens one and one hears that Britain herself has lost an arm or a leg.[20a] I have been expecting a deluge, and a famine, and such casualties as enrich a Sir Richard Baker[21]—but we have all King David's options at once! and what was his option before he was anointed, freebooting too.

Drowned as we are,[22] the country never was in such beauty; the herbage and leafage are luxurious; the Thames gives itself Rhone airs and almost foams; it is none of your home-brewed rivers that Mr Brown makes with a spade and a watering-pot[23]—apropos, Mr Duane like a good huswife in the middle of his grass plot[24] has planted a pump and a watering trough for his cow, and I suppose on Saturdays dries his towels and neckcloths on his orange trees—but I must have done or the post will be gone—

To LADY OSSORY, Tuesday 1 October 1782

Address: To the Countess of Ossory at Farming Woods, Northamptonshire, by Thrapstone bag. *Postmark:* ISLEWORTH. OC.

Oct. 1, 1782.

SO far from being your gazetteer, Madam, I believe I shall be nothing but your echo, for I can only repeat or reply to the paragraphs you send me. I know nothing new, nay, nor anything old that is new. Mr Churchill and my sister have been with me; I made a little assembly for them and lighted up my gallery, but the terrors of highwaymen are so prevalent, that I could muster but two cribbage, and one commerce table. If partridge-shooting is not turned into robber-shooting, there will be an end of all society!

20. Prince Alfred (b. 22 Sept. 1780, d. 20 Aug. 1782) was actually the fourteenth child of George III and Queen Charlotte.

20a. Cf. *ante* 23 June 1780, n. 4.

21. In his *Chronicle,* 1643.

22. 'We have had the most deplorably wet summer that ever I remember' (HW to Mann 30 Aug. 1782).

23. In *A Note Book of Horace Walpole,* ed. W. S. Lewis, New York, 1927, p. 33, is a note under the year 1782: 'A home-brew'd River,—water in a garden to look like a river.' HW also refers to 'home-brewed rivers' in a letter to Harcourt 7 Sept. 1782.

24. At his villa at Twickenham.

I admire Lady Westmorland's[1] delicacy in her toasts. Indeed I am so ignorant in the fashions of the world that *is* come, that I thought toasting was quite left off, except by the volunteers in Ireland,[2] and by some of your parsons who probe venison and calculate how many stone of fat will come to their share—but fashions alter! I should not wonder if it grew the *ton* to sell bargains.

I know not whether the Episcopal Earl[3] had any hand in ordaining *Lord Russel*[4] for the stage,[5] but I conclude Dr Cumberland had; at least I am sure he had undertaken to correct it.[6] How curious must the produce be of frenzy steeped in laudanum![7]

Cecilia[8] I did read, but, besides its being immeasurably long, and written in Dr Johnson's unnatural phrase, I liked it far less than *Evelina*. I did delight in Mr Briggs, and in the droll names he calls the proud gentleman, whose name I forget. Morris too is well, and Meadows tolerable and Lady Something Something and Miss Something; but all the rest are *outrés*. The great fault is that the authoress is so afraid of not making all her *dramatis personas* act in character, that she never lets them say a syllable but what is to mark their character, which is very unnatural, at least in the present state of things, in which people are always aiming to disguise their ruling passions, and rather affect opposite qualities, than hang out their propensities.[9] The old religious philosopher is a lunatic, and contributing nothing

1. The Dowager Countess, mentioned *ante* 10 June 1780, or Sarah Anne Child (1764–93), only child and heir of Robert Child the banker (*ante* 29 June 1777), m. (20 May 1782) in Scotland (a runaway match) John Fane, 10th E. of Westmorland, 1774.

2. 'Not a glass of wine is drank in Ireland without first naming the toast. Victor i. 158' (Cunningham's MS note in his edition of HW's letters, now wsl, viii. 284). The quotation, slightly modified, is from Benjamin Victor, *History of the Theatres of London and Dublin*, 1761; HW's copy is Hazen, *Cat. of HW's Lib.* 2973.

3. Frederick Augustus Hervey, 4th E. of Bristol, 1779; Bp of Derry, 1768. He had sent HW the MS of the play mentioned below (MASON ii. 223).

4. *Lord Russell, a Tragedy*, first acted at Drury Lane 20 Aug. 1784; ran for four nights (Genest vi. 303); privately printed,

Dublin, ca 1794; by the Rev. Thomas Stratford (1735–86), rector of Gallstown, co. Westmeath, for whom see MASON ii. 223–5, 233–5, 273.

5. A premature report that the play 'is to be brought out this season at Drury Lane Theatre' had appeared in the *London Courant* 18 Sept. (MASON ii. 273 n. 3). The *London Chronicle* 17–19 Sept., lii. 275, reported that the tragedy 'has been presented and accepted at . . . Drury Lane.'

6. As Stratford had told HW in April 1782 (MASON ii. 233).

7. Stratford's 'frenzy'; Cumberland's 'laudanum'; see MASON ii. 233, 273.

8. *Cecilia, or Memoirs of an Heiress*, 5 vols, published 12 June; by Frances Burney (1752–1840), m. (1793) Alexandre d'Arblay (Joyce Hemlow, *History of Fanny Burney*, Oxford, 1958, p. 151; Hazen, *Cat. of HW's Lib.* 2812).

9. Cf. CHATTERTON 256.

to the story, might be totally omitted, and had better be so. But I am most offended at the want of poetical justice. The proud gentleman and his proud wife ought to be punished and humbled—whereas the wife is rather exhibited as an amiable character. To say the truth, the last volume is very indifferent.

The vindication of the Governor of Barbadoes[10] was quite lost upon me, who had never interested myself in his story, nor even know of what he was accused. I am a prodigious economist of my memory, and never load it with details about people and things for which I do not care a straw. This is meant with no disrespect for your Ladyship's information, for which I am obliged, as you see it has furnished me with five lines; a great object in my present sterility! My barrenness is much increased by shutting my ears to politics, to which I never will listen more. I was accustomed to a flourishing free kingdom; I had extended my ideas to empire—I cannot contract them to a fragment of a bankrupt island, which has gamed away its fortune, and learned all the tricks of a ruined gamester. We are totally degenerated in every respect, which I suppose is the case of all falling states. In what do we shine? Saving the respect that I have for youth, I do not think the present blossoms are entertaining. They may amuse themselves very well, but surely they are not ingenious nor contribute to enliven us. I think I could still be diverted if the complexion of the times furnished matter, but I certainly cannot divert your Ladyship, when my own mind stagnates for want of something to put it in motion.

Princess Amelie told Lady Margaret Compton two days ago that Mr Morice has recovered the use of his legs—I don't know how her R[oyal] H[ighness] heard it.

I have now replied paragraph by paragraph to your letter, Madam, as if saying my catechism, and given reasons of the faith that is in me; but as good boys are commonly dull, perhaps you would prefer a correspondent that played truant and told you a few fibs.

Have you seen in the papers[11] the excellent letter of Paul Jones to Sir Joseph Yorke? *Elle nous dit bien des vérités!* I doubt poor Sir

10. Maj.-Gen. James Cunningham; see *ante* 9 Jan. 1781. On 2 July 1782 the General Assembly of Barbados had passed a resolution thanking Shelburne for recalling Cunningham, 'by which our country has been most happily released from an arbitrary and oppressive system of taxation, established by that officer for his own emolument . . . for thirteen weeks successively' (*London Chronicle* 15–17 Oct., lii. 372).

11. Not identified.

Joseph cannot answer them! Dr Franklin himself I should think
was the author.[12] It is certainly written by a first-rate pen, and not
by a common man-of-war. The *Royal George* is out of luck!

I have told a lie; the *Royal George* is *in* luck. I have this minute
received a letter[13] from Gen. Conway with these words,

I have a piece of good news to tell you, which is the complete and entire
defeat of the long meditated attack on Gibraltar, which began on the
13th at 3 P.M., and before midnight all the famous floating batteries
were either burnt or sunk by our red-hot balls. They lost, it is said, 1500
men, but none of distinction named. They saved some in their own
boats, and Gen. Elliot some in those he sent out.

Well, Madam, is not this General Elliot the Old Man of the Mountain[14] who destroyed enemies with his *feu grégeois?*[15] It was very
obliging too in him to enliven my tame letter by such a gay conclusion—if one is to smile at the destruction of 1500 men! I did smile
inwardly, for two persons came in as I was reading my letter, and
as I naturally said I hoped this event would facilitate peace, one of
them said, 'it is very uncertain what effect it will have on the King
(of Spain): he has a sort of head that may persist the more for a thing
being impossible'—now we must wait to see whether the combined
fleets will be obstinate too and attack Lord Howe, or let him victual
Gibraltar.[16]

12. Franklin was the author of the
alleged letter of John Paul Jones to
Yorke, dated 'Ipswich, New England,
March 7, 1781,' and printed at Franklin's
press at Passy as 'Numb. 705. Supplement
to the Boston Independent Chronicle,'
written before 22 April 1782 (Luther S.
Livingston, *Franklin and His Press at
Passy*, New York, 1914, pp. 59–63, with
facsimile). Number 705 of the Boston *Independent Chronicle and . . . Universal
Advertiser*, which Franklin imitates, had
been published 28 Feb. 1782.

13. Missing. For further details of the
battle, see the *London Chronicle* 28 Sept.–
3 Oct., 9–12 Nov., liii. 320, 322, 458; W.
M. James, *The British Navy in Adversity*,
1926, pp. 373–4.

14. Hasan ibn-al-Sabbah, known as the
Old Man of the Mountain, founded in
Persia in 1090 a military and religious
sect, the Assassins, finally suppressed in
the thirteenth century; see *post* 4 Sept.
1792.

15. 'Greek fire,' a firebrand capable of
burning on the water, used by the Greeks
in the Middle Ages to set fire to ships.
See J. R. Partington, *A History of Greek
Fire and Gunpowder*, Cambridge, [1960].
HW in his letter to Conway 16 Sept. 1781
applies that term to Lord George Gordon.

16. The combined fleets, though superior in numbers, did not attack Howe;
see W. M. James, op. cit. 372, 374–7, 450–
1.

To Lady Ossory, Sunday 3 November 1782

Strawberry Hill, Nov.[1] 3, 1782.

OUR mutual silence, Madam, has had pretty nearly the same cause, want of matter, for though my nominal wife Lady Browne has not left me like your Lord, I have led almost as uneventful a life, as your Ladyship in your lonely woods, except that I have been for two days in town[2] and seen Mrs Siddons.[3] She pleased me beyond my expectation, but not up to the admiration of the *ton*, two or three of whom were in the same box with me, particularly Mr Boothby,[4] who, as if to disclaim the stoic apathy of Mr Meadows in *Cecilia*,[5] was all *bravissimo*. Mr Craufurd too asked me if I did not think her the best actress I ever saw? I said, 'By no means; we old folks were apt to be prejudiced in favour of our first impressions.' She is a good figure, handsome enough, though neither nose nor chin according to the Greek standard, beyond which both advance a good deal. Her hair is either red, or she has no objection to its being thought so, and had used red powder.[6] Her voice is clear and good, but I thought she did not vary its modulations enough, nor ever approach enough to the familiar—but this may come when more habituated to the awe of the audience of the capital. Her action is proper, but with little variety—when without motion, her arms are not genteel. Thus you see, Madam, all my objections are very trifling

---

1. HW first wrote 'Oct.'

2. 28–29 Oct. (n. 3 below; HW to Harcourt 29 Oct.).

3. Sarah Kemble (1755–1831), m. (1773) William Siddons. HW saw her on 28 Oct. in the title role of *Isabella* (Garrick's version, 1757, of Southerne's *Fatal Marriage*, 1694). Following her failure in 1775–6, she had returned to Drury Lane in this rôle on 10 Oct. 1782 and was acting it for the eighth time when HW saw it with *Robinson Crusoe* (see below; GM 1782, lii. 464; *London Courant* 28 Oct., where the casts for both are given).

4. HW's third cousin, Charles Boothby Skrymsher (Clopton after 1792) (ca 1740–1800), known as 'Prince Boothby' (BERRY ii. 201 n. 16; MANN v. 431 n. 14).

5. Mr Meadows is described in Fanny Burney's *Cecilia* (Book IV, Chapter II) as 'a man of the *ton*' for whom 'nothing is entertaining . . . for two minutes together.' 'I hate everything that requires attention.' 'Always some drawback! nothing ever perfect.'

6. She later discontinued the use of powder. 'Sir Joshua [Reynolds] often honoured me by his presence at the theatre. He approved very much of my costumes and my hair *without powder*, which at that time was used in great profusion, with a reddish-brown tint and a great quantity of pomatum, which, well-kneaded together, modelled the fair ladies' tresses into large curls like demicannon' (*Reminiscences of Sarah Kemble Siddons 1773–1785*, ed. Van Lennep, Cambridge, Mass., 1942, p. 19).

—but what I really wanted, but did not find, was originality, which announces genius, and without both which I am never intrinsically pleased. All Mrs Siddons did, good sense or good instruction might give. I dare to say, that were I one-and-twenty I should have thought her marvellous[7]—but alas! I remember Mrs Porter and the Dumesnil —and remember every accent of the former in the very same part.[8] Yet this is not entirely prejudice—don't I equally recollect the whole progress of Lord Chatham and Charles Townshend, and does it hinder my thinking Mr Fox a prodigy?—Pray don't send him this paragraph too[9]—I am not laying a courtly trap, nor at sixty-five, projecting, like the old Duke of Newcastle, to be in favour in the next reign.[10] My real meditations are on objects much more proper to my age. A letter[11] I have just received from Lord Buchan[12] in-forms me of, probably, much more splendid courts than the little tottering ruined palace in St James's Street. Somebody at Bath (whose name I cannot read)[13] has made a telescope that magnifies a celestial object *6450* times,[14] by which he finds that the new planet[15] (which I did not see in town like Mrs Siddons) is *160* times bigger than our little football;[16] and as the inventor expects to improve his instrument much farther, I suppose, the new planet will improve in proportion. Perhaps I do not talk like an optician or astronomer —but think, Madam, what exquisite glasses the new planetarians must have, before they can have any idea of our existing at all! Well,

7. Cf. HW to Mason ?ca 21 Jan. 1783, MASON ii. 282.

8. Mrs Porter played Isabella in Sou-therne's *The Fatal Marriage* from 1717 until 13 March 1742, the year before her retirement (Genest ii. 601, iv. 8, 447).

9. See *ante* 7 July 1782.

10. See *ante* 13 July 1776, n. 27.

11. Missing.

12. David Steuart Erskine (1742–1829), 11th E. of Buchan, 1767; styled Lord Cardross 1747–67; founder (1780) of the Society of the Antiquaries of Scotland. HW's reply to Buchan 5 Nov. 1782 is in DALRYMPLE 165–8.

13. The astronomer, William Herschel (1738–1822).

14. Herschel wrote to Watson 7 Jan. 1782: 'I do not suppose there are many persons who could even find a star with my power of 6450' (*Scientific Papers of*

Sir William Herschel, 1912, i. p. xxxiii). 'Mr Herschel's large improved telescope is 8 feet long, and magnifies 6500 times' (GM 1782, lii. 520).

15. On 13 March 1781 Herschel had discovered the planet Uranus, which he at first thought was a comet, and then called the 'Georgium Sidus' or 'Georgian planet.' His paper announcing the dis-covery was read at the Royal Society 26 April 1781 and was printed in the *Philo-sophical Transactions* for 1781, lxxi pt ii. 492–501. See also *The Herschel Chronicle*, ed. Constance A. Lubbock, Cambridge and New York, 1933, pp. 78–86; DALRYM-PLE 167–8, 188.

16. Actually Uranus is 64 times the size of the earth; Herschel computed it to be 5.45 times the size of the earth (J. B. Sidgwick, *William Herschel*, 1953, p. 144).

but as those 160-times-bigger folks may have remained in as profound ignorance as Sir Joseph Banks's friends or Capt. Cooke's,[17] how clever is it in *us* invisible pismires to have invented telescopes and calculated *their* size! I have often asked myself whither the myriads that are continually swept from our earth are to be transported?—now, as human pride concludes that the universal system was made for little us, here is a receptacle large enough—at least, that planet may know of others within reach, and not above some millions of millions of miles off. Now stoop, Madam, as many millions of miles as all these distances make, and let us talk of Gibraltar—Oh! what an atom! how can one figure it little enough, compared with what we have been talking of? Common sense is lost in the immensity; I am forced to look at my window, and persuade myself that Richmond Hill is a large object, before I can dismount from the stirrups of the telescope, and talk the usual language of the world.

I am glad to hear so good an account of Hatfield from our Lord. I have been invited thither—but I have done with terrestrial journeys. I have not philosophy enough to stand stranger servants staring at my broken fingers at dinner. I hide myself like spaniels that creep into a hedge to die—yet having preserved my eyes and all my teeth, among which is a colt's, not yet decayed, I treated it and my eyes, not only with Mrs Siddons, but a harlequin farce—but there again my ancient prejudices operated—how unlike the pantomimes of Rich,[18] which were full of wit! and coherent, and carried on a story! What I now saw was *Robinson Crusoe*[19]—how Aristotle and

17. James Cook (1728–79), Capt. R.N., 1775, the circumnavigator whom Banks had accompanied on the voyage of 1768–71.

18. John Rich (ca 1682–1761), pantomimist, introduced into his pantomimes of Harlequin (a rôle he always played) and Columbine 'a variety of surprising adventures and tricks, which were produced by the magic wand of Harlequin; such as the sudden transformation of palaces and temples to huts and cottages; of men and women into wheelbarrows and joint-stools; of trees turned to houses; colonnades to beds of tulips; and mechanics' shops into serpents and ostriches' (Thomas Davies, *Life of Garrick*, 1780, i. 92).

19. *Robinson Crusoe, or Harlequin Fri-*

day, a pantomime first acted at Drury Lane 29 Jan. 1781, when it was described in the *London Chronicle* 27–30 Jan., xlix. 103, and in a cutting inserted by HW in his 'Collection of Prologues and Epilogues . . . from the Year 1780' (he also inserted a song from it, cut from the *Public Advertiser* 1 Feb. 1781). 'This is said to be contrived by Mr Sheridan, whose powers, if it really be his performance, do not seem adapted to the production of such kinds of entertainment. The scenery, by Loutherbourg, has a very pleasing effect, but considered in every other light it is a truly insipid exhibition' (David Erskine Baker, *Biographia Dramatica*, new edn, 1782, ii. 312). The attribution to Sheridan, mentioned also

Bossu, had they ever written on pantomimes, would swear! It was a heap of contradictions and violations of the costume. *Friday* is turned into Harlequin, and falls down at an old man's feet that I took for Pantalon, but they told me it was *Friday's* father[20]—I said, 'Then it must be *Thursday*'—yet still it seemed to be Pantalon. I see I understand nothing from astronomy to a harlequin-farce!

Your new visitor,[21] I hope Madam, has carried you to Drayton. It is a most venerable heap of ugliness with many curious bits. There is a modern colonnade erected by Sir John Germayne, the pillars of which, according to his usual ignorance, were at first, as Lady Suffolk told me, set up with their capitals downwards, supposing them pedestals.[22]

I condole your loss of an old servant—I know no more of Gibraltar than you have seen in the papers. My Russians[23] did come to breakfast, but understood Strawberry so little, that I thought it never before was so much the nurse—

—of Goths, of Alans, and of Huns.[24]

I am very uncertain when I shall settle in London, but think I must in a fortnight,[25] when Mr Duane will. He replaces Mr Morice for Cav. Mozzi. Mr Bull,[26] whom I saw in town, tells me poor Morice is not at all better, and thinks of Naples.[27] I direct to Ampthill.

in the *London Courant* 24 Oct. 1782, is generally accepted; see Sheridan's *Plays and Poems*, ed. Rhodes, Oxford, 1928, iii. 337–41; HW had none of the printed versions: *A Short Account of the Situations and Incidents*, 1781; *The Overture Comic-Tunes and Song*, [1781]; *Robinson Crusoe or Harlequin Friday*, Newcastle, [1791].

20. Friday's father is in the cast as listed in a letter by Sybil Rosenfeld, *Times Literary Supplement*, 4 March 1944, p. 120, describing a performance in 1790. After the first act, which follows Defoe to some extent, Friday and his father become Harlequin and Pantaloon.

21. Not identified.

22. 'The Inner Court [at Drayton] has been modernized by Sir John, very richly, but not in good taste, with two colonnades at each end, like the Inner Court at Hampton Court' (*Country Seats* 55, *sub* 1763).

23. The Saltykovs (*ante* 31 Aug. 1782).

24. 'The North by myriads pours her mighty sons,
    Great nurse of Goths, of Alans, and of Huns!'
(Pope, *Dunciad* iii. 89–90).

25. HW went to London 18 Nov. (*post* 16 Nov. 1782, the last letter for this year written from SH).

26. Richard Bull (ca 1725–1805), M.P. Newport 1756–80; HW's occasional correspondent. He had houses at Ongar in Essex, Shorwell, Isle of Wight, and in Stratton Street, Piccadilly. He and Anthony Morris Storer were the chief 18th-century collectors of HW's works and SH publications. He was also 'among the half-dozen principal collectors in England of engraved portraits' (W. P. Courtney in *Notes and Queries*, 1913, 11th ser., vii. 170–1). See DALRYMPLE 161 n. 14 for a biographical note.

27. He planned to leave Lausanne for Naples around 1 Sept. 1783 (HW to Mann 10 Sept. 1783, Mann to HW 10 Oct. 1783).

PS. Lord Buchan, who tells me a vast deal about *our* Antiquarian Society at Edinburgh,[28] and generally asks me many questions about past ages, has sent me two franks, that my knowledge may cost him no more than it is worth.[29] Does your Ladyship know that Lord Monboddo[30] has twice proposed to Mrs Garrick?[31] She refused him; I don't know whether because he says in his book that men were born with tails,[32] or because they have lost them.

The following is an extract (I think you will like it) from a letter of Lord Mansfield[33] to Monsieur Limon,[34] who, Gerbier[35] being ill, pleaded and carried the cause of Miss Hamilton[36] against Parson Beresford,[37] and sent his *plaidoyer*[38] to his Lordship. 'Vous avez pris,

28. On 29 Jan. 1781 HW had been elected an honorary member of the recently founded Society of the Antiquaries of Scotland. Buchan was its chief promoter (DALRYMPLE 150 and n. 2).

29. HW does not mention the franks in his reply to Buchan 5 Nov. (DALRYMPLE 165–8).

30. James Burnett (1714–99), lord of session as Lord Monboddo, 1767; author of *Ancient Metaphysics*, 6 vols, 1779–99, and *Of the Origin and Progress of Language*, 6 vols, 1773–92, of which the first three volumes had appeared in 1773, 1774, and 1776.

31. On 28 June 1783 'Mrs Garrick gave us [Mrs Walsingham, Miss Boyle, and Miss Hamilton] high entertainment by showing us Lord Monboddo's letter with an offer of his hand; the style and proposals I cannot well forget' (*Mary Hamilton* [Mrs Dickenson], *Letters and Diaries*, ed. Anson, 1925, p. 137). Cf. HW to Mason 4 Aug. 1782, MASON ii. 271.

32. Monboddo merely asserts 'that there have been individuals in Europe, with tails, is, I think, a fact incontestable,' and that 'it is at least probable . . . that there is a race or nation of men with tails' (*Of the Origin and Progress of Language*, Book II, Chapter III, i. 258). The most quoted remark about Monboddo is perhaps Johnson's that Monboddo was 'as jealous of his tail as a squirrel' (Boswell, *Johnson* v. 111).

33. As Lord Chief Justice of the King's Bench.

34. Geoffroy de Limon (d. 1799), known as the Marquis de Limon, afterwards con-

trôleur général des finances to the Duc d'Orléans, 'qui a été attaché à Monsieur [as intendant des finances] . . . n'ayant d'avocat que le titre' (Louis Petit de Bachaumont, *Mémoires secrets*, London, 1777–89, xx. 142, 169, *sub* 13, 28 March 1782; NBG; Gouverneur Morris, *Diary of the French Revolution*, Boston, 1939, ii. 177, 184; Talleyrand, *Mémoires*, ed. Broglie, 1891–2, i. 178–9; *Almanach royal*, *passim*; Jacob-Nicolas Moreau, *Mes souvenirs*, 1898–1901, ii. 286). On 11 Nov. he and his brother were in the Court of King's Bench 'and sat upon the Bench a long time by the judges. Lord Mansfield and his brethren paid particular attention to these gentlemen and conversed in French with them a good deal' (*London Courant* 12 Nov.).

35. Pierre-Jean-Baptiste Gerbier (1725–88), a well-known French barrister.

36. Sidney Hamilton (ca 1766–1827), dau. of Gawen Hamilton of Killyleagh Castle, co. Down, by Jane Rowan, m. (1780) Rev. Benjamin Beresford, and died in Great Quebec Street, London (GM 1827, xcvii pt ii. 646; Burke, *Landed Gentry of Ireland*, 1904, p. 239).

37. Benjamin Beresford (?1750–?1819), son of James Beresford; tutor and chaplain to the Duke of Bedford; rector of Bedford; 'simple chapelain, fils d'un cordonnier, et maître d'école d'un village'; translator of German works; British chaplain at Moscow (Foster, *Alumni Oxon.*; Bachaumont, op. cit. xx. 140–1, 165–71, 180–1, 256–9, *sub* 13, 27–9 March, 4 April, 23 May 1782; Boswell, op. cit. iii, 284; Venn, *Alumni Cantab.*, *sub* Beresford,

Monsieur, le rôle destiné à Monsieur Gerbier, et vous l'avez remplacé. On ne s'est point aperçû de l'absence d'Atlas, quand le fardeau a été soutenu par Hercule.'

The French, I conclude, Lord Stormont's—and the thought too perhaps—it is *pensé à la française.*

I have seen the *plaidoyer;* it begins with setting forth that Mr Hamilton,[39] the father of Miss, is in the line of succession to the crown of Scotland—and in three lines more I found that this Scottish princess lived at Pinner[40]—a village vulgar enough for so highborn a heroine!

To Lady Ossory, Tuesday 5 November 1782

The postscript is here first printed.
Address: To the Countess of Ossory at Ampthill Park, Bedfordshire. *Postmark:* ISLEWORTH. 5 NO.

Nov. 5, 1782.

I BEG your Ladyship's pardon, but I cannot refrain from sending you a codicil to my last. I have taken to astronomy, now the scale is enlarged enough to satisfy my taste, who love gigantic ideas—do not be afraid; I am not going to write a second part to the *Castle of Otranto,*

Hamilton Sidney; BM Cat.; B. Q. Morgan, *Critical Bibliography of German Literature in English Translation,* 2d edn, Stanford, Cal., 1938, p. 635). He eloped with the 15-year-old heiress 1 Nov. 1780, married her at Gretna Green 3 Nov. and again in London 11 Dec. 1780, and (when her mother carried her away to France) brought suit in the French courts for her return. For details, see the *plaidoyer* mentioned below and Beresford's *Narrative of Circumstances Attending Mr B's Marriage with Miss Hamilton,* 1782, and his *Appendix to Mr B's Narrative,* 1788; *Rambler's Magazine,* Jan. 1783, i. 40).

38. *Question de droit public. Plaidoyer pour Messire Gawen Hamilton . . . contre le Sieur Benjamin Beresford,* 1782. Beresford won this cause but was later

harassed by Mrs Hamilton and her friends and hirelings. HW's copy is now in the British Museum (Hazen, *Cat. of HW's Lib.* 2050. 24).

39. Gawen   Hamilton   (1729–1805) (Burke, *Landed Gentry of Ireland,* loc. cit.). In the *Question de droit public* (p. 1) the title styles him 'Messire Gawen-Hamilton, des Comtes de Clambrasil, descendant des Comtes d'Arran, héritiers du royaume d'Écosse au défaut d'enfant de Marie, Reine d'Écosse, et Reine douairière de France, seigneur des terres de Killeleagh et Killinghy.'

40. In Middlesex. 'Madame Hamilton, qui demeure les hivers à Londres dans un hôtel qui lui appartient, rue de Marlboroug, passe les étés à sa maison de campagne de Pinner, à cinq lieues de la capitale' (ibid. 12).

nor another account of the Patagonians[1] who inhabit the new Brobdignag planet;[2] though I do not believe that a world 160 times bigger
than ours, is inhabited by pigmies—they would do very well for our
page, the moon.

I have been reading Lord Buchan's letter[3] again. He tells me that
Mr. What-d'ye-call-him[4] at Bath says that the new planet's orbit is
80 of our years. Now if their days are in proportion to their year, as
our days are to our year, a day in the new planet must contain 1920
hours—and yet I dare to say, some of the inhabitants complain of the
shortness of the days. I may err in my calculations, for I am a woeful
arithmetician, and never could learn my multiplication table—but
no matter: one large sum is as good as another. How one should
smile to hear the Duchess of Devonshire of the new planet cry, 'Lord,
you would not go to dinner yet sure! it is but fifteen hundred o'clock!'
or some Miss, 'Ah! that superannuated old fright, I'll lay a wager
she's a year old'—but stay—here I don't go by my own rule of proportion—I ought to suppose their lives adequate to their size. Well, any
way one might build very entertaining hypotheses on this new discovery.

The planet's distance from the sun is 1,710 millions of miles—
I revere a telescope's eyes that can see so far! what pity that no Newton should have thought of improving instruments for hearing too!
if a glass can penetrate seventeen hundred millions of miles beyond
the sun, how easy to form a trumpet like Sir Joshua Reynolds's, by
which one might overhear what is said in Mercury and Venus that
are within a stone's throw of us! Well, such things will be discovered
—but alas! we live in such an early age of the world, that nothing is
brought to any perfection! I don't doubt but there will be invented
spying-glasses for seeing the thoughts—and then a new kind of stucco

1. A reference to HW's *An Account of
the Giants Lately Discovered; in a Letter
to a Friend in the Country*, 1766, a satire
on the newspaper accounts of the Patagonians (said to be nine or ten feet high), as
reported by Hon. John Byron, captain of
the *Dolphin* (COLE i. 126 n. 4). In its
penultimate paragraph HW writes, 'Oh!
If we could come at an heroic poem
penned by a giant! We should see other
images than our puny writers of romance
have conceived; and a little different from
the cold tale of a late notable author, who

did not know better what to do with his
giant than to make him grow till he
shook his own castle about his own ears'
(pp. 29–30). HW has noted in   copy,
now WSL, 'Castle of Otranto by the author
of this pamphlet.'

2. Uranus. In *An Account of the Giants*
HW twice alludes to Swift's Brobdingnag
or Gulliver (*Works* ii. 94, 97).

3. Ca 29 Oct. 1782, missing. For HW's
reply, 5 Nov., see DALRYMPLE 165–8.

4. Herschel.

for concealing them—but I return to my new favourite, astronomy. Do but think, Madam, how fortunate it is for us that discoveries are not reciprocal. If our superiors of the great planets were to dabble in such minute researches as we make by microscopes, how with their infinitely greater facilities, they might destroy us for a morning's amusement! They might impale our little globe on a pin's point, as we do a flea, and take the current of the Ganges or Oroonoko for the circulation of our blood—for with all due respect for philosophy of all sorts, I humbly apprehend that where people wade beyond their sphere, they make egregious blunders—at least we do, who are not accustomed to them. I am so vulgar, that when I hear of 17 millions of miles, I fancy astronomers compute by *livres* like the French, and not by pounds sterling, I mean, not by miles sterling. Nay, as it is but two days that I have grown wise, I have another whim. I took it into my head last night that our antediluvian ancestors who are said to have lived many hundred years, were not inhabitants of this earth, but of the new planet, whence might come the account, which we believe came from heaven. Whatever came from the skies where the new planet lives, would in the apprehensions of men at that time be deemed to come from heaven. Now if a patriarch lived ten of their years, which may be the term of their existence, and which according to our computation make 800 of our years, he was pretty nearly of the age of Methusalem; for what signifies a fraction of an hundred years or so?—Yet I offer this only as a conjecture; nor will I weary your Ladyship with more, though I am not a little vain of my new speculations.

Apropos to millions, have you heard, Madam, of the Prince de Guemené's[5] breaking for 28 millions of *livres?*[6] Would not one think it was a debt contracted by the two Foleys?[7] I know of another Prince

5. Henri-Louis-Mériadec de Rohan (1745–1802), Prince de Guéménée (Jacob-Nicolas Moreau, *Mes souvenirs*, 1906–7, ii. 237).

6. For this bankruptcy see Louis Petit de Bachaumont, *Mémoires secrets*, London, 1777–89, xxi. 155–6, 161, 166–7, 184–5, 198, 212–13, 24–5 of second pagination, *sub* 30 Sept., 5, 11, 23, 30 Oct., 8 Nov., 1 Dec. 1782; du Deffand v. 32–3.

7. The debts of the Foley brothers in 1778 'are supposed to amount to near £220,000' (*Journals of the House of Lords* xxxv. 467); 28,000,000 livres, with the livre valued at a shilling (cf. OED, Johnson's *Dictionary*, *sub* livre), would amount to £1,200,000. To pay the interest the Foleys 'had bound themselves to pay annuities . . . that amounted to £17,540 a year' (*Last Journals* ii. 135) or £17,450 (Mason i. 392).

de Guemené,[8] who lived, I think, early in the reign of Louis Quatorze, and had a great deal of wit. His wife[9] was a *savante*. One day
he met coming out of her closet an old Jew (not such as the present
Prince and the Foleys deal with but) quite in rags, and half stark.
The Prince asked, who he was? The Princess replied scornfully,
'Mais il me montre l'hebreu'—'Eh bien,' said the Prince, 'et bientôt,
il vous montrera son cul'— I hope this story, if you did not know it,
will make amends for the rest of my rhapsody.

PS. I fear some planet or other out of contempt for our impertinent curiosity has emptied its jordan on our heads—why, Madam,
if Tonton lifts his leg over an ant's hill, do you think the pismires
don't say, 'It rains terribly'?

To Lady Ossory, Sunday 10 November 1782

Strawberry Hill, Nov. 10, 1782.

I AM very happy that they amused your Ladyship and Lady Anne
for a moment in our Lord's absence; but I do not intend to over-
load you with my illustrations of the new planet—which you call
anonymous; but I assure you the inventor has christened it 'the
Georgian'[1]—whether in imitation of the constellation named
'Charles's Wain,'[2] or to console his Majesty with new dominions in
lieu of those he has lost, I do not know. I was happy to be *planet-
struck,* as you so properly call it; for having totally abandoned politics
and authorship, I catch at any whim that will occupy me for a day or
two, and stop a gap in my correspondences. Lord O. asks very reason-

8. Probably Louis de Rohan (1598–1667),
Prince de Guéménée, Duc de Montbazon;
his wit is noticed by Louis, Duc de St-
Simon, *Mémoires*, ed. Boislisle, 1879–1930,
v. 231 n. 1, 233, xxiii. 112, 185.

9. Anne de Rohan (1604–85) m. (1616)
the Prince de Guéménée; she was well
known as a *précieuse* (ibid. v. 228 n. 7,
233 n. 4).

1. In honour of George III, Herschel
called the planet *Georgium Sidus* or 'Georgian planet'; 'The Georgian' was the name
used in the British *Nautical Almanac* up
to 1850. 'Uranus,' the name now accepted,
was suggested by the German astronomer,
Johann Elert Bode. See *ante* 3 Nov. 1782,
n. 15.

2. 'The name appears to rise out of the
verbal association of the star-name *Arcturus* with *Arturus* or Arthur, and the legendary association of Arthur and Charlemagne; so that what was originally the
wain of *Arcturus* . . . . became at length
the wain of Carl or Charlemagne' (OED).
'In England it goes by the name of "King
Charles' Wain"' (OED, quotation dated
1876).

ably why I correspond with Lord B.[3]—because I cannot help it now and then: I am his Tom Hearne, and he *will* extract from me whatever in the course of my antiquarian dips, I have picked up about Scottish kings and queens, for whom in truth I never cared a straw. I have tried everything but being rude to break off the intercourse; and sometimes go as near the line as I can by smiling. My last answer was of that kind: I humbly pointed out an error of the press in the first number of the memoirs of their Society[4] which he sent me. On the reverse of a medal of their Vestal Martyr Queen Mary,[5] they have printed *Satyr* for *Saltyr*[6]—and I terrified myself lest it should be construed into an intended aspersion![7]

My last diversion has been of a different nature from star-gazing. Mrs Hobart last Friday invited me to her play at Ham Common. I went, because Mr Conway and Lady Ailesbury and Mrs Damer were for that purpose at Lady Cecilia Johnston's, and I had not seen them for an age. I was extremely pleased especially with the afterpiece. The play was *All in the Wrong*,[8] and a vile thing it is: there are three couple, all equally jealous,[9] with no discrimination of character.[10] It is like two looking-glasses that reflect each other without end. Mrs Hobart[11] played admirably and most genteelly, which was

3. HW's correspondence with Buchan lasted 'for more than thirty years' (DALRYMPLE, p. xxxii).

4. William Smellie's *Account of the Institution and Progress of the Society of the Antiquaries of Scotland*, Edinburgh, 1782; a second part appeared in 1784. This work does not appear in the SH records: HW wrote to Buchan 5 Nov. 1782 that he had 'lent the tract.' Cf. Hazen, *Cat. of HW's Lib.* 1609:42.3. William Smellie (1740–95), printer and naturalist, had been appointed keeper of the Society's museum in 1781.

5. A gift from Sir John Dick included fourteen coins of base silver of Mary Queen of Scots, on all of which appeared the 'saltyr' (Smellie, op. cit. 50–1).

6. Saltire: a heraldic term for a St Andrew's cross. The error in Smellie's *Account*, p. 51, was corrected on the errata sheet which appeared with 'Part Second' of the *Account*, Edinburgh, 1784.

7. 'This blunder may make some of her Majesty's censors smile' (HW to Buchan 5 Nov. 1782, DALRYMPLE 166).

8. By Arthur Murphy; HW's copy, 1761, is now WSL (Hazen, *Cat. of HW's Lib.* 1810.2.7; H. H. Dunbar, *The Dramatic Career of Arthur Murphy*, New York, 1946, pp. 125–32; J. P. Emery, *Arthur Murphy*, Philadelphia, 1946, pp. 66–70; Genest iv. 616–17; HW to Lady Ailesbury 13 June 1761).

9. In the Advertisement to the play, 'Nov. 15, 1761,' Murphy wrote: 'Though jealousy, in all its appearances, has been frequently exhibited on the English stage, yet it was imagined that a plan, which should delineate all the varieties of that passion, whether subsisting between lovers or in the matrimonial life, and blend them together in one piece, would not be unacceptable to the public.'

10. 'Acted by professionals the characters were properly discriminated, and the play was still acted on the London stage as late as 1835' (Dunbar, op. cit. 129).

11. As Lady Restless.

very refreshing, as one never sees anything like a woman of fashion on the stage.[12] Her three daughters[13] all did well. A Mr Fury[14] is cried up as a miracle: he was not so in my eyes. Col. Gardiner,[15] who is not liked, was, I thought, little inferior, yet but middling—but in *The Guardian*,[16] all was perfect. The eldest Miss Hobart, so lovely and so modest, was not acting, she was the thing itself.[17] There was an Irish Mr Arabin,[18] from Sir William East's[19] theatre,[20] incomparable in the uncle.[21] His own brogue added exceedingly, and a Colonel Tims,[22] being a very well-looking man, and playing most justly,[23] made the story very probable.

There was a great deal of good company collected from the environs and even from London, but so armed with blunderbusses,

12. Cf. HW's remark on Miss Farren and Mrs Abington, *post* 12 Dec. 1786, 14 June 1787.

13. The three eldest: Albinia Hobart (1759–1850), m. (1784) the younger Richard Cumberland; lady of the Bedchamber to the younger princesses 1796–1812; Henrietta Anne Barbara Hobart (ca 1760–1828), m. (1789) John Sullivan; and her twin Maria Frances Mary Hobart (ca 1760–94), m. (1785) George Augustus North, styled Lord North 1790–2, 3d E. of Guilford, 1792 (BERRY ii. 196 n. 7; Collins, *Peerage*, 1812, iv. 372; George Kearsley, *Peerage*, [1796], i. 108; John Debrett, *Peerage*, 1817, i. 251; Burke, *Peerage*, 1928, p. 386; ibid., 1953, p. 2029; GM 1794, lxiv pt i. 390; 1798, lxviii pt ii. 730; 1828, xcviii pt ii. 572).

14. Possibly Peregrine Furye (d. 1792), one of the gentlemen of the King's Privy Chamber ca 1780–92; lived in Upper Grosvenor Street (*London Chronicle* 14–16 Feb. 1792, lxxi. 157; GM 1792, lxii pt i. 184; *Royal Kalendar* 1779–92).

15. William (Neville) Gardiner (1748–1806), Lt-Col., 1778; Lt-Gen., 1799; diplomatist. A satirical print of 'A Modern Fine Gentleman,' 1783, may be of him (BM, *Satiric Prints* v. 776, No. 6342).

16. An English translation of Fagan's *La Pupille*, 1734, with alterations by Garrick, 1759.

17. As the heiress, Miss Harriet.

18. William John Arabin (ca 1751–1828); Maj., 1782; Gen., 1814; friend of Boswell (GM 1828, xcviii pt ii. 284).

19. Sir William East (1738–1819), cr.

(1766) Bt, of Hall Place, Hurley, Berks.

20. At Hall Place. A detailed account of the third performance there of Congreve's *The Mourning Bride*, 12 April 1782, appears in the *London Chronicle*, 13–16 April, li. 363. Arabin apparently was in charge of arrangements for the production, and he spoke the epilogue, written by Edward Topham (*London Chronicle*, loc. cit. and 16–18 April, li. 375). In HW's 'Collection of Prologues and Epilogues . . . from the Year 1780,' now WSL, is a newspaper cutting (dated by HW 'April 16, 1782') similar to that in the *London Chronicle*, and also a cutting of Topham's epilogue, dated by HW 'April 1782.'

21. Sir Charles Clackit. The account in the *London Chronicle* refers to Arabin's 'great comic talents.'

22. Richard Timms (d. 1785), nephew of John Elwes, the miser; of Orchard Street, Portman Square, 2d Lt and Lt-Col., 1779; 'He was a great encourager of theatrical merit, and had convinced the world of great abilities . . . at Sir William East's theatre, where, whilst he amused himself, he excited every tender, every generous feeling in his audience' (GM 1785, lv pt i. 405; Edward Topham, *Life of the Late John Elwes*, 6th edn, 1790, *passim*).

23. In the role of Heartly, the guardian of Harriet, who is in love with him. For his acting in *The Mourning Bride* he was praised in the *London Chronicle* (see n. 20): 'except on the public stage, there never was exhibited . . . a finer or more complete piece of acting.'

that when the servants were drawn up after the play, you would have thought it had been a midnight review of conspirators on a heath. There were Lord and Lady North and their family, the Seftons, Lucans, Duncannons,[24] Lady Maries Coke and Lowther,[25] Lords Graham and Palmerston, Lady Bridget Talmache and her sister,[26] the T. Pitts and the two Storers. There too I saw Mrs Johnstone[27] the Portugu-Englishwoman, that was called such a beauty: she is a fine figure but not handsome, though too good for such a brutal swine.

You are very kind about my nieces, Madam; but I do not believe there was the least intention of hurt to them. The gentlemen were cleaning their pistols at the window of the Toy,[28] and discharged them as the girls were going by. Mrs Keppel[29] took an alarm; and much less falling on such a soil as Hampton Court will bring forth lies an hundred fold.[30] Lady Chewton looked remarkably well at her return from Weymouth;[31] I know nothing of her since.

Berkeley Square, 12th.

I had begun this letter at Strawberry on Sunday night just before I went to bed—my *reveil* was shocking—an express brought me news of the death[32] of Lady Hertford! I truly loved her, she had been invariably kind to me for forty years. She had been seized on the preceding Sunday with a violent cough and spitting of blood, and left Ditton on the Tuesday[33] for fear of being confined in that damp spot, which has been her death.[34] Lady Ailesbury saw her on Friday

24. Henrietta Frances Spencer (1761–1821) m. (1780) Frederick Ponsonby, styled Vct Duncannon to 1793, 3d E. of Bessborough, 1793.

25. Lady Mary Stuart (1740–1824) m. (1761) Sir James Lowther, 5th Bt, 1751, cr. (1784) E. of Lonsdale.

26. The youngest and only unmarried sister, Lady Elizabeth Henley (1757–1821), who m. (1783) Morton Frederick Eden, cr. (1799) Bn Henley.

27. Deborah Charlotte Dee (d. 1813) m. 1 (31 Jan. 1782) at Lisbon, Commodore George Johnstone; m. 2 (1790) Charles Edmund Nugent, Capt. R.N., later Admiral (BERRY ii. 81 n. 18; Burke, *Peerage*, 1953, p. 1152).

28. A 'well known inn near the bridge'

at Hampton Court (Daniel Lysons, *Historical Account of Those Parishes in . . . Middlesex*, 1800, p. 75).

29. After the death of her husband in 1777 she was given lodgings in Hampton Court Palace (Mrs Keppel's correspondence with Anne and Jane Clement 1778–9, MSS WSL).

30. HW alludes to this incident in his letter to Harcourt 29 Oct. 1782.

31. She had miscarried in August.

32. On 10 Nov.

33. To go to her house in Lower Grosvenor Street, London, where she died.

34. According to Lady Mary Coke, she 'got her death by attending' Lord Beauchamp's son. 'She had then a cold upon her and getting up in the night when the

morning and thought her very ill, and I had determined to come to her yesterday morning—but heard the cruel event before I could set out—it was an inflammation in her bowels—but as on Friday she had had no physician, I could not conceive her in danger. The moment I arrived I sent to know if Lord Hertford would see me— he said he would in the evening. I went—but met his son Henry in the hall, who said his father could not bear the interview—alas! this was a relief to me—I had amassed resolution to go, as it was right I should—but I behaved so wretchedly at the sight of the son that it was well I did not see the father! His loss is beyond measure. She was not only the most affectionate wife but the most useful one, and almost the only person I ever saw that never neglected or put off, or forgot anything that was to be done. She was always proper, either in the highest life or in the most domestic. Her good humour made both sit easy; to herself only she gave disquiet by a temper so excessively affectionate. In short I was witness to so many virtues in her, that after my Lord and her children, I believe nobody regrets her so sincerely as I do. Her house was one of my few remaining habitudes —but those drawbacks on long life make its conclusion less unwelcome!

To Lady Ossory, Saturday 16 November 1782

Address: To the Countess of Ossory at Ampthill Park, Bedfordshire. *Postmark:* ISLEWORTH. 16 NO.

Strawberry Hill, Nov. 16, 1782.

YOUR Ladyship, as ever, is good to me both in inviting and in excusing me. Could I wait on you, the great misfortune of losing poor Lady Hertford, should not detain me; for as Lord Hertford will be in Suffolk,[1] I could be of no use to him; and to be at Ampthill would be much more agreeable than to be in London, where I have lost the house to which for forty years I went the oftenest— but to London I must go on Monday on different businesses. One is

---

child was ill brought that inflammation upon her which put an end to her life' ('MS Journals' 15 Nov. 1782).

1. At his seat, Sudbourne Hall, near

Orford (HW-Hertford Correspondence, especially Hertford to HW 27 Sept. 1759). Lady Hertford was buried on 20 Nov. at Arrow, Warwickshire.

to meet Lord Orford's lawyers[2] with Mr Duane, whom I have obtained to replace Mr Morice as referee for the suit between my Lord and his mother's residuary legatee,[3] who has been treated scandalously[4] and put off to this moment. I have another affair to settle with the children of Mr Bentley[5] who is dead, and for whom (the children) I had placed a very small sum in the funds,[6] which I am now to transfer to them. I will say nothing of myself, though, without being confined, I cannot at present take a journey. I should be very glad to meet Lady Chewton whom I have not seen a great while. I do hear she is very well, but grown extremely thin.

Lord Hertford I am certain will be extremely sensible of your Ladyship's attention. Any mark of regard for Lady Hertford's memory will be dear to him. Every word he utters is an encomium on her. Indeed his grief is as rational as it is deep: it is an uninterrupted funeral sermon on her. Yet though he is so devout, it was not tinged with any of the commonplace litanies, with which pious people often colour their want of feeling. His concern is too sincere and too desponding to use any expressions that are not genuine. Lady Hertford was his wife, friend, clerk and steward, and was as active as she was attached. Her affection and zeal attended to everything, and her good sense made everything easy to her—but I forget, and am indulging my own sensations, while I meant only to do justice to those of Lord Hertford.

I hope Lord Ossory adjusted the squabbles of his regiment to his satisfaction.

---

2. Of whom Charles Lucas was one. Joshua Sharpe may have been another; see *ante* 17 July 1781.

3. Mozzi.

4. HW inserted 'treated,' then struck it out.

5. Richard Bentley (1708–23 Oct. 1782), miscellaneous writer and artist; HW's correspondent; lived in Abingdon Street, Westminster, at the time of his death (Foster, *Alumni Oxon.*; GM 1782, lii 504). He had several daughters and one son: Thomas Richard Bentley (ca 1759–1831), who was admitted to Lincoln's Inn in 1779 and called to the bar in 1785 (*Old Westminsters*).

6. Probably about £200. On 28 July 1780, William Cole was told by Bentley 'that he translated into English the part of Hentzner which was printed at Strawberry Hill, and that Mr W. was so pleased with it, that immediately he told him that he should have the profit of it: yet he would not suffer him to make any bargain with a bookseller; but Mr W. himself agreed with one for £100 which he told Mr Bentley should lie for a nest egg for him: so it did till last year, when he put him in mind of it, being now about £200 yet he refused to let him have it till after his death, though it would have been convenient for him with his family' (Cole's account of Bentley, in Sir Egerton Brydges, *Restituta*, 1816, iv. 385).

PS. As I was going to seal this, I received your Ladyship's second kind note—I wish the character[7] could comfort Lord Hertford—but it is no momentary satisfaction that can close such a wound—which every incident that reminds him of his loss, will open. It is justice to him to tell you that the very morning Lady Hertford expired, his first thought was to have this tribute paid to her. I found a note from him on my table in town, which I could scarce read, to beg it,[8] and in an hour he wrote again.[9] It is as just to her to say that they were my immediate thoughts, and consequently the true; that I set them down, transcribed and carried them at seven that evening, and gave them to his son Henry, when my Lord was not able to see me himself—thus your Ladyship sees there could be no art, study or preparation in them.

Lady Lucan has just called and told me what I am very sorry for too, though in no proportion, that Sir Joshua[10] Reynolds has had a stroke of palsy[11]—I finish—lest I should moralize—

To Lady Ossory, Friday 29 November 1782

In Kirgate's hand.
Address: To the Countess of Ossory at Ampthill Park, Bedfordshire. *Postmark:* 29 NO. GC.

Berkeley Square, November 29, 1782.

THE hand tells your Ladyship that I cannot write with my own: I have been extremely ill; in point of fever, I think, worse than I ever was; for though I have the gout in five places I have had but little pain.[1] I trust the disorder is turned, for I am so low today that

7. Of Lady Hertford. At the request of Lord Hertford, HW wrote and sent it to the newspapers. It was printed in the *London Courant* 18 Nov. See also the HW-Hertford Correspondence.

8. See Hertford to HW 11 Nov. 1782, 'past 12': 'Her character with a sketch of it drawn by you and inserted in a public print, will give me a satisfaction I cannot express.'

9. See Hertford to HW 11 Nov. 1782 *bis*, in reply to HW's missing letter of condolence.

10. 'Reynolds' blotted and struck, then rewritten in MS.

11. Or paralysis. Sent by his physician to Bath, he had recovered by the end of the month (Dr Johnson to Reynolds, 14 Nov. 1782, in Johnson's *Letters*, ed. R. W. Chapman, Oxford, 1952, ii. 515, and Boswell, *Johnson* iv. 161–2).

1. HW to Mann 26 Nov. 1782: 'I suppose I caught cold on my coming to town [18 Nov.], for in three days I was seized with the gout, and have it now from the

the fever must be in a manner gone, and I have no new pain anywhere; therefore your Ladyship will be so good as not trouble yourself about my gout, which will cure itself in due time.

It was not pleasant, when I was so ill, to have all my windows
broken for that vain fool Rodney, who came out of his way to extend
his triumph.[2]

I am very happy, Madam, with what you say of Lady Chewton:
she is an extremely good young woman, of a very grave turn and
extreme sensibility; she very seldom is in high spirits, but always
more affected by sorrow than joy. I had a note[3] from her this morning, and expect to see her, and I hope Lord Chewton, tomorrow.
I have heard that Lady Waldegrave is very ill,[4] but that my Lord
was returned from Bath much better.[5]

I have been so entirely shut up for this week, that I know nothing,
and my voice is too weak to dictate much if I did. As I take a great
many killings, more than a Hercules, I shall probably be well again in
a few days, and able to write myself.

To Lady Ossory, Saturday 14 December 1782

In Kirgate's hand.
Address: To the Countess of Ossory at Ampthill Park, Bedfordshire. *Postmark:* 14 DE. GC.

Berkeley Square, December 14, 1782.

I HAVE been so extremely ill, Madam, that I was utterly incapable of dictating two lines, nor could I give you any account of
myself but what was as bad as possible. Since yesterday morning I am

top of my left shoulder to the ends of
my fingers.'

2. For details, see HW to Mann 26 Nov.
1782. On Saturday, 23 Nov., at his house
in Hertford Street, Rodney was thanked
by a Committee of the Common Council
for 'the great and signal victory obtained
. . . over the French fleet, commanded by
the Count de Grasse, on the 12th of April.'
Afterwards there was a dinner for him at
the London Tavern. 'At night many
houses . . . were illuminated' (*London
Chronicle* 19–26 Nov., lii. 493, 506; GM
1782, lii. 549).

3. Missing.

4. Lady Mary Coke mentions 'great de-
jection of spirits as she had last year' ('MS
Journals' 30 Nov. 1782), 'a fit of a bad
nature, a repetition of which may prove
fatal' (ibid. 6 Dec. 1782), and her continuing 'in a very low state, but the report
of her having made an attempt upon her
life I don't believe is true' (ibid. 26 Dec.
1782). On 12 Nov. 1783, 'Poor Lady Waldegrave is as ill as she was last year but I
am told there is now a proper person
about her to prevent any bad consequence'
(ibid.).

5. On 3 Oct. Lady Waldegrave told
Lady Mary Coke she was going to Bath,

certainly out of all manner of danger, but my breast is still so weak
that I cannot speak to be heard without uneasiness, and therefore
I must beg your Ladyship will excuse my saying any more now. You
shall have a better account as soon as I am able to give it.

To Lady Ossory, Wednesday 25 December 1782

Address in Kirgate's hand.
Address: To the Countess of Ossory at Ampthill Park, Bedfordshire. *Postmark:* 26 DE. GC.

Berkeley Square, Christmas night, 1782.

I AM as persevering as Whittington in 'Chevy Chace,' who fought
with his stumps, for I am now undertaking to write to you without
a finger, Madam. My hand is still swaddled in the bootikin, yet it
is less irksome than to dictate. I am wonderfully recovered, and
could walk about my room without a stick, if Tonton did not caper
against me and throw me down, for I have no more elasticity in my
joints than the tail of a paper kite. Sleep is my great restorative; no
dormouse beats me. Nay, I do not even look so ill as I have a right to
do, though to be sure I might be admitted at the resurrection, without being rejected for a counterfeit corpse—but I cut short details
about myself; the gout is a subject of no variety.

I cannot repay your Ladyship's story of *L'Amant voleur.*[1] We
continue to have robbers of the public and of individuals, but their
passions are all instigated *par les beaux yeux d'une cassette.*[2] However I have had an adventure not unentertaining. T'other day I received a letter from Lady Aldborough,[3] an Irish countess, whom I
never saw in my days but for one quarter of an hour seven years ago
at old Lady Shelburne's. All she desires of me is, to select, correct,

and Lady Mary notes on 30 Nov. her return. The *London Courant* 19 Oct. 1782
reported: 'Bath, Oct. 16. Arrived here Earl
of Waldegrave.' A year later he 'has had
another stroke of the palsy which he has
recovered for the present but in his weak
state it cannot be for long' (Coke, op. cit.
3 Oct., 30 Nov. 1782, 11 Dec. 1783).

1. Evidently someone who attempted
to abduct a lady; not explained.

2. Harpagon in Moliere's *L'Avare,* V.
iii: 'Les beaux yeux de ma cassette!'

3. Barbara Herbert (1742–85) m. (1765)
Edward Augustus Stratford, 2d E. of Aldborough, 1777. Her letter is missing; HW
mentioned her request in his letter to
Pinkerton 18 Aug. 1785, CHATTERTON
276–7. In GM 1829, xcix pt i. 207, she is
said to have been born in 1739.

and print a sufficient number of her father's[4] poems[5] (whom she vulgarly calls *the Honourable* Nich. Herbert) to make a quarto pamphlet, as she does not care to *give* or *sell* them to a bookseller; and then she concludes I will admit him into my catalogue of *Noble Authors.* Her Lord,[6] she says, is too much engaged in politics when at Dublin, and with improvements of his estate when in the country[7] (which I am told he has improved to none at all)[8] to assort the poems —and then, as ladies are abominably said to tell their mind in the postcript, she orders me to enclose my answer to her Lord *that it may come to her free.* Thus I may lay out £30 or £40 for her, and she would not give sixpence[9] to know whether I will or not. I have sent a most respectful No,[10] and have saved her the sixpence—which is all I shall save her.

I have received a much more flattering compliment, and as disinterested as her Ladyship's was the contrary. Mr Bull, to amuse me when I was ill, sent me my *Royal and Noble Authors*[11] let into four sumptuous folios in red morocco gilt, with beautiful impressions of almost all the personages of whom there are prints.[12] As they

4. Hon. Nicholas Herbert (ca 1706–75), of Great Glemham and Farnham, Suffolk, and Upper Brook Street, Grosvenor Square; son of the 8th E. of Pembroke; M.P. Newport 1740–54, Wilton 1757–75; secretary of Jamaica 1765–75 (CHATTERTON 277 n. 7, but his monument, cited GM 1829, xcix pt i. 207, indicates that he died 1 Feb. 1775, aged 67).

5. No other reference to them has been found.

6. Edward Augustus Stratford (ca 1740–1801), 2d E. of Aldborough, 1777; M.P.; a governor of County Wicklow, 1778; F.R.S., 1777.

7. His chief estates were at Belan, co. Kildare, at Baltinglass, co. Wicklow, and at Mount Neale, co. Carlow.

8. He founded Stratford-upon-Slaney, co. Wicklow, besides greatly improving Baltinglass. He, with others, also built Stratford Place, Oxford Street, and Aldborough House in London ca 1775–80 (Wheatley, *London Past and Present* iii. 327–8). In 1783 he offered land for 'New Geneva,' proposed for Swiss emigrants to Ireland (*London Chronicle* 1–3 May 1783, liii. 418).

9. The charge for a single letter 'Between London and Dublin, by way of Holyhead' (*New Complete Guide to All Persons Who Have Any Trade or Concern with the City of London*, 16th edn, 1783, p. 105).

10. HW's letter is missing.

11. Second edition, 1759.

12. On 22 Dec. HW showed the volumes to Lady Mary Coke, who mistakenly thought Bull had given them to HW (Coke, 'MS Journals'). When Bull died in 1805 the volumes went to his daughter Elizabeth and on her death in 1809 to Bull's stepson R. H. Alexander Bennett, whose descendant, the 5th Lord Burgh, sold them at Sotheby's 28–29 June 1926, lot 273A, for £220 to 'Mason.' (For the descent, see *Notes and Queries*, 1913, 11th ser., vii. 170–1; Burke, *Peerage*, 1953, pp. 311–12). According to the auction catalogue there were 'some hundreds of portraits in mezzotint, line, stipple, and woodcut, also many portraits in water-colours, by J. Strutt, G. P. Harding and others.' When WSL bought the volumes in 1949 many of the prints had been removed. The volumes, each with Bull's bookplate and a

came when I was at the worst, I sent him word,[13] that if I might compare little things with great, he put me in mind of Queen Elizabeth, who laid an Earl's robes on Lord Hunsdon's death-bed.

Mrs Siddons continues to be the mode and to be modest and sensible. She declines great dinners, and says her business and the cares of her family[14] take up her whole time. When Lord Carlisle carried her the tribute-money from Brooks's, he said she was not *maniérée* enough— 'I suppose she was grateful,' said my niece Lady Maria.[15] Mrs Siddons was desired to play Medea[16] and Lady Macbeth[17]—no, she replied, she did not look on them as female characters. She was questioned about her transactions with Garrick; she said he did nothing but put her out; that he told her she moved her right hand when it should have been her left—'In short,' said she, 'I found I must not shade the tip of his nose.'

Have you seen the two last volumes of Bachaumont's *Mémoires secrets*,[18] Madam? If you have not, don't give yourself the trouble; there is but one tolerable trait, but that is charming. They have hung a room at Ferney with portraits of Voltaire's friends.[19] Under

specially printed title-page, were rebacked between 1926 and 1949.

13. No letter to Bull at this time has been found.

14. She had three children living at this time: Henry (1774–1815), Sarah Martha (1779–98), and Maria (1779–98). A fourth, Frances Emilia, had been born in 1781 and had died in infancy (Mrs Clement Parsons, *The Incomparable Siddons*, 1909, pp. xviii–xix *et passim*).

15. Lady Charlotte Maria Waldegrave.

16. Although Genest (viii. 308–12) does not list Medea among Mrs Siddons's characters, there is a print of her in the part (Richard Glover's *Medea*) by J. Thomthwaite, published by J. Bell, British Library, 18 Feb. 1792.

17. She had played Lady Macbeth at Bath 18 Nov. 1779 (Genest vi. 161, 164); her first London performance in the role, one of her greatest, was for her benefit on 2 Feb. 1785. In that season alone she played the part nine additional times (ibid. 336–8, 342). For her 'Remarks on the Character of Lady Macbeth,' see Thomas Campbell, *Life of Mrs Siddons*, 1834, ii. 10–39. The only portrait of her

as Lady Macbeth, by G. H. Harlow, is reproduced in Mrs Clement Parsons, op. cit., facing p. 145.

18. *Mémoires secrets pour servir à l'histoire de la république des lettres en France depuis 1762 jusqu'à nos jours*, 36 vols, 'Londres' [?Amsterdam], 1777–89. The first four and a half volumes were by Louis Petit de Bachaumont (1690–1771); the continuation was by Mathieu-François Pidansat de Mairobert (1707–79), who prepared the first eight volumes (1777) for the press, and others. HW had at least nine volumes of the set; see Hazen, *Cat. of HW's Lib.* 3030, 3128; BM Cat.; DU DEFFAND iv. 478; MASON i. 324–5. HW's 'two last volumes' refers to vols xv and xvi, 1781 (see n. 21), but vols xvii and xviii had appeared in Paris on 1 Sept. 1782 (*Mémoires secrets* xxi. 101, *sub* that date).

19. The 'chambre du cœur de Voltaire.' In the *Description générale et particulière de la France*, 1781–96, is an engraving of this room with its portraits, drawn by Duché and engraved by Née (DU DEFFAND iii. 325, vi. 215; Thieme and Becker, *sub* Duché de Vancy).

the Abbé de Lille²⁰ the translator of Virgil, they have placed this happy application,

Nulli flebilior quam tibi, Virgili.²¹

They again talk much of peace—Oh! let it come! We have lost territories enough, and got heroes enough in their room. If it is a bad peace, at least we shall not be fools for making it, as we have always been, when we have been masters to make as good an one as we pleased. I don't suppose our enemies will be as obliging idiots.

You cannot imagine, Madam, how long I have been engraving this letter. I am in debt for some others, but my Secretary of State²² must answer them, for I find our royal breast is as tired as our hand.

YO EL REY.

To Lady Ossory, Tuesday 7 January 1783

Address in Kirgate's hand.
One sentence is here first printed; see below.
Address: To the Countess of Ossory at Ampthill Park, Bedfordshire. *Postmark:* [?] JA. GC.

Berkeley Square, Jan. 7, 1783.

THOUGH the newspapers have advertised a book called, *Every Man His Own Letter-Writer*,¹ I doubt it will not keep me so long. I really have no movement in any finger of my right hand, but my thumb; and with so serious an excuse, should employ my sec-

20. Jacques Delille (1738–1813), Abbé, author of *Les Jardins*, 1782, and *La Pitié*, 1803; translator of Virgil's *Georgics*, 1769, and *Ænëid*, 1804, and of Milton's *Paradise Lost*, 1805.

21. Horace, *Carm.* I. xxiv. 10: 'But no one mourns more than thou, O Virgil.' In an extract of a letter from Ferney 6 Feb. 1780 the 'chambre du cœur' at Ferney is described: on one wall portraits of prelates; opposite them some ladies, including Mme de Sévigné and Mme du Deffand; on another wall, 'des beaux esprits,' including Delille; and opposite them, 'Les amis sont les plus voisins du cœur' (*Mé-*

moires secrets, xv. 56–7, or, in some copies, pp. 46–7, *sub* 14 Feb. 1780).

22. Kirgate.

———

1. *Every Man His Own Letter-Writer; or, the New and Complete Art of Letter-Writing Made Plain and Familiar to Every Capacity*, by 'Rev. James Wallace, D.D., and Charles Townshend, A.M.' It was advertised as 'A Real New and Original Work . . . In a handsome pocket volume, Price 1s. 6d. sewed, or 2s. neatly bound in red . . . Containing a collection of upwards of 200 original letters, on the most interesting, important, and instruc-

retary, if I were not more ashamed to dictate my nonsense, as Lady Anne justly calls it, than to write it. It is no more uneasy to write than to speak the first foolish thing that comes into one's head—but to oblige a third person not only to hear but transcribe it, is being such a simpleton in cool blood, that if I write by proxy, my letters will have no more nonsense or sense, than those which royal personages send to one another from the Secretary's Office on births and deaths.

I have taken the air and might have done so a week ago, but was in dread of a relapse—however, as I am all recovered but my hand, and as I fear there is no chance of that ever being well again, I must determine to carry it about in its nightgown, or stay at home for my short forever.

I know nothing—at least nothing that your Ladyship would care about more than I do. The peace seems like the kingdom of Heaven, for though Mr Townshend[2] and St Paul announced them to the City[3] and to the Corinthians as believing them near at hand,[4] they both seem to have had more faith than inspiration.[5] I have a general notion about treaties of peace, which the present has not hitherto contradicted. It is, that when peace is necessary to the mutual views of two prime ministers of two hostile nations, it is clapped up in an instant, the material articles being postponed, to be adjusted afterwards by commissaries—but that if they go into discussions, the same causes remain for dispute and quarrel, that made the war—and then the treaty breaks off. I hope that is not the case at present—I am very willing not to be a prophet in my own country.

On prétend, that certain invisible machines, of which one heard much a year or two ago, and which were said to be constructed of cork, and to be worn somewhere or other behind, are now to be transplanted somewhere before, in imitation of the Duchess of Devonshire's

tive subjects, which may serve as copies for writing letters on all occasions. . .' (*London Chronicle* 8–10 Oct. 1782, lii. 351).

2. Thomas Townshend (1733–1800), cr. (6 March 1783) Bn and (1789) Vct Sydney; M.P.; secretary for war March–July 1782; home secretary (succeeding Shelburne) July 1782–April 1783 and Dec. 1783–June 1789.

3. As home secretary, Townshend had written to the Lord Mayor of London on 22 Nov. and 3 Dec. (and to the governors

and directors of the Bank of England on 23 Nov.) announcing the approach of peace and asking for the prevention of gambling in the funds. See *London Chronicle* 21 Nov. 1782 – 2 Jan. 1783, lii. 504, 536–7, liii. 7; GM 1782, lii. 548, 595.

4. John the Baptist and Jesus, rather than St Paul, announced 'the kingdom of Heaven is at hand' (St Matthew 3.2, 4.17, 10.7, and St Mark 1.15, 'kingdom of God').

5. This sentence is here first printed.

pregnancy,[6] as all under-jaws advanced upon the same principle.[7] Apropos, Lady Jersey[8] desired Mr Stonhewer to order me to ask Mr Hayley, what had cured him when his head was disordered,[9] her Ladyship having a relation in that situation. I sent her word, that I not only was not acquainted with, but had never seen him, yet I could tell her his nostrum; he had been put into a course of breast-milk, and sucked the nine Muses, and is now as tame as a lamb.

As this letter, Madam, is written entirely *in usum*[10] of the Dauphiness Anne, it is long enough—at least my hand finds so, which has not attempted a quarter so much, since I had the honour of writing to your Ladyship last,[11] and now aches a good deal.

To Lady Ossory, Wednesday 22 January 1783

Address: To the Countess of Ossory at Ampthill Park, Bedfordshire. *Postmark:* 26 IA. GC.

Berkeley Square, Jan. 22,[1] 1783.

I HAVE had so little to say, Madam, and so much to do in making visits of thanks to the charitable who visited me in my illness, that I have not been so correspondent as usual. I have also been for two days at Strawberry, where it snew most of the time. In truth I have still a more real cause for silence, the lameness of this hand, which can

6. Her first child was born 12 July 1783: Lady Georgiana Dorothy Cavendish (d. 1858), m. (1801) George Howard, 6th E. of Carlisle, 1825.

7. The Duke of Devonshire's under-jaw is accentuated in a satirical print reproduced in Iris Leveson Gower, *The Face without a Frown*, 1944, facing p. 113: 'The Duke and Duchess of Devonshire Viewing the Camp at Dover.'

8. HW's *apropos*, linking the Duchess and Lady Jersey, may be suggested by their connection with the Prince of Wales; see, for example, BM, *Satiric Prints* v. 644, 730–1, Nos 6115, 6263; Sir Nathaniel Wraxall, *Memoirs*, 1884, v. 368–372; Robert D. Bass, *The Green Dragoon*, New York, 1957, pp. 135, 197, 236. According to Wraxall, the Prince was particularly solicitous during the Duchess's second pregnancy in 1785.

9. In *An Essay on Epic Poetry; in Five Epistles to the Rev. Mr Mason. With Notes*, 1782 (published 22 June), pp. 91–4, Epistle IV, ll. 439–93, Hayley, in lines admired by Gibbon and Lamb, thanks his mother for her care during his illness as a child. See Morchard Bishop, *Blake's Hayley*, 1951, pp. 29–33; Hayley, *Memoirs*, ed. John Johnson, 1823, i. 15–25, 137–8; Mason ii. 255 n. 1.

10. From *in usum Delphini*, 'for the use of the Dauphin,' in reference to the Delphin classics published in 1674.

11. Between 25 Dec. and 7 Jan. no letters from HW are known to exist.

1. The date is unclear: apparently HW wrote 22, then changed it to 25; see the second section of the letter.

write but a few lines at a time, and must rest every quarter of an hour; so that the expedition with which I used to dispatch my letters is quite gone, and they are become a pain instead of an amusement.

You know to be sure, Madam, that the peace is arrived.[2] I cannot express how glad I am. I care not a straw what the terms are, which I believe I know more imperfectly than anybody in London. I am not apt to love details—My wish was to have peace, and the next, to see America secure of its liberty. Whether it will make good use of it, is another point. It has an opportunity, that never occurred in the world before, of being able to select the best parts of every known constitution—but I suppose it will not, as too prejudiced against royalty to adopt it even as a corrective of aristocracy and democracy; though *our* system has proved that every evil had better have two enemies to contend with than one, as the third may turn the scale on every emergence; but when the one defeats the only other, it is decisive. In short it is necessary there should be government, but that government should be checked as much as those it controls; for one man, or a few, or a multitude, are still men, and consequently not fit to be trusted with unlimited power. The misfortune is, that men cannot be trusted with the power of doing right, without having the power of doing wrong too, and the more you limit them, the more they pant for greater latitude. However, the more they are limited, the farther they have to go before they acquire the boundless latitude they long for. These are some of my visions, which the experience of all ages and countries have shown are such as scarce ever have been realized.

Saturday, 26th.[3]

I had written the above on Wednesday; but on seeing our Lord on Thursday,[4] did not finish it. Well, Madam, you must hate only

2. Unofficial notice reached London on 21 Jan. that the preliminary articles of peace between Great Britain and France and Great Britain and Spain had been signed 'on Saturday the 18th' (Grantham to George III 21 Jan., *Corr. Geo. III* vi. 217); they were signed at Versailles on 20 Jan. 1783 (articles with the United States had been signed 30 Nov. 1782); the official courier did not arrive in London until

Thursday evening, 23 Jan. See HW to Mann 23 Jan. 1783; *Last Journals* ii. 476; *London Chronicle* 23–25 Jan., liii. 81. For the text, see ibid. 28–30 Jan., liii. 97–9; *Journals of the House of Commons* xxxix. 113–18, *sub* 27 Jan.

3. Saturday was the 25th.

4. Parliament had met, after the recess, on Tuesday, 21 Jan. (*Journals of the House of Commons* xxxix. 39).

the Dutch.[5] The French and Spaniards are our good friends, and you may *lawfully* speak well even of the Americans, without being called a rebel and republican, as I was by Marie Alacoque.[6] I know few of the terms of the preliminaries, but that Gibraltar, or Rock-Elliot,[7] is still in the parish of St Martin's in the Fields.[8] When I do learn all the articles, I intend to like all, for I must be so fair as to say that they will be better than I expected we should ever obtain. Nay, if the French had not been as great blunderbusses as we, they might have reduced us much lower long ago. If Ireland has slipped out of our yoke too,[9] the French have no title to boast, who might have had it themselves, if they had thought of it before the Volunteers.[10] Now I hope it will be a perpetual thorn in their sides.

As one is always open to new calamities on the cessation of the old, I now expect that one shall be robbed and murdered two or three times a day, aye, and a night, more than ever, on disbanding the army —and then we shall have such swarms of French, yes, and insolent ones too! What is that to me? Oh! a great deal, Madam; they will come to see Strawberry, perhaps have recommendations, and I must ask them to dine! Is that nothing to a poor superannuated invalid?

I know no news—nay, news are but beginning; news out of Parliament-tide are fruits out of season, have not the true flavour. Besides, when Lord Ossory is in town, I am like a vice-chancellor, who is nobody, when his principal is on the spot—I shall therefore not trespass any longer on his office, but wish your Ladyship good night.

5. With whom no preliminaries had been signed, 'only a suspension of arms' (*Last Journals* ii. 476).

6. Lady Mary Coke; a comparison with St Margaret Mary Alacoque (1647–90). See MASON i. 402 and n. 23.

7. HW uses the phrase also in his letter to Mann 23 Jan. 1782. For Elliot's defence of Gibraltar, see *ante* 1 Oct. 1782.

8. See *ante* 26 Oct. 1781, n. 36.

9. The repeal in 1782 of the Declaratory Act of 6 Geo. I (1719), c. 5, not having satisfied the Irish, Townshend, the home secretary, moved, 22 Jan., for leave to bring in a Bill 'for removing and preventing all doubts which have arisen, or might arise, concerning the exclusive rights of the Parliament and courts of Ireland, in matters of legislation and judicature, and for preventing any writ of error, or appeal, from any of his Majesty's courts in that kingdom, from being received, heard, and adjudged in any of his Majesty's courts in the kingdom of Great Britain' (*Journals of the House of Commons* xxxix. 43; Cobbett, *Parl. Hist.* xxiii. 328, 322–42, 730–57). This Renunciation Bill (23 Geo. III, c. 28) was passed.

10. Several companies of Volunteers (First Armagh Volunteers, Belfast Volunteer Company, etc.) had sent addresses to Lord Beauchamp asking for 'a British law, that Great Britain renounces forever, all claim to bind this kingdom, externally or internally, in any case whatever' (*London Chronicle* 18–21 Jan., liii. 68). Similar addresses appear ibid. 21 Jan.–1 Feb. 1783, liii. 75–6, 84, 95, 109.

To Lady Ossory, Thursday 30 January 1783

Address: To the Countess of Ossory at Ampthill Park, Bedfordshire. *Postmark:* 30 IA.

The Martyrdom,[1] 1783.

THIRDLY, Madam, if I never was to write to your Ladyship, till I have the full and free use of every finger of my right hand, I should never write again, for I certainly shall recover none of the four; and if I could not move the joint of the thumb, I should not be able to use a pen at all. As you perceive I can, I hope you will not disband the four invalids for the sake of old Colonel Thumb, who begs to die in your service.

Secondly I do rejoice in the peace, and will, though I find it grows very unpopular—and fourthly I will not correct my historic errors: I am not apt to recant my tenets, nor will give up the only king that I have defended;[2] especially as I shall never enter the *sanctum sanctorum,* where one's religion like a chameleon takes the hue of the place the instant one enters it. One quality of the chameleon I have, and rejoice in having; the orbit of my eye allows me to look backward—other creeping things only see before them, and think but of advancing: I keep my eye on what I have always been, and choose to be uniform. It will not be difficult now to hold out a little while longer.

I was last night at Mrs Montagu's to hear Le Texier read *Le Bourgeois gentilhomme,* and was tired to death, for though it had merit at first in the infancy of comedy, it is mere farce, and has no characters. But the famous phrase[3] struck me as applicable to Cumberland, who has just produced a tragedy in prose;[4] he has thought that he had

1. 30 Jan., the anniversary of Charles I's death.

2. Richard III.

3. 'M. Jourdain: Par ma foi! il y a plus de quarante ans que je dis de la prose sans que j'en susse rien' (*Le Bourgeois gentilhomme,* II. iv).

4. *The Mysterious Husband,* 'A Play in Five Acts,' first performed at Covent Garden 28 Jan. 1783, and published a few days later (*London Chronicle* 28–30 Jan., 8–11 Feb., liii. 102, 142). 'The plot . . . was suggested by Walpole's *Mysterious Mother,* which deals with similar events veiled in the decent obscurity of an earlier age' (S. T. Williams, *Richard Cumberland,* New Haven, 1917, pp. 193, 194–8; Mason ii. 286). There is no record that HW saw the play or owned a copy of it.

often written verses, and did not know that he had all his life been writing prose.

We are going to suffer an inundation of French. It is better at least than an invasion of them, which I cannot conceive why they have not committed. Have you seen his Majesty of Prussia's intimation to the Dutch that he intends to saddle them with the House of Orange for the sake of preserving their *liberty?*[5] I remember a story of a lady who had a favourite plump lark, of which she was very fond. On going out of town, she gave strict orders to her housemaid to take the tenderest care of it. The woman promised—'No, I am sure you will neglect it and starve it'—'Lord! Madam, how can your Ladyship think so? I assure you'—'No, I know you will starve it—come, I know what I will do; I'll kill it and eat it.'

There is an insurrection at Portsmouth of a Scotch regiment[6] who will not go and plunder the remainder of the Indies;[7] and Lord George Gordon, who is excellent at putting out fires, has offered to go and appease them[8]—how can anybody say that there is a dearth of virtue and patriotism?

PS. Madame de Virri is dead suddenly, as she was just coming to England.[9]

5. In a letter dated from The Hague 22 Jan. 1783 and addressed to the States General of Holland, Baron de Thulemeyer, envoy extraordinary from Frederick II, demanded, in Frederick's name, that internal dissension be quelled and that the Stadtholdership and the established form of government be maintained. The text of the letter is in the *London Chronicle* 25–28 Jan., liii. 93. The envoy had also presented the King's views 17 Dec. 1782; see ibid. 26 Dec.–2 Jan., lii. 621, liii. 6; GM 1782, lii. 597–8; *Nieuwe Nederlandsche Yaarboeken*, 1782, pp. 1551–2; 1783, pp. 53–6.

6. The 77th Regiment of Foot, or Atholl Highlanders, which had been stationed in Ireland before it was ordered to the East Indies (*Army Lists*, 1782).

7. 'Mutiny at Portsmouth of the 77th regiment, who pleaded having been promised dismission [after three years of service or at the end of the war], and yet were to be sent to the East Indies. They

shot one man, wounded their Lieutenant-Colonel, and would have killed the Duke of Athol, and Murray, their Colonel, had they appeared. *Lord George Gordon* offered Lord Shelburne to go and pacify them. They were quieted' (*Last Journals* ii. 478, *sub* 29 Jan. 1783). The mutiny was discussed in the House of Commons on 29 and 31 Jan.; on the second day 'General Conway [Commander-in-Chief] said that the 77th should not be ordered for India, or any other Highland regiment' (*London Chronicle* 28 Jan.–1 Feb., liii. 103–4, 110–11; GM 1783, liii pt i. 89–90; HW to Mann 3 Feb. 1783).

8. Lord George Gordon's letter, dated 'Eleven o'clock, Tuesday night, Welbeck Street, Jan. 28, 1783,' and Shelburne's reply of the 29th are printed in the *London Chronicle* 30 Jan.–1 Feb., liii. 107.

9. She 'died [on her husband's estate in Savoy] of an apoplexy occasioned by excessive corpulency' (Lord Harcourt, 'Por-

To Lady Ossory, Saturday 8 February 1783

Address: To the Countess of Ossory at Ampthill Park, Bedfordshire. *Postmark:* 8 FE. D.

Berkeley Square, Feb. 8, 1783.

YOUR dryads must go into black gloves, Madam: their father-in-law, Lady Nature's second husband, is dead! Mr Brown dropped down at his own door yesterday.[1] The death of the second monarch of landscape[2] is a considerable event to me, the historian of that kingdom—the political world, I believe, is more occupied by the resignation of Lord Carlisle[3]—but the petty incidents of the Red Book[4] are much below my notice, and I care not who is grubbed up or transplanted. The American war is terminated to my great satisfaction, and there end my politics! I cannot tap a new chapter; but am returned to all my old studies, and read over again my favourite authors on times past. You must not be surprised if I should send you a collection of Tonton's *bons mots:* I have found a precedent for such a work. A grave author[5] wrote a book on the hunt of the Grand Sénéchal of Normandy, and of *les DITS du bon chien SOUILLARD, qui*

trait of Henrietta Jane Speed, Countess de Viry,' in *Harcourt Papers* viii. 3, quoted in *Gray's Corr.* i. 332 n.).

---

1. The day before yesterday: 'Lancelot Brown, gardenist, died February 6, 1783, at his son-in-law Holland's door in Hertford Street, aged 67, of an asthma' (*Anecdotes of Painting*, Vol. V, ed. F. W. Hilles and P. B. Daghlian, 1937, p. 182; 'Book of Materials' 1771, p. 84; *A Note Book of Horace Walpole*, ed. W. S. Lewis, New York, 1927, pp. 29–30).

2. William Kent (1684–1748) was the first ('On Modern Gardening,' *Works* ii. 534–41, 544).

3. On 5 Feb. 'Lord Carlisle resigned the place of lord steward, giving out that he disapproved the sacrifice of the American Loyalists. . . . But the true reasons were supposed to be, that Lord Carlisle had wished to go ambassador to Paris . . . that Eden had wrought on Carlisle, who might

also wish to get back to Charles Fox, as the extreme unpopularity of Lord Shelburne made it probable that he would not be able long to keep his power . . . Lord Carlisle had quitted Ireland abruptly on the change of the ministry; had been made lord steward by Charles Fox. . . . On Fox's resignation immediately after, Lord Carlisle deserted him' (*Last Journals* ii. 479). In the coalition ministry of Fox and North, Carlisle became lord privy seal; to him, 'who had now changed sides three times in one year, and whose resignation had been the signal for blowing up Lord Shelburne,' the King did not speak on 2 April, when the coalition came in (ibid. ii. 509). See also HW to Mann 3 Feb. 1783.

4. 'A popular name for the "Royal Kalendar, or Complete . . . Annual Register" (published from 1767 to 1893)' (OED).

5. Jacques de Brézé (ca 1430–94).

fut au Roi Loy de France onzième du nom.[6] Louis XII, the reverse of his predecessor of the same name, did not leave to his historian to celebrate his dog, *Relais,* but did him the honour of being his biographer himself—and for a reason that was becoming so excellent a king. It was, *pour animer les descendants d'un si brave chien à se rendre aussi bons que lui, et encore meilleurs.*[7] It was great pity that the Cardinal d'Amboise[8] had no bastard puppies, or to be sure his Majesty would have written his prime minister's life too for a model to his successors.

As this is a very gossiping letter about nothings, I will tell your Ladyship an incident that struck me the other night. Lady Beaulieu thought Lady Albemarle mourned too long for Lady Vere;[9] Mrs Hussey[10] said, 'Madam, they were cousin-germans.' I scoffed at Mrs Hussey, thinking them removed by two or three generations—but she was in the right; Lady Albemarle is daughter of the first Duke of

---

6. *Le Livre de la chasse du grant seneschal de Normandie. Et les ditz du bon chien Soulliart: qui fut au roy Loys de France, XI, de ce nom,* printed at Paris by Pierre le Caron, ca 1494. The only copy known was in 1783 listed as No. 2131 in *Catalogue des livres de la bibliothèque de feu M. le duc de la Vallière . . .* [to be sold] *dans les premiers jours du mois de Décembre 1783,* Vol. I, 2d part, 1783, pp. 598–9. The work was reprinted at Paris in 1858, ed. Baron Jérôme Pichon, then owner of the unique copy. See also J. Thiébaud, *Bibliographie des ouvrages français sur la chasse,* 1934, p. 130, where the title-page is reproduced.

7. In 'Epitaphe du bon Relay,' a poem of 140 lines, which appeared in Guillaume du Sable, *La Muse chasseresse,* 1611, is the passage:

'Car ma vie est par luy escrite et redigée,
Dont ma race à jamais luy demeure obligée.
Courage aussi donnoit à mes postérieurs
D'estre bons comme moy, ou estre encore meilleurs.'

(*Le Livre de la chasse,* ed. Pichon, 1858, p. 42, the entire poem at pp. 37–43 and in *La Muse chasseresse,* 'avec une notice par Paul Lacroix et des notes par Ernest

Jullien,' 1884, pp. 29–35. Louis XII's life of Relay has not survived; the epitaph may indeed be the 'life' (Pichon edn, pp. xv–xvi, 42 n.).

8. Georges d'Amboise (1460–1510), cardinal, Archbishop of Narbonne and of Rouen 1493–8; chief minister under Louis XII and director of his foreign policy 1498–1510.

9. Mary Chamber or Chambers (d. 21 Jan. 1783) m. (1736) Lord Vere Beauclerk, cr. (1750) Bn Vere. 'Lady Vere flourishes, the death of poor Lady Blandford has given her a great deal more company. Mr Walpole I'm told goes there more frequently, as does the Dowager Lady Albemarle' (Coke, 'MS Journals' 5 Nov. 1779).

10. One of Lord Beaulieu's four sisters died at his house in London in 1794, 'in her 84th year' (GM 1794, lxiv pt i. 485). She may have been Mabel, Elizabeth, Frances, or Mary Hussey (Mary m. James Hussey of Galtrim), but it is possible that HW refers to his own cousin the Hon. Mary Walpole (d. 1840), m. (1777) Thomas Hussey, Lord Beaulieu's 4th cousin once removed (Sir John B. Burke, *Genealogical History of the Dormant . . . and Extinct Peerages,* 1866, p. 294; Sir Bernard Burke and A. P. Burke, *Landed Gentry of Ireland,* 1904, p. 279).

Richmond,[11] and Lord Vere was son of the first Duke of St Albans;[12] yet Charles II has been dead 98 years—nay, Lady Albemarle or the Bishop of Hereford[13] may mourn some years hence for the other.[14] Lady Albemarle supped at Lady Ailesbury's on Sunday night, drank two glasses of champagne, and stayed till past one in as good spirits as ever I saw her.[15]

There has been a more rapid succession in another family. Several years ago, when Lord Strafford and I were at Lord Thomond's,[16] we walked to Walden Church, and were shown in a vault there the coffins of eleven Earls and Countesses of Suffolk that had died since 1700.[17] With this last Earl[18] there have been seven more since that time[19]— you will not wonder, Madam, that I know no modern news, when I am so deep in the lore of obituaries! Your other correspondents will tell you *les dits et gestes du siècle;* it is more seemly for me to concern myself about past generations than about the rising one.

11. Charles Lennox (1672–1723), illegitimate son of Charles II by Louise Renée de Penancoët de Kéroualle, Ds of Portsmouth; cr. (1675) D. of Richmond.

12. Charles Beauclerk (1670–1726), illegitimate son of Charles II by Nell Gwynne; cr. (1684) D. of St Albans.

13. Lord James Beauclerk (1702–87), Bp of Hereford, 1746; seventh son of the 1st D. of St Albans, Lord Vere being the third (Burke, *Peerage,* 1953, pp. 1841–2; Foster, *Alumni Oxon.*).

14. The Bishop died on 20 Oct. 1787, Lady Albemarle on 20 Oct. 1789.

15. On Sunday evening, 22 Dec. 1782, at Lady Ailesbury's, Lady Albemarle 'said old as she was she could not resist temptation, and made her words good for she eat a large quantity of cold partridge pie and drank champagne, after which she was very cross' (Coke, 'MS Journals').

16. At Shortgrove Hall, Essex; HW had been there in 1762 (*Country Seats* 33; MONTAGU ii. 30).

17. They died between 1703 and 1745, the last being the 10th Earl, the son of HW's friend and correspondent; see GEC xii. 469–75. The widow of the 4th Earl was buried in Enfield, Middlesex (ibid. xii. 470–1).

18. Thomas Howard (1721 – 3 Feb. 1783), 14th E. of Suffolk, 1779; M.P.

19. Between 1757 and 1783 died eight earls and countesses of Suffolk, none of whom (except possibly Lady Suffolk mentioned above) was buried at Saffron Walden. If HW's visit of 'several years ago' refers to 1762, he could count seven deaths from 1762 to 1783, although the death in 1762 occurred on 13 Feb. before his visit to Lord Thomond in May.

To Lady Ossory, Tuesday 18 February 1783

Address: To the Countess of Ossory at Ampthill Park, Bedfordshire. *Post-mark:* 18 FE.

Berkeley Square, Feb. 18, 1783—a great-grandchild of 1688.[1]

PRAY, Madam, do not imagine that I pretend to send you a cool newspaper, when probably you have had my intelligence anticipated by a courier—oh! dear, no—but as gazetteers think it their regular duty to specify everything that happens, as well as everything that does not, though all the world may know both, I acquaint your Ladyship that at eight this morning (which eight o'clock was part of yesterday, Monday) the administration was defeated on the very same field[2] where another administration was routed about this time twelvemonth[3]—and, which makes the victory more memorable, the general who was beaten last year,[4] and one of the generals who beat him,[5] had joined their forces to fight the general,[6] who had had a share over the vanquished one of this time twelvemonth.

This is all that is necessary to be told by me, who have ceased to be *an Examiner,* and am only *a Spectator.*[7]

I will not distract you with any other news foreign to the big event of the day. You would listen to nothing else, except conjectures; and those, though one cannot help forming them, would be so entirely coined by my own brain, that they would not assist you. I will not even answer any paragraph of your Ladyship's last, except one word about the loyalists. As I always apply my reflections to my own way of thinking, that is, consider what operation any great event will have

1. In upholding the power of the Commons. See below.

2. The House of Commons. By a vote of 224 to 208, Lord John Cavendish's motion against Shelburne on the preliminary articles of peace was carried. The House divided at 7:30 A.M. on Feb. 18. See Cobbett, *Parl. Hist.* xxiii. 436–93; *Last Journals* ii. 481–5. Shelburne resigned on 24 Feb. (ibid. ii. 487, 509).

3. North announced his resignation in the House of Commons on 20 March 1782 (ibid. ii. 422). For the defeats which preceded his resignation, see *ante* 23, [28] Feb. 1782.

4. North.

5. Fox.

6. Shelburne.

7. In *Last Journals* ii. 411–12, *sub* 27 Feb. 1782, HW notes the imperfection of his chronicle for 1782 and 1783: 'age and indolence have unfitted me for taking pains to inform myself.' He makes clear, however, that he has authentic sources for the information he does record. In his letter to Mann 2 March 1783, at the end, after forecasting a new era, he says: 'You may depend upon it that I shall have nothing to do with it; and consequently shall know nothing but outlines. I with-

in *my* system, I draw some sweetness from the dereliction[8] of the
loyalists.[9] I do pity sincerely the conscientious among them, but I
trust that this example will a little cure people of the distemper of
loyalty. If the more zealous, *the Rubiconians,* and those whose cause
they promote against the general happiness, would ever read, or ever
profit by what they might read, what a lesson would the American
war be against aiming at extending power! *Quieta non movere* was
the maxim of a man,[10] whom I, who have seen a good deal, do not
think wanted common sense; Lord Chatham, no doubt, bought us
more glory—but very dearly. We have paid still dearer for losses and
disgrace. My Quiet Statesman was called the Father of Corruption,
though his political parents and children, had been and have been
full of the same blood. Was it a capital crime to bribe those *on sale*
to promote the happiness of themselves and others, to bribe them
to preserve the constitution, and make the commerce of their country
flourish? Very different experiments have been tried since—I beg
your pardon, Madam, for wandering back to my own ideas—but
when a revolution happens, it is natural to reflect on those one has
seen. I am a Methusalem from the scenes I have seen—yet t'other
day I made an acquaintance with one a little my senior—yet we are to
be very intimate for a long time, for my new friend is but ninety-
four. It is General Oglethorpe[11]—I had not seen him these 20 years,
yet knew him instantly. As he did not recollect me, I told him it was a

draw myself more and more from the
world, have few connections left.'

8. Abandonment, 'Now rare except in
legal use' (OED).

9. Article V of the preliminary articles
between Great Britain and the United
States of America, signed 30 Nov. 1782,
provided that Congress would 'earnestly
recommend' to the states a conciliatory
policy toward the loyalists but provided
no guarantee of amnesty and compensation for them. This provision, although
attacked by both loyalists and many disinterested Englishmen, was 'the utmost
attainable in the treaty,' and England later
'proved honourable and generous in the
highest degree by compensating the loyalists out of her own treasury' (C. H. Van
Tyne, *The Loyalists in the American Revolution,* New York, 1902, p. 288 *et passim;*
Cobbett, *Parl. Hist.* xxiii. 468; BM, *Satiric*

Prints, v. 679–80, No. 6182; *A Full and
Faithful Report of the Debates in Both
Houses of Parliament* [17, 21 Feb.] *on the
Articles of Peace,* n. d., pt i. 38–40, HW's
copy, marked and annotated, now WSL;
*The Case and Claim of the American
Loyalists,* 'Printed by Order of Their
Agents,' 1783).

10. Sir Robert Walpole: 'The great
principle on which Walpole conducted
himself, seems to have been his favourite
motto, *quieta non movere,* not to disturb
things at rest' (William Coxe, *Memoirs of
. . . Sir Robert Walpole,* 1798, i. 753; see
also *Walpoliana* i. 88; *Last Journals* ii.
265).

11. Gen. James Edward Oglethorpe
(1696–1785), the philanthropist and col-
onist of Georgia, was in his eighty-seventh
year. HW recorded anecdotes 'from General Oglethorpe (aged 91) Feb. 16, 1783' in

proof how little he was altered, and I how much. I said I would visit him; he replied, 'No, no, I can walk better than you; I will come to you.' He is alert, upright, has his eyes, ears and memory fresh. If you want any particulars of the last century, I can procure them, but I know nothing of what is to happen *tomorrow*.¹²

PS. I have just seen in the *Public Advertiser*¹³ a passage in a letter from the Emperor to the Pope, which informs me how little the delegates of Heaven have occasion to *read*. Cæsar tells St Peter, 'that *he* possesses in his own breast a voice which tells what as legislator and protector of religion, he ought to pursue or desist from; and that voice, with the assistance of Divine Grace, and the honest and just character which he feels in himself, can never lead him into error'—There! Madam, there is Imperial Infallibility to some purpose! Henry VIII undoubtedly felt the same inspiration when he became head of our Church—and I dare to say that the Earls of Derby and the Dukes of Athol, till they sold the Isle of Man,¹⁴ had exactly the same unerring feelings. That inward voice, which the Greeks called *gastromuthos*,¹⁵ prattles to every monarch before he can speak himself, and did so to Henry VI in his cradle, though he lived to lose everything.

To Lady Ossory, Tuesday 11 March 1783

Address: To the Countess of Ossory at Ampthill Park, Bedfordshire. *Postmark:* 11 MR ⟨G⟩C.

March 11, 1783.

I HOPE, Madam, you have been rejoiced at the appointment of every new prime minister that we have had for this last fortnight, Mr W. Pitt,¹ the Duke of Portland,² Lord Temple,³ Lord Gower⁴ and

---

A Note Book of Horace Walpole, ed. W. S. Lewis, New York, 1927, p. 48.

12. Written in large letters.

13. 18 Feb.: 'translation of a letter from the Emperor to the Pope, privately handed about at Rome.'

14. Granted by Henry IV, 1406, to Sir John de Stanley; grant confirmed to the 6th E. of Derby, 1609; remained in the Stanley family until 1736, 'when it passed through an heiress to the family of Murray, Dukes of Atholl' (GEC iv. 205, 213). In

1764 the 3d D. of Atholl, whose wife, Charlotte Murray, had inherited the sovereignty, sold the Isle of Man to the Government 'for £70,000 and an annuity of £2,000 for their joint lives, reserving, however, their landed interest' (GEC i. 318, 320; *Scots Peerage* i. 490).

15. Literally, word of the belly.

———

1. William Pitt, the younger. 'The offer has been made to Pitt of the Treasury, with *carte blanche;* which, after two days'

Lord Thurlow. There may have been more for aught I know; as it is no business of mine, and as Lord Ossory is in town, I left it to him to make the several notifications—and it is well I did, or I might have distracted you, as I should perhaps have sent you one administration and he another by the same post. At present there is no premier at all, at least there was not a quarter of an hour ago—nay, they say there never is to be another; and, as I am the only unadulterated Whig left in England, I am prodigiously glad of it. You cannot imagine how much better things go on. Seconds, and thirds and fourths execute all business without molestation; for as every man thinks himself fit to be first, nobody condescends to oppose seconds and thirds: and as seconds and thirds never presume to do more than their duty, nobody has any fault to find—and no mortal ever finds fault without cause. The only present grievance is, the want of levees and drawing-rooms. All the world is eager to pay court to their sovereign on the abolition of the odious office of prime minister—but as all the world have thronged to offer their compliments on the accession of every new premier, their present contradictory homage is justly disdained—and as we can go on without a first lord of the Treasury, we certainly might exist without levees or drawing-rooms—why do people go to them, but because they hope to be rewarded by a first lord of the *Treasury?* In the East, where all are excellent subjects, they scarce

deliberation, he has this day refused' (W. W. Grenville to Temple 26 Feb., in *Memoirs of the Court and Cabinets of George III*, ed. 2d D. of Buckingham and Chandos, 2d edn, 1853–5, i. 168; Charles James Fox, *Memorials and Correspondence*, ed. Russell, 1853, ii. 40).

2. Portland told Gen. Cunninghame that, on 4 March, George III asked Lord North 'if *they* (meaning Mr Fox and his associates) would be satisfied with a neutral person being at the head of the Treasury: his Lordship replied, they would only be satisfied with the Duke of Portland' (Cunninghame to Temple 5 March, Buckingham, op. cit. i. 173). On 12 March ('this morning and not before') the 'King sent for Lord North, and desired him to acquaint the Duke of Portland that he was desirous of forming an administration, and had no objection to his being at the head of it' (Fitzpatrick to Fox 12 March, Fox, op. cit. ii. 58; see also *post* 13 March 1783, n. 1).

3. George Grenville (1753–1813), 2d E. Temple, 1779; cr. (1784) M. of Buckingham; son of the prime minister (1763–5) George Grenville; lord lieutenant of Ireland 15 Sept. 1782 – 3 June 1783, 1787–9; secretary of state 19–23 Dec. 1783 (on the formation of the Pitt ministry); K. G., 1786 (*Daily Advertiser* 23 Sept. 1782, 11 June 1783). His brother wrote to him 28 Feb.: 'Today the prevalent report was that you had been sent for. This I know to be otherwise, in present, though I think it not unlikely to happen; as I know the King's wish—at all events to exclude Fox and North, and particularly the first' (Buckingham, op. cit. i. 169).

4. Who 'had not resolution enough to accept' (HW to Mann 2 March 1783). On 7 March Gower was summoned by George III 'to form an administration' (*Corr. Geo. III* vi. 265); Thurlow was employed as negotiator (ibid. vi. 263–72).

ever see their monarch, except at the mosque or at an oratorio. In short, whether Whig or High-Churchman, one must be pleased with the present dispensation—I am only afraid that, such is our levity, we shall grow tired of this mundane theocracy, when the novelty is over; and like the frogs, neither be content with the log, nor the stork, nor the stagnant pool.

I am grown prodigiously older within these two days, Madam. I have been for some time the patriarch of a long line of nephews and nieces, and of great-nephews and -nieces—yet still when I had a mind to give myself juvenile airs, I could say, 'I have been to see my aunt.' Alas! that consolation is gone! The old Lady Walpole[5] died on Sunday at eighty-seven. Did I ever tell your Ladyship a trait of her, that was very respectable? She was daughter of a French refugee staymaker.[6] When ambassadress,[7] the late Queen of France[8] was surprised at her speaking French so well, and asked her how it happened? She replied, 'Madame, c'est ce que je suis française.'—'Vous!' said the Queen, 'et de quelle famille?'—'D'aucune, Madame,' replied my aunt. Would not one rather have made that answer, than have been able to say, a Montmorenci? The French ambassadress[9] here at the same time, who was the tally[10] of my aunt too in birth, and in quickness of reply, though not of such sublime modesty, was an heiress also of very low extraction. The Maréchal de Broglie,[11] her husband, talking of his children,[12] and to what professions he destined them, said, 'Et pour le

5. Mary Magdelaine Lombard (ca 1695–1783) m. (1720) Horatio Walpole, cr. (1756) Bn Walpole of Wolterton; died in White-hall (Mann ii. 47 n. 2; *London Chronicle* 8–11 March, liii. 234).

6. Peter Lombard (1643–1725), tailor (H. S. Vade-Walpole, 'Notes on the Wal-poles,' *Genealogical Magazine*, 1898–9, ii. 390–1).

7. Her husband was a special envoy to France, 1723; envoy extraordinary, 1724; ambassador extraordinary 1724–7; ambassador extraordinary and plenipotentiary 1727–30 (Horn, *Diplomatic Representatives* 17–18).

8. Marie-Catherine-Sophie-Félicité Lesz-czyńska (1703–68), m. (1725) Louis XV, K. of France. This anecdote is also in HW to Mann 20 Sept. 1772 and (without the 'Montmorenci' sentence) in 'Book of Materials' 1759, p. 42.

9. Thérèse-Gilette Locquet de Grand-ville (d. 1763), dau. of 'Charles, Sieur de Grandville, armateur de Saint-Malo,' m. (1716) François-Marie de Broglie, later Duc de Broglie (La Chenaye-Desbois).

10. HW first wrote 'counterpart.'

11. François-Marie de Broglie (1671–1745), Duc de Broglie, Maréchal de France, 1734; ambassador to England 1724–33 (ibid.; NBG; L. G. Wickham Legg, *List of Diplomatic Representatives and Agents, England and France 1689–1763*, in *Notes on the Diplomatic Relations of England and France*, ed. C. H. Firth, Oxford, 1909, p. 42).

12. His two older sons (here under discussion) entered the army, as did the third, while the fourth became a cardinal; his daughter married an army officer (La Chenaye-Desbois).

cadet, je l'aurais fait Chevalier de Malte,[13] mais Madame,' pointing to his wife, 'nous a fermé toutes les portes'—She replied, 'Oui, jusqu'à celles de l'hôpital.'[14] Apropos of *bons mots,* has our Lord told you that George Selwyn calls Mr Fox and Mr Pitt *the idle and the industrious apprentices?*[15] If he ⟨has not,⟩ I am sure you will thank me, Madam.

—Oh! stay, there is a prime minister just made—not indeed at the head of the Treasury, nor one that has either salary or perquisites, but who consequently would be much more in earnest in declining the honour, if he dared—in short, alas! your Ladyship's gazetteer is grown such a favourite at a certain tiny court in Cavendish Square,[16] that he is called to sit at the board[17] three nights in a week. I really think that I should *accept,* if I was sent for to the Queen's house, if only to recover my liberty, as Lord North[18] set a precedent of being as idle as one pleases.

To Lady Ossory, Thursday 13 March 1783

Address: To the Countess of Ossory at Ampthill Park, Bedfordshire. *Postmark:* 13 MR. GC.

March 13, 1783, New Style.

I CONCLUDE in the language of the day that our Lord has been *sent for,* and that I shall tell your Ladyship very stale news when I acquaint you that the Duke of Portland is minister.[1] I should tell

13. In France, 'the statutes and the present practice require that the presentee [candidate for admission to the order] prove his great-grandfathers by the father's and the mother's side were gentlemen by name as well as arms' (René-Aubert de Vertot, *The History of the Knights of Malta,* 1728, ii. 120, 115–23). Some knights 'descended of fathers of noble extraction but of mothers of ignoble or plebeian birth' were known as 'knights of grace' (ibid. ii. 115).

14. The Knights of Malta were originally known as Hospitallers.

15. In Hogarth's 'Industry and Idleness,' 1747, a series of twelve prints il-

lustrating the lives of Thomas Goodchild and Thomas Idle, based on the play by Chapman, Jonson, and Marston, *Eastward Hoe,* 1605. HW repeated the bon mot in his letter to the Duchess of Gloucester 13 March 1783.

16. Princess Amelia's. Cf. *post* 4 Nov. 1786.

17. The loo-table.

18. When first lord of the Treasury 1770–82.

———

1. This announcement was premature. The King had agreed on 12 March to accept Portland as prime minister, but many difficulties had to be resolved be-

you more than I know if I added another promotion, for though I heard that last night, it is now past four in the afternoon, and simple as I sit here, I have not learnt, nay not inquired a syllable more, nor have seen a two-legged creature today but a crooked painter.[2] Perhaps there is not another gentleman or gentlewoman in London equally ignorant. Nay, as I go again to *my* Court[3] this evening, where we have not the best intelligence in the world, it may be tomorrow morning before I know whether the Old Duchess of Portland[4] or Lord Guilford is to be Queen Dowager—the most important point to *me*, as they are my play-fellows. I sat with the former candidate till past eleven last night at Mrs Delany's,[5] and had a mind to ask for Margaret my housekeeper to be necessary woman[6] instead of Jenkinson,[7] with a pension of only a thousand a year, which, according to Colonel Barré's way of calculating,[8] she might have had, if my father had continued prime minister to this time.

I think your Ladyship may now steal into Grosvenor Place, without hearing *Odd Man*[9] called over the way.[10] As soon as all the sorties and entrées have been made and the several parties have visited reciprocally, things will fall into their usual channel, and the nearest rela-

fore he was officially appointed on 2 April (*Daily Advertiser* 3 April); he and six others of the new cabinet were ordered to St James's by George III 'to kiss hands this day, by half hour past one' (George III to North 'April 2nd, 1783 8 h. A.M.,' *Corr. Geo. III* vi. 331).

2. Not identified.

3. Princess Amelia's.

4. Margaret Cavendish Harley (1715–85) m. (1734) William Bentinck, 2d D. of Portland, 1726.

5. Mary Granville (1700–88) m. 1 (1718) Alexander Pendarves; m. 2 (1743) Patrick Delany, Dean of Down, 1744. Her house was in St James's Place. HW saw her frequently in London, and she left him a miniature of Liotard by himself, now wsl (Mason i. 197 n. 19). Part of the time she lived with the Duchess of Portland.

6. 'Under the Master of the Robes are . . . necessary women' (John Chamberlayne, *Magnæ Britanniæ notitia*, 38th edn, 1755, pt i. 105). In this, and other government offices, they rendered 'necessary or useful services' (OED), apparently in

connection with cleaning and supplying.

7. The 'chief' of 'the few' advisers the King trusted (*Last Journals* ii. 494). On 24 March in the House of Commons Jenkinson 'did in effect own that he was the secret minister, though he protested he had never gone to the King but when sent for' (ibid. ii. 503; Cobbett, *Parl. Hist.* xxiii. 664–8, 670–2).

8. In defending himself on 9 July 1782, when his proposed pension of £3200 was debated (*ante* 4 Aug. 1782), Barré 'pleaded having lost his commission in the army for having opposed the Court from conscience; and urged that, had he remained in the service, he might by that time have been a General, and have had a regiment and government equal in value to his pension' (*Last Journals* ii. 456; Cobbett, *Parl. Hist.* xxiii. 156–7).

9. '. . . calling, *Odd man!* as the hackney chairmen do when they want a partner' (HW to Mann 14 Feb. 1746 OS, Mann iii. 213).

10. By Lord Shelburne, who lived in Berkeley Square, 'over the way' from HW.

tions will not hate one another more than usual. Nay, *amidst the changes and chances* of this mortal life (a phrase which one should think had been coined at Brooks's) the reverse of an old proverb has just taken date. *The dearest friends must part* was an obvious and trite old saying—*The bitterest foes may embrace* is newer,[11] and not so trist a reflection: I love gay and good-humoured maxims. If the refinements of society have corrupted the heart, they have at least improved the temper. There are no deadly feuds now. People love and hate one another so often, that they go into friendship or out, as easily as into or out of mourning; and within this twelvemonth, for almost as short a time. Pray, Madam, don't be so vulgar as to stay in the country because there is somebody or other here that you are afraid of meeting. What an old-fashioned prejudice! Does one like anybody the less, because one dislikes that person? There is not a monarch in Europe that cannot conquer his aversion in *seventeen days;*[12] and shall a subject be allowed greater latitude? I know your Ladyship's are not antipathies, but very contrary awkwardnesses—but you must get over them. Lions and lambs, doves and serpents now trot in the same harness, and it does one's heart good to see them. They will all go into the Ark together on Monday, the sun will shine, and some evanescent rainbow will promise that the Ministry shall never be drowned again.

Here ends the first chapter of Exodus, which in Court Bibles always precedes **Genesis.**

To Lady Ossory, Tuesday 18 March 1783

Dated 16 March in earlier editions.
Address: To the Countess of Ossory at Ampthill Park, Bedfordshire. *Postmark:* 18 MR.

March 18, 1783.

WHEN Lord Ossory is in town, Madam, I shall certainly not pretend to send you politics—no, not even abortions of them. At any time I know none but what I learn by sitting here behind the bar

11. An allusion to the coalition of Fox and North.

12. 'When the inter-ministerium had lasted seventeen days, the King' agreed to accept the Duke of Portland; before arrangements were completed, however, the King made another offer to Pitt (*Last Journals* ii. 499, 501-4).

of my own coffee-house. Indeed I only write now to say that you extended the ideas of my last farther than I meant—I only alluded to a house very near me,[1] whither I thought it might be awkward to you to go just at this turn of the tide. I shall say nothing more on any such subject. You ought to and must judge by your own feelings.

I do not well recollect how I applied *Exodus before Genesis* in my last, and believe it was too far fetched, as it appeared an enigma. I think it was used on the change of the ministry, and that I referred to the derivation of the two words which are Greek. *Exodus* signifies *a going out,* and *Genesis* a *generation:* now a new ministry cannot be born, till the old is gone out; and therefore in the Red Book or Court Bible, Exodus must precede Genesis—I find that *much learning had made Paul mad,*[2] and that I talked nonsense by talking Greek. I will not be so apostolic again when I am speaking on heathen topics.

As I have not much faith, Madam, in sentiments after matrimony, I suspect that your Bedfordshire husband who would not go to see Mrs Siddons without his wife, is a hypocrite, and meant to persuade her that he never saw any woman *in Drury* Lane without her being present.

I don't know whether I ought to afflict your Ladyship with the dreadful account I received last night from Sir Horace Mann[3] of the devastation of Sicily and Calabria,[4] nor where you will find horror enough adequate to the calamity! What do you think of one hundred and thirty-two cities, towns and castles totally destroyed![5] This is literally sweeping

Towns to the grave, and nations to the deep![6]

1. Shelburne House, in Berkeley Square.

2. 'Festus   said . . . Paul, . . . much learning doth make thee mad' (Acts 26.24).

3. See Mann to HW 25 Feb. 1783, which included a printed account dated from Naples 17 Feb.

4. Reports of the earthquake and storm on 5–6 Feb. had appeared in the *London Chronicle* 11–15 March, liii. 242, 245, 256, before Mann's letter arrived; more detailed reports followed ibid. 15–20 March, liii. 264, 265, 266, 271–2. In what follows,

HW combines Mann's report with accounts from London newspapers; some accounts had appeared in the daily newspapers earlier than in the *London Chronicle.*

5. Not mentioned in Mann's account. 'Naples, Feb. 19. . . . it is said that the number of cities, castles, and towns amount to one hundred and thirty-two' (ibid. 18–20 March, liii. 272).

6. 'Towns to one grave, whole nations to the deep' (Pope, *Essay on Man,* i. 144).

There are vanished besides, two islands[7] and a whole river![8] one Cala-brian prince[9] has lost seventeen manors!—Mr Swinburne[10] is become an antediluvian historian: 'Nunc seges est ubi Troja fuit!'[11] How diminutive does a change of ministry appear, when Nature overturns two countries in a couple of nights!

To Lady Ossory, Saturday 5 April 1783

Address: To the Countess of Ossory at Ampthill Park, Bedfordshire. *Post-mark:* [Date mark blurred.] GC.

Berkeley Square, April 5, 1783.

YOU know I do not wait for answers, Madam, when I have any-thing worth telling you. In truth I go so very little into the world, that unless I hear news in my own room, I know but a small part of what is passing. Of late I have been quite tired of rumours and false reports; nor could give accounts of an egg that might be hatched or addled the next hour; and which though set under a brood hen, I could not tell but might produce a goose or a guinea fowl. Besides, Lord Ossory could give you much quicker intelligence than I, and more authentic: nor at this moment can I specify the preferments but of those who have actually kissed hands. Yet of one thing I am sure, which is, that General Conway[1] is delighted with Mr Fitzpatrick's being secretary at war,[2] and will do everything he can to accommodate him.

7. Lipari and Strongoli (Mann's account).

8. 'The river Pietra is become entirely dry' ('Extract of a letter from Naples, Feb. 18' in *London Chronicle* 13–15 March, liii. 256; also mentioned as 'river Petrache' in 'Extract of a letter from the Baron de Choiseul, ambassador from France at the Court of Sardinia, March 1,' ibid. 15–18 March 1783, liii. 264).

9. The Principe di Cariati's loss of 17 *feudi* is mentioned in Mann's account; the Principe may have been Scipione or Carlantonio Spinelli, Principe di Cariati (*Fortgeseszte neue genealogisch-historische Nachrichten*, Vol. VII, Leipzig, 1768, p. 649; Conte Berardo-Candida Gonzaga,

Memorie delle famiglie nobili, Naples, 1875–83, v. 198).

10. Henry Swinburne (1743–1803), trav-eller, author of *Travels in the Two Sicilies in the Years 1777, 1778, 1779, and 1780,* 1783–5. Vol. I is reviewed in GM June 1783, liii pt i. 508–9. For HW's copy, see Hazen, *Cat. of HW's Lib.* 2961.

11. Ovid, *Heroides,* I, i. 53; for *Nunc* read *Iam.* Cf. *post* 6 Dec. 1789.

———

1. Who remained as commander-in-chief until he resigned at the fall of the Port-land ministry in Dec. 1783.

2. His appointment was announced in the *London Chronicle* on 5 April and in the *London Gazette* No. 12430, 8–12 April,

I hope you was not alarmed at the attempt on your house. I do expect that we shall neither be safe at home or abroad. Everything proves that man is an aurivorous[3] animal, and will have its food wherever it grows.

I heard and saw the Misses Fitzpatrick[4] t'other night, and they assured me your Ladyship will be in town at the end of this month. I own, as you have stayed so long, I doubt it—but shall be happy to be mistaken.

The weather is so delicious that I propose going to Strawberry next week for some days, and unless it changes to cold, to be chiefly there. I grow so antiquated, and superannuated, that I am fit for nothing but to be laid up in my own Gothic collection. My politics ended with the American war; I shall tap none more. The greatest folly in my eyes is that of old people who cling to the last plank, when they may be washed off by the next wave.

To Lady Ossory, Thursday 17 April 1783

Address: To the Countess of Ossory at Ampthill Park, Bedfordshire. *Postmark:* 17 AP. GC.

Berkeley Square, April 17, 1783.

I AM a little of your Ladyship's opinion, that the new administration is not founded upon a rock—however, if they fall, I see no reason for expecting any other to be more permanent. The cards have been so thoroughly shuffled, that it will require several deals, before they get into suits again.

I know nothing, Madam, that will make a paragraph. I have been for three days at Strawberry, which does not brighten my intelligence —but you are coming yourself, and I believe will not find that I am particularly ignorant. All I have heard, except politics, of which I am

---

sub 'Whitehall, April 12'; he kissed the King's hand 11 April (*London Chronicle* 3–15 April 1783, liii. 328, 352, 354).

3. Gold-devouring. This is the earliest use cited in OED. HW used the phrase to Mann 30 April 1783. It appears in *A Note*

Book of Horace Walpole, ed. W. S. Lewis, New York, 1927, p. 47, and in 'Detached Thoughts,' *Works* iv. 368.

4. The daughters of Lord Ossory's uncle, Hon. Richard Fitzpatrick (*ante* 27 June 1771).

tired, is that Lady Frances Scott is to be married[1] to Mr Douglas, The Douglas. She was a great friend of Lady Lucy,[2] and it is a proof of *his* sense, that he can forgive her person in favour of her merit.

In a dearth of English novelties, perhaps, Madam, you may be willing to learn the latest mode at Paris. It is, to speak broken French —not to ridicule Britons, but in lowly imitation of us—I conclude the Duke of Manchester will be elected into the French Academy on the recommendation of his barbarisms.[3] Well, it is consolatory in our fall, to be still admired and aped! The Duc de Chartres is coming to study us,[4] as Pythagoras and Solon travelled to Egypt, and I hope will carry back every monkey-worship that he finds established on the banks of the Thames—oh! I fib; Lord Mount Edgcumbe has just been here and says the King of France, He in France, will not allow the Duc de Chartres to come hither, as the Comte d'Artois has the same ambition of improving himself,[5] and no King can like to be out-shone by all the younger branches of his family. I am sorry Lady Anne will not see those two Rajah-pouts driving themselves in gigs to Ranelagh.[6]

---

1. On 13 May 1783, at the house of her brother Henry, 3d D. of Buccleuch, in Grosvenor Square.

2. Douglas's first wife: Lady Lucy Graham (1751 – 13 Feb. 1780) m. (1771) Archibald James Edward Douglas, cr. (1790) Bn Douglas.

3. The Duke of Manchester was ambassador extraordinary and minister plenipotentiary at Paris in 1783–4 (Horn, *Diplomatic Representatives* 25–26). He had kissed hands 9 April (*London Gazette* No. 12430, 8–12 April).

4. It was reported that 'the Duke de Chartres . . . and his Duchess arrived on Wednesday [9 April] at the Royal Hotel, Pall-Mall' and that 'they have engaged 30 English servants in their suite, and intend residing here for two months' (*Daily Ad-* *vertiser* 12 April); he arrived in London 4 May and left London for Paris 5 June according to the *London Chronicle* 6 May–5 June, liii. 434, 528, 538.

5. Since the Duc de Chartres actually came, this report is questionable. The Comte d'Artois, however, was reported to have startled the courtiers at a dinner, early in the year, when 'il propose de boire à la santé des Anglais' (Louis Petit de Bachaumont, *Mémoires secrets*, 1777–89, xxii. 23, *sub* 9 Jan.). He had wanted to go to America during the Revolution, and had briefly joined the army at Gibraltar in 1782 (J. Lucas-Dubreton, *Le Comte d'Artois, Charles X*, 1927, p. 29).

6. Whither the Duc de Chartres went with the Prince of Wales, 2 June (*London Chronicle* 3–5 June, liii. 530).

To LADY OSSORY, Friday 25 April 1783

Address: To the Countess of Ossory at Ampthill Park, Bedfordshire. *Postmark:* 25 AP. GC.

Berkeley Square, April 25, 1783.

UNLESS you have a mind to be Bishop of Norwich,[1] Madam, I can give you no reason for hastening your arrival before Monday—not that I should fling cold water on your coming sooner were I to be in town myself; but I shall go to Strawberry tomorrow, though the weather is as bitter as it always is in Newmarket week, and not return but for my Princess's Monday; and consequently shall not have the honour of kissing your Ladyship's hand till Tuesday. It is not I, but young Mr Horatio, who has kissed hands for a place in Chelsea College,[2] for though *I* am much fitter for an hospital, it is not my intention to go to one through Court. Another of my kin is arrived, Mr Robert Walpole[3] from Portugal, and has brought a wife[4] who is to efface all Venuses and Helens past or present. I have not yet seen her, but mean to do so soon, lest she should be poisoned by some of the reigning beauties who have views on the Prince of Wales.

I have just heard that Lord Hardwicke is dead.[5] I am not sure it is true, yet it is probable. Soame Jenyns, whom I saw last night at Mrs Delany's, said he was very ill and kept his bed. They were talking of the new administration; Jenyns said he hoped it would last at least as long as it had been in forming—In truth I question whether it will be very vivacious. If satirical prints could dispatch them, they would

1. Philip Yonge (ca 1709–83), Bp of Norwich since 1761, had died on 23 April at his house in Upper Grosvenor Street (Venn, *Alumni Cantab.*; *London Chronicle* 22–24 April 1783, liii. 392).

2. 'On Wednesday last [23 April] the Hon. Horatio Walpole kissed his Majesty's hand at St James's, on being appointed secretary and register to Chelsea Hospital, in the room of Samuel Estwick, Esq., resigned' (ibid. 24–26 April, liii. 394). Walpole was appointed 17 April, and on 25 Dec. was replaced by his predecessor Estwick (C. G. T. Dean, *Royal Hospital Chelsea*, 1950, p. 314).

3. Hon. Robert Walpole (1736–1810),

4th son of HW's uncle Horace; secretary of embassy at Madrid 1767–8; secretary of embassy 1768–9 and minister plenipotentiary 1769–71 at Paris; envoy extraordinary and plenipotentiary at Lisbon 1771–1800 (*Eton Coll. Reg.*; Horn, *Diplomatic Representatives* 23–4, 101, 136; Collins, *Peerage*, 1812, v. 673–4).

4. Diana Grosset (d. 24 July 1784), dau. of Walter Grosset, Scottish merchant of Lisbon, m. (8 May 1780) Hon. Robert Walpole (Burke, *Peerage*, 1953, p. 2161; *London Chronicle* 1–3 June 1780, xlvii. 536; HW to Mann 29 May 1783).

5. He lived until 1790. 'Lord Hardwicke lies dangerously ill at his house in St

WALPOLE'S ANNOTATED COPY OF 'RAZOR'S LEVEE'

be dead in their cradle; there are enough to hang a room.[6] The last I think the best; it is called, 'Heads of a New *Wig* Administration on a Broad Bottom.'[7] It is better composed than ordinary, and has several circumstances well imagined. The designer is one Sayer,[8] a Norfolk lawyer, who drew the single figures of several members of Parliament.[9] The woman[10] who keeps the printshop in Bruton Street[11] whence these hieroglyphics issue, says she has engraved all the drawings that are sent to her, and that she gets by them, one with another, ten pounds apiece. I hope you was charmed, Madam, by the figure of the young maiden in Mr Bunbury's 'Robin Gray.'[12]

I rejoice that our correspondence ends here for this season, Madam —how glad I shall be on Tuesday to say 'Go to Grosvenor Place!'

To Lady Ossory, Friday 20 June 1783

Berkeley Square, June 20, 1783.

I DID suspect, Madam, from the *sort* of commendations that I heard bestowed, and from the *sort* of persons who bestowed them, that I should not be much edified by the *improvements* of Hatfield.

James's Square' (*London Chronicle* 22–24 April, liii. 392).

6. In BM, *Satiric Prints* v. 676–704, 37 prints (dated 28 Feb. – 25 April 1783) connected with the coalition are described.

7. 'Razor's Levee, or Ye Heads of a New Wig Ad-------n on a Broad Bottom,' 'Published 21st April 1783 by Thomas Cornell, Bruton Street.' 'J[ames] S[ayers] f[ecit]' (ibid. v. 700–1, No. 6217). See illustration.

8. James Sayers (1748–1823), son of the master of a trading vessel; articled as clerk to an attorney at Yarmouth; became member of the borough council; left the law on inheriting a small fortune from his father; came to London ca 1780; espoused the cause of Pitt vs Fox in vigorous caricatures.

9. See BM, *Satiric Prints* v. 525, 623–30, Nos 5882–3, 6052–63, 6065–73, 6075–7. All but the first two (which appeared 8 Aug. and 23 Nov. 1781 and are doubtfully assigned to Sayers) were published 6 April – 3 July 1782, and all were published by Charles Bretherton.

10. Presumably Mrs Thomas Cornell.

11. The shop of Thomas Cornell in Bruton Street near Bond Street. In BM, *Satiric Prints,* the first print with his name as publisher is dated 16 March 1780 and the last 21 Dec. 1792 (v. 388, No. 5650; vi. 942, No. 8144). In 1785 he was listed as 'Cornell, Stationer to the Prince of Wales, 7, Bruton Street' (John Pendred, *The Earliest Directory of the Book Trade . . . 1785,* ed. Graham Pollard, 1955, p. 10). In 1790 he gave his address as 'Bruton Street, Berkeley Square' (title-page of the Countess of Carlisle, *Thoughts in the Form of Maxims,* 2d edn).

12. Engraved by Bartolozzi after Bunbury, published 10 Feb. 1783 by 'W. Dickinson, Engraver and Printseller, No. 158 New Bond Street.' A quotation from the ballad 'Auld Robin Gray' serves as title:

'My Faither urged me sair, my Mither did nae speak,

But she look'd in my Face till my heart was like to break.'

The girl is in anguish in the centre, her mother on her right and her father on

The Earl and Countess[1] did me the honour of inviting me to see them two years ago,[2] but as I neither love to flatter nor disoblige, I have not been—and *two years* have certainly not made me more of a *going* disposition. Brocket Hall[3] I never did see, and nothing has made me more going *thither*. When I play for green gowns with fair nymphs, *they* are not of the coterie of the nymphs and swains that I should meet there,[4] *il s'en faut beaucoup*. Lord Chewton won the prize,[5] and consequently there would be no gallantry in the case.

I came to town yesterday, expecting, like Cibber, *to meet the Revolution,*[6] but I am told that all is readjusted.[7] I am glad of it; I wish the present administration to last, which is not often the colour of my inclination towards ministries.

The month of June has been as abominable as any one of its ancestors in all the pedigree of the Junes. I was literally half drowned on Sunday night. It rained through two stories and into the Green Closet at Strawberry, and my bedchamber was wet to its smock. The gutters were stopped or could not carry off the deluge fast enough. Margaret prayed to St Rainbow, but as he never appears till it is too late, we were forced to have recourse to mortal help and litter all the floors with hay to soak up the inundation.

I had a worse woe the next night. The house of De Guines[8] had notified to Lady Ailesbury their intention of visiting Strawberry, and she had proposed to bring them to breakfast. At first I refused, but reflecting that they might invade me unawares like the Duc de Chartres,[9] I had agreed that she should bring them yesterday—but lo! on

her left. HW's copy of the print (coloured) is now WSL.

———

1. Of Salisbury.

2. See *ante* 3 Nov. 1782.

3. In Hertfordshire, near Hatfield; seat of Vct Melbourne.

4. A reference to the connection between the Prince of Wales and Lady Melbourne.

5. Lady Chewton. Lady Melbourne had caused the breaking of Lord Egremont's engagement to Lady Charlotte Maria Waldegrave, Lady Chewton's sister.

6. Heading to Chapter III of Cibber's *Apology* (MANN iii. 92 n. 14). HW's annotated copy is Hazen, *Cat. of HW's Lib.* 450.

7. The coalition administration was al-

most overthrown when the King, disliking the plans of the ministry to allow the Prince of Wales £100,000 a year on his coming of age, was supposed to have offered Lord Temple the administration on 13 June, but changed his mind three days later. When the ministers were on the point of resigning, the King begged Portland to continue. 'The miscarriage of this change certainly was a great step towards a much firmer establishment of the administration' (*Last Journals* ii. 524–7).

8. With him were his daughters, and the Comte de Charlus, his son-in-law (*London Chronicle* 17–24 June, liii. 581, 594).

9. This visit, which HW mentions in his letter to Harcourt 5 Aug. 1783, occurred between 31 May – 1 June (when

Monday morning Lady Pembroke wrote to me that she would bring them to drink tea that evening. I told her my arrangement, but left it to her option to do as she pleased. From dinner-time I sat at the window watching for them, and taking every old woman with a basket on her head for a coach and six. It rained all the time as it had done the preceding evening. At last, at half an hour after seven, as I had left it to their option, and the night was so bad and dark, I concluded they had given it up, and called for my tea—but alas! at a quarter before eight the bell rang at the gate—and behold a procession of the Duke, his two daughters,[10] the French ambassador[11] (on whom I had meant to sink myself[12]), Lady Pembroke, Lord Herbert and Lord Robert.[13] The first word M. de Guines said was to beg I would show them all I could—Imagine, Madam, what I could show them when it was pitch dark! Of all houses upon earth mine, from the painted glass and overhanging trees, wants the sun the most, besides the Star Chamber and passage being obscured on purpose to raise the gallery. They ran their foreheads against Henry VII[14] and took the grated door of the Tribune[15] for the dungeon of the castle. I mustered all the candlesticks in the house, but before they could be lighted up, the young ladies, who by the way are extremely natural, agreeable and civil, were seized with a panic of highwaymen and wanted to go. I laughed and said, I believed there was no danger, for that I had not

HW wrote to Mason that he had not seen one of the French visitors) and 5 June, when the Duc left London for Paris (MASON ii. 306; ante 17 April 1783, n. 4).

10. Marie-Louise-Philippine de Bonnières de Guines (d. 1796) m. (1778) Armand-Charles-Augustin de La Croix, Comte de Charlus, later Marquis and Duc de Castries; Marie-Louise-Charlotte de Bonnières de Guines (d. 1792) m. (1782) Charles-Philibert-Gabriel LeClerc, Comte, later (1807) Marquis de Juigné (A. Révérend, *Titres . . . de la Restauration*, 1901–6, iv. 127, 250–1; DU DEFFAND v. 53; *La Grande encyclopédie*).

11. Jean-Balthazar d'Azémar de Montfalcon (1731–91), Comte d'Adhémar; ambassador to England 1783–7. He had delivered his credentials to the King on 14 May (*London Chronicle* 17–20 May, liii. 474). On 31 May 1784 he again visited SH (BERRY ii. 221).

12. HW had intended to become in-

visible to the new ambassador to avoid acquaintance with 'anything that comes from France' (HW to Mason 31 May 1783, MASON ii. 306; OED, *sink*, verb, IV. 25b).

13. Lord Robert Spencer, Lady Pembroke's brother.

14. In the Star Chamber, on a mahogany cabinet, 'a bust of Henry VII, in stone, a model in great taste for his tomb, by Torreggiano' ('Des. of SH,' *Works* ii. 454). HW paid £10.10.0 for it (his MS note in 1774 'Des. of SH,' now WSL, p. 57); sold SH xvii. 96 for £27.6.0; in 1940, in the possession of William Randolph Hearst.

15. 'The grated door was designed by Mr Thomas Pitt,' cr. (1784) Lord Camelford ('Des. of SH,' *Works* ii. 471). A photograph in *Country Life*, 12 July 1924, lvi. 60, Fig. 10, shows the door, and part of it appears in W. S. Lewis, 'The Genesis of SH' 77, Fig. 25.

been robbed these two years. However, I was not quite in the right; they were stopped in Knightsbridge by two footpads, but Lady Pembroke having lent them a servant besides their own unique, they escaped—and so much for the French and the rain—I wish the latter were as near going as the former! Tomorrow I dine at Gunnersbury, and then I hope my troubles will be over for the summer.

I called on Lady Frances Douglas, but could not deliver your Ladyship's commands, for she was just going to town to be presented[16] and did not let me in.

To Lady Ossory, Tuesday 15 July 1783

Strawberry Hill, July 15, 1783.

I WAS in town last week, Madam, and just as I was returning, was told poor Mr Morice was dead, and Miss Howe has heard so too;[1] but as I have not seen it yet in the papers, I would flatter myself it is not true, for the only truths which the newspapers tell, are those which will give concern to anybody.

I am sorry your Ladyship has suffered so much by the heat. For me, I am below all weather, for none affects me. If it could, it would during the two days I passed in London, where I was forced to meet Lord Orford's lawyers.[2] Indeed, as much as I love to have summer in summer, I am tired of this weather—

The dreaded east is all the wind that blows,[3]

it parches the leaves, makes the turf crisp, claps the doors, blows the papers about, and keeps one in a constant mist that gives no dew, but might as well be smoke. The sun sets like a pewter plate red hot, and then in a moment appears the moon at a distance of the same complexion, just as the same orb in a moving picture[3a] serves for both. I wish modern philosophers had not disturbed all our ideas! two

16. At the Queen's Drawing-Room 19 June (Coke, 'MS Journals' 12, 19 June 1783).

———

1. On 12 July, 'Mrs Howe mentioned the death of Mr Morrice thinking I [Lady Mary Coke] had known it . . . she said the account arrived the day before yesterday . . .' (Coke, 'MS Journals'). This false

report was corrected in the *London Chronicle* 16–19 Aug., liv. 170.

2. In connection with Mozzi's affairs.

3. Pope, *The Rape of the Lock*, iv. 20.

3a. In 1781–2 and again in 1786 Loutherbourg (*ante* 30 Dec. 1773) presented his 'Eidophusikon,' moving pictures within a proscenium, with lights, coloured gauzes, etc., to represent various times of the

hundred good years ago celestial and terrestrial affairs hung together, and if a country was out of order, it was comfortable to think that the planets ordered or sympathized with its ails. A sun shorn of his beams, and a moon that only serves to make darkness visible,[4] are mighty homogeneal to a distracted state; and when their ministry is changed every twelve hours, without allaying the heat or mending the weather, Father Hollinshead would have massed the whole in the casualties of the reign, and expected no better till he was to tap a new accession.

As I have meditated so profoundly on the season, you will perceive, Madam, that I had nothing else to talk of, and consequently did not write till I had some answer to make. With your letter I received one from Lord Chewton to tell me the birth of his daughter,[5] for which event I was anxious. I do not mean that I wished it a girl, nor affect the apathy of the Duke of Devonshire,[6] for though Lord Chewton is no King of the Peak, a boy can shift better than a poor girl.[7] However, dear Lady Chewton is perfectly well, and I am easy.

News I have heard none this month but the deaths of Irish peeresses Lady Middleton[8] and Lady Gage;[9] but as Hibernian peers spring up like mushrooms, or are mushrooms, I suppose there will be as great plenty of ermine in that country as ever—perhaps soon of their own growth, without a drawback from *our* Custom House! *Here,* I am told, no more is to be issued—As the *sun's* train is much curtailed,[10] I suppose he thinks he has stars enough around him—but to change the topic, I was glad that the late Chancellor and his virtue were dragged through the kennel.[11]

day, shipwreck, Satan and Pandemonium, etc.; music and sound effects accompanied the pictures. Reynolds, Gainsborough, and many others praised the performance. See Austin Dobson, *At Prior Park and Other Papers,* 1912, pp. 111–17, 277–81. HW pasted into his 'Book of Materials' 1771, p. 72, an undated newspaper advertisement for the Eidophusikon and a four-paragraph newspaper account of this 'new species of public spectacle and entertainment' which had begun on 'Monday evening last'; HW has dated the cutting 'Wednesday Feb. 28, 1781.'

4. *Paradise Lost* i. 63.

5. Maria Wilhelmina Waldegrave (14 July 1783–1805), first child of the Chewtons, m. (1804) Nathaniel Micklethwait of Taverham Hall, Norfolk (GM 1805, lxxv pt i. 285; BERRY ii. 50 n. 9; George Kears-

ley, *Peerage,* [1796], i. 100; John Debrett, *Peerage,* 1817, i. 238).

6. Whose daughter, Lady Georgiana Dorothy Cavendish, had been born on 12 July (*ante* 7 Jan. 1783).

7. HW refers again to Lord Chewton's lack of fortune *post* 19 June 1784.

8. Frances Pelham (1760 – 28 June 1783) m. (1778) George Brodrick, 4th Vct Midleton.

9. Elizabeth Gideon (ca 1739 – 1 July 1783) m. (1757) William Hall Gage, 2d Vct Gage, cr. (1780) Bn Gage (*London Chronicle* 1–3 July, liv. 13).

10. By the loss of the American colonies.

11. Thurlow had resigned at the insistence of Fox in April with a pension of £2,680 and the reversion of a tellership in the Exchequer. On 4 July 'Lord J.

I must shift the subject once more, and talk of another no better, myself, or finish my letter. I have given one or two dinners to blue-stockings,[12] and one pedigree dinner to my cousin the Portuguese beauty,[13] and her husband and his two nephews Horatio[14] and Thomas;[15] and I have been again commanded to Gunnersbury, where I found Prince William.[16] He had been with the Princess in the morning, and returned of his own accord to dinner. She presented me to him, and I attempted, at the risk of tumbling on my nose, to kiss his hand, but he would not let me. You may trust me, Madam, who am not apt to be intoxicated with royalty, that he is charming. Lively, cheerful, talkative, manly, well-bred, sensible, and exceedingly proper in all his replies. You may judge how good-humoured he is, when I tell you that he was in great spirits all day, though with us old women —perhaps he thought it preferable to Windsor!

Another day the Jerninghams[17] brought to see my house—whom do you think?—only a *Luxembourg*,[18] a *Lusignan*,[19] and a *Montfort!*[20] I never felt myself so much in the Castle of Otranto. It sounded as if a company of noble Crusaders were come to sojourn with me before they embarked for the Holy Land[21]—Still I was a very uncourteous *châtelain*—I did not appear—in short, Mr Mason, whom I had

Cavendish's bill for reform of Exchequer places' was debated, and 'Rigby proposed by a clause to put the Chancellor Thurlow upon the same foot with the other tellers.' 'He had bragged much of not taking it, and had thrown out hints as if such grants were illegal: but the reason was said to be, that he did not care to insert his son's name in the patent, whose legitimacy was doubtful. Charles Fox, whom he had lately termed a bankrupt, violently opposed the clause, as did Sheridan, and [on 7 July] it was rejected by a majority of eight [57 to 49], and with great disgrace to Thurlow' (*Last Journals* ii. 529; Cobbett, *Parl. Hist.* xxiii. 1061–91).

12. One dinner was on 5 July. See the account by Mary Hamilton in MORE 206.

13. Mrs Robert Walpole; see *ante* 25 April 1783.

14. Eldest son of the 2d Bn Walpole (*ante* 22 April 1777).

15. Thomas Walpole (1755–1840), eldest son of Hon. Thomas Walpole; of Stag-

bury Park, Surrey; minister plenipotentiary 1784–8 and envoy extraordinary and plenipotentiary 1788–96 to the Court of the Elector Palatine at Munich; HW's correspondent (Burke, *Peerage*, 1953, p. 2160; Horn, *Diplomatic Representatives* 43, 62).

16. On 4 July (*London Chronicle* 3–5 July, liv. 21).

17. One of them was Charles (1742–1814), the Chevalier (HW to Harcourt 5 Aug. 1783; BERRY i. 67 n. 41).

18. Possibly Anne-Charles-Sigismond de Montmorency-Luxembourg (1737–1803), Duc de Luxembourg (DU DEFFAND iii. 129).

19. Perhaps Hugues-Jacques de Lezay (1749–1814), Marquis de Lusignan (Henri Jougla de Morenas, *Grand armorial de France*, 1934–49, iv. 457).

20. Perhaps Philogène-Charles de Montfort (b. 1733) or his son Jean-Louis (b. 1763) (ibid. v. 96).

21. The Lusignans were Kings of Cyprus at the time of the Crusades; the

not seen for a year, was at dinner with me, and was to pass but that one day with me[22]—*cedant arma togæ*[23]—I preferred the *Heroic Epistle* to a troop of heroes—that is, the supposed author of the one to what I do not suppose the others.

You bid me watch my purse, Madam, when I am in good company. In truth I am not apt to watch it: yet without my taking the smallest precaution to guard it, it has escaped through two *houses*[24] full of the *best* company in England, and in which there were *bishops* too.

Alas! here is half my letter about myself, and half of that about what I have *not* been doing. It shows how antiquated I am and how little I know. To complete my personal journal, I send you a vile pun of my own making. Miss Pope[25] has been at Mrs Clive's this week, and I had not been able to call on them. I wrote a line of excuse, but hoped very soon to salute Miss *Pope's eye*[26]—Excuse my *radotage*—but what better can you expect?

To Lady Ossory, Wednesday 23 July 1783

Address: To the Countess of Ossory at Ampthill Park, Bedfordshire. *Postmark:* ISLEWORTH. 24 IY.

Strawberry Hill, Wedn[esday] evening, July 23.

AS YOUR Ladyship interests yourself about Mr Morice, these are to certify you that he is alive—and I dare to say, merry. Mr Towneley,[1] uncle of the statuarist,[2] and with whom I once dined at

Comtes de Montfort were eminent Crusaders.

22. This visit is not mentioned in the HW-Mason Correspondence. It was before 4 July, when Mason wrote from Bill Hill, Berks, where he was visiting the Dowager Countess Gower, that he would 'proceed to Nuneham tomorrow' (photostat now WSL of original in the possession of Canon R. A. Wilson).

23. Cicero, *De Officiis,* I. xxii. 82. 'Let wars yield to peace.'

24. Parliament. HW's 'office of Usher of the Exchequer has not only been alleged in the House of Commons [on 17 June] as an expensive one, but as a bar to the correction of great waste' (HW to Lord Shelburne 19 June 1783, in which HW defends himself). Pitt's bill for re-

form in the public offices was debated in the House of Commons on 2, 17 June and was passed 19 June without a division but was rejected in the House of Lords on 30 June by a vote of 40 to 24 (Cobbett, *Parl. Hist.* xxiii. 945–59, esp. 951–5, and 1106–14).

25. Jane Pope (1742–1818), actress at Drury Lane 1756–1808.

26. HW thought well enough of this 'vile pun' to repeat it in his letter to Harcourt 5 Aug. 1783: 'I am to eat your Lordship's health at Cliveden, in your own venison, . . . and to drink Miss *Pope's eye.*'

———

1. John Towneley (1731–1813) (MORE 204 n. 3). He had a house at Chiswick,

the Grove, came to see my house yesterday, and left word that Mr Morice is not only not dead, but better, and at Lausanne, and purposes to winter at Naples;[3] which methinks is risking his life at least as much as trying to preserve it, for the earthquakes do not seem at all to have retired into their own channel.[4]

I have been in town to see Lady Chewton,[5] and found her excellent well, and suckling her infanta without mercy. I believe she will be a more staid nurse than the Duchess of Devonshire, who probably will stuff her poor babe[6] into her knotting bag, when she wants to play at macao, and forget it.

More French are just come to see the house, a Vicomte and Marquis de St Chamant[7] and a Baron de Montesquieu.[8] I could not leave the Blue Room to their sight, for I have the gout today both in my ankle and left hand,[9] but I think it will not be a fit, for the pain is already gone, though it came but in the night. Are not you prodigiously glad, Madam, that somebody whom you never saw, is dead at the farthest end of the globe? My neighbours at Twickenham are overjoyed at the death of Hyder Ally,[10] who I suppose they think lived in Lombard Street.[11]

near Morice's The Grove (DNB, *sub* Towneley, Charles).

2. Charles Towneley (1737–1805), collector of classical antiquities. His marbles and terra cottas were purchased by the British Museum in 1805 and his bronzes, coins, gems, and drawings in 1814.

3. Lady Mary Coke mentions on 29 Nov. 1783 a letter from him at Naples (Coke, 'MS Journals').

4. Morice wrote Lady Mary Coke that 'there are still frequent shocks felt in Calabria' (ibid.), as the newspapers also reported (*London Chronicle* 29 April – 31 July, liii, liv. *passim*).

5. Her London house from 1782 to 1786 was in Mansfield Street, as appears from her letters (now WSL) to Anne Clement.

6. Lady Georgiana Dorothy Cavendish, born 12 July (*ante* 7 Jan. 1783). Much was made of the Duchess's suckling her own infant; see, for example, the *Rambler's Magazine*, Aug. 1783, i. 318, May 1784, ii. 113–14, with print (described in BM, *Satiric Prints* vi. 78, No. 6490) facing p. 113.

7. Probably Armand de Saint-Chamans

(b. 1754), styled (1778) Marquis de Saint-Chamans, and his brother, Auguste-Gabriel-Louis (b. 1761), Vicomte de Saint-Chamans (Henri de Woelmont, Baron de Brumagne, *Notices généalogiques*, 1923–35, ii. 925–7).

8. Anne-Élisabeth-Pierre de Montesquiou-Fézensac (1764–1834), Baron de Montesquiou, cr. (1809) Comte de Montesquiou-Fézensac (*Rép. de la Gazette* iii. 647; Révérend, *Titres . . . de la Restauration*, 1901–6, v. 164).

9. The gout had attacked HW during his visit to Lord Dacre at Belhus (HW to Hon. Thomas Walpole and to Lady Browne 23 July 1783, MORE 204; to Conway 27 July 1783).

10. Ḥandar Shāh, or Hyder 'Ali (ca 1722 – 7 Dec. 1782), Khan Bahādur; Nawab of Mysore; allied with the French and Mahrattas against the English; invaded the Carnatic, 1780; defeated by Sir Eyre Coote at Porto Novo, 1781. His death 'in . . . December last' was announced in the *London Gazette* No. 12459, 19–22 July. See C. E. Buckland, *Dictionary of Indian Biography*, 1906, pp. 213–14, 424;

My visitors are gone already—it is literally true that they arrived while I was writing the last paragraph but one, and went away as I finished the last, though I certainly do not write slowly. They are gone to Hampton Court, and return to France tomorrow. Don't you like seeing a house in the time one can write eight lines, and a country in less than one can wash one's hands?—I wish all who come to see my house stayed no longer.

To Lady Ossory, Monday 4 August 1783

Strawberry Hill, Aug. 4, 1783.

IT IS shameful, Madam, to keep a letter unanswered that came kindly to ask how I did—but, good Lord! I hate to write, when I have no other, no better topic than myself. My last was filled with nothing else; for alas a day! it is all I know! and never was anything less worth knowing or repeating! The sultry season did me a great deal of good and a great deal of harm. It agreed with me like a charm; but the nights were so hot, that I left off or kicked off all covering, and first I caught the gout in my ankle, then the rheumatism in my shoulder, and so was exceedingly well, except that I could not move hand or foot. Still I love to have summer in summer, and as our doggest days never produce earthquakes nor make us swallow shoals of insects with every mouthful, I never complain of them—not but I do think I felt an earthquakeling a fortnight ago between four and five in the morning,[1] but it was a poor rickety thing, and could not have thrown down a house of cards. I hope the plague with which we are threatened *de par le Roi*[2] will prove as arrant a miscarriage. The Semiramis of the North,[3] the devil take her, has fetched it to this side of the globe,[4] and

Cambridge History of India, Vol. V; BM Cat.; MASON ii. 123.

11. Of 48 bankers listed in *The New Complete Guide to All Persons Who Have Any Trade or Concern with the City of London*, 1783, p. 332, 14 were in Lombard Street.

1. Slight earthquakes in April and August 1783 are mentioned by Charles Davison, *A History of British Earthquakes*, Cambridge, 1924, p. 16.

2. The *London Gazette* No. 12462, 29 July – 2 Aug., starts with an official procla mation from St James's, 25 July: 'Present, the King's most excellent Majesty in Council. Whereas information has been received from . . . his Majesty's ambassador at Constantinople, that the plague had begun to spread . . . his Majesty doth hereby require and command all the officers appointed for the service of quarantine to use their utmost care.'

3. Catherine II of Russia. 'M. de Voltaire ne perd aucune circonstance de faire sa cour à la Czarine, qu'il appelle la

it may be added to the catalogue of her great exploits which the French Academicians so much admire. I know, the plague is not so horrid a thing as some people imagine—at least, Boccace chose such a period as a delicious one for telling stories. He makes a select company of young gentlemen and ladies shut themselves up in a country house and relate novels to pass away the time, while all their relations and friends were swept away by cartloads in the city.

Have you seen Lord Carlisle's tragedy,[5] Madam? he has been so good as to send it to me. It has great merit; the language and imagery are beautiful, and the two capital scenes are very fine.[6] The story is Sigismonda and Guiscard,[7] but he has much improved the conduct, and steered clear of the indelicacy and absurdity of the original, which did not stop Dryden,[8] who knowing that he could tell anything delightfully, did not mind what he told—or how could he have thought of making an old king sleep behind a bed instead of upon it? There are some parts that might be mended, and a situation or two too like what has been seen on the stage—yet I am sure your Ladyship will admire most of it. Do not imagine that I am prejudiced by the compliment of its being sent to me. I have read it twice carefully, and liked it better the second time than the first.

I hear often of Lady Chewton and perfectly good accounts, but I have not seen her since the first week,[9] for I should be burnt as black as an Etruscan vase, if I went to my house in Berkeley Square in this weather—no disrespect to this day sennight, surely, Madam, last Saturday was still nearer to the torrid zone. I begin to think that the Rumbolds[10] and Co. have robbed the Indies of their climate as well

---

Semiramis du Nord' (Louis Petit de Bachaumont, *Mémoires secrets*, 1777–89, xix. 5–6, *sub* 24 July 1768).

4. 'And whereas . . . the plague . . . now rages . . . in the country which is called the Tartary . . . and in the Crimea, and . . . upon the frontiers of Poland: and his Majesty . . . doth thereupon judge it probable, that the infection may be brought into this kingdom from Dantzick, or some port or place in royal and ducal Prussia or Pomerania; his Majesty doth therefore . . . order, that all ships . . . do make their quarantine for forty days' (*London Gazette*, loc. cit.).

5. *The Father's Revenge, a Tragedy,*

1783. HW's copy is at Harvard (Hazen, *Cat. of HW's Lib.* 3222.20.2).

6. HW repeats the sense of this sentence in his letter to the Earl of Strafford 11 Oct. 1783.

7. In Boccaccio's *Decameron* iv. 1.

8. In 'Sigismondas and Guiscardo. From Boccaci,' the third story in his *Fables Ancient and Modern*, 1700.

9. After the birth of her daughter; see *ante* 23 July 1783.

10. Sir Thomas Rumbold (1736–91), cr. (1779) Bt; governor of Madras 1777–80. In 1782–3 his conduct in India and the amassing of an immense fortune there were the subject of an ineffectual Parlia-

as of their gold and diamonds, and brought it home in ingots. You hoped that Hyder Ally would have extirpated our banditti—do not fear, Madam; I believe it will not be long before we are outcasts like the Jews, and become pedlars like them up and down the earth, with no country of our own.

I saw Captain Waldegrave at Lady Chewton's, and he was quite re-covered of his accident; but I know nothing of him since.

I must tell you an excellent reply of a person your Ladyship scarce knows, and I, not at all. Lord Lewisham lately gave a dinner to a certain Electoral Prince,[11] who is in England, and at which *à la mode de son pays* they drank very hard. The conversation turned on matri-mony: the foreign *Altesse* said he envied the Dukes of Devon and Rutland, who, though high and mighty princes too, had been at liberty to wed two charming women whom they liked—but for his part he supposed he should be forced to marry some ugly German B—— —I forget the other letters of the word—and then turning to the Irish Master of the Rolls,[12] asked what *he* would advise him to do? —'Faith, sir,' said the Master, 'I am not yet drunk enough to give advice to a Prince of —— about marrying.' I think it one of the best answers I ever heard. How many fools will think themselves sober enough to advise his Altesse on whatever he consults them!

Apropos to matrimony; I want to consult your Ladyship very seri-ously: I am so tormented by droves of people coming to see my house, and Margaret gets such sums of money by showing it, that I have a mind to marry her, and so repay myself that way for what I have flung away to make my house quite uncomfortable to me. I am sure Lord Denbigh[13] would have proposed to her, had he known of her riches;[14]

mentary inquiry. See the references cited in Mason ii. 35 n. 26.

11. The Prince of Wales, whose father was Elector of Hanover. This passage was first elucidated by 'L' in *Notes and Queries*, 1857, 2d ser. iii. 42–3.

12. Richard Rigby, Master of the Rolls in Ireland 1759–88.

13. Basil Feilding (1719–1800), 6th E. of Denbigh, 1755; master of the Royal Harriers 1761–82; a lord of the Bed-chamber 1763–1800; 'the lowest and most officious of the Court-tools' (*Last Journals* i. 175, *sub* Feb. 1773).

14. At Court on 17 July the King told Lady Mary Coke 'that Lord Denbigh had come to him last week dressed remarkably well, upon which he said to him, "Lord Denbigh, you are so dressed out I believe you are going to tell me of a marriage." " 'Tis just so, Sir," replied his Lordship; "I came to acquaint your Majesty that I am going to be married to Lady Hald-ford, a lady of Leicestershire that has seven and twenty hundred a year and but forty years of age." What charms rank must have in Lady Haldford's eyes when with near three thousand pounds a year

and I doubt Margaret could not have resisted the temptation of being a Countess more than Lady Halford.[15] She certainly can never have a more disagreeable suitor;[16] and therefore I grow every day more in danger of losing her and all her wealth. Mr Williams said this morning that Margaret's is the best place in England, and wondered Mr Gilbert[17] did not insist on knowing what it is worth. Thank my stars he did not! Colonel Barré or Lord Ashburton would propose to suppress housekeepers, and then humbly offer to show my house themselves,[18] and the first would calculate what he had missed by not having shown it for the last ten years, and expect to be indemnified,[19] for Virtue knows to a farthing what it has lost by not having been Vice. Good night, Madam; my poor rheumatic shoulder must go to bed.

To Lady Ossory, Wednesday 27 August 1783

Address: To the Countess of Ossory at Ampthill Park, Bedfordshire. *Postmark:* 27 AV. [Second mark blurred].

Strawberry Hill, Aug. 27, 1783.

I AM sorry to hear, my Lady, that the plague is broke *loose* in Bedfordshire; it has been here and now rages much. I heard so many histories of it t'other night at Twickenham Park, that recollecting I had eaten a vast deal of fruit, I stopped at the apothecary's as I came home and made him give me a glass of peppermint-water. I don't know why I thought my own disorders preferable, or why one more

she marries Lord Denbigh at sixty-three' (Coke, 'MS Journals').

15. Sarah Farnham (1741–1814) m. 1 (1769) Sir Charles Haldford, 7th Bt; m. 2 (21 July 1783) Lord Denbigh (GM 1769, xxxix. 318).

16. 'How,' HW asked Lord Strafford 1 Aug. 1783, 'could a woman be ambitious of resembling Prometheus, to be pawed and clawed and gnawed by a vulture?' Lady Mary Coke noted on 12 May 1785 that Lord Denbigh 'is so blind he did not know his own lady' at the Drawing-Room ('MS Journals').

17. Thomas Gilbert (?1719–98), M.P. Newcastle-under-Lyme 1763–8, Lichfield 1768–95. He had recently taken part in the inquiry into the value of pensions and

patent places, including HW's and Rigby's (*Last Journals* ii. 129–30; *Quarterly Review*, 1848, lxxxiii. 114–15; *ante* 15 July 1783).

18. Dunning, through Shelburne's influence, had been created Bn Ashburton on 8 April 1782 and had been 'made Chancellor of the Duchy of Lancaster, receiving some £4,000 *p.a.*, though always loud against pensions and sinecures' (GEC). There were sixty to seventy parties of visitors (each party limited to four) admitted to SH each year, and it was customary for each visitor to give Margaret Young, HW's housekeeper, a gratuity, often of a guinea.

19. As explained *ante* 13 March 1783.

should signify—I have a constant rheumatic fever every night which ruins my sleep, though almost all I have lived upon for a century—but how can one talk of one's self after you have told me such a tragical story![1] and when half Italy is smoking in ruins! Even my Lilliputian earthquake was true, for others felt it. I don't know how I missed seeing the meteor and its young ones,[2] for I was sitting over against the window. We were better in our old-fashioned summers when sitting up to our knees in rain.

If your Ladyship makes apologies for writing of weather and epidemic illnesses from Bedfordshire, I ought to make them tenfold from Twickenham, where our old marketwomen used to have other commodities to traffic with—and yet I know no more than a county club—except that Craufurd has been robbed in Oxford Road in a hackney-coach at ten at night—He lost twenty guineas and his pocket-book; and as he has always presence of mind enough to be curious, Hare says that he said to the highwayman, 'You must have taken other pocket-books; could not you let me have one instead of mine?'

I believe part of my fever is owing to being disturbed every morning: I do all I can to be forgotten, but my wicked house, like a fine tomb, draws crowds hither, without letting me rest in it. The complexion of my latter days is certainly not of the hue I proposed; it was not in my plan to live with princes and princesses, or to keep an inn. A Prince de Hessenstein[3] has lately been to dine here. My first acquaintance with him was odd; he was then only called Count. The last time but one[4] that I was at Paris, and with Madame du

1. On 14 Aug. 'a most terrible fire broke out in the market town of Potton, in the county of Bedford, about two in the afternoon; which, in . . . four hours, entirely consumed more than one half of the said town.' The loss not covered by insurance amounted to 'thirty thousand pounds and upwards.' A subscription was started to relieve the sufferers (Lord Ossory, Lord Lieutenant of the county, headed the committee); £946.9.0 had been collected by 22 Aug., and approximately £900 more had been subscribed when the advertisement was inserted in the *London Chronicle* 9–11 Sept., liv. 255. See also ibid. 14–19 Aug., liv. 168, 174: 'no human lives were lost. . . . More than 100 houses were burnt down.'

2. 'Monday night [18 Aug.], about nine o'clock, a body of fire, or some other luminous matter, took a horizontal direction from north to south across the firmament, and in its transit, which seemed to continue about four seconds, emitted light, nearly as vivid as the rays of the sun at noon-day; it . . . had a tail something resembling a kite, with variegated colours' (ibid. 19–21 Aug., liv. 180).

3. Fredrik Wilhelm (1735–1808), Furste von Hessenstein, natural son of Fredrik I of Sweden by Hedvig von Taube (*Nordisk familjebok*, Stockholm, 1923–4; DU DEFFAND ii. 280–1 n. 15 *et passim*). He took leave of George III, 14 Aug., 'previous to his returning home' (*London Chronicle* 14–16 Aug., liv. 162).

4. That is, 1771; but HW's memory is at fault: he met the elder Hessenstein

Deffand, they announced as I thought Monsieur le Comte d'Estain
—I was rejoiced to see a man of whom I had heard so much. A *cordon
bleu* entered. When he was gone, I said he was a very different kind
of man from what I had expected—'and what did you expect? and
why did you expect anything?' said Madame du Deffand. I explained
my reasons; she said, 'this was not Comte d'Estain, but de Hessenstein,[5] a natural son of the old King of Sweden'[6]—very well—Two
years afterwards the same thing happened, and a different *cordon
bleu* entered. Now I thought I was quite sure I had got the true
D'Estain—but lo! this second was another son of the same king—and
this is he that has been here.

Since my letters are forced to live upon old stories, I will tell you
another, Madam, that I had from Mr Cambridge this morning. A Sir
Blundel Carlton[7]—as great a fool as the outset of his Christian name
seemed to promise, was addressed for charity by an old woman, who
had nursed him. He would give her nothing—She urged her care and
tenderness and how well she had brought him up. He fell into a
passion, and swore she had been his greatest foe—'They tell me,' said
he, 'that I was the finest child in the world, and that you changed me
at nurse.'

I hope Lady Ella Fitzpatrick[8] was a changeling too; I should be
mortified to have had any genuine Fitzpatrick escape me, who have
the honour of being genealogist to the family, and who have studied
the MSS of O'Bull King-at-Arms to the Milesian monarchs, before
they had any arms, or he could write or read. I beg George Selwyn
would confine himself to his own province, and concern himself only
with those upstarts the Howards and Douglases, and not meddle with
the Fitzpatricks, who are so ancient that the best Irish antiquaries
affirm that they reckoned many generations before the first man was

in 1767 and again in 1771, and the
younger in 1769, the year of his death
(DU DEFFAND v. 319, 328, 333, 336).

5. Carl Edvard von Hessenstein (1738–
69), Comte von Hessenstein (*Nordisk familjebok*, Stockholm, 1923–4; DU DEFFAND v.
328, *sub* 2 Sept. 1769: 'Passed whole day
at Mme du Deffand's . . . Comte Hessenstein the younger there').

6. Fredrik I (1676–1751), King-Consort
of Sweden 1718–20, K. of Sweden 1720–
51; Landgrave of Hesse-Cassel.

7. Sir Blunden Charlton (ca 1682–1742),

3d Bt, 1729 (Foster, *Alumni Oxon.;* E.
Kimber and R. Johnson, *Baronetage of
England,* 1771, ii. 491).

8. Although Lady Ella Fitzpatrick is
not mentioned in John Lodge, *Peerage
of Ireland,* ed. Mervyn Archdall, 1789,
she may be one of the following: Ellice,
granddaughter of Fynin (or Florence) Fitzpatrick, 3d Lord; Elan Shortall, who married Dermoid (or Darby) Fitzpatrick, son
of Thady (or Teige), 4th Lord; Ellen
(died young), dau. of Bryan, 6th Lord
(op. cit. ii. 338–43).

created—but I will command my passion, lest I should not have a good night's rest.

To Lady Ossory, Tuesday 9 September 1783

Strawberry Hill, Sept. 9, 1783.

I DOUBT my answers to your Ladyship's questions will be a little stale as well as unsatisfactory, for I have been absent eight days, in order to try change of air for my nightly fever. I began to fancy that Strawberry did not agree with me, and went to Park Place,[1] but to no purpose, but to convince myself that if Twickenham does not suit me, no other *country* air is better, the only two good nights I have had these six weeks being two I passed in London[2]—nor is this the first experience I have had of the kind, as I never am out of order, but I mend much sooner in town than anywhere else—no very grateful discovery, after having meant this place for my latter days, and trimmed it accordingly.

Be assured, Madam, that the story of the pocket-book was Mr Hare's—at least not mine. He has a great deal too much wit for me to presume to deck myself in his plumes, I who am a jackdaw to him. Lady Di told me the story. Of Sir Blundel I reported all I knew, and my author too. I almost wish you had not paid me with the catastrophe of Mrs Hesse's[3] family—I have lately heard but too many tragedies. Sir William Hamilton was at Park Place, and gave us the full details of the Calabrian devastation, and more than he chose to insert in his book:[4] of which one dreadful instance shall suffice—Many crushed wretches perished, because the priests insisted on having the rubbish of churches removed first to deliver the consecrated wafers, who, they ought to have supposed, were capable of helping themselves.

1. On Tuesday, 2 Sept. (HW to Mann 27 Aug. 1783).

2. 'I was there for two nights a fortnight ago and slept perfectly well' (HW to Strafford 12 Sept. 1783).

3. Not identified; she may have been among those who suffered losses in the fire at Potton, alluded to in the preceding letter.

4. *An Account of the Earthquakes in Calabria, Sicily,* Colchester, [1783]; Italian translation, Florence, 1783. There is no record that HW owned a copy of either, but he would have been familiar with Hamilton's account communicated to the Royal Society and reprinted in newspapers and magazines, for example, in the *London Chronicle* 6–11 Sept., liv. 244–6, 252; *London Magazine. Enlarged and Improved,* 1783, i. 220–8, 295–304.

I must be negative too, Madam, to all your other queries. I was not well enough ⟨to⟩ go to Lady Chewton's christening.⁵ I have not seen the Princess⁶ since her nephew⁷ dined with her,⁸ though like you I have heard how great a favourite he is. I know nothing of Mrs Johnson's⁹ letter, nor of the mock royalty at Hatfield,¹⁰ but what you are so good as to tell me. George Lord Bristol used to play at drawing-rooms in the same manner at Ickworth,¹¹ and ask if the parsons and neighbours loved walking or riding—I do not wonder that people are servile courtiers, when they delight in aping the insipidity of levées themselves. One must reverence an *ignis fatuus,* if one should be glad to be a glowworm one's self.

There is little good that is new in Atterbury's pieces,¹² Madam, as you have found yourself by this time. Blair's¹³ criticisms I have not seen—Beattie's¹⁴ nauseated me. Of the Dauphin's life¹⁵ I have not heard. Of the lives of abortive kings I had a surfeit too in Birch's *Life*

5. Of Maria Wilhelmina Waldegrave.

6. Amelia.

7. The Prince of Wales.

8. On Monday, 28 July, at Gunnersbury. According to Lady Mary Coke, Princess Amelia 'has invited the Duke and Duchess of Portland, Lord and Lady Southampton, Mrs Howe, and Mr Walpole' ('MS Journals' 26 July 1783). On 29 July she records that 'Lord Duncannon and Lady Clermont were of the party . . . which Mrs Howe says went off extremely well; they played two pools at commerce in the evening and the Prince of Wales took his leave at ten o'clock. Perhaps he would turn them all into ridicule the next day.' Although in none of his known letters does HW say that he attended this dinner, he reports one incident from it, between Lady Clermont and Princess Amelia, in his letter to Harcourt 5 Aug. 1783.

9. Not identified.

10. Presumably Hatfield House, Herts, seat of the E. of Salisbury.

11. Ickworth Park, seat of the Earls (later Marquesses) of Bristol near Bury St Edmunds.

12. Francis Atterbury, *Epistolary Correspondence, Visitation Charges, Speeches, and Miscellanies,* ed. Nichols, 3 vols,

1783–4. Vols I, II were published 1 May 1783 (*London Chronicle* 22 April – 1 May, liii. 388, 411). HW's copy, 3 vols, now WSL, contains several of his MS notes (Hazen, *Cat. of HW's Lib.* 2791).

13. Hugh Blair (1718–1800), divine, Regius Professor of Rhetoric and Belles Lettres at Edinburgh University 1762–83, author of sermons and of *Lectures on Rhetoric and Belles Lettres* (to which HW refers), 2 vols, 1783, published ca 7 June (*London Chronicle* 24 May – 7 June, liii. 503, 542). There is no record that HW owned a copy.

14. James Beattie (1735–1803), poet, essayist, and moral philosopher, author of *Dissertations Moral and Critical,* published ca 17 May (ibid. 3–17 May, liii. 428, 470). For HW's copy, see Hazen, *Cat of HW's Lib.* 3289. Cf. HW to Mason 9 June 1783, Mason ii. 309–10.

15. Two lives of Louis XVI's father were published in 1777; *Mémoires pour servir à l'histoire de Louis, Dauphin de France,* by Henri Griffet (1698–1771), and *Vie du Dauphin, père de Louis XVI,* by Liévain-Bonaventure Proyart (1743–1808). The latter was reprinted in 1782, and is probably the one mentioned by Lady Ossory (Catalogue of the Bibliothèque Nationale).

of Prince Henry.[16] A Black Prince[17] happens but once in a millennium.

As at Park Place I was within eighteen miles, I made a visit to Lord and Lady Harcourt, and was much pleased with poor Browne's alteration of the house,[18] and improvements of the place,[19] as much as I could see of them, for there was such a tempest during the two days and half that I was there, that I could stir out of the house but for one hour—but I went to my passion, Oxford, and saw Sir Joshua's 'Nativity'[20]—but alas! It is just the reverse of the glorious appearance it made in the dark chamber in Pall Mall.[21] It is too high, the antechapel where it is placed is too narrow to see it but foreshortened, and the washy Virtues[22] round it are so faint and light, that the dark shepherds and the *chiaroscuro* that are meant to relieve the glory, child and angels, obscure the whole. I foresaw long ago that Jarvis's colours being many of them not transparent, could not have the effect of old painted glass.[23] Indeed to see his window tolerably, I was forced

16. *The Life of Henry Prince of Wales*, 1760, by Thomas Birch (1705–66), historian and biographer; secretary of the Royal Society 1752–65. For HW's copy and for the use HW made of the book, see Hazen, *Cat. of HW's Lib.* 1666.

17. Edward (1330–76), eldest son of Edward III; P. of Wales, 1343. *The Life and Glorious Actions of Edward Prince of Wales . . . the Black Prince*, 1740, by Arthur Collins (ca 1682–1760) was in HW's library and is now WSL (Hazen, *Cat. of HW's Lib.* 1674).

18. In 1778 Brown designed 'rectangular, three-storey wings placed to north-east and south-east of the main block [of Nuneham], and linked to it by two-storey curved corridors. The structural work was carried out under the supervision of Henry Holland' (Dorothy Stroud, *Capability Brown*, 1950, p. 188).

19. For these, see ibid. pp. 47, 187–91, 206.

20. The upper portions of the west window of New College Chapel, painted by Thomas Jervais or Jarvis (d. 1799), 1777–87, from Reynolds's 'Nativity,' exhibited in 1779 (when HW saw it) at the Royal Academy Exhibition. Jervais's painted-glass window of it, in a compartment

10 x 18 feet, contains thirteen figures, including Reynolds and Jervais as shepherds. See Graves and Cronin iii. 1177–88, iv. 1458–9.

21. HW wrote to Mason 11 May 1783: 'Jarvis's window from Sir Joshua's "Nativity" is glorious. The room being darkened and the sun shining through the transparencies, realizes the illumination that is supposed to be diffused from the glory, and has a magic effect' (MASON ii. 301).

22. Faith, Hope, and Charity had been in the Royal Academy Exhibition in 1779, Justice in 1780, Temperance and Fortitude in 1781 (Graves and Cronin, loc. cit.).

23. See HW to Cole 12 July 1779, COLE ii. 170. HW's copy of *Anecdotes of Painting*, Vol. IV, 1780, now WSL, contains HW's MS note, apropos of the necessity to darken the room when Liotard's coloured glass was exhibited: 'There is the same defect in the glass-paintings of Jervais; most of his colours are not transparent, and their great beauty is produced by the strong lights in the spots for the sun or moon in opposition to the darkness surrounding them: thence his paintings cannot serve like the ancient painted win-

to climb into the organ-loft, by such a pair of stairs, that not having broken my neck, I can almost believe that I could dance a minuet on a horse galloping full speed, like young Astley[24]—for I have seen young Astley, when I was in town last—and henceforth shall believe that nothing is impossible; nay, shall wonder if flying is not brought to perfection, and if Bishop Wilkins[25] does not prove as great a prophet of arts as Sir Francis Bacon. How awkward will a dancer be for the future that has not consummate grace on a plain firm floor!— but though Mercury did not tread the air with more sovereign agility than the son, it was the father that I contemplated with most admiration! What a being, who dared to conceive that he could make horses dance, and any horse dance, and that men, women and children might be trained to possess themselves, on, over, round the rapidity of two, three, four racehorses, and neither tremble for their necks, nor forget one attitude that is becoming! When he can collect whole troops of such agents; form and command them; I look on him with the reverence that I should have for the legislator of society in its infancy, for a Mango Capac, or a Zoroaster. Dr Franklin and Marshal Washington will sink in my esteem if the Congress and the Colonies are not rendered as docile as Astley's Hounhyms.[26] A master genius, I see, can do anything. Impossibilities are difficulties only to those who want parts.

dows to illuminate a church or chamber' (p. 91).

24. John Astley (ca 1767–1821), son of Philip Astley, equestrian performer (*ante* 22 Dec. 1781); succeeded his father in the management of equestrian performances; died at Paris (DNB, *sub* Astley, Philip; GM 1821, xci pt ii. 476). His dancing 'sur des chevaux qui courent la poste' was especially noted as new in equestrian performances. 'Il exécute principalement le menuet de Devonshire, de la composition du Sieur Vestris, pendant le sejour à Londres de ce grand choréographe en 1781' (Louis Petit de Bachaumont, *Mémoires secrets*, 1777–89, xxi. 29, 70; xxiii.

279–81, *sub* 19 July, 16 Aug. 1782, 3 Nov. 1783).

25. John Wilkins (1614–72), Bp of Chester, 1668; one of the founders and first secretary of the Royal Society; author of *The Discovery of a World in the Moone, or a Discourse Tending to Prove That 'Tis Probable There May Be Another Habitable World in That Planet*, 1638, to the third edition, 1640, of which he added a 'Discourse concerning the Possibility of a Passage Thither.'

26. That is, *Houyhnhnms*, the rational horses in Swift's *Gulliver's Travels*, Book iv.

To Lady Ossory, Saturday 27 September 1783

Address: To the Countess of Ossory at Farming Woods near Thrapston, Northamptonshire. *Postmark:* ISLEWORTH. 27 SE.

Strawberry Hill, Sept. 27, 1783.

THE last I heard of the plan of their Highnesses of Gloucester was that they intended to winter in Provence:[1] if they have changed their purpose, it is more than I know. The Churchills were delighted with Nancy;[2] but then I think King Stanislas was living[3]—now, I conclude, both Nancy and Lunéville[4] are fallen into the state of other little capitals that have become appendixes to greater,[5] are grown poorer, and keep up a melancholy kind of pride in lamenting the better days they remember—but, Madam, why are you inquisitive about Nancy?—I fear you cast a look that way![6]—I shall be very sorry! It is the sad lot of long life to outlive one's friends—but must I part with them before I go!—well! the less one has to regret, perhaps the easier is the passage—indeed *my* pleasures are already not too ecstatic!

The bark, as your Ladyship says happened in your neighbourhood, did cure my fever—indeed like a spell—I took a dose but two hours before I went to bed, and yet slept all night. I cannot say my rheumatism is as tractable—It maintains its post like General Elliot, and I suppose will not remove till superseded by Governor Gout.

I never saw Apthorpe,[7] Madam, nor is your account inviting. Old

1. The Duchess of Gloucester wrote to Anne Clement from Strasbourg 15 Aug. 1783, and from Nice 26 Jan., 17 Feb. 1784 (MSS WSL).

2. They lived chiefly at Nancy from 1764 until 1771.

3. Stanislas I (Leszczyński) (1677–23 Feb. 1766), K. of Poland 1704–9, 1733–5. Following his abdication in 1735 (retaining the title of King of Poland), he became (1737) Duke of Lorraine and Bar and lived in Lorraine until his death.

4. The seat of Stanislas's court, though Nancy was the capital.

5. On the death of Stanislas, the duchies of Lorraine and Bar became part of France.

6. Lady Mary Coke, 'MS Journals' 21

Nov. 1783: 'I was told Lord and Lady Ossory talk of going abroad. I wonder she has not brought this about before, as no doubt it will introduce her into company, and I never thought she would have been so easy in retirement so many years. She is certainly not worse than many others who by some means or other go into many houses where I confess I am surprised to see them, but there is little difference now made between the most exemplary characters and those who have not a single virtue.' The Ossorys did not go abroad.

7. Apethorpe Hall, Northants, part of it dating from the reign of Henry VII; seat of the Earls of Westmorland. For an illustrated account of it, see H. Avray Tip-

mansions papered and laid open, are like modern ancient ladies in polonaises and with bare necks: they are neither respectable nor comfortable, but make one wish them demolished and changed for younger structures. The façade of Peterborough is noble and in great taste; I have seen it twice.[9]

I did not know who were the competitors for the vice-embassy:[10] the papers named Mr Storer. Mr Gibbon I heard was going abroad for three years[11]—but as you see, Madam, I can only answer your questions by pleading ignorance—I should not be less informed if I lived in Siberia; nay *there* new exiles would at least tell me what had passed since *my* time—but the strangers that visit my dwelling I do not even exchange a word with—and whatever the papers tell me, rather creates in me disbelief. I remember how false they were when I lived in the world[12] and I have not yet fallen into that common practice of the ancient, to believe them only because I know nothing more true. Indifference and content, I believe are as well as age the causes of my want of curiosity: I like the present administration and would not have it changed—but the humiliated state of this country makes me rather avoid all thoughts of politics. My English or selfish pride is mortified at seeing the decadence of our empire. While I was angry at the authors, resentment served for spirits—now I am numbed and careless.

Others, I find, have not contracted my torpor, nor is it natural that the young should. They seem as eager for honours as when we were at our meridian—but I could not help smiling at the King's showering Irish peerages.[13] Is not it a little like the Old Pretender

ping, *English Homes*, Period III, Vol. II, 1927, pp. 1–20; part of this paragraph from HW's letter is quoted at p. 18.

9. On 24 July 1763 and 5 Aug. 1772. The first time he wrote: 'The front of the Cathedral light and superb. The inside has no beauty but from its vastness' (*Country Seats* 59, 71; to Montagu 25 July 1763, MONTAGU ii. 91).

10. George Maddison, secretary of the embassy at Paris, had died there 27 Aug. 1783. Gibbon had applied for the post, but it went to Anthony Morris Storer (Horn, *Diplomatic Representatives* 26). The Duke of Portland wrote to the Duke of Manchester 4 Sept. 1783: 'Gibbon, Dudley Long, Tom Walpole's son [the younger Thomas], Mr William Ponsonby,

Mr Charles O'Hara, and [William Everard] Fawkener . . . were all objects of our discussion.' Fox wrote the Duke of Manchester 21 Sept. that 'it was impossible for [me] to avoid naming Mr Storer' (Hist. MSS Comm., 8th Rep., App. ii, 1881, p. 133).

11. Gibbon lived in Lausanne from Sept. 1783 to April 1793, except for a visit to London in 1788 to see Vols IV–VI of his *Decline and Fall* through the press.

12. This word is written above 'old,' which HW apparently struck out, but he may have intended to write 'old world.'

13. The creation of nine Irish baronies was announced in the *London Gazette* No. 12476, 17–20 Sept.

comforting himself for the loss of a crown by bestowing pinchbeck coronets?[14] I wish some of the engineers of the American war were to be created Dukes of New England and Earls of Boston and Charlestown; and that since they have been so unlike the Romans who acquired the titles of Africani for conquering hostile countries, our Machiavels were to be denominated from the provinces that they have lost.

Have you seen Lord Aldborough's foolish and contemptible pamphlet,[15] Madam? As his wife could not persuade me to print her father's[16] works, and though no peer, enrol him amongst the noble authors, I suppose she determined her Lord should be one in spite of my teeth, and in spite of Nature's too. She is welcome, for I am out of the scrape; I keep no register of living scribblers. The sextons of next age may bury the dead of this.

To Lady Ossory, Thursday 9 October 1783

Strawberry Hill, Oct. 9, 1783.

MADAM my Lady, you have set me a task that poses me, and I must go and rub up my memory—no wonder I did not speak of the *Walpoliana*[1]—why, it is two or three years since it was printed; and I had quite forgot it. I saw it on a person's table, and was interrupted before I had finished the last two pages. I found it such a flimsy thing, that I never inquired after it more. I can now not recollect enough to give you much account of it. All I do recollect is that I thought it like all the other water-gruel that Lord Hardwicke has published,[2] only with this merit, that the former insipid messes were

14. Between 1701 and 1760 he created 55 peerages; see the list in GEC i. 483–8.

15. *An Essay on the True Interests and Resources of the Empire of the King of Great Britain and Ireland,* Dublin, 1783; London, 1783. Dedicated to the King, the pamphlet supports the King's prerogative and argues that the loss of the American colonies will be to the advantage of England. No copy is recorded in Hazen, *Cat. of HW's Lib.*

16. Hon. Nicholas Herbert's; see *ante* 25 Dec. 1782.

———

1. By Philip Yorke, 2d E. of Hardwicke; HW's copy, 1781, with numerous annota-

tions, is now at King's School, Canterbury (COLE ii. 261–2 n. la; Hazen, *Cat. of HW's Lib.* 3924). A new edition and a supplement appeared in 1783.

2. Hardwicke had edited *Letters from and to Sir Dudley Carleton,* 1757; *Miscellaneous State Papers* from 1501 to 1726, 1778; and had written some of the *Athenian Letters,* privately printed in small editions in 1741 and 1781. HW, in his copy of *Walpoliana,* facing p. 3, comments: 'As the great and almost only business of the second Lord Hardwicke's life was to collect, purchase, amass state-papers and anecdotes, and as he has published three ample quartos filled with the most un-

doled about in leaden kettles, and this is contained in a pewter firkin. It is told with the gossiping importance of an old story-teller, who loves to repeat what he has seen or heard, without judging whether his anecdotes are worth hearing. The only passage of consequence that I remember is the manner of my father's getting the better of Lord Wilmington[3] at the late King's accession;[4] and that is represented with the utmost ignorance of all the circumstances that made it curious.[5]

If it was Lord Grantham[6] that wanted to know my opinion, pray don't tell him how poor a dab I think it, for I like Lord Grantham, and do not want to acquaint him, that I think, as he must do in his heart, that his papa is an old goody, and never was any better—which he may not suppose—besides the thing is a very harmless thing, and would really be very well for any old servant of my father to have written, who was proud of boasting of what his master had said to him or before him.

I rejoice to hear that your Ladyship's *équipée* to Nancy is not determined—however I will not lose my *de tristibus,* that I had prepared on the occasion. I remember a Mr Seward[7] (father of the present Muse of Litchfield),[8] who was travelling governor to Lord Charles

important rubbish, and as this little piece is a proper codicil to those tomes, by being equally insignificant; his head seems to have resembled a sieve so fine, that though it may take up a mass of stones and dirt, yet transmits nothing but dust and the most minute particles. H. Walpole.'

3. Spencer Compton (ca 1674–1743), K.B., 1725, K.G., 1733, cr. (1728) Bn Wilmington and (1730) E. of Wilmington; Speaker of the House of Commons 1715–27; succeeded Sir Robert Walpole as first lord of the Treasury, 1742.

4. 'On King George the 1st's death, the succession to the ministry was thought doubtful for a few days, between him and Lord Wilmington: Sir Robert soon fixed himself by applying immediately to the Queen. At a dinner, where Lord Chesterfield was present, his Lordship slyly said, I was at Court today, the crowd was great, but they did not make way so readily for Sir Sp——r C——n as before. "Why," replied Sir Robert (very indiscreetly and too coarsely), "I do not wonder at that; he took the wrong sow by the ear (Lady S——k), I the right," meaning the Queen' (Lord Hardwicke's *Walpoliana,* p. 6; George II's mistress was Mrs Howard, later Lady Suffolk). Sir Robert obtained £100,000 a year for the Queen from the civil list; 'No one but Walpole could have hoped to get such grants through the Commons' (J. H. Plumb, *Sir Robert Walpole. The King's Minister,* 1960, p. 168).

5. HW's version of this affair is in his copy of *Walpoliana,* facing pp. 6–7, and, in greater detail, in *Reminiscences, Written in 1788,* Chapter V (*Works* iv. 294–7; *Reminiscences,* ed. Paget Toynbee, Oxford, 1924, pp. 48–53). According to HW, who makes no reference to money, the Queen's choice of Sir Robert was based on merit.

6. Hardwicke's son-in-law (*ante* 29 June 1780).

7. Thomas Seward (1708–90), canon of Lichfield and Salisbury; friend of Dr Johnson.

8. Anna Seward (1747–1809), the 'Swan of Lichfield.'

Fitzroy,[9] who falling dangerously ill at Genoa, and being saved, as Mentor thought, by Dr Shadwell,[10] the governor whipped up to his chamber and began a complimentary ode to the physician—but was called down before it was finished, on his pupil's relapse, who did die —however the bard was too much pleased with the début of his poem, to throw it away, and so finished it, though his gratitude had been still-born. My lamentation is no ode; and though I hope its foundation will be still-born too, yet being perfected before I knew so much, you shall have it, as I believe it much superior to Mr Seward's Pindaric. Mine is *des couplets*, in imitation of Monsieur de Coulanges,[11] who had a marvellous facility of writing foolish songs and epigrams on any or no occasion, and I flatter myself that I have caught his manner very happily.

1.

I love and hate Nancy,
Because my dear Nancy
Has taken a fancy
To leave me for Nancy.

2.

Mais puisque il est ainsi,
Je n'aimerai Nancy,
Que quand ma chère Nancy
Reviendra de Nancy.

3.

Till then I'll sob and sigh;
Unless that perchance I
Should find a new Nancy;
And then I will fancy,
That in hers I'm more dear than I was in my Ann's eye.

My dear old Frenchwoman would have asked me to what tune it was set, and would have insisted on my singing it. I should have told her, to *Colin's Complaint*[12] or *All in the Downs;*[13] and that though I

9. (1718–39), 4th son of Charles, 2d D. of Grafton.

10. Sir John Shadwell (1671–1747), Kt, 1715; physician to Queen Anne, George I and II; withdrew from practice and retired to France 1735–40.

11. Philippe-Emmanuel (1631–1716), Marquis de Coulanges; cousin and correspondent of Mme de Sévigné; 'un gour-

mand, et bouffon médiocre' (DU DEFFAND ii. 139–41). Several of his songs and short poems are quoted in Mme de Sévigné's *Lettres,* ed. L.-J.-N. Monmerqué, 14 vols, 1862–6.

12. The tune and words are in J. Ritson, *Select Collection of English Songs,* 2d edn, 1813, i. 64–6, iii. 31–2.

13. From the opening line of Gay's

could not sing, Mr Craufurd could, and then she would be charmed with it. If your Ladyship is not, I will make you amends by a story, with which I defy you not to be delighted.

At the neighbouring village of Teddington lives a Captain Prescott,[14] who is not only a tar, but pitch and brimstone too. Two or three years ago, he is near fifty, he married a beautiful sensible young woman,[15] daughter of the minister of Portsmouth,[16] who gave her £2500.[17] Trincolo soon used her inhumanly, beat her, had a child[18] by her, thrashed her again,[19] she was again three months gone with child,[20] and then he beat her so unmercifully, that a young footman[21] who had lived five years with him, could not bear to be witness to so much brutality, left him, and has since lived a year with Mrs Clive, who finds him the best servant she ever had. Poor Mrs Trincolo's sufferings continuing, she resolved to run away, and by the footman's assistance did, and got to London.[22] Her father and friends came up,

ballad, 'Sweet William's Farewell to Black-Eyed Susan,' which appears as a glee 'harmoniz'd by Francis Ireland' (i.e., Francis Hutcheson) in Thomas Warren's *A Thirteenth Collection of Catches, Canons, and Glees . . . Inscribed to the Noblemen and Gentlemen of the Catch Club at the Thatch'd House Tavern, St James's*, ca 1770.

14. Isaac Prescott (1737–1830), Capt., 8 April 1778, Rear-Adm., 1795, Vice-Adm., 1799, Adm., 1805 (GM 1830, c pt i. 559; DNB *sub* Prescott, Sir Henry). For details of his cruelty to his wife, see *The Trial* ['in the Consistory Court at Doctors Commons'] *of Isaac Prescott, Esq. . . . for Wanton, Tyrannical, Unprovoked, and Savage Cruelty, towards Jane Prescott, His Wife*, 1786, a trial 'unprecedented in the line of brutality' (*Rambler's Magazine*, 1785, iii. 318). He had moved to the house in Teddington in July 1782 (*Trial . . .* , p. 98).

15. Jane Walter (ca 1752–1840), m. (1779) Isaac Prescott; left him in 1782 and in 1783 'was divorced from bed, board, and mutual cohabitation with her husband, by reason of cruelty; and the court has adjudged ninety pounds per annum, to be paid her by Mr Prescott, during her natural life' (*Trial . . .* , p. 111; GM 1840, n.s. xiii pt i. 555).

16. Richard Walter (ca 1718–85), chaplain of Anson's ship *Centurion* 1740–2 on voyage round the world; chaplain at Portsmouth Docks 1745–85 (Venn, *Alumni Cantab.; Trial . . .* , pp. 28–9).

17. £2,000 (*Trial . . .* , p. 29, from Walter's own deposition).

18. The first child was born dead in January 1780 (*Trial . . .* , pp. 6–8, 72). A son (ca 1781–1806), 'an officer in the East India Company's service . . . was drowned when returning to England, in 1806' (GM 1830, c pt i. 559; William R. O'Byrne, *A Naval Biographical Dictionary*, 1849, p. 922).

19. ' "For love and war take turns like day and night" Lotharia' (HW). The passage is from Nicholas Rowe's *Fair Penitent*, 1703, IV. i. 100.

20. Her son, Sir Henry Prescott (4 May 1783–1874), C.B. in 1815, K.C.B. in 1856, and G.C.B. in 1869, became an admiral in 1860.

21. John Sith (b. ca 1761) 'became servant to . . . Isaac Prescott' when the latter was 'appointed to the command of . . . the *Queen*,' Sith 'having been the servant of the former commander of the said ship, and he quitted his service about nine months ago' (Sith's deposition, 8 Oct. 1783, in *Trial . . .* , p. 91; pp. 9–100). He lived with the Prescotts from their marriage until Mrs Prescott left in Nov. 1782.

22. Her father deposed 12 Aug. 1783 that Mrs Prescott left her husband 'on or

and made her swear the peace against her husband. The cause was heard before Lord Mansfield.[23] Mrs Clive's servant was summoned as a witness. The Chief Justice asked him if he had not been aiding and abetting to his former mistress's escape. He said, yes, he had. 'You had!' said my Lord; 'what, do you confess that you helped your master's wife to elope?' 'Yes, my Lord,' replied the lad, 'and yet my master has never thanked me.' 'Thanked you!' said Lord Mansfield, 'thanked you! what, for being an accomplice with a wife against her husband!' 'My Lord,' said the lad, 'if I had not, he would have murthered her, and then he would have been hanged.' The Court laughed, Lord Mansfield was charmed with the lad's coolness and wit —and if your Ladyship is not, I hope you will never hear anything better than M. de Coulanges's poetry.

PS. I never saw the present Duc de Bouillon;[24] I knew his wife, then Princesse de Turenne;[25] a grave sensible woman, who I believe is dead. I am glad when any French arrive and expose themselves here, that we may have something to set against all the articles that they can produce against our fools.

To Lady Ossory, Saturday 18 October 1783

Address: To the Countess of Ossory at Ampthill Park, Bedfordshire. *Post-mark:* 18 OC. GC.

Berkeley Square, Oct. 18, 1783.

I NEVER think myself in the wrong in writing nonsense. Sense seldom turns to any account, especially to a writer. Your Lady-ship strengthens me in my opinion. I sent you some exceedingly foolish

about the 6th day of November last, and went to the deponent's sister . . . at Brentford, where, as soon as the deponent was informed thereof, he went to and received her under his protection' (*Trial . . .* , p. 32).

23. Presumably on 8 Oct., when Sith's deposition was made; the depositions range from 11 Aug. to 23 Oct. (ibid., *passim*).

24. Godefroy-Charles-Henri de la Tour d'Auvergne (1728–92), Prince de Turenne, Duc de Bouillon, 1771. Fanny Burney heard an anecdote from George Cambridge

'upon the Duke de Bouillon, who tries to pass for an Englishman, and calls himself Mr Godfrey. "But I think," says Mr Walpole, "he might better take an English title, and call himself the *Duke of Mutton Broth*"' (Frances Burney d'Arblay, *Diary and Letters*, ed. Barrett and Dobson, 1904, ii. 237). He appears as 'Sir Zealous Godfrey' with Fox and North in a print published 7 April 1784 (BM, *Satiric Prints* vi. 86, No. 6508).

25. Louise-Henriette-Gabrielle de Lorraine (1718–84) m. (1743) the Prince de

rhymes, and they produced very pretty ones in return, and full of meaning. Do you think I will not adhere to my tenet? I only write this to thank you; not to *agacer* you again. I have nothing to say—and our correspondence shall lie dormant if you please till I have something to tell you that you might not hear otherwise. I will answer your question on omens, and bid you good night.

Omens I do not pretend to explain, and for this very good reason, that I cannot expound that which you have sent me. If they have any mean*ing*, they must have had a mean*er*—now if the meaner does not speak to be understood, I take him to be a very silly agent, and I conclude so the more, because the silliest persons are those who guess his meaning; as Charles II said of a fool,[1] who was a popular preacher in his own parish, 'I suppose his nonsense suits their nonsense'—but though I cannot guess the meaning of a thing without meaning, I can easily tell how Lady Grantham would interpret the omen, for a silly ugly prude must know what she would do, if she was her grandmother's[2] picture, and could do the only thing that can be in a picture's power, tumble down, when your Ladyship was present. I have a female relation[3] who is a mighty dealer in those winks which she thinks Providence tips her upon every occasion; and though they never come to pass, she does not suspect that Providence is making a fool of her—or rather made her so once for all.[4] I wonder I am not

Turenne, Duc de Bouillon. HW had supped with her at Hénault's 11 April 1766 (DU DEFFAND i. 73 n. 4, v. 313).

1. Edward Wolley (ca 1604–84), chaplain to Charles I and II, rector of Toppesfield, Essex, 1662–4; Bp of Clonfert, 1665 (MANN vi. 57 n. 43). HW uses the same anecdote in his letters to Mann 31 July 1762, and 22 Oct. 1774, and to Harcourt Oct. 1779. A slightly different version is in *Walpoliana* i. 57.

2. Lady Grantham's paternal grandmother was Margaret Cocks (d. 1761), m. 1 John Lygon, m. 2 (1719) Philip Yorke, cr. (1733) Bn Hardwicke and (1754) E. of Hardwicke. Her maternal grandmother was Amabel Grey (d. 1727), m. (1718) John Campbell, 3d E. of Breadalbane.

3. HW's niece, Mrs Keppel. Lady Waldegrave to HW 7 Feb. 1785: 'I do not pretend to the gift of prophecy like Mrs Keppel . . .' When Bishop Keppel, against

the advice of his physicians, wished to drink the Sunning Hill waters, Mrs Keppel said, 'as I am superstitious, I looked upon it as a dictate of Nature' (Mrs Keppel to Jane Clement 24 July [1777], MS WSL). 'I have expected this bad news [the serious illness of the Duke of Gloucester], for t'other night I dreamed I saw his funeral, and the night before last I dreamed Mr Walpole told me H.R.H. had broke a tubercle upon his lungs and was suffocated' (Mrs Keppel to Jane Clement 9 Sept. 1777, MS WSL). 'By my dreams and my eyes itching I'm sure there will be a pretty piece of work about it' (Mrs Keppel to Jane Clement ca 18 Feb. 1776, MS WSL).

4. The lack of sympathy between HW and Mrs Keppel is suggested by her letter to Jane Clement 6 March 1797 (MS WSL). After outlining the chief provisions of HW's will, including bequests of £500 to herself and to each of her children, she adds: 'I am very much obliged to him for

a greater adept at interpretation, as she has told me what everything in the world *signifies,* except itself; for expounders of prophecies never allow a prognostication to have any first meaning, though always a second.

I came to town on Wednesday to get rid of a rheumatic fever, which had returned with more violence—and I have found the nostrum succeed. It is most unfortunate for me, but I am convinced that country air is too sharp or too damp for me. If I am in the least out of order, I cannot recover but in London. It is at this moment a most unpalatable medicine—I have nowhere to go, and have sat almost alone for the whole four days. I shall return to Strawberry on Monday, and then settle here at the very beginning of next month. Mr Selwyn comes on Tuesday.

PS. I direct this to Ampthill, as I conclude, if you are not there, it is less likely to miscarry, than if it went to Farming Woods and should not find you there.

To Lady Ossory, Saturday 8 November 1783

Address: To the Countess of Ossory at Ampthill Park, Bedfordshire. *Postmark:* 8 NO. [Second mark illegible].

Berkeley Square, Nov. 8, 1783.

I DOUBT, Madam, that when I do go to Strawberry, I shall not be able to discover the lady who owns the tree and five of hearts. It seems to be a German coat of arms, and my heraldry does not extend so far. If I knew the name of the village where the building, that sounds as if designed for a chapel, stands, one may perhaps find some mention of it in Dugdale[1] or Tanner.[2]

having remembered me and my children at all, though I should have been as well pleased if he had left me five thousand, and Sir Horace Mann five hundred. . . . As to myself, I have more than I expected, for I know there has been much pains to prejudice him against me, and I never paid him any court. Others have slaved thoroughly. Lady Euston I daresay *now* thinks she has thrown much of her time away. I bought new mourning before I knew he had left me anything . . . I

never can be furious against a person one minute and change so very violently the next minute.'

1. Sir William Dugdale (1605–86) and Roger Dodsworth, *Monasticon Anglicanum,* 1655–73.

2. Thomas Tanner (1674–1735), *Notitia monastica,* Oxford, 1695. It is remarkable that neither work appears in the SH Library records; the books may have been in his London house.

My rheumatism and its appendages are much better, thank your Ladyship, for the warm atmosphere of London. They made me afraid to venture to Mrs Hobart's play,[3] for though I have always been brave about the gout, the rheumatism has made me a great coward. The first goes, when it has had its swing, and does not return, till, like a comet, it has made its revolution. The other may never leave one, or come back the day after it has disappeared—however, as mine seems to be put upon the establishment, I shall talk no more of it.

The town is so empty, or rather, I have lost so many of my acquaintance, that I have scarce seen anybody since I came. I have not heard a word of Lord Spencer's will,[4] nor of the relict, but that she is retired to St Albans.[5]

My chief entertainment has been in reading the mutual philippics of Messieurs Flood and Grattan,[6] who, if you believe their accounts of each other, are *very honourable men*. There is a little book, which you would not read if you could, called, *Elegantiæ Latini sermonis*.[7]

3. *The Wonder! A Woman Keeps a Secret*, by Mrs Centlivre (cf. *post* 14 June 1787, 15 Dec. 1787), and *Three Weeks after Marriage*, by Arthur Murphy, performed at her villa, Sans Souci, on Ham Common on 3, 5, and 7 Nov. Lady Mary Coke, Lady Greenwich, Mrs Clive, and Mrs Abington were there on 5 Nov. (Coke, 'MS Journals' 14, 26 Oct., 5 Nov. 1783).

4. Lord Spencer, aged 48, had died 31 Oct. at Bath, after a long illness. His will, dated 30 July 1772, was proved 13 Dec. 1783. On 13 Nov. 1783 Mrs Howe told Lady Mary Coke 'Lord Spencer's will was made in the year '72, since when he has added nothing to it. He left Lady Spencer all his personal estate excepting the furniture of his three great houses, Althorpe, Wimbledon, and the house in town . . . The present Lord Spencer . . . [offered her] any house she had a mind to . . . but whether, she has accepted the house at St Albans I have not heard, though I am told she intends staying there some time' (Coke, 'MS Journals' 13 Nov. 1783).

5. Cf. *ante* 12 Sept. 1780. 'She lived [and died] at Holywell House (now demolished) built by the great Duke of Marlborough when he purchased the estates of his wife's family, the Jenningses, at Sandridge, near St Albans' (Toynbee).

Lord Spencer was buried at Brington, Northants, on 9 Nov.

6. On 28 Oct. in the Irish House of Commons, 'Violent abusive altercation between Mr Flood and Mr Grattan, which the House bore for an hour and half. They were to have fought, but were prevented, and bound by Chief Justice in £20,000 apiece' ('Mem. 1783–91' *sub* Oct. 1783). This quarrel ended a friendship of twenty years. Gillray's print, 'The Irish Patriots,' described in BM, *Satiric Prints* v. 736–7, No. 6272, gives the most spirited invective from the debate. See also DNB, *sub* Flood; *London Chronicle* 6–8 Nov., liv. 450–2.

7. Mentioned by HW to Mann 7 Jan. 1742 OS (MANN i. 273 and n. 24): *Joannis Meursii elegantiæ Latini sermonis. Aloysiæ Sigeæ Toletanæ satyra sotadica de arcanis amoris et Veneris*, Lyon, ca 1658–60. This example of erotica has no connection with the two authors named in the title-page; it is generally attributed to Nicholas Chorier (1612–92), of Grenoble. Three editions (1757, 1774, and 1781, the last with a fictitious London imprint), with additions, had recently appeared when HW wrote. There is no record of the work in his library. For bibliographical details, see the sources in MANN, loc. cit.; J.-M. Quérard, *Les Supercheries littéraires*

Hibernian elegance is not a whit behind it in displaying naked truth, though of another kind. Well! I am very glad there is so much animosity amongst them—alas! for these eight or ten years one has been forced to wish for mischief, lest worse mischief should happen. In short, I have found out that the love of one's country makes one a wicked animal, and hope for plagues in all the rest of the world.

Would not one think, Madam, that there was evil enough toward, and that quiet I might escape in the hurlyburly? Yet this morning at breakfast I was saluted with the first scene of my old tragedy,[8] all sugared over with comfits like a Twelfth-cake.[9] I have been writing to Mr Woodfall, to beg to buy myself out of his claws, and to lecture him for his gross compliments. I have ever laughed when I have seen little men called *great,* and I will not bear to be made ridiculous in the same way.

I fear you will hear melancholy accounts of poor Lady W.[10] but it is not a subject for a letter.

You say, *we* shall be found at Ampthill till after Christmas, probably. I am very sorry for it, though a little comforted by the *probably,* which at least is not a definitive term. The long evenings before Christmas are just the time when I most wish your Ladyship here, as then one can have a little society without a mob. In spring everybody is running after everybody, or waiting till supper-time for those they expect to dinner. Though you say *we,* I depend on seeing our Lord next week,[11] and though I hope his individuality will not be absolutely necessary, yet surely the more numerous the appearance the better.[12] Nay, I should hope your Ladyship's zeal would rather accompany him, than keep a drawback to Ampthill. It is in every light so serious

dévoilées, 2d edn, ed. Brunet and Jannet, n.d., ii. 1129–33; W. T. Lowndes, *Bibliographer's Manual,* ed. Bohn, 1865–78, vi. 1540.

8. *The Mysterious Mother,* from which extracts appeared in the *Public Advertiser* (HW to Woodfall 8 Nov. 1783). The play had been reprinted in London in 1781 (see Hazen, *SH Bibl.* 82–3, for HW's comments); extracts from it were quoted in the *St James's Chronicle* 8–10, 15–17 Nov. 1781, and in the *Public Advertiser* 21 Nov. 1781.

9. 'A large cake used at the festivities of Twelfth-Night, usually frosted and

otherwise ornamented and with a bean or corn introduced to determine the "King" or "Queen" of the feast' (OED). A source cited ibid. gives the ingredients as flour, honey, ginger, and pepper.

10. Waldegrave, whose illness was mental. See *ante* 29 Nov. 1782.

11. When Parliament opened on 11 Nov., Lord Ossory moved the Address in reply to the King's Speech from the Throne (Cobbett, *Parl. Hist.* xxiii. 1132–56).

12. That is, the Portland ministry, with its coalition of Fox and North, needed to show as much strength as possible.

a moment, that I could almost chide you for having philosophy enough to look at it from a distance. I who hang but by a thread, and from whom no threads hang, could not be so indifferent.

To Lady Ossory, Tuesday 30 December 1783

Address: To the Countess of Ossory at Ampthill Park, Bedfordshire. *Postmark:* 30 DE. [Second mark illegible].

Dec. 30, 1783.

I AM not such a buzzard, Madam, but that I did guess from your Ladyship's silence and *other circumstances,* that my last letter or two were not to your taste. I was and perhaps shall be a prophet; but as that is a profession never honoured in its own country (as I can say with truth and a little vanity I have often found), I shall touch on nothing you do not like. I obeyed your silence, lest I should say what you wished me not to say; and now you bid me write again, I am ready to talk nonsense rather than sense, being sure that I have much more talent for the one than the other. News I know none, but that they are crying peerages about the streets in barrows, and can get none off.[1] Lord Chesterfield[2] is named ambassador to Spain[3] to pay off the old debt of sending us Gondomar,[4] and the Foundling Hospital[5] is to be converted into an Academy of Politicians.

1. 'I have mentioned reasons enough for despondency in the new ministers [Pitt's ministry, which replaced Portland's on the failure of Fox's East India Bill]. When they found they could gain no converts by great offices, they profusely squandered offers of peerages—they too were rejected' ('Mem. 1783–91' *sub* Dec. 1783). According to a correspondent of the *London Chronicle* 27–30 Dec., liv. 632, the following offers had been rejected: 'to the Earl of Hertford a dukedom; to the Earl of Surrey, Lord Clive, Lord Delaval, Lord Newhaven, Sir Francis Basset, Sir Tho. Dundas, and Mr Pelham, English peerages; to Sir Charles Bunbury, Sir Peter Burrell, Mr Bowes, Mr Delmé, and several other gentlemen, Irish peerages.'

2. 'A worthless young man, universally despised' ('Mem. 1783–91' *sub* Dec. 1783).

3. Chesterfield was nominal ambassador to Spain from 1 Jan. 1784 until 1787, when he resigned, but he never went to Madrid. See Horn, *Diplomatic Representatives* 138; Sir N. W. Wraxall, *Historical and Posthumous Memoirs,* ed. Wheatley, 1884, iv. 245–50.

4. Diego Sarmiento de Acuña (1567–1626), Conde de Gondomar, ambassador to England 1613–18, 1619–22; hated by many of the English for his share of responsibility for the execution of Sir Walter Raleigh and for his influence on James I's foreign policy; the Black Knight in Middleton's *A Game at Chesse,* 1625.

5. Founded in 1739 by Capt. Thomas Coram for 'exposed and deserted children'; now the Thomas Coram Foundation for Children. See Wheatley, *London Past and Present* ii. 72–3; R. H. Nichols and F. A. Wray, *The History of the Foundling Hospital,* 1935.

I did mean to pass my holidays at Twickenham, but the weather is so severe I did not venture. I have been so perfectly well since I came to town, that I will not risk another rheumatism.

American news may now be a neutral article; Washington, *qui, il me semble, tranche un peu du Roi,* has instituted a military order, and calls it the Order of Cincinnatus,[6] *ce qui tranche un peu du pedant.* He sent it to La Fayette,[7] and it made an uproar in Paris. As the *noblesse* spell only by the ear, they took it for the order of St Senatus. They had recourse to the calendar, and finding no such saint in heaven's almanac, they concluded it was a new canonization at Boston, and were enraged that Washington should encroach on the papacy as well as on the diadem. It may offend even the Bishop of Derry who has renounced all religions, to qualify himself for being a cardinal.[8] Lord Edward Fitzgerald[9] told me last night that he fears the volunteers are very serious—*sans compter* the spirits which the late revolution here may give them—but I had better break off, lest I offend by sliding into politics which you dislike.

6. The Society of the Cincinnati, an association of American and French officers who had served in the late war, was instituted 10 May 1783 by Gen. Knox, with Washington as president general. This anecdote appears also in HW to Mason 30 Dec. 1783, MASON ii. 323.

7. See Washington to La Fayette 20 Oct. (Washington, *Writings,* ed. Fitzgerald, xxvii. 202). On 18 Dec. Louis XVI had issued a decree permitting La Fayette and others to accept the order (MASON ii. 323 n. 7).

8. HW noted in 'Mem. 1783–91' that 'Lord Bristol was a jealous advocate for toleration of them [papists]' (Oct. 1783). 'Of the 40,000 volunteers, probably two thirds papists. The Earl-Bishop of Derry living like a cardinal, with a band of music.

If an army of volunteers carry a reform of Parliament, will an army stop there? A popish army, fine reformers of a Protestant constitution' (ibid.). 'It was now known that Lord Bristol's extravagant behaviour proceeded from his having twice asked and been refused, to be Lord Lieutenant of Ireland—as if a bishop had ever been so' (ibid.). 'Nov. 10. Bishop of Derry entered Dublin at head of two troops of horse; declared for rooting out the Church, which supported legal hypocrisy and superstition' (ibid. Nov. 1783).

9. (1763–98), 5th son of 1st D. of Leinster, joined the United Irishmen in 1796, was wounded while resisting arrest for high treason 19 May 1798, and died of his wounds in Newgate Prison, Dublin, 4 June 1798.

TO LADY OSSORY, Monday 19 January 1784

Address: To the Countess of Ossory at Ampthill Park, Bedfordshire. *Postmark:* 19 IA. G⟨C⟩.

Berkeley Square, Jan. 19, 1784.

I CAN never suspect your Ladyship of want of goodness: you would not choose a moment of tenderness for showing indifference. Indeed, though the six last days of my brother's life[1] were most afflicting to behold, I had cause for nothing but satisfaction from the instant he expired; nor even before, could I have shut out the sight. He had passed a very long life with every enjoyment he chose, with almost equal health; he did not wish to live longer; he leaves nobody he loved in distress; he died without suffering, though his case ought to have been excruciating; it was beyond the power of remedy; and his indifference, unabated firmness, his gaiety at moments within two days of his exit, and his unaffected heroism, are all subjects of consolation—and the tranquillity of his mind, enviable—yet, I assure you, Madam, that death is so much more tiresome a thing than I had imagined, that I had far rather that mine should be extempore, than philosophic. I do not like the apparatus at all, and hope I shall know no more of my going out of the world, than I did of my coming into it. Life is a farce, and should not end with a mourning scene.

Lord Ossory will tell you much more than I could, Madam, of the world's bigger features. I was in the chambers of death on the *12th* when the battle was fighting, which has not yet proved decisive,[2] though the generals were so unequally matched,[3] nor even the forces.

1. Sir Edward Walpole died 12 Jan., aged 77. For details of his illness, see HW to Mann 8, 13 Jan. 1784. A post-mortem report on Sir Edward is among the Farr MSS at the library of the University of California.

2. 'This [12 Jan.] was the great day of expectation in the House of Commons, which sat till a quarter before seven of next morning when the ministers [Pitt's ministry] were beaten by *239,* to *193'* ('Mem. 1783–91'). The vote on Fox's motion for 'resuming the Committee on the State of the Nation' was actually 232

to 193, a majority of 39 for the Fox-North forces; see Cobbett, *Parl. Hist.* xxiv. 268–99. HW and others doubted that the Pitt ministry could continue; on 16 Jan. Lord Charles Spencer's motion 'for the removal of ministers' had passed by 205 to 184, a majority of 21 (ibid. xxiv. 360–80).

3. HW refers to 'Mr Fox's, General Conway's, Mr Rigby's and Mr Sheridan's excellent speeches. . . . Pitt answered Conway angrily and poorly, talked high prerogative, called himself minister of the *Crown,* hinted at dissolution (perhaps to awe members to vote with him for fear

The vanquished[4] still hold out, though the language of the commanders is desponding enough to make their soldiers disband. The want of pay is yet more disheartening;[5] and the late vapour of a benevolence[6] betrays the lowness of the military chest,[7] which was to have raised a new army;[8] the thought of which is now said to be given up; at least Mr Pitt's friends and those of the Chancellor[9] affectedly proclaim *their* aversion to the measure, and lay all blame on *superior* obstinacy,[10] which alone forbids Mr Pitt's resignation; as on the other side the whispers from the backstairs lament the latter's irresolution —I know not what foundation either have for what they give out; nor whether both do not speak to shift off the disgrace of a defeat from themselves.

To Lady Ossory, Friday 6 February 1784

Berkeley Square, Feb. 6, 1784.

I AM very sorry, Madam, to have occasion so soon to return your Ladyship's kind condolence on my brother's death. It is more difficult to speak on your loss,[1] though I am persuaded you feel it more sensibly than I did mine, who was prepared for it, and saw it so gradual and so little grievous to himself, that I admired more than lamented. Yet your Ladyship, I hope, will have a consolation that I could not receive—I do not mean in point of fortune, though as you

of it) and made a very poor figure' ('Mem. 1783–91' 12 Jan. 1784).

4. Pitt's administration.

5. Money for the Army for 1784 had not been voted before the fall of the Portland ministry in Dec. 1783. On 22 March 1784, preceding the dissolution of Parliament on 24 March, £2,360,992.0.9 was voted for Army Extraordinaries (Cobbett, *Parl. Hist.* xxiv. 768–74).

6. 'Much talk of [Alderman Thomas] Harley and merchants advancing a million to King without security. This would be a benevolence and illegal: yet the Duke of Richmond, who last year condemned Sir J. Lowther giving a ship as a benevolence, approved this. Harley and Drummond [banker] and Sir J. Lowther had talked, but did nothing' ('Mem. 1783–91' *sub* 14 Jan. 1784).

7. In the House of Commons on 12 Dec. Minchin had referred to the heavy ordnance debt of more than £850,000 and to the present 'time when the state of public credit was so low, and the finances in such disorder' (Cobbett, *Parl. Hist.* xxiv. 117).

8. On 10 Dec. 1783 Fitzpatrick, secretary at war, proposed to the House of Commons (in committee of supply) 17,483 men, including 2,030 invalids, but the money for them was not voted before the fall of the Portland ministry. See ibid. xxiv. 111–17.

9. Thurlow.

10. The King's.

___

1. Her father, Lord Ravensworth, had died 30 Jan. 1784.

have children, you cannot be indifferent to a great accession, as the town says, you are likely to have,[2] and which I most sincerely wish—but in reality you will, instead of losing a parent, I trust, recover one.[3] *That* I most heartily hope will happen both for your sake and hers! —but it is not proper to say more—yet I could not help telling you how much I have considered your present position under all its faces —and having done so, I will mix nothing else with it—though without any Pindaric transition, one might easily slide into a variety of reflections, which however foreign to the theme, would be all serious.

Your Ladyship's most devoted

H.W.

To Lady Ossory, Tuesday ca April 1784

As indicated in a note to the preceding letter, Lady Ravensworth and Lady Ossory were reconciled soon after the death of Lord Ravensworth 30 Jan. 1784. This letter is tentatively dated in that year, although it might have been written somewhat later. The handwriting suggests 1784–6.

Tuesday night.

I WAS excessively mortified, Madam, when I found I had kept your Ladyship so inconveniently from going to Lady Ravensworth. Indeed by Lord Palmerston's staying I had concluded you were not going out, and having seen so very little of you this year, I was glad to indulge myself. I am sure you are good enough to excuse so involuntary a fault.

Your purse is so pretty, that I should like it, if it had no superior merit: it has no rival in my estimation but another work of the same fingers, your Ladyship's kind note. When written to such a decrepit skeleton, I should think it mere charity, had you not always been too partial to me. Still it is pleasant, when one has outlived one's self, not to have survived the kindness of one's friend's; and I will not think that age and pain are terrible evils, when they have neither shaken your friendship, Madam, nor weakened my memory of the gratitude I owe you.

2. The chief family estates at Ravensworth, Co. Durham, did not go to Lady Ossory but to her father's nephew, the 5th Bt.

3. Lord Ravensworth had been estranged from Lady Ossory since her divorce and remarriage in 1769. After his death, Lady Ravensworth and Lady Ossory were soon reconciled.

To Lady Ossory, Saturday 19 June 1784

Address: To the Countess of Ossory at Ampthill Park, Bedfordshire. *Post-mark:* ⟨ISLE⟩WORTH. 19 IV.

Strawberry Hill, June 19, 1784.

YOU are very obliging, Madam, to embrace any opportunity of reviving our correspondence, and still more kind on that you have taken. I am indeed very happy in Lady Chewton's safety. I am pleased too that she has a boy,[1] as it pleases her and Lord Chewton; nor do I wish her to encumber him with a bevy of indigent infantas[2] —but alas! what is an heir, where there is so little to inherit? Lord Chewton has every amiable virtue that man can have; but virtues are like the pipkins used by chemists in search of the philosopher's stone, which are very worthy utensils when employed in humble offices, but mighty apt to crack in pursuit of gold—and therefore I neither believe nor desire that he would go upon the process. I went to town on Tuesday to inquire after her—and that is all I know of London. I have been constantly here where there is nothing to know, but that it is cold when it should be hot, and that there is as great plenty, as if a board of seasons could carry on the business, and let the place of first commissioner be a sinecure to their principal, the sun. My absence from London has been the reason of my not waiting on Lady Ravensworth;[3] which I certainly will on the first opportunity. If she could do me the honour of visiting Strawberry, it should be made as easy to her Ladyship as I could contrive; nor are there more than fifteen steps in two flights up to the Blue Room, and three more only to the Star Chamber. Will you, Madam, be so good as to negotiate this for me; and to say that in any case, the young lady (whose name I don't know) may command a ticket for any morning she pleases, on giving me notice two or three days before, for you must know that I have been so tormented with visitants, and demands of breach of my rules, and explanations, etc., that I have been forced to print a

1. George Waldegrave (13 June 1784–94), styled Vct Chewton 22 Oct. 1784–9, 5th E. Waldegrave, 1789; drowned in the Thames at Eton 29 June 1794.

2. She had two daughters, her first child

(*ante* 15 July 1783) and her last (*post* 9 Oct. 1789), and four sons. See George Kearsley, *Peerage,* [1796], i. 100; Burke, *Peerage,* 1953, p. 2151.

3. At 13 St James's Square (GEC).

regulation, or in fact a memorial,[4] in which I have positively declared I will not depart from my method. All my mornings are disturbed, and the money I have laid out to make my house agreeable to myself, has almost driven me out of it. Lady Ravensworth on the contrary, if she comes herself, will have the contrary effect, for I will have the honour myself of showing it to her.[5]

Capt. Cooke's voyage[6] I have neither read nor intend to read. I have seen the prints—a parcel of ugly faces with blubber lips and flat noses, dressed as unbecomingly as if both sexes were ladies of the first fashion; and rows of savages with backgrounds of palm-trees. Indeed I shall not give five guineas and half—nay, they sell already for nine,[7] for such uncouth lubbers: nor do I desire to know how unpolished the north or south poles have remained ever since Adam and Eve were just such mortals. My brother's death has made me poor,[8] and I cannot now afford to buy everything I see. It is late to be sure to learn economy, but I must do it, though a little grievous, as I never was able to say the multiplication table—well! before I come to the Rule of Three, it will be all over—and then an obolus will serve to pay the ferry-man—how he will stare if I cry, 'No, stay, I cannot give you that, it is a Queen Anne's farthing!'

I rejoice in Lady Gertrude's recovery, who I really thought looked very ill. I cannot say so of Lord Ossory, and yet I am glad he is better, if he wanted to recover—though he is so healthy, that I believe he only took his anxiety for her for an ague. The young and robust are surprised at any uneasy sensation and conclude it illness. On the contrary we ancient invalids try to persuade ourselves that any cessation of pain promises an entire cure—and so we die, just when we imagine we have taken a new lease.

---

4. See illustration.

5. Her name is not in HW's 'Book of Visitors' (Berry ii. 219–52).

6. Cook's third voyage, *A Voyage to the Pacific Ocean . . . In . . . the Resolution and Discovery. In the Years, 1776, 1777, 1778, 1779 and 1780*, in 3 vols 'royal quarto' and 1 vol. folio (plates), vols i and ii by Cook, and vol. iii by James King (1750–84), second lieutenant and astronomer on the voyage, who succeeded to the command of the *Discovery* 22 Aug. 1779, on the death of Captain Charles Clerke, and was promoted to captain 3 Oct. 1780. It

was published on Friday, 4 June (*London Chronicle* 22–25 May, lv. 499).

7. The work was published at £4.14s.6d. in boards (*Monthly Review*, June 1784, lxx. 460). 'On the third day after publication, a copy was not to be met with in the hands of the bookseller; and, to our certain knowledge, six, seven, eight, and even ten guineas have since been offered for a set' (ibid. 474).

8. HW's income was diminished by £1400 a year. See *post* 18 Jan. 1792; Mason ii. 327–8; Gray i. 15.

Mr. *Walpole* is very ready to oblige any curious Perfons with the Sight of his Houfe and Collection; but as it is fituated fo near to *London* and in fo populous a Neighbourhood, and as he refuses a Ticket to nobody that fends for one, it is but reafonable that fuch Perfons as fend, fhould comply with the Rules he has been obliged to lay down for fhowing it.

Any Perfon, fending a Day or two before, may have a Ticket for Four Perfons for a Day certain.

No Ticket will ferve but on the Day for which it is given. If more than Four Perfons come with a Ticket, the Houfekeeper has pofitive Orders to admit none of them.

Every Ticket will admit the Company only between the Hours of Twelve and Three before Dinner, and only one Company will be admitted on the fame Day.

The Houfe will never be fhown after Dinner; nor at all but from the Firft of *May* to the Firft of *October*.

As Mr. *Walpole* has given Offence by fometimes enlarging the Number of Four, and refufing that Latitude to others, he flatters himfelf that for the future nobody will take it ill that he ftrictly confines the Number; as whoever defires him to break his Rule, does in effect expect him to difoblige others, which is what nobody has a right to defire of him.

Perfons defiring a Ticket, may apply either to *Strawberry-Hill*, or to Mr. *Walpole*'s in *Berkeley-Square, London*. If any Perfon does not make ufe of the Ticket, Mr. *Walpole* hopes he fhall have Notice; otherwife he is prevented from obliging others on that Day, and thence is put to great Inconvenience.

They who have Tickets are defired not to bring Children.

June 1784.

To Lady Ossory, Thursday 19 August 1784

Address: To the Countess of Ossory at Kingsgate, Kent. *Postmark:* 18 AV.

Strawberry Hill, Aug. 19, 1784.

I WAS not alert, I own, Madam, in answering your Ladyship's last note, and I thought, for tolerable reasons. I am so superannuated, so antiquated, that it is impossible my letters should entertain you, and I did suspect that with all your civility *you* felt what *I* know. You might have other reasons too for letting a correspondence languish which my unreasonable length of life has protracted longer than you could expect. I am always ready to do justice on myself, and should always remember your past goodness, and approve your abridging it when it grows a tax rather than an amusement.

You did mention your intention of going to Kingsgate,[1] but I had not heard of that journey taking place. I am not surprised at your liking it, for it is certainly singular and in no light disagreeable. The situation is uncommon and cheerful, and the buildings and erections so odd, and so little resembling any one ever saw, that a view might to those who were never there, be passed for a prospect in some half-civilized island discovered by Capt. Cook, and, with leave of the editors, more novel than any in the new pompous publication. I am as little surprised that the place, after the first impression, should have excited a thousand less pleasing reflections[2]—*There's room for meditation.*[3]

The verses[4] that Lady Ravensworth has in MS have been frequently

1. In Kent, near Margate, where 'Charles Fox's father scattered buildings of all sorts, but in no style of architecture that ever appeared before or has since, and with no connection with or to one another, and in all directions—and yet the oddity and number made that naked, though fertile soil, smile and look cheerful' (HW to Mary Berry 27 Sept. 1794, Berry ii. 110; see also ibid. ii. 112, 124–5).

2. To pay gambling debts, Charles James Fox had sold the large house to John Powell, who committed suicide in 1783 (Berry ii. 125 n. 11; HW to Mann 29 May 1783).

3. 'Meditation even to madness' as quoted in *Emma, or the Unfortunate Attachment,* 1773 (Warren H. Smith, *Architecture in English Fiction,* New Haven, 1934, p. 89).

4. Gray's bitter 'Impromptu, suggested by a view, in 1766, of the seat and ruins of a Deceased Nobleman [Henry Fox], at Kingsgate, Kent,' printed in the *New Foundling Hospital for Wit,* 1769, iii. 34–5; GM 1777, xlvii. 624 (stanzas 1–3); GM 1778, xlviii. 88 (stanzas 4–6), with corrections in GM 1782, lii. 39, 75 (C. S. Northup, *Bibliography of Thomas Gray,* 1917, pp. 163, 250; Berry ii. 110–11 n. 25).

printed in magazines since, nay, and before Mr Gray's death. I was very sorry that he wrote them, and ever gave a copy of them. You may be sure I did not recommend their being printed in his works; nor were they.[5]

I am glad your society is improved by Lady Ravensworth's company, and I hope all the three generations will return much amended in health. Though I am too indolent ever to try it, I have the highest opinion of sea air, and always in every illness determine to go to the coast—and as constantly neglect it when I am better, as if it was a qualm of conscience, that was dissipated by health. At present I am scandalously well, considering what a winter and what a summer there have been. Except three days at Park Place, I have not stirred hence. If I did, I should not sojourn in an inn at Margate! I have a notion my friend Mrs Vesey is there,[6] but I have no more intelligence from London than from Indostan. Florence is the nearest spot whence I hear any news. The dying Pretender[7] has acknowledged his natural daughter Lady Charlotte Stuart,[8] and created her Duchess of Albany, and declared her his heiress.[9] I heard a report some time ago in town, that his Queen,[10] as soon as she is Dowager, intends to come to England and marry Alfieri,[11] who is or was here,[12] being sent out of Rome

5. They first appeared in a collected edition of Gray's poems in 1882, in Edmund Gosse's edition (Northup, op. cit. 163).

6. She had arrived in Margate shortly before 14 Aug. See *Delany Corr.* vi. 222, 224, 227; *A Series of Letters Between Mrs Elizabeth Carter and Miss Catherine Talbot,* ed. Pennington, 1809, iv. 344–7; *Letters from Mrs Elizabeth Carter to Mrs Montagu,* ed. Pennington, 1817, iii. 222, 224, 227–8.

7. Mann had written 24 July 1784 that the Pretender 'decays so fast that it seems dubious if he should live to see the completion' of his plan to have his daughter come to live with him and marry her to 'a Florentine cavaliere.'

8. Charlotte Stuart (1753–89), dau. of Charles Edward, the 'Young Pretender,' by Clementina Maria Sophia Walkinshaw; legitimated by her father as Duchess of Albany, by deed dated 30 March 1783 and recorded in the Parliament of Paris 6 Sept. 1784. Many documents relating to her and

her parents are described in Hist. MSS Comm., 10th Report, Appendix vi, *Braye MSS,* 1887, pp. 222–52. See also Mann to HW 24 July 1784; *London Chronicle* 13–15 Jan. 1789, lxv. 54.

9. In his will dated 23 March (with codicil dated 25 March) 1783 and in his last will dated 22 Oct. 1784. See GEC i. 86 n. (a); Mann to HW 24 July 1784; Hist. MSS Comm., op. cit. 235.

10. See *ante* 2 Jan. 1781.

11. Vittorio Alfieri (1749–1803), the poet, whose attachment to the Countess of Albany lasted from 1777 until his death. They were never married, but she was buried beside him in Santa Croce in Florence, despite the fact that she had taken another *cavaliere servente* shortly after Alfieri's death.

12. The Countess of Albany's intrigue with Alfieri becoming known, 'Alfieri was sent out of Rome by the interest of the Cardinal of York, and came again to England in 1783, and it is said that the Princess of Stolberg, called Countess of

at the instance of the Cardinal of York.[13] I don't know whether her Royal Highness Lady Mary Coke will visit her after such a *mésalliance*, though having quarrelled with most of the sovereigns of Europe, it would be refreshing to have an intimacy with a royal relict.[14]

Have you seen the *Mémoires of Marshal Villars*,[15] Madam? the two first volumes have many entertaining passages.[16] The two latter are a little tedious, but to *me* very interesting, for they abuse my father—stay, let me account for this satisfaction. The Opposition wrote volumes to accuse him of being a tool to France, and governed by Cardinal Fleury—Marshal Villars is so good as to rail at the Cardinal for being governed and duped by my father.[17] It is not living to no purpose, when I have reached to this vindication.

Albany from her husband, will come to England if he dies, and marry Alfieri' (HW's note on Mann's letter of 24 July 1784, in 'Book of Materials' 1771, p. 106). Alfieri came to England in 1783 to buy horses.

13. Henry Benedict Maria Clement Stuart (1725–1807), younger brother of the Young Pretender; styled D. of York; cardinal, 1747, and thenceforth known as Cardinal York or Cardinal of York. On the death of his brother in 1788 he assumed the title of Henry IX.

14. For Lady Mary's unhappy experience with royalty, especially Maria Theresa, see *ante* 10 Aug. 1775, 12 Sept. 1781; HW-Coke correspondence in MORE; MANN, *passim*.

15. *Vie du Maréchal Duc de Villars*, written by himself, ed. Louis-Pierre Anquetil, 1784 (Hazen, *Cat. of HW's Lib.* 3387). Claude-Louis-Hector (1653–1734), Duc de Villars, Marshal of France, became president of the war council in 1715 and a member of the council of regency in 1718. He was especially active in diplomatic affairs after 1723.

16. HW noted in his 'Book of Materials' 1771, p. 107: 'Two remarkable passages in the life of Maréchal de Villars published at Paris in four volumes in 1784.

'In vol. 2, p. 373. "L'intention du feu Roi [Louis XIV—HW's insertion] avait été de lui [the Pretender—HW's insertion] donner les moyens de remonter sur le trône; c'était aussi le dessein de la Reine Anne sa sœur, et il y avait diverses

mesures *déjà* [HW's italics] prises pour le rétablir dans ses états."

'The second, is an account of a traitor one Douglas who followed the Pretender when he set out to embark for Scotland in 1716, and was taken near Dreux in Normandy with a musket that would discharge 8 or 10 bullets at a time, and was *released* at the *requisition* of Lord Stair the ambassador from George I.' This account is in ii. 375.

17. In his 'Book of Materials' 1759, p. 44, HW wrote: 'The opposition to Sir Robert Walpole accused him of being duped and influenced by France. It appears by the authentic memoirs of the Marshal de Villars published in four volumes in 1784, that the Marshal who was of the French Cabinet Council was convinced that Cardinal Fleury was governed, and as he says [iv. 307, *sub* 1733], duped by Sir Robert and his brother Horace the ambassador in France. It appears from the same book [vols 3–4, *passim*] that while the Marshal was endeavouring to unite France and Spain, and to prevent Spain from joining the Emperor, that Sir Robert and his brother dexterously balanced the French politics: and sometimes supported Spain and sometimes the Emperor, kept England out of war, and till the death [1 Feb. 1733] of Augustus second King of Poland prevented any union amongst those three great powers, that would have been prejudicial to England. This defence out of the mouth of an enemy so well in-

This summer has afforded me *two* such *amendes honorables*. In my earlier time I was almost proscribed for my contempt of the Duke of Newcastle and Mr Pelham. Lord Melcombe's[18] *Diary*[19] does not prove that I was so much in the wrong.[20] It is comfortable to find that one does not *always* form judgments ill-founded! and that one's opinions may grow fashionable when one is dead.

To Lady Ossory, Thursday 26 August 1784

Address: To the Countess of Ossory at Kingsgate House, Kent. *Postmark:* ISLEWORTH. ⟨?⟩ AV.

Strawberry Hill, Aug. 26, 1784.

I MUST reply a few words, Madam. I was so far from thinking that you had any *double* meaning in your congratulation on the *Fitzroyal* match,[1] that I had not, when I received your Ladyship's letter on that subject, ever heard that there could be a *double* meaning in that expression.[2] It is a delicate subject no doubt,[3] as indeed the sub-

formed, is the highest panegyric of Sir Robert Walpole.' See also the index to Villars' *Mémoires*, ed. Marquis de Vogüé, 1884–1904; *Walpoliana* i. 37.

18. George Bubb Dodington (1691–1762), cr. (1761) Bn Melcombe; a lord of the Treasury 1724–40; treasurer of the Chamber to the Prince of Wales 1749–51; treasurer of the Navy 1744–9, 1755–6, 1757. HW wrote an account of him in *Mem. Geo. II.* i. 437–42.

19. *The Diary of the Late George Bubb Dodington . . . From March 8, 1749, to February 6, 1761*, ed. H. P. Wyndham, Salisbury and London, 1784. For HW's copies, see Hazen, *Cat. of HW's Lib.* 429, 2837. HW noted in 'Mem. 1783–91' 18 May 1784: 'Lord Melcombe's diary published.'

20. When Melcombe wrote (p. 151) that Pelham 'spoke a little Pelham, but intelligible enough to those who are acquainted with the language,' HW wrote in his copy: 'i.e., that Pelham meant himself and his brother, and cared for little else.' On p. 157 Melcombe interprets a remark of Pelham as 'saying in effect, that he would take a blow from a strong man, but not from a weak one'; HW comments: 'a most

just character of Mr Pelham.' On Melcombe's reference to Newcastle as 'such a creature' (pp. 323–4), HW asks, 'Did not Dodington know, after an experience of 30 years, what a creature the Duke was, till the last transaction?' (HW's notes, copied into the *Diary* formerly in the possession of Lord Holland, and now WSL). See also Sir Charles Hanbury Williams, *Works*, with notes by HW, 1822, i. 21–4.

———

1. HW's grand-niece, Laura Keppel, m. (2 July 1784) George Ferdinand Fitzroy (1761–1810), 2d Bn Southampton, 1797; army officer; Groom of the Bedchamber to the Prince of Wales, 1783; M.P. They had been married before in Scotland (HW to Mann 8 July 1784). Both were descended from Charles II: 'Lord Southampton [father of the groom] was grandson of the [first] Duke of Grafton [son of Charles II]; the Bishop of Exeter's mother [the bride's grandmother] was Lady Anne Lennox, daughter of the first Duke of Richmond [son of Charles II]' (HW's note on his letter to Mann 8 July 1784).

2. In the nineteenth century, there was a rumour that the Hon. Charles Fitzroy,

ject always is where the fate of a young woman is at stake. However on my own part I can speak with the utmost truth and simplicity, for I have nothing to disguise or conceal. I remember you thought me mysterious on a *royaller* match;[4] and yet it proved that I had been totally out of the secret till it was publicly divulged.

It is most strictly fact, that I live so totally out of the world and know so little of what is passing in it, that going to town to see Lady Chewton on her lying-in,[5] as I was leaving her, I said, 'Is it true that Mr Fitzroy likes Laura?'—'Likes her!' replied she—'why, have you heard nothing?' 'Yes,' said I, 'I was told at Twickenham that they were much together'—'Bless me!' said she, 'don't you know that they ran away yesterday!'

I was still more in the dark about volume the second;[6] I had not even so much as heard that the parties had ever been supposed to like[7] —nay, the proposal had been made to the Duke,[8] before even common fame that knows everything, had told me what she had told to everybody else—and when everybody else told it, till it reached even

with whom the younger Princess Amelia was in love, was George III's natural son (W. S. Childe-Pemberton, *The Romance of Princess Amelia*, 1910, p. 212 n. 1; D. M. Stuart, *The Daughters of George III*, 1939, p. 333). If a similar rumour existed about George Fitzroy, who was Charles's elder brother, it may explain HW's cryptic remark; the rumour was almost certainly untrue.

3. And made more delicate because the bride's mother was the illegitimate daughter of Sir Edward Walpole.

4. The marriage of the Duke and Duchess of Gloucester.

5. 'I went to town on Tuesday [15 June] to inquire after her' (*ante* 19 June 1784).

6. The engagement of Lord Euston, Lady Ossory's son, to Lady Charlotte Maria Waldegrave; they were married 16 Nov. 1784; see *post* 17 Nov. 1784. Lady Mary Coke on 20 July 'heard a piece of news that surprises me, if it is reasonable ever to be surprised with a marriage. Lord Euston it seems was at Lord Westmoreland's at Easter when the Lady Waldegraves were there but it is not Lady Horatia he fell in love with (that would not have been surprising, as she is handsome), but it is the poor distempered Lady

Maria, who has neither beauty or health, so bad a humour about her that she is often quite lame; yet she is the person he has taken the fancy to and is as I am told to marry, though 'tis believed the Duke of Grafton very much disapproves. 'Tis extraordinary the fortune of some people in this world. Lord Euston is handsome, sensible, well spoke of by everybody, and heir to the first rank and fortune in this kingdom and the lady has small pretensions; yet she obtains this prize' ('MS Journals' 20 July 1784). HW to Mann 2 Dec. 1784 refers to this as 'another Fitzroyal match in my family': Lord Euston was descended from the first Duke of Grafton, and Lady Maria from Henrietta Fitzjames (d. 1730), natural daughter of James II and wife of Henry, 1st Bn Waldegrave.

7. At the Keppel-Fitzroy marriage on 2 July, 'Mrs Keppel did not mean that anyone should be present but Lady Albemarle; however, my sisters insisted that they would be there, and when they were all assembled Mr Fitzroy sent for Lord Euston' (Lady Chewton to Anne Clement 16 July 1784, MS WSL).

8. Of Gloucester, Lady Maria's stepfather.

me, I did not ask a question about it of those who must know something of the matter—and it was quite accidentally that it has been mentioned to me at all: nor can I at all judge whether there is any likelihood of its taking place. I have not varied in a tittle from the most minute veracity; though as your Ladyship cannot conceive the extreme ignorance in which I live, you may perhaps think my account inexplicable, or imagine that there is some coldness between me and my family; though there is not the smallest. I believe my nieces love me as much as they can love an old obsolete uncle, for I am always in good humour with them and never preach; but I do not wonder that they do not run to me with their histories, who never interfere in them, nor give my advice unless they ask it.

The new Duchess of Albany, the only child the dying Pretender ever had,[9] was by a Mrs Walkinshaw,[10] sister of the Woman of the Bedchamber to the late Princess of Wales.[11] The mother and daughter lived in a convent at Paris on a moderate pension from the Cardinal of York.[12] They formerly went to Rome, but were sent back.[13] The mother died a year or two ago;[14] the daughter is about nine-and-twenty.[15] The House of Fitzjames[16] fearing their becoming a burthen

9. The Young Pretender signed a declaration at Florence 11 March 1785 that she was his only child (Hist MSS Comm., 10th Report, Appendix vi, *Braye MSS*, 1887, p. 236). F. J. A. Skeet in his *Life and Letters of H.R.H. Charlotte Stuart, Duchess of Albany*, 1932, pp. 3, 8–9, accepts this statement as true but discusses other claimants at pp. 158–60. See also GEC *sub* Albany.

10. Clementina Maria Sophia Walkinshaw (ca 1726–1802), dau. of John Walkinshaw, of Comlachie and Barrowfield, Lanarkshire, by Katherine Paterson; cr. (before 22 July 1760) Countess of 'Alberstroff' by Francis I (GEC *sub* Albany suggests that 'Alberstroff' is a corruption of Albertsdorf). Her liaison with the Young Pretender began either late in December 1745 at Shawfield House, Glasgow, or early in January 1746 at Bannockburn (Skeet, op. cit. 4–5, 153–5, 159).

11. Catherine Walkinshaw (ca 1716–94), Bedchamber Woman at £200 per annum in the household of Augusta, Princess Dowager of Wales, from 1768 to 1772 (Skeet, op. cit. 6; *Royal Kalendar*, 1768,

p. 90; *Court and City Register*, 1772, p. 91; BERRY ii. 43 n. 4).

12. The two lived from 1760 to 1766 as paying guests at the Couvent de la Visitation de Ste Marie, Rue du Bac. Upon the Old Pretender's death (1 Jan. 1766) Clementina's pension of 6000 livres a year was cut to 5000 by Henry, Cardinal York, and mother and daughter moved to the Abbaye de Notre Dame at Meaux (Meaux-en-Brie), where they lived until they went to Rome in the winter of 1772 (Skeet, op. cit. 29–30, 32–5, 41–2; Mann to HW 24 July 1784).

13. They were forced to return to Paris in the summer of 1773 without having seen either the Young Pretender, who had been married on 17 April 1772, or Cardinal York (Skeet, op. cit. 42–3).

14. HW makes the same mistake in annotating Mann's letter of 24 July 1784 in 'Book of Materials' 1771, p. 106; the mother died in 1802.

15. Baptized 29 Oct. 1753, she was almost thirty-one.

16. The Young Pretender's cousins, the descendants of James Fitzjames (1670–

to themselves, prevented the acknowledgment of the daughter.

I have sent for the Memoirs of Cromwell's Family,[17] but as yet have only seen extracts from it in a magazine.[18] It can contain nothing a thousandth part so curious as what we know already; the inter-marriage in the fourth descent of Oliver's posterity and King Charles';[19] the speech of Richard Cromwell[20] to Lord Bathurst in the House of Lords;[21] and Fanny Russel's[22] reply to the late Prince of Wales on the

---

1734), cr. (1687) D. of Berwick, natural son of James II by Arabella Churchill. In 1784 the heads of the family were James Francis Edward Stuart-Fitzjames (1718–85), titular 3d D. of Berwick, 1738; and Charles Fitzjames (1712–87), Duc de Fitzjames.

17. *Memoirs of the Protectorate-House of Cromwell*, Birmingham, in two volumes (the second is entitled: *Memoirs of Several Persons and Families . . . Allied to, or Descended from, the Protectorate-House of Cromwell*), by Rev. Mark Noble (1754–1827), later HW's correspondent. HW's copy, now WSL, containing notes, corrections, etc., is Hazen, *Cat. of HW's Lib.* 2913. HW and Lord Ossory subscribed to the second edition, 1787, the title of which reads . . . *Protectoral-House . . .* ; HW is alluded to as 'an honourable and most learned gentleman' on pp. x–xi of the first volume.

18. The work was reviewed in the *European Magazine*, July 1784, vi. 41–7, which was in HW's library (Hazen, *Cat. of HW's Lib.* 3338.3).

19. In his 'Strange Occurrences,' dated 'Dec. 28, 1782,' and printed in *Works* iv. 363–7, HW lists (p. 364) as the third 'strange occurrence': 'The descendants of Charles I and Oliver Cromwell married in the fourth generation;

Charles II	Lady Falconberg,
Lady Litchfield	Lady Russel,
Earl of Litchfield	Sir Thomas Frankland,
Earl of Litchfield [m.]	Diana Frankland.'

Since Lady Fauconberg died without issue, the Cromwell descent should read Lady Russell, Lady Frankland, Sir Thomas Frankland, Diana Frankland; Dinah Frankland (ca 1718–79) m. (1745) George Henry Lee (1718–72), 3d E. of Lichfield, 1743 (GEC vii. 646 n. e; Coke, *Journals* iii. 110–11 n. 5). In Noble, op. cit. ii. 423, HW wrote in

his copy: 'This was a most memorable match, for as the Countess [of Lichfield] was descended in the fourth degree from Oliver Cromwell, so was the Earl in the same degree from King Charles I.'

20. (1626–1712), third son of Oliver Cromwell and his successor as Lord Protector 1658–60.

21. 'Richard Cromwell, second protector, it is well known, was produced as a witness at the age of near ninety, in Westminster Hall, in a civil suit. It is said that the counsel of the opposite party reviled the good old man with his father's crimes, but was reproved by the judge, who ordered a chair to be brought for the venerable ancient; and that Queen Anne, to her honour, commended the judge for his conduct. From Westminster Hall, Richard had the curiosity to go into the House of Lords; and standing at the bar, and it being buzzed that so singular a personage was there, Lord Bathurst, then one of the twelve new created peers [He became Bn Bathurst 1 Jan. 1712], went to the bar and conversed with Mr Cromwell. Happening to ask how long it was since Mr Cromwell had been in that house—"Never, my Lord," answered Richard, "since I sat in that chair"—pointing to the throne' (HW's note to 'Strange Occurrences,' *Works* iv. 364–5). HW's source is mentioned in his MS note in Noble, op. cit. i. 227: 'See a most remarkable story in the anecdotes preserved by Dr Newton, Bishop of Bristol, and printed with his *Works* of Richard . . .' In Hazen, *Cat. of HW's Lib.* 317, the remainder of HW's note is quoted. Thomas Newton (1704–82), Bp of Bristol, 1761, relates the anecdote in his *Works*, 1782, but Noble, op. cit., 2d edn, i. 175–6, prefers a version somewhat different from Newton's or HW's. See also William Seward, *Anecdotes of Some Distinguished*

30th of January.[23] They are anecdotes, especially the two first, worthy of being inserted in the *History of Mankind,* which, if well chosen and well written, would precede common histories, which are but repetitions of no uncommon events.

I did read the *Lettres de cachet;*[24] but like the *Tableau de Paris*[25] they shocked me far more than they amused me. I hate to read or hear of miseries that one knows it is out of one's power to remedy. The earthquakes in Naples and Sicily last year were of that kind. When I glance in a newspaper on an article of a report on convicts, I hide the paragraph with my finger, that I may not know the day of execution, and feel for what wretches, whom I cannot help, are feeling. The knowledge of woes that one can alleviate, ought never to be avoided—when they are too big for my weak grasp, I fly to the gayer side of the picture—and there one can always find food for smiles. I have often said that this world is a comedy to those who think, and a tragedy to those who feel!—but I have wandered beyond the bounds of a reply, and will wish a calm to Kingsgate, and fair weather everywhere. Were Homer alive who made gods and goddesses commissaries

Persons, 1795–7, i. 264, where the anecdote is given but Bathurst is not named.

22. Frances Russell (1699–1775), eldest dau. of John (3d son of Sir John Russell, 3d Bt, by Frances, youngest dau. of Oliver Cromwell), m. John Revett of Chequers Court, Bucks; bedchamber woman to Princess Amelia ca 1727–75, and to Princess Caroline ca 1727–57 (Noble, op. cit. ii. 397, 2d edn, ii. 415; John Chamberlayne, *Magnæ Britanniæ notitia,* 1728, pt ii. p. 267, the earliest edition in which 'Frances Russel' is listed as 'Dresser' to the two princesses; *Court and City Register* to 1775; George Lipscomb, *History . . . of . . . Buckingham,* 1847, ii. 196–7).

23. 'One 30th of January [the date of Charles I's execution] as Mrs Russel was dressing the Princess, Frederick Prince of Wales came into the room, and to tease Mrs Russel, said, "Fanny, why are [you] not at church; you should be praying and mortifying for the sin committed by your [great-]grandfather Oliver on this day." —"Mortifying!" replied she; "do you think, Sir," replied she, "that it is not mortification enough for a granddaughter of Oliver Cromwell to be pinning up your sister's

tail?"' (HW's MS note in Noble, op. cit. ii. 397). For Gray's version of the anecdote, as told to him by HW, see D. C. Tovey, *Gray and his Friends,* Cambridge, 1890, p. 286. Lady Mary Coke recorded 11 July 1769 that Mrs Revett did 'value herself upon her descent. . . . The late Prince, she said, used to tell her she ought to be whipped every thirtieth of January, which she thought very unreasonable' (*Journals* iii. 110; see also ibid. 301, iv. 458, which quotes another version of the story from *The Book of Days*). The *London Chronicle* 26–28 Oct. 1784, lvi. 412, gives the story as an 'Original Anecdote.'

24. *Des Lettres de cachet et des prisons d'état,* Hamburg, 1782, by Honoré-Gabriel Riquetti (1749–91), Comte de Mirabeau, who had been imprisoned by means of a *lettre de cachet.* The book is not listed in the SH records (Hazen, *Cat. of HW's Lib.* 3031).

25. By Louis-Sébastien Mercier (1740–1814), dramatist and miscellaneous writer; twelve volumes appeared under this title 1781–8. HW's copy, 8 vols, was published in Amsterdam, 1782–3 (ibid. 3031).

and contractors to kings, I suppose he would tell us that Ceres having favoured the English with exuberant plenty, Juno who was on the French side, sent deluges to drown all harvest. Good night, Madam.

To Lady Ossory, Saturday 23 October 1784

Strawberry Hill, Oct. 23, 1784.

IT IS very true, Madam; we are robbed in the face of the sun, as well as at the going down thereof. I know not how other districts fare, but for five miles round us, we are in perpetual jeopardy. Two of our justices[1] returning from a cabinet-council of their own at Brentford, were robbed last week before three o'clock at the gates of Twickenham[2]—no wonder: I believe they are all hoodwinked like their Alma Mater herself, and consequently, as they cannot see, it is not surprising that both she and they should often weigh out their goods with uneven scales.

Being perfectly secure of not having given your Ladyship any cause of offence, I did conclude that one reason of your silence must be the topic to which you allude,[3] and on which you could not like to write, after you knew that I had absolutely nothing to do in the affair. I was certainly as little desirous of renewing a theme, which terminated as I had foreseen,[4] and as, in the only conversation I had with the person

1. William Heckford (d. 1797) and Stephen Cole (ca 1707–90), both J. P. (R. S. Cobbett, *Memorials of Twickenham*, 1872, pp. 74, 104).

2. 'Last Tuesday [12 Oct.] at noon-day a most daring robbery was committed within twenty yards of Twickenham, in the sight of many people passing along. As William Heckford and Stephen Cole, Esqrs, were returning home to dinner, from Brentford, where they had been to hold a Sessions, they were attacked by two highwaymen, well mounted, armed with horse pistols, and their faces covered with handkerchiefs, who, with dreadful imprecations and a brutality of behaviour unwarrantable (as no resistance whatever was made), demanded their money, watches, rings, etc., which they took from them, and rode hastily towards Isleworth. When highway robberies are arrived at

that pitch to be committed at noon-day, in a public road, in the sight of several passengers, who is safe from their depredations? Sunshine is now no security' (*London Chronicle* 14–16 Oct., lvi. 371).

3. The marriage of Lord Euston and Lady Maria Waldegrave; see following letter.

4. The Duke of Grafton opposed the marriage. Some of the difficulties are suggested in Lady Chewton's letter to Anne Clement 6 Oct. 1784: Lord Euston 'appears to have more hopes of an union . . . between Maria and himself than he had when they met in town. . . . I find that Mr Walpole [HW] is very angry with Lord Euston and is of opinion that he has behaved ill; I do not think he has acted quite right, though I am convinced whatever he did, he did it from good motives and that he really is very much in love

concerned I foretold it would; the last words I said to her, being to warn her to be prepared for such an event. You may then well believe, Madam, that it cannot be my wish to revive a subject so little agreeable.

I am acquainted with Mrs Allanson,[5] and have very great esteem for her, and could tell your Ladyship her history, were it not too long for a letter. Her conduct has been noble, and reasonable—her patroness's, in my opinion, preposterous at least.[6] The female disciples of that school, which is not that of Pythagoras,[7] the mistress resembling him in nothing but in a thigh of solid gold,[8] are loud in her defence. I hope Mr Pulteney[9] will protect Mrs Allanson by the same substantial arguments.[10]

I cannot unlock Mr Powys's[11] charade. It may be a very good something, but does not seem to be a charade, which used to be formed of a first part, a second, and a whole—now I did not know that *character* was the whole of anybody or anything.

Balloons is a subject I do not intend to tap.[12] If they can be improved into anything more than Brobdignag kites, it must be in a

with her—she is so much attached to him that I am sure she will never be happy till they are married.'

5. That is, Alison: Dorothea Gregory (ca 1755–1830), dau. of Dr John Gregory of Edinburgh University, on whose death in 1773 she went to live with his friend Mrs Montagu; m. (14 or 19 June 1784) Rev. Archibald Alison, later (1790) the author of *Essays on the Nature and Principles of Taste* (DNB *sub* Alison, Archibald; *Mrs Montagu 'Queen of the Blues,'* ed. Reginald Blunt, Boston and New York, 1923, i. 148, ii. 172 *et passim*).

6. For Mrs Montagu's view of the marriage, which she thought imprudent because Alison was impoverished, see her letter to the Duchess of Portland 20 June 1784 in Hist. MSS Comm., *Bath MSS* (at Longleat), 1904–8, i. 353–5. She had wished for her nephew to marry Dorothea Gregory, but after his marriage in 1785 Mrs Montagu resumed friendly relations with her (Blunt, op. cit. ii. 172, 186, 191 *et passim*).

7. That is, of wisdom.

8. One of the legends about Pythagoras was that one of his thighs was of gold,

and that he exhibited it at the Olympic games. Mrs Montagu was said to have an income of £10,000 a year.

9. William Pulteney (1729–1805), formerly Johnstone, 5th Bt, 1794; M.P.

10. Pulteney had expected to provide Alison (then incumbent of Sudbury, Northants) a living of £150 a year and a house. Unable to provide the living at the time of the marriage, he gave the couple meanwhile £150 a year, and they were to live in the parsonage at Sudbury; in 1790 he gave Alison the perpetual curacy of Kenley, in Shropshire, and in 1794 the vicarage of High Ercal; other preferment followed (Blunt, op. cit. ii. 171–7).

11. Probably Sir Horace Mann's nephew-in-law Thomas Powys (1743–1800), cr. (1797) Bn Lilford; M.P. Lord Ossory's seat, Farming Woods, was near Lilford Hall, and both Ossory and Powys were in opposition at this time. Toynbee's suggestion (xiii. 201) of the Rev. Thomas Powys (1736–1809), rector of Fawley, and a neighbour of General Conway, is less likely.

12. See HW to Mann 2 Dec. 1783 for HW's first reference to balloons.

century or two after I shall be laid low. A century in my acceptation means an hundred years hence, or a year or two hence, for after one ceases to be, all duration is of the same length; and everything that one guesses will happen after one's self is no more, is equally a vision. Visions I loved, while they decked with rainbows, or concealed the clouds of the horizon before me; but now that the dream is so near to an end, I have no occasion for lesser pageants—much less for divining with what airy vehicles the atmosphere will be peopled hereafter, or how much more expeditiously the East, West, or South, will be ravaged and butchered, than they have been by the old-fashioned clumsy method of navigation.

It is true, I do not shut my eyes to the follies actually before them. I smile at the adoration paid to these aerial Quixotes; and reflect, that as formerly men were admired for their courage in risking their lives in order to destroy others; now they are worshipped for venturing their necks *en pure perte*—much more commendably I do allow; yet fame is the equal object of both. I smile too at the stupidity that pays a guinea for being allowed to see what any man may see by holding up his head and looking at the sky:[13] and I observe that no improvements of science or knowledge make the world a jot wiser; knowledge, like reason, being a fine tool that will give an exquisite polish or finishing to ornaments; but is not strong enough to answer the common occasions of mankind.

To Lady Ossory, Friday 12 November 1784

Part of the second to last paragraph is here first printed.

Strawberry Hill, Nov. 12, 1784.

IT HAPPENS to me now, Madam, as I suppose it does to most who have intervals in their correspondence: when they come to write, their letters must be a patchwork of discordant affections—if affections

13. A similar view is in HW to Mann 30 Sept. 1784. At this time HW had seen at least two balloons; see HW to Conway 30 June 1784, 15 [16] Oct. 1784. For Lunardi's ascent on 15 Sept., tickets to the Artillery Ground sold for one guinea, half a guinea, and five shillings. 'About five hundred people paid . . . very few of whom sat in the half-guinea seats, and still fewer in the guinea ones' (*London Chronicle* 7–18 Sept., lvi. 247, 273). Tickets for Blanchard's ascent on 16 Oct. sold for half a guinea, a crown and a half-crown (ibid. 16–19 Oct., lvi. 377). See also J. E. Hodgson, *The History of Aeronautics in Great Britain*, Oxford, 1924, pp. 117–24, and illustrations of tickets.

they have; so chequered are the events of human life! if I turn to one side of my mind, it is all sunshine and joy, on the Queen's goodness to Lord Waldegrave[1]—if to the other, what true sorrow for the death of Lady Drogheda![2] She was really as perfect as a mortal could be. Her piety though rigid, was so sweet! her understanding she had cultivated herself; it was as deep as it was improved. She had a concise and comprehensive eloquence, that summed up the newest and most just reflections in the compass of a short sentence; from the mouth of an ancient sage they would have been handed down as maxims. The gentle and harmonious tone of her voice, the captivating graces of her manner, and the blushes that accompanied all she said, for her resolution of speaking when it was proper, was forever combating her bashfulness, made such an assemblage of attraction, that she appeared more beautiful than she was in reality—but it was the beauty of a modest saint. Her firmness was equal to her other qualities: perceiving that in fondness to her son[3] she equalled her mother,[4] she sent him from her to England for his education.[5] She has been carried off in six days by a bilious disorder, leaving a miserable husband, whom, though doting on her, she could not preserve from ruining his health and fortune by drink and play,[6] four or five daughters,[7] to whom her

1. On 4 Nov. the fourth Earl had kissed hands as Master of the Horse to the Queen (£800 a year), succeeding his father, the third Earl, who had died 22 Oct. (*London Chronicle* 4–9 Nov., lvi. 442, 449). 'The present Lord Waldegrave does not stand indebted to the friendship of ministers for his appointment . . . the act was entirely her Majesty's . . . and founded upon justice: before the death of his father, he held the office of Vice Chamberlain to the King, worth £1200 a year; upon succeeding to the title he lost the appointment, as it cannot be held by a peer, and having but a small patrimonial estate, her Majesty took it into consideration, and when the Minister waited upon her to recommend a Master of the Horse, he was told that her Majesty had already disposed of it to Lord Waldegrave' (ibid. 9–11 Nov., lvi. 463).

2. Anne Seymour Conway (1744 – 4 Nov. 1784), 1st dau. of HW's cousin, Lord Hertford, m. (1766) Charles Moore (1730–1822), 6th E. of Drogheda, cr. (1791) M. of Drogheda; 'died at the Earl's seat at Moore

Abbey' (*London Chronicle* 23–25 Nov., lvi. 509). A drawing by her is in HW's *A Collection of Prints Engraved by Various Persons of Quality*, now wsl.

3. Edward Moore (1770–1837), 2d M. of Drogheda, 1822, who died insane. Her younger son, Henry, was b. 15 March 1784 (Venn, *Alumni Cantab.*).

4. That is, Lady Hertford's fondness for her eldest son, Lord Beauchamp; seven sons of Lady Hertford were living at the date of this letter.

5. The elder son may be the 'Moore' who was at Eton 1781–3 (*Eton Coll. Reg.*).

6. 'A very eccentric character, passionately fond of play, to which he was a victim all his life, and subjected to great pecuniary embarrassments. In his later years his estates were put out to nurse, and a moderate pension was allowed to him by the creditors for his subsistence' (Thomas Raikes, *A Portion of the Journal . . . From 1831 to 1847*, 1856–7, iii. 115). Lady Mary Coke recorded that Lady Drogheda 'has left seven if not eight children. . . . She had the care of everything.

loss is irreparable, a family of brothers and sisters who idolized her, and a most fond father, to whom this blow will recall the death of her mother, exactly at this time two years ago. I never saw General Conway so much struck as when he brought me the news.

This indulgence to my own sensations will not compensate to your Ladyship for the story of Mrs A.[8] but that indeed I am not entirely at liberty to write, as there are some circumstances, which, though highly to her honour, are not proper for the post. In lieu I can tell you a curious anecdote of the King of Sweden.[9] When last at Florence,[10] he found the Count of Albany in a wretched condition, destitute even of an exchequer to pay his household. He imparted his sympathy *at the opera*—to whom, think you, Madam? only to the minister[11] of the Count's rival—who with his usual readiness and propriety replied, that he supposed the subsidy his Majesty said he intended to bestow on his poor compeer, was mentioned to *him,* as a hint to sound whether it would not be offensive to a brother monarch. He accepted that idea—then proposed to make a free gift of £1000—to be followed by a like benevolence in six months, and an annual donative of more than both. You expect next no doubt to hear, Madam, that the good ship Gildenstern arrived at Leghorn loaded with copper money[12]— *pas encore.* The modern Gustavus[13] desired the English Resident to advance the money, for which he would give him a draft on the mines of Dalecarlia.[14] Having received no such instructions, the minister desired to be excused—and somehow or other the treasure is not yet arrived—On the contrary, as the new Duchess of Albany will inherit jewels and effects to the amount of at least an hundred thousand pounds,[15] it is said, that one of the royal Dukes of Ostrogothia or

Lord Drogheda has hurt his circumstances by play, but she by care and management endeavoured to put order into their affairs' ('MS Journals' 12 Nov. 1784).

7. For six daughters living at this time (a seventh, Gertrude, for whom no dates are given, probably died young), see DNB, *sub* Moore, Charles (1730–1822); John Debrett, *Peerage,* 1817, ii. 911.

8. Alison; see preceding letter.

9. Gustav III (1746–92), K. of Sweden 1771–92.

10. At the end of 1783 (Mann to HW 13 Dec. 1783); Mann reported Gustav's offer, 10 Dec. 1783, in his dispatch to the sec-

retary's office (A. C. Ewald, *Life . . . of Prince Charles Stuart,* 1883, p. 410).

11. Sir Horace Mann.

12. HW makes this witticism to Mann 8 Jan. 1784.

13. Gustav III, whom HW considered a tyrant and a usurper (HW to Mann 20 Sept. 1772, Dec. 1783).

14. A mountainous province in Sweden, abounding in copper and iron mines.

15. This sum presumably is based on an estimate of both her father's and uncle's estates. Her will, dated three days before her death in 1789, shows that she had not a great deal to leave her uncle, her uni-

Vandalmania[16] is to marry her—but this I do not warrant. I had the whole story from the younger Sir Horace,[17] who is just come to England. The elder is too discreet ever to send *me* such anecdotes of the porphyrogeniti.[18]

You tell me, Madam, the *humours* of the P[rince] of W[ales] and his new comrade, old Slender[19]—nay, but they are not of my calibre. I kissed the hand of George I, and do not look to the revels of his great-great-grandson. My life has been protracted long beyond the term that my weak frame seemed to promise; yet having lived long, is no reason for expecting to live much longer. I amuse the remnant by recollection, not by guessing at futurity; for though memory is a shadow, [it] is at least a more substantial one than hope or foresight.[20] What diversion could it be to Moses to be carried up a mountain and treated with the prospect of a valley that was to be peopled by the young folks around him when he should be no more? Were I an allegorizing preacher I should treat that story as a moral parable, calculated to teach the ancient the vanity of their visions. They wander forty years in a wilderness, reach the confines of the promised land, when they are decrepit, crawl up a precipice to have a glimpse of something that they are not to enjoy, and leave their bones to be leaped over by a thoughtless tribe, who are pursuing a similar chimera —we are all links of one chain, which is forever carrying on, without being an inch longer, every preceding link decaying as fast as new are added.

I have seen Mr Duane, who is feeble indeed; but his head is clear; and his appetite for buying curiosities still alert—consequently *I* am much more superannuated, for I find *that* passion has taken its flight too!

---

versal heir, and her bequests were not large. For her will, see F. J. A. Skeet, *Life and Letters of H.R.H. Charlotte Stuart, Duchess of Albany*, 1932, pp. 164–70.

16. The Dukes of Sudermania and Ostrogothia were brothers of the King of Sweden: Charles (1748–1818), D. of Sudermania, 1772, regent 1792–6, K. of Sweden 1809–18 (as Charles XIII) and of Norway 1814–18; and Frederick Adolf (1750–1803), D. of Ostrogothia, 1772.

17. Sir Horace Mann (1744–1814), Kt,

1768; 2d Bt, 1786, in succession to his uncle, HW's long-time correspondent.

18. Those 'born in the purple,' or of royal descent.

19. In the *Merry Wives of Windsor*. Probably Lord Clermont, aged 62, is meant (the Prince, 22). Cf. *post* 13 Sept. 1789; BM, *Satiric Prints* iv. 786, No. 4702, 'The Coterie and Newmarket Macaroni,' identified on a copy now wsl as Clermont.

20. The remainder of this paragraph is here first printed.

To Lady Ossory, Wednesday 17 November 1784

Strawberry Hill, Nov. 17, 1784.

NATURALLY, Madam, I should rejoice on a favourite niece[1] being married to a young Lord of the great rank, character, and figure of Lord Euston; and much more, on my family's acquiring the honour of alliance with your Ladyship's—yet that satisfaction is much abated by the circumstance of the Duke of Grafton's disapprobation. I am not fond of matches where any proper consent is wanting. Still I flatter myself, that as my niece's birth, fortune, and character made her in every light a suitable party, except for his Grace's younger children,[2] Lord Euston will not be thought to have made a very ineligible choice; and I do hope that Lady Ravensworth and your Ladyship do not condemn him. It does please me to recollect that I have often talked to you, when I could not have the most glimmering idea of such an event, of the uncommon understanding of Lady Euston. The dignity of her conduct on the wretched behaviour of Lord Egremont, did deserve a man of nobler principles—and fate has amply compensated by giving her one who has acted as honourably as the other meanly. I am not likely to see the consequences—it would grieve me should they prove what are threatened; but I will venture to foretell that if sense and sweetness of temper can constitute the chief felicity of a husband, Lord Euston will not be unhappy. Still, he will do me the justice to say, that in the only interview I have had the honour of having with him since the marriage was in question, I told him, nobody could advise him to risk his father's displeasure. I have most strictly adhered to that declaration; and when I saw my niece the next day (the sole time I have seen her since) I entreated her to break off the connection entirely. This justification I owe to the long friendship, Madam, with which you have honoured me: it is not due to anyone else, nor should I condescend to make it but to you. However flattered I may be by the alliance, I would not have obtained it by staking Lord Euston's fortune, nor by shocking a father's authority, however harshly, and I think, unreasonably, ex-

1. Lady Maria Waldegrave.
2. That is, if Lady Maria had had a great fortune, the Duke would have been able to make better provision for his younger children.

erted. A letter[3] from Lady Waldegrave this morning acquainted me that the marriage was solemnized yesterday.[4]

I am in utter ignorance of anything else that could help out a letter. The papers tell me that the Dutch are drowning their country to save it.[5] It puts me in mind of an old pagan parable. The priests of the god of fire, and those of the god of water, agreed on a duel be tween their principals—what pity *that* etiquette has been disused!— The aquatic champion was clad for armour in a jug, bored with holes stopped by wax. Emperor Flame advanced with all the fervour of his element: Mynheer Neptune received the onset with *sang-froid*— Cæsar pushed on, the wax dissolved, an inundation burst forth— and Vulcan was extinguished—and so be it!—how the imperial vulture of Russia must long to extend a talon, and carry off a limb of another republic!

Since I adjusted the affair between Lord Orford and Cav. Mozzi,[6] I have heard nothing of Mr Morice who was then at Ischia, and better, and as he always is whether better or worse, in good spirits.

Pray, Madam, revere Uncle Methusalem; Lord Euston makes the fifty-sixth of my nephews, nieces, and great-nephews and -nieces. Two Fitzroys[7] will not stop the lengthening of the line, if it does not break off at the other end!

3. Missing.
4. By special licence, at the seat of Lord and Lady Waldegrave at Navestock, Essex.
5. By the Treaty of Munster, 1648, the Scheldt River was closed to Belgian vessels and its freedom reserved for the Dutch navy and merchant marine; subsequent treaties had recognized and supported this provision. Joseph II, wishing to have the river opened to Belgian trade, was sending soldiers into the Netherlands; the Dutch, to protect themselves, were cutting dikes and flooding lands. The *London Chronicle* 13–16 Nov. has three accounts of the flooding: lvi. 473, 477, 480, the last of which mentions a tract 'near twenty miles in circumference under water; in the lower part of which . . . the country is entirely drowned . . .' The dispute was finally resolved by the Treaty of Fontainebleau 8 Nov. 1785, when concessions were made on both sides; see *The Cambridge Modern History*. Vol. VI: *The Eighteenth Century*, Cambridge and New York, 1934, pp. 640–6.
6. See the HW-Mann Correspondence for July 1784.
7. Lord Euston and Hon. Capt. George Ferdinand Fitzroy, the latter recently married to Laura Keppel.

To Lady Ossory, Saturday 20 November 1784

Address: To the Countess of Ossory at Ampthill Park, Bedfordshire. *Postmark:* ISLEWORTH. 20 NO.

Strawberry Hill, Nov. 20, 1784.

IN OBEDIENCE to your Ladyship's commands I write a few words. I certainly cannot disapprove anything you say on the present occasion. Much less do I disagree with you in thinking that any fervour on your Ladyship's part[1] would but do hurt. Indeed the only part I take myself is to recommend perfect silence, which I shall strictly observe myself. I told Lady Euston my opinion, as it was my duty; both when she told me of the proposal, and when I thought it entirely broken off. When anything is over, though contrary to one's opinion, good nature as well as good sense, bids one take the favourable side. My disposition always inclines me to be partial to young people and young passions; and therefore it was no effort to exchange prudence for kind wishes. Mine are so very barren, that I am not even likely to see them fulfilled, should they ever be!

I could only vary my expressions, Madam, if I wrote more on this subject; nor should I have said so much but to you. When one can do no service, silence is the only *succedaneum*.

To Lady Ossory, Thursday 9 December 1784

Address: To the Countess of Ossory at Ampthill Park, Bedfordshire. *Postmark:* 9 DE.

Berkeley Square, Dec. 9, 1784.

I CAN answer Lady Anne's Salique query very easily, Madam—or rather I cannot—but I believe that even when Edward VI died, there was not a single prince living who descended in the direct male line from any king since the Conquest. Numerous as were the sons of

1. To reconcile the Duke of Grafton to Lord Euston's marriage. The Duke 'has assured him he shall never have any part of the unsettled estate, which is far the greatest part' (Coke, 'MS Journals' 17 Nov. 1784).

Edward III, only Thomas Duke of Gloucester[1] continued the masculine line, and I cannot (upon memory only) affirm that.[2] If he did, the Duke of Buckingham[3] beheaded by Henry VIII had, *Saliquely* speaking, the best title to the Crown.[4] The Beauforts[5] are doubly illegitimate, being descended from a bastard of one of John of Ghent's legitimated issue.[6] I doubt therefore whether enacting the Salique law here would not in any period have been a dangerous measure— at least I know nowhere of an uninterrupted male genealogy of genuine princes but in Wales—and it would occasion an inundation of civil wars, before the Herald's Office could settle which Mr Price, or which Mr Williams, or which Mr Philipps is the genuine heir of our true British princes. I am sure I do not mean to arrogate a right in myself, nor pretend to say how near I stand to the Crown; but I have a pedigree of my mother, drawn up by the late Sir John Philipps my cousin,[7] and father of the present Lord Milford,[8] in which it is clear that we are descended from Cadwallader.[9] I really do not believe Sir John had any ambitious views himself, for though he gave himself all that trouble, I believe it was only meant as a compliment to his cousin,[10] the wife of the then prime minister, or at most a hint to her, that so noble a prince ought to be at least a commissioner of the

1. Thomas of Woodstock (1355–97), 6th and youngest son of Edward III; cr. (1385) D. of Gloucester.

2. The Duke's only son, Humphrey de Bohun (ca 1381–99), left no children (GEC v. 729). Of the three daughters of the Duke who survived him, one left issue (ibid.).

3. Edward Stafford (1478–1521, 3d D. of Buckingham, 1485.

4. He was descended from Ann, sister of Humphrey de Bohun and daughter of Thomas, Duke of Gloucester (GEC ii. 388–91); under Salique law his claim through the female line would not be recognized.

5. The illegitimate children (and their descendants) of John of Gaunt, 1st D. of Lancaster, 4th son of Edward III, by his mistress Katharine Swynford, whom he married in 1396.

6. John of Gaunt's four surviving children by Katharine Swynford were legitimated by Act of Parliament in 1397. The eldest son, John Beaufort, cr. (1397) M. of

Somerset, was the ancestor of the earls, marquesses, and dukes of Somerset 1397–1471 (GEC xii pt i. 39–58); his grandson, Henry, 2d D. of Somerset (n.c.), left an illegitimate son, Charles Somerset, cr. (1514) E. of Worcester, who was the direct ancestor of the Dukes of Beaufort (GEC xii pt i. 57 n. b, ii. 52 n. c; Burke, *Peerage*, 1953, p. 165).

7. Sir John Philipps (ca 1701–64), 6th Bt, 1743, of Picton Castle, co. Pembroke, to whom HW was related through his maternal grandmother, Elizabeth Shorter, dau. of Sir Erasmus Philipps, 3d Bt.; HW's mother and Sir John Philipps were first cousins.

8. Sir Richard Philipps (1744–1823), 7th Bt, 1764, cr. (1776) Bn Milford; M.P.; Lord Lieut. co. Pembroke 1781–1823.

9. Cadwaladr (d. 682), 'last king of the Britons' (GRAY i. 81 n. 1). The pedigree, now WSL, is described in MONTAGU i. 69 n. 14, with two misstatements: it is written on two sheets of paper joined, and it measures 19" x 52".

10. HW's mother.

customs; and I am the more inclined to acquit his Royal Highness my cousin of any intention of disturbing the established succession from personal views, as (from no resentment I believe for not obtaining a place in the Custom House), he became a very zealous and active Jacobite, and at last died in very good odour with his present Majesty.[11]

Thus you see, Madam, whichever way I turn myself, I have royal or Fitzroyal connections; and yet, however beneficial it might be to me and my relations on Cadwallader's side, I cannot come into your Ladyship's scheme of a Salique law here. At least I hope you will repeal the Marriage Act[12] first—for two reasons—one, that our present princes may have as many lawful male heirs as possible; and the other, that our princesses may not be forced to scamper to Gretna Green, in order to supply the Crown with heirs—which they would not do, if their children [were] not *habile* to succeed.

I luckily arrived in town the eve of dreadful yesterday.[13] I came for my *waiting* tonight in Cavendish Square,[14] and did mean to return to Strawberry tomorrow, and thence go on Saturday to Park Place: but since Boreas and Eolus and all the demons of the air are let loose, I shall keep myself as warm as I can, and not venture being laid up with the gout and compounded in snow as I was some years ago at Ampthill,[15] and then forced to have a track hewn for me by the charity of my hosts.

May I beg to consult your Ladyship on a case of conscience? I think I ought to wait on Lady Ravensworth on a late event[16]—and yet I am so afraid of doing a wrong or seemingly impertinent thing, that I have not ventured yet. Pray tell me seriously whether I should or not.

I have neither seen *The Carmelite*[17] nor Holman,[18] nor anything

---

11. Probably a reference to George III's Tory sympathies; Sir John Philipps became privy councillor, 1763.

12. The Royal Marriage Act, 1772 (12 Geo. III, c. 11), stipulated that no member of the royal family under the age of twenty-five could marry without the consent of the Crown; any marriage contracted without this consent was null and void. See Cobbett, *Parl. Hist*, xvii. 383–424; *Last Journals* i. 23–4, 27–71; *English Historical Documents* [Vol. X] *1714–1783*, ed. D. B. Horn and Mary Ransome, 1957, pp. 107–8.

13. Snow had blocked most of the roads

(*London Chronicle* 7–9 Dec., lvi. 560).

14. At Princess Amelia's.

15. See *ante* 22 Jan. 1776.

16. The marriage of her grandson, Lord Euston.

17. A tragedy by Richard Cumberland, first acted at Drury Lane on 2 Dec. 1784, with Mrs Siddons as Matilda. HW's copy, not traced, is listed in Hazen, *Cat. of HW's Lib.* 1810: 37.2.

18. Joseph George Holman (1764–1817), actor and dramatist, had made his first professional appearance (he had done considerable amateur acting) at Covent Gar-

or almost anybody else. You don't consider that I was a cotemporary of Dugdale and Ashmole,[19] that I am or ought to be superannuated, and that I know no more of the present generation, than if Deucalion and Pyrrha had just tossed them over their shoulders and restocked the earth—Alas! I have lost most of those that used to inhabit it in my days! and a teacup full of deluge would wash me away too.

To Lady Ossory, Monday 27 December 1784

In Kirgate's hand.
Address: To the Countess of Ossory at Ampthill Park, Bedfordshire. *Postmark:* 27 DE.

Berkeley Square, Dec. 27, 1784.

I AM told that I am in a prodigious fine way; which, being translated into plain English, means, that I have suffered more sharp pain these two days, than in all the moderate fits together that I have had for these last nine years: however, Madam, I have one great blessing, there is drowsiness in all the square hollows of the red-hot bars of the gridiron on which I lie, so that I scream and fall asleep by turns like a babe that is cutting its first teeth. I can add nothing to this exact account, which I only send in obedience to your Ladyship's commands, which I received just now: I did think on Saturday that the worst was over.

To Lady Ossory, Monday 3 January 1785

In Kirgate's hand.
Address: To the Countess of Ossory at Ampthill Park, Bedfordshire. *Postmark:* 3 IA.

Berkeley Square, Jan. 3, 1785.

I AM much obliged to your Ladyship and Lord Ossory: I am essentially better, and quite contented, for my pains are gone. It is not so easy to recover what I had not, strength; and, consequently, I

den 25 Oct. 1784 as Romeo. On 12 Nov. he had appeared as Macbeth and on 3 Dec. in his first rôle in comedy as Don Felix in Susannah Centlivre's *The Wonder* (*London Chronicle* 11–13 Nov., 2–4 Dec., lvi. 470, 544).

19. Elias Ashmole (1617–92), antiquary, founder of the Ashmolean Museum at Oxford.

am as low and languid as possible; but having no occasion for myself, I am very indifferent about the little progress I make. I return your Ladyship's New Year's compliments with wishes, I hope, better founded.

To Lady Ossory, Thursday 13 January 1785

Address in Kirgate's hand; misdated 1784 by HW.
Address: To the Countess of Ossory at Ampthill Park, Bedfordshire. *Postmark:* 13 IA.

Jan. 13, 1784[5].

I CAN just use one hand enough slowly to scratch out a few thanks to your Ladyship for your very kind notification.[1] Indeed I had heard the agreeable news yesterday; and also that the Duke has sent word to Lord Euston by Mr Pratt[2] that he will continue his allowance.[3] I am heartily glad; not being of so romantic an age as to believe that love and a cottage compose very durable felicity. The Duke of Grafton has certainly acted very temperately. It would be most unjust to say that a father has not cause to be displeased at his child's marrying against his consent. That he will be satisfied with Lady Euston, if she ever has the happiness of being known to him, I am persuaded. I do not know so perfect a young woman; she has all her father's sense and temper, and the utmost discretion. They who spread absurd stories about her, had not one of the three. I know some of them; they are hags of high rank; they bestow Sunday mornings on church, and the rest of the year on scandal, malice, envy, and lies of their neighbours—and their neighbours are those of the Gospel, the first that falls in their way. Three of those pious Furies are

1. Of the reconciliation between the Duke of Grafton and Lord and Lady Euston.

2. John Jeffreys Pratt (1759–1840), styled Vct Bayham 1786–94, 2d E. Camden, 1794, cr. (1812) M. Camden. His father and the Duke of Grafton had been friends for many years.

3. 'His allowance from the Duke . . . is only £800 a year, and upon this trifling sum he has . . . maintained his rank without entering into the fashionable vice of annuities and *post obits*. In a young nobleman who is heir to 25,000 a year, this is very singular. He has now married a most accomplished lady. . . . Their present fortunes joined, not amounting to more than 1600 a year' (*London Chronicle* 23–25 Nov. 1784, lvi. 512). Lady Ravensworth's letter to Lady Ossory, endorsed 8 Jan. 1785, indicates that the Duke of Grafton had offered to continue the allowance of £800 (National Library of Ireland: Fitzpatrick MSS).

sisters, and their names, the Ladies Tisiphone, Megæra, and Alecto.[4]

I can say today, Madam, that I do believe my gout is going. One of the fogs, or the eternal fog, gave me cold last week, and my pains returned a little. From being foolhardy, I am grown such a coward, that I do not believe I shall venture to moult a single wrapper this age.

You see the Airgonauts have passed the Rubicon.[5] By their own account they were exactly birds; they flew through the air, perched on the top of a tree, some passengers climbed up and took them in their nest[6]—The smugglers, I suppose, will be the first that will improve on the plan. However, if the project is ever brought to any perfection (though I apprehend it will be addled like the ship that was to live under water and never came up again)[7] it will have a different fate from other discoveries, whose inventors are not known. In this age all that is done (as well as what is never done) is so faithfully recorded, that every improvement will be registered chronologically. Mr Blanchard's[8] *Trip to Calais*[9] puts me in mind of Dryden's *Indian Emperor,*

4. HW's Furies may be Lady Mary Coke, Lady Greenwich, and Lady Betty Mackenzie; for the last, see Berry i. 35 n. 40. Lady Greenwich is 'Tisiphone,' *post* 10 Aug. 1785. All three, especially the first two, were known as gossips, had summer residences in the neighbourhood of Strawberry Hill, and were in HW's circle of acquaintance in London.

5. On 7 Jan. 1785 Blanchard (see below) and Dr John Jeffries (1745–1819), American physician and scientist, made the first crossing of the English Channel in a balloon, starting from Dover Castle and landing at Guines, near Ardres (DAB; John Jeffries, *A Narrative of the Two Aerial Voyages* [30 Nov. 1784, 7 Jan. 1785] *of Doctor Jeffries with Mons. Blanchard; with Meteorological Observations and Remarks*, 1786, reprinted in facsimile, New York, 1941; *London Chronicle* 1–13 Jan., lvii. 11, 36, 48).

6. Jeffries' letter from Calais 8 Jan. appears in the *London Chronicle* 11–13 Jan., lvii. 48: 'we descended most tranquilly into the midst of the forest *De Felmores*, almost as naked as the trees, not an inch of cord or rope left, no anchor. . . . My good little captain begged for all my exertion to stop at the top of the first tree I could reach. I succeeded . . . [in] holding

the top of a lofty tree, . . . the balloon playing to and fro over us . . . We soon heard the wood surrounded by footmen, horsemen, etc., and received every possible assistance from them. . . . We were invited to the château or seat of Monsieur de Sandrouin, where we received every polite attention.'

7. The 'sole projector,' J. Day, planned 'a method of sinking a vessel under water, with a man in it, who should live therein for a certain time, and then, by his own means only, bring himself up to the surface.' After experimenting for a time and getting a patron who placed bets that he would succeed, Day entered his vessel and sank it on 27 June 1774 in about seventeen fathoms of water at Plymouth. He did not bring his vessel to the surface at the end of twelve hours, as he had agreed to do, and attempts to recover the vessel and his body were unsuccessful (*London Chronicle* 30 June–1 Sept. 1774, xxxvi. 8, 16, 36 *et passim*; GM 1774, xliv. 304–5; *London Magazine*, 1774, xliii. 354–5.

8. Jean-Pierre Blanchard (1753–1809), one of the most famous of early aeronauts, made over fifty balloon ascensions before he fell from his balloon and was killed at The Hague.

9. A play on the title of Foote's comedy

What divine monsters, O ye gods, are these,
That float in air, and fly upon the seas![10]

Dryden little thought that he was prophetically describing something more exactly than ships as conceived by Mexicans. If there is no air-sickness, and I were to go to Paris again, I would prefer a balloon to the packet-boat,[11] and had as lief roost in an oak, as sleep in a French inn, though I were to caw for my breakfast like the young ravens.

This is a volume for me, Madam, and my hand must lie down and take a nap.

To Lady Ossory, Saturday 5 February 1785

Address: To the Countess of Ossory at Ampthill Park, Bedfordshire. *Postmark:* 5 FE.

Berkeley Square, Feb. 5, 1785.

I HAVE not written lately, Madam, because I relapsed, and have been so very ill, the gout falling on my lungs, that I did not know whether before my letter could set out for Ampthill, I should not be obliged to add a postscript from another world, and send you a new direction—but I am recovered, and have even been out twice to take the air. This time indeed my recovery was a little artificial, and not entirely owing to my own management and to my Herculean weakness. Sir John Elliot[1] had happened to attend my housemaid[2] and would not take a fee—to prevail, I pretended to talk on my own gout, and he was so tractable, and suffered me to prescribe to him what he should prescribe to me, without giving me powder of volcanos and other hot drugs, that I continued to see him, and I do believe that at the crisis, I should not have conducted myself quite so judi-

A *Trip to Calais*, written in 1776, satirizing the Duchess of Kingston (as Lady Kitty Crocodile), through whose influence the Lord Chamberlain prohibited it; revised and acted as *The Capuchin*. HW had a copy of the two plays printed together, 1778 (Hazen, *Cat. of HW's Lib.* 1810:27.5).

10. Act I, scene ii.

11. Pilâtre de Rosier, tired of waiting for a favourable wind to take his balloon from Boulogne to England, went to Calais, 'where he embarked in a packet boat, which he thought a less dangerous vehicle than a balloon at this season of the year, and arrived in London' (*London Chronicle* 4–6 Jan., lvii. 21).

1. Sir John Elliott (1736–86), Kt, 1776, cr. (1778) Bt; M.D. St Andrews, 1759; physician to the Prince of Wales.

2. Perhaps Martha Fare, to whom in his will, 1793, HW left £100; she sent a visitor to SH in 1792 (SELWYN 362; BERRY ii 240).

ciously as he did.[3] This is making very honourable *amende* to the college whom I have always treated with contempt; but as I love my own veracity still more than my own way, I do not haggle about confessing the truth.

As I don't know that your Ladyship is particularly devoted to Hippocrates, perhaps I have tired you by my recantation—but I had nothing of more worth to tell you, and only wrote to excuse my silence.

Your aunt Lady Dowager Gower[4] is dying of a similar accident to poor Lady Strafford's,[5] in whom the mortification is said to be begun. As much as I shall pity Lord Strafford, it is impossible to be sorry for her. She had burnt off one ear, part of the other, and was likely to lose one of her eyes.

The news of my coffee-house, since I began my letter, is, that Lady Strathmore[6] eloped last night, taking her two maids[7] with her—but no swain is talked of.[8] The town, they say, is empty—it certainly does

3. HW wrote to Lord Sandwich ca 26 Jan. 1785 'that Sir John Eliot has forbidden his seeing anybody for a few days.'

4. Lady Mary Tufton (1701 – 12 Feb. 1785), m. 1 (1718) Anthony Grey, Lord Lucas, styled E. of Harold; m. 2 (1736) John Leveson-Gower, cr. (1746) E. Gower. 'On Friday last [4 Feb.] as the Countess Dowager of Gower, who resides at Bill Hill [in Berkshire], about 30 miles from town, and who is aged upwards of 80, was standing too near the fire, her clothes were caught by the flames; her cries alarmed the family, and the butler was the first who entered the room and instantly rolled her up in the carpet; but she was so terribly burnt that her recovery is not expected' (*London Chronicle* 5–8 Feb., lvii. 136; her death is noted ibid. 19–21 Feb., lvii. 179). She was Lord Ossory's step-grandmother, not his aunt, his mother being a child of Lord Gower's first marriage.

5. She died 7 Feb. 'after nine weeks of dreadful sufferings from falling into the fire in a fit' (HW to Thomas Walpole the younger 19 Feb. 1785; *London Chronicle* 10–12 Feb., lvii. 148). 'The servants, on opening her dressing-room door, one winter's day, discovered her lying senseless against the grate, too much burned for

recovery, although she lingered. . . . This manner of dying was shocking; the event itself not to be regretted, as her intellects were already impaired by the epileptic disease, and she would probably have become utterly imbecile had she lived a very little longer' (Lady Louisa Stuart, *Selections from Her Manuscripts*, ed. Hon. J. A. Home, Edinburgh, 1899, p. 46).

6. Mary Eleanor Bowes (1749–1800) m. 1 (1767) John Lyon (from 1767, Bowes), 7th E. of Strathmore; m. 2 (1777) Andrew Robinson Stoney (from 1777, Bowes), from whom she separated in 1785. He abducted her 10 Nov. 1786, but she escaped from him and obtained a divorce 3 March 1789.

7. Mrs Mary Morgan, widow, Lady Strathmore's 'own woman' since 1784, and Ann Parkes, the housemaid (*A New Collection of Trials for Adultery*, 1799, containing the trial of 'the Countess of Strathmore and her husband Andrew Robinson Stoney Bowes, Esq.,' pp. 24–9; *The Trial at Large* [30 May 1787] *of Andrew Robinson Bowes, Esq. . . . for a Conspiracy against Elenor Bowes, Commonly Called Countess of Strathmore*, 'taken in shorthand by J. Johnson,' n.d., pp. 6–7).

8. Lady Strathmore on the night of 3–4 Feb. left her house in Grosvenor Square,

not produce its usual complement of extravagances, when one solitary elopement of a veteran madwoman is all that is at market.

To Lady Ossory, ca March 1785

Written before Princess Amelia's death in 1786, possibly in May 1783 when the younger Mme d'Andlau (MANN vi. 176, n. 16) was apparently in London (GM 1783, liii. 446). HW's hand and tone suggest a later date.
Address: To Lady Ossory.

IF IT is possible that Madam d'Andelot should know that there is such an antediluvian as I remaining, why would not your Ladyship be so good as to say that Strulbrugs are dispensed with from making visits?—if I must, I must—so the first dark night, I will order my coffin and pair, and *appear* to her.

I want to ask when your Ladyship will do me the honour to dine in my burying-ground—but till I have been at the Princess's, tonight, I do not know when I shall be at liberty to take up my bed and walk. I wish it might be this day sennight, but I will send to your Ladyship tomorrow morning and settle it.

To Lady Ossory, Tuesday 7 June 1785

Address: To the Countess of Ossory at Ampthill Park, Bedfordshire. *Postmark:* 7 IU.

Berkeley Square, June 7, 1785.

THOUGH you had declared yourself on the wing, Madam, you took your flight before I was aware, or I should have attempted to make you a parting bow. People, who *have* paid their bills, are not apt to fly from town so rapidly. You have time to cool indeed, perhaps not to dry yourselves, for June, that is not often in debt for rain, seems likely to discharge all his arrears. I question however whether

and on 7 Feb. 'exhibited articles of the peace in the Court of King's Bench against her husband, for ill treatment of her person: her Ladyship desired to have the protection of one of the tip-staves to her house, which was complied with' (*London Chronicle* 5–10 Feb., lvii. 136, 142). 'He procured ample bail' and kept the peace until he had her abducted on 10 Nov. 1786; see *post* 1 Dec. 1786; *London Chronicle* 21–23 April 1785, lvii. 386; *The Trial at Large . . .* , p. 2. On 28 Feb. 1785 she sued him for divorce on the grounds of adultery and cruelty (ibid. 4).

a deluge will replace the leaves before the mid-summer shoots: the tops of all my elms are as naked as in the first days of November; chafers and nabobs—I mean, caterpillars, have stripped them stark.

Mr B.[1] wrote, I conclude, when he was mad or drunk, probably the latter, for he seems to have had sober intervals enough to flatter every man who is or may be a minister. His advertisement[2] is of a piece with Miss Bellamy's.[3]

The poor milkwomans'[4] poetry is published,[5] and the charity, I

1. James Boswell, whose *Letter to the People of Scotland, on the Alarming Attempt to Infringe the Articles of the Union, and Introduce a Most Pernicious Innovation, by Diminishing the Number of the Lords of Session* had just appeared (*London Chronicle* 31 May–2 June, lvii. 524; F. A. Pottle, *The Literary Career of James Boswell*, Oxford, 1929, pp. 108–12). For HW's copy, now wsl, see Hazen, *Cat. of HW's Lib.* 1609: 47. Boswell's presentation copy to Lord Ossory is now owned by Mr and Mrs Donald F. Hyde.

2. In the *London Chronicle*, loc. cit., appeared an advertisement which Professor Pottle considers 'certainly of Boswell's writing': 'This day was published . . . *A Letter to the People of Scotland* . . . Topics.—The security of the Union destroyed; the Presbyterian kirk in danger . . . Mr Dundas's prodigious power . . . sketches of the Lord High Chancellor Thurlow, Earl of Lonsdale, Earl of Upper Ossory, Lord Palmerston, Lord Advocate of Scotland, Hon. Colonel James Stuart, Sir Matthew White Ridley, Mr Burke, Mr Lee, Mr Wilkes, Captain M'Bride, Mr Fox, Mr Pitt, a Great Personage.' Of Lord Ossory Boswell says in *A Letter* . . . : '. . . I am very vain to sit at the table of FITZPATRICK: the respect for whose ancient and noble blood is not lessened, but increased, by the character of its present representative; which, as I feel, is saying a great deal. I flatter myself FITZPATRICK was convinced [by Boswell's previous argument]. If he was—I'll answer for it, all the world shall not make him flinch' (pp. 68–9).

3. George Anne Bellamy (1731?–88), actress, author of *An Apology for the Life of George Anne Bellamy, Late of Covent Garden Theatre*, 'Written by Herself,' and said to be edited by Alexander Bicknell;

five volumes had appeared in January and had reached a third edition in March; and a sixth volume was published 21 May (*London Chronicle* 17–21 May, lvii. 477, 487). For both the five volumes and the sixth, elaborate advertisements listed the complete index of names; for the five volumes the advertisement was over two columns and for the sixth almost one column. See the *London Chronicle*, Jan.–June, lvii. 69, 103, 152, 198, 294, 487, 503. Advertisements for Boswell's pamphlet and the sixth volume of the *Apology* appear ibid. 31 May–2 June, lvii. 524.

4. Ann Cromartie (1752–1806) m. (1774) John Yearsley; known as 'Lactilla' or 'the Bristol Milkwoman'; befriended in 1784 by Hannah More, who was instrumental in getting a distinguished list of subscribers for her poems. See MORE 218 *et passim*.

5. *Poems, on Several Occasions*, 'By Ann Yearsley, a Milkwoman of Bristol,' published 'in the first week of June,' 1785, with two editions later in the year, and the fourth edition in 1786 (J. M. S. Tompkins, *The Polite Marriage*, Cambridge, 1938, p. 198). HW is listed among the subscribers, and one poem is addressed to him: 'To the Honourable H——E W——E, on reading *The Castle of Otranto*. December 1784,' pp. 87–96. HW's copy is now at Harvard, with 'June' written by HW on the title-page (Hazen, *Cat. of HW's Lib.* 3222:20). In the *London Chronicle* 4–6 Jan., lvii. 19, the discovery of a 'literary phenomenon,' Ann Yearsley, is reported, and 'The Primate of Ireland, the Bishop of Salisbury, Hon. Horace Walpole, Mrs Montagu, and other distinguished characters, have taken this extraordinary genius under their patronage, and are raising subscriptions for settling her in a boarding school.'

imagine, equal whether by subscribing or buying the book. She seems to have a conscious dignity of mind, which I like better than her verses, and which is a greater rarity than middling poets, or even than middling poetesses—I am a little sick of the Hayleys and Miss Sewards, who are like common milkwomen who borrow tankards and flowers of all their acquaintance for May-day.[6]

You tell me, Madam, that you only wrote to receive a letter—you do receive only your own letter back again, paragraph by paragraph. In truth I am superannuated, and know nothing, do nothing, am fit for nothing. I have been three days alone at Strawberry, and nowhere else but to dine at Gunnersbury last Friday, with the Conways, Harcourts, Mount Edgcumbes and Mrs Howe. I expected that Lady Harcourt[7] would every now and then say *your Majesty* instead of *your Royal Highness*. My Lord too is quite Count Castiglione[8] the perfect courtier.[9] General Conway, who never remembers what anybody is or was, asked him, on speaking of Handel's music at Westminster Abbey,[10] whether his Lordship had been in waiting! concluding he was a lord of the Bedchamber.[11]

This is all my journal contains, Madam—but what better can you expect from a Strulbrug? and one so insipid as to be content with being so?—nay, it is not an unpleasant state. Having outlived all one's passions and pursuits, and not having acquired avarice in lieu, one sits down tranquilly like an old sailor that has been in many storms, and sees the crowd bustling and jostling or playing the fool, and feels the comfort of idleness and indifference, and the holiday

6. For the May Day celebration of milkwomen and chimney-sweeps see P. J. Grosley, *A Tour to London* . . . , 1772, i. 183–4; Samuel Curinen, *Journals and Letters,* New York, 1845, p. 54; a print (reproduced in W. S. Lewis, *Three Tours through London,* New Haven, 1941, p. 78) is in the *Wit's Magazine,* 1784.

7. Who had been lady of the Bedchamber to the Queen since 7 Aug. 1784 (*London Gazette* No. 12566, 3–7 Aug. 1784). She held the post until the Queen's death in 1818 (GM 1818, lxxxviii pt ii. 561).

8. Count Baldassare Castiglione (1478–1529), author of *Il Libro del Cortegiano,* 1528.

9. HW later wrote that Lord and Lady Harcourt 'became a proverb even to courtiers, of the most servile attachment to their Majesties, though both had forsworn St James's, on the King's and Queen's neglect of them on the unfortunate death of the Earl's father' (MASON ii. 322). After Lady Harcourt's appointment, 'Lord H. was constantly dangling in the Drawing-Room' (ibid. 348).

10. On Thursday, 2 June, the first of four Handel concerts given in 1785, following the success of the commemoration in 1784. See GM 1785, lv pt i. 484; *London Chronicle* 21 April – 14 June, lvii. 388 (which lists all three programs).

11. Harcourt was Master of the Horse to the Queen 1790–1809, his only Court appointment.

luxury of having nothing to do. Don't you think the retired trades-man, whose journal is in the *Spectator*,[12] was a happy being? He played with his cat,[13] and strolled to Mother Redcap's,[14] if the weather was fair, and had no uneasiness, but when his friend the politician (I forgot his name)[15] prognosticated war. There I am happier: I am past and below political apprehensions, and have so little time left, that the events of all futurity might as well disturb my imagination, as, perhaps, the next that are to happen. Even returns of pain, of which I have suffered so much, have little terror for me—I cannot feel a quarter of what I have felt, I mean in point of duration; and should they be violent, I have not strength to struggle with them—but I beg your pardon, Madam, though I can but smile with thinking how you will be disappointed on receiving, instead of a letter, the reflections of a Strulbrug on his own inanity. When Swift drew the character, he did not know it—poor man! the turbulence of his own temper, and the apprehensions of his own decay, made him conceive it as a miserable condition—on the contrary it is almost a gay one, when one can be sensible of it and of all its enjoyments. I would tell you more of it, Madam, if it were capable of any variety; but as its uniformity is one of its felicities, you people of the world who have no taste for sameness, would not be diverted with the particulars: 'Tomorrow, and tomorrow, and tomorrow'—all alike. Tonton is as principal an actor as the tradesman's cat, but he has more vivacity, though he is not mad, as your Ladyship apprehended when he bit Lord Ossory's finger; indeed he can bite but little more than your obedient servant his master.

To Lady Ossory, Monday 20 June 1785

Address: To the Countess of Ossory at Ampthill Park, Bedfordshire. *Post-mark:* ISLEWORTH. 21 ⟨IU⟩.

Strawberry Hill, June 20, 1785.

I GIVE your Ladyship a thousand thanks for the crown of laurel you sent me: I tried it on immediately; but it certainly was never made for me; it was a vast deal too big and did not fit me at all; it

12. No. 317.
13. No cat is mentioned.

14. Mother Cob's.
15. Mr Nisby.

must have been designed for one of double my size—besides as I never wear so much as a hat, it would make my head ache—and then too, as nobody in the village has worn a sprig of laurel since Mr Pope's death, good Lord! how my neighbours would stare, if I should appear with a chaplet, to which I have no more title than Lord de Ferrers to the Earldom of Leicester.[1] I will not be such a bear as to send back your Ladyship's favour; but if you would give me leave to present it to poor Mr Hayley or Mr Cumberland, who ruin themselves in new laurels every day, it would make them as happy as princes; and I dare answer that either of them would write an ode upon you, not quite so good perhaps, yet within an hundred thousand degrees as excellent as Major Scott's,[2] and at least better than Mr Warton's.[3] However though I am no poet yet, I don't know what I may come to, if I live. I have just written the life of a young lady in verse, in which perhaps I have too much affected brevity, though had I chosen to spin it out by a number of proper names, more falsehoods, and a tolerable quantity of anachronisms, there was matter enough to have furnished as many volumes as Miss Bellamy's Memoirs.[4] Mine I have comprised in these four lines,

> Patty was a pretty maid;
> Patty was of men afraid;
> Patty grew her fears to lose,
> And grew so brave she lost her nose.[5]

1. George Townshend (sometime El-lerker) (1753—1811), 4th Bn Ferrers and Bn Compton, 1770; cr. (1784) E. of Leices-ter; 2d M. Townshend, 1807; F.S.A., 1777; F.R.S. 1781; President of the Society of Antiquaries 1784–1811. For his descent 'from the old Earls of Leicester of the house of Beaumont,' see GEC vii. 561–2 n.

2. John Scott (1747–1819), major in the service of the East India Company; M.P. West Looe 1784–90; zealous but tactless agent for Warren Hastings. HW refers to 'Number XII.' Ode, by 'Major John Scott, M.P., &c. &c.,' in Probationary Odes for the Laureateship, 1785, a work by several authors, including Richard Fitzpatrick. (It was 'No. X' when reprinted in the European Magazine, June 1785, vii. 434–5). For HW's copy, see Hazen, Cat. of HW's Lib. 2318. The ode attributed to Scott is said to have been written by Lord John Townshend (The Rolliad, 22d edn, 1812,

now WSL, with identifications from a copy given by R. B. Sheridan to Alderman Combe and from the publisher Ridgway's copy).

3. Following the death of Whitehead on 14 April 1785, Thomas Warton had been appointed poet laureate 27 April (London Gazette No. 12642, 26–30 April 1785). His first official performance was his 'Ode for His Majesty's Birthday, June 4, 1785,' printed in the London Chronicle 2–4 June, lvii. 533, and reprinted verbatim in Proba-tionary Odes for the Laureateship, No. XXIII.

4. The length and style of Bellamy's Apology, six volumes, led the authors of Probationary Odes for the Laureateship to quote her testimony in favour of Sir Cecil Wray supposedly from the 'Ninth volume of Mrs George Anne Bellamy's Apology, now preparing for the press.'

5. These lines, titled 'Epigram,' are in

As the world is now so overstocked with anecdotes, I don't know whether it will not be advisable for future English biographers to aim at my conciseness, and confine themselves to quatrains. Dr Johnson's history, though he is going to have as many lives as a cat, might be reduced to four lines; but I shall wait to extract the quintessence, till Sir John Hawkins,[6] Madame Piozzi[7] and Mr Boswell[8] have produced their quartos.[9] Apropos, Madam, t'other night I was sitting with Mrs Vesey; there was very little light; arrived Sir Joshua Reynolds, and a person whom I took for Mr Boswell. I sewed up my mouth,[10] and though he addressed me two or three times, I answered nothing but Yes or No. Just as he was going away, I found out that it was Mr Richard Burke,[11] and endeavoured to repair my causticity. I am not quite in charity with Sir Joshua; he desired to come and see my marvellous Henry VII[12]—when he saw it, he said, 'It is in the old hard Flemish manner.'—for hard, it is so bold, that it is one of the great reasons for doubting its antiquity; and for Flemish, there is nothing Flemish in it, except a chiaroscuro as masterly as Rubens's— but it is not surprising that Sir Joshua should dislike colouring that has lasted so long!

I went last week to see a new piece[13] by Okeeffe, my favourite author next to Major Scott. Harry Fox was in the box; I asked him if he

HW's 'Book of Materials' 1786, p. 62 (first numbering) with 'modest' instead of 'pretty.'

6. His *Life of Samuel Johnson, LL.D.* was published in 1787. HW's copy, now wsl, is described in Hazen, *Cat. of HW's Lib.* 412.

7. Hester Lynch Salusbury (1741–1821) m. 1 (1763) Henry Thrale; m. 2 (1784) Gabriel Piozzi. Her *Anecdotes of the Late Samuel Johnson, LL.D. during the Last Twenty Years of His Life* was published in 1786 (see *post* 27 Jan. 1786; HW to Mann 28 March 1786); for HW's copy, now wsl, see Hazen, op. cit. 3826.

8. His *Life* did not appear until 1791. HW's copy, now in the Dyce Collection in the Victoria and Albert Museum, is described ibid. 3294.

9. The first two are in octavo, the last in quarto.

10. 'Lord Holland, speaking of Boswell, whom he remembered, said that whenever he came into a company where Horace Walpole was, Walpole would throw back his head, purse up his mouth very significantly, and not speak a word while Boswell remained' (C. R. Leslie, *Autobiographical Recollections*, 1860, i. 155).

11. (1733–94), younger brother of Edmund Burke.

12. 'On the window-side' of the Great North Bedchamber at SH: 'Henry VII, a most capital portrait on board, and incomparable for the truth of nature, expression and chiaroscuro' (*Works* ii. 498). 'Mr Walpole convinced himself that this portrait was painted by Mabuse' (Kirgate's notes in 'Des. of SH,' *Works* ii. 498, transcribed in copy owned in 1821 by C. M. Hodges and now wsl). The picture was sold SH xx. 89 to Lord Holmsdale (2d E. Amherst, 1857) for £31.10.0. Sir Joshua's objection to the 'stiff drapery' of the picture is mentioned in *Walpoliana* i. 23.

13. *A Beggar on Horseback*, first acted at the Haymarket 16 June (gm 1785, lv pt i. 470).

had ever seen *The Agreeable Surprise*. He said No; I cried it up to the heavens—He was much surprised at *The Beggar on Horseback*, and asked me if *The Beggar on Horseback* was like *The Agreeable Surprise*. The new piece is very low to be sure, and yet it diverted me —but you know I like extremes, and next to perfect wit, perfect nonsense, when it is original. A sort of folly I do not admire is air-balloons—but I believe their reign is over;[14] they say Monsieur Pilatrier[15] and another man[16] have been burnt to cinders;[17] and Mr Sadler[18] has not been heard of yet.[19]

The old mad drunken Duke of Norfolk[20] is going to be married again to a Miss Eld,[21] who is forty years old and a Protestant.[22]

14. 'It is thought the melancholy exits of M. Pilâtre de Rosier and his . . . companion will in some measure check the too-soaring ideas of the many candidates for aerial fame' (*St James's Chronicle* 18–21 June).

15. Jean-François Pilâtre de Rozier (1756 – 15 June 1785), the first to ascend in a balloon, 1783, died in attempting to cross the Channel from Boulogne to England. He had been in England in May and early June and had dined with Lord Orford at Epping 4 June. He was engaged to an Englishwoman, Susan Dyer (*London Chronicle* 21 May – 23 June, lvii. 490, 587, 592, 600; GM 1785, lv. 565; J. E. Hodgson, *The History of Aeronautics in Great Britain*, Oxford, 1924, pp. 160–1 *et passim*).

16. Pierre-Ange Romain (ca 1761 – 15 June 1785), attorney and aeronaut; 'ancient procureur au bailliage de Rouen' (Auguste d'Hauttefeuille and L. Bénard, *Histoire de Boulogne-sur-mer*, Boulogne-sur-mer, 1860, ii. 37–9; *London Chronicle* 5–7 July, lviii. 19; *La Vie et les mémoires de Pilâtre de Rozier, écrits par lui-même*, ed. Tournon de la Chapelle, 1786, p. 66).

17. *London Chronicle* 16–18 June, lvii. 578: 'Wednesday [15 June] a balloon was launched from Boulogne in France, which took up Monsieur Pilâtre du Roziere and another gentleman; when they were at an amazing height, the balloon took fire, burnt the cords by which the car was suspended, and the above gentlemen were dashed to pieces in a manner too shocking to mention.' Further details appear ibid. 25–28 June, lvii. 611.

18. James Sadler (1753–1828), of Oxford, who made his first ascent there 4 Oct. 1784, 'the first Englishman to pilot an aeronautical machine through the air.' See J. E. Hodgson, *The First English Aeronaut: James Sadler, of Oxford*, privately reprinted (from the *Cornhill Magazine*, April, 1928), 1928, *passim*; *London Chronicle* 7–9 Oct., 13–16 Nov. 1784, lvi. 352, 476; *European Magazine*, 1785, vii. 384, 386–7.

19. Sadler 'has been missing, and is supposed lost in the German Ocean . . . Sadler, whom I thought lost, is come to light again' (HW to Mann 24 June 1785).

20. Whose wife had died 21 Nov. 1784. In the *Town and Country Magazine*, Oct. 1785, xvii. 513–16, he appears as 'The Venerable Admirer' of 'The Captivating Miss J[a]rv[i]s,' a woman of the town who came to the Duke of Norfolk.

21. Perhaps Catherine Eld who m. Dr Kirby of Dorking; she was dau. of John Elde (ca 1704–96) of Dorking, and sister of Francis Eld (1736–1817) of Seighford Hall, Staffs (Burke, *Landed Gentry*, 1952). The Duke of Norfolk's branch of the Howard family was from Dorking. The marriage did not take place. Lady Mary Coke heard the rumour at the Duchess of Montrose's 13 June 'of many marriages, some of which are too improbable to make them worth naming, but one that is affirmed to be true, however ridiculous, is the Duke of Norfolk and a Miss Elde who I have not seen for many years but remember about twenty years ago, a tall thin person with a neck like a swan, black

Tuesday.

I could not finish my letter yesterday, for Lord Sandwich who was to breakfast with me, arrived sooner than I expected. He brought Mr Noble with him, the author of the history of the Cromwells,[23] and Mr Selwyn came to dinner with us, and the latter stayed all night. Lord Sandwich has taken the patronage of Mr Noble, as Hinchinbrook was the residence of Oliver,[24] and the second edition will be much more accurate and curious than the first.[25] I could but look with admiration at the Earl, who at our age[26] can enter so warmly into any pursuits and find them amusing! It is pleasant to have such spirits, that after going through such busy political scenes, he can be diverted with carrying a white wand at Handel's jubilee[27]—and for two years together! Do you think Lord Lansdown would be content with being master of the ceremonies at Bath? The papers tell a different story from mine of poor Pilatrier's exit. I hope it will prevent Mr Fitzpatrick from such an expedition.[28] It would be silly to break one's neck in going no whither; don't you think so, Madam?

hair, and not a dust of powder. She is as is said about forty-four or -five . . .' ('MS Journals' 14 June 1785).

22. The Duke of Norfolk's son, who succeeded him in 1786, had renounced the Roman Catholic faith in June 1780 at the time of the Gordon Riots.

23. HW at Sandwich's request took his annotated copy of the book to London (HW to Sandwich 1 Jan. 1785). The correspondence between Sandwich and Noble is now in the Bodleian (Eng. Misc. d. 150, 151). Sandwich forwarded HW's letter to him of 1 Jan. 1785: 'I enclose a letter which I think will give you no small pleasure; the approbation and assistance of so eminent a character in the literary world as Mr Walpole, cannot but be extremely flattering and advantageous to you.'

24. Not the Protector, but his uncle Sir Oliver lived at Hinchingbrooke. HW makes the same mistake in Montagu ii. 79. It was the seat of the Cromwell family from 1538 to 1627, when Sir Oliver sold it to Henry Montagu, 1st E. of Manchester, who sold it to his brother Sir Sydney Montagu, ancestor of the Earls of Sandwich, Viscounts Hinchingbrooke (GEC, sub

Sandwich). For HW's description of the house and its pictures, see *Country Seats* 49–50; HW to Montagu 30 May 1763, Montagu ii. 79.

25. The first edition was severely handled by Richard Gough in the preface to his *Short Genealogical View of the Family of Oliver Cromwell*, 1785, pp. v–xviii, *Bibliotheca Topographica Britannica*, Vol. VI, and both editions are criticized in GM 1787, lvii pt i. 516–18, and by William Richards of Lynn in *A Review of the Memoirs . . . in Which the Errors of Those Memoirs Are Pointed Out*, Lynn, 1787. W. C. Abbott, *A Bibliography of Oliver Cromwell*, Cambridge, Mass., 1929, p. 189, calls it 'a mine of minor information' and quotes DNB: 'some useful facts amid a mass of error.'

26. HW was thirteen months older than Sandwich.

27. In 1784 for the Handel commemoration Sandwich was one of five directors, in 1785 one of four honorary vice presidents, and in 1786 the honorary president (*London Chronicle* 25–27 May 1784, 21–23 April 1785, 18–20 April 1786, lv. 512, lvii. 388, lix. 372).

28. See *post* 30 June 1785.

To Lady Ossory, Thursday 30 June 1785

Strawberry Hill, June 30, 1785.

Icarus Icariis nomina fecit aquis—[1]

THANKS to the powers of the air that Mr Fitzpatrick has not
new-christened the Thame or the Isis! nor dyed the Saxon White
Horse black! Why did he ascend from Oxford?[2] He should have left
the laureate[3] to get another fall from *the White Horse*.[4] Mr Fitzpatrick had given ample proofs of his spirit before, and therefore
I hope he will now lie on his arms.

As to me, Madam, if I gathered a chaplet and crowned myself, at
least your Ladyship planted the tree, of which I plucked a branch.
You did not utter the words *crown of laurel,* but you did say I was
reposing under my own laurels, therefore I may justly plead with our
prime ancestor that *the woman tempted me and I did eat*—yet I did
not swallow a leaf—but no more of that!

I can make as just a defence on my omission of Lord Barrington,[5]
of which here is the simple narrative. As he was an obscure Pres-

1. Ovid, *Tristia* I.i.90: 'Icarus, æquoreas
nomine fecit aquas' (Icarus gave a name to
waters of the sea).

2. On 24 June, 'behind Corpus Christi
College,' Sadler's balloon was inflated. 'At
two o'clock . . . Col. Fitzpatrick and Mr
Sadler seated themselves in the car, when
the balloon was found incapable of ascending with both the passengers, and the
Colonel being resolved not to quit his seat
. . . after receiving the flag and proper
instructions from Mr Sadler, he ascended
alone. . . . The Colonel manifested a cool
intrepidity . . . He descended near Kingston Lisle, opposite the White Horse Hills,
Berks' (*London Chronicle* 25–28 June, lvii.
611). This is 'probably the earliest instance
in England of an amateur balloonist
undertaking a solo flight with no more
than a few verbal instructions received the
moment before ascending' (J. C. Hodgson,
The First English Aeronaut: James Sadler,
1928, p. 12).

3. Thomas Warton.

4. Fitzpatrick had descended near the
White Horse of the Saxons near Uffington,
Berks. The last squib in the preliminaries
to *Probationary Odes for the Laureateship*
(see preceding letter) is 'A Full and True
Account of the Rev. Thomas Warton's
Ascension from Christ-Church Meadow,
Oxford (in the balloon of James Sadler,
Pastry-Cook to the said University), on
Friday, the 20th of May, 1785, for the pur-
pose of composing a sublime Ode in hon-
our of his Majesty's Birth-Day; attested
before John Weyland, Esq. one of his
Majesty's Justices of the Peace for the
County of Oxford.' At the end of this supposed account, Warton is made to refer
to himself as 'the first Literary Aeronaut
of these kingdoms.'

5. John Barrington (1678–1734), cr.
(1720) Vct Barrington; M.P. until expelled
from the House of Commons, 1723, for
having promoted the lottery of Harburg.
A brief version of the anecdote which follows is in *Walpoliana* i. 44.

byterian writer,[6] I had never heard of him when I published my first edition.[7] Being then told of him, I asked his son, the present Lord, for a list of his works. His Lordship, conscious that his parent, who had been a great rogue, had better be forgotten, desired as a favour that I would *not* repair the omission—and therefore I did not. His brother the Bishop of Salisbury,[8] who was not so discreet, and who did not like to lose the authorship out of the genealogy, inserted his father's life in the new *Biographia,*[9] and in grateful return for my *noli pro-sequi,* ascribed the punishment of his own father's knavery to an act of revenge in mine. In short, the late Lord Barrington was expelled the House of Commons for being concerned in a gross bubble called *the Hamburgh Lottery,*[10] and the Bishop pretends (which his father himself never did) that the expulsion was procured by Sir Robert Walpole, because Lord Barrington, who twice sold the Presbyterians to the Court, had been attached to Lord Sunderland[11]—Lord Barrington in the next edition of the *R[oyal] and N[oble] Authors* will find his proper place,[12] though he did not in the first edition—nor in the pillory.

6. For more than a dozen works by him, chiefly religious, but also philosophical and political, see DNB and BM Cat.

7. Of *Royal and Noble Authors,* 1758. Barrington was called to HW's attention late in 1759 or early in 1760; see CHATTERTON 370.

8. Hon. Shute Barrington (1734–1826), Bp of Llandaff, 1769, of Salisbury, 1782, and of Durham, 1791 (BERRY i. 288 and nn. 30–1).

9. *Biographia Britannica,* ed. Andrew Kippis, five volumes and part of a sixth, published 1778–95. Joseph Towers, author of the biography of Barrington (i. 624–8), acknowledges assistance from the Bishop of Llandaff, 'who hath obligingly communicated to us some of the facts above mentioned, as well as several pieces written by his Lordship's father, and which have been enumerated in this article' (p. 628). See also HW to Cole 10 Sept. 1778, COLE ii. 120–3.

10. So in MS; HW's slip for *Harburgh.* A £1,500,000 lottery (£1,000,000 in prizes), advertised in the *Flying Post, or Postmaster* 2–4 Dec. 1722, and launched by the Harburgh Company, of which George I's grandson, Prince Frederick, later Prince of Wales, was governor and Barrington sub-governor. A Parliamentary inquiry found it to be 'an infamous and fraudulent undertaking' upon evidence that of the £500,000 profits arising from the lottery only £210,000 were intended for capital stock, the balance to be accounted for under 'managing the lottery' (*Journals of the House of Commons* xx. 115–25, sub 1 Feb. 1722/3).

11. Charles Spencer (ca 1674–1722), 3d E. of Sunderland, 1702; Sir Robert Walpole's predecessor as first lord of the Treasury 1718–21. The account of the Harburg lottery comes not from Bishop Barrington but from Sir Michael Foster (1689–1763); first printed in *Biographia Britannica* i. 625–6.

12. HW inserted a brief account of Barrington in the 1770 edition of *Works* (printed but not published), p. 523; after the appearance of the first volume of *Biographia Britannica,* 1778, he defended Sir Robert in a much longer account, pp. 546–51 (printed in 1787). For the dates of printing, see Hazen, *SH Bibliography* 89. Both accounts were first published in *Works,* 1798, i. 523, 543–8.

I beg you will send for a new book called *Letters of Literature* by Robert Heron Esq.[13] It is an extraordinary work, in which there is a variety of knowledge and a great mixture of parts. There are several things to which I do not at all agree—others much to my mind—but which will not be popular. I never heard of *Robert Heron* before, but he does not seem to design to remain in obscurity, nor averse to literary warfare, whence I conclude he is young; and you will see from every page, Madam, that he will not want antagonists.[14]

I have been for two or three days in town, where I heard two Hessian French horns,[15] who are reckoned super-eminent. They are as reasonable as March[16] the tooth-drawer, they ask BUT ten guineas for an evening. I heard too what diverted me more, an impertinence of Mr Hastings[17] when he was last in England.[18] Lord Huntingdon by way of acknowledging him, told him he believed they were related —'No, my Lord,' said Hastings, 'I am descended from Hastings Earl of Pembroke'[19] meaning that he was of the elder branch[20]—judge

13. The pseudonym of John Pinkerton (1758–1826), antiquary and historian, whose correspondence with HW is printed in CHATTERTON 251–328. The *Letters* were published 11 July (*Morning Chronicle* 11 July 1785). For HW's copy of *Letters of Literature*, now in the Boston Public Library, see Hazen, *Cat. of HW's Lib.* 3825. On p. 342 Pinkerton refers to 'Mr Walpole, in his admirable *Catalogue of Royal and Noble Authors*,' and on p. 384 to 'Mr Walpole's account of his *Castle of Otranto* being a translation from the Italian . . . wherein strict truth is sacrificed to the pleasure of the hearer.'

14. For the attacks and Pinkerton's replies, see HW to Pinkerton 17 Sept. 1785, CHATTERTON 278–80 and nn. 1–3.

15. Presumably Johann Palsa (1752–92) and Karl Türrschmidt (1753–97), duo players, who appeared as soloists in a 'Concerto for French Horns' 2 March 1786 of the following season, in one of Salomon's subscription concerts at the 'Assembly Rooms, Hanover Square' (*Morning Herald* 2 March 1786), and 'had . . . played previously at the Anacreontic Society' (W. T. Parke, *Musical Memoirs*, 1830, i. 63, *sub* 1786). From 1770 to 1783, Palsa and Türrschmidt were in the service of Jules, Prince de Guéménée, on whose bankruptcy

in 1783 they were engaged by Friedrich II, Landgrave of Hesse-Kassel; in 1786 they entered the Berlin Royal Orchestra (R. Morley-Pegge, *The French Horn*, 1960, pp. 157–8; Sir George Grove, *Dictionary of Music*, 5th edn, ed. Blom, 1954; C. F. Pohl, *Joseph Haydn*, Leipzig, 1878–1927, ii. 143; Arthur Schurig, *Wolfgang Amadeus Mozart*, Leipzig, 1913, ii. 191).

16. See *ante* 26 Nov. 1780, n. 39.

17. Warren Hastings (1732–1818) had landed at Plymouth 13 June 1785.

18. From 16 June 1765, when he reported to the Directors of the East India Company his arrival in England, until late in March 1769, when he sailed from Dover (Keith Feiling, *Warren Hastings*, 1954, pp. 53, 61).

19. Laurence de Hastinges (1320–48), cr. (1339) E. of Pembroke, by virtue of his descent from the eldest sister of Aymer de Valence, E. of Pembroke.

20. According to Feiling, op. cit. 1–4, and A. Mervyn Davies, *Strange Destiny A Biography of Warren Hastings*, New York, 1935, pp. 7–9, Warren Hastings was descended from neither the Pembroke nor the Huntingdon line, but from an equally old but humbler branch of the Hastings family, which came to England with the Conqueror.

how the blood of Clarence[21] boiled! 'I thought,' said the Earl, 'that there were no descendants of that branch left but the Marchioness of Grey'[22]—and turned on his heel. I wish he had replied, 'I thought *you* was only of the branch of green Hastings.'[23]

I am now settled on my hill, a melancholy widower—Lady Browne has left Twickenham.[24] As she was my newsmonger, I shall know even less than I used to do. All this morning I have been busy in placing Henry VII in the State Bedchamber and making a new arrangement of pictures. It is really a very royal chamber now and much improved. Besides the family of Henry VIII over the chimney as before,[25] and Queen Maintenon over one of the doors,[26] there are Henry VII[27] and Catherine of Braganza,[28] on one side of the bed; Henry VIII[29] and Henriette Duchess of Orléans[30] on the other.[31] There will be a much

21. George Plantagenet (1449–78), cr. (1461) D. of Clarence, brother of Edward IV and Richard III; his great-grand-daughter had married the 2d E. of Huntingdon.

22. Jemima Campbell (1722–97), Marchioness Grey, 1740, in succession to her maternal grandfather Henry Grey; m. (1740) Philip Yorke, 2d E. of Hardwicke, 1764. For her descent from the Hastings family, see GEC, *sub* Grey of Ruthin; Kent (earldom and marquessate); and Hastings, especially Chart A, which shows that Marchioness Grey was descended from a daughter of the first Lord Hastings.

23. Hasting, 'an early-ripening fruit or vegetable' (OED).

24. See HW's letters to her 1785–90 for her various residences (MORE, *passim*).

25. 'Over the chimney, a large picture of Henry VIII and his children; bought out of the collection of James West, Esq. in 1773. *See a description of this curious piece in the Anecdotes of Painting*' ('Des. of SH,' *Works* ii. 494; for the description, *Works* iii. 115n.). See also HW to Cole 7 April 1773, COLE i. 305 and n. 10; the picture, now attributed to Hans Eworth (fl. 1547–73), is in the possession of Mrs Brocklehurst, Sudeley Castle, Glos (Lionel Cust, 'The Painter HE,' in the *Walpole Society, 1912–1913*, ii. 1–44, and especially pp. 39–40 and Plate XXII).

26. Also as before: 'Over the doors . . . Madame de Maintenon' (*Works* ii. 496);

sold SH xx. 107 (attributed to Mignard) to Lord Northwick for £42.

27. Which had been 'On the window side' (*Works* ii. 496, 498).

28. It had been 'On the window side. . . . Over the glass, the original portrait of Catherine of Braganza, that was sent from Portugal previous to her marriage with Charles II and from which Faithorne scraped his print: a present from Richard Bull, Esq.' (*Works* ii. 496); 'it was found at a lodge in the New Forest in 1778 in a very dirty condition, and serving as a cover to a table, by Rich'd Bull Esq. who gave it to Mr W.' (HW's MS note in his copy of *Des. of SH,* 1774, now WSL). It was sold SH xx. 94 to Lord Holmsdale (2d E. Amherst, 1857) for £33.12.0.

29. Moved from the Holbein Chamber: 'Henry VIII, three quarters; a present from the Reverend Mr Pennicott' (*Works* ii. 460); sold SH xxi. 12 (then in the Round Tower: 'A valuable portrait . . . the dress elaborately worked to represent embroidery, a remarkably fine and undoubted picture by this extraordinary master. Holbein') to Norton for £50.8.0; Lot 63 in the John Hugh Smyth Pigott, Brockley Hall Sale 8 Oct. – 7 Nov. 1849.

30. Henrietta Anne (1644–70), dau. of Charles I, m. (1661) Philippe, Duc d'Orléans. Her portrait was moved from 'The Round Bedchamber, Two Pairs of Stairs': 'Henrietta Duchess of Orléans, as Pallas; bought at Lady Suffolk's sale'

prettier room soon at the other end of the village: Lady Di is painting another,[32] with small pictures framed with wreaths of flowers—

—Flowers worthy of Paradise![33]

there is already a wreath of honeysuckles, surpassing her own lilacs,[34] and such as she only could paint and Milton describe; and there is a baby Bacchus so drunk! and so pretty! borne in triumph by bacchanalian Cupids.[35] Twickenham does not vie with the pomps of Stowe, [36] but like the modest violet, 'qui se cachoit sous l'herbe,'[37] has its humble sweets.

(*Works* ii. 506); sold (attributed to Mignard) SH xx. 119 to Emanuel for £23.2.0; sold (owner not given, 'different properties') Christie's 12 Feb. 1926, lot 81, to Willis for £60.18.0.

31. The pictures HW replaced were 'On one side of the bed, a whole length of Henry Vere Earl of Oxford, in his robes. . . . On the other side, Robert Walpole, second Earl of Orford; whole length, in robes of the Bath; by Vanloo' (*Works* ii. 495). At the time of the SH sale in 1842 the first was on the 'Landing and Stairs' near the Round Tower (xxi. 18); the second, which HW 'bought at Sir Everard Falkener's Sale, £3.3.0' (HW's note in his copy of the 1774 *Des. of SH,* now WSL), is not in the Sale Catalogue. According to MS notes by both Kirgate and Mrs Damer in their copies of the *Des. of SH,* it was 'Since given to Mrs Keppel.'

32. In her villa, Little Marble Hill, which she occupied until 1789 (HW's note quoted below; BERRY ii. 36 n. 4; R. S. Cobbett, *Memorials of Twickenham,* 1872, pp. 245–6; *Gazetteer and New Daily Advertiser* 22 Feb. 1791; HW to Thomas Walpole the younger 8 April 1786; Mrs Steuart Erskine, *Lady Diana Beauclerk,* 1903, pp. 109, 199, 244 *et passim*).

33. Milton, *Paradise Lost* iv. 241.

34. In a room she had painted earlier. See HW to Mason 4 Aug. 1782, MASON ii. 272 and nn. 11–14; BERRY ii. 252 and n. 3.

35. 'After Mr Beauclerk's death she bought the small but most beautifully

situated house next to Marble Hill, and opposite to Ham House. There she painted in the boldest style, though in watercolours, a room hung with green paper, which she adorned with large festoons of lilacs, and the surbase with wreaths of different plants, in a style superior to the greatest flower-painters. She afterwards painted another room there on brown paper with lunettes of peasants and children, chained together by garlands of different flowers, which were still more excellent and natural than even the lilacs. . . . She left that house in 1789, and bought another, next to the Duke of Montagu's, at the foot of Richmond Hill, and there painted another room with flowers on treillage in a style equally natural and masterly. The paintings on brown in the second room she gave to her sister the Countess of Pembroke. For her brother Lord Robert Spencer she painted a whole room in panels on velvet in Berkeley Square' (HW's MS note to the Postscript to 'The Parish Register of Twickenham,' in his *Des. of SH,* 1774, now WSL).

36. In Buckinghamshire; the great house of the Grenvilles.

37. 'Madame de Sévigné in her letter to Madame de Grignan of Sept. 1, 1680, refers to Madame de la Vallière as "cette petite *violette qui se cachoit sous l'herbe,* et qui était honteuse d'être maîtresse, d'être mère, d'être duchesse" ' (Toynbee; see Sévigné, *Lettres,* ed. Monmerqué, 1862–6, vii. 52–3).

To Lady Ossory, Monday 4 July 1785

Strawberry Hill, Monday night, July 4, 1785.

I WRITE again so quickly, Madam, not to detain Mr Fitzpatrick's letter, for which I give you many thanks, and which you must value, as it is so very sensible and unaffected an account of his aerial jaunt, and deserves to be preserved in your Milesian archives;[1] for whether aerostation becomes a professional art, or is given up with the prosecution of the Tower of Babel and other invasions on the coast of Heaven, an original letter under the hand of one of the first airgonauts will always be a precious curiosity.

I have just been reading a work by a new noble authoress, a princess of the blood of Clarence, and a lady deeply versed in the antiquities of the country where the great Brian Mac Gill Patrick was seated,[2] as well as of the Phœnicians, Egyptians, Gauls, etc. It is the present Countess of Moira[3] whose letter to her son[4] is in the new seventh volume of the *Archæologia,* and gives an account of a skeleton and its habiliments lately discovered in the county of Down and Barony of Linalearty.[5]

Oh! but I have better news for you, Madam, if you have any patriotism as a citizen of this world, and wish its longevity. Mr Herschell

1. Vernon Smith's note ii. 225: 'I am sorry it is not, at least, I cannot find it.' Fitzpatrick's letter to William Windham, written from 'Grosvenor Place, London, June 27, 1785,' describes his flight (*The Windham Papers,* 1913, i. 81–2, reprinted, with slight omissions, in J. E. Hodgson, *The History of Aeronautics in Great Britain,* Oxford, 1924, pp. 147–8).

2. Ireland. See *ante* 4 Dec. 1771 (to Lord Ossory), n. 8.

3. Elizabeth Hastings (1731–1808), who, as dau. of the 9th E. of Huntingdon, was descended from George, D. of Clarence, m. (1752) John Rawdon, cr. (1762) E. of Moira. Her literary and social merits are described in the *Annual Register,* 1808, pp. 150–1, of the 'Chronicle.' HW did not include her in *Royal and Noble Authors, Works,* 1798. He apparently had not seen two letters by her on experiments in the making of cloth from flax, or the two in *Transactions of the Society . . . for the Encouragement*

of Arts, Manufactures, and Commerce, 1783, i. 202–13, although he was a member of the Society; see following letter.

4. Hon. John Theophilus Rawdon (1757–1808), her 2d son; M.P. Appleby 1791–6, Launceston 1796–1802 (John Debrett, *Peerage,* 1817, i. 371, gives 1756 as date of birth).

5. 'Particulars relative to a Human Skeleton, and the Garments that were found thereon, when dug out of a Bog at the Foot of Drumkeragh, a Mountain in the County of Down, and Barony of Kinalearty, on Lord Moira's Estate, in the Autumn of 1780. In a Letter to the Hon. John Theophilus Rawdon, by the Countess of Moira; communicated by Mr Barrington. Read May 1, 1783,' *Archæologia,* 1785, vii. 90–110. Lady Moira refers to the Phœnicians on p. 107, the Egyptians or Egypt on pp. 101, 107, and the Gauls on pp. 96–8, 101, 105. HW's copy, now WSL, contains no annotation.

has found out that our globe is a comely middle-aged personage, and has not so many wrinkles as several stars, who are evidently our seniors.[6] Nay, he has discovered that the Milky Way is not only a mob of stars,[7] but that there is another dairy of them[8] still farther off; whence I conclude comets are nothing but pails returning from milking, instead of balloons filled with inflammable air, which must by this time have made terrible havoc in such thickets of worlds, if at all dangerous—now I shall descend, as if out of a balloon, from the heavens to the milkwoman.[9] It is no doubt extraordinary that the poor soul should write tolerably—but when she can write tolerably, is not it extraordinary that a Miss Seward should write no better? I am sick of these sweet singers, and advised that when poor Mrs Yearsley shall have been set at her ease by the subscription, she should drive her cows from the foot of Parnassus and hum no more ditties.[10] For Chatterton, he was a gigantic genius, and might have soared I know no[t] whither. In the poems, avowed for his,[11] is a line, that Rowley nor all the monks in Christendom could or would have written, and which would startle them all for its depth of thought and comprehensive expression from a lad of eighteen—

Reason a thorn in Revelation's side![12]

I will read no more of Rousseau; his *Confessions* disgusted me beyond any book I ever opened.[13] His hen, the schoolmistress, Mad-

---

6. This conclusion was presumably an unpublished utterance by Herschel; it does not appear in the contemporary *Philosophical Transactions of the Royal Society* nor in his collected scientific papers. In 1789, Herschel 'saw quite clearly where this conception of the degree of condensation as an index of age [of nebulæ] was leading him' (J. B. Sidgwick, *William Herschel*, 1953, p. 184). 'The papers since 1784 contain numerous indications that ideas on the evolutionary aspect of the cosmos were stirring in Herschel's mind' (ibid. 189).

7. 'On applying the telescope to a part of the *via lactea*, I found that it completely resolved the whole whitish appearance into small stars' (Herschel's 'Account of Some Observations Tending to Investigate the Construction of the Heavens,' read before the Royal Society 17 June 1784 and

printed in his *Scientific Papers*, 1912, i. 158).

8. 'One of these nebulous beds is so rich, that in passing through a section of it, in the time of only 36 minutes, I detected no less than 31 nebulæ' (ibid. i. 160).

9. Ann Yearsley.

10. See HW to Hannah More 13 Nov. 1784, MORE 220–1, where this advice is less bluntly stated.

11. *Miscellanies in Prose and Verse*, 'by Thomas Chatterton,' 1778, and *A Supplement to the Miscellanies*, 1784.

12. 'Vide Chatterton's "Defence," p. 36, in the *Supplement* to his *Miscellanies*, Becket, 1784' (HW in 'Book of Materials' 1786, p. 11). HW placed an asterisk opposite this line in his copy (now WSL) of Chatterton's *Miscellanies*.

13. Hazen, *Cat. of HW's Lib.*, lists no copy of the *Confessions*.

ame de Genlis,[14] the newspapers say is arrived in London.[15] I nauseate her too; the eggs of education that both he and she laid, could not be hatched till the chickens would be ready to die of old age.[16] I revere genius; I have a dear friendship for common sense; I have a partiality for professed nonsense; but I abhor extravagance that is given for the quintessence of sense; and affectation that pretends to be philosophy. Good night, Madam!

PS. Pray tell me where your new library is placed. The parson of Teddington[17] and his wife[18] were robbed at half an hour after nine last night by three footpads with pistols at my back gate. My housekeeper heard the bustle from her room that is over the Holbein Chamber. I was in the library, but knew nothing of the matter till today—It is agreeable to have banditti at one's door!

To Lady Ossory, Saturday 9 July 1785

The first paragraph is here first printed.

Strawberry Hill, July 9, 1785.

THE *Letters of Literature* are to be had of G.G.J. and J. Robinson[1] in Paternoster Row.

I am sorry Lord Ossory has any Irish difficulties great or small.

I made no commentary on General Oglethorpe's death, Madam,

14. Stéphanie-Félicité Ducrest de Saint-Aubin (1746–1830) m. (1763) Charles-Alexis Brulart, Comte de Genlis, later Marquis de Sillery; dramatist and educational writer; mistress of the Duc de Chartres (Duc d'Orléans from 18 Dec. 1785) and 'governor' to his children.

15. No newspaper paragraph announcing her arrival has been found. She got to London about 25 June and returned to Paris 27 July (Amédée Britsch, *La Jeunesse de Philippe-Égalité*, 1926, pp. 413–16).

16. Her educational theories, partly derived from Rousseau, had been presented in the *Théâtre à l'usage des jeunes personnes* (later called *Théâtre pour servir à l'éducation*), 1779–80; *Adèle et Théodore, ou Lettres sur l'éducation*, 1782, English tr., 1783; *Veillées du château*, 1784. No

work by her is listed in Hazen, *Cat. of HW's Lib.*

17. John Cosens (1736–91), D.D. Edinburgh, 1769; vicar (perpetual curate) of Teddington 1761–91; tutor to the Princess Royal, to whom he addressed *Windsor: An Ode* (Hazen, op. cit. 3222:16.26; Venn, *Alumni Cantab.*; BM Cat.; Halkett and Laing; BERRY ii. 233; Daniel Lysons, *Environs of London*, Vol. III, 1795, p. 511).

18. —— m. 1 —— Hart; m. 2 (1774) John Cosens, she being at that time 'of Brentford'; m. 3 (1797) 'at Finmere, the Rev. Mr Harvest, rector of Milbrook, Hants' (GM 1774, xliv. 238; 1797, lxvii pt ii. 1069).

————

1. George, George the younger, James, and John Robinson.

because his very long life was the great curiosity; and the moment he is dead, the rarity is over; and as he was but 97,[1a] he will not be a prodigy compared with those who reached to a century and half. He is like many who make a noise in their own time from some singularity, which is forgotten when it comes to be registered with others of the same genus but more extraordinary in their kind. How little will Dr Johnson be remembered, when confounded with the mass of authors of his own calibre!

I said no more on the Duchess of Bedford's broken wrist, because I did not know of it. The Duchess of Montrose told me she was said to have broken her leg, but that it was not true; and that she had given a public breakfast the next day, but did not appear at it herself, so I concluded she had only miscarried of a broken leg[2]—but ah! Madam, when old folks break their wrists by tottering out of their own houses, is not it a just reason for my not daring to think of clambering up ladders to range books at Ampthill, though I should have more pleasure in it, than the Duchess could have at a ball at five in the morning? I could delight too in playing with Lady Anne's orrery, and I could prattle on the planet that rolled under your Ladyship's feet[3]—but when I am sensible of the lameness of my feet, why should I be more indulgent to my head? I talked nonsense enough on astronomy in my last, and I will not again violate a maxim that I have laid down to myself, and which I believe so true, that it ought to be repeated daily to old people, like Saladin's *Remember thou art mortal!*[4] This is my maxim, 'When a man's eyes, ears, or memory, decay, he ought to conclude that his understanding decays too, for the weaker it grows, the less likely he is to perceive it.'

When you send for Mr Heron's book, you may write too for the seventh volume of the *Archæologia,* in which you will find a few pages

1a. 'He died July 1, 1785, aged 97' (HW's note in his copy, now WSL, of *Archæologia,* 1785, vii. 59). He was only eighty-eight, but estimates of his age ranged as high as 104.

2. 'The Duchess of Bedford has broke her arm in coming down the stairs at Bolton House last Monday [4 July]. She was to have a great breakfast on Wednesday and would not put her company off, so they all came. But her Grace could not receive them. She is, however, in a good way' (Coke, 'MS Journals' 9 July 1785). 'Her late accident . . . was a violent sprain of her wrist and a fracture of the smaller bone in the forearm' (*Morning Chronicle* 12 July).

3. HW is recalling her appearance as Cleopatra at the Duke of Richmond's masquerade, 6 June 1763, 'when you looked like the Empress of the Universe' (*ante* 3 June 1778).

4. 'Remember you grow old' (*ante* 22 Sept. 1776).

amusing, amongst several that don't know their own meaning. I early translated the title of these volumes, *old women's logic*,[5] and seldom do they contradict me, witness the first dissertation in the present,[6] *cum multis aliis*—but there is a very sensible discourse p. 303, on the religion of the Druids,[7] in which the writer,[8] unlike his companions, demolishes fantastic reverence for barbarians,[9] instead of discovering arts and sciences amongst rude nations, who had nothing but labour, and time to spare, and who put one in mind of Lord Abercorn's[10] answer to the gentleman who complimented him on the growth of his trees, 'They had nothing else to do.'[11] I have lately dipped into D'Ancarville's[12] two volumes,[13] in which he ascribes universal knowledge and invention to the Scythians, as Bryant did to the Lord knows whom;[14] but with all my pertinacity in reading

<hr>

5. For HW's use of this title 1771–7, see COLE i. 218–19, 270, 304, and MASON i. 239, 319. HW resigned from the Society of Antiquaries 13 July 1772 (H.S. Kingsford to WSL 30 July 1937).

6. 'Observations on an Inscription on an Ancient Pillar now in the possession of the Society of Antiquaries,' *Archæologia*, 1785, vii. 1–18.

7. 'A Dissertation on the Religion of the Druids. Addressed to Governor Pownall. By Edward Ledwich, LL.B. Vicar of Aghaboe, Queen's County, Ireland; and Member of the Antiquary Societies of London, Dublin, and Edinburgh. Read November 11, 1784,' pp. 303–22. On p. 303 HW noted in his copy, now WSL, 'This is a very sensible dissertation. H.W.'

8. Edward Ledwich (1738–1823), of Trinity College, Dublin (B.A. 1760, LL.B. 1763); vicar of Aghaboe 1772–97; friend of Richard Gough and Francis Grose.

9. Ledwich attacks several writers who glorified the Druids.

10. James Hamilton (1712–89), 8th E. of Abercorn, 1744.

11. At Duddingston House, Abercorn's seat near Edinburgh, 'Dr [William] Robertson, the celebrated historian, not aware . . . [that Lord Abercorn was 'highly offended if any person presumed to visit him without the formality of a card of invitation'], went to pay his respects . . . and found him walking in a shrubbery which had been lately planted. The Doctor, wishing to pay a compliment to the

soil, observed the shrubs had grown considerably since his Lordship's last visit; "They have nothing else to do," replied his Lordship; and immediately turning on his heel, left the Doctor without uttering another word' (GM 1789, lix pt ii. 961).

12. Pierre-François Hugues (1719–1805), called D'Hancarville; antiquary; compiler of *Collection of Etruscan, Greek, and Roman Antiquities from the Cabinet of the Honble Wm Hamilton*, Naples, 1766–7, 4 vols folio (Hazen, *Cat. of HW's Lib.* 3536; NBG).

13. *Recherches sur l'origine, l'esprit et le progrès des arts de la Grèce; sur leurs connections avec les arts et la religion des plus anciens peuples connus; et sur les monuments antiques de l'Inde, de la Perse, du reste de l'Asie, de l'Europe, et de l'Égypte*, London, 1785, 2 vols quarto, with 74 plates. 'Le livre est resté incomplet, parce que l'auteur, piqué des critiques dirigées contre les deux premiers volumes, ne l'a pas achevé. Le troisième volume est un supplément [1785] en réponse aux censures' (A.–A. Barbier *et al.*, *Dictionnaire des ouvrages anonymes*, 1872–9, iv. 31). There is no record that HW owned these volumes (Hazen, *Cat. of HW's Lib.* 3536).

14. In his *A New System, or, An Analysis of Ancient Mythology: Wherein an Attempt Is Made to Divest Tradition of Fable . . . In This Work Is Given an History of the Babylonians, Chaldeans, Egyptians, Canaanites, Helladians, Ionians,*

quartos, I could not wade through the tautology and impertinence of D'Ancarville's, though he has lately been here to draw a bronze I have of Ceres with a bull in her lap;[15] and because I have this ugly morsel, I suppose he will call me, *the ingenious and learned,* as Mr Daines Barrington[16] does[17]—and I had rather they would box my ears, for it is calling one a fool that has taken his degrees. Now I declare I have no more regard for the Phœnicians, Pelasgians, Vics, Egyptians, Edomites, Scythians and Gentoos, than I have for Madame de Genlis. I read such books as I do Mrs Bellamy's, and believe in them no more.[18] The one nation worth studying was the Greeks. In the compass of two or three centuries half a dozen little towns, or rather one town, scarce bigger than Brentford, discovered the standard of poetry, eloquence, statuary, architecture and perhaps of painting and music—and then *the learned* have the impertinence to tell one that the Grecians borrowed from the Egyptians, Tartars, Indians, etc. That is, they stole the genuine principles of all beauty and all taste from every idea of deformity and absurdity! The Apollo and the Venus from mummies and idols with four heads, more hands, and two legs as immovable as oaks in an avenue! I concentre my admiration in the few centuries of Greece, and for that marvellous period in the Roman history, when five excellent princes, though possessed of absolute power, succeeded to one another, Nerva, Trajan, Hadrian, and the two Antonines[19]—This is not learning: the learned are busied in inquiring how long the world has blundered without discovering what was worth knowing.

Leleges, Dorians, Pelasgi: Also of the Scythæ, Indo-Scythæ, Ethiopians, Phenecians, 3 vols quarto, 1774–6. HW's copy is listed in Hazen, *Cat. of HW's Lib.* 3161. HW mentioned to Cole, 25 April 1775 (COLE i. 368), that Bryant in this work was 'sublime in unknown knowledge.'

15. In the Gallery; sold SH xxiii. 109 to Cope for £73.10.0; sold at Christie's 7 June 1872, lot 52 (property of Charles Cope, Esq., deceased) for £15.0.0 to Calvetti; engraved from D'Hancarville's drawing in Richard Payne Knight, *An Account of the Remains of the Worship of Priapus,* privately printed, 1786, Plate VIII, Fig. 1, with a reference to it on p. 124: 'In an ancient bronze at Strawberry Hill this goddess is represented sitting, with a cup in one hand, and various sorts of fruits in the other; and the bull, the emblem of the power of the Creator, in her lap.'

16. Hon. Daines Barrington (1727–1800), son of 1st Vct Barrington; antiquary and naturalist; correspondent of Gilbert White.

17. In the postscript to his 'On the Progress of Gardening. In a letter from the Hon. Daines Barrington to the Rev. Mr Norris, secretary. Read June 13, 1782,' *Archæologia,* 1785, vii. 113–30 (reprinted in the *European Magazine,* July, Aug. 1785, viii. 66–9, 97–100): 'that learned and ingenious antiquary.'

18. Cf. *Walpoliana* i. 67–8: 'To my certain knowledge one half of it [Bellamy] is false; and I therefore believe the whole is in the like predicament.'

19. HW similarly refers to these five

Sunday.

PS. After writing my letter, I learnt that by the new arrangement of the post, it would only have lain in town, and could not depart the same night as usual.[20] For this letter it is no matter; I wrote it merely to give your Ladyship the bookseller's direction, though when my pen began gossiping, it could not stop. When I came from Lady Dysart's last night, I found on my table the annual transactions *de l'Académie* of Arts and Sciences,[21] in which the gold medal to our Lord is recorded,[22] and his gardener's letter,[23] which says he could not make Lombardy poplars grow in wet ground.[24] The lawn beyond my flower-garden was a morass, that I was forced to have drained, yet before the drains were made, Lombardy poplars grew there astonishingly; and the first I ever saw in England General Conway planted at the foot of his mountain close to the Thames, and in three years it was of an amazing height.[25]

emperors in letters to William Robertson 4 March 1759 (DALRYMPLE 50) and to Chute 5 Aug. 1771.

20. With the introduction of John Palmer's mail coaches, beginning in 1784, the mail left London at 8 p.m. instead of midnight. The mail to Ampthill was delivered by mail coach beginning 25 July 1785 (DNB *sub* Palmer, John; Kenneth Ellis, *The Post Office in the Eighteenth Century*, 1958, p. 103; *London Chronicle* 5–8 Feb., 23–26 July, lvii. 136, lviii. 85).

21. *Transactions of the Society . . . for the Encouragement of Arts, Manufactures, and Commerce*, Vol. III, 1785. HW had been a member of the Society (founded in 1754; since 1908, the Royal Society of Arts) since 24 March 1762, was a 'contributing member' who paid three guineas a year instead of the usual two, and owned the *Transactions* 1783–96 (GRAY i. 37; *Transactions*, 1783, i. 306; Hazen, *Cat. of HW's Lib.* 2957). Lord Ossory is listed among the 'contributing members elected since the publication of the first volume of the Society's *Transactions*'; as a 'perpetual member' he paid 20 guineas 'at one payment' (*Transactions*, 1783, 1784, i. 278, ii. 260).

22. 'In . . . 1782, the Society were informed a large plantation of wood has been made, by . . . the Earl of Upper Ossory, near Ampthill in Bedfordshire; and although no application had been

made to the Society for any premium offered on that subject, yet they judged proper to inquire into the nature and extent of those improvements; and after receiving the information contained in the following letters, presented to the Earl of Upper Ossory their GOLD MEDAL, as a mark of their approbation of the extensive plantations made by his Lordship near Ampthill' (p. 4).

23. Robert Gibbs, the gardener, wrote two letters, 12 Jan. and 22 Dec. 1783, describing the recent planting of 46 acres at Ampthill Park with 184,000 trees of several kinds (pp. 6–12). In the *Universal British Directory*, 1791–[1798], ii. 47, Gibbs is listed as a freeholder of Bedfordshire.

24. 'I have planted some Lombardy poplars in a poor sandy soil, which do very well, but thrive much better in a moist loam, on which I planted some about seventeen years ago, and they are now near sixty feet high; but in a very wet ground I cannot get them to grow at all' (2d letter, p. 11). The Society offered in 1783, 1784, and 1785 its gold medal for 'planting . . . the greatest number of the Lombardy Poplar or Po Poplar ['called by some the Pine Poplar'], properly fenced and secured, for raising timber' (*Transactions*, 1783–5, i. 78, ii. 283, iii. 231).

25. See also HW to Conway 25, 29 Dec. 1770; BERRY i. 146 and n. 24; Percy Noble,

To Lady Ossory, Saturday 23 July 1785

Address: To the Countess of Ossory at Ampthill Park, Bedfordshire. *Postmark:* ISLEWORTH.

Strawberry Hill, July 23, 1785.

I AM very sorry to hear that the war of bad seasons which has lasted eight months, has affected your Ladyship too. I never knew so much illness—but as our natural season, rain, is returned, I hope you will recover from your complaints. English consumptions are attributed to our insular damps; but I question whether justly. The air of the sea is an elixir, not a poison; and in the three sultry summers which preceded the three last, it is notorious that our fruits were uncommonly bad, as if they did not know how to behave in hot weather. Nay, it is certain, that in our camps there was scarce any sickness when the tents were swimming; whereas in those Italian summers the contrary was fact. I hope I shall not be contradicted by the experience of last night. Mrs Keppel had, or rather was to have had all London at her beautiful villa at Isleworth.[1] Her Grace of Devonshire was to have been there, aye—you may stare, Madam! and her Grace of Bedford too. The deluge in the morning, the debate in the House of Commons,[2] qualms in the first Duchess,[3] and I don't know what, certainly not *qualms,* in the second, detained them, and no soul came from town but Lady Duncannon, Lady Beauchamp,[4] the two Miss Vernons,[5] the Boltons,[6] the Norths,[7] Lord William

---

Park Place, 1905, pp. 61–2, and illustration facing p. 61.

——

1. The house purchased in 1781 by Sir Edward Walpole and inherited by Mrs Keppel at his death in 1784 (*ante* 17 July 1781).

2. The chief topic of debate was the commercial resolutions between Great Britain and Ireland. For this and other matters, see the *London Chronicle* 21–23 July, lviii. 78–9; Cobbett, *Parl. Hist.* xxv. 934–42.

3. Who gave birth to her second daughter 29 Aug.: Lady Harriet Elizabeth Cavendish (1785–1862) m. (1809) Lord Granville Leveson-Gower, cr. (1815) Vct and

(1833) E. Granville; 'Hary–O' in the family circle; author of *Letters 1810–1845,* ed. Hon. F. L. Gower (her son), 1894.

4. Isabella Anne Ingram Shepheard (1760–1834) m. (1776) Francis Seymour-Conway, styled Vct Beauchamp 1750–93 and E. of Yarmouth 1793–4, 2d M. of Hertford, 1794.

5. Lord Ossory's half-sisters, Caroline Maria and Elizabeth; see the last sentence of this paragraph.

6. Harry Powlett (1720–94), 6th D. of Bolton, 1765, m. (1765), Katharine Lowther (ca 1736–1809).

7. Lord and Lady North and perhaps some of their children.

Russel,[8] Charles Windham,[9] Col. Gardiner and Mr Aston,[10] and none of these arrived till ten at night. Violins were ready, but could not play to no dancers—so at eleven the young people said it was a charming night and went to paddle on the terrace over the river, while we ancients to affect being very hot too, sat with all the windows in the bow open, and might as well have been in Greenland! Miss Vernon did not know her brother was set out.[11]

You surprise me, Madam, by saying the newspapers mention my disappointment of seeing Madam de Genlis[12]—how can such arrant trifles spread? it is very true, that as the Hill would not go to see Madame de Genlis, she has come to see the Hill. Ten days ago Mrs Cosway[13] sent me a note[14] that *Madame* desired a ticket for Strawberry Hill.[15] I thought I could not do less than offer her a breakfast, and named yesterday sennight. Then came a message that she must go to Oxford and take her Doctor's degree[16]—and then another, that I should see her yesterday, when she did arrive with Miss Wilkes and Pamela,[17] whom she did not even present to me, and whom she has educated to be very like herself in the face. I told her I could not

8. (1767–1840), 3d son of Francis, M. of Tavistock; M.P. Surrey 1789–1807, Tavistock 1807–19, 1826–30; murdered by his valet (*Old Westminsters*).

9. Hon. Charles William Wyndham (1760–1828), 3d son of Charles, 2d E. of Egremont; secretary and clerk of the enrolments in Jamaica 1775–1816; M.P. Midhurst 1790–5, New Shoreham 1795–1802, Sussex 1807–12 (*Old Westminsters; Royal Kalendar* 1775–1817).

10. Henry Hervey Aston (d. 1798), son of Henry Hervey Aston, of Aston Hall, Cheshire; army officer (*Scots Peerage* v. 19; Collins, *Peerage*, 1812, iv. 152–4; GM 1799, lxix pt i. 527; Foster, *Alumni Oxon.; Army Lists*).

11. Lord Ossory was on a tour; see *post* 19 Aug. 1785.

12. This notice has not been found.

13. Maria Louisa Catherine Cecilia Hadfield (1759–1838) m. (1781) Richard Cosway the miniature-painter; known for her own miniatures, drawings, and etchings, and for her elaborate concerts and entertainments, which HW occasionally attended. From 1781 to 1784 the Cosways lived at 4 Berkeley Street, Berkeley Square; from 1784 to 1791 at Schomberg House, Pall Mall (George C. Williamson, *Richard*

Cosway, R.A., 1905, *passim;* Berry i. 285 and n. 14).

14. Missing.

15. Since he entertained her himself, HW did not list her in 'Visitors,' Berry ii. 223.

16. Mme de Genlis in her *Mémoires,* Brussels, 1825, iii. 314, says that 'M. Burke me conduisit à Oxford, où nous passâmes deux jours.' HW's facetious remark is questioned by M. Wahba, 'Madame de Genlis in England,' *Comparative Literature,* 1961, xiii. 227, n. 14. She was at Beaconsfield 16 July (William Windham, *Diary,* 1866, p. 56), and was back in London 22 July, after the Oxford visit (her letter of thanks to Jane Burke, 22 July, in the Fitzwilliam MSS at Sheffield).

17. Pamela (ca 1773–1831), supposed natural dau. of the Duc de Chartres, later Duc d'Orléans, by Mme de Genlis (see *post* 19 Aug. 1785); m. 1 (1792) Lord Edward Fitzgerald; m. 2 (1800) Joseph Pitcairn, American consul at Hamburg. For a full discussion of her birth and parentage, the details of which have never been settled, see Lucy Ellis and Joseph Turquan, *La Belle Pamela (Lady Edward Fitzgerald),* 1924; Amédée Britsch, *Lettres de L.-P.-J. d'Orléans Duc de Chartres à Nathaniel*

attribute the honour of her visit but to my late dear friend Madame du Deffand.[18] It rained the whole time and was dark as midnight, so that she could scarce distinguish a picture—but you will want an account of her, and not of what she saw or could not see. Her person is agreeable, and she seems to have been pretty. Her conversation is natural and reasonable, not *précieuse* and affected and searching to be eloquent, as I had expected. I asked her if she had been pleased with Oxford, meaning the buildings, not the wretched oafs that inhabit it. She said, she had had little time; that she had wished to learn their plan of education, which, as she said sensibly, she supposed was adapted to our Constitution—I could have told her that it is directly repugnant to our Constitution, and that nothing is taught there but drunkenness and prerogative, or, in their language, Church and King.[19] I asked if it is true that the new edition of Voltaire's works[20] is prohibited; she replied, severely[21]—and then condemned those who write against religion and government, which was a little unlucky before her friend *Miss Wilkes*.[22] She stayed two hours, and returns to France today *to her duty*. I really do not know whether the Duc de Chartres is in England or not[23]—She did lodge in his house in Portland Place[24]—but at Paris I think has a hotel[25] where she educates his daughters.[26]

Parker Forth, 1926, pp. 4–5 and n. 2, *et passim*).

18. Mme du Deffand's opinion of Mme de Genlis and Mme de Genlis's account of Mme du Deffand are in DU DEFFAND iv. 293, v. 212, 219, vi. 62–5.

19. Cf. *ante* 12 Sept. 1761, Selwyn's bon mot.

20. *Œuvres complètes*, ed. P.-A. Caron de Beaumarchais *et al.*, [Kehl], 70 vols. Some copies of early volumes are dated 1784; others 1785; the last volume (dated 1789) appeared in 1790 (Georges Bengesco, *Voltaire. Bibliographie de ses œuvres*, 1882–90, iv. 121, 137 *et passim*). HW owned this edition (Hazen, *Cat. of HW's Lib.* 3057).

21. See also HW to Thomas Walpole the younger 25 Oct. 1786. Attempts to hinder, discredit, and prohibit the sale and publication of the edition are discussed in Bengesco, op. cit. iv. 118–21.

22. Whose father had attacked and satirized both in his *Essay on Woman* and the *North Briton*.

23. 'On Saturday [16 July] . . . the Duke de Chartres arrived at his house in Portland Place from France' (*London Chronicle* 16–19 July, lviii. 57). His visit to Sir Henry Fetherstonhaugh at Uppark is recorded ibid. 26–28 July, lviii. 96. Most of the time on this, his third visit to England in 1785, he spent at Brighton with the Prince of Wales. He returned to Paris early in August (Amédée Britsch, *La Jeunesse de Philippe-Egalité*, 1926, pp. 412–13, 478–9).

24. In 1789 he advertised this house to be let or sold (*World* 1 Oct. 1789).

25. Mme du Deffand had written HW 4 April 1780 that the Duc de Chartres 'a fait bâtir une maison [for Mme de Genlis and his daughters] dans un terrain contigu et appartenant à Bellechasse; vous savez que c'est presque à ma porte' (DU DEFFAND v. 219).

26. In 1779 Mme de Genlis was appointed governess to Mlle d'Orléans (1777–82) and her twin sister Louise-Marie-Adélaïde-Eugénie de Bourbon d'Orléans,

Mr Horace Walpole (not myself) called on me yesterday morning, when no will of the Duchess of Portland[27] had been found.[28] He thinks the bulk of the collection will be sold, but that the Duke will reserve the principal curiosities—I hope so, for I should long for some of them, and am become too poor to afford them—besides that it is ridiculous to treat one's self with playthings, when one's eyes are closing.[29]

I hope the visit to Lady Ravensworth and fresh grass will restore your Ladyship's health and looks—I send this response to Ampthill as you have given me no direction.

To LADY OSSORY, Wednesday 10 August 1785

Endorsed in an unidentified hand: I send you this on account of the paragraph about Lady Euston. I forgot to do so before. You will be so good to return them all.

Address: To the Countess of Ossory at Ampthill Park, Bedfordshire. *Postmark:* ISLEWORTH. 10 AU. 11 AU.

Strawberry Hill, Aug. 10, 1785.

I WAS just getting into my chaise with Mr Jerningham to go to Park Place on Friday when I received the honour of your Ladyship's letter, and consequently could not answer it so punctually as I generally do. We saw the new bridge at Henley,[1] which is complete

(1777–1847) called Mlle de Chartres (DU DEFFAND iv. 469, v. 165; MASON ii. 302). In 1782 she became 'gouverneur' of the Duke's sons as well, an unprecedented appointment which caused considerable comment (MASON ii. 181; [A.-G.-L. Pellepore], *La Vie privée du Duc de Chartres, aujourd'hui Duc d'Orléans,* 'Par une Société d'Amis du Prince,' 1790, pp. 73–5).

27. Who had died 17 July at Bulstrode.

28. After reporting on 24 July that the will could not be found, Lady Mary Coke in her 'MS Journals' wrote 26 July 1785: 'The Duchess . . . made a will and has given to the Duke [her son] all the best pictures which she had bought and are at Bulstrode. She has likewise given him all her jewels, a cabinet of valuable medals, and a cabinet left her by her father full of gems, and other valuable curiosities to

which she added. She has left to Lady Wallingford a hundred a year for her life. To Mrs Delaney two snuff boxes and a picture, the legacy she had told the Duke she desired. She then makes Lady Weymouth, Lady Stamford, and Lord Edward Bentinck executors and residuary legatees. What they will get cannot at present be told; her personal estate must be great, and everything is ordered to be sold. Money I have not heard she has left, but there are no debts, and eight thousand pounds due to her from her estates. You may depend on this account as I had it from Lady Bute.'

29. For HW's purchases at the sale, see *post* 5 July 1786.

1. 'This beautiful bridge was built [that is completed] in 1787, from designs of a

on one side, and is most beautiful; the bend of the arch was regulated by General Conway himself on three centres, and for grace does not veil the bonnet to the Ponte di Trinità at Florence. His daughter's head of the Thame is placed and has charming effect—the Isis is fixed too, but not yet uncovered.[2] They are going—not the Thame and Isis, but the father and daughter, with the Duke of Richmond to Jersey,[3] and I hope the sea air will be of service to her, for I think her far from well.

I had heard, Madam, of Lady Euston's felicity in being agreeable to Lady Ravensworth,[4] and of my niece being charmed with her Ladyship. This was no flattery, for it came to me indirectly from a letter[5] to her sister Horatia. Indeed I trust that Lady Euston's calm temper and good sense, which resemble her father's, will always answer to the character I have constantly given of her, and which is just the reverse of what that Tisiphone Lady Greenwich coined for her—or rather lent her from her own superabundant fund of bad qualities.

I have heard since my return that Sir William Hamilton's renowned vase,[6] which had disappeared with so much mystery, is again

---

Mr Hayward; it cost £10,000, and consists of five elliptical arches with balustrades of stone' (Percy Noble, *Anne Seymour Damer*, 1908, p. 80).

2. For illustrations of the masks of Thame and Isis, see ibid. facing p. 79. Noble refers to these masks as the 'most widely known, perhaps, of Mrs Damer's works' (ibid. 79). 'The two faces on the centre arch are the sculpture of Mrs Damer. . . . The arch measures 43 feet across. The enormous stones facing it, and with such a noble effect, were brought from fourteen different countries. The iron cramping them together weighs two tons. The expense was £2,000' (*World*, 23 Oct. 1787).

3. 'I've had a letter from Lady Ailesbury to let me know Mr Conway was returned; contrary winds would not let either the Duke of Richmond or him make the Island of Jersey, and as the Duke had no time to lose they are returned back, and the expedition at an end for the present' (Coke, 'MS Journals' 22 Aug. 1785).

4. On 3 May Lady Mary Coke 'passed the evening with the Duchess of Beaufort. The Dowager Albermarle . . . told us that Lady Ravensworth had sent Lord Euston

five hundred pounds and told him he might draw for the same sum every year, but whether she can assure him that money longer than her life I should doubt' (ibid.). In her will Lady Ravensworth left 'Lord Euston one thousand pounds, and five hundred a year till he is Duke of Grafton, and two thousand pounds apiece to his little girls' (Lady Elizabeth Laura Waldegrave to Anne Clement 22 June 1794, MS wsl).

5. Missing.

6. '. . . some few months before her death she [the Duchess of Portland] was tempted by the celebrated Barberini Vase, imported [in 1784] by the noted virtuoso Sir William Hamilton, minister at Naples, who had purchased it and the head of Jupiter Serapis in basaltes, of Byers [Byres] a cicerone at Rome. The Princess of Palest[r]ina, mother of Prince Barberini, had during her son's minority, to pay her gaming debts, sold these curiosities to Byers for £500 and Byers had resold them to Sir William, as it was also said, for £1000. The Duchess gave £2000 to Sir William for them, a fine cameo of Augustus, and a fragment of an intaglia of Hercules' (HW, *The Duchess of Portland's Museum,*

discovered—not in the tomb, but in the treasury, of the Duchess of Portland, in which I fancy it had made ample room for itself. He told me, it would never go out of England—I do not see how he could warrant that. The Duke and Lord Edward have both shown how little stability there is in the riches of that family[7]—and *mine* has felt how insecure the permanency of heirlooms![8] Lawyers, though so like in many points, are, in respect of their own code, the reverse of churchmen, and set it aside just as they please.

A mightier potentate,[9] who sets aside codes too without ceremony, is going to sell part of his plunder by auction at Brussels. I have seen the catalogues of the jewels[10] and pictures[11] that are to be sold—and I took the trouble of counting them. Of pictures there are above three hundred and thirty—yet by some numbers left in the margin, it looks as if there were not half a quarter of the forfeitures, though I can scarce believe that his Imperial rapacity loves the arts better than money. Sir Joshua Reynolds is gone to see them;[12] yet there are but

ed. W. S. Lewis, New York, 1936, p. 7). At the Duchess of Portland's sale in 1786 the Portland Vase, as it has since been known, was sold to the Duke of Portland for £1029, and HW noted: 'As the Duchess paid £2000 for the Vase, the Jupiter, the Augustus and the Hercules, and the Duke bought the Vase and the Augustus for 1265, and as the Jupiter and Hercules produced but £220, the Vase and Augustus really cost the family £3045' (MS note in HW's copy of the Sale Catalogue, 1786, now WSL, p. 194). It has been in the British Museum since 1810, when the Duke of Portland lent it for exhibition. For an account and illustration of the vase, see GM 1786, lvi pt i. 97–8 and Plate I.

7. The Duke's 'fortune . . . had been noble; but obscure waste, enormous expense in elections . . . and too much compassion for an idle and worthless younger brother [Lord Edward Bentinck] . . . had brought him into great distresses' (*Last Journals* ii. 448; MASON ii. 265; COLE i. 229 n. 6). Lady Mary Coke recorded in her 'MS Journals' 23 Dec. 1777: 'Last night it was said at the Princess Amelia's that there had been an execution in the Duke of Portland's house. I don't affirm this . . . to be true; yet a few days ago I heard he did not pay the Duchess his mother what

he had engaged to pay, and this I had from the best authority.'

8. An allusion to the sale of the pictures at Houghton; see *ante* 1 Feb. 1779.

9. Joseph II, Emperor of Germany.

10. *Catalogue de diamants roses et autres, rubis . . . et autres pierres, ainsi que de perles*, Brussels, 1785; sold 21 July 1785 in 134 lots (Hazen, *Cat. of HW's Lib.* 2303; Lugt 3925).

11. *Catalogue d'une collection de tableaux de plusieurs grands maîtres . . . provenant des maisons religieux supprimées aux Pays-Bas, dont la vente se fera au couvent des ci-devant Riches Claires*, Brussels, 1785; sold 12 Sept. 1785 and following days in 270 lots of pictures and 1 lot of sculpture (Hazen, *Cat. of HW's Lib.* 2303; Lugt 3938).

12. He left London 20 or 21 July and returned before 10 Aug. (the date of this letter), when Boswell breakfasted with him (F. W. Hilles, *The Literary Career of Sir Joshua Reynolds*, Cambridge, 1936, pp. 73–7; Reynolds, *Letters*, ed. Hilles, Cambridge, 1929, pp. 131–5; *London Chronicle* 21–23 July, lviii. 80). Reynolds 'was much disappointed in the pictures of the suppressed religious houses; they are the saddest trash that ever were collected together. . . . I was shown some of the pictures

three of Rubens, two of Vandyck, one of Snyder, and half a dozen of Jordan. The rest are of old Flemish masters, and most being large altar pieces and too big for private houses, I should think would not sell well. It is said that the Catholics will not purchase such sacrilegious goods—but we virtuosos are seldom so scrupulous.

Of pearls there are more than seventeen thousand—probably small, and four thousand and six hundred diamonds, all roses, besides table diamonds. I used to imagine that most of the precious stones one sees in churches were false, concluding priests were too wise to lose the interest of their treasures. However, this sale confirms a contradictory opinion that I formed long ago, which was that the bushels of diamonds, rubies and pearls with which the portraits of Henry VIII and Queen Elizabeth are so gorgeously decked, had been embezzled from convents. The present profusion will lower their own value.

Cæsar is said to have already realized three millions sterling by the suppression of monachism[13]—and by that wealth he will purchase a deluge of blood!—*Such reformers* make one regret Popery! Indeed Mother Reformation herself was too dearly purchased. Had I been Luther, and been really conscientious, which I doubt whether he was, and could have foreseen by what torrents of gore the Church was to be purified, I should have asked myself whether for the benefit of any number of future millions of souls, I had a right to occasion the slaughter of a present million of lives—I should have hesitated on my mission—and I believe not have taken out my patent.[14]

I have been told that when this Austrian bird of prey set about his reform, the nobility of Flanders presented a memorial to him, observing that most of the monastic had not been royal foundations,

which were reserved by the Emperor, which were not a jota better than the common run of the rest of the collection' (Reynolds to the Duke of Rutland, 22 Aug. 1785, *Letters*, p. 134).

13. After the death of Maria Theresa, 29 Nov. 1780, Joseph II lost no time in beginning his reforms, fostering religious tolerance by the edict of tolerance 13 Oct. 1781, and suppressing the monasteries of the 'contemplative Orders, which he condemned as useless, allowing only the Congregations occupied with the care of the sick and with teaching to remain. At the end of his reign [1790], 700 out of 2000

convents had disappeared, and the number of monks had been diminished by 30,000' (Eugène Hubert, 'Joseph II,' in *Cambridge Modern History*, ed. Sir A. W. Ward *et al.*, Vol. VI, 1934, p. 636). In Ludwig, Freiherr von Pastor, *Geschichte der Päpste*, Freiburg, 1886–1933, xvi pt 3. 343–4, the number of suppressed houses is said to be only 413, consisting of two thirds of the women's convents, and one third of the men's.

14. This view of Luther and the Reformation appears in HW to Mason 9 June 1780 (MASON ii. 61), to Strafford 26 June 1790, and *post* 1 July 1789, 9 Dec. 1790, 30 April 1791, 10 Sept. 1792.

and therefore they hoped from his Imperial Equity that he would restore to the respective families the lands which their ancestors had given away from their posterity to the Church—Cæsar made no reply —for he could make none that had common sense—but he did not seize an acre or a ducat the less.

Don't imagine that I am changing sides, Madam, because I have some *high church* qualms. It is laudable to suppress convents; but it ought to be done by forbidding any more persons to be professed.[15] It is inhuman to turn those adrift who either entered conscientiously, or are too old to seek a new livelihood by new professions.[16] Besides, when those dear friends the Crown and the Church fall out, I adhere to the latter. Priests get their wealth or power by sense and address; monarchs by force and bloodshed—I am for sharpers against cut-throats.

To Lady Ossory, Friday 19 August 1785

Address: To the Countess of Ossory at Ampthill Park, Bedfordshire. *Postmark:* ISLEWORTH. 20 AU.

Strawberry Hill, Aug. 19, 1785.

I AM glad your Lord is returned so soon, Madam, and has dispatched so many prospects, and recovered of a law-suit, with which I did not know he was afflicted. His expedition and success would qualify him for an ambassador, if to be qualified for an office were a recommendation. I have oft been puzzled to guess why so many fools are sent about Europe on that employment, which seems to demand the utmost sagacity, shrewdness and industry. At last I conceived this solution of my wonder: the incapacities selected are doubtless chosen for the resemblance they bear to the characters of the august personages they are to represent—an observation that

15. Which is the course Joseph II followed in his edict suppressing the Mendicant Friars in the Austrian Netherlands: 'Finally, we strictly enjoin, till our pleasure is further known, that no novice be in future admitted into your order, without the express consent of our Governor General, to whom you may apply on the subject whenever you shall think it indispensable to admit such novices in any of the said monasteries' (*London Chronicle* 18–21 Dec. 1784, lvi. 599).

16. 'Civis,' in a letter from 'Sarum, Dec. 30,' 1784, discusses this view, among others, concerning the suppression of monachism (ibid. 6–8 Jan. 1785, lvii. 31).

escaped the great Wicqfort[1] himself—but perhaps he adapted his precepts to the wise remark of a Spanish grandee to one of the Philips: 'Your Majesty's self is but a ceremony'[2]—Consequently the copy ought not to be of more value than the original.

The newspapers told us of Mr Murray's[3] elopement.[3a] Pray is not it too juvenile a prank at his time of life? And how came the nymph[4] to overlook that circumstance?—a Scot too to commit a disinterested imprudence! Strange!

The Duchess of Portland was a simple woman, but perfectly sober, and intoxicated only by *empty* vases. Other duchesses, it seems, can grow tipsy with lemonade. *The* vase, the two-thousand-pounder, is I hear to be sold again—but who is to buy it? Lady Frances Douglas tells me from the present Duchess of Portland,[5] that there are great

1. Abraham van Wicquefort (1606–82), ambassador and historian; author of *Mémoires touchant les ambassadeurs et les ministres publics*, Cologne, 1676; *L'Ambassadeur et ses fonctions*, The Hague, 1680–1, translated into English, 1716. HW in his 'Book of Materials,' 1759, p. 14, refers to 'Wicqfort's Embassador' for information on Sir Robert Shirley, but there is no record that either work was in HW's library. HW mentions him to Mann 14 June 1769, as the authority on ambassadors.

2. Lord Herbert of Cherbury in his *Life*, SH, 1764, p. 141 (ed. Sir Sidney Lee, 2d edn, rev., n.d., pp. 110–11), *sub* 1619, tells 'the answer a Spanish ambassador made to Philip II King of Spain, who, finding fault with him for neglecting a business of great importance in Italy, because he could not agree with the French ambassador about some . . . pundonore [point of honour] . . . , said to him . . . "How have you left a business of importance for a ceremony!" The ambassador boldly replied to his master . . . "How, for a ceremony? Your Majesty's self is but a ceremony."'

3. James Murray (1727–99) of Broughton, co. Wigtown, and of Cally in the Stewartry of Kirkcudbright; M.P. Wigtownshire 1762–8, Kirkcudbright Stewartry 1768–74; receiver general of land tax, of duties on houses, windows and lights, and of duties on inhabited houses in Scotland 13 Aug. 1783–22 July 1784; receiver

general of land rents and casualties and paymaster in Scotland 12 Sept. 1783–20 Aug. 1784. He resigned all these offices (information kindly supplied by Mr David Erskine: *Scots Peerage* iv. 166; P. H. McKerlie, *History of the Lands and Their Owners in Galloway*, Edinburgh, 1877, iii. 496).

3a. '*Extract of a letter from Edinburgh:* The conversation of the *bon ton* is much engrossed at present by an incident not very usual on this side of the Tweed. Mr M——, of Broughton, a Gentleman of great fortune and connections, and who is moreover on the wrong side of fifty, it is said, has lately made an excursion of gallantry with a young lady of a respectable family, leaving his own lady, the daughter of the E. of G. to sigh alone, and to think of what's past' (*Morning Herald* 12 Aug.; *Morning Post* 13 Aug.; Mr David Erskine).

4. Grace Johnston, dau. of Alexander Johnston of Carnsalloch by Janet Gordon. She bore Murray four children—Grace (b. 4 Nov. 1785), Euphemia (b. 12 Jan. 1788), Alexander (b. 11 Sept. 1789), James Wentworth (b. 24 April 1796)—and survived him (information kindly supplied by Mr David Erskine from the Broughton and Cally Muniments, Register House Accession 1421/440, in the Scottish Record Office).

5. Dorothy Cavendish (1750–94) m. (1766) William Henry Cavendish Bentinck, 3d D. of Portland, 1762.

uncertainties about the will, and that they find it difficult to distinguish what is to be sold, and what not—so probably the lawyers may get more than the auctioneer.

The Bristol lunatic's[6] is a more moving story even than the Heliconian milkwoman's.[7] Miss Hannah More, who is humanity itself, has laboured in the service of both; but the former's case is desperate.[8]

I am much flattered, Madam, by Lady Ravensworth's reading a book[9] on my recommendation, and more by her liking it. I have read it three times, and admired the sensible parts more the last time than the first. If the author can arrive at judgment enough to winnow his grain from the chaff, I think he will make a great figure. He might be bold without being extravagant. What I most dislike in so eccentric and daring a writer is his patience in translating a whole Spectator into his gibberish.[10] Patience is of all others the virtue that seems the least congenial to genius: perseverance is nearer allied to madness than to originality.

As this is a letter of scraps and replies, I will add an answer that I forgot to make to a former question of your Ladyship. Pamela is a child which Madame de Genlis gives out is an English girl, and which she is said to foster with more attention than her own children, or than the princesses of Orléans[11] to whom she is governor, for so she is styled.[12] Sceptics pretend that Pamela is both her own child and a spurious Orléannaise. For fondness, I did not perceive the least: the resemblance is less obscure.

6. Louisa, 'the maid of the haystack'; see HW to Mary Hamilton, Mrs Dickenson, 7 Oct. 1783, 19 July 1785, MORE 207, 233. Additional references are in GM 1801, lxxi pt i. 280–1; European Magazine, 1785, viii. 114–15, 295. Freeman O'Donoghue and Henry M. Hake, Catalogue of Engraved British Portraits . . . in the British Museum, 1908–25, iii. 92, lists a portrait of her, 1788, by W. Palmer, engraved by P. W. Tomkins.

7. Mrs Yearsley, in her 'Clifton Hill. Written in January 1785,' ll. 205–301 (Poems on Several Occasions, 1785, pp. 121–7), relates the story of Louisa and praises Hannah More for her humanity and generosity in helping Louisa.

8. Hannah More had written a 'Tale of Real Woe,' first printed in the St James's Chronicle 10–13 Nov. 1781, and later as a broadside to be used in soliciting subscriptions for Louisa, who was placed in a private asylum in Bristol and later, when she was found to be incurable, in Guy's Hospital (MORE 207).

9. Pinkerton's Letters of Literature.

10. Pinkerton presents (pp. 254–63) Spectator No. 159, 'The Vision of Mirza,' 'in the improved language which I would propose.' The opening sentences: 'When I waz ato Grand Cairo, I picked up several orientala manuscripta, which I havé still by me. Among othera, I met with oné entitulen, Thea Visiona of Mirza, whica I havé redd ové with great pleasuré.'

11. Only one of whom was alive at this time; see ante 23 July 1785.

12. That is, governor of all the Duke's children; see ante 23 July 1785, n. 26.

The Irish propositions[13] seem to me to be brooding a storm. Methinks we have a strange propensity to gaming for our own dominions! France, like an old blackleg, sits by, till the parties are heated, and she can strip the winner. I believe I shall live till we have not a whole island left to our back!

Friday night.

I wrote my letter after dinner before I went to the Duchess of Montrose. The moment after I arrived, Mr Cambridge, who rather than not be the first to trumpet a piece of news, would tell anybody the most disagreeable news, sent a card to acquaint the Duke[14] and Duchess, that after a long debate Mr Orde[15] had withdrawn his Irish bill.[16] This occasioned a consternation, and then a dead silence. I don't believe the officious intelligencer will be thanked—however, I trust this defeat will have saved us from another civil war!

To Lady Ossory, Monday 29 August 1785

Address: To the Countess of Ossory at Ampthill Park, Bedfordshire. *Postmark:* 30 AU. GC.

August 29, 1785.

IT IS flattering and too flattering to me, Madam, to be supposed the author of the *Letters of Literature*. The writer[1] has much more variety of knowledge, and of useful knowledge, and a sounder under-

---

13. On 2 Aug., following debate on the 'Irish Commercial Propositions' from February through July, Pitt introduced a bill for 'regulating the intercourse and commerce between Great Britain and Ireland, on permanent and equitable principles.' For a copy of the bill at this stage, considerably changed from the form earlier passed by the Irish House of Commons, see the *London Chronicle* 4–6 Aug., lviii. 121–4; for the debates, see Cobbett, *Parl. Hist.* xxv. 311–985, *passim*.

14. William Graham (1712–90), 2d D. of Montrose, 1742.

15. Thomas Orde (Orde-Powlett, 1795) (1746–1807), cr. (1797) Bn Bolton; M.P. at this time both Harwich in England, and Rathcormick in Ireland; secretary to the Lord Lieutenant of Ireland 1784–7.

16. As chief secretary for Ireland, he moved, 12 Aug., for leave to bring in a bill 'for effectuating the intercourse and commerce between Great Britain and Ireland on permanent and equitable principles'; his motion passed, 127 to 108, and on 15 Aug. he presented the bill, which was read and ordered to be printed (*Journals of the House of Commons . . . of Ireland* xxii. 586–7). It was based on the 'eleven propositions voted by both houses of the Irish Parliament,' and altered into twenty propositions by the English Parliament; Orde withdrew it because of strong opposition (*London Chronicle* 16–20 Aug. lviii. 167–8, 175–6; 'Mem. 1783–91' *sub* Aug. 1785).

———

1. John Pinkerton.

standing than I have; though I do not think that even thirty years ago I should have written so rashly as he has done, nor so fantastically. Far was it ever from my thoughts to admire Dr Akenside[2] (and to commend him in a work that excommunicates imitators!)[3] or to depreciate Boileau,[4] or not to think Molière a genius of the first water.[5] Who upon earth has written such perfect comedies? for *The Careless Husband*[6] is but one—*The Nonjuror*[7] was built on the *Tartuffe;* and if *The Man of Mode*[8] and Vanbrugh are excellent, they are too indelicate—and Congreve who beats all for wit, is not always natural; still less, simple. In fact I disagree with Mr Heron, as often as I subscribe to him; and though I am an enthusiast to original genius, I cannot forget that there are two classes of authors to be venerated: they who invent, and they who perfect: who has been so original, as to exclude improvements?

Well, Madam, but I not only am not the author of the *Letters,* but *upon my veracity,* I never saw a line of them, nor knew such a work was in embryo, till it was left at my house in full impression.

Should a doubt remain with any man (your Ladyship I flatter myself will not question my truth) I will give him an irrecusable proof of my not having had a hand in these letters, if he will have patience to wait for it—and that is, that the author will write better than he has done, twenty years after I shall be under ground. In short, it is a capacity that will improve by maturity, for it will be corrected by opponents; if it is not hardened into the defence of paradoxes, by defending them too ingeniously; as was the misfortune of Rousseau; who might have excelled by writing good sense, but found that there

2. Mark Akenside (1721–70), Doctor of Physic (Leyden), 1744, classed by Pinkerton among English lyric poets, along with Waller, Milton, Cowley, Dryden, Collins and Gray: 'Though Akenside, considered as a lyric writer, wants richness of images and melody, his style will ever render what he has done in this way valuable' (pp. 130–1). Letter IV (pp. 21–32) is devoted to Akenside's corrections to *The Pleasures of the Imagination,* 'deservedly one of your most favourite poems' (p. 21); Letter IV is referred to on p. 426.

3. In Letter XLI (pp. 356–64) Pinkerton refers to 'the unjust esteem in which Imitation is held' and calls it 'only a decent and allowed plagiarism. When it appears in a certain degree, it is pronounced literary theft, and justly held infamous: in other degrees, and in certain forms and dresses, it is called honourable: but in fact it only differs in the degree of disrepute' (p. 356).

4. Pinkerton calls Boileau 'the very ape of the ancients,' etc. (pp. 129–30).

5. 'Molière, in attempting to introduce laughter into the French comedy, has blundered upon mere farce' (p. 42).

6. By Colley Cibber.

7. Also by Cibber.

8. *The Man of Mode, or, Sir Fopling Flutter,* 1676, by Sir George Etherege (ca 1634–ca 1691).

was a shorter path to celebrity by climbing the precipice of absurdity.

I cannot make the same excuse for the pious editors of Dr Johnson's *Prayers*[9]—See what it is to have friends too honest! How could men be such idiots as to execute such a trust?[10] One laughs at every page, and then the tears come into one's eyes when one learns what the poor being suffered,[11] who even suspected his own madness![12] One seems to be reading the diary of an old almswoman; and in fact, his religion was not a step higher in its kind. Johnson had all the bigotry of a monk, and all the folly and ignorance too. He sets himself penances of reading 200 verses of the Bible per day;[13] proposes to learn High Dutch[14] and Italian[15] at past sixty, and at near seventy *begins* to think of examining the proofs (p. 160) of that religion,

9. *Prayers and Meditations, Composed by Samuel Johnson, LL.D. and Published from His Manuscripts,* advertised 'This day was published' in the *London Chronicle* 11–13 Aug., lviii. 147. HW's copy, now WSL, has a number of pencil marks in the margins but no notes (Hazen, *Cat. of HW's Lib.* 1609:48). The Rev. George Strahan (1744–1824), 2d son of William Strahan the printer (see Boswell, *Johnson, passim*) was the sole editor: Johnson, 'on my visiting him by desire at an early hour . . . put these papers into my hands, with instructions for committing them to the press' (pp. iv–v). Strahan's 'heavy editing' is described in the Yale Edition of the Works of Samuel Johnson, ed. Allen T. Hazen: Vol. I, *Diaries, Prayers, and Annals,* ed. E. L. McAdam, Jr. with Donald and Mary Hyde, New Haven, 1958, pp. xvii–xviii.

10. 'Strahan printed many parts of Johnson's diaries which Johnson would certainly have omitted as having no relevance to the book of prayers which he had in mind' (ibid. xviii). Boswell reports a talk with HW 25 April 1788: 'He said the sentiment which Johnson produced was pity, he was so miserable. It was cruel to publish his Diary [*Prayers and Meditations*]. I said there was no man whose diary would not have weak and foolish things in it. "Yes," said he, "and therefore I wonder how any man should choose to review his own life"' (*Boswell Papers,* xvii. 102).

11. Cf. HW's remark to Joseph Faring-ton 24 July 1796 'that he felt great compassion for the wretched state of Johnson's mind in his last illness. The relation one can scarcely read without horror' (DALRYMPLE 332–3).

12. See, for example, pp. 75, 181, 190, 199, 202; W. B. C. Watkins, *Perilous Balance The Tragic Genius of Swift, Johnson, & Sterne,* Princeton, 1939, *passim.*

13. Johnson's resolutions to read the Bible and his actual reading are mentioned *passim,* and on p. 94 he writes: 'The plan which I formed for reading the Scriptures, was to read 600 verses in the Old Testament, and 200 in the New, every week. . . . This day I began to read the Septuagint, but read only 230 verses, the nine first chapters of Genesis.'

14. 'July 22,—73 . . . Between Easter and Whitsuntide . . . I attempted to learn the Low Dutch language; my application was very slight, and my memory very fallacious' (p. 123). 'Sept. 24, 1773 . . . I tried in the summer to learn Dutch, and was interrupted by an inflammation in my eye' (p. 125). He resumed the study of Dutch in 1782 (Yale Edition of Johnson, i. 158, 333–55).

15. 'July 25, 1776 . . . When I purposed to apply vigorously to study, particularly of the Greek and Italian tongues' (p. 145). Johnson had known Italian for many years; as early as 1737 he offered to translate an Italian work into English for Edward Cave (Boswell, *Johnson* i. 107, 115 *et passim*).

which he had believed so implicitly.[16] So anile was his faith, that on a fast-day he reproaches himself with putting a little milk into his coffee inadvertently![17] Can one check a smile when in his old age, one might say his dotage, he tried to read Vossius on baptism?[18]— no wonder he could only *try!* but one laughs out, when about a dozen years before his death he confesses he had never yet read the Apocrypha, though when a boy he had heard the story of Bel and the Dragon[19]—I wonder he did not add, and of Jack the Giant-killer— for such blind faith might easily have confounded the impressions of his first childhood, which lasted uninterrupted to his second—

Methinks this specimen, and Rousseau's *Confessions,* should be lessons against keeping journals, which poor Johnson thought such an excellent nostrum for a good life[20]—how foolish might we all appear, if we registered every delirium! Johnson certainly had strong sense at intervals—of how little use was it to himself!—but what drivellers are his disciples, who think they honour him by laying open his every weakness!

If the Cardinal de Rohan[21] has any biographers, or *sincere friends,* the narrative will be very different. He is in the Bastile[22] for forging

16. 'My purposes are to study divinity, particularly the Evidences of Christianity' (p. 160, with HW's pencil mark). In Boswell's *Journal of a Tour to the Hebrides,* published 1 Oct. 1785, p. 41, Boswell refers to 'Dr Johnson, who had thought it ['scepticism in morals and religion'] all over, and whose vigorous understanding was fortified by much experience.' HW's note on this passage: 'This does not appear from his diary subjoined to his prayers, where at 60 he proposed to examine the evidences of his religion.'

17. On Easter Day, 7 April 1776, 'I fasted, though less rigorously than at other times. I, by negligence, poured milk into the tea, and, in the afternoon, drank one dish of coffee with Thrale' (pp. 140–1, with HW's pencil mark on p. 140).

18. After tea on Easter Day, 19 April 1778, Johnson 'tried Vossius de Baptismo. I was sleepy' (p. 163). Johnson's copy of Vossius, *De baptismo disputationes XX,* Amsterdam, 1648, was presumably one of the six dissertations by Vossius, 'Amst. 1642 &c.,' lot 423, sold 18 Feb. 1785, to King for 2s. (*Sale Catalogue of Dr John-*

son's Library, 1925; Yale Edition of Johnson, i. 291 n.).

19. On 26 April 1772, 'I have never yet read the Apocrypha. When I was a boy, I have read or heard Bel and the Dragon, Susanna, some of Tobit, perhaps all; some at least of Judith, and some of Ecclesiasticus; and, I suppose, the Benedicite. I have some time looked into the Maccabees, and read a chapter containing the question, *Which is the strongest?* I think in Esdras' (p. 112, with HW's mark beside 'Bel and the Dragon').

20. Johnson's resolutions to keep a journal range from 1760 to 1781. On p. 126, he says, 'My hope is, for resolution I dare no longer call it, to divide my time regularly, and to keep such a journal of my time, as may give me comfort in reviewing it.'

21. Louis-Réné-Édouard   (1734–1803), Cardinal-Prince de Rohan-Guéménée, implicated with Cagliostro and Mme de La Motte in the affair of the Diamond Necklace.

22. He had been arrested 15 Aug. 1785.

the Queen's signature to obtain a collar of diamonds[23]—it is supposed, for a present to some woman, for his Eminence is very *galant*
—He is out of luck—He might not have been sent to Newgate here
for using the Queen's name to get diamonds.[24]

Lady Waldegrave, I flatter myself, is very well, Madam; she is at
Navestock.[25]

To Lady Ossory, Saturday 17 September 1785

No address or postmark, but the letter was addressed to Farming Woods,
Northants, as appears from the first sentence and last paragraph.

Strawberry Hill, Sept. 17,[1] 1785.

I DID conclude, Madam, that the shooting campaign being opened,[2]
you would be pitching your tents in Northamptonshire. Joseph
II who is as keen a sportsman as Lord Ossory, is going to shoot in
Holland; Lord Rodney who is just arrived from Spa, brings [word],
that forty thousand men are on their march.[3] Others add, that this
imperial murderer is in danger from a swelling in his side[4]—I hope

23. For a picture and description of 'the
Diamond Necklace,' consisting of 579
stones, valued at the time at 1,600,000
livres or £64,000, see J. D. Chamier, *The
Dubious Tale of the Diamond Necklace,*
1939, frontispiece and pp. 91–3, 285–6. On
1 Feb. 1785 the Cardinal had shown to the
jewellers what purported to be an agreement to purchase signed by Marie Antoinette, but he gave them only a copy when
he took possession of the jewels (ibid. 94–5,
118–20).

24. 'I heard this story of Sir T. Rumbold.
It is the custom in the East Indies to make
presents of whatever is commended. A
nabob there had a magnificent diamond
ring; Sir Thomas often praised it, but it
was so large, the nabob did not care to
offer it. At last, he . . . gave him the
ring; but next morning repenting, he
wrote to Sir Thomas that it was a family
ring and he begged to have it again, saying he would give so many thousand
pieces, of which he sent him part . . . Sir
Thomas kept both the earnest money and
the ring. The nabob, determined to be
revenged, wrote to Sir Thomas that he

meant the ring for the Queen of England,
and would send her word that Sir Thomas
had it for her; as he did. The Queen however had difficulty to get it, but being not
less eager than Sir Thomas he was forced
to give it up, and sent it over by his son
who delivered it' ('Mem. 1783–91' *sub* Oct.
1784). Warren Hastings and his wife were
also rumoured to have given diamonds to
the Queen, who was supposed to be greedy
for them; see BM, *Satiric Prints, passim.*

25. Where her second son had been born
31 July 1785 and baptized 25 Aug.: John
James Waldegrave (1785–1835), 6th E.
Waldegrave, 1794. HW was asked to be
godfather; see Lord Waldegrave to HW
14 Aug. 1785.

———

1. HW first wrote '16.'
2. The partridge season opened 1 Sept.;
cf. Cole i. 263.
3. War is reported as 'inevitable, as well
with Prussia as with Holland' in *London
Chronicle* 15–17 Sept., lviii. 268.
4. This is not mentioned by his biographers.

he will die soon! His death would save two hundred thousand lives to Europe at least.

A thousand thanks to your Ladyship for the communication of Lady Ravensworth's letter,[5] which I return. She has expressed in two words the idea that I have tried to give you in many of Lady Euston's disposition: calm sweetness and good sense describe her exactly. I hope they will always make her worthy of Lady Ravensworth's goodness and Lord Euston's partiality. Mr Fitzpatrick's for me is not so justly founded—yet I am flattered by it, as perhaps one always is, when rated too highly—at least that is the common opinion; though I confess, I imagine that I am humbled in my own eyes, when I feel conscious of not deserving what is said of me.

Will not humility look affected, Madam, when in the same breath I ask how I may send you a new book printed here, which might blow up some fumes of vanity in a head that had not been so severely disciplined by the owner as mine. It is the translation of my *Essay on Modern Gardens* by the Duc de Nivernois.[6] I believe I mentioned it to your Ladyship. You will find it a most beautiful piece of French, of the genuine French spoken by the Duc de la Rochfoucault and Madame de Sévigné, and not the metaphysical galimatias of La Harpe and Thomas, etc., which Madame du Deffand protested she did not understand. The versions of Milton and Pope are wonderfully exact and poetic and elegant, and the fidelity of the whole translation, extraordinary. Some passages, not quite tender to his country, I was surprised that he did not cashier.[7]

Of the Cardinal de Rohan I know nothing new, but that he absolutely now denies the charge.[8] Indeed I am not at all *au fait* of the story—but I hear that Gray the celebrated cutler,[9] happening to be

---

5. Missing.

6. Hazen, *SH Bibl.* 129–32; *Journal of the Printing-Office at Strawberry Hill*, ed. P. Toynbee, 1923, pp. 20, 67–9. Lady Ossory's copy has not been traced.

7. References to French practice and taste appear at pp. 6, 18, 22, 24, 44, 52n., 60, 80, 90. Two passages are slightly softened: HW's 'every walk is buttoned on each side by lines of flower-pots' becomes 'chaque allée est bordée des deux côtés d'une rangée de pôts de fleurs' (pp. 23–4); 'in a very affected phrase' is omitted in the translation (pp. 79–80).

8. That is, he protested that he had been imposed upon, that he thought the Queen's signature was genuine.

9. Robert Gray (d. 1788), jeweller, goldsmith, and cutler of 13, New Bond Street, and of Twickenham (Mann v. 295, n. 1; More 84). Associated with him was his son William, who succeeded him and who in April–May 1785 had bought some of the diamonds from the Count de La Motte, had set others for him, and had sold him pearls, two swords, etc. (*Pièces justificatives pour M. le cardinal de Rohan, accusé*, 1786, *passim*; J. D. Chamier, *The Du-*

lately at Paris, was near being sent to the Bastile, as they suspected he was concerned in transmitting some of the stolen jewels, which are in England.[10] Some say the whole was a plot of the Queen and Monsieur de Breteuil[11] her creature—but how or why I am ignorant.

Have you heard the history of our Madame de Maintenon? *There* I am of the best authority—I know many particulars from her own mouth. In short, *La Veuve* Delany, not Scarron,[12] sent her woman[13] to Windsor to get by heart the ichnography of the hotel granted to her.[14] When she had made herself mistress of details, she went to dine at the White Hart. She was recalled by a page to Miss Goldsworthy,[15] who told her it was his Majesty's command that she should bring down nothing but her lady's clothes, and the boxes of her maids, for Louis *le Grand*[16] is very considerate—She must bring no plate, china, linen, wine, etc., etc., etc., etc., all would be ready—and when ex-

bious Tale of the Diamond Necklace, 1939, pp. 170, 217; *Memoirs of the Countess de Valois de La Motte*, 1789, pp. 194–206, 285–6). Sir Ambrose Heal, *London Goldsmiths 1200–1800*, Cambridge, 1935, p. 163, lists Robert Gray 1777–92, Robert and William Gray in 1792, and William Gray 1792–1825, but Robert and William Gray are listed in the *Universal British Directory*, 1791–[1798], i. 161, and in *A London Directory*, n.d. (but 1794 or later, as appears from a date on p. 10), p. 63. The newspapers reported that the Count de La Motte had killed William Gray in a duel in Brussels in Aug. 1791; Gray printed an advertisement to deny the rumour (*London Chronicle* 20 Aug.–17 Sept. 1791, lxx. 179, 272).

10. The Count de La Motte's narrative shows clearly that Gray knew nothing of the jewels before La Motte brought them to London (*Memoirs of the Countess of Valois de La Motte*, 1789, pp. 194–206).

11. Louis-Charles-Auguste Le Tonnelier (1733–1807), Baron de Breteuil; ambassador to Naples, 1772, and to Austria, 1774; minister for the Court and Paris 1780–7; succeeded Necker as Director-General of Finance 11–14 July 1789; emigrated to Brussels, then to Switzerland, then to England. In 1790 Louis XVI appointed him his 'secret agent and informal ambassador to the courts of Europe.' He became a member of the Queen's inner circle through the influence of the Du-

chesse de Polignac. The belief 'that the Queen [and Breteuil, also the Cardinal's enemy] got up the whole affair in order to be revenged upon the Cardinal . . . appeals to very few' (BERRY i. 36 n. 44; Chamier, op. cit. 5, 70–1, 107, 276 *et passim*).

12. Mme de Maintenon m. 1 (1652) Paul Scarron (1610–60), novelist, dramatist, and satirist; m. 2 (1684) Louis XIV.

13. Anne Astley (living 1832), later married to —— Agnew, to whom Mrs Delany in her will dated 22 Feb. 1778 and a codicil dated July 1785 left most of her wearing apparel and body linen, and 'her own silver hand-candlestick' (*Delany Corr.* vi. 479–83, 489, 498; the name as given on p. 483, 'Ann Motley,' is apparently a misreading).

14. 'As Mrs Delany's summer visits to Bulstrode ceased on the death of the Dowager Duchess of Portland, the King and Queen presented her with a house at Windsor, together with a pension of £300 a year to meet the expense of her new establishment' (Toynbee; *Delany Corr.* vi. *passim*).

15. Martha Carolina Goldsworthy (1740–1816), dau. of Burrington Goldsworthy; sub-governess to the daughters of George III, 1774 (Warren H. Smith, *Originals Abroad*, 1952, pp. 31–75, *passim*; MANN i. 306 n. 18 *et passim*).

16. George III.

hausted, she must not acquaint Mrs Delany—but the aforesaid page. Louis himself pointed out where Mlle Daubigny,[17] the great-niece, should sleep—'And that room her nephew[18] may use.' When the new favourite arrived, Louis himself was at the door to hand her out of the chaise[19]—there ends my journal—Others say that after a short visit, *Elle le renvoyait triste, mais point désespéré.*[20] Lady Harcourt will be as jealous as the Montespan[21] was.

My own history and gazette will both be very brief. Dr Burney[22] and his daughter Evelina Cecilia have passed a day and half with me.[23] He is lively and agreeable; she, half and half sense and modesty, which possess her so entirely, that not a cranny is left for affectation or pretensions—Oh! Mrs Montagu, you are not above half as accomplished!

Next, I have been two days in town to meet Mr Conway and Lady Aylesbury. We went to see the Prince's new palace in Pall Mall;[24]

17. Georgina Mary Ann Port (1771–1850), dau. of Mrs Delany's niece Mary Dewes by John Port of Ilam, Derbyshire, m. (1789) at Bath, Benjamin Waddington of Dunstan Park, Berks, and Llanover, Monmouthshire. Her daughter edited Mrs Delany's *Correspondence (Delany Corr.* iv. 359 *et passim,* with portrait of her, aged 16, vi. facing 455; GM 1789, lix pt i. 275; GM 1850, n.s. xxxiii. 337; Burney, *Diary* iv. 265 *et passim;* George Paston, *Side-Lights on the Georgian Period,* 1902, pp. 3–56, with portrait facing p. 17). Mlle Daubigny was the niece and heiress of Mme de Maintenon.

18. Although Mrs Delany's will (see *Delany Corr.* vi. 483–92) mentioned various nephews and great-nephews, the reference may be to George Rowe Port (ca 1775–94), Georgina's favourite brother, called 'Little Vandyke' by Mrs Delany from his resemblance to a portrait of that painter. He entered the Charterhouse on the presentation of Queen Charlotte (ibid. vi. 5, 388, 448 *et passim*).

19. 'I arrived here [6 Sept.] about eight o'clock in the evening, and found his Majesty in the house ready to receive me. I threw myself at his feet . . . he raised and saluted me, and said he meant not to stay longer than to desire I would *order every thing* that could make the house comfortable and agreeable to me, and

then retired' (*Delany Corr.* vi. 280, 286).

20. 'La nouvelle favorite, Madame de Maintenon . . . écrivait un jour [à propos du Roi] à Madame de Frontenac, sa cousine, en qui elle avait une entière confiance: "Je le renvoie toujours affligé, et jamais désespéré" ' (Voltaire, *Siècle de Louis XIV,* ch. xxvii; Toynbee).

21. Louis XIV's mistress, supplanted by Mme de Maintenon: Françoise-Athénaïs de Rochechouart (1641–1707) m. (1663) Henri-Louis de Pardaillan de Gondrin, Marquis de Montespan.

22. Charles Burney (1726–1814), Mus. D., Oxford, 1769; friend of Dr Johnson; HW's occasional correspondent.

23. They spent the night of 8 Sept. at SH (HW to Charles Burney 6 Sept. 1785). In Fanny Burney's account of HW in her *Memoirs of Doctor Burney,* 1832, iii. 64–70 (reprinted in her *Diary,* ii. 483–8), she calls this 'a visit of some days' in 1786.

24. Carlton House, formerly the residence of the Dowager Princess of Wales, was assigned to the Prince of Wales in 1783, when he was given a separate establishment. The architect in charge of alterations was Henry Holland (1745–1806), whose connection with Carlton House ended in 1805. See Wheatley, *London Past and Present* i. 331–2; DNB *sub* Holland, Henry; Dorothy Stroud, *Henry Holland,* 1950, pp. 21–6 (with most of this paragraph

and were charmed. It will be the most perfect in Europe. There is
an august simplicity that astonished me. You cannot call it magnificent; it is the taste and propriety that strike. Every ornament is
at a proper distance, and not one too large, but all delicate and new,
with more freedom and variety than Greek ornaments, and though
probably borrowed from the Hôtel de Condé,[25] and other new palaces,
not one that is not rather classic than French. As Gobert,[26] who was
a cook, and who was going to play the devil at Chatsworth and
painted the old pilasters of the court there pea green, designed the
decorations, I expected a more tawdry assemblage of fantastic vagaries
than in Mrs Cornelys's[27] masquerade rooms—I beg his pardon—the
Black Prince would not have blushed to banquet his royal prisoner[28]
in so modest a dwelling. There are three most spacious apartments
all looking on the lovely garden, a terreno,[29] the state apartment and
an attic. The portico, vestibule, hall and staircase, will be superb,
and, to my taste, full of perspectives—the jewel of all, is a small
music-room, that opens into a green recess and winding walk of the
garden—in all the fairy tales you have been, you never was in so
pretty a scene, Madam—I forgot to tell you how admirably all the
carving, stucco, and ornaments are executed—but whence the money
is to come, I conceive not—all the tin mines in Cornwall[30] would not

quoted at pp. 23–4), 29, 68–77. A 'View'
appears in the *European Magazine*, Nov.
1788, xiv., with explanation at p. 384.

25. Dorothy Stroud refers to the 'pre-
dominantly French influence of the first
phase in the palace's decoration . . . Holland had been assimilating this influence
for some time, allying it to a new interpretation of classical forms in which Greek
and Roman forms were blended. . .
Whether Holland had yet crossed the
Channel himself is doubtful . . . his style
was based less on personal observation
abroad than on a close study of French
publications such as those of Peyre, Patte,
and Gondoin; and on the assistance of
talented French artists and craftsmen'
(p. 22).

26. Guillaume Gaubert, 'principal foreman at Carleton House. Horace Walpole
speaks of him as "Gobert, who was a cook,"
but he is described in official reports as
"Maker of Ornamental Furniture," and
from the earliest stages he supervised all
the decorative work' (Stroud, op. cit. 23).

27. Theresa Cornelys (1723–97) opened
Carlisle House, Soho Square, in 1760 for
assemblies, balls, and masquerades. She
continued there until 1772 (when she was
declared a bankrupt) and again briefly in
1776. Carlisle House was pulled down in
1788.

28. Jean II (1319–64), K. of France 1350–
64, captured by the Black Prince at the
Battle of Poitiers, 1356; a prisoner in London until 1360.

29. 'A ground-floor; also, a parlour'
(OED).

30. 'The revenues of the Duchy of Cornwall vest in a Prince of Wales the moment
of his birth—On the lowest possible estimate, the annual receipts are £10,000 a
year' (*The People's Answer to the Court
Pamphlet: Entitled A Short Review*, 3d
edn, 1787, p. 43); the *London Chronicle*
26–28 April 1787, lxi. 403, also placed the
net income of the Duchy of Cornwall at
£10,000 a year. The Prince did not formally
apply in 1785 for the arrears (*The People's
Answer* . . . , p. 44); in the debates on his

pay a quarter.[31] How sick one shall be, after this chaste palace, of Mr Adam's gingerbread and sippets of embroidery![32]

You have heard of all the late deaths and self-murders to be sure, Madam. I am very sorry for my cousin Edward Conway,[33] who was a most amiable young man—but his case has long been thought desperate. His sister Lady Bel is going to be married[34] to a Mr Hatton[35] in Ireland.

I shall divert you more by my conclusion than by this long letter —though it may serve, as you are in the woods, and I am alone in a dark wet evening, and therefore will make no excuses—well! but my conclusion! oh, Sir Harry Englefield[36] told me of a new parody of the Christcross row,[37] of which he could remember but the first line and I have forgotten the author—but that first line is worth a whole poem. You recollect, Madam, don't you? that

A was an archer, and he shot a frog.

What think you of

A was an archer—and painted her face![38]

financial problems in 1795 it was brought out that the revenue of the Duchy accumulated during his minority amounted to £233,764, exclusive of interest. The King had retained the entire income (DNB, sub George IV).

31. The original estimate in 1784 for additions and alterations was £30,000. 'The Prince's extravagancies during the season following his marriage to Mrs Fitzherbert [15 Dec. 1785] plunged him into debts amounting to £250,000, and brought the work to a temporary standstill in 1786. A commission was set up to investigate the situation and in 1787 Parliament agreed to produce £161,000 towards settling the debts, and £60,000 for completing Carlton House' (Stroud, op. cit. 22, 24).

32. This sentence is quoted by A. T. Bolton in The Architecture of Robert and James Adam. 1922, i. 100, as an example of HW's malice and critical ineptitude.

33. Edward Seymour Conway (1757 – 29 Aug. 1785), 4th son of Lord Hertford; rector of Sudbourne-cum-Orford, Suffolk; canon of Christ Church, Oxford, 1783; died 'at Lyons, in France, of a decline' (GM 1785, lv pt ii. 747; Foster, Alumni

Oxon.; Miscellanea genealogica et heraldica, 1890, 2d ser., iii. 1–2).

34. On 9 Oct. (GM 1785, lv pt ii. 918) or 19 Oct. (Lady's Magazine, 1785, p. 671).

35. George Hatton (b. ca 1761), of Wexford, Ireland; M.P. Lisburn (Parliament of Ireland) 1790–7, 1798–1800, and (Parliament of the United Kingdom) 1801–2.

36. Sir Henry Charles Englefield (1752–1822), 7th and last Bt, 1780, of White Knights, Sonning, Berks; F.R.S., 1778; F.S.A., 1779; antiquary and astronomer.

37. 'The alphabet; so called from the figure of a cross being prefixed to it in horn-books' (OED).

38. Sarah West (1741–1801) m. (1761) Andrew Archer, 2d Bn Archer, 1768. In his 'Book of Materials,' 1771, p. 61 bis, HW refers to her as 'a young peeress, remarkable for her tawdry dress and a prodigious quantity of rouge.' For a few of the many references to her excessive rouge, see the Westminster Magazine, 1773, i. 463, for her great use of 'fiery rouge'; London Chronicle 14–16 Oct. 1773, xxxiv. 373, where she heads the list of 'The Most Eminent Painters of Our Age'; ibid. 20–23 May 1775, xxxvii. 485, 'the ruddy Lady

The finishing Touch.

LADY ARCHER, BY JAMES GILLRAY, 1791

What a crop of new wits and new poets we have in our caducity! Old people, they say, admire nothing but what was flourishing in their youth—I am sure, in my youth there was nothing like the present constellation. Once in a year or two Pope after many throes was delivered of an imitation of Horace, and Swift now and then sold you a bargain in short verses—for the rest of our time we lived upon Thompson's[39] and Mallet's[40] blank tragedies, and Lord Lyttelton squirted out ballads to Delia[41] no better than what are sung at Vauxhall.[42] I hope this revival of wit is not lightning before death—nay, I do not recollect that other tottering empires threw out the brightest sparks at their extinction—*Speriamo!*

To Lady Ossory, Thursday 27 October 1785

Address: To the Countess of Ossory at Farming Woods near Thrapston, Northamptonshire. *Postmark:* ISLEWORTH. 27 OC.

Strawberry Hill, Oct. 27, 1785.

YOU are very gracious, Madam, in calling yourself in debt, when I was in yours too; but I have had the best or the worst reason in the world for not writing, the having nothing to say. I know nothing, do nothing, but write explanations of my house not being visible after the month of October[1]—I have had an intercourse of letters[2] with Sir Ralph Payne about some Poles who would have ridden into

---

Archer'; *Modern Characters from Shakespear* [sic], 1778, p. 3, where *Hamlet* V. i. ('Now get you to my lady's chamber . . .') and III. i ('I have heard of your paintings . . .') are applied to her; and *Rambler's Magazine*, 1784, 1785, ii. 238–9, iii. 238–9. She appears in several caricatures painting her face, notably in Nos 7301, 7437, 7973, and 8174 in BM, *Satiric Prints*, and in G. M. Woodward, *Elements of Bacchus*, 1792, facing p. 47. See illustration.

39. James Thomson (1700–48), author of *The Seasons* and of five blank-verse tragedies published 1730–49.

40. David Mallet (ca 1705–65), author of three tragedies published 1731–63. Mallet and Thomson collaborated on *Alfred, a Masque*, 1740.

41. Such as his 'Song Written in the

Year 1732,' beginning 'When Delia on the plain appears'; 'Song Written in the Year 1733,' 'Damon and Delia,' etc. (Lyttelton's *Works*, ed. Ayscough, 2d edn, 1775, pp. 591–4). 'The Progress of Love: in Four Eclogues' (the third of which is addressed 'To Edward Walpole Esq.') also related the affairs of Damon and Delia (ibid. 555–67). Cf. Hazen, *Cat. of HW's Lib.* 3173.

42. The words to the songs sung at Vauxhall appear in the newspapers and magazines of the period.

1. The 'Book of Visitors' 1784–96 (BERRY ii. 221–52) shows that HW made few exceptions to the rule of admitting no visitors after the first of October.

2. Missing.

my hall sabre in hand,[3] as if it was the Diet of Grodno, and they a people still[4]—but I suppose they considered that we are not!

Though these invasions, which keep me in hot water for five months, rankle in my mind, I would not torment your Ladyship with them, if I had not occasion to beg your mediation. As this month of October is the only comfortable one I have (and I cannot reckon on many more) I am determined to keep it to myself, and have printed rules[4a]—nay, on the 1st, I unfurnish it as much as I can for an excuse for not showing it. To my sorrow Lady Lansdown wrote to me,[5] after that day, for a ticket for some of her acquaintance. Had it been for herself, I should have begged the honour of showing it to her myself, a dispensation I reserve in my own breast for those I respect, as I most certainly do Lady Lansdown. Unluckily I had but two days before refused a ticket to Marchioness Grey for herself, and did not offer to be my own housekeeper, as I owe no particular attentions to the House of Yorke. However, I could not personally affront a lady, as I should have done if I had obeyed Lady Lansdown, and therefore trusted her Ladyship would excuse me, which I beg, Madam, you will repeat to her, and tell her my case and concern.

Now, Madam, do you wonder I do not *write?* instead of lamentations on Kirby,[6] I can think of nothing but the groans of Strawberry —in verity, instead of *writing*, could time be recalled, I never would be an author. I am sick of my own trumpery, and if humility were not the mask of vanity, I would tell you why—but they would all be vain or selfish reasons—and so, no matter what they are—

I condole with your Ladyship and Lady Ravensworth on the loss of the good General,[7] and I am glad Lord Ossory tripped up the blacklegs.[8]

3. On 13 Oct. HW admitted '5 Polish gentlemen' (Berry ii. 224).

4. An allusion to the partition of Poland; cf. *ante* 3 Oct. 1775 *et passim*.

4a. See *ante* ii. 436 (illustration).

5. Her letter is missing.

6. Kirby Hall, Northants, was in need of repairs; see *post* 30 Aug. 1786.

7. Lord Ravensworth's first cousin, Gen. Cuthbert Ellison (1698–11 Oct. 1785), of Hebburn, co. Durham; Gen., 1772; M.P. Shaftesbury 1747–54; died 'at his house in King Street, St James's Square,' 'the second general officer on the establishment' (*London Chronicle* 10–13 Oct., lviii. 360; Burke, *Landed Gentry*, 1952, p. 754; GM 1785, lv pt ii. 836; Robert Surtees, *History*

. . . *of Durham*, 1816–40, ii. 79; Edward Hughes, *North Country Life in the Eighteenth Century The North-East, 1700–1750*, Oxford, 1952, *passim*, with portrait facing p. 88). He represented the Duchess of Grafton (Lady Ossory) in arranging her separation from the Duke (HW to Hertford 3 Dec. 1764). Several letters from him to Lady Ossory (including one to her as Duchess of Grafton, 1764) are in the Fitzpatrick MSS in the National Library of Ireland, as well as a letter from Lady Ravensworth to Lady Ossory 12 Oct. 1785 to notify her of his death the preceding day.

8. Black-leg, 'a turf swindler' (OED). Lord Ossory's horses had recently run at Lin-

I have had and still have a sad scene before my eyes; my poor honest servant David is dying of a dropsy, has been tapped twice, suffers dreadfully, wishes it over, and does not care for the trouble of another operation—so if Queens or Dukes of Wirtemberg come to see my house, nobody will send them away!9 What a wonderful contrast between poor David and Dubois, a valet-de-chambre of Louis Treize, who has given an account of that monarch's death, which has just been lent to me!10 After receiving the Sacrament *avec de grosses larmes,* the slave adds, *et des élévations d'esprit, qui faisaient connaître évidemment un commerce d'amour entre leurs majestés divines et humaines.*11 I suppose the poor reptile expected that Louis would in heaven take place of the first prince of the blood!—when human folly, or rather French folly, can go so far, it would be trifling to instance a much fainter silliness—but do you know, Madam, that the fashion now, is not to have portraits but of an *eye?*12 They say, 'Lord! don't you know it?' A Frenchman is come over to paint eyes here.

I am not so partial as not to like the retort of Charles V.13 I would not advise Mr Mason to go to Court, if Charles were living—nor will I go to Vienna—When General Johnstone14 returned a fortnight ago, I told him I hoped he had left everybody well in Germany but

coln, 7 Sept., and at the first and second October meetings at Newmarket, 5, 21 Oct. (James Weatherby, *Racing Calendar,* 1785, xiii. 106, 128, 139–40).

9. On 3 Aug. 1764, HW's Swiss servants Favre and Louis turned away the Prince of Mecklenburg and Queen Charlotte because HW was in bed. 'See what it is to have republican servants!' (HW to Hertford 3 Aug. 1764). On 7 April 1776 David turned away Karl Eugen (1728–93), D. of Württemberg 1737–93, for the same reason (HW to Mason 8 April 1776, MASON i. 258).

10. See HW to an unknown correspondent 27 Oct. 1785 and Hazen, *Cat. of HW's Lib.* 3006. *Curiosités historiques, ou recueil de pièces utiles à l'histoire de France, et qui n'ont jamais paru,* Amsterdam, 1759, contains the passage HW quotes, ii. 74, *sub* 12 May 1643, two days before the King's death. Dubois's complete account, beginning 21 Feb. 1643, is at pp. 44–92.

11. HW makes slight changes in the quotation, both here and in his letter to the unknown correspondent 27 Oct.

12. Cosway painted four eyes: one each of Mrs Fitzherbert, the Prince of Wales, Emma Lady Hamilton, and 'a lady' (G. C. Williamson, *Richard Cosway,* 1897, pp. 111, 116, 158, 159). The Dowager Countess Spencer wrote to the Duchess of Devonshire 6 Feb. 1786 about the Prince of Wales's carrying Mrs Fitzherbert's 'picture (or her eye), which is the same thing, about and showing it to people' (Shane Leslie, *Mrs Fitzherbert,* 1939–40, i. 61–2, with Cosway's paintings of the Prince's and Mrs Fitzherbert's eyes at i. 60). On 6 Dec. 1787 Lady Eleanor Butler was shown 'An eye, done at Paris and set in a ring. A true French idea, and a delightful idea, which I admire more than I confess for its singular beauty and originality' (*Hamwood Papers,* ed. Mrs G. H. Bell, 1930, p. 65).

13. (1500–58), Holy Roman Emperor 1519–58.

14. James Johnston (ca 1721–97), Lt-Gen., 1777; Gen., 1793; the husband of Lady Cecilia Johnston (MONTAGU i. 28 n. 19; BERRY, *passim*).

the Emperor—the postman stays—not that I can pretend to have a
word more to say—

To Lady Ossory, Wednesday 16 November 1785

Address: To the Countess of Ossory at Ampthill Park, Bedfordshire. *Postmark:* 16 NO.

Berkeley Square, Nov. 16, 1785.

BY COMING hither an hour ago, I am so fortunate as to be able
to thank your Ladyship instantly for your most kind letter on
Lady Euston's delivery.[1] I am still more pleased with the very proper
manner in which it was notified to you. Lady Horatia, who is with
her sister, tells Miss Keppel that Lord Euston is delighted with his
daughter; it was for a daughter he wished—there certainly is no danger of the line of Fitzroy failing for want of an heir male.[2]

I am in debt, Madam, for another letter which I received at Park
Place, where I have been for some days—but Park Place furnished
me with no more events than Strawberry Hill; and I must own that
when I can tell nothing that will amuse, which seldom happens to
me now, living as I do out of the world, and having outlived so many
of my friends and acquaintance, I am shy of writing—for why should
one write when one has little or nothing to say? I cannot *compose*
letters like Pliny and Pope.

Your Ladyship's query I can answer by heart. Richard Duke of
York,[3] who was supposed murdered in the Tower, was, though an
infant, married solemnly by his father Edward IV to Anne Mowbray
Duchess of Norfolk,[4] and the heiress of that house, and still more a
baby than himself.[5] She died very soon; probably, though I could
never find exactly when, before the King,[6] for it was in right of having

1. Maria Anne Fitzroy (3 Nov. 1785–
1855) m. (1810) Sir William Oglander, 6th
Bt, 1806 (Collins, *Peerage*, 1812, i. 220, 564;
Burke, *Peerage*, 1953, p. 907). Lord Euston's
letter to Lady Ossory 9 Nov. informing her
of the birth is in the National Library
of Ireland: Fitzpatrick MSS.

2. Lord Euston, had one brother and
five half-brothers living at this time; see
Collins, *Peerage* 1812, i. 219–20.

3. Richard Plantagenet (1473–ca 1483),

cr. (1474) D. of York; 2d son of Edward
IV. That he was murdered by order of
Richard III is one of HW's 'doubts' in
Historic Doubts.

4. Anne Mowbray (1472–81), *suo jure*
Countess (not Duchess) of Norfolk, 1476,
on the death of her father, John, 4th D.
of Norfolk, m. (1478) Richard, D. of York.

5. She was eight months older.

6. She died in 1481; Edward IV died
9 April 1483.

married, or having been son of, her aunt (I forget which), that John Howard was created Duke of Norfolk[7] by Richard III—and was the Jocky of Norfolk[8] slain at Bosworth—you now see, Madam, why I know so much of the matter offhand.

I am come to town for two or three days on a little private business of my own, and to quit a horrid scene. My poor honest Swiss David has been dying of a dropsy for seven or eight months, and has suffered dreadfully. I have seen him but once since my return, as he has been speechless—and I flatter myself senseless, since last Saturday; but he groans shockingly; and though I trusted to hearing he was gone this morning, he was still alive but motionless. I shall not go back to Strawberry till he is buried. As your Ladyship says Lady Ravensworth is in town, I shall endeavour to pay my duty to her. I am much pleased with the good old General's[9] legacy; and don't wonder your Ladyship is so, though it will scarce purchase half an acre of a modern hat.

As the ashes of the Cecils are rekindling,[10] perhaps a Phœnix may arise! I remember Lord Hervey saying that everything degenerated and dwindled, and instancing in the last Lord Salisbury,[11] who he said was the cucumber of Burleigh—well then, as matters when they can go no lower, may mount again, who knows what may happen, Madam? Some melon-seeds, that have been neglected and not cultivated in the hot-house of a great family, may fall on good ground and bring forth brave melons. Thus *my father* sprung from a granddaughter of Lord Burleigh[12]—and then dwindled to the gherkin

H.W.

---

7. John Howard (ca 1430–85), cr. (1470) Lord Howard and (1483) D. of Norfolk; his mother, Margaret Mowbray (wife of Sir Robert Howard), was great-aunt of Anne, Cts of Norfolk (see above and GEC ix. 601–4, 610–12).

8. 'Jockey of Norfolk' (*Richard III* V. iii. 305).

9. General Ellison's; see preceding letter.

10. The head of the family, James, 7th E. of Salisbury, held various offices and was created M. of Salisbury in 1789. HW may also refer to the pregnancy of Lady Salisbury, which was common knowledge

(a daughter was born 20 March 1786) (GEC iii. 480; Coke, 'MS Journals' 11, 18, 26 Nov. 1786).

11. James Cecil (1713–80), 6th E. of Salisbury, 1728; in the seventh generation of descent from Lord Burghley. His addiction to driving a stagecoach and his profligacy are mentioned in MONTAGU i. 349, ii. 348; GEC xi. 410.

12. Lady Dorothy Cecil (d. 1613), dau. of Burleigh's son, Lord Exeter, m. Sir Giles Allington, and was Sir Robert Walpole's great-great-grandmother (see COLE i. 374).

To Lady Ossory, Friday 18 November 1785

Address: To the Countess of Ossory at Ampthill Park, Bedfordshire. *Post-mark:* 18 NO.

Berkeley Square, Friday 18th.

AS I could mean *only* respect, Madam, on your Ladyship's telling me Lady Ravensworth was in town, I am glad you have prevented my troubling her with a visit, which I should have made this evening; and which as I return to Strawberry tomorrow, will be as well made by the intention. My breeding *de vieille cour* makes me attend to certain ceremonials; but the slightest dispensation quiets the etiquette of my conscience, especially if it can give any kind of disturbance to anybody.

A marriage is agreed on between Mr Pratt and Miss Molesworth;[1] but as there is still a moment between the cup and *her* lip, it may not yet be recorded in Fate's parish-register.[2]

My poor servant died in a few hours after I left him. Mr Morice I hear is dead too,[3] which must be as great a deliverance.

---

1. They were married 31 Dec. 1785, in a 'great wedding,' the bride 'a most beautiful young lady . . . and a fortune of nearly £40,000' (Mrs Caroline Powys, *Passages from the Diaries*, ed. Climenson, 1899, p. 222) or £45,000 (Coke, 'MS Journals' 18 Nov. 1785). 'Miss Molesworth is at last married to Mr Pratt—her fortune is £45,000. I pity Lord Lucan, as it was thought he had cheated her, and it has proved quite the contrary, as Sir William Molesworth cheated her of all but £30,000, and Lord Lucan has nursed it up to £45,000' (Charlotte Augusta Keppel to Anne Clement 5 Jan. 1786, MS WSL).

2. 'Everybody told us it would never take place, as three matches with noblemen had been broken off; but I've often heard the lady's reason for refusing each. I always thought our friend Pratt had a better chance than either of the trio. The first, she said, never entertained her with anything but politics, but a dry topic for courtship; the second made a horrid husband to his first wife; and the third had not sixpence in the world, from his own extravagance. She was not wrong in refusing all three!' (Powys, op. cit. 223). Lord Shelburne was the first of the trio (*ante* 17 Jan. 1778; 22 June 1779). Lady Mary Coke records in her 'MS Journals' 17 Dec. 1779 the rumour of a marriage between Miss Molesworth and Lord North's eldest son, who became 3d E. of Guilford in 1792; he may be the third.

3. At Naples 18 Oct. 1785.

To Lady Ossory, Monday 16 January 1786

Vernon Smith and Cunningham followed HW's mistake in date and placed the letter in 1785; Toynbee placed it correctly in 1786.

Address: To the Countess of Ossory at Ampthill Park, Bedfordshire.

Berkeley Square, Jan. 16, 1785.[1]

I AM always thanking you, Madam, I think, for kind inquiries after me; but it is not my fault that I am so often troublesome! I would it were otherwise!—however, I do not complain—I have attained another resurrection; and was so glad of my liberty, that I went out both Saturday and Sunday, though so snowy a day and so rainy a day, never were invented—yet I have not ventured to see Mrs Jordan,[2] nor to skate in Hyde Park—we had other-guess winters in my time! fine sunny mornings, with now and then a mild earthquake, just enough to wake one, and rock one to sleep again comfortably. My recoveries surprise me more than my fits; but I am quite persuaded now that I know exactly how I shall end—as I am a statue of chalk, I shall crumble to powder, and then my inside will be blown away from my terrace, and hoary-headed Margaret will tell the people that come to see my house,

> One morn we miss'd him on the custom'd hill[3]—

When that is the case, Madam, don't take the pains of inquiring more—as I shall leave no *body* to return to, even Cagliastro[4] would bring me back to no purpose[5]—by the way, is not it curious, that

1. HW's mistake for '1786.'
2. Dorothy Bland (1761–1816), who took the name of Mrs Jordan (and later became the mistress of the future William IV), was praised as an actress by Hazlitt, Lamb, Hunt, and others. She had made her London début 18 Oct. 1785 at Drury Lane as Peggy in *The Country Girl*, Garrick's adaptation of Wycherley's *Country Wife* (BERRY i. 352 n. 10). For her rôles to this date, see Genest vi. 374–81.
3. Gray's *Elegy*, l. 109.
4. Giuseppe Balsamo (1743–95), impostor who, after using various names and titles, assumed the name of Conte Alessandro di Cagliostro. Arrested a week later than the Cardinal, he was tried and acquitted in the affair of the Diamond Necklace. HW's copy of Cagliostro's *Lettre . . . au peuple anglais*, [London?], 1786, is listed in Hazen, *Cat. of HW's Lib.* 1609: 48.
5. Among his various schemes and cures was a plan for the regeneration of the soul or body. For a brief description of the procedures involved, see Peter Wilding, *Adventurers in the Eighteenth Century*, New York, 1937, pp. 292–3. He had performed a miraculous cure on the Cardinal de Rohan's kinsman, the Prince de Soubise,

when credulity and superstition are so far exploded, that even a Cardinal[6] is abandoned by bishops and clergy, and left to the civil power,[7] there should still be dupes to such a mountebank as Cagliastro? I have been told that Prince Ferdinand himself had faith in him. I know that our late King, though not apt to believe more than his neighbours, had no doubt of the existence of vampires and their banquets on the dead. Dr Johnson seems to have been the representative in epitome of all the contradictions in human nature.

Your Ladyship may be sure I am happy in Lady Euston's good fortune, not only in the Duke's being reconciled,[8] but in obtaining Lady Ravensworth's favourable opinion. It has always been mine, that her paternal understanding and temper would pierce at last through all clouds. She still in my eyes wants one essential boon from fortune[9] to complete her felicity; and though I may not live to see that moment, I hope your Ladyship will then allow that I gave a just character of her, when I could have no idea of what has happened since.

Most of the diversions that I have given up, cost me no regrets—but I own I should have enjoyed the play at Ampthill[10]—indeed you might have made me a little amends by sending me the prologue, epilogue,[10a] instead of a charade which I shall never guess. In revenge here is one, which I hope you will all find as uncrackable: General Conway, who never rests till he has mastered one, miscarried: 'ma première partie fait aller, ma seconde fait reculer, mon tout fait rire et pleurer.'[11]

General Burgoyne's *Heiress*,[12] I hear, succeeded extremely well,

and it was rumoured that Cagliostro raised the illustrious dead to converse with them (ibid. 307–8, 316). 'Ce fameux charlatan, qui se vantait très sérieusement d'avoir assisté aux noces de Cana, en Galilée, s'était emparé de l'esprit du cardinal [Rohan], au point de lui persuader qu'il le faisait souper avec Voltaire, Montesquieu, etc.' (Jean-Louis Giraud Soulavie, *Mémoires historiques et politiques du règne de Louis XVI*, 1801, vi. 84).

6. Cardinal de Rohan.

7. When Louis XVI offered a choice between throwing himself on the King's mercy or being tried by the Parliament of Paris, the Cardinal chose the latter. The trial began 11 Jan. 1786 with questioning of the Cardinal, and on 31 May he was acquitted (J. D. Chamier, *The Dubious*

Affair of the Diamond Necklace, 1939, pp. 104–20, 142–63, 264–6).

8. 'Lord Euston is gone to his father, who has written a letter with the highest approbation of Lady Euston' (HW to Lady Browne 14 Dec. 1785, MORE 238). The 'Duke of Grafton has seen Lady Euston, and treated her very kindly' (HW to Thomas Walpole the younger 25 Oct. 1786).

9. A son: Henry Fitzroy (10 Feb. 1790–1863), 5th D. of Grafton, 1844.

10. The play has not been identified.

10a. This word is written above 'prologue.'

11. Vapeur ('Lindis' in *Notes and Queries* 1874, 5th ser. i. 385, 475).

12. At Drury Lane 14 Jan. 1786 (Genest vi. 381).

and was besides, excellently acted.[13] Have you had patience, Madam, to wade through Mr Hayley's *Old Maids*?[14] I could not—and can you guess why he wrote them, unless to sell *three* volumes? That sot Boswell is a classic in comparison.[15]

You know to be sure, Madam, that Lady Brudenel is dead[16]—everybody laments her, for she was perfectly unexceptionable. I have lost a very old friend, one of my oldest, and a most worthy man, Lord Dacre[17]—but after forty years of miserable sufferings, his death was charming, and not two hours in duration from his seizure. We who are dead in equity, though not in law, should hope for such conclusions, and have former preludes discounted.

Sir William Hamilton I am told, has been probing Vesuvius and announces a more dreadful explosion than ever.[18] Lord and Lady Spencer have ascended the mountain while the lava boiled over the opp⟨osite⟩ brim: I should have no thirst for such bumpers.

My hand, you see, Madam, has obeyed you very debonairly; I am

13. It 'was well acted, and was the best new C[omedy] since *The School for Scandal* . . . the language is peculiarly good . . . *The Heiress* was acted all the month, except the 18th—and 30 times in the course of the season' (ibid., where the cast is also given).

14. *A Philosophical, Historical, and Moral Essay on Old Maids*, 'By a Friend to the Sisterhood,' 1785, in three volumes octavo (Hazen, *Cat. of HW's Lib.* 3104); dedicated to Elizabeth Carter, who was not pleased (Montagu Pennington, *Memoirs of the Life of Mrs Elizabeth Carter*, 3d edn, 1816, i. 34; Morchard Bishop, *Blake's Hayley*, 1951, pp. 89–90, 104, 132–5).

15. Boswell's most recent book was *A Journal of a Tour to the Hebrides with Samuel Johnson, LL.D.*, 1785, 'Boswell's most absurd enormous book . . . the story of a mountebank and his zany' (HW to Conway 6 Oct. 1785). In HW's copy (now wsl), p. 524, is an 'Epigram' in his hand:

'When boozy Bozzy belch'd out Johnson's sayings,
And half the volume fill'd with his own brayings,
Scotland beheld again before her pass
A brutal bulldog coupled with an ass.'

Cf. Hazen, *Cat. of HW's Lib.* 3069.

16. She died 12 Jan. (*London Chronicle* 12–14 Jan. lix. 46).

17. Though his death is dated 12 Jan. in *Daily Adv.* 18 Jan., it is dated 13 Jan. in *Scots Magazine*, 1786, xlviii. 81, and GM 1786, lvi pt i. 84; it is 6 Jan. in GEC. 'He contracted a disorder that deprived him of the use of his limbs for several years before his death' (GM loc. cit.), and he was a hypochondriac as early as 1749 (MANN iv. 84).

18. Hamilton had published in 1772 *Observations on Mount Vesuvius, Mount Etna, and Other Volcanos: In a Series of Letters Addressed to the Royal Society* and had continued his observations. 'Some Particulars of the Present State of Mount Vesuvius . . . In a Letter ['Naples, January 24, 1786'] from Sir William Hamilton . . . to Sir Joseph Banks' appeared in *Philosophical Transactions*, 1786, lxxvi. 365–81: The eruption of Vesuvius from November 1784 to about 20 Dec. 1785 'has afforded much amusement to travellers unacquainted with this operation of nature' (p. 365). Hamilton's private letters to Banks in 1785 also mention the eruption of Vesuvius, and the letter of 8 Nov. refers to signs of greater activity (British Museum, Natural History, *The Banks Letters*, ed. W. R. Dawson, 1958, pp. 383–4; cf. GM 1786, lvi pt i. 74).

⟨sorry I⟩ had no better materials. I have straws enough, but I don't find that ⟨I make⟩ good brick.

PS. ⟨I am no⟩t such a *blockhead*, as I thought I was. ⟨I be⟩lieve *that* is the key to your charade. My French one is as just.

To Lady Ossory, Friday 27 January 1786

Berkeley Square, Friday night, Jan. 27, 1786.

AS THE first part entertained your Lady- and Lordships,[1] it is but a sort of duty to send you the second. I received a little Italian note[2] from Mrs Cosway this morning to tell me that as I had last week met at her house[3] an old acquaintance without knowing her, I might meet her again this evening *en connaissance de cause* as Mlle la Chevalière d'Eon,[4] who, as Mrs Cosway told me, had taken it ill that I had not reconnoitred her,[5] and said she must be strangely altered—the devil is in it if she is not!—but alack! I have found her altered again! adieu to the abbatial dignity that I had fancied I discovered—I now found her loud, noisy and vulgar—in truth I believe she had dined a little *en dragon*.[6] The night was hot, she had no muff or gloves, and her hands and arms seem not to have participated of the change of sexes, but are fitter to carry a chair than a fan. I am comforted too about her accent. I asked Monsieur Barthélemy[7] the French secretary, who was present, whether it was Parisian and good French: he assured me, so far from it, that the first time he met her, he had been surprised at its being so bad, and that her accent is strong Burgundian.[8] You ask me, Madam, why she is here? She says, *pour ses petites affaires*—I

1. HW refers to his letter of 23 July 1785 containing the account of Mme de Genlis, whose visit to SH had been arranged by Mrs Cosway.

2. Missing.

3. Schomberg House, Pall Mall (*ante* 23 July 1785, n. 13).

4. Charles-Geneviève-Louis-Auguste-André-Timothée de Beaumont (1728–1810), Chevalier d'Éon, transvestist (DU DEFFAND ii. 494 *et passim*). He lived in England 1762–77 and 1785–1810; during the second period he dressed as a woman (BERRY i. 68 nn. 45, 47), having been ordered to do so by a covenant between him and Beaumarchais 5 Oct. 1775 (J. B. Telfer,

Strange Career of the Chevalier d'Éon, 1885, pp. 243–52).

5. HW had entertained d'Éon at SH in 1763 (MONTAGU ii. 70).

6. D'Éon had held the rank of captain of dragoons in the French army (BERRY i. 68 and n. 47).

7. François Barthélemy (1747–1830), cr. (1800) Comte and (1815) Marquis de Barthélemy; secretary to the French embassy in London 1785–7, minister plenipotentiary 1787–8 (Robert Beatson, *Political Index* 3d edn, 1806, ii. 429).

8. D'Éon was born at Tonnerre in Lower Burgundy and lived there until he was sent to school at Paris.

take for granted, for the same reason that Francès was here two years before he was known.[9]

Nor was this all my entertainment this evening. As Mlle Common of Two's reserve is a little subsided, there were other persons present, as three foreign ministers besides Barthélemy, Lord Carmarthen, Count Oghinski,[10] Wilkes and his daughter, and the chief of the Moravians.[11] I could not help thinking how posterity would wish to have been in my situation, at once with three such historic personages, as D'Éon, Wilkes, and Oghinski, who had so great a share in the revolution of Poland,[12] and was king of it for four-and-twenty hours.[13] He is a noble figure, very like the Duke of Northumberland in the face, but stouter and better proportioned.

I remember many years ago making the same kind of reflection. I was standing at my window after dinner in summer in Arlington Street, and saw *Patty Blount* (after Pope's death) with nothing remaining of her immortal charms but her *blue eyes*,[14] trudging on foot with her petticoats pinned up, for it rained, to visit *blameless Bethel*,[15] who was sick at the end of the street.[16]

9. 'Francès, a man of middling birth, was exceedingly shrewd, and perhaps better acquainted with this country than any Frenchman living. Before his appearance as Du Châtelet's confidential secretary, he had privately, obscurely, and unknown, resided here three years in the City, and by that time had made himself perfectly master of our language and affairs' (*Last Journals* i. 521, *sub* Feb. 1776; a similar account is in *Mem. Geo. III* iv. 137, *sub* 1770, where HW also says 'three years').

10. Michal Kasimierz (1731–1800), Prince Ogiński, hetman of Lithuania and candidate in 1764 for the throne of Poland (*Encyklopedja powszechna*, Warsaw, 1930–, viii. 40–1). HW showed him SH 27 Aug. 1786 (BERRY ii. 226).

11. Presumably the Rev. Benjamin Latrobe (ca 1728–86), head of the Moravians in England 1765–86 (J. E. Hutton, *History of the Moravian Church*, 2d edn, 1909, pp. 438–40; GM 1786, lvi pt ii. 1094). He was a friend of Hannah More (Hutton, op. cit. 440).

12. In 1771, Ogiński, incited by France, raised some four or five thousand men in Lithuania, and as 'liberateur de la patrie' joined the Confederation of Bar to oppose

Stanislas II of Poland and the Russians. He was defeated by Suvorov, at Stolowicze, and fled to France (*Encyklopedja powszechna*, loc. cit.; *Mémoires du roi Stanislas-Auguste Poniatowski*, St Petersburg, 1914–24, i. 665–6).

13. Presumably in the election for the crown of Poland in 1764, when Ogiński's candidacy was supported by French propaganda and by Osten, the Danish minister, who sent him to seek Catherine II's support (Jean Fabre, *Stanislas-Auguste Poniatowski*, 1952, pp. 244, 618 n. 32).

14. 'When those blue eyes first open'd on the sphere' (Pope, Epistle II, 'To a Lady [Martha Blount] On the Characters of Women,' l. 284). This passage in HW's letter is frequently quoted to illustrate Pope's line.

15. Hugh Bethel (d. 1748), M.P. Pontefract 1715–22; 'one of Pope's oldest and most esteemed friends,' called 'Blameless Bethel' in *An Essay on Man* iv. 126. See John Butt (ed.), Pope, *Imitations of Horace*, in the Twickenham Edition of Pope's Poems, iv (2d edn, 1953) 346–7.

16. HW told this anecdote to Malone sometime between Feb. 1792 and Aug. 1795: 'Patty Blount was red-faced, fat, and

Early in the evening I had been, according to your Ladyship's leave, to wait on Lady Ravensworth.[17] Her cough is very frequent, but it seems entirely from her throat, and not in the least from her breast.

After treating your Ladyship with some of the dramatis personas of modern story, I beg leave to enclose[18] a Venus of the present hour in her *puris* non *naturalibus*. The drawing[19] was made by a young lady at Bath[20] and was given to me by my sister. It diverted me so much that I gave it to Kirgate with leave to have it engraved for his own benefit, and I should think he would sell hundreds of them.[21]

Miss Hannah More, I see, has advertised her *Bas Bleus,*[22] which I think you will like[23]—I don't know what her *Florio* is. Mrs Frail Piozzi's first volume of *Johnsoniana*[24] is in the press and will be published in February[25]—There is published another kind of *Ana*

---

by no means pretty. Mr Walpole remembered her walking to Mr Bethell's in Arlington Street, after Pope's death, with her petticoats tucked up like a sempstress' (James Prior, *Life of Edmond Malone,* 1860, p. 437).

17. At her house in St James's Square.

18. 'Not enclosed in the MSS' (Vernon Smith's note, ii. 255).

19. See illustration (from HW's Satiric Prints, now in the New York Public Library). The line drawing of 'A Modern Venus' clothed is by Lady Ossory; see *post* 10 Feb. 1786.

20. 'By Miss Hoare of Bath,' as HW has noted on his copy of the print (see illustration). She was daughter of William Hoare, R.A., of Bath (known as Hoare of Bath). She exhibited at the Society of Artists, 1761, and the Free Society 1761–4 (Algernon Graves, *The Society of Artists . . . The Free Society of Artists,* 1907, p. 118; Thieme-Becker, *sub* Hoare, William; Joseph Farington, *The Farington Diary,* ed. James Greig, 1923–[1928], v. 63).

21. Among HW's Satiric Prints in the New York Public Library is a copy of the print, with the same caption and quotation as appear on the drawing, except that *1785* is changed to *1786.* HW's copy gives no name of designer, engraver, or printseller, but that in the British Museum has a notation 'in a contemporary hand,' 'Published as the Act Directs by E. Yardley,

New Inn Passage, Clare Market' (BM, *Satiric Prints* vi. 989–90, No. 8257, where the similarity of this print to No. 7100 in the same catalogue is pointed out).

22. *Florio: a Tale, for Fine Gentlemen and Fine Ladies: and, The Bas Bleu; or, Conversation: Two Poems,* advertised 'In a few days will be published' in the *Morning Herald* 25 Jan. and as published 'This day' ibid. 10 Feb. 1786. *Florio* was dedicated to HW, *The Bas Bleu* addressed to Mrs Vesey. HW had two copies, one now in the Harvard Library, with notes by him, and another sold London 1038 (Hazen, *Cat. of HW's Lib.* 3222:20). For Hannah More's dedicatory letter, 27 Jan., and HW's reply 9 Feb. 1786, see MORE 239–42. In *The Bas Bleu,* ll. 52–3:

'For polish'd WALPOLE shew'd the way, How wits may be both learn'd and gay.'

23. As Hannah More pointed out in the Advertisement to *The Bas Bleu* (p. 66), the poem had circulated in manuscript: 'But copies having been multiplied . . . she has been advised to publish it, lest it should steal into the world in a state of still greater imperfection.' Fanny Burney heard it read 'again' in Nov. 1783 (Burney, *Diary* ii. 229).

24. *Anecdotes of the Late Samuel Johnson . . .*

25. It was not published until 25 March (HW to Mann 28 March 1786; James L. Clifford, *Hester Lynch Piozzi,* Oxford,

'A MODERN VENUS,' 'BY MISS HOARE OF BATH,' 1785

called *Silva,* by a Dr Heathcote,[26] on which I advise your Ladyship not to throw away five shillings as I did[27]—yet I could not read half-a-crown's worth—it is a heap of dull commonplace.

To Lady Ossory, Friday 10 February 1786

In Kirgate's hand.

Friday night, Feb. 10, 1786.

AS YOUR Ladyship announced your speedy arrival in town; and as I suppose few read the second edition of a book after reading the first, I forbore to send you a second edition of my gout; yet I have had a black-letter one. My healed finger opened again, and for this week my surgeon[1] has been picking chalk-stones out of both hands as if he were shelling peas. The gout returned too into my right hand and elbow, and swelled both. In short, since Wednesday was sennight[2] I have been prisoner a second time, and when my durance will end, I do not guess.

When you do come, Madam, you will not hear much of Mr Eden[3]

1941, p. 263). The manuscript did not reach England until the end of 1785; and there were various delays, discussed fully ibid. 255–63.

26. *Sylva, or, The Wood, Being a Collection of Anecdotes, Dissertations, Characters, Apothegms, Original Letters, Bons Mots, and Other Little Things.* 'By a Society of the Learned.' It was advertised ('This day was published') in the *Morning Herald* 19 Jan.; 2d edn enlarged, 1788; 3d edn enlarged, Dublin, 1789. The author was Ralph Heathcote (1721–95), D.D. Cambridge, 1759, who had written *A Letter to . . . Mr Horace Walpole Concerning the Dispute between Mr Hume and Mr Rousseau,* 1767 (dated by HW in his copy, now WSL, 9 Dec. 1766). Part of *A Letter* is reprinted in *Sylva,* pp. 300–15.

27. The book is not listed in the SH records; cf. Hazen, *Cat. of HW's Lib.* 1609: 16.

---

1. Henry Watson (d. 1793), of Rathbone Place; sometime warden of the Corporation of Surgeons and member of the Court

of Examiners; surgeon to the Middlesex Hospital, and later to the Westminster Infirmary; F.R.S., 1767 (BERRY i. 180 n. 2 *et passim*). He gave HW 'The Virgin and Child, and two angels holding tapers: an ancient carving in ivory,' in the Breakfast Room at SH, sold SH xviii. 78 to James Dolman for £3.3.0; and 'Venus and Cupid in ivory, finely drawn and executed, but in the Flemish style,' in the closet in the corridor near the Great North Bedchamber, sold SH xvi. 115 to William Knight for £5.5.0 (*Des. of SH,* 1784, pp. 22, 91; *Works* ii. 427, 494). 'Mr Walpole seems perfectly to adore Mr Watson—and so does Lady Albemarle, for she says if anything is ever the matter with her she will instantly send for the little Watson, as he has showed so much skill about Mr Walpole' (Charlotte Augusta Keppel to Anne Clement 5 Jan. 1786, MS WSL).

2. 1 Feb.

3. 'Mr Eden's desertion [of Fox and North for Pitt] has been the chief topic of politics' (HW to Mann 13 Feb. 1786; 'Mem. 1783–91,' *sub* Nov. 1785). In No-

or Mrs Jordan, or of *The Heiress*,[4] which, by the way, I went through twice in one day, and liked better than any comedy I have seen since *The Provoked Husband;*[5] I like the prologue[6] too very much; the epilogue[7] is unworthy of both—Oh! but the hubbub you are to hear, and to talk of, and except which, you are to hear and talk of nothing else, for they tell me the passengers in the streets of all ranks talk of it, is, a subject[8] to which I suppose your letters have already attuned you, and on which I alone, for certain reasons,[9] will say nothing; but if you don't guess, Madam, I will give you a clue: don't you remember that after Louis Quatorze had married the Maintenon and the Dauphin Mlle Chouin,[10] the Duchess of Burgundy[11] said to her husband, 'Si je venais à mourir, feriez-vous le troisième tome de votre famille?'[12] —You may swear that my mysterious silence is not dated from any privity or knowledge; I do not know a tittle from any good authority; and though a mass of circumstances are cited and put together, they command no credit: whoever believes, must believe upon trust. The

vember Eden had gone over to Pitt and in December had become a member of the Committee of Council relating to Trade and Plantations (which had replaced the Board of Trade) and (at £6000 a year) a special envoy for concluding a commercial treaty with France, which was signed in September 1786. Rowlandson's print, 'The Loss of Eden,—and Eden, Lost,' published 21 Dec. 1785, equates Eden's apostasy with that of Benedict Arnold (BM, *Satiric Prints* vi. 244–5, No. 6815).

4. Burgoyne's *The Heiress. A Comedy in Five Acts*, had been published on 4 Feb. (*Morning Herald* 23 Jan., 4 Feb.). The dedication to the Earl of Derby is dated 1 Feb. 1786.

5. HW also liked *The School for Scandal* 'much better than any [comedy] I have seen since *The Provoked Husband*' (HW to Mason 16 May 1777, MASON i. 309).

6. 'By the Rt Hon. Richard Fitzpatrick,' pp. vi–vii.

7. 'The epilogue [*The Heiress*, pp. 111–12] was written, as we understand, on the spur of the moment, in consequence of a disappointment of an epilogue by another hand, by General Burgoyne' (*London Chronicle* 14–17 Jan., lix. 53; *Morning Herald* 16 Jan.). In the Preface, p. v,

Burgoyne says it, 'from an accident, was much too hastily written in some parts, and in others pieced together with a like insufficiency of time.'

8. The marriage of the Prince of Wales to Mrs Fitzherbert on 15 Dec. 1785. Maria Anne Smythe (1756–1837) m. 1 (1775) Edward Weld; m. 2 (1778) Thomas Fitzherbert; m. 3 (1785) George Augustus Frederick, P. of Wales, later (1820) George IV. For details of the marriage and a summary of the current rumours concerning it, see Shane Leslie, *Mrs Fitzherbert*, 1939–40, i. 2, 43–72.

9. The marriage of his niece to the Duke of Gloucester.

10. Louis (1661–1711), son of Louis XIV, was supposed to have married, ca 1695, Marie-Émilie Joly de Choin (ca 1670–1732) (*Dictionnaire de biographie française*, 1933– , viii. 1190).

11. Marie-Adélaïde (1685–1712) of Savoy, dau. of Victor Amadeus II, D. of Savoy, later K. of Sardinia, m. (1697) Louis (1682–1712), D. of Burgundy, Dauphin in 1711–12. He was devoted to his wife, whom he survived only six days.

12. A variant of this anecdote is in Saint-Simon's *Mémoires*, ed. Boislisle, 1879–1928, xxii. 287.

rest must be the work—or the explosion, of time—though secrecy does not seem to be the measure most affected.

To divert the theme, how do you like, Madam, the following story? A young Madame de Choiseul[13] is in-loved with by Monsieur de Coigny[14] and Prince Joseph of Monaco.[15] She longed for a parrot that should be a miracle of eloquence: every other shop in Paris sells mackaws, parrots, cockatoos, etc. No wonder one at least of the rivals soon found a Mr Pitt, and the bird was immediately declared the nymph's first minister: but as she had two passions as well as two lovers, she was also enamoured of General Jackoo at Astley's:[16] the unsuccessful candidate offered Astley ingots for his monkey, but Astley demanding a *terre* for life, the paladin was forced to desist, but fortunately heard of another miracle of parts of the Monomotapan[17] race who was not in so exalted a sphere of life, being only a *marmiton*[18] in a kitchen, where he had learnt to pluck fowls with inimitable

13. Gaston Maugras (*Le Duc de Lauzun et la cour de Marie-Antoinette*, 1895, pp. 347–8) gives this anecdote, but says that the lady was Mme de Valentinois. The Duchesse de Valentinois and the younger Duchesse de Choiseul were both sisters-in-law of Prince Joseph of Monaco, and were both subsequently divorced by their husbands. The former was Louise-Félicité-Victoire d'Aumont de Mazarin (1759–1826), m. 1 (1777) Honoré-Aimé-Charles-Maurice Goyon-de-Matignon de Grimaldi, Duc de Valentinois, later Prince of Monaco (she remarried 4 times; see DU DEFFAND ii. 438 n. 6). The Duchesse de Choiseul was Marie-Stéphanie de Choiseul-Stainville (1763–1833), m. (1778) Claude-Antoine-Clériadus-Gabriel de Choiseul-Beaupré, Comte (Duc, 1785) de Choiseul (ibid. i. 226 n. 14a).

14. François-Marie-Casimir de Franquetot (1756–1816), Marquis de Coigny (DU DEFFAND iv. 159; Maugras, op. cit. 186–7, 347–8).

15. Joseph-Jérôme-Marie-Honoré Goyon-de-Matignon de Grimaldi (1763–1816), younger son of the Prince of Monaco and known as 'Prince Joseph of Monaco.' He had m. (1782) the younger sister of the Comtesse (later Duchesse) de Choiseul. HW was to send him a sword in 1771

(DU DEFFAND i. 226 n. 14a, v. 416; Albert, Vicomte Révérend, *Titres . . . de la Restauration*, 1901–6, iii. 243).

16. 'Last night the little monkey, General Jackoo, from the fair of St Germaine at Paris, made its first appearance [of the season at Astley's amphitheatre, Westminster Bridge]. . . . He first appears in regimentals as a Prussian hussar; being asked where he is going, he pulls a letter from his pocket, which . . . being read, appears to be a furlough . . . he . . . draws his sword, which he flourishes, and returns in the scabbard . . . He is then dressed as a rope-dancer, and performs on the tight rope, dancing quite erect with a balance pole. . . . This little animal has been the admiration we hear of all Paris these two years past' (*Morning Herald* 5 April 1785; Ralph Heathcote, *Sylva*, 1786, pp. 254–5). Astley's amphitheatre at Paris was in the 'Rue et Fauxbourg du Temple' (Louis Petit de Bachaumont, *Mémoires secrets*, 1777–89, *passim*).

17. From the East African district of Monomotapa, 'un grand état de la basse Éthiopie' (C. Maty, *Dictionnaire géographique universel*, Amsterdam, 1701, p. 672).

18. Kitchen scullion (OED).

dexterity. This dear animal was not invaluable, was bought, and presented to Madame de Choiseul, who immediately made him the *sécretaire de ses commandements.* Her caresses were distributed equally to the animals, and her thanks to the donors. The first time she went out, the two former were locked up in her bed-chamber: how the two latter were disposed of, history is silent—Ah! I dread to tell the sequel. When the lady returned, and flew to her chamber, Jackoo the Second received her with all the *empressement possible* —but where was Pol—found at last under the bed shivering and cowering—and without a feather, as stark as any Christian. Pol's presenter concluded that his rival had given the monkey with that very view, challenged him, they fought,[19] and both were wounded; and an heroic adventure it was!

I have not paper or breath to add more, Madam, but to thank you for inverting the story of Pol and feathering my Venus.[20] I hope I shall have occasion to send you no more letters; but that if I cannot wait on you, you will have charity enough to come and visit the chalk-pits in Berkeley Square.

To Lady Ossory, Wednesday 5 July 1786

Strawberry Hill, July 5, 1786.

IT is no wonder, Madam, that I durst not recommence, who know that I ought to think of nothing but finishing. Your Ladyship tells me of my *lively ideas,* and the newspapers flatter me that I am a *well-preserved veteran;*[1] but my weak fingers, my tottering steps, and above all my *internal* looking-glass, are more faithful monitors, and whisper certain truths to one ear, that the sycophant self-love at the other ear cannot obliterate. Indeed I had nothing to write; I know nothing, and the sameness of summers makes me afraid of repeating

19. In Jan. 1786 (Maugras, op. cit. 347). Coigny was 'grièvement blessé' (ibid. 348).

20. Lady Ossory's drawing of 'A Modern Venus' with her clothes on; see *ante* 27 Jan. 1786 and illustration.

———

1. 'The illustrious monarch of Prussia, the venerable chief of the Court of King's-Bench, and Mr Macklin, the comedian, have been often mentioned as instances in whom the mental faculties, as well as the corporeal powers were unimpaired by age. Should we not add to these the Veteran of Strawberry Hill and Col. Lascelles, the latter of whom particularly still enjoys society with all the vivacity of youth' (*Morning Herald* 30 June). HW also mentioned this to Selwyn and Dr Burney.

'A MODERN VENUS' CLOTHED, BY ANNE, COUNTESS OF
UPPER OSSORY, 1785

what I may have said twenty times. The great lines of my little life are indeed (very contrary to my intentions and to all the colour of my progress) marked with red letters like the almanac, that is, tinged by princes and princesses. Princess Amelie breakfasted here last[2] week, and I have dined again at Gunnersbury,[3] where were the Prince of Wales and the Prince of Mecklemberg;[4] and that dinner produced an event which composes my whole annal. They went to drink tea at the dairy. I did not choose to limp so far, and stayed behind with Lady Barrymore, Lady Clermont and Mrs Howe. However I was summoned and forced to go. It was to command me to write verses on Gunnersbury—'Lord! Madam,' said I, 'I am superannuated.' She insisted. 'Well, Madam, if I must, your Royal Highness shall have an ode on your next birthday.' All would not save me, though I protested against the rigour of the injunction. As it happened, the following trifle came into my head in the coach as I returned home:

1.

In deathless odes for ever green
    Augustus' laurels blow;
Nor e'er was grateful duty seen
    In warmer strains to flow.

2.

Oh! why is Flaccus not alive
    Your fav'rite scene to sing?
To Gunnersbury's charms could give
    His lyre immortal spring.

3.

As warm as his my zeal for you,
    Great Princess, could I show it—
But though you have a *Horace* too—
    Ah! Madam, he's no poet.

I sent it next morning to her breakfast, and received this gracious and genteel answer;

'I wish I had a name that could answer your pretty verses. Your

2. MS reads 'lasted.'

3. On 16 June (HW to Conway 18 June 1786, which contains HW's verses and Princess Amelia's letter quoted below, as well as some details not in the letter to Lady Ossory).

4. Karl Ludwig Friedrich (1741–1816), as Karl II, D. of Mecklenburg-Strelitz, 1815–16; next older brother of Prince Ernst (*ante* 4 Dec. 1771).

yawning yesterday opened your vein for pleasing me, and I return
you my thanks, my good Mr W. and remain sincerely your friend

AMELIE.'5

To explain this, your Ladyship must know that the ancient laureate
gaped in the evening at the commerce-table, which I can tell Miss
Burney is a great sin on any Palatine hill.6 The moment the Princess
came hither t'other morning and spied the shield with Medusa's head
on the staircase,7 she said, 'Oh! now I see where you learnt to yawn.'

I am glad for *her* interest, but sorry for my own that Evelina and
Cecilia are to be transformed into a Madame de Motteville,8 as I shall
certainly not live to read her memoirs, though I might another novel.9

I readily believe that Lord Euston's little girl10 is a fine child,
Madam; I never saw her, but she has good claims: nor do I know
where Lord Euston is absent. My nepotism is so very extended, that
I cannot follow their sojournings through the maps of so many counties, nay, nor of countries.

This summer may be very fine, but it is not quite to my taste: the
sun never appears till as late as the fashionable people in town; and
then has not much more warmth. However he has made me amends
in hay: I asked why they were so long mowing one of my meadows?
they said it was so thick they could not cut it. I have really double the
quantity of any other year—yet I doubt these riches will not indemnify me for the Portland sale!11—however, here my collection closes:

5. The original letter, signed 'Amelia,'
is in the Princeton University Library.

6. On 19 June Fanny Burney had agreed
to succeed Mrs Hagerdorn as Second
Keeper of the Robes to Queen Charlotte;
see HW to Dr Burney 6 July 1786; Burney,
Diary ii. 361 ff. She began her service on
17 July 1786 and retired from the position
on 7 July 1791.

7. 'Two shields of leather, for tourna-
ments, painted by Polidore; one has the
head of Medusa, the other of Perseus: on
the insides are battles in gold. They came
out of the collection of Commendatore
Vittoria at Naples, and were sent to Mr
W. by Sir W. Hamilton' ('Des. of SH,'
Works ii. 439). See HW to Hamilton 22
Feb., 19 June 1774. The shield depicting
Medusa was sold SH xix. 87 to the E. of
Charleville for £5.5.0.

8. Françoise Bertaut (ca 1621–89) m.
(1639) Nicolas Langlois, Seigneur de Motteville; author of *Mémoires pour servir à
l'histoire d'Anne d'Autriche*, 1723.

9. On her accepting the position HW
entered in his 'Book of Materials' 1786,
p. 19: 'For Miss Burney. Qui se donne à
la cour, se dérobe aux talents. Life of
Voltaire.'

10. Lady Maria Anne Fitzroy (*ante* 16
Nov. 1785).

11. At which he spent £359.3.6. As HW
has noted in his copy (now WSL; Hazen,
Cat. of HW's Lib. 3902) of *A Catalogue of
the Portland Museum, Lately the Property of the Duchess Dowager of Portland*
[sold 24 April – 8 June 1786], he bought
seven items, the most important of which
were, 27th day, lot 2952: 'A most beautiful
missal, illuminated . . . by the famous

I will not buy sparks, since I have acquired such a bulse of jewels—adieu! Madam, the *modern* post goes out so early,[12] that I shall scarce save it—

To Lady Ossory, Saturday 22 July 1786

Address: To the Countess of Ossory at Ampthill Park, Bedfordshire. *Postmark:* ISLEWORTH 22 IY.

Strawberry Hill, July 22, 1786.

IN your last, Madam, you sent me a list of topics, on which we are not to talk for fear of disagreeing. It would be exceedingly difficult for me to disagree with your Ladyship on all of them, as of some I know no more than a babe unborn; nor of the rest more than the newspapers, which are not my rule of faith, tell me. Moreover, as I neither love disputation, nor have any zeal for making converts, I shall certainly tap no subject, on which I might be likely not to be of your Ladyship's sentiments. As far as I know what your political sentiments are, I should rather imagine that we do agree, for I am sure you are in the right, and I am not quite ready to think that I am in the wrong, as we neither of us ever think or act from partiality, prejudice, or motives of personal affection or resentment: and principles being less subject to be warped than our passions, it is probable that our opinions are perfectly consonant; and when that is the case, it is still more useless to discuss topics on which we already know each other's mind. A neutral person perhaps would conclude that one of us at least must be very determined to think everything right on one side, and wrong on the other, when on a medley of questions of the most heterogeneous natures, we dare not touch one for fear of squabbling. But such a person would be strangely in the dark, from not knowing that I am always ready to change my opinions in conformity to yours; and that you are so persuaded of my deference to your sentiments, that out of generosity you will not start a thought

Don Julio Clovio . . .' £169.1.0, with HW's note: 'Mr Udny assured Mr. W. he had seen six more by the same hand, but none of them so fine or so well preserved,' sold SH xv. 90 to Earl Waldegrave for £441; and 37th day, lot 4154: 'The head of Jupiter Serapis, cut out of green ba-

saltes . . .' £173.5.0, with HW's note: 'It was a mere head; Mrs Damer has since added to it the bust in bronze,' sold SH xiii. 82 to Hume, Berners Street, for £78.15.0; illustrated in BERRY i. facing p. 29.

12. At 1 p.m. (*post* 9 July 1788).

that might at first sight create a doubt in me, and that at the next minute I might adopt as being yours, before I was clearly convinced of its being well founded: though I should indubitably find it[1] so on knowing the grounds of your reasoning. At present I am so totally in the dark on all that is passing, and whatever does happen is of so little importance to one of my age, and who has no children who will be interested in the consequences, that to save myself the trouble of uneasy prospects, I determine to think with Pope that

Whatever is, is right,[2]

and in that composure I am secure of not disagreeing with your Ladyship.

I wish this district supplied me with any matter that would entertain you; but a village near the capital has only the news and the fish that have been hawked about in town. Poor Lord Grantham is dead, I do believe though the papers say so; but I heard two days ago that he could not outlive the night.[3]

I hope our daily oracles lie, according to their laudable practice, about the Whiteboys;[4] at least I flatter myself that our Lord's domains[5] are unmolested by them. I am surprised they are not quieted and all made peers![6]

I shall go to London next week to see Mrs Damer, who is expected from Paris.[7] If the weather continues as cold as it has been these two last nights, I will settle for the winter.

---

1. HW first wrote 'them.'

2. *Essay on Man* iv. 145.

3. He died 20 July at Grantham House, Putney Heath, Surrey.

4. 'The risings of the White Boys, or, as they are now pleased to term themselves, *Right Boys*, are much more frequent than has been known these many years past' ('Extract of a letter from Cork, June 23,' *London Chronicle* 29 June – 1 July, lx. 2, where appears almost a column describing their activities). For other accounts, see ibid. 6–22 July, lx. 29, 40, 45, 70, and especially 77, giving a summary of activities from 21 May to 15 July.

5. Grantstown Manor and Lisduff in Queen's County; in 1883 these estates totalled 22,510 acres (GEC iii. 102).

6. In 1785, '16 new Irish peers made or advanced in rank' ('Mem. 1783–91' *sub* July 1785) or given special remainders, and one was restored. No other Irish peerages were granted until 1789 (Robert Beatson, *Political Index*, 3d edn, 1806, iii. 174–6).

7. She and Caroline Campbell had left for the Continent on 30 Oct. 1785 and had been in Florence and Rome (HW-Mann Correspondence, *passim*).

To LADY OSSORY, Wednesday 2 August 1786

Address: To the Countess of Ossory at Ampthill Park, Bedfordshire. *Postmark:* ISLEWORTH. 2 AU.

Strawberry Hill, Aug. 2, 1786.

YOU would have been very unjust, my dear Lady, which you are not, if you had been *seriously* angry with me for joking with you on your politics. You said you would not name them lest we should disagree: I on my side with the same good and peaceable intention, and who, you really know, never do dispute about anything, replied jesting. Now it would have been hard, if you had been offended at my listing under Democritus,[1] when you yourself had pointed out to me to avoid Heraclitus.[2] I had rather be ready with Dr Warton to panegyricize everything; but when he himself is reduced to generals, and can find no particular theme for encomium, it is fair for me to resort to one of the other three divisions; for politics must range under one of the four: one must admire, lament, laugh at, or be indifferent about, whatever happens. My time of life and the multitude of events I have seen, dispose me to indifference —but to keep up good humour, when you was afraid of our being too grave, I preferred smiling—and there I hope the matter will rest. It is for this reason I reply so soon, and because you are going to wander, and I might not know where to overtake you.

I have heard that the Duke of Bedford has ordered Mr Palmer[3] to have all his palaces ready for him;[4] which is considered as an expulsion of the Queen Dowager.[5] If it is only to make room for another

1. The 'Laughing Philosopher.'

2. The 'Dark' or 'Weeping Philosopher.' Bentley ca 1755 drew HW standing between Democritus and Heraclitus as a frontispiece for his 'Memoirs of George II'; see W. S. Lewis, *Horace Walpole*, 1961, pp. xxi, 85.

3. Robert Palmer (d. 1787), of Otes, near High Laver, in Essex, and Great Russell St, Bloomsbury; solicitor to and executor of the will of Edward Wortley Montagu; 'trustee,' 'guardian,' 'steward,' or 'principal agent to the Duke of Bedford . . . maintained an universally good character' (GM 1787, lvii pt i. 94; J. Curling, *Edward*

Wortley Montagu, 1954, *passim*; Coke, 'MS Journals' 10 June 1776; *London Chronicle* 13–15 Jan. 1785, lvii. 55; Anthony Pasquin [John Williams], *Life of the Late Earl of Barrymore*, 3d edn, 1793, pp. 109–11).

4. The Duke had come of age on 23 July. He had arrived at Bedford House, Bloomsbury Square, on 31 Aug. (*London Chronicle* 31 Aug.– 2 Sept., lx. 218). On 10 Oct. was published his *Descriptive Journey through the Interior Parts of Germany and France, including Paris* 'by a young English peer . . . just returned from his travels' (*Morning Chronicle* 10 Oct.).

5. The Duke of Bedford wrote to Lord

antique, old woman for old woman, I should think one's own grandmother might be preferable to one that for many reasons might be grandmother of half London[6]—but, as about politics, I leave everybody to judge for himself, nor is it any business of mine whether young Hamlet *speaks daggers* to Gertrude or not.

The vase for which your Ladyship is so good as to interest yourself was not the famous cat's *lofty vase*,[7] nor one of any consequence, but a vase and dish of Florentine faience, that stood under the table in the Round Chamber;[8] nor had I the least concern but for the company who were so grieved at the accident—With the troops that come, I am amazed I have not worse damage—however I am sometimes diverted too. Last week a scientific lady was here,[9] and exactly at the

Ossory 15 Aug. from Plombières: 'I was very much surprised at receiving a letter from the Duchess informing she meant to give me up Woburn in October and one from Palmer (to whom I had wrote to take possession of my houses . . .) to say that if I was in a hurry she would contrive to go to Blenheim a little sooner. I intended being in England by this time had Woburn been given up. It has made me put off my journey for about a fortnight . . . I shall immediately come and pay you a short visit and then return to London to settle my affairs. I shall avoid going to Woburn after my first visit as I am sure the Duchess will do nothing but pester me to let her live there and if not that to let her take away half the furniture' (National Library of Ireland: Fitzpatrick MSS). The Duchess took a 'ready-furnished house in Pall Mall ['within two doors of Carlton House'], the same Lord Cowper had when he was in England . . . Her grandson has not . . . taken or given her a country house . . . This is no good mark of his disposition' (Coke, 'MS Journals' 25 Oct., 19 Dec. 1786).

6. Lady Maynard (Nancy Parsons), former mistress of the Duke of Grafton, the Duke of Dorset, and others had become the mistress of the Duke of Bedford. On 31 Dec. 1784 the Duchess of Bedford told Lady Mary Coke 'she was extremely glad the Duke . . . had fallen into Lady Maynard's hands as she was sure she would improve him very much' (Coke,

'MS Journals'). 'The Duke of Bedford is so entirely governed by Lady Maynard that his family don't think he will return to England when he comes of age, unless she chooses to reside at Bedford House or at Woburne' (ibid. 6 Oct. 1785). 'The young Duke of B—— is about 19, his *lovely Nancy* about 42; but his Grace has a taste for the *antique*, and gratifies it in an *antick* manner' (*Rambler's Magazine*, March 1785, iii. 120).

7. In Gray's 'Ode on the Death of a Favourite Cat Drowned in a Tub of Gold Fishes.' 'The blue and white china tub in which Selima was drowned stood on the pedestal in the Small Cloister, on the north side of the house'; sold SH xix. 32 to Lord Derby for £42; now at Knowsley Hall (Hazen, *SH Bibl.* 209, where the label printed at SH is described).

8. 'A large round vase and cover, and a dish to it, of Roman faience' stood under a table (*Des. of SH*, 1784, p. 55; *Works* ii. 470) and 'a large vase of Florentine faience, with the arms of the Great Duke,' was under a Japan cabinet in the Round Drawing Room (*Des. of SH*, 1784, p. 55; *Works* ii. 470). The first, or possibly its replacement after the accident here mentioned, was described in the SH Sale as 'A very choice specimen of the Raphael or Faenza ware, in the form of an urn, with cover and dish,' sold xxiii. 43 to Webb for £7.7.0; the second was sold SH xxiii. 51 to W. M. Smith for £22.1.0.

9. Five groups totalling twenty people

moment that I opened the cabinet of enamels, she turned to a gentle-man who came with her, and entered into a discussion of the ides and calends. Another gentlewoman was here two days ago who has seen a good half century;[10] she said, 'Well I must live another *forty* years to have time to see all the curiosities of this house.' These little incidents of character do not make me amends for being the master of a puppet-show, for though I generally keep behind the scenes, I am almost as much disturbed as if I constantly exhibited myself—and

E'en Sunday shines no Sabbath-day to me![11]

PS. I am told that this has been a fine summer—and in one respect I allow it, for it has brought the winter so forward already, that my grate was in full blow on Monday night with a good fire!

To Lady Ossory, Wednesday 30 August 1786

Address: To the Countess of Ossory at Ampthill Park, Bedfordshire. *Postmark:* ISLEWORTH. 31 AU.

Strawberry Hill, Aug. 30, 1786.

HOW the Israelites contrived to make bricks without straw, I cannot tell; though to be sure there are succedaneums for every-thing. Letters I know can be made of lies, as well as newspapers; and we have large manufactures at Richmond and Hampton Court wrought by old ladies themselves, as they used to make japan, by cutting prints to pieces, and daubing them over with colours and varnish; and they are so generous that they give their wares to any-body that will retail them. But though I am hard driven to keep up a correspondence in these halcyon days, when there are no more events than in Paradise, not even a new peer made,[1] I neither care to coin nor clip—by the way I wonder what people will do in the next world for want of newspapers, where everything will be settled to all eter-

were at SH 21–27 July (BERRY ii. 226); the 'scientific lady' and the 'gentleman' here mentioned have not been identified.

10. 'Mr and Mrs Russel' were at SH 31 July (ibid.); not further identified.

11. Pope, 'Epistle to Dr Arbuthnot,' l. 12.

1. There had been ten new creations in August; for the titles, see Robert Beatson, *Political Index,* 3d edn, 1806, i. 142–3. Cf. *ante* 22 July 1786.

nity, and where we know there is to be no marrying or giving in marriage, and then of course there will be no lyings in, no Gretna Greens, etc., etc. Pray, Madam, do you think there will be any change of fashions? Do angels always wear the same patterns for their clothes? oh! I find I could make a letter long enough, if I were to indulge all the questions that rush into my head—but I will return to earth, and grovel, as I generally do, within the bounds of my own parish. I have indeed been for a few days at Park Place,[2] and seen the delight of my eyes, the new bridge at Henley;

A Senator of Rome, while Rome survived,[3]

would have allowed it worthy of the Tiber—and it traverses a river a thousand times more beautiful; and some Verres I suppose some time or other will strip it of Mrs Damer's colossal masks and transport them to the capital of Europe, or America, or wherever that is to be. The Emperor to be sure intends it shall be Vienna, now the King of Prussia is dead.[4] As I hate both those heroes, and all such captains of banditti, I shall *go up* to Berlin with no address of condolence —not that I disdain knighthood on a good occasion, and have offered to accept it, if my *addresses* are accepted. You must know, Lady Charleville[5] has taken a house between my niece Mrs Keppel[6] and the Duchess of Montrose.[7] That dowager has buried Captain Mayne, her second consort, whom she married in an arbour by moonlight,[8]

2. HW to Strafford 29 Aug. 1786 gives further details of this visit.

3. Addison, *Cato*, V. iv. 88.

4. On 17 Aug.; the news of his death reached London on 28 Aug. (*London Chronicle* 26–29 Aug., lx. 208).

5. Hester Coghill (d. 1789) m. 1 (1737) Charles Moore, 2d Bn Moore, cr. (1758) E. of Charleville; m. 2 (in or after 1764) Maj. John Mayne (d. 1785), who assumed the name of Coghill (1779) and was cr. (1781) Bt; M.P.

6. The house on the Thames at Isleworth which she had inherited from her father Sir Edward Walpole (*ante* 17 July 1781, n. 4).

7. 'Next to Mrs Keppel's is a house where about 40 years ago resided three maiden ladies, Lady Judith Coote, Mrs Sambrook and Mrs Paucefort. After them it was purchased and enlarged by Mrs

Cavendish, daughter of Lord James Cavendish; then by a Mr Brown, and then by the Countess Dowager of Charleville [who died there], and her second husband Captain Mayne, who had assumed her maiden name of Coghill, but he dying before her, her Ladyship bequeathed her villa to her relation Lord Muncaster. He let it to Mary Stuart Countess Dowager of Bute, who died there in 1794' (HW's MS note to p. 100 of Lysons, *Environs of London*, Vol. III, 1795, now WSL; cf. Lysons, *Supplement to the First Edition of the Historical Account of the Environs of London*, 1811, p. 203).

8. They were married at Drumcondra House, near Dublin, in an arbour within the Temple, a classical building (now in ruins) said to have been imported from Italy and partly re-erected, without a roof (J. P. Campbell, 'Two Memorable Dublin

and whom she obliged to take her family name of Coghill, that he might be her heir, as he was certainly fitter to be her son than her husband; and she remains possessed of £6000 a year, but no *child* —*Therefore* I have commissioned my two friends above mentioned to propose *me,* and to offer that I will condescend to be Sir Horatio Coghill; and if she will waive the arbour scene, she being still more gouty than I am, I engage, that like old Jack Harris[9] and his first wife,[10] I will ring the bell and order the grooms of the chambers to wheel us to one another, when we have a need to kiss.[11] You shall know, Madam, if the treaty succeeds, and may depend on having a favour.

I admire the Duchess Dowager for holding out Woburn to the last moment.[12] We shall now see which of the venerable matrons triumphs. I hope Duchess Nancy will not call in Mr Hastings—He would turn the old Begum into the highway in her pattens, and boast of it when he had done.[13]

I conclude your campaign in Farming Woods is now opening, Madam. Mr Hatton,[14] I hear, intends to refit Kirby, and inhabit it, and as he has the true patina of the Finches,[15]

Houses,' *Dublin Historical Record,* 1940, ii. 141–55, especially pp. 151–2, where this passage from HW's letter is quoted).

9. John Harris (ca 1690–1767) of Hayne, Devon; M.P.; his second wife was HW's cousin, Anne Seymour Conway (MANN i. 486 n. 18).

10. Margaret Tuckfield (d. 1754) m. 1 (ca 1704) Samuel Rolle (by whom she was the mother of Lady Orford, HW's sister-in-law); m. 2 (after 1719) John Harris (MANN i. 486 n. 19).

11. For other references to Harris's gout, see HW to Montagu 7 Jan. 1755, MONTAGU i. 167; HW to Conway 7 Aug. 1760, 31 Dec. 1774.

12. 'The Duke of Bedford is now in town. When he first came to England he went to Woburn Abbey and passed' a day or two with 'the Duchess of Bedford, since which he stays in town. . . . It is said he has wrote to the Duchess . . . to let her know that it will be convenient in a little time that she should quit Woburn Abbey. . . . The Duchess . . . was to come to Blenheim the end of this month for that she has no house to go to' (Coke, 'MS

Journals' 13, 22 Sept. 1786). 'Lady Maynard is now at Woburn with the Duke of Bedford' (ibid. 28 Oct. 1786).

13. Burke's charge of Hastings's treatment of the Begums of Oudh and Hastings's defence are in Burke's *Articles . . . against Warren Hastings . . . Presented to the House of Commons, on the 4th Day of April 1786,* 1786, pp. 86–152, and Hastings's *Minutes . . . of What Was Offered . . . at the Bar of the House of Commons upon the . . . Charges of High Crimes,* [1786], pp. 75–89. HW's copies are Hazen, *Cat. of HW's Lib.* 1609.50.2 and 3. See also Keith Feiling, *Warren Hastings,* 1954, pp. 259–78, especially p. 273.

14. George Finch-Hatton (1747–1823), of Eastwell Park, Kent, and of Kirby, Northants; grandson of the 7th E. of Winchilsea; M.P. Rochester 1772–84 (Venn, *Alumni Cantab.; Old Westminsters;* Burke, *Peerage,* 1953, p. 2254).

15. 'The black funereal Finches'; 'all my Finches,/With their black funereal face' (Sir Charles Hanbury Williams, 'A New Ode to a Great Number of Great Men, Newly Made,' 1742, quoted in HW

Will breathe a browner horror on the woods.[16]

I like the restoration of those ancient palaces, and I suppose it will now be accessible, as this age has invented good roads, which our worthy ancestors did not think at all a necessary ingredient in living comfortably. We are so effeminate that we hate being jolted to death, or dug out of a hollow way—but every thing degenerates!

Mr Fox, I am told, is at Cheltenham entirely occupied with taming a young rabbit—This is Mr Hare's account—but he is partial—for my part I suspect that he is teaching it to exercise that terrible weapon, a dessert-knife—but whether he is or not, I think there ought to be an Act of Parliament against eating any thing but spoon-meat.

Lady Charleville has just sent me a flat refusal; so that if I have a mind to have children of my own to inherit Strawberry, I must look for

Arbutei fœtus alibi[17]—

This is a little disappointment—but when one has threescore nephews and nieces, one cannot want heirs. Nay, I still want a month of sixty-nine—*nous verrons.*

To Lady Ossory, Thursday 28 September 1786

Addressed to Farming Woods, Northants; see following letter.

Strawberry Hill, Sept. 28, 1786.

AS I conclude, Madam, that by this time you are at least as real an inhabitant of the woods as Peter the Wild Boy,[1] or that guileless savage the Marquis of Lansdown,[2] who would make one believe,

to Mann 11 Sept. 1742 OS, Mann ii. 51; HW's 'Reminiscences,' *Works* iv. 276 n.; and 'Squire Sandys's Budget Open'd,' in Williams, *Works*, with notes by HW, 1822, ii. 195).

16. 'And breathes a browner horror on the woods' (Pope, 'Eloisa to Abelard,' l. 170).

17. 'Young strawberries elsewhere,' adapted from Virgil, *Georgics* i. 55, 'ar-borei fetus alibi,' 'young trees elsewhere.' Cf. Ovid, *Metamorphoses*, i. 104.

————

1. (ca 1712–85), an idiot found in the woods near Hanover in 1725, presented to George I and brought to England in the following year (DNB; GM 1785, lv pt i. 236, pt ii. 851–3).

2. At this time living in retirement at Bowood. Cf. *ante* 20 June 1785.

like Biddy Tipkin in *The Tender Husband*,[3] that he lives on hips and haws, and is mighty fond of pignuts,[4] I direct to Farming Woods rather than to the honour of Ampthill. I should have answered your last sooner, but had nothing to tell you; and at present all my gleanings would not load a parish girl's little paw. Except the sad deaths of two happy young women Lady Graham[5] and Lady Harriot Elliot,[6] I know no event but the death of Mr Charles Hamilton,[7] one of my patriarchs of modern gardening,[8] who has been killed by Anstey, author of *The Bath Guide*. Mr Hamilton, who had built a house in the Crescent,[9] was also at 83 eager in planting a new garden, and wanted some acres, which Anstey his neighbour, not so ancient, destined to the same use. Hamilton wrote a warm letter[10] on their being refused; and Anstey, who does not hate a squabble in print, as he has more than once shown,[11] discharged shaft upon shaft against the poor veteran, and

> The grey goose quill that was thereon
> In his heart's blood was wet,[12]

for he died of the volley, as even a goose quill will do the feat at eighty-three, and surely, since the *first* edition of *The Bath Guide*, never was a duller goose than Anstey! This is a literary anecdote, not much known, I believe, in the coffee-houses on Parnassus.[13]

3. By Sir Richard Steele.

4. Biddy Tipkin to Humphry Gubbin in Act III: 'Don't you love blackberries, haws, and pig-nuts mightily?'

5. Lady Jemima Elizabeth Ashburnham (1762 – 18 Sept. 1786) m. (1785) James Graham, styled M. of Graham to 1790, 3d D. of Montrose, 1790.

6. Lady Harriot Pitt (1758 – 25 Sept. 1786), sister of William Pitt the younger, m. (1785) Hon. Edward James Eliot (GEC xi. 309).

7. Hon. Charles Hamilton (1704 – 11 Sept. 1786), 9th son of James, 6th E. of Abercorn; M.P. Truro 1741–7; of Cobham and Painshill, Surrey, both of which estates he sold before his death at Lansdown Hill, near Bath (*Scots Peerage* i. 61; Mon-tagu i. 71 n. 32).

8. In 'On Modern Gardening' (*Anecdotes of Painting*, SH, 1762–71, iv. 145; *Works* ii. 541) HW praises Painshill as

'a perfect example' of 'the forest or savage garden.'

9. Hamilton's house was on Lansdown Road, near but not a part of Lansdown Place or Lansdown Crescent. Since 1770 Anstey had lived at No. 5, Royal Crescent, about a quarter of a mile southwest of Hamilton's house. A considerable portion of the land between had had no houses built upon it. See R. E. Peach, *Historic Houses in Bath*, 1883, pp. 113–15; *A New Plan of the City of Bath*, published 1 Jan. 1789, 'sold by W. Taylor and W. Meyler, Booksellers, in Bath.'

10. Missing.

11. Cf. *ante* 14 June 1774.

12. A paraphrase of *Chevy Chase*; cf. *ante* 23 July 1775; MASON i. 309, ii. 85.

13. W. C. Powell, *Christopher Anstey*, Philadelphia, 1944, pp. 212–13, quotes this passage from HW's letter, 'the only version' of the incident. 'There is no hint of

I was last week of a small party at Lady Clifford's[14] at Richmond, and half of the company consisted of pinchbeck royalties, for there were the grandmother Princess Dowager Mrs Molyneux,[15] her son-in-law Mr Smyth[16] father of Inés de Castro,[17] his sister Lady Langdale[18] and I. Lady Mary Coke, who envies us for having mixed our alloy with the standard, when her own counterfeit is but a Birmingham shilling[19] that never had the impress and titles on it,[20] would swear that we met to hatch a new Gunpowder Plot. It is incredible how she has toiled tooth and nail to couple Inés with Margery Nicholson.[21] For my part the rencounter put me in mind of Lady Dorchester,[22] who meeting the Duchess of Portsmouth[23] and Lady Ork-

such a quarrel in Anstey's correspondence nor in the Hamilton obituary notices. Nor is there any extant poem which can be associated with the incident. But . . . we have little reason to doubt Walpole's story. Indeed, the supposition that this is true is increased by another incident of the same kind, perhaps involving the very same land. In 1790 Anstey was given notice to abandon his garden near St James's Square since the ground was to be built upon. In his anger the poet addressed an epigram to his fellow citizens.'

14. Apollonia Langdale (ca 1755–1815), whose mother, Bns Langdale, was dau. of Sir John Smythe, 3d Bt, m. (1780) Hugh Edward Henry Clifford, 5th Bn Clifford, 1783; she was Mrs Fitzherbert's first cousin.

15. Mrs Fitzherbert's grandmother: Maria Leverly (ca 1709–95), dau. of James Leverly of London, m. 1 Joseph Griffin (d. 1728), of Bickmarsh, Warwickshire; m. 2 (1734) John Errington (d. 1741), of Beaufront, Northumberland; m. 3 (1746) Hon. Thomas Joseph Molyneux (1689–1756), of Croxteth Hall, Lancashire, by whom she was mother of the 1st E. of Sefton (ante 29 June 1780; BERRY ii. 149 n. 3; A History of Northumberland, Newcastle-upon-Tyne, 1893–1940, iv. 189; GEC, sub Sefton).

16. Walter Smythe (d. 1788), of Brambridge, Hants, 2d son of Sir John Smythe, 3d Bt. He had married (1755) Mary Errington, Mrs Molyneux's daughter by her second husband (GM 1788, lviii pt i. 85; E. Kimber and R. Johnson, Baronetage of England, 1771, ii. 168; A History of Northumberland, Newcastle-upon-Tyne, 1893–1940, iv. 194).

17. Mrs Fitzherbert, paralleled with Inés de Castro (d. 1355), a Spanish noblewoman whom Pedro, the son of Alfonso IV of Portugal, said he had married after the death of his wife. Inés de Castro was killed by order of Alfonso IV.

18. Constantia Smythe (d. ca 1792) m. Marmaduke Langdale, 5th Bn Langdale of Holme (Catholic Record Society, Obituaries, 1913, p. 41).

19. I.e., a counterfeit shilling; see OED, sub Brummagem.

20. Lady Mary Coke's infatuation with Edward, D. of York, led her to think of herself as his widow. See Lady Louisa Stuart's account in Coke, Journals i. lxxxii–xcix et passim.

21. Margaret Nicholson (ca 1750–1828) on 2 Aug. 1786 attempted to stab George III as he arrived at St James's Palace from Windsor. Declared insane, she was sent to Bedlam, where she died. Lady Mary Coke first heard of the attempt on 3 Aug.: 'If it [the report] proves true, can anyone doubt but that the Roman Catholics are at the bottom of it? Mrs Fitzherbert a bigoted papist; pray God preserve the King's life.' Similar entries appear in her 'MS Journals' 3–12 Aug. 1786.

22. Catherine Sedley (1657–1717), cr. (1686) Cts of Dorchester by James II, whose mistress she had been for many years; m. (1696) Sir David Colyear, 2d Bt, cr. (1699) Bn Portmore and (1703) E. of Portmore.

23. Louise-Renée de Penancoët de Kéroualle (1649–1734), cr. (1673) Ds of Portsmouth; mistress of Charles II from 1671; retired to France in 1688, but visited England early in 1716.

ney[24] in the drawing-room at Windsor in the beginning of George I, cried out, 'God! who would have thought that we three royal whores should meet here!'[25]

Oct. 1.

I began my letter three days ago, and it was barren enough, so I postponed it on a prospect of imperial recruits. I had notice that the Archduke[26] and Archduchess[27] desired a ticket to see

My gothic Vatican of Greece and Rome,[28]

and that I would name the day. I replied,[29] I could not presume to send a ticket or name a day, but that their R.R.H.H. might command me and my nutshell whenever they pleased, if they would be so good as to excuse such a reception as a decrepit old man could give them—Accordingly I made no preparation but of coffee, tea and chocolate; and as I am a courtier of the old rock, *only two cups* were set for their Arch Highnesses in the Round Chamber, and none for their suite. In two days I could not make an entertainment,[30] nor do I pique myself on vulgar ostentation, nor could light up the garden with coloured lamps by daylight, and when the leaves are falling and my orange trees gone into winter quarters. It was intimated that I

24. Elizabeth Villiers (d. 1733), sister of Edward, 1st E. of Jersey, m. (1695) her distant cousin Lord George Hamilton, cr. (1696) E. of Orkney; the only English mistress of William III.

25. This anecdote is also in HW's 'Reminiscences, Written in 1788,' *Works* iv. 316 n., and in his notes to Lady Mary Wortley Montagu's letters, which he sent to Lady Ossory (Fitzpatrick MSS, National Library of Ireland). See Appendix 9.

26. Ferdinand Karl Anton Joseph (1754–1806), Archduke of Austria, titular D. of Modena, 1803; third surviving son of Maria Theresa. He and the Archduchess arrived in London at a house taken for them in Dover Street on 4 Sept., left 4 Oct., and sailed from Dover to Calais 7 Oct. (*London Chronicle* 31 Aug.–12 Oct., lx. 223, 232, 335, 354).

27. Maria Ricciarda Beatrice (1750–1829), of Este, grand-daughter of the D. of Modena, m. (1771) Archduke Ferdinand. Cf. MANN vi. 125–6.

28. An adaptation of Pope's *Dunciad* i. 125–6 ('A' Text), i. 145–6 ('B' Text):

'A Gothic Vatican! of Greece and Rome
Well purged . . .'

'The Gothic Vatican of Greece and Rome' is in one of HW's notebooks, 1786 (BERRY ii. 261), and he applied the phrase to SH in his *Des. of SH*, SH, 1784, Preface, p. 3 n. (*Works* ii. 397 n.).

29. Both the 'notice' and HW's reply are missing.

30. 'The Archduke and Duchess are to be at Strawberry Hill on Tuesday morning [3 Oct.], which I imagine makes Mr Walpole very happy. It is certainly unlike most other places and contains many curious and fine things and therefore I am glad they see it' (Coke, 'MS Journals' 29 Sept. 1786). 'It was this morning [1 Oct.] or tomorrow that the Archduke and Duchess were to visit Strawberry Hill. Not being sure which day must be very inconvenient to Mr Walpole, as I conclude he must prepare a breakfast' (ibid. 1 Oct. 1786).

might expect them today. The morning was of the best October gold, and the sun himself came to do the honours of my house—however I began to fear they would serve him as they did at Hampton Court and not arrive till six o'clock; but at near two as I sat watching for Heyducs and Pandours to come powdering down my avenue,[31] I saw a gang of foot passengers in boots and riding dresses strolling from Twickenham, holiday folks as I thought—but at last one of the troop ran before, who I perceived was the Venetian Resident[32]—I hurried down to the gate, and the Resident named the Archduke and Madame—and Prince and Princess Albani,[33] etc., in short they were eleven[34]—Well! they have been here above an hour, were exceedingly civil, totally unceremonious, commended everything, were really charmed with the situation and views, especially the Archduke; and Prince Albani, who does know, marked the right pictures,[35] and they all fell pell-mell on the biscuits and bread and butter, but tasted nothing liquid. The Archduke is rather a little man, and if Mr Hare was to ask, as he did Garrick, whether he looked much like an eagle,[36] I could not say Yes. The Archduchess is not a beauty but better than I had heard, seems sensible, and is very conversant in our history. I had rummaged that old garret my memory for recollections of the month I passed at the Fair of Reggio with the Archduchess's grandsire and grandam the Duke and Duchess of Modena[37] in the year of our Lord one thousand seven hundred and forty-one. I had recalled the

31. HW was expecting a large suite since the *Morning Chronicle* 4 Sept. had reported that 'Forty beds were bespoke at Dessein's, at Calais, for the retinue and suite of the Archduke . . .'

32. —— Soderini replaced Torniello as Venetian Resident at London, ca 1786, and remained until ca 1789 (*Royal Kalendar* 1786–9, p. 105). He was probably Giulio Maria Soderini (Francesco Schröder, *Repertorio genealogico delle famiglie . . . nelle provincie Venete*, Venice, 1830–1, ii. 278–9). He was at Oxford with the Modenese party (*Daily Adv.* 19 Sept.).

33. The Archduchess's first cousin and lord high steward was Carlo Francesco Saverio Giuseppe Albani (b. 1749), Principe di Soriano, m. (1783) Teresa, Contessa Casati; he was the son of Orazio Francesco Albani (1717–92) by Maria Anna Matilde Cybo (1726–97), Princess of Massa, sister of the Archduchess's mother (*Europäisches genealogisches Handbuch*, ed. C. F. Jacobi,

Leipzig, 1800, pt i. 565–6; MANN iii. 475 nn. 9–12).

34. Probably including some of those who accompanied the Archduke and Archduchess to Oxford: 'the Marchioness Cosani, of Milan, Lady of Honour to the Archduchess; . . . the Chevalier Rosales . . . the Prince Rezzonico, Senator of Rome; . . . Prince Lichenstein; and Reviczky, the Imperial Ambassador' (*London Chronicle* 16–19 Sept., lx. 278).

35. 'Of all the Roman nobility, Prince Albani is reckoned the best judge, as well as the most liberal encourager of the fine arts' (*Morning Chronicle* 5 Oct.).

36. See HW to Mason 27 Feb. 1777, MASON i. 285.

37. Francesco III (Francesco Maria d'Este) (1698–1780), D. of Modena 1737–80, m. (1720) Charlotte-Aglaé de Bourbon d'Orléans (1700–61), dau. of Philippe, Duc d'Orléans, Regent of France.

serene Duke's figure with a mound of vermilion on the left side of his forehead to symmetrise with a wen on the right;[38] and his sister the Princess Benedict,[39] who was painted and peeled like an old summer-house, with bristles on her chin sprouting through a coat of plaster—but I did not intend to draw these portraits; and above all things put a gag on my tongue lest it should blurt out the dreadful compliment I blundered on to the Duchess of Modena on her own mother's[40] jealousy of her[41]—but I had no occasion for my caution; there was such a babel of Italian dialects, and the Archduke has such a very sharp *faussette,* that my meek voice could not be distinguished —Well! it is happily over—they expressed satisfaction, and at least were better pleased than with their *no* reception at Blenheim[42] by the Prince of Mindleheim.[43]

This detail, which I might have given in fewer words and was not worth giving at all, may fill up a chink in an evening after a whole morning's shooting.

---

38. Cf. HW to Mann 17 May 1749 OS, and Mann to HW 25 July 1749 NS, MANN iv. 57, 75.

39. Benedetta Ernestina d'Este (1697–1777) (GRAY i. 242 and n. 8).

40. Françoise-Marie de Bourbon (1677–1749), called Mlle de Blois, dau. of Louis XIV by Mme de Montespan, m. (1692) Philippe de Bourbon, Duc de Chartres, later Duc d'Orléans, Regent of France. Horace Mann mentions her hatred of her daughter, to HW, 4 Feb. 1744 NS, MANN ii. 385.

41. 'The Duke of Orléans, Regent of France, was too familiar with both his daughters, afterwards duchesses of Modena and Berry. In consenting to the marriage of the latter, he is said to have bargained for a day or two of her company every week. When I was in Italy, in my youth, I went to a ball at Reggio, and was placed next the Duchess of Modena. This circumstance, and my being known as the son of the English minister, engaged me to say something polite, as I thought, to the Duchess. I asked her the reason why she did not dance. She answered, that her mother always said she danced ill, and would not allow her to join in that diversion. "I suppose," replied I in complete innocence, "that your mother was jealous of you." Her face was all scarlet in an instant, and she seemed ready to sink into the ground. I very hastily withdrew, and took my politeness along with me' (*Walpoliana* ii. 97–8). HW's letter to West 10 May 1741, N.S. ('A daughter of the Regent's, that could please him . . .') indicates that the incident had occurred before that date (GRAY i. 242, 241 n. 1).

42. 'I am told the Archduke and Duchess were much pleased with their tour to Oxford [12–16 Sept.] and the places they saw in their journey, particularly with Stow [14 Sept.] and their reception; at Blenheim [13 Sept.] something happened that was not so well. The Duke of Marlborough has a very fine observatory which he had not shown; the Archduke being very curious desired to see it, and the report is the Duke of Marlborough sent a footman to show it him. I hope it is not true' (Coke, 'MS Journals' 19 Sept. 1786; *London Chronicle* 16–19 Sept., lx. 278).

43. On 28 Aug. 1704 the Emperor Leopold created the first D. of Marlborough, his children, heirs, and lawful descendants, male and female, Princes of the Holy Roman Empire, and on 18 Nov. 1705 Joseph I gave him the Principality of Mindelheim in Swabia, which he exchanged in 1713 for the county (then erected into a principality) of Mellenburg in Upper Austria (GEC viii. 493–4).

PS. The Austrian ovation came to me from Pope's,[44] whence they had sent their coaches to the inn.[45]

TO LADY OSSORY, Friday 13 October 1786

Address: To the Countess of Ossory at Ampthill Park, Bedfordshire. *Postmark:* ISLEWORTH. 13 OC.

Strawb[erry Hill], Oct. 13, 1786.

FAR be it from me, Madam, to think that you ought to answer my letters incontinently. They very seldom contain anything that requires or deserves a reply. Your own last lay long before I wrote again. In fact this only comes to ask if you did receive one that I sent on Monday was sevennight directed to Farming Woods, where the time of year made me conclude you was. If it lies there till this time twelvemonth, it will not signify; but I would not have your Ladyship think that I have been still more remiss than I really have been. Though indolence would be very excusable at my age, want of matter is oftener the cause of my silence. Therefore, when I have spun three pages out of nothing, I like to have the merit of the deed; and as you will give me credit for the assertion, your gamekeeper is welcome to light his pipe with my epistle.

TO LADY OSSORY, Saturday 4 November 1786

Strawberry Hill, Nov. 4, 1786.

WHEN I in the heart of these populous villages can glean so little worth repeating, I do not wonder, Madam, that Farming Woods are still less productive—and without events and news or business, what idle, affected and unnatural things are letters! I sent a postscript after mine because I thought, as did happen, that the direction was wrong. Now I can only reply to a few paragraphs, and

44. About a quarter of a mile from SH; at this time owned by Welbore Ellis (cr., 1794, Bn Mendip), who had inherited the house through his first wife, dau. of Sir William Stanhope, the purchaser of it in 1744 (GEC, *sub* Mendip; R. S. Cobbett,

Memorials of Twickenham, 1872, pp. 284–6).

45. The George Inn, near the intersection of Cross Deep and Church Street. See 'A Plan of Twickenham . . . 1784,' frontispiece to Edward Ironside, *The History*

return thanks for the charades;[1] but easy or difficult, I have solved neither: people without teeth can no more eat an apple than crack a nut. I did guess at the more mysterious one, and thought it might be a *spelling-book,* but that solution is so awkward, that I think the enigma would not be worthy of Mr Fitzpatrick. For Mrs West's[2] verses, I do not think I shall tap them. The milkwoman at Bristol has made me sick of mendicant poetesses. If deep distresses and poverty cannot sow gratitude in the human heart, nor balance vanity and jealousy, these slip-shod Muses must sing better than they do, before I will lend an ear to them. Miss Hannah More is the best of our numerous Calliopes; and her heart is worth all Pindus. Misses Seward and Williams[3] and half-a-dozen more of those harmonious virgins, have no imagination, no novelty. Their thoughts and phrases are like their gowns, old remnants cut and turned.

Mr Selwyn had a bad fever in Gloucestershire, but is recovered and returned to Richmond.[4] My good old friend Sir Horace, whom your Ladyship is so kind as to mention, was alive when those scalping assassins the newspapers killed him.[5] I scarce dare affirm that he is so now, as his excellent nephew, the younger Sir Horace, who posted to him on hearing of his danger, gives me small hopes of his lasting[6] —but why should I hope it? He suffers, is eighty-five,[7] and perfectly resigned to his fate!

of *Twickenham,* 1797, reproduced as the back endpaper to More.

————

1. Both by Fitzpatrick, and both quoted in HW to Conway 29 Oct. 1786:

1. 'In Concert, song, or serenade,
   My first requires my second's aid.
   To those residing near the pole
   I would not recommend my whole.'

2. 'Charades of all things are the worst,
   But yet my best have been my first.
   Who with my second are concern'd
   Will to despise my whole have learn'd.'

2. Jane West (1758–1852), born in London, at the age of eleven moved with her father to Northamptonshire; m. Thomas West, a yeoman farmer of Northamptonshire; self-taught author of poems, plays, and novels. Her works published before this date are *Miscellaneous Poems, Translations, and Imitations,* 1780; *Miscellaneous Poetry. Written at an Early Period of*

Life, 1786. No work by her is listed in Hazen, *Cat. of HW's Lib.*

3. Helen Maria Williams (1762–1827), whose collected *Poems* appeared in 1786. HW, Hannah More, Anna Seward, and 'Mrs West' are among the many subscribers to *Poems* (Hazen, *Cat. of HW's Lib.* 2989). Living chiefly in France from 1788, she wrote with enthusiasm of the French Revolution.

4. Near the D. of Queensberry's; see *post* 1 Dec. 1786.

5. 'Letters from Florence bring advice of the death of Sir Horace Mann, K.B.; envoy extraordinary and minister plenipotentiary to that Court' (*London Chronicle* 17–19 Oct., lx. 384). He died 6 Nov.

6. The younger Sir Horace had written to HW on 25 Sept.; probably there was a later missing letter.

7. 'The age of 80 which I think the next month will complete' (Mann to HW, 8 July 1786).

It is being very fickle to go out of the fashion when the fashion adapts itself to me; yet except one day's lameness, and constant chalky rills from my fingers, I have had no gout this summer. If the Duchess of Devonshire has, and retains the diadem of fashion still (a long reign in so unstable a kingdom) I suppose the ladies of her court will recall their chins, and thrust out a shoe wadded with flannel. Then it will be an easy transition to the 'Béquille du Père Barnabas!' I recommend the tune to Colonel Fitzpatrick.

Lord and Lady Waldegrave have been with me two or three days,[8] and today have sent me a confirmation[9] of several of Princess Amelie's[10] legacies as you have seen in the papers; but thus particularly:

To Ladies Eliz.[11] and Caroline Waldegrave,[12] each £4000 *in money*. This she told me, on Lady Waldegrave's death,[13] she intended, and so she did to this Lord. To the two brothers[14] of the Landgrave of Hesse £20,000 apiece, and they are to be residuary legatees.

To Lady Anne Howard—£5000 ⎫
    Lady Barrymore—£3000 ⎬ —Stock
    Lady Templetown[15]—£2000 ⎭

To Lady Anne Noel[16] the interest of £5000 for life.[17]

8. 'We went first to Strawberry Hill; then we went to town for Princess Amelia's funeral . . .' (Lady Waldegrave to Anne Clement 22 Nov. 1786, MS WSL). 'We dined at Strawberry Hill on Thursday [2 Nov.] to meet the Waldegraves. They both looked remarkably well' (Charlotte Augusta Keppel to Anne Clement 7 Nov. 1786, MS WSL).

9. Missing.

10. Princess Amelia had died on 31 Oct.

11. Lady Elizabeth Waldegrave (1758–1823) m. (1791) James Brudenell, cr. (1780) Bn Brudenell, 5th E. of Cardigan, 1790; lady of the Bedchamber to the Princess Royal and to the Princesses 1783–91; and to Queen Charlotte 1793–1809 (BERRY i. 241; *Royal Kalendar; London Chronicle* 21–23 April 1791, lxix. 387).

12. (1765–1831), lady of the Bedchamber to the Princesses 1791–8, and to the Dowager Queen of Würtemberg, 1827 (BERRY i. 349 n. 8; *London Chronicle*, loc. cit.).

13. In 1784. 'What the house in town sells for is to be the legacy destined for the Lady Waldegraves' (Selwyn to Lord Carlisle, 6 Nov., *Carlisle MSS* 650).

14. Charles (1744–1836), Prince of Hesse-Cassel, regent of Schleswig-Holstein; and Frederick (1747–1837), Prince of Hesse-Cassel; sons of Princess Amelia's sister Mary. Princess Amelia was 'much pleased with her nephew Prince Frederick of Hesse' (Coke, 'MS Journals' 4 Oct. 1775).

15. Elizabeth Boughton (d. 1823) m. (1769) Clotworthy Upton, cr. (1776) Bn Templetown; lady of the Bedchamber to Princess Amelia, April, 1786, succeeding Lady Henrietta Vernon, who d. 12 April 1786 (Coke, 'MS Journals' 26 Apr., 26 Oct., 2 Nov. 1786; GM 1786, lvi pt i. 353).

16. (b. 1737), dau. of Baptist, 4th E. of Gainsborough; lady of the Bedchamber to Princess Amelia (George Kearsley, *Peerage*, [1796], i. 74; Collins, *Peerage*, 1779, iv. 51; Coke, *Journals* and 'MS Journals,' *passim*).

17. 'I am afraid [this legacy] is fifty pounds a year less than she [Princess Amelia] gave her, for when she resigned her place the Princess said she should have the half of her salary' (Coke, 'MS Journals' 5 Nov. 1786).

Small legacies to all her servants.[18]

To her executors Lords Besborough and Pelham £1000 stock.

Her jewels to the Duchess of Brunswic.[19]

Gunnersbury and her house in town to be sold.[20]

Lord Besborough not being well enough, and Lord Pelham not in town, Lord Duncannon went to the King to know if he chose to be present at the reading of the will, which he declined;[21] but has since sent Lord Sydney to one of the ladies of the Bedchamber[22] to ask if previous to her death she had expressed any wishes not inserted in her will, and to say he would fulfil whatever had been her desire.[23] The Princess is to be buried this day sevennight[24] at the King's expense, and the mourning to commence the next day.[25]

The will seems to me a proper and a kind one; and surely neither her life nor death deserved the infamous abuse of the newspapers, which is as false as the exaggeration of her wealth.[26] History, I be-

18. For details, see the *London Chronicle* 31 Oct. – 11 Nov., lx. 431, 447, 455, and ('Authentic Particulars') 459.

19. Her niece; sister of George III (*ante* 14 Dec. 1771).

20. Gunnersbury House (and grounds) was sold in 1788 for £12,000 ('very cheap indeed . . . It certainly cost the late Princess Amelia above thirty thousand pounds') to 'Colonel Ironside, who sold it again in 1792 to Walter Stirling, Esq., the present proprietor' (Daniel Lysons, *Environs of London*, Vol. II, 1795, p. 226; Coke, 'MS Journals' 31 May 1788). 'Mr Morley, a floor-cloth manufacturer, purchased Gunnersbury House and grounds, on speculation in . . . 1800 or 1801. The house was soon afterwards pulled down, and sold piecemeal, and the land (being 83 acres enclosed within a wall) in lots' (Lysons, *Supplement to the First Edition of . . . the Environs of London*, 1811, p. 128). Her town house in Cavendish Square at the corner of Harley Street was bought by her after George II's death, and sold by auction 8 Feb. 1787; it was purchased in succession by the Earl of Hopetoun, Watson Taylor, and Viscount Beresford (Wheatley, *London Past and Present* i. 342; *Morning Chronicle* 3, 8 Feb. 1787).

21. Duncannon asked if 'the will should be opened at the Queen's house. The King said, "By no means; I have nothing

to do with the will; I only desire a copy of it" ' (*Carlisle MSS* 650).

22. Lady Anne Howard (Coke, 'MS Journals' 5 Nov. 1786).

23. 'I am sorry to say she did not deserve such attentions from him, as she never did him justice' (ibid.).

24. In Henry VII's Chapel in Westminster. For a description of the funeral, see the *London Chronicle* 9–14 Nov., lx. 463–4, 466–7; GM 1786, lvi pt ii. 1000–1. 'She is already embalmed, cered, and coffined; her body is wrapped in I do not know how many yards of crimson silk, and she, they tell me, looks like a silkworm in its outward case. Warren saw her embalmed, Potts attended, but I suppose that Hunter embalmed her' (Selwyn to Carlisle, 6 Nov., *Carlisle MSS* 650).

25. As announced in the *London Gazette* No. 12800, 31 Oct.– 4 Nov. (*London Chronicle* 4–7 Nov., lx. 442).

26. The *London Chronicle* 31 Oct.– 2 Nov., lx. 431, after mentioning her will, her 'munificence, and extensive charities,' continued: 'Her Highness died immensely rich.' George II 'left her £100,000 . . . and the Duke of Cumberland a very considerable sum. Her annual income from Government . . . was besides much beyond her expenditure.' In the same newspaper 2–4 Nov., lx. 440, it is said that the bequest 'to the Prince of Hesse-Cassel

lieve, seldom contains much truth;[27] but should our daily lying chronicles exist and be consulted, the annals of these days will deserve as
little credit as the *Arabian Nights*.

To Lady Ossory, Friday 1 December 1786

Strawberry Hill, Dec. 1, 1786.

OH! yes, Madam, I am ready to continue playing at questions
and commands if you please, since you are content with such
answers as I simple man can send you. I have no character to sustain,
and don't care a straw how silly my letters are, if you find they fill
up some of your idle moments. I am sure I have nothing better to
do, and it was for your sake that I proposed *passing eldest*.[1]

No, I am not at all struck with the letter of Beaumarchais,[2] except
with its insolence. Such a reproof might become Cato the Censor in
defence of such a tragedy as Addison's on his descendant—but for
such a *vaurien* as Beaumarchais, and for such a contemptible farce as
Figaro,[3] it was paramount impertinence towards the Duke,[4] and

amounts to near three hundred thousand pounds in the funds,' but in 4–7 Nov., lx. 447–8, some of these rumours are called 'erroneous,' and the total value of her estate is said to be '£110,000—£75,000 of which is certainly all . . . [she] had in the stocks.' The above accounts also criticize her for leaving so much money outside England.

27. On 15 March 1789 HW told Malone that, after Sir Robert Walpole's retirement, HW, 'considering that his father had been long engaged in public business, proposed to read some history. "No," said Lord Orford, "don't read history to me; that can't be true"' (Sir James Prior, *Life of Edmond Malone*, 1860, p. 387). Cf. *post* 26 Oct. 1791.

1. A phrase used in loo and other games (MONTAGU i. 181 n. 20). Lady Ossory had apparently sensed that HW was beginning to weary of the correspondence.

2. 'Réponse à quelqu'un qui me rend une grande loge pour en avoir une petite, en disant que c'est pour des femmes qui craignent d'être vues à ma pièce.' It begins: 'Je n'ai aucune considération,

Monsieur le Duc, pour des femmes qui se permettent de voir un spectacle qu'elles jugent malhonnête, pourvu qu'elles le voient en secret.' Louis Petit de Bachaumont, *Mémoires secrets*, 1777–89, Vol. XXVI 1786, *sub* 18 July 1784, gives a text from which Lady Ossory may have taken her copy; see following letter. The text quoted in Grimm (not printed until after HW's death) xiii. 530, *sub* May 1784, is slightly different. Betsy Sheridan sent a copy of the letter, said to be addressed to the Duc d'Aumont, to her sister Alicia 4–6 May 1785 (*Betsy Sheridan's Journal*, ed. Le Fanu, 1960, p. 47).

3. *La Folle journée, ou Le Mariage de Figaro*, first publicly performed in Paris at the Théâtre français 27 April 1784; completed in 1778 but hitherto suppressed by the King. HW's only copy was Holcroft's adaptation, *The Follies of a Day; or, The Marriage of Figaro*, 1785 (dated by HW on the title-page, 'February'; see Hazen, *Cat. of HW's Lib.* 1810:37.5), an adaptation made before the first editions in French were published later in 1785.

4. Louis-Alexandre-Céleste d'Aumont (1736–1814), styled Duc de Villequier 1759–

gross ill-breeding towards the ladies. Besides I abhor vanity in authors; it would offend in Milton or Montesquiou; in a Jack-pudding
it is intolerable. I know no trait of arrogance recorded of Molière
—and to talk of the *Marriage of Figaro* as *instructive!*[5] Punch might
as well pretend to be moralizing when he sells a bargain. In general,
the modern *gens de lettres* in France, as they call themselves, are complete puppies. They have beaten up their native pertness with the
brutality of the ancient philosophers, and would erect themselves
into a tribunal of dictators: they lay down laws impertinently, and
employ affronts and insults as penalties. The *literati* on the revival
of learning were less intolerable, for they only threw dirt and called
names in coarse Latin, which nobody but a Roman scavenger could
have understood. The present fry are saucy, and quaint and distorted,
and void of all simplicity—What a forced affected phrase is *bégueules
mitigées!*[5a]

The history of Lactilla[6] of Bristol is worse; she is a *bégueule* not
mitigée. Her ingratitude to Miss More has been superlative. The
latter laboured unweariedly to collect subscriptions[7] for her, and
was at expense herself for the publication; and lest the husband,[8]
who is a dolt, should waste the sum collected, placed it out at interest
for her as trustee,[9] besides having washed and combed her trumpery
verses and taught them to dance in tune.[10] The foolish woman's head

1814, although he succeeded his brother
as Duc d'Aumont in 1799; 'premier gentilhomme de la chambre du roi,' 1782 (BERRY
i. 259 n. 13; *Dictionnaire de biographie
française*, 1933–). According to Grimm
xiii. 530–1, 'd'abord on la disait adressée
à M. le duc de Villequier, ensuite à M. le
duc d'Aumont. Elle a été sous cette forme
jusqu'à Versailles, où on l'a jugée, comme
elle méritait de l'être, d'une impertinence
rare.' See also Bachaumont, op. cit., *sub*
8 July 1784.

5. Grimm's text says, 'J'ai donné ma
pièce au public pour l'amuser et non pour
l'instruire,' while Bachaumont's reads
'pour l'instruire.'

5a. The second sentence of Beaumarchais's letter (n. 2 above), said that he did
not give his play 'pour offrir à des
bégueules mitigées le plaisir d'en aller
penser du bien en petite loge.'

6. A name Anne Yearsley applies to

herself in her *Poems*, 1785, pp. 106, 108
et passim.

7. There were over 1000 subscribers to
the first edition.

8. John Yearsley (d. 1803), 'a man who
is said to be honest and sober, but of a
turn of mind very different from' his
wife's; described in 1784 as 'of no vice but
little capacity' (Hannah More, 'Prefatory
Letter' to Mrs Yearsley's *Poems*, 1785, p.
iv; J. M. S. Tompkins, *The Polite Marriage*, Cambridge, 1938, pp. 62, 101, 203).

9. About £500 (£350 from the first edition, £150 from the second) was invested
in the Funds, with Mrs Montagu and
Hannah More as trustees. Before the end
of 1785 Hannah More's position became
untenable and she relinquished the trust
(Tompkins, op. cit. 69–76).

10. 'If her epithets are now and then
bold and vehement, they are striking and
original; and I should be sorry to see the

turned with this change of fortune and applause; and concluding that her talent which was only wonderful from her sphere and state of ignorance, was marvellous genius, she grew enraged at Miss More for presuming to prune her wild shoots, and in her passion accused her benevolent and beneficent friend of defrauding her of part of the collected charity. In short she has abused Miss More grossly, has written a volume of scurrility against her,[11] and is really to be pitied, as she is grown extravagant and ostentatious—am I in the wrong, Madam, for thinking that these parish Saphos had better be bound 'prentices to mantua-makers, than be appointed chambermaids to Mesdemoiselles the Muses!

I am sorry the Knight of the Brush has also now and then some human delinquencies[12]—but alas! everybody has a heel or a finger not dipped in Styx—⟨o⟩r rather I think we should say, that has been dipped in Styx. I went t'other day when I was in town to see the Sacraments of Poussin that he has purchased from Rome for the Duke of Rutland.[13] I remember when I saw them there a thousand years ago[14] that I was not much enchanted—I rather like them better now

wild vigour of her rustic muse polished into elegance, or laboured into correctness. Her ear is perfect. . . . She abounds in false concords, and inaccuracies of various kinds; the grossest of which have been corrected' (Hannah More, op. cit. pp. vii–viii).

11. Mrs Yearsley's narrative, dated 12 Oct. 1786, 'To the Noble and Generous Subscribers' to the first two editions (the third and fourth had no list of subscribers) of her *Poems*; printed in her *Poems*, 4th edn, 1786, pp. xviii–xxxi. Some of the abuse that HW mentions was probably oral; see Tompkins, op. cit. 68–76.

12. Three letters of Sir Joshua Reynolds to Lord Ossory, 10, 17 July, 5 Sept. 1786, relate to a picture of Venus and Adonis, said by Reynolds to be 'a copy by Titian himself from that in the Colonna palace,' but in such poor condition that it 'can never be successfully repaired,' and 'the picture cleaner will only make it ten times worse.' Although Reynolds offered Lord Ossory an exchange for it, Lord Ossory had it sent to Benjamin Van der Gucht for repair and cleaning (Reynolds, *Letters*, ed. Hilles, Cambridge, 1929, pp. 153–6, 158–9). HW's comment suggests that, de-

spite Reynolds's forebodings, Lord Ossory was pleased with the result. When Reynolds died, Lord Ossory chose from his paintings one by Reynolds himself on this subject; Lord Castletown sold it at Christie's 18 July 1924.

13. James Byres, agent in Rome for the Duke of Rutland and others, had arranged (by substituting copies) for the purchase for £2000 of Poussin's 'The Seven Sacraments' (really eight pictures) in the Boccapaduli Palace. They were sent to Reynolds's house in Leicester Fields, the D. of Rutland being in Ireland. For details of the purchase, and Reynolds's comments on the pictures, which are still at Belvoir Castle, see Reynolds, op. cit., *passim*. The pictures are described by J. J. Le Français de Lalande, *Voyage en Italie*, 2d edn, 1786, v. 291–2, *sub* 'Palazzo Boccapaduli,' with the footnote 'Un amateur m'assure en 1784, que des sept tableaux . . . il n'y en a plus que deux qui soient originaux, que les autres sont à Paris, et ont été remplacé par des copies.' They are depicted by Otto Grautoff, *Nicolas Poussin*, Munich and Leipzig, 1914, i. 155–60.

14. HW's letters from Rome in 1740 do not mention the palace or the pictures,

than I expected,[15] at least two or three of them—but they are really only coloured bas-reliefs, and old Romans don't make good Christians. There are two of Baptism;[16] Sir Joshua said, what could he mean by painting two? I said, I concluded the second was Anabaptism. Sir Joshua himself has bought a profile of Oliver Cromwell, which he thinks the finest miniature by Cooper[17] he ever saw—but all his own geese are swans, as the swans of others are geese. It is most clearly a copy and not a very good one; the outline very hard, the hair and armour very flat and tame. He would not show me his Russian Hercules[18]—I fancy he has discovered that he was too sanguine about the commission, as you say.[19]

The town was ringing about your old neighbour of the north Countess Strathmore,[20] and the enormous barbarities of her husband,[21] who beat her for six days and nights

but HW's eagle was dug up in 'the gardens of Boccapadugli' in 1742 (MANN iii. 66 n. 10).

15. Reynolds had had the pictures lined and cleaned; they 'are now just as they came from the easel' (Reynolds to D. of Rutland 4 Oct. 1786, Reynolds, op. cit. 163).

16. 'I expected but seven pictures, but there are eight. The sacrament of Baptism is represented by Christ baptizing St John, but that picture, which does not seem to belong to the set (though equally excellent with the rest) is St John baptizing the multitude' (Reynolds to D. of Rutland 7 Sept. 1786, ibid. 161, 163–4). Lalande, loc. cit., says that the picture of Christ being baptized by St John is inferior.

17. Samuel Cooper (1609–72) painted several miniatures of Cromwell and members of his family. This one was 'sold by Lady Cornwallis to Sir Joshua . . . for 100 guineas. He bequeathed it to Richard Burke, who left it to Frances, Lady Crewe, from whom it descended to her granddaughter, Lady Houghton, by whom it was exhibited' in 1865; it then descended to Lady Houghton's son, the Marquess of Crewe, who died in 1945 (J. J. Foster, A List . . . of Works of English Miniature Painters of the XVII Century, 1914–16, p. 139; C. R. Leslie and Tom Taylor, Life and Times of Sir Joshua Reynolds, 1865, ii. 496 n.). It 'had long remained concealed

. . . in the false bottom of a gold snuff-box' (Samuel Felton, Testimonies to the Genius and Memory of Sir Joshua Reynolds, 1792, p. 59).

18. 'I have received a commission from the Empress of Russia to paint an historical picture for her, the size, the subject, and everything else left to me. . . . This subject I have fixed on . . . is Hercules strangling the serpents in the cradle, as described by Pindar' (Reynolds to D. of Rutland 20 Feb. 1786, Reynolds, op. cit. 149; cf. HW to Thomas Walpole the younger 8 April 1786; Leslie and Taylor, op. cit. ii. 482–4, 516; Graves and Cronin iii. 1160–4, iv. 1480AAA). The painting is now in the Hermitage Museum, Leningrad.

19. Reynolds had written to Lord Ossory 17 July 1786: 'My mind at present is entirely occupied in contriving the composition of the Hercules' (Reynolds, op. cit. 155).

20. She was the daughter and sole heiress of George Bowes of Streatlam and Gibside in the county of Durham; the estates of Lady Ossory's father were in the same county.

21. Andrew Robinson Stoney (from 11 Feb. 1777, Bowes) (1747–1810), of Coldpig Hill, co. Durham; M.P. Newcastle-upon-Tyne 1780–4 (GEC, sub Strathmore; Sir Lewis Namier's Parliamentary lists).

round Stainmore's wintry wild,[22]

for which the myrmidons of the King's Bench have knocked his brains out—almost.[23] This and Lady Cathcart's[24] long imprisonment ought to make wealthy widows a little cautious of Mac-Philanders—but the Lord knows whether it will.

Lord Chewton is perfectly well. He was here lately with his parents. Soon after my neighbour Sir Robert Goodere[25] made me a visit, and said he had been a little doubtful whether he might come, as he heard the Princess Elizabeth[26] was come to Strawberry Hill for the air— 'Jesus! Sir Robert! what can you mean? Princess Elizabeth with me? you must dream, or imagine that Princess Elizabeth Lutterel[27] is

22. 'Oft too on Stanemore's wintry waste' (David Mallet, *Edwin and Emma*, stanza 14). HW uses another variant of this line in Montagu ii. 307.

23. On 10 Nov. 1786 Bowes, who was separated from his wife and who had been sued by her for divorce (*ante* 5 Feb. 1785), had Lady Strathmore abducted in London and brought to Highgate, where he joined her and the abductors and went with them to her estate, Streatlam Castle. After holding her there until 13 Nov., he attempted to take her to Ireland, then to Scotland, but about 18 Nov. he was captured by a constable, and she was returned to London. His purpose was to force her to drop divorce proceedings, she having, under duress, made over all her property to him on 1 May 1777. See *The Trial at Large of Andrew Robinson Bowes* [Court of King's Bench, 30 May 1787] . . . *for a Conspiracy against Elenor* [sic] *Bowes, Commonly Called Countess of Strathmore.* Bowes and his colleagues were found guilty of conspiracy and were 'sentenced on 26 June 1787 to a fine of £300, imprisonment of three years, and to find securities for good behaviour for fourteen years' (DNB, *sub* Bowes, Mary Eleanor). Gillray's satirical print, showing Bowes 'apparently very ill' as he was brought into court on 28 Nov. 1786 to answer his wife's charges, is described in BM, *Satiric Prints* vi. 335, No. 7012. The *Morning Chronicle* 29 Nov. 1786 suggests that his dress and actions in court were assumed to evoke sympathy.

24. Elizabeth Malyn (1691–1789) m. 1 James Fleet; m. 2 (ca 1734) Capt. William Sabine; m. 3 (1739) Charles Cathcart, 8th Bn Cathcart; m. 4 (18 May 1745) Hugh Maguire (d. 1766), of Castle Nugent, co. Longford, Ireland, an officer in the Hungarian service, afterwards (1742–ca 1750) Lt-Col. in the British army. According to her testimony in a lawsuit, he kept her a prisoner in Ireland for twenty years, 1746–66 (Selwyn 84–5 nn. 13, 15).

25. (ca 1720–1800), Kt, 1762; lieutenant of the Band of Gentlemen Pensioners 1762–72; water bailiff of the Thames above Staines, 1760, 1762. He and Lady Goodere were HW's tenants at Cliveden or Little SH from 1785 (the death of Mrs Clive) until 25 Dec. 1790; they were succeeded by the Berrys (Berry i. 124 n. 19).

26. (1770–1840), dau. of George III, m. (1818) Frederick Joseph Louis, Landgrave and Prince of Hesse-Homburg. Her health had been the subject of many newspaper paragraphs for the past year.

27. Lady Elizabeth Luttrell (d. 1799), sister of the Duchess of Cumberland. She 'distinguished herself by her high-bred superiority of carriage, magnificent style of life, and dissipation' (GM 1799, lxix pt ii. 998–9); 'played high, and cheated much. She was commonly called the Princess Elizabeth.' Thrown into gaol, 'she gave a hairdresser £50 to marry her; her debts then becoming his, she was discharged. She went abroad, where she descended lower and lower; till, being convicted of picking pockets at Augsburgh, she was condemned to clean the streets, chained to a wheelbarrow; in that miserable situation she terminated her existence by

with me'—at last I found out that he had seen Lord Waldegrave's servants in the Queen's livery here,[28] and the rest was the product of his own reasoning upon that phenomenon—Such is the birth of half the stories circulated—and had he communicated his conjecture to the village before I set him right, in three days that vision would have been in the newspapers.

I went yesterday to see the Duke of Queensberry's palace at Richmond,[29] under the conduct of George Selwyn the *concierge*.[30] You cannot imagine how noble it looks, now all the Cornbury pictures from Amesbury[31] are hung up there. The great hall, the great gallery, the eating-room and the corridor are covered with whole- and half-lengths of royal family, favourites, ministers, peers and judges of the reign of Charles I—not one an original, I think, at least not one fine, yet altogether they look very respectable, and the house is so handsome, and the views so rich, and the day was so fine, that I could only have been more pleased if (for half an hour) I could have seen the

poison' (Sir Robert Heron, *Notes*, 2d edn, 1851, p. 293). See also *Last Journals* i. pp. xix–xx; *The History of White's*, ed. Algernon Bourke, 1892, i. 136. She had been on the Continent with the Duke and Duchess of Cumberland and had returned to London with them on 20 Oct. (*Morning Chronicle* 21 Oct.).

28. Lord Waldegrave was Master of the Horse to the Queen (*ante* 12 Nov. 1784).

29. Queensberry House or Queensberry Villa, built by George, 3d E. of Cholmondeley, HW's brother-in-law, 'above 30 years after' 1708 (HW's note on p. 444 of Daniel Lysons, *The Environs of London*, Vol. I, 1792, now WSL), and subsequently owned by the E. of Warwick; Sir Robert Lyttelton; John, Earl Spencer, who gave it to his mother, Lady Cowper; the 3d and 4th Dukes of Queensberry. It was pulled down in 1830 (Estella Cave, *Memories of Old Richmond*, 1922, pp. 293–7; E. B. Chancellor, *Historical Richmond*, 1885, pp. 249–54).

30. Selwyn had a house near Queensberry House and spent much of his time there: 'The Duke dines with me when he is here, a little after four, and when we have drank our wine, we resort to his great hall . . . to drink our coffee, and hear quintettos' (Selwyn to Lord Carlisle 25 Oct. 1786, *Carlisle MSS* 646).

31. In 1751 Lord Hyde (formerly styled Vct Cornbury) sold Cornbury, Oxon, to Charles, D. of Marlborough. The pictures collected by the first Lord Clarendon were allowed to remain there until 1763, when, after a lawsuit, they were divided. Half went to Catherine Hyde, Duchess of Queensberry, who took hers to Amesbury, Wilts, whence the 4th Duke of Queensberry had recently brought them to Richmond; on his death in 1810 they were removed to Bothwell (V. J. Watney, *Cornbury and the Forest of Wychwood*, 1910, p. 191). For a list of the pictures in 1751, before their division, see ibid. 235–44. HW had first seen them at Cornbury in 1736 (MONTAGU i. 5; MANN iv. 182; HW to Bentley Sept. 1753). In his copy of Archibald Robertson, *A Topographical Survey of the Great Road from London to Bath and Bristol*, 1792 (now in the British Museum), i. 36, HW notes: 'The Duke of Q. has transferred hither a large portion of the collection of portraits in the reign of Charles I, assembled by Lord Chancellor Clarendon, formerly at Cornbury, and since at Amesbury, whither they are entailed to return.' Selwyn's letter cited in the preceding note indicates something of the arrangement of the pictures.

real palace that once stood on that spot,[32] and the persons represented walking about!—a visionary holiday in old age, though it has not the rapture of youth, is a sedate enjoyment that is more sensible because one attends to it, and reflects upon it at the time—and as new tumults do not succeed, the taste remains long in one's memory's mouth.

PS. I was told t'other night that Lady Cathcart, who is still living, danced lately at Hertford, to show her vigour at past fourscore[33]— ware an Abbé de Gedoyn![34] She would risk another incarceration[35]— it is woeful to have a colt's tooth when folks have no other left!

To Lady Ossory, Tuesday 12 December 1786

Address: To the Countess of Ossory at Ampthill Park, Bedfordshire. *Postmark:* 12 DE.

Berkeley Square, Dec. 12, 1786.

I PRETEND to neither judgment nor taste, Madam, and I am sure I am in the wrong when I dislike what Lady Ravensworth, Lord Ossory and Mr Fitzpatrick approve; and yet, instead of condemning contrary to my opinion, I rather doubt whether your Ladyship does not commend more than you think the letter[1] deserves, for your unalterable good humour makes you always set everything in the best light possible. *Modified brimstones,* I own, did sound to me too harsh an expression to be used of women of quality in a country that piques itself on being the standard of good breeding—but one every day learns to correct one's original ideas, which are generally the fruits of

32. Richmond Palace, built by Henry VII after the old Palace on the same site was destroyed by fire ca 1498. Most of it was pulled down in 1703 (Chatterton 73–4 nn. 2, 10).

33. She was now 95. 'She danced at Welwyn [Herts] assembly, with the spirit of a young woman, when she was past 80' (GM 1789, lix pt ii. 767).

34. Nicolas Gédoyn (1667–1744), abbé, lover of Ninon de Lenclos when she was past eighty, according to HW's account in the *World*, No. 28, 12 July 1753 (*Works* i. 173). In Lillian Day, *Ninon. A Courtesan*

of Quality, New York, 1957, p. 251, the liaison is assigned to 1690, when Ninon was seventy and the Abbé Gédoyn twenty-three.

35. She 'was not encouraged, by his [her fourth husband's] treatment of her, to verify her resolution, which she inscribed as a poesy on her wedding ring,— *If I survive, I will have five*' (GM 1789, lix pt ii. 766).

———

1. Of Beaumarchais; see *ante* 1 Dec. 1786.

ignorance. I imagined that the ladies scarce gave as a reason for asking for Beaumarchais's box that they supposed his play was indecent— at least I know that that is not the object of *loges grillées,* nor could be for this plain reason, that the French stage does not allow of indecencies. *Des loges grillées,* I believe, are for the purpose of going undressed, and are used at all the chastest old plays: I know I have been in one at a *tragedy* with Mesdames de Luxembourg and du Deffand;[2] and therefore I was naturally enough led into the mistake of thinking that Beaumarchais had given himself an impertinent air on a very common occasion. If his farce was reckoned indelicate, it was he that had offended the custom, not the ladies—*mais peut-être qu'on a changé tout cela;* and the austere Beaumarchais, like stern Lycurgus, may insist on ladies descending stark naked into the arena and wrestling with gladiators, to show that genuine modesty does not wear a mask.[3]

When I have said thus much, I know how much I am guided by prejudices: I have an aversion to the dictatorial pertness of the modern French authors, and cannot conceive that their very flimsy talents can entitle them to an importance that would misbecome Racine himself. In truth, except for such a predominant genius as Shakespeare or Milton, I hold authors cheap enough: what merit is there in pains and study and application, compared with the extempore abilities of such men as Mr Fox, Mr Sheridan, or Mr Pitt? What puerile matters are the orations of Cicero composed, corrected and rewritten at fifty or sixty years of age, in comparison of what start and flow and overflow from our prodigies the moment they are men? It is from being so proud of my countrymen that I betrayed so much contempt of the frogs of the French Hippocrene; and I hope I have a little disculpated myself for the disrespect I showed to what your Ladyship liked and was so good as to send me.

I came to town the middle of last week to quit the damps that made

2. HW went with the Duchesse de Luxembourg and Mme du Deffand 14 Dec. 1765 to see a comedy, Michel-Jean Sedaine's *Le Philosophe sans le savoir,* 'in Prince of Conti's box' ('Paris Journals,' DU DEFFAND v. 285). No record of their seeing a tragedy together has been found.

3. Lycurgus's 'method of training up children, was extremely proper to make them good soldiers; but he extended it too far, because he would oblige the young maidens to perform the same exercises as the youths; to dance stark naked before them; and . . . the youths danced stark naked before them' (Pierre Bayle, *A General Dictionary,* 1734–41, vii. 276–7, with supporting evidence in the notes from Plutarch, Euripides, etc.).

me much out of order,[4] but the smoke of London soon recovered me. I dined with the Duchess of Bedford on Sunday, as she was to have no company but the two Misses Pelham,[5] Miss Loyd and Admiral Pigot[6]—yet though three misses sound very young, your Ladyship is sensible it was not a very callow party. I shall be more juvenile tonight, for I am going to Mrs Cowley's[7] new play,[8] which I suppose is as *instructive* as the *Marriage of Figaro,* for I am told it approaches to those of Mrs Behn in Spartan delicacy;[9] but I shall see Miss Farren,[10] who in my poor opinion is the first of all actresses.[11]

Of news I have not heard a tittle since I arrived. To give them their due the houses in London are of themselves as quiet good sort of houses as any in the universe, and it is only when they are brimful that they produce so many strange scenes every day.

4. 'Mr Walpole was here [at Mrs Keppel's house at Isleworth] last night; he talks of going to London this day sennight as he has got a cold and is afraid of the gout' (Charlotte Augusta Keppel to Anne Clement, Thursday 30 Nov. 1786, MS WSL). 'Mr Walpole went to town last Wednesday [6 Dec.] which is a great loss to the Montrosy [the Duchess of Montrose's] parties, as now, poor little woman, she has nobody to come to her but us' (the same to the same 11 Dec. 1786, MS WSL).

5. Frances Pelham (*ante* 1 June 1762) and Mary Pelham (1739–94), youngest dau. of Henry Pelham (Montagu ii. 72 n. 15).

6. Hugh Pigot (1722–92), brother of Bn Pigot (*ante* 17 Jan. 1778), entered the navy at an early age; Admiral of the Blue, 1782, and commander-in-chief in the West Indies 1782–3.

7. Hannah Parkhouse (1743–1809), dau. of a bookseller, Philip Parkhouse, of Tiverton, Devon; m. (ca 1768) —— Cowley, a captain in the East India Company's service; dramatist and poetess.

8. *A School for Greybeards; or, The Mourning Bride: A Comedy, in Five Acts,* first presented at Drury Lane 25 Nov. 1786; published 28 Dec. 1786; adapted from Aphra Behn's *Lucky Chance,* 1687 (Genest, vi. 426–9; *London Chronicle* 23–30 Dec. 1786, lx. 616, 629; *A School for Greybeards,* pp. vii–viii). HW saw the fourth performance (*Morning Chronicle* 12, 14 Dec. 1786). HW's copy of the play, now WSL, has notes on p. 42 correcting *Philip* to *Gasper* and *Phil.* to *Gasp.* (three times).

9. After the first performance of the play, 'one of the papers recorded,' 'with many cruel remarks,' all the passages that were considered objectionable. 'In the following pages they are *all* restored; that the public AT LARGE may have the power to adjudge me' ('An Address,' in *A School for Greybeards,* 1786, p. iv). On p. 72 is a speech of Don Sebastian ('No, Sir—*I* am the arbiter of her [Viola's] lot;—however, I confirm half your punishment; and a dark chamber she shall certainly have') on which Mrs Cowley comments in a footnote: 'This is the expression, I am told, which had nearly proved fatal to the comedy. I should not have printed it, but from the resolution I have religiously kept, of restoring every thing that was objected to.' See also Genest vi. 427.

10. Elizabeth Farren or Farran (b. 1759 or 1763, d. 1829) m. (1797) Edward Smith-Stanley, 12th E. of Derby, 1776, (Berry i. 64 n. 13). As Donna Seraphina, the second wife of Don Alexis (one of the greybeards), she also spoke the epilogue.

11. 'When she left the stage, genteel comedy became extinct' (Richard Edgcumbe, 2d E. of Mount Edgcumbe, *Musical Reminiscences,* 3d edn, 1828, p. 21).

To Lady Ossory, Friday 15 December 1786

Berkeley Square, Dec. 15, 1786.

INSTEAD of being too prolix, I think you are very condescending, Madam, to enter into my cavils and discuss them with me—but you are not so gracious when you suspect my *douceurs* of irony, which would reduce me to weigh my words, and then I should have no satisfaction in chatting with you. I set down the first thing that comes into my head, foolish or not—for instance, the moment I had written the last paragraph of my last, I knew it was silly, but I could not take the trouble of writing my letter again—and in truth, I have a little partiality for nonsense. We are so much in the dark about most things, that when we attempt to reason, we often fall into great absurdities; but giving the reins to nonsense, it is heads or tails, whether we do not light upon sense.

Anti-Gallican I was literally, when I found fault with Beaumarchais's epistle, but not politically so, God knows, nor in a fury. At past sixty-nine my tow and tinder are pretty well exhausted, and I should be ashamed to go out of the world in a fury about anything. About the commercial treaty[1] it is impossible I should be in one, for it is most strictly true that I have not read a single article, and for this plain reason, that I should not understand a syllable of it. I understand trade no more than I do Coptic, and being much disposed to amuse myself for the little time I have left, I waste none of it on what I do not comprehend. Many years ago a person[2] who was never sorry to tell me my truths, said to me, 'You understand several out-of-the-way things, but you know nothing that is common or useful.' This was true then, and alas! is so to this hour, and will continue so for a few more; and therefore good or bad, the commercial treaty could have no share in my censure of the letter, nor will occasion a wrinkle on the surface of my thoughts. All I can say on the subject, is, that the treaty

1. The Treaty of Navigation and Commerce between Great Britain and France, signed by William Eden and J.-M. Gérard de Rayneval at Versailles 26 Sept., had reached London 2 Oct. Abstracts, summaries, and eventually the complete 47 articles were published in the newspapers (*London Chronicle* 3 Oct.–21 Nov., *passim*). The complete text is in *Journals of the House of Commons* xlii. 266–73. In 'Mem. 1783–91,' *sub* October, HW noted: 'Eden's treaty of commerce with France arrived by his secretary.'

2. Not identified.

being good, he must be a bad Whig that is angry at it, let who will have made it.³

I know nothing of the milkwoman's new edition,⁴ and certainly shall not send for it.⁵ When people disappoint me and prove very worthless, I have done with them, and suppose they don't exist.

The Greybeards have certainly been chastised, for we did not find them at all gross. The piece is farcical and improbable, but has some good things and is admirably acted.⁶ *Cœur de Lion*⁷ did not answer; nor was I much charmed with the music; but my ear is too bad to judge at first hearing. The scenes are excellent, Mrs Jordan⁸ is quite out of her character, and makes nothing of the part;⁹ and the turning the ferocious Richard¹⁰ into a tender husband is intolerable. If an historic subject is good but wants alteration, why will not an author take the canvas, cut it to his mind, but give new names to the personages? It only makes a confusion in one's ideas to maim a known story.

You guessed rightly, Madam: I certainly should have been distracted to have risked my letters to Sir Horace¹¹ being printed. Though I could not write very freely through the gutters of so many post offices, I did not desire Europe should see what I thought of its sovereigns, who were chiefly our dramatis personæ—Sir Horace the nephew brought away my letters at different times; and as he was there at his dear uncle's death, he will secure the rest, which are not a dozen.

For the new edition of Shakespeare,¹² it did not at all captivate

3. The treaty was negotiated by William Eden, for whom HW had little respect.

4. In Felix Farley's *Bristol Journal* 25 Nov. 1786 were advertised the fourth edition of Ann Yearsley's *Poems, on Several Occasions,* and her forthcoming *Poems, on Various Subjects,* 1787.

5. The only work by her which is in Hazen, *Cat. of HW's Lib.,* is the first edition of *Poems, on Several Occasions,* 1785.

6. An opinion confirmed by Genest vi. 427.

7. *Richard Cœur de Lion. An Historical Romance. From the French of . . .* [Michel-Jean] *Sedaine,* 1786; first acted at Drury Lane 24 Oct. and published the following day; by Gen. John Burgoyne; music by Grétry, adapted by Thomas Linley (Allardyce Nicoll, *History of Late*

Eighteenth-Century Drama, Cambridge, 1927, p. 241 *et passim; Morning Chronicle* 24, 25 Oct.). A rival work of the same name, by Leonard MacNally, had opened at Covent Garden 16 Oct. 1786 (Nicoll, op. cit. 285).

8. As Matilda, in love with Richard.

9. 'Mrs Jordan . . . acted very well' (Genest vi. 425).

10. Played by John Philip Kemble.

11. Mann.

12. As advertised in the *Morning Chronicle* 29 Nov., John and Josiah Boydell and George Nicol proposed to publish by subscription 'a most magnificent and accurate edition of the plays of Shakespeare in eight volumes of their largest quarto size . . . the text to be regulated . . . by George Steevens, Esq. To accompany this

me. In the first place, I did not subscribe for my heirs and executors,[13] as it would have been, when the term of completion is twelve years hence[14]—but I am not favourable to sets of prints for authors: I scarce know above one well executed, Coypell's *Don Quixote*[15]—but mercy on us! *Our* painters to design for *Shakespeare!* His commentators have not been more inadequate. Pray, who is to give an idea of Falstaffe, now Quin is dead?—and then Bartolozzi,[16] who is only fit to engrave for the *Pastor fido*,[17] will be to give a pretty enamelled fan-mount[18] of Macbeth![19] Salvator Rosa might, and Piranesi[20] might dash out Duncan's Castle—but Lord help Alderman Boydell[21] and the Royal Academy![22]

work, Messieurs Boydell also intend to publish by subscription a series of large and capital prints after pictures to be immediately painted by the following artists . . . Sir Joshua Reynolds [and twelve others named] . . . To be engraved by Mr Bartolozzi [and eight others named]. As soon as they have all been engraved they will be hung up in a gallery, built on purpose, and called the Gallery of Shakespeare.'

13. HW later subscribed to the prints: he had two incomplete sets (11 numbers, with 55 plates), one a subscriber's set; subscribers were to receive copies printed in the order in which subscriptions were placed (Hazen, *Cat. of HW's Lib.* 3904; *Morning Herald* 29 Nov.).

14. According to Condition VI of the proposal, Boydell was to deliver at least one number annually, but probably two, each to consist of at least four prints; at an average of six prints a year, seventy-two prints (the number mentioned in the advertisement) would require twelve years (*Morning Chronicle* 29 Nov.). Actually 100 large prints (plus two frontispieces and two title-page vignettes) were provided and 100 illustrations for Steevens's edition.

15. *Les Principales aventures de l'admirable Don Quichotte, représentées en figures par* [Charles-Antoine] Coypel [1694–1752] *Picart le Romain, et autres,* The Hague, 1746 (Hazen, *Cat. of HW's Lib.* 3081).

16. Francesco Bartolozzi (1727–1815), engraver, born in Florence; came to England as engraver to the King, 1764; an original member of the Royal Academy.

17. The pastoral drama, 1585, by Giovanni Battista Guarini (1537–1612). For

HW's appreciation of Bartolozzi's success in the pastoral tradition, see MASON i. 386.

18. For Bartolozzi's fan mounts, see A. de Vesme and A. Calabi, *Francesco Bartolozzi,* Milan, 1928, pp. 551–6, Nos 2216–26.

19. Bartolozzi engraved only one picture, by William Hamilton, for the large prints: Plate XXXII, for *Twelfth Night,* V. i, published 24 June 1791.

20. Giovanni Battista Piranesi (1720–78), engraver and architect. 'The sublime dreams of Piranesi, who seems to have conceived visions of Rome beyond what it boasted even in the meridian of its splendour . . . yet what taste in his boldness! what grandeur in his wildness' (*Anecdotes of Painting, Works* iii. 399). 'Piranesi has a sublime savageness in his engravings like Salvator Rosa. He sees Rome in its glory and in its decay, with the same eyes with which Salvator considered nature' ('Book of Materials,' 1759, p. 148). HW owned Piranesi's *Le Antichità Romane,* Rome, 1756; 4 vols folio (Hazen, *Cat of HW's Lib.* 3543).

21. John Boydell (1719–1804), engraver, print publisher; alderman for Cheap Ward 1782–1804; sheriff (1785) and lord mayor (1790–1) of London. He paid well for 170 works (including three pieces of sculpture), for his Shakespeare illustrations, which were executed by 33 painters and two sculptors (Thomas Banks and Mrs Damer). In 1804, forced to dispose of his property by lottery, he received enough money to pay his debts but died before the drawing.

22. HW first wrote 'Family'; see *post* 22 Dec. 1786.

Lord Maccartney I have seen twice;[23] he is quite well; I was at Lady Maccartney's last night; I told them of your Ladyship's inquiries. They have got a charming house in Curzon Street and cheap as old clothes. It was Lord Carteret's, and all antiqued and grotesqued by Adam,[24] with an additional room in the court four-score feet long,[25] then dedicated to orgies and now to books.

Thus I have answered all your Ladyship's questions *tant bien que mal;* and now after telling you a short story, will take my leave.

Lady Louvain[26] wished to see Mademoiselle Deon, and Mr Dutens[27] invited her. The lady asked her if she had ever been at Dijon, and said, she herself had lain in there.[28] 'I have been there,'[29] said Miss Hector, 'but did not lie in there, *car je suis vierge, et pour que les vierges accouchent, il faut qu'elles aillent à Jerusalem'*—It was impertinent to Lady Louvain, and worse in a clergyman's house—but women of fashion should not go aboard Amazons.

To Lady Ossory, Friday 22 December 1786

Berkeley Square, Dec. 22, 1786.

YOUR Ladyship is so apt to refine, that, give me leave to say, your penetration sometimes a little overshoots itself. You tell me that Lord Ossory says you *must* believe that I have not read the commercial treaty, which rather implies that you was not so disposed. Now I

23. Macartney had arrived in London from Calcutta on 9 Jan. 1786 (*London Chronicle* 7–10 Jan., lix. 32). He had more recently been in Ireland. Lady Portarlington, his sister-in-law, described him as he appeared on 7 Sept. at Dawson Court, Queen's County: 'He is not as much altered as I expected, and seems in very good spirits, and I think much more agreeable, as he has left off the sneering way he had' (to Lady Louisa Stuart, 7 Sept. 1786, in *Gleanings from an Old Portfolio*, ed. A. G. C. Clark, Edinburgh, 1895–8, ii. 61).

24. For Adam's alterations of Carteret's house in Curzon Street, No. 30, see Arthur T. Bolton, *The Architecture of Robert and James Adam*, 1922, ii. 36.

25. Apparently not Adam's (ibid.).

26. Isabella Susanna Burrell (1750–1812), sister of Peter, 1st Bn Gwydir, m. (1775)

Algernon Percy, 2d Bn Lovaine, 6 June 1786, cr. (1790) E. of Beverley.

27. Louis Dutens (1730–1812), antiquary, diplomatist and man of letters, a 'French Protestant clergyman who was chaplain in the family of the Duke of Northumberland. . . . He wrote an itinerary of Europe (the first book of that kind), *Les Mémoires d'un voyageur qui se repose*, etc., etc.' (Mary Berry, quoted in BERRY i. 35 n. 41).

28. Her second child, Elizabeth Percy, was born at Dijon 31 March 1777 and died in London 28 April 1779 (Collins, *Peerage*, 1779, ii. 487).

29. At Bath on 29 April 1785 Charlotte Brooke told Betsy Sheridan 'she had seen Mademoiselle D'Éon at Dijon and was delighted with her' (*Betsy Sheridan's Journal*, ed. Le Fanu, 1960, p. 46).

do not see what credit was to result to me from not having read it. Most people would think that I ought to have examined a matter of national importance; and few men perhaps would have owned so frankly, that my reason for not reading it was, that I could not understand it. Yet so the whole fact was; and though I think it less despicable to affect ignorance than to pretend to know what one does not, there was not a grain of affectation or untruth in the case. I have lived too long not to despise art, which is the filigraine of a little mind; and were I to grow cunning now, I should probably be underground before my *finesse* could achieve any *tour* of legerdemain.

Had you been content with less shrewdness, Madam, you would not have slid into another error. You saw, that I had first written *Family* for *Academy,* as was very plain I had—and then you concluded that I had substituted the latter word out of prudence, for it seems that in your Ladyship's eyes I am grown all on a sudden a miracle of circumspection, but had you considered a moment you would have seen that it was impossible I could ever have meant to write *Family,* and that my pen by inattention must have written *Royal Family* from the greater familiarity of the phrase; for, I beseech you, are the *Royal Family* to design the prints for Shakespeare? With all my respect for nonsense, I never mean to write one word for another, which would not be to be foolish but drunk; and I must have swallowed two bottles before I could lament that the royal family were incapable of giving a just drawing of Macbeth. I might as well have said that I did not read the treaty because Mrs Siddons had negotiated it.

You will perhaps, Madam, discover some close policy, when I tell you that I have not even seen the new volume of Lord Clarendon's papers[1]—yet it is what I must say if I answer you with truth. Nay, I even never did look into the former volume.[2] I was tired of those times before they appeared. I had read and written as much as I chose about Lord Clarendon,[3] and I did not care to return to the subject. Mere personal amusement is all I seek now, and I would sooner re-

1. Edward Hyde, 1st E. of Clarendon, *State Papers,* Vol. III, ed. Thomas Monkhouse, Oxford, 1786; folio (Hazen, *Cat. of HW's Lib.* 426).

2. Volumes I, II, ed. Richard Scrope, Oxford, 1767, 1773. HW forgets that he had cited this work in 'Book of Materials' 1759, pp. 6 (2 references), 14. Cf. Hazen, op. cit. 3229.

3. In *Royal and Noble Authors,* SH, 1758, ii. 13–20; *Works* i. 385–90, with some additions, chiefly in the list of works and in the notes, but with no mention of the *State Papers.*

turn to Mother Goose's tales than to the gravity of the former century. Gout and pain and confinement have made me hate everything serious, and I try to paint all my thoughts *couleur de rose*,[4] which is *my* philosophy.

I am not surprised that there should be a great party for the milkwoman. The wise people of Bristol have taken it into their heads that they have a manufacture of original genius *chez eux*,[5] and the less foundation they have for their credulity, the stronger their faith is, as always is the case of fools. Great was the Diana of the Ephesians, though they made the image themselves.[6] If Lactilla puts gin into her milk and kills herself, she will be immortal, and Mr Hayley[7] and Mr Cumberland[8] will write hymns to her—with all my heart.

Lady Anne's good sense and just observations are not only doubly hereditary, but the consequence of the very rational education you give her, Madam. Truth is natural to youth, and I believe would produce a good portion of sense too, if they did not hear and see so much falsehood as they find by degrees in the commerce of the world, and which they receive with respect, because it comes from elder persons, who they conclude act rightly. People are afraid of trusting the indiscretion of their children and do not tell them, such a gentleman is a rascal; such an one, a fool—nay, I can recollect having believed that several persons were sensible, because I heard others say they were so; and I had not then learnt to ask silently[9] the leading question, 'How do *you* know whether they are sensible or not?' Lady Anne seems to do so already, and therefore will not easily be a dupe. Commonly we have not a stock of experience, till it is of little or no

---

4. In imitation of Mme de Matignon (MANN i. 140).

5. Chatterton and Ann Yearsley. A concert in commemoration of Chatterton had been given at Bristol in 1784 (CHATTERTON 351, 363; E. H. W. Meyerstein, *Life of Thomas Chatterton*, New York, 1930, p. 476).

6. Acts 19. 23–41.

7. Who had written on Chatterton's suicide in *An Essay on Epic Poetry; in Five Epistles to the Rev[eren]d Mr Mason*, 1782, pp. 81–2, Epistle IV, ll. 219–48); HW's copy, with notes, is now at Harvard. A 'fond adviser' to a young poet warns him not to expect fame and wealth; Chatterton is 'Young genius struggling with ma-

lignant fate!' (l. 224). Having taken poison,

'And stung to madness by the world's neglect,
He, in abhorrence of the dangerous Art,
Once the dear idol of his glowing heart,
Tears from his Harp the vain detested wires,
And in the frenzy of Despair expires!'
(ll. 244–8).

8. HW had ridiculed Cumberland's odes, particularly the ones to Gray and Dr James (HW to Mason 11 March 1776, MASON i. 252). He makes a similar comment on Hayley and Cumberland *ante* 20 June 1785.

9. HW first wrote 'myself.'

use. We want it most when we are coming *into* the world. Sages, who are proud of it when they do not want it, are sometimes so generous as to bequeath their hoard to posterity—and posterity value it no more than a mourning ring.

I have lost another old acquaintance, Lady Beaulieu.[10] As there are not above half a dozen persons left now who were on the stage to my knowledge when I became a spectator, I should be weak indeed if I interested myself much in what happens on a theatre where the principal actors are twenty, thirty, or forty years younger than I am. My old remembrancer the gout, who never lets me forget myself long, is come, since I wrote the former part of this last night, into my left hand, and I must suspend my manœuvres I suppose for some weeks, for he seldom makes his visits superficially, so I can only be a *visitée;* and the weather is so sharp, that I am not sorry to remain in my own chimney-corner.

To Lady Ossory, Tuesday 9 January 1787

Berkeley Square, Jan. 9, 1787.

THE post is come in so late (past three) and I am forced to dine so early, Madam, that I could say but a few words, were I able; but I have been out, leaving my name, by way of airing, at doors of How-d'yes, and it tired me so much, that I was forced to leave half upon my conscience and come home to rest till another day—however I am recovered of my gout, have been abroad three evenings, and wish myself much joy of far the shortest fit I have had these twenty years (only for a fortnight) so that if I live another century, I may hope to have worn out the mines of chalk, and to be very healthy and robust too.

I must not only thank your Ladyship for your most obliging inquiry, but for your great condescension in making most unnecessary apologies. It was indeed my head was hurt at a soupçon of untruth, not my heart which can only be answerable to itself; but on the verge of seventy I should be liable to the imputation of dotage if I were grown either affected or artful—what! make the undertaker laugh at me!

10. She died 20 Dec. in Dover Street, London.

I am charmed with your theatre,[1] and only wish I could be a spectator. I extremely approve your good humour in dancing and acting, for I should hate gravity, dignity or austerity in one's own house in the country. Who had not rather see Scipio playing at leap-frog with his children at his Ampthill, than parading to St Paul's to sing Te Deum! Would to the Muses too that I were capable of being your poet epilogate—not that I would if I could, when you have the best epilogue[2] as well [as] prologue-maker[3] in the whole county of Parnassus at your elbow—how the deuce, Madam, should I fifty years ago have been able to write an epilogue worthy of waiting on a prologue of Mr Fitzpatrick? I am foolhardy enough when I send you a dab of prose,[4] and yet I would not venture that, if it were not a curiosity— that is, almost a *true* novel—at least, I have not, as you will find, attempted to add one romantic circumstance, rather the contrary. The little French ditty, *said* to be written by an English earl, I am sure will please you for its tender simplicity.

I have printed but forty copies, and merely for presents, which I only mention from my ambition that Lord Ossory may have a complete set of my editions; and as I have appropriated all the rest, I shall not have another copy but my own left.

I must finish for every reason, *as per above*, and am

The Most Obedient Servant

of the Whole *DRAMATIS PERSONÆ.*

1. 'During the Christmas recess, an elegant ball was given by the Earl of Ossory, at Ampthill Park, Bedfordshire . . . and on two other evenings, were performed the farces of *The Guardian* [by Garrick], and *The Mayor of Garratt* [by Samuel Foote], by part of the company' (*Northampton Mercury* 27 Jan.). The actors, listed ibid., included Lord Holland, Lord W. Russell, Lady Gertrude and Lady Anne Fitzpatrick, the Hon. Mr St John, George Robinson, and the Hon. Miss Fox. Lord Ossory was 'manager and prompter.'

2. 'Epilogue, written by the Countess of Ossory, and spoken by Lord Holland' (ibid.).

3. 'Prologue, written by Col. Fitzpatrick, and spoken by Lady G. Fitzpatrick' (ibid.). The Prologue, of 16 lines, begins 'When hoary Christmas binds in icy chain.'

4. His *Postscript to the Royal and Noble Authors*, SH, 1786; reprinted in *Works* i. 553–61. See also Hazen, *SH Bibl.* 135–7. The *Postscript* gives an account of Christine de Pisan (*post* 15 Sept. 1787) and John de Montacute or Montagu (ca 1350–1400), 3d E. of Salisbury, 1397, whose 'amour' HW mentions to Cole 27 Feb. 1780 (Cole ii. 195).

To Lady Ossory, Sunday 21 January 1787

Address: To the Countess of Ossory at Ampthill Park, Bedfordshire. *Postmark:* 22 IA.

Strawberry Hill, Jan. 21, 1787.

YOUR Ladyship's letter followed me hither, and I give you many thanks for complying with my suit for the epilogue,[1] which was very proper for the occasion, simple and unaffected. In fact those overtures and adieus are very difficult, especially when the pieces are not new—nor can I in general approve them. If a prologue, like the contents prefixed to cantos of a poem, opens the plot, it anticipates it. If it does not, why is it there? An epilogue is essentially as useless: will people have liked a play, if they have not liked it, though the poet begs they will have done so, or thanks them though they have not? Dryden talked politics or controversy, or of anything passing in town, in *his* prefaces and postfaces—Addison and classic authors talked of Sophocles and Euripides—in their prologues—and in their epilogues, as if the whole audience were to sup at the Rose Tavern.[2] Garrick's essays were like medley overtures, drew characters of different classes, which diverted the pit and galleries, answered his purpose, showed his mimicry, and will not do without it. In short, prologues seem never to have been necessary but to Shakespeare, whose plays often comprehending half a century and half Europe, it was impossible for the spectators to conceive at once from the mere shifting of the decoration (or from not shifting it, as was a little the case in his time) that the actors were one moment in the street at Venice, and the next in a bedchamber in Cyprus[3]—but I did not mean to write a dissertation, and shall leave the practice to the will of the world to be continued or omitted as it pleases—which I believe is the wisest way in most things, when one's opinion does not sail with the current. I dip so little in that tide, that I did not know of Mr Craufurd's new passion:[4] I have seen him but once this six weeks.

1. Written by Lady Ossory; see preceding letter.
2. In Russell Street, Covent Garden, adjoining Drury Lane Theatre (Wheatley, *London Past and Present* iii. 170–2).
3. As in *Othello.*
4. Not explained.

Lord Waldegrave has taken, for six months, the ready-furnished house in Dover Street over against Lord Ashburnham's,[5] which is very agreeable to me, as being so near me. I saw them on the eve of the Birthday.

Lord Carmarthen's dinner[6] answered the expectation of nobody; except Mr Fox, General Conway and Lord Maccartney, I think there was nobody but foreign ministers.[7] Though his list of invitations was as promiscuous as the company that Noah carried into the ark, the pairs were not quite so well sorted. The Marquis and Earl of Buckingham would not have been a very loving couple[8]—In truth I thought the whole congregation, had it met, would have been so distressed and awkward, that it would have been like a dinner that the late Duke of Montagu[9] made at Bath of all the people he could find there that stuttered. The three that did go, were the fittest in the world for a heterogeneous mixture; Mr Fox and Lord Maccartney are easy with anybody; and Mr Conway never knows with whom he is, nor perceives there is anything political or uncouth amongst any set of people. He had forgotten the dinner the next day, till I asked him about it.

5. Ashburnham House, built for him at No. 8, Dover Street (*Royal Kalendar*, 1787, p. 21); later renumbered (Wheatley, *London Past and Present* i. 517); demolished between 1885 and 1910 (GEC i. 273 n.c.).

6. 'Given on Thursday [18 Jan.], in honour of her Majesty's birthday, by the Marquis of Carmarthen, at the house of his father, the Duke of Leeds, in St James's Square' (*World* 20 Jan. 1787, with list of 32 guests 'present at the dinner'). 'Lord Carmarthen, [foreign] secretary of state [1783–91], surprised everybody by inviting on the Queen's birthday, when he always gave a dinner, all who had been in the Home Department of secretary (except Lord Bute and Lord Mountstewart) and all who had been our ministers abroad. This would have been an assemblage of Court and Opposition; of Mr Pitt, Mr Fox, Lord Lansdown, the Marquis of Buckingham, the Earl of Buckingham[shire], and etc.—It was supposed that Lord Carmarthen knew or apprehended that he was to be dismissed, and meant to affront the Court.—It is certain that few days before he had been to wait on the Prince of Wales. None however of the Opposition went but Mr Fox; and General Conway, who though he had resigned, was very indifferent to the Opposition, and took no part in it' ('Mem. 1783–91' *sub* Jan. 1787).

7. That is, foreigners accredited to England, as opposed to the guest list (n. 6 above) which consisted largely of English who had been diplomats abroad. Seventeen foreign diplomats are listed in the *World*, loc. cit., as present. 'I saw one who dined at Lord Carmarthen's, a foreigner, who told me the only English at the table were the Duke of Manchester, Lord Stormont, and Mr Fox. 'Tis really too extraordinary to be explained and has very much surprised the other ministers' (Coke, 'MS Journals' 19 Jan. 1787). On 18 Jan. Lady Mary Coke heard that the Duke of Manchester and Lord Lansdown had 'sent their excuse' (ibid. 18 Jan. 1787).

8. Political differences aside, they would have been incompatible: the Earl of Buckinghamshire resented the Marquis's choice of title in 1784, as Lady Mary Coke's 'MS Journals' for 1785 make clear.

9. John Montagu (1690–1749), 2d D. of Montagu, 1709.

Are not you sorry, Madam, that the King of Prussia's bigamy is not true?[10] It diverted me exceedingly; it would have been quite new to have three queens at once,[11] one that is not his wife, one that is, and one that cannot be. I fear too that the Prince of Anhalt[12] is not so complete a courtier as was reported; it was said that in compliment to his sovereign he had doubled his matrimony too. Kings should strike novel strokes; *they* can give a fillip to the world, and turn it out of its old humdrum ways. Nobody minds individuals—the Duchess of Kingston and Mr Madan[13] aimed in vain at introducing polygamy; but when Solomon countenanced it, the Queen of Sheba went to admire his wisdom; and I dare to say at her return had as many husbands, as his Hebrew Majesty had wives—she never went so far on mere speculation.

10. 'Since his accession to the throne, he has become enamoured of a young lady of the highest rank and of the most exquisite beauty. Having already a Queen and several children, and the object of his affection possessing . . . virtue . . . he was determined, if possible, to repeat the rites of marriage, and give her an equal rank with his Royal Consort.' The clergy told him 'his intentions were impossible,' and there was no precedent for it. ' "Then," exclaimed he, "I will establish a precedent myself, and teach the world, that a passion like mine ought not to be circumscribed by any laws whatever." He has since publicly married the young lady, and allowed her to share the honours of his former Queen. Such an instance of polygamy will afford matter of curious speculation for all Europe' (*London Chronicle* 6–9 Jan., lxi. 32, contradicted ibid. 13–16 Jan. lxi. 53). The *General Evening Post* 9–11 Jan., identifies the 'young lady of the highest rank' as 'daughter to his minister, the Count of Finkenstein.' In 'Book of Materials' 1786, p. 20, *sub* 6 Jan. 1787, HW refers to 'the marriage of William New King of Prussia with Mlle Finkenstein, his Queen living.'

11. Frederick William II had married (1765) Elizabeth (1746–1780) of Brunswick-Wolfenbüttel, whom he divorced, 1769, when he married Frederica (1751–1805) of Hesse-Darmstadt (Wilhelm Karl, Prinz von Isenburg, *Stammtafeln*, Berlin, 1936, i. taf. 63). 'Mlle Finkenstein' was Amalie

Elisabeth von Voss (d. 1789), cr. (1787) Gräfin Ingenheim, daughter of Friedrich Christoph Hieronymous von Voss. Her brother Otto Karl Friedrich had m. (1780) the daughter of Graf Fink von Finkenstein, Frederick the Great's first minister (*Genealogisches Taschenbuch der deutschen gräflichen Häuser*, Gotha, [1848], p. 316; C. F. Jacobi, *Europäisches genealogisches Handbuch*, Leipzig, 1800, ii. 204; Eduard Vehse, *Geschichte des preussischen Hofs und Adels*, Hamburg, 1851, v. 31–5; *Allgemeine deutsche Biographie*, Leipzig, 1875–1912, xl. 352, 363; in the last two sources she is called Julie von Voss. According to Mirabeau, 'Le mercredi, 22 [Nov.] . . . fut le jour remarquable où Mademoiselle de Voss accepta la main du Roi, et lui promit la sienne. Il fut résolu qu'on serait agréer à la Reine le plan d'un mariage du côté gauche' (letter of 2 Dec. 1786, in Honoré-Gabriel Riquetti, Comte de Mirabeau, *Histoire secrète de la cour de Berlin*, 'Londres,' 1789, ii. 187–8), The issue of this 'marriage,' Gustav Adolf Wilhelm, Graf Ingenheim, was b. 2 Jan. 1789.

12. Leopold III (Leopold Friedrich Franz) (1740–1817), Prince, 1751, of Anhalt-Dessau; Duke, 1807 (MANN vi. 418 n. 9).

13. Rev. Martin Madan (1726–90), author of *Thelyphthora; or, A Treatise on Female Ruin*, 1780, in which he advocated polygamy, using the Mosaic law as support. HW's copy, now WSL, is described in Hazen, *Cat. of HW's Lib.* 3244.

To Lady Ossory, Thursday 1 February 1787

Address: To the Countess of Ossory at Ampthill Park, Bedfordshire. *Postmark:* 1 FE.

Berkeley Square, Feb. 1, 1787.

THOUGH you announced Lord Ossory,[1] Madam, I did not expect to see him so soon as the next day, when he was so good as to call on me. His appearance prevented my immediate reply, as he can now shoot news flying, and I only gather up a few scattered feathers—and at present have not picked up one *pen*-feather, nor should write but to explain the ballad you wot of,[2] and which I never saw in its own person,[3] though I know its birth and parentage, aye, its father and mother.

It was written by the late Lord Melcombe, on a Mrs Strawbridge,[4] whom I knew, and who was still a very handsome black woman; she lived at the corner house going to Saville Row over against the late Duke of Grafton's.[5] The Lord, then Mr Doddington, fancied himself in love with her, and one day obtained an assignation. He found her lying on a couch;—but whether he had not expected so kind a reception, or was not so impatient to precipitate the conclusion of the romance, he kneeled down, and seizing her hand—cried, 'Oh! that I had you but in a wood!'—'In a wood!' cried the astonished Statira—'what would you do? rob me?'—however, then, or afterwards, that interlude produced an arrangement, and he gave her a bond of ten thousand pounds to be paid if he married anybody else. He did marry Mrs Behan,[6] with whom he could not own his marriage till Mrs Strawbridge died.[7]

1. For the opening of Parliament on 23 Jan.

2. 'Ballad on Mrs Strawbridge. By Geo. Budd Doddington, afterwards Baron Melcombe,' printed in Appendix 10 (*post* iii. 262) from HW's MS copy in his *Des. of SH*, 1774, now WSL. In his letter to Bentley 17 July 1755 HW refers to it as 'Rowe's ballad on Dodington's Mrs Strawbridge.'

3. That is, HW never saw the original copy of the ballad.

4. Who died in 1742; see n. 6 below.

5. Charles Fitzroy (1683–1757), 2d D. of Grafton, 1690; grandfather of the 3d D.

of Grafton. His house was in Old Bond Street (*Court and City Register*, 1757, p. 20), and Mrs Strawbridge's house presumably was at the corner of Vigo Lane and Old Bond Street.

6. Katherine Behan (d. 1756) m. (1725) George Budd Dodington, cr. (1761) Lord Melcombe, Bn of Melcombe-Regis. Until November, 1742 (when Mrs Strawbridge died and Dodington acknowledged the marriage), she was known as Mrs Behan and was considered his mistress.

7. On 7 June 1784 HW wrote a slightly different version of this anecdote (printed

As I cannot precisely ascertain the date of the ballad, I am not sure that *Mrs Masham* was the famous *Lady Masham*,[8] though perhaps it was, as by the mention of the Kit-Cats, it was probably written in Queen Anne's time, when her Majesty's favour might have stamped that gentlewoman for a beauty. *The little Whig* was most certainly the beautiful Lady Sunderland,[9] the D[uke] of Marlborough's daughter. There never was but one Duchess of Shrewsbury,[10] the Italian, mentioned in Lady Mary Wortley's first pastoral[11]—and there never was a Duke of Beaufort that made it worth knowing which duke it was.[12] Who the witty Sir Harry was, it is impossible to guess now: it might be the wittiest Sir Harry then alive, or the foolishest—for the expression rather seems ironic.

The pamphlet[13] I have read, Madam; but cannot tell you what

in *Mem. Geo. II* i. 439–40) in his copy of Lord Melcombe's *Diary*, then recently published. See also MANN ii. 104–5, 391–2, 424.

8. Since HW's notes on the ballad (Appendix 10, iii. 262) identify 'her Majesty' as Queen Anne, he clearly, when he wrote the notes, identified 'Madam Masham' as Lady Masham (*ante* 13 July 1776).

9. Anne Churchill (1683–1716), 2d dau. of John, 1st D. of Marlborough, m. (1700) Charles Spencer, 3d E. of Sunderland, 1702. She was 'the general toast by the name of The Little Whig' (obituary notice in *The Political State* for 1716, quoted in Cunningham ix. 91 n. 3). 'Lady Sunderland was a great politician; and having, like her mother, a most beautiful head of hair, used, while combing it at her toilet, to receive men whose votes or interest she wished to influence.' She was the 'most beautiful of her [Duchess of Marlborough's] four charming daughters' (HW, 'Reminiscences,' *Works* iv. 314; ed. P. Toynbee, Oxford, 1924, p. 88).

10. Adelaide Paleotti (d. 1726) m. 1 Alessandro Roffeni; m. 2 (1705) Charles Talbot, 12th E. of Shrewsbury, 1668, cr. (1694) D. of Shrewsbury; lady of the Bedchamber to Caroline, Princess of Wales 1714–26 (Vittorio Spreti, *Enciclopedia storico-nobiliare italiana*, Milan, 1928–36, v. 53).

11. 'Roxana, or The Drawing Room' (first published in 1716), the first poem in Lady Mary Wortley Montagu's *Six Town*

Eclogues. With Some Other Poems, 1747, pp. 5–8. HW's copy, now WSL, contains notes of identification; cf. Hazen, *Cat. of HW's Lib.* 3363:2. Coquetilla, identified by HW as 'Ds of Shrewsbury,' is mentioned on pp. 7–8. Cf. Robert Halsband, *Life of Lady Mary Wortley Montagu*, Oxford, 1956, pp. 50, 242, *et passim;* GRAY ii. 38–9 n. 40; MANN iii. 449 n. 10.

12. Mentioned in the ballad is Henry Somerset (1684–24 May 1714), 2d D. of Beaufort, 1700; 'a staunch Tory' (GEC).

13. *A Short Review of the Political State of Great Britain at the Commencement of the Year One Thousand Seven Hundred and Eighty Seven*, published anonymously, 18 Jan. (*Morning Chronicle*); by Nathaniel William Wraxall (Wraxall's *Historical . . . Memoirs*, ed. Wheatley, 1884, i. xxiii–xxiv, iv. 372–5, where Wraxall dates the publication as 22 Jan.; cf. n. 15). It went through eight editions during the year, the sixth published 30 Jan. (*Morning Chronicle*). In HW's 'Tracts of George III,' although he had two answers to it, 'This [*A Short Review* is] wanting.' For the answers, see Hazen, *Cat. of HW's Lib.* 1609:50. The *World* 18 Jan. mentioned that 'Wraxall . . . is talked' of as the author; two days later it commented, 'It may not be fair to publicly conjecture the name of the author. Various writers are guessed at—Wraxall, Horace Walpole, Tickell, and Sheridan himself,' and on 23 Jan. added Wilkes to the list of possible authors.

would have been my opinion of it, because my opinion was influenced before I saw it.[14] A lady-politician ordered me to read it and to admire it, as the *chef d'œuvre* of truth, eloquence, wit, argument and impartiality; and she assured me that the *reasonings* in it were unanswerable —I believe she meant the *assertions,* for I know she uses those words as synonymous.[15] I promised to obey her, as I am sure that ladies understand politics better than I do; and I hold it as a rule of faith

> That all that they admire is sweet,
> And all is sense that they repeat.

How much ready wit they have, I can give you an instance, Madam, that I heard last night. After the late execution of the *eighteen* malefactors,[16] a female was hawking an account of them, but called them *nineteen.* A gentleman said to her, 'Why do you say *nineteen?* there were but *eighteen* hanged.' She replied, 'Sir, I did not know *you* had been reprieved.'

The *Letters of Henry VI's Reign,* etc., are come out, [17] and *to me*

14. HW's considered opinion appears in 'Mem. 1783–91' *sub* Jan. 1787: 'A very extraordinary pamphlet was published at this time, called *The Present Political State.* It affected great impartiality, but was very favourable to the King and Mr Pitt, and very far from being so to the Prince. The heroes of it were Lord Rodney (supposed for a blind), and Mr Hastings, who seemed to be the real object. It looked like the performance of a young man, but inspected by the Court, perhaps by Jenkinson. It seemed afraid of Sheridan and the authors of the *Rolliad,* to whom it made great court. Was very false in several points, sunk many, many others notoriously true, and contradicted the apparent enthusiasm of a young man, who might be charmed by the beauties of the *Rolliad,* and the eloquence and advancement of Mr Pitt, by recommending *corruption* to the latter, which was more likely to be the object of Jenkinson, than of a virtuous young politician. Not a word was said of royal duplicity, of the bad education of the son, of the latter's noble retrenchment in order to pay his debts, nor of Mr Pitt's blundering measures, whose every bill had been forced to be corrected by subsequent acts. As great

silence was observed on the choice of the Parliament, purchased by the money of the East India Company. The ridiculous addresses procured by the Court on Margaret Nicholson and by the profusion and hopes of knighthoods, were ascribed to affection for the King, though at first heard with general indifference.'

15. Lady Mary Coke, if not the lady-politician HW refers to, would have agreed with her: 'There is a pamphlet published, the best wrote which I have seen for some years, and the most impartial; though more might have been said to the King's advantage with the strictest truth. It was sent me yesterday morning to read and I returned it in an hour' ('MS Journals' 16 Jan. 1787).

16. On 9 Jan., 'before the Debtors-door in Newgate.' For the names and crimes of the malefactors, see the *London Chronicle* 6–18 Jan., lxi. 32, 58, and (the account slightly condensed) GM 1787, lvii pt i. 84–5.

17. The Paston letters: *Original Letters, Written during the Reigns of Henry VI, Edward IV, and Richard III,* ed. John Fenn (1739–94), Kt, 23 May 1787, HW's correspondent; vols i–ii published 1 Feb. (*Morning Chronicle*); vols iii–iv, 1789, vol

make all other letters not worth reading. I have gone through above one volume, and cannot bear to be writing, when I am so eager to be reading. There is one of *Sir John Falstaff*,[18] in which he leaves his enemies to *White Beard* or *Black Beard,* that is, says he, to God or the Devil.[19]

There are letters from all *my* acquaintance,[20] Lord Rivers,[21] Lord Hastings,[22] the Earl of Warwick;[23] whom I remember still better than Mrs Strawbridge, though she died within these fifty years—What antiquary would be answering a letter from a living countess, when he may read one from Eleanor Mowbray Duchess of Norfolk?[24]—

To Lady Ossory, Friday 9 February 1787

Address: To the Countess of Ossory at Ampthill Park, Bedfordshire. *Postmark:* 9 FE.

Berkeley Square, Feb. 9, 1787.

T HOUGH I sigh for your Ladyship's coming to town, I do not know whether I shall not be a loser, for what news don't you send me? that Lord Salisbury is a poet,[1] is nothing to your intelligence that *I* am going to turn player[2]—nay—perhaps I should, if I were not too

v, with letters from the reigns of Edward V and Henry VII, ed. William Frere, 1823. Cf. Hazen, *Cat. of HW's Lib.* 3251.

18. Sir John Fastolf (ca 1378–1459), K.G., 1426; warrior and landowner of Norfolk.

19. Letter XII, Fastolf to Sir Thomas Howes, Parson of Castlecomb, 27 May 1450: 'And if they will not dread nor obey that ['Law and Reason'], then they shall be quiet by Blackbeard or Whitebeard, that is to say, by God or the Devil' (i. 53, in Fenn's modernized text; for complete text, see i. 52–5).

20. Because they appear in his *Historic Doubts on the Life and Reign of King Richard the Third,* 1768.

21. There are no letters from or to Lord Rivers, but two men with this title are mentioned: Richard Wydevill (d. 1469), cr. (1448) Bn de Ryvers and (1466) E. of Ryvers, mentioned in letters of 1459, i. 185, 187–9; his son, to whom HW refers, Anthony Wydevill (ca 1440–83), 2d E. Rivers, 1469; beheaded at Pontefract 25

June 1483 after Richard Duke of Gloucester (later Richard III) had procured his arrest; mentioned in 1459, i. 185, 187–9, and 1471, ii. 75, 89, 115, 157.

22. William Hastings (d. 1483), cr. (1461) Bn Hastings; arrested by order of Richard Duke of Gloucester and beheaded for high treason. Two of his letters (1473, 147–) are in ii. 152–5, 296–9.

23. Richard Neville (1428–71), cr. (1450) E. of Warwick; 6th E. of Salisbury, 1460; 'the King-Maker'; slain in battle at Barnet. Two letters by him (1455, before 1460) are in i. 84–91; and one to him (1470) is in ii. 40–3.

24. Eleanor Bourchier (d. 1474), great-granddaughter of Edward III, m. (1424) John de Mowbray, 3d D. of Norfolk, 1432. A letter from her (before 1460) is in i. 195–7, and another, possibly by her (no date) is in i. 96–7.

————

1. See *ante* 9 Jan. 1787.
2. At Richmond House; see below.

young for the company!—You tell me too, that I snub and sneer—I protest, I thought I was the snubbee.

For *The Way to Keep Him*[3]—I did not imagine it would come to anything—and so it has proved—however I was enjoined secrecy; and though I knew it could not remain a secret, I did not choose to be the reporter—I should have been a very premature one, for the *dramatis personæ* were not filled by two or three; one of the principal actresses has already declined—and there is an end of it.

For sneering, Lord help me, I was as guiltless—every day I meet with red-hot politicians in petticoats, and told your Ladyship how I had been schooled by one of them, and how docile I was. If you yourself have any zeal for making converts, I should be very ready to be a proselyte, if I could get anything by it. It is very creditable, honourable and fashionable—but alas! I am so insignificant, that I fear nobody would buy me; and one should look sillily, to put one's self up to sale and not find a purchaser. In short, I doubt I shall never make my fortune by turning courtier or comedian; and therefore I may as well adhere to my old principles, as I have always done, since you yourself, Madam, would not be flattered in a convert that nobody would take off your hands. If you could bring over Mr Sheridan, you would do something—he talked for five hours and half on Wednesday, and turned everybody's head—one heard everybody in the streets raving on the wonders of that speech—for my part I cannot believe it was so supernatural, as they say—do you believe it was, Madam?[4] I will go to my oracle, who told me of the marvels of the pamphlet, which assures us that Mr Hastings is a prodigy of virtue and abilities[5]

3. Arthur Murphy's comedy, first performed in three acts at Drury Lane, 1760; enlarged to five acts and performed at Drury Lane 10 Jan. 1761. The play was acted later this year at Richmond House; see *post* 14 June, 4 Oct. 1787.

4. On 7 Feb.: 'In the committee for the impeachment of Hastings, Sheridan made the longest and most admired speech ever heard, and was complimented by Pitt and all parties. His speech lasted five hours 20 minutes. Pitt moved to adjourn to consider till the next day, when [Feb.] 8, with many softenings he condemned Hastings and the committee voted by *175* to *63* [i.e., 68], in which majority were

Pitt and his friends, that he deserved to be impeached' ('Mem. 1783–91'). For the 'substance' of Sheridan's speech, and the debate 7–8 Feb., see the *London Chronicle* 6–10 Feb., lxi. 134–5, 137–43; Cobbett, *Parl. Hist.* xxvi. 273–342. Two pamphlet versions of the speech appeared, but neither is in the SH records.

5. Hastings is a 'very distinguished and very illustrious person . . . selected by party violence, for its most inveterate attacks.' His services have 'been attended with the most solid and beneficial consequences'; 'from the boundless resources of his own mind' he opposed in India 'the efforts of domestic faction, of interior

—and as you think so too, how should such a fellow as Sheridan, who has no diamonds to bestow, fascinate all the world?—yet witchcraft no doubt there has been, for when did simple eloquence ever convince a majority? Mr Pitt and one hundred and seventy-four other persons found Mr Hastings guilty last night, and only sixty-eight remained thinking with *the pamphlet* and your Ladyship, that he is as white as snow—well, at least there is a new crime, sorcery, to charge on the opposition! and till they are cleared of that charge, I will never say a word in their favour, nor think on politics more, which I would not have mentioned, but in answer to your Ladyship's questions—and therefore I hope we shall drop the subject, and meet soon in Grosvenor Place in a perfect neutrality of good humour.

To Lady Ossory, Thursday 14 June 1787

Strawberry Hill, June 14, 1787.

THOUGH your Ladyship *gave me law* (a very proper synonym for delay) I should have answered your letter incontinently, but I have had what is called *a blight* in one of my eyes,[1] and for some days was forced to lie fallow, neither reading nor writing a line; which is a little uncomfortable when quite alone. I do begin to creep about my house, but have not recovered my feet enough to compass the whole circuit of my garden. Monday last was pleasant, and Tuesday very warm; but we are relapsed into our east-windhood, which has reigned ever since I have been here for this *green winter,* which I presume is the highest title due to this season, which in southern climes is positive *summer,* a name imported by our travellers, with grapes, peaches and tuberoses; but as we cannot build hot-houses for our whole latitude, our summers seldom come to maturity. However, most of my senses have enjoyed themselves, my sight with verdure, my smell by millions of honeysuckles, my hearing by nightingales, and my feeling with good fires—tolerable luxury for an old cavalier in the north of Europe! Semiramis of Russia is not of my taste, or she

rebellion, and of external hostility'; he acted 'with celerity and decision' (N. W. Wraxall, *Short Review,* 4th edn, pp. 60–2).

1. '*Blight in the eye:* extravasation of blood under the conjunctive membrane' (OED).

would not travel half round the Arctic Circle[2]—unless she means to conquer the Turks and transfer the seat of her empire to Constantinople like its founder. The ghost of Irene[3] will be mighty glad to see her there—though a little surprised that the Grand Duke her son[4] is still alive. I hear she has carried her grandchildren[5] with her as hostages[6]—or she might be dethroned, and not hear of it for three months.

The Duke and Duchess of Buccleugh,[7] they say, came through Holland, and going to visit a chief burgher, found cannon planted before his door—and did not stay to leave a card.[8] How Lord George Gordon must long to be there and burn a street or two![9]

Most of Mr Cunningham's anecdotes[10] to be sure are not new at present, Madam, but they would have been so twenty years ago, and at least confirm much of what has come out recently. Some, I doubt, have been castrated;[11] indeed I have heard so—nay, am sure, for in one paragraph a siege or town is mentioned and refers to the

2. She had begun in February her journey to Cherson and Sebastopol to see her newly acquired territories. The conqueror Potemkin was her guide.

3. (ca 752–803), Byzantine empress, m. (769) the emperor Leo IV; regent (780–90) for her son Constantine VI, whom she plotted against after her regency ended, and whom she dethroned, blinded, and had put to death in 797; deposed in 802.

4. Who succeeded her as Paul I and was murdered in a palace revolution in 1801.

5. Alexander I (1777–1825), emperor of Russia 1801–25; and Constantine (1779–1831), who, except for his renunciation of the throne in 1822, would have become emperor in 1825.

6. They did not go with her. She particularly wished Constantine to see the borders of Turkey, which she thought of as his future kingdom.

7. Elizabeth Montagu (1743–1827) m. (1767) Henry Scott, 3d D. of Buccleuch, 1751, and 5th D. of Queensberry, 1810.

8. 'You will see a strange paragraph in the papers relating to them [the D. and Dss of Buccleuch], that when they rose in the morning at Amsterdam they saw ten men hanging before their windows; there were riots, but nobody hanged but one who was already dead' (Coke, 'MS Journals' 17 June 1787; London Chronicle 12–14 June, lxi. 561, which reports they saw '21 men hanging in the marketplace'). 'Holland was in . . . tumult owing to the endeavours of the so-called patriotic party to depose the Stadtholder, and to declare his office not hereditary in the House of Orange' (Toynbee).

9. He had been convicted on 6 June for a seditious libel against the government and for a libel against the French ambassador and Marie-Antoinette. Instead of appearing to be sentenced on 13 June, he went to Amsterdam but was sent back by the magistrates (London Chronicle 5–26 June, lxi. passim).

10. In The History of Great Britain: from the Revolution in 1688, to the Accession of George I, by Alexander Cunningham (1654–1737); published for the first time on 24 March 1787 in an English translation by William Thomson from the Latin (Dalrymple 193–4; London Chronicle 22–24 March, lxi. 285; Morning Chronicle 24 March; World 24 March).

11. HW voiced his fear of mutilation before the book was published (HW to Buchan 11 Feb. 1787, Dalrymple 194).

WALPOLE'S ANNOTATED COPY OF 'THE WAY TO KEEP HIM,' 1787

preceding paragraph in which not a syllable of it is said[12]—clumsy enough.

I am very far from tired, Madam, of encomiums on the performance at Richmond House;[13] but I by no means agree with the criticism on it that you quote,[14] and which I conclude was written by some player from envy. Who should act genteel comedy perfectly but people of fashion that have sense? Actors and actresses can only guess at the tone of high life, and can*not* be inspired with it. Why are there so few genteel comedies, but because most comedies are written by men not of that sphere? Etheridge, Congreve, Vanbrugh and Cibber wrote genteel comedy, because they lived in the best company; and Mrs Oldfield[15] played it so well, because she not only followed, but often set the fashion. General Burgoyne has written the best modern comedy[16] for the same reason; and Miss Farren is as excellent

12. For instance, i. 177, where a paragraph begins: 'Brisac being delivered up to the Emperor, he raised new regiments . . .' This comes immediately after a long discussion of Louis XIV's marriage to Mme de Maintenon, in which the Jesuits are blamed.

13. Murphy's *The Way to Keep Him* was performed, under Miss Farren's direction, at Richmond House 20, 30 April and 4, 17 May by a cast that included Lord Derby, Richard Edgcumbe, Major Arabin, Sir Harry Englefield, Mrs Damer, and Miss Campbell (*World* 14, 21 March, 21 April). Accounts of it appear in the *Morning Chronicle* 23, 26 April and in the *London Chronicle* 21–24 April, lxi. 387, reprinted in GM 1787, lvii pt i. 361–2. See also Lord Auckland's *Journal and Correspondence*, ed. 3d Bn Auckland, 1861–2, i. 409: Anthony Morris Storer names the cast to Eden in his letter of 10 April 1787 and comments, 'How Mrs Damer got there is a difficult matter to explain. Mr Walpole says she will act excessively well.' 'Perhaps upon the whole no *private play* was ever better acted—certainly *none* better managed in point of scene and stage arrangement' (*World* 21 April). Genest vi. 463–4 says 'the play was really well acted, particularly by the ladies.' The *World* 18, 21 May describes the performance on 17 May for the King and Queen; the prologue, written by Conway and spoken by Mrs

Hobart, and the epilogue, written by Gen. Burgoyne and spoken by Mrs Damer, are given, including special passages inserted on the opening night for the Prince of Wales and on the last night for the King and Queen. Cf. Hazen, *SH Bibl.* 274–5. HW had a satirical print of 'The Way to Keep Him as Performed at the Richmond Theatre &c. Act V' (now in the New York Public Library), published 23 April 1787, described in BM, *Satiric Prints*, vi. 439, No. 7215. See illustration.

14. Possibly from the *World* 21 April, which devoted almost a column to 'the scenes of high life acted by the professors of it' the day after the first night. 'It may be asked, should *they* be criticized? But do they not invite the public—court applause—and are gratified by it? . . . but then they are *amateurs* only—and yet we have heard some who say—"nothing so *easy as acting, and that gentlemen alone can represent polished life*" . . . and we wish we *could* say it too. . . . Perhaps as an *amateur* it would not be easy to find a representation of the vivacity and the *nonchalance* of the Widow better portrayed than by Mrs *Hobart*. . . . Miss Cambell in Lady *Constant*—had not much room for effect . . . Mr Edgcumbe's *Sir Brilliant* was certainly not fortunate,' etc.

15. Anne Oldfield (1683–1730).

16. *The Heiress*.

as Mrs Oldfield, because she has lived with the best style of men in England; whereas Mrs Abington can never go beyond Lady Teazle, which is a second-rate character, and that rank of women are always aping women of fashion without arriving at the style. Farquhar's plays talk the language of a marching regiment in country quarters; Wycherley, Dryden, Mrs Centlivre,[17] etc., wrote as if they had only lived in the Rose Tavern—but then the Court lived in Drury Lane too and Lady Dorchester and Nel Gwyn were equally good company. The Richmond Theatre, I imagine, will take root. I supped with the Duke at Mrs Damer's[18] the night before I left London, and they were talking of improvements on *the local*,[19] as the French would say.

Apropos, Mrs Damer has given me her eagle,[20] which I call *the spoilt child* of my antique one,[21] it is in such a passion. I hope your Ladyship will approve of the motto I design for it. Do you remember the statue at Milan with this legend,

Non me Praxiteles, sed Marcus finxit Agrati![22]

Mine is to be this pentameter,

Non me Praxiteles finxit, at Anna Damer.

17. Susannah Freeman (ca 1667–1723) m. (ca 1706) Joseph Centlivre, principal cook to Queen Anne and George I; actress and dramatist; author of nineteen plays, including *The Gamester*, 1705, and *The Busy Body*, 1709. HW had a copy of *The Gamester*, 4th edn, 1736, and *The Ghost*, 1767, an adaptation of her *The Man's Bewitched*, acted 1709, printed 1710 (Hazen, *Cat. of HW's Lib.* 1810:11, 1908:2).

18. In Sackville Street, where she lived from 1778 until late 1794 or early 1795 (BERRY i. 8 n. 6 *et passim*; Coke, 'MS Journals' 13 Oct. 1778).

19. 'To the room which is called the *Play-house* you enter from a large saloon, through a great doorway, raised on temporary steps, the descent from which again in the other room forms the gradation of seats down to the stage. In the bow window of the *Play-house room* a very curious little gallery is formed, holding about fourteen people' (*World* 20 April).

20. In the Library at SH: 'The fishing eagle [or osprey], modelled in terra cotta, the size of life. This bird was taken in Lord Melbourn's park at Brocket Hall ['before Christmas 1786'], and in taking it one of the wings was almost cut off, and Mrs Damer saw it in that momentary rage, which she remembered, and has executed exactly. She has written her own name in Greek on the base, and Mr W. added this line, *Non me Praxiteles finxit, at Anna Damer*, 1787' ('Des. of SH,' *Works* ii. 445; BERRY ii. 272; *Hamwood Papers*, ed. Bell, 1930, p. 117, *sub* 26 July 1788). See illustration. It was sold SH xix. 1 to Sir Alexander Johnston for £7.7.0.

21. One of HW's most prized possessions, a marble eagle found at Rome in 1742; described in DU DEFFAND i. 405 n. 4, MANN iii. 66 n. 10, with illustration of it facing p. 66.

22. For *Agrati* read *Agrates*. 'Not Praxiteles but Marco d'Agrate made me.' The marble statue of 'St Bartholomew Flayed,' 1562, by Marco Ferreri d'Agrate (fl 1540–ca 1570), is in Milan Cathedral (Thieme-Becker; *Enciclopedia universal ilustrada*, Barcelona, [1907–33], iii. 427, with illustration; *Dizionario enciclopedico italiano*, Rome, [1955–61], i. 182).

James Roberts del. Portrait Painter to his Royal Highness the Duke of Clarence.

John Jones sculp.

The OSPREY,

or Fishing Eagle,

Taken in Lord Melbourne's Park at Brocket Hall in Hertfordshire in 1786.
One of the Wings was almost cut off in seizing it.
Mrs Damer was present, and caught the Idea in that moment of its rage.

Publish'd as the Act directs, June 28. 1790, by James Roberts, Hogarth's Passage, Oxford;
and J. Jones, No 75, Great Portland Street, London.

Non me Praxiteles finxit, at Anna Damer, 1787.
H. W.

THE OSPREY, OR FISHING EAGLE,
BY ANNE SEYMOUR DAMER

I left Lady Waldegrave in town, not quite well, though I never saw her better than when she arrived, and her complaints, I believe, are merely the consequence of her situation.[23] I asked her little girl[24] whether she had a Waldegrave or a Walpole temper, but in more intelligible phrase to her, a gentle or a violent one? She replied, 'A middling one.'

Friday night, 15.

Today has contradicted all I wrote last night. The Cadogans and Churchills have dined with me, and the south wind came to meet them, and we drank tea out of doors and sat there till half an hour after eight, Strawberry never looking in greater beauty. Mr Trevis[25] the Jew came with them, of whom Lord Cadogan is as fond as the Prince. Lord Hertford is to give his Royal Highness a ball on Monday,[26] to which I am asked—but I have sent my excuse; dancing and the next reign are not in unison with seventy and limping. Lady Pembroke is to bring the Princess Lubomirski[27] hither tomorrow to

23. Her third son was born on 29 Aug. 1787: Hon. Edward William Waldegrave (1787–1809), drowned at sea on his return from Spain 22 Jan. 1809 (Burke, *Peerage*, 1953, p. 2151).

24. Lady Maria Wilhelmina Waldegrave (*ante* 15 July 1783).

25. Pellegrine Treves (1733–1817), born at Venice, settled in London in 1760; friend of the P. of Wales. 'In the meridian of life he was the companion of royalty, and the wit of society' (GM 1817, lxxxvii pt ii. 91; Alfred Rubens, *Anglo-Jewish Portraits*, 1935, p. 115; Lucien Wolf, *Essays in Jewish History*, 1934; Sylvester Douglas, Bn Glenbervie, *Diaries*, ed. Francis Bickley, 1928, i. 250). In a satirical print described in BM, *Satiric Prints* vi. 291–2, No. 6929, the man pushing the Prince of Wales toward Mrs Fitzherbert is identified as Fox; HW identified him as 'Trevis the Jew' on his variant copy of the print, now in the New York Public Library.

26. 'Lord Hertford gives a great ball next Monday to the Prince of Wales. At his time of life and with no lady, to be giving those sort of entertainments appears very extraordinary . . . I greatly suspect the company will chiefly be taken from the Opposition, which will be highly

improper but not unlike Lord Hertford, who always studies his interest, and if he thinks it will be agreeable to the Prince of Wales he will certainly do it. . . . The ball at Lord Hertford's was very fine. The Prince of Wales was there and stayed till twelve o'clock, but his health would not allow him to sup' (Coke, 'MS Journals' 14, 19 June).

27. Who visited SH on 23 July and breakfasted with HW 25 July; in that month Mrs Damer did a bust of her nephew 'young Prince Lubomirski' (BERRY ii. 228, 273; HW to Conway 17, 24 June 1787 and to Mrs Boyle Walsingham 26 July). The Princess Lubomirska, who had been at Bologna in Nov. 1785 on her travels, was Isabelle [Elizabeth] Helene Anne Czartoriska (1736–1816), m. 1 (1753) Stanislaus (1722–83), Fürst Lubomirski; m. 2 (Feb. 1786) Michael, Graf Oginski; she was sister-in-law of the Princess Czartoriska (Elizabeth Berkeley, Cts Craven, *A Journey through the Crimea to Constantinople*, 2d edn, 1789, pp. 89, 121; Wilhelm Karl, Prinz von Isenburg, *Stammtafeln*, 2d edn, Marburg, 1957–60, iii. taf. 153; *Europäisches genealogisches Handbuch*, ed. C. F. Jacobi, Leipzig, 1800, pt i. 519, 531). Rosalja, a more famous Princess Lubomirska,

breakfast,[28] which I cannot avoid—but I will not begin the chapter of grievances on the people that come to see my house; I should be as tiresome to your Ladyship, as they are to me—yet you do deserve a little chastisement. What a string of lofty words have you applied to a poor old creature who never was entitled to one of them! Honour! Value! Admiration!—for what! of what!—mercy on me! I look into my heart, I look into my head, and find nothing in either that does not make me blush, and reject thoroughly mortified such unmerited compliments. Honour and value Mr Howard,[29] Madam; admire Mr Sheridan; but scatter no flowers on a skeleton, who is hasting to the land of oblivion, and may be well content, if his faults accompany him thither!

To Lady Ossory, Thursday 28 June 1787

Address: To the Countess of Ossory at Ampthill Park, Bedfordshire. *Postmark:* 28 JU 87.

Strawberry Hill, June 28, 1787.

I BEG your Ladyship to forgive my asking you what will sound like an impertinent question: it is whether you received an answer from me, dated the 16th,[1] to one I had the honour of receiving from you a day or two before. My reason for asking it is, that a letter[2] I wrote on business by the same post did actually miscarry, and has given me some trouble. We have no posthouse at Twickenham, but a boy from Isleworth fetches them, and I suppose sometimes twists them to the tail of a paper-kite. If he made that use of my last to your Ladyship, perhaps you will have thought that as you gave me holidays, and told me I need not write soon, I have been flying a kite too—but

was only 19 at this time (Casimir Stryienski, *Deux victimes de la Terreur*, 1899, pp. 54, 114).

28. On Saturday 'at half an hour after two, nobody came but a servant from Lady Pembroke, to say her Polish altitude had sent her word she had another engagement in town that would keep her too late. So Lady Pembroke's dinner was addled . . .' (HW to Conway 17 June 1787).

29. John Howard (ca 1726–90), prison reformer and philanthropist, had recently refused to countenance the Howardian Fund, a subscription fund designed to pay for a statue of him. See, for example, GM 1787, lvii pt i. 101–2; D. L. Howard, *John Howard: Prison Reformer*, 1958, pp.135–50.

1. The preceding letter, dated 14 and 15 June, but sent on 16 June, since the second part was written on 'Friday night, 15,' too late for the post of that day.

2. Missing.

my second childhood does not enable me to gambol; and if it did, you are one of the last persons from whom I would play truant.

I have been sending some layers of clove-carnations to Lady Ravensworth, for which Lady Euston wrote to me.[3] I had not so many as I wished, the severe weather of last year having killed most of mine, and my gardener[4] is so bad, that he does not restock me soon. I offered him an annuity some years ago, if he would leave me; but he desired to be excused, as it was not so good as his place, and he knew nobody else would take him—so I have been forced to keep him, because nobody else will.

As this is only a codicil to the letter I doubt you never received, Madam, it shall not be longer.

To Lady Ossory, Thursday 6 September 1787

Strawberry Hill, Sept. 6, 1787.

I WILL not make a feigned excuse, Madam, nor catch at the pretence you kindly offer me of a lost letter—no, I confess honestly that I knew I owed you one—but was too conscientious to pay my just debts with the base currency of Richmond and Hampton Court —and I have no other specie. I know nothing, do nothing, but repeat the same insipid round that I have passed for so many summers, if summer this has been to be called. The dowagers of my canton pick up and dress up tales of what is done in London and at various watering places; but I hold it a prudery becoming old men (the reverse of that of old women) not to trouble myself about or censure the frolics of the young; and for my cotemporaries, so few of them are left, that unless by living to the age of Old Parr or Jenkins, we are not likely to commit anything remarkable. I have seen none of the French, Savoyard or Lorrain princes and princesses,[1] sterling or pinchbeck; I broke off my *commercial treaty* with France, when I was robbed of half Madame du Deffand's papers,[2] and care no more for their *bonne*

3. Her letter is missing.
4. John Cowie, who died in 1795.

———

1. 'Yesterday Prince d'Onbal was presented to the King at St James's by the French secretary' (*Daily Adv.* 19 July). The Princesse de Lamballe 'with her suite'

arrived 10 July in London (GM 1787, lvii pt ii. 733). HW's reference to 'Lorraine' might imply that her sister-in-law, who was of that family (and widow of the P. of Savoy-Carignan), was with her.

2. In 1780–1, after Mme du Deffand had died, bequeathing her papers to HW. Her

compagnie, than for their convicts Monsieur de Calonne[3] and Madame de la Motte.[4]

Under such a negative existence, what could I write, Madam? I
have heard nothing for these two months worth telling you but this
little story. There lives at Kingston a Mrs Barnard,[5] a very wealthy
hen-Quaker: she has a passion for beautiful black and white cows,
never parts with a pretty calf, and consequently has now a hecatomb
as striped and spotted as leopards and tigers. The Queen happened to
see this ermined drove, and being struck with the beauty of their
robes, sent a page to desire to purchase one. Mrs Barnard replied,
she never sold cows, but would lend her Majesty her bull with all her
heart—apropos to Court, it is not a recent story, I believe, but did
you ever hear, Madam, that Mrs Herbert, the Bedchamberwoman,
going in a hackney-chair, the chairmen were excessively drunk, and
after tossing and jolting her for some minutes, set the chair down,
and the foreman lifting up the top, said, 'Madam, you are so drunk,
that if you do not sit still, it will be impossible to carry you.'

To prove how little I had to say, I will empty my bimensal memory with the only other scrap *I* have collected, and which I may send
in part of payment for the four lines of *Latin* of Archbishop Tenni-
son,[6] which I have received from your Ladyship. Mine is an ancient
Latin law, which proves that the famous bulse[7] was a legal escheat to

nephew, the Marquis d'Aulan, withdrew
certain MSS on the grounds that they were
not included in the catalogue. Mme de
Choiseul and the Abbé Barthélemy withdrew their own letters, and the Prince de
Beauvau apparently withheld other papers
(DU DEFFAND i. pp. xliii–xlv).

3. Charles-Alexandre de Calonne (1734–
1802), *avocat général* to the Council of
Artois, *procureur général* to the parliament of Douai, later (1763) *maître des
requêtes.* As Louis XVI's *contrôleur général des finances* 1783–7, he was responsible for an enormous deficit, for which he
was dismissed 9 April 1787 and exiled to
Lorraine. He had come to England before
14 May 1787, where he lived intermittently
until a month before his death, when he
was allowed to return to France (BERRY
i. 43–4 *et passim; Dictionnaire de biographie française,* 1933– , vii. 922–4).

4. Jeanne de Saint-Rémy de Valois
(1756–91), orphan and beggar befriended

by a nobleman, m. (1780) Marc-Antoine-
Nicolas Lamotte, a young policeman. Implicated in the affair of the Diamond
Necklace, she was sentenced to be branded
and imprisoned for life, but she escaped
in June, joined her husband 4 Aug. 1787
in England, and died in London of injuries
received when she jumped from a two-story
window to avoid arrest for debt (BERRY i.
4–5 n. 3).

5. Mrs Anna Barnard (d. 1792), who
visited SH 22 Sept. 1786 (BERRY ii. 227,
281).

6. Thomas Tenison (1636–1715), Abp
of Canterbury, 1694.

7. The Nizam of Hyderabad had sent
to Hastings, to be presented to the King,
a bulse containing a 'prodigiously large'
diamond. It was presented on 14 June 1786
by Lord Sydney at the levee, Hastings
being present. 'Hastings, who had had the
diamond in his possession three weeks,
was suspected of giving it at that moment,

the Crown. In the new volume of the *Archæologia* is an essay on the state of the Jews in England in former times;[8] and there it is said, 'Judæus verò nihil possidere potest, quia quic-quid acquirit, acquirit regi'[9]—I suppose, nobody will dispute Mr Hastings being a Jew— or if you please, for *Judæus* you may read *Indicus,* so like are the words and the essence.

Many thanks for the advertisement which is curious indeed! I have not visited Mr Herschell's giant telescope, though so near me.[10] In truth, the scraps I have learnt of his discoveries have confounded me: my little head will not contain the stupendous idea of an infinity of worlds—not that I at all disbelieve them or anything that is above my comprehension. Infinite space may certainly contain whatever is put into it; and there is no reason for imagining that nothing has been put into it, but what our short-sighted eyes can see! Worlds, systems of suns and worlds may be as plenty as blackberries—but what can such an incredibly small point as a human skull do with the possibility of Omnipotence's endless creation? Do but suppose that I was to unfold to a pismire in my garden an account of the vast empire of China—not that there is any degree of proportion in the comparison—proceed; suppose another pismire could form a prodigious, yet invisible, spying-glass that should give the student ant a glimpse of the continent of China—Oh! I must stop—I shall turn my own brain, which while it is launching into an ocean of universes, is still admiring pismire Herschell—That he should not have a *wise* look, does not surprise me—he may be stupefied at his own discoveries—or to make them, it might require a head constructed too

and so publicly, to show resentment to the King for his having been given up.' The censure of Hastings by the House of Commons in Feb. 1787 'revived the story of the famous bulse given the last year to the King' ('Mem. 1783–91' *sub* June 1786, Feb. 1787; GM 1786, lvi pt i. 524). It was rumoured also that the diamond was really from Hastings, a gift intended to bribe the King (A. M. Davies, *Strange Destiny. A Biography of Warren Hastings,* New York, 1935, p. 410).

8. John Caley (ca 1763–1834), 'On the Origin of the Jews in England,' read 15 March 1787, *Archæologia,* 1787, viii. 389– 405. In his copy of *Archæologia* (now WSL), HW made no notes or marks on this essay.

9. 'Judæus vero nihil proprium habere potest, quia quicquid acquirit, non sibi acquirit, sed regi' (ibid. viii. 398, with Caley's footnote reference: 'Bracton, 1569, lib. v. tract. 4. cap. 6. sect. 6'). See also BERRY ii. 262 and n. 46.

10. On 3 April 1786 Herschel and his sister had moved from Clay Hall, near Windsor, to Slough, also near Windsor, to a house afterwards known as The Herschels. In 1787 he was using a twenty-foot telescope but was constructing a forty-foot one, for which George III had given him two grants of £2000 each. See Constance A. Lubbock, *The Herschel Chronicle,* Cambridge, 1933, pp. 144–68, and the illustration facing p. 167.

simply to contain any diversity of attention to puny objects. Sir Isaac Newton, they say, was so absorbed in his pursuits, as to be something of a changeling in worldly matters—and when he descended to earth and conjecture, he was no phenomenon.[11]

I will alight from my altitudes, and confine myself to our own ant-hill. Have you seen, Madam, the horrible mandate of the Emperor to General Murray?[12] Think of that insect's threatening to sacrifice thousands of his fellow pismires to what he calls *his dignity*! the dignity of a mite, that, supposing itself as superior as an earwig, meditates preventing hosts of its own species[13] from enjoying the happiness and the moment of existence that has been allotted to them in an innumerable succession of ages!—but while scorn, contempt, hatred, kindle against the imperial insect, admiration crowds in for the brave pismires who so pathetically deprecate their doom, yet seem resigned to it! I think I never read anything more noble, more touching, than the remonstrance of the Deputies to Prince Kaunitz.[14]

11. Cf. Bishop Atterbury on Newton: 'Indeed in the whole air of his face and make, there was nothing of that penetrating sagacity which appears in his composures . . . I see M. Fontenelle [in his *éloge* of Newton] speaks warily as to the MSS relating to Antiquity, History, and Divinity, which Sir Isaac left . . . I fear . . . that he will be found to have been a great master only in that one way to which he was by nature inclined. It is enough for us poor limited creatures, if we remarkably excel in any one branch of knowledge' (Atterbury to Thiriot in Atterbury's *Epistolary Correspondence*, 1783–4, i. 180–1, a passage marked by HW in his copy; Hazen, *Cat. of HW's Lib.* 2791; now WSL).

12. Joseph Jacob Murray (1718–1802), Graf Murray de Melgum, officer in the Austrian army; commanding general in the Netherlands, 1780, and governor of the Austrian Netherlands 1785–7 (Constant von Wurzbach, *Biographisches Lexikon des Kaiserthums Oesterreich*, Vienna, 1856–91, xix. 467–70). On 15 Aug. 1787 'the States of Austrian Flanders appeared before' the Emperor 'to justify their conduct . . . His Majesty's answer was stern, ungracious, and unconciliating.' His orders of 16 Aug. list seven stipulations, the first

of which is 'that in all the provinces of the Low Countries everything should be restored to the footing on which it stood before the first of April of this year.' 'My dignity renders all these preliminary re-establishments absolutely indispensable, . . . But if it shall happen against all expectation, that any one shall dare to oppose this restitution . . . I authorize you . . . to employ for this purpose all the means of authority which I have confided in you, and which, but with much regret, though I find it to be necessary, I am obliged to augment as far as the occasion shall require' (*London Chronicle* 4–6 Sept., lxii. 228; GM 1787, lvii pt ii. 825, the translation differing slightly).

13. MS reads 'specie'; cf. OED, *sub* specie, 76.

14. Wenzel Anton Kaunitz (1711–94), Graf von Rietberg, Fürst Kaunitz; chancellor and chief minister 1753–92, under Maria Theresa, Joseph II, and Leopold II (MANN i. 37 n. 2 *et passim*). The memorial to Kaunitz, which had no immediate effect on Joseph II (although he later relaxed his demands), urged Joseph not 'to revenge himself' for 'his insulted dignity' (*London Chronicle* 4–6 Sept., lxii. 228; GM 1787, lvii. pt ii. 826).

If tyrant dignity is ready to burst on Brabant, appearances with us seem also too warlike.[15] I shall be sorry if it arrives—I flattered myself that in our humiliated state, the consequence of *our dignity,* we should at least be tame and tranquil for the remnant of my time—but what signifies care about moments? I will return to your letter, which set me afloat on the vasty deep of speculation, to which I am very unequal and do not love. My understanding is more on a level with your ball, and meditations on the destruction of Gorhambury,[16] which I regret. It was in a very crazy state, but deserved to be propped; the situation is by no means delightful.

I called at Sir Joshua's, while he was at Ampthill, and saw his Hercules for Russia;[17] I did not at all admire it: the principal babe put me in mind of what I read so often, but have not seen, *the monstrous craws:*[18] Master Hercules's knees are as large as, I presume, the late Lady Guilford's.[19] *Blind* Tiresias[20] is *staring* with horror at the ter-

---

15. Under Sept. 1787 HW records in 'Mem. 1783–91': 'Del Campo, Spanish minister here, was made their ambassador, and at the same time presented a memorial saying, his master pretended to be a party to settling the disputes in Holland, and was arming. We armed too, and 1500 men were pressed.' In July France had 'declared she would not interfere in the affairs of Holland, but if any other power did, she should look on herself as at liberty, and would take a part' (ibid. *sub* July 1787).

16. Two miles NW of St Albans, Herts; built by Sir Nicholas Bacon 1563–8; described by HW ca 1760 in *Country Seats* 21–2, when it belonged to the 2d Vct Grimston; pulled down by the 3d Viscount, who 'built the present mansion at Gorhambury 1777–84 . . . a ponderous edifice in the Palladian style' (GEC vi. 206 n.c.); now the seat of the E. of Verulam.

17. Reynolds was at Ampthill the 'last three days of August' (C. R. Leslie and Tom Taylor, *Life and Times of Sir Joshua Reynolds*, 1865, ii. 511). The Infant Hercules 'is the grand picture, according to the grander order of the Czarina, in which the painter was unlimited in subject and in price . . . This may not be the most engaging of his work, but unquestionably it ranks among his best! It is nearly finished, and in a week or a fortnight, probably it will be open to common inspection.'

The infant Hercules is 'in the act of strangling the serpents. One in his right hand, the other in his left' (*World* 23 Aug.).

18. 'To the Nobility, Gentry, and others. To be seen, at Mr Becket's, trunkmaker, No. 31, Haymarket . . . three wild human beings; each with a Monstrous Craw, being two females and a male, of a very small stature, and odd form, with natural large craws [caused by goitre] under their throat, full of big moving glands, which astonishingly play all ways within their craws, according as stimulated by either their eating, speaking, or laughing. They have been admired by all Princes, celebrated anatomists, etc., to whom they have been shown since, saved from a wrecked ship near Trieste. Admittance two shillings each. Children half price' (*Morning Chronicle* 29 Jan. *et passim;* the same or a similar advertisement appeared in other newspapers). A print of them was published by C. Bowles 14 May, and HW owned a satirical print by Gillray, 'Monstrous Craws, at a New Coalition Feast' (now in the New York Public Library), published 29 May, showing the King and Queen with monstrous craws and the Prince with none (BM, *Satiric Prints* vi. 417, No. 7166).

19. Katherine Furnese (d. 1766) m. 1 (1736) Lewis Watson, 2d E. of Rocking-

rible spectacle. If Sir Joshua is satisfied with his own departed pictures, it is more than the possessors or posterity will be. I think he ought to be paid in annuities only for so long as his pictures last. One should not grudge him the first fruits.

Mr Gibbon's three volumes[21] I shall certainly read: I am fond of quartos; and I dare to say he has laboured these, and I shall be quite satisfied if they are equal to the first tome. The 'Long Minuet'[22] you may be sure I have, as I get everything I can of Mr Bunbury's.[23]

Though I have wandered into another sheet, I will not be so unconscionable as to fill more of it, and make your Ladyship repent your condescension of having awakened me. I will only ask whether you have heard that the Duchess of Kingston has adopted the eldest Meadows,[24] paid his debts, given him £600 a year, and intends to make him her heir?[25] Methinks this is robbing Peter to pay *Peter*.[26]

Stay, I forgot to tell you, Madam, that Miss Boyle[27] has designed

ham; m. 2 (1751) Francis North, 3rd Bn Guilford, 1729, 7th Lord North, 1734, cr. (1752) E. of Guilford. She was very large; see GEC vi. 213–14.

20. 'I have understood that Sir Joshua told a friend that the attitude and expression of the prophet Tiresias . . . were taken from those in which he had occasionally seen his friend Johnson' (James Northcote, *Memoirs of Sir Joshua Reynolds*, 1813, p. 331; Graves and Cronin iii. 1161; Derek Hudson, *Sir Joshua Reynolds*, 1958, p. 198).

21. Vols IV–VI of *The Decline and Fall of the Roman Empire*, completed in June, 1787, but not published until 27 April 1788.

22. 'A Long Minuet as Danced at Bath. Longa Tysonum Minuit [annotated by HW: 'Tyson was Master of the Ceremonies at Bath.'] Quid Velit et posit rerum concordia discors. Horace'; engraved (after Bunbury) and published 25 June 1787 by 'W. Dickinson, Engraver, Bond Street.' For a description of this 'strip design [8 9/16 x 84 5/8 inches] of ten couples in different stages of the minuet,' one of Bunbury's two 'most famous' designs, see BM, *Satiric Prints* vi. 444–5, No. 7229. HW's copy (now WSL) lacks the Latin inscription above the design (*Bos, Fur, Sus, atque Sacerdos*) that is in the BM copy.

23. See *ante* 13 July 1776 for HW's col-

lection of Bunbury's prints and drawings. For other works by Bunbury, some of which HW acquired after this date, see Hazen, *Cat. of HW's Lib.* 3905, 3913, 3914.

24. Evelyn Philip Medows (*ante* 1 Oct. 1773). 'The unlooked-for reconciliation is that of the Duchess of Kingston with Mr Meadows, her quondam opponent. He is now with her, all in all; is going with her into Russia, where she has bought a large estate, and which estate, in all form, and no doubt for value received, she has settled on Mr Meadows' (*World* 19 June).

25. According to the Baroness d'Oberkirch, the Duchess heard of him at Metz, living in misery and unable to pay his debts; she interceded for him with the King, paid his debts, and set him up in a house near Paris (Henriette-Louise d'Oberkirch, Baroness d'Oberkirch, *Mémoires*, 1869, ii. 286). When the Duchess made her will 7 Oct. 1786, he was 'of Chaillot near Paris' (Lewis Melville [L. S. Benjamin], ed., *Trial of the Duchess of Kingston*, 1927, p. 314).

26. That is, the money would remain in the Medows family. The Duke of Kingston had disinherited Evelyn Philip Medows, leaving everything to the Duchess for her life and then to Medows's younger brother Charles (*ante* 1 Oct. 1773; GEC vii. 309 n. b).

27. Charlotte Boyle (1769–1831), dau.

and carved in marble three medallions of boys for a chimney-piece at Ditton.[28] Lady Di has done two pictures for *Macbeth* and *Lear;*[29] the latter with the madman is very fine. Now I have finished indeed.

To Lady Ossory, Saturday 15 September 1787

Strawberry Hill, Sept. 15, 1787.

OF such of my editions, Madam, as you say Lord Ossory has not, I am sure I had no doubt but I had given him all but one.[1] The last time I was at Ampthill[2] I did desire his Lordship to look if he had all my publications, and told him I would, as far as I could, perfect his set, as I will now do; and I am glad to know which he wants, that I may supply him while I can. ·

Pray excuse me, if I say a little more on this occasion, though it will only be collaterally.

I have been long vexed at the ridiculous prices given for my editions. It could not be flattering to the vainest author or editor upon earth; for their dearness is solely to be attributed to their scarcity; and a collector who pays extravagantly for a rare book, will never read *in* it, or allow anybody else, for the virgin purity of the margin is as sacred with him as the text.

When the *Anecdotes of Painting* became so ridiculously dear,[3] which happened by collectors of portraits cutting out the prints, and using the text, I suppose, for waste paper, I printed a small edition without prints, at half-a-crown a volume,[4] that painters and artists

and heir of Hon. Robert Boyle Walsingham, m. (1791) Lord Henry Fitzgerald; *suo jure* Bns Ros or Roos; by royal license 6 Oct. 1806 took the name of De Ros after her husband's name.

28. At her mother's house, Boyle Farm, at Thames Ditton, Surrey. See HW to Hon. Mrs Boyle Walsingham 26 July 1787, to Lord Strafford 28 July 1787.

29. Mrs Steuart Erskine, *Lady Diana Beauclerk Her Life and Work*, 1903, pp. 224, 248, assumes that these were done for Boydell's Shakespeare Gallery, but she notes that 'No mention of them is to be found in Boydell's Catalogue.'

1. *Des. of SH;* see the seventh paragraph of this letter.

2. In Jan. 1776 (*ante* 22 Jan. 1776).

3. See Hazen, *SH Bibl.* 56–7.

4. Both 'The third edition, with additions,' (Vol. IV, 'Second edition'), 5 vols, octavo, 1782, and 'The fourth edition, with additions' (Vol. IV, 'Third edition'; *Catalogue of Engravers*, 'Second edition'), 5 vols, octavo, 1786, were published 'without cuts,' and both sets sold for '15 *s.* sewed' (*London Chronicle* 28–30 May 1782, 4–7 Nov. 1786, li. 518, lx. 445). The advertised price of the first edition (*Anecdotes*, Vols I–III and *Catalogue of Engravers* was £3; of the second edition, with additions, £3.3.0; Vol. IV, dated 1771 but not published until 1780, presumably sold for 15s., but Bell's advertisement in the *London Chronicle* 7–10 Oct. 1780, xlviii.

might purchase them cheaply, and that nobody might pay dearly, unless by choice. This is all I can do to remedy a folly I did not certainly intend to occasion. Those *Anecdotes* are the only thing I ever published of any use; and if I reprinted my other trumpery, nobody would buy them; and I cannot afford to put myself to great expense to save the money of foolish virtuosos.

I am sorry too on many accounts that this idle list has been printed[5] —but I have several reasons for lamenting daily that I ever was either author or editor. Your Ladyship has often suspected me to continue being the former, against which I have solemnly protested, nor except the little dab[6] on Christina of Pisan[7] (on which I shall tell you one of my regrets) I have not written six pages on any one subject for some years. No, Madam, I have lived to attain a little more sense; and were I to recommence my life, and thought as I do now, I do not believe that any consideration could induce me to be an author. I wish to be forgotten; and though that will be my lot, it will not be so, so soon as I wish—In short (and it is pride, not humility that is the source of my present sentiments), I have great contempt for middling writers. We have not only betrayed want of genius, but want of judgment—how can one of my grovelling class open a page of a standard author, and not blush at his own stuff? I took up the first part of *Henry IV* t'other day, and was ready to set fire to my own printing-house. 'Unimitable unimitated Falstaffe!' cried Johnson in a fit of just enthusiasm;[8] and yet amongst all his repentances, I do not find that Johnson repented of having written his own *Irene*.

Well! I should grow tedious on this subject, Madam, if I gave a loose to my own reflections on that ground—I will only add two circumstances. Not designing to add 'Christina,' as I found Lord Salis-

339, does not give the price; cf. *post* 6 Feb. 1789.

5. A list of books printed at SH; see n. 15 below. The list has not been found. HW's MS 'List of Books printed at Strawberry Hill' (now wsl) contains 28 items, the last of which is 'Hieroglyphic Tales . . . Octavo, 1785'; the 'List' as printed in *Works* ii. 515–16 (26 items) concludes with 'Description of Strawberry-Hill; royal quarto, 1784: 200 copies.'

6. *Postscript to the Royal and Noble Authors*, SH, 1786 (*ante* 9 Jan. 1787).

7. Christine de Pisan (ca 1363–ca 1431),

dau. of Thomas de Pisan, councillor of the Venetian republic and astrologer to Charles V; voluminous writer of prose and verse; m. Stephen Castel.

8. 'But Falstaff unimitated, unimitable Falstaff, how shall I describe thee?' (Johnson's comments at the end of *Henry IV*, Part II, in his edition of Shakespeare, *Plays*, 1765, iv. 356; ed. Johnson and Steevens, 1785, v. 647). According to Hazen, *Cat. of HW's Lib.* 1360, HW in 1787 had no edition with Johnson's notes; he later purchased Malone's edition, 1790.

bury was *not* a noble author,[9] I printed only forty copies. For this I have been abused and called illiberal, for not letting all the possessors of my *Noble Authors* have that scrap. Nay, a Mr Ireland,[10] a collector (I believe with interested views), bribed my engraver[11] to sell him a print of the frontispiece,[12] has etched it himself, and I have heard, has reprinted the piece[13]—and I suppose will sell some copies as part of the forty—I could tell you twenty of these foolish grievances; one of which leads to my second circumstance.

In the list for which Lord Ossory asks, is the *Description* of this place; now, though printed,[14] I have entirely kept it up, and mean to do so while I live for very sound reasons, Madam, as you will allow. I am so tormented by visitors to my house, that two or three rooms are not shown to abridge their stay. In the *Description* are specified all the enamels and miniatures, etc., which I keep under lock and key. If the visitors got the book into their hands, I should never get them out of the house, and they would want to see fifty articles which I do not choose they should handle and paw. The mention of the *Description* came out by two accidents. I gave an imperfect account of my collection to an old Mr Cole a clergyman of Cambridge many years ago,[15] and on his death it was sold to a bookseller.[16] It set some gossip-

9. In the last paragraph of the *Postscript*, p. 18, HW wrote, 'In a word . . . I cannot on such doubtful characteristics admit the Earl into the choir of English poets.' Although there is evidence that he wrote poems, almost certainly in French, none has survived; cf. DNB, *sub* Montacute or Montagu, John; HW, *Catalogue of Royal and Noble Authors*, enlarged and continued by Thomas Park, 1806, i. 183–4.

10. Samuel Ireland (d. 1800), author and engraver, father of William Henry Ireland, forger of Shakespeare manuscripts.

11. Not identified.

12. 'Reason, Rectitude & Justice appearing to Christina de Pisan, and promising to assist her in writing *La Cité des Dames*. From an illumination in the Library of the King of France'; later used in *Works* i. facing p. 288.

13. 'Despite [this rumour] . . . no spurious printing of the *Postscript* has ever been identified.' Probably 'HW intended to refer only to the frontispiece: this may very well have been duplicated, since HW reported as fact and not as

rumour that Ireland had copied the engraving' (Hazen, *SH Bibl.* 135).

14. For a description of the 1774 and 1784 *Des. of SH*, as well as the shorter version of the 1774 edition, see Hazen, *SH Bibl.* 105–10, 123–9.

15. On 29 Oct. 1774 HW gave Cole one of the six large-paper copies of the *Des. of SH*, 1774, now WSL, into which Cole entered the notes from HW's copy and added others, including (on the verso of p. 119) a 'List of the Books [18 items] printed at Strawberry Hill,' at the end of which Cole noted, 'Copied this at Strawberry Hill from a paper in Mr Walpole's own writing. Wm Cole. 1774.'

16. Benjamin White (1725–94), 'Bookseller, at Horace's Head, in Fleet Street, London,' issued *A Catalogue of the Entire Libraries of Charles Hedges, Esq. . . . and of the Rev. William Cole, the Eminent Antiquary* . . . ('The sale will begin on Tuesday, February 3, 1784'), but the *Des. of SH* is not included (DNB, *sub* White, Gilbert; H. R. Plomer, *et al.*, *A Dictionary of the Printers and Booksellers . . . in*

ing virtuosos on inquiry: Mr Gulston[17] bribed my engravers[18] to sell him some of my prints; Mr Gough,[19] without asking my leave, published a list of ten of those engravings in his *Topography*,[20] and has occasioned my being teased for specimens, which I have refused. The list of my editions was procured by some of these *liberal* artifices—and yet is not complete—yet I am sure I have said enough, Madam, to convince you how much cause I have to regret having exposed myself to the paltry fame that belongs to an Aldus or an Elzevir, without having deserved myself to be printed by either of them!

To others these calamities must sound comic, and I own I am happy not to have more ponderous: but it is the consequence of living much alone: one must grow occupied by one's own trifling aches, when vacant of graver matter. The worst is that solitary people are apt to grow peevish. I hope I am not so—indeed on stating my mishaps, I see how insignificant they are, and laugh at them—I hope, Madam, you will do so too, and at me, if you please.

So little do I remember what I write, that I cannot for my life recollect what I said in my last to which your Ladyship replies 'that Lord Ossory thinks Hercules will fail.' If you trouble yourself to explain, tell me if you know a conundrum I heard t'other day; 'Why is a bad wife better than a good one?'—the solution is good, though not very civil to Eves[21]—Oh! it has just started into my head that Hercules is Sir Joshua's—I doubt my poor memory begins to peel off —it is not the first crack I have perceived in it. My brother Sir Edward made the same complaint to me before he died, and I suggested a comfort to him, that does not satisfy myself. I told him the memory

England . . . 1726 to 1775, Oxford, 1932, p. 261; GM 1794, lxiv pt i. 284). Thomas Barrett of Lee Priory, Kent (*ante* 23 Aug. 1780), acquired the book after Cole's death, and it remained in the possession of his descendants until 1859 (Hazen, *SH Bibl.* 110), when it was bought by Lord Waldegrave, whose descendant sold it to wsl in 1948.

17. Joseph Gulston (? 1744–86), collector and connoisseur, who had appropriated many prints from Cole (COLE i. 287–8 n. 5 *et passim*).

18. That is, Richard Bernard Godfrey (1728–ca 1795), who engraved ten plates for the *Des. of SH;* see COLE ii. 211, 249, 274.

19. Richard Gough (1735–1809), antiquary; HW's occasional correspondent.

20. *British Topography*, 1780 (a revision of his *Anecdotes of British Topography*, 1768), i. 571*; the passage is printed in COLE ii. 249 n. 8. On the passage HW noted in his copy, now in the Huntington Library (Hazen, *Cat. of HW's Lib.* 33): 'There is but one drawing by Marlow; the others are by Sandby and Pars, and the chimney-pieces by Mr R. Bentley; and the prints were made for the only edition intended.'

21. The solution has not been found.

is like a cabinet, the drawers of which can hold no more than they can. Fill them with papers; if you add more, you must shove out some of the former. Just so with the memory; there is scarce a day in our lives that something, serious or silly, does not place itself there, and consequently the older we grow, the more must be displaced to make room for new contents. 'Oh!' said my brother, 'but how do you account for most early objects remaining?'—why, the drawers are lined with gummed taffeta; the first ingredients stick; those piled higgledy-piggledy upon them are tossed out without difficulty as new are stuffed in—yet I am come to think that mice and time may gnaw holes in the sides, and nibble the papers too.

To Lady Ossory, Thursday 4 October 1787

Oct. 4, 1787.

NAY, Madam, I know not how to steer between Mistress Scylla, impudent vanity, and Madam Charybdis, affected modesty! You reprove me for being decently humble, and then tell me you show my letters to Mr Fitzpatrick. Do you think I can like that? and can I help suspecting that you are laughing at me for a credulous old simpleton? Indeed I do suspect so, and am not such a gudgeon as to swallow the hook with which you keep me in play. Mr Fitzpatrick has too much sense and taste to be amused with the gossiping babble of my replies to the questions you put to me; and I can have no satisfaction in scribbling the trifles I send you, if they are to be seen, or if I am to ponder, and guard them against being downright dotage—and how shall I discover that they are not so, if they are? Where is the touchstone on which old age is to try its decays? It will strike seventy tomorrow,[1] and who will be so much my friend as to tell me that it might as well strike fourscore? With these convictions staring me in the face, do not imagine, my good Madam, that I suppose I can entertain one of the liveliest young men in England, and who passes his time with Mr Fox, Mr Sheridan and Mr Hare. It will not be kind in you either to show my letters, or to believe that I write them to be admired. I have long been honoured with your correspondence; I lead a most insipid life, and when I hear from an old acquaintance, I own frankly I am

1. HW was born on 24 Sept. 1717 OS, 5 Oct. NS.

glad to chat and throw off all the foolish things that have floated last on my mind, and that have served to amuse me for want of better employment. My letters are only fit to be seen by those who have no more rational diversions.

Your Ladyship asks me why Mr Fitzpatrick's *Dorinda*[2] is not specified in the catalogue of my impressions—recollect if you please, that I told you that the list was an imperfect one, and not such as I avow —but I let newspapers and magazines say what they please of me without setting them right. Whoever trusts them must thank himself for being imposed on in points indeed so unimportant, that it matters not whether they possess truth or falsehood. This very month a magazine has republished a tale which I do not remember, and of which I will swear part is false. It is, that many years ago I gave Mr Beauclerc my tragedy with injunctions not to show it to Garrick or Dr Johnson.[3] I doubt the fact very much, but am sure the reason assigned for not communicating it to the former is absolutely false, viz., because Garrick was such a goose as to prefer *Agis* to *Douglas*[4]—goose, and *goosissime* he was if he did, but I will take my death I never heard he did; nor do I believe that anyone ever did, unless the author did, who was such a goose too, as to write *Agis*, aye and all his other plays after having written *Douglas*.[5] If there is a grain of truth in the tale, it may have arisen from what I may have mentioned and which was true, that Home the author showed me *Agis* in MS and never

2. *Dorinda, A Town Eclogue*, SH, 1775; 300 copies printed (Hazen, *SH Bibl.* 112–14).

3. 'This dramatic piece [*The Mysterious Mother*] was . . . distributed among his particular friends, but with strict injunctions that it should never be shown to Mr *Garrick* or Doctor *Johnson*. Mr *Walpole* could by no means stoop to the judgment of the former, who had preferred *Agis* to *Douglas*; and of the rigorous criticism of the latter he would seem to have encouraged the most unreasonable apprehensions' (*European Magazine*, Sept. 1787, xii. 191, giving Act I, Scene i of HW's play). Beauclerc is not mentioned in the account (pp. 191–3), which 'appears to have been intended as an article in the *Biographia Dramatica* [by David Erskine Baker and Isaac Reed, 2 vols, 1782]; but why it was suppressed, and an inferior

one, in every point of view, substituted in its place [op. cit. ii. 247–9], we are unable to give any information' (p. 191). The passage, written by George Steevens, appears on one of the cancelled leaves of *Biographia Dramatica* preserved in Edmond Malone's copy in the Bodleian Library (L. F. Powell, 'George Steevens and Isaac Reed's *Biographia Dramatica*,' *Review of English Studies*, July 1929, v. 288–93, esp. p. 292).

4. Both by John Home. Garrick rejected *Agis* in 1747, but accepted and played in it at Drury Lane 21 Feb. 1758, after the success of *Douglas* (which he had also rejected), first performed at Covent Garden 14 March 1757 (Home, *Works*, Edinburgh, 1822, i. 34–59; Carola Oman Lenanton, *David Garrick*, 1958, pp. 184–7 *et passim*).

5. Home wrote *Agis* before he wrote *Douglas*.

visited or bowed to me afterwards, because I was too sincere to commend (I think it was not *Agis*, but) his *Siege of Aquileia*.[6] I doubt too the truth about Johnson; you know, Madam, I never reverenced him, yet had no reason to be in terrible fear of his criticisms, for he really, as far as I have heard, always spoke civilly of my publications.[7]

For another copy of the tragedy, your Ladyship shall have it if you please, but not the Strawberry edition, of which I have not one left.[8] I printed an edition, when the surreptitious one was advertised;[9] but on advertising my own,[10] it stopped the pinchbeck one, and so I avoided publishing it at all[11]—Oh! these would be pretty details for the eye of Mr Fitzpatrick!—indeed I ought to blush at sending them to Lady Ossory—but if you will converse with a printer, what can he tell you but the anecdotes of his shop?

Oct. 5th.

I began this in town where I have been for two days to see Lady Cadogan, who has lain in,[12] and had not time to finish it. Neither the egg of war nor the egg of peace is hatched yet; so probably the old hen of negotiation may sit on both till spring, and then the chick of the former, being true game, may burst its shell—but in truth I know

6. A tragedy produced by Garrick at Drury Lane 21 Feb. 1760 (DALRYMPLE 65–6 and n. 5). No letters between HW and Home have been found.

7. 'Talking to me of Horry Walpole . . . Johnson allowed that he got together a great many curious little things, and told them in an elegant manner' (Boswell, *Johnson*, iv. 314, *sub* June 1784). In his journal 16 Aug. 1773 Boswell quotes Johnson's reference to 'Horace Walpole, who is read with pleasure' (*Boswell Papers* ix. 272).

8. There is a mystery here. Of the 50 copies of the SH *Mysterious Mother* only about a dozen have been traced (Hazen, *SH Bibl.* 79–85). There were only two copies in Kirgate's sale and it is possible that HW destroyed a sizable proportion of the edition.

9. In 1781 *The Mysterious Mother* was advertised for publication with HW's name but without his permission. The advertisement has not been found. See Hazen, op. cit. 82–3; MASON ii. 139–40, 143–4, 148.

10. 'Speedily will be published by the author (to prevent spurious editions which have been advertised without his consent) *The Mysterious Mother*, a Tragedy. Printed for J. Dodsley in Pall Mall' (*Public Advertiser* 30 April 1781).

11. HW retained the whole impression (the number of copies is not known) and presented some copies to friends; 'thirty-one copies of it were in Kirgate's Sale in 1810 and fourteen in the SH Sale in 1842' (Hazen, op. cit. 83). Dodsley was still making use of this impression when he advertised in 1796: 'A spurious edition ['Reprinted for J. Roe, and Sold by Ann Lemoine, White Rose-Court, Coleman Street . . . Price One Shilling'] of the *Mysterious Mother* being advertised, an authentic and correct impression may be had at Mr Dodsley's in Pall Mall, with an apology by the author. Price 1s. 6d' (*London Chronicle* 24 June 1796, lxxix. 531).

12. Hon. (from 1800 Lady) Louisa Cadogan (b. 1 Sept. 1787) (John Debrett, *Peerage*, 1817, i. 313).

nothing, and saving compassion for the follies and woes of mankind, care very little about the matter. I know one loves one's country, because one has done it the honour of being born in it, and one takes the religion that happens to be in waiting at the time of one's birth, for much the same wise reason; but bating those grave prejudices, I am grown tolerably indifferent about Europe's bloody noses, and cannot love and hate just as treaties cross over and figure in.

I am equally in the dark about any acting that has been at Park Place;[13] and for the report of a match between Lady Constant and Sir Brilliant,[14] I believe it no more than the story of St George and the Dragon.

Monsieur Le Chauvelin's[15] verses I think I have seen, and do like prodigiously, especially 'La Gourmandise,' 'L'Orgueil,' 'La Paresse,' 'L'Envie'—in short—all, though 'Avarice' the least.[16]

Thus I have answered, Madam, and prosed according to custom, and will only tell you more that I dined last Monday at Bushy (for you know I have more *penchant* for ministers that are out than when they are in) and never saw a more interesting scene. Lord North's spirits, good humour, wit, sense, drollery are as perfect as ever—the unremitting attention of Lady North[17] and his children, most touching; Mr North leads him about, Miss North sits constantly by him, carves his meat, watches every motion, scarce puts a bit into her own

13. Mrs Hobart told Lady Mary Coke at Court on 25 Oct. 'she heard from good authority a play was getting up by Mrs Damer, the Duchess of Devonshire, Miss Campbell, etc., but that neither herself or Mrs Bruce had heard anything of it, so she supposed they were not to be of it' (Coke, 'MS Journals' 26 Oct. 1787, 8 Dec. 1787). That play, however, was planned for Richmond House.

14. That is, Caroline Campbell and Hon. Richard Edgcumbe, who had played those parts in Murphy's *The Way to Keep Him* at Richmond House (*ante* 14 June 1787, n. 13). Lady Mary Coke also doubted the rumoured match but thought that Lady Ailesbury was encouraging it ('MS Journals' 2, 7 Jan., 5 Aug., 26 Oct., 18 Nov. 1788).

15. Claude-François (*alias* Bernard-Louis) Chauvelin (1716–73), Marquis de Chauvelin, soldier, diplomatist, and poet;

friend of Mme du Deffand, but HW had not met him because Chauvelin had not been in Paris during HW's visits (DU DEFFAND ii. 64, iii. 433 *et passim;* Louis Petit de Bachaumont, *Mémoires secrets,* 1777–89, vii, *sub* 24, 29 Nov., 13 Dec. 1773; MANN iv. 353 n. 28).

16. 'Sept jolies femmes s'étant trouvées à un souper ensemble [at L'Isle Adam, the seat of the Prince de Conti], on les a comparées aux sept péchés mortels; chacune a tiré le sien par le sort, et M. Chauvelin a consacré ce nouveau genre de galanterie par ces vers.' The poems, each of four lines, with the name of the lady representing each sin, are in Grimm iii. 512–13, *sub* May 1758.

17. 'Lord North is with his family at Bushy. He takes the air constantly in a post-chaise or a low phaeton, in which Lady North drives' (*World* 11 Oct.).

lips; and if one cannot help commending her, she colours with modesty and sorrow, till the tears gush into her eyes—if ever loss of sight could be compensated, it is by so affectionate a family. Good-night, Madam.

To Lady Ossory, Monday 3 December 1787

Address: To the Countess of Ossory at Ampthill Park, Bedfordshire. *Postmark:* [Illegible.]

Berkeley Square, Dec. 3, 1787.

YOUR Ladyship ought not to blame my silence, which you certainly occasioned yourself. Could I be such a coxcomb as to write letters on purpose that they might be shown? I have scarce ever failed to answer yours instantly, and chiefly to questions you have asked; and in that careless hurry, have scribbled the first trifle or nonsense that presented itself. I should be ashamed of doing so, were my letters to be shown; and more ashamed of *preparing* them for inspection— in short, I cannot write fine letters, nor would if I could—I am too old to care a tush for reputation; and on the other hand cannot in cold blood invite people to laugh at me. Living in a very confined circle, I rarely hear news till stale; and thus disqualified for the easiest and best part of a correspondent, I was not at all unwilling to give up an employment that could entertain you so little. It was no shadow of disrespect to you, Madam, that silenced me; but just so much regard to myself, as preserves me from silly vanity, and the appearance of it.

Though I received your Ladyship's letter on Saturday, and began this reply incontinently, yet I could not find a minute for finishing it, for being confined by a slight attack of gout, I can be denied to nobody, and so many people came in, and their hour of dressing being so much later than mine of dining, they were so good as to bestow their vacant time on me, their idleness being of much more consequence to them, than my obsolete regularity, and consequently my dinner and the post clashing, and Sunday and the post being alike incompatible,[1] I was forced to defer this till today.

The return of the Duke and Duchess of Gloucester[2] engaged me

1. That is, the post did not leave London for Ampthill on Sunday.

2. '10 [Nov. 1787]. Duke and Duchess of Gloucester landed at Dover, after an

but the first two or three days, for etiquette is grown so antiquated in five years and half, that though the Duke does not think forms and ceremonies the least delectable part of the rubric, he is forced to relax, and they both now return visits in a morning and go to assemblies in an evening; in course my presence is little necessary, and I can lay myself aside, as Polonius would do, though not shocked as he would be at the dereliction of good old customs. However if courts have lost their energy, it is made up to the world by the community of princes. Besides the goodly display at St James's, there are half a dozen royal personages somewhere or other every night.

In France their Highnesses of Orléans and Bourbon[3] are banished[4] —as far as Knightsbridge and Kensington. The monarch sat from nine in the morning till five in the evening to hear philippics[5]—and may see louis d'ors representing him like Corniger Ammon:[6] the Duke of Gloucester has actually brought over one of them—after such a chapter on demi-gods, it would be profane to mix mortal affairs, and luckily I know nothing of this nether earth.

Your Ladyship's, etc.,

H.W.

---

absence of five years and half' ('Mem. 1783–91'). They 'arrived at Gloucester House' 'on Sunday night [11 Nov.]' (*World* 14 Nov.).

3. Louis-Henri-Joseph de Bourbon (1756–1830), Duc de Bourbon, later Prince de Condé; son of the Prince de Condé mentioned *ante* 18 Aug. 1775 (DU DEFFAND, *passim*).

4. On 20 Nov. the Duc d'Orléans was exiled to his seat at Villers Cotterêts, about 15 to 18 leagues from Paris, because on 19 Nov. he had vigorously protested the King's registering an edict. It was falsely rumoured that the Duc de Bourbon had been exiled also, 'for having seconded the protestations of the Parliament after the King's departure' (*London Chronicle* 24 Nov.– 8 Dec., lxii. 511, 520, 524, 531, 546).

5. Most of the day was spent in discussing the King's edict concerning a new loan 1788–92; a second edict pertaining to the rights of Protestants was partly read but not discussed. The King invited discussion 'without restraint,' but he ordered the edict concerning the loan registered although no vote had been taken and counted. 'The meeting . . . lasted from nine o'clock in the morning till half past five in the evening. His Majesty remained the whole time in the House' (ibid. lxii. 511, 524).

6. Horned Ammon, 'originally the god of the city of Thebes in Egypt,' was portrayed in Greece on coins, etc., usually 'with a head of Zeus to which the curling ram's horns of Ammon were added' (*Oxford Classical Dictionary*, ed. M. Cary, *et al.*, Oxford, 1949). Cf. also Ovid, *Metamorphoses*, v. 17, xv. 309, for 'corniger Ammon.' The coin or medal showing Louis XVI with horns was 'struck at Strasb[ourg]' ('Mem. 1783–91,' *sub* Dec. 1787).

To Lady Ossory, Saturday 15 December 1787

Berkeley Square, Dec. 15, 1787.

I AM so shocked, Madam, at the account I have this instant received from your Ladyship of the fire in your house,[1] that I must for a while postpone what relates to myself. I heartily congratulate the escapes of your persons and the preservation of your dwelling; but I do see that you have still a terrible calamity left, your suspicions, which seem too well founded. Nor can I suggest any comfort, but the hope that, as you think no discovery probable, there was no internal villainy, but that it was an attempt at plunder by *outward* banditti, who had no opportunity of firing the house within. They seem to have meant to draw attention to the stables, and then to have conveyed combustibles to the top of the house, perhaps by ladders—but as I am not master exactly of the locale, I don't know whether my conjecture was a probable one. Indeed it is horrid to be exposed at all to such violence; yet it is much lighter than to be distracted between the dread of having execrable servants, and the horror of suspecting the innocent. I remember when Gen. Conway's house in Warwick Street was set on fire,[2] I was persuaded, though I did not utter a word, that his own *maître d'hôtel* was the criminal. He turned livid, looked wrapped in thought, and would scarce speak a syllable. He was a most worthy honest creature, and as the sole criminal,[3] who was taken

---

1. 'About the hour of their all going to rest [on 12 Dec.; see postscript below] a great cry and screaming was heard, which came from the stables which were on fire. Water engines were procured and the fire was extinguished. The family was then going to bed when fortunately they discovered that the house, which is at a considerable distance from the stables, was burning in two places. Help being ready at hand, it was put out, but nobody went to rest the remainder part of the night, as it was very certain it must be some of the servants who had the wicked intention of burning the house; but think of the terrible situation they must be in, for if there is not any strong suspicion falls on anyone, they must for their own safety turn away all, though many must be innocent' (Coke, 'MS Journals' 18 Dec. 1787). 'I have not heard whether they have discovered at Ampthill the author of the shocking attempt of burning the house, though they have every reason to believe it must be one of their servants, for Lady Ossory wrote to Mr Walpole that previous to the attempt Lord Ossory had lost prints from his library and Lord Holland had five guineas taken from his bureau' (ibid. 25 Dec. 1787).

2. 2 March 1768 (HW to Mann 8 March 1768, MANN vi. 587–8).

3. James Sampson, convicted at the Old Bailey 14 April 1768 'for stealing [from Conway] . . . several bank notes, value £925, and to conceal the theft, most un-

and confessed everything and was executed, absolutely removed every tittle of suspicion from the *maître d'hôtel,* it proved that the poor man, being necessarily interrogated, could not support the idea of a possibility of guilt lighting on him. It had been a young secretary of Richmond House,[4] who having frequently copied papers for Mr Conway and had married Mrs Damer's maid,[5] was familiar in the house, had entered it in the evening unnoticed, and had concealed himself in a back room till five in the morning, when he broke open and robbed Mr Conway's drawers, and then set fire to a number of letters and papers that lay on them in the library under Mr Conway's and Lady Ailesbury's bedchamber. I hope at least, Madam, that you will discover some such extrinsic villain.

I must particularly thank your Ladyship for recollecting your charge against me in such an hour of distress; your goodness in telling me your misfortune and your saying you know how much I should interest myself in it, as I do most cordially, proves, I trust, that you neither really blame me, nor suspect me of becoming less attached to you than I have been for so many, many years—No, Madam, you do know, I am sure, that it is my own vanity and pride that has made [me] grow a less punctual correspondent. You have often heard me declare how jealous I am of growing superannuated, and how much I dread exposing myself in the dregs of life. I have not those happy spirits of some ancients, who totter on to the last, and do not find out what everybody else does, that they are ridiculous. Why should I suppose that when every limb is decayed, my inside should remain more sound? My head never was strong enough for me to trust to its defying the buffets of seventy years—within this hour I have experienced its weakness. Lord Carmarthen called on me in the midst of my letter, and I have almost lost the post, by keeping him with telling

gratefully set fire to the house of his best benefactor,' and hanged at Tyburn 11 May 1768 (MANN vi. 587–8; *Complete Newgate Calendar,* ed. G. T. Crook, 1926, iv. 51–4; *London Chronicle* 1–3, 8–10, 17–19 March, 14–16 April, 10–12 May 1768, xxiii. 214, 238, 270, 363, 454; *Whitehall Evening Post* 8–10 March 1768).

4. The Duke of Richmond employed him for drawing (copying), 'and employed masters properly qualified to afford every possible improvement to his fine genius. Afterwards the Duke warmly recommended

Sampson to the patronage of . . . Conway, who appointed him one of the draughtsmen to the Tower' (*Complete Newgate Calendar,* iv. 52).

5. 'Having married an upper servant in the General's family, he appeared to live in a state of great felicity; but unfortunately he maintained an illicit intercourse with some women of debauched principles, whose extravagances involved him in many embarrassments' (ibid. iv. 52).

him stories of his great-grandfather,[6] whom I remember. I can therefore say nothing now of the future play at Richmond House,[7] or of
that at Ampthill;[8] but you shall not lose a very good-humoured story
of Lord North—Col. Barré made him a visit lately; Lord North said,
'Colonel Barré, nobody will suspect us of insincerity if we say, that we
should always be overjoyed to *see* each other.'[9]

PS. Pray acquaint me if you make any discovery.

Postscript to my Saturday's letter.

Dec. 16, [17]87.

On considering your Ladyship's account of your conflagrations
more deliberately, I perceive that I mistook, and thought the *top*
of the faggots had been at the *top* of the house—Now I conceive, or
at least guess how the event happened. I conclude some villains who
knew something of your seat, but had not entrance, set fire to the
stables to draw the whole attention of the family; and that lurking at
a little distance in the dark, one of them, seeing their plan succeed,
and all the doors of your house left open by the servants hurrying
to the stables, slipped in, and set fire to the faggots, intending to
plunder plate in the double confusion.

This, detestable as it was, I hope was the case.

You did not say, Madam, whether the stables were burnt down, nor
what the house suffered.[10]

6. Peregrine Osborne (1659–1729), 2d D.
of Leeds, 1712; styled E. of Danby 1689–
94, M. of Carmarthen 1694–1712. HW
added a brief account of him in *Royal
and Noble Authors*, *Works* i. 535; cf. *Royal
and Noble Authors*, enlarged by Thomas
Park, 1806, iv. 116–17.

7. See the postscript.

8. Not identified.

9. HW expanded this anecdote in his
'Book of Materials' 1786, p. 63 (first numbering), *sub* 1790 'When Lord North
and Col. Barré, who were of different
parties, were both gone blind, the latter
went to visit the former. Lord North said
to him, "Col. B. everybody will believe us
both sincere, if we said, we should always
be glad to see each other." ' Barré had

been 'totally blind' since 1782 (*London
Chronicle* 28 Sept.– 1 Oct. 1782, lii. 318).

10. 'Late on Wednesday night [12 Dec.]
a fire broke out in the Earl of Ossory's
stables at Ampthill Park, which burnt
down one stable, and greatly damaged two
others, before it was got under, which was
about two o'clock in the morning. And
no sooner had the flames in the stable
subsided than another fire broke out in
the house, which was fortunately got under
with little damage. It is supposed that both
the fires were wilfully occasioned' (*Northampton Mercury* 15 Dec., reprinted in the
London Chronicle 15–18 Dec., lxii. 584;
and *World* 18 Dec.). The fire broke out
between 9 and 10 p.m., and, during it,
'another part of the said stables (totally

The play at Richmond House is to be *The Wonder*,[11] with *The Guardian.* The new performers are Lord Henry Fitzgerald,[12] who never played in comedy before, but is good in tragedy; a Miss Hamilton,[13] niece of Lord Abercorn, and a Capt. Merry,[14] Mrs Hobart[14a] does not play in those pieces, but is to choose her own part in the next. In return I shall expect a detail of the theatre at Ampthill.

I have had no formal gout, but several skirmishes with it that have confined me for two or three days at a time; yet I have been once at the opera,[15] and was tired to death; and though I came away the moment it was ended, did not get home till a quarter before twelve. The learned call the music good,[16] but there is nothing to show the humour and action of the Storace[17] and Morelli.[18] I bought the book[19]

unconnected) appeared to be in flames' (advertisement in the *Northampton Mercury* 29 Dec.).

11. *The Wonder! A Woman Keeps a Secret,* by Mrs Centlivre.

12. (1761–1829), 4th son of 1st D. of Leinster; succeeded to the estate of Strangford, co. Down; M.P. (Ireland) Kildare borough 1783–90, city of Dublin 1790–7, and (United Kingdom) co. Kildare 1807–14 (BERRY i. 266 n. 37, where additional information is given). He played Don Felix in *The Wonder* (*World* 27 Dec.).

13. 'The beautiful Miss Hamilton is added to the charming group of private acting at Richmond House. This Lady is the niece of Sir William, the daughter of the Dean' (*World* 22 Dec.). She was Jane Hamilton (d. 1810), daughter of Frederick, archdeacon of Raphoe; m. (1798) George Halman or Holman (John Anderson, *Historical and Genealogical Memoirs of the House of Hamilton*, Edinburgh, 1825, p. 153; GEC, *sub* 3d E. of Aldborough; GM 1798, lxviii pt i. 169; GM 1810, lxxx pt i. 672). She played Donna Isabella in *The Wonder* (*World* 27 Dec.). Lord Abercorn was not her uncle but her father's first cousin.

14. Charles Merry (ca 1759 – after 1789), brother of Robert Merry ('Della Crusca'); Capt. 1782, in 79th Foot, in 52nd Foot 1786 – ca 1790; friend of Sir Charles and Lady Hotham; matriculated at Balliol College, Oxford 29 Nov. 1776, aged 17, but did not graduate (Foster, *Alumni Oxon.; Army Lists;* A. M. W. Stirling, *The Hothams*, 1918, ii. 227–8, 247–51, 253; *World*

13, 14 Dec.; Hester Thrale Piozzi, *Thraliana*, ed. Balderston, Oxford, 1951, ii. 756). He played Lissardo in *The Wonder* and Sir Charles Clackit in *The Guardian* (*World* 27, 31 Dec.).

14a. 'Inis—Mrs Hobart,' in cast of characters of *The Wonder* (*World* 27 Dec.; see, however, *post* 15 Jan. 1788, n. 34) and 'Mrs Oakley—Mrs Hobart' 'in the second play . . . *The Jealous Wife*' (*World* 31 Dec.).

15. *Il Re Teodoro in Venezia: or, Theodore (King of Corsica) at Venice*, 'a serio comic opera in two acts' (*World* 8 Dec.) or 'dramma eroicomico'; text by Giovanni Battista Casti (1724–1803); music by Giovanni Paisiello (1741–1815); first performed in London 8 Dec. 1787, opening the season at the Opera House, and repeated on 11 and 15 Dec. and thereafter (*World* 8–22 Dec.; Alfred Loewenberg, *Annals of Opera 1597–1940*, 2d edn, Geneva, 1955, i. 411–12).

16. 'This opera . . . has a fault, for which no excellence can atone—that of being too long. One half hour removed from it would make the rest the better. The airs are formed with that originality and science which are not the least of Paesiello's praise; and the only doubt about them is, whether they most surprise from novelty of contrivance, or please from the force of effect' (*World* 10 Dec.).

17. Anna Selina Storace (1766–1817), English soprano who had made her debut at the Opera House in London 24 April 1787 as Gelinda in Paisiello's *Gli schiavi per amore*; m. (ca 1784) John Abraham

to read at home, because the Emperor paid £1000 for the piece as a satire on the King of Sweden[20]—how the Lord knows. The plot is taken from Voltaire's deposed kings at Venice in his *Candide*,[21] of whom only two are introduced, King Theodore[22] and Sultan Achmet.[23] The words are ten times stupider, than our operas generally are; nor do I yet know that the King of Sweden, to whom I am no more partial than Cæsar is, was ever deposed[24]—In short, if it is a satire on any mortal, it is one on Cæsar himself for having paid so dear for such unintelligible nonsense.

My elderly cousin Mr Thomas Walpole has espoused the sister of Monsieur Francès, Madame de Villegagnon,[25] at Paris, who is no infant neither—but that is their affair.

I am going to tell you a story, Madam, that perhaps you have heard better from Mr Fitzpatrick, who was one of the company. Lord Wescote wrote lately to Lord North, that as his Lordship was in so deplorable a condition, he, Lord W. should go over to Mr Pitt. Soon after, the Speaker,[26] not knowing of that missive, invited Lord W. to dinner with a set of the Opposition, who did know a little more of the matter, though pretending ignorance. The conversation soon fell on Lord George Gordon's Mosaic beard[27]—on which one of the com-

Fisher, from whom she soon separated (*London Chronicle* 24–26 April, lxi. 394; *World* 23, 24 April; Sir George Grove, *Dictionary of Music*, 5th edn, ed. Blom, 1954).

18. Giovanni Morelli (fl. 1787–1812), basso, who made his first London appearance in Paisiello's *Gli schiavi per amore* 24 April 1787. He had been 'running footman' to Lord Cowper at Florence.

19. *Il Re Teodoro in Venezia. A New Comic Opera, in Two Acts*, 1787 (Hazen, *Cat. of HW's Lib.* 3448).

20. Casti, the librettist, had been in Joseph II's service since 1773 (Herman van den Bergh, *Giambattista Casti*, Amsterdam, 1951, pp. 27–9). Joseph disliked Gustav III of Sweden, calling him 'un homme sans caractère, faux et qui, avec un vernis d'esprit et de connaissances, n'est qu'un fanfaron et petit-maître manqué' (Joseph II to Leopold II 13 Nov. 1783, *Joseph II und Leopold von Toscana*, ed. Arneth, Vienna, 1872, i. 179); Leopold II alludes to Gustav III's shabby quarters and entourage at Pisa (to Joseph II 10

Nov. 1783, ibid. i. 178); hence Teodoro's opening words in the opera most appropriately apply to Gustav III.

21. In Chap. 26 Candide and Martin sup with six dethroned kings.

22. Theodore (1694–1756), Bn de Neuhoff, proclaimed K. of Corsica April–Sept. 1736 (MANN ii. 145 n. 1; GRAY i. 28, ii. 170).

23. Achmet (or Ahmed) III (1673–1736), Sultan of Turkey 1703–30; forced to resign; died of poison in prison.

24. He had not been deposed.

25. Jeanne-Marguerite Batailhe de Montval (1731–1821) m. 1 (1755) —— Durand, Marquis de Villegagnon; m. 2 (1787) Hon. Thomas Walpole. HW had met her in Paris and had entertained her at SH in 1769 (DU DEFFAND ii. 336 *et passim*; H. S. Vade-Walpole, 'Notes on the Walpoles,' *Genealogical Magazine*, 1898–9, ii. 433).

26. Charles Wolfran Cornwall (1735–89), Speaker of the House of Commons 1780–9.

27. Lord George Gordon, having been forced to leave Holland, had returned to

pany said, it was lucky when *converts* wore distinguishing marks by which they might be reconnoitred—and the whole dinner was carried on in the same tormenting style.[28]

You will not be less diverted with an anecdote of your aunt.[29] She had a mind to go to Gloucester House, but declared she could not till an affair was arranged, for she had had a quarrel with the Duchess of Gloucester in the year *One*—no mortal could guess what she meant, nor do I know yet, for her Grace of Bedford herself was not born in 1700, nor the Duchess of Gloucester till 1735.[30] The latter said, they never could have had a quarrel, for they never had been intimate enough. This anachronism (in her Grace's memory) has somehow or other been rectified, and she has been at Gloucester House.[31]

This is an inordinate postscript, and I will add no more, but that Strawberry has felt many a twitch since the fire at Ampthill.

Dec. 17, 1787.

I was at a rehearsal[32] last night, and amazed: Lord Henry is a prodigy, a perfection—all passion, nature and ease; you never saw so genuine a lover—Garrick was a monkey to him in Don Felix—then he is so much the man of fashion, and is so genteel—in short, when people of quality can act, they must act their own parts so much better than others can mimic them—Mr Merry is an excellent Lissardo too.

England. On 7 Dec. 1787 he was arrested at Birmingham and the following day was returned to London to await sentence on two convictions (*ante* 14 June 1787). 'It is supposed . . . [he] has resided above three months at Birmingham, in the character of a Jew, during which time he has not been shaved; his beard being at present near four inches long' (*London Chronicle* 8–11 Dec., lxii. 558). For prints and portraits showing his 'Mosaic beard,' the earliest ('The Birmingham Moses') dated 12 Dec., see Alfred Rubens, *Anglo-Jewish Portraits*, 1935, pp. 47–50, Nos 134–41, with illustration facing p. 48; BM, *Satiric Prints, passim*).

28. A long account of the dinner, with the guests listed as Fox, Fitzpatrick, Sheridan, Adam, Lord George Cavendish, Welbore Ellis, Hare, and Lord Westcote

(whose name alone is printed in small capitals), is in the *World* 22 Dec., with supplementary pleasantries about Westcote on 24, 28 Dec. and later.

29. The Dowager Duchess of Bedford.

30. 10 July 1736.

31. 'The Duchess of Bedford notwithstanding all her dislike of the Duchess of Gloucester intends going to her next Wednesday [5 Dec.]. At seventy-four she has not enough houses to go to; 'tis a misfortune at that time of life to have spirits enough to do silly things and expose oneself to ridicule' (Coke, 'MS Journals' 29 Nov. 1787).

32. At Richmond House. 'The rehearsals go on every night at Richmond House . . . Miss Farren is to preside, as before' (*World* 18 Dec.).